Contemporary Literary Criticism

Guide to Gale Literary Criticism Series

When you need to review criticism of literary works, these are the Gale series to use:

If the author's death date is:	You should turn to:
After Dec. 31, 1959 (or author is still living)	**CONTEMPORARY LITERARY CRITICISM** for example: Jorge Luis Borges, Anthony Burgess, William Faulkner, Mary Gordon, Ernest Hemingway, Iris Murdoch
1900 through 1959	**TWENTIETH-CENTURY LITERARY CRITICISM** for example: Willa Cather, F. Scott Fitzgerald, Henry James, Mark Twain, Virginia Woolf
1800 through 1899	**NINETEENTH-CENTURY LITERATURE CRITICISM** for example: Fedor Dostoevski, George Sand, Gerard Manley Hopkins, Emily Dickinson
1400 through 1799	**LITERATURE CRITICISM FROM 1400 to 1800** *(excluding Shakespeare)* for example: Anne Bradstreet, Pierre Corneille, Daniel Defoe, Alexander Pope, Jonathan Swift, Phillis Wheatley **SHAKESPEAREAN CRITICISM** Shakespeare plays and poetry

---

Gale also publishes related criticism series:

CONTEMPORARY ISSUES CRITICISM

Presents criticism on contemporary authors writing on current issues. Topics covered include the social sciences, philosophy, economics, natural science, law, and related areas.

CHILDREN'S LITERATURE REVIEW

Covers authors of all eras. Presents criticism on authors and author/illustrators who write for the preschool to junior-high audience.

Contemporary Literary Criticism

Excerpts from Criticism of
the Works of Today's Novelists,
Poets, Playwrights, Short Story
Writers, Filmmakers, Scriptwriters,
and Other Creative Writers

Jean C. Stine
Editor

Bridget Broderick
Daniel G. Marowski
Associate Editors

Gale Research Company
Book Tower
Detroit, Michigan 48226

STAFF

Jean C. Stine, *Editor*

Bridget Broderick, Daniel G. Marowski, *Associate Editors*

Lee Ferency, Jeanne A. Gough, Roger Matuz, Jane E. Neidhardt,
Jane C. Thacker, Debra A. Wells, Robyn Young, *Assistant Editors*

Sharon R. Gunton, Sharon K. Hall, Phyllis Carmel Mendelson, *Contributing Editors*

Robert J. Elster, Jr., *Production Supervisor*
Lizbeth A. Purdy, *Production Coordinator*
Denise Michlewicz, *Assistant Production Coordinator*
Eric F. Berger, Michael S. Corey, Paula J. DiSante,
Serita Lanette Lockard, Amy T. Marcaccio, Janet S. Mullane,
Yvonne Robinson, Gloria Anne Williams, *Editorial Assistants*

Linda M. Pugliese, *Manuscript Coordinator*
Donna Craft, *Assistant Manuscript Coordinator*
Rosetta Irene Simms Carr, Colleen M. Crane, Maureen A. Puhl, *Manuscript Assistants*

Karen Rae Forsyth, *Research Coordinator*
Jeannine Schiffman Davidson, *Assistant Research Coordinator*
Victoria Cariappa, Anne Marie Dadah, Kathleen Gensley, Barbara L. Hammond,
Robert J. Hill, James A. MacEachern, Kyle Schell, Mary Spirito,
Margaret Stewart, Carol Angela Thomas, Valerie Webster, *Research Assistants*

L. Elizabeth Hardin, *Permissions Supervisor*
Filomena Sgambati, *Permissions Coordinator*
Janice M. Mach, *Assistant Permissions Coordinator*
Patricia A. Seefelt, *Assistant Permissions Coordinator, Illustrations*
Margaret Chamberlain, Mary P. McGrane, Anna Maria Pertner,
Joan B. Weber, *Permissions Assistants*
Elizabeth Babini, Virgie T. Leavens, *Permissions Clerks*

Copyright © 1983 by Gale Research Company

Library of Congress Catalog Card Number 76-38938
ISBN 0-8103-0109-1
ISSN 0091-3421

Contents

Preface

Literary criticism is, by definition, "the art of evaluating or analyzing with knowledge and propriety works of literature." The complexity and variety of the themes and forms of contemporary literature make the function of the critic especially important to today's reader. It is the critic who assists the reader in identifying significant new writers, recognizing trends in critical methods, mastering new terminology, and monitoring scholarly and popular sources of critical opinion.

Until the publication of the first volume of *Contemporary Literary Criticism* in 1973, there existed no on-going digest of current literary opinion. *CLC,* therefore, has fulfilled an essential need.

Scope of the Work

CLC presents significant passages from published criticism of work by today's creative writers. Each volume of *CLC* includes excerpted criticism on about 65 authors who are now living or who died after December 31, 1959. Since the series began publication, more than 1,500 authors have been covered. The majority of authors covered by *CLC* are living writers who continue to publish; therefore, an author is frequently covered in more than one volume. There is, of course, no duplication of reprinted criticism.

Authors are selected for inclusion for a variety of reasons, among them: the publication of a critically-acclaimed new work, the reception of a major literary award, or the dramatization of a literary work as a movie or television screenplay. For example, the present volume includes John Cheever, who wrote his last book, the critically-acclaimed *Oh What a Paradise It Seems,* during a fatal illness; Elias Canetti, who won the 1981 Nobel Prize in literature; and James Clavell, whose novel *Shōgun* became a popular television mini-series. Perhaps most importantly, authors who appear frequently on the syllabuses of high school and college literature classes are heavily represented in *CLC.* Saul Bellow, John Dos Passos, and John Berryman are examples of writers of this stature in the present volume. Attention is also given to several other groups of writers—writers of considerable public interest—about whose work criticism is often difficult to locate. These are the contributors to the well-loved but nonscholarly genres of mystery and science fiction, as well as writers who appeal specifically to young adults and writers for the nonprint media, including scriptwriters, lyricists, and cartoonists. Foreign writers and writers who represent particular ethnic groups in the United States are also featured in each volume.

Format of the Work

Altogether there are about 750 individual excerpts in each volume—with an average of about eleven excerpts per author—taken from hundreds of literary reviews, general magazines, scholarly journals, and monographs. Contemporary criticism is loosely defined as that which is relevant to the evaluation of the author under discussion; this includes criticism written at the beginning of an author's career as well as current commentary. Emphasis has been placed on expanding the sources for criticism by including an increasing number of scholarly and specialized periodicals. Students, teachers, librarians, and researchers frequently find that the generous excerpts and supplementary material provided by the editors supply them with all the information that they need to write a term paper, analyze a poem, or lead a book discussion group. However, complete bibliographical citations facilitate the location of the original source as well as provide all of the information necessary for a term paper footnote or bibliography.

A *CLC* entry consists of the following elements:

- The **author heading** contains the author's full name, followed by birth date, and death date when applicable. Pseudonyms and other forms are also listed.

- A **portrait** of the author is included when available.

• A brief **biocritical introduction** to the author and his or her work precedes the excerpted criticism. However, *CLC* is not intended to be a definitive biographical source. Therefore, *cross-references* have been included to direct the user to other useful sources published by the Gale Research Company: the *Contemporary Authors* series now includes detailed biographical and bibliographical sketches of nearly 73,000 authors; *Children's Literature Review* presents excerpted criticism on the works of authors of children's books; *Something about the Author* contains heavily illustrated biographical sketches on writers and illustrators who create books for children and young adults; *Contemporary Issues Criticism* presents excerpted commentary on the nonfiction works of authors who influence contemporary thought; and *Dictionary of Literary Biography* provides original evaluations of authors important to literary history. Previous volumes of *CLC* in which the author has been featured are also listed.

• The **excerpted criticism** represents various kinds of critical writing—a particular essay may be normative, descriptive, interpretive, textual, appreciative, comparative, or generic. It may range in form from the brief review to the scholarly monograph. Essays are selected by the editors to reflect the spectrum of opinion about a specific work or about an author's writing in general. The excerpts are presented chronologically, adding a useful perspective to the entry. All titles by the author featured in the entry are printed in boldface, which enables the user to readily ascertain the work being discussed.

• A complete **bibliographical citation** designed to facilitate location of the original essay or book follows each excerpt. An asterisk (*) at the end of a citation indicates the essay is on more than one author.

Other Features

• An **Appendix** lists the sources from which material has been reprinted in a volume. Many other sources have also been consulted during the preparation of the volume.

• A **Cumulative Index to Authors** lists the authors who have been included in previous volumes of *CLC*—more than 1,500 of the best-known creative writers in the world today.

• A **Cumulative Index to Critics** lists the critics and the author entries in which their work appears.

• A list of **Authors Forthcoming in *CLC*** previews the authors to be researched for future volumes.

Acknowledgments

The editors wish to thank the copyright holders of the excerpted articles included in this volume for permission to use the material and the photographers and individuals who provided photographs for us. We are grateful to the staffs of the following libraries for making their resources available to us: Detroit Public Library and the libraries of Wayne State University, the University of Michigan, and the University of Detroit. We also wish to thank Walter Abish, Jascha Kessler, and Robert Lecker for their editorial assistance; and Jeri Yaryan for her assistance with copyright research.

Authors Forthcoming in *CLC*

With the publication of *Contemporary Literary Criticism,* Volume 12, the series expanded its scope to encompass songwriters, filmmakers, cartoonists, scriptwriters, producers, and other creative writers whose work is often evaluated from a literary perspective. These writers take their place with the novelists, poets, dramatists, and short story writers who will continue to be the primary focus of *CLC.* The material presented in Volume 26 will be selected on the basis of its appeal to young adults. Volume 27 will include criticism on a number of authors not previously listed and will also feature criticism on newer works by authors included in earlier volumes.

To Be Included in Volume 26

Ralph Bakshi (American animator and film-maker)—His animated films treat subjects that fascinate young adults: fantasy, urban street life, and the world of popular music.

Robert Frost (American poet)—His adherence to traditional verse forms and his masterful use of nature imagery make Frost one of the best-known figures in twentieth-century poetry.

Virginia Hamilton (Black American novelist)— Highly individualistic in style and rich in symbolism, Hamilton's fiction portrays young people coming to terms with themselves and the world around them. Her young adult novel *M.C. Higgins the Great* received both the Newbery Medal and a National Book Award in 1975.

Thor Heyerdahl (Norwegian nonfiction author)—Beginning with his now classic *Kon-Tiki,* Heyerdahl's writing chronicles his adventures and discoveries as an anthropologist.

Rosa Guy (West Indian-born American novelist)—Her popular and respected novels for young adults present the experiences of her adolescent protagonists as they struggle for self-realization and independence.

Billy Joel (American songwriter)—He has been one of the most popular songwriters and performers in American pop/rock music since the late 1970s.

John Knowles (American novelist)—Written in the same mode as his renowned *A Separate Peace,* Knowles's recent novel *Peace Breaks Out* has generated new discussion of his work.

Colleen McCullough (Australian novelist)— Set in Australia, her popular novels *The Thorn Birds* and *An Indecent Obsession* are stories of love and the testing of honor and courage.

Farley Mowat (Canadian novelist, short story writer, and nonfiction writer)—His work is often based on his own experiences and reflects his love of the Canadian wilderness.

Richard Pryor (Black American comedian)— His perceptive, irreverent portrayals of contemporary persons and situations have made Pryor's work a critical and commercial success.

Paul Schrader (American scriptwriter and director)—He has written scripts for several major films, including *Taxi-Driver* and *Raging Bull.*

Rosemary Sutcliff (English novelist)—She is a writer of acclaimed historical fiction for young adults.

To Be Included in Volume 27

John Barth (American novelist and short story writer)—The recent publication of his novel *Sabbatical: A Romance* has generated new discussion of the theories and techniques of this innovative and critically controversial author.

Hilda Doolittle (H.D.) (American poet and novelist)—Her work and life as one of the leading Imagist poets is commanding new attention with the posthumous publication of *End to Torment* and *HERmione.*

Gabriel García Márquez (Colombian novelist, short story writer, and scriptwriter)—A major figure in both Latin American and world literature, García Márquez was awarded the 1982 Nobel Prize in literature. He has recently published *Chronicle of a Death Foretold,* a novel that explores the death of a young man and the minds of his murderers.

Geoffrey Hartman (German-born American literary critic)—His work, notably *Criticism in the Wilderness,* presents and defends critical expression as a creative literary act.

Kazuo Ishiguro (Japanese novelist)—His first novel, *Pale View of the Hills,* won praise for its success in capturing the emotional turmoil of post-war Nagasaki.

Thomas Keneally (Australian novelist)—His growing reputation as an important international writer is reflected in the reception of *Schindler's Ark,* the 1982 winner of the prestigious Booker McConnell Prize.

Helen MacInnes (Scottish-born American novelist and dramatist)—She is a prolific and bestselling author of novels of international intrigue that are noted for being well-researched and suspenseful.

Bernard Malamud (American novelist and short story writer)—His recent novel *God's Grace* is dramatically different from his previous works in both setting and approach. In this novel, Malamud writes of the destruction of the world by thermonuclear warfare.

Paule Marshall (Black American novelist and short story writer)—Long neglected by critics, her novels, including *Brown Girl, Brownstones* and the recent *Praisesong for the Widow,* blend her West Indian heritage and urban American experience.

Marge Piercy (American poet and novelist)—Her recent novel *Braided Lives* continues Piercy's activist attempts to raise social consciousness through fiction that merges the political with the personal.

Muriel Rukeyser (American poet)—Her death in 1980 ended a long career of political activism and innovative poetic expression.

Boris and Arkadii Strugatskii (Soviet science fiction writers)—Combining Boris's scientific background and Arkadii's literary expertise, the Strugatskii brothers produce science fiction of high quality that has won acclaim in both the Soviet Union and the West.

Alice Walker (Black American novelist, poet, and short story writer)—Her recent and much acclaimed novel *The Color Purple* is a moving portrait of a rural black woman's struggle for identity.

Martin Walser (German novelist and dramatist)—A recipient of the prestigious Georg Büchner Prize, Walser is one of Germany's foremost authors.

James Wright (American poet and translator)—The posthumous publication of his last poems in *This Journey* enhances Wright's reputation as one of America's finest contemporary poets.

Arthur Adamov

1908-1970

Russian-born French dramatist, essayist, editor, and translator.

Adamov was an important figure in the French theater of his time. Though his plays eventually moved away from the Theater of the Absurd, Adamov, along with Samuel Beckett and Eugene Ionesco, originally helped shape this idiom on the stage. Adamov also contributed to the theater the importance of visual impact in expressing a play's meaning. He treated stage space as a visible representation of meaning and physical movement on stage as a language to communicate meaning to the audience. Adamov's dramas, therefore, cannot be easily read and understood; they must be seen.

Three periods are generally observed in Adamov's career but he consistently strove to convey his view of the intensity of human isolation and of the loss of significant human communication. He did so by developing only slight plots and by presenting unrealistic characters who often acted like machines and spoke in a mechanical language laden with clichés. These characters are portrayed as victims of forces beyond their control, driven to withdrawal and eventually, to suicide.

In the early plays, during his "absurdist" period, Adamov is concerned with universal situations that are removed from any specific realistic setting. His characters are nearly symbolic and his plays take place in a dream world, often a nightmare. These plays are said to have arisen from the dramatist's personal fears and obsessions. *Le Professeur Taranne (Professor Tarrane)* is singled out as the best work of this period. In his middle plays, during his "Brechtian" period, Adamov turned to plays of social realism set in the contemporary world, evidencing a conscience outraged by the social injustices of modern political and socio-economic systems. Critics have noted in these dramas an unusually strident tone, which often detracts from their effect. *Le Ping-Pong (Ping Pong)*, called Adamov's masterpiece, is from this phase. In his final period, Adamov attempted to blend the work of his previous two phases. These plays show his growing disillusionment with social action as an effective way to change social systems and his lack of faith in the individual's ability to create personally meaningful values. Adamov's last play, *Si l'été revenait (If Summer Should Return)*, is seen as a statement of his ultimate despair.

(See also *CLC*, Vol. 4; *Contemporary Authors*, Vols. 17-20, Vols. 25-28, rev. ed. [obituary]; and *Contemporary Authors Permanent Series*, Vols. 1-2.)

CARLOS LYNES, JR.

In an age in which the theatre remains primarily literary, psychological, or philosophical, Arthur Adamov stands almost alone in France—along with Samuel Beckett and Eugène Ionesco—in the effort to renew the ancient tradition of the drama as the imitation of an action and to create a modern art of the theatre appealing to the "histrionic sensibility" through direct means which no other art possesses. (p. 48)

It would be vain to outline the "plot" of an Adamov play or analyze the "psychology" of the characters, for these terms—at least in their conventional meanings—simply do not apply to the "univers créé" which Adamov brings to the theatre. Even the complete printed texts of the plays, with the detailed notes on mise-en-scène, are more like musical scores than traditional "literary" or "psychological" dramas; they can be "read" by anyone with the necessary skill and imagination, but they cannot be fully grasped apart from actual performance. (p. 50)

In *La Parodie* [*The Parody*], with its brief prologue and twelve rapid scenes, we are in the anonymous "waste land" of a contemporary European city. . . . [We] encounter a variety of characters in whom we find the absurd, the tender, the grotesque, the naïve. There is no "story"—these people meet, engage in various activities, speak to one another with apparent conviction, suffer or laugh; there is no order or coherence in their world or their lives, only solitude and the absurd. This play is, of course, the *parody* of meaningful human life; when it is over, we may suspect that we too are living just such a parody.

The characters in [*La Parodie*] have a kind of fixed, mechanical rigidity in bearing, action, and speech, which is maintained throughout and which manifests *literally* the pathetic absurdity of their fate. They meet without really seeing one another, they speak but their language remains opaque, even to themselves. Everything is rendered directly, by the use of the specific, non-verbal "language" of the theatre; in *La Parodie* we can see for once, as Adamov remarked on the eve of the first performance, "the characters of a play act in keeping with their real situation, exposing before everyone's eyes the shrieking spectacle of their blindness." (pp. 50-1)

La grande et la petite manoeuvre [*The Great and the Small Maneuver*] . . . , like *La Parodie*, takes place in the nightmarish atmosphere of a contemporary police-state city. Here the disorder and brutality are in sharper focus, for the conflict between revolutionary action and dictatorial repressive measures comes close to the center of the stage. Yet this is no political play; we are not asked to take sides as between the brutal agents of authority and the platitude-mouthing revolutionary who sacrifices human sympathy to blind party discipline. . . . The real protagonist of the play is caught in "la petite manœuvre," that is, the political and social disorder of the day; but above all, he is caught—like the rest of us—in "la grande manœuvre," this is, the human condition itself. . . . The world of this play is like the world of ancient tragedy, for some of the characters seem to be agents of an implacable, cosmic malevolence, while others are victims. In the end, however, all are victims. . . . (p. 52)

Of all Adamov's plays, *La grande et la petite manœuvre* comes the closest, perhaps, to the author's idea of a modern theatre which, by its firmness and clarity, its force and immediacy, would constitute an autonomous art in which every element contributes to the total effect. From the rhythmic handclapping in the darkness and the derisive brutality of the policemen at the beginning to the mocking laughter of Erna as she pushes the armless, legless protagonist in his wheelchair out into the violence of the street at the end, the ten scenes of this play move with the irrational but relentless efficiency of the machine in Kafka's *Penal Colony*. In *La grande et la petite manœuvre*, as in Adamov's other works, there are no lyric outbursts, no psychological probings, no metaphysical disquisitions. This theatre is characterized by a kind of rigor in the dramatic progression, by the refusal of rhetorical embellishments, by a certain pure and naked violence rendered in action and in the simple language of everyday life stripped only of its triviality and surface "realism." (pp. 52-3)

Tous contre tous [*All Against All*], like Adamov's other plays, is a play about victims. Here there is a new note of courage and energy, however, for several of the victims transcend the passive, masochistic, Kafkaesque attitude of the protagonist of *La grande et la petite manœuvre* by the manner in which they meet death. There are no speeches on revolt or human dignity or love here, but there are simple actions which are directly meaningful in the total context of the play. For the first time, at the end of *Tous contre tous*, there is a very faint glimmer of light, there is a bit of pure air that we can breathe.

All of Adamov's plays to date rest upon the author's poignant apprehension of man's solitude and on his deep-seated feeling that "whatever he undertakes, man runs head on into the impossible," that "there is . . . no remedy for anything except for bagatelles." But the *word* "solitude" is never spoken in the plays, there are no disquisitions on metaphysics, no discursive conclusions. Everything is directly rendered in movement, gesture, sounds, objects, and in words which, as in our own lives, are but imperfect vehicles for communication. These things fill the physical space of the theatre and are grasped by

the spectator through his "histrionic sensibility" and his imagination. . . . (pp. 54-5)

One may feel, however, that in spite of his idea of the theatre as action literally expressed, Adamov's metaphysical "keys" are sometimes a bit too much in evidence and that they unlock a narrow domain which has been too often explored in our age, a dark, Kafkaesque tunnel which may prove to be a blind alley unless Adamov, whose gifts as a dramatist are outstanding, can find a way of widening or breaking out of the narrow passage. (p. 55)

Carlos Lynes, Jr., "Adamov or 'le sens litteral' in the Theatre," in Yale French Studies (copyright © Yale French Studies 1955), No. 14, Winter, 1954-55, pp. 48-56.

LEONARD CABELL PRONKO

Arthur Adamov has recently turned his back upon the avant-garde and upon his early plays that embodied more than those of any other dramatist the revolutionary principles expressed by Artaud in *The Theater and Its Double*. Adamov's last play, *Paolo Paoli* . . . , indicates a turning to the drama of social implications with a message, written in a quasi-realistic style. (p. 131)

[Adamov's early plays] are in great part an exorcism of private terrors. . . . [*La Parodie*, *La Grande et la petite manoeuvre*, *Le Sens de la marche* (*The Direction of the March*), and *Tous contre tous*] are such plays, long, loosely constructed, almost episodic works revealing the nightmare existence within a frightening and incomprehensible police state.

In an effort to correct certain excesses of his first play, Adamov turned from *La Parodie* to a work on a more specific subject, with a small cast and a more controlled technique. The result was *L'Invasion* [*The Invasion*] . . . , the first of four plays revealing an equally perplexing, but perhaps less frightening universe than the police state plays [*Le Professeur Taranne*, *Comme nous avons été*, and *Les Retrouvailles* (*The Recoveries*)]. . . . (pp. 131-32)

La Parodie is an attempt to embody in a crude and *visible* manner the themes of solitude and absence of communication suggested by the most common of everyday scenes. Like the other "police state" plays, *La Parodie* is an outgrowth of a close personal contact with Artaud the man and with his radical criticism of the conventional theater. In spite of Adamov's later skepticism regarding the value of Artaud's ideas, it is quite clear that the author of *The Theater and Its Double* has exercised an enormous influence on him. Adamov follows Artaud in his rejection of psychology, in his acceptance of the basic idea of a "theatre of cruelty," and in his utilization of the theater above all as a space to be occupied. . . . A play of Adamov must be seen to be appreciated, for the text is only a scenario, describing in rather great detail the physical movement that is to take place, and will constitute the major impact and the principal means of communicating with the audience. Dialogue has been reduced to dry and frequently dull platitudes without any of the humor or verve of Ionesco, or the naked, suggestive poetry of Beckett. The characters are often ciphers, represented by letters ("N" in *La Parodie*) or by generic names (The Mother, The Sister, The Happiest Woman, and so on). It is only with difficulty that we become involved in their plight, for they are rarely alive enough to elicit pity or sympathy.

The treatment is episodic rather than linear, and we must sometimes follow many characters with various symbolic values through a series of short tableaux with little apparent connection. . . . Adamov's works tend to be stillborn because they depend too exclusively upon the visual element, they are moving pictures, but they do not move in any particular direction (and this is, of course, part of the point). *Le sens de la marche* is nowhere, and we have no sense of beginning, middle, or end. The theater is indeed a scenic space to be filled, but it is much more than that, and by doing away with what Vilar whimsically calls the "lacework of dialogue and plot," Adamov has done away with two essentials of any dramatic production. . . . [The] spectator is usually not seized by a play of Adamov: there is too great a distance between actor and spectator, no warmth is generated by the characters, no interest fostered by the episodic treatment which lacks the minimum plot required to give form to the action of the play. Although what I have said can be pretty well applied to most of Adamov's theater, it is particularly true of what I have called his police state plays, typifying most radically the anti-theatrical play which renounces traditional dramatic categories. (pp. 132-34)

[The exorcism of Adamov's personal demons through his early plays] no doubt gives a certain immediacy and pathos to these plays, but at the same time it fills them with private symbolism and meanings which are so highly particular that they are not always easily transferable to the majority of spectators. Like the nightmares of others, we can view them objectively without being gripped ourselves. (p. 135)

The police state plays, however, . . . betray a social awareness and a political turn of mind. No matter how abstract they become, the characters are not inhabitants of the nonpolitical universe of Ionesco, or the asocial one of Beckett. On the contrary, they belong to a state that controls, dominates, and oppresses them, and they are aware of the social relationships existing between the people within the state, whether they be political leaders and refugees, or fathers and sons. (p. 137)

L'Invasion strikes me as one of Adamov's most satisfactory plays, because he has . . . conserved here the minimal plot that the spectator seems to require, and presented characters who are able to interest us as human beings rather than simply as allegorical figures with no human warmth. . . . At the same time, *L'Invasion* does not reject the technique which is Adamov's most original contribution to the avant-garde theater: his preoccupation with the stage as a space to be occupied, filled with *visible* meaning. In this one long play it seems to me he has hit that happy middle ground where we are both interested and challenged, where there is enough of traditional dramatic technique to keep us going, and enough that is new, or that is mysterious or incomprehensible at first, to keep us from relaxing into a passive attitude.

The reviewer of *Tous contre tous* in *France Illustration* sums up quite well the theater of Adamov when he says, "Few dramatists have cared less about pleasing than has M. Adamov." For Adamov during his experimental period and before his defection to the social theater, in protesting against the conventional theater of psychology went so far in the other direction that it was often difficult to join him at any point. Particularly in the police state plays, but also to some extent in the others of the same period, he rejected plot more completely than have either Beckett or Ionesco, spurned characterization, and relegated dialogue to a minor role in his universe where characters rarely say what they mean, and never succeed in really communicating with each other. Instead of cracking

and exploding dramatically, as does Ionesco's language, instead of dropping "like leaves, like sand," in an intense lyric overflow as does Beckett's, Adamov's dialogue simply drags along. Stressing the visible resources of the stage, he reminds us that drama is more than literature and that a play is only a play when it is presented on the boards before spectators. But the same may be said of ballet and pantomime, and it has been Adamov's error to deny certain essentials that distinguish drama from other genres in order to stress the importance of an element that is equally essential. Any theatrical revolution based uniquely upon the visible elements of theater will necessarily be a partial (and probably an abortive) revolution, for the simple reason that theater is a great deal more than a physical space to be filled. (pp. 138-40)

Leonard Cabell Pronko, "Theater and Anti-Theater," in his Avant-Garde: The Experimental Theater in France *(copyright © 1962 by The Regents of the University of California; reprinted by permission of the University of California Press), University of California Press, 1963, pp. 112-53.**

JACQUES GUICHARNAUD

Early in the 1950s any discussion of the current French stage was concentrated on three names uttered in the same breath—Ionesco-Adamov-Beckett—and in tones of surprised delight or indignation. (p. 196)

Today, however, the Ionesco-Adamov-Beckett trinity has lost its meaning. . . . Adamov defected: after having written a few plays comparable to those of Ionesco, situated in what he himself calls the no-man's-land of the theatre of the absurd, he repudiated the genre and moved in the direction of a Brechtian theatre. He thus set himself up as the head of a new "critical" drama, whose objective is the portrayal of a collective destiny, clearly situated in history. (p. 197)

[The] works of Arthur Adamov consist entirely of plays that surpass one another in a truly dialectical manner. Furthermore, he has written, parallel to his theatre, a body of texts made up of explanations, discussions, political and aesthetic stands—and remorse. His meditations on Strindberg, Chekhov, and Brecht, each of whom influenced him in turn, have the distinction of always being sharply critical, even when they are admiring and enthusiastic. In fact, the debate now dividing French playwrights into Marxists and anti-ideologists would be far more fruitful if Ionesco, in his theoretical texts, displayed as much intelligence as Adamov, who knows how to go beyond invective and self-defense and really come to grips with the basic questions concerning the future and essence of the theatre. What counts more than the debate, however, is the series of theatrical experiments—however unequal in value—that constitute Adamov's theatre.

Having begun with a theatre of dreams, Adamov moved off in the direction of documentary dramas (*Le Printemps 71* [*Spring 71*] being an extreme example) and then reintegrated his dream world, or what he calls "neurosis," into works which "would be *forced* always to take place on the borders of individual life and collective life" and which would express "everything that . . . links man to his own ghosts, but also, but as well, to other men and hence to their ghosts, and all of this within a given era, which is not a bit ghostly." Finding the no-man's-land of the plays during the 1950s too limited because it obliged the writers to go round in circles within their eternal commonplaces, Adamov wanted to give man a more complete and more concrete image—that is, to restore his social and historical dimensions by means of a synthesis of the two visions, thus achieving a total portrayal of man's condition. Obviously, his evolution consists less in repudiating past experiences than in criticizing them, in order to recover them for use on another level.

For this reason, certain constants are characteristic of Adamov's works as a whole. The most striking is the use of fantasies—private fantasies, reconstructed fantasies, or fantasies borrowed from psychiatric works. In *Le Printemps 71* . . . they are replaced by an objective form—political allegories inspired by Daumier's drawings—but this was merely an intellectual detour, reabsorbed into *Sainte-Europe* [*Holy Europe*] . . . , in which allegorical cartoons and the imagination's dreams are synthesized in the nightmarish behavior of characters who are at once Ubuesque monsters, medieval figures, and politicians of the Common Market. Essentially, Adamov's devices are drawn from the realm of dream, obsession, and delirium. (pp. 198-99)

Whether [his] plays belong to the traditional absurd or have some precise political significance, they are always objective representations of fantasy: the absurd, nonsense, nightmares, and madness are free of the blurred effects that would make them "ghostly." As in Ionesco, all that happens on stage is presented naïvely as a solid reality, not as a floating dream. *Le Professeur Taranne* is based on a shameful and very common fantasy—that of finding oneself suddenly nude or in some obscene posture in public. But the play relates the fantasy in terms of an event experienced in the waking state. . . . [Beyond] the impression of nightmare, yet because of it, the spectator—who has not been enchanted by any great display of poetic whimsey—is struck by an impression that reflects on the normal world: that of the instability of the real, the possibility of ordinary situations taking unforeseeable directions with the same apparent necessity as they are generally accorded, and the resulting terror.

Neurosis, then, has a double value in Adamov's theatre. Being real, it can be presented in terms that are used for other realities, but it is at the same time a reflection or, as it were, a way of living parallel to what is usually considered the normal world. Scenically, it legitimately represents that world, and by transposing a mental image into outer reality, the playwright both remains faithful to reality and presents it with a theatrical distance. Adamov was Brechtian before even meditating on Brecht.

Within this general phantasmagoria one particular motif persists throughout Adamov's works—that of the object. Here again comparisons can be made with the proliferation of things in Ionesco's plays (*L'Invasion,* for example, where Adamov's characters are drowned in piles of unreadable papers, the archives of a dead man, trying obstinately to give them some meaning), for Adamov is obviously haunted by objects—their unjustified presence, the meaning society gives to them, and questions as to their real meaning. (pp. 199-200)

Thus, while Adamov derided the metaphor in Ionesco's *Le Nouveau Locataire,* he himself makes use of a similar obsession. He tries, however, to avoid the ontological stalemate created by it. Eliminating the absurd from the substance of his plays if not from the form, he *explains* the obsession in sociopolitical terms, relating it to a collective state of consciousness created by the modern world. In *Ping-Pong,* for example, the pinball machine is a product deliberately exploited by a consortium; in other words, if certain men founder in futility

and the absurd, it is because they are the indirectly brainwashed victims of profiteers. (p. 201)

On this level, *La Politique des restes* [*The Politics of Waste*] is perhaps Adamov's most modern play—not so much in form (the trial of a white South African who has killed a black man is presented through traditional flashbacks) as in his use of an object psychosis, which does not naïvely explain the protagonist's racism but is structurally parallel to it. Little is said during the trial to indicate that one is the cause of the other; there is simply a constant crisscross of the two themes—an obsession with the refuse of the world (cigarette butts, old torn-up tickets, kitchen peelings, and so on) and a fear of the expansion of the black population. It is not until the play is over that the spectator sees the significant relationship between the two and realizes that the racist murderer grasps the accumulation of civilization's refuse and the multiplication or political rise of the blacks in one act of consciousness, feeling equally and identically threatened by them both. Without foundering in a demonstrative discourse, the play is a gripping metaphor of one vision of the modern world, in which a proliferation of refuse and a proliferation of human beings leads to the same terror.

The two motifs also lead to a specific judgment. Most of Adamov's plays clearly establish, deductively or structurally, the equivalence of the profitable exploitation of objects and of man. (pp. 201-02)

The theme of the man-object as a victim is the second constant in Adamov's works. Once again his point of departure is an existential anguish typical of the theatre of the fifties. More expressionistic or Germanic in form than Ionesco's or Beckett's, his plays point up the tragedy of conscious and irreplaceable subjectivity being incomprehensibly massacred, humiliated, or mutilated by the world. The form is more expressionistic because his imagery not only is painted with bold strokes but suggests the world more in terms of social universality than in terms of cosmic universality. In Adamov's absurd plays, as in all the plays of that school, what the spectator sees onstage is at first given as no more than what he sees. The difference comes when the spectator tries to set up a parallel with the perceived reality of his own life. . . . [With Adamov], one pole of the conflict is a social specificity, the other being the individual, of course, but the individual situated socially. If the individual is a victim, it is because the social system can be maintained only by an anti-Kantian procedure. Adamov's plays are all centered on that blind victimization (*La Grande et La Petite Manoeuvre,* for example) or on a refusal of it (*Le Printemps 71*) as well as on an aesthetic revenge: the playwright himself transforms into objects—that is, into puppets—the social forces that feed on the dehumanization of man.

Adamov's theatre is thus committed and openly Marxist—and hence is unacceptable, on principle, to a great number of French critics. Their judgments, however, must be largely dismissed, for what really matters is Adamov's dramatic experimentation—the manner in which he began with the absurd and expressionism, absorbed them, and then went beyond them, without actually repudiating them. For him that which is concerned only with "eternal" situations, is idealistic in nature and thus futile. What really interests him is that the modern form of his theatre have a practical significance "here and now." . . . (pp. 202-03)

Adamov's plays are not altogether didactic. They are primarily a theatrical transposition of "mechanisms." In the early plays the universal mechanisms of the dream that paralyzes the individual and the totalitarianism that mutilates people or chooses scapegoats are not linear; their horror comes largely from the dialectic of the fallacious hope and the real despair that they impose on the individual, the better to crush him. At the other extreme, *Le Printemps 71,* which demonstrates the failure of the first proletarian revolution, is concerned not with a universal mechanism of society but with a specific event unique in history—the Commune. Indeed, all of Adamov's plays are haunted by the workings of human affairs. He shows how, mechanically (and dialectically), the individual is crushed as a Negro is killed, a revolution comes to grief, or a Holy Alliance is formed (an economic alliance, since this is the twentieth century). In fact, Adamov is the theatrical poet of mechanisms.

Adamov has been faced with a serious dilemma, however, for while each mechanism may have dramatic potential, it is primarily an object of science. Reconstruction—boring even during the period of Romanticism and local color . . .—requires a juxtaposition of details and a fidelity to all kinds of trifling vicissitudes that may be fascinating in a history book but are monotonous on stage. If the playwright transposes or poetizes, his only recourse is allegory, which may charm the imagination but which, since it reflects an intellectual study of the problem, obscures the historical event more than it adds the distance necessary for criticism. Adamov is still hesitant about the means to establish that distance: he has tried the contrast between an imaginary anecdote and the interjection of historical documents (*Paolo Paoli*), the contrast between a fresco of revolutionaries' daily lives and allegorical interludes (*Le Printemps 71*), the almost medieval transpostition of a contemporary political mechanism (*Sainte-Europe*), and, perhaps most successfully, the parallel that may exist between an individual psychosis and a collective attitude (*La Politique des restes*). In the last case the double game of participation (we who belong to a world that is essentially racist are hypocritically urged to commit racist murder) and distance (the racist murderer in the play is mad by any standards—that is to say, a creature separate from us, who bears the weight of our intellectual and objective judgment) is convincing. Adamov simultaneously dissects two mechanisms, remaining faithful both to his own temperament and to his ideology. Influenced by Brecht—not as a disciple but as a critic—he might create a new and significant committed theatre if, beyond his defection from the no-man's-land of the absurd, he continues to resist copying Brecht and avoids the oversimplified and tortuous intellectualism of *Sainte-Europe.* (pp. 204-05)

> *Jacques Guicharnaud, "Dialectic Continued," in his* Modern French Theatre *(copyright © 1967 by Yale University), revised edition, Yale University Press, 1967, pp. 157-212.**

RICHARD E. SHERRELL

To show in a theatrical event, as largely and visibly as possible, human solitude and the absence of communication—this became Adamov's goal in turning to the theatre. (pp. 110-11)

Adamov's characters do not really communicate with one another. Human understanding is very problematic. He consciously creates a dialogue in [*L'Invasion*] which makes the characters speak past each other. . . . In writing for the theatre a dialogue that "drags along," he is thereby intensifying an image which sees man unable to transcend his situation through flights of language. We must also note that it is precisely the language of the manuscript that is so problematic for Pierre [in *L'Invasion*]. No single word is unambiguously identifiable and thus capable of carrying a precise meaning. A language which does not communicate, which limps along, which is even obscure in being written down, is a language that intensifies Adamov's vision of man who cannot do without language, but who also cannot fulfill his life through language. (pp. 120-21)

Pierre is presented as a member of a group which is engaged with him in the task he personally feels most reponsible for. His sense of reponsibility, with its attendant compulsions and pressures upon Agnés, together with his method of procedure, in time drives a wedge between him and his colleagues. An open question is whether he willingly withdraws from community or whether he is forced into withdrawal by his commitment. While his individuality is heightened in his withdrawal, we do not see much evidence of it because he is in isolation in his room off stage, and eventually completely isolated in death. . . . He is man *in situ,* without a history, a future except as his task be pursued. The meaning of his existence is the nonmeaning of the manuscript which has invaded his life, leaving him an "occupied territory" without even a "provisional government" which can administrate within the tension presented by an unfulfillable and inescapable task. (pp. 122-23)

[The Professor in *Professor Taranne* also] discloses himself to be an exceedingly self-centered man. He has no relationships with anyone which would indicate concern and interest in others. Except insofar as the actions of others directly concern what he thinks is his own welfare, he is totally unconcerned with them. The one possible exception might be his sister, Jeanne. He does relate to her as something of an equal, but her essential relationship to him is merely that of the bearer of his final betrayal as unself-knowing at best, and as carping hypocrite at worst. We know nothing of her as a person; she is the last in a devastating series of mediators of self-knowledge to Taranne. (p. 126)

It is by no means clear whether Professor Taranne is a free agent confronted with a monstrous conspiracy of circumstances bent upon his destruction or whether he is a fraud by some inner compulsion, who is at last exposed for what he really is. That he is alone is undoubted. He shares in no meaningful community with anyone. . . . In the face of an apparently absurd world, he opts to enact his guilt [through indecent exposure], thus becoming guilty existentially. This final gesture of guilt-acceptance grants a kind of tragic stature to Taranne. We are left with an image of isolated man whose only means of asserting his identity is a gesture, and in this case a gesture by which he intensifies his isolation and guilt.

Adamov's man is alone, bewildered by the circumstances of his existence, bound by a sense of responsibility, though incapable of effectively discharging it, unable to achieve significance through language, and finally reduced to a gesture of alienation and withdrawal as the sole means of asserting identity. Both Pierre and Professor Taranne feel a responsibility toward their vocations: deciphering the manuscript in the case of Pierre, and university lecturing in the case of Taranne. In differing ways, they both come to the realization that language fails them. Their final gestures are made in silence and are gestures of self-alienation from their worlds. (pp. 127-29)

In Adamov's vision, man is affirmed as a creature who has responsibility, who is guilty in the face of failure to discharge his responsibility, but who is caught in a metaphysical situation in which neither language nor reason can save him. All efforts come to the same end: radical isolation and death. Man's final act is a gesture of resignation. But this is a theatrical gesture, enacted in an event of the theatre and on a stage taken by Adamov as a space to be filled. Thus man's gesture of resignation takes on both the qualities of an artistic resolution to his envisioned condition, as well as the symbolic values of a metaphysical assertion. . . . In Adamov's vision, man is revealed as both responsible and guilty, as isolated from his world and finally reduced to a gesture which intensifies his exile. (p. 129)

> *Richard E. Sherrell, "Arthur Adamov," in his* The Human Image: Avant Garde and Christian *(© 1969 by M. E. Bratcher; reprinted by permission of the author), John Knox Press, 1969, pp. 110-29.*

D. M. CHURCH

With his last play, published posthumously, Adamov has come full circle; *Si l'été revenait* is primarily an exposition of a psychological nature, not a call to revolutionary action such as we have come to expect. (p. 180)

[While] Adamov's early plays present psychological subjects in something of a vacuum—semi-archetypal characters moving through a dream world that bears little relation to any specific real place—*Si l'été revenait* attaches the dreams to a quite solid reality—credible individuals moving in the definite and specific context of present-day Sweden. What is constant is the use of dreams to reveal otherwise hidden psychological truths. The vision in the early plays was relatively comprehensible, for the dream was Adamov's own and the distortions imposed by the device were at least consistent. This last play, however, is quite obscure, primarily because we see, in four dreams, events distorted from the points of view of four different dreamers: Lars, a young man who has been expelled from Medical School; his sister Thea, with whom he has an incestuous relationship; his wife Brit, and their friend Alma, whose androgynous nature links her to both Lars and Brit. Three other important characters—Mme Petersen, mother of Lars and Thea; Viktor, a friend somewhat older than the others, and the Rector of the Medical School—remain even more enigmatic because, since they do not dream, we do not see their points of view; they seem almost to exist only on a symbolic level.

Si l'été revenait is not a play of development but one of exposition. Instead of a traditional plot we see different events in jumbled and varying chronological order from the four points of view. All the dreams seem to come long after the facts detailed in them, even after the deaths of two of the dreamers. The only progression in the play is the growing awareness of the multiple facets of the characters and their relationships, the gradual exposition of their ambivalent feelings of love, hate, guilt, gratitude, and dependence. A recurrent image of various characters swinging while others push the swing seems to represent a summer of bliss for which all are nostalgic but which remains unattainable since their complex relationships always destroy the cooperation needed to make the swing work.

The play does contain socio-political elements, underlined by the setting in Sweden, where liberal socialism would seem to provide the best chances for social justice. But each time a character tries to engage in social action he fails, largely because of his own sado-masochistic neuroses. The result is a feeling of bitter disillusionment that perhaps indicates Ada-

mov's own feeling. *Si l'été revenait* does not represent a total surprise; each of Adamov's plays after *Le Printemps 71* shows hints of the return to the beginnings. Psychological elements and the use of dreams appear with increasing frequency in the later plays, accompanied by a growing sense of pessimism and disillusionment with social action. It is significant that Adamov chose to republish *L'Aveu,* the early exposé of his personal neuros, along with other later tales of desolate eroticism as *Je . . . ils . . .* in 1969 and that the penultimate play *Off-limits* shows social action resulting in defeat and suicide. In the final analysis, *Si l'été revenait,* with its disillusionment and multiple suicides, is probably less revealing of the characters in the play than of the final developments of Adamov's own life. (pp. 180-81)

> *D. M. Church, "Reviews: 'Si l'été revenait'," in* The French Review *(copyright 1971 by the American Association of Teachers of French), Vol. XLV, No. 1, October, 1971, pp. 180-81.*

MARGARET DIETEMANN

In *Le Ping-Pong* an electric pinball machine holds the diverse strands of the action together. Arthur and Victor, the play's protagonists, waste their lives planning and executing improvements on it. The machine is not, however, a symbol of the complexity of the social system. Rather, it is a source of conversation. . . . It elicits religious, aesthetic, philosophic, and social response from all those who come in contact with it. The machine is, above all, however, a sexual fetish. Indeed, its magnetic attraction for all the characters in the play has clearly marked sexual overtones. The language with which they discuss its operation, its rods, corridors, flippers, bumpers, the ecstasy of winning, the despair of losing, is a coded language instantly decipherable to the spectator. It is a game which all must play—artist, professional, schoolgirl, old or young, willing or not.

Because the machine is there, the characters in the play must talk about it, and in Adamov's world the word always precedes the act, stimulates it, in fact. But the words at the disposal of the characters are nothing but clichés, stereotypes, and truisms which can only produce mechanical response in mechanically conditioned individuals. The tragedy one feels in Adamov's theatre comes from the fact that its characters mean what they say. Furthermore, like the spectators who watch them, they have a limited vocabulary which must suffice to denote an unlimited reality. The language of a basic mechanism, the sex drive, has long been the one used to designate the social processes of production and consumption of goods and services. A cursory examination of the prose of modern advertising is ample evidence of this fact. Thus the lyrical response of Arthur and Victor to the joys of the machine is a pitiful attempt to say what cannot be said, because the meaning of the words they must use hopelessly oscillates between their essential sexual need and the acquisitive commercial need that has been grafted on to it. (pp. 49-50)

Le Ping-Pong is the first of a series of plays with an essentially political slant. The machine generates around itself a sort of miniature social structure. From a Marxian viewpoint it contains its own antithesis, in that it destroys the strength and enthusiasm of those who might perpetuate it. More importantly, it permits the characters in the play to interract socially, and allows them an existence which is more than a mirror of the psychological struggles within the author.

Moreover, since they interract in a pattern determined by the possibilities latent in the linguistic stimuli generated by the machine, and since these stimuli are both sexually and socially conditioned, the characters behave both psychologically and socially. Adamov obviously intended this dramatic demonstration to force his spectators to respond to the sexual stimuli of the language, while they react intellectually, and therefore politically, to his grotesque tableaux of an essentially trivial game played in dead earnest.

This interaction of mechanically conditioned individuals within a miniature system has of course generic implications. While Adamov's characters were under the control of monstrous and cosmic forces, their actions took on tragic, or at least melodramatic, stature. Their struggles against the forces that controlled them were at best frightening, and at the least, pitiful. But if, as Bergson suggested, the comic is the mechanical grafted upon the human, then these mechanically conditioned creatures are comic. . . . [Adamov] was aware . . . that he had moved into the time sequence of comedy in exchanging a closed and deterministic world for one which admits a dialectical movement. Where there is choice and the creatures on stage make choices that the audience perceives as being stupid or silly, then the laughter of superiority and derision will break out at the spectacle on stage. In this play Adamov had begun his breakthrough into the genre of social satire.

In *Paolo Paoli* Adamov attempted for the first time a political satire of the twentieth-century world. . . . This play is a new genre for Adamov, tragic farce. For its message is that from such farcical behavior came the tragedy of World War I. In it Adamov treated pre-1914 society as if it were a work of art in which any part must contain the image of the whole. And in a society whose ideal was conspicuous waste, the most conspicuously wasteful activities must have been the most representative.

In structure *Paolo Paoli* is a transformation of Adamov's early theatre. Although there are again two protagonists, Hulot-Vasseur and Paolo Paoli are not two parts of a single consciousness but the necessary poles of a system of exchange. . . . [The] circular and repetitive actions which we again see portrayed are no longer the activities of a frightened soul repeating fetishistic gestures to ward off an undefined threat. They are the activities of people caught in a network of social demands that forces them to an endless exchange of goods, in which the exchange process itself is its own end. Here the patterns of reaction are meant to reflect outer and not inner reality. Adamov transposed to the stage a lesson which he had recently learned from Mao. Like Mao, Adamov believed that an economic system which pushes each nation to continue to widen its area of exchange must inevitably push it to vie with other nations for the same markets and resources, leading to class struggle and international war. And through the highly selective realism of his play he was trying to use the theatrical form itself to illustrate and persuade. . . . It is Marxist theatre. (pp. 50-2)

Le Printemps 71 is, as its title suggests, a play about time. Adamov's favorite object, paper—in this case the newspaper *Le Cri du peuple*—is the focus of the action. In every scene we see it being written, diffused, read, and discussed. It circulates through the Commune as blood circulates through an organism, for the newspaper is an embodiment of the time that provokes this drama, that is to say, the time gap between event and knowledge. (p. 52)

Nine "guignols" or allegorical interludes are interspaced within the twenty-six tableaux which comprise the action. (pp. 52-3)

[These] "guignols" are meant to be such inhuman caricatures of men that no identification can be possible, yet they must retain enough human characteristics so that they cannot be mistaken for superhuman or metaphysical forces beyond the control of men. The audience must see them as grotesquely perverted humans, historical monsters. Thus Adamov's spectators today can at once reject their perversion and learn, as the contemporaries of Thiers and Bismarck did not, ways of controlling their destructiveness. Adamov was thus attempting to modify an avant-garde technique and give it a new function in his theatre. (p. 53)

Technically, the "guignols" are dramatized history lessons which eliminate necessity for lengthy exposition within the narrative portion of the play. The "guignols" are Adamov's answer to the problem of spectator participation in epic drama. The spectator asks nothing better than to identify with the actors on stage; yet it is difficult to identify and still maintain the rational critical stance which Adamov believed is the one that the spectator should be led to take. Therefore Adamov broke his play into a parallel form intended to alternately attract and repel, to permit empathy while provoking judgment. (pp. 53-4)

[With *La Politique des restes,* Adamov] returned to the type of play he had favored in his "absurd" period. Its plot is double: we enter into the psychological fears of the protagonist, Johnny Brown, whose neurotic terror of the proliferation of dirt and waste has focused on a black man, Tom Guiness, whom he has murdered. We also witness the agony of a society, white society, which sees a threat to its supremacy in the higher birth rate and increasing claims for social justice of the Negro. Thus the Negro is the center of this drama, that point where the psychological and the social intersect. The universe of the play resembles Adamov's old one, where fear is the motor of all activity. But here it is no longer metaphysical dread, but rather the fear of those who realize the precariousness of the structure of their society and the tenuousness of their social domination. In fact, the neurosis of the madman Johnny Brown is different only in intensity from the mental state of the "sane" members of his society. (p. 54)

If we place this play in a structural continuum starting with *La Parodie* and going on through *La Grande et la Petite Manoeuvre* and *Tous contre tous,* we can see how it is the ultimate statement of a series of theatrical essays which progressively seek to investigate the nature of the fear that pervades our society. In the first, the social basis of personal terror is present only in an embryonic state (police whistles, sirens, faceless crowds). In the second, individual and collective conditions are shown as parallel but not necessarily interrelated ("Le Mutilé" is destroyed by interior voices and "Le Militant" by social actions); *Tous contre tous* shows both psychological and social life to be controlled by a single inexorable mechanism, the circular nature of apparent change. *La Politique des restes* at last explores the nature of that circularity—and discovers that individual neurosis and collective injustice are mutually reactive, one causing and perpetuating the other. (pp. 54-5)

[*Sainte Europe*] is an allegory in which places, characters, and ideas shimmer back and forth between the medieval and the modern worlds. . . . The theme of the crusade against the east, a medieval creation, connects the two time periods, although here it is shown to be a diversionary tactic of the establishment (keep the colonels busy) or part of neocolonial diplomacy (hold on to a market for manufactured goods).

The play has a triadic structure which conforms to Adamov's view of the triple reality of our time. He believed that power, religion, and money are united in a last desperate holding action against the legitimate aspirations of the disenfranchised. (pp. 55-6)

In this play the dream is not so much an expressionistic technique for revealing interiority as a satirical device for pointing out the discrepancy between gesture and motivation, and for provoking in the spectator an awareness of the imprint of objective reality on psychological processes. The dream sequences in *Sainte Europe* have this in common with the "guignols" of *Le Printemps 71:* they are distancing devices and allegorical commentaries upon the narrative. They also underline the layers of disguise in which modern political reality conceals itself. For the play is a masquerade superimposed upon a masquerade. The culminating scene of the masked ball shows the characters donning medieval disguises. . . . (p. 56)

But we are constantly made aware that outside this phony world is a real world, suffering and angry. We hear of floods, fires, murder, cancer, torture, insurrection, strikes. But this world is not primarily threatening to us, as were the noises off stage in Adamov's first plays. Rather, it threatens the monsters on stage. It is a distillation of the anger that Adamov believed would sweep away these grotesque puppets, which we are led to laugh at derisively.

The language of the play is as grotesque as the action. And similarly, it shimmers back and forth between the medieval and the modern. . . . (pp. 56-7)

But most striking is the way in which the language of the play alternates between . . . inflated rhetoric and doggerel verse. Here rhetoric is obviously the tool which the establishment uses to prevent others from seeing the social reality it conceals, while the real thoughts of the characters are so degraded that only doggerel can express them.

Thus this is a theatre of indirect reference whose every structure is meant to remind the spectator that he is expected to make a critical judgment of a time, his own. The medieval-modern poles of language, action, and characterization are Adamov's distancing device, his mechanism for provoking thought. (p. 57)

[*M. le modéré* offers] evidence of Adamov's desire to give new meanings to the techniques of the "avant-garde," which he had come to despise. . . . M. le modéré is preoccupied with self, not because he is a frightened victim at the mercy of forces beyond his control, but because he is the representative of a social order whose illness is a diseased egotism. His paralysis is both a symbol of his guilt—he has tortured and killed to retain power—and a symptom of his basic uselessness; he contributes nothing to society. His sexual aberration indicates the historical extent of his depravity. (p. 58)

[The] great difference between *M. le modéré* and the early plays, which it superficially resembles, lies in its point of view. This play is a "clownerie," a parade of clowns, individuals with no interior life, no psychology. It is a masque of fools with whom there can be no spectator identification. M. le modéré's itinerary is not a projection of an inner quest, but an allegorical rise and fall of a petty politician who moves from proprietor of a sleazy hotel to dictator, and ends in the political refuse heap of a London exile. He begins as a cheat, becomes a bully, and ends a sniveling drunk. The geographic signposts

along his route underline the fact that this is a political and not a metaphysical journey. In Paris he is a parvenu, in Switzerland the pawn of American imperialism, and in London the impotent spectator of a round of games: tennis, croquet, and archery fill the empty and useless days of his mindless circle. (pp. 58-9)

[Adamov] adapted the characters, language, and generative objects that he first created as projections of his personal anguish to a theatre asking pertinent social questions. (p. 59)

> *Margaret Dietemann, "Departure from the Absurd: Adamov's Last Plays," in* Yale French Studies *(copyright ©Yale French Studies 1971), No. 46, 1971, pp. 48-59.*

JOHN FLETCHER

Nearly all [Adamov's] plays are political in one way or another, being derived from his experience as a rootless intellectual who, in a very human way, was subject to terrifying dreams of injustice and persecution. His early work, written and performed around 1950, is undoubtedly his finest achievement, since it springs with such intensity from his personal sufferings and fears. His very first play, *La Parodie,* . . . is a depressing but impressively claustrophobic image of modern life. . . . The play as a whole shows little development (except that N, who had masochistically craved death at Lili's hands, is in fact run over by a car); it is a simple *constat d'échec,* an intense, personal, rather naked, and perhaps narrow, vision of things. In an understated, unexplicit play such as this, the dramatic power generated arises from the initial situation projected; the problem for the playwright is then to harness this energy and get it to drive the play forward. Like Genet, who is faced with a similar difficulty in some of his work, Adamov does not quite solve the problem in *La Parodie,* which remains a grey, rather drab play. . . . (p. 194)

L'Invasion . . . is clearly better; it has more of a recognisable plot, and is set in a more readily indentifiable milieu. Pierre is editing the papers of his dead brother-in-law, and himself dies in the attempt. His wife runs off with Le Premier Venu (puckishly called so in the play); this, and the chilling presence of Pierre's mother, who insinuates herself between husband and wife and proffers reactionary opinions about the immigrants she reads of in the papers, are the themes which recur in the next two plays, *La Grande et la Petite Manoeuvre* and *Tous contre tous.*

Like *L'Invasion,* they are about fear, about pressure and influence, and about the weakness of the individual who attempts to resist. Whereas, though, *L'Invasion* was almost a *pièce mondaine* (not unlike Cocteau's *Parents terribles,* in fact), with only a hint about politics in the mother's remarks, these works deal explicitly with such menaces as police repression and political chicanery. So far, however, the politics remains undirected. . . . (pp. 194-95)

[A] play like *Tous contre tous,* which is one of Adamov's best, constitutes a ruthless exposure of intolerance, cowardice, the abuse of power by racial minorities as well as by racial majorities, and of the dishonest hollowness of the kind of political rhetoric which covers such abuses and blatantly excuses self-interest. . . . The play, whose title is well-chosen, is in fact about the cruelty of all political life: the 'réfugiés' are alternately harried and courted, with cynical opportunism, according to the political needs of the moment. Adamov projects a world . . . in which we witness the disgusting treachery of those who are politically afraid, and in which we observe the shifting quicksands of political fortune, of anarchy and disorder, of rhetoric and menace, and the consequential spinelessness of those involved. The conclusion is lucid and detached: in such a climate only the shrewdest opportunists survive, like Darbon; the rest, both the genuine and courageous like Noémi, or the shabby and grovelling like the loathsome Mother and the refugee Zenno, go under. The play ends with one of the most effective codas in all political theatre: the stage is cleared and four shots ring out, the last of which silences the Mother. (pp. 195-96)

Adamov's best work is that which arises from his personal fears and obsessions, and his worst from an over-ambitious if well-meant attempt to write plays that would turn away from those fears to the injustices of the social universe. It is a pity that such an honest and likable man, who exposes himself, without vanity if not without silliness, in *Ici et maintenant,* was not able to achieve his ambition of writing a committed drama. . . . The truth is that Adamov was more successful in dealing in broad symbolic terms with the human condition, its miseries, anxieties and acts of self-deceit, than he was in showing up the iniquities of a given politico-economic system.

If Adamov's contribution to the permanent repertoire should in the end turn out to be slender, there is no doubting his historical importance in vitally assisting, at a certain moment in time, in the fixing of the idiom of [a] new theatre. . . . (pp. 196-97)

What one misses is a certain playfulness . . . , the conception of his drama is rarely witty. Like all dream plays, Adamov's draw their strength from the power of evocation through unassigned symbols in which universal but vague anxieties are figured in stage action; this is not devoid of a certain ponderous monotony, for which, in the end, one does not feel the originality of the manner and the technical smoothness and efficiency (such as the trick of achieving transitions through a momentary darkening of the stage) really compensate. It now seems clear that for all his intelligence and sensitivity, Adamov was only a relatively minor dramatist. (pp. 197-98)

> *John Fletcher, "Conclusion: Towards a New Concept of Theatre, Adamov, Beckett and Arrabal," in* Forces in Modern French Drama, *edited by John Fletcher (copyright © 1972 by Hodder & Stoughton Ltd., formerly University of London Press, Ltd), University of London Press, 1972, pp. 188-210.**

JOHN H. REILLY

Adamov's writing is a desperate attempt to relate to the world around him, to find a way of adjusting to the nightmare of living. The dramatist himself is the subject of his plays, and every one of his works, whether a part of his personal theater or of his political commitment, is a representation of the deep and vital concerns of the playwright. Looked at in their totality, his plays are an extraordinary account of a man and his alienation and separation, for, basically, this is a theater of separation. (p. 153)

It is not by accident that his plays . . . are, in one form or another, dream plays, which come from the world of nightmares, the real world of the dramatist. In all of his writings, the characters are people who have lost or are about to lose the battle with life. In this mélange of masochism, remorse, frustration, and hostility, Adamov's figures continually experience one sentiment: fear, especially fear of death. From

his first play to his last, his characters are confronted with and surrounded by death. At times, as in the case of "N," this becomes a sign of the futility and hopelessness of living and simply the final destruction of a life that has already been destroyed. At other moments, it is a means of escape, as in Pierre's suicide or Sally's and Jim's willful death. Death can also be brought about by man's inhumanity to his fellowman as in *Spring 71.* In the overall context, it is evident that the "incurable" aspect of life [as Adamov calls the anguish of existence] is always at the basis of each one of Adamov's plays. While the "curable" side of existence [as Adamov calls the social and political aspects] provided him with a temporary diversion or a sort of life raft to which to cling, the playwright never forgot his primary image of the helplessness of man adrift in the universe. (pp. 153-54)

[We] can see a pattern in Adamov's writings in which he struggled to cope with life, attempted to achieve a sense of maturity. . . . All of his plays deal with justice or injustice in one form or another, accompanied by masochistic guilt feelings as well as a desire to blame others. The real development can be seen in the manner in which Adamov handled these feelings and, in that respect, came to limited terms with reality.

In the first plays, the dramatist was concerned with the nameless, frightening forces which prevented him from functioning as a human being. Sometimes these forces came from an indifferent fate, with everybody sharing the same final destiny, death. Other times, as in *The Maneuver* [or *The Great and the Small Maneuver*], fate turned out to be man's own psyche, his obsessions and neuroses having taken control. In *Professor Taranne,* his best play in this early period, Adamov continued to explore this theme: man as the victim of unknown opponents, either within himself or within the universe. Eventually, he tried to trace the responsibility to more specific sources. At first, he placed the blame on the family: Father, mother, sister all share the responsibility. It was probably necessary that he put some of the burden on their shoulders, if only to alleviate the terrible guilt feelings which he felt toward all three. . . . With the father, mother, and sister figures, the Adamov hero alternates between an almost incapacitating sense of guilt and a rejection of this burden placed upon him, moving from a masochistic acceptance of recrimination to a rebellion against the people responsible.

A similar ambivalent, love-hate relationship applies as well to the playwright's treatment of women. In *The Parody,* the writer established his concept of the eternal female: faithless, flitting from one man to another, cruel, indifferent. Later, in *The Maneuver,* the woman becomes as emasculating as the mother, rendering the man helpless and ineffective, inevitably having her share of the responsibility for the central character's incapacity to deal with the adult, mature world. At the same time, however, woman is also the source of most of his hope for the future. While Pierre in *The Invasion* recognizes that Agnès brings disorder and chaos into his life, he also realizes that she is the basis of his creativity and that a relationship with her is the only means at his disposal to a reasonable, sane acceptance of life. (pp. 154-55)

If his theater is any indication, Adamov did find a period in his life when his personal neuroses were under some sort of control, thereby allowing him to turn his attention to another area of interest—the political and socioeconomic systems of the capitalist enterprise. In effect, however, this new phase was really only a logical extension of the feeling of injustice and persecution which was at the base of all of his works. This time he directed it against the capitalist system. . . . *Paolo Paoli* and *Spring 71* were strongly and clearly political plays, expressing the author's outrage over social injustices, and indicating his concern for his fellow human beings, notably those of the working class. Curiously, in spite of his proclaimed affection for the workers and his intent to write for them, many of his succeeding plays had little to do with the laboring class, since the dramas were situated in a bourgeois, middle-class atmosphere.

In this second phase of his writing, Adamov had evidently come to more rational terms with himself. The somewhat irritating plaint of the victim had disappeared, but had been replaced with a didactic, strident voice. Now man could find a measure of hope in taking action, committing himself, solving the "curable" problems of life; he was no longer totally the helpless plaything of fate. At the same time, the dramatist was acutely aware that his theater could not ignore life's "incurable" matters. In *The Politics of Waste,* he began to forge a link between the individual's obsessions and society's neuroses. It was this attempt that led him into his third phase in which he tried to find a balance between the realm of the neurosis and the structure of the world in which one lives, the merger of the personal and the political. (pp. 155-56)

The playwright's personal situation and its expression are the most important aspects of Adamov's theater, but not the only part worthy of consideration. His theater is also an innovative, inventive use of the stage and, while not totally successful in this respect, it is nonetheless a fascinating experiment in drama. If the term "theater of the absurd" can apply to the dramatist at all, it is most appropriately used in referring to his bold use of the acting area. . . . Like Artaud, Adamov held the view that the stage was a treasure house of unique interrelationships between dialogue, mime, setting, lighting, music. The stage was to be a visual, concrete representation of the theme to be expressed. "N.," lying prone on the floor, can suggest his real situation more clearly than words in this case; the step-by-step mutilation of the *Mutilé* conveys more stunningly than dialogue the frightening disintegration which the playwright wanted to express; the physical disorder in Pierre's house is a vivid realization of the disorder in his inner being. Objects also assumed a vital importance: The preeminence of the mother's chair in *The Invasion* powerfully emphasizes her control over her son; the woman's bicycle in *The Reunions* [or *The Recoveries*] expresses clearly the protagonist's inability to function as a man; the seesaw in *If Summer Should Return* is a vivid example of the desire for balance and equilibrium; and the pinball machine in *Ping-Pong* becomes a major symbol of man's foolishness and wastefulness. (pp. 157-58)

Most of Adamov's plays lack the normal plot structure. From the sketchy, schematic arrangement of *The Parody* to the nightmarish mosaic of *If Summer Should Return,* the dramatist never adopted the conventions of the well-made play.

Language was always an important, often major, element in his writings. He never adopted the nonsequitur quality of the theater of Ionesco, for example. In general, his dialogue follows its own inner, but always understandable, logic. Adamov did, however, attempt numerous experiments with language. In *The Invasion,* he thought that he had developed a new technique when he used indirect dialogue, the characters expressing one idea but really meaning another, only to discover that Chekhov had already preceded him. In *Ping-Pong,* language was to be played against the action in order to obtain the full value of the pomposity and artificiality of the characters. In

Holy Europe and *Off Limits,* the language varied according to the effect desired, at times involving doggerel verse to express the playwright's contempt and, at other times, approaching a freer, more liberated form of poetry to convey the depths of the soul. No one style dominates, and each individual play has its own particular expression of the author's obsessions. Within all of this, there is an undeniable absurdity, incongruity, and iconoclasm. It would be very difficult, however, to view Adamov's theater as truly humorous or comical; what might pass for humor comes out of the illogical situations and the exaggerated actions. Even in his more "comical" plays, there is too much bitterness, too much hatred. Adamov's satire, which does indeed exist, is too strong to provoke much laughter; it demands reflection and ultimately provokes sadness. (pp. 158-59)

Since Adamov's plays cannot really exist without an understanding of the dramatist, they are consequently often too hermetic to be appreciated, too secretive to be understood. It is probably this quality which requires us to place the dramatist into the ranks of the important, but secondary writers in French literature. Adamov generally did not succeed in taking the step that would move him from the personal to the universal; when he did turn to the world around him, as in *Paolo Paoli* or *Spring 71,* he became unnecessarily limited in perspective, partial in view, and strident in tone. Later, when he attempted to combine neuroses and social comment, the potential was present for a truly unique theatrical expression—an expression never realized in a cohesive, fully-developed vision. (pp. 159-60)

Nevertheless, while Adamov will never achieve the ranks of the outstanding writers, he will remain a significant and important figure of his period. Some of his works will stand up relatively well: *The Invasion* is an effective cry of anguish; *One Against Another* [or *All Against All*] is a vivid expression of persecution; and *Paolo Paoli, Spring 71, Off Limits,* and *Holy Europe* all contain powerful scenes which, for one reason or another, do not sustain that power in their totality. However, it seems likely that two plays by Adamov will stand the test of time: *Ping-Pong* and *Professor Taranne.* The former achieves that difficult balance which the dramatist pursued. It is a careful blend of the personal foolishness of man linked with discreet comments on the oppressive nature of the social system. The connection of the personal and the public is well formulated in the work, the point is subtly made, and the stage becomes a concrete image of man and his folly. *Professor Taranne* is a truly fine realization of the nightmare and anguish of living. Perhaps because it is a transcription of a dream, the play has ironically a terrifying reality, a reality which comes from the truths of the subconscious. Man's quest for his identity, the confused torment of existence, and man's eventual submission and defeat are made compelling and valid. It is not by chance that both of these works achieve their effectiveness from a carefully-controlled and somewhat restrained expression of theme and structure. The hermeticism and exaggerations which mar the other plays are thankfully nonexistent and, in these two works, Adamov shows the power of his writing.

Curiously, though, the most telling work may very well have been his first, *The Confession,* the haunting reflections about his life. This revealing work may possibly outlast his theater. In spite of his many innovative theatrical techniques, Adamov never seemed entirely comfortable with the restrictions which the dramatic form imposed. The journal, with its individualistic, less restrictive style of writing seems to have been more suitable for him. In this highly personal form he was often able to achieve the universality that he rarely attained in his theater. (pp. 160-61)

John H. Reilly, in his Arthur Adamov *(copyright © 1974 by Twayne Publishers, Inc.; reprinted with the permission of Twayne Publishers, a Division of G. K. Hall & Co., Boston), Twayne, 1974, 177 p.*

JOHN J. McCANN

The common denominator of Adamov's last five plays [*La Politique des Restes, Sainte Europe, M. le Modéré, Off Limits,* and *Si l'été revenait*] . . . is that their dimensions are essentially social. All five plays are principally concerned with the social systems of alienated modern society, their viciousness, perversions, degradation and inauthenticity. (p. 122)

The five plays are penetrated with the prevailing despair of the times. Their latent thematic identity proceeds from modern man's failure to create a new unifying myth to fill the void in a world of absence, absence of *a priori* values, absence of communication, absence of personal dignity, and in these plays most especially, the absence of man's awareness of and concern for his fellow man as they live together in society. . . .

Another unifying factor in this final phase of Adamov's theater is the thrust of these five plays towards a more authentic reconciliation of the divergent forms of his work. Having developed to their fullest in *Le Printemps 71* the epic-realist possibilities announced in *Paolo Paoli,* Adamov's ensuing theater re-examines and re-incorporates certain formal considerations of his earlier work. (p. 123)

[In] abandoning the purely ethical protest of his earlier work in favor of a developing political conscience in the transitional plays, Adamov's theater falls victim in the political plays to a certain timidity of form and conformity in language, an excess of "realism" inimical to his talent. It is a type of strait-jacket self-imposed, a protection against the anarchistic energies of his absurdist view that might impinge upon and obscure the ideology he espouses and wishes to express. (pp. 123-24)

In his final five plays Adamov succeeds in reconciling not only the formal divergencies of "avant-garde" and epic-realist dramaturgy, but the thematic duality of "absurdist" and "political" orientation. He moves, as in his masterpiece, *Le Ping-Pong,* towards a synthesis of form and content, a union of style and view that is particularly his own, like no other, and that takes into account both man in the universe and man in society. (p. 124)

[*Off Limits*] is the fullest expression of [Adamov's] vision of the contemporary world and its systems as the "temps de l'ignominic." By using an America sick with imperialistic war and inner conflicts revealed by racism and abuse of drugs as the setting for his play, Adamov succeeds in describing the anguish of a modern society in crisis and its paralyzing effects on a cross section of the people making up and perpetuating that society. (p. 141)

The play is divided into five tableaux and an epilogue. Each tableau represents a party or reception; each tableau repeats with slight variations and increasing intensity the empty frenzy of a group of New York intellectuals, media people, and young drug addicts bent on self-destruction. Whatever revolt they can muster against the established order, with its vacuity, degradation and oppressive war in Vietnam, is smothered by their self-pity, vanity, selfishness, eroticism and alcoholism. Their

flirtations, drunken accusations, staged "happenings," petty conceits and enmities vary little from party to party, revealing each participant to be both a victim and perpetrator of a destructive social order which permits only the illusion of escape. The momentary release of their pent-up aggressiveness and frustrated anguish at drunken parties makes them only more aware of their incapacity to act, to break with the system. (p. 142)

Jim and Sally represent a threat to the noisy chaos and changing hostilities that dominate the drunken parties of the first four tableaux. They embody the two constants which are the nuclei of individual and societal redemption: (1) the genuine love they feel for each other, and (2) their intense hatred of the oppressive war in Vietnam. (pp. 142-43)

The structure of *Off Limits* is one of gradual and then rapid disintegration of the play's universe by the intensification by repetition of the prevailing inauthenticity of values. The sterility, impotency and puerile revolts of the "chic" New York intellectuals exhibited in the first four tableaux contrast sharply with the young couple's genuine love for each other and mutual hatred for the oppression of war. Ultimately these contrasts drive Jim and Sally to their act of defiance and death.

The play's universe further disintegrates in the fifth tableau after the death of the young couple, when the second party at Humphrey's fails to have its usual narcotic effect, fails to dull the minds of the participants and erase Jim and Sally's repudiation of a life to which the others have grown accustomed. Thus they are driven to the final desperation of the Epilogue, an attempt to create for television a false but harmless drama out of defiance and death, to confiscate by falsification an authentic act of revolt. (pp. 146-47)

Off Limits combines, although in a less integrated fashion than *Le Ping-Pong,* the two dominant directions of Adamov's dramaturgy, the theater of dream, neurosis and futility and the Brechtian theater of realistic social criticism. While the play is principally concerned with the social systems of alienated modern society and their resultant oppressive war, it unites and integrates the personal or individual dramas of Jim and Sally, George and Dorothy, Humphrey and Lisbeth and the others within the general destructive socio-political fabric. Personal neurosis and societal malaise, escapism and war, drugs and racism intermingle to create a nightmarish world.

The play is more than a simple reportage. Not only does it succeed in portraying the inauthentic way of life as lived according to the ethic of evasion and rationalization, but it projects the very vertigo and confusion felt by the characters themselves. By the use of certain avant-garde techniques—*images fixes,* staged happenings, transitions between tableaux, self-critical *Récitatifs* in free verse form, symbolic décor, etc.— the play recreates the chaotic nightmare that it seeks to criticize. (pp. 147-48)

Off Limits depicts and condemns the social system of alienated modern society in America, its viciousness, perversion, degradation and inauthenticity. As in the other plays of this final phase of Adamov's theater, the accent is placed here on the absence of man's awareness of and concern for his fellow men as they live together in society. Moreover Adamov reconciles not only the thematic duality of "absurdist" and "political" orientations, but the formal divergencies of "avant-garde" and epic-realist dramaturgy. He moves towards a synthesis of form and content, a union of style and view that is particularly his own, that takes into account both man in the universe and man in society.

Having exposed America in **Off Limits** as the ultimate expression of contemporary emptiness and inauthenticity, Adamov in his final play **Si l'été revenait** . . . , reveals as false the "new myths" of a liberated, socialist Sweden. . . . [The play] is perhaps Adamov's most desperate image of modern man lost in a maze of selfishness, frustration, guilt, fear and impotency. Having failed to create an authentic unifying myth to fill the void of their existence, the characters of **Si l'été revenait** are reduced to performing in a dream world that is not always of their own making. It is Adamov's ultimate statement on absence, for in this play the absence of a spiritual dimension leads directly to the absence of life itself. There is no exit save dream or suicide.

Moreover, like the penultimate **Off Limits**, Adamov's final play depicts a world where socio-political action is continually stifled by the self-pity, vanity, selfishness, eroticism and masochism of its characters. And as in the other plays of this final cycle the accent in **Si l'été revenait** shifts from the political to the social, specifically to the failure of its characters to maintain the coherent and cooperative interdependence necessary for their survival. The play is a study in complex relationships threatened at their core by the characters' sadomasochism and guilt, by their inability to deal with ambivalent emotions of love and hate, dependence and dominance, faith and fear, gratitude and scorn, devotion and resentment. The play is primarily a psychological exposition, but unlike the archetypes of the early plays, the characters of **Si l'été revenait** are "realistic," living out their dreams in the specific context of contemporary Sweden. Thus, in its concern for the individual as well as for man's failure to build together as a social unit, **Si l'été revenait** comes full cycle and bears witness to the consistency of Adamov's theater. (pp. 149-50)

Si l'été revenait is a play about absence. In an advanced socialist country where there is no hunger and practically no crime, man still fails to bridge the gap between himself and others. The "new myths" of the "smiling girl in a bathing suit" are hollow and fail to create the unifying dimension necessary to fill the void in a world of absence, absence of communication, absence of innocence, and especially absence of man's awareness of and concern for his fellow man. (pp. 152-53)

The very title of the play intimates a lost or "absent" summer, a nostalgic longing for a unity that once was but is forever gone. The central image of the play, a recurrent motif of various principal characters riding a swing together while others push, represents a cohesive solidarity no longer attainable because the characters are incapable of cooperating to keep the swing going. (p. 153)

Si l'été revenait is a fitting end-piece to a collection of plays that fused, better than any other contemporary theater, the divergent trends of French drama in the 1950's and 1960's. By mixing realism with fantasy, by superimposing variant dream-sequences for which there is no objective version, the play creates a world where psychological and socio-political elements coalesce into a highly theatrical language of visual as well as auditory images, of psychical distancing as well as direct involvement, of avant-garde as well as epic-realist techniques. The play is a complex metaphor which demonstrates Adamov's consistent vision of the "social" failure of modern man to relate to his fellow travelers as directly resulting from the absence of an interior, unifying spiritual dimension. The void without is a direct result of the void within. (p. 154)

John J. McCann, in his The Theater of Arthur Adamov, *Chapel Hill, 1975, 168 p.*

Anna Akhmatova

1888-1966

(Pseudonym of Anna Andreyevna Gorenko) Russian poet, translator, and essayist.

Akhmatova is often seen as Pasternak's successor in the Silver Age of Russian poetry and is generally considered the finest woman poet Russia has produced. Participating with the Acmeists in a reaction against symbolist poetry, she wrote in a concise and accessible style. Words are used logically, imagery is concrete. Hers is an intimate and authentic poetry, showing a love of nature, of Russia, and of love itself.

Akhmatova's early collections of poetry, notably, *Vecher (Evening)*, *Chotki (Rosary)*, and *Belaya Staya (The White Flock)* contain lyric self-portraits and intensely personal reflections on love and love's sorrows. They nevertheless grope towards the making of universally true statements and do so, in the opinion of many critics, with admirable success. Critics acclaim Akhmatova's ability to reach the general through her own experiences. Written in the clear and exacting style for which she is renowned, Akhmatova's early works are often seen as the chronicle of a passionate woman's movement from love through pain and bitterness to a restoration of faith in love and life.

Although Akhmatova continued to write, after the publication of her *Anno Domini MCMXII* in 1921, she did not publish another collection until her *Iz shesti knig (From Six Books)* appeared in 1940. In this period of silence, she suffered great personal tragedy. Akhmatova's first husband, the poet Nikolai Gumilev, was executed as a counterrevolutionary and their only son was sentenced to a prison camp. He was not finally released until after the death of Stalin. Akhmatova's work of this period reflects her anguish over these events and shows a more overt love of country than her earlier works. As war and revolution spread through Russia, Akhmatova wrote of both her own losses and those suffered by all Russian people.

Akhmatova was expelled from the Writer's Union in 1946 and her work was banned from publication until after Stalin's death. She nevertheless continued to record the terrors of his regime in her poetry and speaks compelling of them in the acclaimed poem cycle, *Requiem*. After Stalin's death Akhmatova was allowed to travel abroad. In 1965, she received an honorary doctorate from Oxford University. She was also elected to the governing board of the Writer's Union. Akhmatova worked up to her death and her works are still being translated.

(See also *CLC*, Vol. 11; *Contemporary Authors*, Vols. 17-20, Vols. 25-28, rev. ed. [obituary]; and *Contemporary Authors Permanent Series*, Vol. 1.)

LEONID I. STRAKHOVSKY

[In *Vecher*, Akhmatova's first book of poems, she] speaks about simple earthly happiness and about simple intimate and personal sorrow. Love, love's parting, unrequited love, love's betrayal, clear and serene confidence in the lover, feelings of grief, of loneliness, of despair—all the things that everyone

Gabriel D. Hackett, NY

might feel and understand, though perhaps less deeply and personally than the poet—such are Akhmatova's themes, told with a remarkable frugality. . . . (p. 57)

[In Akhmatova's second book of poetry, *Chyotki*,] her themes remained the same. . . . Akhmatova was consistent in her femininity. (pp. 60-1)

[In Akhmatova's poetry there are] unexpected but convincing, illogical but fine psychological transitions from words of emotion to words of description, from the soul to nature, from feeling to fact. She assembles artistically the particulars of a given moment which are often unnoticeable to others; she notices everything anew so that her internal world is not merely framed by the external world, but they combine into one solid and organic wholeness of life. . . . She often compares the present with the past, and the recollections of her childhood create nostalgic moods. . . . (pp. 62-3)

Akhmatova is essentially an urban poet, primarily a poet of St. Petersburg. . . . Yet there is something foreboding in the way she speaks about the city of Peter: "Sumptuous, granite-clad city of glory and woe"; "dark city by a terrifying river"; "the city loved by a bitter love." There are also other cities in Akhmatova's poetry and they are brighter, sunnier: "Hilly Pavlovsk," "brilliant Tsarskoye Selo," "golden Bakhchisarai."

All told, cities predominate in Akhmatova's poetry. It seems that man-made structures attract her more than nature's land-scapes. (p. 64)

As [World War I] progressed, a strong religious feeling appears in Akhmatova's verse. She was always deeply religious with a strong, almost primitive, simple faith. And now that death was rampant in the wake of war . . . there was no other recourse than to turn to God for succour. At the first news of the war, Akhmatova, covering her face with her hands, implored God to kill her before the first battle, and exclaimed that the day of declaration of war has made everyone one hundred years older. And now, when she writes about the death of a loved one, she does not rebel at the cruel fate, but merely states that a new warrior has been added to God's own host. "Thy image, thy righteous sacrifice I shall cherish until my hour of death." (pp. 69-70)

It was not until 1917, after the first revolutionary rumble of that year had rolled over Russia, that Akhmatova published her next book, **Belaya Staya**. . . . Most of her themes remained the same as before, but her artistry had become more per-fect. . . . [Her] themes are more fully carried out within the limits of a given poem. . . . (pp. 70-1)

On the whole, **Belaya Staya,** reflecting the years of war and revolution, reveal Akhmatova's "brittle voice" as somewhat subdued, having lost some of the sharpness of **Chyotki,** but mellowed by a religious fatalism so characteristic of a Russian woman.

Four years had passed since the publication of **Belaya Staya.** The turmoil of revolution and civil war was gone, but not forgotten. And then Akhmatova published [**Podorozhnik (Buck-thorn)**]. . . . This pathetic little volume marks a turning point in Akhmatova's poetry. Although the theme of love still pre-dominates, it has now a tragic note. It marks the end of the love of two poets, the end of Akhmatova's marriage to Gum-ilyov which had culminated in divorce in 1918, after which Gumilyov remarried. Although Akhmatova herself remarried in later years, her first love remained the stronger. (pp. 72-3)

In a way [Akhmatova's next book, **Anno Domini MCMXXI** is her] swan song, as it is the record of how a woman's love can turn to hate. Its pathos is really tragic and the poetess chose as its epigraph these utterly despairing words: *Nec sine te, nec tecum vivere possum* (Neither without you nor with you can I live). Hapless, tragic love, "love full of evil," marks most of the poems in this book. It is the outcry of a woman abandoned by her lover for another. . . . But her hate is only another form of her love, yet there is nothing now she can hope for and so she sighs: "Oh, life without tomorrow!" . . . Only in the last poem of this book does there appear a note of religious sub-missiveness, reminiscent of Akhmatova's war poems, which seems to indicate an exit out of the "accursed circle." (pp. 75-6)

Years went by, but Akhmatova's "brittle voice" remained silent. And then in 1940 there appeared a collection of her selected lyrics under the title *Iz Shesti Knig* . . . , which in-cluded an entire new section entitled *Iva* (**The Willow**). . . . It was still the same Akhmatova, only one endowed with greater wisdom and mellowed by the years, by years of want and of suffering. Her voice was now reduced almost to a whisper and her eyes were dimmed as she looked at the present through the mirror of the past. But her mastery was still the same. . . . (p. 77)

On the whole [in *Iz Shesti Knig*] Akhmatova's emotions are more controlled now and the ideological content is deeper than before. She is more sure of herself and of her medium. But there is a note of nostalgia which appears here and there, as in a remarkable poem about Lot's wife, who "gave her life for one look." (p. 78)

During World War II, Anna Akhmatova's poetry appeared in the leading journals of the Soviet Union. . . . Of these poems, some (obviously written for the occasion) are almost trite. . . . On the other hand, there are some as remarkable as the best that Akhmatova has ever written. (pp. 79-80)

Anna Akhmatova—the poetess of tragic love—has stirred the hearts of readers of Russian poetry for thirty-five years and she is still writing, but again not publishing, because she en-countered the wrath of the leaders of the Soviet Union. In a decree of the Central Committee of the All-Union Communist Party of Bolsheviks dated August 14, 1946, her poetry was condemned in the following words: "Akhmatova is a typical representative of empty poetry lacking in ideas and alien to our people. Her poems, permeated with the spirit of pessimism and decadence and expressing the tastes of old 'salon' poetry, which grew out of the position of burgeois-aristocratic aes-theticism of 'art for art's sake' and which does not desire to keep in step with the people, do harm to the work of educating our youth and cannot be suffered in Soviet literature." This was followed by her expulsion from the Union of Soviet Writers on September 4, 1946. Although Akhmatova's voice has been silenced again, perhaps permanently, what she has said so far not only places her ahead of all living Russian poets, but assures for her a preëminent place in Russian poetry of all time as the greatest woman-poet the Russian nation has produced. (p. 82)

Leonid I. Strakhovsky, "Anna Akhmatova: Poetess of Tragic Love," in his Craftsmen of the World, Three Poets of Modern Russia: Gumilyov, Akhma-tova, Mandelstam *(copyright © 1949 by the Presi-dent and Fellows of Harvard College; excerpted by permission), Cambridge, Mass.: Harvard University Press, 1949 (and reprinted by Greenwood Press, Publishers, 1969), pp. 53-82.*

ANDREI SINYAVSKY

For many years Anna Akhmatova's poetry appeared to her contemporaries as if it had frozen within the restricted limits laid down by her first books: **Evening, Rosary, White Flock.** . . . It seemed that the poetess, submerged in the past, in the world of intimate reminiscences and in her own tradition of versifi-cation, would never tear herself away from the captivity of her beloved themes, familiar images, and established intonations. Even in the twenties critics had written that Anna Akhmatova was doomed to "repeat herself," and, unfortunately, such a view of her poetry is still current even today in her readers' minds.

If one turns, however, to the Akhmatova of today and reads carefully everything that she has produced during the last three decades, then extraordinary, at times decidedly new notes are perceptible, and unexpectedly bold developments and turns are noticeable in a lyrical view which was fully developed long ago and of which we are still quite conscious. (p. 72)

While not ceasing to be herself, Akhmatova rejects herself, or to state it more precisely, she casts off and broadens the es-tablished image of herself which classified her only as a poet of pre-revolutionary times who is locked within her narrow limits, in one unchanged river-bed. Her civic poetry of the thirties and of the war years, so full of tragic power and courage, testifies to this most of all. Akhmatova argues against those who would like to see in her only a "peripheral" phenomenon, alien to the life of her native country, indifferent to the fate of its people. . . .

In her lyric poetry during the Second World War the idea of the unity of the poet and the citizen and the high pathos of struggle and sorrow rang out loud and clear. (p. 73)

[As indicated by her poem **"Courage,"** written in 1942, the] very structure, the tonality itself is changed in Akhmatova's lyric poetry. We used to consider it soft, exquisite, womanly fragile, and we used to follow the play of details, of "microscopic trifles," of barely audible and scarcely perceptible modulations. Who would have believed that this "Muse of Tsarskoye Selo" could speak out so loudly, so powerfully, using colloquial language, and all this not about just anything, but about her Tsarskoye Selo, thrice celebrated in songs, which for a long time now has become the symbol of the exquisite poetry of the past? (pp. 73-4)

Unlike many of her literary colleagues and contemporaries, Akhmatova was reluctant to use abrupt stylistic shifts, radical changeovers, and was more inclined toward the traditional forms of poetry, toward classical exactness and clearness of language, and toward the harmonious language of [A. S.] Pushkin and [Yergeny Abramovich] Baratynsky. She still favors poetical reminiscences, which again and again perform the function of parallel mirrors, creating in her work a perspective in depth and thus bringing subjects remote from one another into closer relationship. . . . Names of literary importance, epigraphs, dedications, and gestures of good-bye to the past . . . , the settling of old accounts with herself and her memory: all this does not impede, but rather facilitates the task of evoking in a small section of poetical text the feeling of great spaciousness, of moving within it with great ease, of exchanging greetings with voices of other epochs and other spheres of existence. Owing to the breadth of her scope the entire world can become the mediator in the author's conversation with her imaginary interlocutor, and the fact that this exchange of thoughts is carried on in a low voice or happens silently no longer presents difficulties. Silence and calm in Akhmatova's poems usually speak not of the absence but rather of the presence of that which is all-embracing and magnificent. (pp. 74-5)

The new features of Akhmatova's latest lyric poetry force us to take a different view also of her literary autobiography and to reconsider certain traditional ideas about the early stages of her poetry. It is worthwhile to ask a question about her possibilities: is it possible that already in the initial "salon" period of her development there existed potentially and secretly those features which served at first only as a starting point and then later on came to fruition?

Akhmatova has always been the recognized master of the lyric self-portrait, a portrait which recreated the gestures and mimicry of the living face with such ease and clarity that it almost burst the frame of the poem like a relief. . . . [She] possesses the gift of compressing into the framework of a four-line poem man's fate with all the psychological complications and secrets of the inner life. (p. 75)

In addition to being filled with ideas and concrete subject matter Akhmatova's early poetry is frequently able to astonish us with the sweep of its intonation, with the power and energy of her voice, which also, as [Osip] Mandelshtam once wrote in a

poem dedicated to her, "frees the depths of the soul." . . . In the most intimate spheres she possesses the art of the exalted, heroic and tragic, both in word and gesture. (pp. 75-6)

One could . . . feel the diapason of her lyric talent rather early in the poems which are permeated with the consciousness of patriotic duty and personal and communal responsibility for the fate of the motherland. Noteworthy in this respect is the poem by Akhmatova written in 1917 which sounded like a reproof to all who intended to leave a Russia caught in the conflagration of revolution. In those circumstances (notwithstanding the fact that contemporary life was presented by her mainly in dark colors) it was the very choice made by Akhmatova in favor of her beloved country that was important. This is why (according to K. I. Chukovsky) Alexander Blok, who loved this poem and memorized it, assigned to it such a programmatic significance. "Akhmatova is right," he said, "this is an unworthy way of talking. To run away from the Russian revolution is shameful." (p. 76)

From a barely perceptible whisper to flaming oratory, from shyly cast-down eyes to thunder and lightning—such is the range of her feeling and her voice. It may be that one has to look for the sources of that development which blossomed later on and gave Akhmatova's poetry the possibility of turning into a new riverbed—one which can accommodate between its shores both patriotic pathos, the calmness of high metaphysical contemplations, and the loud, many-voiced arguments of the living and the dead. (p. 77)

Andrei Sinyavsky, "The Unfettered Voice" (originally published under a different title in Novy mir, *No. 6, 1964), in his* For Freedom of Imagination, *translated by Laslo Tikos and Murray Peppard (copyright © 1971 by Holt, Rinehart and Winston; reprinted by permission of Holt, Rinehart and Winston, Publishers), Holt, Rinehart and Winston, 1971, pp. 72-7.*

THE TIMES LITERARY SUPPLEMENT

[Anna Akhmatova's **Selected Poems**] ranges from whispers to anguished screams, from personal happiness to the most acute personal distress. It is lyrical, modest, feminine, narrow in tone and form. The sensibility of many passages is admirable, and has encouraged scores of young "unofficial" poets in Russia, brought up to despise sensibility, nevertheless to give expression to their own.

In her youth Akhmatova was capable of turning out sentimental trash such as **"The Grey-Eyed King"**: the triteness of this ballad is difficult to appreciate unless one actually hears the tum-tee-tee, tum-tee-tee of the original Russian; but the fact that it was set to even triter music by the émigré chansonnier Vertinsky, and sung at moments of boozy nostalgia in those countless Russian restaurants and cafés that abounded in at least three continents during the 1920s and 1930s, speaks for itself. At her worst, Anna Akhmatova was less good than any English-language poetess who is taken seriously anywhere today.

The historical events which took her away from the parks and beaches, poets' gatherings and lovers' quarrels of her early years and placed her in the queue of women waiting endlessly outside the gates of a Leningrad prison for news of husbands or sons also eliminated every trace of false sentiment from her writing. In **Requiem** (1935-1940), which describes this experience, she reached the peak of her powers. But the subject called for something at once simpler and more austere than Akhmatova the poetess seems to have been capable of. That is why, to this reader at least, the most moving lines in the whole volume are not in the poetry at all but in the short prose piece which prefaces *Requiem*. . . .

The history of Akhmatova's generation of Russian poets is well known. Let us recite it once again. Gumilev was executed, Yessenin and Mayakovsky committed suicide. Osip Mandelshtam, the great stoic classicist—as unique among Jewish poets as Isaac Babel, the Jewish storyteller of genius, had been unique among the rough riders of the Red Cavalry—perished in a concentration camp. Marina Tsvetayeva hanged herself. Pasternak, the sources of his poetic inspiration poisoned and ultimately exhausted, turned to producing mediocre prose. It was the fact of her miraculous survival as a poet, not the inherent quality of her verse, that made it true to say in 1963 that Anna Akhmatova was then the greatest living Russian poet. Paradoxically, the finest poems in this volume are precisely those which lament the cruelties, the idiocies, which caused the deaths of other artists and ordinary human beings and made it possible for the title of "greatest living Russian poet" to be justly bestowed upon her at the end.

"Lyrics of Survival," in The Times Literary Supplement *(© Times Newspapers Ltd. (London) 1969; reproduced from* The Times Literary Supplement *by permission), No. 3515, July 10, 1969, p. 751.*

JOSEPH BRODSKY

Akhmatova is a traditional poet, in the highest sense of the word. . . .

Traditional verse more vividly than free verse emphasizes the banal, or the basic, in what is said. The contrast of traditional form to so-called contemporary content gives the work greater scale and tension. The principle is extremely simple: here is a normal person, with arms and legs, properly dressed, a tie and stickpin, but just look at the way he talks! Remember how the author of *The Waste Land* dressed, or imagine an automobile rushing straight toward you in your lane, and you will discover the function of the traditional verse line in Russian nineteenth-century poetry.

But Akhmatova is traditional in yet another respect. If an explosion takes place as a result of the contrast of form and content on paper, then what happens to the reader before whose eyes the poet himself stifles this explosion? Most of Akhmatova's poems are written with falling intonation toward the end, as if nothing special has happened. Whether she is calming herself or the reader is unimportant; what is important is the fact that she does this, and it is even more important to know why she does it. (p. 9)

One of the main characteristics of Russian poetry is its restraint. Russian poets (I am speaking of the best of them) never allow themselves hysterics on paper, pathological confessions, spilling ashes over their heads, curses aimed at the guilty, no matter what the character of the events which they become witness to, participants in, or, sometimes, victims of. Akhmatova was a profound believer, and therefore she understood that, more or less, no one is guilty. Or more precisely, that the guilty exist, but that they are also human beings, just like their victims. I think that she knew the ambivalence of consciousness characteristic of all Russians. As a rule ambivalence leads to one of three things: cynicism, wisdom, or complete paralysis,

i.e., an inability to act. Akhmatova achieved wisdom. Therefore her verse is extremely simple, restrained, and at times, like all real wisdom, it sounds banal. . . .

[*Poems of Akhmatova*] is a good book . . . [despite some translation flaws], and to a certain degree it does represent Akhmatova. Even if it is in profile which corresponds to the dust jacket, Akhmatova lived a long life and wrote much. The selection done for this book is a bit strange and one-sided. Akhmatova furiously opposed the tendency of many native and Western literary scholars to interpret her as a chamber poetess of the Teens or as a "fighter against the regime." She is an extremely profound and diverse poet. She is a lyric poet and a chronicler, but hers is the lyricism and chronicling of a person who "like a river, was reversed by the cruel epoch." Meditativeness and surrealism are characteristic of her, however it is the meditation not of a prophet sitting under a tree but of a person whose sufferings make her speak in a hoarse, almost disembodied voice; and her surrealism is not esthetic, but psychological, i.e., the madness of philosophy. The poetry is very musical, very rich phonetically, and the phonetics communicate a metaphysical reality to the information given in the text.

For all this she is an extremely restrained poet, almost simple. But her simplicity is like the "simplicity" of Robert Frost, to whom, in my opinion, she is extremely close stylistically in her **"Northern Elegies."** . . .

Akhmatova is still a very Russian poetess. Russian not in the sense of "baring the soul" or of a landscape with gold cupolas . . . , but in the psychological sense, in the depth of penetration into any character—whether a beloved or an executioner. This is a characteristic of Russian psychological prose, out of which Akhmatova came. . . . (p. 10)

Joseph Brodsky, "Translating Akhmatova," translated by Carl R. Proffer, in The New York Review of Books *(reprinted with permission from* The New York Review of Books; *copyright © 1973 Nyrev, Inc.), Vol. XX, No. 13, August 9, 1973, pp. 9-11.*

AMANDA HAIGHT

In Akhmatova's poems we are faced with three images of the poet: the one arising out of the facts of her biography; the one created by Russo-Soviet criticism of the poems; and the one she created of herself in her work. The third image emerges initially from many different versions of 'I'. Slowly, during the course of her life, the word and the person giving the word utterance ceased any longer to be divided, so that the voice of the person Akhmatova can be heard speaking to us directly through her poetry, without intermediary and with the awesome authority of complete integrity. But in the poems of her youth we find the poet searching for heroines who can reflect a part of her own personality and set it in a larger context, freeing her experience from the purely private.

The figure of the village woman, with her structured culture of Orthodox beliefs and her ritualistic way of life, was to provide at least a partial solution to this problem of how to enrich and deepen her poetry and relate it to the events shattering and recreating her country around her, while remaining true to their reflection in her own life. The use of this woman as one of her heroines was the beginning of that 'extension of personal feelings to a wider sphere' which her critics demanded—a process which culminated in her cycle **'Requiem'**, written during the Terror, when finally the loss of the son by the mother becomes the loss experienced by Mary at the foot of the Cross.

Looking at Akhmatova's early poetry, it is easy to fall into the confusion of seeing her as the village woman, beaten by her husband, or the pale sorrowing face, so like the Annenkov portrait in *Anno Domini,* examining itself in the mirror, or even the tall girl wearing a shawl, reciting her poetry as she was later to do in the poets' night club, the Wandering Dog. In fact she is all three of these. Those of her friends and admirers who left Russia in the twenties and who wished to crystallize her as the Akhmatova of the early love poems and those critics who took the religious village woman of *Evening* as an expression of the poet's values and her Christianity, misunderstood equally the sources from which Akhmatova's poetry springs. Forced by her very nature only to write of her own personal experience, she uses external 'props' in her attempt to reach the universal through the particular.

The circumstances of Akhmatova's life were to lead her over and over to consider why she wrote poetry and whether it was important to her. Little by little, her understanding of herself, of what she felt to be her role in the larger life of her nation, and her position as a poet among poets of the world, both past and present, made it possible for her to rise above the circumstances of her own life and of her day and age and to see the patterns behind the events, the links that, close up, seemed to be divisions. Then she was able to say that she looked down at everything 'as from a tower'. . . . But although this process of growth and integration was reflected from the start in her poetry, in *Evening* poetry is not yet seen as anything bringing a solution to the poet's problems. It will not, for instance, stop her heart breaking—on the contrary, death will stop her poetry. She describes herself as a cuckoo clock which sings when wound up. She sees nothing enviable in this: 'You know I can only wish an enemy such a fate'. (pp. 21-2)

[In] *Rosary* the poet is beginning to understand how to survive. (p. 30)

The past is losing its hold on her and soon she will be free. When her lover leaves her or she leaves him, life becomes empty but also bright. Poetry now has a positive role to play in this freedom from bondage, for what she writes at this time is 'happy' and if her lover knocks on the door she may not even hear. (p. 31)

[In *White Flock*] it is through the mouth of the village woman or pilgrim that Akhmatova is able to express her deepest feelings about [World War I]. She sees it as a wounding of the body of Christ and uses imagery related to that of early Russian folk poetry, showing sensitivity to the land as to something alive. When not making use of this persona, she approaches the subject with greater difficulty as if finding it almost impossible to express her grief and horror. Her first reaction is to cover her face with her hands and ask God to take her as a sacrifice, but this is not allowed. As a poet she has a duty to perform and God's command is that her memory, emptied of passion and song, become the 'terrible chronicle of news of the storm'. . . . (pp. 47-8)

Akhmatova, however, had not yet reached the stage where she could use her gift to inspire people and strengthen them, as she was able to do in the Second World War. Although it is wrong to say that she avoided mention of the war in her poems, her approach was, as always, a personal one. As for many of her countrymen, the reasons for the war did not seem to her clear-cut, but the result, the death of her contemporaries, was

only too painfully clear. It is not surprising, therefore, to find that despite the war by far the greater number of poems in *White Flock* deal with what had up till now been the poet's central obsession, the theme of love. (pp. 50-1)

The poems in *Plantain* and *Anno Domini* cover the period from the end of the war on through the February and October revolutions and the civil war. To say, as her critics later did, that nothing about these great historic events can be found in Akhmatova's poetry is simply not true. Nor can it be held that her response to the revolution was entirely a pessimistic one. It was an honest one and she managed to keep it so by dealing, as always, only with her own experience. (p. 60)

A poem written in the summer of 1917, **'The river flows slowly along the valley'** . . . , might seem at first to have absolutely no connection with what was happening. But noting the date, the words 'And we are living as they lived in Catherine's day / Going to church and waiting for the harvest' can be appreciated in their full irony. (p. 61)

In **'Requiem'** Akhmatova no longer needed to use a heroine as a means of linking her own life with that of other women. It was enough to formulate her own private suffering. This voice coming out of the silence was sufficient, for little by little what was happening to the country was stripping off false values, until even the blindest person was forced to realize that 'only blood smells of blood'.

But for Akhmatova to give form to this suffering she had to live through it, and because it was that of a mother it inevitably led to an understanding of the archetype Mary. The poems of **'Requiem'** trace the stations of her suffering to the foot of the Cross. Lev Gumilyov's arrest for little reason other than having had herself and Gumilyov as parents could again be laid to her failure as a mother. But most awe-inspiring in **'Requiem'** is Akhmatova's understanding of the inevitability, almost necessity, that all this had to happen: that at the Crucifixion 'A choir of angels glorified that hour'. . . . While Mary Magdalene sobbed, 'No one dared to cast a glance to where the Mother, silent, stood alone.'

Mary the Mother is set in opposition to Mary Magdalene who has lost Christ and will only find Him again when He appears to her after His resurrection. The Mother's suffering is a reflection of that of Christ, who endures the Crucifixion to fulfil what He has been sent to do and whose suffering is not lessened but, if anything, heightened by understanding this necessity. He has no comforting illusions to place between Himself and the feeling of having been forsaken by God. And Mary, His mother, must watch Him, knowing that one cannot help anyone else, however great one's love, and that His suffering is necessary if God's purpose is to be fulfilled.

In this poem Akhmatova uses religious language to a very different purpose than years before at the time of the First World War. There is none of that feeling of suffocation that overcame her when she felt that to believe in the after life implied that it was wrong to grieve over death. . . . There is nothing gentle or comforting about this Mary. She is the other half of Christ: the woman who bore Him and who understands that the Crucifixion is the greatest moment in history. And as with the women of the Old Testament, Akhmatova is not observing Mary from outside. She is looking at the world through her eyes.

'Requiem' is not just a series of short poems strung together, but an organic unit documenting a precise progression through all the stages of suffering to this point and clearly set by the poet in the larger context of her life and work. The four-line poem with which it opens, written in 1961, is in a sense a triumphant vindication of a conviction Akhmatova had first formulated in 1917, that it was right and necessary for her to stay in Russia and die with her country if need be. (pp. 99-100)

The women to whom **'Requiem'** was dedicated were drawn together by the fact that in their suffering they were completely alone. In the ten poems forming the main body of the cycle Akhmatova is no longer speaking *about* those others like herself who made up a multitude, but *for* them. She does this by speaking of that single woman, herself. Passing through that suffering she is at one with all other women forced to do the same. (pp. 101-02)

In the two poems of the **'Epilogue'** Akhmatova turns from the depiction of the woman alone in sorrow who becomes universal by becoming one with Mary the Mother of Christ, to describe again the many Marys to whom she has dedicated these poems. The first poem is about what fear and suffering do to people. . . . This is now the other side of the coin. The understanding of the Cross produces, not a passive acceptance of horror, but rather the ability to look at it with both eyes open, full in the face. Here is no prayer for it all to be covered over with black cloth or, as long ago, with the Virgin's cloak. Nor is there any question of not understanding what has happened. The poet understands only too well. She can face up to it because she has taken suffering to its limit and so there is nothing to fear. Whereas Pushkin still prayed, 'Lord, don't let me lose my mind', Akhmatova no longer fears even madness. She has passed through it, surrendered herself to it, to learn, miraculously, that all the props to which she desperately clung for strength were not strength at all and that when they were gone and nothing more could be taken from her, she was stronger than she had ever realized was possible.

In the second poem of the **'Epilogue'** her voice is stern. . . . (pp. 106-07)

Here remembering is not a consolation, something to cling to when all is lost, nor its opposite, the memory that must be killed so that one can go on living. It is the cry of fury from the woman whose husband is taken away at dawn: 'Not to forget!' Akhmatova consents to a monument only if it is to be an everlasting reminder of the horror, of the old woman's cry 'like a beast that was hurt'. And in a sense **'Requiem'** is itself this monument. It is not raised to herself, the poet, but to the women who stood in the queues outside the prisons. If the suffering she and her contemporaries had been forced to live through were to be forgotten or glossed over that suffering might be repeated. Only by creating something more lasting than the short memory of man with his tendency to forget pain quickly, can Akhmatova carry out her vow not only not to forget but also: *not to allow to be forgotten.*

'Requiem' is a map of a journey leading through hell into the light and it is as accurate as any chart. The poet's position as map-maker, as formulator, is seen to be all-important, his responsibility to the word absolute. Only by speaking the truth can his words bring healing. Misuse of the word, the lie, the half-truth, the omission, are crimes against all those whose lives have been their only formulation and who rely on the artist with his peculiar gift of cutting across the barriers of time to reflect this in truth, so that what has been learnt can be passed on to later generations. Not to do this, to be silent, becomes a crime against humanity. (p. 108)

'The Way of all Earth', one of Akhmatova's few long poems, she referred to as the most *avant-garde* work she had written. Much shorter than the **'Poem without a Hero'** and certainly much less complex, it is however so condensed in style that it seems longer than it actually is. In **'Requiem'** Akhmatova expressed the fate of the suffering mother. In **'Poem without a Hero'** she was to explore that of the poet of the 'True Twentieth Century'. In this poem, set between the two, she deals with her own fate as a poet and as a person and with the reasons for her existence. The answer here is not so much the 'I can' spoken to the woman outside the prison, as that acceptance of whatever life may bring of 'Already madness with its wing'. As then she had learnt that even when she had given up everything, all was not lost, so now she knows that she has come from somewhere else to this world of misery and trouble and that one day she will return 'home'.

This poem is not, however, about escape from life, but one which expresses faith in the most profound sense of the word. Strength here stems from the recognition that the poet has come from God and will one day return to Him, and that she must make her way through time to the place where there will be none. (p. 116)

Akhmatova's longest work, the beautiful but extremely difficult and complex **'Poem without a Hero'**, was written over a period of twenty-two years. She began it in Leningrad before the war, continued it in Tashkent and in postwar Leningrad and Moscow, and was not finally to admit that it was finished until 1962. It is a work written on so many levels and so rich in reference and quotation both to the poet's life and times and to the literature of western Europe that interpretation is difficult—the more so because of the piecemeal way in which it was published, so that many readings have been based on faulty or incomplete texts. (p. 148)

On the literal level the theme of the poem would certainly seem to be what time or history did to a specific group of people, mainly poets, the friends of Akhmatova's 'hot youth', people who include the person she was then and to whom she refers as her 'doubles'. But even to penetrate thus far we have actively to participate with the poet in recreating time past. (p. 151)

At no point does Akhmatova simply offer us material for our passive reception. The beauty of the words and the extraordinary power of the poem's rhythm force us to study its 'code': find out who the people actually were to whom it is dedicated, consider the significance of its many epigraphs, follow up its oblique references. (p. 152)

In the **'Poem without a Hero'** Akhmatova seems to have gained conscious control over a world of symbol and allegory shared by all poets and in which they too play out their symbolic roles. Thus she becomes able to take their words and re-use them: sometimes it seems her poem could be taken as an answer to all those literary statements which have concerned her, while at other times, as she suggests, their voices seem to mingle with her own as her verse echoes theirs. But most important of all is the way in which she not only sees the friends of her youth as 'natural symbols'—much as Dante had seen his contemporaries in the *Divina Commedia*—but also as playing roles in an allegorical masque, linked with characters from fiction, mythology, history, and fairy tale until what she has created is a series of psychological types connecting literature, allegory, and symbol with life. . . . People become symbols and symbols become people. (pp. 156-57)

Having understood on one level that she and her contemporaries were playing out their roles on a stage set for the coming destruction of their world in 1914, as she probes deeper into the reason for it all Akhmatova comes to questions of fate, of guilt, and of the understanding of what is outside the normal structure of our lives. The criss-crossing of time, the mingling of dream and reality, which at first confuse, are seen to be an important device freeing us from the bonds of ordinary time and space. (p. 157)

Constantly we return to the same point: the role of the poet in the 'True Twentieth Century' and of Akhmatova in particular is self-vindicating. The poet-lawmaker, guiltless on one level, bearing the guilt of others on another, is the creator or tool of the thing that can overcome death, the Word. It is this that makes a poet's silence something shameful, what earns Akhmatova's departing shade a bunch of lilac from the hands of an unknown man in the future. It is as a poet that she conquers space and time, understands her contemporaries, shares the world of Dante, Byron, Pushkin, Cervantes, Oscar Wilde. Formulation is the bridge that crosses time and space and provides the entry into another world in which we walk usually unaware and where we are all living symbols 'manifesting forth a greater reality'.

If a poet can be said to have a philosophy then ['**Poem without a Hero**'] is Akhmatova's: it is the prism through which she looks forward and back. . . . The completion of a structure large enough to contain all her experience and knowledge allowed her to be at one again with those of her contemporaries from whom she had been estranged, it linked her with other poets through her use of their work in hers, and freed her from the necessity to try and formulate a further explanation of her life. In the '**Poem without a Hero**' Akhmatova found that explanation, in an affirmation of the necessity both for things to be as they are and for them to change. In her mirror the 'True Twentieth Century' becomes not unendurable chaotic suffering, but a strange and beautiful, and yet cruel and horrible drama in which not to be able to play a role is seen as a tragedy. (pp. 158-59)

> *Amanda Haight, in her* Anna Akhmatova: A Poetic Pilgrimage *(© Oxford University Press 1976; reprinted by permission of Oxford University Press), Oxford University Press, London, 1976, 213 p.*

D. M. THOMAS

[Akhmatova's] incorruptibility as a person is closely linked to her most fundamental characteristic as a poet: fidelity to things as they are, to 'the clear, familiar, material world'. It was Mandelstam who pointed out that the roots of her poetry are in Russian prose fiction. It is a surprising truth, in view of the supreme musical quality of her verse; but she has the novelist's concern for tangible realities, events in place and time. . . . In all her life's work, her fusion with ordinary unbetrayable existence is so complete that only the word 'modest' can express it truthfully. When she tells us (*In 1940*), 'But I warn you, / I am living for the last time', the words unconsciously define her greatness: her total allegiance to the life she was in. She did not make poetry out of the quarrel with herself (in Yeats's phrase for the genesis of poetry). Her poetry seems rather to be a transparent medium through which life streams. (pp. 9-10)

In Akhmatova all the contraries fuse, in the same wonderful way that her genetic proneness to T. B. was controlled, she said, by the fact that she also suffered from Graves' disease, which holds T.B. in check. The contraries have no effect on her wholeness, but they give it a rich mysterious fluid life, resembling one of her favourite images, the willow. They help to give to her poetry a quality that John Bayley has noted [see *CLC*, Vol. 11], an 'unconsciousness', elegance and sophistication joined with 'elemental force, utterance haunted and Delphic . . . and a cunning which is *chétif*, or, as the Russians say, *zloi*.'

Through her complex unity she was able to speak, not to a small élite, but to the Russian people with whom she so closely and proudly identified. Without condescension, with only a subtle change of style within the frontiers of what is Akhmatova, she was able to inspire them with such patriotic war-time poems as *Courage*. It is as though Eliot, in this country, suddenly found the voice of Kipling or Betjeman. The encompassing of the serious and the popular within one voice has become impossible in Western culture. Akhmatova was helped by the remarkable way in which twentieth-century Russian poetry has preserved its formal link with the poetry of the past. It has become modern without needing a revolution, and has kept its innocence. In Russian poetry one can still, so to speak, rhyme 'love' with 'dove'.

Akhmatova herself, with her great compeers, Mandelstam, Pasternak and Tsvetaeva, must be accounted largely responsible for the continuity of Russian poetic tradition. Together, they made it possible for the people to continue to draw strength from them. (pp. 11-12)

> *D. M. Thomas, in his introduction to* Way of All the Earth *by Anna Akhmatova, translated by D. M. Thomas (translation copyright © D. M. Thomas 1979; reprinted by permission of Ohio University Press, Athens), Ohio University Press, 1979, pp. 9-13.*

NIKOLAI BANNIKOV

Anna Akhmatova's personality was phenomenal. It was not given to any woman in Russian poetry before her to express herself with such convincing, lyrical power, to speak out so independently that her voice added once and for all a special—Akhmatovan—note to the art of the Russian poetic word. Akhmatova triumphed in competition with many poets of the early twentieth century who were then regarded as leading figures in poetry and who occupied the center of the stage. Akhmatova's word did not grow dull with the years. None of the accidents of circumstance in which that word was born deadened it, killed it with the flight of time, as occurs with some poets. Countess Rostopchina, Karolina Pavlova, Iuliia Zhadovskaia, and Mirra Lokhvitskaia—all the Russian women poets of the nineteenth century were no more than undergrowth among mighty trees, among the giants of Russian poetry. Akhmatova was the first woman to rise to the heights in the writing of lyrical poetry. "I taught women to speak," she said as far back as the '30s, with reference to the unprecedentedly headlong development of female poetic creativity, which began in our century and in which the influence and example of Akhmatova were a most important factor.

From the very outset the profoundly psychological character of Akhmatova's verse did not flow in the channel of Russian Symbolism and Acmeism. Despite the passionate and high evaluation of "The Cypress Casket" . . . by Akhmatova, traces of lessons learned from the poetry of Innokentii Annenskii are barely detectable in her work, which took shape in an entirely independent fashion. The influence of Alexander Blok was of a purely general nature. Of course, in Akhmatova's eyes he was the highest embodiment of poetry among her contemporaries and its leading figure, and his many-faceted strophes could not but feed her thoughts. But who would dare assert that Blok was a leader she followed in poetry?

The proposition that the roots of the psychological in Anna Akhmatova's poetry were to be found in Russian prose, the Russian novel of the previous century, arose, in its general outlines, as early as the 1920s. To this day that exceedingly complex process of interaction and transformation has not been fundamentally investigated by anyone, nor has it been refuted; but it would seem that only there can an explanation of the genesis of Akhmatova's poetry be found. This in no way does away with our responsibility to take a closer and more vigilant look at older Russian poetry. Russian poetry is full of every conceivable kind of anticipation of what followed, in the matter of style as well. We also underestimate the purely psychological saturation of older Russian poetry, which often manifested itself even among lesser, secondary practitioners. But when Academician Zhirmunskii propounded his thesis that the creativity of Anna Akhmatova was the connecting link, the bridge between the Russian classics of the nineteenth century and the new art, the art of the twentieth century, Russian classical poetry was not the last thing in his mind. Pushkin's harmony, compelling one to recall the art of the ancient Greeks, hangs over Akhmatova's best work, And in this one feels her deep adherence to the legacy of the classics. But some of the cells, some grains of Akhmatova's style, can also be found in secondary poets of the past. (pp. 43-4)

[Although influenced to some degree by the poetry of the century], Akhmatova would not have been a major poet if her work had not shown traces, manifestations, of the gains made by Russian art, particularly poetry, in our century. Above all, this is a new ability to master color, hues, the ability to describe an object sparingly but expressively, to render the plastic nature of things seen; and—in intimate unity with all this—there was a new, considerably greater burden of meaning in the word, its density, its lapidary polishing. In this respect Akhmatova was an outstanding master. She developed and kept her own style while living alongside powerful poetic personalities at a time when various "schools" of poetry existed and functioned. Her characteristic rhythms alone always make Akhmatova's poetry distinguishable, identifiable in the flood of poetry written at the beginning of the century. (pp. 44-5)

Anna Akhmatova lived a long life, and her work underwent considerable evolution. In her late years, as is not rare with poets, she condemned and did not like much that she had written in her youth. Faced with the enormous social cataclysms that developed, Anna Akhmatova tried to embody a view of history in her words. The awesome tread of history was combined in her late verse with lofty ethical demands, a real judgment of the past, evidence of which is her **"Poem without a Hero."** . . . The maximalism of spirit that had long since appeared in Akhmatova became a constant feature of her poetry. (pp. 45-6)

In the difficult years of World War II, and even somewhat earlier, active civic notes could be clearly heard in Akhmatova's poetry. In her **"Courage"** . . . , written in February 1942, which was pasted up as a poster on the house walls of besieged Leningrad, one heard, as it were, the soul of the people in its wrath, defending its right to life and freedom . . . This was the path traced by the poet from closed literary circles and esthetic artists' cafes to the many millions of Soviet readers, to the people as a whole.

Native land: how much those words meant to this Russian poet grown gray and wise with the years, who held herself with great dignity, preserving to her very death the alertness in her light green eyes! Her talent did not age. Each new poem was fresh and bore a poetic discovery. In the phrase of Nikolai Rylenkov, her "will to self-resurrection" and profound awareness of the mission of the poet responsible to her native country and people, her humanism, were the soil that fed the marvelous creativity of Akhmatova for almost an entire half-century. The "Fountain House" in the city on the Neva, where she lived for many years, singing its granite embankments, awaits a memorial plaque in her honor. Her name is written in enduring letters in the chronicle of Russian literature. One need not doubt that Anna Akhmatova's poetry will always be needed. (p. 46)

Nikolai Bannikov, "On Anna Akhmatova: On the Ninetieth Anniversary of Her Birth" (originally published as "Ob Anne Akhmatovoi: K 90-letiiu so dnia rozhdeniia," in Literaturnaia Rossiia, *June 22, 1979), in* Soviet Studies in Literature *(translation © 1980 by M. E. Sharpe, Inc., Armonk, NY 10504), Vol. XVI, No. 1, Winter, 1979-80, pp. 42-6.*

RONALD HINGLEY

[The] young Akhmatova shuns the obscurity so characteristic of avant-garde verse. When she published her first poems, Russian readers had long been accustomed to expect new poetry not to yield its secrets as easily as hers does. True, her lyrics normally convey no more than an elusive and vague impression of emotions that are themselves elusive and vague. But they are otherwise largely free from obscurity, their originality being that of startling simplicity. The language is straightforward, conversational—at times even prosaic. The mystery lies more in the poet's personality than in her way of expressing herself.

She writes without obtrusive stylistic devices, most lyrics consisting of three or four four-line stanzas, with regular metre, often iambic, and with alternate rhyming lines. But this seeming lack of adventurousness conceals much elegant workmanship, and owes some of its success to surprise; it was not what readers had come to expect in an age when art often consisted less of concealing art than of flaunting artifice.

Despite her obsession with love Akhmatova is no erotic writer. (p. 24)

Though the reader [of Akhmatova] can indeed sense . . . "tumultuous passions," he is also conscious of the discipline and control with which the poet deploys them. The general tone is cool, and so the comparison with Sappho sometimes made . . . can be misleading. If Akhmatova is seized by convulsive trembling, if she is paler than grass, nigh unto death with frozen tongue and fire flickering under her skin (to quote a few Sapphic images), she manages to convey those experiences in a more clinical, less vibrant spirit than does the bard of Lesbos. (p. 25)

The early Akhmatova did not offer, as was claimed by Aleksandra Kollontay (a leading early Bolshevik and famous apostle of free love) "an entire volume of the female soul." Still less was she—at least in her earlier years—"concerned with the necessity of giving voice to the woman's point of view". . . . It is hard to see Akhmatova as a typical woman or a typical anything. She did not regard herself as the mouthpiece of collective womanhood, natural though this impression may be in view of her status as the first Russian woman writer to attain such prominence. She expressed *a* woman's point of view, but for *the* woman's point of view her readers had to wait for

Requiem, written many years later. She was not an apostle of feminism, however justifiably that cause had been preached in Russia since the mid-nineteenth century, being perhaps too self-possessed to feel that she needed to assert herself, either ''as a woman'' or in any other capacity. Nor was she the kind of mean spirit that chiefly sees itself as the representative of a social or sexual category. But her self-possession was combined with great vulnerability: here is a leading paradox among the many that lend her fascination.

Vulnerable or not, Akhmatova displays control and inner strength in her writing from the beginning. This claim is not contradicted by the tragic, pessimistic, gloomy sentiments that she often voices. They are not the wailings of self-pity. They are rather a dispassionate adverse diagnosis of the human condition offered by one free from illusions who believes in her need and capacity for a great love that (she knows, even as she craves for it) can never be anything but transitory and disappointing. Hers is an unruffled appraisal of a complex situation, not a cry of pain. (pp. 25-6)

Ronald Hingley, ''Torture by Happiness,'' in his Nightingale Fever: Russian Poets in Revolution *(copyright © 1981 by Ronald Hingley; reprinted by permission of Alfred A. Knopf, Inc.; in Canada by Weidenfield (Publishers) Limited), Knopf, 1981, (and reprinted by Weidenfield and Nicolson, 1982), pp. 18-44.**

Edward Albee

1928-

American dramatist and screenwriter.

With his first play, *The Zoo Story,* **Albee established himself as an avant-garde dramatist with great potential. His succeeding works,** *The Death of Bessie Smith* **and** *The American Dream,* **remained off-Broadway, but contributed to his growing reputation as one of the leading American figures in absurdist theater. With the Broadway production of** *Who's Afraid of Virginia Woolf?,* **Albee received international recognition.**

Albee's work addresses the problem of effective intimate communication in a world of increasing personal remoteness and emotional callousness. Critics have praised Albee's ability to use common speech and idiom to generate dramatic tension. In his later plays, however, such as *Tiny Alice* **and** *Seascape,* **the language has been heard as rather artificially elaborate and formal. Albee's recent play,** *The Lady from Dubuque,* **disappointed many critics by its unfocussed meaning. This new play, however, does employ the cocktail party setting, verbal asperity, and violence which contributed to the power of** *Who's Afraid of Virginia Woolf?.*

(See also *CLC,* **Vols. 1, 2, 3, 5, 9, 11, 13;** *Contemporary Authors,* **Vols. 5-8, rev. ed.;** *Contemporary Authors New Revision Series,* **Vol. 8; and** *Dictionary of Literary Biography,* **Vol. 7.)**

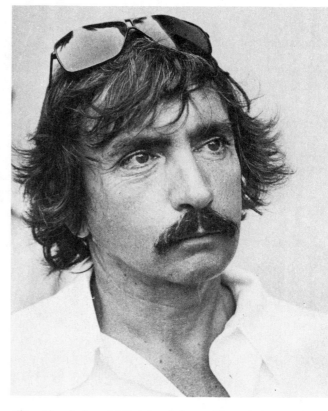

RICHARD A. DUPREY

It is incredible to consider that on the basis of four plays, one little more than a fragment, Edward Albee, the *enfant terrible* of America's *avant garde,* is being seriously considered in many quarters as a genuinely important playwright. The same critics and theorists who deny Thornton Wilder his legitimate right to be called a great playwright because he has written so little are ready to canonize young Albee as the greatest thing in modern drama.

This neatly tailored young man, who sounds quite rational and even personable, writes like a bomb-carrying anarchist. Without benefit of beret and red armband he seems to be principal among the new iconoclasts in our theatre. This group, claiming some inspiration from Ionesco, causing many a theatre-goer to shake his head in helpless bewilderment, seek, it seems, to shake the contemporary theatre to its roots, to put mystery back on a stage that has become enamored of fact and completely captivated by obvious *formulae*—a theatre which to them has become ossified.

The idea, on the surface, sounds quite commendable. Our American theatre has certainly been guilty of a narcissism that has disgusted many of its patrons and practitioners. Inbred, obsessed with its own fancied significance, prudently unoriginal and technique-ridden, it is overdue for the guillotine of meaningful revolt.

There is little doubt that the American theatre needs change and there's little doubt that such change will be forthcoming. . . . But then, we mustn't be too precipitous in praising just *any* change, for the theatre is the art of man, the art through which he most triumphantly asserts his humanity, his ration-

ality, his glorious birthright of free will, and the wondrous circumstances of his creation. The *avant gardist,* in his eagerness for change, in his fever for the joyous madness of demolition, does not offer this. He does not promise us that any such great theatre will arise from the ashes of the old. Instead he offers a collage of marginal comprehensibility, a collection of carefully collated contemporary inanities, devoid of order or any hint that beyond mystery's dark veil an unchanging truth may lie hidden. He offers only incongruity, the perverse and bizarre, and the unexpected. He offers no hint of a criteria for normalcy. (pp. 74-5)

Undoubtedly the *avant gardist,* and Albee here provides a fortunate case in point, has an axe to grind. He is original— terrifically original—and in his originality, extreme as it may often be, lies his strength. Nevertheless, it is difficult to peer through the smokescreen of paradox to see whether or not he really has something to say. In the theatre the audience doesn't *bother* to comprehend unless the playwright, within the generally accepted and known conventions of the stage, says what he has to say in a reasonably overt manner. No audience can sit happily guessing as to what the playwright means. (pp. 75-6)

Peculiarly enough, the *avant gardist* talks about man's failure to communicate. He notes the lack of love and understanding in the world and he stands up and howls dismally that men are horrible walled islands shut up within themselves, fated never to break loose from their bleak isolation. The terrible pair in *The Zoo Story* talking *at* each other instead of *with* each other, never genuinely touching each other in communication, likely embody this point of view as clearly as anything Albee has written. . . .

The *avant gardist* despairs of the modern theatre's technique and it is at this point we can scream derision at the precocious band who would level our theatre and render it a grotesque playground of their own devising. One needn't argue with their position that our modern world is a piteous place, constipated with egocentricity and bilious with smugness. We can accept this analysis and we can cheer any sincere and well-chosen efforts taken to better it. We *can* question the *means*, however, and it is in the means that the commendable objectives of some of the *avant gardists* (like Albee who does not appear a nihilist) are tragically betrayed.

In these cases, and let's use Albee for an example, we can note that he neither lectures interestingly like Brecht, delights and outrages like Shaw, nor sings like O'Casey as he slings his thunderbolts into the world's teeth. He fails dismally in getting his audiences up and outside themselves. He only slaps them back into the lonely cell of ego where they must dwell unfulfilled and in spineless terror. Albee is too busy indulging in private ironies to share with the humble generosity that is inevitably present in an artist who is earnest and true. (p. 76)

Albee's theatre gives nothing. It seeks attention in return for the dry crust of a spurious mystery. A concatenation of the same *non sequiturs* and banalities one hears on the street are poor payment indeed for those who come to the theatre.

One must not infer, in all of this, that theatrical experimentalism is to be questioned. Only through reasonable experimentation, with the erosive testing of ideas and execution in the acid-filled retort of performance and rehearsal and subsequent criticism, through the labor pains of the innovator who has given birth to the new idea and ideal, can the old theatre regenerate itself. (p. 77)

There is a relevant point in the classic fairy-tale, *The Emperor's New Clothes*, in which everyone fears to cry out the obvious truth that the Emperor is bare. Everyone fears to be called stupid for failing to see the clothes which are, as a matter of fact, not there. This damnable fear is ever the protection of the faddist.

Edward Albee, brash young novice, has torn off the white veil of humility and is confidently belching in the sanctuary of art. He writes for the narrow audience, an audience far removed from the broad pastures of grassroots participation where great plays are grown. His *Zoo Story*, following the hysterical indictments of conformity and self-isolation contributed by some of the European *avant gardists*, really paves the way for a new and insidious kind of conformism—one in which personal responsibility and the inexorable obligations occasioned by man's social nature are trampled under by the *new* herd.

The type of freedom extolled in *The Zoo Story* . . . is a perverted concept and Albee manifests . . . a frightening confusion between freedom *for* principle as opposed to freedom *as* principle. The difference is crucial and marks the boundary line where responsible human liberty leaves off and the tyranny of license begins. Albee, along with the others, recognizes no such distinction and would likely ridicule the idea that "The truth will make you free."

The Death of Bessie Smith provides us with the sight of another level of Albee's mendacity. This short play, set in a small hospital of the American South, seems a murky visitation to a world of abnormality—a hooded world of psychological aberration where man's motives are never clear and clean, but ever murky, never stemming from rationality, but from a sort of blind impulse. This sort of treatment vitiates the purpose of drama which involves the operation of the volitional man in a rational framework of purpose. All the play manifests is some talent for aping down-to-earth, repetitive dialogue true to his setting. A tape recorder can do nearly as much. Poor Bessie, planted anonymously in a Philadelphia grave, is ignored, despite the play's promising title.

The Sandbox, which is rather misleadingly described as a *play* in one scene, reaches new heights in obscurity with a middle-aged couple popping a senile granny into a child's sandbox at the shore. The old woman finds herself mightily attracted to the Angel of Death disguised as a muscle-bound beach boy. After some nearly incoherent theatrical tradespoofs in which the scene itself is mocked, the woman apparently dies, though it's difficult to be sure. Walter Kerr has referred to this piece as a "single, oddly satisfying sigh" and given it some cautious praise, seeming to approve Albee's clever impudence. One suspects, however, that in making the evaluation, Kerr is speaking as much from the ranks of theatre buffs who can enjoy a joke now and then as he is for the critical fraternity. (pp. 77-8)

It is a sad thing to see a young man—even one as intellectually complacent and self satisfied as Albee appears to be—given . . . adulation so early. Adulation that allows him to evade, even within himself, the problem of self-justification. Many a potential talent has been ruined by the flush of early success, and though to this date Albee has achieved only limited production in small theatres and under one management, he has been widely lionized as the champion of the new stage form, as the beardless young prophet who will deliver our theatre from the old nasty ways.

Perhaps if he takes the trouble to master his craft, if he builds endurance for his short-winded muse, if he correlates his natural ear for modern speech to something rational and truly dramatic, he will in time become a playwright to reckon with. He may even become the theatrical Messias for which the American theatre stands waiting. (pp. 79-80)

Richard A. Duprey, "From Pilate's Chair," in his Just off the Aisle: The Ramblings of a Catholic Critic *(copyright © 1962 by The Newman Press), The Newman Press, 1962, pp. 65-80.**

WALTER KERR

There are two Edward Albees, and they are both in *The Zoo Story*. In *The Zoo Story*, you will remember, a quiet man who is minding his own business, merely reading his newspaper on a park bench, is accosted by an unkempt, garrulous, desperately contemporary fellow who is determined to make contact at any cost. The neatnik on the bench is evasive; the beatnik circling him is fiercely direct. At play's end, the passive figure has killed the challenging one; the intruder has arranged things that way as a last resort. (p. 203)

Edward Albee #1 is the invader, the unsettler of other men's tidy little worlds, the unexpected noise on a summer day, the uninvited improviser. Not having been asked to speak, not having been offered any sort of subject for conversation, he bridles, invents, mocks, lashes out.

In this mood he can start from nowhere and in no time make a scene. *Virginia Woolf,* for instance, lunges forward for two long acts, emptying its lungs violently, without our having the least notion of the true nature of the quarrel. Its energy is boundless and gratuitous. . . . We do not understand why Martha and George behave so savagely toward one another, certainly not before the last act and, strictly speaking, not even then. But the savagery nourishes our need to be engaged as it does theirs. It is a felt presence, like heat slowly filling a cold room and imperceptibly altering the disposition we make of our bodies. We were numb; we don't know why the heat was turned on; but we are anything but numb now.

So long as Mr. Albee is forcing to the surface something that seems not to have been preshaped, so long as he is prodding for response like the aggressor in the park, he is free with his tongue and adroit with his whip. Practically speaking, it would appear that his creative imagination snaps to attention whenever there *is* no ready-made scene to be played. He may be concealing his ultimate intention, and so forced to feint; perhaps sometimes he does not even have one. But if the situation is open or even empty, and if two people can be persuaded to walk out onto the stage, he instinctively knows what to do. He makes the two people scratch at one another to see what may peel off. Inside a mystery at least malice may be real, and with malice there is thrust and counterthrust, evasive action and headlong action, heads and shins cracking together. If no relationship exists, Mr. Albee will make one. His unleashed intuition runs beyond his intellect, and fury forms before our eyes.

But that is Edward Albee #1, the playwright writhing with great intensity toward a pattern that may never come; the writhing is the play, and as writhing it has authority. Edward Albee #2 is the passive reader on the bench, the man who doesn't want to be bothered looking into other people's lives, the creature of the cut-and-dried. In *The Zoo Story* the indifferent man has everything accounted for—nights and days, beliefs and rejections, what does and does not belong to the Schedule. That is why he is indifferent. He has no need to speak because his bed is made, his movements are planned, his course is foreseen. The outline of his life has a certain prefabricated animation; but he is inert, having abdicated in favor of the outline.

The resemblance between this chap and Albee the Second asserts itself in several different ways. It may turn up, as it does in *Tiny Alice,* when a play is so schematically conceived, so rooted in a philosophical predisposition, that the figures onstage have all they can do to keep up with the marching propositions. It is as though they had all read Mr. Albee's timetable. . . . (pp. 203-05)

And the Other Albee turns up, most noticeably, in his adaptations. Between original plays Mr. Albee likes to tinker with novels he admires, first Carson McCullers' *Ballad of the Sad Café* and then James Purdy's *Malcolm.* But tinkering is the strongest word that can be applied here; Mr. Albee does not feel obliged to question too deeply the novelist's appointed rounds, he does not like to interfere with the Schedule.

Malcolm is meant to record the impact of adult life upon an innocent. (p. 205)

During his journey of discovery, Malcolm has presumably played out scenes with each of these people, suffering an injury here, a shattering illumination there. But in fact he has played no scenes. As Mr. Albee has fashioned the play, Malcolm drifts—literally, on a treadmill—into one environment after another,

observing relationships that are only standstill illustrations, and then drifts off again, reportedly withering along the way. But he has not entered these environments to play a role. (pp. 205-06)

No connections are made. . . . In some way Mr. Albee is not challenged to discover scenes, not impelled to scrape or to badger or to probe. He has accepted another man's outline for the evening—rather as though Mr. Purdy had employed him and told him to be there from eight till closing—and, like a good bourgeois and unquestioning square, he has filed everything dutifully and minded his manners. The play is written by wristwatch, composed of cursory glances to make certain no chore has been neglected; one feels that, having done the required typing, Mr. Albee, primly satisfied, has retreated behind his newspaper on *The Zoo Story*'s park bench. . . .

It is perfectly possible that the passive Albee, pursuing schema rather than invention for too long a time, may kill off the active Albee, the restless, eruptive, run-on interloper—though of course that would make *The Zoo Story* much too prophetic and ironic. Albee #1 is the man to count on and to hope for. Starting from scratch he can scratch; and that, very possibly, is his mission. (p. 206)

Walter Kerr, "Albee, Miller, Williams," in his Thirty Plays Hath November: Pain and Pleasure in the Contemporary Theater *(copyright © 1963, 1966, 1969 by Walter Kerr; reprinted by permission of Simon & Schuster, a Division of Gulf & Western Corporation), Simon & Schuster, 1969, pp. 203-30.**

GARETH LLOYD EVANS

[The] most brilliantly effective user of the American language in drama is Edward Albee. He has achieved as much fame in England as have Miller and Williams. In his case there might seem to be a special relationship with European drama for he has frequently been dubbed an 'absurd' dramatist. The claim of his alleged affiliation to this essentially European cult was based largely on the play *The Zoo Story.* On the evidence, however, of a more substantial and longer work—*Who's Afraid of Virginia Woolf?*—the claim seems to have an uncertain validity.

Absurdism, in so far as it relates to drama, has two main aspects—the point of view expressed in and by the play, and the method and means of expression. (p. 196)

The language of an 'absurd' play is just as distinctive as the vision which one senses or observes in it. Indeed what marks off Pinter, Ionesco, Beckett, in particular, from their non-absurdist colleagues is the amount of attention the language they use demands (because of its uniqueness) from the playgoer and the critic. To a very high degree, the language is the focus of the vision. To try and separate meaning and speech in an absurd play is to enter far into misrepresentation or into bafflement. In absurd drama language is used poetically, in the sense that however much it may seem to be a naturalistic version of real speech, closer examination shows that it is using the resources of poetry, to a degree. (p. 197)

An absurd play is . . . an image of human existence. It uses the sense-data provided by the so-called everyday world . . . but, in the long run, the spatial boundaries of an absurd play are not to be found in 'real' life, but in an inexplicable universe and a relentless eternity.

Edward Albee, in *The Zoo Story,* seems to partake of some of the characteristics of absurdism. The language is apparently inconsequential at times; the relationships are unsure or inexplicable; motivations both for speech and action seem governed less by rational processes than by a meaningless spontaneous reflex, the 'meaning' is elusive and, like so many absurd plays, there is 'no beginning, no middle, no end'.

This seems a formidable collection of evidence, but it may be suggested that, qualitatively, it is spurious. Almost every item seems too mechanically arrived at, contrived by a 'clever' writer. All the figures are correct, but the answer is not the right one. There are two main reasons for placing doubt on the claim for Albee's absurdism.

The first is the absence of the characteristic absurdist vision. This is absent from all of his plays, including the chief candidate for acceptance—*The Zoo Story.* In that play the frenzy, the change of mood, the menace, seem to be less an attribute of character than an exercise of quixotic theatricality. Apart from this, we find ourselves eventually wondering whether this sort of episode happens often in Central Park—in other words the play is less an image than a brilliant piece of quasi-naturalistic guignol.

The second arises from the degree of 'naturalism' which is present in Albee's plays and which, finally, separates him from the absurdists. Both the degree and its extent is rooted in Albee's sensitive, almost nervy feeling for contemporary American society. He is a superb demonstrator and explicator of certain aspects of Americanism. In order to align him with Pinter we would have to say that in Pinter we find the best mirror of certain aspects of British society today—and nothing else.

It is Albee's commitment to a surgical analysis of certain aspects of American society which debars him from acceptance as a complete and pure absurd dramatist. It is easy to see why he has been associated with these dramatists, because some details of attitude which he takes up towards his society are reminiscent of the typical absurdist vision. *The American Dream, Who's Afraid of Virginia Woolf?, The Zoo Story,* in particular, exhibit the meaninglessness of certain habits of behaviour, speech, *mores,* cults, myths. Again, all three plays, to a degree, brilliantly dissect certain sterile usages of speech. *The Zoo Story,* especially, is redolent of Pinter's concern with human isolation and the dark wastes of non or partial communication. It might be said that Albee's apparent preoccupation with an inability to beget children (in *The American Dream* and *Virginia Woolf*) as an image of sterile futility is, in itself, an 'absurdist' point of view.

But, in all this, there is not the characteristically absurdist miasma of menace, sometimes terror, the sense of unfathomable contexts behind the immediate world of the play, the implacable atmosphere of a-morality, the curiously paradoxical use of language in a 'poetic' fashion to demonstrate, often, the futility of language itself. Indeed it is in the use of language that we can find the distance from European absurdism and the closeness to Americanism. In Albee, too, is perhaps the clearest proof, if not the deepest, that the American language is not the same thing as the English language.

He is amazingly versatile in his deployment of language forms and styles, but there are two broad areas in which he excels—they occupy . . . extreme positions from one another. The one may be called literary/dramatic—an eloquent, rhetorical, philosophically inclined mode, the other is demotic/dramatic—in which the usages of contemporary American speech are employed with exciting variety and effect. In *The Zoo Story* he uses both types, in *Who's Afraid of Virginia Woolf?* he concentrates, though not exclusively, on the second, *A Delicate Balance* is almost monopolized by the first. His handling of the demotic/dramatic is much surer, and the results are decidedly more dramatically and theatrically credible than his attempts in the other mode. There, echoes of Eliot, traces even of Charles Morgan and a ghostly assembling of literary forefathers petrify the drama. . . . (pp. 197-99)

Albee is revealed as a dramatist of stature in his use of his 'alternative' language. He owes something to Miller in his deployment of certain characteristics of American speech but, in the long run, his is a more precise and searching mode. The most obvious affinity to Miller is in the use of repetition, but the effect is different. With Miller we feel that repetition is used in order to heighten the effect of the language—to take it one degree over naturalistic statement. With Albee we are aware that the repetitions fit more closely into the matrix of characterization; indeed they are often used, as in *Virginia Woolf,* self-consciously by characters with that kind of brittle, conscious verbosity apparent when the scotch-on-the-rocks set has reached the cocktail hour and its tongue is becoming loose. (p. 200)

One of the most conspicuous characteristics of absurdist writing is the extent to which dialogue—often using repetition—mirrors emptiness and futility. That emptiness separates and isolates the participants in the dialogue as certainly as a thousand miles of ocean. . . . The emptiness is, largely, imposed upon the participants, first and foremost by the nature of existence, but also by the particular situation and by their respective personalities. The crucial factor, however, is the first one—the strong sense of a blank force beyond control.

Albee very rarely gives this impression. The gaps and emptinesses that fall between his characters when they speak habitually convey the impression that they could be filled but, more often, they are filled almost as soon as we are aware of them—not by words, but often as efficaciously in the circumstances. Albee, unlike the absurdists, is less dominated by 'mal d'existence' than beguiled by 'mal de psychologie'. His silences and gaps are filled very quickly by material which comes straight out of the personality of the participants, goaded by the situation or event. (pp. 200-01)

Albee's métier as a dramatist of society and man's self-created tensions within it, and his versatility with words are shown, too, in his remarkable manipulation of the language of situation. Again, he uses repetition, but with a very much greater sense of using a technique; at times he reminds one of the Restoration penchant for drawing attention to the very fabric of language and to the cleverness with which it is spun. *Virginia Woolf,* again, provides the best evidence. (p. 202)

Albee, generally, seems to be very much more deliberately conscious of the technicalities of using words and takes more delight in employing them for dramatic and theatrical effect than other twentieth-century American dramatists. He seems to have a fastidiousness in his make-up which impels him to look at and to listen to the way his countrymen speak with a rare attention to detail. . . .

In his deployment of American speech Albee, especially in *The Zoo Story* and *Virginia Woolf,* shows that same compulsion towards the rhetorical [noticeable] . . . in Miller and Williams and which seems to be a characteristically American predisposition. Albee seems more aware than his colleagues of its dangers—of sentimentality and sententiousness—and he attempts to disguise these in different ways. In *A Delicate Balance* where he uses a sophisticated language which has the flavour of the more cerebral long speeches in *A Family Reunion,* he tries to moderate the effects by the occasional use of an idiomatic phrase. (p. 203)

Albee, like Miller and Williams, is at his best when he is not attempting to create a 'literary' language. The American penchant for over-dramatization, over-explicit statement, sentimentality of expression, overcomes them all when they try to invent a poetry of language. All three, but particularly Albee, succeed when they exploit the resources of American spoken speech, not when they try to make one up. This can be put in another way. When American dramatists, either consciously or unconsciously, try to achieve an English classicism they fail. When they write out of the dialect or dialects of their own American tribe, they succeed. (p. 204)

> *Gareth Lloyd Evans, "American Connections—O'Neill, Miller, Williams and Albee," in his* The Language of Modern Drama *(© Gareth Lloyd Evans, 1977), Everyman's University Library, J M Dent & Sons Ltd, 1977, pp. 177-204.**

JOHN SIMON

In *All Over,* Edward Albee wrote about a man dying offstage; in *The Lady From Dubuque,* he writes about a woman dying more or less onstage. Otherwise, there is not much difference: *All Over* was the worst play about dying until Michael Cristofer's *The Shadow Box; The Lady From Dubuque* is the worst play about dying since *The Shadow Box.* It is also one of the worst plays about anything, ever.

Jo is dying of cancer as her valiant husband, Sam, stands lovingly by. . . . [Much of the first act covers] that heavily worked-over Albee territory, the closed-circuit bitchery he steadfastly puts into the mouths of his married and unmarried couples. . . . What had some freshness, acerb wit, and propulsion in *Who's Afraid of Virginia Woolf?* is here the ultimate in witless nastiness, gratuitous offensiveness, and, above all, psychological nonsense and verbal infelicity. . . .

[Furthermore], Albee turns cancer into a sort of sick joke. Apparently privileged by the fact that she is dying, Jo is beastly to everyone. . . . Now, there is no need for someone doomed and in pain to be that bestial to everybody, or for everybody to tolerate and thus encourage it, but it permits Albee to practice his only skill, however moribund—insult comedy. . . .

[After] much multidirectional animosity and nonstop imbibing . . . , Jo, in acute pain, is carried upstairs to bed by Sam. Forthwith, an elegant, elderly woman in a red coat arrives in the company of an elegant, middle-aged black; we don't know who they are, how they got in, and why, but they seem to know exactly what is going on and take possession of the place as the curtain falls. In Act II, Sunday morning, Sam comes down in his nightshirt . . . and, understandably shocked, asks the intruders who they are. The woman launches on an interminable, teasing tirade with which she evades the question, while Sam asks a dozen times, "Who *are* you?"—a variation, I suppose, on Twenty Questions. Then the black joins in in a game of sadistic obfuscation, until it finally dribbles out that the woman, Elizabeth, is Jo's mother, unheard from for years, and Oscar, the black, her "friend." (p. 74)

The harrowing account from Act I about the horrors of slow dying . . . [is] wiped out by an Elizabeth and Oscar *ex machina.* Everybody leaves, and Elizabeth tells Sam a dream of hers about a series of distant, silent atomic explosions. When Sam identifies this as the end of the world, Elizabeth notes they had been talking about nothing else all along.

So ends the play, and Albee's last claim to being a dramatist, and no significant part of the world. *The Lady From Dubuque* is a lot of desperate pretensions and last-ditch attitudinizing about nothing, borrowed for the most part from previous Albee catastrophes. Let me enumerate the strategies for streching out nothing into two acts. (1) Repetition. Roughly one fourth of the dialogue is multiple repeats, e.g.: "I suppose you should know." "I suppose I should know." "I suppose you should." . . . (2) Asides. After a character has spoken to another, he will repeat the same point to the audience, thus: "I like your friends. *(To audience)* I like his friends." About one thirteenth of the play is redundant asides. (3) Not answering simple questions. This, drawn out beyond endurance, supposedly creates suspense. (4) Irrelevant but grandiose political or metaphysical mouthings. So Marx and Engels are trotted out repeatedly. . . . If Albee has read even one chapter of *Das Kapital,* I'll eat the others. (5) Obscenity. When all else fails, bring on the four-letter words. Albee, apparently, takes this to be still daring; but, then, he is always a couple of decades behind. Which leads to (6) *Ex post facto* liberalism. Oscar revels in ironies at the expense of racism as if they were boldly new; they have been heard on Broadway (and elsewhere) for 30 or 40 years. (7) Running gags that, though unfunny, keep running; thus variations on "No offense!" "None taken!" pop up a half dozen times. (8) Mystification. Is Elizabeth Jo's mother, or are she and Oscar angels of death? Obviously Albee himself doesn't know; he has publicly stated that they are not, yet how else . . . could they get past the locks of an expensive Manhattan apartment? But mystification obviates the need for characterization, which is beyond Albee. (pp. 74-5)

One last point. Albee is sometimes described—most often by himself—as a word-wizard, a stylist. No. He shares his characters' subliteracy. (p. 75)

> *John Simon, "From Hunger, Not Dubuque," in* New York *Magazine (copyright © 1980 by News Group Publications, Inc.; reprinted with the permission of* New York *Magazine), Vol. 13, No. 6, February 11, 1980, pp. 74-5.*

BRENDAN GILL

If it should prove to be the case that I like Edward Albee's new play, **"The Lady from Dubuque,"** . . . less well than other people do, one reason may be that the play is of a sort that I find particularly unsympathetic. Mr. Albee's intentions and my prejudices confront each other with an immediacy that has, if nothing else, the virtue of appropriateness, for in Albee's oeuvre a confrontation, usually within the bonds of a formally affectionate relationship, soon leads to collision, out of which a pinch of painful truth is expected to emerge. In the present instance, the truth *I* think I see emerging can be stated as a dictum: Plays that begin in a naturalistic vein risk losing credibility and the interest of their audiences if at the halfway mark they suddenly introduce characters who turn out to be personifications of states of mind or conditions of existence . . . , not unlike Sloth and Gluttony in some medieval morality play. I resent the insertion into a play about real people—about people, that is, whom we have been invited to pay attention to because they share with us the burden of being human—of creatures who pretend, for reasons that they may or may not consent to reveal, to be of our species but who are, we gradually perceive, embodiments of Death, or Life-in-Death, or one of a hundred other tiresome hand-me-down literary abstractions. Death is the harshest fact we know, not to be mitigated for us by the presence of superior Others from Out There; my intelligence, as well as my good nature, is taken advantage of when death is depicted as a creaky knight in armor, or a nice old man in a tree, or (who knows?) a lady from Dubuque who is neither a lady nor from Dubuque. (p. 63)

Brendan Gill, "Out There and Down Here," in The New Yorker *(© 1980 by The New Yorker Magazine, Inc.), Vol. LV, No. 52, February 11, 1980, pp. 63-5.**

GERALD CLARKE

[Every line of *The Lady from Dubuque*] bears the name of Edward Albee. It is not only fine theater, savagely funny and affecting. But it is also his best work since *Who's Afraid of Virginia Woolf?* nearly 18 long years ago. The curtain rises on that familiar Albee landscape, a living room late on a Saturday night. Three young couples have been playing Twenty Questions, or, more accurately, Who Am I? Sam, the host, . . . is up, and though everybody else is tired of the game, he refuses to quit. He wants an answer. His wife Jo . . . stops him, however, with a game of her own. One by one she tells their friends exactly who and what they are. . . . But everyone forgives Jo because she is visibly dying of cancer and is just radiating a part of her own intense pain. . . .

The lady from Dubuque enters only . . . after the guests have left and Jo and Sam have gone upstairs to bed. Her title is derived from Harold Ross's famous statement that he was not editing *The New Yorker* for "the little old lady in Dubuque." Albee uses it ironically, and his mysterious lady . . . is a figure of commanding presence. . . . [She] is, it seems, an angel of death, or some other instrument of mercy, who has arrived to relieve Jo of her misery.

With daylight, last night's guests return to make up. They automatically accept the fact that [the lady] is Jo's mother and tie Sam up when he impotently protests. Even Jo, half delirious with painkillers, is drawn to her, finally begging the black companion to carry her to bed, and to death. As Sam gives up his role as husband and protector, so he loses his identity. The shape of our lives, Albee is saying, is created by the needs of those around us. When those needs disappear, so, in a sense, do we. Jo's pain is physical and therefore transitory; Sam's is spiritual and therefore endless.

For almost two decades, Albee often buried his plays under metaphor and meaning, sometimes forgetting that drama, by definition, demands a clash of living characters, as well as ideas. In *The Lady from Dubuque,* he has returned to the style of *Virginia Woolf.* This is a smaller play, shorter and less emotionally demanding. But it is a major work nonetheless, and like the enigmatic lady of the title, Albee is very much in control.

Gerald Clarke, "Night Games," in Time *(copyright 1980 Time Inc.; all rights reserved; reprinted by permission from* Time*), Vol. 115, No. 6, February 11, 1980, p. 69.*

HAROLD CLURMAN

[*The Lady From Dubuque*] baffled me. It begins with a party of friends who play games around the hostess, a dying woman whose malignancy is matched by the festering poison which issues from the hostile stupidity of her (and her husband's) guests. Such a group . . . could never be collected in one room and could never remain together for more than a few moments after the initial exchange of insults. Are these people supposed to represent our middle class? Are we to take them as "real" people or as gargoyles inspired by a sickened imagination?

And then after a long scene of random venom, two mysterious figures—a gracious "lady from Dubuque" and a cultivated black man—enter. The supposedly real characters confront the two symbolic ones who are, I presume, minions or heralds of death.

This entrance is followed by a barrage of wisecracks and sententious utterances on a range of unrelated subjects. From this we are to gather that the main question in life is "Who am I?"; it is also asserted that when we die the world comes to an end, etc., etc. Normally I might insist that such thoughts are idle or false, but in this instance there would be no point in doing so because they emerge from a vacuum and go nowhere; they float about in a virtually nonexistent context. Albee has not only lost his bearings but also cuts us off from our own, leaving us with no way to argue with him. He has created no dramatic body and therefore cannot make any dramatic or ideological statement.

Harold Clurman, "Theatre: 'The Lady from Dubuque'," in The Nation *(copyright 1980 The Nation magazine, The Nation Associates, Inc.), Vol. 230, No. 7, February 23, 1980, p. 221.*

ROBERT BRUSTEIN

Whenever I review a play by Edward Albee, I worry about the distribution of his royalties. He has such a perfect gift for theatrical mimicry that I begin to imagine August Strindberg, Eugene O'Neill, and T. S. Eliot rising from their graves to demand for their estates a proper share of *Who's Afraid of Virginia Woolf, Tiny Alice,* and *A Delicate Balance.* Even living authors like Samuel Beckett, Eugene Ionesco, and Harold Pinter might be contemplating a case against Albee, not so much for expropriating their plots and characters as for borrowing their styles. In his latest play, *The Lady From Dubuque,* . . . the playwright has gone to an unusual source—namely himself. I can see a lawsuit coming—Albee v. Albee—where the younger accuses the older writer of plagiarism, perhaps even alienation of affection and breach of promise.

Albee certainly has breached his promise in his last 11 plays, not excepting *The Lady From Dubuque.* It is really quite an awful piece, drenched with those portentous religious-philosophical discharges about death and truth and illusion that have been swamping his work ever since he got the preposterous idea in his head that he was some kind of . . . prophet and metaphysician of our disorders. I felt acutely embarrassed for actors charged with saying things like "Everything is true . . . therefore nothing is true . . . therefore everything is true." If *that* is true, then they ought to stop talking altogether. Unfortunately, they don't. And the characters they are given to play are not much improvement on their dialogue.

Collected together in a living room that looks more like the first-class lounge on the SS *United States* are three mismatched couples who spend the opening minutes of this two-hour evening bitching at each other, when they are not looking around . . . for their lost identities. . . . [Basically, the characters] are your average run-of-the-mill Albee scorpions, and while they are depositing some diluted venom into each other's necks, the heroine (who is dying of cancer) curls up every so often in a question mark of pain and screams. . . .

Still, Albee faking Albee is better than Albee faking Eliot, if you're measuring degrees of fakery. I found enough faint echoes of the old ripper in the play to keep my eyelids from closing—as they did . . . in *All Over,* and Albee's other boring discourses on mortality. Every so often, a little wave of energy courses through the dead electrical circuits of the work, as when a character says, "My cup runneth over," and another replies, "Right, but watch the rug." A little more of this stuff, and I might have snapped awake entirely, but Albee's heart is no more in the bickering of his couples than in the suffering of his heroine. Perhaps the ghastly reception and quick closing of this play will get him angry enough to give up the metaphysical gush and get back to his proper work—cutting the jugulars of his unfortunate American contemporaries. (p. 26)

Robert Brustein, *"Self-Parody and Self-Murder"* (reprinted by permission of the author; © 1980 by Robert Brustein in The New Republic), Vol. 182, No. 10, March 8, 1980, pp. 26-7.*

STANLEY KAUFFMANN

Fate has not been kind to Edward Albee. I don't mean only the bitterness of early success and subsequent decline, though that's hard enough. Worse: He was born into a culture that—so he seems to think—will not let him change professions, that insists on his continuing to write plays long after he has dried up. . . .

Look at Albee's career since its peak, which I take to be *Who's Afraid of Virginia Woolf?,* produced 18 years ago. Three adaptations, *The Ballad of the Sad Cafe, Malcolm,* and *Everything in the Garden,* all deplorable. . . . Then *Tiny Alice, A Delicate Balance, All Over,* and *Seascape,* a long torpid decline interrupted only briefly by a pair of short, passable attempts at the Absurd, *Box* and *Quotations From Chairman Mao Tse-Tung.* What marked the full-length plays, right after the realism of *Virginia Woolf,* was Albee's use of mysticism and death. I mean use, utilization, not inquiry or dramatization. The big words and ideas became weapons to club us into awe of the works' profundity, a conclusion that was inescapable because the works themselves were so tenuous, even silly. Allegory (*All Over*) and symbolism (*Seascape*) were also called into service, creakingly. Overall, Albee seemed compelled to write plays just to prove that he is still a playwright, and he grabbed at sonorous subjects and august methods to cloak his insufficiencies.

The bottom, so far, is reached in his latest play, *The Lady From Dubuque.* There *is* a lady from Dubuque in it, or she says she is, only so that the title could refer to Harold Ross's remark that the *New Yorker* wasn't edited for the little old lady from Dubuque. Which has nothing to do with the play. Which, in pertinency, lines up the new title with *Virginia Woolf.* Even more strained is Albee's attempt once again to place himself at the center of mysteries, though again he ends up in the center of gas.

Lady begins realistically with party games (once again!) in a living room, with Albee's latter-day salty language that offends because it's so self-consciously salted on. The realism is mechanically lightened with an ancient dramaturgic device: The actors know they are in a play, and they address the audience from time to time. Since no reason, narrative or textural, is

ever adduced for the device, we soon realize that it's Albee who is addressing us, not the actors, assuring us that he is a clever-deep master of the stage. (p. 34)

Inarguably death is haunting Albee's mind. One way or another, death has figured in all his long plays since *Virginia Woolf*—but to no artistic end. It may be critically overwhelming but it's thematically apt to raise the name of this age's prime dramatist of mortality, Samuel Beckett. Unlike Beckett, Albee can't face death without a lot of spiritualist's hokum, let alone add to our apprehension—any kind of apprehension—of the idea. . . .

Albee is now 52. What will become of this intelligent, valuable man? He has a third of his life left—more than that, I hope—plenty of time for another career if misconstrued pride doesn't deter him. I've long thought that he would make a first-class dramaturg . . . in the European tradition that is beginning to prosper at American institutional theaters—an in-house critic (Albee's writing and interviews show sharp critical acumen about everyone but himself), a literary manager and production adviser, and occasionally a director. . . .

It's not a matter of renunciation. Why should he flatly renounce playwriting? But the evidence of the last 18 years doesn't justify Albee's investment of all his remaining life in his own plays. What a courageous act it would be for him to opt for dramaturgy. How helpful to a theater, to other writers he can advise, to the changing of a cultural pressure that is wasteful, to the fullest use of his own gifts. Will he insist instead on serving out the term to which, presumably, he has let our culture sentence him? (p. 35)

Stanley Kauffmann, *"Edward Albee: All Over?"* in Saturday Review (© 1980 Saturday Review Magazine Co.; reprinted by permission), Vol. 7, No. 6, March 15, 1980, pp. 34-5.

BEN CAMERON

Evaluating Edward Albee's *Lolita* solely on the basis of injustices done to the Nabokov novel is a disservice to the play; such evaluation misses Albee's larger, more theatrical intent. The drama at best uses the novel as a departure point, adopts its narrative framework, exploits certain of its verbal and visual images. Albee unsuccessfully attempts something more ambitious than mere adaptation; his departures from the novel are calculated to facilitate his own theatrical and spiritual sensibility. Comparing the play and the novel makes such a sensibility manifestly clear. The Nabokov book should be examined to illuminate Albee's work; it should not be used as a sacrosanct standard by which to judge the quality of an adaptation.

Even enthusiastic admirers of the novel may forget the brief introduction that precedes the journal of Humbert Humbert. The manuscript has passed from Humbert to his legal counsel and subsequently to an editor after Humbert's death. Even now, certain precautions have been taken to insure that involved parties will not be identified. . . . This preface pretends to lift *Lolita* beyond the realm of fiction. . . . (p. 77)

Albee's *Lolita* opens with the appearance of "A Certain Gentlemen"—the theatrical descendant of the editor. He too introduces the pedophilic mania of Humbert and establishes a framework for Humbert's appearance, but here his resemblance to Nabokov's editor ceases. For A Certain Gentleman is a writer, an artist who claims responsibility for the creation that appears before us; he does not merely offer the work of another man. Nor does he withdraw and leave us alone with Humbert. On the contrary, he takes an active role: he remains visible throughout the evening, conspires with the other characters in Humbert's absence, and jokes with the audience during Humbert's love scenes. His presence, instead of suggesting that the story has happened (or could happen), reminds us that this version is totally fictitious, the product of his imagination; this Humbert, fantastic and remote, cannot demand confrontation and is safe, laughable, distant.

The play follows the novel's basic narrative path. (pp. 77-8)

The picaresque structure of the Nabokov novel carries us more and more deeply into the unique psychological world of Humbert, while using Humbert's passions to stand for larger, more universal human passions and obsessions. Puritanism tempers the pedophilic, moral rigor matches prurience, a black grimness of humor and purpose balances a surprising frailty. Such combinations account for much of the novel's power. . . . These alliances of light and dark, of universal and idiosyncratic are the crucial determinants of Humbert's character, yet these alliances are severed in Albee's adaptation.

Albee's Author embodies the moral force, the restrainer who must confound Humbert. When sensual encounters border on the graphic, the Author drops a large curtain and obscures the lovemaking, he encourages Clare Quilty's attempts to lure Lolita from Humbert; he even calls a halt to Humbert's call for pedophiliacs in the audience and curtails the graphic description of seduction. Humbert willingly relinquishes such moral restraint but thereby loses any sensitivity, sense of love, or moral presence that could deepen and enrich the character. Albee confines Humbert's obsessive passions to the sexual, and reduces his love to mere pedophilic lust.

This bifurcation of Nabokov's Humbert maims any growing moral tension. The Author and Humbert enjoy a congenial relationship. They treat Humbert's love as amusing, inevitable, perhaps even as logical, but never as obsessive or alarming; Freudian vaudeville replaces passion. Even the normally stern Author allows himself to slide into sleaze after the seduction of Lolita. . . . Albee's *Lolita* is sterile, passionless, and his protagonist is a satyr, not a sufferer.

But perhaps Albee's *Lolita* is not supposed to be about passions at all. Indeed, adapting *Lolita* for the stage has incurred a host of new problems that alone may account for such a switch in focus. In the novel, Lolita is never seen except through Humbert's eyes. Even in her most difficult moments, his epithets of passion bathe her in a beatific glow, incarnate her as a divine "nymphet"; she never vanishes from our minds. This technique of perpetual presence and its importance to the themes of obsession are more difficult, though not impossible, to achieve onstage; indeed, Lolita's stage appearances undermine our response to Humbert's passion. Embodied by an actress, Lolita attains precisely the independence of persona that Nabokov denies her. Humbert's paeans to sensuality are contradicted by the corporeal presence of a gangly, foul-mouthed girl with jutting elbows and knocking knees. Her every move strains any belief in Humbert's "light of my life, fire of my loins," and when she exits, she vanishes—totally. A tension is automatically established between Humbert's possessed perceptions of Lolita and the audience's more objective, detached ones. The commonplace Lolita cannot match the ethereal one Humbert describes; her pretensions to any eroticism beyond mere carnality become solely inventions of Humbert's. And because he is reduced to a one dimensional, amoral omnivore, she cannot really affect him by provoking any inner conflict

or confusion; she can only satisfy his sexual appetite. From god-life *figura,* she has descended to mere creation.

This concern with creator and creation dominates Albee's play. A superstructure has been imposed on the novel, one that emphasizes the Author as *figura* as the Humbert-Author relationship supercedes the Humbert-Lolita one. In the play, Albee creates a surrogate presence, A Certain Gentleman. This second Author in turn creates Humbert, who in turn creates Lolita. . . . Such a structure holds fascinating potential on various moral, social, psychological, even theological planes.

But Albee does not carry this structure beyond its inception; there is no consistent development of ideas. . . . [Nothing] that Albee accomplishes in *Lolita* suggests any fascination, indeed any involvement, with his characters or with this new emphasis on the created and the creator. Deprived of passions and true feelings, his characters can reveal nothing about love; stripped of moral dimension, the play can neither indict nor condone social mores; tentative in its understanding of the connection between art and artist, the play cannot manipulate the distance between audience and actor or between author and play. *Lolita* does not have to be about Humbert's passion for Lolita, but neither can it be a work totally devoid of passion. The dramatic Author(s), in denying any passionate involvement with their creations, undercut the ultimate source of literary life and energy. Albee's *Lolita* is born of inertia, tedium, and it frequently discloses its parentage. This passionless center only emphasizes Albee's own lack of vital connection with the theater and compounds the problems of adaptation.

For *Lolita* traps as well as inspires Albee. The idea of adaptation frees Albee for his new focus; in dealing with situations and themes already created, he can more fully manipulate certain distances and structures. But Albee never demonstrates a need for using *Lolita* as his source; hundreds of other novels could have served his purposes just as easily. Nabokov's plot, a reaction to social attitudes of the 1950's, cannot meet certain demands of the 1980's, especially when forced into the present and stripped of its passionate underpinnings. Albee nonetheless tries to update the novel by merely adding four letter words, stale jokes about the Shah, and lame references to early morning television. Such vulgarizations cannot move *Lolita* into the present. Indeed, this additional profanity clearly violates Nabokov's sense of propriety and stunning verbal economy, while highlighting Albee's verbal flabbiness. "Is this a lecture?" the Author asks. "An exegesis. The briefest of exegeses," Humbert replies. Such hair-splitting demonstrates the turgid, untheatrical nature of the text. (pp. 78-9)

Ben Cameron, "Who's Afraid of Vladimir Nabokov?: Edward Albee's 'Lolita'" (reprinted by permission of the author), in Theater, *Vol. 12, No. 3, Summer, 1981, pp. 77-80.*

FRANK P. CALTABIANO

American playwrights and screenwriters seem to have run out of timely issues and borrowed subjects and, since the late seventies, to have hit upon one which the great world dramatists have treated for centuries with greater insight and less arrogance and glibness: death. With *The Lady from Dubuque* Edward Albee takes his place among a cadre of recent Americans who have focused on this ultimate of passage rites.

Sam and his wife Jo, a victim of some terminal form of cancer, give parties for and play parlor games with a seemingly masochistic group of friends. The play opens during one such gathering. (p. 473)

The second act focuses on the appearance of the mysterious Elizabeth, an angel of death—cum-mama who, with her black friend Oscar, takes over the house with several brilliantly executed acts of psychological terrorism. . . . After repeated postulations of the question "Who are you?" throughout the play (most tellingly by Elizabeth in the second act), Sam, as a result of this symbolic sacrifice, discovers who he is and learns finally that his emotional dependence on Jo was robbing him of his individuality.

If the above sounds a bit familiar, it is because much of the work borrows from past successes while it leaves the craft to stand alone and naked, an empty echo of the depth and sensitivity found in *The American Dream, Who's Afraid of Virginia Woolf, Tiny Alice* and *A Delicate Balance.* Many of the old concerns are resuscitated: the disintegration of American society, the quest for human identity in the face of inexorable technology, the call for individualism in a pluralistic and threatened society. Skeletons which have had Americans scurrying with guilt-ridden tails between their legs are flashed before us. Communism, racism, the bomb, pathologically excessive momism, consumerism and even New Jersey (which Albee seems to loathe) receive their share of attention. It would appear that in dealing with these past themes in the light of the present subject of death, Albee seeks to point to what he sees as a society in its death throes. He offers as the only alternative, the sole means for survival, a retreat into the self, a world in which trust and dependence are placed entirely in the individual self. Hence the recurring question: "Who are you?" becomes the thematic leitmotiv.

Many of the elements of an important work are clearly present. One notes immediately the classic use of ritual and symbol, the near-Aristotelian cleanliness of arrangement and the command of language so familiar to Albee's admirers. It is unfortunate for *Lady from Dubuque* that these do not suffice. For despite its moments of brilliance and poetry, the play is marred by an extreme self-consciousness as reflected in the dialogue, in the dredging up of old causes and personal dislikes, in the rehash of old characters and techniques and in the ill-advised use of the direct audience address, which fails miserably in this instance. But most of all it suffers from a lack of any real penetration of character or situation beyond what is needed to convey Albee's dicta. *The Lady from Dubuque* may be exciting theatre, but it cannot be counted among Albee's great works. To fashion one that can, he will have to abandon formulae and explore the human condition from a new, uncluttered, less didactic point of view. (pp. 473-74)

Frank P. Caltabiano, "Theatre: 'The Lady from Dubuque'," in World Literature Today *(copyright 1981 by the University of Oklahoma Press), Vol. 55, No. 3, Summer, 1981, pp. 473-74.*

DAN SULLIVAN

"The Man Who Had Three Arms," is about a man who had three arms.

That is to say a man who *once* had three arms, the extra having gradually sprouted from his back in midlife, like an angel's

wing or a unicorn's horn or a late-blooming talent, bringing him fame, fortune and appearances on all the talk shows.

But as unexpectedly as his new limb grew, it shrank and when the man went back to having two arms again nobody wanted to interview him on TV any more. There was, however, still the Midwest lecture circuit: afternoon talks to blue-haired ladies thrilled to meet even the formerly famous.

Albee's play takes the form of such a lecture. . . .

Will "**The Man Who Had Three Arms**" be another "**Virginia Woolf**"? No. It's not the big play that one keeps hoping Albee will come up with, the play he needs to climb back into contention in today's theater. Neither, though, does it have the stillborn feeling of his later plays—"**All Over,**" say. There is some juice in this one, even if it is mostly bile. . . .

The first half of the play is a game of keep-away. The lecturer will tell us what it was like to have a third arm in a moment, but first he wants to tell us about some other things. Such as what he thinks of the morbid celebrity-hunting exorcise that his appearance represents. Such as what he thinks of our pathetic faces staring up at him. (Just kidding.) Such as what he thinks of killer lady newspaper reporters. . . . But first why don't we call an intermission, so I can have a drink and a cry? Ten minutes.

So far, not bad. Albee's capacity for informed scorn gives the lines real energy, and [it is] . . . clear that the speaker is in real pain, not just doing riffs on the bourgeoisie. Maybe we will get to the nub of the pain in the second act. . . .

Surprisingly the story of how that third arm came and went is less vivid than the prologue. As with Philip Roth's novella about a man who turned into a female breast, it's a little hard to picture the anatomy being described. . . .

Obviously we are supposed to take the hero's extra limb as a symbol of specialness and strangeness, not wished-for but profited from—and then disastrously lost. It is also a phallic symbol, "Old No. 3 with a will of its own," its loss a symbolic unmanning, always a threat in Albee's plays.

One admits the implications, but the image on the first level doesn't prove out as vigorously as it should, probably because Albee didn't want his audience to visualize the arm too strongly, fearing giggles or groans. Too bad he didn't take the risk. Any freshman playwright can invent a symbol. I wanted to believe in that arm.

You do believe in Albee's description of what being "celebrated" (for whatever) brings a man these days—the big bucks, the willing playmates, the reporters who think they own you— and the things it takes away, such as love. When fame recedes, the love does not necessarily reappear and this is the box [the hero] is in as the curtain falls on his lecture, howling for us to love him for himself, not for his phantom limb. "I am you!" he screams—we whom he's been belittling for two hours. Yet we pity him.

For all its problems, this play is written from the gut. It could be something of a catharsis for Albee, putting him on a more vital theatrical track than his latter dramatic essays in pseudo-Henry James prose on the failures of others to encounter reality.

Dan Sullivan, "Albee Presents 'Three Arms' in Chicago," in Los Angeles Times *(copyright, 1982, Los Angeles Times; reprinted by permission), October 24, 1982, p. 38.*

A(rchie) R(andolph) Ammons

1926-

American poet.

Because of his poetic adaptation of natural forces, forms, and phenomena in the American landscape, some critics consider Ammons, more so than Whitman, the fulfillment of Emerson's call for an American bard.

Although his first book, ***Ommateum with Doxology***, was a commercial and critical failure, Ammons has since received much favorable recognition, including a National Book Award in 1973 for his *Collected Poems: 1951-1971*. Harold Bloom has stated that, "No contemporary poet, in America, is likelier to become a classic than A. R. Ammons. . . ."

Remarkably prolific, Ammons has produced three new volumes of poetry *(The Snow Poems, A Coast of Trees*, and *Worldy Hopes)* and two collections of selected poems in the past five years.

(See also *CLC*, Vols. 2, 3, 5, 8, 9; *Contemporary Authors*, Vols. 9-12, rev. ed.; *Contemporary Authors New Revision Series*, Vol. 6; and *Dictionary of Literary Biography*, Vol. 5.)

PETER STITT

© Rollie McKenna

When A. R. Ammons goes wrong, I think the problem is primarily one of voice. At his best, he is an objective poet who speculates on the nature of reality and its possible underpinnings. There is an observer present in such poems, to be sure, but his explicit role is a small one. Ammons is at his best when he most follows Emerson's inspired standard: "I become a transparent eyeball." In such cases, little or no attention is drawn to the speaker-observer. In *The Snow Poems*, however, all attention is consciously directed at the speaking character himself, and this fact accounts, I think, for the book's monumental failure. Good confessional poetry achieves its success by drawing on the tensions, neuroses, and self-destructive impulses of the poet's own life. Judging from *The Snow Poems*, Ammons lives an altogether too sane and ordinary life for him to operate successfully in this mode. The book has the form of a versified journal in which Ammons talks endlessly about the weather and professional football. The forms are pedestrian, as if the author's prose diary entries had simply been broken into lines. Occasionally, the words that comprise the lines are further broken down into letters, so that we think we are reading concrete poetry [but] . . . it is not good concrete poetry either. (pp. 944-45)

Happily, Ammons' other recent volume, ***The Selected Poems 1951-1977***, is more than good enough, although it does not begin on a particularly strong foot. The book is arranged chronologically, and so the first poems that we encounter are the Ezra poems from Ammons' first volume, ***Ommateum***. The problem with the speaking voice mentioned above is once again present here, though in a different way. These poems are written not in the disastrous confessional voice of *The Snow Poems*, not in the objective-meditative voice of Ammons' best poems, but in the voice of the biblical figure, Ezra. One of the recent vogues in American poetry is the portentous mythic or pseudo-

mythic poem which purports to give modern man sage advice drawn from a less complicated but more spiritually authentic time. We ought to be the wiser for having read such poems, and for a time perhaps we were. But the mode now seems predictable and obvious, even dated, and one longs to meet no more shaggy prophets bearing sonorous aphorisms from the loneliness of an empty desert. Ammons thus opens his second ***Selected Poems*** (the first appeared in 1968) in a common, conventionalized voice not characteristically his own.

Beginning somewhere around the twentieth page, however, we find ourselves in more comfortable surroundings. Ammons has been widely praised as an Emersonian Transcendentalist—optimistic, somewhat mystical, a lover of nature. The connection between the two writers is most certainly there, and does appear in these areas. What is equally—and perhaps more importantly—striking, but far less widely recognized, is the Platonic basis or bias of Ammons, which may again be traced to Emerson. At the beginning of the sixth section of his most famous work, "Nature," Emerson sends a seismic shock through his reader by asking—and this after describing and praising physical nature for five long and complicated sections—whether nature actually, that is, physically, exists. He concludes that probably nature does *not* outwardly exist, though, since we believe that we perceive it, we can proceed as though it does exist. At heart, Emerson is a Platonist—the ideal forms, the abstract, spiritual laws that lie behind the things of this world, are of greater reality and importance to him than the things of this world themselves. That is one reason, among others, why Emerson hired Thoreau to spade his garden, despite his own idealistic praise of gardening; and it is why he really preferred meditating in his study to going with Henry on nature walks.

In Ammons we find a deep and abiding love for nature constantly being expressed. But through it all, Ammons is always searching for the general within and behind the specific, for the abstract, spiritual laws that govern and actuate physical reality—and it is the abstract realm that most deeply engages his interest and attention. Where Emerson felt able to identify the spiritual principle behind reality as the Oversoul, Ammons—while convinced that some such thing exists—is unsure of its exact nature or identity. Thus he could accurately be called a speculative poet, as he openly pursues unseen reality through his poems. As he says in **"Snow Log"**: "there's some intention / behind the snow snow's too shallow / to reckon with: I take it on myself."

The poem **"One: Many"** may be Ammons' fullest expression of this theme, and once again the perspective is decidedly Emersonian. Unity, he decides, cannot be imposed upon diversity from above. . . . Variety, and the freedom implicit in variety, are themselves aspects of the principle of unity. (pp. 945-46)

Elsewhere, Ammons is less complicated, in poems that praise and describe nature for what it is without searching out the principle of unity. Poems like **"Cascadilla Falls," "Rectitude," "Eyesight," "Bonus,"** and especially the very remarkable **"Jungle Knot"** are supremely beautiful and rewarding works. It was wise of Ammons to follow the disaster of **The Snow Poems** so closely with the triumph of **The Selected Poems 1951-1977**. Our faith in his powers is restored. (p. 947)

> *Peter Stitt, "Book Reviews: 'The Snow Poems' and 'The Selected Poems 1951-1977'," in* The Georgia Review *(copyright, 1978, by the University of Georgia), Vol. XXXII, No. 4, Winter, 1978, pp. 944-47 [the excerpt of Ammons's poetry used here was originally published in his* The Selected Poems 1951-1977 *(reprinted by permission of W. W. Norton & Company, Inc.; copyright © 1977, 1975, 1974, 1972, 1971, 1970, 1966, 1965, 1964, 1955 by A. R. Ammons), Norton, 1977].*

ROBERT McDOWELL

After he has published a "major" collection, a poet can be excused for some time. A few may groan a little, but nobody will long lament if he never approximates that height again. They will think that you were lucky to have been there once. It would be still more rare for a poet, in the span of seven years, to follow *two* "major" collections with a *third*. But in his new book, **The Snow Poems**, that is exactly what A. R. Ammons has done. In **Collected Poems: 1951-1971**, in **Sphere: The Form of a Motion**, and in **The Snow Poems** this prolific poet shows no signs of letting up.

In an age when most poets have pulled in their claws to confront us with mushy, probing soft paws, Ammons comes at us with his talons bared, aiming at the Universal Heart. The man's drive is unique in that it does not produce bulk at the expense of quality. Few poets match his productivity or his level of excellence. When we sit down to Ammons we need never grieve about warmed leftovers. With a painter's eye for color

and detail he writes about the things he sees. You will not catch him astride the dark merely imagining—he reports *and* imagines. This way, for the true poet, is the one way. The risks and rewards are infinitely greater. There are pitfalls, but they are overshadowed by sustained periods of unbridled flight. Even when Ammons stumbles, even when he makes mistakes, he is never sloppy or less than completely honest about himself. He appears to be riding the crest of a wave with no descent in sight. In that state of grace it looks as if he could go on forever.

The Snow Poems contains 119 poems in which an admirable craftsmanship is indisputable. But taken together the poems also read as one long poem. The sense of the book is best assimilated through this approach. It is refreshing to encounter a contemporary long poem that is not just another self-indulgent joke, another tedious and forgettable specimen of "literature." How tired we are of encountering poems in which there is nothing more substantial than random words on a page. **The Snow Poems** has little to do with such a tradition.

Ammons brings to his new work familiar concerns: the on-going, minute examination of his inexhaustible world, the continual reduction and reconstruction of the Self. There are new wrinkles as well: encroaching middle age (the poet's fiftieth year) and the gradual deterioration of memory. All are linked together by the symbolic snow. It is an apt device that functions ably on two levels. There is the level that Melville pondered in the whiteness of the whale, the sacred, white dog of the Iroquois, the white bear of the polar ice, the white stallion of the plains. "This elusive quality it is," Ishmael says, "which causes the thought of whiteness, when divorced from more kindly associations, and coupled with any object terrible in itself, to heighten that terror to the furthest bounds." For Ammons the "object terrible in itself" is the oblivion of which Death is the gatekeeper.

Snow also functions on a more prosaic level that reminds the poet of the shutdown of exterior exertion. He finds himself deep in a severe East Coast winter. People anxiously watch the weather forecasts and bear confinement with that gritty patience familiar to those acquainted with the harshness of winter. In such a claustrophobic schema the Self cannot be ignored. The frigid solitude spurs Ammons into interior monologues, the extensive periods of talking to one's Self, into the face-to-face encounter with the terror that is the whiteness of the whale.

Conflict is at the center of poetry. No poem can be successful without it. The poem must do more than settle for a presentational approach. It is not enough to say, "this is conflict—I'm done." A poet has to work it out in an objective way that comprehends both sides. A poet must be Cain and Abel. Therein tension lies, and that makes the poem go.

The ability to create tension and sustain it is sadly missing from much contemporary poetry. Whether poets have forgotten how to develop tension in their work or whether they even recognize it in themselves I cannot say. It is enough for me that Ammons is not plagued by this difficulty. . . . [The poem **"This Is"**] is an Ammons trademark: the toughminded treatment of the modern, suburban man. It is no subjective observation from a poet hunched in a corner, drooling with self-pity, pounding a gavel to certify each arbitrary notion that comes to mind. His compassion is unquestionable. Even the most skeptical reader must see that Ammons fully comprehends both sides [of every conflict]. (pp. 203-04)

In the hands of this poet there is a poignant grandeur, far from pity, that marks [the] peculiar American inability to make contact. . . . We make money. We take out the garbage and never quite feel that we are doing it correctly. We pull out weeds and drive our children to school. We attend meetings and watch television and make more money . . . and we are terribly alone. Ammons feels the weight of this dilemma and yet, he heroically transcends it. It is the major Whitmanesque achievement of an uncommonly big-hearted man who embraces his country and sees in it the material for a still better place.

How does Ammons do it? . . . Often he will write in the conversational modes he is used to hearing. The language is simple, clear and pliant. It is occasionally wrenched by contemporary words of science, words like "Curvature," "Numeration," "interpenetrations," "discontinuity," and "differentiation." Normally, such words in a poem make me shudder. But when Ammons uses them I merely quiver cozily like a fawned-over aspic. In short, we see this poet doing the things that you or I do every day. But he also does some things that maybe we don't do. He sits at the window, for instance, and watches a bird in a tree. . . . Or he watches the snow fall, transforming the houses. He watches and "snow / ghosts stand up / and walk off the roof." With Ammons' help we can see them, too. . . . [Ammons'] gift does not simply aim for the breadbasket. It impresses the ear as well. For Ammons has always been a first-rate lyricist. The more I read his work the more I am convinced that he can (and will) do anything with the language that he wants. He is just that precise. He has that much control and, bless him, he has an ear. Nowhere is this more obvious than in his brazen and brilliant word play. (pp. 204-05)

The overall achievement of *The Snow Poems* becomes more remarkable when I consider that encroaching age is a recurrent, central concern. The poet has reached his fiftieth year and must contend, in a furious winter, with the ominous implications. The comfortable promises of youth have faded. He is haunted by ghosts. . . . Surrounded by material gain and artistic accomplishment, by fifty years of experience and the necessity, born of instinct, to make something worthwhile out of his remaining years, Ammons meets the lonely struggle with perfect honesty. Perceiving the limitations in whatever he attempts, the poet expresses himself with the graceful ease of an eloquent river. . . . Ammons knows himself. What emerges is an indomitable spirit forged in conflict, tempered by compassion, ready to advance on a questionable future with confidence and delight. Richard Eberhart said on accepting last year's National Book Award: "Poets should not die for poetry but should live for it." Nobody better personifies this sentiment than Ammons. He is as huge as the country he inhabits, as compassionate as it would like to be. . . . (p. 205)

> Robert McDowell, "The Spirit in Mid-Winter Rises," in The Hudson Review (copyright © 1978 by The Hudson Review, Inc.; reprinted by permission), Vol. XXXI, No. 1, Spring, 1978, pp. 202-06.

STEPHEN YENSER

Although they shade off into one another, there are basically three kinds of poem in [A. R. Ammons's *The Selected Poems: 1951-1977*], and they all have to do with nature. First there is the quasi-imagist poem that usually describes a scene or develops a single metaphor while doing so ("**Rectitude**," "**Right On**," and "**Winter Scene**," for example). These poems are the slightest, on the whole, but usually charming. Then there is a parable, distinguished from the preceding by the promi-

nence of the moral and, often, by a dialogue between the poet and his favorite solitary, the wind, or some crusty gulch or sage old mountain ("**The Wide Land**," "**Terminus**," "**Dunes**"). In this mode Ammons can be as winsome as Cummings and as pithy as Frost. The wonder is that he can be both at once. The meditation on nature differs from the parable by virtue of the sweep of the vision, the scope of the speculation, and, sometimes, simple length and a left-hand margin that traces out a "waterline, waterline inexact, / caught always in the event of change" ("**Corsons Inlet**," "**Expressions of Sea Level**," "**Identity**"). This is the most provocative Ammons, the man who puts you in mind of Emerson, Whitman, D'Arcy Thompson, and Whitehead, and whose language and movements are still unpredictable as jumping beans. (p. 96)

It is wonderful how Ammons's poems work, which is as much like the world he loves as possible. As he defines it in "**Summer Session**," too long to be included in this selection, "the problem is / how / to keep shape and flow:"—a problem momentarily resolved in those lines by the speech unit-line coincidence and the eye rhyme, on the one hand, and the asymmetrical stanza and the characteristic colon, the one punctuation mark that urges forward, on the other. Ammons tries to merge form and flux, to make himself "available / to any shape." If nature continuously changes, he will not come to a full stop during a poem; but if in nature "through change / continuities sinuously work," he will develop a poem in which the *idea* of shape continues through a series of unique stanza forms. Things in nature are "separate particles" yet related in a "'field' of action," so that is the way they will appear in his poems. (p. 97)

"The structure of poetry and the structure of reality are one": Stevens's dictum could gloss the unity of vision that accounts for much of the vitality and the "widening / scope" of Ammons's work. Sometimes it even seems that he is trying to expand his work until it is coextensive with reality. He wants "no conclusions" and "no boundaries," wants to be as indulgent as "the radiance" he describes in "**The City Limits**," where he is a wealthy spendthrift of lustrous phrases. . . . (pp. 97-8)

So it comes as rather a shock to realize that these poems are after all limited. They are limited especially in terms of subject matter, for they have almost no people, no human relationships, and thus a restricted range of emotions. Awe, exultation, bemusement, and mild disappointment we have aplenty—but of such passions as love (excepting two very short "love songs"), grief, and pity, we hear next to nothing. . . . But it would be ungrateful, in view of all that we have here, to dwell on what we do not have. Besides, Ammons, one aspect of whose outflanking genius is that his poems forecast their possible marginalia, long ago redeemed his own "omissions" when he wrote that "it is not that words *cannot* say / what is missing: it is only that what is missing / cannot / be missed if / spoken."

Those lines are from "**Unsaid**," which will indeed be missed. Everyone who knows Ammons's work will discover that at least a couple of favorites have been passed by ("**Coon Song**" is not here either), but that is inevitable. Going through the short poems in *Collected Poems: 1951-1971*, from which all but three of these come, one is in the frustrating situation of the tourist visiting the huge collection of small gold pieces from Mycenae: Stunning, but look at that one, and isn't *that* one exquisite. . . . The advantage of a reduced selection is that one finds things previously neglected somehow: "**The Wide Land**," perhaps, or "**Project**" or "**The Quince Bush**." On the other hand, in spite of a gesture or two in the direction of a quest for essence (see the opening third of **"The Arc Inside and Out,"** which will bear any comparison with Stevens it provokes), the preference of this "periphery riffler" has always been for inclusion rather than exclusion. And for that reason the **Collected Poems** represents him more faithfully: it comes closer to the ideal plenitude. As he says wryly in **"Cut the Grass,"** "less than total is a bucketful of radiant toys." (pp. 98-9)

Stephen Yenser, "Recent Poetry: Six Poets," in *The Yale Review* (© 1978 by Yale University; reprinted by permission of the editors), Vol. LXVIII, No. 1, Autumn, 1978, pp. 83-102.*

DAVID KIRBY

Ammons is hard to read, not because he is hard to understand, but because his vatic poems make the reader want to get everything from them. Ammons's usual persona is a prophet in the sense that E. M. Forster meant the word—not that he predicts outbreaks of war or encounters with handsome strangers but that he speaks as though inspired. A glance at some of the shorter poems (using the texts in **Selected Poems 1951-1977** and **Diversifications**) bears this out. In an early one, **"Bees Stopped"**, the persona derives complete satisfaction from his understanding of nature's quiet but ceaseless activity. . . . In another early poem, **"The Wide Land,"** nature's noisier aspects are broached, but still the persona is happy. The wind blinds him and then apologizes, yet the doughty persona is unflappable. . . . Bee song or blizzard: anything nature throws his way is fine with him.

Lest this persona seem smug and overweening, a third poem from roughly the same period should be cited as evidence that he is taking his vatic duties seriously. In **"Choice"** the persona comes to a stair that goes in both directions. He spurns "the airless heights" and sinks into what seems to be "the inundating dark", but there is a surprise in store. . . . Though he tries to descend, the persona ends in a place much like the airless heights he wanted to avoid. The idiot happiness of the two earlier poems is absent here; the persona takes seriously his struggles with a deceitful god and reveals that he is aware of the serious and possibly dangerous implications of "loose stones" and "sudden alterations of height".

The persona's awareness of his awareness grows as Ammons's career develops. In **"Dunes"** and **"Center"** he says "Firm ground is not available ground" and "nothing gets/caught at all". A superb short poem entitled **"Mountain Talk"** . . . , combines the persona's joy in nature (which characterizes **"Bees Stopped"** and **"The Wide Land"**) with his understanding of his inability to apprehend nature (as seen in **"Dunes"** and **"Center"**). . . .

[In such short poems as **"Mountain Talk"**, it] is clear that Ammons is bearing out William James's belief that you ought not to distinguish where you cannot divide, yet sometimes you must. Temperatures have to be taken, cuts to be made. The trick is to cut cleanly, and there are few surgeons tidier than Ammons. His short lines, his overall brevity, his avoidance of punctuation marks other than the occasional comma and that quick stop-and-go colon are the hallmarks of his minimalism, his exquisitely unencumbered technique. **"For Harold Bloom"**, the last poem in **Selected Poems 1951-1977** and one of the longest poems in the book (though it is only a page), expresses the persona's struggle with the central paradox of Ammons's

poetry, namely, that it is necessary to distinguish though never adequate. The poem that expresses best the poet's (especially the prophet-poet's) need to continue is **"Measure"**, which says that the objects of nature "promote the measure" and that there is no "other measure but man". The trick is to measure in the most judicious and subtle way.

For some reason the critics who have attempted to take Ammons's own measure have been prone to use other writers as their yardsticks. His thought and art has been compared to that of Henry Vaughan, Sir Thomas Browne, D'Arcy Thompson, Emerson, Thoreau, Whitman, Gerard Manley Hopkins, Pound, Eliot, Wallace Stevens, William Carlos Williams, Roethke, Dylan Thomas, and Robert Creeley. A list of such length of poets of such brilliance almost precludes additional comparisons, but perhaps its self-evident appropriateness will permit the suggestion of one more name: that of Stephen Crane. His other roots notwithstanding, Ammons characteristically writes like Crane at his best (though Crane was not at his best very often, at least as a poet). . . . What makes Ammons's poetry technically closer to Crane's than anyone else's are not only its minimalist characteristics but also the recurrent and perhaps conscious sophomorisms on which both writers rely. Both of them have personae who wrestle with gods and talk to the wind. Both use words like "foreverness" (Ammons) and "impenetrableness" (Crane). Both have in common the stock poetic situations, the abstractions, the poems so brief that they seem more the jottings of the apprentice who wants to be known as poet than the attempts of the maturing artist who wants to perfect his craft. The odd thing is that both writers, and especially Ammons, manage to pull it off. All great ideas are simple, as Tolstoy said, but he might have added that it takes a great artist to present great ideas simply. Ammons is such an artist, which is why he is one of a handful of American lyric poets meant to be read again and again.

[As indicated by the recently published **Selected Longer Poems,** his] achievement as a writer of long poems is another matter, however. Not that any writer of long poems has it easy. Even the best of us have a built-in resistance to length in literature. . . . But literature abounds with splendid long poems: in America alone there is Whitman's *Song of Myself*, Hart Crane's *The Bridge*, Williams's *Paterson*, Stevens's *Notes Toward a Supreme Fiction*, Eliot's *Four Quartets*, Pound's *Cantos*, W. D. Snodgrass's *Hearts Needle*, Ginsberg's *Howl*, and Alvin Greenberg's marvellous but little-known *In/Direction*. With one exception, though, none of these poets uses the sophormoric language that Ammons employs so successfully in his short poems. (The exception is Whitman, who makes up for the sophomoric language in his long poetry with sheer energy and who, paradoxically, fails when he uses the same language in his short poems, which are often flaccid and tired.) And that is the problem. Ammons is a prophet, a vatic poet. Yet oracular utterances are gnomic, not windy; when they become windy, we lose interest and turn away. In Ammons's short poems, sophomoric language resonates long after we finish reading; in the long poems, the resonances come one upon another, and the effect, if there is any effect at all, is discordant and finally numbing. Someone with some *Sitzfleisch* may find Ammons's **Essay on Poetics,** one of the poems in [**Selected Longer Poems**], a masterpiece, but I found it "a project" (as Ammons calls it in the last line) that helped the poet while away a snowstorm.

And yet one of these five longer poems is a work of sustained artistry that ranks with any on the list above. In **Summer Ses-**

sion, Ammons's persona is a teacher whose gentle ruminations range from wry advice to his students . . . to voluptuous reminiscences of picnics alfresco. . . . What sets this longer poem apart from the others is its use of sophomoric language comically . . . and its avoidance of it otherwise. . . .

Alas, that leaves the *Essay on Poetics* and three other poems like it which are "projects" for the snowbound poet. Prophecy is essentially a Mediterranean art; perhaps poets who don't live in sunny climes should realize that there is nothing wrong with writing novels and cook-books.

> David Kirby, *"The Measure of Man," in* The Times
> Literary Supplement (© *Times Newspapers Ltd.*
> *(London) 1981; reproduced from* The Times Literary
> Supplement *by permission), No. 4073, April 24, 1981,*
> *p. 466.*

VERNON SHETLEY

A. R. Ammons means to be a meditative poet, but he keeps getting distracted. He would, like Wallace Stevens, write the poems of the mind in the act of finding, but what he finds, as often as not, is natural appearance or natural fact. He is thus led around to a conflicting tradition, that of Frost, in which ideas are presented not directly but through the medium of natural imagery. His poems shuttle back and forth between image and abstraction, description and discursion, even seeming, on occasion, to blur those distinctions. Confusing those opposites, Ammons at times successfully accommodates both; when he attempts to compromise, he more often falls down between them.

"A Coast of Trees" shows Ammons working in the vein of such earlier volumes as **"Briefings"** and **"Uplands,"** short lyrics annotating a single perception or enclosing a single inflection of thought. The voice Ammons assumes in these new poems, that of the reflective, perambulatory naturalist, is familiar from his earlier work, as is the peculiar mix of lofty argument and plain wordplay; botany, metaphysics, punning and alliteration tumble freely one after another through the poems. If anything, Ammons's characteristic inwardness and reticence are more than usually pronounced in this volume. Proper names and pronouns other than "I" scarcely appear, and the rhetorical eruptions Ammons has occasionally indulged in are absent. Familiar, too, is the goal toward which these poems, however obliquely, work: an acceptance of the two harsh faces nature shows to man, that of change and corruption and that of a cold, mechanical order. Ammons endeavors, if not to praise, at least to admit of those aspects of nature.

This is high matter indeed, and one can hardly accuse Ammons of wanting ambition. Yet he draws back from elevating his style to the height of his argument, as if he had bankrupted his supply of daring on his conceptions and had none left to spend for their execution. Too often the force of thought in these poems is dissipated in the comfortable abstractions that embody it. . . . Too fond of the chance congruities between the mind and the world it inhabits, he hesitates to set the mind against that world. Ammons certainly delivers real satisfactions of one kind, but he raises without satisfying expectations of another order altogether. In that gap lies the difference between a fluent, interesting poet and a great one. (p. 12)

> Vernon Shetley, *"Nature and Self," in* The New
> York Times Book Review (© *1981 by The New
> York Times Company; reprinted by permission), May 10,*
> *1981, pp. 12, 41.**

ROBERT PHILLIPS

Ammons' work is almost always about man in nature, attempting to make the visible yield the visionary. His writing, Harold Bloom reminds us, confirms his "vital continuities with the central Whitmanian tradition of our poetry."

I could take issue with the Whitman parallel. Of course Ammons writes pastoral poetry, of the common man, and frequently achieves the mystical. But Ammons' voice and line and vision are ultimately anti-Whitmanesque. His poems are nearly always brief, his lines nearly always narrow. He does not conduct self-interviews, and he never sermonizes. Moreover, he has never attempted a real epic. (His longest poems are his lightest.) Rather than attempt to change the reader's life, he is content to report, vividly, what he has felt and seen.

This makes Ammons sound simple. He is not. Often, in the course of a brief poem, he will zig-zag wildly away from a linear thought construction (—but he always returns!). While his language is usually of the simplest kind, the poems deal with the complex. (p. 429)

A Coast of Trees collects Ammons' most recent shorter poems written since *The Snow Poems* and *Highgate Road*. It contains several that rank with his best. These include **"Swells"** (which reveals his intense interest in science, as if we didn't know), **"Rapids"** (beginning with a case for the superiority of autumn over spring and ending in the nature of the universe 100-million years from now—all within 12 lines!), **"Parting"** (atypical: about a stroke victim and the illness's effect upon a marriage), **"Sweetened Change"** (also atypical: a Williamsesque poem on a marriage and a hospital), and **"Persistences"** (about man's indomitability).

In all these poems, the mind is seeking truth. . . . Yet Ammons maintains his light touch. He is also, alas, capable of parodying himself—perhaps unintentionally. Any poet who has published sixteen collections in twenty-six years runs a risk of repetition, of stating a felt concern less well the third or fourth time. (pp. 429-30)

Ammons does continue to renew the language of the tribe by making verbs of nouns: In one poem an argument is said to "thruway." His occasional tendency to sound like Frost, as in his early sand dune poem and **"Visit,"** is repeated . . . in **"Range,"** a meditation on divine order inspired by observing a spider, a poem which inevitably recalls Frost's "Design." Ammons even becomes as folksy as Frost. . . .

On the positive side, in this tidy book there is less abstraction, more people, and a continuation of Ammons' explorations of light, color and radiance. It is a fine place to begin for any reader not yet familiar with this poet who is determined to capture the shape and flow of the universe and to untell its dreams. (p. 430)

> Robert Phillips, *"Poetry Chronicle: Some Versions
> of the Pastoral," in* The Hudson Review (*copyright
> © 1981 by The Hudson Review, Inc.; reprinted by
> permission), Vol. XXXIV, No. 3, Autumn, 1981, pp.
> 420-34.**

IRVIN EHRENPREIS

Ammons deals with his world immediately. The macrocosm and microcosm of nature occupy his imagination, and he defines himself by his way of facing these ultimate challenges. In his engaging new collection [*A Coast of Trees*] he has some exquisite love poems and a couple of tender descriptions of old men trying to look after their frail wives. He also has an elegy on his own boyhood.

But as usual, nine-tenths of the poems invite us to stand with the speaker isolated in a landscape, sharply observing some particulars of the scene while responding with quasi-didactic reflections. The most densely populated of the poems is centered on a graveyard.

As if to make up for the lack of human agents, Ammons regularly personifies the features of landscape that hold his attention. Sometimes this habit can give sharpness to an image, as when a thawing brook "steps" down a ledge; . . . But when the poet exchanges opinions with a mountain (as in **"Continuing"**), I balk.

Selfhood, for Ammons, means the establishment of healing continuities in the face of unpredictable, often withering disruptions. So it is restorative for him to notice how the elements of landscape survive and establish a new balance after destructive assaults. On such images of change, loss, and restoration he concentrates an attention sharpened by scientific training.

Ammons's handling of free verse evokes the process he celebrates. One characteristic of the normally short lines is what might be called radical enjambment, or the ending of lines after words that demand an object or complement—adjectives, prepositions, transitive verbs, conjunctions. Another peculiarity is the repetition of a few key words, often three times or more. In spite of the apparent freedom of form of the whole poem, Ammons generally returns at the end to an image prominent at the start, to which he then gives new depth; and the poem often turns formally on the movement from observation to reflection. The effect of the enjambments, the repetitions, and the circular form is to suggest the disruptions, continuities, and resolutions of the flow of our emotions. The short poems of Ammons have more power than the long, because he tends to neglect shape and point when he becomes discursive.

An invitation to misread the poetry is the surface of calm in Ammons's work. Strangers may suspect him of complacency. But like Stevens and Bishop—two other poets obsessed with landscape—Ammons has only a slight hold on his hard-won moments of tranquillity. The bleakness of human life breaks out in phrases like "the many thoughts and / sights unmanageable, the deaths of so many, hungry or mad." . . .

The underlying sadness rises to anguish in **"Easter Morning,"** the longest poem of the book. Here the lonely poet expresses his bitterness over the deformations produced in a child like himself by the imperviousness of adults who die before they can recognize and redeem their errors. Mourning for the person he might have been, the poet faces the graveyard in which are buried those people—teachers, relations, parents—who could have saved him from becoming a man more at ease with brooks and hills than with human society. The power of the poem springs from the central conceit of the isolated individual standing before the sociable dead.

But he does not see his crucifixion as unique. . . .

In the last third of the poem, the theme of resurrection emerges, in the shape of two large birds seen flying together. When one veers from the straight way, the other notices and joins him. Then both return to the original route. The watcher admires their possession of free patterns which they may companionably leave and return to, unlike the rigidity of his own development;

and he admires the beauty of the "picture-book, letter-perfect" morning. (p. 46)

Irvin Ehrenpreis, "Digging In," in The New York Review of Books *(reprinted with permission from* The New York Review of Books; *copyright © 1981 Nyrev, Inc.),* Vol. 28, No. 15, October 8, 1981, pp. 45-7.

HELEN VENDLER

Ever since Schiller distinguished naive from sentimental poetry, we have been worried by the pathetic fallacy (as Ruskin named it). It is the aesthetic version of the tree falling in the woods; does it make a sound if nobody is there to hear it? Is nature hospitable of itself to meaning (by its rhythms and its orders, its catastrophes and its variety) or are our symbolic uses of it truly abuses, a foisting of our sentiments onto an inert and indifferent scenery? This question has become one that no modern "nature poet" from Wordsworth on can avoid addressing in a perfectly conscious way. (p. 26)

In Ammons, the question of the pathetic fallacy is raised again and again, most luminously and painfully in his great poem **"Grace Abounding,"** where the title makes explicit his claim that in states of inchoate feeling he finds a relief so great in the clarification offered by a visual image chanced upon in nature that the feeling corresponds to that which Bunyan named "grace abounding." We recall that in the Biblical formulation, where sin abounds, grace will the more abound: in Ammons's frame of things, the emphasis changes from sin to misery. In the poem, where he is trapped in a vise of misery, the sight of a hedge completely encased and bound down by ice so strikes him that he realizes that it is an image, perfectly correspondent, of his inner anguish, the more anguishing because it had as yet remained unimaged, unconceptualized, and therefore indescribable. The relief felt when the hedge strikes his eye, and his state is at last nameable, is grace—not offered by Ammons as an "equivalent" to Bunyan's grace, but as *the same thing*, a saving gift from an external source. A poet who has felt that unexpected solace will seek it again.

Ammons looks literally for sermons in stones, books in the running brooks. He has been reproached for the minuteness of his detail, for scrutinizing every letter of the natural alphabet, even every syllable in the genetic code, seeking to extract from each item its assuaging human clarification. If a hedge of ice can explain him to himself, why so can a pebble (and it has) or a wave (and it has). **"Grace Abounding"** is a critical poem in Ammons's canon because it tells us his habitual state—one of a mute congestion of burdened feeling that must go abroad, baffled, letting the eye roam aimlessly, if minutely, until it feels the click that tells it, when it sees the hedge of ice, that that visual form is the mirror of its present feeling. (pp. 27-8)

[Ammons's new collection, **Worldly Hopes,** reminds us that he] is always oscillating between his expatiations and his "briefings" (as between, from another angle, his hymnody and his nihilism). The short poems here are more of Ammons's experiments in the minimal. The question is how few words can make a poem, and how densely can a few words be made to resonate. (pp. 29-30)

If these brief forms seem constricting at times, it is because we know Ammons's discursive amplitudes. I have not found any poem in this book to equal the sublime **"Easter Morning"**. . . . There are new versions here of themes Ammons has touched before: they range from the artist's defense of his life . . . to exercises in pure verbality. . . . Science, as always, provides apt metaphors . . . and the antagonisms of writing are made ever more cunning.

In Ammons, the compulsion to form lurks as a danger. When he says that a poem "begins in contingency and ends in necessity" he is of course right, but necessity need not always wear a necessitarian aspect; it can assume an openhanded stance too, as it sometimes does in Williams or Stevens. . . . As Ammons packs words ever more densely and punningly, perhaps necessity begins to usurp some of the place of contingency.

If we step back, after reading Ammons's account of the alternate burgeoning and collapse of "worldly hopes" (as religion would call them) as well as his hymns of thanksgiving for "grace" . . . , we can see in him a representative figure for the persistence of the Protestant vein in American poetry. He uses the strategy of religious language with much of Dickinson's attachment to it, but he preserves, as Dickinson did not, the tonality of genuine prayer (resembling in this Stevens above all). If this were all he offered—religious language, religious tonality—Ammons would be simply a poet of religious nostalgia, a whited sepulcher. That he is not, we must attribute to two virtues of style which coexist with the religious elements and counterbalance them. One is the grounding of reality in the seen (like Williams, he finds his ideas in things). And the other is his stubborn inclusion of the recalcitrant detail, the hard ragged edge resisting the spherical sheerness of ultimate religious vision. In his naturalist speech, in his untroubled admitting of the psychic origins of the pathetic fallacy, Ammons is modern; in his willingness to substitute the word "grace" for the poetic experience of nature in lieu of the words "pathetic fallacy," he argues, like all poets, for the primacy of feeling in the naming of inner response. If the clarification conferred by the natural world—there is one in almost every poem by Ammons—feels like what Bunyan named "grace," then it *is* grace. What does not feel like a fallacy cannot be truthfully called one. Ammons is sure that the number of fluid inner states is infinite, and that the only matrix of possibility ample enough to correspond with the inner world is the massively various outer world. And the only mediating instrument between the liquid currents of mind and the mountains and deserts of matter is language, that elusive joiner of rivers to rock. . . . (pp. 31-3)

> *Helen Vendler, "Spheres and Ragged Edges," in* Poetry *(© 1982 by The Modern Poetry Association; reprinted by permission of the Editor of* Poetry*), Vol. CXLI, No. 1, October, 1982, pp. 26-33.*

CHARLES FISHMAN

Few human beings inhabit the typical Ammons landscape—indeed, the poems that home toward the center of his visions *are* landscapes: either literal mappings of place and event or philosophical graphs of the questing mind and spirit. The powerful imprint of a primal communion between poet and place that informs ***Tape for the Turn of the Year*** is never entirely erased from Ammons' pages, no matter how quickly they are written and gathered into books. That Ammons must remember one-ness and is forced—by inner compulsion as well as by conscious choice—to measure each new walk, each new moment, against those "blackcherry" days gives his voice both its great particularity and its pathos. (p. 4)

Surely no poet actively writing today observes with Ammons's precision—he captures each flick and rustle with clean, indelible strokes. Yet, faced with displays of such meticulous calibration of mainly transient phenomena, we may properly recall Ammons' injunction for us to pay heed to what he has "left out," to what has fallen outside his gaze. And here we will wish to turn back once more toward an earlier Ammons, toward the author of **"Corsons Inlet,"** who could still both record and praise. . . . (pp. 4-5)

In **"Corsons Inlet,"** Ammons walks the shore-edge of possibility, at the extreme and shifting border of the sea which, alone—in this austerely beautiful but, for Ammons, forever alien landscape—can offer wholeness: absolute loss and gain. For certainly it is true that **"Corsons Inlet"** is the poem, above all others up to this point in his career (1965), in which Ammons reiterates the course of his poetic enterprise. It is an inlet into the ungraspable sea of being and event, a summing up of the main current of the journey. In this "overcast" seascape, says Ammons, he was "released from forms." This kind of release has always been a requirement for spiritual travel, for embarking on a visionary quest. And it is the impossibility of sustaining this delicate balance-point of spiritual and artistic freedom that is the chief precipitator of the poet's despair. . . . Driven by this knowledge that, in the world he lives in—which is not the lost Eden of his emptiest hopes—"terror pervades but is not arranged," Ammons vows to meet the challenge of loss with courage: "I will try," he declares, "to fasten into order enlarging groups of disorder. . . ."

Unfortunately, this fastening of "enlarging groups of disorder" into the eddying lines of his longer and more complex poems is precisely what they cannot bear. For Ammons is a lyric poet (often despite himself) who is most poignant and most sure of his voice when he sings in a celebratory or elegiac key. As a metaphysical or philosophical writer, he is consistently inventive and engaging, but he can rarely achieve the coherence he seeks. What is most forceful and arresting in both the longer poems, like **"Essay on Poetics"** and **"Hibernaculum,"** and the shorter, more obviously lyric pieces, are what [David] Kalstone calls the "lightning weddings of the self to the outside world." This sense that momentary harmony may be achieved—that a bridge may be built between inside and outside, between mind and nature—is nearly always present in Ammons' strongest work, as is the corollary: the bridge must collapse. This perception is cleverly articulated in *Tape for the Turn of the Year:*

> just as the
> whole fell
> together it
> fell apart.

Even more suggestive is Ammons' characterization, early in this 205 page poem, of the precise nature of his personal venture: "running to catch up: to/be at the /crest's break, the/ running crest, / event becoming word:" The problem, for Ammons, is that this struggle to "catch up" is foredoomed. As he laments, also in *Tape for the Turn of the Year,*

> we can approach
> unity only by the loss
>   of things—
> a loss we're unwilling
> to take—

Despite this terse summation of the danger there are a few poems at the center of Ammons' work that were given shape by his willingness—his daring—to ''approach unity,'' to take this great risk, to experience this great loss. **"Hymn"** is a special case, almost but not quite unique, in Ammons' poetry, in which a kind of balance is reached between the poet's knowledge of the doomed nature of his mission and his obsessive search for the sacred in the fragmented past and partially fragmented present. For clearly the true yearning in this poem proceeds from Ammons' search for the ''deposed'' god and from his never-to-be-satisfied hunger for the lost home, the lost ground of being where he first felt himself enwombed by that sacred present. Ammons has never been more clear or affecting than here, in this magical poem that articulates his loss and his questing after this nameless deity and the place where he held sway over being. Ammons knows that if he should succeed in finding this lost god, he will cease to be a poet: that he ''will have to leave the earth / and go on out / . . . up farther than the loss of sight / into the unseasonal undifferentiated empty stark.''

But to be drawn out of earthly being is only half—the expected half—of the terror. . . . Ammons knows there is an equal, if less awesome, danger: that he will not transcend earthly existence but, instead, will be condemned to follow an increasingly narrow spiral of perceptions, that he ''will have to stay with the earth,'' and with all the minutiae of temporal being. What Ammons sees is that, if God *is,* if God can be ''found,'' he is to be found in each separate fragment of created matter, in each electron, in each subatomic particle of the energy-field we call the universe. This is the ultimate dimension of the problem, the final ambivalence, which is as fully biochemical and phenomenological as aesthetic or metaphysical in origin. The "you" that Ammons seeks—has always sought—is "everywhere partial and entire." (pp. 5-7)

Although it is not obvious in the **"Hymn"** sequence that Ammons includes in the *Collected Poems,* **"Still"** is clearly intended to stand side by side with **"Hymn"** in any final ordering that may be brought to Ammons' poems. Like **"Hymn,"** **"Still"** is given over to the mystical and visionary. But here we see Ammons drawn away from ''the empty stark.'' Although he flirts with the idea of unity, he is no longer centered but has moved into an eccentric orbit, in which he searches not for a bridge to the ''not me'' but, instead, and with intentional irony, for ''what is lowly,'' for ''a ready measure of my significance.'' The fact that Ammons is unable to track down even one living organism that is not ''magnificent with existence'' leads him to the essential recognition that ''there is nothing lowly in the universe'' and that nothing in nature is intended to serve him as a gauge of his own worth. (p. 8)

In seeing ''lowly'' organisms like the moss and the tick as ''magnificent,'' Ammons shows himself to be a man who properly values the ''separate leaves'' of creation. In perceiving the love that shakes the mutilated body of the ''lowly'' beggar, he demonstrates his compassion and empathy. But when he recognizes that his own anguished, lonely, yearning self also partakes of the magnificence of being, Ammons achieves a close encounter with the lost home, with the deposed god of the sacred place that lingers in his memory and imagination. In **"Still,"** the mystical union is nearly attained in a vision of significance-in-being. He realizes that nothing in Nature can

be *his* place because *he* is his place: in him, in the self, is the holy ground; in him, only, can he discover home, wholeness. But this great knowledge is, as we have seen, fatal knowledge—fatal, that is, to the progress of the work. For, in bringing him home, to center, it would also bring to a close the journey that is the necessary spur and momentum behind the art. In **"Still,"** at ''one sudden point,'' the forward motion appears to stop; briefly, briefly, a bridge between the physical and spiritual appears to rise up in the empty spaces of the poem, between the bounding limits of language. For one moment, Ammons seems to be home, which—for the poet—is to be in ''the mouth of Death.''

One other poem in the *Selected Poems* appears central to me, if we are to know Ammons as he has directed us to know him—in his silence. I am thinking of **"Expressions of Sea Level,"** which stands with **"Corsons Inlet"** as a major poem of what Richard Howard has called the ''littoral'' imagination. Here, as in **"Still,"** Ammons walks the naked edge of possibility, seeking a complete vision of the cosmos. However, in **"Expressions of Sea Level,"** there is no single moment when revelation comes, when the troping stops, when the journey turns in upon itself like a spiralling galaxy or whorled shell. Here the abiding question must once more be asked: ''is there a point of rest where / the tide turns: is there . . . an instant when fullness is.'' Yet this poem, which is perhaps not ''a statement perfect in its speech,'' is nevertheless a showing-forth of the all-but-invisible. In this masterful poem, Ammons gives form to his yearning to express the flow of event and being with the precise nuances evident in the natural language the wind and sea inscribe on the shore, where ''broken, surf things are expressions: / the sea speaks from its core. . . .'' Ammons, too, wishes to speak with the force and exactness and centrality of the sea. But, as he concedes in a later poem, **"Plunder,"** human language appropriates things in a way the ''core'' language of the sea does not. At the poem's center is a wonderfully accurate metaphor that explains this distinction. Ammons focuses on a clam shell that ''holds smooth dry sand, / remembrance of tide: water can go at / least that high.'' If, Ammons assures us, we were to come ''at the right time'' to observe the process—how the sea turns and fills the shell's shallow cup, marking off in granules the depth of its penetration—we would witness that, in nature, things are not displaced; they are the record of their being-in-the-world and bear the clear marks of their presentness, which is also their history. (pp. 8-9)

In this, one of his most physically rooted poems, we see Ammons at his most mystical, Romantic, visionary. Here, he shows us—as did the early Romantics, Blake and Wordsworth in particular—that wholeness is recovered in a whole view of the universe. (p. 9)

Charles Fishman, ''A. R. Ammons: The One Place to Dwell,'' in The Hollins Critic *(copyright 1982 by Hollins College), Vol. XIX, No. 5, December, 1982, pp. 2-11 [the excerpts of Ammons's poetry used here were originally published in his* The Selected Poems 1951-1977 *(reprinted by permission of W. W. Norton & Company, Inc.; copyright © 1977, 1975, 1974, 1972, 1971, 1970, 1966, 1965, 1964, 1955 by A. R. Ammons), Norton, 1977].*

John (Lawrence) Ashbery

1927-

American poet, novelist, dramatist, critic, and editor.

Ashbery is often considered by critics to be a "poet's poet," because of the difficulty his poetry presents to the average reader. The typical Ashbery poem thwarts the reader through its shifting viewpoint, non sequitur associations, and hyperconscious preoccupation with the writing process itself. Poetry, or poetry making, is the predominant theme of Ashbery's work.

Throughout his career, Ashbery, like others in the New York school of poetry with which he has been associated, has been strongly influenced by developments in other artistic media, particularly abstract painting and experimental music, notably that of John Cage, who inspired the long poem, "Litany."

Ashbery received three of poetry's highest honors in 1976: a National Book Award, a National Book Critics' Circle Award, and a Pulitzer Prize, for his collection *Self-Portrait in a Convex Mirror*. In his recent book, *Shadow Train*, Ashbery adapts the tight structure of a sonnet sequence to demonstrate his elliptical poetics.

(See also *CLC*, Vols. 2, 3, 4, 6, 9, 13, 15; *Contemporary Authors*, Vols, 5-8, rev. ed.; and *Dictionary of Literary Biography*, Vol. 5.)

© Lütfi Özkök

DAVID SHAPIRO

[*The observations in Shapiro's essay are based substantially on interviews with John Ashbery, 1964-72.*]

Ashbery was a connoisseur of [the French author Raymond Roussel] and began a doctoral dissertation on him but decided not to go through with it, although characteristically he collected many minute particulars about that grand eccentric. Thus the modulated parodies of narration in *Rivers and Mountains* may be associated with the labyrinthine parentheses of Roussel's poems and novels; this contagion of the parodistic tone seems to lead structurally to a "chinese box" effect or play within a play. . . . [In later works] Ashbery wittily employed another device of Roussel: the specious simile, "The kind that tells you less than you would know if the thing were stated flatly." . . . In lieu of the organic and necessary simile, Ashbery learned from the French master an extravagance of connection that leads one nowhere. . . . Ashbery is also a master of the false summation, the illogical conclusion couched in the jargon of logic and reminiscent of the false but rich scholarship of Borges. . . . (p. 17)

John Ashbery can properly be called a child of the muse of Rimbaud. In the somewhat unenthusiastic tones of the introduction to *Some Trees*, W. H. Auden also placed him in the tradition of Rimbaud's *dérèglement de tous les sens*. Contrary to Auden's expectations, Ashbery denies French poetry as a major influence. He does, however, acknowledge the influence of Pierre Reverdy. . . . He admires "the completely relaxed, oxygen-like quality of Reverdy," whose cadences he likens to "breathing in big gulps of fresh air." . . . (p. 18)

[Raymond Roussel] is a very "prosy" poet, and Ashbery also is interested in the poetic possibilities of conventional and banal prose, the prose of newspaper articles. Many of his poems of the '60s and '70s are particularly works that function by proceeding from cliché to cliché, in a "seamless web" of banality transformed, by dint of combination and deformation, into a Schwitters-like composition in which the refuse of a degraded quotidian is fused into a new freshness. . . . The use of prose elements in poetry, as in William Carlos Williams and Ezra Pound, is so common a heritage and so diffused a technique as rarely to provoke sensations of novelty, but Ashbery's intense employment is an adventure. The prosaic elements in the early poetry of W. H. Auden influenced Ashbery, as did the touching qualities of ordinary speech, journalism, and old diaries in Auden's *The Orators*. . . . Collage elements for Ashbery's poem **"Europe"** were taken from a book for girls written at the time of the First World War. The book, William LeQueux's *Beryl of the Bi-Planes*, which he picked up by accident on one of the quais of Paris, is one reason for much of the placid plane imagery of **"Europe."** . . . At the time, Ashbery was "collaging" a great deal as a symptom of an imagined "dead-end" period in his writing; living in France, he felt cut off from American speech. . . . He often received American magazines and manipulated their contents as a stimulus and pretext for further poetry. The grand collapses often noted in Ashbery's **"Europe,"** its dashes and discontinuities, are one result of this *collagiste* direction. Though Ashbery's poetry leads most recently to a calm clearness, it truly began with the presentation of ''objects'' and ''idioms'' in explicitly dislocated form. . . . His dislocated poetry had something of the pathos of obscurity, and the ''pathos of incomprehensibility'' was very much part of the mystique of such writing, though Ashbery always pointed towards principles of cohesion by discontinuity. . . . Gertrude Stein furnished a specimen source for the opacities of **''Europe.''** . . . But Ashbery has a very full palette, and one must distinguish between grammatical anomaly, unexpected dream imagery, and the nonsensical. Ashbery is one of the poets who senses an epoch's rule system for sense itself and revolts against it with wit. His theme of ''unacceptability'' is allied always to related concepts of absurdity, stupidity, and the unreal. (pp. 18-21)

The self-conscious mid-progress shifts of narration in Ashbery's *collagiste* poems . . . are distinctly and masterfully of the age in which Jackson Pollock threw himself on the canvas, a proof and *permission*. Even though Ashbery unexpectedly characterizes himself as more aural than visual, his participation in the art world as critic has been a constant source for his critical poetry.

The influence of psychoanalysis, also, permitting a more or less watery relationship with the unconscious and everyday mind, and corollary devices of ''dipping into'' an almost completely associational stream . . . is another common heritage of technique Ashbery shares with the abstract expressionists and surrealists. (p. 21)

Ashbery's work, begun with kinds of *disjecta membra*, coalesces at certain periods in big coherent works: **''Europe,'' ''The Skaters,'' ''The New Spirit,'' ''The System,''** and **''The Recital.''** The development from collage of seemingly despairing fragments to unbroken paragraphs of de Chirico-like prose (Ashbery admits to de Chirico's prose and not painting as an influence . . .) is likened, by the author, to the development of one of Ashbery's favorite composers, Busoni. ''Busoni wrote a piano concerto, entitled 'The Turning Point,' and all his subsequent music fittingly seems different from earlier pieces.'' . . . Similarly in Ashbery's poetry the disjointed and indecisive has the look, at least, of a highly unified music. Ashbery's larger compositions achieve this ''look'' of compositional unity while remaining what may be a ''multeity.'' Composition in these works is not random but rather more a matter of parsimonious distribution of disparate images, tones, and parodies than of unifications and harmonizings. One may find a tone of Pope in **''The Skaters,''** and the mock-heroic here does sometimes bear resemblance to the highly polished surface of *The Rape of the Lock*. The highly polished surface in Ashbery, however, is less a social hint than a *memento mori* of a world of manufactured objects and smooth, unbroken concrete. **''The Skaters''** may be thought of as a radiant porphyry of a variety of rhetorics, including imitations of Whitman, Baudelaire, science textbooks, translations of Tu Fu, Theodore Roethke, and John Ashbery. He has described his intentions in respect to **''The Skaters''** as trying ''to see how many opinions I had about everything.'' . . . The most alarming feature of this style is the way it keeps upsetting our charming equilibrium and understanding of tone. . . . To some, his meditations upon or within meditations of self-laceration add to the absurdity of the universe rather than interpret it, but these are ultimately friendly satires which point to the fact that unity, as we dream of it, is not realizable. One dreams of the perfect language within the fallen universe. Ashbery's decep-

tive drifts and accumulations of parody always erupt in the dramatic return which surprises and regulates, as in Proust. By his grand multeity in unity, his surprising simultaneity in unity, and a type of probabilistic unity, he achieves something of the misery and joy of a Jacques Callot baroque. He has always avoided the vanity that derives from purely random techniques. But the spectre of indeterminacy and uncertainty shadow his structural convolutions and involutions, if only in the numerous self-lacerating dwarfs that appear and disappear throughout his poems. (pp. 22-3)

Ashbery has been most extreme in his reluctance to pad his poetry with what he calls the ''stuff of explanation,'' just as he has been reluctant to be anything but a ''practical critic'' or ''anecdotal'' critic of the arts. . . . However, one of his central themes is the breakdown of causality in the nineteenth-century sense. His discontinuities tend to throw us most clearly into the middle of the century of the Uncertainty Principle, one in which the poet and scientist expunge false *copulas* for a truer style. The montages of Eisenstein and Ezra Pound's clear, cinematic Oriental translations are part of this lucid tradition of juxtaposition. Most of the best passages in Ashbery's poetry, moreover, as in Stevens' work, still deal with the practitioner's point of view and *praxis* itself, however veiled. His poetry, though not vulgarly explanatory is, in the manner of the ''action'' painters, a criticism of poetry itself as much as of life. A dice-playing God does indeed reign over the aesthetics of Ashbery's kingdom. (pp. 23-4)

There is a kind of simultaneous irony and depth to Ashbery's work, as if a critic paused to announce that he was invalidating all his critical statements including the present one he was making and yet continued. His simultaneity is also that of chamber music, in which the ''narration'' of four voices can seem, as in Haydn, to recreate the comic possibilities of a domestic quarrel over a dish-towel. His domesticity and Firbankian penchant for prosy gossip can be seen further enlarged in his collaborative venture, *A Nest of Ninnies*. His **''Pantoum''** . . . , inspired by Ravel, is another example of a witty use of an arbitrary and musical form. Again, it is music, and not the rhyming dictionary . . . that inspires Ashbery's poetry. He is averse to ''melodious poetry'' though not to melody itself. He is most interested in sound as it joins and flies apart from the meaning of the words, and his disjunction is reminiscent of Anton Webern's practice of setting a poem with a meagre amount of imitative music. (p. 25)

One must remark, if parenthetically, that though Ashbery's own intellectual music is associated journalistically with Frank O'Hara and Kenneth Koch, the discrimination of their differences is equally useful. At first they were pragmatically and conspiratorially joined against poets of a different aesthetic (Richard Wilbur, for example); but though they share a common *tradition* of French surrealism, a taste for the Russian poets of revolution, Pasternak and Mayakovsky, and a somewhat similar procedure of montage, the characteristic Ashbery tone is not that of the others. He is neither as celebratory as Koch nor as urbane and political as O'Hara. To lump the poets of the so-called ''New York School'' as contemporary Chaucerians is inaccurate. The meditations of Ashbery are piously pluralist, perhaps impious to some.

As for the subject of poetic influence, Ashbery has indeed digested both the influence of Wallace Stevens and Walt Whitman. He particularly loved the long poems of Stevens. . . . His own ubiquitous third-person narrator might very well have derived from Wallace Stevens as a way of ''entering'' the poem. . . . Ashbery is "more spellbound by the technical virtuosity of Whitman than the spontaneous image of the bard mumbling in his beard." . . . Ashbery's marvelous catalogues—like that of musical instruments in **"The Skaters"** . . . also derive from Webern's "Cantata," where things "go bumping and rumbling for a time after you thought they were going to stop." . . . Certain elements of Ashbery's *catalogue raisonné* also can be associated with the noisiness of Whitman's poetry and prose. (pp. 25-6)

Ashbery's own work is much concerned with a true solicitude for the bitter impressions of meaninglessness, and this poetry which speaks of the fundamental religious absence of our day should certainly be appraised for what it is rather than for what it is not. After all, with its flourescent imagery, disjunction, collages, two-dimensionalisms, innovations in the traditional forms of sestina, and "simultaneous" use of an aggregate of styles, John Ashbery's poetry today constitutes a revitalization movement in American poetry.

Ashbery's poems are unclear; they are mysterious and seem meant to be so. Throughout this study [*John Ashbery: An Introduction to the Poetry*] I shall attempt to show *how* they are unclear, and how Ashbery values the unclear, and what is gained and lost by this species of opacity. Some of the poems are filled with dissociated elements that teasingly suggest different meanings. Humor is a large element throughout Ashbery's work: the humor of polysemy.

The poet tends to use paradox and "nonsense" to achieve, not so much an ambiguity of the kind analyzed denotatively and connotatively by "The New Critics," as a pointing to *logos* by its extreme absence. This theme of the absence of meaning and a concomitant style of concealments and opacities is the central and abiding metaphor within the specimen texts. . . . One finds that his techniques of dissociation, his use of the banal, the antipoetic, the discontinuous, and the arbitrary all yield clues to possible states of wholeness. I view the work of the '70s, moreover, as the extreme attempt to escape from the bleaker aspects of "the unacceptable" in "nonsense" and to calculate the possibility of a conversion to the heavy requirements of love and belief, which are however mercilessly parodied.

One might take the famous catalogue of I. A. Richards and C. K. Ogden [*The Meaning of Meaning*] and disrupt their definitions of *meaning* to indicate what a palette of "meaninglessness" might be, and how congruent this is with the central theme and style of Ashbery. If "meaning is an intrinsic property," meaninglessness in Ashbery's work is conjured up by an utter denial of intrinsic *logos*, by his lacerations of any such pathetic fallacy in his "colorless indifferent universe." . . . (pp. 29-30)

If meaning is "a unique unanalysable relation to other things" . . . , then meaninglessness in Ashbery is evoked by the constant scrutiny of disrupted rapports and the loss of any coherent relation between Nature, Man, and Divinity. If connotation is meaning, then Ashbery's poetry, like Gertrude Stein's, attempts utter meaninglessness by attempting to strip the word of any of its usual configurations and connotations.

If meaning is an "essence," then Ashbery like Sartre is existentialist and presents an absurdist impasse without essence. If meaning is "an event intended" . . . then Ashbery takes from the world this species of coherence by presenting a world of blank contingency, funny and unfunny unexpectedness.

If meaning is the place of anything in a system, Ashbery evokes a world where "the system" is almost an utterly unsystematic stream in which usual places, indeed any *locus*, is seen to be deprived. Only an absence of locus remains, as in the astronomer's concept of an extremely weighty black hole.

If meaning is "practical consequences" . . . then Ashbery by dint of *non sequitur* tends to shatter any sense of causality. (p. 31)

If meaning is "emotion aroused by anything," Ashbery's flatness attempts an affectless pose and poise to lance the sense of any arousal or emotion. If meaning is "what anything Suggests" . . . , Ashbery often attempts paradoxically to suggest "nothing," to present a blank configuration of words in which any interpretation may be an overinterpretation, and the circumference of meaning is either seen to be zero or practically infinite.

If meaning is "that to which the User of a Symbol refers," Ashbery is peculiarly evocative of meaninglessness when he tries to employ words without a seeming concern for the referential, as in his collaged bits and fragments. The white spaces between his words seem to remain as suggestively referential as the words themselves, with the whole pointing mystically, or insidiously, nowhere.

If meaning is that "to which the user of a symbol Ought to be referring," then Ashbery mocks the reader into a meaninglessness of an antinomian bent by consistently employing a theme that tends against any but the most chaotic obligations. Experimentalism, metrical betrayals, betrayals of syntax: all go to show that Ashbery rejects this category of "meaning."

If meaning is, finally, "that to which the interpreter of a symbol either refers, or believes himself to be referring, or believes the User to be referring" . . . , then Ashbery's "puzzle pictures" lead maddeningly into a labyrinth of possible denotations and possible lack of denotations.

These are some of the meanings of meaninglessness. In Ashbery's poetry, there is much confidence in a new threshold for incoherence and randomness, leading to affirmations of freedom. The poet avoids any transcendental defense for his usages of contingency, but in his work order is wilfully and painstakingly rescued from disorder. Conventional orders and meanings are parodied sharply and starkly. (pp. 31-2)

[Ashbery] has gained authority in all of his work of the '70s because of his tolerance for negativity. (p. 33)

> *David Shapiro, "The Meaning of Meaninglessness" (originally published in a different form in* Field, *No. 5, Fall, 1971), in his* John Ashbery: An Introduction to the Poetry *(copyright © 1979 Columbia University Press; reprinted by permission of the publisher), Columbia University Press, 1979, pp. 15-33.*

HELEN VENDLER

It seems time to write about John Ashbery's subject matter. . . . It is Ashbery's style that has obsessed reviewers, as they alternately wrestle with its elusive impermeability and praise its power of linguistic synthesis. There have been able descriptions of its fluid syntax, its insinuating momentum, its generality of reference, its incorporation of vocabulary from all the arts and all the sciences. But it is popularly believed, with some reason, that the style itself is impenetrable, that it is impossible to say what an Ashbery poem is "about." An alternative view says that every Ashbery poem is about poetry—literally self-reflective, like his **"Self-Portrait in a Convex Mirror."** Though this may in part be true, it sounds thin in the telling, and it is of some help to remember that in the code language of criticism when a poem is said to be about poetry the word "poetry" is often used to mean: how people construct an intelligibility out of the randomness they experience; how people choose what they love; how people integrate loss and gain; how they distort experience by wish and dream; how they perceive and consolidate flashes of harmony; how they (to end a list otherwise endless) achieve what Keats called a "Soul or Intelligence destined to possess the sense of Identity." . . .

[Ashbery] is a generalizing poet, allegorizing and speculating and classifying as he goes, leaving behind, except for occasional traces, the formative "world of circumstances," which, as Keats says, by the trials it imposes proves the heart, alters the nature, and forms a soul. Ashbery turns his gaze from the circumstances to the provings and alterations and schoolings that issue in identity—to the processes themselves. He has been taking up these mysteries with increasing density in each of his successive volumes.

I was only one of many readers put off, years ago, by the mixture of willful flashiness and sentimentality in **"The Tennis Court Oath."** . . . And I was impatient for some time after that because of Ashbery's echoes of Stevens, in forms done better, I thought, and earlier, by Stevens himself. Ashbery's mimetic ear, which picks up clichés and advertising slogans as easily as "noble accents and lucid inescapable rhythms" (as Stevens called them), is a mixed blessing in the new book [*As We Know*] (which has undigested Eliot from the "Quartets" in it), as in the earlier ones. But though some superficial poems still appear in these new pages, poems of soul-making and speculative classification . . . have been in the ascendant. . . . (p. 108)

Increasingly, Ashbery's poems are about "fear of growing old / Alone, and of finding no one at the evening end / Of the path except another myself," as the poem **"Fear of Death"** (from **"Self-Portrait"**) rather too baldly puts it. The distinct remove of his subject matter from immediate "experience" also concerns Ashbery. . . . Something—which we could call ruminativeness, speculation, a humming commentary—is going on unnoticed in us always, and is the seedbed of creation. . . . Intuition, premonition, suspicion, and surmise are the characteristic forms of Ashbery's expression. Otherwise, he would not be true to the stage of spiritual activity in which he is interested. . . .

[Misgivings] and questionings are often put quite cheerfully by Ashbery, in a departure from the solemnity with which truth and beauty are usually discussed. The chaos we feel when one of the truths we hold to be self-evident forsakes us is generally the source of lugubrious verse; for Ashbery, for whom a change of mood is the chief principle of form, "the truth rushes in to fill the gaps left by / Its sudden demise so that a fairly accurate record of its activity is possible." In short, a new truth sprouts where the old one used to grow, and the recording of successive truths is what is on Ashbery's mind. (p. 110)

An eminent scholar told me recently, more in sorrow than in anger, that he had read and reread the poem **"Houseboat Days"** and still he could not understand it. This can happen, even as people read Ashbery with good will, because Ashbery has borrowed from Stevens a trick of working up obliquely to his

subject, so that the subject itself makes a rather late appearance in the poem. The poem begins with a thought or image that provides a stimulus, and the poet works his way into the poem by an exploratory process resembling, Ashbery has said, philosophical inquiry. The beginning, Ashbery modestly adds, may eventually not have very much to do with the outcome, but by then it has become enmeshed in the poem and cannot be detached from it. If a reader proceeds past the rather odd and off-putting beginning of **"Houseboat Days,"** he will come to a meditation, first of all, on how little either the mind or the senses finally give us. In youth, we are appetitive, mentally and physically, and are convinced we are learning and feeling everything; as we age, we find how much of what we have learned is corrupted by use, and how fast the surge of sensual discovery ebbs. . . . After the next meditation (on the insusceptibility of our inmost convictions to reason and argument) comes a meditation on the ubiquitous presence, no matter what your convictions make you praise or blame in life, of intractable pain. . . . Oddly enough, our first response to emotional pain all around us, down in the cisterns, up in the gutters, is to deny we are feeling it; it is, Ashbery muses, "as though a universe of pain / Had been created just so as to deny its own existence." In the manifesto that follows, Ashbery sets forth a Paterian ethics of perception, introspection, memory, art, and flexibility. He argues, given the nature of life, against polemic and contentiousness. . . . (pp. 112, 114, 116)

Life for Ashbery, as everyone has noticed, is motion. We are on boats, on rivers, on trains. Each instant is seen "for the first and last time"; each moment is precious and vanishing, and consequently every poem is unique, recording a unique interval of consciousness. This is a consoling aesthetic, since by its standards every utterance is privileged as a nonce affair; it is also mournful, since it considers art as fleeting as life. In an interview he gave to the *New York Quarterly* (reprinted in "The Craft of Poetry," Doubleday, 1974). Ashbery spoke unequivocally on various topics—his subject matter, his supposed "obscurity," his method of writing, his forms, his influences. . . . The entire interview is a revealing one, and links Ashbery conclusively to the Western lyric tradition. In short, he comes from Wordsworth, Keats, Tennyson, Stevens, Eliot; his poems are about love, or time, or age.

And yet it is no service to Ashbery, on the whole, to group him with Stevens and Eliot; when he echoes them most compliantly, he is least himself. In any case, though he descends from them, he is not very much like them: he is garrulous, like Whitman, not angular, like Eliot; he is not rhetorical, like Stevens, but, rather, tends to be conversational, for all the world like Keats in his mercurial letters. The familiar letter, sometimes the familiar essay are his models now that he has forsaken the formal experiments of his earlier books. We open **"As We Know"** already included, by its title, in a complicity of recognition and inquiry. The book clarifies itself over time, and is itself the clearest of all Ashbery's books; his special allusiveness, a private language perfected over the past twenty years, appears in it, of course, but there are long stretches of accessible table talk, so to speak. These appear chiefly in **"Litany,"** a long poem written in double columns, in what I find a somewhat trying imitation of the bicameral mind. It is full of perfectly intelligible and heartfelt ruminations on soul-making in art, life, and criticism. On the whole, it wonders why— placed, as we are, on this isthmus of our middle state—we go on living and doing the things we do: inventing, imitating, and transforming life. (pp. 116, 120, 122)

Ashbery, like Coleridge, who found all life an interruption of what was going on in his mind, lives in the "chronic reverie" of the natural contemplative. As often as not, his contemplation is chagrined, reproachful of the world that promised us so much and gave us so little. At times, he even doubts whether we are doing any soulmaking at all. . . . (p. 122)

Ashbery has said that his long poems are like diaries, written for an hour or so a day over long periods, and "Litany"—a "comic dirge routine," like so many of his poems—has to be listened to as well over a long stretch of time. Such a form of composition, he says in a poem at the end of "Houseboat Days," has to do with "The way music passes, emblematic / Of life and how you cannot isolate a note of it / And say it is good or bad." Nor can a line, or a passage, or an inception or conclusion from Ashbery be isolated as good or bad. . . . It is our wish to isolate the line as touchstone which makes us at first find Ashbery baffling; once we stop looking for self-contained units we begin to feel better about our responses, and soon find a drift here, a meander there that feels, if not like our old beloved stanzas or aphorisms, at least like a pause in the rapids. (pp. 122, 124)

"Houseboat Days" is the volume containing Ashbery's most explicit short accounts of his own intent. His model there is a tapestry done in the form of a Möbius strip; this metaphor, with its (literal) new twist on an ancient figure for the web of art, coexists with the metaphor of the litany, the chain of words, the sequence of lessons in the heart's hornbook. . . . As things are reduced, once leafless, to the harsh geometry lesson of winter, we learn the diagrammatic forms of life, and chant its repetitive and lengthening chant. Such is the mournful view. On the other hand, Ashbery is irrepressibly sanguine. Something will always turn up to change the mood as it does in a sonata. (p. 124)

Not only is Ashbery perennially hopeful, he is perennially generous, especially toward the whole enterprise of art—its origins in experience, the collecting of data that might help it along, its actual, stumbling efforts, its stiffening into print or onto canvas, its preservation by the academies. In "Litany," he is quite willing, for example, for the academy and the critics to exist. After all, his fresco or his "small liturgical opera," this litany, will be preserved by the academy, described by critics, long after the author dies, and even while time threatens to devour everything. . . . (pp. 124, 127)

As for critics, they are there, like the poets, to keep reminding people of what is in fact happening to them. . . . (p. 127)

The best moments in Ashbery are those of "antithesis chirping / to antithesis" in an alternation of "elegy and toccata," all told in a style of "ductility, its swift / Garrulity, jumping from line to line, / From page to page." The endless beginnings and endings in Ashbery, the changes of scenery, the shifting of characters ally him to our most volatile poets—the Shakespeare of the sonnets, the Herbert of "The Temple," the Keats of the letters, the Shelley of "Epipsychidion." He is different from all but Keats in being often very funny. . . . (pp. 127-28)

The rest of "As We Know"—forty-seven short lyrics—is not any more easily summarized than "Litany." There are poems (I begin this list from the beginning) about growing up, about fidelity, about identity, about death. . . . One could go on, listing the subjects of all forty-seven poems. They are all "about" something. Some are carried off better than others; some seem

destined to last, to be memorable and remembered—none more so than the calmly fateful "Haunted Landscape."

"Haunted Landscape" tells us that we all enter at birth a landscape previously inhabited by the dead. We all play Adam and Eve in the land; we then suffer uprootings and upheaval. . . . Life is both a miracle and a non-event. At the end, we die, and become part of the ground cover and the ground; we become ghosts, as we are told by an unknown herald that it is time to go. The transformation takes place without our knowing how, and our history becomes once again the history of earth's dust. This is the "plot" of "Haunted Landscape"; there is no plot more endemic to lyric. (p. 130)

Ashbery is an American poet, always putting into his poems our parades and contests and shaded streets. He sometimes sounds like Charles Ives in his irrepressible Americana. . . . There is nonetheless something monkish in [the poems of As We Know] which, in spite of their social joy and their hours of devoted illumination in the scriptorium, see a blank and blighted end. The poem with the portmanteau title "Landscapeople" sums up our dilemma—the intersection of humanity and nature. It tells us, in brief, all that Ashbery has to say at this moment about our lives, a summary both scarred and sunlit. . . . At the close of "Landscapeople," Ashbery thinks of Wordsworth's "Immortality" ode, and of his own art as a Rilkean Book of Hours. . . . (pp. 134-35)

I have been [referring to] chiefly the more accessible parts of Ashbery, but it is possible to explain his "hard" parts, too, given time, patience, and an acquaintance with his manner. It is possible also to characterize that manner. . . . It is within our grasp to schematize his practice, categorize his tics—opaque references, slithering pronouns, eliding tenses, vague excitements, timid protests, comic reversals, knowing clichés. We can recognize his attitudes—the mania for collection, the outlandish suggestions, the fragrant memories, the camaraderie in anguish. If we ask why the manner, why the tics, why the attitudes, and we do ask it . . . , the answer, for a poet as serious as Ashbery, cannot be simply the one of play, though the element of playfulness (of not being, God forbid, boring or, worse, bored) always enters in, and enters in powerfully. The answer lies in yet another of Ashbery's affinities with Keats. Keats said that the poet had no identity of his own but, rather, took on the identities of other things—people, animals, atmospheres—which pressed in upon him. "I guess I don't have a very strong sense of my own identity," said Ashbery in the *New York Quarterly* interview. "I find it very easy to move from one person in the sense of a pronoun to another and this again helps to produce a kind of polyphony in my poetry which I again feel is a means toward greater naturalism." "A crowd of voices," as Stevens called it, is spoken for by the single poet; as we feel ourselves farther and farther from uniqueness and more and more part of a human collective. . . . What the poet can do is remind us of "the gigantic / Bits and pieces of knowledge we have retained," of that which "made the chimes ring." If anything, in Ashbery's view, makes a beautiful order of the bits and pieces and the chimes ringing, it is poetry. . . . (pp. 135-36)

Helen Vendler, "Understanding Ashbery" (© 1981 by Helen Vendler), in The New Yorker, *Vol. LVII, No. 4, March 16, 1981, pp. 108-36 [the first excerpt of Ashbery's poetry used here was originally published in his* As We Know *(copyright © 1979 by John Ashbery; reprinted by permission of Viking Penguin Inc.), Penguin Books, 1979; the second excerpt originally appeared in his* Self-Portrait in a Convex

DAVID YOUNG

[**Shadow Train**] is endearing and exasperating in the same ways that all of Ashbery's poetry is. It reflects his great strengths as a writer: endless inventiveness, superb mimicry, artistic transformations of the banal into the beautiful. And it demonstrates his weaknesses as well: a certain preciousness, an absence of self-criticism, an artistic program that allows the manufacture of poetry almost at will and without inspiration. The problem of excessive length that sometimes mars Ashbery's most ambitious efforts is here neatly solved: since each section of **Shadow Train** is a poem in its own right, as in a sonnet cycle, the reader who experiences tedium can pass on to the next poem without much loss or guilt. The loose structure, formally pleasing, also invites browsing and skimming.

Indeed, I have always found skimming and skating to be the best means of enjoying Ashbery, which is not the admission of deficiency it might be in another writer. Since Ashbery works with surfaces, like a painter, reading him too closely or thinking too much about his content is missing the point. One of the poems in this sequence is called **"Corky's Car Keys."** If you imagine a character named Corky and start worrying about his car keys, you go right past the play on sound that is the real point. Similar earnestness will give you similar difficulties with other titles too, e.g., the inspired **"Untitled,"** and **"Indelible, Inedible."** A friend of mine recently said "old tomato" and I heard "ultimatum." Out of such chance collisions and freak likenesses Ashbery derives a poetry of brilliant surfaces, where the verbal gestures—narrative, assertion, lament, conjuration—are often poses for stylistic fun rather than purposive parts of some coherent whole.

How, given this fact, does Ashbery's poetry manage to seem so profound and meaningful? The answer lies in his canny manipulation of our incessant, helpless, pursuit of meaning. Even when we know that Corky is not a character and that his car keys are only a strange rhyme, we can't help imagining both. . . . [In] **"The Ivory Tower,"** we may labor awhile, with dutiful concentration, to make good sense of "Those thirsting ears, / Climbers on what rickety heights have swept you / All alone into their confession . . ."—until we realize that the metaphor is hopelessly mixed and stop to acknowledge with a grin that the poet has once more tricked us into the generation of meaning, an earnest belief in ears that climb and sweep and confess.

This kind of thing can only work if meaning comes and goes, of course, and in the best poems of **Shadow Train** that is precisely the case. (pp. 4, 8)

To some, this playing at pseudo-poetry, anti-poems, will come as a disappointment, and they will presumably seek consolation among more serious and "responsible" poets. Certainly there are emotional and musical limitations to what Ashbery is doing, but I wish to applaud his air of quiet enchantment and wide-eyed fun. I find pleasure in his felicitous metaphors ("The surprise box lunch of the rest of his life") and his evocations of mood . . . that melt away before we quite grasp them.

Constant speculation will keep us upright in Ashbery's world, and certainty will send us sprawling. Laughter and melancholy give the air its bracing tingle. If you take **Shadow Train** in the proper spirit, you can strap on your skates, put your hands behind you, let your scarf float out in the breeze, and give yourself up to some real enjoyment. (p. 8)

David Young, "John Ashbery: At Play in the Fields of Poetry," in Book World—The Washington Post *(©1981, The Washington Post), June 7, 1981, pp. 4, 8 [the excerpt of Ashbery's poetry used here was originally published in his* Shadow Train *(copyright © 1980, 1981 by John Ashbery; reprinted by permission of Viking Penguin Inc.), Viking Penguin,*

PHOEBE PETTINGELL

[**Shadow Train**] is a sustained experiment with a new short form. . . . In the past, Ashbery's lyrical strengths were best exemplified by his long poems, but now he seems able to move just as freely in a briefer space. His work has an operatic air, entertaining us with a variety of cadenzas performed against pleasantly tacky backdrops. The actual sense of the action is elusive, as in opera, and one hardly cares, coming away with a comfortable feeling that the tone has somehow carried all the important meaning. Much has been said about Ashbery's polite evasion of any attempt to synopsize "plot" in his poems and certainly there are many mysterious passages in his verse. . . .

Ashbery carries the old saw that "poetry is its own subject" to its limit. **"Paradoxes and Oxymorons"** claims to be "concerned with language on a very plain level. / Look at [the poem] talking to you." We dutifully look, but the trick seems to have misfired. "You miss it, it misses you." Ashbery scratches his head, pretending to consider what went wrong, all the time keeping up his professional patter like a magician whose rabbit has gotten stuck in the hat. . . . Then he suddenly turns on the reader. "I think you exist only / To tease me into doing it, on your level, and then you aren't there / Or have adopted a different attitude. And the poem / has set me softly down beside you. The poem is you." Despite its paradoxes (not to mention oxymorons), this seems relatively clear on reflection: Poems address an audience that the author has dreamed up as he works, so that both are, in a sense, his creation. Meanwhile, the actual reader must make something for himself out of the poem's solipsism, so that he, too, recreates it as his own. Somewhere in between, poet and reader make contact. Although such a bald summary sounds platitudinous, Ashbery makes his thesis both playful and profound in his poem. Yes, it really does work like that.

Sometimes Ashbery can be willfully frivolous in his unseriousness, especially in his annoying habit, picked up from Wallace Stevens, of silly titles: **"Penny Parker's Mistake," "The Image of the Shark Confronts the Image of the Little Match Girl," "Corky's Car Keys."** At its best, though, his playfulness becomes a way of sidestepping banality, and puts solemn subjects in perspective by protecting them from overstatement. . . . Beneath the clowning, it turns out, Ashbery too has a certain monkish detachment. His more consistent underlying view is that life is benign. . . . What he calls "one's private guignol" of horrors is only part of the interior theater we impose upon ourselves.

Ashbery's reliance on ellipsis is not an attempt to play coy with his readers (at least, not most of the time). He seeks to capture "the truth inside that meaning" that prevents poetry's reduction to a paraphrase, and perhaps that is why his romantic affirmations about our passions are never flattened into mawkishness or half-truths. A grave poet like Ammons makes each wrinkle on every leaf his own; Ashbery absorbs the ebb and flow of the interior landscape and lets his poetic scenery dissolve into personification. . . . In finding language to depict ''The weather of the soul,'' John Ashbery has few equals. (p. 15)

Phoebe Pettingell, ''Outer and Inner Landscapes,'' in The New Leader *(© 1981 by the American Labor Conference on International Affairs, Inc.), Vol. LXIV, No. 13, June 29, 1981, pp. 14-15 [the excerpt of Ashbery's poetry used here was originally published in his* Shadow Train *(copyright © 1980, 1981 by John Ashbery; reprinted by permission of Viking Penguin Inc.), Viking Penguin, 1981].*

ROBERTA BERKE

If the New York poets are each as individual as New York taxi drivers, then with Frank O'Hara at the wheel we cruise through Greenwich Village with occasional side trips out to Fire Island. John Ashbery drives us down deserted back streets between huge locked warehouses with occasional glimpses of the harbor, then stops and soliloquizes about his driving, his poor sense of direction and the tricks perspective can play and asks us if we really want to go to the destination we had requested. . . . O'Hara is casual, open, revealing. . . . Ashbery can be formal, hermetic, secretive: he often slides a deliberate barrier between himself and his readers like the glass shield protecting a New York taxi driver from his passengers.

In Ashbery's poems there are constant echoes of other, secret dimensions, like chambers resounding behind hollow panels of an old mansion rumored to contain secret passages (which our guide emphatically denies exist). Ashbery both hunts for these secrets and tries to conceal them. . . . A heretic among contemporary poets who glory in ''confessional'' poetry, Ashbery even questions the value of ''openness.''

Often these secrets are conveyed in code, secret messages hidden in the everyday. Code is a metaphor for the special language of poetry, into which Ashbery ciphers his secrets. He outlines two of his main methods of coding: ''I thought if I could put it all down, that would be one way. And next the thought came to me that to leave it all out would be another, and truer, way.'' ''Leaving out'' is a method which he frequently uses in earlier poems, where the connections among diverse apparent topics of his poems seem to have been erased. . . . He compares his literary method of ''leaving out'' to the natural process of forgetfulness which has its own concealed logic.

Ashbery's other method of coding, ''putting it all down,'' also has a parallel in a natural process of the mind: dreams, which often seem like cluttering an attic with everything imaginable. This use of ''dream-work'' gives Ashbery, like other New York poets, an affinity with the Surrealists. Ashbery's abrupt shifts from topic to topic detail the reader's logical expectations. Dreams use the same method to short-circuit the censorship of the waking mind. Ashbery has said: ''[In poetry] I would also like to reproduce the power dreams have of persuading you that a certain event has a meaning not logically connected with it, or that there is a hidden relationship among disparate objects.'' Dreams, then, are *active* and, despite their apparently rag-bag inclusion of bits and pieces, reveal a secret code, a

''hidden relationship among disparate objects.'' In this way dreams are like poems, particularly many of Ashbery's poems, which require the reader to relax and let the images flow over him or her, and yet at the same time to stay alert for hidden connections and look for the secret code. In another heresy (for his time), Ashbery even says that dreams, and perhaps poems, with their satisfactions of desire, may be preferable to transitory sex.

How can Ashbery reveal to a reader this secret code which is in his poetry without feeling vulnerable? . . . One way is to focus intensely on the present, on ''our moment of attention.'' Ashbery's later work has often had the tone of a letter—a form which seems to have released him from certain inhibitions. . . . This one-to-one (and ephemeral) form allows Ashbery to reveal himself without making his private life a public spectacle. While introspective and autobiographical, Ashbery is not ''confessional'' in the way that Lowell, Plath and Ginsberg are.

What secrets does Ashbery reveal in poems that use devices similar to forgetfulness, dreams and letters? Until recently, the secrets we might have expected at the culmination of most ambitious poems on philosophical questions would have been some revelation of the divine. But, as Auden pointed out in his foreword to *Some Trees,* Ashbery is a poet in a secular age. Now, when atheism is orthodox, theology has become as abstract and figureless as an Abstract Expressionist painting. Although Ashbery calls to the ''old heavens,'' he does not expect an answer. . . . Ashbery's secrets, so painfully and tortuously unveiled, are not one single, concrete truth and will vary from reader to reader; indeed he often contradicts himself, even within the same poem.

One secret Ashbery discloses is the very fact that secrets exist: not only is our age scientific and secular, but much of our poetry, particularly that influenced by Williams and by the New York poets, is emphatically grounded in the commonplace, the ordinary. Ashbery's concern with the mysterious and the transcendental, in addition to the everyday, contrasts with the poems of his friend, Frank O'Hara. When the sun, representing the source of O'Hara's poetic inspiration, speaks to him, it uses the jocular voice of another guy trying to wake him up. In Ashbery's poems, the fluid changes of subject signal to us that the hermetic glass bubble within which we try to contain ''the real world'' artificially is fragile and distorted. . . .'' By pushing us beyond our assumptions about reality, Ashbery moves decisively out of bounds.

At the same time as he affirms the sharply focused convex mirror which represents the ordering force of art and its opening of mystical dimensions, Ashbery turns away from its demands which impede life and he questions the restrictions art imposes on life, which is untidy. Sometimes Ashbery has attempted to reproduce the randomness of life through surreal automatic writing in books such as *Vermont Notebooks* and *The Tennis Court Oath.* However appealing automatic writing may be in theory, the result is not poetry: *Vermont Notebooks* is a relentlessly banal collection of lists and trivia, and most readers will punctuate *The Tennis Court Oath* with oaths more commonly heard on tennis courts when one's partner persists in serving outside the line.

In addition to revealing that secrets exist, Ashbery questions the process of our perception through poetry and reveals the secret of that perception by showing himself at work on the poem. This is both the subject and central metaphor of his long poem **"Self-Portrait in a Convex Mirror,"** which is partly a description of the strange painting in which Parmigianino copied his reflection onto a wooden hemisphere the same size as his convex mirror. When the reader is allowed backstage, into the cluttered studio, and the poet reveals himself at work, there is always a risk of breaking the spell. . . . Ashbery avoids this by constantly turning his curious mirror to shift its focus and keep us hypnotized. (pp. 97-100)

This simple reality, the ordinary world before it was distorted, Ashbery nominates as another of his secrets. . . .

Certainly an important secret which Ashbery is very anxious to conceal, yet which constantly obsesses him, is his own self-portrait and what it reveals about him. The world for Ashbery is a hall of mirrors whose polished surfaces continually reflect, magnify and fragment his own image. These mirrors attract him, yet he feels compelled to shatter even their pleasantest illusions. . . . His awareness of illusion enables him to endure it, to face the potentially grotesque and terrifying images of himself in the distorting mirrors, and even to look again. . . . (p. 101)

Perhaps the ultimate secret for Ashbery is poetry itself: a code as mysterious in its source as the snowflakes which represent it [in **"The Skaters"**]. . . . What is significant is not each single flake or the entire storm but the rhythm of the shifting focus between the two. This shift is invisible and elusive, like the secret code that crystallizes into Ashbery's poetry.

Having decoded some general outline of these secrets within Ashbery's thicket of contradictions, the reader is entitled to ask: "How much work should I reasonably be expected to do before enjoying a poem? How obscure can a poet be when 'illustrating opacity' without confounding his readers?" The danger of boredom and exasperation is a real one, particularly when Ashbery's style, while pleasant enough, is not outstandingly musical and relies on imagery for its effects. Sometimes his exposition of abstract philosophical issues is rather bloodless. Yet in his mature work his quicksilver images fascinate us, and his lines pace forward with inevitability and authority.

By exploring intellectual questions deeply and attempting to discover an artistic order, Ashbery has taken a stand against the neo-Dadaists of the sixties; he is a very traditional poet who has affinities with Stevens and Rilke. Yet by moving beyond . . . traditional ideas of form and opening his poetry to the voices of forgetfulness, dreams, letters and secret codes, Ashbery is at the same time one of our most experimental and unrestricted poets. He has the ingenuity of a renaissance alchemist who can perform the boldest experiments because he claims the authority of the most ancient texts. (pp. 101-02)

> *Roberta Berke, "Neon in Daylight: The New York Poets," in her* Bounds Out of Bounds: A Compass for Recent American and British Poetry *(copyright © 1981 by Roberta Berke; reprinted by permission of Oxford University Press, Inc.), Oxford University Press, New York, 1981, pp. 90-106 [the excerpts reprinted here were revised by the author for this publication].**

DANA GIOIA

Shadow Train will change no one's mind about Ashbery's merits as a poet. His admirers will praise the new-found discipline and concentration in this collection of sixteen line, "sonnet-like" poems. His detractors will grumble about the emperor's new briefs. And the rest will continue to play Pontius Pilate washing their hands of the whole matter. Yet *Shadow Train* is an interesting book that can give a careful reader a new understanding of Ashbery's strengths and weaknesses as a poet.

Part of the pleasure of reading Ashbery comes from the variety of words, images, moods, and styles he can fit so seamlessly into his work. He continually surprises one with things not usually found in a poem. *Shadow Train* encompasses everything from Warren G. Harding to the Keystone Kops, from the idea of God to the **"Image of the Little Match Girl."** He can move convincingly from pathos to low humor in the same stanza or turn a piece of slang into a remarkable metaphor. Yet sometimes this diversity works against him. He often indulges in gross sentimentality, and though he tries to distance it with an ironic title, as in **"Some Old Tires,"** the burden of his clichés sometimes sinks the entire poem. . . .

[But] these obvious lapses are rare. Ashbery's pervasive sentimentality is usually better balanced by flashes of wit or at least the pleasant chiaroscuro of deliberate ambiguity. . . . His usual style is nostalgic but in a suave and worldly way—the tone of a man who has seen it all stoically looking back on life. (p. 587)

As *Shadow Train* demonstrates, Ashbery still has a good ear for spoken language. While there is not much traditional music in his recent poetry, it bristles with striking lines and phrases. This gift for felicitous, natural phrasing is the key to Ashbery's unique sound. Whereas most poets use the stressed word or the metrical foot for their rhythmic unit. Ashbery uses the larger unit of the phrase. This choice gives his verse its speed and distinctively supple rhythms. This practice also has its dangers. In his longer poems it can allow Ashbery's complex syntax to run away with him. The self-imposed limits of *Shadow Train* (fifty short poems of identical length) keep Ashbery from spinning the elegant camouflage that typifies his longer work. Here one can see how Ashbery's imagination works. Since the poems are short enough to be seen as a whole, their underlying structure, usually so elusive, becomes clearer than before. The abrupt transitions from scene to scene, image to image, are now easier to follow. They may still seem arbitrary, but at least now one can hold both unrelated parts in mind for comparison. (p. 588)

[Ashbery] is still not a poet one would recommend without reservations, but at least this volume provides a manageable introduction to his prolific and difficult work. If one is prepared to approach him uncritically, he is very entertaining, but his work must not be read so much as overheard—like an attractive voice talking at another table. Under scrutiny, however, his graceful elegant poems often seem arbitrary and overlong. Their unity is mainly stylistic. Their meaning is in their method.

Ashbery is a discursive poet without a subject. Although he deals indirectly with several recurrent themes, themes which have become increasingly dark and personal as he has grown older, the poems are mainly the surface play of words and images. One never remembers ideas from an Ashbery poem, one recalls the tones and textures. If ideas are dealt with at all, they are present only as faint echoes heard remotely in some turn of phrase. Ideas in Ashbery are like the melodies in some jazz improvisation where the musicians have left out the original tune to avoid paying royalties. They are wild variations on a missing theme with only the original chord changes as a clue. This sort of music can be fun as long as someone doesn't try to analyze it like a Beethoven symphony. A skillful and sympathetic critic like Helen Vendler can trace major themes in Ashbery [see excerpt above], but somehow in reading him, even repeatedly, one does not see the deeper side of his work emerge so satisfactorily. Despite the awards and attention, he lacks the weight of the major poet his defenders claim he has become. Paradoxically his work becomes more pleasurable and interesting the less claims one makes for him. He is a marvellous minor poet, but an uncomfortable major one. (pp. 588-89)

> Dana Gioia, *''Poetry Chronicle'' in* The Hudson Review *(copyright © 1981 by The Hudson Review, Inc.; reprinted by permission), Vol. XXXIV, No. 4, Winter, 1981-82, pp. 579-94.**

ROBERT RICHMAN

Helen McNeil, a British critic writing in the *Times Literary Supplement,* has said that ''since the death of Robert Lowell, the title of most important American poet has been on offer to John Ashbery.'' Countless other critics have registered similar judgments. And as if all that were not enough, the government of the United States commissioned Ashbery to write a poem for the bicentennial. Ashbery responded, with all due mockery, with **''Pyrography.''** . . .

Ashbery's famous ''difficulty'' . . . has not seemed to pose an obstacle to his acclaim. This is partially due, no doubt, to the cachet difficult poems have had recently (the less one understands a poem, the better it must be), but mainly to his incredible perseverance: Ashbery's latest book, **Shadow Train,** is his tenth in under twenty years. His seemingly immaculately planned career is, as he says in two telling lines from a poem in this book, ''too perfect in its outrageous / Regularity to be called to stand trial again.''

If Ashbery had ever been on trial in the past, it was because his method was not understood. Once one grasps that method—as well as its philosophical sources and influences—one understands how the poetry is generated (although not what it is about). As Ashbery himself once noted, rather than dealing specifically with problems, issues, or feelings, his method seeks to reproduce ''the actions of a mind at work or rest.'' A typical Ashbery poem attempts to focus attention on its own content—formless, arbitrary, free-associational fragments—rather than on any ostensible subject matter or point. Ashbery once claimed that he rarely rewrites, for the poetry's craft and ''meaning'' are automatically ''there'' in the words first put down on paper. He also claims to begin often with a title, since ''there are many ways of getting pushed into a poem and they're all valid.'' The lines of an Ashbery poem seem less the natural products of an emotion or idea than insertions, and the overall result is, as other commentators have noticed, similar to an abstract expressionist painting—fractured and indistinct. (p. 62)

An Ashbery poem is sometimes as discontinuous in its style as in its logic. Syntactical contortions, endless parenthetical remarks, and ellipses are typical—as if the linear requirements of grammar were too constricting for the poet's roller-coaster of associative thoughts. Often Ashbery abruptly changes tense or person. . . . Ashbery likes to be interrupted in the act of composition—by the telephone, by an advertisement on the radio—so he can incorporate these extraneous snippets to vary the poem's music. Indeed, all of Ashbery's language seems taken from other sources, making the poems sound oddly rehearsed. Even symbols and literary allusions, when they are

used, refer more to their secondhand nature than to any fresh poetic idea. Ashbery's typical tone is flat, nasal, unenthused: the emotions, like the images, seem to be used or false—certainly of no great consequence to the poet himself.

In the early 1950's, after a period of intense depression and inactivity, Ashbery attended a concert of John Cage's *Music of Changes* with his friend and fellow poet, the late Frank O'Hara. Ashbery recalls: ''It was a series of dissonant chords, mostly loud, with irregular rhythm. It went on for over an hour and seemed infinitely extendable. I felt profoundly refreshed after hearing that. I started to write again shortly afterwards. I felt that I could be as singular in my art as Cage was in his.'' This inspiration resulted in, to use the title of an Ashbery poem written a few years later, a ''new realism,'' which, like Cage's music, rejects the laws of perspective, logic, and narration in favor of randomness and discontinuity.

The roots of this ''new realism,'' however, were in the (then) thirty-year-old French artistic movement known as surrealism, which, under the auspices of the writers André Breton, Paul Eluard, and Guillaume Apollinaire, and the painters René Magritte, Giorgio de Chirico, and Salvador Dali, fostered outrageous blends in their art of the familiar and the improbable. . . . What particularly caught Ashbery's attention, however, was the surrealists' (especially de Chirico's) poeticization of the banal and subordination of the crafting or organizing sensibility. As Breton, the acknowledged leader of the movement, declared, true literary art should consist of ''[a] monologue that flows as rapidly as possible on which the critical spirit of the subject brings no judgment to bear . . . and which will reproduce as exactly as possible spoken thought.''

Toward such a goal each verbal unit (images as well as words) of ''spoken thought'' has equal value and, more importantly, has value in and of itself rather than in relation to other verbal units or to any overarching (read: oppressive) poetic idea. Hence no ''correct'' balance exists between the particular and the general, or between abstraction and detail, and the resulting disjunct verse contains no specific meaning, at least the kind one would expect. As David Shapiro writes in a recent book on Ashbery [see excerpt above], ''If meaning is 'what anything suggests,' Ashbery often attempts paradoxically to present a blank configuration of words'' that not only are interpretation-proof but offer a ''labyrinth of possible denotations and possible lack of denotations.''

What, then, does this poetry concern itself with? The answer is: itself—its inconclusiveness, its antinomianism, its absurdism, and, above all, its deep distrust of language that naively attempts statements about reality and reality's possible meaning. Ashbery's poetry is, in a word, self-referential. (pp. 62-3)

Bits of self-reflexiveness occur in Ashbery's first book, **Some Trees,** published originally in 1956. But essentially this book consists of, in the words of Shapiro, ''parodies of narration'' in which the cadence and look of typical narrative poetry are used in the service of poems which, if they are not meaningless altogether, at least attempt to undermine their ''announced'' subjects. For example, in the apparently autobiographical poem, **''The Portrait of Little J. A. in a Prospect of Flowers,''** clarity of image and smooth linguistic simplicity reveal absolutely nothing substantial about the poet's childhood, which one vaguely senses was full of importance (particularly regarding his sexual development). Instead, Ashbery writes around his life, and then at the end of the poem comments on this process, capping it with a slice of jarringly false nostalgia. . . .

Ashbery snubs the standard poetic contemplation of youth by ironically "rescuing" his past by means of extraneous images and a cool remove that scants the pain and urgency of childhood. The more traditional effect of reminiscence (such as forcing the poet to reevaluate his present life or reconcile it to the past) is replaced with the unexpected one of reevaluating the method of the poem itself. These lines supply a foretaste of Ashbery's later, more ambitious self-reflexive experiments. . . . (p. 63)

Ashbery's quarrel with causality and referentiality takes a different form in his second book, *The Tennis Court Oath* (1963). Instead of modulated ironic narratives and false limpidity Ashbery resorts to the syntactically, grammatically, and metaphorically disjunct poetry of collage. . . . Following the lead of the painter Robert Rauschenburg, Ashbery admits everything into [the long poem] "Europe": stray bits from newspapers, lopped-off phrases from children's books, bad poetry, and loose thoughts from the back of the poet's mind—all frosted over with an equalizing emotional deadness. Like the pieces of a painter's collage, the words refer to themselves and to the "idea" of collage. Entrance requirements for the poem are gratuitousness and error. . . . About "Europe" Ashbery remarked, "I didn't know what I wanted to do, but I did know what I didn't want to do."

In his next two books, *Rivers and Mountains* (1967) and *The Double Dream of Spring* (1970), the title of which is taken from a painting by de Chirico, Ashbery moves back from opaque collage to the smooth ironic cadences of his early poems. But there is a wider range of feelings that are the butt of his irony. . . .

In these volumes Ashbery still writes radically anti-causal verse. In a note to one group of poems in *Double Dream* the poet says that he wrote them first "in French and translated them myself into English, with the idea of avoiding customary word-patterns and associations." He also depends heavily on clichés, as in "**Decoy**," which uses a good number of the pseudo-political, or particularly banal industrial-newsletter, type. . . . The entire poem, couched in such jargon, leads nowhere . . . and ends with [a] false conclusion. . . .

Ashbery's world of irony and parody continues full-steam in his next book, comically titled *Three Poems* [1972], for the book actually consists of three long free-associational prose works ("I don't know what poetic means," says the poet)—"antinomian confessions" in the Christian tradition, as Shapiro points out, but, of course, contemporary ones of "discontinuity and revolt." (p. 64)

This most obscurely private of Ashbery's books was followed, in 1976, by his most accessible, the award-winning *Self-Portrait in a Convex Mirror*, which contains more reflexive "guides" to the poetry than any other collection. In fact, the title poem's statements of method intrude more and more as the poem proceeds—until they become the poem itself. . . . [This poem discusses] its own verbal "flatness," anti-logical bias, condescension to "old" subjects, and the poet's refusal to reveal anything below the surface of the poem. . . . (p. 65)

In a rare moment in *Self-Portrait* Ashbery deals expressly with an issue: his inability, as a poet, to have a "traditional" transcendent experience, and the result ["**As I Came from the Holy Land**"] is probably the best thing in the book. . . . This poem, the title of which is taken from Sir Walter Raleigh's haunting poem about the durability of the *idea* of love, as opposed to its earthly variation, poignantly expresses the poet's "lateness"

in history in the same way "**Answering a Question in the Mountains**" in *Some Trees* does ("It is late to be late."). But here Ashbery dispenses with irony, parody, and the usual drabness of feeling. For once, the poem's rhythm is synchronized to its emotional level. It seems as if the proximity of the transcendent experience inspired Ashbery to share his vision rather than preempt it for a discourse on method.

In *Houseboat Days* (1977), however, Ashbery returns to writing poems that profess their own nonproductivity. . . . In "**Litany**," from *As We Know* (1979), Ashbery goes back to his disjunct style, this time in the form of a two-columned poem designed to be read simultaneously and aloud, creating a disharmonious jangle. The poem's two private voices perhaps most aggressively indicate Ashbery's belief in the insurmountable separateness of two minds. The rest of *As We Know* resembles *Houseboat Days* (the latter is perhaps slightly more inspired) except for a group of poems the titles of which are longer than the actual poems; parodies, it would seem, of the worst of Richard Brautigan (for what reason, one can only guess).

Shadow Train, Ashbery's new book, parodies the national mood of retrenchment and specifically the new conservatism of form and representation in the arts (notably painting) with a tidy package of fifty poems of identical length (sixteen lines) and structure (four stanzas). But beneath the surface the poet is up to the same old tricks—only worse. (pp. 65-6)

The poet's concern with the autonomy of language takes on an especially jejune cast in *Shadow Train*. . . .

On the whole the book casts a bleak, if sometimes comic, shadow—more diffuse than usual (one is less sure in this book *why* the poet is so obscurely despairing), but then, Ashbery never promised things would get better, or, for that matter, clearer.

If the foregoing successfully describes the curious and unique nature of John Ashbery's poetry, it would certainly seem a non sequitur to say that his work is Romantic, in the line of Keats, Wordsworth, and Tennyson. Yet Helen Vendler . . . says just that [see excerpt above]. (p. 66)

[Miss Vendler contends that Ashbery] "comes from Wordsworth, Keats, Tennyson, Stevens, Eliot; his poems are about love, or time, or age."

What can be said for this view? One thing that Ashbery's free-associational technique and surrealism allow, as we have seen, is freedom of form and content. The fact that anything gains admittance to the poem, as well as the fact that Ashbery's linguistic resources are quite deep, will make for a wide range of words that *could* be construed to be "about" love, time, or age. (It should be pointed out in passing that in this essay, as in Miss Vendler's, only Ashbery's understandable lines have been quoted; at least 80 percent of the total are not readily graspable at all.) But does an obscure or unintegrated utterance amid self-reflexive ruminations and misleading metaphors—"yellow flowers," or "bed"—mean the poem is a love poem? . . .

The Romantics' obsessive investigation of their political, moral, and imaginative relation to the external world is profoundly opposed to Ashbery's self-reflexive tap dance. Ashbery's "contradictoriness"—another supposed likeness to the Romantics—is not couched, as it is for them, in dialectic. The Romantic poets bartered with the world; Ashbery, with himself. Whether it is the early automatism or the later poems constructed from slogans, TV news, and doggerel, there is no imaginative interaction with the sensual world—not even any moments of illumination; his banal objects remain brutally dull. . . .

The single point that connects Ashbery with the Romantics is his attempted creation of a "new world." Yet would Wordsworth or even Stevens approve of something so disharmonious, denigrating, without energy, lacking transcendental effect, and, to most readers, utterly incomprehensible? (p. 67)

Ashbery's quick cutting from one thought to another is, according to Miss Vendler, part of a "consoling aesthetic, since by its standards every utterance is privileged as a nonce affair; it is also mournful, since it considers art as fleeting as life." This rather somber consideration does not take into account the unconsoling thought, suggested by Ashbery's poetry, that nothing could (or presumably should) be looked into at all. . . . Ashbery himself has admitted that at times he does not know where he is going in a poem, and lacks a subject—how is this to be reconciled with Miss Vendler's assertion that Ashbery has "borrowed from Stevens the trick of working up obliquely to his subject, so that the subject itself makes a rather late appearance in the poem"? Miss Vendler's own generous "deep trust" of Ashbery's associative processes—necessary in a critic—is hardly paid back in kind.

In a bold attempt to vindicate Ashbery's emotional coldness, Miss Vendler writes: "Oddly enough, our first response to emotional pain all around us, down in the cisterns, up in the gutters, is to deny we are feeling it." If this startling remark were true of our poets, their art would soon die for lack of blood. Fortunately, this is in general not the case. It is too true, however, that one vainly searches in Ashbery's poetry for some verbal correlative to the pain of loss, disillusion, unrequited love, or, on the positive side, to the warmth of friendship. . . . Instead, one finds the isolation of self-reflexivity. . . . (pp. 67-8)

Miss Vendler finds Ashbery's poetry hopeful. . . . Yet the more one of his poems says, the more embarrassed and the *less* hopeful it becomes. Also, the more knowledge it imparts, the less it succeeds; the more it displays the poet's learning, the less it educates; and the more the poetry resembles the voice of a living, breathing man, the less it is "itself." One would think that, if anything, Ashbery's poetry of non-production—involving endless linguistic copulation with no creation—threatens to destroy the enterprise of art altogether. Like the surrealists, who frightened even Sartre for this reason, Ashbery's radicalism is purely negative. Self-referentiality breaks down the vital link between the object and the world; the idea that the mind is a conduit breaks down the attachment between the object and thought. Artaud could have been referring to Ashbery when he said that the "surrealist despairs of attaining his own mind," for Ashbery replaces mind—represented in poetry by a strong and stable "I"—with a theory or code.

One might say this is, to one degree or another, true of all poets. With Ashbery, however, a serious claim has been entered that the importance lies entirely in the theory and not in what rises out of it. "It is as though poetry were incompetent to see its own image until reflected in the discursive language of criticism," says Miss Vendler. "And it may be so." Shapiro agrees: "The best poetry of our day is . . . a form of literary criticism." Such gross absurdities could only be uttered in an age that has little use for poets.

The "dark idolatry of the self" which Shelley feared has become a reality in contemporary art, and its poetic avatar of the

moment is John Ashbery. His impressive linguistic inventiveness, and his unique voice, have been placed in the service of what Shapiro honestly calls an "icy, autocratic humiliation of the reader." Only a critic still anxious, as Helen Vendler is, to *will* some connection between poetry and human life and the human world could write of Ashbery that he "makes us feel more and more a part of a human collectivity," when the truth is more nearly the opposite. But as a young woman poet said to me when *Shadow Train* appeared: "It's like Marxism. You lie often enough and people will believe you." (p. 68)

Robert Richman, "Our 'Most Important' Living Poet," in Commentary *(reprinted by permission; all rights reserved), Vol. 74, No. 1, July, 1982, pp. 62-8.*

VERNON SHETLEY

[One] might caution the reader that *Shadow Train* is by no means the best place to start in reading Ashbery, as it occupies a curious position in the evolving body of his work. This collection . . . marks another peculiar twist in a protean career, another of the seemingly willful swerves from his natural predispositions that discomfit his admirers almost as much as his detractors. Ashbery's previous book, *As We Know,* while it contained a number of poems as brief as one line apiece, nevertheless presented him in one of his freest, most expansive moods, particularly in "**Litany,**" a poem long and discursive by almost any standards. *Shadow Train* comes then as something of a counter-move to the magnificent sprawl of "**Litany,**" a book rigidly suited up in an unvaried form, a steady march of quatrains through fifty poems on pages numbered 1 through 50. Ashbery has never shown a particular aptitude for sonnet-length poems, and *Shadow Train* is of course something of a sonnet sequence; he has always been most comfortable in those fixed forms, like the sestina, whose spurious, exoteric nature seems to mock and comment on itself almost without the poet's help. The sonnet had seemed simply too short, seemed to afford too little space for the vast spiraling, ranging, or redoubling movements that are the best part of Ashbery. The decision to write a book of sonnet-length poems shows him again intent on testing his limits, moving antithetically against his most recent achievement. (pp. 237-38)

[Though] Ashbery certainly succeeds in hollowing out his chosen form, he does not always seem completely comfortable in it. His characteristic amplitude gives way at times to a curious kind of halting or truncation, in which sentences or whole lines of argument that had seemed destined to spin themselves playfully out were compressed into unnaturally small compass. So these poems frequently leave the reader without the sense of roundedness, that peculiarly traditional feeling of lyric closure, that most of Ashbery's best poems deliver. They further strike the reader as uncharacteristically premeditated; one has less often the intoxicating sense that Ashbery is making it up as he goes along, the feeling of shock and freshness upon arriving at destinations that seem as totally unexpected to the poet as to the reader. One on occasion even glimpses a narrative concealed through an extended metaphor, as in the peculiar detective-story plot (*Columbo,* it seems) that runs through "**Every Evening When the Sun Goes Down.**" . . . (pp. 238-39)

Whether the form enforces or follows the particular inflection of attitude, *Shadow Train* shows Ashbery at his most limiting, most in the mode that Harold Bloom has referred to as the "failed orphic." Each of the poems plays out a little drama of emptying and restitution, but while the pain of loss is shrugged off throughout with a deadpan humor, it nevertheless is real, and informs many of even the best poems in the book. . . . (p. 239)

One might say that **Shadow Train** partakes more of Ashbery's tragic mode, where past and future empty one another, or empty themselves into one another, than his romance mode, where a future gathers and restores the fragments, however altered, of today. . . . The pathos is muted by an offhand irony, in contrast to the almost unmediated intensity of much of Ashbery's work, but muted, it seems, because the restitutive hope is similarly muted and curtailed. Even the most confident of fulfillments seem hesitant, curiously noncomittal. . . . The reader accustomed to Ashbery's characteristic extravagance and largesse may at first be put off by the flat, evasive quality of so many of these poems. But Ashbery may by this time be trusted to know better than the reader who would have him continue to yield familiar pleasures, and **Shadow Train** shows him, if not at his most daring and expansive, certainly at his most masterful. In its fecundity of trope, its enormous humor, and the perfect accuracy with which it reflects and enlarges the spirit of our age, **Shadow Train** is a permanent addition to American poetry. (pp. 240-41)

Vernon Shetley, "Language on a Very Plain Level,"
in Poetry (© 1982 by The Modern Poetry Association; reprinted by permission of the Editor of Poetry), Vol. CXL, No. 4, July, 1982, pp. 236-41.

Margaret (Eleanor) Atwood

1939-

Canadian novelist, poet, critic, and short story writer.

Since the publication of her first collection of poetry, *Double Persephone*, in the early sixties, Margaret Atwood has been recognized as an outstanding poet. The publication of *The Edible Woman* several years later initiated her reputation as an important novelist—a reputation confirmed by her feminine quest novel, *Surfacing*, judged by many to be a contemporary classic. Although Atwood writes well in either form, most critics maintain that her true gift lies in poetic expression because of her spare, controlled, and direct style.

As a spokesperson for the culture and psyche of her native Canada and, also, for the feminist point of view, Atwood frequently uses dual themes and images. A favored combination is the search for identity coupled with a journey motif, especially a journey into the wilderness, such as the one outlined in an early collection of poems, *The Journals of Susanna Moodie*. Atwood advocates a return to a simpler, more natural way of life, in order to shed the roles imposed upon people by commercial culture. She aims to find the real, hidden self and to regain the lost past. This attempt to break out of role-playing, survive the accompanying pains, and establish relationships without illusions, is the basis for *Dancing Girls and Other Stories* and the novel, *Bodily Harm*. A recent collection of poetry, *True Stories*, also emphasizes the importance of self, bolstered by the instinct for survival. But despite her often solemn subject matter, Atwood infuses her writing with satiric wit, and both *The Edible Woman* and *Lady Oracle* are regarded as comic novels.

Although most of Atwood's writing has been widely acclaimed, there is one point upon which many critics agree: that her characterizations lack depth. Her males in particular are stereotypical, representing only negative and destructive elements. In addition, critics note that the constant re-use of her themes, images, and narrative styles has tended to make her work somewhat predictable. Nevertheless, such techniques as direct address, dramatic monologue, and the use of personal and historic events allow Atwood to achieve a uniquely personal style and voice. She has the ability to present the ordinary in extraordinary ways, giving the reader new options for re-evaluating those things previously taken for granted.

(See also *CLC*, Vols. 2, 3, 4, 8, 13, 15; *Contemporary Authors*, Vols. 49-52; and *Contemporary Authors New Revision Series*, Vol. 3.)

DOUGLAS HILL

Margaret Atwood's stories [in *Dancing Girls*], taken as a whole, express the urban intellectual sensibility of the Canadian sixties with a comprehensiveness and finality that her novels don't attain (and don't attempt). If it's true also that Atwood's lyrics, rather than the novels and criticism, are the main prop upon which her critical reputation should rest—upon shorter rather than longer forms, that is—then it should be no surprise to find this a thoroughly challenging and rewarding volume. . . .

© Lütfi Özkök

[All of the stories] are remarkably approachable—well-crafted, focussed, unfailingly interesting even when not especially brilliant. They're traditional in form, only modestly experimental, unselfconscious realism that now and then pushes unalarmingly into the terrain of serious fantasy or the surreal. . . .

A full selection of Atwood's prose is on display, from straightforward exposition to Lardneresque monologue to her most characteristic voice—elliptical, flat, spare, filled with disjunctions—the one that sounds as if it's coming at you from under the rug. More than a third of the fourteen stories are first-person narratives; an equal number employ the run-on sentence of *Surfacing*, a device that in Atwood's medium has the curious effect of damping intensity while it provides the illusion of creating it. Although there is humour in all the stories—sardonic, cynical, the usual deflations of ego and expectation—it seems least successful, perhaps only by comparison, at its most deliberate. The gum-cracking one-liners of **"Rape Fantasies"** wear a bit thin after the first reading.

The whole book might well be viewed as a collection of rape fantasies, if it were understood that the image of the physical act is most often a metaphor for profounder violations, far more dangerous forcible entries into the cubicle of selfhood. The majority of the stories are about fear, anxiety, self-defense: if the hypothetical—and thus comic—attackers are often Oriental exchange-students ("persons of another culture"), the real and serious enemy, the one that threatens actual annihilation, is simply Men. The male antagonists all seem stamped from the same die. Like Joe in *Surfacing* (the buffalo on the nickel), they are lamely creative, insensitive, stolid, stupid—aging unidealistic dropouts from the sixties who turned on but couldn't tune in. One is tempted, after a while, to call them all stereotypes, and shrug off Atwood's offensive—her feminism—for being too simplistic, too easy. One hesitates at last to do this, because of the nagging possibility that she has hit the mark dead centre. . . .

From the time—around 1970—when it became obvious to everyone that Margaret Atwood's career was to be an extraordinary one, her intelligence, the perspicacity and vigour with which she whirls across the Canadian literary landscape, has caused problems for her reputation as a serious artist. There have been charges of opportunism from one direction, of sterile intellectual cleverness from another. *Surfacing* and *Survival* the same year: what does she *mean*? If anyone should still need proof at this late date that Atwood's intelligence deserves neither apologists nor debunkers, then *Dancing Girls* should give it in abundance. The stories themselves are good, a few are fine. More important, they are ordered in a volume of considerable yet always coherent range. Most important of all, the book reflects—and in turn illuminates—the complex unity of idea and attitude that Atwood has established through her previous work. *Dancing Girls* is no hothouse forcing of thin stock, but the bloom from a solid, confident, and organic talent.

Douglas Hill, "Violations," in The Canadian Forum, *Vol. LVII, No. 677, December-January, 1977-78, p. 35.*

R. P. BILAN

Margaret Atwood's first collection of short stories [*Dancing Girls*] . . . centres on the relationships between men and women. . . . Atwood writes mainly of the struggles between men and women, of painful failures and of equally painful readjustments. Atwood's women tend to suffer the most in these relationships; their male friends have affairs, or simply leave them, and the women have to shore up their defences just to get by. . . . [Atwood's stories] range in tone from cool detachment, to suppressed hysteria, to the lightly ironic and humorous. And Atwood's considerable ability as a poet is often evident in the stories in the vividness of phrasing and imagery. The use of suggestive imagery to convey meaning is in fact one of the most distinctive features of the best stories—'**Under Glass**' and '**Polarities**,' for instance.

By the standard of Atwood's own best fiction—*Surfacing*, that is—*Dancing Girls* is a reasonably good, but not major work. It may be unfair or even inappropriate to compare a collection of short stories with a novel, but none of the stories has the reach or depth of *Surfacing*. Further, many if not most short-story collections are of uneven quality, and Atwood's is no exception; her stories, it is true, do not differ radically in quality, but distinctions between them can be made. The stories of sexual politics, nearly all told in the first person from the woman's point of view, achieve varying degrees of success. '**Under Glass**,' for instance, is successful because the narrator is fully individualized, and, even as she considers that ultimate defence of Atwood's heroines, withdrawal and a retreat from all pain, she shows an appealing sense of humor. In '**The Grave of the Famous Poet**,' on the other hand, the central situation is simply never brought to life. The story portrays the typical Atwood battle: the characters fight for the role of victim, es-

tablish a truce, resume the battle. The format is familiar, but we never really see the characters; they never become individualized, realized, alive. (pp. 329-30)

'**The Resplendant Quetzal**,' one of the finer stories in the book, has a mellow tone unusual in Atwood, and while the story may lack the sheer emotional power found in Atwood's presentation of the savage hostility between David and Anna in *Surfacing* or in the bitter warfare of the lovers in *Power Politics*, her balanced, sympathetic portrayal of the problems of both the husband and the wife has a compensating gentleness, humaneness. Atwood, however, occasionally presents her tales of men and women in a much lighter manner. In one story she creates the voice of an unsophisticated working-class woman who is recounting her rape fantasies; another more or less comic tale focuses on a rather ordinary, not particularly attractive girl whose only moment of glory comes when she is suddenly 'courted' by a strange foreigner. These stories successfully achieve what they attempt but they are light, and they are not the essential Atwood; they relate to the world of *Lady Oracle* rather than to that of *Surfacing*.

Sexual politics, of course, is only one of Atwood's major concerns; extreme alienation, both from society and from oneself, as in '**The War in the Bathroom**,' is another. Atwood is expert at mapping out feelings of alienation, but there is an aspect of her dealings with these experiences that needs to be questioned. The problem that arises can be seen most obviously in '**A Travel Piece**.' The main character increasingly feels a sense of unreality about her own life and waits longingly for some 'real' event to occur. When the plane she is on crashes into the sea, even the accident doesn't seem real to her until some of the other survivors in the raft think of slitting the throat of one of the others to get his blood to quench their thirst. This act, or the possibility of it, the woman takes to be definitive of 'reality.' Although there is an obvious distance between Atwood and the main character, we can't say that this is simply the character's view of reality; the third-person narrator—Atwood—seems, to some degree, to share it. Certainly in other stories we encounter the sense that only the grotesque, the bizarre, the disordered are 'real.' Undoubtedly much of the strength of Atwood's work comes from the intensity with which she explores this vision of reality, but it is in itself a narrow, partial vision.

In '**Polarities**,' which I think is the best story in the book, Atwood to some extent goes beyond this limited vision. . . . Atwood doesn't sentimentalize her portrayal of Louise, who is presented as being virtually 'mad,' but also partly a visionary, and the story at least points to possibilities beyond a totally alienated view of reality. And the story doesn't merely portray and accept alienation, inner paralysis, but diagnoses it. The main male character, Morrison, makes some effort to help Louise but he's trapped by his essential inability to respond, by his 'chill interior, embryonic and blighted.' In a stunning ending Atwood gives us a surrealistic image of the land that expresses the emptiness of Morrison's emotional life. . . . Here we have an example of Atwood's art at its best, and, in her analysis of alienation, of her insight. (pp. 330-31)

R. P. Bilan, "Letters in Canada: 'Dancing Girls'," in University of Toronto Quarterly *(© University of Toronto Press 1978; reprinted by permission of University of Toronto Press), Vol. XLVII, No. 4, Summer, 1978, pp. 326-38.*

TOM MARSHALL

Atwood is a swimmer. The familiar Canadian "underwater" motif, the notion of the self and Canada itself trapped underwater like Atlantis, occurs in the first poems of her first full collection and is repeated throughout her work, reaching a kind of climax in the novel *Surfacing*. The notions of inner order and outer space, garrison and wilderness, the issue of perspective and of the ways of seeing also recur, as they do in the work of Avison, Page and numerous other writers. Like Al Purdy and others, she has a concern for ancestors and for evolution, even for the geological past. There is the familiar Canadian identification with animals and a sense of fierce native gods. There is both social satire and an interest in the metaphysics of landscape, as in the work of P. K. Page. . . . [But] Atwood utilizes Canadian traditions in an apparently more conscious way than most writers of her generation. She taps Canadian culture's most important concerns. And she brings to traditional materials her own sensibility, her own way of saying things: the famous cool, apparently detached tone, the canny disposition of loaded words in short, punchy lines without much heightening of rhythm. It is a style highly distinctive both in its limitations and its strengths. Atwood attempts, for better and/or worse, and certainly to her immediate advantage with readers, to clarify what is complex and difficult, to get right to what she regards as the essential point.

Metaphysics and metaphor: the search for ways in which to find one's whole self, to find identity with one's body, one's instincts, one's country—in this emotional pioneering Atwood moves to the centre of national concerns. (pp. 154-55)

The Journals of Susanna Moodie enlarges upon the national theme; as a poem sequence it enlarges Atwood's scope and is highly successful, indeed an advance on her two earlier books [*The Circle Game* and *The Animals in That Country*], which were uneven though often striking. In the person and experience of Susanna Moodie the poet finds an appropriate objective correlative for her own thoughts and emotions. The book is both personal and objective, both nationalist and universal in its metaphysical enquiry. . . .

Procedures for Underground presents family poems, the deep well of childhood memories, the bush, Canada under water, the descent into the earth to recover the wisdom of the spirits of place, alienation in cities, travel, and marriage. It is a quieter book of individual poems with a quieter and, for some, a more enduring appeal than the one that follows. *Power Politics* is, as they say, something else again—an account of grim sexual warfare that restores all the Atwood bite and mordant humour. It makes surreal black comedy out of the historic difficulties of women and the destructive games, projections and illusions of modern lovers in a world built on war and the destruction of the environment. But in *You Are Happy,* which can be regarded as a kind of sequel, the Atwood protagonist moves forward toward a new country of relationship without false hopes, promises, defences, evasions, mythologies. The singularity, the uniqueness of things, of people, in the flux: this is something nameless, beyond language, as in *Surfacing*. One gives oneself to the flux. (p. 157)

Her first two novels, *The Edible Woman* and *Surfacing,* are enlargements upon the themes of her poems. In each of them a young woman is driven to rebellion against what seems to be her fate in the modern technological "Americanized" world and to psychic breakdown and breakthrough. But they are quite different in tone and style.

The Edible Woman is delightfully, wickedly funny. It is feminist, certainly, but it provides a satirical account of the absurd ways of Canadian men *and* women. It is kindly in its irony: never so fierce in its assault as is *Power Politics*. There is anger but there is also good humour. The major characters are satirized—they represent various undesirable ways of existing in the modern consumer society—but they are also seen sympathetically as human beings, even the pompous Peter and the pathetic Lothario Leonard. They are not grotesque caricatures like David and Anna in *Surfacing*. (p. 158)

[*The Edible Woman*] is a largely successful comic novel, even if the mechanics are sometimes a little clumsy, the satirical accounts of consumerism a little drawn out. It is skilfully written, shifting easily from first to third person and back again to convey the stages of Marian's mental travels, her journey into self-alienation and out again. Of Atwood's three novels it is least a poet's novel. . . .

Surfacing introduces a young woman far more fearful, desperate, and alienated from her true self than Marian McAlpin. The atmosphere is correspondingly tense and eerie, for this is a psychological ghost story like *The Turn of the Screw,* in which the ghosts, the young woman's parents, are lost parts of herself that she must recover. She has been unable to feel for years, even though she had a good childhood, much of it spent on an island in northern Quebec. She believes (as the reader does for much of the book) that she has been married and divorced, abandoning a child. Her encounter with the gods of place and, apparently, with the corpse of her drowned father when she returns to the scene of her childhood reveals the truth—that she had in fact had a traumatic abortion—and this drives her to a healing madness, a descent to animal simplicity and a rejection of the destructive, mechanical "civilization" that has wounded her and of all its works, even words. (p. 159)

The first-person point of view combined with the evocative description of setting makes it possible for Atwood to get away with a certain shallowness of characterization; only the narrator seems at all complex. But this is not something that interferes with the powerful flow of the novel as one reads it.

Still, it is evident here, as it is more seriously in *Lady Oracle,* the third novel, that characterization is not Atwood's strong point. And it is revealing that much of her fiction, including her shorter fiction, employs the first person. Everything must be filtered through the mind of the Atwood protagonist, who is usually supposed to be both shrewd and confused, a combination that is possible but which tends in certain cases to put some strain on the reader's credulity. In this respect *The Edible Woman* is a more balanced novel than *Surfacing,* and yet it is *Surfacing,* the poet's novel, that more powerfully engages the reader's emotions.

In *Surfacing* the repeated imagery of bottled, trapped and murdered animals builds powerfully to the key scene in which the father's corpse and the aborted foetus are encountered. . . . In *Lady Oracle,* however, a similar patterning of images, metaphors, and ideas fails to compensate for the fuzzy personality of the narrator, even if this last is part of the author's point. Nor is there the power of language found in the latter part of *Surfacing*. Indeed, the female-picaresque *Lady Oracle* is decidedly thinner than the other novels and lacking in over-all shape or focus, even if it is in places very interesting and enjoyable and even if it offers some rewarding insights into the need for and nature of art and the fantasy life. It is just that all of this seems too intellectually worked out, too far removed from any very deeply felt or imagined experience of the kind that "stood in," so to speak, for any very searching exploration of human character in *Surfacing*. Though a serious emotional resonance seems quite clearly intended, it is not achieved, mainly because recurrent poetic imagery is finally no substitute for depth of characterization. This is the major limitation of Atwood the novelist. Also, the reader may suspect that Atwood is indulging herself a little in this book, even to the extent of succumbing somewhat to the old-style "woman's fiction" she parodies. . . . (pp. 160-61)

It is in *Surfacing,* where a considerable emotional power is allowed to develop (as in *The Journals of Susanna Moodie,* another excursion into "large darkness" and out again), that Atwood's vision and gifts may be seen to best advantage. Here she has given the theme of quest into darkness and the journey to wholeness, a theme that she shares in recent Canadian fiction with Klein, LePan, Watson, Cohen, and MacEwen, its most overtly Canadian expression, and this is no doubt one reason for her considerable success at a time when this great and universal theme has a special significance for a rapidly developing and "surfacing" Canadian consciousness. (p. 161)

> Tom Marshall, "Atwood Under and Above Water,"
> in his Harsh and Lovely Land: The Major Canadian
> Poets and the Making of a Canadian Tradition (©
> The University of British Columbia 1979), University
> of British Columbia Press, 1978, pp. 154-61.

SHERRILL GRACE

Margaret Atwood has remarked that her poetic tradition is Canadian. . . . [Her nearest of kin] are James Reaney and, possibly, Jay Macpherson. (p. 129)

Influenced by Frye, both Reaney and Macpherson believe in the power of the imagination to create autonomous poetic worlds. Atwood, while celebrating the imagination, often in disturbing images that recall, for example, Reaney's *The Red Heart* . . . or Macpherson's *Welcoming Disaster* . . . , is aware of its dangers. In her poetry physical reality constantly assails imagination, challenging its proud autonomy so that the poet must adopt an ironic eye and an ambivalent attitude towards both realms. Atwood further resembles Reaney in the emphasis she places upon perception, although she is again less willing than he to trust the eye of the beholder, the individual's inner vision. Her use of myth owes much to Reaney's theories in *Alphabet,* . . . because Reaney provided a model for the intersection of immediate experience and myth. Macpherson's *The Boatman,* published in 1957, was one of Canada's first series of poems artistically shaped as a book instead of a collection. With *Double Persephone, The Circle Game, The Journals of Susanna Moodie,* and to a lesser degree in other volumes, Atwood creates comparable unity—poems inter-related through theme and image to create a structural and imaginative whole.

Atwood's differences from Reaney and Macpherson underline her affinities with poets like Al Purdy and Dennis Lee. Both write about personal experience and historical event in a style that relies less on myth, symbol, or imaginative structure than on colloquial speech rhythms and statement. Though fascinated by the power of imagination and the independence of a verbal universe, Atwood remains committed to social and ethical perspectives in her art. As well, her style is one of direct personal address or dramatic monologue which involves a deft use of colloquialisms; even the most ordinary words, "this" or "but", carry startling importance. Because the theory of art as mirror or map, outlined in *Survival,* is basic to her writing, one should

admire the beauty of the mirror, the colour and complexity of the map, without neglecting the social relevance of poem or novel, the connection between art and life.

This connection indicates the central dialectic and tension in Atwood's work, the pull towards art on one hand and towards life on the other. How does one capture living forms in imaginative and verbal structures? How does the artist work from life to art and still reflect life? Atwood asks these questions repeatedly. . . . The tension that exists between art and life informs the subject/object dialectic as well. Atwood's artistic world rests upon a Blakean world of contraries and William Blake is, I suspect, the most significant non-Canadian influence upon Atwood's imagination. (pp. 129-30)

More important than Atwood's relationship to other poets is the development of her own voice and style. While a cool, acerbic wit, ironic eye and laconic phrase are characteristic of her poetry, she continues to explore new forms. Up to and including *You Are Happy,* the combination of detachment and irony coupled with cut-off line and duplistic form dominates her poetry. *Selected Poems* marks a plateau in this development. (p. 131)

As a fiction writer Atwood's tradition is tenuous. Her novels are best read in the context of twentieth-century fiction where first person narrators, ironic self-reflexive narratives, and symbolic or even mythic structures, are common. There are, however, elements that place her within a broadly-defined Canadian tradition: Atwood's emphasis on the past and the individual's need to be part of a social context, as well as her treatment of victimization and struggle for survival, are common features in [Canadian] novels. In *The Edible Woman* and *Lady Oracle,* Atwood consciously draws upon the tradition of Canadian satire from Haliburton to Leacock and Davies. This satire is heavily ironic and self-critical, while affirming fundamental human values. . . . (pp. 131-32)

Although Atwood's published fiction is polished and enjoyable, it is as a poet that she is truly distinctive and commanding. There are several reasons for this distinction between the power of her poetry and prose. Some of these are matters of voice and style. The sense of challenge and tension so effective in the poems is harder to maintain in a narrative. Moreover, the ironic exploration of self, a constant Atwood theme, is more successful in the poems because the irony of first person narration in the novels too often blurs. The poems are more dramatic vehicles for the exploration of the self because of the possibilities they provide for abrupt juxtaposition of points of view or creation of hallucinatory distortions of a solipsistic eye. With the exception of *Surfacing,* Atwood fails to sustain in her fiction the eerie, disembodied voice that rivets our attention in the poetry. Beckett's experiments with voice in *Molloy, Malone Dies,* and *The Unnameable* resemble the voice in Atwood's poetry, but in general the novel form cannot avoid some sense of ego, of particularized individuality. Certainly, it is in her poetry that Atwood best combines voice and style in order to explore perception, the philosophical extremes of solipsist and materialist, and her concept of the self as a place where experiences intersect.

The closest Atwood comes to resolving the paradoxes of self and perception is in terms of duplicity. Duality is neither negative nor ambivalent. Duality, whether of structure or metaphor, is not the same as polarity. But the human tendency to polarize experience, to affirm one perspective while denying the other, is deeply ingrained, and this makes choosing to live with duality very difficult. (p. 132)

For Atwood the dynamic of violent duality is a function of the creative act. From **Double Persephone**, to **Lady Oracle** and now **Two Headed-Poems,** she has continued to explore the inescapable tension between art and life, the two immortalities. . . . She is constantly aware of opposites—self/other, subject/object, male/female, nature/man—and of the need to accept and work within them. To create, Atwood chooses violent dualities, and her art re-works, probes, and dramatizes the ability to see double. (p. 134)

> *Sherrill Grace, in her* Violent Duality: A Study of Margaret Atwood, *edited by Ken Norris (© copyright Sherrill Grace, 1980), Véhicule Press, 1980, 154 p.*

DAVID MACFARLANE

The most obvious and compelling strength of **True Stories** is that, like much of Atwood's verse, it seems to grow naturally and with ease from a personal vision no less articulate for its privacy. Reading Atwood has always been like following a guide's brilliant flashlight through an eerie but not entirely unfamiliar cellar. In **True Stories** the guide has emerged to the light of day only to find the world no less frightening a place. Gestures of love and family and day-to-day life jive in a *danse macabre* with the incomprehensible and chaotic lunges of poverty, torture, and imprisonment. Familiar and foreign become indistinct, and Atwood's remarkable sensibility finds itself the choreographer of two strange partners. . . .

In many ways, **True Stories** is a collection of anti-travel poems, dismissing our assumptions of both home and away as facile and ridiculous. "The palm trees on the reverse / are a delusion," she writes on a postcard, and one senses that Atwood is bent on decrying a great many delusions, about herself as much as anything else. . . .

Throughout the collection the juxtaposition of false tranquillity and real terror weave irony after bitter irony. Even the most gruesome poems—"Torture," "A Women's Issue," and "Spelling"—possess a grim, sardonic awareness of the cruel and absurd co-existence of love and hate. Poverty and affluence are seen as torturously entangled as the pleasures of sensuality and the pain of rape. The two worlds meet in a place that Atwood maps out in one of the most disturbing and potent poems in the book, **"Notes Towards a Poem That Can Never Be Written."** . . .

If there is not much that is pretty here, there is a great deal that is beautiful. Atwood's language and understanding of the power of language work together in careful harmonies. At times the effect is, like a chant, magical. . . .

Margaret Atwood has a level-headed sense of compassion that strips all the potential radical chic and romantic fashionability from the causes she espouses. She does not react to issues so much as create them, finding them within herself. Even the subtle humour she employs is used to keep any nonsense from creeping into her poetry. . . . **True Stories** is a remarkable book.

> *David Macfarlane, "A Terrible Beauty," in* Books in Canada, *Vol. 10, No. 3, March, 1981, p. 10.*

MARK ABLEY

[**True Stories**] is centred on **Notes Towards a Poem That Can Never Be Written,** a sequence about present-day torture and the brutality of the past. . . . At moments, Atwood seems damaged by her own security; unable to shut her eyes on "darkness, drowned history," she knows prison cells and death camps by a recurrent ache of the imagination. Some poems are painful to read, for she doesn't flinch from showing us the methods and effects of evil. . . .

Not all her poems are explicitly political, though many inhabit a borderland between private and public unease. As ever, Atwood moves with brilliant fluency from objects to emotions; her ideas often take shape and force from sharp physical details such as "cooking steak or bruised lips" and "mouthpink light." That famous cool intelligence can be sardonic with a vengeance. . . . In **True Stories,** however, the abrasiveness is subdued by tenderness, a surprising vulnerability and her consciousness of our need for love (an impossible word to define, an impossible word to do without). It's a measure of Atwood's stature as a poet that the sheer excellence of the writing can be almost taken for granted. Because it is blooded by political comment, **True Stories** may not be one of her most immediately appealing books of poetry, but it's among her best. (p. 52)

> *Mark Abley, "Bitter Wisdom of Moral Concern," in* Maclean's Magazine *(© 1981 by Maclean's Magazine; reprinted by permission), Vol. 94, No. 13, March 30, 1981, pp. 52-3.**

GEORGE WOODCOCK

[Much] of **True Stories** consists of a kind of poetic actuality, a continuing oblique comment on the world that is our here and now. It is perhaps the best verse Atwood has written, honed down to a stark directness, an accuracy of sound, yet imbued with the visual luminosity that makes poetry more than a verbal exercise. It tells us not only of the abdication of reason, but also of the tyranny of the senses and the cruel proximity of violence and love.

One of the striking aspects of **True Stories,** which it shares with much of the poetry in Atwood's previous volume, **Two-Headed Poems,** is the metamorphic process by which thoughts merge into sensations, so that the mind seems imprisoned in its flesh, yet things in a curious and compensating way become liberated into thought. . . .

The constant interplay between the sensual and the intellectual, between things and thoughts, provides the kind of formal remoteness from which Atwood can, like Auden's "Just," exchange her messages. For these are poems that, even while they warn us not to rely too much on reason, nevertheless tell us factual things about the world in which love exists on sufferance, threatened by kinds of violence and injustice that none of our theories or our codes of conduct can comprehend.

The poems assembled in the middle section of the book— **"Notes towards a poem that can never be written"**—read often like a verse abstract of the more harrowing sections of Amnesty International reports. They depict a condition of unreasoning barbarity, where cruelty and death are no longer tragic but merely gratuitous, absurd in their horror. (p. 55)

These poems may not—cannot—portray the rational, yet they are some of the most intensely moral writing I have read in recent years, and not less so because they savage romantic notions of love, motherhood, etc., and show how such myths can imprison and, indeed, destroy.

Yet **True Stories** is not all negation; its very moral intensity makes that impossible. It is about human cruelty and human love, and the two are far less necessarily intertwined than they were in earlier Atwood poetry. . . . (p. 56)

George Woodcock, ''Love and Horror'' (copyright © 1981 by Saturday Night; reprinted by permission of the author), in Saturday Night, Vol. 96, No. 5, May, 1981, pp. 55-6.

JUDITH FITZGERALD

Although *Bodily Harm* is a gripping and horrific narrative (complete with CIA and spy vs. spy reinforcement) it is not merely a suspense-filled adventure thriller set in the Caribbean for an added touch of exotic flair. It is the story of Rennie Wilson, an ''options open'' drifter who takes a seemingly harmless vacation in St. Antoine to escape the pressures and perversions of her life. . . .

My first impulse was to dismiss the ineffectual and introspective hold that Rennie has on her life, but nothing is that simple, a fact that becomes all too clear as Rennie attempts to escape from an essentially middle-class environment. The novel possesses the unrelenting sub-surface terror of *Under the Volcano*, the irony and condemnation of innocence and *laissez-faire* that can be found in *The Quiet American*, and Atwood's own unflinching belief in her characters' ability to bring the story home, in all its violence and nightmare reality. The book is also concerned with that same violence, magnified several times, that major political forces effect in their race for oil, for power, for control. St. Antoine is a devastating example of what that cold and brutal mentality can do both against a country and its citizens.

Bodily Harm is an overwhelming novel; it goes for the hands (the motif is used frequently) and arrives at the throat, possessing Atwood's usual ability to harness the energy of language and implication.

Judith Fitzgerald, ''Fiction: 'Bodily Harm','' in Quill and Quire (reprinted by permission of Quill and Quire), Vol. 47, No. 10, October, 1981, p. 34.

LINDA W. WAGNER

For Margaret Atwood, life is quest, and her writing—particularly her poetry—is the charting of that journey. Atwood's journey is seldom geographical. . . . Unlike Charles Olson, Atwood does not dwell on location, physical presence, details of place. Her search is instead a piercing interior exploration, driving through any personal self-consciousness into regions marked by primitive responses both violent and beautiful. Atwood is interested in the human condition, a condition which exists independent of sex; and she plays a variety of games in order to explore that condition fully.

The strategies Atwood uses in her poems are similar to those of her fiction: personae described in terms of such basic biological functions as eating and sleeping; myriad patterns of disguise, whether literal or anthropomorphic; duality presented as separation, as in relationships between lovers (the hints of Jungian traits suggest that Atwood's ''males'' could represent the rational side of her female characters as well as their own selves); praise for life simplified, closer and closer to the natural; and a stark diction and rhythm, meant to be as far from the ''literary'' as Atwood's own ideal life is from the conventionally ''feminine.''

Whether the Atwood persona is a Circe, a Lady Oracle, a Susanna Moodie, a Marian MacAlpin, or the unnamed heroine of *Surfacing* [1972] she is a questioning and often bitter woman, at first resisting the passions that eventually lead her to knowledge. She pits accepted roles of womanliness, with all their final ineffectuality, against those of outraged non-conformity. . . . (pp. 81-2)

Ironically, given the tools of the writer, Atwood finds that the most significant knowledge comes without words. . . . Atwood's poetry and fiction teem with characters who fail, consistently and harshly, in expressing themselves; and she often comments on the ineffectuality of purely rational knowledge. . . .

By her 1974 collection, *You Are Happy,* however, Atwood has stopped lamenting and instead shows her acceptance of the nonverbal. . . . One learns because one senses in the blood/heart/hands—centers of touch and emotion rather than intellect. And one is happy, without qualification, only when she, or he, has accepted that resolution of the quest. Self-knowledge must go deeper than fragile, temporal self. It must include an other. . . . (p. 82)

Atwood's progression to this new and apparently satisfying resolution is clearly drawn through her first six books of poetry. While the poems of *The Circle Game* in 1966 appeared to be direct, cutting in their perceptions, the personae of those poems never did make contact, never did anything but lament the human condition. . . . Relationships in these poems are sterile if not destructive. . . . The lovers in ''Spring in the Igloo'' are touching the edge of drowning; the lover in ''Winter Sleepers'' has already gone down. The female persona in ''A Sibyl'' admits her ''bottled anguish'' and ''glass despair.''

Even in this first collection, however, the problem as Atwood sees it is more than personal. There are complex reasons why love between a man and a woman is tenuous—cultural, philosophical, anthropological reasons, many of which grow from mistaken values in modern living. Because contemporary people judge in terms of technology and scientific progress, they value ''improvements,'' devices, the urban over the rural, the new over the timeless. Much of Atwood's first collection is filled with her arguments against these attitudes. . . . (p. 83)

This dissatisfaction with the modern milieu, and the ethos it has spawned, leads Atwood first to the immediate move away from urban life. . . . ''Pre-Amphibian'' reinforces that tactic, and in the three-part poem ''Primitive Sources'' she studies ancient beliefs about god-systems, magic, and other devices for understanding the process of life—and a sentient human being's place in it. (p. 84)

Although most of the attention in the poems of *The Circle Game* falls on personae other than the female character, the book can easily be read as her portrait. The collection opens with ''This Is a Photograph of Me,'' which describes the landscape surrounding the lake in which the heroine has recently drowned. In Atwood's wry directions to the viewer lies her admission of the long and difficult process that ''surfacing'' is to be. First one must realize the need to surface. Identity comes after that, and full definition much later. . . . As the last lines [of ''This Is a Photograph of Me''] imply, part of that full definition must also come from the viewer/reader/lover. Attention in *The Circle Game* tends to be given more regularly to the male persona—he may be disappointing but he is the authority, the determinant. Atwood is not yet able to draw her female characters as if they had distinctive qualities. They are instead mirrors, listeners, watchers. . . . Atwood's eventual development from woman as pupil to the authoritative protagonist of *Lady Oracle* [1976] illustrates well the journey to self-definition.

That Atwood has excluded so many of these poems first published in *The Circle Game* from her 1976 *Selected Poems* suggests that—for all their thematic accuracy—she finds them less satisfying as poems than some later work. Perhaps the very directness and flat diction that in the sixties appeared to be strengths had grown comparatively uninteresting, for Atwood later set her direct statements in more metaphorical contexts, and often avoided making statements at all, unless they were ironic. She also began the search for poetic personae other than the woman-lover of the poems in *The Circle Game*.

In *The Animals in That Country* [1968] she wrote about anthropomorphic characters who seemed to represent the human types already drawn in her early poems. Metaphor suffuses these poems. . . . The young feminine persona remains submissive, coerced into action, dissatisfied with what choices do exist—and with her decisions about those choices. Repeatedly, she wrongs herself, whether she takes in **"A Foundling"** or blurs into the obliging lover (''more and more frequently the edges / of me dissolve and I become / a wish''). (pp. 85-7)

Her experiments here with varying rhythms and tones probably equipped her to catch the ambivalent persona of the book-length sequence of poems, *The Journals of Susanna Moodie* (1970). Her achievement in this collection is to present a protagonist believable in her conflicts. Through Moodie/Atwood, we experience hope, anguish, fear, joy, resignation, and anger. It may be more important for the thematic development of Atwood's poetry that we experience the paradox of Canadian nationalism. Like Atwood, Moodie wrote enthusiastically about life in Canada yet her journals also showed her real fear of the wild, the primitive, the untamed. (p. 87)

The character of Susanna Moodie becomes a perfect mask for the journey to self-exploration that Atwood attempts. Her statement ''Whether the wilderness is / real or not / depends on who lives there'' sounds much like Atwood's later surfacer. **"Looking in a Mirror"** and **"The Wereman"** repeat this theme of unwitting metamorphosis, identity shaped by the wilderness and its arduous living. Not all changes are negative, however; and one of the results of this acrid confrontation with natural forces is an acceptance of dream knowledge. . . .

Published in the same year as the Susanna Moodie collection, Atwood's *Procedures for Underground* has as central persona a pioneer woman, whose memories seem to be given voice as she looks at old photographs. Her family, the old cabin, hard winters, her husband—she speaks with a spare wisdom, moving easily between fact and dream, myth and custom. In **"Procedures for Underground"** she speaks as a Persephone who has gone below, been tested, learned ''wisdom and great power,'' but returns to live separate, feared, from her companions. Knowledge of whatever source is the prize for Atwood's persona, and many of the poems in the collection play with the definition of truth, fact, knowledge, the ''search for the actual.'' In some of the poems Atwood moves to present-day Canada and continues the theme of search through the sexual power conflict that is to be the subject of her 1971 *Power Politics*. (p. 88)

Power Politics is Atwood's comic scenario of the themes she had treated with relative sombreness in *Susanna Moodie* and *Underground*. If the former was an exploration of a sentient woman character, caught in and finally able to acknowledge ''the inescapable doubleness of her own vision,'' then *Pro-*

cedures for Underground is a survival manual for the kind of learning that a perceptive woman would have to undertake. Handicapped as she is (with her head resting in her ''gentle'' husband's sack), she must make use of emotion, dream, the occult, the primitive, even the animal to find her way. In *Power Politics* the assumption that any woman's protective male *is* her handicap becomes a given, and the fun in the book comes through Atwood's myriad inventive descriptions of the power struggle—as politics, war, physical waste, innuendo, sly attack. (pp. 88-9)

One of the changes Atwood made in choosing work for *Selected Poems* was to omit many of the poems in *Power Politics* that were titled as if for stage directions: **"He reappears,"** **"He is a strange biological phenomenon,"** **"He is last seen."** By emphasizing instead poems about the two people in the relationship, and often the woman, she manages to reverse the expected power positions. In *Selected Poems* the male ego is less often central. The collection as represented in the 1976 book thus meshes more closely with Atwood's earlier poems, in which the female persona often moves independently on her search for self-awareness, although in her omissions Atwood has deleted some poems important to thematic strains. **"Small Tactics,"** for example, a seven-part sequence in *Power Politics*, relates the war games described in this collection to those of **"The Circle Game,"** but here the feminine voice laments, ''Let's go back please / to the games, they were / more fun and less painful.'' . . . More often, in [**Selected Poems**], the woman is wise and loving, ready to admit her own necessary anger, but not misshapen by it. (p. 90)

Atwood's reasons for deleting [the] powerful poem [**"He is last seen"**] with its important recognition of dual emotions remain unexplained, but the poem does picture the male as dominant—decisive, aggressive—in ways that tend to contrast with the transformation and Circe poems of *You Are Happy*. In tone, however, in the strong balance of antipathy and desire, it leads [towards the poems of *You Are Happy*] with its somewhat richer diction and more varied rhythms.

The ironically generous central persona of *You Are Happy* is Atwood's fully-realized female—maker, poet, lover, prophet—a Circe with the power to change all men into animals, all men except Odysseus. Her capacity to control and yet give marks her as truly royal; her sometimes coy reluctance to accept praise suggests her basic awareness of the futility of bucking convention. Her powers may be dramatic, as the poems of **"Songs of the Transformed"** indicate, but they are limited to the physical, and fragile compared to the ''wrecked words'' Circe laments. Powerful as she is, Circe still cannot create words, and it is words for which her people beg. (pp. 92-3)

Circe differs from Atwood's earlier protagonists in that she is more aware of inhibiting mythologies. Her great understanding—of individuals as well as of patterns and cultural expectations—sharpens her perception but does not make her less vulnerable. (p. 93)

As Odysseus' dissatisfaction [with Circe] grows (his basic greed is impossible to satisfy), he thinks often of Penelope, and Circe realizes the wife's power to draw him back. . . . At the base of reality is the word. Despite omens and auguries, fire signs and bird flights, happenings return to the word, as Odysseus did:

> You move within range of my words
> you land on the dry shore
>
> You find what there is . . .

Atwood changes the image of conquering male into the image of man lured by a subtler power. Verbal magic bests physical force; feminine wiles and words convince the male persona—no matter what the circumstance—that "you are happy." The ambivalence of the opening poem, **"Newsreel: Man and Firing Squad"** suggests the transitory and often indefinable quality of any happiness. One learns to say *No* to the most unpleasant of life's experiences; one counters fate and myth with strategy; one develops powers of his or her own kind and value, and for the poet, those powers are verbal. . . .

Atwood's poems suggest that the range of human promise is wide, that exploring that range—for woman, man, artist, or lover—should be a primary life experience: "To learn how to live," "to choose," "to be also human," and, as culmination, "to surface." (p. 94)

> Linda W. Wagner, "The Making of 'Selected Poems', the Process of Surfacing," in The Art of Margaret Atwood: Essays in Criticism, edited by Arnold E. Davidson and Cathy N. Davidson (copyright © 1981, House of Anansi Press Limited; reprinted by permission of the publisher), Toronto: House of Anansi Press, 1981, pp. 81-94.

FRANK DAVEY

[In] Margaret Atwood's new novel, **Bodily Harm**, . . . readers of her previous comic novels will find much that is familiar. Here again is the opposition between a superficial world of social convention and a subsurface one of unconscious will, physiological need and barbaric impulse. Again the narrative pattern is that of Shakespearean comedy—alienation from natural order (Rennie's Toronto career), followed by descent into a more primitive but healing reality (cancer and Caribbean violence), and finally some reestablishment of order (the concluding insight). Rennie, the point-of-view character, is another of the self-preoccupied female participants in intellectual Toronto that one encounters in **The Edible Woman, Surfacing** and **Lady Oracle;** although carrying a different history, she has the same general vocabulary, ironic wit and speech patterns of the earlier characters. . . .

Atwood has consistently used the human body as a metaphor for surface and depth; concern for the skin as in Anna's make-up in **Surfacing,** Joan's weight-loss in **Lady Oracle,** Rennie's fashion stories here in **Bodily Harm,** have stood for repression of organic reality. The body itself has stood for that reality, refusing to eat in **The Edible Woman,** being stripped of make-up and clothing to reveal itself in **Surfacing,** and here asserting its mortal flesh and blood nature through Rennie's cancer.

The central irony of **Bodily Harm** is that this cancer, which Rennie fears may reappear and kill her, is the principal agent of her spiritual healing. The cancer forces Rennie to turn her attention from the surface beauty of her body (and of herself as sexual package) and toward her body's inner nature; she becomes dissatisfied with her superficially affectionate relationship with Jake and seeks a man to whom she can be willingly "open." It leads her to the Caribbean island where she will transcend her glib condescension toward those who suffer ("everyone gets what they deserve") and come to experience true compassion. Cancer heals. (p. 29)

Bodily Harm is overall a more satisfying novel than its forerunners. The recurrent Atwood argument that the chic veneer of civilization conceals and even apologizes for unspeakable barbarism is much more persuasive when the consequences of such concealment are not merely the bourgeois ones of unhappy liaison and neurotic despair but are instead torture, disfigurement and death. The book is stronger also because its conclusion—the comic return to society and healthful reintegration into it—is related in the future tense (either by Rennie or the unidentified third person narrator—the point of view is unclear here) only as a fantasy prediction, possibly Rennie's wish, of what may happen. The transformation and salvation of Atwood's three earlier comic heroines was less than totally credible because so abruptly achieved in the concluding pages. Here it is not achieved; we know not whether her captors will permit her return nor whether Rennie herself is capable of living out her new vision of life in a Canadian context. We know only that she has experienced a new vision, which for the novel's structural requirements is enough.

I am troubled by the similarity between the narrators of the four novels—several times I had the eerie feeling I was once again reading **Surfacing** or **Lady Oracle.** Also troubling is Atwood's re-use of the narrative structure of the earlier three books. One wishes the general patterns were less obvious so that one's primary experience of the book could be its own events. Similarly, the surface imagery of fashion, packaging, cosmetics, jewellery and furniture, the subsurface organic imagery of blood, wounds, dirt, insects and openness, as well as the numerous mirrors that reflect back the false doppelganger of illusory surface, have after appearing in four novels become predictable and lack the power they had when the author originated them. In short, Atwood doesn't risk much with this book; it is constructed almost entirely out of well-tested elements. These reservations aside, **Bodily Harm** is still a pleasure to read. (pp. 29-30)

> Frank Davey, "Life After Man," in The Canadian Forum, Vol. LXI, No. 714, December-January, 1981-82, pp. 29-30.

EVE SIEGEL

[**True Stories**] is a worthy successor to [Atwood's] previous works. As in an earlier book of poetry, **The Journals of Susanna Moodie,** the poet stakes a claim in the world against natural, human and inhuman forces of uncontained, inexplicable oppression. . . .

Through a personae of professional torturers, seen as artistic *poseurs,* Atwood probes for clues to the insanity and irrationality that mock the life principle. Again, the truth varies and wavers, takes on plausible and implausible facades. In **"Notes Towards a Poem That Can Never Be Written"** (dedicated to poet Carolyn Forche, whom Atwood admires for her courage as a political journalist in El Salvador), her linguistic control and detachment convey more horror than any overwrought, "social conscience" poetry. . . .

Atwood's strength derives from the fact that she seems to know exactly where she has come to at any stated point. The lay of the land is visible to her through a myriad of perspectives. The "true story" is not a constant, but kaleidoscopic and relative to its originator or the objects it encompasses. Truth, like happiness, is not a goal, but the result. . . . Dynamic tension is always present, inducing a springy, taut rhythm to the language itself.

Atwood's message in **True Stories** seems to be an assertion of the importance of self, whether alone on an island, beaten in prison, or sharing experiences with the beloved. Like the protagonist in her novel, **Surfacing,** Atwood escapes the pervasive, spiritual takeover of mass culture and slick ad campaigns. She pares away the extraneous and reveals herself naked but independent, offering only her self in the immediate moment. This is the only relationship or pact which the poet can genuinely offer, the only thing that matters. . . .

In *Surfacing,* Atwood's writing tends more towards the poetic as the protagonist retreats further and further from a society victimized by the invidious effects of cultural imperialism. However, *True Stories* carries some of the imperative of prose in that the author moves from the language of personal isolation to that which confronts the reality of widespread politically/sexually-based torture. This extends Atwood's range of expression and enables her to capture a more representative slice of humanity's contemporary conditions. In other words, Atwood makes the transition from personal to political worldview carefully, avoiding the pitfalls of polemicism by adhering to her craft. . . .

Atwood's use of bold, primal imagery conjures up echoes of Sylvia Plath. But Atwood steps beyond the confines of what she described at a recent seminar as the way critics stereotype modern women poets possessed of strong voices. Either they are neurotic, suicidal Plaths/Sextons or else hysterical, repressed Dickinsons. In Atwood's cosmology there is a need to define a new model of the assertive, articulate poet with a feminist perspective who can step away from the wholly personal to a more powerful, universal language. In earlier times the words or ''spells'' of some women were powerful enough to be feared by men, who labelled them witches. In more recent times there is still fear of women's words when they speak out against inequity and outright repression. But poets like Atwood are conscious of their power as writers and are determined to wield it. . . .

With *True Stories* Margaret Atwood demonstrates that the Canadian instinct for survival in precarious environments prevails again. This poet has torn the gag irrevocably from her mouth, and her message is clear: a poem after a poem after a poem from a committed poet, if they can be heard, is power.

> *Eve Siegel, ''Poetry: 'True Stories','' in* San Francisco Review of Books *(copyright © by the* San Francisco Review of Books *1982), January, 1982, p. 21.*

JONATHAN PENNER

Bodily Harm, a constantly diverting novel, fairly breathes narrative grace and skill. (p. 1)

The novel has flaws. One is narrative design run riot. There are first-person sections, set in Canada, told in the past tense, with un-quote-marked dialogue; and there are third-person sections, set on St. Antoine, told in the present, with dialogue in quotes.

So far so clear: But one understands near the end that the first-person sections are being *told* by Rennie to Lora in the jail cell they share; and that this setting is also the justification for the several first-person passages from *Lora's* point of view—passages that have had the reader rapping the walls for secret passageways. Logically, and in hindsight, it all hangs together, but fiction ought to cohere in the reading, not in the reading explained.

A more serious flaw is that the novel-of-adventure element is permitted to run so far that this wonderful book becomes hard to take with full seriousness. As it thickens with drastic events, the foreshortened plot leaves less and less room for character,

often squeezing it out of the story entirely. Rennie becomes a passive observer, a narrative convenience, now posted and now moved wherever she can see the action best.

Rennie's character (who she is, the choices she makes) doesn't affect the plot; and in turn the plot, though it sweeps her up along with everyone else, finally affects her least of all (only she can fly away from it). A close relationship of mutual influence between plot and character is what distinguishes literary from genre fiction. The perfect brilliance of the writing insists that this novel is by birthright literary, but it finally sells that birthright for a delightful mess of delicious plottage. (p. 2)

> *Jonathan Penner, ''Plots and Counterplots,'' in* Book World—The Washington Post *(© 1982, The Washington Post), March 14, 1982, pp. 1-2.*

DANA GIOIA

Margaret Atwood's *Two-Headed Poems* are full of interesting ideas, memorable images, and intelligent observations. She has a deep understanding of human motivation, and her poetry deals naturally with an intricate sort of psychology most poets ignore. Her poems are often painfully accurate when dealing with the relationships between men and women or mothers and daughters. And yet with all these strengths, Atwood is not an effective poet. She writes poetry with ideas and images, not with words; her diction lies dead on the page. Her poems have a conceptual and structural integrity, but the language itself does not create the heightened awareness one looks for in poetry. The problem centers in her rhythms, not only the movement of words and syllables within the line, but also the larger rhythms of the poem, the movements from line to line and stanza to stanza. While the pacing of her ideas works beautifully, her language never picks up force.

One notices the curious neutrality of Atwood's language most clearly in her sequence of prose poems, ''**Marrying the Hangman,**'' which obliquely tells the story of Françoise Laurent, a woman sentenced to death for stealing, who legally avoids punishment by convincing the man in the next cell to become a hangman and then marrying him. (Atwood uses a real historic incident here, but the plot seems like something out of a Mascagni opera.) The language in these prose poems is qualitatively no different from the language of her verse, except that it has no line breaks. It most resembles a passage of ''elevated'' prose, like an excerpt from Joan Didion's histrionic *Book of Common Prayer.*

The few times in *Two-Headed Poems* that Atwood's language condenses into genuinely arresting rhythms, the results are fresh and convincing, as in ''**Foretelling the Future.**'' . . . But these moments are rare. Imaginative in conception, these *Two-Headed Poems* are mostly flat and perfunctory in execution. If images and ideas alone could make poetry, Atwood would be a major poet. (pp. 110-11)

> *Dana Gioia, ''Eight Poets,'' in* Poetry *(© 1982 by The Modern Poetry Association; reprinted by permission of the Editor of* Poetry), *Vol. CXL, No. 2, May, 1982, pp. 102-14.**

JULIA O'FAOLAIN

[''**Bodily Harm**''] bristles with intelligence and is often so witty that I wondered why I wasn't enjoying it more. The trouble may lie with the tropes. These are clever but obtrusive and can make the story seem to be no more than a hook for hanging symbols on. Atwood's metaphors are deft, but there are just too many of them: almost anything can stand for something else. When Rennie's untidy lover fails to throw out empty containers and keeps glancing at her blouse, it is because Rennie has had a mastectomy and the blouse too is an empty container.

The mastectomy itself—bodily harm—prefigures worse to come and may be an emblem of the harms wreaked by the consumer society. . . . Reification is rampant. We are objects for each other's skills and jokes—the most painful being inadvert, as when Rennie's doctor, just before diagnosing cancer, asks whether she's ready yet to have babies and adds, 'You're heading for the cutoff point.'

Rennie is not, however, allowed to wallow in wise-cracking self-pity. The author has shock therapy in store: a visit to a Third World country with an unstable régime in whose eruptions she becomes engulfed. Ever since Graham Greene used revolutionary Mexico as a metaphor for hell, such settings have served novelists for harrowing souls. When Rennie finally escapes she has been sufficiently politicised to plan some serious reporting—and has learned that there are worse things than cancer. The neat conclusion suggests that the revolutionary country is a purely contingent place, devised to bring Rennie to her moment of truth. **'Bodily Harm'** is an imaginative, thoughtful novel, but perhaps over-controlled.

Julia O'Faolain, "Desperate Remedies," in The Observer *(reprinted by permission of The Observer Limited), June 13, 1982, p. 31.**

NANCY RAMSEY

Margaret Atwood, the Canadian novelist, has one of current fiction's more detached voices. Her tone toward her characters reflects the nature of the characters themselves: women who are divided into separate personae—one half defined by the role they feel society has thrust upon them, the other, their true self (insecure and amorphous as it is) trying to break out. Like many other characters in recent fiction, their lives are directionless; they drift in and out of relationships and find little satisfaction in work. Atwood doesn't treat them as whole persons, but rather as fragmented parts of a human being. Consequently, it's often difficult for the reader to gather much sympathy for them—they're too much the victims of every current neurosis. Her last novel, *Life Before Man,* examined the lives of three narcissistic, shallow individuals; although the novel progressed along a linear time span, and set out to analyze the characters' changing over time, we saw almost no change in their lives, and little of redeeming value to justify such a detailed presentation of their neuroses.

But in *Bodily Harm,* her most recent novel, by placing Rennie Wilford, her protagonist, on a Caribbean island in the throes of revolution, and adding a scare with cancer to her life, Atwood has, in a sense, saved Rennie from the stagnant fate of her other novels' characters. The stakes are higher; survival, one of Atwood's favorite themes, is no longer a 1970s term tossed around at cocktail parties. Death, rather than the modern sense of ennui, threatens Rennie and the people around her, and ultimately gives her life a meaning she hadn't known before. . . .

The structure of the novel effectively plays off Rennie's Toronto life against her Caribbean life. Her experiences in the Caribbean are interrupted by flashbacks from her childhood, growing up among an oppressive mother and grandmother— the standard background of Atwood's women—and her life around the time of her mastectomy. The sections in the Caribbean move more quickly than do those in Canada; the latter often producing a sense of frustration in the reader, since its stagnancy is juxtaposed with the urgency of the Caribbean scenes. When one has confronted life-and-death situations and people constantly living on the edge, it's difficult to turn back to people who wonder what trend to follow next. Let's hope Atwood's next novel continues along the same lines, for this is her most readable to date.

Nancy Ramsey, " 'Bodily Harm'," in San Francisco Review of Books *(copyright © by the* San Francisco Review of Books *1982), Summer, 1982, p. 21.*

LINDA ROLENS

"In a way I admire her, she gets through the days." That is what Margaret Atwood's characters do—get through the days. In other stories by other writers, these characters would commit suicide or join support groups and we would be forced to recognize them as contemporary victims/heroines. . . .

Margaret Atwood does not write that kind of story. She looks deeper and sees more clearly and she insists that the reader see as well. The stories in **"Dancing Girls"** are painful and subtle, for Atwood's characters do not thrash but suffer quietly in ways they do not quite understand. Most are women too alone to realize their own aloneness. . . .

Each is unsure of herself as a woman, somehow incomplete. They suffer from wounds too deep to acknowledge and they give off the desperation of the unloved.

Though Atwood's characters yearn for love, they suffer from an odd insistence on being hurt. Most are best at experiencing loss; it is what they know and somehow it solaces them. These characters almost seek loss and make bad choices or choices that keep them small. They linger in the prolonged adolescence of graduate school; they pick men who will betray them.

Margaret Atwood's attitude makes these dark stories extraordinary: She trusts her characters and knows they are survivors. No one here is going to stick her head in an oven or gas herself in the garage. They survive by the force of strengths they do not understand.

The momentum of this collection is much like that of a novel and, by the final stories, the heroines have developed wry senses of humor and ways of moving through the world without damaging themselves. . . . These last women have pieced themselves together and grown from vulnerable to tender.

Atwood's prose is poet's prose, full of startlingly accurate images, much of it rich enough to be relined as verse. She has a poet's sense of how deep to lay open her characters.

If Hemingway is correct and "good books are truer than if they really happened and that after you are finished reading one you will feel that it all happened to you," then this is such a book. Margaret Atwood is one of our finest contemporary writers.

Linda Rolens, "Women Too Alone to Realize Their Aloneness," in Los Angeles Times Book Review *(copyright, 1982, Los Angeles Times; reprinted by permission), October 17, 1982, p. 3.*

Enid Bagnold

1889-1981

English dramatist, novelist, autobiographer, and poet.

Although not a major writer, Bagnold's work is considered important for the insights it gives into the lives of the British. Usually affluent and urbane, her characters are examined from both a comic and a serious point of view. Bagnold's play, *The Chalk Garden*, for instance, contains a portrait of a young girl's painful acceptance of truth that is alternately humorous and somber. Many of Bagnold's later works, including her *Autobiography*, portray the mixed pleasures of growing old.

A notable exception to Bagnold's stories of the upper class is *National Velvet*, a novel about a butcher's young daughter whose childhood dream comes true. Made into an inspiring movie, this book is acclaimed for its realistic depiction of family life among the British working class. *National Velvet* is also an indication that Bagnold's craft is not limited by her subject matter. Witty, entertaining dialogue and sharp observations of life are characteristic of most of her work.

(See also *Contemporary Authors*, Vols. 5-8, rev. ed., Vol. 103 [obituary]; *Contemporary Authors New Revision Series*, Vol. 5; *Something about the Author*, Vols. 1, 25; and *Dictionary of Literary Biography*, Vol. 13.)

© *Jerry Bauer*

THE TIMES LITERARY SUPPLEMENT

The devastated areas would strike most people as a singularly unpromising scene in which to place an idyll, yet Miss Enid Bagnold has performed this feat with striking success [in "**The Happy Foreigner**"]. The very incongruity between the little human romance and gloomy, uncomfortable reality in which it is enshrined is pleasing; and one is not sure whether one admires more the author's skill in keeping the love passage—which is the idyll—light, delicate, and fleeting, though poignant, or the descriptive power and poetic feeling with which the ruins left by war and the workers engaged on clearing them up are represented.

On the whole, we should give our vote for the descriptive power, which never flags. . . .

Miss Bagnold seems to see [the postwar action] with a personal detachment which blends with an intense sympathy for others: for the French who starve their prisoners, as they starve themselves, but will not shoot them: for the Americans who are generous with food and ruthless with rifles: for a Scotsman left with pale Chinamen to tidy a vast cemetery: for conquered Germans, and for all suffering and all courage. . . . If Miss Bagnold is rather irritatingly fascinated by the fragmentary style, for which we have to thank Miss Dorothy Richardson, her power of getting to the heart of things carries her through. She has a splendid equipment for a novelist.

> *"New Novels: 'The Happy Foreigner'," in* The Times Literary Supplement *(© Times Newspapers Ltd. (London) 1920; reproduced from* The Times Literary Supplement *by permission), No. 963, July 1, 1920, p. 422.*

KATHERINE MANSFIELD

If Miss Bagnold had chosen that her heroine [in '**The Happy Foreigner**'] should lead the most sheltered and protected life that is left for a young woman to endure, we are confident that there would have blossomed within its narrow boundaries flowers as rich and as delicate as those which Fanny gathered on the strange roads of France. For she understands how it is vain to seek adventure unless there is the capacity for adventure within us. . . . '**The Happy Foreigner**' exists for a proof of how she ventured, and to tell how great was her reward. (p. 232)

Fanny, an English girl, goes to France at the end of the war and drives a car for the French Army. She falls in love, but it comes to nothing, and the end might be the beginning. That is all. Who Fanny is, what her life has been up till the moment she is discovered for us 'stretched upon the table of the Y.W.C.A.' in Paris, on her way to Bar-le-Duc, we are not told. She remains from first to last an unknown young woman, secret, folded within herself, a 'happy foreigner.' She is almost without fear; nothing can overwhelm her or cast her down, because it is her nature, and unchangeable, to find in all things a grain of living beauty. We have the feeling that she is, above all, unbroken. . . . Praise be to Miss Bagnold for giving us a new heroine, a pioneer, who sees, feels, thinks, hears, and yet is herself full of the sap of life. (p. 233)

Katherine Mansfield, "A Hymn to Youth" (originally published in The Athenaeum, *July 16, 1920, No. 4707), in her* Novels and Novelists, *edited by J. Middleton Murry (copyright 1930, copyright renewed © 1958 by Alfred A. Knopf, Inc.; reprinted by permission of The Society of Authors as the literary representative of the Estate of Katherine Mansfield),* Knopf, *1930, pp. 232-34.*

THE SPECTATOR

The Happy Foreigner is quite as ingenious as **A Diary Without Dates,** and has none of the qualities that made that book so curiously detestable. Miss Bagnold has still the same almost uncanny perceptiveness for the things of sight and sound, smell and touch, the same cold desire for experience, the same objective aloofness. But this time she does not display the inhuman lack of sympathy of her first "Anatomy of Nursing." . . . Nowhere is the new sympathy which Miss Bagnold has found more apparent than in her treatment of the relations between the American Army and the French. She has the courage to affirm what we are all more or less aware of—*i.e.,* the bad feeling which existed between them—and she has insight enough to sympathize with both sides. (p. 278)

The love story that runs through the tale, unlike most of such narratives which are put in to "brighten" what is really a personal experience, is admirably sentimental and most convincing. (p. 279)

> *"Books: 'The Happy Foreigner','' in* The Spectator *(© 1920 by* The Spectator; *reprinted by permission of* The Spectator), *Vol. 125, No. 4809, August 28, 1920, pp. 278-79.*

RAYMOND MORTIMER

[**National Velvet**] is the story of a girl of fourteen with a passion for horses who obtains in a shilling raffle a piebald gelding, with which she wins the Grand National, owner up. This super-daydream is the skeleton of the book, its flesh is enormously English humour about children, animals and the lower middle classes. I cannot imagine a more repulsive recipe for a novel—and the result is one of the jolliest, raciest, books I have read in years. Miss Bagnold, except in one or two purplish passages, is entirely unsentimental. What amuses her in children is not their naiveté . . . , but their slyness, their egotism, their terrifying determination. To use the word "Dickensian" about Miss Bagnold would be misleading, for she is not a poet; she always remains in complete control of her characters; and she never lapses into caricature—the trouble is that I don't know how to suggest a mint-sauce and crisp Yorkshire pudding atmosphere, which is conveyed without a hint of offensive heartiness. The fact that books and pictures and musical compositions have to be classified as high and middle and low brow is profoundly depressing. It is therefore with something like a whoop that I recommend **National Velvet** as a novel calculated to sell by the ton, and at the same time likely to be gobbled up by the most fastidious.

> *Raymond Mortimer, "Books in General: 'National Velvet','' in* The New Statesman & Nation *(© 1935 The Statesman & Nation Publishing Co. Ltd.), Vol. IX, No. 215, April 6, 1935, p. 489.*

HARRIET COLBY

In no sense a fantasy, ["**National Velvet**"] is still the kind of book which it is best not to try to resist; it should be allowed to cast its spell with the full consent of the reader. Rightly and high-handedly allowing no room for quibbles as to whether the events described were probable, the author merely gives them a lucid actuality—saying take it or leave it, here it is. Wise readers will take it and like it. . . .

Velvet does not walk or run; she trots or canters. Her love for horses has the huge single-minded concentration of genius, revealing itself in a passionate concern for the most minute and technical details of care and equipment. It is a fever and a dream. . . .

So fierce a love as Velvet's demands something more substantial to feed on than daydreams and paper horses; Miss Bagnold's obliging world provides it in the shape of the wild and restless Piebald. . . . On the day of the raffle [for Piebald] she goes to deliver meat to the squire, and something of her consuming passion communicates itself to the tired old man. He shows her his stables, asks for paper and pencil and Velvet's signature, retires behind the corner of the barn and blows his brains out, leaving Velvet heir to five horses. Sick with excitement, she goes home to find she has won Piebald.

But this is too much, you say; this is fantastic. It is only the beginning, and as final argument against all improbability there is the author's inspired matter-of-factness and there are the Browns themselves. Here are no pallid figures of the imagination but characters so vividly alive as to give reality to whatever they experience. In the midst of lovely incongruities they persist in a humorous normality. Velvet is indeed a child of fourteen, on whom the excitement of a dream so suddenly and abundantly realized has its natural effect: she is sick. Mrs. Brown, stalwart and unsurprised handles the situation with immemorial calm. Mr. Brown pursues his patient, obscure existence, mildly asking, now and then, why a man who left five horses to a butcher's daughter couldn't have left something to keep them with.

But Velvet . . . has begun to have a larger dream, terrifying in its enormity. It is the Grand National, nothing less, for The Piebald, a vision of glory not for Velvet but for the horse, a fulfillment of his splendid destiny. Her efforts to realize this dream bring mystery, conspiracy, sick excitement into the story. And when the roaring dies away Velvet is just what she was before—a little girl with a horse.

"**National Velvet**" is no wistful story of a child's world. There is in it no false tenderness, no maudlin "understanding." Its realism is sustained, uncompromising and completely adult. Unforeseen in subject and manner, it is full of small, quick surprises—in the uneven rhythm of its prose, in the crystal, tonic freshness of its language, in its unique and irrepressible humor. Sudden and lovely, it breathes and lives in the unexpected.

> *Harriet Colby, "A Girl and Her Horse: A Sudden, Lovely Book,'' in* New York Herald Tribune Books *(© I.H.T. Corporation; reprinted by permission), April 28, 1935, p. 5.*

CHRISTOPHER MORLEY

With the loveliest humor and feeling, with words that are alive, fresh, simply and unwaveringly accurate, Enid Bagnold puts [the Browns of "**National Velvet**"] before us. . . . With never an overplus word, no slackening of pace, with loving magic power, she puts us inside in. We *are* the Browns. We *are* Velvet. . . . I do not know where you would go in recent fiction to find a family interior more superbly captured, made real; every line of dialogue true, moving, progressive, relevant to plot. And this is not accident or a mere gush of charm; Enid Bagnold knows well that if we are to accept and be ravished by the fantastic wish-fulfilment story to come we must be set solidly in the actual. And so we are. Her pages have the clear lightsome freshness and candor of the first day of spring: even the million times battered and fatigued mind of the adult reader capitulates to her magic. By the time we've read three chapters we accept anything. . . . In its own vein, and for those who can ride the flying trapeze of fancy, this is a masterpiece. Should we say something solemn and sociological? Very well then: you can learn more about the mind of childhood from this book than from many volumes of pedology. The mind of childhood, zigzag, indolent, unblemished by the subjunctive mood, is the mind of any great artist. Disregard the dull dutiful attempt of any critic to praise this lovely escapade. Read it for its humble magic. Read it to be one of the Browns.

> *Christopher Morley, "Wishes Were Horses," in* The Saturday Review of Literature *(© 1935, copyright renewed © 1962, Saturday Review Magazine Co.; reprinted by permission), Vol. XII, No. 1, May 4, 1935, p. 6.*

JANE SPENCE SOUTHRON

["**National Velvet**"] is a book that is rich with life that has been lived amply and with gracious easiness and that has eventually spilled over irresistibly into art. You may speak of it as escape literature if you like, for it in no way impinges on the problems that are tearing the heart of today's humanity; but it will be more fittingly thought of as a reminder of those eternal human amenities that invariably survive political and social cataclysms. . . .

The book abounds in wit and in scores of passages that the reviewer would have liked to include here for their startling appositeness. There are delectably funny bits, like that midnight scene when the mountainous Araminty "rose like a sea monster from its home," battling furiously for her daughter's dream. There is Don, the 4-year-old, as dirty, exasperating and natural a brat as ever got onto paper. It is, all in all, one of the sanest and most amusing light novels we have had from England in a long while.

> *Jane Spence Southron, "A Light of Unusual Quality," in* The New York Times Book Review *(© 1935 by The New York Times Company; reprinted by permission), May 5, 1935, p. 6.*

EDITH H. WALTON

Except for its sharpness of observation and its delicate humor, there is little to connect the author of "**National Velvet**" with this informal diary, written when Miss Bagnold was 19. For reasons which now seem incomprehensible, the publication of "**A Diary Without Dates**" produced a flurry in wartime England and caused Miss Bagnold's dismissal from the military hospital where she was working as a V.A.D. It is true that her book . . . shows a certain hostility to the sisters who were Miss Bagnold's superiors, but otherwise it could only have been offensive in that it was too clearheaded and realistic to please contemporary patriots.

Considering her youth, considering the feverish emotions of the period, one is amazed at Miss Bagnold's immunity to the traditional bunk about war. Her book is not sentimental, nor does it babble of heroism and glory. She records, merely, the impressions of a very sensitive young person who can never accustom herself to the pain—nor to the stupidity—which she sees all around her. . . . It is the merit of her book that it is fresh, unsparing, honest. She feels no necessity to sentimentalize the wounded, whose sufferings affect her so keenly.

As to the actual material in her diary, there is nothing new or particularly remarkable about it. . . . Where she surpasses the average is in her pungent vignettes of eccentric or amusing patients, and in her general capacity to dramatize both sides of hospital life, the tragic and the comic. Despite its brevity and its apparent casualness, her book captures the living quality of a major experience.

The answer, of course, is that Enid Bagnold, even at 19, had two important assets. She could feel, and she could write. Simple as her prose is, it has an exquisite economy and exactness which presage her later work. After two decades and a plethora of war literature "**A Diary Without Dates**" is still worth reading and reprinting. Entirely unpretentious, it communicates emotion directly and poignantly; it makes one share the impact of war and suffering upon a youthful, intelligent and very receptive mind.

> *Edith H. Walton, "The Wartime Diary of Enid Bagnold," in* The New York Times Book Review *(© 1935 by The New York Times Company; reprinted by permission), November 24, 1935, p. 11.*

CHRISTOPHER MORLEY

[In "**The Door of Life**"] Enid Bagnold gives us, with candor and subtlety, an inward-gazing study of the companionship between a woman and her child, in the days just before and just after birth. At a time when so much of the world's attention is upon the destruction of life, this tender and explicit revelation of lifegiving is a thrill to enjoy. But I fear it probes too clinical, too frank, too tender, to please maternal readers. A deep and I daresay a wise instinct usually withholds the creators of life from articulate comment on the dreamy strangeness of its process.

For fathers, however, this is superb. Hardly since the famous childbirth in the Shandy family has the drama of a household in parturition been so astonishingly rendered. But in this story the father is appropriately removed from the scene; he has gone off on a three months' business trip to Bombay, and his magnificent madonna is in charge of the household. . . .

[This] book has much humor. Even anyone who has never kept house in Britain or read Margaret Halsey will relish Enid Bagnold's innocent revelations of the British Stately Home. The gaiety that delighted us all in "**National Velvet**" is here in full measure; and the same masterly delineations of the different children, each sharply identified and understood. The same quality of acute observation and freshly vitalized writing is here. Passage after passage, some of beauty and some of clearest intuition, plead for quotation. . . .

But beyond humor this book explores deep beauty and universal feeling. The character of the Squire—so the mother is called in the absence of the titular head of the house—is livingly before us. For the moment, in the crisis of these few weeks, she is scarcely of either sex but is the fundamental stuff of all humanity. . . .

Enid Bagnold has remarkable powers; not least of them a sharply substantive sense of *things*. With no laborious contriving she makes the house and all its surroundings suggestively actual, influential. And she shows the delight and despair of the human spirit which finds itself so incomprehensibly mixed up with all these tangibles and carnals. She has dared a dangerous job, and gazed "with eye serene, at the very pulse of the machine." It seems to me a notable success; a cry in praise of life in a world bent upon death. It really is a Book of Genesis.

> *Christopher Morley, "Book of Genesis," in* The Saturday Review of Literature *(© 1938, copyright renewed © 1965, Saturday Review Magazine Co.; reprinted by permission), Vol. XVIII, No. 23, October 1, 1938, p. 7.*

ROSEMARY BENET

Readers who complain that the shadow of futility and frustration hangs over the modern novel, should read **"The Door of Life"**. Here is no wishy-washy inhibited heroine, but a vigorous lady, full of zest for life.

She rules her own world, the typical large English household. . . . She has four strong and interesting children, and is awaiting the birth of the fifth with a brooding pleasure that verges on ecstasy. It is around the idea and the expectancy of birth that the whole household revolves during that warm, still summer. . . .

Though the core of the book is the birth, the background is clear and well drawn. The four other children are very alive for Miss Bagnold has a rare gift for describing children. She makes them talk and walk and act like children, not literary phenomena. . . . It is a particular achievement to have created Boniface, for the remarkable child is hard to do. Written down, he becomes merely precocious or queer. Not so, Boniface, "resolved to lead the life of a man, before he was fit to leave babyhood for childhood." . . .

The only person who seemed unreal to me, is one undoubtedly drawn from life, the Scotch midwife or nurse. She is too remote, and mystical, and too much the High Priestess to come alive to me, even if she does exist somewhere. . . .

In this book, Miss Bagnold reminded me of Colette. One is as French as French, the other typically English. Each has a fine and careful style. The resemblance is still more in the vigour and vitality of their writing and their feeling for the rhythms of nature. Finally each has done an excellent—though very different—portrait of a middle-aged woman, a woman by no means through with emotion, who has stopped midway to ponder over emotion. . . .

["**The Door of Life**"] is feminism at its best. It combines vitality with sensitivity, an excellent combination.

> *Rosemary Benet, "Rich Mystery of Birth," in* New York Herald Tribune Books *(© I.H.T. Corporation; reprinted by permission), October 2, 1938, p. 4.*

LEO LERMAN

Miss Bagnold's special talent has ever been the telling of stories set in the milieu which she seems to know best; and this milieu has several faces. One is that of the world dedicated to high life, the haut monde still to be found in the *mondaine* places, be they Manhattan, Morocco, or a villa upon some conveniently remote island. This world has a painstakingly assembled face.

Another of the Bagnold faces is the weathered and seamed one of outdoor folk: sportsmen, racing people, county gentry. And, naturally, she knows her servants, the people up in the garrets, down in basements, behind counters. She even knows those anonymous persons in streets, undergrounds, on omnibuses— those who make the big city roar.

That Miss Bagnold's men and women of fashion [in **"The Loved and Envied"**] continue, despite their new recherché lives, to hold the reader's attention is a measure of her novelistic ability. (p. 5)

The world of Miss Bagnold's novel is precisely that international one whose members are publicized incessantly in society columns and in magazines of high fashion. . . . If you look beneath the immaculate surface of the carefully assembled face on the fashion magazine page, if somehow you can see the face without the photographer's retouching, you will see the people in Miss Bagnold's book as she sees them and as she ultimately shows them to you and to themselves.

You will also know why she has taken the time and the prodigious trouble to write this intricately designed fan of a book, folding and unfolding some fifty years of life, manipulating the highly colored fan so that the people and places depicted upon its surface shift in time: are one moment to be seen piecemeal, the next exposed totally, and ultimately unfurled all together—the whole elaborate design revealed.

The picture upon this fan is that of a cohesive and meaningful community—aging and doomed. Since Enid Bagnold has been able to execute this picture, it becomes not merely a novel of high life, but a charting of the death of many hearts. It is another one of those reports that are being written by those who realize that their worlds are dying and know exactly why. (pp. 5, 14)

> *Leo Lerman, "Some People and Places," in* The New York Times Book Review *(© 1950 by The New York Times Company; reprinted by permission), December 31, 1950, pp. 5, 14.*

ANTHONY WEST

[Insofar as **"The Loved and Envied"**] is about people and emotions, it is a very good book. . . . **"Serena Blandish,"** [Miss Bagnold's second novel, was] an extraordinarily exact, lucid, and, in a wholly feminine way, strong account of the experiences that turn a girl into a woman. It was a brilliant start, which promised at least an English Colette. What followed, however, was a long silence, broken, finally, by ["**National Velvet,"**] an agreeable middle-brow comedy. (About her next novel, **"The Door of Life,"** which was concerned largely with the glories of motherhood and the maternal instinct, the less said the better; it might have been written by a man.) But now, after more than twenty-five years, Miss Bagnold has abruptly turned back to the line of development she began with **"Serena Blandish"** and has to a considerable extent fulfilled its promise.

What **"The Loved and Envied"** does, and does extremely well, is create an atmosphere of maturity. Since the triumph of the literary movement—or, to be more accurate, drift—initiated by Hemingway, which is devoted to celebrating the dumb ox above all other kinds of men, the focus of writing has been more and more on violent death and perpetual adolescence. The average novel treats the crisis through which people pass on their way to maturity as a matter of the final solution of problems of relationship. When characters over forty appear at all, they repeat, without any gain in experience, fundamentally adolescent situations. . . . The great virtue of Miss Bagnold's book is that it is a clear break away from this sort of inanity. Most of her characters are between fifty and sixty. They have behind them experience appropriate to their age, which has taken them beyond a fumbling confusion about sex, and they have digested that experience into ideas about living that have some richness. The main business of the book is the discovery of the emotional poverty of a woman in her fifties who has lived so entirely to herself that love has died around her without touching her, and its contrast to the emotional wealth that love of one kind or another has brought to the people in her circle of acquaintance. There is an imaginative abundance in the number of complete lives, and in the variety of situations, that have been brought into the story, but what is truly impressive is the manner in which the relationships are shown in development, from uncertainty to certainty, from passionate urgency to friendship and constancy, and away from it to estrangement. There is a description of the loss of emotional contact between a woman and her parents that amounts to a *tour de force*; it is done, with a beautiful economy, in terms of a slow ebbing of intensity that shows up the ordinary *Sturm-und-Drang* account of the process, done in terms of adolescent rebellion, for the crude personal fantasy it usually is. The economy is accompanied by grace and wit, so that although mortuary thoughts are never very far off, there is no feeling about the book of gloomy snuffling around the doors of the charnel house.

These merits are substantial, but it has to be said that **"The Loved and Envied"** has one major defect. Like so many British writers, Miss Bagnold dearly loves a lord. A sour whiff of snobbery comes from her pages. . . . Miss Bagnold's Italo-Anglo-French aristocracy is transparently and tediously fraudulent; characters whose psychological and physical construction is as convincing as it could conceivably be are knocked clear into dreamland by the pretense that they are vicomtes, dukes, and so forth. (pp. 86, 88)

Anthony West, "Three Novels," in *The New Yorker* (©1951 by The New Yorker Magazine, Inc.), Vol. XXVI, No. 49, January 27, 1951, pp. 86, 88.*

ROBERT KEE

The central character of [Enid Bagnold's ***The Loved and Envied***] is Lady Ruby Maclean, a beautiful, rich, 33-year-old Parisian socialite, who "for a quarter of a century has been more fun than anyone else," and who is now making the transition from that quarter of a century to the next. "The old," she says, "are a bit sad, but it's like rheumatism—one can do nothing about it and they grow used to it." This sweet creaking of joints is the main theme of the book. . . . One should not let oneself be too much put off by the woman's magazine ring of the names or some of the sentences, or the slightly unreal atmosphere of a moneyed closed shop which pervades the book. These are merely the points at which the disguise is flaking off most clearly.

In fact, there is a good deal of moving and sensitive treatment of the theme. There is a deep and genuine feeling for the pathos of human life, often expressed with the ease of a first-class writer. A phrase such as that which describes a room in the flat where Rose, the Vicomte's mistress, has lived for thirty years ("the backroom was as though they had never quite got there") sometimes conveys the sadness of human transitoriness with a success which one would expect only from a better writer. (pp. 165-66)

But the success is limited. It is confined to an expression of the *general* pathos of human decay. The characters, as individuals and not just as pegs for hanging old age on, leave only a faint impression, which is perhaps why they have to be such very *grand* people. It is as if their money and grandness were there to bolster them up. But money and grandness will not do the work of a creative writer for him. ***The Loved and Envied*** is also given away by occasional simple technical faults. There are one or two annoying instances of recapitulation of incident, caused by dipping back into the memories of more than one old person. And, granted that sudden deaths are more pardonable in a novel concerned with old age than most, the number of them in ***The Loved and Envied*** (four) seems excessive. (p. 166)

Robert Kee, "New Novels: 'The Loved and Envied'," in The New Statesman & Nation (© 1951 The Statesman & Nation Publishing Co. Ltd.), Vol. XLI, No. 1040, February 10, 1951, pp. 165-66.

WALTER F. KERR

The dramatist who would convey one of the essential secrets of her play by having two of her characters sit down in the second act and simply ask one another twenty questions is quite a daring one. The dramatist who can, while engaging in this pretty game, make us all lean forward and hang suspended on every curious word must be a very good one.

I say "must be" because . . . ["**The Chalk Garden**" is] baffling on quite a few counts. . . .

Gleams of some kind of truth flash back and forth across the stage somewhere between the words that are spoken and the glances that are evaded. Tea goes on being served, flowers go on being transplanted, the conversation grows brighter and brighter. Spurts of wild humor cascade without warning over the darkening landscape; epigrams that would do credit to Ivy Compton-Burnett leap unpredictably out of sober, even savage, clashes. Whatever is being communicated is communicated elliptically, around psychological corners, with the impulsiveness of thunderbolts out of clear blue skies. It is as though Miss Bagnold had wanted to dramatize what one of her characters calls "the shape and shadow of life, with the accidents of truth taken out." Truth is an accident, and cannot be discovered until eleven o'clock.

But what is truly baffling about ["**The Chalk Garden**"] . . . is that, out of all that is circuitous and eccentric and delightfully left-field, something very real is communicated. At the last the defiant picture slips gently, almost imperceptibly, into focus: this particular world rests on a soil of chalk, and nothing can grow in it; only someone who has brushed death and earned detachment can penetrate the underbrush of daily living, weed out the simple facts, and save a couple of souls.

It should be obvious enough that Miss Bagnold has not written a play, or used a method, that is likely to have vast popular appeal. She has done one thing, though: she has had a vision of what a very fresh and personal kind of play could be like and she has seen it through with wit, literacy, and an almost unearthly integrity. A special taste, no doubt; but, on its level and of its kind, extraordinarily tasty.

> Walter F. Kerr, "Theater: 'The Chalk Garden'," in New York Herald Tribune (© I.H.T. Corporation; reprinted by permission), October 27, 1955 (and reprinted in New York Theatre Critics' Reviews, Vol. 16, No. 20, October 31, 1955, p. 229).

RICHARD WATTS, JR.

It was my disturbing impression [while watching **"The Chalk Garden"**], . . . that Enid Bagnold, its author, had perhaps written the wrong play. She introduced some odd and interesting characters, provided them with a provocative situation, revealed signs of an original sense of humor and demonstrated that she is the possessor of a graceful and intelligent prose style, but it seemed to me that the resulting drama . . . rarely came to life in the fashion it kept hopefully suggesting. . . .

Since Miss Bagnold seemed to regard all of [her characters] with freshness of humor and to write about them with amused appreciation, I thought it appeared likely that she was going to offer us an entertainingly, mad comedy concerning their curious interrelationships. And there was every indication that she had just the proper style for it. But it wasn't long before it became evident that she was up to more serious matters. There was, for instance, that garden, which, it proved, was made of chalk and was highly symbolic.

It was this symbolism, it seemed to me, that got in her way. . . . Instead of adding point to the play, it resulted in a stubborn refusal of the narrative to remain properly alive.

> Richard Watts, Jr., "A Play with a Symbolic Garden," in New York Post (reprinted from The New York Post; © 1955, New York Post Corporation), October 27, 1955 (and reprinted in New York Theatre Critics' Reviews, Vol. 16, No. 20, October 31, 1955, p. 229).

BROOKS ATKINSON

Enid Bagnold is "the lady of quality" who once wrote a novel from which S. N. Behrman wrote a drama of quality, **"Serena Blandish."** It was warmly admired by a few people in 1929.

The episode is recalled here because she has now written another drama of quality, **"The Chalk Garden."** . . . It has been put together in the same off-center fashion, witty lines popping off at tangents, non-sequiturs rambling brightly through the dialogue, everything more or less upside down, nothing leading directly into the next point of the story.

Miss Bagnold gives the impression of being a severe writer with a sharp mind who disdains pencil, paper and all the materials of her craft, and has small patience with logic and what is known in the trade as "the obligatory scene." **"The Chalk Garden"** is like a piece of sparkling cut glass. . . .

[The] plot is the least interesting item in **"The Chalk Garden."** Miss Bagnold's eccentric manner is everything. . . .

In **"The Chalk Garden"** it is a sound rule not to pay much attention to Miss Bagnold when she is developing her story. But pay attention to the lines she throws away. A perverse writer, she squanders all her talent on the things that do not matter. . . .

"The Chalk Garden" is an odd, unyielding comedy by a witty writer with a highly personal style. There's a keen mind behind it, and one that is not intimidated by either the theatre or the world.

> Brooks Atkinson, "The Theatre: Sparkling Cut Glass," in The New York Times (© 1955 by The New York Times Company; reprinted by permission), October 27, 1955 (and reprinted in New York Theatre Critics' Reviews, Vol. 16, No. 20, October 31, 1955, p. 227).

KENNETH TYNAN

Enid Bagnold's *The Chalk Garden* . . . may well be the finest artificial comedy to have flowed from an English (as opposed to an Irish) pen since the death of Congreve. Miss Bagnold's style recalls Ronald Firbank's *The Princess Zoubaroff;* it has the same exotic insolence, the same hothouse charm. We eavesdrop on a group of thoroughbred minds expressing themselves in speech of an exquisite candour, building ornamental bridges of metaphor, tiptoeing across frail causeways of simile, and vaulting over gorges impassable to the rational soul. . . .

Miss Bagnold evokes a world full of hard, gem-like flamethrowers, a little room of infinite riches. . . . [There] is nothing affected, or snobbish, about Miss Bagnold, unless verbal precision is a mark of snobbery. (p. 127)

Something is being said about the necessity of rescuing young people from the aridity of a rich, irresponsible life; but it is being said wittily, obliquely, in a manner that one would call civilised if one thought civilisation was worthy of the tribute. (pp. 127-28)

> Kenneth Tynan, "The British Theatre: 'The Chalk Garden'" (1956), in his Curtains: Selections from the Drama Criticism and Related Writings (copyright © 1961 by Kenneth Tynan; reprinted with the permission of Kathleen Tynan), Atheneum, 1961, pp. 127-28.

WALTER KERR

I find myself touched by **"The Chinese Prime Minister"** and I don't think it is because [the play is] . . . about the end of things coming so soon after they have just begun. I am touched, I think, because I have seen one whole play in which there is not a single careless line.

There are careless scenes, oh, yes. Quite a large portion of the middle act is taken up with a crossfire of family quarreling that has as its purpose the badgering of [the main character] until [she] is pushed into a vital, and mistaken, decision. The sequence is ratchety enough to badger you, too, and to make you wonder whether the silken strands of the evening can be gathered into one steady hand again. But even here "carelessness" is not quite the right word. For playwright Enid Bagnold never does anything simply because she cannot think of anything better to do. Whatever she does, she does on impulse, inspiration, with a jump and with a dagger in her hand, eyes gleaming. The gleam, the mad glint of her inspiration, may indeed flash out of the untidiest of corners. But in itself it is marvelously pure.

The obvious word for a lofty, detached, unpredictably witty play of this sort is "civilized." But I think we should do Miss Bagnold the justice of trying to avoid obvious words. **"The**

Chinese Prime Minister'' might more nearly, more properly be called humanely barbaric.

Its comedy is barbaric in the sense that, for all the elegance of elbow-length blue gloves and for all the urbanity of precise syntax sounded against deep chocolate drapes, the minds of the people who make the comedy are essentially brutal minds, minds capable of caring for themselves. . . .

The play deals with "the fascination and disaster of growing old" with a steady, open, impish and boldly questioning gaze that will not take sentiment for an answer. As a result of its unflinching smile and its emotional reserve, it earns sentiment. (p. 395)

[All] who speak Miss Bagnold's brisk, knobby, out-of-nowhere lines somehow or other become admirable. For the lines are thoughts, not echoes, not borrowings. And they are so often so very funny because they come not from the stage or from remembered literature but from a head that has no patience with twilight cant.

Miss Bagnold does not construct a play that all audiences will settle to easily. . . . [But it] shimmers on the stage—and wavers there, too—like a vast, insubstantial spider's web, strung with bits of real rain. It is not conventional, and it is not altogether secure. But it is written. And what a blessing that is. (p. 396)

> Walter Kerr, "'The Chinese Prime Minister' Bows In,'' in New York Herald Tribune (© I.H.T. Corporation; reprinted by permission), January 3, 1964 (and reprinted in New York Theatre Critics' Reviews, Vol. XXV, No. 1, January 20, 1964, pp. 395-96).

HOWARD TAUBMAN

Grow old along with Enid Bagnold. The last of life, like the first of it, is full of crotchets and ironies as she contemplates both parts in **"The Chinese Prime Minister."**

In this new comedy, . . . the author of **"The Chalk Garden,"** that model of elliptical humor and wisdom, is writing again with civilized wit and the kind of mature understanding that forgets little and forgives nearly everything. In a theater accustomed to simplemindedness, if not downright barrenness, it is exhilarating to hear an urbane, yet affirmative voice that can be both teasingly subtle and joyously direct.

There are eight characters, and they have, after a fashion, identities. All but one, the main one, have names; she is simply She. And there, one suspects, is a clue to Miss Bagnold's intent. For she has not written a conventional comedy of manners, but using the form, she has composed a delicious fantasy on the nature and promise of old age, which should amuse any age.

"The Chinese Prime Minister" is short on action. If you do not find stimulation in the good talk of spirited minds, Miss Bagnold's play, particularly part of its second act, may seem drawn out. But if you rejoice in the unexpected turn of thought felicitously phrased, you will not be troubled by the fact that little is happening and a lot is being said about it. . . .

"The Chinese Prime Minister" cares most about the interplay of good talk. Age has no terrors when looked at with such musing speculation and such amusing, vital maturity.

> Howard Taubman, "Theater: 'Chinese Prime Minister',' in The New York Times (© 1964 by The New York Times Company; reprinted by permission), January 3, 1964 (and reprinted in New York Theatre Critics' Reviews, Vol. XXV, No. 1, January 20, 1964, p. 393).

ROBERT BRUSTEIN

A play about old age should not itself be tired, but the writing in *The Chinese Prime Minister* is sometimes more enfeebled than its subject matter. Enid Bagnold, I am informed, was seven years about it. That's too long, especially when the work still lacks plot, or focus, or clear intention. I would guess that the author spent the major portion of those years honing up her dialogue, for each line has been sharpened to a fine edge. But she has grown too sage, and the epigrams tend to come out homilies. Take, as typical, this sentiment, which I assume to be the theme of the play: "The only way to enjoy death is to exhaust life." Note how Miss Bagnold has structured the thought; note the Latinate balance, the euphuistic contrasts, the rhetorical antitheses. Note also that, for all its formal finish, the sentence offers purely routine wisdom. This may be a personal prejudice, but the *carpe diem* motif has begun to strike me as a commonplace and sentimental notion. There is something contradictory in these self-conscious exhortations to instinctual pleasure—and something useless, too, since how does one decide to follow such advice? Miss Bagnold is too tasteful to tell her audience to enjoy, enjoy, live life to the fullest, realize every golden moment. . . . Still, one senses her wrestling with a like temptation; and there is a quality in her play which is as banal as the proverbialism in a fortune cookie.

In short, *The Chinese Prime Minister* lacks the poetic suggestiveness that so distinguished Miss Bagnold's previous drama, *The Chalk Garden*. And though it employs many of the same characters . . . , these characters now seem very isolated and disjunct, lost in the separate corridors of the author's mind. As if aware of this, Miss Bagnold has shaped them to a Chekhovian design, while borrowing that loose, eccentric structure that Shaw used in *Heartbreak House*—the play wanders, lurches, and ambles according to the author's fancy. In *The Chalk Garden*, the action was built around a suspenseful plot; here, it is built around a 70-year-old actress on a latter-day quest for identity. But the character is simply not interesting enough to justify the loss of narrative. (p. 28)

> Robert Brustein, "Mid-Season Gleanings" (reprinted by permission of the author; © 1964 by Robert Brustein), in The New Republic, Vol. 150, No. 5, February 1, 1964, pp. 28, 30.

NORA SAYRE

Almost everyone's childhood is boring—except one's own and Enid Bagnold's. At 80, she has written a splendid memoir [**"Enid Bagnold's Autobiography"**], which seethes with a fledgling's energy, lunging back and forth among the decades. . . .

Gleefully aware of her own "self-delight," greedy for praise, she hurtled into experiences that were scarce for girls of her generation. . . .

Eventually, she was bullied into marriage by Sir Roderick Jones, the head of Reuters. . . . The evocations of their brawling marriage—"the truces, the fun, the love, the rage"—and her years with four children, two houses, stacks of servants, infinite (often unwanted) guests, and the necessity of writing for three hours every day, truly make family-life sound worth-while—as some can hardly believe it is today. . . .

[The] attendant elegance (and the frank snobbery) will make some readers uneasy. The footnotes are unsettling, thus: Nöel* / Nöel* Coward; Juliet Duff* / *Lady Juliet Duff. And the dining room with pillars, sofas with dolphins and angels and garlands, Dresden mirrors, all that poshness and privilege can prompt the rebellion that many now feel against possessions, plus the suspicion of roots, and the recoil from blood-relations. Still, these reactions oddly heighten the value of these memoirs—as history. . . .

Throughout, Miss Bagnold's friends and acquaintances leap to life in a few words: Edith Evans as "a stupid genius," or the unnamed director who had "the swift, offended fury of a man who had been wounded before in his life. His scars flushed easily." . . . Her descriptions of madness are painfully brilliant, as a character snaps out of sanity and can't return.

There are devastating passages on failure in the theatre—"The Observer critic (a nice man, I hear) wrote as though he had seen vomit on the stage"—and reflections on the compulsion to keep going. . . . Some of her paragraphs are too rich for quotation: they ought to be recited.

As in **"The Chinese Prime Minister,"** she has "written of age as a special landscape; . . . curious, not devoid of pleasure, a time for adventure (when the duties got less)." Nearly all of her pages suggest further essays or chapters: one hopes that many more will follow, in her style of "conveying the incredible as though it was credible—or conveying the truth as though it was *incredible*."

Nora Sayre, " 'Enid Bagnold's Autobiography','' in The New York Times Book Review *(© 1970 by The New York Times Company; reprinted by permission), August 30, 1970, p. 4.*

MARTIN GOTTFRIED

It is not often these days that a play is written with grace in pursuit of intelligence. Both seem out of fashion. **"A Matter of Gravity"** . . . is hardly in the class of her wonderful **"The Chalk Garden,"** or the lesser **"The Chinese Prime Minister,"** but time spent with even an untidy Enid Bagnold play is time spent in the company of intellectual finesse. . . .

[**"A Matter of Gravity"**] is about a very rich, very aristocratic and devastatingly bright old English lady who is living alone in a grand country house. She is alone, that is, except for a cook who has the disconcerting habit of rising into the air now and again. . . .

[Mrs. Basil has] outgrown faith in science and so the choice between believing what she sees—the floating cook—and what makes sense, ultimately concludes with a final philosophy: "There are things to which I am tied that need loosening." She abandons the house to find new knowledge with the cook.

That doesn't make sense, besides which, nothing happens onstage to convince us that the cook or anyone else can levitate, which is the play's first order of reality. But then these are only the most obvious of the play's confusions.

The play's sociological points are in equal abundance and confusion. The handsome country home . . . is a fulsome symbol of everything that was refined, tasteful and civilized in British life. It is coming apart at the seams, destroyed by a modern age of homosexuals, interracial marriages and other disturbers of the past, toward whom Bagnold's liberalism is unconvincing. At the play's start the lady is left to living only in the front of the house. By its end, even that is crumbling. The end of elegant living. . . .

Bagnold writes with such wit, and such sense, that she makes wisdom and civility seem like long lost treasures that must be returned to our lives at once, lest we die of stupidity. Even when nothing is happening, which is most of the time, the flow of observation and humor is invigorating. And though it is actionless there is a theater of language to the play. . . .

[The] charm and wisdom of this play [is not] to be dismissed out of hand. . . . **"A Matter of Gravity"** is not mere matinee theater. It may not be first rate but it is certainly first class.

Martin Gottfried, " 'Gravity': A High for Katharine the Great," in New York Post *(reprinted by permission of the New York Post; © 1976, New York Post Corporation), February 4, 1976 (and reprinted in* New York Theatre Critics' Reviews, *Vol. XXXVII, No. 2, January 26, 1976, p. 375).*

CLIVE BARNES

They say that to understand is to forgive, but I am not sure that I understood Enid Bagnold's new play **"A Matter of Gravity."** . . .

An eccentric Englishwoman, with bird's-nest hair, glittering eyes, a forthright tongue that can never quite decide whether to be blunt or forked, and a style of dress that froze immediately after World War I and never thawed—we know the type. We know also the fat cook with a taste for liquor and an ingratiating manner, but there are differences. . . .

Mrs. Basil is, for all her vigor and animal vitality, an old woman and she fears death as passionately as she has embraced life. She does not believe in God, or in a future. She is a materialist with humor. But suddenly she sees a miracle. She sees, with her own eyes, Dubois rise in the air as stately as a zeppelin, and bounce off the ceiling with plaster in her hair. Now she knows. As she puts it: "If only there were a mystery it would be the ladder to all mysteries." Mrs. Basil and Miss Bagnold are absolutely right. But do you believe in Mary Poppins?

Mind you, some might have literal doubts about the Ghost of Hamlet's father, but there is more in Shakespeare than has ever been dreamed of in Miss Bagnold's philosophy. Her play—which has a bittersweet ending by the way—is full of crosscurrents of motivation and whirlpools of thought.

There is a lot of levitation offstage and a certain amount of levity on, but it never adds up. The characters are all equally unlikely, and apart from Mrs. Basil equally disagreeable. The writing consists chiefly of maimots, semi-epigrams and portentously ponderous sayings such as: "The State of the world depends upon one's newspaper." What havoc Oscar Wilde wreaked on the British playwright attempting cultivation!

Clive Barnes, " 'A Matter of Gravity' Enshrines Hepburn," in The New York Times *(© 1976 by The New York Times Company; reprinted by permission), February 4, 1976 (and reprinted in* New York Theatre Critics' Reviews, *Vol. XXXVII, No. 2, January 26, 1976, p. 374).*

ALAN RICH

[*A Matter of Gravity*] is not so much a play . . . as a series of patches from several plays that connect only in having the same cast in each. One patch concerns an elderly woman, crusty and conservative (in all but her apparent passion for heavy green eye shadow), going somewhat to pieces at her grandson's marriage to a girl of partially black parentage: proposition, conflict, and, need we add, reconciliation. Another concerns the housemaid of said grandmother, a slovenly sort, but given to levitation, and the grandmother's decision to join the maid in a mental institution so that she, too, can learn to levitate. (I am *not* making this up.) A third concerns the breakup of two homosexual matings, one male and one female, identical in their May-December configurations and in the clumsy self-delusions of both Decembers. . . .

There is no pace to Ms. Bagnold's play, no movement, no action overt or inward. More depressing yet, from a writer of her wonted exquisiteness, is the lurid witlessness of some of her individual lines. . . . ''I'm so rich it's like having cancer.'' Or, from another character: ''Sex is an old carrot, used by God to get children.'' What—beyond the easy, momentary titter—can any of this mean?

Alan Rich, ''The Old Ladies Show Their Muddles,''
in New York *Magazine (copyright © 1976 by News*
Group Publications, Inc.; reprinted with the per-
mission of New York *Magazine), Vol. 9, No. 7,*
February 16, 1976, p. 71.

Saul Bellow

1915-

Canadian-born American novelist, short story writer, essayist, dramatist, editor, and translator.

Bellow is, perhaps, the most important writer to have emerged in post-World War II America. Thoughtful yet humorous, his work pursues the timely question of what it is to be fully human in an increasingly impersonal and mechanistic world. Bellow firmly rejects the modern concept of the absurdity of human existence. Instead, his protagonists—sensitive, observant, intensely individualistic intellectuals—although sometimes despairing and alienated, are never totally so. Their struggle is for a kind of spiritual balance to enable them to exert the will and imagination necessary to control their lives.

Bellow favors a prose style in which he can "talk his characters into existence," reflecting his casual dependence on plot and his emphasis on dialogue, monologue, and "inner voice". As his protagonists speak to each other and to themselves, the reader is drawn into their struggles with self and society.

Taking his place beside other "Bellow Heroes" (Augie March, Henderson, Herzog, and Mr. Sammler) is Albert Corde, the middle-aged academic of Bellow's recent novel, *The Dean's December*. Critical reaction to this newer work varies, with some critics being reluctant to applaud yet another of Bellow's autobiographical creations. Nonetheless, Bellow maintains a stature shared by few writers of fiction. A recipient of three National Book Awards, he also won both the Pulitzer Prize in fiction and the Nobel Prize in literature in 1976.

(See also *CLC*, Vols. 1, 2, 3, 6, 8, 10, 13, 15; *Contemporary Authors*, Vols. 5-8, rev. ed.; *Dictionary of Literary Biography*, Vol. 2; and *Dictionary of Literary Biography Documentary Series*, Vol. 3.)

© Nancy Crampton

V. S. PRITCHETT

Saul Bellow has the most effusive intelligence of living American novelists. Even when he is only clever he has a kind of spirited intellectual vanity that enables him to take on all the facts and theories about the pathetic and comically exposed condition of civilized man and distribute them like high-class corn so that the chickens come running to them. That is the art of the novelist who can't resist an idea: to evoke, attract that 'pleasing, anxious being', the squawking, dusty, feverish human chicken. Aldous Huxley could always throw the corn but nothing alive came fluttering to it.

But immensely clever novelists have to beware of self-dispersal when they run to great length. I enjoy Saul Bellow in his spreading carnivals and wonder at his energy, but I still think he is finer in his shorter works. *The Victim* was the best novel to come out of America—or England—for a decade. *The Dangling Man* is good, but subdued; *Seize the Day* is a small grey masterpiece. If one cuts out the end, *Henderson the Rain King* is at once profound and richly diverting in its fantasy. These novels had form; their economy drove their point home. By brevity Bellow enhanced our experience. And, to a European reader—though this may be irrelevant—he seems the only

American of this generation to convey the feel and detail of urban America, preserving especially what is going on at the times when nothing is going on: the distinctive native ennui, which is the basic nutriment of any national life.

It is when he turns to longer books, chasing the mirage of 'the great American novel', that Bellow weakens as he becomes a traveller, spreading the news and depending on the presence of a character who is something like a human hold-all, less a recognizable individual than a fantastic piece of bursting luggage. His labels, where he has been, whom he has met in his collision with America are more suggestive than his banal personal story. (pp. 146-47)

Structurally and in content, the story of *Herzog* is unsustaining. But what Herzog sees, the accidental detail of his experience, is very impressive. Here he grows. He really has got a mind and it is hurt. It is a tribute to Mr Bellow's reserves of talent that the novel survives and over-grows its own weaknesses. The muddle Moses is in, his sense of victimization, are valuable. His paranoia is put, by Mr Bellow, to excellent use. If the theme is lost, we have the American scene. Moses is not really exposed, but his New York and Chicago are. Mr Bellow has something like a genius for place. There is not a descriptive insinuator of what, say, a city like New York is like from minute to minute who comes anywhere near him. Some novelists stage it, others document it; he is breathing in it. He knows how to show us not only Moses but other people, moving from street to street, from room to room in their own circle of uncomprehending solitude. Grasping this essential of life in a big city he sees the place not as a confronted whole, but continually askance. His senses are especially alive to *things* and he catches the sensation that the *things* have created the people or permeated them. This was the achievement of *The Victim,* and it is repeated in *Herzog.* A wanderer, he succeeds with minor characters, the many small figures in the crowd who suggest millions more. The dialogue of a Puerto Rican taxi driver, a Chicago cop, a low lawyer, a Jewish family, people brash, shady or saddened by the need of survival and whose ripeness comes out of the dirty brick that has trapped them, is really wonderful. It is far superior to Hemingway's stylized naturalism: Bellow's talk carries the speaker's life along with it. Their talk makes them move. They involve Moses with themselves and show him living, as all human beings do, in a web spun by others as well as by himself.

The habit of seeing things askance or out of the corner of his eye has given Mr Bellow an even more important quality: it keeps alive a perpetual sense of comedy and feeds his originality. There is sometimes talk of a taste for elegance in his book; spoken of like that, as a sort of craving or innate possession, it sounds very nearly vulgar. But there is an implicit elegance of mind in his writing: it sharpens the comic edge and dares him to spirited invention. As far as the comedy is concerned it has all the fatality of Jewish comedy, that special comedy of human undress and nakedness of which the Jewish writers are the world's masters. The other gift of Mr Bellow is his power of fantastic invention. . . . [Herzog] is absurd yet he is fine; he is conceited yet he is raw. He is a great man yet he is torpedoed by a woman who 'wants to live in the delirious professions'—trades in which the main instrument is your opinion of yourself and the raw material is your reputation or standing. At times he lives like a sort of high-class Leopold Bloom, the eternal Jewish clown; at others he is a Teufelsdröckh; again he is the pushing son of the bewildered Polish-Jewish immigrant and failed boot-legger, guilty about his break with the past, nagged by his relations, his ambitions punctured.

As a character Moses is physically exact—we know his domestic habits—but mentally and emotionally amorphous. Any objection to this is cancelled by his range as an observer-victim. It is a triumph that he is not a bore and does not ask our sympathy. (pp. 148-51)

> V. S. Pritchett, "Jumbos," in his The Tale Bearers: Literary Essays *(copyright © 1980 by V. S. Pritchett; reprinted by permission of Random House, Inc.; in Canada by Literistic, Ltd.), Random House, 1980, pp. 146-55.*

HUGH KENNER

A genre has long since defined itself, Nobel-certified: the Saul Bellow Novel. This is the Novel as First-Draft Dissertation: a rumination on the sorry state of the world, insufficiently formal for the Committee on Social Thought at the University of Chicago, however well it may translate into Swedish, but not unworthy of that Committee's encouraging noises. About the sorry state of the world there is nothing to be done save accept it, as every Bellow protagonist must learn for himself the way Job did. And since the Bellow Novel is obdurately protagonist-centered, what the reader gets to do is share his learning process.

In *The Dean's December,* the Dean—not a Jewish Dean from the Bellow Repertory Company, not at bottom an *echt* dean at all but a mere dean of students, moreover a moon-faced French-Irish ex-newspaperman named Albert Corde who has drifted into academe, and don't confuse him with his fox-faced creator—the Dean, if I could just finish this sentence, is stranded in communist Rumania waiting for his mother-in-law, Valeria, to die.

His wife, Minna, née Raresh, is an astrophysicist of the Palomar caliber; he cannot understand a thing she does, save that she brings together "a needle from one end of the universe with a thread from the opposite end." Here, Minna being preoccupied with her mother, he gets little solace from her. And it's cold and he speaks no Rumanian: plenty of time to ruminate. Herzog, left in solitude, wrote letters. Corde can simply run on, third-person imperfect. (p. 62)

[At one point in his life, Bellow might] have judged *The Dean's December* dreary: a book (for one thing) so remote from reliance on idiom that there's nothing save the regime to impede a Rumanian version.

For along the way Bellow has acquired an alter ego named Herzog, who first surfaced in the 1964 novel of that name and promptly addled his creator's head. . . . (p. 64)

Not that *The Dean's December* lacks all touch of as skilled a fabulist as you might want. Its opening is rich with possibility.

"Corde, who led the life of an executive in America—wasn't a college dean a kind of executive?—found himself six or seven thousand miles from his base, in Bucharest, in winter, shut up in an old-fashioned apartment."

In the bundle of worries he spends long hours unpacking, Chicago dominates, a place of terminal craziness: its rich without point, its poor without hope, its ongoings rife with jagged violence and sexual hysteria, its very jails full of rats and sodomizings and stabbings. There fate assigns each denizen his place in one or the other of two anarchies: the legitimate, the illegitimate. No melioration of Chicago seems thinkable.

Is there life after Chicago? If so, Bucharest seems to emblematize it. Bellow's Bucharest is neither a Lower Slobovia of ludicrous privations nor a Len Deighton playground for adventurous free-world spirits. It's a suitable limbo for Corde's introspections. . . . (pp. 64-5)

[In] this way station for his stunned soul Corde has nothing to do but wait: for one more hospital visit, arranged by bribery; for Valeria to die; for a grim day at the crematorium; for the flight home. Not that when he does have, or will have, things to do (in Chicago) does *doing* any longer seem to signify. In his morass of seeing-all-sides, acts are irrelevant.

So his plight—killing time in limbo—is rather close to the plight of his author, who must fill a book with sheer inaction and has consequently piped in what's been all too fluent for him of late years, the Herzogian vitality to be gotten from *opinions.* . . .

And [Corde's] drear December has left his creator bereft of occasion for the sort of comic epiphany that can salvage all: scenes like the miniature Noah's Flood in *Mr. Sammler,* or the page near the end of *Henderson the Rain King* . . . where the hero (you have to believe this) climbs into a roller coaster with a mangy old trained bear, too old to ride a bike anymore.

*And while we climbed and swooped and dipped
and swerved and rose again higher than the
Ferris wheels and fell, we held on to each other.
By a common bond of despair we embraced,
cheek to cheek. . . . I was pressed into his long-
suffering age-worn, tragic and discolored coat
as he grunted and cried to me.*

That's a high Saul Bellow moment, one of the highest. Devoid
of reflections, it prompts them. It would have been understandable to the author of the Book of Job, who envisioned Leviathan
drawn out of the sea with a kind of Hebrew safety pin, and
tethered on a leash for laughing maidens. Impossible to imagine
it in Latin. (p. 65)

> *Hugh Kenner, "From Lower Bellowvia," in* Har-
> per's *(copyright © 1982 by* Harper's Magazine; *all
> rights reserved; reprinted from the February, 1982
> issue by special permission), Vol. 264, No. 1581,
> February, 1982, pp. 62-5.*

KATHA POLLITT

As long as Bellow gave us fictional richness, one would have
had to be stern indeed to resist his charm merely because he
gave away, every now and then, that he too found himself
charming, like a hypnotist who puts himself along with his
subjects into a trance. But what happens when the fictional
juices run out, when a novelist becomes so convinced of his
own wisdom, his grasp of the Big Subjects—Western Civilization, The Modern Condition, The Future of Humanity—that
fiction seems too fragile a bark to carry all his intellectual
cargo? Well, if he's Tolstoy, he decides that fiction is evil, a
trick, and gives away all his money. If he's Solzhenitsyn, he
turns himself into a witness to history and an ideologue. If he's
Bellow, he veers off into nonfiction (**To Jerusalem and Back**),
autobiography (**Humboldt's Gift**) and sociopolitical tirades disguised as novels (**Mr. Sammler's Planet**).

And so, here we are, at last, with **The Dean's December,** a
novel as flat as the paper on which it is printed, for all Bellow's
literary energies have been swallowed up in pontification. This
is a book so bitter, so self-infatuated, so boring, as to make
one wonder if his earlier books could really have had the intellectual weight ascribed to them at the time. (p. 66)

[In **The Dean's December**] Albert Corde, a middle-aged journalist and dean of a Chicago college, has gone to Bucharest
with his beloved Rumanian astronomer wife, Minna, because
her mother is dying. Corde has recently published a series of
articles about Chicago, detailing the corruption of the political
and judicial systems and the true scope of inner-city—that is,
black—degradation and criminality. These articles have offended everybody, as has Corde's insistence on bringing to
prosecution a black ex-con and a black prostitute who have
murdered a white student.

Corde has a lot of time to think in Bucharest, and among his
concerns are: the corrupting influence of journalists, himself
excepted; the cowardice of American intellectuals, himself excepted; the moral squeamishness of white liberals, himself *not*
excepted (since he is no liberal); and the failure of humanists
to face issues raised by scientists—himself excepted, since he
is considering writing a piece about a geologist who attributes
the craziness of modern folk in general, and poor blacks in
particular, to lead poisoning. What has happened to "the American idea," Corde wonders. Here in Bucharest, the government
is tyrannical, but the people are warm and help each other. In

America, the government is less evil, but the well-off are
corrupt and selfish, the poor close to bestial. Go figure.

In due time, the old lady dies, the two blacks are convicted,
and Corde loses his job. His literary rival, a famous journalist,
publishes a piece about Corde in which he attributes to Corde
a remark equating tenured professors to welfare mothers—free-
loaders both—and the provost of the college suggests that perhaps Corde is not cut out for academic life. The book ends
with Minna star-gazing at Mount Palomar and Corde wandering
around the drafty observatory, promising himself another go
at explaining to humanity how far astray it has gone.

The most puzzling question raised by this very puzzling book
is, why did Bellow write it as a novel? Corde compliments
himself, in the traditional Bellovian manner, on his "poetic"
apprehension of complex realities, his intuitive grasp of character—"What a man he was for noticing!"—but this time out,
Bellow doesn't deliver. His people barely exist, although we
learn a lot about their complexions, hairstyles and noses. (Corde
himself is fully inventoried every 20 or 30 pages, as though
we might have forgotten what he looked like. And so we have.)
Minna is a pleasant cipher. Her mother is a standard matriarch,
all warmth and dignity. Corde's enemies—his radical nephew,
his journalistic rival, his cousin the dishonest lawyer who is
defending the two blacks in court—are grotesque cartoons.

Corde spends a lot of time in Bucharest rereading his piece on
Chicago, which is quoted at length. One glimpses the old
Bellow in Corde's sketch of the cynical elderly lawyers hanging
out at the courthouse, waiting to pick up work; the dilapidated
county hospital, where the corridors are lined with bloodstained
stretchers and, down in the basement, elderly blacks lie drows-
ing on kidney dialysis machines; the ex-murderer who runs a
detoxification center in an abandoned warehouse. These passages are so much more vivid than the novel that surrounds
them, one wishes Bellow had simply given us a nonfiction
book about Chicago. At least it would have been well-written.

It would also have been infuriating. Bellow deserves credit for
denouncing Chicago's corruption and its writing-off of destitute
black neighborhoods, although neither point is the revelation
he thinks it. But the only aspect of the black condition that
really engages him is the one that affects middle-class whites
directly: crime. About crime, from purse-snatching to the most
horrendous murders, Bellow waxes powerfully wroth. It is
animalistic. It is insanity of an order hitherto unknown in history. It presages a whole new stage in human affairs, characterized by "universal stupefaction, a Saturnian, wild, gloomy
murderousness."

This is surprising indeed, coming from a man who has spent
the better part of his literary career romanticizing gangsters
and crooks. (pp. 66-7)

People are losing their humanity, Bellow tells us, and no one
is exempt but himself and a chosen few. Academics are cowards. Criminals are animals. Politicians? Forget it! Students?
Behind those preppy demeanors lurk raunchy, low-down drives.
Scientists are mostly antihumane. Humanists are universally
ignorant. Radicals are fools. Journalists do nothing but offer
degraded language and bastardized nonideas to a populace that
has lost its sense of reality. (This is a bit thick coming from
someone who speaks of "the American idea," but let that
pass.) America is saturated with violence, sexual license, incoherence and rudeness. Chicago is ruined. Bucharest is hideous. December is cold and damp.

Our only hope, Bellow seems to be saying, is to undertake a national moral awakening, the nature of which is unspecified but which apparently consists largely of listening with great attention to Bellow himself. He wants very badly to play Jeremiah and philosopher-king to the American establishment, and if he has to strangle the sources of his best fiction to make himself credible in the part, he seems, alas, eager to do so. The wish to be taken seriously as a sociopolitical thinker within the highest circles of punditry and power explains, perhaps, why he has made his latest protagonist-spokesman, Corde, a colorless, buttoned-down, responsibly married Midwesterner, instead of a flamboyant, sexually irresponsible Jew like Herzog, whose testimony might seem tainted by ethnicity and neurosis.

This is a sad development indeed. There was knowingness and humanity in the old Chicago *ganef* in **Humboldt's Gift,** who dismissed sexual kinks with a shrugged "For a funny foot, you need a funny shoe." There is only bile in Corde's sour claim that Americans now go to S-M shops the way they used to go to beauty parlors. Could it be that winning the Nobel Prize has awakened in Bellow this urge to issue grandiose pronouncements of impending doom? I hope not. One Solzhenitsyn is enough. (p. 67)

> *Katha Pollitt, "Bellow Blows Hot and Cold," in* Mother Jones *(copyright © 1982 by the Foundation for National Progress; reprinted by permission of the author), Vol. VII, No. II, February-March, 1982, pp. 66-7.*

DIANE JOHNSON

Like the earlier Mr. Sammler's, Corde's mission is to be at the moral center of [*The Dean's December*], the worried and thoughtful person. And at that he is splendid. (p. 6)

[While in Rumania to attend the deathbed of his wife's mother] Corde is following the progress, back home, of a court case involving the murder of a student. Two blacks are accused of pushing him out of a window to his death. They claim he fell, and that he had anyway been asking for trouble. Corde has encouraged their prosecution, but without his interest the case would probably have gone the way of other such cases—postponement after postponement until the witnesses died or moved away, and eventual freedom for the killers. Some, including his nephew Mason, feel that Corde is failing to allow for the social conditions which led to the depravity of the accused blacks. Increasingly appalled by what he has been finding out about the legal system, hospitals, slums, social conditions generally, and the outlook for black people, Corde has written some controversial articles in *Harper's* telling what he sees.

The action of the novel proceeds simply, without suspense. The mother dies, is cremated, family members gather. Minna and Corde return to Chicago. If the blacks had not been found guilty, Corde would have been in difficulty at the university. But the accused have been tried, convicted, and given sixteen years. Nevertheless Corde resigns his academic post and plans to devote himself to journalism.

His *Harper's* articles are mostly descriptive. Detectives shoot an escaping young prisoner ten times in the head. In the slum housing project, people, "being afraid to go at night to the incinerator drop on each floor," drop their garbage down the toilets and break them. There are "young men getting on top of the elevator cabs, opening the hatch and threatening to pour in gas, to douse people with gasoline and set them afire."

Snipers, rapes, revolting murders, terrible despair—a huge American underclass which is not attached to life, and no one can suggest how to attach it (n.b., "Corde").

People don't want to read about this. The *Harper's* subscribers are angry. Student militants demand an apology to "Black, Puerto Rican and Mexican toilers" for making them look like "animals and savages." Corde observes that in our society the truth-teller needs a lead apron against the radiation and shock waves set off by mere objectivity—and the complicated formal arrangement of the novel is perhaps Bellow's lead apron.

If there is a lie at the heart of the book it is here, in assuming or pretending that there would be a great public reaction to objective descriptions of American social conditions. Perhaps we are beyond outrage. People do try to write angry descriptive articles and outcries are seldom raised. It's wishful thinking to imagine that one commentator, even Albert Corde, speaking of "superfluous populations," "written off," "doomed peoples," might get through to the rest of us, but it's an honorable wish, and the novel an honorable outcry. . . . In a sense, Bellow has written a novel about how nobody will read or accept the novel he is writing, any more than the people Corde talks to believe *him*. . . . (pp. 6, 8)

[Corde's] is the Arnoldian view that people can be attached to life by culture—but there is no culture in the city, in the wasteland. He is defending humanistic Western culture against the conventional liberal institutions that have failed to maintain it. "Public discussion is threadbare." The communications industry "breeds hysteria and misunderstanding," academics make no effort to lead the public, "the intellectuals have been incapable of clarifying our principal problems."

John Updike's recent novel *Rabbit Is Rich* is a picture of the moral and spiritual situation of a modern middle-class American man. Bellow's novel is only a picture of a man thinking about the spiritual situation and its actual correlatives; that is, it is abstracted by a process of diffraction through the minds of Corde, of his friend Dewey, of other people he talks to. It would have been possible to dramatize the Chicago novel another way. The dean is awakened one night to learn of the murder of one of his students. He enlists the help of the university in seeing that the killers are brought to justice—and attempts are made to dissuade him from seeing justice done. His ambitious cousin Max is attorney for the defense, etc.

This would have provided a dramatic, active, involving novel with a climactic courtroom scene, or whatever. But it is not the novel Bellow, a masterly novelist, chose to write, perhaps because it would have deprived him of Rumania, and the implicit contrast of a regimented society with our chaos, but also perhaps because this more conventional structure would have required a resolution, some ending, unhappy or happy, to suspense; and that in turn would provide a satisfaction that would belie the view of contemporary life he is taking here. If the formal success of a work of art lies in part in the resolution of the tensions and problems with which it deals, if only in the form, then this novel could be said to fail. Yet to resolve the huge problems that engage Corde, by prescription on the one hand or catharsis on the other, would produce a reassuring work. Perhaps art is meant to be reassuring at the same time that it disturbs. But reassurance, more suited to the matters of the individual soul than to the body politic, would falsify the subject here. So Bellow has chosen a strategy more akin to that of an essay, which leaves questions, and his language is the plain meditative language of thought, in place of the exuberant language he has commanded elsewhere.

Perhaps Corde overstates the failure of press and academy, but it doesn't seem so. The American novel, which has always waxed private and public in turn, has been stuck for three decades in a mode of private confession now very worn, or of experiment, the more vital strain with too few practitioners. Breaking away, as he does, from the confessional mode, Corde is perhaps, as he puts it, "objectivity intoxicated." But he seems nowhere wrong. If the role of art is somehow, as Arnold Hauser suggested, to make you feel that you must change your life, then this novel succeeds by recommending—no, by showing (for novelists are always being enjoined to show, not tell, and Bellow has not forgotten this injunction)—an American in the first stages of change, that is, the describing stage, the stage of admitting how things really are in the world beyond the self. (p. 8)

> Diane Johnson, "Point of Departure," in The New York Review of Books (reprinted with permission from The New York Review of Books; copyright © 1982 Nyrev, Inc.), Vol. XXIX, No. 3, March 4, 1982, pp. 6, 8.

MELVYN BRAGG

The Dean's December might not be vintage Bellow but then he probably grew bored with vintage Bellow. It is new ground, seeking to retrieve, most boldly, the territory of social description and prescription so largely abandoned by novelists during this century. Bellow has always been conscious of the European literary heritage—whether it was bringing in the rhythms of Yiddish or digesting the intellectual currency of Paris; here it is Dostoevsky he seems to turn to; and if he falls short, then, who does not? In the attempt there are riches: the failures are so easy to spot that a reviewer must beware, Bellow is an exceptionally clever man. He would not "fail" so simply or seem to fail for no good purpose. . . .

As an intellectual round-up [*The Dean's December*] has all Bellow's force—made even more forceful by the comparative plainness of the prose he chooses to employ in this case. . . .

What is worrying is the concept of Corde himself and the organisation of the novel. Corde, the Huguenot Dean, does seem in his nerve-ends to be much more a man from the labyrinthine lands of American-Jewish-Intellectual-Ambitious-Questioning-Family than from the long, laconic tradition sketched in for Corde. It will not do to say Corde should have been Bellow because Bellow himself wrote articles on the underclass of Chicago and Bellow himself has a Rumanian wife, (a mathematician) and Bellow himself has expressed some of Corde's thoughts. As a novelist he has often chosen to sail brilliantly close to the autobiographical/documentary winds without capsizing the fiction. In this case, though, I cannot quite understand the necessity for *such* a distancing.

Similarly, the novel is organised largely as a series of flashbacks. Therefore, some of what is significant is reported by Corde who has a wrapped-up view on it, and his is the only view. This gives us less than usual of the variety of perspective or the vivacity of narrative story telling to which Bellow has so often treated us. Again, I cannot work out why he saw the necessity for this.

Except—and this could answer both worries—that he has said that *The Dean's December* is the first of a series of novels which will centre on and explore Chicago and, to paraphrase, will be a new sort of fiction for him. Therefore we could be seeing a structure and a character whose ultimate validity will

be shown later. Or, he wanted this shape to give clearance for the hammer blows he aims at today's America.

However that might be, there is in *The Dean's December* enough thought and matter for ten other contemporary novels. . . .

> Melvyn Bragg, "Eastword Ho!" in Punch (© 1982 by Punch Publications Ltd.; all rights reserved; may not be reprinted without permission), Vol. 282, March 31, 1982, p. 536.

STEPHEN MILLER

If Updike is the narrator-as-preacher, nudging his readers to speculate about what it all means, and Nabokov is the narrator-as-aesthete, insisting that his readers pay close attention to his exquisitely detailed observations, Bellow is the narrator-as-taxi driver, telling his readers to cut the nonsense and stop taking this or that fashionable idea seriously. Even though some of his novels are in the third person and others are in the first, it does not seem to make much of a difference; we hear Bellow talking in all of them, hear the voice of a writer who is in turn amused, exasperated, and angered by the way we live now.

As a worldly-wise taxi driver—one, moreover, who has read all the Great Books—Bellow is not afraid to pursue his own reflections while the plot languishes. He is our most essayistic novelist; his main characters are always struggling with ideas—getting angry at them or, more often than not, being confused by them, befuddled by the profusion of ideas on the loose in the modern world.

The dangers of Bellow's essayistic approach to fiction are obvious. At times his novels veer too close to monologue; we do not know who is doing the struggling with ideas—the main character or the novelist. Bellow is most successful when he creates characters who are not intellectuals, such as Tommy Wilhelm of *Seize the Day*, Hattie of **"Leaving the Yellow House"** (a short story), and Woodrow Selbst of **"The Silver Dish,"** a recent short story that is one of Bellow's most powerful works of fiction. But even novels such as *Herzog* and *Humboldt's Gift*, which have intellectuals as central characters, are generally successful despite their garrulity and gimcrack plots because Bellow makes them farcical as well as serious. He doesn't endorse his central characters' opinions; he merely offers them for inspection. . . .

It would be easy to jump to the conclusion that [Chicagoan Albert Corde in *The Dean's December* is] simply a spokesman for Bellow, because Bellow has always made much of his Chicago connection. And because Bellow often has trouble distancing himself from his main character, it is hard to know what to make of Corde's opinions. But the problem with *The Dean's December* is not simply that Bellow is, so to speak, too close to Corde; the problem is that Bellow takes Corde all too seriously. He is not a farcical figure. Far from it, he is a hero of sorts, but his heroism is not sufficiently tested in the novel. Only one other character—an old school pal who is now a famous columnist—acts as a foil to Corde, but Bellow never gives the columnist a chance to challenge Corde's views. Corde comes through the novel with flying colors—getting high marks for insight, decency, moral seriousness. The result is a novel brimming with important ideas yet inert as a work of fiction. (p. 33)

Yet the ideas themselves are compelling. Despite its limp central character, *The Dean's December* is in the best sense a disturbing novel, disturbing because Bellow confronts the problem of the black underclass—refusing to blink at it, to make easy sense of it by invoking the "deep" explanations of psychology and sociology. Corde realizes that in order to see what life in the underclass is like you have to "recover the world that is buried under the debris of false description or nonexperience." He refuses, for example, to collaborate with an eminent scientist who explains the conduct of the underclass by the pervasiveness of lead poisoning in the slums. Following the train of Corde's thoughts, we sense that Bellow has thought deeply about a subject that is on the minds of most Americans—not bureaucracy, alienation, or the other fashionable subjects most American novelists wine and dine on, but crime. And in this novel he has grimly observed that if in the East the danger comes from above—from the Stalinist bureaucracy with its secret police and informers—in the West the danger comes from below, from an underclass out of control. But Bellow has not imagined the subject fully. One hopes he will return to the question again, for he—more than any other American novelist save, perhaps, Ralph Ellison—has the imagination, intelligence, and knowledge to write a novel that will make us *see* the question. (pp. 34-5)

> Stephen Miller, "Book Reviews: 'The Dean's December'," in The American Spectator (copyright © The American Spectator 1982), Vol. 15, No. 4, April, 1982, pp. 33-5.

DAVID EVANIER

[In *The Dean's December*] we have the bare bones of Bellow: the novel as essay, stripped of the whimsey and decoration of character and fanciful prose. Bellow at his worst. This book has the disquieting effect of encountering an old friend—a good friend—who has undergone some startling decline.

But the symptoms and patterns have been there from the mechanical beginnings in *Dangling Man* and *The Victim*. They have persisted, notably in the metaphysical obsession with the anthroposophy of Rudolf Steiner that virtually took over the latter part of what was supposed to be a portrait of poet Delmore Schwartz in *Humboldt's Gift.*

The truth of the matter is that Bellow's passion for cerebration has weighed down and sometimes canceled out his interest in fiction. No novelist except Thomas Mann has been able to carry such heavy excess baggage without being crushed by it. Bellow's enduring achievements are his short novel *Seize the Day* (his only fully fictional work, free of ideas and opinions), the excellent recent story "A Silver Dish" . . . , the fictional sections of *Herzog,* the collection of earlier stories entitled *Mosby's Memoirs,* and his fully realized novel, *Henderson the Rain King.* "I have no literary interests, but am made of literature," Kafka wrote. "I am nothing else, and cannot be anything else." Bellow, alas, is a mix of things. Only a book as bad as *The Dean's December* could occasion a reassessment at this point in the career of a writer considered to be America's most important living novelist.

Bellow's erraticism is a fact, and a prior awareness of it could give the reader a more sober estimate of this dismal book, where stale ideas are unalloyed with narrative brilliance. *The Dean's December* is not primarily a comedown symptomatic of decline, but really another manifestation of Bellow's multiple careenings as a writer. For Bellow is not only seduced by ideas (as here). When Norman Podhoretz wrote of the willed, forced quality of affirmation of *The Adventures of Augie March,* this was a true insight, which can be related to the gallery of

overblown characters (bigger than life: yet really balloon-like) in *Humboldt's Gift.* For Bellow is a "literary" writer in two senses of that slippery word. Sometimes his prose brilliantly invents reality on a deeper level. At other times his words run away from (rather than toward) him, and the reality he presents glossily outstrips and supplants a felt reality. Nevertheless, Bellow has shown a feeling for the possibilities of life that has lifted his work to high planes of achievement.

The Dean's December has the odd tone of having emerged from (or been exhumed from) a time-chamber; there is a musty feeling of removal and unreality in its stilted language ("rum" as an adjective is used eight times; there are phrases like "a dumb matching a dumb," "shut in like a birdie in a cage," "the generality-mind," "He felt like a pity-weirdo") and the tired nature of the subject matter: a stereotyped radical student out of the Sixties, ossified reflections on the decline of the inner cities and black crime. The dialogue does not help. When the dean tells his wife he has lost his job, she says, "But how disagreeable for you, Albert." (pp. 364-65)

The writing is pale, wooden, flat; the characterizations evaporate into air after the reading. (p. 365)

Beyond the creaky plot, thin characterizations, boring cerebration, and poverty of style, there is one further thing that needs to be brought up about this novel. Every writer at some point in his career is involved in a project that goes totally, inexplicably wrong: the tone is not what was intended, the characters remain woodenly in place, the anticipated excitement is absent. *The Dean's December* is such a book. It certainly has some of Bellow's worst traits. But primarily it should be seen not as a harbinger, a roadmark, or a symptom of Bellow's status now—but as an aberration. (pp. 365-66)

> David Evanier, "Bare Bones," in National Review (© National Review, Inc., 1982; 150 East 35th St., New York, NY 10016), Vol. XXXIV, No. 6, April 2, 1982, pp. 364-66.

GABRIEL JOSIPOVICI

Since *Herzog* Saul Bellow has been developing his own quite unique kind of novel. Like Virginia Woolf (though he wouldn't thank me for the comparison) he has gradually discovered a form of fiction in which plot counts for extremely little, but which is open enough to include almost everything. Of course Bellow's minimal plots are very different from Virginia Woolf's: instead of house-parties and village fêtes there are divorces, court cases, deaths. The setting is urban—usually Chicago, which is seen as the archetypal modern city—and the cast includes hoodlums, media men, academics and politicians. The "almost everything" also differs from Virginia Woolf's, for it includes all the horrors of slums and big cities, the rapes and muggings and killings, the greed for fame and money, and the monstrosities that go on over the whole world. Bellow wants to get Bokassa and his jewels as well as Idi Amin, Guatemala as well as Czechoslovakia, Vietnam as well as Auschwitz into his books. These must be nothing less than a long hard look at the whole of our civilization as it now stands, or totters.

Some might admire the ambition, others, more cannily, recognise its dangers. For who is Saul Bellow to tell us how we live and how we should live? Why should we listen to him rather than to anyone else? Bellow's speeches *in propria persona* are often no more than the public airing of prejudice; a book such as *To Jerusalem and Back* leaves us predominantly with a sense of the author's bigotry and arrogance. But in fiction all that is changed. Bellow, half-aware of the problem, never gives the impression in his novels that what is being said about the state of the world is being said by himself or is to be taken as the final truth on the matter. Just as important are who is saying it and why, and what pressures the character is under at the time. As with Wittgenstein we cease to listen to what is being said and instead watch the speaker's gestures. For those rantings tell us more about the character than about the objective situation. Indeed, one of Bellow's points, forcibly brought out in *The Dean's December,* is that there *is* no "objective situation", that the journalists—even super-journalists—and the scientists—even marvellously humane and concerned scientists—do not and cannot give it to us "how it is", for "it is" only how we grasp it. And this does not mean that understanding remains irremediably subjective, but that in order really to understand what is going on we must ourselves make an imaginative effort. Understanding will never simply reveal itself, it is never simply information which we can add to our existing stock; it comes only at a cost, as the result of a painful shedding of defences.

In *The Dean's December* the only things that happen are that the Dean's mother-in-law dies and a black murderer is convicted. But it is a far richer book than the sprawling and overlong *Humboldt's Gift,* which actually suffered from having too much plot. . . .

Those who know Bellow will know what to expect. I don't feel that the novel breaks any new ground, except in one respect, which I will come to in a moment. But the ground can't be gone over too often. Bellow manages to make long intellectual speeches, even internal speeches, deeply dramatic; he has an instinct for the ways in which a grey day, the bare furnishings of a room, will colour our thinking, and for the complex interconnections between daily routine and our deepest thoughts and urgings. Auden made poetry capable of bearing intelligence again, and Bellow has done the same for the novel. Yet this time I was not entirely convinced. What were once insights, discoveries, are now in danger of turning into mere tricks of style. But the problem lies deeper than that.

Bellow's heroes are all-too aware of the temptations of imagining that horror and filth are more real than beauty and humanity. They know the romantic pull of the Chicago stockyards and their human equivalent. But Bellow himself appears to have grown curiously ambivalent. In *Humboldt's Gift* he seemed to be trying to force us to admire his immersion in the real—here, he was saying, was a man who hobnobbed with gangsters, who really knew what was what, not an effete ivory tower artist. But is a Chicago gangster any more real than Miss La Trobe? Part of Bellow wants to say, no, of course not, death and loss and the sufferings of the heart are the same everywhere, there are no masses, only millions of individual human beings. But part of him also wants to say: America is where it is really happening, and Chicago is where America is happening, and here am I right in the centre of it and not flinching.

Contradictions don't matter if they are faced and recognised—indeed, the power of Bellow's novels up to *Herzog* was precisely this: his sense that only fiction could hold such contradictions together. But now there is a lack of control, a rift right at the heart of the work. In *The Dean's December,* though, this is almost compensated for by one thing: Bellow has at last created a plausible and likeable woman, and he has done so with wonderful economy. Minna, the Dean's wife, is a famous

astronomer; her dying mother was once Rumanian Minister of Health. This sounds unlikely and unpromising, but Bellow manages to create a woman who is lovable and also—to the doting Dean—often irritating in her absorption in her stars, her failure to listen to him as he puts forward his ideas. Unlike Bellow's other women she is more than a set of theories, she is palpable in her silence and her contradictions; she and her mother and aunt make of the Rumanian scenes something particularly poignant and moving.

Working with so loose a structure, with so little plot and with the possibility of introducing almost anything, via the hero's musings, into the book, Bellow needs to have a particularly firm grasp of inner form. Here his images are never mere symbols, they are real events and objects, but they take on, even if only momentarily, the resonance of something more. They can do this for us because we sense them doing so for the hero. The last brief chapter recounts the trip up to the giant telescope of Mt Palomar undertaken, on her return to America, by the astronomer and her husband. The telescope has been booked for her, and, when they arrive, she gets into her warm suit and enters the lift. It is very cold. The Dean accompanies her and then redescends, leaving her up there, small and determined, to wrestle with her stars. He thinks of that other dome, in the crematorium, half way across the world, where her mother's body disappeared forever. Momentarily he holds the two in balance. He has understood something, and so, mysteriously, have we. Not anything that can be stated in words; rather, the sum of what he and the reader have experienced in the course of the book. This is art of a very high order.

Gabriel Josipovici, *"A Foot in the Stockyard and an Eye on the Stars,"* in The Times Literary Supplement (©Times Newspapers Ltd. (London) 1982; reproduced from The Times Literary Supplement by permission), No. 4122, April 2, 1982, p. 371.

ROBERT R. DUTTON

The themes of Saul Bellow are hardly original: they include the old established counterclaims of the individual versus society and the individual in self-conflict. What Bellow offers is a clarity of vision concerning these issues that is, above all, honest. In all of his writing, Bellow faces squarely the timely issue of personal effacement and consequent degradation that every social trend seems to manifest. He never draws away from the frightening implications of an impersonal, mechanical society.

The distinctive achievement of Bellow, however, lies in his depiction of the individual in such a society, for it is the plight of the man, not society, that is emphasized throughout his work. In Bellow's world, society is rendered in an almost naturalistic manner—as an almost unchanging, indifferent, yet powerful background against which his protagonists in all of their sensitive awareness, their vitality, their frustrating absurdities, are seen. This juxtaposition of a static society and the organic individual informs all of Bellow's novels. That is, how does the individual in all of his individuality, with his dreams, aspirations, and idealism, along with his ever-present awareness of society as a naturalistic reality, find a place for himself, establish a personal and a unique identity, and still maintain an honest integrity of self? (p. 1)

[Bellow's protagonists struggle] to break through to life and to achieve their possibilities; their human potentiality; and, most importantly, their individual potentiality. But they must do so without the loss of a moral and intellectual humanism basic to their views of themselves.

Bellow's heroes, then, find the complexities of their dilemma not only in an alienation from society; they are confronted by a kind of treason within themselves, which creates an even more insoluble problem. (pp. 1-2)

Philosophically, the heroes of Bellow are in the Sartrean position of the *en-soi* versus the *pour-soi*: the being-in-itself versus the being-for-itself. Unlike the stone whose being can never transcend itself, and which is therefore complete and whole in itself, a being-in-itself, man, blessed or cursed with an imaginative consciousness, is forever in a state of self-transcendence, or in a state of being-for-itself, as well as being-in-itself. Through his imagination, man would be something other than what he is or what he seems to be; for what he is, or seems to be, is an irritatingly unsatisfying and discomfiting mystery, a mystery to which depth and breadth are given with every stretch of his imagination. Bellow's novels are narrative dramatizations of the fact of this dilemma of existence; they are a working-out not to a resolution, but to a revelation of a human condition.

Bellow the critic has spoken on this issue. In **"Distractions of a Fiction Writer"** he maintains that novelists in the past have often failed to catch the positive factor in this human equation of the *en-soi* versus the *pour-soi*. He feels that they have too often depicted the consequent seeming absurdity of man. (pp. 2-3)

This is not to say that Bellow is crying out for a new optimism, especially one founded on false postures. But neither would he accept a useless and hopeless pessimism. (p. 4)

What Bellow urges, as well as what he attempts to create in his novels, is a depiction of man as subangelic. But to define what subangelic man is, just what the term means, and, equally important, what it does not mean, it is a difficult task. The difficulty lies in the fact that the term has nothing to do with the figure observed; the meaning is to be found within the observer. Hence, all definition is subjective. "Subangelical," when applied to man, is an attitude toward man, not a description of man.

Bellow speaks of the subangelic as the "nobler assumption" that is based on the concept that man at least has the power to "overcome ignominy" and to "complete his own life." We can conjecture that by "overcome ignominy" Bellow means that any depiction of man should grant him the power to rise above the indignities of complete subjection to unseen and unknown forces, to give him a nature not totally in the chains of a miserable naturalistic impotency. Furthermore, Bellow would say that this power must be granted to man, not only because the lack of it closes debate, and not only because its alternative is unthinkable, but also because there is good reason to believe that man actually has the power to complete his own life. It may be true that this power is difficult to find through a scientific dissection or through an objective, cold analysis: its validity is to be discovered more easily in active man, in man involved. In any case, no matter what a laboratory experiment indicates and no matter what a sociological study might conclude, the nature of man is finally defined by no one but himself, and that definition must include the power of the imagination. (pp. 4-5)

Robert R. Dutton, in his Saul Bellow *(copyright © 1982 by Twayne Publishers, Inc.; reprinted with the permission of Twayne Publishers, a Division of G. K. Hall & Co., Boston) revised edition, Twayne, 1982, 212 p.*

John Berryman

1914-1972

American poet, novelist, biographer, and editor.

Berryman was a key figure in the confessional mode of post-modern poetics. His work is characterized by convoluted syntax and interior, theatrical dialogue with imaginary personae through whom Berryman explores personal concerns and torments. The most significant of these concerns appear to be his father's suicide, self-condemnation based on his break with Catholicism, and an ongoing battle with alcohol. Berryman eventually took his own life.

Although opinion varies regarding the quality of his talent and the importance of his achievement, Berryman won many awards, including the Pulitzer Prize for Poetry in 1965 for *77 Dream Songs* and the 1969 National Book Award for *His Toy, His Dream, His Rest*. His ambiguous poetry presents a universally recognized challenge to literary critics and scholars. *Dream Songs*, a long personal epic consisting of several hundred lyrical poems, is considered his most significant work and continues to be the focus of the criticism written about him.

(See also *CLC*, Vols. 1, 2, 3, 4, 6, 8, 10, 13; *Contemporary Authors*, Vols. 15-16, Vols. 33-36, rev. ed. [obituary]; and *Contemporary Authors Permanent Series*, Vol. 1.)

© Jerry Bauer

WILLIAM MEREDITH

77 Dream Songs is a fine and remarkable book of poems by any standards. (p. 27)

It is a book of powerful originality, almost of eccentricity, and it presents difficulties at first. In the remarks that follow I will try to point out what I think are its chief distinctions and delights, and also to suggest what may stand, temporarily, between these poems and a new reader. . . . Berryman has long been famous as a poet's poet, with the contradiction that that forlorn phrase carries. This book should make him famous with everyone who uses modern poetry at all.

Two statements by the author about the Dream Songs are suggestive of how the poems are meant to be taken. Reading some of them in public two years ago he said, and has since allowed to be printed: "The poem is about a man who is apparently named Henry, or says he is. He has a tendency to talk about himself in the third person. His last name is in doubt. It's given at one point as Henry House and at other points as Henry Pussy-cat. He has a friend, moreover, who addresses him regularly as Mr. Bones, or some variation on that. Some of the sections . . . are really dialogues." In the present book he adds: "These are sections, constituting one version, of a poem in progress. . . . Many opinions and errors in the Songs are to be referred not to the character Henry, still less to the author, but to the title of the work."

In both cases the poet speaks of the poems as a single work, in spite of the fact that the eighteen-line Songs are often self-contained lyrics. And by calling attention to the dubious identity of "a man apparently named Henry," . . . Berryman suggests that the unity of the work lies in its being the dream-autobiography of the central character. Whether this character calls himself *I* or *he*, Henry or Mr. Bones, his identity doesn't change. What does shift, with dreamlike uncertainty, is the relationship of the dreamer to his dream self. . . . (pp. 27-8)

The discovery of Henry's whole identity, by him and by us, comprises the plot of the poem. It is a narrative poem and, as is true of a lot of literature, to discover its unity is to discover its meaning. (p. 28)

Henry gradually emerges . . . as a wholesome clean-cut American Proteus, a man with as many selves as our dreams confer. He commands the idiom, rhythm and experience of a jazzman, both old-style New Orleans and hipster-junkie. He is equally at home with—or, more exactly, he can adapt himself with alcohol or Eastern philosophy to—a meeting of the Modern Language Association. . . . He has read a lot more than I have and is more implicated in what he reads. He is generous, moral and manic, but also lecherous, alcoholic and depressive. Three songs treat directly with insanity. . . . But through all the changes of his dreams the character and the voice remain so individual that you would no more mistake a song of Henry's, finally, than you would a meditation of Leopold Bloom's.

Henry's agonizing and beautiful energy is like that of Joyce's hero in another respect: it is profoundly, essentially humorous. The subconscious, which is chiefly what *Ulysses* and the Dream Songs record, knows no deliberate mode. It is not serious or joking, tragic or comic. It combines but doesn't rationally select, so that rational incongruity, a source of humor, is its habit. . . . (pp. 28-9)

Henry is an imaginary Negro . . . and the poems draw on the several levels of humor that we owe to the Negro. Some of it runs deep and bitter, as it does in the blues, where only language and rhythm remain playful and even the word-play bites. . . . (p. 29)

Some of Henry's dreams are monologues and dialogues in the dialect of Negro vaudeville, a double-edged joke where the Negro plays it both cunning and obsequious, like an Elizabethan Fool, to amuse both himself and his slower-witted master. But Henry, being only an imaginary Negro, speaks mostly in a black-face parody of this, the vaudeville dialect of The Two Black Crows and Stepin Fetchit—a speech that has a rich, shrewd, rather brutal history in our national humor. Berryman refers once . . . to Henry's "burnt-cork luck." The phrase could be applied to the success with which this dialect gets at the truth in a world where the Negro's situation is both a symptom and a metaphor of our failure. The world is acutely perceived, in all its wonderful incomprehensibility, in this dialect. . . . But against this perception is set the cliché of rational, white man's speech and the oversimplified, disastrous culture which that speech accommodates. . . . (p. 30)

But these Negro masks are only one of Henry's identities. It would be more accurate to describe the hero of this poem as an imaginary madman. He identifies himself easily and completely with every sort of person and situation, even some that are totally unsympathetic. He has the inability of the insane to distinguish between things that are merely alike, and it is this that charges his metaphors with so much force. They are no longer implied comparisons but terrible uncertainties of identity. . . . [Berryman often] holds to an insane accuracy of colloquial idiom and low image at moments when a sane man would be driven naturally to a more formal rhetoric. . . . (pp. 31-2)

Madman and black-face are real identities of the "man who is apparently named Henry," who is looking for wisdom and truth along with his identity. He insists on *wording* himself and his world exactly, as though the mystery might lie in words. . . . The poems seem to escape mannerism because Berryman never takes his eye off the scene, the event, the mood of Henry's dream. A grand style, or its parody, is frequently used. . . . As various as they are, we learn to recognize Henry's characteristic ways of wording himself and together they make a character. (p. 32)

77 Dream Songs seems to me to deserve [a place at the top of Berryman's accomplishments]. Moving forward with the intensity of vision that characterized *Mistress Bradstreet* and with the range of common experience of *The Dispossessed,* this work is free of the slight air of bookishness that hovered over Berryman's earlier work. (It is an air that hovers over all but the luckiest of modern poems.) The Dream Songs use a diction of their own, one that owes little to the familiar though flexible diction of current poetic practice. The language seems to spring naturally from the gusto (insane? holy?) with which Henry makes the human scene. . . . (p. 33)

> William Meredith, "*Henry Tasting All the Secret Bits of Life: Berryman's 'Dream Songs',*" in Wisconsin Studies in Contemporary Literature (© 1965, Wisconsin Studies in Contemporary Literature), *Vol. VI, No. 1, Winter-Spring, 1965, pp. 27-33.*

CLIVE JAMES

If the contention is accepted that an excess of clarity is the only kind of difficulty a work of art should offer, John Berryman's *Dream Songs* . . . have been offering several kinds of unacceptable difficulty since they first began to appear. It was confusedly apparent in the first volume of the work, *77 Dream Songs,* that several different personalities within the poet's single personality (one doesn't suggest his "real" personality, or at any rate one didn't suggest it at that stage) had been set talking to and of each other. These personalities, or let them be called characters, were given tones of voice, even separate voices with peculiar idioms. The interplays of voice and attitude were not easy to puzzle out, and many reviewers, according to Mr. Berryman and their own subsequent and sometimes abject admissions, made howlers. With this new volume of 308 more dream songs comes a rather impatient corrective from the author pointing out how simple it all is.

Well, the first book was not simple. It was difficult. In fact it was garbled, and the reviewers who said so and later took it back are foolish. *His Toy, His Dream, His Rest,* this new and longer book, is simpler, with many of the severally voiced conversational devices abandoned. Its difficulties are more of texture than of structure: the plan is less schematic but the indulgences are proportionately greater, eccentricity proliferating as the original intellectualized, constructional gimmicks fold up under the pressure of released expression. There are passages that are opaque and likely to remain so. Some of the language is contorted in a way designed to disguise the platitudinous as a toughly guarded verity. The range of reference is very wide (the *Dream Songs,* like dreams in sleep, draw freely and solidly on the cultural memory), but there are some references which go well beyond the legitimately omnivorous curiosity of the poetic intelligence and achieve impenetrable privacy through not being, like most of the rest, explained by their general context.

This last, the general context, is the true structure of Berryman's complete book of 385 individual, but not isolated, lyrics. It is not wise to contend that the ambitions of Structure (with a capital "S") can go hang, the individual lyrics being all that matters. In fact, the lyrics mostly explain each other's difficulties—sometimes across long distances—by tilting themes to a different angle, revisiting a location, repeating a cadence or redefining a point. It was Yeats's way and for that matter it was Petrarch's—the long poem as an arrangement of small ones. One proof that this is the operative structure in the *Dream Songs* is that the work feels more comfortable to read as one gets further into it. But if it is not wise to say that the structure is nothing and the individual lyric everything, it is still less wise to say that the work is unintelligible without a perception of its grand design. It is unlikely that a clear account of such a grand design will ever be forthcoming. . . . It will probably not be possible to chart the work's structure in the way that the *Divine Comedy,* for example, can be charted out in its themes, zones and stylistic areas. The development of the *Dream Songs* is much more a development by accretion: Ezra Pound and William Carlos Williams are the two obvious models. An indication of this is the already mentioned fact that the multi-voiced interplay of *77 Dream Songs* is in these later ones not so much in evidence: as a device it has yielded to ideas more productive, especially to the unabashed elegiac strain, sonorous as lamenting bagpipes, which in many ways makes this new book a convocation of the literary ghosts. One feels at the end of this new volume that there is no reason, except for the necessary eventual loss of inspiration, why the work shouldn't go on literally for ever—just as the *Cantos,* whose material is *un*digested information (Berryman digests his), could obviously go on to fill a library. The work has no pre-set confining shape to round it out, and one doesn't see why the 385th song need absolutely be the last one—not in the way one sees that the last line of the *Divine Comedy,* for many previously established reasons, must bring the poem to an end.

In brief, with the **Dream Songs** Berryman has found a way of pouring in everything he knows while still being able to tackle his themes one, or a few, at a time. Attacking its own preliminary planning and reducing it to material, the progressive structure advances to fill the space available for it—a space whose extent the author cannot in the beginning accurately guess at but must continue with the poem in order to discern.

The **Dream Songs** are thus a modern work, a work in which it is possible for the reader to dislike poem after poem and idea after idea without imagining that what he likes could have come into existence without what he dislikes. (pp. 53-5)

[**Dream Songs** have] a structure, and will continue to have it even when the scholars say they do. That is the thing to remember, that and the fact that the structure is inside rather than overall. Especially when a long poem is such a present to the academics as this one is, the humane student is engaged in a fight for possession from the very outset: he needs to remember that to be simplistic is to lose the fight. He must admit complication—certainly here, for the **Dream Songs** are extremely complicated, having almost the complexity of memory itself. They depend on the perception that the mind is not a unity but a plurality, and by keeping the talk going between these mental components, by never (or not often) lapsing into a self-censoring monologue, they convey their special sense of form. It's even possible to say that the poorest sections of the work are the sections where the poet's sense of himself is projected into it as a pose—where an attitude is struck and remains unquestioned in a work of art whose unique quality is to question all attitudes through the critical recollection of their history and a sensitive awareness of all the clichés attendant on the concept of the creative personality. And the personality in play is, all along, the creative one: the central motive of the **Dream Songs** can be defined as an attempt by a poet to examine himself without lapsing into self-regard. (pp. 55-6)

[Obviously,] in what is mainly the story of a poet who is currently writing a poem which sounds remarkably like the one the reader is reading, the poet *is* the hero, a fact readily ascertainable from the amount of autobiographical material being used, some of which would be embarrassing if not rendered neutral by the poem's universalizing mechanisms, and some of which is not rendered neutral and consequently *is* embarrassing. The question is always being turned up, as the reader ploughs on, of whether the author *knows* that every so often a certain insensitivity, a certain easily recognizable "creative" belligerence, is getting through unqualified to the page. Here and only here is the central character "me" in the raw sense: in the refined sense the "me" is representative of all artists and hence of all men in their authentically productive moments. The embarrassments are probably best accepted as a contributory quality, a few turns of the stomach consequent upon the many thrills. The poem's devices of voicing are not meant to distance personality but to reveal it: the doubts begin when we suspect that attitudes are reaching us which the poet has not analysed, that he does not realize he is being revealing in a crude sense. But really there are bound to be these. The important thing to say here is that the personality in the poem,

manifold, multiform and self-examining in an obsessive way, keeps all one's attention. The language never settles into anything less than readability, and even when the restlessness becomes a shaken glamour in which one can see little, it is evident that something is being worried at: we are not just being dazzled with an attempt to churn meaning into existence. There is not much fake significance, though quite a lot of blurred.

Thematically, these new songs are first of all a disorderly, desperate and besotted funeral for Berryman's literary heroes, who might be called, following the author's own terminology, the "lovely men." Of these, Delmore Schwartz is easily the star. His decline is convincingly (one hopes fairly) illustrated. There are sketches towards blaming this writer's collapse on society at large, but there is also a more powerful evocation of a sheer inability to cope. . . . In the new book the simple admiration for the masters continues, but in Schwartz's case (and to a lesser extent in Randall Jarrell's) it goes a long way beyond admiration, and a good deal deeper than craft, into a disturbed exploration of the artist's way of life in America now—and this concern again, through the internalizing way the poem has, is referred back to the condition of the poet-narrator, a condition of physical crack-up and a fearful but no longer postponable facing of the unpalatable truths. (pp. 56-7)

A lack of "good taste" is one of Berryman's strengths, in the sense that he can range anywhere for images without a notion of fitness barring his way. But positive *bad* taste is one of his weaknesses. His tough, anti-intellectual line on the American virtues can bore you in an instant by the insensitivity of delivery alone. There are moments when Berryman writing sounds a bit like John Wayne talking. For all his absorptive capacity for the fine details of life, Berryman's conception of America and of civilization itself seems cornily limited, and even the book's elegiac strain, its congested keening for the gifted dead, edges perilously close to an elementary romanticism whose informing assumption is the withdrawal of support by the gods. Waiting for the end, boys. But at their best the **Dream Songs** are a voice near your ear that you listen to, turn towards and find that you must turn again; a voice all around you, unpinnable to a specific body; your own voice, if you had lived as long and could write in so condensed a way; a voice not prepossessing, but vivid and somehow revivifying. (pp. 57-8)

Clive James, "On John Berryman's 'Dream Songs'" (originally published in The Times Literary Supplement, *No. 3513, June 26, 1969), in his* First Reactions: Critical Essays, 1968-1979 *(copyright © 1974, 1980 by Clive James; reprinted by permission of Alfred A. Knopf, Inc.; in Canada by Literistic, Ltd.),* Knopf, 1980, pp. 53-8.

ROBERT PHILLIPS

"These Songs are not meant to be understood, you understand. / They are only meant to terrify & comfort," John Berryman wrote in his 366th Dream Song. And understood many have not been. Packed with private jokes, topical and literary allusions . . . , they boggle many minds. . . . The situation was considerably beclouded when, four years [after the first **77 Dream Songs** were published in 1964,] Berryman dumped on the world a truckful of 308 additional Dream Songs, under the title **His Toy, His Dream, His Rest.**

This latter title could apply to all the Dream Songs. At once Berryman's plaything, hope for immortality, and major achievement, after which he could repose, the cycle consists of 385 impossible dialogues by Berryman with his possible selves. Daydreaming and nightmaring on the printed page, Berryman broke from his earlier, academic, Audenesque verse into confessions of over-drinking, over-smoking, over-sexing, pill-popping, whathaveyou. That these poems are confessions is undeniable—though Berryman claimed they are about a character named Henry. (p. 92)

Of the two volumes, the second and fatter is the superior. For this reader, **77 Dream Songs,** with its twisted syntax, Negro minstrel-show dialogue . . . , and the sheer sloppiness of its several sequences has not worn well. . . . **His Toy, His Dream, His Rest** is more coherent, and the minstrel friend is kept in the wings for most of the performance. Moreover, many of the second set of Dream Songs give off a great shimmer of beauty.

The difference is the difference in the poet at the time of composition. **77 Dream Songs** seems the work of some randy contender, youthful despite his years. **His Toy, His Dream, His Rest** is mellow, sad, and at times maudlin. Death in the first book is discussed in detail only in several poems centering on Robert Frost . . . and in one brief stanza on his father's suicide. The second collection, on the other hand, is filled with accounts of friends' deaths and suicides, events which took their toll on Berryman's psyche. . . . These personal losses were experienced during a time of great public loss as well: John Kennedy, Robert Kennedy, Martin Luther King, Ernest Hemingway, William Faulkner. Yet none of these personal or public deaths figure so importantly in the volume as the suicide of Berryman's father which is, in one sense, the sole subject of the latter collection.

What these losses did to Berryman the man can be deduced from the great number of poems on death or contemplated suicide. . . . Indeed the first fourteen Dream Songs of the second volume are designated as ''op. post.,'' as if written after the fact of the poet's death. Only one Dream Song in all, number 259, seems directly counteractive and assertive of joy in life: ''My desire for death was strong / but never strong enough. I thought: This is my chance, / I can bear it.'' That the desire for the grave became stronger and overcame the desire to accept the chance and bear up to life, was tragically made public on January 7, 1972, when spectators saw Berryman jump from a bridge onto the ice of the Mississippi River. (pp. 93-4)

[Though] both collections are confessional, the second is far more personal, bearing greater witness to Berryman's attempt to confront his past. (p. 94)

Berryman was a long time coming to a method which would allow him to expiate his guilt, to confront his demons if not exorcize them. His earliest verse was . . . elegant, his mentors Auden, Housman, Hopkins, and Yeats. Only when he wrote **Homage to Mistress Bradstreet** (1956), a long, intricate and anguished poem, did he break with literary tradition and find his own quirky style. . . . But using Mistress Bradstreet as self-spokesman was only partially satisfactory or satisfying, and it was through Berryman's later development of the *personae* of Berryman/Henry/Mr. Bones that the poet was able to let go.

And let go he did, for 385 Dream Songs' worth. . . . It is this third-person singular device which struck a necessary note of

distance in the Dream Songs. Whereas Anne Sexton's best work is her most personal . . . , the reverse is true of Berryman. So long as Berryman does not wallow in the first-person singular, he is capable of striking, if not important, poetry; after the completion of the Dream Songs, unfortunately, he chose to do so. . . . His last works are his least. In them, something seems to have happened to the poet or the poet's method; the two books which came after **The Dream Songs—** **Love & Fame** and **Delusions, Etc.**—were derived from the same imagination and the same life; but the result was altogether different. (pp. 96-7)

[**Love & Fame** is] the most blatantly self-aggrandizing sequence of autobiographical poems. . . . [In it] Berryman clearly came to equate fame with money. The book also demonstrates that for him love had become equated with lust. It is this self-aggrandizement and lack of compassion which make Berryman's late confessions a series of false notes. Instead of confessing for therapeutic or purgative purposes, he appears to have done so to gratify his formidable ego. . . . Rather than displaying moral courage, these poems display instead immoral callowness. In place of love and fame, we have lust and notoriety.

These tendencies were present in **The Dream Songs,** of course, but were held in check by Berryman's use of the Henry *persona*. When in **Love & Fame** he abandons altogether the third-person singular fiction, he gifts us only with unprecedented breast-beating. The Dream Songs are motivated by the ego; **Love & Fame** is sheer vanity. Berryman tries to make himself egoistic, but in fact becomes egotistic—which is why his confessions seem false. (p. 97)

[**Love & Fame** reveals] much of what is wrong with bad confessional poetry, and can educate us to what makes a confessional poem go wrong. (p. 98)

Mr. Berryman, alas, was toting up his relative successes in the game of love and the game of fame. And about love Mr. Berryman seemed to know sadly little, though of lust he wrote a lot. The poems literally attest to his status as a ''sexual athlete.'' . . . We would suggest that [his] catalog of sexual performances, without passion or personal commitment to other values than satisfying the itch, is indicative of the poet's total lack of commitment to other higher values as well.

About fame Mr. Berryman is equally boastful, and the matter-of-fact attitude toward celebrity found in Dream Song 133 . . . has vanished. (pp. 98-9)

Being famous, of course, provides opportunities for the poet to meet others famous. Berryman, I fear, is guilty of dropping names as readily as he says he drops his trousers, and always on a first-name basis so that the reader can see how very well he knows them. . . . The truth seems to be, Berryman is guilty of the sin of *hubris*, a sin which has been the downfall of greater men than he. Here he brags as much about his friendships as he does his money. Berryman's *hubris* is not a trait as in the Aristotelian hero's fall. The reader will neither thrill with horror nor melt with pity at what takes place. He might be a little disgusted though. (p. 99)

[Berryman also] writes about receiving ''elephant checques'' for his readings and books. . . .

If the amount of money a poet makes seems a supremely trivial topic for poetry, it is absolutely Olympian when compared to some of Berryman's others. He writes of losing the vice-presidency of his class in school. . . . One poem is on getting a

C in a course at Columbia. . . . These could be topics for poems, of course: ironic or spritely light verse by John Betjeman or deliberately deprecating and played-down lines by Philip Larkin. But in Berryman's heavy hands they are mawkish at best. . . . Is the poet guilty of overwriting or, worse, of failing to see through the personal experience to the poetic experience? This can be seen as a major fault of bad confessional poetry, and time and again Berryman seems unwilling to sacrifice the personal meaning to the poetic.

Berryman's questionable topics are at times elevated by superior poetics, as they indeed are in certain of the Dream Songs. But in fact his rhetoric and glib abbreviations and slang here help not at all. (p. 100)

Moreover, there seem to be no memorable images or metaphors in *Love & Fame*. . . . Weighing the six hundred pages of his last four books, Berryman might have done well to heed Ezra Pound's dictum: "It is better to present one image in a lifetime than to produce voluminous works."

All that has gone wrong can be examined in the book's first poem, **"Her & It."** The "it" ultimately is fame, and how it gets in the way of the poet's recovering his past. But initially "it" is also the vagina of a girl the poet once knew; or, as Berryman indelicately puts it, "a gash." The poet in times past seems to have been in love with a disembodied female organ, if one trusts the poem. In stanza one he conjectures that this "gash" must now have "seven lousy children," though why the children should be lousy is not indicated. (pp. 100-01)

The second stanza is offensive for a different reason: the poet wishes the girl would now write to him. . . . The famous poet boasts about his correspondence. . . . Stanza three continues the *hubris*. . . .

The fourth stanza contains the offensive description of Berryman's "elephant checques," plus the observation that his Dream Songs are selling well in Tokyo and Paris, and that his publishers are very friendly both in New York and London. . . .

In the fifth stanza the poet compares his reputation to that of Saul (Bellow, of course, but with Poundian pride unidentified). Berryman further lets the reader know he himself was in *Time* magazine the year before. . . . (p. 101)

The poem concludes with the promising line, "She muttered something in my ear I've forgotten as we danced." Promising, because for the first time in a poem titled **"Her & It"** we finally have a portrayal of the "her" in a human (as opposed to dehumanized, disembodied, anatomical) way. The poem's missed potentialities are for a moving contrast between human relations when one is an unknown lover and when one is a famous poet. But all the bravura and insecurity of the narrator have stood between him and the unrealized poem.

Berryman in his last poems seems to have eschewed [syntactical and rhetorical synthesis completely]. . . . (p. 102)

Which is not to say the entire collection is ragged. Part four [of *Love & Fame*], subtitled **"Eleven Addresses to the Lord,"** reveals (briefly) a Berryman capable of contemplation, reminding us of the religious poet of Dream Songs 194 and 234. It was a mode he was to continue in the first section of *Delusions, Etc.* as well. In these eleven short lyrics *hubris* is displaced by what would appear to be a genuine humility. . . . The self-aggrandizement gives way to a search for salvation.

The poet here admits he does not know all the answers, but is willing to commend his spirit into the hands of the Lord, and "Whatever your end may be, accept my amazement." Berryman's choice of the word "amazement" is fresh and vital within this context, and the entire sequence possesses imagery and insight superior to the callow autobiography which precedes it. . . . (pp. 102-03)

Delusions, Etc., which, unlike the posthumous books of Sylvia Plath, was given order by the poet himself and seen in proof before he died, shows the extroverted poet to have assumed a new tone of humility in his final years. If *Love & Fame* was Berryman's loudest work, *Delusions, Etc.* is surely his quietest. The pathetic boasting and glory-seeking somehow segued into movements of melancholy and finally of cold despair. (p. 104)

The fame so touted in the former book is now seen, perhaps more realistically, as only "half-fame." The lust which has supplanted love is now replaced by tenderness for a wife and worship of God. Berryman was surely moving in these directions with the **"Eleven Addresses to the Lord"** which conclude *Love & Fame.* Beginning where that book left off, *Delusions, Etc.* opens with a group of eight meditations. But a return to Catholicism is not to save the poet, any more than a return to the origins of his boyhood and youth had done in the previous volume. All are, as the title testifies, delusions, etc. He is still sick in life and more than ever haunted by death. . . . Berryman seems more forgiving than before, now calling his father merely a man who was "not . . . very able." It is as though, in his own new-found humility, Berryman was finally able to forgive others. Even his suicidal father.

This humility is best expressed in the opening section, **"Opus Dei."** . . . (pp. 104-05)

The third section is a mixed bag of thirteen poems on various personal, theological, and historical topics. A fourth, arranged as a scherzo, briefly) reintroduces the figure of Henry (from *The Dream Songs*). Henry's randyness has turned to pure despair. **"Henry By Night"** depicts Berryman's insomnia, night sweats, and shakes, concluding, "Something's gotta give." **"Henry's Understanding,"** a companion piece, presents the poet's certainty that some day he will take his own life. . . . (p. 105)

The fifth and final section, meditations and reflections, culminates in **"The Facts & Issues,"** the true climax to the book and to Berryman's life ("*Let this be it.* I've *had* it. I can't wait"), though a short poem (**"King David Dances"**) follows as a sort of coda. In David's dance before the Ark, as in Beethoven's death, Berryman perceives a joyful triumph after trial and adversity. In the Beethoven poem we find identification by the poet with the composer; let us hope that in his vision of the survival of art after the death of the maker ("You're all over my wall! / You march and chant around here! I hear your thighs") Berryman saw and believed in a probable parallel in his own life and work. *Delusions, Etc.* is not Berryman's best book. But it redeems his reputation, tarnished so badly by the offenses of *Love & Fame.* (pp. 105-06)

Robert Phillips, "Balling the Muse," in The North American Review *(reprinted by permission from* The North American Review; *copyright © 1971 by the University of Northern Iowa), Vol. 257, No. 4, Winter, 1971-72 (and reprinted as "John Berryman's Literary Offenses," in his* The Confessional Poets, *Southern Illinois University Press, 1973, pp. 92-106).*

ARTHUR OBERG

The Dream Songs are distracting and distractions. They are *His Toy, His Dream, His Rest*, as Berryman indicates in the title of the second volume of poems which, together with *77 Dream Songs*, form the long work. [In addition to refusing to yield what they are about, Berryman's poems] are distracting in other regards as well, especially in the insistence and self-consciousness from which they proceed. The 385 poems, or songs, draw attention to themselves in every possible way: by their sheer number, by their language, by their range in knowledge, thinking and feeling, and style. The poems build toward an elliptical long poem that seems unwilling to end. . . . Through the voices assumed in the poems, the poet becomes his own public relations man, as well as a man at the mercy of the public relations of literary reputations. Berryman, who in life could manage a loud speaking voice, finds comparable pitch and volume in many of the dream poems. The poems display the paraphernalia of mikes, broadcasts, spotlights, gramophones, P.A. systems, televisions, radios, telephones, and box-office attractions. Repeatedly, Berryman's voices are scored for bravura and brass. (pp. 49-50)

As the dream songs alternate between manic and depressive maneuvers, perhaps a modern equivalent of Thomas Nashe's "queerly schizophrenic" style, Berryman complicates both extremes by similar, paradoxical impressions. (p. 53)

Berryman composes out of a love which never seems adequate to or in expression. At times, this love takes on the sexual-aesthetic dimensions of the work of Walt Whitman or Hart Crane. Significantly, these poets are among the artists most prominent throughout the dream songs.

"It's a matter of love." But Berryman uses every imaginable device to deflect that fact, however simpler the syntax of the later poems became. The poet gains distance by proceedings that assume the force of a method and a dialectic. The poems . . . insist upon coming to their world obliquely. The poet distances his material through the persona of Henry and, in turn, through Henry's ability to shift person and voice, face and style; through lending things the impersonality of anecdote and bad joke and tale; and through devoting whole poems or strategic portions of poems to forestalling criticism of *The Dream Songs* as a long poem.

Berryman also, ironically, achieves distance by "letting out" so much love that a reader or audience has no option at times but to seek invisibility. Pathetic, bathetic moments create their own spaces of reserve, whether or not the poet chooses to point the way back to feeling and however much or little he may feel called on to help. Sometimes, in the course of a poem, Berryman is able to move beyond a heart-rending plea for a "vision of friendlies" to discover a more acceptable and finally more moving lyricism. . . . At home or abroad, Berryman addresses what is a recurrent dilemma for him as a needy, wanting poet and man.

Berryman's deflection in the dream songs, then, is not what it might first seem. Evasive poetic ways never completely disguise feeling which the poet often gives the impression of trying to skirt. Attempts at evading feeling by using minstrel blackface and impersonal, slangy idioms work both ambiguously and not ambiguously at all: "— You is from hunger, Mr. Bones," Berryman writes in Dream Song no. 76. The very vulnerability and need, intended for denial, not only are admitted but underlined. Vaudeville turns, introduced to create distance, in part bridge that distance and even can conclude by becoming "hel-

lish." Related to this method, Henry's tales, started about someone else, end by being about a first-person Henry: "So. / I am her." . . . (pp. 53-6)

The distinctiveness of *The Dream Songs* resides in how the crises in feeling recorded by the poet have to be dealt with, moment by moment, as artfully as the poet knows how. . . . The poems break off, resume, only to give way to the welling up of new feeling. Recurrently, emotion gives the impression of beginning *in medias res*. . . . (pp. 56-7)

"Need" and "love" are among the most insistent words and foci in *The Dream Songs*. They are as insistent as Lear's "no"'s and "nothing"'s, and as pathetic as some of the later moments in that play where "need" and "love" also figure so centrally. . . . Need and love extend beyond the particular contexts to assume dimensions which are archetypal. An urgency appears in these songs which the *Short Poems* and the *Sonnets* noticeably lacked. (pp. 57-8)

Considerations of love and need caused Berryman to raise questions that are at once abstract and intensely personal. . . . In the course of *The Dream Songs*, Berryman creates more complications about matters of need and love than he can ever begin to untangle. (pp. 58-9)

Berryman assigns to "the concept 'love'" . . . a weight and an intensity that are inordinate. Such extreme burdens are placed upon love that Berryman significantly surrounds it, as word and as concept, with quotation marks. In the case of the deaths of his father and his friend, Delmore Schwartz, to whose "sacred memory" *His Toy, His Dream, His Rest* is dedicated, Berryman's love is so overwhelming in what it would give and in what it needs to be sufficient that it almost "dies" from him. The rhetoric proves to be more than a stylistic device. It represents a typical, defining movement in all of Berryman's work. Commonly, in the guise of a negative syntax or dialectic Berryman sets down his most mystical, loving words. (p. 60)

For Berryman, an acknowledgement of "overneeds," the need for "extra love" or "surplus love," causes him not to abandon man in the contradictions that surround him. Instead, Berryman begins where he can begin, with what defines man and makes him unique, his capacity for language and love. Love may not last, and need may linger on. But this does not stop Berryman from loving and "versing." Out of this situation, *The Dream Songs* proceed, like self-generated love songs or "Valentines." What the poet seeks is the creation of a community of caring friends, men and women who will share with him their talk and love. (pp. 60-1)

That the Dream Songs are love poems becomes most obvious in the lyric-linguistic bias of Berryman's work. In the elegies and *"Op. posth."* pieces, Berryman insistently links the figure of poet and lover. Love and expression are one. (p. 61)

Versing in *The Dream Songs* . . . joins the sexual to the aesthetic. Berryman's numerous memorial poems link the "heart" and "art" of love; his rhyming "heart" and "art" functions as instructively as his "need" and "seed" does in other contexts. The poet-figures Berryman eulogizes in his poems are remembered for writing well, for crafting poems as an act of love. Translators and translations also become, respectively, workers and works of love.

Berryman joins himself in *The Dream Songs* to poets like W. C. Williams and Randall Jarrell, Delmore Schwartz and Sylvia Plath. These poets, as Berryman views them, also made "a good sound" out of love. That poet-critics like Robert Lowell and William Meredith have written some of the best criticism of Berryman reveals similar connections. Such men entered into the loving, writing community which Berryman so desperately came to depend upon. The community of caring friends which Berryman established in *Homage to Mistress Bradstreet* between himself and that one poet is infinitely enlarged in *The Dream Songs* to range more freely among countries, cultures, and centuries; and this community intently seeks comfort in numbers. (pp. 61-2)

Each Dream Song makes a new attempt at expression and love. Berryman never deceives himself about the labor involved. He knows the risky attractiveness of silence and refuses to turn *The Dream Songs* into dejection odes. . . . But this is the Berryman of *The Dream Songs;* the later poems and books and suicide are still to come. (p. 62)

Berryman draws our attention [to the link between] that of art and of love.

Whether Berryman's poetic expression in *The Dream Songs* will be adequate merges into fears for his sexual potency. Mikes, gramophones, telephones, pens, and pencils link the instrument of expression or communication with phallic strength and length. Berryman's Henry alternately boasts and fears for his sexual-aesthetic self. . . . In the course of *The Dream Songs* no humor is too indecorous for Berryman, whose habit of sexual punning becomes notorious: "whole," "country," "come," "lay," "piece," "stub point," "Venus." But Berryman's puns seldom are indulgent. They often return the reader to what is an important center in the poems. "Venus" can be both Goddess of Love and brand of pencil. "Lay" can be both song and "lovely fuck." Berryman manages to pass so effortlessly from love to art or from woman to poem that the two continually merge, sometimes happily, into one. . . . (p. 63)

In some very intimate way, Berryman may remind the reader of the Calvinist who, although finally uncertain of salvation, must go on to act as if he were to be among the saved. Berryman wrote *The Dream Songs,* aware of the contradictions and ambiguities of man and of man's art. . . . [The] cost involved in that effort helps to explain the continuing distractions along the way: the quirky syntax, extreme topical references and the range of styles included in the poems. (p. 64)

"The horror of unlove." To move from "unlove" to love—this is what these poems are all about. The prefix "un-" recurs throughout the poems. It proves symptomatic both of how the poems proceed and how they must be read (unread?). . . . But, even more important, it is symbolic of the kinds of seemingly contractory movements and maneuvers which take place in so many of the poems. (p. 65)

Lyric by loving lyric, *The Dream Songs* proceed. As separate poems. Yet in the process, Berryman simultaneously moves toward the creation of a long poem, *the* long poem to the extent that his intentions, ambition, and craft will allow. The second volume of the songs, *His Toy, His Dream, His Rest,* reveals increasing attention given to the progress and process of what Berryman has chosen to take on. The procedure assumes the enormity of a life work in art. (p. 66)

Berryman places himself in that long line of American poets who also wrote long poems: Whitman, Crane, Pound, Eliot Stevens and Williams. Pound's "MAKE IT NEW" and Williams's "Invent" consciously figure in Berryman's long poem. . . . (p. 68)

Berryman's concern in writing a long American poem determines many concerns within the work. These are concerns which both join him to and separate him from the poet of the *Cantos.* Berryman reveals in *The Dream Songs* several things: a large fund of Puritanical guilt; a search for an adequate tradition and for ancestors; a preoccupation with "know-how" and with the "labour" that never seems to get done. . . . Work, for Berryman, the born Catholic, amounts to nothing less than Puritan exorcism and prayer.

Berryman complicates a particularly American thrust in the poem by an extension of his work not only to a European and Western humanistic past, but to an Eastern culture he finds attractive as a sensibility and as an art form. (p. 69)

What Berryman seems to intend for *The Dream Songs* is the stature of a work that can manage national and international naive and elitist styles. . . . How the poem should be judged became an obsessive concern for Berryman. Sections of poems hammer away at the would-be critic. . . . In the *Sonnets,* Berryman had also seen the problems involved in the ability or inability of criticism to handle innovative, long works. . . . (p. 70)

Berryman's ambitions for *The Dream Songs* as epic work raise considerations not unlike those of Williams's *Paterson* or Lowell's *Life Studies* or *Notebook* poems. In all these works, there are epic dimensions, just as there are narrative, satiric, and dramatic modes. Yet, in the end, it is as lyric or lyric sequences that these poems most profoundly proceed and succeed, if they succeed at all.

Despite Berryman's use of "Books" and some of the machinery of epic, his long poem continually makes its way and creates its impact by means of lyrical images of loss and love. Successful individual poems stand more autonomously than Berryman might have intended. Lyric power is most in evidence, while Berryman struggles with the epic unity of the work. (pp. 70-1)

The lyrical center of *The Dream Songs,* once located, brings with it considerable problems for the poet and for the reader. The intensities and compressions which involve Berryman commonly result in creating an impression of an impersonal, lyric voice. As with Berryman's ambitions for *The Dream Songs* as epic work, his lyricism runs the risk of pushing language more and more to the foreground at the expense of whatever was to be done or said or sung.

Part of Berryman's dilemma in his long poem derives from a continuing attempt to move toward some pure, ultimate song. . . . (p. 71)

The attraction to some kind of final poetry Berryman often expresses in analogies from music and painting, definitively nonverbal media. And, beyond that, he links such poetry with those moments or achievements in music and painting which seem to him most extreme in their accomplishment, the accomplishment of notes or brush-strokes almost beyond the human reaches of art—the particular intensities of Mozart and Beethoven, Van Gogh and Renoir. Berryman knows the costly effort of his undertaking and of the undertaking of all major, absolute art. . . .

Berryman's program for *The Dream Songs* is at once inclusive and exclusive. It is exculsive in its content and in the elitist, Yeatsean audience it imagines. It is inclusive to the point of having Berryman wish nothing or no one, living or dead, escape from the work. This inclusiveness, instead of being comforting, turns into a nightmare of proliferation where, after endless ledgering, Berryman lets no one go. . . . (p. 72)

The risks of language replacing life never disperse themselves completely in *The Dream Songs*. . . . At times, instead of reverting to Berryman, the construct which we encounter as *The Dream Songs* looks like an inadequate, deflective substitute for life. . . . It is not that Berryman is unaware of the dangers of an implicit, marginal decadence. The humor he can manage in its face can be considerable. . . . But in many of the . . . songs there is less of a conscious, real struggle between the claims of art and life. Too often pen threatens to replace penis. Love and life tend to be kept at too comfortable and safe a distance. What begins as a humorous retelling of a story barely hides what is occurring, namely art replacing sex as source and organ. . . . (pp. 73-4)

In *The Dream Songs* Berryman's language frequently suffers from the masturbatory indulgence we meet in characters and in the language of characters, in Genet and Albee, in Bellow and Salinger and Roth. (p. 74)

Berryman, by giving language a more and more prominent place in his work, necessarily commits himself to the risks of leaving out or obscuring feeling. It is that fund of feeling which major poetry must somehow manage to embrace. From the *Sonnets* to *The Dream Songs*, Berryman's "words," or *"mots,"* "fly," The *Sonnets*, although written about an actual affair, exceed the sonneteers' conventional attention to his poor, inadequate art. And *The Dream Songs* turn a traditional concern of the poet with language into an obsessive, even pathological motif. In theory, the world which Berryman wishes to create in his long poem sounds at once reasonable and ambitious: "the construction of a world rather than the reliance upon one which is available to a small poem." . . . [Yet, Berryman's plan for his long poem looks] like an apology for a decadent aesthetics: life existing and aiming to end in a book.

Just as Berryman deftly passes back and forth between the realms of life and art, so at times he moves toward the establishment of a "style" that is "black jade," a potentially decadent lyric-elegiac mode. In *The Dream Songs*, Berryman is fond not only of "style" as word, but of style, styles, and stylists, as question and meaning. . . . Berryman is aware of a defining style he needs to work out for himself, and, in the case of *The Dream Songs*, for his long poem.

The most triumphant of *The Dream Songs* manage to find that music, a style which can be austere or grand, austere and grand at the same time. (pp. 75-6)

In a very basic sense, what *The Dream Songs* evidences is an unending preparation for death or, more specifically, for executing a death-style adequate to artful dying. . . . (p. 78)

Love & Fame, published in 1970, soon after *The Dream Songs*, offers the same distractions and dangers of that long work: a linguistic center which is potentially evasive, an incipient elegiac decadence, and the sustained impression of a posthumous, prophetic book. And it was not long before *Delusions, Etc.* and the novel *Recovery* appeared, not as metaphorically posthumous books but as literally posthumous facts.

As with *The Dream Songs*, Berryman lends to this new book the force of a stock-taking which becomes part of an artistic and spiritual biography executed before a reader's eyes. At worst, this stock-taking degenerates into another *Advertisements for Myself* or another *Making It*, very much in the American grain.

At a very basic and obvious level, Berryman attempts in *Love & Fame* to address what comes after love and after fame (which he sometimes calls "after-fame"). . . . Also, in the new book he seeks a unity of its own, moving more or less chronologically back to his prep school days, Columbia College, graduate school in England at "the other Cambridge," and up to his days as an established poet. But whatever differences and distance he seeks to establish in this new volume may in the end be superficial. More ghosts, technical and spiritual, linger on in *Love & Fame* than Berryman might have wanted to admit.

Love & Fame reveals familiar Berryman country. Again, there is the poet's need for caring, loving friends or "confrères"; again, the obsession with deaths and suicides of friends, writers, and fathers; again, Berryman's fears for art and love. (pp. 78-9)

[But in *Love & Fame*] he is a man even closer to mortality, more profoundly aware of his own eventual death. (p. 79)

Love & Fame ostensibly moves in its last section, made up of **"Eleven Addresses to the Lord,"** to an art of praise, from the love and fame recorded in the earlier sections to a love of God the Father, in a style complexly echoic of Donne and Herbert and Hopkins. But these addresses, concerned with praise, reveal less sureness of first and last things than he would have liked them to.

What happens in the last section of *Love & Fame,* at least what happens to part of Berryman as he records that part in art, is the expression of a confessional need for a Pauline persona or protagonist. (pp. 79-80)

If anywhere at all in *Love & Fame,* it is in the third section that Berryman writes poems closer to what I consider major Berryman. These poems keep before a reader what the too casual poems of the first two sections and which the willfully sure, tensionless poems of the last section avoid—that horror of unlove which *The Dream Songs* made into a defining music. (p. 81)

[For example, the] short poem **"Despair"** is one of the longest, slowest, most agonizing poems Berryman ever wrote. The other better poems in the third section of *Love & Fame*, which happen also to be the best poems in the book, **"The Search," "Message," "Antitheses," "Of Suicide,"** proceed as unflinchingly as **"Despair."** And they comprise the poems which show the most awareness of the dramatic situation behind the book. . . .

Berryman was most successful and most recognizably Berryman when he was uneasy about the intimate, intricate alignments among life, fame, art, love, death, lyric, and elegy. *Love & Fame* is no exception. In this book, his poems still are his "lovelies." His lyrics still are, in a repeated phrase from the book, "deathwords & sayings in crisis." (p. 84)

Berryman's posthumously published work—his book of poems, *Delusions, Etc.* and his uncompleted novel, *Recovery*—only confirm directions and dangers which I noted in earlier volumes. . . . What we witness in *Love & Fame* is the same irony and pity which distinguished *The Dream Songs* but with more pity and less irony than we had seen before. . . . The complexities of lyric, elegy, blues, ballad, minstrelsy, and vaudeville dwindle to something less than art.

If in *Love & Fame* Berryman did not "entirely resign," he calls one of his poems in *Delusions, Etc.* **"He Resigns."** If in *Love & Fame* he still saw the Blues (and, by extension, poetry as the Blues) as "the most promising mutual drama," *Recovery* descends to A.A. group therapy, which makes the possibility of recovery seem one more delusion along the way. The titles of the two posthumous books are almost beyond irony. *Delusions, Etc.* suggests in its second word the will toward some movement counter to delusion as much as it suggests pure physical, psychological, and artistic exhaustion and spiritual despair. And *Recovery* gives the lie to the emergence of recovery on every page of the book.

Both books are undistinguished. *Delusions, Etc.* has several fine poems in it,, **"Washington in Love," "Beethoven Triumphant," "Scholars at the Orchid Pavilion," "He Resigns," "Henry's Understanding," "Defensio in Extremis,"** but most of the poems are thin and artless. *Recovery* is helplessly, relentlessly bad; Berryman not only was unable to disguise his biography but unable to find the art necessary for any novel at all. Berryman falling apart—drinking himself to death, engaging in failed loving encounters, harboring incestuous desires, fouling himself behind, finding fame the last infirmity or delusion of mind—is the spectacle we never are allowed to bypass or forget. Berryman the man and writer come more and more together, ironically as Berryman comes more and more apart.

Motifs from the earlier books continue—the endless need for "the lovely men" or "unloseable friends," for love in all its forms against loss. (pp. 86-7)

The problem facing the critic in *Delusions, Etc.* and *Recovery*, even if he tries to forget that the books are posthumous and that Berryman finally killed himself, is that the books are full of contradictory impressions. Berryman wants to live and to die. He wants to move from lay artist to Catholic layman at the same time we wonder about his "layman's winter mockup." He wants to move to the love of the Virgin and Christ as the God of Love, while he knows that God the Father and Christ the Son have to be One. And it is easy to transpose. . . . But the problem, as *Recovery* so chillingly sets it forth, is that the saying or hearing of "I love you" . . . evokes in Berryman the most terrifying feelings of all. In part, Berryman's horror of unlove is as much Berryman's horror of love, love too good to be believed. . . .

The poems in *Delusions, Etc.*, like the Twelve Steps of A.A. in *Recovery*, finally prove "maladaptive devices" for the poet and protagonist. (p. 88)

The Dream Songs managed to suggest that there might be another method or music if only the poet could find those loving sounds. By the time of the writing of **"He Resigns,"** however, probably the best and most significant poem in *Delusions, Etc.*, Berryman had written a poem which looked back to poems like **"Snow Line"** and **"Despair"** at the same time that it moved closer to that final dejection ode and its accompanying exhaustion which Berryman had tried so hard to stave off. . . . (pp. 88-9)

> *Arthur Oberg, "John Berryman: 'The Dream Songs' and the Horror of Unlove," in* The University of Windsor Review *(reprinted by permission), Vol. 6, No. 1, Fall, 1970 (and reprinted in a different form as "John Berryman: 'The Horror of Unlove'," in his* Modern American Lyric: Lowell, Berryman, Creeley, and Plath, *Rutgers University Press, 1978, pp. 49-92).*

CAROL AMES

In his uncompleted, posthumous novel, *Recovery*, John Berryman creates a remarkable tension between traditional form

and experimentation. As in Action Painting, the content and the form of *Recovery* are united to present and embody the visions and revisions, the versions and reversions of a suicidal alcoholic struggling with his disease. *Recovery* shows that addition is a major impediment to art, because it infects both language and imagination. In the novel, Alan Severance feels that only the truth can heal, but he discovers that language lends itself less easily to truth, than to wit, metaphor, story, myth, evasion, and delusion. Unlike the poet, the alcoholic confuses the essential differences between language and experience.

In *Recovery*, Berryman creates an original form that reveals the gradual movement of a mind away from delusion, evasion, and showmanship and toward truth and honesty.

"Recovery" implies a conventional plot or narrative with action rising to a climax. The title implies that Severance will follow "The Twelve Steps" outlined by Alcoholics Anonymous, complete treatment, and change—the climax. Because treatment has twice failed, Berryman supplements this impulse toward change with the possibility that the study and discipline necessary to Judaism will insure a lasting change—the denouement.

Against this possible optimistic story with a traditional form, Berryman plays off a pessimistic story with an experimental form. The pessimistic story shows that the alcoholic can never recover his pre-alcoholic self. He can never again have a casual drink or two. He can only become a more-or-less controlled alcoholic, renewing his struggle each day, each moment, in the face of ever-shifting moods, tempting and threatening situations, emotional crises, and whims. . . .

His keeping and rereading [a] diary lead to the split narration of the novel, in which excerpts from Dr. Severance's Journal are interspersed within the third-person narrative. The first-person journal shows Severance struggling with the duplicity of language. . . .

Berryman and his personae, Henry Pussycat and Alan Severance, drink more and more whenever they create, even though alcohol weakens their stamina and makes them suicidal, i.e., willing to sacrifice themselves for the progress of their art.

Creation necessitates being able to imagine and perhaps to verbalize ideas, solutions, and hypotheses that do *not* exist, or do *not as yet* exist, or *can never* exist in actuality. The language of a metaphor joins ideas, objects, situations, and feelings that may otherwise be experienced as separate.

Alcoholic hallucination involves a parallel separation of language from actuality. But the alcoholic behaves as if saying or thinking something is the same as doing it. . . . The poet can write about dying and coming back from the dead, as Berryman does in *The Dream Songs*, **78-91**, which are individually titled **"Op. posth. nos. 1-14."** In contrast to the poet, however, the alcoholic believes he actually possesses any powers he can express in words. . . . Thus, both the imagination of the poet and the hallucination of the addict manipulate language, but the addict confuses the words with the reality. The poet knows the difference.

Recovery draws on Berryman's experience during his third cure, but it is not simply a diary of that experience. Writing it, Berryman, now dry, has to imagine his way into the mind of a drunk who is still hallucinating. Berryman's dry mind has to bypass the later revisions and perceptions to recreate the early moments of detoxification. The writer must maintain the distinctions among his past pain and longing for death, his present lesser pain and longing, and his powerful, imaginative fabrication of the past pain and longing. The task is original and daring. The challenge may have been overwhelming. Berryman committed suicide without finishing his novel.

Nevertheless, the completed portion of *Recovery* succeeds because it develops a compelling tension between a traditional plot moving toward a climax and an experimental ebb and flow of ever-renewed struggle. *Recovery* is important, because fresh, powerful insights about truth, imagination, and language emerge from Berryman's portrait of a suicidal alcoholic.

> Carol Ames, ''The Form and the Language of John Berryman's 'Recovery','' *in* Notes on Modern American Literature, *Vol. IV, No. 1, Winter, 1979.*

DIANE ACKERMAN

In a natural way, John Berryman is oblique, private, elliptical. We seem to overhear him. Locked in a verbal spasm, he has trouble, often enough, in getting out or across, and an essential part of his performance is a rheumatism of the sensibility, in which the grammar is so knotted up that his poems evince the difficulty of getting them written at all. Beginning, he seems not quite to know what is nagging at him; finished, he has allowed into the poem various accidents, concomitants, and ricochets. . . . One of the most ego-ridden poets, he makes authoritative rhetoric out of the nervous tic, and an original voice as well. It is almost out of the question to confuse lines by Berryman with those of any other poet, though like a celebrant magpie he echoes dozens of poets from Pound and Stevens to Hopkins and Cummings. His ''grammaticisms'' alone would identify him, I suppose: his wrenchings or mutilations of grammar are not those of others. In fact, nearly everything about him is manneristic and, at times, he seems almost like an involuntary exercise in the manner of poet as idiosyncratic paradigm. A hard nut to crack, he is a poet fully qualified for exegesis and often badly in need of it.

My purpose here is . . . to consider certain tendencies in *Homage to Mistress Bradstreet* and *Delusions, Etc.* There were times when Berryman verged on the metaphysical mind, although never sustainedly; it seems to have haunted him, the possibility of getting into such a frame of mind (and reference) flickers in his work like morganatic fire. It shows up in *Dream Songs*, I think, in the persona of intervening Mr. Bones, the death-figure who puts awkward questions at the wrong moments only to answer them himself in a weird combination of black lingo and uncouth blues. Henry, the poet figure whose interior biography the Songs jerkily reveal, owns Mr. Bones and, presumably, goes on owning him until Mr. Bones owns him, which is when the Songs end, as they did in 1972. But I don't think it would be right to regard *Dream Songs* as metaphysical. . . [their drift is social]. . . . The entire sequence is an almost spastic search for a self, and it's not a self blurred through transcendental overlap with rocks and stars and trees, it's a self blurred by its own chemistry. If Berryman reaches out in these short poems, it's to bring himself back, not to steal a magic from the universe at large. Psychologically of enormous interest, . . . they are actually a bit short—in voracious interest, in intuited vastness, in empathetic penetration—compared with certain other works. . . . (pp. 141-42)

Homage to Mistress Bradstreet is an imaginary portrait almost in the manner of Walter Pater; indeed, Berryman's real-life alias has more fictional range than does the invented, arbitrary one of Henry. The answer, I think, is that, down the track, there was something precise and vivid to aim at, whereas Henry is too much Berryman himself to have edges. The one poem is a monument, the other a potpourri of broken images. Not that *Homage* isn't a poem of voices; it is, and these include the poet's own. . . . In fact, vocally, it is a polyphonic *tour de force,* sometimes achieving the uncanny effect of what has been presented serially becoming simultaneous: the voice lingers in one's ear and overshoots the next voice that comes along. Most impressive of all, the rhythm of Anne Bradstreet's mind comes boldly through, not only from Berryman's study of her own *Meditations* and his occasional use of phrases from them (some of which she had culled from the Scriptures), but also from his almost involuntary impersonations, which leave her mental gait on the silent white space around the poem like an oral signature. Adroit, subtle, tight, *Homage* . . . is an astonishing feat of invasive homage; her mind breathes again and, courtesy of the later poet, makes new images galore. . . . My point is that, through grammar or ''grammaticism,'' Berryman offers optional readings which, rather than providing us with alternative insights into Anne herself, multiply her world instead, attuning us to things she may not be aware of, but which the intruding poet has supervised. And the motion thus implied, on our part complied with, not only turns the duo Bradstreet-Berryman into the Marcus Aurelius of Massachusetts, but also provides the poem with almost supernatural auspices that . . . turn the whole thing ontological. (pp. 142-43)

[In the verse on childbirth Berryman accomplishes a vivid empathy. How] many male poets have gone so alertly, so keenly, to the core of a female experience? Pain, relish, and disgust come together here to make a shocking, though far from sensationalist whole. The odd thing, as so often in Berryman, is that the means to this effect feels also like the means to something bigger that looms just beyond the stanza's edge. It's not just a woman, a woman poet, it's a human being in a fit of being tweaked by body chemistry, if you like by the matrix of all human life. The apparatus, the cadences, the sheer drops, the psychodramatic speaking of the unspoken in response to the unspeakable, all betoken the sense of being *put upon* by the universe; only—this qualifier will reappear apropos of Berryman—he never quite takes it to the limit. . . . (p. 144)

[Further on, his poetry accomplishes an] iconography of panic, the physical equivalent of a pandemonium which Berryman excels at conveying without, however, getting quite past it into an imaginative survey of its sources. . . . If ever a poem sat on the edge of an abyss, *Homage* does: it teeters, wobbles, falls apart, invites some cosmic power to rend it further, rends itself, comes provisionally together again, and comes to a dead stop. . . . (pp. 144-45)

Berryman, in this long poem at least, [is] the master of the ceremonies of homelessness. Not at home in the universe, he isn't located anywhere else. Unable to sift from cosmic phenomena the one he wants (maybe a personal intervention in his life by a caring God?), he transcribes the froth of wanting. In other words, he uses Anne Bradstreet to delineate the bittersweet, thwarted transcendence of a non-believer who asks only: Why should all this emotional ferment lead to nowhere, have no point? He aspires to a metaphysical habit in almost purely emotional terms without the least reaching out into the cosmic evidence. (pp. 145-46)

Twenty years separate *Delusions, Etc.* from *Homage.* The imagery has widened out, especially the cosmic sort, from references to "the Local Group" (of galaxies, that is), the Hale reflector, Wolf-Rayet stars (which are *extremely* hot ones), to God as "Corpuscle-Donor," "pergalactic Intellect," and such novelties as collapsars and the expanding universe. . . . But the references come out of duty, not enthusiasm. . . . Agile, suave in the extreme . . . , full of cultural and historical allusions, the poems are monuments to a failed religious attitude. As much dares as entreaties, as much acts of defiance as calls for help, they more or less ask the Creator why the hell He hasn't come yet and gotten John Berryman, whose untidy, cussed, bad-mouth waiting is getting on John's overwrought nerves. In the wake of Auden's clinical and public-school "Sir," Berryman comes up with a miscellany of vocatives, from "Your Benevolence," "Thou hard," "Dear," to "You," "in-negligent Father," "Sway omnicompetent," and others; but, although he works dismally hard at his new-found vocation of convert-disciple-prodigal unbeliever—he only keeps running headlong into the old panic which no flip "Okay" is going to mitigate. . . . [Berryman is] a poet of unsignifying pain, whose yearning is as metaphysical as Herbert's, say, whose images are as dishevelled as those of Cowley and Carew, but whose mind just cannot shed ego and hitch an atomic or molecular or electromagnetic lift along one of the avenues of out. It is a sad spectacle, an even sadder sound, when he recites the physique of *Angst*. That is what he does from his beginning to his end and he has few competitors for his demoralized post. Perhaps no one else has done this narrow, yet inescapable thing quite so vividly, knowing that at the end of the line (end of the life-line) there is only sensuous escapism . . . or something unspeakably bleak. . . . (pp. 147-49)

Berryman may not have cut through to the *x* for unknown that he craved and coveted with all his being; the increasing scope of his references has more a look of trophy-hunting than that of awed immersion; he never achieved what a *Newsweek* reviewer incredibly gifted him with (an "austere, level voice . . . so quiet it's sometimes hard to hear him"!); but it is impossible not to recognize the gibbering convulsions of his need. I think of him as a naturally metaphysical spirit, but one unable to sense the wonder that accompanies what he thought the *insult*, the *snub*, behind the nomenclature, almost as if the Local Group . . . were something from which he'd been shut out. That is the least we can say about him, though; the best is that he somehow mustered the courage to face ontological precipices dared by only a few. (pp. 149-50)

Diane Ackerman, "Near the Top a Bad Turn Dared," in Parnassus: Poetry in Review *(copyright © Poetry in Review Foundation), Vol. 7, No. 2, Spring-Summer, 1979, pp. 141-50.*

JAMES E. MILLER, JR.

Berryman has said that it took him two years to get over the writing of his **"Bradstreet"** poem, first published in [1953]. . . . He began work (or planning), then, . . . and lived with the creation of *The Dream Songs* [some thirteen years]. (p. 246)

The mid-1950s, then, was a critical moment in Berryman's career. It was at this time that he made the decision to remake himself as a poet, to give over the Eliotic kind of impersonal or "made" poetry that he had previously written and to launch a personal epic with an open-ended structure in the Whitmanian (or "orbic-flex") manner and tradition. His enthusiastic 1957 essay on "Song of Myself," with its extravagant praise of

Whitman, provides an indirect account of his own poetic turmoil in change.

But it is *The Dream Songs* that provides the spiritual history of that remaking of the poetic self. The epic is in the broadest sense *about* Berryman's personal transfiguration from one kind of poet to another. As a newly committed *personal* poet, Berryman felt able for the first time in his poetry to confront the personal events of his life—as, for example, the earlier suicide of his father. The poetic remaking of the self, then, was in a sense a move to come to terms with the battering events of a difficult life.

Berryman's form, the interior "dream song," enables him to scramble chronology at will (as in a dream). But there is running throughout this work a recognizable "contemporary time" paralleling the time of the writing of the songs, roughly 1955-68, a period that provides the basic frame. But many poems break out of this frame into various levels of the past, treating those events that continue to haunt the poet.

Moreover, *The Dream Songs* has a symmetry of form in spite of its chaotic appearance. The first three books (*77 Dream Songs*) look back from the "contemporary time" frame to focus on the poet's life up through his first (or Eliotic) poetic identity. These books sketch in the long foreground of the poet before the radical change or remaking (death, resurrection) that comes in Book IV. They carry the poet not lineally but cyclically or spirally, to the point of publication of his poetry previous to writing of *The Dream Songs*, including *Homage to Mistress Bradstreet*. The short Book IV (**"Op. posth. nos. 1-14"**), the only book with a title, dramatizes the death of the old and the birth (or self-resurrection) of the new (or Whitmanian) poetic identity. . . . The new being that comes "back" to life in Book IV is clearly the poet who will embark on *The Dream Songs*, written in a style radically different from that of all his previous poetry. The last three books of the work, balancing the first three, focus on this new identity—and the problems of writing a long epic poem in the Whitman tradition. These last books carry the poet through significant stages of his later life to a deeper awareness of some of his most persistent personal problems (or recurring nightmares), to resolution of them or resignation to their endurance.

The "narrative" outlined above is embedded in a cyclic or spiral structure encrusted with a multitude of themes—those that enter the poet's consciousness over the years of the poem's writing (1955-68), carrying the poet from his forty-first year to his fifty-fourth; themes supplemented by memories and imaginative extensions, memories of past years (especially the poet's all-important boyhood) and imaginative re-creations of national or world events. (pp. 246-47)

The most vital event of *The Dream Songs* is one which occurred long before the time of the loose "narrative frame" of the poem, but which haunts it throughout and provides its most deeply obsessive theme. Berryman was no doubt referring to it when he mentioned in his prefatory Note that Henry had "suffered an irreversible loss": the suicide of his father when the poet was only twelve years old. . . . [Berryman had a theory that ordeal was necessary for great artistic achievement and his] ordeal for *The Dream Songs* clearly was his father's suicide. (p. 260)

It is perhaps impossible to ferret out the entire presence of this event in *The Dream Songs*. But it is easy to guess that it exists behind the guilt, [bitterness, and loss of faith] so brilliantly dramatized in [the work]. . . . (p. 261)

If we consider the father's suicide the central theme of *The Dream Songs,* we may imagine the other themes as radiating out from this core and shaped by it. Song 1 ended with an image of continuous, universal death. . . . There is, of course, all of Book IV envisioning Henry's death and burial—and ultimate resurrection. There are many many other songs that touch on death—friends, acquaintances, often unnamed; and there are many poems that touch on death in a general way, often with a personal twist. (p. 265)

More often than not, death is the inescapable horror in *The Dream Songs,* and most frequently the poet draws a personal connection—even envisioning his own death, sometimes even seeming to hope for it, sometimes trying to evade it. (p. 266)

In Song 4, the sex-love theme is introduced in *The Dream Songs*—a theme that seems omnipresent but seldom emotionally dominant. In its context of death, sex seems to get short shrift from Henry, like a passionate spasm followed abruptly by the old familiar agony. (p. 267)

There is a wide range of treatment of the sex-love theme in *The Dream Songs*. . . . This theme is, in a way, put in its place in *The Dream Songs* in Song 311, in which Henry makes an inventory of his desires and needs. . . . A list of needs, and on the list: women. Before them, hunks of bread and raw onion. Well! But the point is made: the poem above all. When the poet goes to pieces, even the pieces will sit up—and write. The poet's creative vitality is to be conserved, not for love, but for the making of poetry.

The personal dimension is so all-consuming in *The Dream Songs* that it is sometimes forgotten that the poem was written in a historical context with a great many historical-political references. The period of 1955-68 was a period of great moment in American and world history, and Berryman includes many songs on topics of the day. (pp. 268-69)

[But nowhere] do we feel the passion of political outrage sustained, as, for example, in Ezra Pound or Allen Ginsberg. It seems clear that Berryman felt uneasy in writing these "political" poems. (p. 271)

The sex-lust-love theme and the political (or topical) themes in *The Dream Songs* by no means go against the grain of the poem; on the contrary, they fill out the "record of a personality" (in the way the various themes in *Leaves of Grass,* Berryman's acknowledged model, put a personality on record). When Berryman described his model as "Song of Myself," he pointed out that Whitman's poem proposed "a new religion," that it was a "wisdom work, a work on the meaning of life and how to conduct it." Berryman said, "Now I don't go that far . . . [in *The Dream Songs*] but I buy a little of it." In short, Berryman believed that, although *The Dream Songs* did not propose a new religion, they were—in some measure—a wisdom work.

And indeed, the poem conveys a strong sense of "questing" throughout, a search for (to use Berryman's words for Whitman) "the meaning of life and how to conduct it." (pp. 271-72)

Henry's imagination—the source of his poetry, the place of his quest—will be his house until his death. The quest has not revealed the secret, but the quest must go on: in the questing itself is life. In a sense, then, Henry is wrapped in the secret he cannot find. To quest is to live, to know, to be. (p. 274)

James E. Miller, Jr., "The American Bard/Embarrassed Henry Heard Himself a-Being: John Berryman's 'Dream Song'," in his The American Quest for a Supreme Fiction: Whitman's Legacy in the Personal Epic *(reprinted by permission of The University of Chicago Press; © 1979 by The University of Chicago), University of Chicago Press, 1979, pp. 234-75.*

G(uillermo) Cabrera Infante

1929-

(Also wrote under pseudonym of G. Cain) Cuban-born novelist, short story writer, screenwriter, journalist, critic, editor, and translator.

Although now a British citizen, Cabrera Infante is often described as one of Latin America's most important writers. Loosely structured and linguistically inventive, his fiction resists traditional literary classifications. It therefore demands flexibility of approach from both critics and readers.

Censored in both Cuba and Spain, Cabrera Infante has written graphic, satiric portrayals of his native country. Among the most acclaimed of these is his *Así en la paz como en la guerra: cuentos,* a composite of stories, sketches, and sociological commentary dealing with the terrors of the Batista regime.

Cabrera Infante is best known, however, for his *Tres tristes tigres (Three Trapped Tigers).* Blending comedy and tragedy, this novel portrays Havana nightlife on the eve of Batista's fall. Written primarily in the language of the Cuban streets and narrated by several speakers, *Tres tristes tigres* pictures a society devolving into physical and spiritual confusion. Within this society, language sounds bizarre as it is reshaped by people struggling for new means of communication. Events are sudden and inexplicable. As the revolution looms, in the words of Raymond D. Souza, Cabrera Infante's characters search for "order in chaos, permanence in a realm of change, infinity in a world of limitations."

(See also *CLC*, Vol. 5 and *Contemporary Authors*, Vols. 85-88.)

© Jerry Bauer

ENRICO-MARIO SANTÍ

[*Vista del amanecer en el trópico (View of Dawn in the Tropics)*]—whether a novel or collection of stories is unclear, or perhaps unimportant, as proven by the use of both terms on the jacket and cover of this edition respectively—seems to be a revision of the fragments Cabrera Infante excised from *Tres tristes tigres* and which were part of an earlier and identically titled manuscript, winner of the Premio Biblioteca Breve in 1964. Censorship prevented the winning manuscript from being published in Spain in its original form. The result, then, has been publication of two books: first, the famed novel, and now this other text.

In comparison with the author's own previous descriptions of *Vista,* this final version is more like a complete rewriting of the socialist realist text he had originally conceived for these fragments. . . . It is a collection of moments in Cuban history whose structure recalls the author's first books and whose characters . . . parade anonymously in historical and anecdotal scenes described in tones that range from pathetic to ironic. Therefore, because of its paradoxical nature, a chronicle silent about the facts, *Vista* necessarily becomes a Borgesian intertextual exercise in reference to both written and unwritten history—the first being Fernando Portuondo's classic school text . . . which is alluded to explicitly throughout the book, and

the second being the insistence upon anecdotes and legends . . . drawn from Cuban lore.

Despite some obvious sentimental weaknesses in the last scenes, the overall result is a dazzling—though by comparison to some of his earlier texts, modest—experiment in the dialectical relationship between history and fiction by one of Latin America's most innovative writers.

> *Enrico-Mario Santí, "Fiction: 'Vista del amanecer en el trópico'," in* Books Abroad *(copyright 1976 by the University of Oklahoma Press), Vol. 50, No. 1, Winter, 1976, p. 123.*

RAYMOND D. SOUZA

In [Lezama Lima's] *Paradiso,* the universe is viewed as an enigma but with a definite design and form, but in *Tres tristes tigres* it is presented as a realm of chance. Chaos is not a frightening condition for Guillermo Cabrera Infante; and one could almost say that he finds it extremely fascinating and with endless possibilities. He regards the universe more as a creative explosion of a continual process of appearance and dissipation. There is a great sense of movement in *Tres tristes tigres,* created by the author's experimentation with language and his radical approach to structure. This movement is enhanced by his humor that delights his readers even though they sometimes suspect that the author's wit is directed at them. As the reader proceeds through *Tres tristes tigres,* he sometimes feels that there is a whimsical imp peering at him from the letters of the text. The universe is presented as a huge comedy rather than an enigma, a gigantic folly perpetrated by some unknown being. (p. 80)

The setting in *Tres tristes tigres* takes place in Havana in the summer of 1958, that is, just a few months before the revolutionary government came into power in January of 1959. However, the work is not a political one, although it does capture an era that is coming to an end and the feeling of disintegration that characterizes an apocalyptic period. The novel opens with the English word Showtime!, and we are exposed to the inane chatter of the master of ceremonies in one of Havana's leading nightclubs. We are immediately thrust into the nocturnal setting that constitutes a major part of the novel, and we are left with the impression of a superficial and casual world that is in a chaotic state. Before the main show begins, the MC introduces several people who are in the audience, and many of them reappear in the novel. After these introductions are made and the MC has had the opportunity to tell several absurd jokes in English and Spanish, the section closes with the words Curtains up! The reader has been introduced to an artificial situation that exists in a real world and yet exercises a strange attraction over him. It is a place where reality and illusion blend and the show is about to begin.

In addition to a Prologue and Epilogue, the novel is divided into eight sections. The novel contains a mixture of several separate story lines, and there are narrators or voices that are not always identified. As a result, the reader gets the impression that the novel has little structure, and the emphasis placed on creative language enhances this sensation. In many respects, *Tres tristes tigres* represents an attempt to capture essence in language itself, and the language of the work is freed from the authority of logic. This freedom gives the novel spontaneity, which is one of the novel's greatest assets, but it also creates a sense of disorder in the reader. The structure of *Tres tristes tigres* is a problem for the critic who tries to be consistent in his traditional methods of analysis, because the different sections in the novel demand diverse approaches. *Tres tristes tigres* is a good example of the difficulties that criticism can have in keeping up with innovative works.

Cabrera Infante's work is a novel to which neither the reader nor the critic can bring traditional concepts of form or structure. The novel, for example, is plotless and could be considered as a collection of many stories or narrations. One critic has classified *Tres tristes tigres* as an open novel, that is, one that the reader can organize or rearrange to his own liking. Whether or not this is the case, the critic's opinion does emphasize the extent to which the novel's structure is experimental and helps to explain why the novel confounds the reader. (pp. 81-2)

Tres tristes tigres demands that the reader be extremely flexible in his approach to the novel, and that he judge it as an artistic creation that has both particular and total effects. The novel's organization causes the reader to confront, as the characters do, the chaos of existence. In this sense, he becomes a participant in the novel's organizational process, imposing order on a fragmented reality.

The best way to approach *Tres tristes tigres* is to appreciate each section for its own merits without attempting to relate it to an overall logical order. The novel is much more rewarding to the reader once he perceives that it is better not to categorize

and organize reality. Organization, of course, gives us security and protects us, at least psychologically, from change. *Tres tristes tigres* defies these tendencies and overwhelms us with explosive bursts of creativity. These bursts expand themselves soon after coming into being and fall back into a formless void, victims of death. . . . Herein lies the ecstasy and tragedy of human existence, and the only salvation is to sustain the continuity of the creative process that allows man to rediscover and redefine himself constantly. (pp. 82-3)

Tres tristes tigres opens and closes with sections that capture or suggest rebellion against a society that has lost its way. It is a society devoid of any sense of purpose and is seriously committed to error. Energies are not released the way they should be, and, as a result, we have substitutes and perversions rather than creativity and genuineness. Like a rudderless ship that is guided by nonexisting lighthouses, its random motion produces a sense of giddiness even as it glides inexorably toward disaster. Cabrera Infante has described the nocturnal festival that his characters engage in as a "communion with deadly night sin." His description explains the attractions and pitfalls of the existence the novel portrays. His work also explores the possibilities of escape offered to the individual by the creative process, and this search is centered on sound and language.

The language of *Tres tristes tigres* is the most authentic that any Cuban writer has ever produced. Only the short-story writer Novás Calvo approaches Cabrera Infante's ability to capture the essence of his characters in the language they use. His language is authentic yet creative. Cabrera Infante accomplishes this without falling into the pitfalls that captured so many of the writers who preceded him, especially those who employed realistic and naturalistic techniques. Those writers were so intent on reproducing the language of their characters that creativity was suffocated. Words for them were individual symbols that defined their characters. They confused duplication with creativity and failed to see that words should not be regarded merely as symbols but as part of a symbolic process. Cabrera Infante succeeds where many did not, because he recognizes that he is capturing a process rather than an end result. Consequently, we see the world as his characters perceive it, as a place of dynamic change rather than static definition. (pp. 97-8)

In terms of sheer enjoyment, it would be difficult to name a work that surpasses *Tres tristes tigres*. It is an easy book to read because of its fresh humor and the continual sense of discovery it imparts. *Tres tristes tigres* contains a unique and successful combination of tragedy and comedy, contributing greatly to the novel's artistic success. This combination appeals directly to our emotions and intellect. However, it is not easy to understand the novel's meaning and significance. The novel's structure is particularly baffling and challenges the reader's concepts of form and order.

The characters in *Tres tristes tigres* search for order in a chaotic world and for meaning in a confused society. The creative force of the language contributes to the fragmentation of the work's structure, and the novel's arrangement is such that the reader experiences this process. There are contradictory forces operating in the novel that are moving the characters simultaneously toward death and rebirth. The fragmentation of form captures the essence of a social order in the process of dissolution, well on the way to destruction. On the other hand, the fragmentation of language can be regarded as the first stage of a new creative art. It is the force that is conjuring up new beings within a waning social order. Destructive and creative forces are operating at the same time, and the vehicle of these processes is language. It creates as it destroys, offers doom and hope, conveys inspiration as it defeats. (pp. 99-100)

> *Raymond D. Souza, "Cabrera Infante: Creation in Progress," in his* Major Cuban Novelists: Innovation and Tradition *(reprinted by permission of the University of Missouri Press; copyright © 1976 by the Curators of the University of Missouri), University of Missouri Press, 1976, pp. 80-100.*

ELIAS L. RIVERS

The tongue-twisting title of *Tres tristes tigres* makes the reader immediately aware, at the elemental phonetic level, of language as an opaque substance, not a classically transparent and fully codified medium. *Tres tristes tigres,* when first published in Spain in 1967, caused a stir in the Spanish-speaking world. While some passages are readily accessible to any reader, others are obscured by Cuban vernaculars in phonetic transcription and by word-plays and allusions of many different kinds. A multiplicity of "voices" engage in narrative, dialogue and soliloquy. It is a text which fascinates as it eludes and frustrates; the over-all narrative sense is by no means obvious. (p. 333)

Language [in *Tres tristes tigres*] is a central theme and problem directly connected with the author's striving to capture a recent past which is still echoing in his mind: the conversational nightlife of Havana shortly before the fall of the Batista régime. Nostalgic attraction and disgust are embedded in an anti-literary language which Cabrera Infante simultaneously transcribes and invents as the basis of his text. He is aware that textual transcription and composition falsify the voices of the street and night clubs; but only in this way can he give permanent, that is written, form to his memories. His caustic inconoclasm and black humor work explicitly against the establishment of an autonomous literary language; at the same time the writer implicitly works at converting a Havana vernacular into an international Spanish "novel." (pp. 333-34)

Despite his orality, this writer is not only a listener, but a reader of cosmopolitan dimensions. He links Cervantes and James Joyce. . . . For him Borges is the great Spanish American classic. . . .

Cabrera "irritates the oyster" of the Spanish language in a much more direct and obvious way than Borges does. One of his main devices is the literal transcription of colloquial peculiarities. . . . [His] Anglo-Cubanism, the substitution of an acoustically equivalent consonant, and the emphatic hiatus (reinforced by glottal stop) between identical vowels, reflect popular speech-patterns which have seldom if ever been caught in writing before. (p. 334)

[The] best introduction to *Tres tristes tigres* is Auerbach's *Mimesis:* when the standard upper-class literary language is suddenly infiltrated by colloquial turns of phrase and thought, the effect may be not simply comic, but potentially revolutionary, bringing the lower classes into the text, recognizing their presence within the social fabric. (pp. 334-35)

> *Elias L. Rivers, "Cabrera Infante's Dialogue with Language," in* MLN *(© copyright 1977 by The Johns Hopkins University Press), Vol. 92, No. 2, March, 1977, pp. 331-35.*

KLAUS MÜLLER-BERGH

[*Exorcismos de esti(l)o*] contains graphic razzle-dazzle and verbal rat-tat-tat [which] masks one of the most innovative and daring experiments with the Spanish language from one of the most significant Latin American writers today. For the potpourri of puns, parodies, pastiches, word squares and other jeux d'esprit belies the intrinsic earnestness of Cabrera Infante's work. . . . [*Exorcismos de esti(l)o* consists of] hilarious parodies of authors, literary genres and schools of criticism: from Plutarch, Shakespeare and Quevedo to St. John of the Cross; fables which Aesop, La Fontaine or Samaniego never dared to write; and painful needling of the Tel Quel group.

As we might guess from sections titled "Acido (P)Rúsico" and "Marxismas," the targets are politically predictable at times and turn out to be prominent figures of the Cuban Revolution, Stalinism, the Moscow trials, as well as the inherent contradictions of Communist party orthodoxy. Occasionally the author waxes METAPHYSICAL/-PHORICAL in dealing with the essence of time, censorship, freedom of thought and expression, art as craft and unalienated activity, the meaning of literature and its role as a mode of cognition. Finally, it is not surprising, for a man who has tasted the bitter bread of exile, that the invocation of the Holy Name which clears the place of evil spirits be CUBA. This is quite apparent in the affectionate remembrance of things past and in the nostalgic silhouette which concludes the book—"The Island," an outline of Cuba literally rising from a sea of words, made from the word *mar*.

> *Klaus Müller-Bergh, "Verse:'Exorcismos de esti(l)o'," in* World Literature Today *(copyright 1977 by the University of Oklahoma Press), Vol. 51, No. 2, Spring, 1977, p. 253.*

ALFRED J. MACADAM

While Cabrera Infante does not share [Julio] Cortázar's didactic attitude toward literature, their texts, *Tres tristes tigres* and *Rayuela*, are remarkably similar in that they overwhelm the reader with an avalanche of fragments, pieces which only cohere after memory links them. Cabrera Infante, unlike Cortázar, does not feel impelled to instruct: he assumes the existence of a public that will appreciate his scrapbook technique and his depiction of a lost milieu. This public would share the archeological tastes of the readers of Joyce or Proust, and would not be jarred by the discontinuities of satire or the need to have a familiarity with pre-Castro Havana. The reader of Latin American satire is under great pressure; to read a book like *Tres tristes tigres* . . . he must not only know a great deal but must also hold his own literary expectations in abeyance, paying close attention to the text's own rhetoric. Only by determining a work's "intrinsic genre" can the reader ever hope to read it fairly, and such a reading will result, in the case of Latin American narrative, in an esthetics of narrative based on satire. (p. 61)

The reader's first task in dealing with *Tres tristes tigres* is reconstruction. He begins by reassembling the text, making sense of what appears to be an agglomeration. He connects the pieces of the characters' lives as they appear in the text, like a quilt-maker constructing a whole out of scraps, until suddenly he sees a kind of nebulous totality, a whole fragment which points to a vast number of new totalities.

Tres tristes tigres, like *Brás Cubas* or *Morel*, is [an] elegiac text. Like the early poetry of Borges, it is concerned with documenting a loss, not only of the object observed but of the observer as well. Cabrera Infante, unlike [Adolfo Bioy Casares], is not as overtly concerned with the phoenix-like death-and-resurrection of the work of art out of the ashes of life, perhaps because he (like his characters) realizes that the two worlds, though tangential, are eternally separate. The world to which the text corresponds is dead, and the text can only be a metaphor, a reality of words with no specific reference to anything palpable.

The basic metaphor on which *Tres tristes tigres* is constructed is the notion that esthetic representation is a betrayal. The work of art cannot be about anything but itself, and since it is a translation of one mode into another, it cannot presume to have any higher status than its subject. Cabrera Infante's satire is a study of the idea of betrayal, both as a form and as a content. That is, one kind of betrayal may be substituted for another: if a translator calls the lions of a particular text sea lions, he has violated a trust; if a friend has lied to his friend, he has broken a bond; if a text pretends to capture scenes from various lives but succeeds only in giving versions of those scenes, then it too has betrayed its "promise" to the "original."

The satirist is, of course, satirized in Cabrera Infante's work. Silvestre, the putative "secretary of history," is his own subject. He must deform what he recalls of himself simply because of what the act of transcription entails. Silvestre is an implacable enemy of oblivion . . . and he is fully conscious of the inevitability of memory, the persistence of the past in its invasion of the present . . . but he himself is defeated because he can only give the shell of what he observes. Like the fruit growing near the Dead Sea, representation is a surface, devoid of real content, always promising something, always "about" something, but never anything. Within the text this emptiness, seen also as a kind of sterility, is reflected in the characters' constant word play.

Puns are a means whereby the characters generate the illusion of action. They create a verbal space, but this space is illusory because it is conceived in the mode of metaphor, of substitution, and not in the metonymic mode of flow. There is literally no place for the characters to go in the text because they have reached the end of their historical and cultural rope. Like Bioy's narrator, they are trapped on an island (Cuba here being as metaphoric as the island in *Morel*), and all their movement is circular, reminiscent also of the protagonists' trajectories in *L'Immoraliste* or *Voyage au bout de la nuit*. Like Bioy's narrator, they too will become art, but it is the cost that receives the emphasis here, a heavy price unmitigated by the love Bioy's narrator feels for Faustine. Individual salvation of the kind Bioy postulates is a poor consolation for Cabrera Infante's characters because it too is tainted by betrayal. There must be an interpreter, a Silvestre or the reader so often addressed by Silvestre. Committing oneself to language, as Borges seems to be saying in texts as disparate as "Borges and I" and "Tlön, Uqbar, Orbis Tertius" confers a provisional immortality on the subject, but it simultaneously subjugates the subject to the interpretations of the reader.

Metaphoric space, which the characters create when they make puns, and in which they reside after Silvestre writes down his version of what he has experienced, is in reality no space at all. It is for this reason that the characters exist only in each other's company; they are all mirror images of one another, reflections of reflections. Much is made of this in the relationship between Cué and Silvestre because other characters point out their being twins, although they in no way resemble

each other physically. They constitute an ironic rejoinder to J. Hillis Miller's statement about characters in the Victorian novel: "In most Victorian novels the protagonist comes to know himself and to fulfill himself by way of other people." Cabrera Infante's characters are shadows no amount of contact can complete.

This condition is exemplified in the text by the death of a character who never actually appears. Bustrófedon, Cabrera Infante's Morelli, is a linguistic wizard, a pun master, and his death provokes an immense crisis in the lives of the other characters. They try to preserve his works (the parodic sequence "The Death of Trotsky Told by Various Cuban Writers Years After—or Before" is his), but, as the characters realize, his works are not he. He is lost forever. Moreover, he becomes a character in their memory, and finally becomes what they all become, words. For the reader, Bustrófedon was never anything but language, and if we never experience him directly he is nonetheless as "real" as Cué or Silvestre. His being absent is a sign of the absence that underlies the existence of all the characters. (pp. 65-7)

Cabrera Infante's text is, or aspires to be, the language of a particular place and time, or at least his version of it, and its being enclosed in a book signifies its being dead. . . . For Cabrera Infante . . . , the creation of the text, the verbal monument to the dead, is another betrayal, the act of having recourse to metaphor, because the actual subject is ephemeral. The text contains the ghost of ghosts, the remains of a language, itself a metaphor.

"Beguiling the hour" seems to be the principal occupation of Cabrera Infante's characters. They are dying with their milieu, like antediluvian beasts on the verge of extinction. Language is the only means left to them to dissimulate their despair. Like the digressions and interpolations in Greek romances, their verbal adventures give the illusion of expanding or widening time, but they are merely decorations. The world of *Tres tristes tigres* is sterile, except as the subject of a work of art, in the same way the world of Encolpius and Giton is a world which acknowledges itself to be without transcendence. Turning night into day, turning words inside out, being constantly in motion are all the means whereby Cabrera Infante's characters deceive themselves. It is just one more betrayal, one which leads both to death and to esthetic resurrection. (p. 68)

> Alfred J. MacAdam, "Guillermo Cabrera Infante: The Vast Fragment," in his Modern Latin American Narratives: The Dreams of Reason *(reprinted by permission of The University of Chicago Press; © 1977 by the University of Chicago), University of Chicago Press, 1977, pp. 61-8.*

DOLORES M. MARTIN

Confrontation and censorship notwithstanding, the '60s were prodigious years for the Latin American novel in general and for the Cuban in particular. Among the most astonishing of these novels was Cabrera's *Three Trapped Tigers*. . . . This work is a dazzling assault on Spanish speech by Cuban street-talk, a delightful dissolving of stony, stodgy Castilian prose into something resembling the nonsense of Lewis Carroll, with the bawdiness of Joyce.

View of Dawn in the Tropics was the original title of a much earlier and very different version of *Three Trapped Tigers* which won a Spanish prize but was nonetheless banned by Franco's government in 1964 just as *Tigers* would be banned by Castro's in 1967. Cabrera has since repudiated the 1964 version of *View of Dawn* by calling it "a book of absolute socialist realism" and emphasizing that "literature must only have to do with literature," and, presumably, not politics. The question, then, is: Why has Cabrera chosen to write this new [1978] version?

Admirers who expect the wonderful exuberance, humor and inventiveness of *Tigers* will be disappointed. The new *View of Dawn* is a curiously austere and bitter book, far more reminiscent of the author's early style. His short stories of the '50s . . . were separated by 15 historical vignettes which reported with exemplary economy and detachment the atrocities of the Batista regime. *View of Dawn in the Tropics* stretches the same form to the limit with more than 100 sketches tracing the history of Cuba from the dawn of man to the dawning of the Revolution. However, the fragile craft of the vignette sinks under so much intention that one wonders if this is the same writer who warned readers of *Tigers* that "any similarity between literature and history is accidental."

The impact of Cabrera's vignettes of the '50s hinged upon the Cuban reader's recognition of the unnamed victims of Batista's atrocities. But what is the non-Cuban reader to make of such cryptic references in *View of Dawn* as "the son of a Spanish dancer and a mulatto barber," "the bald little man with the big moustache," or "the big black general"? Even those somewhat familiar with Cuban history may wonder whether one character is Marti and another Maceo or whether the appalling gangster-style killing reported on page 63 is one in which the young Fidel Castro was allegedly involved.

Perhaps Cabrera does not wish his reader to bother with who is who or what is what, but to read on inexorably towards some grim moral about the unchanging venality and brutality in Cuban history. My suspicion is that the fatalism and pessimism of this version of *View of Dawn* is the reversal, indeed the mirror image, of the socialist realism and optimism of that earlier version. Instead of the heroic guerrillas and liberating progress of 1964, we now have the villainous commissars and despotic regression of 1974.

Nevertheless, some of the sketches . . . have the paradoxical immediacy of good photographs, the illumination of a presence serving to emphasize the shadow of its essence. The vignettes are vivid but, somehow, their ultimate effect is ephemeral. Unlike the images of a good film whose overall impact is cohesive and cumulative, the impression left by these sketches is random and sporadic.

> *Dolores M. Martin, "Fictional Vignettes of Cuba's History," in* Book World—The Washington Post *(© 1979, The Washington Post), January 28, 1979, p. L4.*

PAUL T. HORNAK

[*View of Dawn in the Tropics*] is a history of Cuba in sketches that draw upon fact but read like fiction. The sketches run at longest three pages; the shortest is 15 words. Characters—many of them historical personages—have no names. Scenes are set in the mountains, in the city, on the highway, without further identification. They are placed in time only by their references to engravings as opposed to photographs, and by the appearance of machine-guns. The past is a mystery, Cabrera Infante contends; it comes clear not through analysis but through imagination. Thus he has cast his imagination back to the moment Cuba rose from the sea. From the very first it reminds

him of bloodshed: Cuba is like "a long green wound." . . . The sketches in *View of Dawn* are almost exclusively portrayals of senseless death. Conquistadores turn a feast into a massacre because, receiving a friendly reception from the Indians, they "thought that so much courtesy was intended to kill them for sure." A young man running along a rooftop is shot by a soldier. From the days of the Spaniards through Castro the bloodshed has not ceased. But Cabrera Infante never descends into rationalization. For him it is enough that people have died. In drumming the theme of incessant violence, however, Cabrera Infante communicates more than outrage. He is mortified by what he has found in the histories and in the latest news. . . . But he is also bored by the inability of his countrymen to break free of the urge to slaughter. His country's history can be narrowed, as he shows in *View of Dawn,* to a single theme. He has no hope that the Cubans will turn around. One can only smile ironically, he says, and admire the island itself, "surviving all disasters, eternally washed by the Gulf Stream: beautiful and green, undying, eternal."

> *Paul T. Hornak, "Books in Brief: 'View of Dawn in the Tropics'," in* National Review *(© National Review, Inc., 1979; 150 East 35th St., New York, NY 10016), Vol. XXXI, No. 13, March 30, 1979, p. 434.*

KLAUS MÜLLER-BERGH

Guillermo Cabrera Infante's [*La Habana para un infante difunto*]—autobiography, novel, biography or erotic fantasy of a precocious Cuban don Juan—is a tropical *education sentimentale* defying generic classification. If nine-year-old New Yorkers rob banks, their uninhibited Latin American counterparts father children, or dream about it. Feminism may be alive and well (and living in Argentina), Severo Sarduy may idolize an Indian friend in the pages of *Vuelta* . . . , but *machismus* is far from *moribundus*. . . . In any case, Latin American literature certainly does present some of the more viable, heroic, heterosexual alternatives, from Macondo's exuberant Amaranta Ursula and Aureliano Buendía to *La guaracha del macho Camacho,* Puerto Rico's national saga of the *guachafita,* and now the work of the Cuban Quevedo.

Be this as it may, Cabrera Infante's latest effort decidedly has a lot of *Bildung* and a little of *Roman,* although it ultimately never comes across as a combination of both terms but rather as a requiem for a child wise in the ways of the street, as well as a requiem for everything gone with the wind, for the Havana that time has swept away. In other words, it narrates the adolescence and early manhood of a nameless *pícaro* of dubious identity and even more dubious aspirations, who might be Guillermo Cabrera Infante. If such is the case, it is an author bigger than life, fictionalized and subtly transformed by time and nostalgia. . . . Cabrera Infante's last name clearly appears in the title *La Habana para un infante difunto* (Havana for a Dead Infant[e] or Prince), a pun that parodies Maurice Ravel's piano piece "Pavane pour une infante défunte" (1909). The play on words is even stronger in Spanish, since *pavana* is only a phoneme removed from *Habana.*

Another formidable protagonist that appears in the title is Old Havana, probably the city between 1941 and 1948. . . . This time frame is roughly a decade before that of *Three Trapped Tigers* (1965), the author's other remembrance of things past, which focuses largely on the decade of the fifties and the night life of Cuba's capital. Other emblems that grace the black-and-white cover are photography, cinema, voyeurism, a passion for language and politics, as well as eroticism. The photo of the urban square of Havana's Parque Central contains a still shot with the portrait camera of an aging park photographer, the monument of José Martí in the far background, and a cast iron flagpole. As in *Un oficio del siglo XX* (1963), film is often a vehicle of narration as well as a metaphor of life, ultimately determining the circular structure of a "función continua" (continuous showing) limited by the "Aquí llegamos" (Here's where we came in) that opens and closes a brilliantly written, sad, hilarious, bawdy book. (pp. 435-36)

> *Klaus Müller-Bergh, "Fiction: 'La Habana para un infante difunto'," in* World Literature Today *(copyright 1981 by the University of Oklahoma Press), Vol. 55, No. 3, Summer, 1981, pp. 435-36.*

JORGE H. VALDÉS

Highly reminiscent of the grimness of both Goya's *Caprichos* (from which the opening epigraph is taken) and *Los desastres de la guerra*, [*View of Dawn in the Tropics*] is a personal view of the history of Cuba from a time well before that of the first inhabitants down to the present. It is a tragic, fatalistic, ironic, sarcastic, and, at times, humorous account of a series of events linked by violence and suffering, such as the massacre of the native Indians by the Spanish conquistadores, the bloody suppression of uprisings of slaves and peasant workers against the landowning establishment, the arduous struggle for independence and the political tortures and murders of the national governments which followed, the Castro-led revolutionary movement against the tyranny of Batista, the perilous exodus of anti-Castro Cubans, and the violations of the human rights of conterrevolutionary political prisoners.

In an attempt to be both moving and convincing, Cabrera Infante has compiled a sequence of vignettes based on a variety of sources—photos, engravings, historical data, telephone conversations—whose authenticity he sometimes questions and which he presents with apparent objectivity. The illusory detachment is an artistic means used by the author to impress his personal and, at times, highly fictionalized view of past and recent events on the reader. Moreover, Cabrera Infante's seemingly objective approach, in combination with a careful selection and structuring of the material, allows him to make a convincing case for his dire view of Cuban history as a repetitive and often accidental course of events always leading to an unhappy ending.

> *Jorge H. Valdés, "Fiction: 'View of Dawn in the Tropics'," in* Best Sellers *(copyright © 1981 Helen Dwight Reid Educational Foundation), Vol. 41, No. 9, December, 1981, p. 326.*

Elias Canetti

1905-

Bulgarian-born English novelist, essayist, and dramatist.

Canetti has been recognized as an important and original thinker by European critics for several decades. Only in the last ten years has he received a significant amount of attention in the United States. American critics are now analyzing Canetti's work and find him to be an intriguing literary figure whose work commands respect and careful scrutiny.

Canetti, who fled Austria with his parents and moved to London in 1938, was deeply disturbed by the social climate in Europe before the Second World War. He eventually became obsessed with "the conflict between culture and the mass mind." His acclaimed sole novel, *Die Blendung (Auto-da-Fé*, also published as *Tower of Babel)*, is a social and political satire on the greed, cruelty, and intolerance of the mass mind for the individual who is both alienated from and victimized by it. The book was originally intended to be the first of eight dealing with madness and the distortion of reality in the contemporary world. Canetti later decided that *Die Blendung* sufficiently stated his views and the remaining volumes were never written. *Masse und Macht (Crowds and Power)* is, however, often described as a companion volume to *Die Blendung*. This treatise on the psychology of the masses is one of Canetti's most important works. It attempts to explain the origins, behavior, and significance of crowds as a force in society with an imaginativeness and forcefulness that led critics to read his other works with intense interest. Among these works is *Der andere Prozess: Kafkas Briefe an Felice (The Other Trial: Kafka's Letters to Felice)*, an examination of Kafka through his letters to his fiancee, and a book of sketches entitled *Der Ohrenzeuge: Fünfzig Charaktere (Earwitness: Fifty Characters)* which collects personality traits into monstrous exaggerations as a protest against inflexible social attitudes.

Canetti's recently published autobiographical volumes, *The Tongue Set Free* and *The Torch in My Ear* deal with family influences upon Canetti during his childhood and adolescence and with the literary influences of his early adulthood, notably Karl Kraus and Franz Kafka.

Although some critics find Canetti's work over-detailed and unscientific, most believe that he writes in an original and compelling manner, incorporating metaphor, irony, and symbolism into his aphoristic style. Canetti won the prestigious Georg Büchner Prize in 1972 and the Nobel Prize in literature in 1981.

(See also *CLC*, Vols. 3 and 14 and *Contemporary Authors*, Vols. 21-24, rev. ed.)

IRIS MURDOCH

To deal adequately with *Crowds and Power* one would have to be, like its author, a mixture of historian, sociologist, psychologist, philosopher and poet. One is certainly confronted here with something large and important: an extremely imaginative, original and massively documented theory of the psychology of crowds.

© Lütfi Ö-kök

Using heterogeneous and very numerous sources, Dr. Canetti has built a structure which has the clarity, simplicity and explanatory flexibility of a metaphysical system. His view will not prove easy to 'place' in any familiar pattern or genealogy of ideas; nor has he himself given any help to would-be 'placers.' He quotes the most diverse and esoteric writers, but the names of Freud and Marx occur nowhere in his text (Freud is mentioned once in a note). This particular reticence, which reminds one of Wittgenstein, is the mark of the artist and of the confident, truly imaginative thinker. . . .

The book falls roughly into two halves. The first half analyses, with an amazing wealth of illustration, the dynamics of different types of crowds and of 'packs,' a term used to denote a smaller, more rigidly structured and purposive crowd. The second part, which discusses how and why crowds obey rulers, deals with the psychology of the despot. The key to the crowd, and to the crowd's master, Canetti finds in his central theory of 'command' and 'survival.' . . .

In the last part of the book, Canetti introduces another concept, that of 'transformation.' This specifically human talent has many uses but is most primitively a kind of protection. It is a danger to any would-be despot, whose corresponding passion is 'to unmask.' The book ends with a discussion of the case of Schreber, a paranoiac who wrote a detailed memoir of his delusional life. In this account Canetti finds all the character-istics of power and its relation to crowds which he has been analysing. 'It is only a step from the primitive medicine man to the paranoiac and from both of them to the despot of history.' . . .

I think Canetti's theory throws a great deal of light and precisely illuminates places which have hitherto been very dark. Marx has told us much about the dynamics of society. Freud has told us much about the human heart. But neither of them provides us [as does Canetti] with a satisfactory theoretical explanation of Hitler or an explanation, say, of the political power of a church over its adherents. (p. 337)

Ideally a 'theory' should be both centripetal and centrifugal, and this I think Dr. Canetti's theory triumphantly is. His book is full of starting points, embryo theories, sudden independent illuminations. When he says of Christianity, for instance, that it is a 'religion of lament' in which the 'hunting pack' expiates its guilt by turning into a 'lamenting pack', or when he speaks of the 'frenzy of increase' which in modern capitalism under-mines the religion of lament, he is giving us new means of thinking which, as it were, contain their own ambiguities. Dr. Canetti might be the first to agree that concepts as well as men should enjoy the privileges of transformation. Rich concepts have histories. And precisely because Dr. Canetti's concepts are so rich I do not think we should be in too much of a hurry to see them as rigidly systematic.

This problem of the 'necessary incompleteness' of systems occurs to one particularly in relation to the 'moral' of *Crowds and Power.* Canetti speaks of power as fundamental to human nature and he analyses power with predominantly 'political' imagery. . . . Our most pressing need, as Canetti very mov-ingly and convincingly argues at the end, is to control the 'survivor mania' of our rulers, and the key to this is 'the humanisation of command.' But how is command to be hu-manised? Canetti has not given us a psychology with which to picture the humanisation of command. Here rival science and indomitable morality stand ready to enter the argument. (pp. 337-38)

[We] have here that rare sense of being 'let out' into an entirely new region of thought. Canetti has done what philosophers ought to do, and what they used to do: he has provided us with new concepts. He has also shown, in ways which seem to me entirely fresh, the interaction of 'the mythical' with the ordinary stuff of human life. The mythical is not something 'extra'; we live in myth and symbol all the time.

Crowds and Power, one may add, is a marvellously rewarding book even if one were to read it without any theoretical interests at all. It is written in a simple, authoritative prose . . . , and it is radiant with imagination and humour. There are hundreds of memorable things. . . . The book is full of entertainments and provocations to thought. It is also a great original work on a vitally important subject, and provides us with an emi-nence from which we can take a new look at Marx and Freud. A large work of scholarship which is also a completely new work of theory is rare enough: and we should remind ourselves that in the obscure and disputed field of 'the study of human nature' we cannot rely only upon the piecemeal efforts of teams of merely competent scientists. We need and we shall always need the visions of great imaginers and solitary men of genius. (p. 338)

Iris Murdoch, "Mass, Might and Myth," in The Spectator (© 1962 by The Spectator; reprinted by permission of* The Spectator)*, No. 7002, September 7, 1962, pp. 337-38.*

THE TIMES LITERARY SUPPLEMENT

Between 1942 and 1948, Elias Canetti kept a kind of psycho-logical and moral breviary, jotting down thoughts, feelings, nightmares forced on him by war and exile. Having denied himself recourse to imaginative writing, and turning more and more to the mythography and sociology of *Crowds and Power,* this fiercely intelligent, self-fascinated man sought to under-stand . . . the nature of the political catastrophe and of his own marginal condition. He wrote down his meditations only for himself, "in order not to suffocate".

Naturally enough, the result [*Aufzeichnungen 1942-1948 (The Human Province)*] is rather a rag-bag. There is a sprinkling of witty maxims. . . . There are various somewhat Kafkaesque germs for future stories or plays. . . . Then there are lengthier notes, sketches of consequent argument, dealing mainly with the soul-rending effect of war and of the destruction of central European values on Elias Canetti the writer and the Jew. . . .

Mr. Canetti wondered also about the continued viability of literature, about the place of poetic form in an age of bestial turbulence. . . . A good deal of what Elias Canetti jots down about the intolerable weight of vain words, about the root mystery of the existence of different languages, about the dan-ger of living a life in which verbal abstraction is master, is acute and moving. He touches on a central nerve when he remarks: "As a profession, literature is destructive: one should have greater *fear* of words." But being so incomplete, and at times banal, these *Aufzeichnungen* suggest that there is no great gain in making public, in solemnizing, what was meant to be intimate and provisional, a necessary striving to keep aloud the echo of the threatened self.

"Canetti's Cahiers," in The Times Literary Sup-plement (© *Times Newspapers Ltd. (London) 1965; reproduced from* The Times Literary Supplement *by permission), No. 3306, July 8, 1965, p. 577.*

THE TIMES LITERARY SUPPLEMENT

In [*Die Stimmen von Marrakesch (The Voices of Marrakesh)*] Mr. Canetti appears as a traveller, and one would expect this traveller to combine the anthropological preoccupations of the author of *Masse und Macht* with the literary sophistication of *Die Blendung.* Yet he has written the straightest of travelogues, whose very virtue lies in the absence of theoretical disquisition, stylistic bravado or any other accretion that might have made this book a contribution either to science or to fiction.

Each of the short sections that make up the book concentrates on a particular aspect or experience of the Moroccan city which the author visited in 1954; each makes its impact by the vivid and direct rendering of things observed and heard—of camels and donkeys, streets and houses, men, women and children, beggars, merchants and artisans, Arabs, Berbers and Jews. The observer's and narrator's responses are part of the account, so that the book also complements Mr. Canetti's diaries as a biographical record; but whereas the diaries revealed his in-tellectual interests and speculations, the new book reveals emo-tional involvements and sympathies. The persona of the trave-logue is not a *fort espirit* but almost a *coeur simple,* with an extraordinarily warm and spontaneous response to the most basic phenomena of human life and animal life.

Basic is the word, since Marrakesh provided abundant instances of animals and human beings reduced to little more than hunger, endurance and lust. It is the celebrations of the life urge in those conditions—often with a dignity *in extremis* not to be found in more advanced societies—that animates and unifies all the sections that constitute this book. Although Mr. Canetti does not leave out his personal reactions to the cruelty, piety, greed and stoicism that he found in Marrakesh, a true gift of empathy has enabled him to enter deeply into a primitive order alien to his assumptions, and to affirm it simply by letting its phenomena speak for themselves. What he gives us is something quite different from the long awaited second novel; but it is a fascinating and moving book.

"Life Urge in Extremis," in The Times Literary Supplement *(© Times Newspapers Ltd. (London) 1968; reproduced from* The Times Literary Supplement *by permission), No. 3479, October 31, 1968, p. 1219.*

IDRIS PARRY

In *Der Ohrenzeuge* Elias Canetti has gone back to a literary form at least as old as Theophrastus. He describes fifty "Characters" or types. He too is protesting against the rigidity of outlook which can turn a human creature into a pathetic or dangerous insect. Not that he raises his voice in protest. He never raises his voice; the dagger effect of these studies comes from detachment and the restraint of prose, unsurprised as absurdity follows absurdity. Like several other recent German writers, Canetti is a scientist by academic training. This comes out in his work. There is no stated moral judgment; the facts are left to speak for themselves. We seem to be reading through a handbook of scientific information, told in the simple prose which occasionally occurs in handbooks of scientific information. No names are given, no personal names, only strange generic titles, male and female, for specimens pinned and delineated. . . .

This literary form depends on the existence of fixed ideas—and Canetti is a specialist in the observation of fixed ideas, as we know from the protagonists of his novel, *Die Blendung*. He is fascinated by the delusions of people who live in capsules. Now, in different words and different people, he presents fresh variations on the selective blindness of Peter Kien and the paranoia of Therese and Pfaff in that novel.

If the prose of this primer seems appropriately naive, the "facts" are extraordinary. . . .

Canetti furthers the alliance between science and art as he realizes the utmost potential of any visible situation and finds the unsuspected behind the familiar. He is an admirer of Gogol. In these portrayals we find a similar touch of mad exuberance, like the Gogol description of a character who gets up from the gaming table and stands for a while "in the posture of a man who has no handkerchief in his pocket". Such writers surprise us into belief, largely because they show no surprise at all. They are merely telling us the irrational facts of their life. In such moments we can believe there are vibrations which have always existed but have not been registered up to now: we needed instruments of new-found sensitivity called writers.

Idris Parry, "Unsuspected Vibrations," in The Times Literary Supplement *(© Times Newspapers Ltd. (London) 1975; reproduced from* The Times Literary Supplement *by permission), No. 3801, January 10, 1975, p. 38.*

MARION E. WILEY

Since reflective thought is of central importance in Canetti's writing, this discussion regards his prose as provocative reflections—provocative in a dual sense—first, to Canetti, who intentionally writes to stimulate his thought; and secondly, to readers reacting to his observations. (p. 130)

The element of reflection is especially visible in the notations, the *Aufzeichnungen,* where Canetti covers innumerable topics in a variety of concise forms. The provocative quality stems most directly from the dialectical structure of the short commentaries, with Canetti seeking new ideas by means of opposing suppositions. Each notation can stand alone as an independent, excursive observation, but collectively the notations constitute intellectual explorations of diverse regions. The fifty sketches included in *Der Ohrenzeuge* . . . and the recollective narrative of *Die Stimmen von Marrakesch* . . . are also explorative. Like the *Aufzeichnungen* they investigate human motives and attain a timelessness which transcends but does not ignore intellectual questions of contemporary concern.

As is true of most reflective writing, his prose requires the concentration of the reader and would therefore not appeal to the casual erudite. . . . The prose appeals rather to the analytical reader who reacts to Canetti's observations and then formulates a personal commentary. Canetti also writes in this additive manner, developing his ideas in response to his initial thoughts and to the observations of others. (pp. 130-31)

Still Canetti's prose demands more of the reader than concentration and analysis; a receptivity to the thematic and structural diversity of his prose is also a prerequisite. In addition to his familiar themes of power, the masses, death, and transformation, the reader also encounters general observations on language, religion, culture, and aspects of contemporary life, such as the implications of lunar exploration and the position of the poet in modern society. . . .

Canetti's prose thus covers a wide range of topics, which he often develops dialectically or by tangential digression. (p. 132)

[Other] factors suggest that Canetti has written a prose of provocative reflections. His diverse approaches to a given topic, for example, attest to his purposeful communication of reflective thought. He can be succinct, shocking, humorous, or contradictory; and sometimes he is all of these at once. . . . (p. 134)

Yet Canetti's numerous commentaries on any one topic are not simply repetition but rather continuations of discussions. His frequent reflections about death fall in this category, for they are deliberate attempts to widen his perception of the subject. In steadily pursuing topics over the years Canetti also practices his belief in the continuous examination of crucial issues. It is apparent, however, that he views his reflections in a larger context. His aggressive rejection of death is a case in point: rejection of death is essential to a full exploration of life. His preoccupation with death is then related to his belief in the possibility of intellectual growth and subsequent change. . . . Since he does not consider death in the sense of mental deterioration to be inevitable, he relentlessly rejects intellectual decline in principle and in practice. His remarks about death are thus part of his energetic support of life, which he defends against life's most formidable opponent, death.

Equally striking is the extent of Canetti's respect for life. He does not limit his concern but extends his sympathy to all living beings from the rabid camel to the human bundle crouching on the ground, two extreme cases vividly depicted in *Die Stim-*

men von Marrakesch. . . . His concern for human beings is also the motivating force behind his character sketches, where he exposes individuals committed only to self-aggrandizement. Canetti is concerned about them and recognizes the need for objective awareness of their existence. . . . At the same time his belief in the potential of mankind enables him to criticize with a measure of moderation. He is able to reveal imperfection without irreversibly indicting the individual or condemning mankind to its imperfect state. Canetti's reluctance to draw premature conclusions thus stands the individual in good stead, allowing, as it does, for the further development of character.

In much the same way the critic of Canetti is reluctant to draw final conclusions about Canetti's evolving prose. . . . [The] critic accustomed to the desperate confusion reflected in the literature of the later twentieth century may be moved to note that the reflective writing of Canetti is a stimulating and complementary addition to contemporary prose. It is stimulating to share ideas with an author who verbalizes his thoughts with clarity, frequent wit, and appropriate compassion. It is also encouraging to encounter the refutation of inevitability and the advocacy of spirited inquiry. In this respect Canetti is the antipode to the writer who records primarily the spiritual malnutrition of contemporary society and the resulting loss of illusions. Canetti possesses a view of life which impels him to search for alternative approaches to existence. (pp. 135-36)

Canetti's commitment to the investigation of existence is perceptible in all of his writings, and in his essay *Der Beruf des Dichters* . . . he directly discusses the position of the poet in modern society. In his opinion authors must assume responsibility for the condition of man even though they can not necessarily prevent disasters by means of their words. This sense of responsibility, nourished by learning and compassion, serves as an example and helps mankind to seek its own transformation. He leaves no doubt about the obligation of the poet. . . . [Canetti maintains that] the poet must resist the ambassadors of nihilism and fight them with all his strength. In place of capitulation Canetti sets exploration, and the goal is the comprehension of life's multiplicity, including both its chaotic defeats and its victories. . . . (p. 136)

Canetti thus views the poet as a responsible and committed explorer of life, a description which we may appropriately apply to Canetti himself. In doing so we also acknowledge his main communication, namely, that mankind is still alive and capable of discovering, perhaps even saving, itself. This type of discovery interests Canetti, and his reflective prose attests to the success of his intellectual explorations. In respect to this achievement his prose is a unique contribution to contemporary writing, and his belated reception in the seventies is a noteworthy entry for a history of German literary reception. (p. 137)

Marion E. Wiley, "Elias Canetti's Reflective Prose" (a revision of a presentation made at the Modern Language Association meeting on December 28, 1977), in Modern Austrian Literature (© copyright International Arthur Schnitzler Research Association 1979), Vol. 12, No. 2, 1979, pp. 129-39.

MICHAEL WOOD

"The Voices of Marrakesh" is a terse and sensitive record of a visit to Morocco. **"Earwitness"** is a set of fantastic character sketches, a human bestiary containing creatures like the Bittertangler, the Never-must, the Name-licker, the Corpse-skulker, the Long-changer, the Narrow-smeller, the God-swanker, the

Moon Cousin, the Bequeathed Man and 40-odd more. Both books reveal Mr. Canetti's talent for what he calls precise exaggeration. . . . Of the two, **"Earwitness"** points us more clearly toward Mr. Canetti's other works. Its characters are weakest when they are closest to recognizable types and strongest when they gather scattered human traits into composite monsters. . . .

This tells us something, I think, about the virtues and liabilities of Mr. Canetti's imagination, and it helps us bring the laborious **"Auto-Da-Fe"** into proper focus. The exaggerations of this schematic story of a man who loved books and hated women are not precise, they are simply methodical. The novel has one or two grand and lurid epigrams—"Man is the only deformity"—but its ironies keep freezing into whimsy, and we are left with the dogged pursuit of stereotypes like the scholar and the harpy and the vengeful dwarf. There is nothing in the book that has the force or the edge of Mr. Canetti's later, more casual jottings. . . . (p. 11)

[The] best portrait we have of Mr. Canetti is **"The Human Province,"** a selection from 30 years' worth of notes, many of them made while he was writing **"Crowds and Power,"** which he regards as his "life's work." Only here do we get a clear sense of this prickly, ambitious, intelligent and sometimes silly man. The other books are more secretive, and a lot more solemn. . . . (pp. 11, 58)

[It] is in **"The Human Province"** that he reveals his doubts and makes his jokes. He is fascinated by anthropology, he says, because "I think I have truth itself in my hands. . . . It is the mirage of the greater clarity of relatively simple conditions." More than half of **"Crowds and Power"** rests without hesitation or apology on this very mirage, the belief that primitive life will disclose all of civilization's secrets. . . .

"Crowds and Power" is the most *displaced* book imaginable: its real subject, the masses of this century and the dictators associated with them, constantly being buried among Moguls and Mongols and all sorts of ethnological lore. Partly this is a matter of tact: Mr. Canetti expects us to remember horrors closer at hand, and doesn't wish to blackmail us with them. Partly it is a result of the enormity of the subject, which drives the student back on analogies, sends him to the massacres of another time and place. But mainly, I think, the displacement comes from Mr. Canetti's method. He wants to know what crowds *really* are, what power *really* is, and he won't stop until he has a single, reductive answer.

This urge is what produces the frequently circular logic of the book—Mr. Canetti decides what a crowd is and then excludes all deviant crowds on the ground that they are not the real thing—as well as its insistent regressions. Having described dozens of mobs without having come up with more than a handful of banalities . . . , he retreats to the notion of the *pack*, and begins a new taxonomy (the hunting pack, the war pack, the lamenting pack, the increase pack, with further subdivisions among them).

Mr. Canetti is absolutely undaunted by the obvious . . . , but he will not deceive himself, and he knows his method cannot give him what he wants. Yet he won't abandon the method, he just moves it from territory to territory, and so the principal effect of **"Crowds and Power"** is that of a fascinating, example-packed book that keeps getting lost.

When it is lost, it indulges in all sorts of nonsense—sees teeth as the first manifestation of order, for example, and the mouth as the model of a prison. . . . It can scarcely be [wrong or right] because we are in a realm of speculation that lies beyond all possibility of argument. This is worth insisting on, because as Mr. Canetti *in fact* suggests, he is not at all clear on the point himself.

In one passage he contends that "no social event whatever, of any kind" can be understood without a knowledge of the ways his different packs turn into one another. Mr. Canetti's schemes cannot help us to an understanding of social events, because social events are the book's material, the building blocks with which Mr. Canetti constructs his lofty imitation of a collective human mind. . . .

"Crowds and Power," then, is allegorical even when it is not lost; it's more elusive than it looks. But it is time to turn to the principal arguments of this troublesome book—I mean *troublesome*, as Mr. Canetti would no doubt take it, as a compliment. After his descriptions of crowds and packs and the toothy excursion into fantastic biology, Mr. Canetti offers an account of the figure he calls the *survivor*. A survivor, for Mr. Canetti, always survives someone. He must contemplate the corpses of those he has outlived. . . . [We] all get the feeling, Mr. Canetti insists, in any graveyard. It is as if we had defeated the dead. Heroes are people who try to pile up such moments of survival, and tyrants are people who live for them. "To be the last man to remain alive is the deepest urge of every real seeker after power." (p. 58)

There are all kinds of things wrong with this argument, not the least of which are its rather excited cynicism and its indifference to the fact that people have been known to want to die. But it is not a trivial argument, and a film such as "The Deer Hunter," with its image of war as a form of Russian roulette, in which fortune and survival are simply equated, reminds us that the argument needs long and careful inspection.

The other principal argument of **"Crowds and Power"** concerns command. After some dubious guessing about the animal origins of the phenomenon, Mr. Canetti arrives at his human thesis: A command that is obeyed leaves its sting. Life for most of us is full of commands, and consequently we are riddled with stings, ruled by our stings. . . . The command, Mr. Canetti says, in his usual strident tone, is "the most dangerous single element in the social life of mankind."

What are we to do? We must stop apologizing for power, and where we can we must stop obeying commands, because disobeyed commands leave no sting. . . . Mr. Canetti's formulations are far too hectic and simple. For the moment it will do if we see that we cannot argue with him without *defending* power, and that should slow us down a little.

But as Mr. Canetti suggests, his published arguments are not his life; and his life . . . is what matters. His life *as a writer,* that is, his career as a man committed to language, hating death and cruelty, a man who never excepted himself from his own indictments, and who did not give up on a task that must have seemed endless. He is a man, if I may reverse [a phrase of his], whom the century grabbed by the throat. (pp. 58-9)

Michael Wood, "The Precise Exaggerator," in The New York Times Book Review (© 1979 by The New York Times Company; reprinted by permission), April 29, 1979, pp. 11, 58-9.

SUSAN SONTAG

Auto-da-Fé—the title in German is *Die Blendung* [*The Blinding*]—depicts the recluse as a book-besotted naïf who must undergo an epic of humiliation. The tranquilly celibate Professor Kien, a renowned Sinologist, is ensconced in his top-floor apartment with his twenty-five thousand books—books on all subjects, feeding a mind of unrelenting avidity. He does not know how horrible life is; will not know until he is separated from his books. Philistinism and mendacity appear in the form of a woman, ever the principle of anti-mind in this mythology of the intellectual: the reclusive scholar in the sky marries his housekeeper, a character as monstrous as any in the paintings of George Grosz or Otto Dix—and is pitched into the world.

Canetti relates that he first conceived *Auto-da-Fé*—he was twenty-four—as one of eight books, the main character of each to be a monomaniac and the whole cycle to be called "The Human Comedy of Madmen." But only the novel about "the bookman" (as Kien was called in early drafts), and not, say, the novels about the religious fanatic, the collector, or the technological visionary, got written. In the guise of a book about a lunatic—that is, as hyperbole—*Auto-da-Fé* purveys familiar clichés about unworldly, easily duped intellectuals and is animated by an exceptionally inventive hatred for women. It is impossible not to regard Kien's derangement as variations on his author's most cherished exaggerations. "The limitation to a particular, as though it were everything, is too despicable," Canetti noted—*The Human Province* is full of such Kien-like avowals. The author of the condescending remarks about women preserved in these notebooks might have enjoyed fabulating the details of Kien's delirious misogyny. And one can't help supposing that some of Canetti's work practices are evoked in the novel's account of a prodigious scholar plying his obsessional trade, afloat in a sea of manias and schemes of orderliness. Indeed, one would be surprised to learn that Canetti doesn't have a large, scholarly, but unspecialized library with the range of Kien's. This sort of library building has nothing to do with the book collecting that Benjamin memorably described, which is a passion for books as material objects (rare books, first editions). It is, rather the materialization of an obsession whose ideal is to put the books inside one's head; the real library is only a mnemonic system. Thus Canetti has Kien sitting at his desk and composing a learned article without turning a single page of his books, except in his head.

Auto-da-Fé depicts the stages of Kien's madness as three relations of "head" and "world"—Kien secluded with his books as "a head without a world"; adrift in the bestial city, "a world without a head"; driven to suicide by "the world in the head." And this was not language suitable only for the mad bookman; Canetti later used it in his notebooks to describe himself, as when he called his life nothing but a desperate attempt to think about everything "so that it comes together in a head and thus becomes one again," affirming the very fantasy he had pilloried in *Auto-da-Fé*.

The heroic avidity thus described in his notebooks is the same goal Canetti had proclaimed at sixteen—"to learn everything"—for which, he relates in *The Tongue Set Free*, his mother denounced him as selfish and irresponsible. To covet, to thirst, to long for—these are passionate but also acquisitive relations to knowledge and truth; Canetti recalls a time when, never without scruples, he "even invented elaborate excuses and rationales for having books." The more immature the avidity, the more radical the fantasies of throwing off the burden of books and learning. *Auto-da-Fé,* which ends with the bookman immolating himself with his books, is the earliest and crudest of these fantasies. Canetti's later writings project more wistful, prudent fantasies of disburdenment. A note from

1951: "His dream: to know everything he knows and yet not know it."

Published in 1935 to praise from Broch, Thomas Mann, and others, *Auto-da-Fé* was Canetti's first book (if one does not count a play he wrote in 1932) and only novel, the product of an enduring taste for hyperbole and a fascination with the grotesque that became in later works more static, considerably less apocalyptic. *Earwitness* . . . is like an abstract distillation of the novel-cycle about lunatics Canetti conceived when he was in his twenties. This short book consists of rapid sketches of fifty forms of monomania, of "characters" such as the Corpse-Skulker, the Fun Runner, the Narrow-Smeller, the Misspeaker, the Woe Administrator; fifty characters and no plot. The ungainly names suggest an inordinate degree of self-consciousness about literary invention—for Canetti is a writer who endlessly questions, from the vantage of the moralist, the very possibility of making art. "If one knows a lot of people," he had noted years earlier, "it seems almost blasphemous to invent more." (pp. 186-88)

Canetti's ideals of patience and his irrepressible feeling for the grotesque are united in his impressions of a trip to Morocco, *The Voices of Marrakesh*. . . . The book's vignettes of minimal survival present the grotesque as a form of heroism: a pathetic skeletal donkey with a huge erection; and the most wretched of beggars, blind children begging and, atrocious to imagine, a brown bundle emitting a single sound (*e-e-e-e-e*) which is brought every day to a square in Marrakesh to collect alms and to which Canetti pays a moving, characteristic tribute: "I was proud of the bundle because it was alive."

Humility is the theme of another work of this period, *"Kafka's Other Trial,"* written in 1969, which treats Kafka's life as an exemplary fiction and offers a commentary on it. Canetti relates the drawn-out calamity of Kafka's engagement to Felice Bauer (Kafka's letters to Felice had just been published) as a parable about the secret victory of the one who chooses failure, who "withdraws from power in whatever form it might appear." He notes with admiration that Kafka often identifies with weak small animals, finding in Kafka his own feelings about the renunciation of power. In fact, in the force of his testimony to the ethical imperative of siding with the humiliated and the powerless, he seems closer to Simone Weil, another great expert on power, whom he never mentions. Canetti's identification with the powerless lies outside history, however; the epitome of powerlessness for Canetti is not, say, oppressed people but animals. Canetti, who is not a Christian, does not conceive of any intervention or active partisanship. Neither is he resigned. Incapable of insipidity or satiety, Canetti advances the model of a mind always reacting, registering shocks and trying to outwit them.

The aphoristic writing of his notebooks is fast knowledge—in contrast to the slow knowledge distilled in *Crowds and Power*. "My task," he wrote in 1949, a year after he began writing it, "is to show how complex selfishness is." For such a long book, it is very tense. His rapidity wars with his tenacity. The somewhat laborious, assertive writer who set out to write a tome that will "grab this century by the throat" interferes with, and is interfered with by, a concise writer who is more playful, more insolent, more puzzled, more scornful. (pp. 189-90)

Most of Canetti's entries take up the aphorist's traditional themes: the hypocrisies of society, the vanity of human wishes, the sham of love, the ironies of death, the pleasure and necessity of solitude, and the intricacies of one's own thought processes.

Most of the great aphorists have been pessimists, purveyors of scorn for human folly. ("The great writers of aphorisms read as if they had all known each other well," Canetti has noted.) Aphoristic thinking is informal, unsociable, adversarial, proudly selfish. "One needs friends mainly in order to become impudent—that is, more oneself," Canetti writes: there is the authentic tone of the aphorist. (pp. 190-91)

Despite having much of the aphorist's temperament, Canetti is anything but an intellectual dandy. (He is the opposite of, say, Gottfried Benn.) Indeed, the great limit of Canetti's sensibility is the absence of the slightest trace of the aesthete. Canetti shows no love of art as such. He has his roster of Great Writers, but no painting, theater, film, dance, or the other familiars of humanist culture figure in his work. Canetti appears to stand rather grandly above the impacted ideas of "culture" or "art." He does not love anything the mind fabricates for its own sake. His writing, therefore, has little irony. No one touched by the aesthetic sensibility would have noted, severely, "What often bothers me about Montaigne is the fat on the quotations." There is nothing in Canetti's temperament that could respond to Surrealism, to speak only of the most persuasive modern option for the aesthete. Nor, it would seem, was he ever touched by the temptation of the left.

A dedicated enlightener, he describes the object of his struggle as the one faith left intact by the Enlightenment, "the most preposterous of all, the religion of power." Here is the side of Canetti that reminds one of Karl Kraus, for whom the ethical vocation is endless protest. But no writer is less a journalist than Canetti. To protest against power, power as such; to protest against death (he is one of the great death-haters of literature)—these are broad targets, rather invincible enemies. Canetti describes Kafka's work as a "refutation" of power, and this is Canetti's aim in *Crowds and Power*. All of his work, however, aims at a refutation of death. A refutation seems to mean for Canetti an inordinate insisting. Canetti insists that death is really unacceptable; unassimilable, because it is what is outside life; unjust, because it limits ambition and insults it. He refuses to understand death, as Hegel suggested, as something within life—as the *consciousness* of death, finitude, mortality. In matters of death Canetti is an unregenerate, appalled materialist, and unrelentingly quixotic. (pp. 191-92)

In *The Tongue Set Free* Canetti is eager to do justice to each of his admirations, which is a way of keeping someone alive. Typically, Canetti also means this literally. Displaying his usual unwillingness to be reconciled to extinction, Canetti recalls a teacher in boarding school and concludes: "In case he is still in the world today, at ninety or one hundred, I would like him to know I bow to him."

This first volume of his autobiography is dominated by the history of a profound admiration: that of Canetti for his mother. It is the portrait of one of the great teacher-parents, a zealot of European high culture self-confidently at work before the time that turned such a parent into a selfish tyrant and such a child into an "overachiever," to use the philistine label which conveys the contemporary disdain for precocity and intellectual ardor. (pp. 192-93)

Canetti gives a complex account of that extraordinary process which learning is for an intellectually precocious child—fuller and more instructive than the accounts in, say, Mill's *Autobiography* or Sartre's *The Words*. For Canetti's capacities as an admirer reflect tireless skills as a learner; the first cannot be deep without the second. As an exceptional learner, Canetti has an irrepressible loyalty to teachers, to what they do well even (or especially when) they do it inadvertently. The teacher at his boarding school to whom he now "bows" won his fealty by being brutal during a class visit to a slaughterhouse. Forced by him to confront a particularly gruesome sight, Canetti learned that the murder of animals was something "I wasn't meant to get over." His mother, even when she was brutal, was always feeding his flagrant alertness with her words. Canetti says proudly, "I find mute knowledge dangerous."

Canetti claims to be a "hear-er" rather than a "see-er." In *Auto-da-Fé*, Kien practices being blind, for he has discovered that "blindness is a weapon against time and space; our being is one vast blindness." Particularly in his work since *Crowds and Power*—such as the didactically titled *The Voices of Marrakesh, Earwitness, The Tongue Set Free*—Canetti stresses the moralist's organ, the ear, and slights the eye (continuing to ring changes on the theme of blindness). Hearing, speaking, and breathing are praised whenever something important is at stake, if only in the form of ear, mouth (or tongue), and throat metaphors. When Canetti observes that "the *loudest* passage in Kafka's work tells of this guilt with respect to the animals," the adjective is itself a form of insistence.

What is heard is voices—to which the ear is a witness. (Canetti does not talk about music, nor indeed about any art that is non-verbal.) The ear is the attentive sense, humbler, more passive, more immediate, less discriminating than the eye. Canetti's disavowal of the eye is an aspect of his remoteness from the aesthete's sensibility, which typically affirms the pleasures and the wisdom of the visual; that is, of surfaces. To give sovereignty to the ear is an obtrusive, consciously archaizing theme in Canetti's later work. Implicitly he is restating the archaic gap between Hebrew as opposed to Greek culture, ear culture as opposed to eye culture, and the moral versus the aesthetic.

Canetti equates knowing with hearing, and hearing with hearing everything and still being able to respond. The exotic impressions garnered during his stay in Marrakesh are unified by the quality of attentiveness to "voices" that Canetti tries to summon in himself. Attentiveness is the formal subject of the book. Encountering poverty, misery, and deformity, Canetti undertakes to hear, that is, really to pay attention to words, cries, and inarticulate sounds "on the edge of the living." . . . The voice for Canetti stands for irrefutable presence. To treat someone as a voice is to grant authority to that person; to affirm that one hears means that one hears what must be heard.

Like a scholar in a Borges story that mixes real and imaginary erudition, Canetti has a taste for fanciful blends of knowledge, eccentric classifications, and spirited shifts of tone. Thus *Crowds and Power* . . . offers analogies from physiology and zoology to explain command and obedience; and is perhaps most original when it extends the notion of the crowd to include collective units, not composed of human beings, which "recall" the crowd, are "felt to be a crowd," which "stand as a symbol for it in myth, dream, speech, and song." (Among such units—in Canetti's ingenious catalogue—are fire, rain, the fingers of the hand, the bee swarm, teeth, the forest, the snakes of delirium tremens.) Much of *Crowds and Power* depends on latent or inadvertent science-fiction imagery of things, or parts of things, that become eerily autonomous; of unpredictable movements, tempos, volumes. Canetti turns time (history) into space, in which a weird array of biomorphic entities—the various forms of the Great Beast, the crowd—disport themselves. The crowd moves, emits, grows, expands, contracts. Its options come in pairs: crowds are said by Canetti to be quick and slow,

rhythmic and stagnant, closed and open. The pack (another version of the crowd) laments, it preys, it is tranquil, it is outward or inward.

As an account of the psychology and structure of authority, *Crowds and Power* harks back to nineteenth-century talk about crowds and masses in order to expound its poetics of political nightmare. . . . But whereas earlier writers had been content to assert the crowd's pathology and moralize about it, Canetti means to explain, explain exhaustively, for example, the crowd's destructiveness ("often mentioned as its most conspicuous quality," he says) with his biomorphic paradigms. And unlike Le Bon, who was making a case against revolution and for the status quo (considered by Le Bon the less oppressive dictatorship), Canetti offers a brief against power itself.

To understand power by considering the crowd, to the detriment of notions like "class" or "nation," is precisely to insist on an ahistorical understanding. Hegel and Marx are not mentioned, not because Canetti is so self-confident that he won't deign to drop the usual names, but because the implications of Canetti's argument are sharply anti-Hegelian and anti-Marxist. His ahistorical method and conservative political temper bring Canetti rather close to Freud—though he is in no sense a Freudian. Canetti is what Freud might have been were he *not* a psychologist: using many sources that were important to Freud—the autobiography of the psychotic Judge Schreber, material on anthropology and the history of ancient religions, Le Bon's crowd theory—he comes to quite different conclusions about group psychology and the shaping of the ego. Like Freud, Canetti tends to find the prototype of crowd (that is, irrational) behavior in religion, and much of *Crowds and Power* is really a rationalist's discourse about religion. For example, what Canetti calls the lamenting pack is just another name for religions of lament, of which he gives a dazzling analysis, contrasting the slow tempos of Catholic piety and ritual (expressing the Church's perennial fear of the open crowd) with the frenzied mourning in the Shi'ite branch of Islam.

Like Freud, too, Canetti dissolves politics into pathology, treating society as a mental activity—a barbaric one, of course—that must be decoded. Thus he moves, without breaking stride, from the notion of the crowd to the "crowd symbol," and analyzes social grouping and the forms of community as transactions of crowd symbols. Some final turn of the crowd argument seems to have been reached when Canetti puts the French Revolution in its place, finding the Revolution less interesting as an eruption of the destructive than as a "national crowd symbol" for the French.

For Hegel and his successors, the historical (the home of irony) and the natural are two radically different processes. In *Crowds and Power,* history is "natural." Canetti argues to history, not from it. First comes the account of the crowd; then, as illustration, the section called "The Crowd in History." History is used only to furnish examples—a rapid use. Canetti is partial to the evidence of historyless (in the Hegelian sense) peoples, treating anthropological anecdotes as having the same illustrative value as an event taking place in an advanced historical society.

Crowds and Power is an eccentric book—made literally eccentric by its ideal of "universality," which leads Canetti to avoid making the obvious reference: Hitler. He appears indirectly, in the central importance Canetti gives to the case of Judge Schreber. (Here is Canetti's only reference to Freud—in one discreet footnote, where Canetti says that had Freud lived a bit longer he might have seen Schreber's paranoid delusions in a more pertinent way: as a prototype of the political, specifically Nazi, mentality.) But Canetti is genuinely not Eurocentric—one of his large achievements as a mind. Conversant with Chinese as well as European thought, with Buddhism and Islam as well as Christianity, Canetti enjoys a remarkable freedom from reductive habits of thinking. He seems incapable of using psychological knowledge in a reductive way. . . . (pp. 195-200)

His protest against seeing historically is directed not just against that most plausible of reductionisms. It is also a protest against death. To think about history is to think about the dead; and to be incessantly reminded that one is mortal. Canetti's thought is conservative in the most literal sense. It—he—does not want to die.

"I want to feel everything in me before I think it," Canetti wrote in 1943, and for this, he says, he needs a long life. To die prematurely means having not fully engorged himself and, therefore, having not used his mind as he could. It is almost as if Canetti had to keep his consciousness in a permanent state of avidity, to remain unreconciled to death. . . . Recurrent images of needing to feel everything inside himself, of unifying everything in one head, illustrate Canetti's attempts through magical thinking and moral clamorousness to "refute" death. (pp. 200-01)

[Plausible] doom is just what Canetti cannot admit. He is unperturbed by the possibility of the flagging of appetite, the satiation of desire, the devaluation of passion. Canetti gives no thought to the decomposition of the feelings any more than of the body, only to the persistence of the mind. Rarely has anyone been so at home in the mind, with so little ambivalence.

Canetti is someone who has felt in a profound way the responsibility of words, and much of his work makes the effort to communicate something of what he has learned about how to pay attention to the world. There is no doctrine, but there is a great deal of scorn, urgency, grief, and euphoria. The message of the mind's passions is passion. "I try to imagine someone saying to Shakespeare, 'Relax!'" says Canetti. His work eloquently defends tension, exertion, moral and amoral seriousness.

But Canetti is not just another hero of the will. Hence the unexpected last attribute of a great writer that he finds in Broch: such a writer, he says, teaches us how to breathe. Canetti commends Broch's writings for their "rich store of breathing experience." It was Canetti's deepest, oddest compliment, and therefore one he also paid to Goethe (the most predictable of his admirations): Canetti also reads Goethe as saying, "Breathe!" Breathing may be the most radical of occupations, when construed as a liberation from other needs such as having a career, building a reputation, accumulating knowledge. What Canetti says at the end of this progress of admiration, his homage to Broch, suggests what there is most to admire. The last achievement of the serious admirer is to stop immediately putting to work the energies aroused by, filling up the space opened by, what is admired. Thereby talented admirers give themselves permission to breathe, to breathe more deeply. But for that it is necessary to go beyond avidity; to identify with something beyond achievement, beyond the gathering of power. (pp. 203-04)

Susan Sontag, "Mind As Passion" (originally published in a different form in The New York Review of Books, *Vol. XXVII, No. 14, September 25, 1980),* in her Under the Sign of Saturn *(reprinted by permission of Farrar, Straus and Giroux, Inc.; copyright © 1980 by Susan Sontag), Farrar, Straus and Giroux, 1980, pp. 181-204.*

ANATOLE BROYARD

Though Kafka's "Letters to Felice" chronicles one of the most bizarre love affairs in the entire history of that emotion, it is not every reader who can get through its 600 pages. We ought to be grateful, then, to Elias Canetti . . . , for in **"Kafka's Other Trial"** he summarizes the letters, interprets them in the light of Kafka's character and relates them to his books.

According to Mr. Canetti, Kafka's "trial" with Felice closely parallels his novel "The Trial." His engagement becomes Joseph K.'s arrest in the first chapter. And what his letters call the "tribunal"—a meeting with Felice and her parents in which they agree to end the engagement—corresponds to the final scene in "The Trial" when Joseph K. is executed. . . .

"Any life is laughable," Mr. Canetti observes, "if one knows it well enough. It is something serious and terrible if one knows it even better." In **"Kafka's Other Trial,"** both these aspects, the comic and the tragic, are present. What is amazing is that Kafka himself, who had a brilliant sense of humor, did not see the comedy of his five-year engagement to Felice.

Though Mr. Canetti's interpretations of Kafka's letters to Felice are certainly interesting, it does seem that it required no great acumen to arrive at them. One leaves **"Kafka's Other Trial"** feeling rather hungry, sensing that there is much more that might have been said.

Anatole Broyard, "Letter-Writing Lover," in The New York Times *(© 1982 by The New York Times Company; reprinted by permission), February 27, 1982, p. 15.*

ALFRED KAZIN

"The Torch in My Ear" is the second volume of [Canetti's] autobiography; the first was **"The Tongue Set Free: Remembrance of a European Childhood."** . . . The most arresting passages in both books deal with his mother and the long battle between them. But neither book is as important as **"Auto-Da-Fé"** or **"Crowds and Power."** As the very titles indicate, Canetti is more at ease writing cultural history than offering us personal revelation.

"The Tongue Set Free" was about his literary ambitions and his efforts to avoid the business career that his wealthy relatives all over Europe designated for him after the sudden death of his father as a young man. **"The Torch in My Ear"** refers to the overwhelming influence on the young Canetti of the powerful satirist Karl Kraus, who not only wrote every word in his own magazine, Die Fackel (The Torch), but gave public readings that spellbound young intellectuals in Vienna. . . .

My complaint about Canetti as an autobiographer is that he is analytic about many individuals in his life who did not have the emotional influence on him of his strident mother and intrusive relatives. He seems to be so reclusive by nature that he is not only hostile to crowds but unwilling to report any erotic relationships in life. He is so dedicated to the analysis of marginal personalities—a type with which he must identify—that too many pages of the autobiography are concerned with strangers, oddballs and freaks, who are presented not because they had any marked effect on him but because he is proud of being able to confront them sympathetically. He is too much the cultural historian to be interested in such powerless people; he is just setting himself up as a rival to Freud. Ironically, it is Freud the physician and not Canetti the novelist who really captures this sort of person on the page.

Canetti is significantly memorable about people he considers stronger than himself [such as Karl Kraus]. (p. 11)

The most vivid character in both of Canetti's volumes of autobiography, his mother, was also strong enough to dominate him. She was a constant reader, a constant hysteric after her husband's early death, a devotee of Strindberg and a snob. If she had not taught her son the best kind of German and insisted on his keeping up the highest standards in it, he might not have become the writer he did. At the same time, she tried to keep him from a literary career and was constantly at him to see the world in less theoretical and bookish terms. Yet arresting as this portrait is, it is somehow never whole; he reproduces her in bits and pieces, outburst by outburst, as if he had never quite recovered from her impact.

Recalling the 20's in Berlin, Canetti also gives us slashing portraits of Bertolt Brecht and Georg Grosz, neither of whom ever tried to be a nice fellow by Canetti's standards and who appear in this book as tyrants. The one totally sympathetic writer in Canetti's portrait gallery of the time is Isaac Babel, with whom Canetti identified not as a writer or as a Jew but because Babel, who came from the Russian city Odessa on the Black Sea, seemed to connect with Canetti's birth in a country that also bordered on the Black Sea. Which goes to show you what Bulgaria, of all places, finally did for the strangely gifted Elias Canetti, whose autobiography is as odd as the circumstances of his life. (pp. 11, 34)

> Alfred Kazin, "A Bookish Man's Book of Himself," in The New York Times Book Review (© 1982 by The New York Times Company; reprinted by permission), September 19, 1982, pp. 11, 34.

GARY GIDDINS

Despite a few gossipy portraits of writers and artists in 1920s Berlin, Elias Canetti's *The Torch in My Ear*—the second volume in a remarkable autobiography—can hold only marginal interest for readers unfamiliar with the scope of his work. Canetti has published relatively little in 50 years, but as with other models of literary diligence, notably Proust and Joyce, his books are of a piece. Almost every chapter of the autobiography presumes intimacy with the two great books that made Canetti's reputation, the novel *Auto-da-Fé* and the treatise *Crowds and Power*. As a third pinnacle, the memoirs sharpen and enrich the vision of the first two, while embodying Canetti's conviction that the "public and the private can no longer be separated." Until about 15 years ago, the private Canetti was a cipher even in Europe. But his recent books, culminating in the still incomplete memoirs (640 pages covering only 26 years), seem intent on giving the writer parity with his writings.

As novelist, philosopher, and autobiographer, Canetti, the intransigent moral witness, offers no moral codes, utopian dreams, or escape hatches for "our monstrous century." The only code to which he adheres absolutely—a writer's code—is to stand in undaunted opposition to his time. . . . He restates his ambition in one of the aphorisms collected in *The Human Province:* "To find the path through the labyrinth of one's own

time without giving in to one's own time, and without jumping out." The autobiographical writings represent a third way of not jumping out, a third angle from which to ponder a lifetime's obsession with paranoia and power, the individual and crowds, death and God, the self and the world. Writing with the Flaubertian relish he admires in Kafka ("nothing is trivial so long as it is right"), he reinvents himself as a literary character, ruthlessly mining memory for clues to the enigma that is Elias Canetti. (pp. 1, 10)

Canetti's emotional and intellectual involvement with his mother is the central drama of his youth [covered in *The Tongue Set Free* (volume one of the autobiography)]. (p. 10)

The Torch in My Ear details the making of a writer, or at least the making of a writer's obsessions. Its relationship to the earlier books is complex; although Canetti carefully signposts the revelations and illuminations that put him on the trail of crowd psychology, he never draws connections between the events of his life and the plot and symbology of *Auto-da-Fé*. Part of the great pleasure to be had in this sometimes perversely detailed memoir is the experience of coming across bits of cloth that eventually became the fabric of the novel. . . . [Until] *The Torch in My Ear,* it was impossible to realize how much *Auto-da-Fé* was grounded in the reality of his boyhood observations—a reality shaken by fires, inflation, madness, and crowds, as well as a number of impressive people. Canetti came to worship Karl Kraus, the editor and sole writer of the polemical journal *Die Fackel (The Torch).* Constant attendance at Kraus's histrionic lectures helped Canetti develop his gift for parody and mimicry, but Kraus's activism seems to have been beyond his grasp. During a brief stay in Berlin, he came to admire Grosz (though the painter's lechery at a party offended him), hate Brecht (for a lover of Aristophanes, Canetti's dismissal of *Three-penny Opera* is unconvincing), and worship the owlish perceptiveness of Isaac Babel.

The most haunting people in this installment of Canetti's life, however, are his mother, with whom he is locked in a struggle much less paralyzing but no less constrained than Kafka's with his father, and Veza, an intelligent and rather mysterious woman whom Canetti later married. *The Torch in My Ear* concludes unsatisfactorily, in that the mother and Veza disappear from the narrative before those relationships are in any way resolved. He never mentions his marriage, or the response of either woman to the novel (though there are clues to his mother's astonishment in *The Tongue Set Free*). Presumably, these matters will be taken up in the third installment, yet they make this volume a less tidy work than its predecessor. Moreover, the account of his writing of *Auto-da-Fé* is strangely elusive, omitting several important facts that appear in *The Conscience of Words.*

The Torch in My Ear is filled with minutely observed recollections of incidental figures and scenes. . . . [The] Flaubertian zeal to get things right tells us something important about Canetti. . . . [In many passages], especially those concerning his teachers and schoolmates, he exhibits his humanism, his ability to really hear what people say. "With Kafka," Canetti wrote in *The Human Province,* "something new came into the world, a more precise feeling for its dubiousness, a feeling, however, that is coupled not with hatred, but with respect for life." As with so many of Canetti's tributes, the words rebound to the author. Nowhere is that respect more manifest than in these incidental vignettes. Another of Canetti's tributes, however, seems even more relevant—the one to Stendhal in *Crowds and Power.* The 1981 Nobel Prize in Literature has secured

Canetti an international audience, but in the 1950s, when his novel was little read and his life was consumed by a 20-year project, he must have identified with Stendhal, who "was concerned to write for a few . . . certain that in a hundred years he would be read by many." He concluded: "But whoever opens Stendhal will find him and also everything which surrounded him; and he finds it *here,* in this life. Thus the dead offer themselves as food to the living; their immortality profits them." In this regard the diligent, plodding earwitness Canetti has beaten death after all. (p. 11)

Gary Giddins, "A Face in the Crowd," in VLS *(copyright © 1982 News Group Publications, Inc.), No. 11, October, 1982, pp. 1, 10-11.*

John Cheever

1912-1982

American short story writer and novelist.

Cheever's fictional world is suburban New York and New England, and his typical characters are of the upper middle class. This closed, serene social milieu often contrasts sharply with the chaos and despair experienced by his characters. Overall, Cheever is a humanist; he believes in the rejuvenative power of love and treats his protagonists with compassion. Wit and elegance are consistently present in his prose.

Cheever received his first significant critical attention for *The Wapshot Chronicle*, which won the National Book Award in 1958. *The Stories of John Cheever*, a collection of all of Cheever's previously published short fiction and some new material, reenforced his reputation as a major American writer. This volume won several major literary awards in 1979, including a Pulitzer Prize and a National Book Critics' Circle Award.

Cheever's last work, *Oh What a Paradise It Seems*, written before his recent death, is a novella which addresses familiar Cheeveresque themes of redemption and rejuvenation. Although critical reception of this recent book is varied, the consistent quality of the Cheever canon has indisputably placed Cheever among the ranks of America's great storytellers.

(See also *CLC*, Vols. 3, 7, 8, 11, 15; *Contemporary Authors*, Vols. 7-8, rev. ed., Vol. 106, rev. ed. [obituary]; *Contemporary Authors New Revision Series*, Vol. 5; *Dictionary of Literary Biography*, Vol. 2; *Dictionary of Literary Biography Yearbook: 1980*.)

© Nancy Crampton

CHARLES NICOL

Cheever is placed just before Chekhov, another fine writer of short stories, in the fiction section of your public library, and the tempting criticism of the Wapshot novels is that they sometimes seem to be paste-ups of minimally connected stories. *Bullet Park*, a novel with a clean plot line, the convergence of hammer and nail, resists this temptation to digress. We are nevertheless ultimately disappointed, for while Cheever's writing retains its brilliance, his plot is not at all convincing, depending as it does upon the motivation of Hammer, a most unsuccessful character. Hammer's madness is apparent only in his plans for an absurd murder. Can it be Cheever's intention to argue that murder involves little aberration in a man's personality, or is there a previously unsuspected limitation to Cheever's imagination? This lack is made far more obvious when Hammer, for a third of the novel, tells his own story. From Poe through Faulkner and Nabokov, American authors have delighted in projecting variant images of the world through the eyes of the child, the idiot, and the lunatic. Yet the world of Hammer is pretty much the same as the world of Cheever in the rest of the novel. Nothing seems to have been gained through that first-person interlude, and a lot has been lost, including our confidence in the motivation of the character most crucial to the plot. No doubt Cheever intends to show that experiences today are fragmentary and that people no longer possess—if they ever did—a unified personality, yet if Hammer has only the vaguest of notions about why he wanted to commit

murder, and discusses his actions with both detachment and distaste, we may justifiably ask why we should listen to him at all.

Curiously, the novel is more than half finished before the main plot and the character of Hammer begin to be important, and this first half is the more pleasant part. It is always strange to read a novel that weakens toward the end; we blame ourselves for its deterioration. Highly recommended for those who never finish one book before they start another. (p. 98)

> Charles Nicol, "Salvation in the Suburbs," in The Atlantic Monthly (*copyright © 1969, by The Atlantic Monthly Company, Boston, Mass.; reprinted with permission*), *Vol. 223, No. 5, May, 1969, pp. 96, 98*.

GUY DAVENPORT

Mr. Cheever has done a strange thing in [*Bullet Park*]. He has taken the plot of Samuel Beckett's *Molloy* and transposed it to the mortgaged suburbs whose scotch-fuelled denizens he vies with John O'Hara to be the Zola of. Even stranger, he has reached into another Beckett work, the play *Endgame*, and lifted the conceit whereby one of his characters is named Hammer and another Nailles. Thus supplied with a hamper of borrowed stuff, he proceeds with verve to write what might have been a first-rate novel. In Nailles and his wife we have a rich American family that lives in a limbo of spiritual emptiness without suspecting the slightest deprivation. (p. 549)

Mr. Cheever's account of life in suburbia makes one's soul ache. Here is human energy that once pushed plows and stormed the walls of Jerusalem and lifted Chartres to its pinnacles spent daily in getting up hung over, staggering drugged with tranquilizers to wait for a train to rattle one into Manhattan. There eight hours are given to the writing of advertisements about halitosis and mouthwash. Then the train back, a cocktail party, and drunk to bed. Every step one takes is on matter bought with money borrowed from a bank whose sole business is to collect the largest possible interest on the loan for the longest possible time. . . .

Once Mr. Cheever has told his story of Nailles, he turns to the Hammers (as Beckett, after the full measure of Malloy's misery, brings on the sinister Moran), both of whom have apparently been driven mad by life in America. From the Hammers arises an inexplicable force the aim of which is to crush Nailles. It is here that Mr. Cheever ought to have read his Beckett closer, or not borrowed plots from him in the first place. Beckett's *Molloy* makes sense, and lives in one's mind ever after. The same device in Mr. Cheever makes no sense at all; in fact, is embarrassingly awkward and aesthetically wrong. Beckett's Moran is a symbol of malevolence; meanness is his genius. Hammer is a man gone off his rocker, no more interesting than any other lunatic. The end of the novel is therefore false and shockingly inept. (p. 550)

> *Guy Davenport, "Elegant Botches," in* National Review *(© National Review, Inc., 1969; 150 East 35th St., New York, NY 10016), Vol. XXI, No. 21, June 3, 1969, pp. 549-50.**

JOHN GARDNER

When in 1969 John Cheever turned from the lovable Wapshots to the weird creatures who inhabit Bullet Park, most reviewers attacked or dismissed him. They were, it seems to me, dead wrong. The Wapshot books, though well made, were minor. **"Bullet Park,"** illusive, mysteriously built, was major—in fact, a magnificent work of fiction.

One reason the book has been misunderstood is that it lacks simple message. . . . Another reason is that Cheever is right about evil: it comes quietly. . . . Talking of the oldest and darkest evil, Cheever speaks softly, gently, as if casually. Suspense is not something he fails to achieve in **"Bullet Park"** but something he has avoided. The novel moves as if purposelessly, like its bland-minded, not very likable protagonist, and from time to time gives a nervous start at the blow of a distant axe.

Cheever's subject is chance—but more than that. Chance is a vehicle that carries the book into darker country. The opening lines present a setting—a train station—designed to suggest the whole human condition in this mysterious, chance-riddled universe. . . . (But: "The setting seems in some way to be at the heart of the matter," says Cheever, sly. Art, like life, may start with chance, but chance shrouds something darker.) . . .

Cheever reconsiders the idea of chance, remembering psychic and psychological phenomena, the claims of good and bad witches. What emerges is a world where hope does exist (magic is real and can cure or kill), a world in a way even grimmer

than Beckett's because here love and sacrifice are realities, like hope, but realities in flux, perpetually threatened, perishing.

The novel says yes-and-no to existentialists, who can account for all but the paragnost. Cheever, in other words, sees the mind in its totality—sees not only the fashionable existential darkness but the light older than consciousness, which gives nothingness definition. Partly for the sake of this wholeness of vision, Cheever in **"Bullet Park"** abandoned the fact-bound novel of verisimilitude, which is by nature impotent to dramatize the mind's old secrets, and turned to dependence on *voice,* secret of the willing suspension of disbelief that normally carries the fantasy or tale.

Cheever's voice—compassionate, troubled, humorous—controls the action, repeatedly calling attention to itself in phrases like "at the time of which I'm writing." Where his voice fades out, character voices come in. . . .

The decision [of the stranger Hammer to murder Nailles] is without explicit motivation, based mainly on "the mysterious binding power of nomenclature." Cheever could have explained the whole thing, black magic as psychosis (the magic of names), and would have done so in a Wapshot book. But how do you *render* a thing so strange? Instead of explaining, he inserts Hammer's journal. With a mad man's objectivity, Hammer sketches the story of his life.

The coldness of tone (even when the scene is comic), the flat description of his enfeebled quest for relationship, his survival by flight into symbolism (yellow rooms, a dream-castle, pieces of string), explains magically what the fact-bound novel would turn to the dry unreality of a case study. The motive for the projected murder is coincidence—a correspondence of names, two pieces of string. We learn that Paul Hammer has murdered before, without knowing it himself, to get a yellow room. But the rendered proof of his demonic nature is his voice, a quiet stovelid on terror and rage.

As in all first-rate novels, the form of **"Bullet Park"** grows out of its subject. More here than in his earlier writings, Cheever depends on poetic (which is to say, magical) devices—rhythm, imagistic repetition, echo. Instead of conventional plot, an accretion of accidents. Far below consciousness, the best people in Bullet Park are mirror images of the worst: they live by magic, correspondence. (p. 2)

Nailles, a tragicomic fool, is simply lucky. By accidents of his childhood, he is in touch with Nature. . . . Hammer, by accidents of childhood and bastardy, is cut off from Nature and himself. Nailles's blessing is that he is married to a good woman and has a son, whereas Hammer is married to a bitch and is childless. Nailles's luck means that he's faintly in touch with the higher magic of the universe—the magic of love, creative force—whereas Hammer is in touch only with lower magic, correspondence. . . .

Cheever closes: "Tony went back to school on Monday and Nailles—drugged—went off to work and everything was as wonderful, wonderful, wonderful, wonderful as it had been."

There, it may be, is the underlying reason that reviewers were annoyed by **"Bullet Park"**. The novel is bleak, full of danger and offense, like a poisoned apple in the playpen. Good and evil are real, but are effects of mindless chance—or heartless grace. The demonology of Calvin, or Cotton Mather. Disturbing or not, the book towers high above the many recent novels that wail and feed on Sartre. A religious book, affirmation out of ashes. **"Bullet Park"** is a novel to pore over, move around in, live with. The image repetitions, the stark and subtle correspondences that create the book's ambiguous meaning, its uneasy courage and compassion, sink in and in, like a curative spell. (p. 24)

John Gardner, "Witchcraft in Bullet Park," in The New York Times Book Review *(© 1971 by The New York Times Company; reprinted by permission), October 24, 1971, pp. 2, 24.*

SAMUEL COALE

The fictional landscape of Cheever's art includes the social pretensions and moral implications of modern suburbia, the larger patterns of human experience, such as the loss of innocence and the deep spiritual hunger for a golden simpler past, and the discovery of beautiful moments to celebrate within the contemporary wasteland. These themes and ideas occur again and again in the short stories and novels. The way they are organized and detailed reveals the form in which Cheever's fictional landscape is created. (p.115)

[Upon a thin] thread of sensibility, thinner certainly than a sturdy and direct narrative or plot line, are hung the seemingly random episodes of the short stories and novels. Such a method may be overextended in a novel and better suited to the length of the short story, but such is Cheever's method.

The emotional center or vision of Cheever's fiction remains somewhat elusive. His light, ironic style can cut both ways. On the one hand, he seems to be a romantic, yearning for the good old days of yesteryear, far from the madding crowds of the aimless, tasteless contemporary world. On the other hand, he seems to realize the essential futility and unreality of such romantic notions and seems determined to find moments of beauty within the chaotic and graceless contemporary world. Cheever conjures up the romantic past, those glimpses of St. Botolphs, for instance, in some of the most beautiful lyric passages in his fiction. At the same time the contemporary world is regarded comically, almost so absurdly and outrageously that it cannot be taken all that seriously. Yet the ironies of the style deflate the nostalgic pretensions of the romantic past and reveal the real spiritual uncertainty and psychic pain of the chaotic present. In either case Cheever's style can both illuminate and avoid the implications of the situations he writes about. He seems to want his style to be both disarming and protective at once. He seems, finally, to be celebrating his own ability to find delight in both the romantic past, however false, and the contemporary present, however chaotic.

It is essentially Cheever's encounter with experience that we remember, not the encounter of any one of his characters. . . . Cheever is neither concerned with uncovering the complexities within a particular moment of experience nor interested in sounding the depths of an episode. His is more an attempt to translate that immediate experience into the artistic opportunity to display the lyric gracefulness of his style, to focus the reader's attention primarily upon the encounter between the artist and his material. (pp. 116-17)

Such a method basically reveals a comic rather than a tragic encounter, in which the reader and the author are distanced from the painful immediacy of experience and are directed toward the shape or form that the author gives to that experience. The characters perform in a specific social setting, modern suburbia. All their private griefs, sorrows, and joys are enacted in that realm and shaped by it. We can laugh at the exterior situations that engulf these characters, and at the same time we can sympathize with their interior feelings. It is this kind of distanced look—this focusing on outward incident rather than on inward pain—that provides Cheever with his comic angle of vision on the foibles of modern suburban life. It is this essential graceful and comic form of Cheever's style that shapes our lasting impressions of his art.

Cheever's attitudes toward suburbia remain ambivalent throughout. It is no accident that even the names of his suburban sanctuaries contain both good and evil aspects: "Shady Hill," "Proxmire [near the mire] Manor," "Gory Brook," "Bullet Park." Only in **Falconer** did he succeed in overcoming these ambivalent attitudes by choosing to write about a prison instead of suburbia. He observed accurately the worms in the suburban apple without deciding that the entire apple was, therefore, spoiled. He realized that the dream of suburban stability and comfort, however decent and valorous to the middle-class mind, is yet a dream, unreliable, transitory, and easily shattered. To think otherwise is to accept illusion. To replace a truly moral consciousness with a mere appreciation of comfort and affluence is to replace man's unending spiritual quest for self-knowledge and self-transcendence with a closet full of dead, unilluminating objects. Cheever's darker tales conjure up the strange powers that objects may have over the unenlightened mind. His lyric tales celebrate those moments of beauty and spiritual illumination that can occur only within the sound moral framework of an ordered and disciplined way of life. (pp. 117-18)

Samuel Coale, in his John Cheever *(copyright © 1977 by Frederick Ungar Publishing Co., Inc.), Ungar, 1977, 130 p.*

LYNNE WALDELAND

The publication of **Falconer,** with its shockingly new milieu and its unusually violent language, is only the most dramatic proof that Cheever is not afraid to push off from past accomplishments and to work with previously untried materials. But his whole body of work reveals that he has consistently been willing to grow, to extend the range of his subject matter, and increasingly to complicate his recurring themes. One of his early reviewers worried that the main danger for Cheever might be to find himself trapped within the elegant style of his promising early stories, but Cheever has enlarged and refined that style through four novels and several hundred short stories. No two collections of short stories are the same; some obvious development of theme, tone, or style marks each. Even *The Wapshot Scandal,* a sequel, goes far beyond the setting and the perspective of *The Wapshot Chronicle.* **Bullet Park** was different enough from Cheever's previous work so as to be radically misunderstood when it was published, and **Falconer** was an even more startling departure from Cheever's earlier subject matter and style.

At the same time, Cheever does have certain recurrent themes which give a sense of coherence to his career, much as the international theme and the conflict between innocence and experience unify the works of Henry James. One of Cheever's most frequently chosen subjects is family relationships, but he is no simple chronicler or analyst. He has too much respect for the mysterious spaces as well as the successful synapses between husbands and wives, parents and children. He also writes of the relationship between brothers, showing it as intimate and loyal in *The Wapshot Chronicle,* as fratricidal in

Falconer, with many gradations in between in other works. Along with this focus on the family, Cheever incorporates the historical and cultural developments of his times into his fiction. The Depression and World War II figure to some degree in his earliest stories; bomb shelters, the space program, and the sexual revolution appear in his later works. The ground where these dual interests in the internal dynamics of the person and the external convulsions of the world meet is in Cheever's attention to the dailiness of American life, the focus that often gets him characterized as a novelist of manners. Generally, however, in the novel form, he deals with the more extreme experiences of human life; it is more often his stories that really work out the relationships between the inner person and outer world, the present and the past, the best that we dream of being and compromises we continually make.

Cheever's career is varied enough that it is possible to see links between him and a number of American writers and movements. It seems to me, however, that beneath the realistic surface of most of his novels and stories, beneath the careful delineation of manners, a representational American milieu, and historical and cultural facts, Cheever is basically a romantic and a moralist. He is a romantic in that his interest finally is in the individual. . . . And he is a moralist in that despite the comic texture of his works, the toleration for all manner of human foibles, and the general affirmation which most of his works finally reach, he is always aware of right and wrong, better and worse, life-enhancing and life-diminishing qualities both in people and in the world which can thwart the full humanity of his characters. In these qualities he seems most to resemble James and Fitzgerald. . . . There is also a little echo of Hawthorne in Cheever's work in his New England moral toughness, his wish that people reach their best human potential despite a lack of cooperation by society. It seems to me that Cheever in his own time has no close peer. He is less naively romantic than Salinger, less simply a chronicler of manners than Auchincloss, less egocentric than Mailer, less narrowly focused than Malamud or Roth, less gimmicky than Vonnegut. His combination of attention to the individual and awareness of the facts and the power of society connect him more with classic American authors like Hawthorne, James, and Fitzgerald; and despite his own New England background and East Coast life-style, he has resisted the post-World War II tendency of American writers to divert American fiction toward a narrow exploration of their own individual religious, racial, or geographical roots.

Yet, at the same time that Cheever's ability to generalize his materials is clear, his readers are becoming more aware of the genesis of those materials out of his own life. (pp. 141-43)

The single most remarkable aspect of Cheever's career so far is, I think, the beauty and consistency of his style. It is lyrical without being flowery; it is precise without being coldly analytical. . . . Cheever's great contribution to contemporary American literature is that when he brings his formidable gifts of observation and language to bear upon life in our time, he doesn't diminish it but instead leaves us with a sense of increased possibility and even, at times, joy. (pp. 144-45)

> *Lynne Waldeland, in her* John Cheever *(copyright ©1979 by Twayne Publishers, Inc.; reprinted with the permission of Twayne Publishers, a Division of G. K. Hall & Co., Boston), Twayne, 1979, 160 p.*

ANATOLE BROYARD

Of all our major American writers, John Cheever seems to me the most spontaneous. Because that word has been so much abused I'll say that I take it to refer to a talent that appears to be involuntary, that enables Mr. Cheever to see poetic connections where the rest of us would not have, that causes his mind to teem with radical but always concrete images, that keeps his language in a state of excitement.

While Saul Bellow uses a wider frame of reference and John Updike has a firmer control of his effects, John Cheever *seethes* with literature. He seems drunk with it, as if life itself, as well as the wish to write about it, made him happy. He is perhaps our most sophisticated optimist.

In a typical Cheever story or novel, he sends a worldly man out into the world looking for love, beauty, continuity, style, manners, meaning—all sorts of shining things—and follows this man's determined and sometimes hallucinated efforts to find them. . . .

Unlike most of our literary heroes, Mr. Cheever's are not generally sacrificed to irony. Though they may occasionally fall victim to his enthusiasm, or lose their way among his multitudinous inventions, he rarely gives up on them. He's the sort of man who'll go to any lengths for a friend—or for a character. . . .

He's like a crazy millionaire who lavishes his riches not on charities or causes, but on men and women who catch his eye. His romanticism has the toughness of someone who knows better, and he is lyrical in the way that only those who have begun to think about death dare to be.

In **"Oh What a Paradise It Seems,"** Mr. Cheever's felicities and eccentricities are in full spate. Lemuel Sears, his hero, is "old enough to remember the promise of dirigible travel," old enough to notice "that extraordinary preoccupation with innocence that absorbs people on a beach before the fall of darkness," old enough to marvel in "the pleasure of fleetness" as he ice skates on a frozen pond in the suburban town where his daughter lives.

A widower who still considers female company one of nature's bounties, Sears is struck by a woman in line before him at a bank. . . . Whatever else they may be, Mr. Cheever's heroes are always lovers. They work at love, seriously, as other men work at their businesses. Love transfigures them with adrenaline or desire and they throw themselves into gestures. . . .

[Of course, a dozen] things are going on in **"Oh What a Paradise It Seems."** Sears's beloved pond is to be filled in as a site for a war memorial. It is the profit to be made from dumping in the pond that inspires the scheme, and Sears hires a lawyer to fight it. When the woman from the bank abruptly mistreats him, he has a homosexual affair with the elevator operator in her building. . . .

A dog is shot, a man is run down by a car, a woman threatens to poison the food in a supermarket chain. Sears loses his case against the despoilers of the pond when his elegiac letter to the local paper is quoted in court. I'm not sure what happens after all this to the woman from the bank, the elevator operator, or Sears himself, but this, too, is part of Mr. Cheever's spontaneity.

He invents when he wishes and stops where he pleases, as if he were mocking the naïveté and the imaginative timidity of the literal-minded. I can't say that I'm comfortable with the ending of the book, but I gave up some time ago the notion that art was a comfortable affair. I find myself still mulling over **"Oh What a Paradise It Seems,"** still feeling my way through it, and I believe that's what John Cheever intended.

Anatole Broyard, "Books of the Times: 'Oh What a Paradise It Seems'," in The New York Times (© 1982 by The New York Times Company; reprinted by permission), March 3, 1982, p. C28.

JOHN LEONARD

We have been here before, in Cheever country, and it is fine [in **"Oh What a Paradise It Seems"**] to return. Ordinary people, who keep seed in the bird-feeding station and who do not see that playing golf and raising flowers are depraved, undergo an inexplicable test of heart. They are attacked in "that sense of sanctuary that is the essence of love." They dared to imagine that pain and suffering were "a principality, lying somewhere beyond the legitimate borders of western Europe," and then the mountains seem to shift in the space of a night and their children are suddenly refugees, right here on Hitching Post Lane.

There are pluses and minuses when a writer repeats himself. Those of us who were dismayed by the heroin addiction, homosexuality and convenient miracles of **"Falconer"** will be relieved to see him skating again on familiar ice. When Ezekiel ("God strengthens") went to prison for killing his brother, it was as if Chekov—and Cheever *is* our Chekov—had ducked into a telephone booth and reappeared wearing the cape and leotard of Dostoyevsky's Underground Man. Hadn't we had enough of the fire alarms of modernism?

Cheever goes here to the supermarket instead of prison. A woman tries to push too many items through the express checkout, and an old man objects: "I just can't stand to see someone take advantage of other people's kindness. It's like fascism. . . . People like you cause wars."

This is perfect Cheever; it is perfect, period.

And graduate students of the master will be thrilled by "netherness" and "portability," which they can add to "sanctuary" and "trespass" on their list of emotions in the "gypsy culture" of the American exurbs that Cheever anthropologizes. He is, of course, the poet of our displacement, our sense of a lost past and a "sacred grove," our feeling that we came from another country and left a better self behind, like unclaimed baggage. . . .

But Cheever's critics will complain once more of his sweet tooth for the lyrical, of too many nights "where kings in golden suits ride elephants over the mountains." Where is politics? Where is history? The ghetto and the camps? Are the displacements and paroxysms of the exurbs just an accident, a mere failure of luck or charm or nerve? Ought not the bourgeoisie to be punished for sins more grievous than "carnal importunacy"? Who can afford a skating rink so long as there is Bangladesh or the Gulag? And so on.

Certainly, **"Oh What a Paradise It Seems"** is minor art, although many of us will never grow up to achieve it. If Lemuel Sears is more plausible than Ezekiel Farragut, he is less compelling than Asa Bascomb in **"The World of Apples."** He is not, however, a lemon. He doesn't feel that hearing a Brandenburg Concerto in a shopping mall is ridiculous. He is one of the many Cheevers who refuse to give up on "Valor! Love! Virtue! Splendor! Kindness! Wisdom! Beauty!" These Cheevers sometimes try too hard, I agree, and the afflatus can be

embarrassing, but shouldn't we, like Moses in **"The Death of Justina,"** admire decency and despise death?

In Cheever's stories, men drown and fall off mountains, 15-year-old boys commit suicide, a wife shoots her husband as he is about to hurdle the living-room couch. . . . [There] is lighter fluid instead of vinegar in the green salad. In the swimming pool, an undertow; in the liquor closet, skeletons; in the snow, wolves. Why? (p. 25)

Everything is fragile. Chance abides and buffets.

It seems to me that Cheever speaks not so much of failures of luck and charm and nerve as of failures of faith. How to be brave and good? He mobilizes language in the service of decencies and intuitions that are no longer sanctioned at any altar or practiced in any politics. His stories are brilliant prayers on behalf of "the perfumes of life. . . ."

Of course, he wants too much. He wants wisdom *and* beauty, God *and* sex. Don't we all? Didn't Chekhov? (p. 26)

John Leonard, "Cheever Country," in The New York Times Book Review (© 1982 by The New York Times Company; reprinted by permission), March 7, 1982, pp. 1, 25-6.

GEOFFREY STOKES

Though Cheever can still turn a phrase with the best of them, *Oh What* . . . is by any and every standard a bad book, worthy of notice only because he put his name to it. Clumsily lurching back and forth between postmodern and realistic techniques, it botches both. The plot resolves itself by a devil ex machina; the language is flabby ("nether" does not mean "nondescript"), the snobbishness painful. Better you should read the collected stories. Or, best, *The Wapshot Chronicle*, which is truer and more touching a quarter century after its publication than this book is now or ever will be.

Geoffrey Stokes, "Books: 'Oh What a Paradise It Seems'" (reprinted by permission of The Village Voice and the author; copyright © News Group Publications, Inc., 1982), in The Village Voice, Vol. XXVII, No. 11, March 16, 1982, p. 93.

ANN HULBERT

In *Oh What a Paradise It Seems,* [Cheever's] dualistic world of facts and truths, matter and spirit, is suddenly more starkly lit than ever before—the search for spiritual salvation more insistent, material corruption more pervasive. The renowned pungency, diversity, and color of Cheever's writing seem to have faded somewhat; and the nostalgia, ever-present in his narratives about his wandering race, has lost some of its humane, lyric tone and echoes more remotely now.

The narrator of this eerie novella is looking back, as Cheever's narrators usually do, but this time he's not our contemporary taking us back with him to our common recent past—the last several decades of the century. Instead, the narrative voice emanates from the future, observing the close of this second millennium from a distant, and apparently idyllic, vantage point beyond us. The figure in the foreground of the scene is Lemuel Sears as he skates up and down the black ice of Beasley's Pond late one January afternoon. . . . Sears is uneasily beginning to face the facts of approaching old age. But, fleet and graceful on the smooth pond surface, he feels his spirit suddenly braced by "a sense of homecoming. . . ." (p. 43)

For all the familiar Cheever soulfulness with which he is endowed, however, Sears is hardly more than a shadow after the
mere ten pages it has taken to set him off on his spiritual journey
back toward love of nature and woman. As the spare plot
proceeds, it's clear the narrator is more interested in surveying
a culture and an allegorical landscape than in probing his main
character. . . . Like the water, the land has changed beyond
recognition; farms have been paved over by "that highway of
merchandising that reaches across the continent," lane upon
lane of cars blurring by, row upon row of fried-food places
serving up "the food for spiritual vagrants." It was "as if a
truly adventurous people had made a wrong turning and stum-
bled into a gypsy culture"; the country presents "a landscape,
a people . . . who had lost the sense of a harvest." The anthropological imagery abounds, documenting the "barbarity
and nomadism" of a contaminated civilization.

In this habitat, Lemuel Sears is an interesting specimen rather
than a compelling character. The saga of his rejuvenating efforts to purify a dirty pond and pollute a pretty woman is a
schematic spiritual progress, not an absorbing sentimental journey. Cheever's prose throughout is flatter, less highly polished
and graceful than in the past. He is aiming, evidently, to create
a different fictional fabric, strands of which have appeared in
his more recent work; its cut is more contemporary and cool,
with less of the often quaintly elegant style of old.

Thus Sears's love affair is farcical fantasy rather than psychologically compelling romance. . . . Similarly, Sears's ecological mission—ostensibly a traditional suspense story, crude all-
American despoilers versus poetic purifiers—turns out to be
an occasion for surrealistic social satire and meditations on the
state of the planet. Throughout, Cheever's depiction of a contaminated country is successfully alienating, in fact often all
too dispiriting. But his protagonist never becomes a soul lit
from within by a memory of love, by a yearning for some past
bliss of belonging; Sears is not that soft-hearted but stalwart
character of classic Cheever fiction, whom we may know all
too well now but miss nonetheless. (p. 44)

> *Ann Hulbert, "Lonely Nomads," in* The New Re-
> public *(reprinted by permission of* The New Repub-
> lic; © 1982 The New Republic, Inc.), Vol. 186, No.
> 13, March 31, 1982, pp. 42-5.*

JOHN UPDIKE

["**Oh What a Paradise It Seems**"] is too darting, too gaudy
in its deployment of artifice and aside, too disarmingly personal
in its voice, to be saddled with the label of novel or novella;
it is a parable and a tall tale—both sub-genres squarely within
the Judeo-Christian tradition, North American branch. Cheever
has lately taken the mantle of that tradition ever more comfortably upon his shoulders, and now unabashedly assumes the
accents of a seer. . . . Ever more boldly the celebrant of the
grand poetry of life, Cheever, once a taut and mordant chronicler of urban and suburban disappointments, now speaks in
the cranky, granular, impulsive, confessional style of our native
wise men and exhorters since Emerson. The pitch of his final
page is positively Transcendental:

> The thought of stars contributed to the power
> of his feeling. What moved him was a sense
> of those worlds around us, our knowledge how-
> ever imperfect of their nature, our sense of their
> possessing some grain of our past and of our
> lives to come. It was that most powerful sense

of how singular, in the vastness of creation, is
the richness of our opportunity. The sense of
that hour was of an exquisite privilege, the great
benefice of living here and renewing ourselves
with love. What a paradise it seemed!

If such root affirmations ring, in this late age of median strips
and polluted ponds, with a certain deliberate and wry gallantry,
that, too, is accommodated in the tale—in the burlesque of its
consumerism, the ogreish farce of its politics, the chemical
pranks of its natural resurrection. . . . Cheever's instinctive
belief in the purity and glory of Creation brings with it an
inevitable sensitivity to corruption; like Hawthorne, he is a
poet of the poisoned. His American landscape is dotted with
tiny atrocities—back-yard charcoal braziers and "stand-up"
swimming pools and domestic architecture that "was all happy
ending" and in whose sad living rooms people pass one another
"a box of crackers that the label promised would stimulate
conversation." The tinge of snobbishness in his dismay is
redeemed by the generosity with which Cheever feels, like an
American of a century and a half ago, the wonder of this land
of promises.

He loves nature—light, water, human love. Again and again,
the elements are remembered by his paltry suburbanites. . . .
Nature stamps Man at every moment, and litters our lives with
clues to the supernatural:

> When [Sears] was young, brooks had seemed
> to speak to him in the tongues of men and
> angels. Now that he was an old man who spoke
> five or six languages—all of them poorly—the
> sound of water seemed to be the language of
> his nativity, some tongue he had spoken before
> his birth. Soft and loud, high and low, the sound
> of water reminded him of eavesdropping in some
> other room than where the party was.

The party, for now, is here, in this shadow of paradise. Were
Cheever, cosmopolitan as he has become, less a New Englander
than he is, with the breath of Thoreau and Emily Dickinson in
his own lovely quick light phrasing, he might fail to convince
us that a real glory shines through his transparent inventions.
The gap in "**Falconer**" between the circumstantial prison and
the spiritual adventure that it allegorized certainly took a reader's indulgence to bridge. But in "**Oh What a Paradise It
Seems**" there are no more gaps than between the blades of a
spinning pinwheel. All is fabulous from the start; all is fancy,
praise, and rue, seamlessly. Janice, that oddly named village,
receives postcards from all the territories that Cheever's imagination has been happy in—Italy, Eastern Europe, the St. Bo-
tolph's of the Wapshot chronicles, and the Shady Hill and
Bullet Park where America's dream of space and plenty and
domestic bliss has come to so fragmentary a realization. The
paradisiacal elixir has a chalky taste but in this testament survives its contaminants and is served up sparkling. (pp. 189-
90, 193)

> *John Updike, "On Such a Beautiful Green Little
> Planet" (© 1982 by John Updike), in* The New Yorker,
> *Vol. LVIII, No. 7, April 5, 1982, pp. 189-90, 193-
> 97.**

ROBERT M. ADAMS

[*Oh What a Paradise It Seems*] is what Henry James delighted
to call . . . a *nouvelle;* and it would almost seem that the old

master had Mr. Cheever in his mind's eye when he wrote of "the only compactness that has a charm, the only spareness that has a force, the only simplicity that has a grace—those, in each order, that produce the *rich* effect." Though the canvas is small in this new novel, it is not miniature work; it is broad, impressionistic, at its best a poetic narrative.

The book's central figure is a man of some years . . . [who is] shaken by a sense of the fragile beauty of vanishing things. He lives and works in what is clearly New York City, and spends much of his time in what could be the Connecticut suburbs—though really his world is almost limitless because it persistently shades off into vagueness and nondefinition. His actions hint at a parable without ever taking on the symmetry of one; they touch on melodrama, but glancingly. Other characters encountered by the hero are mute, almost inarticulate; with little ado they materialize, and with even less they disappear, as into soft mist.

Lemuel Sears's affair with Renée Herndon occupies a considerable part of the book. . . . Her standard conversational gambit is, "You don't understand the first thing about women"; and about this woman it's certainly true. Sears doesn't understand her, she makes no effort to explain herself so the reader doesn't understand her either; if Cheever does, he isn't letting on. There's an enormous, charming, unreliable vacancy in and around her.

The surface of the book is also charming and unreliable. . . . A speed-reader will sail blithely across the novel's glistening surfaces; if he pauses a moment to look under his feet, the thin ice will be starring out beneath him.

Much of the book's action centers on Beasley's Pond, a deep body of water actually used in winter, by Sears and others, for skating. . . .

The tendency of the solid surfaces to tail off into vagueness counterpoints the way people in the story change their minds abruptly and without explanation, the way crucial developments are determined by coincidence. . . .

[It's] spaced out still further by the narrator's occasional erratic interventions, leisurely and free-floating. The sense of psychic distance, inconsequence, open possibility is enhanced by the vaudeville of Cheever's style, his skill at seeming to tell a simple, unpretentious stry absolutely straight, while introducing patterns of sidestep and evasion. Seeming is the theme of the book, apparent giving and real taking away. . . .

The truth is that Cheever's hero, though he masquerades as a technical specialist . . . is really a poet, with persistent, intuitive feelings for the fresh, the intense, the mortal. . . . An open man, with a sneaking fondness for picturesque, idiotic theories and the exhilarations of a physical moment, his character invites use of the faithless adjective, "human." [He] travels through worlds of outsize or wrong-shaped people, looking for one of his own sort. . . .

It has been said that satiric exaggeration is impossible in a society that already is a grotesque parody of what it pretends to be; also that paranoia in a society like our own is, on the odds, the safest approach to truth. In combining some of these dark perspectives within the frame of an idyll, Cheever has done more to create spacious and lively harmony than one would have thought possible in a small room. The ease and assurance with which the equilibrium is maintained are secondary pleasures of dealing with a practiced storyteller and chance-taker.

Robert M. Adams, "Chance-Taker," in The New York Review of Books *(reprinted with permission from* The New York Review of Books; *copyright © 1982 Nyrev, Inc.), Vol. XXIX, No. 7, April 29, 1982, p. 8.*

ROBERT OTTAWAY

Few swan-songs from any important writer of fiction can have been as well-tuned as [*Oh What a Paradise It Seems*]. In these 100 pages, John Cheever . . . with perfectly pleasurable art provides us with an epitaph to his working life, and the theme that stoked it for 40 years. He once described it as 'the terrible beauty of the world, and the pain of those who reach after it as it disappears'. . . .

The polluting spread of urban greed, and of arid metropolitan attitudes to love and the modes of happiness, was a constant preoccupation of his.

But, lest this should sound portentous and moralising in intent, one must add that Cheever's chief quality in his writing is a distanced irony. He has the sharp eye of a naturalist, and a Jamesian view of manners—the conventional overcoat for surging desires and affections buttoned inside.

This valedictory story has the proportions that he found in his best short stories, but which eluded him in his four longer novels. . . .

[A plot summary of his new book] does distorted justice to Cheever's resonance. First, there is his prose, which is charged like Scott Fitzgerald's, its only flaw a kind of convolution that can jar because the sentences are weighted more than their meaning. Yet it has a sheer pleasure about it that constantly sends one back to reread. It is also aptly digressive, almost Dickensian in its ability to take off into dangerous diversions. . . .

Secondly, the Olympian Cheever doesn't show off his superiority to his characters. . . .

Cheever treats all these people as if he's an observer at a party who doesn't know anyone else there, but is eager to find out. He doesn't invent beyond their capacities, as, say, Nabokov will take off into great flights of fancy, subjecting his creatures to horrors and dilemmas that are exceptional and shocking. Cheever is the chronicler of what Calvin Coolidge called normalcy; it's the ordinary world that his characters can't keep pace with. . . .

His virtues, though they may have been polished to fit the commercial requirements of the magazines which gave him a living, have remained those of a puritanical strain of American writing, going back to Hawthorne and Thoreau.

Robert Ottaway, "Terrible Beauty" (© British Broadcasting Corp. 1982; reprinted by permission of Robert Ottaway), in The Listener, *Vol. 108, No. 2773, August 12, 1982, p. 24.*

BILL GREENWELL

Oh What a Paradise It Seems is very much about marvelling at the environment and at our irreversible pollution of it. There is, as with Barth, some structural chicanery, but Cheever is infinitely more subtle. His disarming narrator tells us, 'This is a story to be read in bed in an old house on a rainy night'. He describes the battle waged by elderly Lemuel Sears to transform the poisoned lake in his home town into the pure, perfect pond of nostalgic memory. . . .

The rug of the plot, however, is gradually and brilliantly pulled from under our feet. For who is the narrator? The seemingly sympathetic voice who guides us through our little idiocies is apparently speaking with casual, intelligent hindsight from some point in the future never exactly defined. He seems to think of our era in the same sentimental manner as his characters. Surely, he has a kindly eye for the absurd? And looks from a time when corruption has been flushed away? It is only suddenly that one leafs back to an early and only moment when we catch a glimpse of him. He is watching a solitary fisherman—*and waiting to assassinate him*. This quiet control of tone and structure marks out Cheever as a master of his craft, as satirist or storyteller. Only 97 pages long, this is one of the most accomplished novels I have ever read. (p. 23)

Bill Greenwell, "Goose Corn," in New Statesman *(© 1982 The Statesman & Nation Publishing Co. Ltd.), Vol. 104, No. 2679, November 23, 1982, pp. 22-3.**

James (du Maresq) Clavell
1924-

English-born American novelist, scriptwriter, poet, and dramatist.

Clavell is known as an entertaining, rather than a "serious" writer. Most critics agree, however, that his stories are riveting and many readers appreciate Clavell's work for its action-packed plots and intriguing Asian settings. His most famous novels are his four Far Eastern historical adventures—*King Rat, Tai-Pan, Shōgun,* and *Noble House.* Of the four, *King Rat* and *Shōgun* have been adapted for the screen.

***The Children's Story,* Clavell's first departure from an Asian setting, is a controversial fable concerning the brainwashing of youth. Published as a magazine story in *The Ladies Home Journal* in 1963, it was reissued in book form in 1981 and also adapted for television.**

(See also *CLC,* Vol. 6 and *Contemporary Authors,* Vol. 25-28, rev. ed.)

GRANVILLE HICKS

["**King Rat**"] is quite unmistakably bad and yet might, one feels, conceivably have been good. . . .

[This] is a novel about the inhabitants of a Japanese camp called Changi, near Singapore. . . .

[Whatever] an author's material, the question is what he is able to make of it, and this is closely related to another question: what attitude does he take towards it? By the end of this book, at any rate, Clavell's attitude can be defined: survival requires a kind of adaptation that controverts most accepted moral codes. . . .

Clavell's approach to his material, then, is serious, at least in intention; but, as everyone knows, a novel is concerned only incidentally with ideas, and primarily with people. The moral dilemma that concerns Clavell is embodied in the lives of many characters, three of whom are of basic importance. Central is "the King," an American corporal who in a community of hunger, filth, and poverty manages, through various ingenious and audacious kinds of skulduggery, to have plenty of food, clean clothing, and money. The King has one great enemy, Lieutenant Grey, provost marshal, who is determined to get him. And he has, in addition to countless underlings and hangers-on, one real friend, Flight Lieutenant Peter Marlowe.

What one feels before one has gone far is that none of these characters is wholly credible, that each of them is more a type than an individual. . . .

In manipulating these characters—not quite puppets and not quite human beings—Clavell is a good deal less than sure of himself, and his uncertainty is revealed in his handling of the point of view. He reserves the right to tell us at any time what any character is thinking and feeling. . . . [Clavell] gives us information that we don't need, withholds information that we have a right to, and some of the time seems to be as much in the dark as the reader about the motives of the characters. If the story had been told from the point of view of Peter Marlowe,

it might have had a firm direction and reached a strong climax. As matters stand, the novel is diffuse and the conclusion weak. . . .

One can analyze a bad novel in many ways—its style, structure, character, and all the other categories discussed in courses in novel writing—but in fact one responds to a novel as a whole, and if the badness is there, one simply feels it. To put my complaint briefly, Clavell's talents aren't worthy of his subject. In the background is physical suffering of the grimmest sort; in the foreground is a chronicle of horrible moral deterioration.

Clearly such themes as these demand a treatment that is consistently serious if not truly tragic. There can be comic episodes (as there are) and there can be episodes that are full of a Hollywood kind of excitement; but the reader should never be allowed to forget the terrible meaning of the experiences about which he is reading. The King himself, of course, is incapable of grasping this meaning, but Clavell shouldn't be. He does grasp it in some degree some of the time, but at other times it gets away from him. Often he takes what seems to me a most unpleasant satisfaction in the King's chicanery and callousness, and this is indicative of his fundamental confusion. But confusion—moral and literary, and of course they aren't wholly unrelated—is what one feels from start to finish.

Granville Hicks, "Powerful POW in Signapore," in
Saturday Review *(© 1962 Saturday Review Maga-*

zine Co.; reprinted by permission), Vol. XLV, No. 32, August 11, 1962, p. 21.

MARTIN LEVIN

James Clavell's blockbuster of a first novel, **"King Rat,"** . . . presents an age-old dilemma against the background of a Japanese prison camp. . . .

[The] chief dramatic interest in **"King Rat"** is not so much the clash of ideals as the unremitting pressure of the Changi compound itself and its effect on the thousands of prisoners living and dying within its boundaries. Some become informers; some rise to new levels of heroism; some are reduced to dithering protoplasm. In Mr. Clavell's story, an unusual friendship arises between moral opposites: the Corporal ("King Rat") and Flight Lieut. Peter Marlowe, who are really not so far apart as their hereditary attitudes would indicate. This friendship and its repercussions—especially the hatred of the British P.O.W. provost marshall, who detests Marlowe for his upper-class origins and King for his classless adaptability—are the core of the narrative. But all personal relationships pale beside the impersonal, soul-disintegrating evil of Changi itself, which Mr. Clavell, himself a Japanese P.O.W. for three years, renders with stunning authority.

Martin Levin, "Reader's Report," in The New York Times Book Review *(© 1962 by The New York Times Company; reprinted by permission), August 12, 1962, p. 24.**

ORVILLE PRESCOTT

[Many] of the most popular contemporary novelists are storytellers. Some of them produce such crude works that they don't seem worth discussion in this space. Others, although their novels are crude also, tell their tales with such compelling force and unceasing narrative drive that they demand critical attention. James Clavell is such a writer.

His first novel, **"King Rat,"** was an utterly engrossing tale of violence and corruption inside a Japanese prisoner-of-war camp. It asked but did not answer important moral questions. Mr. Clavell's second novel, **"Tai-Pan,"** is not nearly so good a book as its fine predecessor; but it is almost an archetype of pure story-telling. It's about the first six months of English settlement on the island of Hong Kong in 1841 and the general atmosphere of violence, intrigue and the clash of European and Asiatic ways of life seem unpleasantly reminiscent of "Hawaii."

Is **"Tai-pan"** only another helping of cold-boiled Michener? The answer is no. James Clavell has his own way with similar material and no matter how grievous his sins against probability, he holds attention with a relentless grip. **"Tai-pan"** frequently is crude. It is grossly exaggerated much of the time. But seldom does a novel appear so stuffed with imaginative invention, so packed with melodramatic action, so gaudy and flamboyant with blood and sin, treachery and conspiracy, sex and murder.

"Tai-pan" certainly isn't art; it is undoubtedly grand entertainment. If it doesn't become a great best-seller all the omens have misled me. And the inevitable movie version will probably be as long as "Gone With The Wind" and just as spectacular. . . .

Mr. Clavell relies on basic ingredients of proved reliability.

But his theatrical gusto and his unflagging ingenuity in contriving unexpected twists of plot are fresh and vigorous.

Sometimes all the feuding and fighting, intriguing and double-crossing, sex and sadism, become a trifle excessive. But these matters alternate with many an interesting exploration of the mysteries of the Chinese concept of "face" and many a neat demonstration of the methods by which business was done in the Orient in the days of the opium trade.

How accurate **"Tai-pan"** may be as to the historical facts of the founding of Hong Kong I have no way of knowing. But since Mr. Clavell has made his hero responsible for everything we can suppose that the facts were rather different. This is not a novel to be taken seriously, although I think Mr. Clavell is serious about some aspects of it—about its general background and about the rudimentary code of honor (rudimentary, indeed) to which Dirk Struan clings.

Like most books of its kind, **"Tai-pan"** is much too long and ought to have been brutally cut. And also like most novels of its kind, its dialogue is rhetorical and stilted. In fact, Mr. Clavell has a tin ear for human speech. . . . There are some anachronisms, too. But why carp at trifles? Hordes of readers will revel in **"Tai-pan."**

Orville Prescott, "The Founding of Hong Kong in Brilliant Technicolor," in The New York Times *(© 1966 by The New York Times Company; reprinted by permission), May 4, 1966, p. 45.*

W. G. ROGERS

In 1841, an Englishman and a Chinaman worked together to secure English rights to the Chinese island of Hong Kong. Only a few years later both were dismissed from their posts, the one (in theory) for getting something of too little worth, the other for getting too little for it. . . .

The historical Englishman and the Chinaman are turned most freely into second-rank characters in [**"Tai-Pan"**], James Clavell's long-drawn-out novel of those turbulent days [of Hong Kong's early development]. In the foreground are the greedy dealers in tea and opium: a couple of deadly foes from England and an American. The book takes its title from the English big-shot (or Tai-Pan), Dirk Struan. (p. 38)

[There is a multitude of] cutthroat business operations, and throats aplenty are cut. That is not the bloodiest part of the novel. A succession of pitfalls, treacheries, piracies, infidelities, murder, rape and whoring constitute the nonstop plot. The author has left out nothing. . . . There are frequent furtive glances to check on Peking, London and Washington, just like today. (pp. 38-9)

Heathen Chinese and pagan or Christian Westerner are taken apart, so you learn what makes them tick. No stone is left unturned, so you can see what's underneath.

"Tai-Pan" is a complete, all-inclusive, economy-size book, from the bound feet of the past to the first railroads—and the steamers to outspeed the clippers on the Far East trade routes. The men who hate each other on page one wait till almost page 590 to settle their scores; some readers will not be so patient. This is a blockbuster in dimensions but not in wallop. If the spaces between the free-for-alls had been contracted, it would have been a bang-up good novel. (p. 39)

W. G. Rogers, "Complete with Scrutable Orientals," in The New York Times Book Review *(©*

1966 by The New York Times Company; reprinted by permission), May 22, 1966, pp. 38-9.

TIME

In his bestselling first novel *King Rat,* James Clavell may have been only clearing his throat for [*Tai-Pan*], which seems every bit as long as it is. Its narrative pace is numbing, its style is deafening, its language penny dreadful. All the characters whirl like dervishes, especially Dirk Struan, a kind of Scottish superman who can borrow $5,000,000 in silver ingots from an Oriental tycoon, invent binoculars, and corner the world supply of cinchona bark, all without breathing very hard. Well, almost. His Scots accent wavers a bit under stress. . . .

It's all nonsense, of course. But there are worse literary crimes than that. Clavell's book can claim kinship to those wonderful lithographs of the Battle of the Little Bighorn that once decorated every barroom. It isn't art and it isn't truth. But its very energy and scope command the eye. (pp. 108, D4)

"Bigger Than Life," in Time *(copyright 1966 Time Inc.; all rights reserved; reprinted by permission from* Time*), Vol. 87, No. 24, June 17, 1966, pp. 108, D4.*

CHRISTOPHER LEHMANN-HAUPT

Not only is **"Noble House"** as long as life, it's also as rich with possibilities. For by the time you're halfway through this fourth installment in Mr. Clavell's fictional history of the Far East—the previous three entries in which were **"King Rat," "Tai-Pan"** and **"Shogun"**—there are so many irons in the fire that almost anything can plausibly happen. It may even be that Mr. Clavell himself loses track of his story. It seems to me that there's a spy or two whose fate is never resolved. And whatever happened to the threat of hepatitis that kept looming over some of the characters?

But for all its complexity of plot—and for all Mr. Clavell tries to teach us about local Hong Kong color, the Asian mind, the Chinese love of gambling, the wonders of free enterprise and the threat of the Soviet Union to the free world's security—what makes **"Noble House"** succeed as an adventure is really very simple. What makes the novel work is simply Ian Dunross, its profoundly middle-class hero.

You really have to hand it to Mr. Clavell. His storytelling is as clumsy as always, with its sudden and arbitrary shifts in point of view, its incredible self-motivating interior dialogues and its onstage whisperings that let you know that something important has happened without revealing yet precisely what. The dialogue is often pure comic-book, and some of the soliloquies are so wooden you could build a raft with them. . . .

But despite the novel's many faults, Mr. Clavell is masterly at manipulating one's identification with Ian Dunross. And this identification occurs because Dunross, though he operates on a heroic scale, is basically the head of a household who, like Thornton Wilder's George Antrobus, is bringing home the bacon and protecting the women and children from the elements. It's interesting that despite the novel's purported anti-Puritanism in sexual matters, Ian Dunross is the only major male character who never comes close to having sex, even with his wife—though of course he's amusingly worldly about everyone else's peccadilloes. Yet we find ourselves rooting for Ian above

all others, and even preferring him to characters much more like ourselves in their foibles and failings.

In short: **"Noble House"** isn't art. It isn't even slick. But it touches a number of nerves. And its scale is occasionally dizzying. At 1,200 pages, it's a book you can get lost in for weeks. In fact, some readers may disappear into it and never be heard from again. (p. 317)

Christopher Lehmann-Haupt, " 'Noble House'," in The New York Times, *Section III (© 1981 by The New York Times Company; reprinted by permission), April 28, 1981 (and reprinted in* Books of the Times, *Vol. IV, No. 7, July, 1981, pp. 316-17).*

WEBSTER SCHOTT

James Clavell's **"Noble House"** is an extravagantly romantic novel for people who really like to spend time reading novels. It's fiction for addicts. . . .

It has 30 or 40 characters—many with interchangeable attitudes, body builds and speech habits. Thus you can concentrate on the dramatic action and tough talk instead of complexities like character and motive. It has so many plot lines—I counted at least 13 plots crisscrossing through the novel—that you can story-hop, like changing TV channels, whenever your interest in one of them wanes. . . .

From start to finish the novel follows the economic war for control of the Noble House; there are shifting alliances, attacks on banks and airlines, partial truces, parleys at lavish parties, and references by all to Sun Tzu's "The Art of War." (p. 13)

Once Mr. Clavell has the Noble House under pressure, he explodes this story into connecting plots involving Hong Kong police swindles, Cold War espionage, the Macao gold trade, a kidnapping, several murders, the U.S. Mafia. . . .

There is another war raging in **"Noble House"** for control of Asian intelligence. It's a three-way struggle between the K.G.B., the People's Republic of China and Britain's M.I.6 and the American C.I.A. With fast plotting and lots of coincidences, Mr. Clavell manages to connect this high-powered cloak-and-dagger story, complete with its own cast, to the power play for the Noble House. . . .

One comes to realize, finally, that **"Noble House"** isn't primarily about any particular story or character or set of characters. It's about a condition that's a place, Hong Kong. Mr. Clavell perceives that city to be a unique setting for extremes of greed and vengefulness, international intrigue and silky romance. Ian Dunross may be Mr. Clavell's hero, but Hong Kong is his protagonist. (p. 42)

Webster Schott, "Lots of Plot in Hong Kong," in The New York Times Book Review *(© 1981 by The New York Times Company; reprinted by permission), May 3, 1981, pp. 13, 42.*

ANNE COLLINS

[In *Noble House*] James Clavell has given us a game or two to play. The first is called pick-the-hero and it isn't so easy because both candidates wear white hats bespattered with the grey mud of Hong Kong. (p. 61)

But let's leave that game for a moment and get on with the next. It's the easier pastime of pick-the-genre, and any answer out of four or five choices is correct. Squeezed into the course of 10 days in Hong Kong in 1963, *Noble House* is an espionage novel along the lines of *Tinker, Tailor, Soldier, Spy,* dealing with KGB and Communist Chinese infiltration of British government and business. . . . There's also a 19th-century Trollope-style chronicle of the manners, mores, business and politics of the embattled British ruling class of Hong Kong. Then there's the pot-boiling dynasty novel, with the Gornt-Dunross rivalry carried out of Clavell's earlier historical best seller *Tai-Pan.* And lastly, the Horatio Alger saga of millions of Chinese intent on scoring (by any means) enough money to raise the "face" of their families permanently. As they say in Hong Kong, *moh ching, moh meng.* No money, no life.

Five into one won't go, though Clavell tries mightily (1,206 pages) to encompass them. Money is his tool, the "fragrant grease" of the plot. Hong Kong reeks of it. Two corporate Americans come to find it, and send Dunross and Gornt into final combat—bank runs and stock market the chosen weapons. With money as its heart, *Noble House* suffers the same fate as the women in the novel, sought for size and configuration rather than qualities of the soul. Though the search for riches was the motivating factor of both Clavell's excellent historical novels, *Shōgun* and *Tai-Pan,* neither were so busily hollow. God, culture, loyalty, nationhood were not yet debased currency, allowing him the layers of meaning necessary to set epics in motion. In *Noble House,* too much money, no life.

To a great extent, that is his point. The governor of Hong Kong, Sir Geoffrey Allison, muses, "greed pride lust avarice jealousy gluttony anger and the bigger lust for power or money ruled people and would rule them forever." But Clavell creates no character who sets up in admittedly foolish opposition to that thought. Which is why it's interesting to play the hero game. Dunross, of course, comes out cleanest—the book *is* called *Noble House.* But he is only better than or different from Gornt in one way: he is the taipan, and suffers none of the insecurity of the also-ran. Gornt in pursuit of power is quite ready to sacrifice anyone. . . . Dunross is the hero because he can take care of his own. The book says grab those dollars and you too will be able to take care of your own. You may as well read *How to Prosper During the Coming Bad Years.* It's shorter. (pp. 61-2)

Anne Collins, "Seeking Fortune in Taipan Alley," in Maclean's Magazine (© 1981 by Maclean's Magazine; reprinted by permission), Vol. 94, No. 19, May 11, 1981, pp. 61-2.

HENRY S. HAYWARD

[In "Noble House" Clavell] has shifted his scene from medieval Japan to the Hong Kong of 18 years ago. But one is still in Asia—where the clash of cultures and ideologies remains as intense in 1963 as in the 1600s.

James Clavell is a master yarn-spinner and an expert on detail. Indeed, one sometimes feels overwhelmed with the masses of information and wishes a firmer editing pencil had been applied. But the author, nevertheless, is in a class with James Michener and Robert Elegant in his ability to handle a massive cast and hold your attention through the intricacies of a 1,200-page plot.

This book should last a weekend reader most of the summer. But since the action is limited to a little more than one week and the chapters are identified by the time of day, the story can be laid down and resumed without too much puzzlement.

Even so, this reviewer was not always certain which character was which—or if all the pieces fitted together. Nor do the British, American, and Soviet spymasters in "Noble House" seem as sophisticated or believable as those in recent works by John le Carré and Graham Greene.

Briefly, this opus has colorful, suspenseful incidents galore—more than enough for another television series. There is the interaction between the few, close-knit Britons and the masses of Chinese, rich or poor, in the prosperous little British Crown Colony. Added to that is the bold intrusion of business-minded Americans, and Russians determined to carry both the East-West espionage race and their bitter rivalry with the emerging China into the Hong Kong arena.

The Noble House is Struan's, a fictional Hong Kong family company, the oldest, biggest, and most powerful one. Struan's origins in the 1840s will be familiar to readers of Clavell's "Tai-Pan." The present tai-pan (supreme leader) of Struan's, Ian Dunross, suddenly finds himself in deep financial trouble, with enemies about to take over his company. Moreover, he must fulfill the ancient pledge by the founder of the trading house to grant "whatsoever he asks" to anyone producing the other half of a certain gold coin. How Dunross maneuvers out of these twin challenges forms the central plot.

Meanwhile, Hong Kong itself provides the backdrop for fascinating characters and violent events. . . .

Mr. Clavell puts the city and its denizens through their paces so competently that one hesitates to quibble about his language. Yet I found some of his unusual contractions hard to take. . . .

A final word about the hero, Tai-Pan Dunross. He comes across as an authentic Hong Kong type who could probably hold his own anywhere in the world. Everyone else is equally ruthless, so you end up hoping he will win out. And, guess what, he does.

Henry S. Hayward, "Epic Yarn from Author of 'Shogun'," in The Christian Science Monitor (reprinted by permission from The Christian Science Monitor; © 1981 The Christian Science Publishing Society; all rights reserved), June 24, 1981, p. 17.

PAUL BERNSTEIN

Despite the enormous success of his Asian books, James Clavell . . . seems equally preoccupied at the moment with American politics. . . . Indeed, his "The Children's Story" . . . has the overtones of a campaign speech on foreign policy; the "speech" has already caused considerable controversy, and can now be expected to cause more. (p. 47)

He wrote it in one "magical" day, compared with an average of three years for each of his last two novels—but then "The Children's Story" is only 96 pages long . . . , and it is a padded 96 pages at that. . . . The story concerns a young, attractive, well-trained teacher who rather effortlessly wins the hearts and minds of her primary-school pupils, shortly after their homeland loses a war, and persuades them to tear the national flag into pieces. One reader's reaction was to suggest that Clavell would be more at home in Pravda. The John Birch Society called him un-American, and called for his impeachment, though from what it did not say.

If the book becomes a success . . . he will have his daughter, Michaela, to thank. As an adult she helped design the [recent] edition; as a child, she inspired the story, when she came home from first grade excitedly reciting the pledge of allegiance. . . . Not only had Michaela's teacher neglected to explain what the words meant, but Clavell found upon asking his adult friends that none of them knew who wrote the pledge, or when it became an obligatory ritual in schools, or why it was considered so important. "It was then that I realized how completely vulnerable my child's mind was—any mind for that matter—under controlled circumstances," Clavell says.

It is curious that the heavy criticism of **"The Children's Story"** should have come then from the right, since Clavell himself sees **"The Children's Story"** as "bluntly and cleanly right-wing." (pp. 47, 88)

[One advance reader] suggests that **"The Children's Story"** will have a greater impact than one of simply affecting current politics. Wouldn't it be ironic, she says, "if this slim, passionate and chilling volume" turned out to be what Clavell was best remembered for? Thus far, however, none of Clavell's other works have riveted the American public's attention as **"Shogun"** has. (p. 88)

> *Paul Bernstein, "Making of a Literary Shogun," in* The New York Times Magazine *(© 1981 by The New York Times Company; reprinted by permission), September 13, 1981, pp. 46-7, 88, 90, 92.*

R. V. WILLIAMS

[*The Children's Story*] represents a new sort of work for the author of *King Rat* and *Shogun*. Frankly didactic and with an explicit moral, it can be read in less than the twenty-three minutes of its action, but during the short duration of the drama, events take place which leave the reader uncomfortably thoughtful about severe current social ills and parental irresponsibility in the intellectual development of their children. *The Children's Story* details the possible consequences of that neglect. (pp. 243-44)

It is no small task effectively to help in the development of a young mind, but Mr. Clavell suggests we must try. Though first, he says, we must care. Failing that responsibility, we condemn children and the adults they become to live with accepted ideas they do not understand, leaving them ripe as potential toadies for the next snake oil merchant who comes to town. (p. 244)

> *R. V. Williams, "Fiction: 'The Children's Story'," in* Best Sellers *(copyright © 1981 Helen Dwight Reid Educational Foundation), Vol. 41, No. 7, October, 1981, pp. 243-44.*

their world, but the main focus is on the more mature and psychologically more successful Monica. By exchanging the local scene for the international and the individual for a more universal theme, it moves beyond the restriction of the first two novels into realms of genuine discovery. (pp. 63-4)

The patterns of growth in *Fifth Business* and *The Manticore* follow veins essentially identical to those in the Salterton novels. The basic obstacle is once again the parental bond which must be broken in order to move from innocence into experience. . . .

With Monica's liberation from her mother's dominance, two important elements were introduced into the struggle: the concept of guilt as an inherent aspect of the loss of innocence, and the ability to come to terms with that guilt by recognizing and accepting its source and integrating the experience in its fullest. The narratives of Ramsay and Staunton are built on this pattern, though the treatment of the theme is considerably more complex and allegorical. (p. 65)

The externalizations of the Magus figures and of the lesser types of Troll, Shadow, Anima/Animus, Friend, and Mentor of *A Mixture of Frailties* appear again in *Fifth Business* and in *the Manticore.* Where the narrative of Monica's artistic and spiritual education gathered together the possibilities and latent patterns of the first two Salterton novels and gave them new significance in a strictly controlled and purposefully directed framework, the two psychological novels refine the externalizations of the psychic forces and elevate them into symbolic realms in two further variations on the theme. (p. 66)

The anguish of existence, which created the dominant atmosphere in *Tempest-Tost* and *Leaven of Malice* but which started to lose its threat in *A Mixture of Frailties,* is finally overcome by the highly introspective and psychologically astute maturation processes of the two protagonists as they move into the realms of enlightenment and fulfilment. The yearning posited in *Tempest-Tost* is fulfilled in the spiritual re-birth of Ramsay and Staunton as they realize the unity of the infinite and the finite which transcends existence and arrive at a deeper understanding of themselves and of their role in the totality of existence. Their leap yields ''some secret, some valuable permanent insight, into the nature of life and the true end of man'' (*Fifth Business*) as they ''learn to know (themselves) as fully human'' and acquire ''a fuller comprehension of (their) humanity'' (*The Manticore*).

Robertson Davies has moved through the levels of externalization of the creative consciousness in the three Salterton novels, in the disguise of Actor, Editor, and Artist, and in that of Scholar and Initiate in the two psychological novels, in his search for the ''flashes of insight (with which a great man) pierces through the nonsense of his time and gets at something that really matters'' (*Tempest-Tost*). Over the course of five novels and a twenty-year process of growth, what really matters to him has clearly emerged and has found increasingly complex and sophisticated expression in the language of his books. It is the conquest of one's Self in the inner struggle and the knowledge of oneself as fully human. It is to be. (p. 67)

> Peter Baltensperger, ''*Battles with the Trolls*'' (reprinted by permission of the author), in Canadian Literature, *No. 71, Winter, 1976, pp. 59-67.*

WALTER E. SWAYZE

Included [in *One Half of Robertson Davies: Provocative Pronouncements on a Wide Range of Topics*] are aspects of Davies'

personal life and habits, beliefs and convictions, aims and intentions that had never been made clear through the person of Samuel Marchbanks, characters in the plays and novels, or the author's own published literary criticism. No totally unsuspected Robertson Davies steps out of these pages, however, and to suggest that these pieces weigh equally with everything that he has published to date will arouse expectations that are not fulfilled.

Even stylistically there are few surprises. In the preface Davies says, ''What is meant to be heard is necessarily more direct in expression, and perhaps more boldly coloured, than what is meant for the reader.'' But in the diversity of styles in which Davies has written for publication direct expression and bold colour have been constant features. Perhaps the most obvious difference between some of these speeches and published essays on similar topics are a less rigorous organization, and a more informal proportioning and linking of parts. Holding an audience with eye and voice, a speaker may indulge himself more readily with a telling personal anecdote, a lengthier plot summary, or more casual transitions than he would permit himself in writing for print.

Regardless of title and proposed distinctions, this collection justifies itself as an unusually varied, provocative, and impressive volume for readers. . . . For many readers these pieces will recall a bygone era. It is hard to believe that people still make speeches like these. The experience is constantly entertaining, heartwarming, and a little sad. There is much allusiveness, much lightly carried erudition and reasonableness, many memorable phrases, much interesting self-revelation. There is also much good advice, which may at times sound dangerously smug and opinionated despite the speaker's obvious efforts to be anything but. . . .

Like John Milton, Robertson Davies is not just one of the boys, and the tension in his writings between attempts to be flamboyantly unique and to be perfectly ordinary is one of the qualities that make him so constantly interesting, so frequently annoying, so unavoidably important, and so difficult to categorize. . . .

Davies gives us profound characterizations and evaluations of differing approaches to literature and literary scholarship, profound insights into the conscience of the writer and the relation between a writer's life and his art, convincing definitions of melodrama and the Victorian novel which account for the lasting significance of both genres, subtle distinctions between *sentiment* and *sentimentality,* and entertaining and lucid comments on a rich variety of authors and works, famous and forgotten, comments which make us envious of the speaker's insatiable catholicity of reading and determined to do something about the limitations of our own energies and the narrowness of our own preconceptions. (p. 25)

Much of what Davies says in this volume about Canadian nationalism, Canadian culture, and Canadian literature he has been saying since the days of Samuel Marchbanks, *Tempest-Tost,* and *Leaven of Malice.* Now he is more likely to be listened to because he says what he has to say more effectively and because through his own career he has demonstrated amply that he has the qualifications to say it. (pp. 25-6)

The lectures are bookish in every sense of the term, good and bad. The good dimensions are obvious in the delight in books and in language. The relation between books and life is movingly explored. . . . But the reader who has just been facing birth and death, good and evil in frightening confrontation in his own life may feel that some of Davies' discussions are literary indeed.

That is not to say that Davies is shallow. Much of what he has said is profound. But there are depths of human experience that his writings have not begun to penetrate. Perhaps another volume will reveal another of his many halves. (p. 26)

Walter E. Swayze, "Improper Fraction," in The Canadian Forum, Vol. LVII, No. 675, October, 1977, pp. 25-6.

JOYCE CAROL OATES

[The] experience of reading *One Half of Roberston Davies* was enlightening—I was forced to realize how close, how astonishingly close, colossal vanity is to pristine innocence. (p. 24)

Of these 22 pieces perhaps five are worth preserving; the others, particularly a "satirical" poem on *Hair,* not to mention a coy, cute animal story written for children but included here because "several people" assured Davies it was really for adults, might have been tossed away without regret. The collection improves as it progresses, though this may be a consequence of Davies's choice of subject matter (Freud, Jung, Trollope, melodrama, ghost stories, Proust, etc.) rather than the actual quality of his writing. . . . On Dickens he writes knowledgeably, if without any particular genius; on Jung he is disappointingly simplistic, and makes statements I would challenge—"For Jung," Davies says, "God was a fact for which evidence existed in the mind of man." And is it true that "Jungians assert the existence of God"? The Jungian position as I understand it is that a *God-experience* of some kind is possible psychologically. But as an empiricist Jung would hardly make the claim that God exists apart from the human psyche.

The collection ends with four conversational lectures on the problems of evil in literature, and one of those essays most Canadian writers have felt compelled to write in recent years, **"The Canada of Myth and Reality."** In this essay Davies repeats what many have said—that Canada . . . is apt to feel self-righteous as a consequence of virtual powerlessness, and to blame the United States for its own problems. I am not altogether convinced, however, that Davies knows, or really cares, where Canada is, or who comprises its population. In his speeches he is careful never to mention the name of any distinguished Canadian contemporary of his, out of indifference—or simply ignorance—or perhaps envy. He speaks as if "the writer" must show Canada to Canadians—as if no writers have yet done so? He will speak learnedly of the supernatural in literature, and confine himself to English writers, ignoring Canadian writers—like Howard O'Hagan, for instance, whose *Tay John* alone is worth the windy rhetorical conventions of all of Davies's books. (pp. 24-5)

It is grossly misleading to bill Davies as Canada's "leading man of letters," and he should certainly not be taken, by non-Canadians, as a "great" Canadian writer. He is, depending upon your taste, a genial storytelling moralizing conservative; or a pompous but charming Tory; or a narrow, exasperating reactionary; or a curmudgeon of the old school whose spite, anger, and vanity have been successfully—or nearly so—hidden behind a persona of bemused old-fashioned courtliness. I read him as possibly the very last image in Canada's collective dream of an older English tradition: a Floating Head whose allegiance is with the Queen (that is, the one who died in 1901), a symbol of all that younger Canadian writers and artists have

been struggling to accommodate, or repudiate, or transcend, or forget. (p. 25)

Joyce Carol Oates, "Books Considered: 'One Half of Robertson Davies'," in The New Republic (reprinted by permission of The New Republic; © 1978 The New Republic, Inc.), Vol. 178, No. 15, April 15, 1978, pp. 22-5.

PATRICIA MONK

In *The Rebel Angels,* morality and hilarity contribute in about equal parts to a story of theft and murder set in the College of St. John and the Holy Ghost (Spook, to its familiars) on the campus of a large Canadian university. Careful readers of Davies will not be surprised by the simplicity of the story-line, the adept management of narrative structure, the lively characterisation, the re-emergence of familiar themes, the acerbic commentary on academic and other forms of life, and the flurry of esoteric information. (p. 578)

The narrative takes the form of two linked first-person accounts, one by Simon Darcourt and one by Maria Theotoky, alternating through the novel. . . . The distinction between them is so neat as to appear almost over-contrived, yet is is thematically appropriate as well as structurally useful, for each of them represents a psychic element of the other which must be reckoned with. Darcourt [an Anglican priest] must come to terms with his physical self, particularly in the form of erotic love and a tendency to put on weight. Maria, whom he loves, must come to terms with her Gypsy inheritance while living in a *gadje* (non-Gypsy) society, represented at its best by Darcourt.

Although Darcourt is an interesting and well-realized character, it is Maria who really occupies the center of the novel, for she is one of Davies' most engaging characters, and certainly his most interesting female character. The female characters of a male writer often attract, not always justifiably, both amusement and abuse from feminist readers. Maria should escape both, for Davies in presenting her shows himself to be informed on the interests and issues of feminism, although not necessarily in agreement with all of it. Maria holds aloof from the women's movement, therefore, and does not have much use for liberation, at least not in the standard definition of the term. But in spite of her unrequited affection for Hollier, a marriage ceremony in which she agrees to obey her husband, and her adoption of two senior males (Darcourt and Hollier) as mentors, Maria manages to be completely herself. (pp. 578-79)

In his presentation of Maria as the development of a feminine personality, Davies is of course re-engaging an earlier theme, in this case the theme of *A Mixture of Frailties.* Other earlier themes and ideas also emerge, notably Jungian psychological theory. If this is not immediately apparent, it is because Davies has moved beyond the now familiar theory of the archetypes, to the more esoteric involvement with the relationship between psychology and alchemy which occupied Jung for many years. In the person of Ozias Froats, the biologist with his shining stainless-steel laboratories and specially designed "buckets" for human excrement, conscientiously deploying statistical methods and microphotographic techniques to the categorization of fecal samples in search of a clue to the temperaments associated with certain categories of sample, Davies explicitly recreates the mediaeval alchemist in modern guise, and through him examines the issue, common to both the alchemist and the modern biologist, of the relationship between soma and psyche.

But the mediaeval alchemists, although the hazards of their lives were numerous and varied, did not have to contend with crusading MLAs calling for their funding to be withdrawn (''Get the Shit Out of Our Varsity'') as Froats does. Confronting Froats with this particular hazard is just one of the ways in which Davies displays his talent for impeccably accurate satiric observation on academic life. (pp. 579-80)

In addition to some rich exhibitions of humour, Davies in each of his novels provides his readers with a display of esoteric knowledge. In *The Rebel Angels,* he offers two. The first is a display of Gypsy life, history, and lore, complete with a sinister Tarot reading and a curse that misfires. But, however esoteric it may seem, this is Maria's inheritance, an inheritance which she must learn to reconcile with the academic world of scholarship into which she has worked her way. Consequently, it forms an important part of the novel's thematic structure. This importance is shared by the novel's other display of esoteric knowledge: the exposition of W. H. Sheldon's constitutional theory of personality, which is at the back of Froats' research, and through which Davies continues to pursue his search for the understanding of human nature. Neither of them is present merely to allow Davies to show off.

The Rebel Angels does not mark a radical change in Davies' development as a writer. Morality and hilarity are still directed to understanding human nature as this presents itself to him. There is some shift in the thrust of his exploration, in that for the first time he seems to be taking an interest in the effects of ethnic and physical factors on human personality. Since Davies seems to work in threes (as witnessed by the Salterton trilogy and the Deptford trilogy), and since it is rumoured that another novel related to *The Rebel Angels* is already on the way, perhaps we should be looking forward to the Spook trilogy. Certainly, *The Rebel Angels,* opening with one death, ending with two more, and packing between them a study of human nature at once hilarious and deeply serious, enjoyable and thought-provoking, is an enticing beginning. (p. 580)

> Patricia Monk, ''Book Reviews: 'The Rebel Angels','' in The Dalhousie Review, Vol. 61, No. 3, Autumn, 1981, pp. 578-80.

SAM SOLECKI

Discussions of Davies' first three novels—the so-called Salterton trilogy—tend to emphasize his comic and satiric vision. By contrast, criticism and discussion of the Deptford trilogy—[*Fifth Business, The Manticore,* and *World of Wonders*] . . .—have focussed on the psychological and religious dimensions of the novels and Davies' substantial debt to the thought of the Swiss analytical psychologist C. G. Jung. Filaments of continuity are evident between the two trilogies but there is no doubt that Davies' reputation as well as his almost unchallenged status as a serious thinker, sage or pundit . . . depends on the later body of work. In this case the common view is at least partly right since there's little doubt that *Fifth Business* is Davies' masterpiece and together with *The Stone Angel, The Scorched-Wood People* and *Coming Through Slaughter,* among the handful of Canadian novels that count. (p. 30)

Davies' concern in his later work has been with man's need to acknowledge the emotional, the irrational and the unconscious side of the self. . . . The central figures of *Fifth Business* and *The Manticore* suffer from an excessive dependence on conscious or rational modes of being, and the action of each novel moves towards a moment of recognition in which we witness the return of what has been repressed/suppressed and the consequent development of an integrated self. . . . Up to a point, the second and third novels repeat, with many entertaining variations, the pattern of *Fifth Business;* each is in the form of a confession, each has essentially the same theme and each borrows its images and symbols from a common store of relatively arcane lore.

In fact, much of the pleasure . . . one gets from reading these later novels, including *The Rebel Angels* derives from the sense of *déja vu* experienced from novel to novel, from the elements of predictability in the whole enterprise. Davies' learning may be arcane and exotic but we expect this from him just as we expect his narrators to explain it in detail, whether dealing with fool-saints (*Fifth Business*), the Jungian anima (*The Manticore*), or body types and the shit cure (*The Rebel Angels*). Similarly the issues posed by, explored and explained in these novels are constant from work to work: the unconscious side of life, the integrated self, the unlived life, and ''the overdeveloped mind and the under-developed heart.'' As well these novels are accessible, even comfortable, in a way that the major works of modernism and post-modernism aren't. To read John Barth is to confront a conjuror doing several illusions simultaneously; Davies, in contrast, is the scholarly and avuncular magician and story-teller who is willing to explain every trick. Even the ostensibly opaque elements in his fiction are ultimately rendered translucent, and therefore knowable and safe.

Yet if the reader derives pleasure from Davies' writing and rewriting of his one story and one story only, there is also the other side of predictability and familiarity, tedium. *Fifth Business* worked because we saw Dunstan Ramsay aging and developing page by page, and because Davies managed to integrate into the theme, style and structure Ramsay's interest in hagiography. The tedium increases between *The Manticore* and *The Rebel Angels* because the novels become increasingly static, cluttered with the flotsam of Davies' store of learning and, surprising in a drama scholar and critic, less dramatic. After *Fifth Business* the scholar-didact has prevailed over the novelist in Davies' fiction.

More than its immediate predecessors *The Rebel Angels* creaks under an excess of intellectual baggage, this time drawn from Rabelais, Paracelsus and gypsy lore. A combination of a murder-mystery novel and comic love story, *The Rebel Angels* is set at a Canadian university and has three related concerns: the search for and recovery of a previously unpublished manuscript and three letters by Rabelais showing him to have been interested in the kabbala and alchemy; Maria Theotoky's desire to acknowledge and understand her gypsy past (her intuitive and emotional side); and the philosopher John Parlabane's return to St. John's College, and his attempt to publish a novel. . . .

The novel's main weakness is that Maria is just too static and undeveloped a character to sustain a novel structurally and thematically dependent on her. Unlike Monica Gall, the appealing heroine of *A Mixture of Frailties,* she never convinces us to take her emotional turmoil, her anxieties, seriously. Her gypsy past is finally just so much costume and scenery. . . . (p. 31)

Much more interesting and more fully realized is the reprobate John Parlabane who specializes in various forms of debauchery and in ''the history of skepticism: the impossibility of real knowledge—no certainty of truth.'' Parlabane is the true rebel angel in that he embodies and exemplifies the repressed-suppressed aspects of the self *talked* about in the rest of the novel.

He is the "Wild Man" whose life and learning can be paradoxically and disturbingly exemplary; while Maria talks about gypsies and studies Rabelais, John Parlabane lives a Rabelaisian life.

Not surprisingly the novel only comes alive when Parlabane is present, as if Davies' imagination responds to his contradictory qualities with a depth and complexity of realization notably lacking in his more staid academic figures; with Parlabane we have the stench of brimstone, with Hollier and Darcourt the grey mustiness of the university common room. Like all of Davies' characters Parlabane talks too much but unlike most of them he doesn't treat living and talking as synonymous terms. His words and actions are the closest Davies has yet come to giving adequate fictional expression to his sense of preconscious or pre-rational modes of being. In the earlier novels we rarely experience the shudder of recognition that should attend an encounter, direct or mediated, with the unknown, the irrational or, in *Fifth Business,* the numinous. Davies' treatment of the emotions, the unconscious, and the religious dimensions in life (often they are identical) is usually unconvincing because it fails to evoke the sense or ambience of the irrational and the unknown. This is partly a matter of an overly controlled even repressive style, partly of characters too obviously intended to represent or symbolize attitudes and modes of being, and partly of a comic mode that may not be a suitable medium for a certain kind of subject.

As a result, Davies' pronouncements on the self and religion tend to sound like good news for modern man, secular (because psychologized) assurances about vaguely spiritual matters. The reader, entertained by an often lively and engaging story, also finds himself sitting through a painless, often entertaining and witty, lecture or sermon. The obvious contrast is with a disturbing novel like Doris Lessing's *Briefing for a Descent Into Hell* in which the encounter with the repressed side of life is made palpable because the style, imagery and plot compel the reader into as direct a confrontation as possible; we experience the novel's reality, whereas in Davies we all too often sense that we have been *told* about it. The telling has been witty, elegant and informed, and the vehicle has been often absorbing and entertaining but there remains a rupture between the potentially disruptive subject matter and the orderly and restrained telling. (pp. 31, 47)

What we have then in *The Rebel Angels,* as in its predecessors, is both an enjoyable novel from a writer who knows how to tell a story in a highly polished style, and another reminder of the extent to which Davies' fiction is seriously divided against itself. (p. 47)

> Sam Solecki, *"The Other Half of Robertson Davies,"* in The Canadian Forum, *Vol. LXI, No. 714, December-January, 1981-82, pp. 30-1, 47.*

JOHN HARRIS

In the main, the heroes and heroines of Robertson Davies' novels, the characters through whom he chooses to tell his stories, are scholars. They are also pedants. They have many opinions, whereas scholars in the strict sense have only a few, closely related to their disciplines. In the course of their conversations and meditations. Davies' heroes and heroines express their opinions expansively and with wide-ranging references to history and literature. Furthermore, since the habit of forming opinions extends most easily into matters of human behavior (politics and propriety), Davies' opinionated scholars are inclined to priggishness. They editorialize extensively and gratuitously on hygiene, university budgets, women's lib, wisdom, contemporary music, and a thousand other subjects.

It's hard to deny a writer his turf, and pedants and prigs are certainly fit subjects for fiction. However, a pedant who remains a pedant can't very easily be a hero and a convincing narrative voice. In a novel, characters and events must seem real. . . . Against the backdrop of real life, in the context of a convincing plot, pedantry must look pathetic. Successful pedantry must look unreal.

Unfortunately, Davies' pedants are eminently successful. They may learn many things, but they are always confirmed in their pedantry and priggishness. They claim to understand the peace that passeth understanding, and they are supported in their claim by events in the stories. The reader begins to realize that the jury is rigged, that the opinions expressed by the characters are meant to be taken as a doctrine, that the novel is really some kind of extended editorial. (pp. 112-13)

Rebel Angels provides alarming evidence that the prig in Davies is still alive and far too strong. In his latest novel, Davies makes the obvious error of permitting the analysis and defense of intellect to proceed almost entirely on the intellect's own terms. The story is told by scholars and they speak retrospectively. That is normal for Davies—but it is a style that he should, perhaps, reconsider. It makes editorializing too easy; since the characters are scholars, and their thoughts and actions are not being presented as they occur but only as they are remembered, the detached, authoritative tone is possible. *Rebel Angels* pushes this event further. All the other characters in the story are scholars, so that even the dialogue is standardized. Furthermore, the narrators do not participate very extensively in the main action; they comment from a distance. In *Fifth Business* the narrator, Dunstan Ramsay, is at the centre of the action. We see his pedantic tendencies develop naturally out of his background and experience, which are representative: life in a small town, the war, etc. We can grasp the deep-rooted emotional needs that are satisfied by his scholarship. There is no such perspective in *Rebel Angels.* Only the intellect gets to take the stand, and the rational analysis and defense of intellect are about as convincing as a police investigation of police corruption.

Davies, I think, was tempted into this story by a desire to explore the superego and to register certain changes that have recently taken place in our social attitudes. But to understand this, and thus to put *Rebel Angels* into its place in the Davies canon and render it more useful and slightly less irritating, we need to examine the theme that Davies has, with some authority, made his own.

I find that I can understand Davies' theme better when I apply basic Freudian concepts. The conscious mind (the intellect or ego) is mysteriously the product of (and has the task of regulating) the two power (emotion) sources of the id (primal wants, traditional evil) and the superego (the social conditioning we all receive from the first day of our lives, traditional good). (pp. 113-14)

As Davies sees the situation, our present "conditioning" is too permissive of emotion in general, but particularly of superego emotions. We are conscience and value-ridden. Of course, this condition only sets the stage for its reversal—the manipulation of the superego by the id that results in so much rationalized, ideological violence in the modern world. Davies is worried that, if this permissiveness ever becomes a fixed passion of the superego, then all hell will, quite literally, break loose.

All hell doesn't break loose in *Rebel Angels,* as it does in *Fifth Business* and that is just the problem. The story is told by two characters, both of whom talk extensively. . . . These narrators are maddeningly detached from the action; the balance beams of their egos are never seriously threatened by id or superego upheaval. The discerning reader will wonder how this could be the case with characters in whom the superego is so obviously on the ascendant. (p. 114)

Maria [Theotoky, a graduate research assistant,] thinks she is in love with her thesis supervisor, Professor Clement Hollier, and indeed, in a flush of scholarly excitement over Maria's revelation of her [family's gypsy] background and her mother's activities in resuscitating old violins (which sets him on the track of new discoveries concerning "filth therapy"), he has, to her great joy, "had" her on the sofa in his office. But Hollier is not interested in Maria, and by way of assuaging his guilt feelings about her, he promises her a valuable manuscript which she can edit. This will establish her reputation in the academic world, a consummation that she greatly desires. . . .

Darcourt is the other narrator of *Rebel Angels,* the hero of the story. He is a rather attractive but preponderantly placid figure, an Anglican priest and student of the Apocrypha. He records much of the action; in fact, he is writing a book about the university and is actively collecting information throughout the story. He plays a subsidiary role in the action, however, and experiences no personal revelations in the course of the story. . . .

The real action involves another character—an old friend of Darcourt's and Hollier's recently returned to campus—John Parlabane. (p. 115)

Parlabane is the only interesting character in *Rebel Angels,* the only character who might legitimately be considered a "rebel." He is left in caricature, however; we can hope that, in another novel, Davies will get into his head and then we are likely to experience another story like *Fifth Business,* for Parlabane is a character who has truly plumbed the depths of depravity and despair and (apparently) fought his way back into the world with great heroism. Parlabane is impressive in the first half of the book; his accounts (to Maria) of his adventures are truly fascinating. Maria is fascinated by him, and he generates powerful responses in her that come straight from the depths of the id. He is her real teacher, as she finally admits . . . ; he promises her the "orgasm of mind" that the rebel angels, in the Apocrypha, provide to "the daughters of men." . . . But Parlabane gets a job from Hollier and a suit from Darcourt and disappears halfway through the story. All we know is that he is working on a novel and has turned into a hopeful bore about it. (p. 116)

Maria talks endlessly about her rejection of her gypsy heritage and consequent immersion in scholarly life. She ostensibly comes to recognize that this is the reason for her infatuation with Hollier. She is then convinced by Parlabane that her background (root) is her strength (crown). But finally she marries a man who, while he says he agrees with Parlabane's comment, represents the epitome of Anglo-Saxon respectability—a self-educated commercial aristocrat who talks pompously about everything from patronage to love. Even Darcourt has some reservations about marrying this couple—"these two were a little too articulate for my satisfaction" . . . , he says. It takes one to know one. There are obviously some spectacular id

fireworks to come from Maria and Arthur in the near future—the basis of a "Massey College" trilogy of novels, perhaps.

One can hope that Davies will change his style before this happens. The editorial voice kills any subtlety of characterization. . . . Darcourt, Parlabane, Maria . . . but really, Marchbanks. And who is Marchbanks but the weak half of Robertson Davies? He is a bit of an ornament in the classroom, on the platform, at the head table, and in the pages of the Peterborough *Examiner*—in all of which circumstances he sometimes masquerades as Robertson Davies. In book form he is a bore. He is certainly not a novelist. Perhaps the rejection of the retrospective mode would drive this squeaky spirit out, so that the novelist in Davies can live again. (pp. 116-17)

John Harris, "A Voice from the Priggery: Exorcising Davies' Rebel Angel," in Journal of Canadian Fiction *(reprinted by permission from* Journal of Canadian Fiction, *2050 Mackay St., Montreal, Quebec H3G 2J1, Canada), No. 33, 1981-82, pp. 112-17.*

JOHN KENNETH GALBRAITH

Davies is a fine writer—deft, resourceful, diverse and, as noted, very funny. But his claim to distinction is his imagination, which he supports by an extraordinary range of wholly unpredictable information. (p. 7)

Fitzgerald, Hemingway and even Faulkner dealt with a world to which the reader feels some connection. Similarly located and circumstanced, one might see what they see. Davies deals with matters far beyond the experiences of his readers; yet, you find yourself taking his word for it, according him full faith and credit. Even if he invents the way a magician practices his art, you have to believe that the invention is at least the equal of the original.

The new novel, **"The Rebel Angels"** . . . yields to none of the others in either diverse and esoteric knowledge or complexity of theme. . . .

The story is told in alternating chapters by Maria Theotoky and Simon Darcourt, and the device allows two different accounts and perceptions of the same flow of events. It is less confusing, once one becomes accustomed to it, than might be expected; in fact, it serves exceedingly well. . . .

There is a convention that, in describing a novel, one should not give away the plot. But the attraction here for me is in the style of the story, the fun, and in the truly massive array of information which the book, like its predecessors, conveys. . . .

It is fair to say that one does not ever come into close proximity with Davies's characters. Maria Theotoky is exceedingly beautiful—so one is repeatedly told. And sexually very compelling. But the reader must take the author's word for it; her beauty and sexuality do not otherwise emerge. And with the others on the stage the reader in the audience is never deeply involved. I do not offer this as a criticism; for me at least it is pleasant to read of people who are immensely knowledgeable and interesting whom I am not impelled either to love or to hate.

Not all of the events in a Davies novel, as distinct from the information, are plausible. . . .

But again, if all novels excluded the unlikely, the production of them would drop rather more severely than new housing starts. . . .

[Davies's novels] will be recognized with the very best work of this century. And they will last. (p. 30)

John Kenneth Galbraith, ''The World of Wonders of Robertson Davies,'' in The New York Times Book Review *(© 1982 by The New York Times Company; reprinted by permission), February 14, 1982, pp. 7, 30.*

PATRICIA MONK

Davies' work reveals a progressive attempt to define human identity in the fullest possible sense. In the development of his work from *Shakespeare's Boy Actors* to *World of Wonders,* he can be seen to examine the possibilities of role-playing, the second self, the autonomous personality of the artist, the Jungian self, the romance hero, and the Magian soul, and to assess each as a possible mythologem of the completed human identity. His exploration of these possibilities is rooted in his deep and long-lasting affinity with Jung, and, for the most part, is carried out within a frame of reference firmly based on Jung's ideas. Nevertheless, Davies eventually moves beyond his affinity with Jung to a more impartial assessment of Jungianism as simply one way of looking at the universe, one myth among a number of others, and finally he is able to present the Jungian self as only one among several concepts of complete human identity.

Each step of his exploration of human identity involves incursions into what Jung calls 'the smaller infinity' . . . , for a definition of human identity can be formulated only in terms of the inner reality of human beings. It is this inner reality which Davies describes as the 'enchanted landscape.' His inner world is not, however, 'the cosy nursery retreat of Winnie-the-Pooh. It is a tough world, and it only seems irrational or unreal to those who have not grasped some hints of its remorseless, irreversible, and often cruel logic. It is a world in which God is not mocked, and in which a man reaps—only too obviously—what he has sown.' It is clear that his concept of the 'enchanted landscape' is broad enough to include not only Jungianism but also the romance myth of the hero and the concept of the Magian soul. It is also easy to see in it a specific analogue of Jung's view of the inner reality, the 'indefinitely large hinterland of unconscious psyche.' . . . Consequently, Jungianism provides an interpretative approach to his enchanted landscape and to Davies' experience of it.

What Jung says of those who undertake the long process of individuation by exploration of their inner landscapes may equally be applied to the writer in search of a myth: 'Nevertheless it may be that for sufficient reasons a man feels that he must set out on his own feet along the road to wider realms. It may be that in all the garbs, shapes, forms, modes, and manners of life offered to him he does not find what is peculiarly necessary for him.' . . . Clearly, what is 'peculiarly necessary' for a writer is the myth which produces the psychosymbolic structures of his or her work. . . . This is to be found in the wider realms of the inner reality, through personal experience of the unconscious within, and because every individual is unique

that experience of the inner reality and the symbolic embodiment of it will also be unique. To remain unique, however, the self must emerge from one individual's experience only, uncontaminated by another's vision. Although Jung speaks of observing an 'untrodden, untreadable' region in many men of importance, both *The Manticore* and *World of Wonders* suggest that such a region exists in every human being. Consequently, with the exception of one particular group of people, experience of the inner reality is private to the individual and 'untreadable' ground to outsiders. The exception is, of course, the group of those we call artists, all of whom have in one way or another the particular gift of being able to share their experiences of the private inner reality with others through the medium of their art. . . . Davies as a writer is an individual who objectifies his own individual experience of the inner reality by relating it to general Jungian psychological theory. He can do this because, although each individual human being is unique, all human beings are members of the human race, and hence to a very large extent similar: their inner reality consequently will have common features. Any objectification of that inner reality by a writer in which the common features are described may, therefore, provide a map of the territory by which anyone who enters his or her own reality may roughly by guided.

It is this role of literary art as a map of inner reality, and the corresponding role of a writer as a map-maker, which prompt Davies, I believe, to describe himself as a moralist: 'I seem to have emerged as a moralist; my novels are a moralist's novels.' He seems to be using the term in a sense which includes, among other elements, a great deal of the Jungian psychological revision of good and evil: personal responsibility for the examination of human conduct (self-examination, it is implied, being the prerequisite for the examination of others), and a Jungian respect for the integrity of the self in others (demonstrated by the refusal to instruct or judge). Hence, the moralist is a map-maker. . . . His work, therefore, is not prescriptive but descriptive—just as a map is descriptive.

It is as a moralist, however, that Davies issues a warning about maps of the inner reality. The map, he insists, is not the territory: Davies' personal experience, however illuminating and significant for his readers in its form of 'a moralist's novels,' remains his personal experience. Just as, in *World of Wonders,* he refuses to substitute Jung's ideas for his own, his readers also must refuse to substitute Davies' experience of inner reality for their own. In moving beyond Jungianism so decisively in this novel, therefore, Davies unambiguously declares that it is the territory we must concern ourselves with, not the map.

The exploration of the 'smaller infinity' which Davies began in his earliest work has, by the end of the Deptford trilogy, reached maturity. It is not finished, and it cannot be finished, precisely because it is the exploration of infinity. Davies has not defined human identity because it is indefinable; he has divined it, because it is, in its true form, that which Jung calls the *imago Dei,* divine. (pp. 182-84)

Patricia Monk, in her The Smaller Infinity: The Jungian Self in the Novels of Robertson Davies *(© University of Toronto Press 1982), University of Toronto Press, 1982, 214 p.*

John (Roderigo) Dos Passos
1896-1970

American novelist, essayist, poet, and journalist.

Dos Passos is best known for his sociopolitical novels of pre-World War II America. His central concerns are social injustices, including the exploitation of the working class, and the injurious emphasis on materialism in American society. The *U.S.A.* trilogy is considered his masterpiece.

Detail and realism are important elements in Dos Passos's work, often emphasized through such innovative means as his "newsreel" and "camera eye" techniques, and the inclusion of biographical excerpts.

Strongly political, Dos Passos moved from his early, left-wing revolutionary philosophy to a later conservatism. The 1950s witnessed a decline in his reputation; however, in recent years scholars have reaffirmed the artistic merit of his innovative methods and re-evaluated his later work.

(See also *CLC*, Vols. 1, 4, 8, 11, 15; *Contemporary Authors*, Vols. 1-4, rev. ed., Vols. 29-32, rev. ed. [obituary]; *Contemporary Authors New Revision Series*, Vol. 3; *Dictionary of Literary Biography*, Vols. 4, 9; and *Dictionary of Literary Biography Documentary Series*, Vol. 1.)

Photograph by Sylvia Salmi; courtesy of Mrs. John Dos Passos

JOSEPH WARREN BEACH

[We] have now had more than twenty years to digest *Manhattan Transfer* and fully ten years to come to terms with the completed trilogy of *U.S.A.* In books like *Journeys between Wars*, *The Ground We Stand On*, and *State of the Nation*, Dos Passos has exhibited his personal outlook upon the world, furnishing us the context in which to consider his "dramatic" representations of life. We should now be in a position to challenge this figure and ask ourselves what and how great is his significance for literary art.

The first thing we can say with a considerable degree of confidence is that his work before *Manhattan Transfer* is negligible, that his volumes of travel and commentary are relatively negligible, and that his place in literature (thus far) must rest on four novels, *Manhattan Transfer* and the three parts of *U.S.A.* The poems are negligible except as a reminder, important for understanding him, that this man is by natural inclination distinctly "esthetic"—drawn to the picturesque, the decorative, the exotic, and to the romantic in the sense in which that term applies to Amy Lowell and John Gould Fletcher. . . . The influence of Sandburg is strongly felt in *Manhattan Transfer* in the language and arrangement of the prose poems prefixed to the chapters. But the influence of Sandburg means a passage from the mere cult of the exotic to a more robust grappling with the familiar,—from the esthetic as evasion to the esthetic as significant composition.

The early fictions are negligible for similar reasons, and equally interesting for the light they throw on the author's temperament. *One Man's Initiation* and *Streets of Night* show us a young man fastidious and sensitive, shrinking from cruelty and ugliness physical and moral, and acutely conscious of the presence of ugliness in war and in sex. *Three Soldiers* . . . is in line with many novels following the first World War in jealous concern for the individual soul trying vainly to save itself from the clutches of the military (the social) machine. One thing more that is clear from these fictions is that their author is not a born story-teller in the traditional sense, being more concerned with the relation of the individual to society than he is with the idiosyncrasy and personal exploits of the individual.

The volumes of commentary on the state of the world are relatively negligible from the point of view of literary art. But they are of great importance for the understanding of Dos Passos' social philosophy, and they have many sturdy merits. They are good reporting in the sense that they render what he has seen—in interbellum Russia, in the United States during the second war, in Spain, in the Pacific—with a minimum of interference by the author. Dos Passos is patient and humble before the facts. He shows no *parti pris*. His ideology is that of one seeking to understand. He is, I suppose, some kind of socialist; which means, in effect, that he abhors the tyrannies and impersonal cruelties of our industrial machine. He can record the feeling of the Spanish peasant that in America men are not able to live their own lives. He is indignant over "justice denied in Massachusetts" or to the Harlan miners. He is sympathetic toward industrial experiments under the New Deal. He is for the American way, but he does not feel that contemporary capitalism favors the ideals of Tom Paine and Roger

Williams. In 1945, in the preface to *First Encounter,* he is as safe in his political pronouncements as a candidate for a college presidency.

> Perhaps the disillusionments of the last quarter of a century have taught us that there are no short cuts to a decent ordering of human affairs, that the climb back up out of the pit of savagery to a society of even approximate justice and freedom must necessarily be hard and slow. The quality of the means we use will always determine the ends we reach.

There is nothing in the style of this to suggest any kind of literary distinction. The only distinction it has is that of earnestness and mild good sense. The last sentence, to be sure, is radical, and if taken seriously would mean a revolution in human behavior, being as it is a reversal of Machiavelli's doctrine. But it is pitched so low that few will hear it, let alone take it to heart. The merit of Dos Passos' own style, when he is not trying for esthetic expressiveness, is the ingratiating humbleness of spirit which it displays. His sole ambition is to be the self-effacing medium of what he has to render. And that is, in his best fiction, a merit of very high order.

The turn from one of these books of commentary to *Manhattan Transfer* or *U.S.A.* is like the turn from Victor Bergen to Charley McCarthy, so much more vivid and colorful is the creature than the creator. (pp. 406-09)

Dos Passos has always been a "collectivist" writer. Of the two sciences that preside over the modern literary heaven he has taken sociology rather than psychology for his guiding star. The individual interests him, but mainly as a member of the social body; and his aim is always to give a cross-section of this body so as to show the structure of its tissues. In *Manhattan Transfer* it is the entire urban center that he shows; in *U.S.A.* the entire country, from Hollywood to Washington, from a Fargo boarding house to a New Orleans garage. In both cases he covers the period from the Boer War to the great boom following the first World War. In *Manhattan Transfer* the system is to present a prodigious number of persons of the most representative groups in short shots, without transition, each going his own way; some of them appearing once, just for the record, some several times over a course of years, some frequently enough to give the impression of leading characters, especially when their orbits cross in marriage, business, or other social contact.

In more or less remote ways they all affect one another; but they hardly seem aware of this, and when they do become more closely involved, this hardly amounts to a plot, with its clearly marked issues, critical scenes, and dramatic resolution. The time element is not there for the sake of a plot, but simply to furnish a measure of process in the social body. What the characters say and do is thematic and illustrative of sociological principles. (pp. 410-11)

In *U.S.A.* there is even less of plot in the conventional sense, but fewer characters are featured and the course of their lives is given in greater detail with less frequent interruptions. Each case is more fully documented. But these *are* case histories for a social worker's filing cabinet. (p. 411)

Many readers object to the unconventionality of Dos Passos' narrative method, as they do to that of Joyce in *Ulysses* and Eliot in *The Waste Land.* The simplest way to meet this objection is to point to the principle of abstract composition as it appears in various schools of post-impressionist painting as well as in poetry and fiction. The object here is not the complete and literal reproduction of a scene now present to the bodily eye and according to the laws of optics. It is rather the assembling within the frame of one picture of representative portions of many scenes related to one another not by their simultaneous presence in the same spot but by mental association—of contrast, analogy, irony, symbolic correspondence—and given significance and esthetic effectiveness by their planned arrangement in the new visual pattern. The application of this principle in the novel obviously does away with the "dramatic" type of narrative (with its neatly articulated "beginning, middle and end") that has dominated fiction from the beginning. There is no reason to suppose that this principle of abstract composition will displace the established tradition in fiction,—which has the advantage of following what we may call the standard or commonsense way of arranging human life in the imagination. It is sufficient to remind readers that Dos Passos is working on a new and in some ways more rewarding line, and suggest that they look for his effects in the direction in which they were sought by him.

The same readers who object to this narrative technique are likely to be repelled by the inconclusiveness of the story, and by the little meaning and little value in the lives presented. Well, that of course is Dos Passos' theme. If he does not offer examples of generous souls pursuing and achieving noble ends, it is because his main impression of contemporary life is of ordinary people caught in the mechanism of a soulless society, and exceptional cases would be irrelevant to the point he is making. If he does not make the point himself in personal commentary, it is because he is a modern objective realist, who does not want to risk the artistic integrity of his performance by mounting the soapbox.

The technical novelties of his narrative procedure are all intended to take the place of personal commentary, as well as to relieve the tedium of the conventional. (pp. 412-13)

The incoherencies of stream-of-consciousness in the Camera Eye [sections of *U.S.A.*] are a perfect rendering of the naïveté of early childhood, the confused gropings of conscious manhood. The tonelessness and uneventfulness of the case histories correspond to the sheer behaviorism exemplified in these lives, which are made up of reaction to stimuli rather than of the voluntary pursuit of significant ends. Perhaps the furthest triumph of art in Dos Passos is the virtually complete submergence of his own personal style in that of his characters. All that is left here of the author-as-author is the somewhat greater concern with color and form in the outward scene than can be plausibly attributed to Mac and Margot. Vocabulary and idiom, rhetoric and grammar are those of the several characters; and above all what may be called the moral tone is that of the people who go through these undramatic adventures. In some cases, where the spiritual confusions are particularly dense, as with Eleanor Stoddard and J. Ward Moorehouse, the effect is an irony all the more destructive because it is free from burlesque ventriloquism. The dialogue has not the point and resonance of Hemingway's, but serves well the rather different purpose of Dos Passos. Here we acknowledge with delight in an objective artist that gift for yielding himself wholly to his subject which, in the volumes of personal commentary, left us with some sense of let-down.

Altogether Dos Passos has given us the most comprehensive and convincing picture of American life in certain highly characteristic phases that is anywhere to be found. And if we shrink from the frosty glitter of the exhibit, we must yield to its fascination as a work of imaginative art. We are held by the teeming fertility of his invention, the colorfulness of his appeal to the senses, and by the bold originality and stark impressiveness of his structural composition.

But this brings us to the most radical of all objections that may be urged against Dos Passos. It may be urged that his representation of human nature is purely external and superficial, that he actually implies as his own philosophy the very behaviorism of which his characters are victims, that he has no conception of anything other than man political and economic. (pp. 414-15)

Dos Passos is not aiming at depth psychology, and must deny himself much of the fascination of a Joyce or Proust. He is not aiming to expose the dialectical complexities of European culture. . . . The only riddle he poses is the simple relation of the individual to the group history of his own time. Above all he has chosen to present men not self-conscious and deliberately seeking for answers and solutions, but men passive to the commonest impulses of instinct. If one's taste is for poetry and metaphysics and for nothing else, one will deny the appeal of Dos Passos and will rate him as distinctly inferior.

But if one's taste is more catholic, one will at least consider the nature of his artistic intention. He has, one may assume, no love for flat souls; but his *theme* is souls made flat by something in the culture-complex in which they have their being. To have presented them in other terms would have been to betray his subject. To complain that his representation is two- or at best three-dimensional is simply to characterize the method and medium which best suit his artistic intention. The thing to note is the brilliant virtuosity with which this method is applied and the inescapable impressiveness of the effect. One can be a passionate devotee of Proust and still admit the esthetic importance of Dos Passos.

But then, one says, his study is not ''religious,'' and he can therefore have no standard of values, no moral sense, without which human nature becomes an unedifying subject of contemplation. Well, that is the moot question of our time, and not to be decided by the testimony of a horde of poets and critics, some of them deliberately unacquainted with the intellectual culture of our age, and many of them inclined to confusing double-talk—employing such terms as religion and myth in senses that would never have been admitted by Dante, Milton, or Swift, let alone St. Augustine or St. Thomas. (pp. 415-16)

There is one quasi-religious concept of which Dos Passos is strongly aware. It is what Kenneth Burke calls ''piety.'' This, he says, is the desire, the impulse of the human being to identify himself with the group. And this, one would suppose, is a human development of what in the lower animals is called gregariousness. Dos Passos' characters, while reasonably gregarious, are singularly lacking in the type of piety that Jesus calls love. But this again is his *theme;* he is depicting a society unaware of what it takes to make a society. And the atomistic lovelessness of his people is a reminder of what he considers the great desideratum. If the reader misses this, it is because he is given objective realism where what might be expected is a tone of obvious satire.

But there is something missing to make these characters full-fledged human beings, and that is the conscious sighting and willed pursuit of ends conceived as having value. Here again we must give Dos Passos the benefit of the doubt and assume that this is precisely what he has in mind. His aim is to depict a society of people passively drifting without benefit of inner controls. His people are for the most part likeable and easily understood, but they are seldom lovable or admirable, and for that reason they are individually unimportant to the reader. And that is the head and front of his offense. His people are not ''sympathetic'' like those of Tolstoi, Dickens, Henry James, or André Malraux. They do not have the psychological interest of Dostoevsky's or Proust's, or the poetic interest of Kafka's. His vision of man is not religious but rationalistic. And most modern readers prefer psychology and the religious vision, along with reasonably sympathetic characters.

The reader will consult his taste, as ever. But tastes change and broaden. Dos Passos is now a standard though unpopular writer, like Henry James. He is an artist of bold originality, ingenuity and dash. He has covered the American scene more adequately than any other novelist. His social commentary is sharply defined and mordant. He has survived some twenty years of critical scrutiny. . . . Another twenty years and he may need no apologia. Our children may positively relish his flavor and take him for granted as an American classic. (pp. 417-18)

Joseph Warren Beach, ''Dos Passos 1947,'' in The Sewanee Review *(reprinted by permission of the editor;* © *1947 by The University of the South), Vol. LV, No. 3, Summer, 1947, pp. 406-18.*

JAMES T. FARRELL

John Dos Passos is one of the few living American writers who is a world figure. Abroad, his books are sometimes cited as criticisms of American capitalism and as novels which expose American claims and propaganda. At home, Dos Passos is now regarded by some of his former admirers as a man who has made a complete turn, and has abandoned liberalism for the extreme right; he has gone from *The New Republic* to *The National Review.* In consequence, he is regretfully considered as writing in a state of *rigor mortis,* and tears—mostly of the crocodile variety—are shed for him. He is a source of shame and danger to the Madison Avenue psychological warriors who would defeat the Kremlin by selling the USA as though it were the biggest cake of perfumed soap in history; his books are not very useful to the People-to-People geniuses and cannot be sent through the gaping holes of the Iron Curtain with as much success as can stamp kits and hobbycraft chat. And he cannot be cited as a novelist of the liberal spirit, fighting reaction and perpetuating the New Deal spirit. Therefore, he is a good man gone wrong. And a good man gone wrong is, *ipso facto,* unworthy of consideration as a man of letters. Dos Passos' liberalism has so decayed that his lifetime of work is not as important as two short stories and one wooden novel by Lionel Trilling. His credentials as a writer might just as well be taken away from him and he might best be forgotten. He is no longer one of us. He cannot write anyway because the new critics do not study him and Mark Shorer probably would not approve of him.

Thus the level of concern for a writer in this Republic after it has come of age, lost its innocence, become a world leader. Thus the destiny of any man who is guilty of the sin of disillusionment. You must be for something, because in both the liberal and the conservative camps, there is no political future for one who is not for something. After some decades of trying, we have failed even in convincing our friends that a novelist does not necessarily have to be for, and that a writer should not be judged in terms of immediate political considerations. It is in vain. Philistinism and self-righteousness are too numerous to be destroyed.

Dos Passos deserves reconsideration and his recent novel, *The Great Days,* helps us to see what he is about. In his own feeling, he is a libertarian. During his long literary career, he has been concerned with bigness. Bigness and liberty are not easily compatible. Dos Passos has always been a novelist of disillusionment, and this is central in his thinking. (pp. 118-19)

Dos Passos' reputation really was established with his novel of post-war disillusion, *Three Soldiers.* To this day, it remains one of the very best of twentieth century American war novels, and it describes the ordinary soldier trapped in the army machine, one of the instruments of the state grown healthy in war. Here, we find the theme of bigness, bigness in which the individual is lost, developed as a cause of disillusion. (p. 119)

The Great Days is a panoramic novel of the Second World War and its aftermath. However, Dos Passos tells the story and unfolds his panorama through the memory, experience and changing fate of a famous journalist. Ro Lancaster is 59, and in the post-war world, he has become a has-been. Drawing all his money, $3000, from the bank, he flies to Cuba with a redheaded gal who is thirty years his junior, physically striking, lost and frigid. Elsa is like a daughter of a character from *USA.* Lancaster seeks to refind love, but he is too old, too marred by experience. The seeds of disillusion are planted deep. The action of the novel ensues on two planes, present and past. Lancaster, going downhill, remembers the Great Days. These are recalled in terms of his own past, his love for his wife, Grace, who died of cancer, their life together, and the scenes and events he has witnessed as a reporter. This permits Dos Passos to describe wartime Washington, war and the functioning of the supply line in the Pacific, the Nuremburg Trials, post-war Paris. And since Dos Passos is an excellent journalist, his description of the Great Days is vivid. (p. 120)

But the Great Days are over and Ro Lancaster is one of yesterday's celebrities. He sees, in the rise of Soviet power, newer and graver dangers than those of the past. His trip to Havana is a mistake and, broke, he puts the girl on a bus in Milwaukee; he sinks into the nondescript crowd in the bus station. A full circle has been travelled. From the soldier caught in the gears of the big army machine of World War I, Dos Passos has pursued the themes of liberty and bigness through to the present; his fading celebrity slips back into a life of commonness and anonymity.

John Dos Passos writes with great ease and he is technically inventive. He has conceived various means to write the story of his times as he sees it. *The Great Days* is a well and even an ingeniously constructed book. It is remarkable to think of how much it takes in, because the novel is only of normal length. Dos Passos has always been best at establishing scenes, rather than in portraying characters with depth and strong individuality. The characters reflect a world that is constantly changing, bringing failure and defeat. (pp. 120-21)

[Dos Passos] has honestly recorded the play of hope and disappointment over four decades. He has done this with dignity and seriousness.

The future will tell how right or wrong he has been, and I personally think and respond differently than he does. From *Three Soldiers* to *The Great Days,* we can see in Dos Passos

the effort of one man of talent and sensibility to take hold of this changing play of forces in our life. It is worthy of new attention and a fresh evaluation. Dos Passos' work is a true, constructive achievement. (p. 121)

James T. Farrell, "How Should We Rate Dos Passos?" in The New Republic *(reprinted by permission of* The New Republic; © *1958 The New Republic, Inc.), Vol. 138, No. 17, April 28, 1958 (and reprinted in his* Literary Essays: 1954-1974, *edited by Jack Alan Robbins, Kennikat Press, 1976, pp. 118-21).*

IAIN COLLEY

The fact has to be faced that in his later fiction John Dos Passos is a failing novelist rather than a novelist of failure: a failing novelist largely because he has ceased to be an effective novelist of failure. It is scarcely possible to believe that the author of *USA* is producing books of which none is a vitalising pleasure to understand and evaluate, but it is true. Worse still, he is a writer whose deficiencies are no longer enlightening objects of critical attention, but one whose art is radically weak even in its most elementary aspects. The novels degenerate not simply in their incapacity to develop fresh thematic energies, but in the restless juggling of technical approaches, in the repetition of over-used and faded material, and in the slackening of the craftsman's hand that used to deal so readily with such fundamentals as the establishment of time, place and mood.

Chosen Country, as the title implies, is a tribute to U.S. civilisation and an announcement that the author has aligned himself with the most authentic tradition of American cultural identity. This is meant to be the Jeffersonian tradition; unfortunately it savours more of the elderly, comfort-loving, *Time*-reading, Republican-voting, stockmarket belt—the thinnest crust of any tradition. The author of *Facing the Chair* creates a hero of Italian descent who, after an early life of waywardness, 'comes home' to the United States. The story is written with a complete disregard for the nature of conviction and personal development and culminates in a section entitled, with supreme vulgarity and despite the fact that much of it is set in Canada, 'O My America My New Found Land'. Jay Pignatelli's rediscovery of his native land is accompanied (needless to say) by his marriage to a girl from an 'old family'. There seems little doubt that the writer considers this arrangement to have *put everything right,* and this belief alone measures the distance he has travelled. (pp. 135-36)

For the first time, Dos Passos offers himself as a novelist of the happy ending, and by doing so relegates his art to the level of the sentimental film or the Norman Rockwell illustration. (p. 136)

Chosen Country is a novel of almost five hundred pages, and because of its length it painfully demonstrates how thin Dos Passos has stretched his material. The absence of dramatic pressure and positively relevant incident, often amounting to even plain tedium, is highlighted by the reduction of the narrative style, for the most part, to a bare sequential recitation. In his effort to restore a measure of vitality to his fiction, Dos Passos makes use of his family history in a manner that has contingent interest but is never fruitfully integrated. The whole of his artistic logic has been inverted to create a fairy tale of error, reform and conversion. (pp. 136-37)

Jay Pignatelli's history is offered as a success-story, and his marriage to an old-stock American implies that the Union has fulfilled its paper promises and discovered a unique strength through blending native and immigrant traditions. Whatever the ultimate merits of this point of view, it is not dramatically validated in *Chosen Country*. Jay's choice is a puppet's twitch. The articulated skeleton of the novelist's former self maintains Jay as the residual legatee of other, more memorable incarnations; it is incapable of realising him as a man making deliberately, out of experience and self-correction, a significant decision. (p. 137)

Purely conventional—even old-fashioned—in form, *Most Likely to Succeed* aims for the most obvious of the ironies suggested by the title. Not only does it miss electrifying the platitude that a man may be a success by all worldly canons yet fail humanly . . . but it sets a positive puzzle for the reader by its inattention to prime requisites of the novel. The failing novelist, himself execrated by the critics and with the fear of professional perdition haunting him, has lost the 'récul esthetique'. He is no longer an intelligible writer in the basic idioms of his craft. For instance the action of 'Morocco' takes place in 1926, as the hero explicitly announces on the first page; prolific allusions to Paris, the Ballet Russe and Dada certainly date it in the twenties. But there is a bewildering lack of temporal actuality. In erasing the landmarks of his own past—here Dos Passos aims at wiping out the New Playwrights' Theatre, as he had earlier wiped out Harvard, Roosevelt, Sacco and Vanzetti—the author has left obscure necessary delineations of circumstance. (p. 138)

[*Most Likely to Succeed*] presents a hero-failure who never convinces in any dimension. It suffocates under a cold-war blanket of hatred. Dos Passos has proved nothing about failure and he has falsified a critical period of history; any consciousness of the giant threat of fascism is absent from *Most Likely to Succeed*. So is the sense of life among ordinary people. Like other anti-Communist revivalists of the fifties, Dos Passos equates Communism with wealthy, parasitic 'elements', and by aiming at this barn-door irony he extinguishes deeper, subtler ironies—and truth. Jed Morris is a total failure. The author say so. But it is not a failure which can touch or persuade the reader, it is contrived. It rings with the infallible false note of the counterfeit.

The remaining two novels published during Dos Passos' lifetime illustrate a further weakening of artistic control, and in each of them a man of about the author's age and with the author's own experience is shown at the end of his tether. Roland Lancaster, in *The Great Days*, comes alive only when he thinks of the past; his affair at the age of fifty-nine, with a much younger girl, is a series of humiliations and cross-purposes. To underscore the contrast, the narrative is divided into two alternating sections. In one, Lancaster gives a first-person account of the key episodes in his life. The other, impersonally narrated in the dramatic present, concentrates on the Cuban trip with Elsa. Lancaster has grown world-weary through the exhaustion of experience: 'Hasn't he always entertained the dream of boxing up his old wornout life and sending it to dead storage?' Elsa embodies his last hope of self-revitalisation, and Cuba the opportunity to mend his professional fortunes as a journalist.

The Great Days partially returns to the use of engrammatic perceptions—Lancaster is used up as a result of a cumulative barrage of assaults on his energy and integrity—but it takes pains also to accommodate Dos Passos' ideological grudges. Potentially the most interesting theme of the later works—reassessment and *apologia pro sua vita* by the aging novelist—

is dissipated. Dos Passos has worked in much of the material from which his later journalism derives, and the positive values are cemented in with egregious reliance on cliché. (pp. 140-41)

The reader is left to draw the conclusion that Roland Lancaster's personal and professional impasses have left him on the edge of nothing, where he can acquire the impetus for a fresh assault on life, repudiating the vanities that have plagued his career. Yet his failure is loosely and rather opaquely described; it is never thoroughly established as a lifelike consequence of impelling circumstances. The depletion of a talent is apparent in nearly every line—not just in the extensive use of unintegrated reportage and the heavy-handed editorialising but in the limpness of characterisation, dialogue and atmosphere. . . .

In *Midcentury* creative exhaustion is terminal: not even a reversion to the manner of *USA* can disguise it. If *The Great Days* is Dos Passos' last attempt to get outside himself, *Midcentury* is his final effort to penetrate society. The penetration is not deep, though: the theme of the book is the extinction of the self-willed individual by the power of large group interests and monopolies but it is expressed in querulous and bigoted accents. (p. 142)

Midcentury is loose, barren, and repetitious. Blackie Bowman is potentially the most interesting character, but his experiences are little more than yet another version of the essential John Dos Passos tale, and they lack scope and density. General MacArthur and Dean are praised for their patriotism, a value now unambivalently good. The Documentaries miss the variety and ironic juxtaposition of the Newsreels in *USA*. The seven abstracts of Investigator's Notes are seven separate pieces of evidence against labour corruption—one would have served, especially as five of the profiles (Bridges, Harry Lewis, Reuther, Tobin/Beck/Hoffa, Senator McClellan) treat the same subject. The lyrical intention of the three prefaces and the epilogue—to warn that 'institutional man' must 'sacrifice individual diversity'—is rendered as a blunderbuss assault on Big Unionism (to a minor extent, on Big Business and Finance); the interplay of tension between social and individual forces is neglected. *Midcentury* is not so much pessimistic as grievance-ridden. (p. 143)

Midcentury, professing to defend the individual against the enveloping institutions that threaten to crush him, only reflects a jaundiced disappointment. Maladroit in its construction, rife with traces of the magazine origins of much of its material, it embodies a sorrowful deterioration.

Dos Passos ends as the fulminating enemy of youth, having begun as its spokesman. Romantic failure is turned into cheap, patriotic self-regeneration and scepticism hardens into dogmatic fetishes of belief and repudiation. Nevertheless, it is an injustice that he should now be widely out of print (at least in Britain), forgotten and despised. The wonder is not that he should have ceased to be a widely respected literary figure, but that he should have left an oeuvre which, despite the relatively small proportion of first-grade work, contains so much that is admirable.

In *Manhattan Transfer* and especially in *USA* Dos Passos had faced up to a universe which bore no objective meaning and in which the existential struggle to create meaning in volitional life-activity itself seemed hopeless. The 'impassioned objectivity' of his manner and his technical resourcefulness helped to make him an author of genuine distinction. Dos Passos at his most accomplished communicates that most frightening sense of a world in which the impedimenta of a human-created civilisation refuse to yield any human meaning for the individual who reaches out to their lethal or recessive profiles. Fitzgerald wrote, wisely, that he spoke 'with the authority of failure', that he could use the phrase suggests how failure is a kind of qualification for making authentic judgements on life—and the significance of the remark is sharpened for Americans. When Dos Passos shows the sickly futility of a life—shows it in the accumulated detail of daily defeat, shows it transformed (to use Sartre's term) into a 'destiny'—he overcomes the ignoble facts by the truth and courage of his portrayal. This task it is the duty and justification of art to perform. That he omits other truths—the transcendence of pervading misery by the intensity of man's perceptions and will to understand; the supremacy of love, however transient its realisation; the deep satisfactions that come out of struggle—no more invalidates his attitude than the existence of happy marriages disproves Hemingway's view of male-female relations. The reader who has shared in the life of our century turns the pages of Dos Passos with the shock of self-recognition.

When the fiction of John Dos Passos ceases to draw energy from a nexus of alienation and doubt it loses artistic cohesion. The persona he chose, or grew into, was increasingly inimical not simply to his earlier purposes as a writer, but to the essential character of his literary ability. When Dos Passos 'came home', when he published crude magazine polemics and volumes of sentimental popular history, he surrendered the insight which underlay his major trilogy and which is so finely expressed by James T. Farrell: 'Time slowly transfigures me just as it transfigures all of us. There is no security in an insecure world. There is no final home on a planet where we are homeless children.' Farrell has also paid tribute to the vitality of the naturalist tradition, including *USA:* 'They have been written in the spirit of truth. If they are part of a tradition, that tradition has had more force and more impact, and has been able to nourish and give more energy to successive generations than any other tradition. This is especially so in America.'

For it remains the case that Dos Passos is an American writer; he had no need to resort to anti-Communist bluster, Barry Coldwater and the *National Review* to assure himself of this. The great American theme of success, from its enshrinement in popular self-help mythology to the beautifully controlled resonances of *The Great Gatsby,* entails its own corollaries of failure, despair and disillusion. Fitzgerald recorded such emotions in typically personal terms: '. . . an over-extention of the flank, a burning of the candle at both ends; a call upon physical resources that I did not command, like a man over-drawing at his bank . . . a feeling that I was standing at twilight on a deserted range, with an empty rifle in my hands and the targets down'. Yet not for nothing is Fitzgerald associated with the *zeitgeist* of inter-war America. What distinguishes his self-analysis is its freedom from rancour or blame; his artist's objectivity served him well. Similarly, the best work of Dos Passos—even where it draws on personal and political sympathies—never identifies a single source of error, a single evil. 'Impassioned objectivity'—more objective in **Manhattan Transfer,** more passionate in *USA*—allows him an exceptional freedom and versatility; antithetical properties (success/failure; radicalism/conservatism; mass institutions/the private consciousness) are deployed with extreme skill and tension. When this tension is dispersed by crude polemicism, the vital framework collapses. A primitive world-view is matched by severe technical regression. Dos Passos' disservice to himself arises not from craft-experiment, but by the sincere yet damaging

change in his viewpoint that persuaded him to re-interpret failure, success, morality and history.

It is especially deplorable that Dos Passos concluded his career as a novelist with a malevolent portrait of American youth. If there is any heroism in our time, any self-denying actions comparable to the heroism of the Spanish workers who fell on the barricades of their murdered republic, much of it has been contributed by a generation of young Americans who denied the limitless power of their government to coerce the individual and who showed their opposition by active resistance. But the great wave of contemporary organised outrage in the West is spent; despite the growth of an international youth counter-culture, one is more aware of fragmentation than of unity or harmony. Here are two themes perfectly in key with the interests of the novelist whose life ended in Baltimore on 28 September 1970. Such a novelist might be the chronicler of a world grown even more complex, uncertain and bewildering in the fifty years since **Manhattan Transfer:** not to point at causes and solutions, but by mirroring our dilemma and frustrations through the medium of art to amplify our awareness of our own situation, to provide us with an alternating focus on ourselves as social and individual beings. The time is due for Dos Passos to be re-read, as he wrote, with both sympathy and impartiality—and above all, with a seriousness equal to the most worthy of his aims and achievements. (pp. 144-46)

Iain Colley, in his Dos Passos and the Fiction of Despair *(© Iain Colley 1978; reprinted by permission of Macmillan, London and Basingstoke), Macmillan, 1978, 170 p.*

LINDA W. WAGNER

Although Dos Passos' writing eventually focused on American themes, his earliest poetry and fiction were more self-conscious than country-conscious. His favorite protagonist was a young, well-educated naif—usually a Brahmin—hungering for all experience simultaneously. There was much fascination with women, with sex (although never explicit), and with travel, all described through a romantic haze of impressionist color. There was also a strong sense of rootlessness, and the most carefully drawn figures are those of the boy's commanding, successful father and his genteel, passive mother.

Dos Passos' early writing is also self-conscious in another sense, in that it illustrates the artistic principles already important to the fledgling author. These were the years of absorption in technique, and most modern writers believed that, in order for any writer to "write straight," he must have some kind of prolegomenon, some set of artistic principles. Dos Passos' beginning aesthetic grew from the contemporary emphasis on the concrete image, the scene—whether in fiction, drama, or poetry—and on the arrangement of those images and scenes into patterns resembling montage or collage. The pose of the objective author became one of his ideals, as did the use of commonplace subjects. (p. 3)

One central premise in the modernist aesthetic revolution was the importance of the image. . . . The concentration on the concrete and the use of free or organic form and of rhythms determined by the spoken phrase rather than the rigidity of the metronome—these principles of imagism were to lay the foundation for most modern poetry and much prose as well. (p. 4)

Dos Passos' poems, finally collected in the 1922 *A Pushcart at the Curb* . . . do seem to have been influenced in some respects by the imagist doctrines. Short poems like **"XV"** from **"Winter in Castile"** are image-centered, highly descriptive, and succinct. . . . Most of the longer poems also emphasize the image, although it may be only one element of a structure determined partly by the musicality of the total poem. (p. 5)

Comparing Dos Passos' poems with those of imagist poets like William Carlos Williams or H.D., however, shows some clear differences. Dos Passos seems to have been closer to the thinking of William Faulkner and Conrad Aiken in his feeling that, whatever its other properties, the modern poem should be "intensely musical." The spare colloquial idiom of the modern American streetwalker or butcher theoretically may be the stuff of art, but Dos Passos had great admiration for the poems of Stevenson, Tennyson, and Swinburne, as well as for the work of Richard Aldington and Ezra Pound. . . . [Frequently] Dos Passos' poems are marked by heavy assonance, one means of creating musicality in language. . . . (p. 6)

From this device, it is only a short step to one of his most pervasive techniques, the repetition of phrase or line, a type of refrain, whether or not conventionally placed at the ends of stanzas. At its simplest, Dos Passos' repetition occurs to create mood, often through color imagery, as in **"V"** from **"Winter in Castile,"** a poem that opens "Rain slants on an empty square" and closes with the mournful "in the grey rain, / in the grey city." In more ambitious poems, Dos Passos uses repetition to vary mood rather than to maintain it. . . . Dos Passos believed in the use of regular poetic forms so long as they achieved desired effects. (p. 7)

Another element of Dos Passos' concept of musicality stemmed from his notion that free verse was never literally free but was "*meant* to have rhythm—it's not the same rhythm as so-called metrical verse; but it's a perfectly definite and sometimes quite *regular* cadence." Line division and line placement in the poems usually help create rhythm or pace; in many places, the division that exists is expected and borders on the uninventive. At other times, however, . . . line arrangement works to create effective montage, a device Dos Passos used throughout his work. . . . [Even] recurring similes (a favorite figure of speech in these early poems) cannot deaden the pace of this juxtaposition, the technique that gives Dos Passos' poetry and prose (as in the Newsreel sections of *U.S.A.* and *Midcentury*) their brisk tempo.

Important as these principles of musicality, the image, and juxtaposition were to Dos Passos' developing aesthetic, one of the essential points of his early credo was the concept of objectivity of presentation. The writer was to aim for the illusion of distance. His role was that of objective conveyor and, although he might use subjective elements in his presentation—indeed, his choices of subjects and details were in themselves subjective—he was to avoid obtrusiveness. Method, more than attitude, was to be objective. Dos Passos' poems follow this directive perhaps too well: nearly all the poems are montages of external details—chandeliers, bells, soldiers, donkeys, children. The people appearing in the poems are also vividly described but always from an external perspective: Dos Passos uses colors and other graphic details but seldom tells his reasons for being drawn to the subjects of the poems. The first person is almost never used, unless it occurs in pastoral poems as a narrative convention. The cumulative effect of *A Pushcart at the Curb* is, then, relatively impersonal: a reader knows more about Tivoli and camel travel than about John Dos Passos. (pp. 7-8)

The few exceptions to these objective presentations are all the more striking for their rarity. Several poems picture the young poet as a classic Prufrock figure—unfulfilled, searching, held back from various kinds of satisfaction because of fear, thinking his life futile. At times the focus for his anguish is a woman (usually slender, dark, shadowy); elsewhere, as in **"Ode to Ennui,"** his malaise is undefined. More frequently, in the somewhat later poems, loneliness itself is the cause of his despair. . . . What some of the strongest of his poems in *A Pushcart at the Curb* seem to suggest is that Dos Passos did carry feelings of frustration and inadequacy into maturity. An isolato for many reasons, he continually tried to overcome his hesitancy about personal relationships. (pp. 8-9)

. . . . .

Much of the "plot" of both *One Man's Initiation: 1917* and *Three Soldiers* concerns the dichotomy between Dos Passos' optimistic acceptance of his fellow soldiers and his later awareness of their sometimes disappointing actions under stress.

A greater part of his excitement about the war, however, seems to have been the accessibility of real experience as subject matter for his writing. (p. 10)

It comes as no surprise that Dos Passos' first two published novels are war novels, written "imagistically" and centered on the searching young protagonists, Martin Howe and John Andrews. What makes the books better than some of his self-conscious technical pronouncements of these years might have indicated is that his emotional energy permeates them and commits him to writing powerfully about experiences and newly developed feelings. Even though he still felt somewhat trapped by what he viewed as the "bell-glass" atmosphere of Harvard and Boston society, his novels convince the reader that war is more than a rhetorical problem or a social one, that the lives of men are valuable, and that Dos Passos' purpose as writer is to present enough of the bones of the experience so that we ourselves can add on the flesh. In *One Man's Initiation*, for example, there is little attention to political events preceding and surrounding the war. Dos Passos' interest, and focus, falls on a few soldiers faced with their first encounter with death—of both physical bodies and cultural ones. The experience of the novel is accordingly immediate and concrete, rather than abstract and philosophical.

What makes the two novels a logical part of the artistic progression Dos Passos' writing career evinces is that the methods he uses in them are very similar to the methods he was then employing in his poetry. Instead of choosing a dramatic structure of rising action-climax-falling action, Dos Passos sets one scene against another, events separated in time become related thematically as they are presented in a nonchronological montage. (p. 11)

Like his poetry, the prose of *One Man's Initiation* is marked by factual detail presented concretely and by a painter's reliance on color. . . . [Contrasting] glimpses of bravado and nervousness take the story quickly from the early tone of comfortable pastiche to the stolid irony of the body of the novel. Throughout *One Man's Initiation,* or *First Encounter* as it was later and intermittently titled, Dos Passos sets the unrelieved horror of physical war against the propagandist version of that war, with snatches of popular songs serving as punctuation. These opposing views of war form the bases for the novel: scenes set in graphic montage to duplicate the effect the sights of war have on Martin Howe's awareness.

Even as the would-be soldiers drink and gamble to allay their fears, these fears surface in their conversation. Dos Passos shows fear in both the abstract and the specific. . . . (p. 12)

[Each] chapter adds another episode to Martin Howe's awakening horror, whether it be the destruction of the picturesque abbey, the slow deaths of the ambulance patients, or the depravity of the soldiers. Each scene is presented graphically, so that separate images stand clear at first and then gradually coalesce into more intense significance. (p. 13)

What is most noticeable about this carefully modulated intensification of horror is that Martin Howe's understanding of the true nature of wounding and death parallels his realizations about other romantic ideals. His concept of the woman he might love differs wildly from the French prostitutes who surround him. His beliefs about the realities of war are also quickly shattered, and the tone of physical outrage and hostility becomes correspondingly dulled and resigned. The image Dos Passos used to represent all the glory of an enlightened culture—that of the abbey—is eventually shelled; its destruction, however, is described with quasi-dreamlike resignation. . . . Similarly described is a macabre crucifixion scene, in which Christ's crown of thorns is replaced with a crown of barbed wire and the physical imagery culminates in the shapeless, sacked bodies of the dead. Instead of pathos or sensationalism, the sight of those unnamed, uncounted dead provokes the narrator to that same ultracontrolled description, focusing on the procession of the "little carts" rather than on the bodies that are their contents.

The progression in the novel to its unrelievedly bitter end—with many of Howe's friends dead or dying and his observing the aftermath of another futile battle—follows effectively from the image clusters placed early in the book. *One Man's Initiation* also has its share of polemic—chance conversations, ironic interchanges, outright diatribe—but even this rhetoric is frequently saved by Dos Passos' graphic use of the language. The propaganda first described as "living, growing flypaper to catch and gum the wings of every human soul" becomes personified in the ideology of the berserk soldier who believes that "to stop the war you must kill everybody, kill everybody."

Such vignettes as this of the mad soldier loosely connected by Howe's presence and central consciousness and by the repetition of images and language create the structure of the book. Relatively free from personal antagonists, Howe moves through the war, often less aware than one might wish of the unending ironies surrounding him. His "initiation" appears to accrue from the gradual accumulation of vivid physical images—colors, flowers, sounds, wounds, fires. Only toward the end of the novel does Dos Passos show Howe trying clumsily to sort through the prevailing attitudes and philosophies about the war. . . . [But events] have proved even the most pessimistic of views too affirmative, and the brisk episodic structure of the book brings the denouement home effectively. (pp. 13-15)

. . . . .

[The theme of an early play, *The Garbage Man*,] is the familiar early one that breaking with familial and other traditions is desirable; the characters Jane and Tom manage to break out of stultifying family "connections" and finally reap romantic and material "rewards." The play's method is the charged, recurring image and quasi-surreal event pattern—heightened by outright fantasy—similar to that of *One Man's Initiation: 1917* and *Streets of Night*. There is also some use of the long-line incantatory rhythm that Dos Passos would use in the Bi-

ography sections of *U.S.A.* The most noticeable device is his reliance on jazz and dance routines. (p. 73)

The Garbage Man included many elements of musical comedy and was one of the New Playwrights Theatre's more interesting productions, despite its jejune philosophy and vapid characters.

Several years later, between 1927 and 1928, Dos Passos wrote a play that, politically, *did* belong on the stage of the New Playwrights Theatre. *Airways, Inc.* is not only his best play; it may also be, as Edmund Wilson suggested, some of his best writing. Proletarian in sympathy and experimental in technique, the play foreshadows *U.S.A.* in its inclusion of events both past and present, act and motivation, and a wide panoply of American characters and cultural problems. In *Airways, Inc.* we see the almost innocent progress of an exploitative culture to its demise, as human values are exchanged for quick profits. The theme is not new, but Dos Passos' presentation of it is fresh and effective. (pp. 74-5)

Airways, Inc. is not a play about the varieties of belief so much as it is a condemnation of capitalism. The play was originally titled *Suburb*, a designation that suggested some urban-suburban difference. Place, however, was not the issue for Dos Passos: *The Garbage Man* is set largely in New York; *Fortune Heights*, in a tiny crossroads community. Dos Passos had seen that the same kind of thinking existed everywhere. What he gained by choosing the title *Airways, Inc.* was an emphasis on the power of business, the profit motivation, coupled with suggestions of the glamour of flying (viz., Charles Lindbergh as national hero) and of flight as an archetypal image of freedom, a commodity none of these characters has enough of. Dos Passos succeeded in locating the blame for American greed squarely where he thought it should lie, with business. . . . (p. 76)

The theme of buying—merchandise, property, business—runs throughout the play, always to the dissatisfaction of the purchaser. Dos Passos shows the ways human considerations are buried under the pressures of finance, whether high or low; money is the pivot for action throughout *Airways, Inc.* (p. 77)

Considering *Airways, Inc.* as a New Playwrights production, intent on some kind of political statement, one of its strongest achievements is that Dos Passos himself does little of the recriminating. The characters, in their quick-paced interaction, give us the analysis and the implied solution for the problems of prejudice, fear, isolationism, but the plot of the play keeps the reader from feeling that he is being subjected to a political treatise. (pp. 79-80)

The main weakness of the play is Dos Passos' turn to violence when he runs out of uses for his characters. . . . Dos Passos may have been influenced by his interest in melodrama, but his reliance on the macabre seems inappropriate for this particular play. *Airways, Inc.* does not pretend to be a comedy; unlike *The Garbage Man* and *Fortune Heights*, it draws its power from its tragic qualities—consistent tone, the threat of impending disaster, human resolution in the face of conflict that determines the action of the central characters, and an inimical and dangerous culture. . . .

By the time of *Fortune Heights* . . . Dos Passos' bitterness about "romance" and "success" was clear. The relationships that exist in that play are hardly "love songs"; they are more often sexual conveniences, with little concern for the other person's needs or desires. Impermanence is the mode and suggests that one person's dissatisfaction with another stems at least partly from an inability to separate fact from fantasy. (p. 80)

Success is as far from the capabilities of the characters as love is, and all the quick juxtapositions of comic and stock characters used in *Fortune Heights* cannot alleviate the impression of disaster. (p. 81)

Fortune Heights attempted less to create any new myth than to debunk all the old American attitudes. . . . [From] the beginning of the play Dos Passos shows us only lost opportunity. (pp. 81-2)

Fortune Heights is an uneven and unlikely mixture of propaganda and vaudeville. The play closes with a series of scenes in which farmers and laborers unite to try to prevent Owen's eviction from his filling station. Dos Passos' "solution" in 1933 to social crises is the action of common men, inarticulate in their rationale but moved by simple, genuinely humanitarian impulses. . . . [The] concluding theme, the "search" for the U.S.A., to find answers to the broken promises and the battered dreams, propels the play to an ending inconclusive in political philosophy. For, finally, cooperation does *not* work. . . . (pp. 82-3)

The chief strength of *Fortune Heights* is Dos Passos' ability to build ironies, especially during the first two acts, through his use of titles for the forty-one separate scenes. Moving much like a vaudeville program, one vignette followed rapidly by the next, *Fortune Heights* develops an expansive structure. Signaled by the captionlike titles, the viewer can accept any kind of action, whether in direct sequence or oblique. (p. 83)

Dos Passos' last play succeeded in the scenes that show characters in . . . poignant realizations, but its melodramatic reliance on foreclosures and evictions, love affairs, robberies and murders as well as its use of a mock-comic speed and tone left its viewers baffled. Because of Dos Passos' technical innovation, the play certainly cannot be judged as part of the "realistic" theatrical tradition, for all the realism of its Depression experience. *Fortune Heights* stands as an imperfect fusion of Dos Passos' interest in experimental theater and the use of American theatrical forms and his desire that drama express meaningful social ideas, a vestige of the New Playwrights era more interesting for its influence on his later fiction than for its own efficacy as theater. (p. 84)

. . . . .

Because the twentieth century has been a period of immense technical innovation in all the arts, it has become natural to study literature as structure, style, epistemological construct. What is in some ways most surprising when Dos Passos' work—fiction as well as nonfiction—is studied from those perspectives is that his style throughout his career did remain relatively constant. At some points, most graphically in *Manhattan Transfer* and the *U.S.A.* trilogy, he used his basic techniques more flamboyantly, in more dramatic patterns, but his writing was based on four tactics that seldom varied.

1. Dos Passos was a character-oriented writer. Regardless of what he was writing, he searched for a person on whom to focus. In his reporting of the United States during World War II, in his coverage of Harlan County, of the Sacco-Vanzetti case, of unemployment in Detroit—his approach to history was consistent. Instead of a study of restrictive Puritanism, he describes Roger Williams as its antithesis; instead of a point-by-point discussion of the Declaration of Independence, he gives us Thomas Jefferson—in three volumes; instead of a political

or military analysis of World War I, it becomes, in vivid outline, *Mr. Wilson's War,* an account laced with individuals who not only represent the common American: they are common Americans. Even the books that might well have become treatises in political science—*The Prospect Before Us* and *The Theme Is Freedom*—are built on portraits of individual people. More and more in his writing, Dos Passos illustrated the centrality of his notion that the primary duty of any governmental system was "growing great people." In parallel fashion, the primary duty of the writer was to capture those people—both great and not so great—as the only sure means of reaching the reader in terms he would be able to understand.

2. This extension of the modernist emphasis on the use of the concrete, the actual, as a way toward the universal occurred because of Dos Passos' conviction that people, characters, were the most important elements in any culture. (pp. 144-45)

3. Because Dos Passos was at heart a skeptical modern no matter how much he wanted to become an eighteenth-century rationalist, he realized that no cause-and-effect arrangement of these details and characters from life would be convincing. Montage, collage, or less sensational forms of juxtaposition thus became his structural basis, and from the days of *Manhattan Transfer* and the *U.S.A.* trilogy forward, nearly everything he wrote was arranged on a variation of that principle. At its simplest, it became the flashback to his life with Grace in *The Great Days;* at its most complex, it was the four-part pattern of *U.S.A.* or *Midcentury;* at its most didactic, it was the interlock of "message" poetry with narrative in the *District of Columbia* books; at its loosest, it was the vignette placed against vignette throughout *The Ground We Stand On* and *Tour of Duty.* Like a true camera (rather than the introspective Camera Eye of *U.S.A.*), Dos Passos' narrative method asks the reader to focus and absorb; then to break (often whimsically, without explanation); then to focus and absorb once again—and leaves the reader with the primary responsibility of assimilating all the information from those various shots into some kind of cogent whole. (pp. 145-46)

4. . . . Dos Passos' choices in language often depended on the characteristic modernist belief that a person could be best described by using his own vernacular. From his book and chapter titles to his descriptions of people to his invectives against the media (first newspapers, then radio, finally—and most violently—television) for its abuses of langauge, Dos Passos worked from the idiom out. (p. 146)

Dos Passos' unquestioning belief that a person's colloquial speech was representative of that person also led to a reliance, narratively, on dialogue. His structuring of narrative segments around scenes depends partly on the success of the dialogue of characters in interaction; when that dialogue works, he can avoid supplemental description.

Besides relying on idiomatic dialogue, Dos Passos also built a basic narrative style out of the vernacular. The language of the *U.S.A.* narratives came to dominate much of his prose, a workmanlike composite of relatively plain American English, whose sentences were more likely to be groups of prepositional phrases than elegantly balanced or periodic constructions. The casualness of American speech had a pervasive influence on what had begun—in the days of *The Harvard Monthly*—as a fairly elaborate syntax.

In contrast to Dos Passos' plain-speaking narrative, which was appropriate for so much of his journalism and fiction, he also worked easily in his prose-poem voice. First apparent in the

U.S.A. Biography and Camera Eye sections, the use of specific poetic techniques within ostensible prose was a contrasting method for expressing views the idiomatic speech could not convey. Visual space, incremental rhythms, conscious repetition, significant line divisions, assonantal language patterns— Dos Passos knew well how to use these devices but so long as he was writing as an average American, the use of these techniques would seem inappropriate. By being able to move— through his fabric of juxtaposed elements—to a section of such contrasting language, Dos Passos could signal the reader that this was the authorial voice. Because it was used sparingly and because, in both early writing and late, it often conveyed the more didactic kinds of expression, readers learned to read Dos Passos' prose-poem sections as important statements of theme. This was as true in the *U.S.A.* Biography sections as it was in the prefaces to the *District of Columbia* novels and *Midcentury.*

So pervasive were these techniques that Dos Passos used them no matter what he was writing. Even the last few books about places—Portugal, Brazil, Easter Island—are written with the same devices and style: focus on character rather than event; attention to physical detail; reliance on juxtaposition of segments; use of vernacular. The qualities of the early *Rosinante to the Road Again,* as well as *One Man's Initiation: 1917,* remain, although Dos Passos has become content with re-creating the randomness of real life instead of trying to impose a construct on events. (pp. 146-47)

Dos Passos' later books of travel share more than technical mannerisms with his late fiction and history. It is increasingly clear that for Dos Passos these books of place should also convey his moral principles, and his choice of characters and detail for his rapportage throughout the books about Brazil (1963), Portugal (1969), and Easter Island (1971) is determined as much by the integrity of their lives as by their color. (p. 148)

When Ro Lancaster wrote in *The Great Days* that the kind of journalism he spent his life writing was "the kind of journalism that's between history and prophecy," he was defining Dos Passos' own mode of narrative. Drawing from the factual bases of history, using a keen sense of prediction and understanding—based largely in people, and alerting readers to the dangers that lay ahead: the astute writer would be more than an entertainer; more, in total, than a craftsman. He would be not just a chronicler; his expertise would also lead him to the crucial art of interpreting. He would give his culture its antennae. That his fate might also be that of a Tiresias or a Cassandra should have been obvious to Dos Passos from the beginning. (p. 150)

. . . . .

Embarrassed as some critics have been about Dos Passos' late insistence that the moral position become explicit rather than implicit in his writing, their attitudes may be more reactionary than his own philosophical positions. For America's contemporary writers—novelists like Norman Mailer in *Armies of the Night,* for example, and countless poets, from W. S. Merwin and Adrienne Rich to Robert Creeley and Denise Levertov— have turned increasingly to writing that is revolutionary, that does show process rather than mask it. Writers today share with their readers their own experiences, convictions, attitudes, uncertainties; the act of reading Creeley's *A Day Book* is the act of coming to know Creeley. The same kind of statement could easily be made about *Century's Ebb.* (p. 172)

The emphasis on stating a moral position, on sharing sentiment, that had been seen in the 1950s as a weakness in Dos Passos' work may have been evidence of his struggling to become more in tune with contemporary thinking. His "contemporary chronicles" really did stay contemporary, not only in themes but also in method. The present demand for a feeling of intimacy in our relationship with a writer, the urge to understand not only the written book but the person responsible for it: Dos Passos was responding to those needs of readers as he wrote some of the *District of Columbia* material and *Chosen Country, Most Likely to Succeed,* and *The Great Days.* The technical problems with these books were chiefly those of a transitional mode of writing, not unlike Hemingway's problems in writing *To Have and Have Not.* Dos Passos knew he wanted different effects, but his methods in *U.S.A.* and *Manhattan Transfer* had been so conspicuous, so many readers had discussed style in commenting on those books, that he naturally decided that to change effect, he should change method. The most obvious tactic seemed to be simplification, in both plot and texture. But Dos Passos' simplification (for all his variety within it) was disappointing. Just as he could never satisfactorily write short stories, so Dos Passos was not at his best working a single story line handled "straight." As a child of the ironic patterns of modern life, Dos Passos wrote best when he could manipulate those countless, unexpected strands of life into some ironic pattern of his own devising.

And so the excellence of the last two novels, *Midcentury* and *Century's Ebb.* Themes had not changed since the *District of Columbia* trilogy, but Dos Passos' use of a montage of techniques was never surer. . . . In addition, in the last novels, through the less disguised use of autobiographical elements, readers feel involved with Dos Passos as person. They are surrounded by the tapestry of the time, a tapestry dominated not only by the larger-than-life saints he had described earlier, but by the equally larger-than-life authorial consciousness. The effect was that writing was taken out of some remote province of "literature" and into the reader's life. Compelling in its intimacy, Dos Passos' late work conveys a sense of the writer that is absent in the early fiction: we are conscious of his intensity, his earnestness, his search—first for America (in the period up to and including *U.S.A.*), then for hero, and ultimately his search for himself. (pp. 172-74)

Because few American writers have remained more consistently optimistic, productive, inventive, and curious than Dos Passos, his closing image in *Century's Ebb* seems more than an accidental choice. For Dos Passos, the landing on the moon was more than a technological feat: it was also some kind of mystical full circle from his earliest romantic dream. . . . In 1917, when he had first worked with that image, no one was predicting a moon landing fifty years later; yet somehow, and from America, the space voyage was launched. Dos Passos' openness to the future, to promise, to the life of the imagination remained his hallmark, and one finds even in his comparatively dour late years, a continuous curiosity. (p. 175)

The essential elements of Dos Passos' art were present early— audacity, subject matter, and an impressionistic craft that defied age. There was also, most importantly, a questioning and rich imagination that understood not only human beings but the patterns of forces with which they had to contend. If some of Dos Passos' last writing is flawed by an overinsistence on opinions readers might not share, we can lament both that overemphasis and those opinions, but, as Joseph Epstein concludes, "It is still possible to recognize a good man behind them." The praise may not, in some final analysis, be so faint as it first seems.

The closing section of *Century's Ebb,* then, is clearly affirmative. Focusing on the journey to the moon is, for Dos Passos, external image, social image, fact-made-personal—a fusion of accessible information and private sensibility, giving any reader insights into the fiction and maintaining as well the continuum of personal meaning that connects all his writing. A half century of work focused on the search for country, hero, and self. . . . (pp. 175-76)

> *Linda W. Wagner, in her* Dos Passos: Artist as American *(copyright © 1979 by the University of Texas Press), University of Texas Press, 1979, 220 p.*

CHARLES MARZ

John Dos Passos records and resists in *U.S.A.* the extinction of the private voice, the invasion of the private space, by the devastating forces of history. The landscapes of the test, like those of *Three Soldiers* and *Manhattan Transfer,* are strewn with that devastation's debris—the residue of character, the remains of narrative. Dos Passos chronicles in the trilogy the voices and the acts of residual men—the echoes, the fragments that compose America.

U.S.A. expands the themes and techniques of *Three Soldiers* and *Manhattan Transfer.* Structurally it is even more artificial and patterned. The usual criterion of realistic style, that it vanishes before the reality of the subject, does not apply to its pages. As in *Manhattan Transfer* Dos Passos deforms the voices of America, the bankrupt speech of anonymous men. . . . *U.S.A.* is not a recording of America. And it is not a story about America. Traditional novelistic unities of character and action are abandoned; beginnings and endings of persons and events are fortuitous. There is little progress, little growth, little development of character; there is no real concern with representation, illusion, or empathy. The trilogy is not held together by any chain of events or "storyline"; it must be apprehended spatially and not sequentially. Sequence yields to a structure characterized by the juxtaposition of disconnected and often incompatible word blocks. *U.S.A.* is a continent and a composition ruled by crisis and collision; it is fragmented, radically incomplete, and as amorphous and incoherent at times as its characters' lives.

The trilogy is a medley of juxtaposed and layered voices. Its meanings are generated by the thematic and structural tensions among its compositional blocks, by the complex and various juxtapositions of Camera Eyes, Newsreels, Narratives, and Biographies. Public and private lives and events constantly intersect; public and private voices collide. Dos Passos records the sound of the collisions, the noise of the public sphere and the silence of the private space during the first thirty crisis-ridden years of this century in America. But as he chronicles he resists the murderous forces of history, the triumph of the world. Neither the composition nor the country disintegrates. The performing voice of the novelist-historian, and his accomplice, the reader, survive the tale told as history and fiction of a world too much with us.

The conflict between the destructive chaos of public voices and the private voice that seeks survival in the world is manifested in the collisions of the Newsreel and the Camera Eye sections of *U.S.A.* The Camera Eye is the last preserve of the sensitive and embattled individual. It is the last remnant of the individual voice—the end product of Martin Howe, John Andrews, and Jimmy Herf—or perhaps the waste product. For the Camera Eye is a residual voice; it is what remains of the intense subjectivity of the early works. (pp. 398-400)

[The] fact that the Camera Eye sections of *U.S.A.* might compose a partially autobiographical history of Dos Passos from the turn of the century to the early thirties is irrelevant to their use and meaning in the trilogy. Matching the life and text of the author is a critical game we need not play. *U.S.A.* is not a *roman à clef.*

The Camera Eye selections in *U.S.A.* contain both historical and fictional materials. They are representations and not samples of a private voice, and their meaning is not autobiographical. It is the manner more than the matter of the telling that is significant. The conversational expression, the direct address of the reader, the unfamiliar allusions, and the paratactic constructions create a sincere and private presence. It gives the appearance of real or natural speech and seems autobiographical, at times even confessional. It remains, however, essentially fictive discourse—the private voice of a fictive self speaking anonymously from the interior of the text. It is a portrait of a Self more than a self-portrait. And the speaker, as in the first Camera Eye, remains the embattled individual, often the stranger, the exile, "The Man Without A Country," the unknown soldier—always the sensitive observer isolated and buried by the world. (p. 400)

The disembodied voice of the Camera Eye represents the slow dissolution of a coherent, private individual. (p. 401)

The Camera Eye chronicles the disappearance, the gradual bankruptcy of the self. It also resists that disappearance. The private voice of the Camera Eye resists subordination—both syntactically and politically. It is expansive and unpredictable; it rebels against order and form, history and society. Violence (linguistic and political) is done to syntax and organization. The world is deformed; it becomes asyntactical. The beginnings and endings that constitute normal historical and narrative order—the "conspiracy" of history we call "plot"—are resisted. And so finally are the echoes and clichés, the headlines and slogans, the word-debris that buries the individual, the noise that silences him. The private voice of the Camera Eye retreats from and resists the world; it is voice haunted by possible complicity, by the deformations of word-slinging and slogan-mongering; it enlists the reader (also complicitous in his aesthetic detachment) in the struggle to find an authentic private voice—a voice that will successfully combat the public noise. (p. 402)

The Newsreels of *U.S.A.* operate at several levels of meaning. Most obviously and, perhaps, least significantly, they mark time chronologically. The panoramic, historical aspect of *U.S.A.* is now a critical given. The Newsreels locate the historical background for the action of the trilogy; they provide its setting; they generate atmosphere; they indicate the passage of time in the world and in the text. It seems also given that the Newsreels may be linked to themes and actions in adjacent narrative, Camera Eye, and biographical passages; they date, comment on, and link the various persons and events in the trilogy. However, even if we could identify the historical source or referent for each of the Newsreel fragments, even if we could "plot" (as "conspiratorial" critics engaged in the "burial" of the text) the chronological progression of the trilogy from Newsreel I to Newsreel LXVIII, we would be no closer to explaining the power of *U.S.A.*, no closer to articulating the significance of the Newsreels. The trilogy must be understood dynamically. Its power and meanings come ultimately from vertical, atemporal, simultaneous events, and not from horizontal, biographical, successive actions. They are not generated by the historical exactness but by the random collisions of voices. The voices in the Newsreels collide with one another and with the rest of the text. These collisions generate grotesque ironies. It is not uncommon in a Newsreel to find juxtaposed celebrations and horrors of America, the dream and the nightmare. Dos Passos resists as he records the noise of history. Random collisions set off random explosions; the novelist is historian and saboteur.

The Newsreels chronicle the voices of the public sphere; they are the most banal, most impersonal, most mechanical registration of persons and events in the trilogy; they are the "nightmare of history," uncolored and uncontrolled by the private voice of the Camera Eye. (p. 403)

In the Camera Eye passage of *U.S.A.*, there is a refusal to abdicate personal control; the embattled individual stands at the center of the world, almost to the exclusion of it; there is an intense—though never transcendent or religious—residual individualism. In the Newsreels, however, the persons exists nearer the periphery of the world. And the subject, the ever-present "I" and "you" of the Camera Eye, recedes. The public voices of the Newsreels are speakerless. They are voices over which men have no control. Individuals are not subordinated—they simply cease to exist. . . . The world of the Newsreels is a lawless, violent world out of control, a world of personalities or celebrities and not characters, personalities whose lives are only as complete as the information available in the headlines. The speakerless world of the Newsreels is a constantly eroding world, a world without human responsibility or moral content. The dispassionate, technological voices of the Newsreels speak constant destruction and violence; they register the nightmare that is history. And in that nightmare the human scale is reduced; things become the locus and power of values. The individual is "heaped" by the world, slowly buried by its objects and its debris. (pp. 405-06)

In the narrative and biographical passages of *U.S.A.* the residual voice of the Camera Eye and the speakerless voice of the Newsreel give way to a voice of the "middle-distance," the performing voice of the chronicler-novelist. The performer and his complicitous audience, the reader, remove themselves from and resist the world by deforming it. Irony becomes the rhetorical strategy most useful in that deformation. It records as it deforms the public voice; it locates the disparity between word and thing; it demands the mutual participation and understanding of writer and reader; and it provides their necessary expiation. (p. 407)

In the biographical passages of *U.S.A.* Dos Passos records the lives and voices of the public space. He chronicles the destruc-tion of America's last heroes—embattled individuals who attempt to hollow out the expanding and consuming public space and preserve an authentic, private voice. And he chronicles and deforms the lives and voices of the survivors, the pseudo-heroes, the word-slingers who contribute to and sustain the public noise—the noise that kills. (pp. 407-08)

The lives and voices of the public space, of the Newsreels and Biographies, penetrate the trilogy. They invade and determine the world and the text in which the narrative characters act and speak. Historical and fictional lives collide. . . . The world and the text interpenetrate; history and fiction blur. Fictional lives, the habitual voices of average Americans, echo the recognizable historical gestures and voices of the public space. In the narrative passages of *U.S.A.*, Dos Passos chronicles the echoing voices and actions of hollow men. Characters are voiceless and nearly invisible. . . . They have no depth; their outlines are often broken; and there is no difference between the space of their interior and exterior lives. (pp. 409-10)

U.S.A. is ultimately an "economic novel of the self." That is not to say that it is simply a commentary or record of the American economy. It is a chronicle of inflated and officious sentiments (public voices), of counterfeit verbal transactions (echoes), of the loss of personal value (private space) in pursuit of the Big Money. *U.S.A.* is the record of the bankruptcy of the self. (p. 411)

Dos Passos refuses to relinquish his voice to the public space. He resists the invasions of history that determine and reduce lives, the public nightmares, the Newsreels. He resists voices that have become public, that demand conformity, that rest in cliché. He refuses to be silenced by the public voice, yet he does not retreat into solipsism. Silence and exile are not viable alternatives. There is only cunning. *U.S.A.* is a chronicle of word-debris, of language betrayals, of treasonous voices. It is also, however, a subversive performance. Its meanings lie neither in documentation (Newsreels), nor in conviction (Camera Eyes). They lie somewhere in between, in that frontier between history and fiction, in the ironic, performing voice of the author in concert with the reader, in their cunning resistance to the public voice, in our controlled deformation of the text and the world. (p. 415)

Charles Marz, "'U.S.A.': Chronicle and Performance," in Modern Fiction Studies *(© 1980 by Purdue Research Foundation, West Lafayette, Indiana 47907, U.S.A.), Vol. 26, No. 3, Autumn, 1980, pp. 398-416.*

G(erald) B(asil) Edwards

1899-1976

English novelist.

Edwards's only novel, *The Book of Ebenezer Le Page*, was published posthumously due to the enthusiastic support of John Fowles, who wrote its introduction. The book is a fictional reminiscence of an elderly bachelor similar to Edwards himself. Set in the Channel Island of Guernsey, it spans nearly eighty years of the twentieth century and details the cultural changes experienced by an island folk accustomed to being isolated. In his "eccentric" voice, Edwards pays tribute to the past, to a place, and to human dignity.

JOHN FOWLES

There may have been stranger recent literary events than [*The Book of Ebenezer Le Page*], . . . but I rather doubt it. It is first of all posthumous, since the author, born a year older than the century, died in 1976. Then it is an only novel, seemingly not begun until he was in his late sixties. Even without those oddities, its voice and method are so unusual that it belongs nowhere on our conventional literary maps. (p. vii)

So far as we know it was not until 1974 that Edwards made . . . any attempt to have **The Book of Ebenezer Le Page** published. He bore the rejections it then received with an at least outward patient obstinacy. . . . If I cannot think much of the judgement of the various eminent London publishers who turned the typescript down in the mid 1970s, at least I can understand why they all seem to have had trouble explaining the rejection. What had landed in their nets was a very strange fish—and one, I suspect, that on a quick reading it was only too easy to place in a wrong literary species, that of the provincial novel.

I think myself that it is no more properly classifiable so than Flora Thompson's famous trilogy, *Lark Rise to Candleford*. Of course any book whose ground is the close observation of a small community risks this damning label of 'provincial'. Yet even if Edwards' account of the life and times of one Channel Islander had to be thus valued, it would still seem to me a remarkable achievement. If Gurnsey feels that it has, since Victor Hugo's famous fifteen years of exile there, been rather left out in the literary cold, it need worry no more. It now has a portrait and memorial that must surely become a classic of the island.

But what Edwards does, as readers will soon realize, is to extend the empire of the book well beyond the confines of one particular island. All small islands conform their inhabitants in markedly similar ways, both socially and psychologically. On the credit side there is the fierce independence, the toughness of spirit, the patience and courage, the ability to cope and make do; on the debit, the dourness, the incest, the backwardness, the suspicion of non-islanders . . . all that we mean by insularity. None of these qualities and defects is special to islands. One might argue that the 'island syndrome' occurs with increasing frequency in many of our embattled inner cities, and very much in the context of what finally becomes the major theme of this book—that is, the impact of new values on old ones, of ineluctable social evolution on individual man.

Edwards' own view is made very clear through his fictional *alter ego*. For him the new values—in local terms, all that has turned Guernsey into tourist resort and international tax haven—are anathema. They have destroyed nearly everything on the island—and by implication everywhere else—that he cherished and celebrates so well and elegiacally, beneath the plain language, in the first half of the novel. Whether Edwards was right or wrong to see more ashes than hope in progress is not, I think, what matters. What does is to have such a richly human account of what it felt like to live through the period of the book, from about 1890 to 1970.

We are still too close to it to realize what an astounding and unprecedented change, unprecedented both in its extent and its speed, has taken place in the psyche of Western mankind during those eighty years. (pp. vii-viii)

It is almost as if in those same eighty years we left the old planet and found a new; and we are all, however brashly contemporary, however much we take modern technology for granted, still victims of that profound cultural shock. One symptom of it is the recurrent recrudescence of conservatism (and in far more than politics) in the second half of this century. We have at least realized we made a very clumsy landing on our new planet, and also left a number of things behind on the old that we might have done better to bring with us—qualities very close to that list of traditional island virtues I mentioned just now.

This inability to forget the old, this querulousness over the new, is what makes Ebenezer Le Page such a convincing portrayal of a much more universal mentality than the matter of the book might at first sight suggest. Edwards himself recognized this when he wrote that Ebenezer 'expresses from the inside out the effects of world events'. His novel is really far more about the impress of recent human history on one fallible but always honest individual than about Guernsey and its traditional manners and mores, fascinating and amusing though those often are to read.

The ubiquitous contempt for England and the English (and outsiders in general, even the sister Channel Island of Jersey) must similarly be taken in a metaphorical way. The encroachment is of infinitely more than ugly holiday bungalows and tourist dross, of greedy entrepreneurs and tax-evaders; it is essentially upon the individual mind, and therefore upon individual freedom. To those who want a homogenized world (because such worlds are easier to manipulate) Ebenezer is an eternal thorn in the side. He may seem an exceedingly unfashionable reactionary about a number of things, including woman. But his saving grace is that he is equally reactionary about anything that tries to occupy, as the Nazis did Guernsey in the last war, the island of the self. He is much more against than he is ever for, and that kind of againstness, or bloody-mindedness, however irritating it may be in some circumstances, is a very precious human (and evolutionary) commodity. Provincialism is not merely lacking city taste in arts and manners; it is also an increasingly vital antidote to all would-be central tyrannies. To give such a convincing illustration of this ubiquitous contradiction, this eternal suspicion at the less articulate base of society, is one of Edwards' major achievements.

Another seems to me a technical one, and that is the creation of such an intensely colloquial speech, with its piquant French undertones, for his hero. Even more remarkable is his almost total reliance on it—how he manages, despite the general absence of normal linear narrative, despite the way characters meander almost haphazardly in and out of his pages, despite the minute stitch of social detail, to carry us through with him, at times to the point where we no longer care how inconsequential or digressive the story becomes, as long as that voice is still speaking. I can think of very few novels where this extremely difficult device, of the prolonged reminiscence, is worked so well. (pp. viii-ix)

[Edwards defined his book's] purpose as 'humanizing'; and to that end, he realized that it had to risk things that no trend-conscious novelist today would care to risk his reputation on, just as in some ways it had to stay resolutely old-fashioned and simple-tongued. But that is precisely what I like most about it. It seems to me, beyond all its more obvious achievements and attractions, beyond its occasional lapses into cantankerousness and sentimentality, an act of courage; and of a kind that can never be old-fashioned if the novel, and the free society of which it is still the deepest artistic expression, are to survive. (p. xi)

> *John Fowles, "Introduction" (copyright © 1981 by J. R. Fowles Ltd.; reprinted by permission of Alfred A. Knopf, Inc.; in Canada by Hamish Hamilton Ltd), in* The Book of Ebenezer Le Page *by G. B. Edwards, Knopf, 1981, pp. vii-xiv.*

GUERNSEY LE PELLEY

A reader need not know of the Channel Islands to enjoy this remarkable book ["**The Book of Ebenezer Le Page**"]. . . . But only a true Guernseyman can feel all its reverberations, and here am I, two generations removed, attempting to share some of them. . . .

Edwards's only book [is] unquestionably unique.

It is a story to be savored carefully, gently, its pervasive wisdom absorbed like the warmth of a jeweled island in the sun. The narrative has no conventional plot or structure. People and names flow in and out like the tides, as they are remembered.

The three copybooks in which Edwards painstakingly crafted the life story of Le Page and from which the novel is made were rendered in the island's quaint, colloquial English, which makes the sorrows and joys of his story cut deeper.

"**The Book of Ebenezer Le Page**" can be read as a many-layered love story. It records the passionate attachment of islanders to their island: the regard a community can have for one another beyond petty hatreds; Ebenezer's poignant, bittersweet enduring love for Liza, a woman he never possessed; and an instinctive longing to understand the underlying truth about the relationship of man to God, which Ebenezer and a few others try to see in the untidy world around them.

What makes the story shine is the treasure of arcane wisdom it contains, spoken offhandedly, or not spoken at all but only implied in the remarks of these quarry workers, seamen, and farmers.

As you read, you understand why island wisdom seems so ageless. Unlike mainlanders, who could leave unfriendly neighbors behind in a flight to a new town, the island people had nowhere to go. Through generations of closeness they had to fashion a suitably tolerant understanding of each other or perish. . . .

The book does not dwell on tragedy or bitterness. It is laced with humor. Readers will chuckle over what seems to be an important island pastime—deciding to whom to leave one's money. In his later years Ebenezer becomes a skillful player at this game. His comic antics in arranging secret tests to determine the worthiness of a potential heir are exceeded only by his startling choice in the end of the most unlikely person of all.

Forming the backdrop for Ebenezer's personal saga is the island itself, becoming less isolated, more open to foreigners over the decades. The starkest drama occurs in the 1940s. The years of German occupation are difficult on Guernsey, but for Ebenezer they offer an opportunity to analyze the sharp emotional divisions that determine right and wrong in wartime. Later, he comes to feel that the occupation, heinous though it was, did less lasting damage to the island than the onslaught of unfriendly Englishmen after the war, swarming to Guernsey in search of an easy, tax-free life.

Through it all, the outreaching, crusty humanity of Ebenezer Le Page makes me love Guernsey even more than my grandfather must have. Though if I were to return I would be one of the dread foreigners; Ebenezer wouldn't like my coming back.

> *Guernsey Le Pelly, "Folksy Wisdom Shines in One-of-a-Kind Novel," in* The Christian Science Monitor *(reprinted by permission from* The Christian Science Monitor; *© 1981 The Christian Science Publishing Society; all rights reserved), March 25, 1981, p. 17.*

ERIC KORN

[*The Book of Ebenezer Le Page* is] the work of a self-exile, magnetically drawn to and held from his homeland, like Joyce Dublin, like a large molecule against a membrane.

Ebenezer's book is the roughly chronological, only incidentally historical or autobiographical recollections of an octogenarian bachelor curmudgeon. . . .

Edwards's great success is in the forging of a character and a diction idiosyncratic in the extreme, but flexible enough for a variety of effects, and so easy on the ear that we don't mind too much what he is saying, or how he goes on (though we do a bit). Ebenezer's speech is a tidied version of Guernsey English, with a few words—too few really—of the Norman-French patois whose use, like that of much that is small and homely and good, has diminished during the period of the book. . . .

There is lots of local colour, but the Chapel and the picturesque drunks and the clogs and the praise of local cuisine . . . should not make us see the novel as the kind of *Sea-Green was my Valley;* though admittedly Edwards's tone resembles Richard Llewellyn's with a gruff intertidal rumble instead of the ingratiating South-Walian lilt. Certainly he memorializes a time past and a place vanished; but he has metropolitan virtues and anxieties. . . .

There are enough quarrels over inheritance and marriage contracts to remind us that Normandy is on the horizon. There is only one happy marriage, which happens to Ebenezer's sister La Tabby; and her husband, like Ebenezer's pal Jim, is killed in the First World War. (Edwards tends to fall into a heavy-breathing Housmanesque about the lads that will never grow old.)

But the impact of the Second War is more fatal to the Islands. During the German occupation there is opportunism, there is collaboration, there is courageous resistance: at the end of the war there was real starvation and those with less than the unkillable ornery greatness of spirit of Ebenezer were as dehumanized as the Ik.

After the war Ebenezer's account becomes dominated by a querulous distaste for change. But the old man learns tolerance of various kinds. . . . The book ends in a sort of sceptical rosy glow as Ebenezer, looking for a suitable heir, finds one in a young painter as cranky and place-proud as himself. If Edwards had gone on to write the two further volumes he planned, the whole trilogy might have tipped over into whimsy and monotony; but this single pillar stands as a fine monument to a particular place, and a particular, solitary and sure-footed skill.

> Eric Korn, ''Getting Down Guernsey,'' *in* The Times Literary Supplement *(© Times Newspapers Ltd. (London) 1981; reproduced from* The Times Literary Supplement *by permission), No. 4069, March 27, 1981, p. 334.*

PHOEBE-LOU ADAMS

The general shape of [*The Book of Ebenezer Le Page*] is plain enough. Le Page, a cantankerous old bachelor who has lived all his life on Guernsey, writes his autobiography, which is full of local details, trivia, anecdotes, Guernsey jokes (incomprehensible to an off-islander), family squabbles, characters who drift in and out to no purpose, and episodes that accomplish nothing. Against all reason these matters become intensely interesting, partly because Edwards had the true storyteller's power to command interest, and partly because the reader soon discovers that what looks like a minor character in a haphazard event can prove, some years and pages later, to be of major importance. In a place as small as Guernsey, where everyone knows everyone else's business and scandals linger for generations, the slightest gestures can be significant and are therefore carefully observed. The reader becomes a Guernsey native, constantly and warily on the lookout. All the rambling minutiae of daily life has, in the end, an application that reaches far beyond the island. Edwards is balancing the value of man's personal independence against the cost of maintaining it despite the inroads of twentieth-century society and female intransigence. (pp. 124, 126)

> Phoebe-Lou Adams, ''Short Reviews: 'The Book of Ebenezer Le Page','' *in* The Atlantic Monthly *(copyright © 1981, by The Atlantic Monthly Company, Boston, Mass.; reprinted with permission), Vol. 247, No. 4, April, 1981, pp. 124, 126.*

GUY DAVENPORT

The passage of time always involves a metamorphosis, and any richly detailed account of a life that spans our paradoxical century of continual advances in technology and savage regressions into violence must, as Edwards so subtly does [in ''The Book of Ebenezer Le Page''], draw a tragic distortion of the human spirit. (p. 1)

A classic bachelor, Ebenezer becomes (without realising it) the classic ironic observer of his constrained, ingrown little society; that is, he becomes a novelist. As if by instinct he buys in old age a blank book and records his life.

The parallel with Proust is suggestive. This is a Proustian work in two senses. It conceals its major theme in a river of sharply observed, seemingly trivial events, and leaves it to us to chart the course of the river and realize its shape, its gesture, on a map of which Ebenezer is necessarily unaware. Like Proust, Edwards can make us feel the passage of time as a tragic force. Like Proust, he has a surprise for us that can only be convincingly revealed in the fullness of time. For this is a novel you must read every word of, or miss the deeply human meaning altogether.

Ebenezer's insignificant, homebody life moves toward a bitter, disappointed old age: such is the red herring carefully laid down for us. He has had one miraculous night of love in all his life, curled beside his friend Jim when they were teen-agers stranded on a peninsula by high tide. This event returns in one unrecognizable ghostly form after another, skillfully disguised by Edwards, until, like time itself, it has undergone metamorphosis enough to emerge as a great happiness, at last understood, at last integrated into a sensibility that has failed to recognize it time and again.

I know of no description of happiness in modern literature equal to the one that ends this novel. The preparation for it has been so cleverly plotted and yet is so psychologically accurate that we wonder if the novel itself is not here returning to its old tricks. . . .

Edwards's understanding of the heart comes, most certainly, from a lifetime of observation, but it is helpful to imagine that he is working out a disarmingly simple remark of Proust's: That a homosexual is a man who wants to be a soldier's best friend. Ebenezer Le Page lives his life wanting to be the best friend of someone like his Jim, whose spirit was killed by a mean and jealous wife before a German bayonet dispatched him for real.

When Ebenezer becomes someone's best friend again, he is old and without illusions, but the friendship happens, and is golden; and we realize that the fable we have been told is a fable of the rarity of selfless love in a world that has degraded everything. . . .

Ebenezer Le Page writes his life in an easy, gossipy, supple English that grows on you as you get the hang of it. . . . Ebenezer does beautifully what most writers would do well to avoid: He writes spoken English, keeping its agility of preposition and adverb, its purity of idiom, its fussy particularity as to what's what.

Technically two writers are at work in first-person narrative. . . .

Ebenezer and Edwards work together without stepping on each other's toes; Ebenezer never gives a thought to the shape of his outpoured memories. Edwards never obtrudes his literary concerns into Ebenezer's restless sorting out of the past.

This is the first novel of a projected trilogy, which will now never exist, but which might have been completed if even one publisher had been perceptive enough to recognize what a masterpiece he was rejecting. (p. 22)

Guy Davenport, "A Novel of Life in a Small World," in The New York Times Book Review *(© 1981 by The New York Times Company; reprinted by permission), April 19, 1981, pp. 1, 22.*

DAVID KUBAL

Despite the bleakness of his theme—or perhaps because of it—G. B. Edwards ends his extraordinary novel [*The Book of Ebenezer Le Page*] so happily that the reader, long accustomed to conclusions of bereavement, paucity, and unforgiving despair, might find himself resisting a gift providing so much pleasure. That one can be suspicious of such generosity may indicate just how far the novel has departed from its origins as the genre of forgiveness and reconciliation. And it may even explain why Mr. Edwards could not find a publisher before his death in 1976 for this his only novel. Like John Kennedy Toole's *The Confederacy of Dunces*, which was also published posthumously after a number of rejections with an introduction by an eminent writer—in his case, Walker Percy—*The Book of Ebenezer Le Page* is presented by John Fowles, a novelist who has expressed his disenchantment with the easy pessimism of contemporary fiction.

Ebenezer Le Page's story is, nonetheless, a melancholy one, telling of the gradual and inevitable absorption of the Isle of Guernsey into the monolithic culture of the twentieth century. (p. 456)

Within the novel, the emotion is fully earned, fought for and gained during a life of anger, deprivation, and austere loneliness. Most painful for Ebenezer is the loss of the male, the severing of that fundamental bond, beginning with the death of his father in the Boer War and continuing with the slaughter of his friends during the two World Wars. But the female and marriage are also his enemies, jealous as they are, in Ebenezer's view, of the independent male self. If these archaic ideas are at odds with contemporary notions of a mature selfhood, they remind us of the great wounds inflicted upon men by the continuous wars of our time and the costs exacted by the therapeutic society. Besides, they are significantly qualified, if not negated, by the love and erotic joy of Ebenezer's legatees. The book remains, then, an anachronism in which the reader can discover all the old rewards of the novel: the voice of an identifiable narrator; affectionate descriptions of nature; the drama of a society told through its manners and domestic rituals; and the celebration of the powers of love and will. (p. 457)

David Kubal, "Fiction Chronicle," in The Hudson Review *(copyright © 1981 by The Hudson Review, Inc.; reprinted by permission), Vol. XXXIV, No. 3, Autumn, 1981, pp. 456-66.**

GEOFFREY GRIGSON

The literal subject [of *The Book of Ebenezer Le Page*] is the passage through life and time—our modern degenerate time—and among neighbors, of [a] rather simple, slightly educated quarryman's son, this Ebenezer, this mouth of patois and old ways. But then what is the subject, when it does not work? Or when it works, or proceeds rather, only through an inadequacy of dull words? Anecdote follows anecdote. Parents, friends, relations, neighbor occur, and occur again, turned round about in new circumstances. Ebenezer is learning. . . . Ebenezer is going to school, Ebenezer goes fishing, Ebenezer is going to the fair, Ebenezer is going after girls (and men eventually), Ebenezer is going round on his bike. Empty clothes instead of people surround Ebenezer who is an emptiness, or a ragbag of the not very consequential.

Subject not being substance, what is encountered, I would judge, is no more than an emptiness all round, which soon becomes the rule of this book. There is war. Ebenezer recalls, Ebenezer quotes. . . .

Particularity of place occurs . . . and Ebenezer acquaints us—in how dull a way—with ormers, garfish, spider crabs, lady crabs, congers; and with interminable particularity of language—how flatly, how much with a turning on and off of a speech faucet, in patois, and in tricks—no doubt Sarnian tricks—of syntax and grammar and the like. . . .

Where the writing should convey its meaning, its message ought in fact to be the substance; and here for substance a curious fumble, a curious uncertainty and intermittency are substituted. Under the patter and the patois, or alongside them, in continuation, the run becomes that of the most uncompelling, the most impersonal or weakly personal ordinariness, as in any other bad novel of less pretension or in any trite extent of journalism. All the time, in the four hundred or so pages, it is this amateurism which shows up, or shows through, clearly. (p. 43)

[According to John Fowles (see excerpt above)] *The Book of Ebenezer Le Page* "must surely become a classic" of his island, making up for Guernsey's literary neglect since Victor Hugo's exile there in Hauteville House. . . . I [do not] believe that this tiresome novel is "undoubtedly a classic of its kind" as well as a classic of Guernsey.

But then what is "its kind"? John Fowles declares, accurately, that "its voice and method are so unusual that it belongs nowhere on our conventional literary maps." Also, unlike the jacketeer, I don't find this novel "reminiscent in its fullness, its nobility of character, its grand simplicity, of the pastoral sagas of Thomas Hardy, and of his literary descendant, John Fowles himself." That is fudge. And I read further that in one newspaper the writer of *The Book of Ebenezer Le Page* has been compared to Proust [see excerpt above by Guy Davenport]; which is also fudge again, and stickier fudge. I wait now to see who after all will now be fooled, in the publishing community, and then in the reviewing community, of the country of G. B. Edwards. (pp. 43-4)

Geoffrey Grigson, "In the Crab Pots," in The New York Review of Books *(reprinted with permission from* The New York Review of Books; *copyright © 1981 Nyrev, Inc.), Vol. XXVIII, No. 17, November 5, 1981, pp. 43-4.*

Paul E(mil) Erdman

1932-

American novelist.

A former economist and banker, Erdman uses his knowledge of international finance to provide his readers with realistic detail. While most commentators admit that his novels are fascinating and hold some relevance for the contemporary layperson, they fault Erdman for stereotyped characterization and far-fetched plots.

Beginning with his first novel, *The Billion Dollar Sure Thing*, Erdman moved to the forefront of the relatively new genre of fi-fi, or finance fiction. Skillful at selecting the commodities which inspire greed and corruption on a global scale, Erdman centered this first thriller around the collapse of the gold market. The plots of his next two books, *The Silver Bears* and *The Crash of '79*, concern the manipulation of silver prices and the oil crisis, respectively. In his recent novel, *The Last Days of America*, Erdman gives readers a glimpse of sinister dealings within computerized corporate America and creates an apocalyptic scenario for the rise of Germany.

(See also *Contemporary Authors*, Vols. 61-64).

© Jerry Bauer

ALFRED L. MALABRE, JR.

One of the troubles with most novels that attempt to treat financial topics is that the people who write them are normally novelists only, rather than novelists-and-financiers, and consequently often don't have much inside understanding of the characters and situations that inevitably arise. This is an unfortunate fact, inasmuch as the world of high—and low—finance should provide fascinating grist for a novel. All too rarely, it does.

This paucity, we are happy to report, has been at least temporarily remedied, for we have a new novel titled **"The Billion Dollar Sure Thing"** from Paul E. Erdman, a man who, however briefly, was in fact a financial insider as well, later, as an insider at a Swiss prison after the Swiss-based bank that he headed failed amid charges of illegal activities at the bank. . . .

Not only does he know banking, particularly the highly secretive Swiss variety, but Mr. Erdman also knows reasonably well how to write in a suspenseful, readable fashion. No work of art, certainly, **"The Billion Dollar Sure Thing"** is nonetheless an absorbing bit of fancy that imagines a situation (is it really that fanciful?) where the President of the U.S. secretly decides to increase the official price of gold to $125 per ounce, roughly triple today's actual official level.

The secret, of course, gets into the wrong hands—a gnomish Swiss banker, a mischievous Russian, a Mafia-linked wheeler-dealer from the U.S. As the date set for the announcement draws nearer, the diverse cast engages in a fascinating variety of financial maneuvers all aimed at cashing in on the massive gold-price boost. . . . Sex, skullduggery and murder come into play. London, Paris, Beirut, Moscow and Washington are among the cities where the action takes place.

But it is in the detailed descriptions of big bankers, their habits and the ways in which they run their banks that Mr. Erdman's novel, his first, rises above many similar fictional efforts involving the world of finance. . . .

The book is liberally sprinkled with . . . delightful glimpses into the world of supermoney. They are not the sort of anecdotes that "outsiders" are very likely to come up with.

As to the plot, it would be unfair to the author and to potential readers to say more than that the suspense builds nicely to a climax that is as swift as it is surprising.

Alfred L. Malabre, Jr., "A Rare Thriller about Banking," in The Wall Street Journal *(reprinted by permission of* The Wall Street Journal, © *Dow Jones & Company, Inc. 1973; all rights reserved), July 11, 1973, p. 12.*

NEWGATE CALLENDAR

"The Billion Dollar Sure Thing" is an exciting novel despite itself. It is not particularly well written. It is loosely organized, and it stops here and there for long-winded explanations of the methods of the gnomes of Zurich and their cousins in Basel. But the concept of the book is tremendous—a Russian raid on the dollar, the manipulations of a sharp American operator all set to make a killing, the theft of a top secret document concerning plans for devaluation and a shift in the price of gold. All that, and a surprise at the end. Or to those who know something about the big-money boys, perhaps not so much of a surprise. Can these things really be? Erdman makes it plentifully clear they can.

Newgate Callendar, "Criminals at Large," in The New York Times Book Review (© 1973 by The New York Times Company; reprinted by permission), August 5, 1973, p. 10.*

R. Z. SHEPPARD

Although [Paul Erdman] is not the James Joyce of high finance, he is not Jacqueline Susann either. His plots and characters tend to be simple, but he combines a zest for the intricate poetry of the big deal with the ability and cheerful willingness to explain it. His first novel, the bestselling *The Billion Dollar Sure Thing,* straightened out the mysterious alchemy of the international gold market. . . .

The Silver Bears deals in a baser metal, but it is just as entertaining and instructive as the first novel. Although names and places have been somewhat altered, the plot is built on the manic-depressive 1968 fluctuations in the price of silver. . . .

Although Erdman does not neglect characterization and the mechanics of storytelling, he is more intent on delivering cold truths. Mainly, that whatever speculators were hearing about the future of silver in 1969, it was largely piped misinformation from a handful of super-sophisticated con men. In his novel, the lords of both the underworld and overworld put aside hurt pride to concentrate on profit by colluding to rig the market. All those dentists, airline pilots and what Erdman gleefully calls "greedy widows" who invested in silver futures never stood a chance. The odds of beating the professionals were about the same as a man in a wheelchair getting a football through the Miami Dolphins' defense.

R. Z. Sheppard, "The Stung," in Time (copyright 1974 Time Inc.; all rights reserved; reprinted by permission from Time), Vol. 104, No. 5, July 29, 1974, p. 65.

NEWGATE CALLENDAR

In Erdman's world, everybody is a wolf. There are big wolves and little wolves, all motivated by one thing only: the pursuit of money—big, big money, of course. Where **"The Silver Bears"** differs from **"The Billion Dollar Sure Thing"** is in its more relaxed manner. . . . Erdman can be quite funny, in a self-deprecating manner, about the money urge, and **"The Silver Bears"** has a few hilarious episodes about financial manipulation and the slavering greed of top financiers.

His relative inexperience as a novelist leads Erdman into one or two dull patches where, not knowing exactly how to weave explanations about high-level financial skullduggery into the action, he pauses to let a character run on like a lecturer at an investment seminar. This does not happen very often, however; and Erdman, who does have a ingenious mind, fulfills his duty as a novelist by keeping interest sustained and by giving the ending a double twist that satisfies the novelistic proprieties as well as the inner man.

Newgate Callendar, "Criminals at Large," in The New York Times Book Review (© 1974 by The New

York Times Company; reprinted by permission), August 18, 1974, p. 23.*

ERIC PACE

This slam-bang novel of international finance and scheming ["**The Crash of '79**"] is largely about greed.

And why not? The author, Paul E. Erdman, is a former international financier and therefore knows the subject intimately. Most of the rest of us may lack his expertise, but we enjoy reading about covetousness—at least the successful practice of covetousness—the way we like reading about more graphic sins. And Erdman eases any guilt we might feel at this pleasure by providing a finale that shows how greed leads to truly dreadful things.

Erdman piles on a lot of factual-seeming detail about international banking, Mideast potentates and so forth. This technique creates some odd technical problems as the book canters along, through world crises and nuclear war scares. Erdman is highly skilled at creating fictive worlds of intrigue and high finance for the lay reader, as he proved with his first two best sellers. . . . But in **"The Crash of '79"** this process of creation involves describing what seems like an awful lot of executive meetings. The reader—this reader anyhow—begins to feel saddle-sore from sitting in on so many meetings—even rousing dramatic ones.

Which brings us to other points. One of the difficulties involved in lacing a novel with current factual material is that the material can get out of date fast. (p. 6)

Instances of [outdated information] suggest that Erdman belongs to the school of thought that holds that what matters in writing commercial action-adventure novels is not factual accuracy but only the semblance of accuracy. . . .

Nonetheless I have no doubt that this Erdman novel, like its two predecessors, will be read with gusto by the Western wheelers and dealers I see hanging out in the lobbies of fancy Persian Gulf hotels. It's a fine read for those who dig the genre. (p. 71)

Eric Pace, "About International Finance, a.k.a. Greed," in The New York Times Book Review (© 1976 by The New York Times Company; reprinted by permission), November 14, 1976, pp. 6, 71.

T. J. BINYON

Bill Hitchcock, [the narrator of *The Crash of '79* and the] sometime chief financial adviser to the Saudi Arabian government, relates the series of events leading up to the great crash of 1979, when the whole economy of the Western world collapses in ruins, a catastrophe brought about by a fatal combination of European weakness, American inefficiency, Iranian aggressiveness, Israeli self-delusion and Swiss greed. The scenario is dolefully convincing: its natural reader would be the confirmed pessimist who always turns first to the financial section of his daily paper. . . . Paul E. Erdman has impressive qualifications as an economist, and the financial detail is correspondingly dense and realistic. Indeed, the dollar, mark, pound, lira and their associates emerge as far more interesting and sympathetic characters than the human beings who, despite a love affair begun in Rome, continued in Teheran and ended in St. Moritz, against a background of luxurious hotels and villas, in which the best bourbon, scotch and champagne flow like the Saudi Arabian sterling reserves, have all the credibility and naturalness of a four-star soap opera.

T. J. Binyon, "Criminal Proceedings," in The Times Literary Supplement (© Times Newspapers Ltd. (London) 1977; reproduced from The Times Literary Supplement by permission), No. 3920, March 29, 1977, p. 536.*

CHARLES WHEELER

In [*The Last Days of America*], Paul Erdman returns to the theme of an earlier book. *The Crash of '79:* the decline of America's will to lead the West and the opportunities this presents to its more irresponsible allies to take the world to the brink of disaster. . . .

Mr Erdman's new book takes us into the later 1980s. . . .

West Germany, feeling uniquely vulnerable to Russian attack, has overcome its national guilt complex and is reverting to type. Willi Brandt and Helmut Schmidt have been discarded. The new saviour is the Bavarian conservative, Franz Joseph Strauss, who, in a comeback as unexpected as Richard Nixon's resurgence in 1968, has been swept into the Chancellorship on a promise to give Germany its own independent nuclear deterrent.

Mr Erdman is a master of timing. His book appears here just as German conservatives have scored their first electoral victory in West Berlin, as Britain considers reducing its forces in Germany, and as Herr Schmidt, following an abortive summit meeting with Mr Reagan in Washington, struggles to head off a revolt among his fellow Social Democrats against the stationing of medium-range nuclear missiles in Europe. . . .

West Germany is about to take its rightful place in the world as a superpower. It is a prospect Mr Erdman finds as distasteful as the personality of the unfortunate Herr Strauss, whom he depicts as an uncouth, malevolent demagogue who only escapes identification with Hitler by virtue of the fact that he is not on record as having advocated the slaughter of Jews.

What Erdman's Strauss does have in common with the Nazi leaders is a belief in Germany's unfulfilled destiny, the cultural and intellectual superiority of its people, and their historic duty to avenge past humiliations. Aided by a consortium of *Wirtschaftswunderkinder* . . . the Strauss regime acquires the capacity to destroy the Soviet Union in a single nuclear strike . . . and with that Mr Erdman's drama slithers to an intriguing if improbable close.

What the real Herr Strauss might make of all this can only be guessed at. . . . Less engaged readers, though, should find Mr Erdman's predictions diverting; he writes with verve and has an admirably sour view of the men who control our destiny.

Charles Wheeler, "Future Shock," in The Times Literary Supplement (© Times Newpapers Ltd. (London) 1981; reproduced from The Times Literary Supplement by permission), No. 4080, June 12, 1981, p. 672.

MICHAEL M. THOMAS

In 1976, *The Crash of '79* established Paul Erdman as a "brand name" author. He quickly became the leading practitioner of "fi-fi" (financial fiction), a genre that has proliferated like money-market funds as big bucks have come to be an important subject for writers, if not a subject for important writers. The novel's apocalyptic title and awesome topicality overshadowed certain deficiencies that appear to have become incidental to the manufacture of best-selling novels: characterization, language, atmosphere, style. The book was a great popular success; parts of the business community hailed it as a fifth gospel.

The title of Erdman's new novel, *The Last Days of America,* also incorporates an inviting frisson of disaster. In this case, the apocalypse involves the surrender of American hegemony to a rearmed German Reich. . . .

Among the moral and factual matters discoursed on by the garrulous protagonist are marital fidelity, the nature of patriotism, the laws of extradition, and the awarding of degrees at the University of Basel. There is also a great deal of simplistic history. Real personages mingle with fictional ones. . . . Languages spoken include several dialects of Swiss-German, Alsatian, French, and German. Places mentioned include backroads Alsace, Knokke-le-Zoute, the Basel-Mulhouse airport (twice), the Black Forest, Stockholm, and the Bohemian Grove (twice). Fiction-guzzlers titillated by the above goings-on and wealth of detail should stop here and rush out to buy the novel.

Last Days asks to be judged as a thinking man's thriller, a Greenean "entertainment." Here, it fails miserably, lacking sufficient force and verisimilitude to engage the reader's belief. Nor does the novel give rise to reflection about the world of political and financial power it seeks to evoke. (p. 46)

While there may be a certain amount of high-level, sinister hanky-panky at the topmost intersections of government and industry in the political and financial capitals of the Free World, the wholesale abdication of mandates implicit in this novel strikes me as far-fetched. To get from A to Z, Erdman presumes an unvigilant, spineless press, a public sector that can be "fixed" from toe to top in a half-dozen nations, and a series of financial gymnastics that are not remotely connected with reality. The thriller of power and place, to which genre this belongs, must be launched from a solid pad of plausibility. In this case, the groundwork is absent. The hopeful reader is left with half-resolved, half-dissolved plot lines, cardboard characters, ersatz technological gabble, and half-baked historical excursuses. There is much of the board game in this book. Plot is reduced to the movement of cardboard figures from one square to another.

Fiction is not parcheesi, however. . . . Tight, credible plotting, which is to this kind of novel what the spinal column is to the human body, has degenerated into a confused mass of unsurely linked ganglia. In place of gripping, believable tales with interesting or glamorous characters whose personalities and motives are vivid and intriguing, we are now served up facts or gossip. Imagination sits in the corner in a dunce cap; its place has been taken by scabrous innuendo retailed by "experts," frequently known liars with an ax to grind, or by information trumpeted as the product of "research."

So, instead of a sense of place, we are given place-names. Characters are not created; names are dropped. Pages are filled with a kind of gossipy, consumerist shorthand. Erdman's book reads like a rough first draft. It looks very much as though he put down whatever came into his head with the view that he, and his editor, presumably, would subsequently knit the plot, give the prose richness, pace, and style, and banish the more unendurable solecisms. That hasn't happened here. The adjectives that come to mind after two close readings of the novel are sloppy, careless, shoddy, awkward.

The narrator seeks to drag the reader into his unmade intellectual bed by presuming a mutual, rib-digging self-satisfaction signaled, as if by neon, with the phrases "of course," or "naturally." The Bohemian Club is "of course" San Francisco's number-two club; in Stockholm one stays, "naturally," at the Grand Hotel; and—my personal favorite—the best asparagus grow, "of course," in "the Calvados region in the South of France." Who cares if the Calvados region is in fact in Normandy, and the best asparagus grow in the Touraine?

This is counterproductive, unattractive pseudo-elitism. Ian Fleming accoutered James Bond with fancy trappings: Morlands cigarettes, Beefeater martinis. But Fleming was a natual aristocrat. In Fleming, Bond's trimmings and trappings seem strangely admirable, as grace to the manor-born always is. Erdman's hero wears his snobbism like someone else's suit.

This book left me with a nasty taste. (pp. 46-7)

> *Michael M. Thomas, "Brand-Name Writing," in Saturday Review (© 1981 Saturday Review Magazine Co.; reprinted by permission), Vol. 8, No. 8, August, 1981, pp. 46-7.*

ROBERT LEKACHMAN

In **"The Last Days of America"** Paul Erdman's exposition is sloppy, careless and ungrammatical. No human voice could conceivably speak his dialogue. It could be composed only by someone immune to the rhythms of ordinary utterance. The hero is in the missile business. He indulges himself in large scale commercial bribery, engages in an episode of breaking and entering, kills a couple of people in passing, and, least forgivable of all, bores anyone who unwisely keeps track of his misadventures to the edge of coma.

> *Robert Lekachman, "Foreign Settings and Domestic Scenes," in The New York Times Book Review (© 1981 by The New York Times Company; reprinted by permission), August 30, 1981, p. 10.*

Roy Fisher

1930-

English poet.

Fisher's poetry is often set in urban landscapes, usually his native Birmingham. His most recognized work, *City,* has been compared with William Carlos Williams's *Patterson* and he has acknowledged his interest in Williams's concept, "no ideas but in things." Fisher's poetic strategy is to present a detached description of phenomenal reality as he perceives it. His observations and insights are rendered in concrete details which transfigure the ordinary. He creates, in the words of critic Deborah Mitchell, "a grammar of sensory experience."

Fisher is also a jazz pianist and his poetry reflects the improvisation, loose structure, and varying tempos associated with jazz. He claims that his poetry is more influenced by music than by literature.

(See also *Contemporary Authors,* Vols. 81-84.)

Photograph by Joanna Voit

THE TIMES LITERARY SUPPLEMENT

Fisher is in many ways traditional, and like most good poets uses tradition for his own ends. He's deeply of the city, an imagist with a vein of childhood reminiscence. *The Ship's Orchestra* was an intermittently fascinating and boring book, a sort of avant-garde *Pinfold* or *Party Going*, gaining from the richness of its fantasies and losing with their pointlessness. Most of the poems in [*Collected Poems 1968*] predate *The Ship's Orchestra* and do not share its extremism. The longest section, called "City", alternates poetry and prose, and celebrates the self-help and cooperation of those Midlands conurbations that Fisher has always lived in. He usually looks for mystery in these house and street scenes but he neither solicits it nor fakes it. . . . While the minutiae of life are justly observed, the total effect is turned aside into mild surrealism—the wind is thought to come only from the next street, gun barrels rolled in lint are under the floorboards, a foetus in the dustbin moves a claw. This is Birmingham as Magritte might have seen it. Fisher's chief fault is a refusal to permit himself the vulgarity of a plain line of development. He insists on the tenuous greyness of reality and will only colour it with fantasy. His poems are all seeing, but he sees with originality and style.

> *"Midland Fantasy," in* The Times Literary Supplement *(© Times Newspapers Ltd. (London) 1969; reproduced from* The Times Literary Supplement *by permission), No. 3517, July 24, 1969, p. 828.**

ALAN BROWNJOHN

Recognition of Roy Fisher's verse . . . is long overdue. In his *Collected Poems* he has a poem called **'The Intruder'** in which the image of a young girl walks in from nowhere onto some idle, arbitrary thought about colours. If the idea is nearly in the Whimsical vein, Fisher has the intelligence to see that no thought is utterly inconsequential, and to perceive that his talent is for catching those moments of consciousness when odd, luminous slants on reality provide insight or understanding. He works this personal seam (though it's one which derives from

William Carlos Williams, even Wallace Stevens a little) very beautifully in poems like **'City'**—surely one of the most consistently interesting experimental poems to come out of the little magazine activity of the last decade? The danger for Fisher is of a kind of detached aestheticism ('working to distinguish an event from an opinion'); but at its best, his precise evocation of the sheer delicate oddness of ordinary things (see **'The Park'** and **'For Realism'**) can be as almost haunting as those ravaged industrial landscapes of the early Auden. (p. 701)

> *Alan Brownjohn, "Subways," in* New Statesman *(© 1969 The Statesman & Nation Publishing Co. Ltd.), Vol. 78, No. 2018, November 4, 1969, pp. 700-01.**

ERIC MOTTRAM

['**City**' from *Collected Poems* can] be said to be a set of ways in which a responsive sensuous man fights off aristocratism in a levelling and mediocre environment. . . . What is so warmly present is Fisher's sense of responsible living possible for the artist who *sees* and whose eyes hold excitement for him, as he uses the technological and human environment, and, as McLuhan would say, makes it visible. (p. 13)

The penetrating mood of '**City**' is not . . . nostalgia but of exploring for relevance to the business of living, working, loving, family. . . .

The Ship's Orchestra is an assemblage, erotic and musical (Fisher's experience with bands and combos penetrates the work). The prose sentences and paragraphs belong to that kind of writing which varies its pitch and tone and cannot simply be called 'poetic prose' or some other such academic slotting. It is certainly a fine instrument. . . . Like listening to jazz changes, reading *Ship's Orchestra* you have to be alert to variants. . . . *Ship's Orchestra* is among other things a description of a way of life: that when the sound stops, the music dies and with it a part of the ongoing life of the band as men and women. . . . (p. 14)

Like '**City**' the book is concerned with the dangers of finding meaning in an environment, of needing to have a larger inclusive meaning into which work and day-to-day living may be fitted. . . . (p. 15)

The space of the work is a music-less ship, with its maze of dark tubes and cul-de-sacs; the form of the work is the waking part of the sexual dream which merges with memories of childhood sexuality. The nightmare of endless and various pipes of connection, communication, organization, evacuation and intake becomes 'the system', a city in itself, out of Fisher's own necessity. Gradually the absence of music becomes the exploration of an absence of essential life—'breath music'. The artistes keep alive the frontiers of activity without actually playing; their instruments are an encumbering collection, fit for disposal, but at least this is not the land, at least the orchestra has a name and a position, at least they may be asked to play together. (p. 16)

The motif unity would be less absorbing if it were not for the startling sense of complete control in the language, the pacing of the cadences, and the timing of the passages coming on as one turns the pages. The interior emotions of '**City**' are exposed here too: the ship is the city as dream of an environment which submits the body to a scattering of the nerves at the mercy of impression and other people. The work's unity has a profound urgency, therefore: an act against the conversion of energy into forms which deplete life. The orchestra may never be asked to play.

The nine '**Interiors**' . . . included in *Collected Poems*, take the relationships of '**City**' and *The Ship's Orchestra* down to intense, disturbing relationships of a man and a woman, in pairs of poems. . . . Fisher returns to a constant theme: the possible insanity of allowing an hallucinatory vision of ordinary things and daily relationships to happen at all: the poet's sacrifice is uncertain of outcome. Compassion between man and woman is generated in the poems by the details of 'interior', which have . . . Robbe-Grillet's obsessive desire for accurate measurement of domestic objects. But here they are like life-savers. These are desperate poems, re-estimating married life, perhaps, and a rare subject for poetry. . . . Fisher has shed reminiscences of other poetry and a certain hovering between description and symbolism, and produced a long work unified with an economy of effect which still uses long-breathed cadences but has cleared up problems of 'modernistic' diction which lingered earlier. His forms and language are his own, with a meticulousness far from the slick magazine styles of contemporary British poetry. '**The Memorial Fountain**', Fisher's most recent work in *Collected Poems,* is not acceptable style for editors. The eye details the urban-suburban without liberalism, like the eye of a man who has just returned from abroad or from incarcerating illness, or prison, startled to find itself registering this object next to that one. . . . No one has recorded the pressures of work inside an impersonalizing society as

Fisher does in '**Seven Attempted Moves**'. . . . His poetry's forms are the orders of a poet who shapes himself with pleasure in what resistance is necessary and possible while being part of community he does not want to lose. He spends a lot of time 'organizing against disastrous breakdowns' in his working life. His opinions are radical, non-ideological and against the authoritarianism of B.B.C., religion, literary punditry. . . . (pp. 17-18)

Eric Mottram, "Roy Fisher's Work," in Stand *(copyright © by* Stand*), Vol. II, No. 1 (1969-70), pp. 9-18.*

RONALD HAYMAN

[Roy Fisher's] *Collected Poems* reveal a very interesting talent. In the pictures he draws of Birmingham, his strong sense of place works hand in hand with his affectionate awareness of people.

Denise Levertov has compared his "**The City**" with *Paterson,* which is flattering to Roy Fisher but not absurd. There is good writing both in the verse and in the prose passages which interlard it. By a careful descriptive focus on parts of the city, Roy Fisher creates an impression of it as a whole, rooting the human lives into the industrial landscape. His rhythms imply sympathy and criticism at the same time and he generates a genuine poetry by crowding unpoetic details together. Images jostle each other like slum buildings and the tone conveys a mixture of resignation and resentment. (p. 91)

Ronald Hayman, "The City and the House," in Encounter *(© 1970 by Encounter Ltd.), Vol. XXXIV, No. 2, February, 1970, pp. 84-91.**

DAVID ZAISS

Roy Fisher's poems are dark and turbulent. One section of [*Collected Poems 1968*], called simply *City,* is exemplary; in it, a poetic conscience corresponding to modernity sets out, in visionary terms, on a journey to its own painful beginnings. With the exception of one poem, *The Entertainment of War,* . . . the section reads like an attempt, on the part of humanity, to come to terms with inhumanity, with the built-in phthisis of the urban situation. However, Fisher's tone is too reserved, and the grand undertaking he may have only felt awaits some future seer. The *City* poems are more vital than visionary, in at least one sense. They speak to an awareness; their dark heat raises an ordinary moment in the mind, so that the images almost crunch. . . . (p. 51)

In general, Fisher seems a bit over-serious, but he avoids the exaggeration and egocentricity that mar most 'serious' poetry. A minimal dependence upon irony gives his voice an unusual plausibility and integrity, if these are virtues. Most of his best delivery sounds like good prose, and throughout this book his use of prose sections is not interruptive. The *City* piece stands out for me, but there are other solid poems in the collection, notably, *The Small Room, Toyland, Chirico* for its drive and defiance, and the long antiphon (as Fisher subtitles it) at the end, *At No Distance.* In this last poem, a conspicuous attempt is made to voluntarize the collisions between voices, and partly due to this, partly due to a coherent sense of timing and image, the poem comes off very well. (p. 52)

David Zaiss, "Perfect Circles," in Poetry *(© 1970 by The Modern Poetry Association; reprinted by per-*

mission of the Editor of Poetry), Vol. CXVI, No. 1, April, 1970, pp. 51-5.*

ALAN BROWNJOHN

[Roy Fisher's *Collected Poems*] made the best case I had seen for an English experimental poetry which drew something usable and interesting out of the work of the American *avant-garde;* his weirdly and delicately observed landscapes of urban desolation offered a slant on things which no one else was providing—at least not with the same wry wit and humanity. *Matrix* . . . was slightly disappointing; and his new volume, *The Thing About Joe Sullivan,* still finds him in rather uncertain form. The ''difficulty'' in these poems is that kind of opacity which results when every image is granted its own individual life and the poet feels inhibited from pulling them together into lumps of paraphrasable material. In **''107 Poems''** he has opted out, and thrown that number of images together into a lively but distinctly pointless heap of iambics. In **''In the Wall''**, which is a virtuoso poem in its own way, carefully and even elegantly crafted, a meaning is groping about somewhere, but it refuses to come clean. . . . But the thing about Roy Fisher is that his best poems blend highly unusual observations and insights with a subtle control which stops *very* far short of banal plotting or artifice. In [*The Thing About Joe Sullivan*], poems like **''At Once''**, **''On the Open Side''** and (in satirical vein) **''Artists, Providers, Places to Go''** show his bizarre and attractive imagination working to excellent effect. (p. 63)

Alan Brownjohn, ''Fascination of What's Difficult,'' in Encounter (© 1979 by Encounter Ltd.), Vol. LII, No. 3, March, 1979, pp. 61-5.*

DEBORAH MITCHELL

Readers of Fisher's *Collected Poems* might be forgiven for believing him to be a poet concerned with realism, albeit a realism used for his own ends. More recently, however, he has developed other aspects of his work and the industrial landscape whose presence was so overpowering in his earlier poems has now been assimilated. . . . [He has come] to believe that in the enumeration of 'realistic' detail there is as much exercise of subjective choice as in other kinds of artistic artifice. This is not of course an original idea; but it is one which he has arrived at in a peculiarly personal way.

The imagination which gave us such evocative detail in *City* was obsessed with the significance of physical reality. There was in *City,* as there still is in his more recent work, an intensity of perception and an insistence on the surface and detail of sensation which I initially connected with his defensiveness towards physical love—which he rejects for 'fear of being able to feel only vertically like a blind wall, or thickly, like the tyres of a bus'. The intensity would seem to be a direct result of sublimation. . . . Equally, we might see this intensity as a rationalization of the discomfort felt at living in an industrial landscape—a way of making this secondhand world interesting, and therefore bearable, to look at. He himself is not sure of his position *vis-à-vis* the physical, hence the ambivalence of such poems as **'Toyland'** or **'As He Came Near Death'**; he knows only that he wishes to perceive fully.

So he has set about formulating a grammar of sensory experience. The objections to lovers or environment, we find, are tangential to the real issues. It is the nature of human perception which denies us knowledge, however 'wary' we are to 'scent the manifold airs'. (pp. 125-26)

To be true to his perception he must show 'clarity and confusion' simultaneously. The structure and syntax of his poems has altered correspondingly; he has moved away from the poem which proposes a simple relation between phenomena and which progresses in a line towards a conclusion. . . . His method now is much more often to cover a 'field' than to make a progressive exposition. (p. 126)

Another correlative of his increasing interest in modes of perception is the change in his use of symbolic language. In his earlier work the symbolic value of the poem's images was brought about gradually as the poem progressed. **'The Poplars'** for instance opens with a factual description; the image of the poplars then develops when he refers to the trees as 'lacunae of possibility' and finally he makes them a point of contrast for his state of mind. . . . There is in this poem, as in another of his rightly praised early poems, **'The Hospital in Winter'**, a simple metaphorical relation between external phenomena and state of mind. Many of the poems in *The Thing About Joe Sullivan,* and also in *Matrix,* however, develop the techniques that he was using only in the prose passages of *City,* that is, of fluctuating between the various levels of meaning that lie between the factual and the symbolic. . . . Indeed the outward references of these and other poems are diffused almost to the point of abstraction; pronouns, for example, which would normally refer back to a previous subject do not or, if they do, represent an image or idea so undefined as to be almost unidentifiable. The syntactic manipulation—particularly repetition of syntactic patterns at points of transition—that he used in the prose of *City* he is also now using in his free verse with great virtuosity. . . . The deliberate confusion of the reader is . . . counteracted by the constant attempt to register actual perception accurately; there are some poems, such as **'The Trace'** and **'The Thing About Joe Sullivan'**, which are devoted solely to this. But, whether originally the cause or result of his beliefs, Fisher's emphasis on sensory detail has left him chronically uncertain of meaning. . . . And while he is exploring ways in which the meaning of language can be broken down to imitate the movements of the mind, he seems at the same time to have lost the impetus 'towards overt feeling' which gave his earlier work coherence and a wider frame of reference. Even the feeling that produced sarcasm has been pushed to one side; his satire is now largely (and entertainingly) concentrated in light verse.

He himself says that his poems are 'propositions or explorations rather than reactions to personal experience'; I feel that when he moves too far away from 'personal' experience into the area of perceptual problems even the symbolic value of his language may be lost in a diction too far removed from actuality to provide a frame of reference. In rejecting realism he sometimes forfeits reality as well. (pp. 126-28)

Deborah Mitchell, ''Modes of Realism: Roy Fisher and Elaine Feinstein,'' in British Poetry since 1970: A Critical Survey, edited by Peter Jones and Michael Schmidt (copyright © 1980 Carcanet New Press; reprinted by permission of the publisher, Persea Books), Persea Books, 1980, pp. 125-30.*

ANDREW MOTION

It's not difficult . . . to see why Fisher has been denied a larger public. For one thing, there's almost no drama in his poems.

He says himself, 'In my poems there's seldom / any *I* or *you*'—which means there's not only seldom any love poetry, but also seldom any individuated human beings at all. Instead, he offers what he calls the 'music of the generous eye': poems which celebrate the phenomenal world by the clarity with which they perceive it. And when people do stray across his field of vision they frequently seem neither more nor less important than the scenery in which they appear. In fact people and objects are often almost indistinguishable—so much so that their functions are sometimes exchanged. . . .

At first glance, this approach to experience might not seem to include much human interest. But, as Fisher meticulously illustrates, his poems do not substitute purity of observation for the pleasures of action and narrative, but make the act of seeing itself dramatic. Throughout his career he has tried to create an absolutely authentic realism, consistently addressing himself to the world with a latter-day kind of wise passiveness. . . .

Nearly all Fisher's poems adopt this distanced but compassionate poetic strategy, notably his long elegy for bombed and brutally redeveloped Birmingham, *City*. And although reading his work in bulk allows its methods to emerge clearly, it also emphasises his limitations. His 'gentle eye' is extraordinarily affectionate and observant, but is rather apt to tyrannise his tone of voice. Fisher obviously realises the danger, and occasionally—and often successfully—abandons his preferred mode in favour of humour or surrealism. But these excursions can't altogether dispel the threat of a rather too-rigorous self-effacement and restraint.

Andrew Motion, ''Clairvoyance,'' in New Statesman *(© 1981 The Statesman & Nation Publishing Co. Ltd.), Vol. 101, No. 2603, February 6, 1981, p. 9.**

PHILIP GARDNER

The map of post-war British poetry is today very much denser and more various than it appeared a decade ago, when the so-called ''Movement'' poets seemed to dominate the 1950s and Ted Hughes and the ''Mersey Beats'' the 1960s. . . . [An] increasing response to other themes and emphases, together with a greater awareness of American poetry, has ensured that a long-neglected poet like Basil Bunting, and such near-contemporaries as Charles Tomlinson and Geoffrey Hill, are now seen as equally valuable practitioners of other modes. It is with these poets, who combine American technical influences with a content strongly English in its sense of locality and history, that Roy Fisher displays his closest affinities. . . .

Where Fisher and Hill are alike is in their attitude to utterance itself: both expend much effort in order to crystallize thought and feeling into hard verbal constructs that resist paraphrase, and are extremely reluctant to make discursive statements. About the only discursive poem in [*Poems 1955-1980*], a recent one entitled **''Paraphrases''**, is in fact a wry, double-edged joke about the poet and his readers, based on some of their letters to him. . . .

''Paraphrases'' is an uncharacteristically prosy poem. Prose itself, however, is a vehicle which Fisher uses seriously, austerely, and with a fine sense of cadence in, and for, some of his longer pieces, though I wish he had not chosen to print last in this volume his longest and most obscure poem, *The Ship's Orchestra*. . . . This, like *The Cut Pages,* is a work ''written on a principle of unpredictability'': that is (to turn the avant-garde into the old hat), a kind of modified surrealism, in which

many individual passages make sense but most are hermetically sealed from the others. . . . The effect of *The Ship's Orchestra* is that of some play for disembodied voices on the Third Programme: well-executed in its way, flatteringly taxing to undergo, but likely to make the audience exit looking puzzled.

That would be a pity. Even though Fisher seems to distrust critics (note the quiet deadliness of **''Critics Can Bleed''**), and in his poem **''The Making of the Book''** describes poetry's purpose as ''constantly to set up little enmities'', he also sees poetry as having a more positive function. ''A poem'', he said in [a] 1973 interview, ''has business to exist . . . if there's a reasonable chance that somebody may have his perceptions rearranged by having read it'', and the reader entering this volume soon finds this happening to him in Fisher's first long poem *City*. . . . Its use of interspersed prose passages, and its location, a Birmingham ''which has already turned into a city of the mind'', anticipates the Geoffrey Hill of *Mercian Hymns*. . . .

City is really an impersonal requiem for Fisher's home town, a nineteenth-century industrial creation altered and emptied by the war, and not yet ready to put on the post-war identity decreed for it by planners. The scene, a ghost-like palimpsest of buildings and people, present and past, was one which no other poet had thought to record. . . . The tone, a curious yet moving detachment, is characteristic of Fisher; but the rhythm has yet to take on the hardness one finds in his spare, mature verse. It is the prose passages, with their sombre sequence of clauses, which look forward to that; and they also transmit a sense, sharp and elusive at once, of the transfiguring of the ordinary, and an uncertainty about that transfiguring, which I take to be Fisher's most valuable ''subversion'' of the reader's way of looking at the world. . . .

The influence of William Carlos Williams, together with a shared response to place and to the visual, links Fisher with Charles Tomlinson and Basil Bunting; and in the 1960s he moved towards more open forms and generally spikier, if not always short, poems. **''In Touch''** specifically invokes Williams's *Pictures from Brueghel*. . . . Fisher stated that, if he had to adopt ''any poetic slogan'', Williams's doctrine ''No ideas but in things'' would be it. In **''The Memorial Fountain''** he describes himself as a ''realist'', who is ''working / to distinguish an event / from an opinion'', and he pursues this self-denying occupation through a number of spare sequences which (together with *City*) are his most important and original contribution to post-war British poetry: **''Matrix''**; the sixteen (once twenty-seven) Birmingham poems called **''Handsworth Liberties''**; the more recent, more mellow **''Wonders of Obligation''**; and the earlier group, set on the North Devon-Somerset border, entitled **''Glenthorne Poems''**. A quotation from any of these may serve to demonstrate how Fisher's cool search for concreteness and objectivity can transcend itself, becoming an intense, perfect blend of observer and ''thing'' observed. . . .

The achievement of . . . the floating of ''real things into a fictive world'' is for Fisher fraught with difficulty. At the end of **''Glenthorne Poems''** he fears that things seen ''are already / three parts idea'', and in **''Wonders of Obligation''** he remarks—with a touch of regret which the reader may find it unnecessary to share—that ''my life keeps / leaking out of my poetry to me / in all directions''. It is significant that the momentary glitter of light on water, the catching of objects edge-on to the air, are recurrent motifs in Fisher's poetry. His chosen task is a balancing act between perception and what it perceives, and his compulsion to keep on attempting it—the subject of **"Cut Worm"**—makes one feel that, at least in terms of basic impulse, the poet with whom Fisher has most in common is Wallace Stevens.

Fisher's range is of course smaller; he makes no claim to cover more than "a fairly limited node of perceptions". . . . Some may find Fisher's poetic territory too rarefied for their liking; for my own part I am sorry he has reduced its extent and its temperature by omitting from this collected volume two such humane poems of place as **"Kingsbury Mill"** [and **"Abraham Darby's Bridge"**]. . . . Nevertheless, Fisher's work has much to offer the reader who is willing to concentrate as the poet himself does. . . .

> *Philip Gardner, "A City of the Mind," in* The Times Literary Supplement *(© Times Newspapers Ltd. (London) 1981; reproduced from* The Times Literary Supplement *by permission), No. 4068, March 20, 1981, p. 314.*

MICHAEL HULSE

Reading *Poems 1955-1980* took on the character of an eye-opener, and although there are still a good many poems in the book which are dead weight, others present an angle on poetry which has taken its bearings largely from American poets (like Williams, or the Black Mountain poets) whose influence on British writers waned during the confessional heyday, but which nonetheless . . . combines strong English and European elements to create something distinctive. (p. 112)

To describe Fisher's affinities is less of a service to the poet than to define his own strengths. He achieves unusually successful counterpoints in his sequences (some of them partly or completely in cadenced prose). Refusing to thrust himself into the foreground, he nevertheless conveys intense personal pleasure, or disappointment, or interest, or sourness, when contemplating landscapes or cityscapes or the actions happening in those landscapes and cities: the sense of direct involvement, to the point of passion, never throttles back. He makes clear but unpretentious statements on aesthetics, in which he does not shy away from reformulating truisms; in **'Releases'**, when he writes 'All structures are mysterious, however the explanation goes', he is re-asserting a tenet apparently simple and commonplace, but one which in fact encapsulates complexities for the writer with a conscience, the writer who wishes (as Fisher clearly does) to be honest. What is more, for all his seriousness Fisher is capable of hilarious wit, as in **'From the "Town Guide"'**. . . . (p. 113)

Fisher's is very much a painter's perception, not only of colour, which he deploys carefully, but also of light. . . . Fisher's mannerism of intensity allows the poet to create patterns of words which paint in language what the eyes saw, at the same time leading the reader further into depths of shadow and light, foliage, grass and earth in the way Charles Tomlinson also does well. Only once in *Poems 1955-1980* (in the description of the farm about halfway through **'Wonders of Obligation'**) does Fisher permit himself a landscape in any way romanticized (the verbs of shining and glowing, the holly hedges and ricks and swinging drays), and there he does so because the description is one recollected from childhood. . . . (pp. 113-14)

Insofar as Fisher's poems can also often be considered in terms of a passage cut through time, they can be looked at from the same angle as the musician's work. The more poetry abjures clear form, the concretions of linguistic space, the closer its

meaning (for want of a better word) can be related to the actual act of progressing through time: that is, the following-on of line after line in continuous sequence. This is an aesthetic primarily American and European (not British), an aesthetic of pared-down primaries and poetic minimalism. To produce work of this type which has value not merely because it prods an experimental finger into traditional flab but also because it is quite simply a pleasure to read is a rare achievement, and I will not pretend that Fisher has managed it in all of his sequences (the **'Handsworth Liberties'**, for example, and **'Matrix'** and **'The Six Deliberate Acts'**, and the prose pieces **'Stopped Frames and Set-pieces'** and **'Metamorphoses'**, I consider to be failures). But in **'The Ship's Orchestra'**, **'Diversions'** and **'Interiors with Various Figures'** he has notched up successes, and in **'City'** a masterpiece.

'City' scales down the pretensions of poetry; it mixes it with prose, too. It noses its way forward through simplicity and elegance, harshness and lyricism, dislocation and repetition, anger and sympathy, in a way which is compendious and wonderful. I suspect that someone more familiar with theory of harmony and counterpoint, someone, in fact, more at home in musical analysis than myself, would understand more clearly the structural principles of the work; it owes little to familiar principles in writing. There are, of course, poems in it which use rhyme, or metre, or echo effects, and there is prose in it urbanely dry and elliptical or surrealistic and crammed. More to the point, perhaps, **'City** also *says* a lot . . . about the character, or lack of character, of the cities we live in, and it says a lot too that can be lifted out, if we wish, and taken to mean more, symbolically, than it seems to say; for there is a wealth of ideas expressed in its things. . . . It is in work like this that the full weight of Fisher's ability is perceived.

No poet has ever been judged only on his flat stuff if he has also written work as fine as **'City'**. If Roy Fisher is to be judged by his best he deserves to be rated highly. (pp. 114-15)

> *Michael Hulse, "Dirty Dramas," in* London Magazine *(© London Magazine 1981), Vol. 21, Nos. 1 & 2, April-May, 1981, pp. 112-15.*

CHOICE

The inclusive nature of [*Poems, 1955-1980*] confronts the reader with the paradoxical problem of being simultaneously exposed to Fisher's enormous versatility as a poet and to his weakness for a falsely elevated urbane wit. At his best (and there are easily 15 poems in this collection that stand among the best of modern and postmodern British poetry), Fisher writes a clear, tense poem that is at once clipped and musical. He is strongest in his long poems, which allow him to spread out his sparse observations of modern dilemmas so that the poems have a cumulative effect. The long poems, **"Handsworth liberties"** and **"Wonders of obligation,"** are remarkable for their sustained vision and their clarity. It is only when Fisher opts for a terse, provincial point of view that the poems become talky and indirect. Fisher stands among the best poets writing in Britain today. . . .

> *"Language and Literature: 'Poems'," in* Choice *(copyright © 1981 by American Library Association), Vol. 18, Nos. 11 & 12, July-August, 1981, p. 1545.*

PETER PORTER

Roy Fisher is a poet strongly bound to experiment and to certain avant-garde expectations. **'The Ship's Orchestra,'** for instance, which is reprinted in **'Poems 1955-1980,'** is a typical work of the 1960s. It is difficult, compacted and surreal; yet it has charm and many flashes of brilliant writing. It seems to me as natural a work as Henry Green's 'Party Going,' which it resembles slightly, but you cannot imagine anyone writing anything like it today, while you can readily enough with the Green novel.

Fisher sees things very sharply. . . . [He] is a fine jazz pianist and many of his poems borrow from jazz the technique of improvisation. This enables him to compose over considerable length: **'Wonders of Obligation,'** for example, is a Coleridge-like soliloquy about death, surprise and survival, in which Fisher starts from a sight in wartime Birmingham, the mass graves dug for the dead expected after air raids. . . .

'Poems 1955-1980' reprints all Fisher's past work other than the Burroughs-like cut ups he published in **'The Cut Pages.'** I have not stressed sufficiently how witty and humane Fisher is. His is a 'Collected' to hang on to.

> *Peter Porter, "Laundromat Lyrics," in* The Observer *(reprinted by permission of The Observer Limited), November 22, 1981, p. 27.**

Thomas (James Bonner) Flanagan

1923-

American novelist, critic, and biographer.

Flanagan, whose four grandparents emigrated from Ireland to the United States, has a great interest in Irish history and literature. His nonfiction work *The Irish Novelists: 1800-1850* demonstrates his mastery of both subjects. This critical study of five Irish novelists of the nineteenth century combines scholarship and creativity.

Flanagan's renown as a novelist derives from his critically acclaimed and popular historical novel, *The Year of the French*. This long, intricately plotted work recounts the abortive French-supported rebellion of Irish peasants against the British in 1798. It also draws parallels between the political and social problems of eighteenth-century Ireland and those of that country today. Flanagan's use of multiple narrative perspectives in *The Year of the French* has been both praised and faulted. Some critics believe that this technique makes the novel ponderous; while others hold that multiple points-of-view provide the reader with a sense of how the same event produces diverse effects. Most, however, praise Flanagan for presenting the events of the rebellion unsentimentally and thus "demythologizing" Irish history.

(See also *Contemporary Authors*, Vol. 108 and *Dictionary of Literary Biography Yearbook: 1980*.)

© Jerry Bauer

VIVIAN MERCIER

[In **"The Irish Novelists: 1800-1850,"** Thomas Flanagan] constantly discriminates among his five chosen authors —Maria Edgeworth, Lady Morgan, John Banim, Gerald Griffin and William Carleton—comparing and contrasting not only their artistic achievements, but also their differing social backgrounds and political viewpoints. The one thing that he sees as uniting them is their common attempt "to come to terms with the experience of life on their maddening island." . . .

The novelists' work is carefully related both to their social and economic status and to the political events of their lifetimes.

It would be very unfair to characterize Mr. Flanagan as merely a sociological critic, however. He proves himself equally skilled as a formal literary critic. Because of the furious political and religious partisanship of Irish life in the years 1800-1850, the novelists often dared to avow their true positions only by means of symbolism—both conscious and unconscious. Some of the most exciting pages in Mr. Flanagan's book contain his explorations of this devious symbolism.

Faced with the quantities of inept or escapist or meanly partisan writing produced in Ireland during the period, Mr. Flanagan wisely decided to be ruthlessly selective. Not that all his novelists are even competent. The appropriate response to Lady Morgan's more high-flown passages is a giggle, but she represents a certain kind of sentimental, pastoral, defeatist Irish nationalism better than any other novelist. . . . The ironies of "Castle Rackrent" make Maria Edgeworth secure in her niche forever, but Carleton, the greatest writer dealt with, has yet to become even a minor classic outside Ireland. This is perhaps the just reward of his venality, for Mr. Flanagan shows that Carleton hired out his pen to any group that would pay him. In writing of Carleton's work, no one finds it easy to be original; Mr. Flanagan must echo Yeats' lavish praise and his great reservations. To be appreciated, Carleton must be read in bulk; each individual work is vitiated by some obvious blemish.

The more one knows about Mr. Flanagan's subject matter, the more exciting his book seems and the better one appreciates his originality. He is never afraid to discard the accepted view in either history or literary criticism; and where, as so often in Irish matters, there is no accepted view, he carves out an intelligent position for himself. **"The Irish Novelists"** is a remarkable pioneering survey.

> *Vivian Mercier, "The Reason Why They Wrote the Way They Did," in* The New York Times Book Review *(© 1959 by The New York Times Company; reprinted by permission), December 20, 1959, p. 5.**

JULIAN MOYNAHAN

The Year of the French, the first novel of Thomas Flanagan, . . . tells an astonishing and terrible story. It is certainly the finest historical novel by an American to appear in more than a decade.

The center of Flanagan's book is a combined French-Irish military venture, with a bright beginning and a deadly close, during a single summer in 1798. Around this Irish rebellion against the British he builds up a complex, brilliantly styled narrative that plays off omniscient survey against the partial views of no less than five contemporary witnesses—a Church of Ireland minister, a Catholic village schoolmaster, a youthful English aide to General Cornwallis, a solicitor member of the Society of United Irishmen, and the solicitor's English wife. Through these marvelously evoked and distinct voices the very complicated and conflicted social realities of late 18th-century Ireland come to life. Dozens of vividly conceived characters of both sexes—Protestant and Catholic fanatics, peasants and poets, landowners and militia men, the historically noted and the nameless obscure—take the stage in his epic drama.

In 1798 in counties Wexford, Carlow and Kilkenny, thousands of country-people, commanded by gentlemen republicans belonging to the United Irish movement of Wolfe Tone, and by some half-mad priests of charismatic character, fought British army regulars and well-armed bands of loyalist yeomenry. There were frightful atrocities committed on both sides before the native insurgents gave way to superiority of arms, numbers, and organization. The next theater of rebellion was in the north, where insurgency failed quickly owing to seeds of distrust between Catholic and Presbyterian rebels. Finally, during that summer of '98, the revolutionary spotlight switched to the remote coast of North Mayo.

There, at Killala, to everyone's surprise, a French expeditionary force of one thousand soldiers under the leadership of the well-known General Humbert came ashore and headed inland. . . .

Humbert, after making contact with local leadership in the United Irish organization and with ''White Boy'' agrarian terrorists, marched to Castlebar where he defeated a large army of British regulars under General Lake. . . .

[But] General Humbert's quixotic, possibly mad adventure ended at Ballinamuck—''the place of the pig''—in a dismal part of County Longford. Hordes of British cavalry surrounded his exhausted and disoriented force. The French immediately surrendered and were escorted to Dublin where they were billeted in comfortable inns before being repatriated to France. But the Irish were not allowed to surrender. Instead they were driven out onto the bog, where the cavalry and foot dragoons had a field day sabering and bayoneting them to death over a period of several hours.

As he masterfully traces the full course of this most brutal and eccentric military campaign, Flanagan avoids partisan myths while deploying his ironies, wryly, compassionately, authoritatively. In part he benefits from the recent harvest of Irish historical scholarship. But *The Year of the French* is itself a permanent contribution to the new, demythologized history of Ireland. Without doubt it will find a wide audience of serious readers here in the United States and in the three European countries from which the book's cast of characters is drawn.

> *Julian Moynahan, ''Historical Fiction at Its Finest,'' in* Book World—The Washington Post *(©1979, The Washington Post), May 13, 1979, p. K5.*

VICTORIA GLENDINNING

Thomas Flanagan is no Tolstoy and he has not written a new ''War and Peace''; but **''The Year of the French''** is suffi-

ciently colored by his intense and informed obsession with place and period for the reader with plenty of time (this is a long, dense novel) to be drawn deep into County Mayo, on the west coast of Ireland, in the year 1798. (p. 12)

Mr. Flanagan's method is mainly documents-with-dialogue, and one of his problems has been that the [French invasion of Ireland in 1798] is fairly well documented. If he had used contemporary accounts verbatim, he would not have been writing a ''novel.'' So he cooked the books a bit. For example, one of the chief sources for what went on in Killala is a manuscript narrative by Bishop Stock, the Protestant prelate whose palace in Killala was used as a headquarters by the French. Mr. Flanagan substitutes for Bishop Stock an imaginary clergyman named Broome, whose house is likewise taken over by the French, and who contributes a similar—but not too similar—narrative. Mr. Flanagan works largely through fictional journal entries of this kind, creating an illusion of authenticity by editorial mock-documentation. Anyone who wants to sift fact from fiction will find the story of 1798 well told in Thomas Pakenham's ''The Year of Freedom.''

Where Mr. Flanagan scores is in his overall historical vision. He has a concept of ''mental maps'' that is the key to his own perspective. The Mayo peasant's map, for example, is bounded by his own fields; for him, ''Dublin, Belfast, Cork, words scattered across the map of a small island, were cities more remote than Rome or Bethlehem.'' Differences in mental geography explain the disjunction of aims. The cultivated leaders of the United Irishmen were ''intellectual'' patriots; they had read Rousseau and Tom Paine, and discussed them in drawing rooms in Dublin, London and Paris. They wanted self-determination for Ireland. . . .

The French general [Humbert] was seeking glory for himself first and for the Revolution second. The Mayo peasants whom he came to lead knew nothing of the French Revolution; their bitterness was not against the English monarchy, or the English Parliament, or even the Dublin Parliament. They knew next to nothing about them. They hated the punishing tithes they were forced to pay, and they could, if worked upon, hate Protestants. They were unlikely allies of the revolutionaries from the clean-linen world of order and ''civilization.'' . . .

It is on the evocation of these dispossessed, fanatical, hungry Mayo peasants that the book stands or falls, and it stands. . . . This was a people trapped in, yet sustained by, their own myth and their own tongue. . . . It is they, whom the French came to ''free'' for their own imperialistic purposes, who were the losers in 1798. Thirty thousand people were killed in Ireland during that year. (p. 35)

> *Victoria Glendinning, ''Mission to Mayo,'' in* The New York Times Book Review *(© 1979 by The New York Times Company; reprinted by permission), May 13, 1979, pp. 12, 35.*

I.M. OWEN

Thomas Flanagan's book **Louis 'David' Riel,** though biographical in form, is not intended to replace George F.G. Stanley's standard biography, which remains indispensable though lamentably pedestrian. Flanagan does tell Riel's life-story, but with less political, military, and legal detail than Stanley gives, concentrating on what was clearly most important to Riel himself: his religion and his mission as ''Prophet of the New World.'' It's a tragic story of a man who might have achieved much if it had not been for a fantasy-life that grew in scope and complexity until it became his only reality. (p. 53)

[In] his last chapter Flanagan attempts to show that Riel's religion is characteristic both of the millenarian Christian cults of the dispossessed that were frequent in the Middle Ages and have continued to appear ever since (as in Jonestown), and the nativistic resistance cults like the Rastafarians and the Black Muslims. For the author, this thesis is perhaps the main point of the book. For the reader, luckily, it isn't. It wouldn't be particularly arresting even if it were sound; but it really doesn't hold water. . . .

[Riel] did confer priesthood on the members of the Exovedate, as he called his provisional government, and they dutifully passed several resolutions on theological and ecclesiastical matters. Gabriel Dumont accepted Riel's military decisions against his own better judgement, in the belief that Riel was inspired by God. But the cult never became a true cult. . . . Hence I don't think Thomas Flanagan makes his point. But he has made a good, readable, funny, painfully sad book. (p. 54)

> I. M. Owen, *"Louis Riel As Religious Prophet"* (copyright © 1979 by Saturday Night; *reprinted by permission of the author), in* Saturday Night, *Vol. 94, No. 5, June, 1979, pp. 53-4.*

DENIS DONOGHUE

The first chapters of [*The Year of the French*] deal with conditions leading up to the [French invasion of Ireland in 1798]. . . . These chapters are recited by an impersonal narrator, the voice of history uttering its disinterested truth. Most of the later events are conveyed from different points of view and in suitably different styles. In certain chapters we hear the voice of history not in complete impersonality but as it yields itself to a particular character. . . . Still other chapters narrate the events through fictitious documents, such as *An Impartial Narrative of What Passed at Killala in the Summer of 1798*, by Arthur Vincent Broome, the local Protestant minister in the novel.

These devices make for variety in a long novel: the several points of view keep the reader sensitive to the proportions of ignorance and knowledge in any account of an experience. Another effect is that the characters and events in the novel are held at a certain distance, as if to prevent the reader from having only an immediate relation to them; he is to see them not only as they were but as they have become. I imagine, too, that Flanagan was reluctant to produce his characters when they had nothing to show for themselves but their bewilderment: he chose to let them stay in the shadow until they had come to understand the various forms of darkness in which they had lived.

I assume that this is what it means for Flanagan to be a historical novelist. Every event, every character, has a dual existence in which past and present are diversely engaged. The reader is not gripped by the events as they occur; his concern is drawn to the events as they have occurred and to the stain of outrage and desolation they have left upon the people who suffered them. Mostly we come upon the events when their form and consequence have already been assessed. There is a loss of immediacy, our interest is not allowed to fasten upon a character as distinct from his role in the story as a whole.

But there is a gain in the depth and resonance of the characters; when we meet them, they have already been changed by their experience. Broome, for instance, is given to us not when he

is in the throes of his suffering but when he has survived it; his tone of bewildered care shows that he has been transformed, driven far beyond the range of qualities he would have produced as the local Protestant minister in a peaceful town. We are interested in him mainly for what he has been through, and for the generosity of his vision, flawed as it is. . . . Each event is seen not only in its immediate light but in the light of the idea it embodied or humiliated: the mediations issue from Flanagan's sense of modern Irish history, the shapes it has taken in his mind.

It is my impression that Flanagan organized the novel in this way not chiefly for the pleasure of managing several viewpoints and styles but to ensure that the conflicts of class, religion, tradition, and self-interest would be disclosed and interrogated. Impartiality is achieved by admitting to the narrative several different forms of partiality. If, as Walter Benjamin remarked, history is invariably recited in favor of those who have won, Flanagan is alert to the fact that in Ireland the narrative of history is still indecisive. His rhetoric does not say that we Irishmen are brothers under the torn skin, or that our differences are the kind that can be sunk. But the many different attitudes in the book at least reveal in the characters motives far more diverse than those proclaimed by our warring ideologies. Given a favorable wind, the book might do something to make the antagonists a little ashamed of themselves, but I do not expect such a wind.

Flanagan's own position in the novel deserves a few words. He does not speak in his own person; nor does he identify himself with the voice of history. Strictly speaking, he does not come into the book at all; but in another sense he is pervasive. . . . [The] novel is handsomely written, but the urge to remark upon its prose arises from the fact that the book is indeed a written thing. We are made aware of the writing, not because the sentences are histrionic or self-regarding but because a pervasive unity of tone suggests that ultimately the prejudices of each style may be reconciled. Since each viewpoint is acknowledged, it is allowed to speak for itself and given an appropriately positive style: one man, one rhetoric. But the tone of the whole book is also felt as issuing from a certain perspective, and the perspective must be pretty high if it is to accommodate every viewpoint decently. None of the styles is transparent, because none can be given the privilege of appearing to issue directly from the events, undarkened by prejudice. Even the voice of history is allowed to sound troubled.

The organization of Flanagan's novel is an act of rhetoric: that is the main point. Prejudices can be entertained only by a style which runs to a certain grandeur of implication: decency, like the historical novel, requires a certain latitude of sympathy. But I must admit that Flanagan favors a rather high style even for the daily purposes of scholarship. He likes a rich mixture of tropes. In a sullen mood, you would accuse him of fine writing: even in a genial mood, you would sometimes tremble for the safety of his soul, so ardently given to the webbing of words. (pp. 21-2)

[Flanagan] insures himself against a sullen reader by ascribing most of the lush passages to the poet MacCarthy. A poet who comes from the Irish bardic tradition, bringing not only the Irish poetry but Ovid and Virgil, can get away with nearly any excess: drink, lechery, high talk. But there are also high passages in which the normally impersonal narrator leans down and gives a helping hand to a character supposedly in need of such assistance. (pp. 22-3)

Flanagan's knowledge of Irish history, mythology, religion, local customs has colored his style, but it would be absurd to ask him to bleach his style or empty his mind. When his poet MacCarthy says, "You were slaves on this land before Christ was crucified," a reader may recall that the last phrase turns up in Yeats, who received it from Frank O'Connor, who translated it from the Gaelic. The recollection doesn't matter, we are not playing the flat historic scale. . . .

The novel ends with the fictitious diary of the local school-teacher, Sean MacKenna, in the summer of 1799. The French invasion and the battle of Castlebar are already moving from fact into mythology. The three French ships that landed at Kilcummin are now fancied by a local peasant to have "masts so tall that you could not see the tops of them and on the tallest mast of all was an eagle called King Lewis." The eagle, so they say, went with the soldiers into the midlands, "but on the night before the battle the eagle flew off and the battle was lost." Flanagan implies that we must go back through lore and mythology to find the motives, noble and shoddy, which provided the events and the need to transform them into poetry. But he is not cynical, he lets the reader see how natural it is that events are transformed, out of need and desire. The facts are not to be thought away, but they cannot be transfixed, arrested in their nature; the novel recognizes the need to transform them from their own nature into ours, so that they become at last indistinguishable from ourselves. (p. 23)

Denis Donoghue, "The Stains of Ireland," in The New York Review of Books *(reprinted with permission from* The New York Review of Books; *copyright © 1979 Nyrev, Inc.), Vol. XXVI, No. 10, June 14, 1979, pp. 21-3.*

DESMOND MORTON

Of Riel as a symbol, enough has been written. Riel as a person remains a troubling enigma. One possible technique is to take him at his own valuation. That is almost exactly what Thomas Flanagan has done [in *Louis 'David' Riel: Prophet of the New World*]. Having edited Riel's diaries, collected his youthful poetry and explored the political theory behind the 1869 Declaration of the Red River colony Metis, Professor Flanagan has now explored the abundant collection of Riel's religious writings. Let us, he suggests, suspend the conventional judgment that the Metis leader was insane. Instead, why not see if he qualifies as a millenarian religious leader?

The resulting book is an impressive and sometimes laborious example of interdisciplinary scholarship. Although a political scientist, Professor Flanagan has applied literary techniques and theological knowledge to an essentially historical problem. His task was made easier by the narrow horizons of Riel's intellectual world but the breadth of Flanagan's erudition is imposing. Biblical references, contemporary allusions and Riel's numerology are painstakingly explained. We may now understand why the papacy will arrive in St. Vital in the year 2333 AD and why, as a result of a vision, Riel could insist that the Indians are descended from the Israelites. (pp. 37-8)

By defining Riel as a millenarian cult leader, Professor Flanagan has justified himself in undertaking a laborious and profitable re-examination of Riel's extensive writings. However, his interpretation is not really at odds with other extensive studies of Riel, particularly the standard biography by George Stanley. We may now understand more about Louis Riel; do we necessarily change our judgment? (p. 38)

Desmond Morton, "Millenarian," in The Canadian Forum, *Vol. LIX, No. 690, June-July, 1979, pp. 37-8.*

JOHN LEONARD

[Thomas Flanagan] has with one exuberant book abolished my prejudice against historical novels. I haven't so thoroughly enjoyed an historical novel since "The Charterhouse of Parma," and "War and Peace." **"The Year of the French,"** consisting of straight narrative, snippets from journals, swatches of invented memoirs, scraps of song, sworn statements to magistrates and subalterns, hindsight and myth, is grand and sad, with ferocious sweep.

There is, necessarily, a poet—the red-haired, whisky-drinking, licentious Owen MacCarthy, a schoolmaster tormented by an image: "Moonlight falling on a hard, flat surface, scythe or sword or stone or spade." He is surrounded, whether he knows it or not, by other people putting pen to paper and equally dismayed by our Celtic Lebanon—a Protestant minister, a clerk to Cornwallis, a lovelorn girl, an ambivalent solicitor, various informers, a historian trying to make sense of the Girondists. Their truths collide with MacCarthy's. His truth is a form of despair. (p. 222)

The image that torments MacCarthy is an idea of poetry itself, the moon on sword and spade. The poem—like the cheap novels and the noble proclamations everybody in **"The Year of the French"** is always reading; like the songs they sing and the prophecies they listen to; like the letters and memoirs and histories they write—is a lie, when the bog runs with blood. Memory, fable, dreams themselves are "tricks of speech," wishful nonthinking.

About the only worthwhile thing England did for Ireland was to foist upon it a language it has used with genius. Mr. Flanagan may not belong with Yeats and Joyce, but he loiters agreeably in their vicinity, and he reminds us of an odd, alien time when, at the very least, we knew the faces of those we killed. We were not cowards with time bombs. (pp. 222-23)

John Leonard, "'The Year of the French'," in The New York Times, *Section III (© 1979 by The New York Times Company; reprinted by permission), May 8, 1979 (and reprinted in* Books of the Times, *Vol. II, No. 5, July, 1979, pp. 221-23).*

CONOR CRUISE O'BRIEN

'The Year of the French' is a novel which does a great deal more than tell [the story of the French invasion at Killala in 1798], though it tells it very well indeed. Its main and absorbing interest is in its picture of the society, or societies, into which the French landed, like men from Mars. . . .

[Mr. Flanagan's] special academic interest is Anglo-Irish literature and he puts this interest to good use in this novel, much of which is built out of brilliant pastiche extracts from various 'diaries' and 'work-books.' It is the work of a man learned in Irish history—as very few novelists are learned—but also emotionally involved in it, tied to it by a strange sardonic yearning. . . .

Mr. Flanagan has a fine ear for Irish speech, and a keen eye for the manifold discrepancies of Irish life and Irish thought: especially for the discrepancies between the life and the thought. These last are particularly relevant to the period and theme of

'**The Year of the French.**' Between the thought of the United Irishmen—the ideological revolutionaries who summoned the French to Ireland—and the life of the country into which they summoned them, there is a discrepancy of the proportions of a chasm. . . .

'**The Year of the French**' is a magnificent and beautifully written historical novel. It can be read with pleasure and profit by people who have no particular interest in Ireland.

Conor Cruise O'Brien, "The Last Invasion," in The Observer *(reprinted by permission of The Observer Limited), No. 9804, July 22, 1979, p. 37.*

TOM PAULIN

The Irish imagination is dominated by the idea of circles and it tends to view history passively as a pattern of cycles. Although this can be a dangerous view to take, it subtly informs Thomas Flanagan's remarkable historical novel [*The Year of the French*]. (p. 61)

Flanagan has an unerring sense of the parallels between the political situation in 1798 and the events in Ulster over the last ten years. Thus the Mayo yeomanry are the shadowy and bigoted forerunners of the ''B'' Specials, the secret society called the Whiteboys of Killala is the Provisional IRA, while the brief ''Republic of Connaught'' parallels Free Derry nearly two centuries later. Flanagan has considerable sympathy for the aims and ideals of the United Irishmen . . . but he is also aware of what happens when ideology is translated into action. . . .

Particularly interesting is Flanagan's presentation of Owen MacCarthy, the Gaelic poet who is caught up in the revolution. Through MacCarthy (he is partly based on Seamus Heaney) Flanagan explores the difficult relationship of poetry to politics in Ireland, and he expresses the historical reality which informs Heaney's powerful conclusion to ''Triptych''. . . .

[Through] the eyes of the sceptical historian, George Moore, we see how Ireland has always been ''a maidservant to others''. . . . [The] French general, Humbert, becomes a prototype of those American congressmen who periodically interfere in Irish politics. Flanagan is also subtly aware of the ''equivocal'' nature of Loyalism, and by admitting every shade of political opinion he builds a rich, intelligent and exciting fiction. Although there are purple passages and moments of costume-drama in this novel, it is a splendid and heartening achievement which must prove influential and enduring. (p. 62)

Tom Paulin, "The Fire Monster," in Encounter *(© 1980 by Encounter Ltd.), Vol. LIV, No. 1, January, 1980, pp. 57-64.**

Carolyn Forché

1950-

American poet, journalist, and translator.

All of Forché's poetry is marked by its identification with place. Forché brings to her poetry a remarkable candidness which compels her to speak of the beautiful and the ugly. Her simple yet deep feelings and astute observations are skillfully crafted in arresting imagery.

In her first collection, *Gathering the Tribes,* Forché recounts the learning experiences of her adolescence in her native Michigan and takes up her travels as a young woman in the North American West. Here, as elsewhere, Forché's interest in the speech of diverse peoples is evident. In poems whose language owes much to her study of Tewa (Pueblo Indian), Forché portrays the American Indian as her spiritual parent. She also finds inspiration in the connection between her life experience and the lives of her Slovakian relations. Within this framework she celebrates and studies nature, rituals of innocence, purification, and sexuality.

Forché's second volume of poetry, *The Country Between Us,* expands the themes presented in the first volume but is also political, being the result of Forché's experiences as a journalist in war-torn El Salvador. Critics note a sense of urgency in this poetry, an artistry aimed at transformation. As Denise Levertov was prompted to say about Forché, "She is creating poems in which there is no seam between personal and political, lyrical and engaged."

(See also *Dictionary of Literary Biography,* Vol. 5.)

Photograph by Andrew Kilgore; courtesy of Carolyn Forché

STANLEY KUNITZ

Kinship is the theme that preoccupies Carolyn Forché. Although she belongs to a generation that is reputed to be rootless and disaffiliated, you would never guess it from reading her poems. Her imagination, animated by a generous life-force, is at once passionate and tribal. Narrative is her preferred mode, leavened by meditation. [In *Gathering the Tribes* she] remembers her childhood in rural Michigan, evokes her Slovak ancestors, immerses herself in the American Indian culture of the Southwest, explores the mysteries of flesh, tries to understand the bonds of family, race, and sex. In the course of her adventures she dares to confront, as a sentient being, the overwhelming questions by which reason itself is confounded: Who am I? Why am I here? Where am I going?

In "**Burning the Tomato Worms,**" a central poem, the narrative focuses on Anna, "heavy sweatered winter woman" seen "in horse-breath weather." She was the poet's paternal grandmother, who spoke a Slovak of the Russian-Czech borderlands and who, with her Old World lore and old wives' tales, profoundly influenced the poet's childhood. . . . Here as elsewhere the local color is vivid and unforced. But the poem is not to be construed as an exercise in sentimentality or ethnic nostalgia: it is woven of two strands, one commemorating a beloved person and place, the other recounting a girl's sexual initiation. The burning of the tomato worms can be read as a ritual of purification. Everywhere in these pages ritual and

litany are close at hand. Even the act of bread making, a recurrent image, assumes a ceremonial aspect. (pp. xi-xii)

Forché's poems give an illusion of artlessness because they spring from the simplest and deepest human feelings, from an earthling's awareness of the systemic pulse of creation. The poems tell us she is at home anyplace under the stars, wherever there are fields or mountains, lakes or rivers, persons who stir her atavistic bond-sense. (p. xii)

She acknowledges a primal sense of the power of words. The power to "make words"—in the mouth, in the heart, on the page—is the same to her as to give substance. Aiming at wholeness, strength, and clarity, she works at language as if it were a lump of clay or dough in her hands. (p. xiii)

[Her poem "**Kalaloch**" is] an almost faultlessly controlled erotic narrative of 101 lines. In its boldness and innocence and tender, sensuous delight it may very well prove to be the outstanding Sapphic poem of an era. (p. xiv)

> *Stanley Kunitz, in his foreword to* Gathering the Tribes *by Carolyn Forché (copyright © 1976 by Carolyn Forché), Yale University Press, 1976, pp. xi-xv.*

WENDY KNOX

In *Gathering the Tribes,* Carolyn Forché gives us voices of people around her. . . . Her mode is generally narrative, slowly spinning out revelation by means of direct references to scenes, people, and natural objects with which she is familiar. Each poem seems to have an exact location drawn for us, and she often moves into a poem by describing the room, geography, or central character objectively. . . .

She also writes with a certain slow descriptiveness and a simple statement that seem very native in character. Wood, sounds, bread, smells, birds, water, aspens, and owls—all seem to speak for her, *through* her, in a way. She has only to mention them, and they evoke other sounds and smells—pine, dust, adobe, or wool. She seems to play the learner in many encounters, the young shaman gathering her trade. (p. 82)

The theme of prophecy or learning from some other person, most often female, recurs throughout the book. These clearly rooted characters: her grandmother, the dulcimer-maker, the old Indian Teles Goodmorning, Alfansa, Rosita, Jacynth in "**Kalaloch**" (which, Kunitz says in his introduction [see excerpt above], "may very well prove to be the outstanding Sapphic poem of an era," and I agree), all these characters seem to be living examples of some natural principle, extensions of the earth itself and the places in which they live. She comes to these people openly . . . and is rewarded with signs at once simple and mysterious. (p. 83)

A close look at [the] stanzas from "**Mientras Dura Vida, Sobra el Tiempo**" brings out two distinct characteristics of Forché's language, one brilliant, one troublesome. First is her tough, almost Hopkins-like use of onomatopoetic speech, alliteration, and rhythms. Her use of plosive consonants cuts edges sharp and deep. In her poem about butchering, "**From Memory**," the *s, p, b, l,* and hard *c* and *k* sounds seem hardly placed by chance but support her feeling and tone. . . . (pp. 83-4)

This "consonant ethic" may come from her Slavic background, as well as from her skill as a linguist. She studies Russian, Spanish, Serbo-Croatian, French and Tewa (Pueblo Indian) and seems to take rhythms and flows from them all. The drawback of this skill, however, is the inclusion of many foreign words that puzzle or distract. In some poems, one can derive that a *fogon* is a stove or fireplace from the context, but often words and clusters like *ma-he-yo, alfansa, mokva,* and *dusha* trip the reader mid-thought, prompting futile backtracking and speculation. If the thought is worth expressing in another language, I'd appreciate some minor glossary or explication to help non-linguists out. This applies to particularly significant acts, rituals, or symbols of native culture not ordinarily recognizable or easily deduced.

Forché's plunges into what Kunitz calls "her atavistic bondsense" remain nonetheless invigorating, a recurrence of power much needed in an over-individualized and disconnected era. When her human shamans are silent, the woods, moose, water, rituals of bread-making, dishwashing, child-feeding, and lovemaking provide a continuity of wordless places in an all-too-verbal and chaotic world. . . . (p. 84)

[In Forché's poetry there is] some of the "nearsightedness" of women's point of view, returning us to mundane miracles we've almost forgotten. The violent beauty of sexuality, the mysterious comforts of memory and known people and places, the terrifying and awesome fecundity and regularity of plants, animals, and natural forces—we turn to these when the glitter of controlled efficiency and voyeuristic titillations runs dry. This world of the earth and the body can be brutal and chaotic, but it is a root from which great power and meaning flows. Dillard, Rukeyser, Kinnell, Lifshin, Muske, Forché—all these

poets seem to be digging in the first gardens and prairies since Whitman to bear real fruit without "chemical" additives, simple and *from* the earth without being simplistic or dull, without leaning on the earth, body, or myth to do their magic *for* them. It's rather sad that a return to the human seems so shocking and courageous to us now. (pp. 84-5)

Wendy Knox, "Relatedness and Ritual," in Moons and Lion Tailes *(copyright © 1976 by The Permanent Press; reprinted by permission of the publisher), Vol. 2, No. 2, 1976, pp. 79-85.**

KENNETH REXROTH

Carolyn Forché is beyond question the best woman poet to appear in the Yale Younger Poet series since Muriel Rukeyser, whom in a special way she somewhat resembles. She is far better educated than most poets, not just in school, but in life. . . . She is also something nobody ever seemed to be able to find in the 30's when they were in demand—a genuine proletarian poet. Her father is a tool and die maker. Most of her later poetry is laid in the Far West, in New Mexico, British Columbia, and Washington and here the identification with place is as intense as in William Carlos Williams or Yvor Winters. . . .

[Forché's *Gathering the Tribes*] is the poetry of a human being in her late 20's moving in perfect freedom and independence (not the same thing) through life experiences that are reserved for young males. . . . Her judgments of her experience are strong and supple, virtues reserved for the male. . . .

[Forché's] prosody is about as far removed from the slick formulas of Charles Olson's "projective verse" as possible. The basic influence is Latin American and American Indian and just possibly Snyder, Whalen, and Rothenberg, all of whom owe much to preliterate poetry and all of whom have shared many of Forché's experiences. . . .

[Her] poems of life in the Pueblos of New Mexico and amongst the Indians of the Northwest have a ceremonial character, rituals celebrating the holiness of all living things. Poems of the unbelievably impoverished original settlers of New Mexico who still persist in calling themselves "Spanish," not "Mexican," certainly reflect Toynbee's "stimulus of harsh environments." Here, not in Harlem, not in Appalachia, is to be found the lowest standard of living and the poorest public health rate of the United States. These are poems of the heroic people that, like all the poor, America keeps swept under the rug. Behind all the other elements of her verse is a mystical pedal note. With few exceptions the poems are religious. . . . They are also poems which should be welcomed enthusiastically by the Feminist Movement and all other groups the press loves to slur with the term "Lib."

Kenneth Rexroth, "On Carolyn Forché" (copyright © 1976 by World Poetry, Inc.; reprinted by permission of Bradford Morrow for the Kenneth Rexroth Trust), in The American Poetry Review, *Vol. 5, No. 6, November-December, 1976, p. 44.*

STANLEY PLUMLY

Carolyn Forché's hold on her material [in *Gathering the Tribes*] is ingratiating if sometimes tenuous. One wants the ambitions of her poems to be realized even when they fail, just as one wants the author herself to emerge even when she refuses to appear. The tribes being gathered here are all local—that is, relative to the poet, whether by blood, as with her Slovak ancestry, or by spirit, as with her Indian "fathers." The locales of her poems, the territories, range from her native Michigan to her adopted New Mexico. The total theme involves the initiation rites of innocence—rituals of conversion to experience. A growth story, a kind of Bildungsroman of consciousness-raising. What is finally learned involves the two-way perception of the spiritual in the carnal, the carnal in the spiritual. Forché is safest in shorter forms. . . . In longer, more self-demanding forms, the poet is forced farther and farther away from her own center of gravity and the confidence of her rhythms. This dilution is particularly in evidence in the central, "Indian" section of the book. The poems of a full page or more too often become awkward, unfocused, and pushed at the reader. The fault is certainly not in Forché's ability with texture—she is especially adept with image, detail, naming, and a complement of languages. What is typically missing, in poems as technically different as **"Ha Chi Je Na I Am Coming"** and **"Alfansa,"** is the clear organizing presence of the speaking voice—or what in fiction is called the narrator. This is another kind of matter altogether from the speaking parts Forché is fond of using, just as the characters are to be distinguished from the storyteller. Forché's signaling device for her "tongues" is italics, but one is hard pressed in several poems (including those mentioned above) to differentiate between speaking part and speaker. The problem seems to lie in Forché's attempt to emulate the ritualistic speech of the territory—whether it be Taos or Tonasket—while reducing her own impulse toward a personal, identifiable rhetoric. She in effect substitutes the language of the tribe for her own. And it becomes much more the language of conversion. . . . Forché creates a shadow voice, one that renders, records, and reports, but never from the center, always at one remove. She either respects or fears her adopted material too much. That is why the first and last sections of her book are superior—familiarity has bred sufficient contempt. The first part deals with her native Slovak heritage, notably Forché's paternal grandmother, Anna, in a poem entitled **"Burning the Tomato Worms."** Here the speaking parts work beautifully. . . . [They do so because] the poet is in primary, not secondary, territory. One's grandmother can have more to offer one's emotional past than one's guru. In the last and best part of her collection, Forché deals with her real, and future, subject, sexual identity. None of the poems here wanders from its source. The power of each begins and ends in the unmitigated voice of the poet, that arbitrating presence that seeks to establish a one-to-one relationship with sensual (all five and country senses seeing) experience, male and female, sky and earth. The rhetoric is hard without being brittle, the narrative sure of itself without being type-cast. **"Kalaloch"** is one poem in particular in which the rhythm of the natural world is realized in counterpart to the carnality of the human . . . in the language of the experience.

Stanley Plumly, "Books: 'Gathering the Tribes'" (copyright © 1976 by World Poetry, Inc.; reprinted by permission of Stanley Plumly), in The American Poetry Review, *Vol. 5, No. 6, November-December, 1976, p. 45.*

CLAIRE HAHN

Audre Lorde and Carolyn Forché are both gifted poets endowed with clarity of inward vision and a willingness and power to project it with often devastating impact. (p. 762)

Like Lorde, Forché writes poetry of pellucid honesty. She too explores the paradoxical freedom and constraint bestowed on her through the blood of her forbears. Her Slavic ancestors bequeathed her rituals of religion and husbandry, customs that were "sacred and eternal." But she presses always to know more, to understand the mystery behind the ritual. . . .

The deepest harmonies Forché discovers [in her *Gathering the Tribes*] are with nature itself. The landscapes and people, not only of the Michigan farm of her childhood, but of New Mexico, British Columbia, and coastal Washington, provide images for her poetry. She writes with a profound sense of the beauty and threat in the rhythms of the seasons and her own bodily needs. Some of her most impressive poetry deals with sexual experience. Perhaps because Forché writes with such deceptive ease, these poems achieve an unadorned eloquence, a seeming inevitability of statement. But Forché is no romanticist; at the most intimate moment a lover can be the enemy. . . . The balanced insight she attains is hard-won, precarious. Her quiet insistence on looking simultaneously at the beautiful and the ugly makes her poetry complex; her technical skill makes it a disciplined art. . . .

[Lorde and Forché] write with authority and intensity. They are artists who, without being "confessional" poets, are not afraid to come to terms with their full experience of life. The voice of American poetry is excitingly alive in their writing. (p. 763)

Claire Hahn, "Books: 'Gathering the Tribes'," in Commonweal *(copyright © 1977 Commonweal Publishing Co., Inc.; reprinted by permission of Commonweal Publishing Co., Inc.), Vol. CIV, No. 24, November 25, 1977, pp. 762-63.*

PAUL GRAY

Carolyn Forché paid extended visits to El Salvador, working as a journalist and human rights advocate. She could not have known that land would be Topic A in the U.S. just at the time her second book appeared; thanks to that coincidence, though, some of the poems in *The Country Between Us* have the urgency of news bulletins. . . . (p. 83)

The brutalities visited on the helpless [in El Salvador] naturally arouse Forché's sympathy and anger. She makes pain palpable. Yet her accounts of antigovernment rebels are neither polemical nor romanticized: "It is not Che Guevara, this struggle." She addresses the guerrillas as friends but tells them what they do not want to hear. . . . [Forché's] is a bleak message, passionately stated. That description holds for the poems in this volume that are not about El Salvador; meditations on Viet Nam, Czechoslovakia, relatives, friends, lovers old and new. . . . What she has seen of the world so far has not made her a reassuring poet; but she is something better, an arresting and often unforgettable voice. (pp. 83-4)

Paul Gray, "Five Voices and Harmonies," in Time *(copyright 1982 Time Inc.; all rights reserved; reprinted by permission from* Time), *Vol. 119, No. 11, March 15, 1982, pp. 83-7.**

JOYCE CAROL OATES

Carolyn Forché, like Neruda, Philip Levine, Denise Levertov and others who have, in recent years, wed the "political" and the "personal," addresses herself unflinchingly to the exterior, historical world. In ["**The Country Between Us**"] her subject is primarily El Salvador, and her news is bleakly and succinctly stated: "What you have heard is true." (p. 13)

Carolyn Forché is blunt, unremitting, candid. There may be readers who object to her somewhat abstract—and apoetic—endorsement of a grief too great to have been experienced by any individual . . . , but her voice is never shrill or strident, and the horrific visions are nearly always contained within fully realized poems. . . .

[In Forché's poetry, El Salvador] is a nightmare country lucidly presented. . . .

Carolyn Forché's first book, **"Gathering the Tribes,"** . . . introduced a poet of uncommon vigor and assurance. **"The Country Between Us"** is a distinct step forward. Though one tends to remember vivid fragments of poems rather than wholes, the cumulative power of the volume is considerable. "In what time do we live," the poet asks, "that it is too late to have children?"—a partial view, but no less compelling, no less authentic. One feels that the poet has earned her bleak and wintry vision. . . . (p. 29)

> *Joyce Carol Oates, "Two Poets," in* The New York Times Book Review *(© 1982 by The New York Times Company; reprinted by permission), April 4, 1982, pp. 13, 28-9.**

KATHA POLLITT

Carolyn Forché's second book [*The Country Between Us*] is interesting both because Forché is a talented poet—her first book was a Yale Younger Poets selection—and because it tackles . . . political subject matter so uncongenial to young poets. The first section, dedicated to the memory of Oscar Romero, the murdered archbishop of San Salvador, is set in El Salvador, where Forché lived for two years and worked as a journalist. Other poems are addressed to old friends from the working-class Detroit neighborhood of Forché's childhood: one has become a steelworker haunted by memories of Vietnam; another, with whom Forché had shared adolescent dreams of travel and romance, lives with her husband and kids in a trailer. Elsewhere in the poems we meet a jailed Czech dissident, the wife of a "disappeared" Argentine and Terrence Des Pres, author of *The Survivor,* a study of the death camps. This is strong stuff, and the excited response *The Country Between Us* has already provoked shows, I think, how eager people are for poetry that acknowledges the grim political realities of our time.

At their best, Forché's poems have the immediacy of war correspondence, postcards from the volcano of twentieth-century barbarism. . . . "There is nothing one man will not do to another," Forché tells us. So shocking are the incidents reported here—so automatic is our horror at a mere list of places where atrocities have occurred ("Belsen, Dachau, Saigon, Phnom Penh")—that one feels almost guilty discussing these poems as poems, as though by doing so one were saying that style and tone and diction mattered more than bloody stumps and murdered peasants and the Holocaust.

This unease, though, should not have arisen in the first place, and it points to an underlying problem: the incongruity between Forché's themes and her poetic strategies. Forché's topics could not be more urgent, more extreme or more public, and at least one of her stated intentions is to make us look at them squarely. And yet, she uses a language designed for quite other purposes, the misty "poetic" language of the isolated, private self. She

gives us bloody stumps, but she also gives us snow, light and angels. (p. 562)

The trouble is, if her images are to bear the burdens Forché places on them and move us in the way she wants, a steel mill can't be a lovely play of light, or bodies dreamlike apparitions, or death either a calm voyage or the sleep of a baby. They have to be real.

When Forché speaks plainly, she can be very good indeed. **"The Expatriate"** is a clever satire on a young American left-wing poet whose idea of solidarity with the Third World is to move to Turkey and sleep with women who speak no English. (pp. 562-63)

Equally memorable is **"The Colonel,"** an account of dinner at the home of a right-wing Salvadoran officer, who, after the wine and the rack of lamb, dumps his collection of human ears on the table: "Something for your poetry, no?" The precise, observed details—the bored daughter filing her nails, the American cop show on TV, the parrot in the corner and the gold bell for the maid—work together to make a single impression, and the colonel himself, with his unpredictable swings between domestic boredom and jaunty brutality, is a vivid character. . . . Interestingly, in view of what I've been saying about Forché's poetics, **"The Colonel"** is written in prose.

Perhaps what I miss in this collection is simply verbal energy. The poems, especially the longer ones, do tend to blur in the mind. Forché insists more than once on the transforming power of what she has seen, on the gulf it has created between herself and those who have seen less and dared less. . . . But how can we grasp the power of this transforming vision when it is expressed in lackluster assertions ("I cannot keep going") and facile caricatures of "American men" as adulterous Babbitts?

Whether or not one admires Forché for stressing the intensity of her responses to the sufferings of others . . . the intensity is vitiated by the inadequate means by which it is conveyed. (p. 563)

The boldness of the promise [to defeat the torturers in **"Message"**] is undermined by the commonplace rhetoric ("hollow of earth" for "grave") and woolly syntax (the hands and lives dig into our deaths *after* the voice is dead?).

On the other hand, to make such a promise is not nothing, either. If poetry is to be more than a genteel and minor art form, it needs to encompass the material Forché presents. Much credit, then, belongs to Forché for her brave and impassioned attempt to make a place in her poems for starving children and bullet factories, for torturers and victims, for Margarita with her plastique bombs and José with his bloody stumps. What she needs now is language and imagery equal to her subjects and her convictions. The mists and angels of contemporary magazine verse are beneath her: she *has* seen too much, she has too much to say. Of how many poets today, I wonder, could that be said? (p. 564)

> *Katha Pollitt, "Poems on Public Subjects," in* The Nation *(copyright 1982 The Nation magazine, The Nation Associates, Inc.), Vol. 234, No. 18, May 8, 1982, pp. 562-64.*

ROCHELLE RATNER

In her recent book of essays, *Light Up the Cave,* Denise Levertov speaks of the need, in the 1960s, to create a new form for political poetry since, in the past, it had been narrative and epic in nature, and those forms were no longer viable. It is fitting, then, that Levertov says of this collection by Carolyn Forche:

> Here's a poet who's doing what I want to do . . . she is creating poems in which there is no seam between personal and political, lyrical and engaged.

Uncommon as blurbs go, there could be no better way to describe *The Country Between Us*. What is crucial here is that it took a poet of the next generation, a decade after the furor of the Vietnam War, to achieve what Levertov, among others, had been aiming for. . . .

Forche has learned she does not have to list the horrors over and over if she can find a few well-chosen incidents which speak for much more than themselves. Despite this knowledge, a poem such as **"Return"** is rhetorical; its four pages could exist for the final section alone, and is nearly saved by an excellent ending. But it proves that she, too, can get caught up in lists of flat description. . . .

What Forche, for the most part, remembers, what too many other political poets have forgotten, is that poetry's ultimate aim is transformation. And that transformation is, by its very nature, subtle. The finest poem is the one which closes this first section, **"Because One Is Always Forgotten."** Here, the political, the repugnant, becomes heightened lyricism. . . .

"The Visitor," describing the man in prison dreaming of his wife, ends "There is nothing one man will not do to another." And on the following page, **"The Colonel,"** a prose poem which can't help but be read as surrealistic, ends with the colonel pouring a sack of human ears on the table and flaunting them before his guests. This image of man as standing for cruelty and torture (a simplistic sensibility which would annoy me were it not for the fact that the poems themselves rise above

it) is strongest in **"Joseph,"** a poem for a childhood boyfriend who has returned from the Vietnam War fascinated by it and cherishing its memories. . . .

In **"As Children Together,"** one of the strongest poems, Forche can speak of childhood innocence without any trace of pretense. . . . The poem ends, two pages later, after describing Victoria's useless, trapped life with the husband mentally broken by the Vietnam War. . . .

By carrying over such images, the identification with friends and relatives at home echoes the attempt to identify with the people of El Salvador, lending a harshness, an urgency, and a sense of failure to the autobiographical poems. At the same time, it gives a calmness and a sense of lifelong continuance to the poems in the first section. . . .

Her craft, or a better word would be *refinement*, is most evident in Part II. One cannot help but think of Philip Levine's work: there is the same long, rambling and semi-conversational poem built around a few carefully chosen images, using the images to convey their final message—. . . .

To read only the poems in Part II, we would be reminded of the best University of Iowa graduates: a poetry extremely well-crafted, revealing a fashionable amount about the author, always promising to do more than it does but, in the final analysis, safe. And yet this same craft is at work in the first section as well, and it is precisely what keeps the poems above the level of rhetoric. Added to this, there is Forche's astute sense of observation, and a tendency to describe things in a way slightly out of the ordinary, so that our heads turn sharply around to look.

Rochelle Ratner, " 'The Country Between Us'," in The American Book Review *(© 1982 by The American Book Review), Vol. 5, No. 1, November-December, 1982, p. 24.*

Athol Fugard

1932-

South African dramatist, novelist, and scriptwriter.

Fugard is South Africa's foremost dramatist. Most of his plays, from *The Blood Knot*, his first major production, to his most recent, *"Master Harold"* . . . *and the Boys*, deal with the consequences of apartheid. They transcend propagandistic protest by their depth of characterization and their sensitive exploration into the pain of racial injustice. Most critics feel that Fugard attains universality in his plays regardless of their specific South African settings.

Fugard is a multi-talented man of the theater having acted in and directed several of his own plays. Of his many efforts to make theater available to black Africans, the most important resulted in the formation of a nonwhite theater company, the Serpent Players. *Sizwe Bansi Is Dead* and *The Island* were written in collaboration with two of the black actors in this company, Winston Ntshona and John Kenil.

Fugard's only novel, *Tsoti*, written over twenty years ago, has recently been published. While some critics find the transformation of its young black protagonist from a hoodlum into a caring human being unconvincing, most agree that Fugard, a white South African, has once again demonstrated his amazing empathy for the plight of his black compatriots.

(See also *CLC*, Vols. 5, 9, 14 and *Contemporary Authors*, Vols. 85-88, rev. ed.)

Photograph by Mary Benson; courtesy of William Morris Agency

JOHN MELLORS

In Athol Fugard's only novel [*Tsotsi*], which has been lying unpublished for 20 years, the protagonist is a murderer because he is a victim—victim of a régime and a philosophy which condemned him to the shanties of Sophiatown, and then virtually orphaned him in a police raid when he was a child of ten.

Tsotsi leads a gang of four young black men. They mug and murder, chiefly for money but also for kicks. . . . One night, he meets a young black woman who hands him a shoebox and runs away. In the box he finds a tiny baby. . . . The baby has the odd effect of triggering off memories in Tsotsi's mind and arousing the youth's curiosity about his own past. As he remembers, he changes character, coming to realise that he can choose whether to kill or not, instead of merely choosing whom to kill. At the end of the book he tries to save the baby's life and loses his own.

Tsotsi is an ambitious novel about the ability of a human being to rise above his environment and aspire to the good life. Squalor and violence are vividly presented. Fugard's indignation and pity are evident. However, the transformation of Tsotsi's character does not carry complete conviction. Too often, the author seems to be forcing his own insights and opinions on to his protagonist. And the climax, when the young man's body is found and 'all agreed that his smile was beautiful, and strange for a tsotsi', is rather too good to be true. (p. 482)

John Mellors, "Dreadful Things" (© British Broadcasting Corp. 1980; reprinted by permission of John Mellors), in The Listener, Vol. 103, No. 2657, April 10, 1980, pp. 482-83.*

CHRIS JONES

Marigolds in August is [a film] about black workers divided against themselves. The crippled Daan . . . works as a gardener in a white seaside village. He has been doing so for years, tending lawns, growing marigolds, but has little security—he hasn't the right papers.

Melton . . . is a farm boy, unemployed and facing eviction. With a child dead from malnutrition and a desperate wife, he arrives in the village in search of work—and is seen by Daan as a threat to his security.

The film begins with some evocative images. Daan, hobbling miles to work, is passed by a white South African on his pre-breakfast jog. The job-hunting Melton, reflected in the window of a bungalow, cannot even attract the attention of the bridge-playing white women inside. The essence of apartheid—apartness—is brilliantly caught.

But having constructed its dramatic dilemma in these clear, bold images, the film fails to resolve it with the same clarity.

Along comes Paulus (Athol Fugard himself), a dropout from the white world, a bicycle-riding philosopher who points out the folly of the two black protagonists.

Images give way to words, actions become heavily symbolic, and the dramatic problem is solved theatrically, not cinematically. The beauty of the early scenes goes, and, for me, much of the interest of the film.

Chris Jones, "Fugard's Images of Apartheid," in Tribune *(reprinted by permission of* Tribune, *London), Vol. 44, No. 29, July 18, 1980, p. 9.*

BRENDAN GILL

The title of Athol Fugard's new play, **"A Lesson from Aloes"** . . . , is so apt that its four words serve as an accurate précis of the entire work and threaten to render some of its more didactic passages superfluous. We are early instructed that aloes are a kind of plant to be found growing on the South African veldt; prickly and not very pleasing to look at, they survive in a hostile climate, and the lesson they furnish is that even against high odds life can assert itself and prove well worth living. Fugard's aloes are at once a metaphor and a model: the three characters who make up the cast are themselves—so we are invited to perceive—a higher form of aloes; if they are allowed to take root, they may be able (in the words of Faulkner's Nobel Prize speech) not only to endure but to prevail. Piet Bezuidenhout is a native white South African. . . . The time is 1963, and Piet, who was once a strenuous adversary of apartheid, has retired from—has perhaps been forcibly retired from—the hurly-burly of political activity. Now he collects aloes and the play begins with his having just brought in from the veldt a specimen that he is unable to identify. Is it a new species, hitherto unknown to science, or is it only a species unknown to him? Is he himself—so Fugard's metaphor insists that we ask—perhaps a new specimen of man, created to outwit the hateful political climate of apartheid?

Occupying the same house as Piet but seemingly light-years away from him is Gladys, his wife, who is suffering from an obscure mental derangement. . . . On this particular evening, Piet and Gladys are awaiting a visit from an old friend and political ally, a black man named Steve Daniels. Newly discharged from prison, Steve is bringing his wife and children to an impromptu farewell dinner before setting out for England and a new life there. . . .

Piet and Steve drink with an uneasy abandon, seeking to regain the camaraderie of a more violent day, while Gladys gloomily bides her time. Something has gone wrong among them, but Fugard is as calculatedly spare a writer as Pinter, and, like Pinter, he chooses to leave unfilled certain crucial gaps in our knowledge of his characters. The audience's nervous, incessant search for some means of bridging these gaps adds a notable degree of tension to the play. No action that we observe onstage is as important as the undescribed actions that have already taken place offstage; it is rather as if we were sitting through a "Hamlet" from which all reference to the murder of Hamlet's father had been omitted.

Suddenly, Gladys accuses Piet of being a government informer—the very informer who was responsible for sending Steve to prison. Steve is quick to join in the accusation. . . . Piet neither admits nor denies the evil of which he stands accused; with a mingling of pride and shame, he confesses only that he has nothing whatever to say. Forsaken by Steven

and by his mad wife as well, Piet sits in the darkening garden as the play ends, staring at the scruffy little aloe that he has yet to identify. Surely he is a good man, but what is the use of goodness if it has left him totally alienated from his fellow-creatures? All he can be certain of is that he is alone, and the weight of that aloneness presses as heavily upon him as the weight of the earth itself.

"A Lesson from Aloes" is a play almost devoid of overt incident, and, as directed by Fugard, is so slow to reach a resolution that I sometimes felt the pins and needles of an unappeasable impatience. My temptation was to exclaim (as I often do with Melville) "Good God, man! Get on with your story!," and it was disappointing for me to discover at last how little story Fugard had had it in mind to tell. His intention had been to wring our hearts by whispers, and I had been mistakenly awaiting loud shouts and the beating of innumerable drums.

Brendan Gill, "Survivors" (© 1980 by Brendan Gill), in The New Yorker, *Vol. LVI, No. 41, December 1, 1980, p. 153.*

TAMAR JACOBY

Very little happens on stage in *A Lesson From Aloes*. . . .

The deep mistrust between the three characters is not created by the action of the play or in any way resolved at its end: much more terrifying, their bitterness and suspicion are simply revealed and then thinly covered over as the work draws to a close. . . .

The people in *A Lesson From Aloes* are victims of South African repression. Yet the play is not a cry of outrage or protest. Fugard's pessimism leaves no room for leftist pieties. . . .

The violence in *A Lesson From Aloes* is suppressed violence, not the violence of revolutionary politics or of a repressive state, but violence that the characters turn against themselves and that divides them from one another: Steve's suspicion of his once-trusted comrade and the bitter envy that passes between Piet and his wife. Fugard is less concerned with South African politics than with the poisoned relations that exist in a certain kind of political climate. It would be too easy to blame the regime for the fear and mistrust that overwhelm the three characters in *A Lesson From Aloes*. . . .

Tsotsi is a somewhat heavy-handed parable about a young black hoodlum who turns away from his gang as he begins to sympathize with the suffering of the people he beats up and robs. His conversion is hard to believe and much of the prose sounds sentimental, but it reveals Fugard's early determination to look as closely and unflinchingly as possible at the violence and ugliness in the black township. In some passages, the setting is described in the emotional but generalized style that Alan Paton and James Agee use to describe poor people. . . .

The intensity of [Fugard's] descriptions is greatly undermined by the writer's habit of stepping in to explain their significance: what he calls "the full meaning and miracle of sharing in another man's suffering." Fugard's story is told in a didactic voice that allows his characters little room to move. Tsotsi's problem was how "to affirm his existence in the face of . . . nullity," the narrator tells us, commenting on "these thoughts, or his equivalents of them." Here and there Fugard looks ironically at the slow-witted hoodlum who thinks he can get anything he wants—even an explanation of God and the ''meaning'' of his life—with a few simple direct questions and a little bullying. But more often Fugard fails to distinguish clearly enough between the young thug and the narrator, sacrificing the story to a rather wooden lesson in his own existentialist beliefs.

Fugard's preoccupation with the tangled intimacy between bully and victim reappears in his first major play, *The Blood Knot*. . . . It is his most winning work for the theater, and has some of the sardonic humor that has marked most of his writing since *Tsotsi*. . . . The hate and fear that passed between the characters in *Tsotsi* are transformed [in *The Blood Knot*] into a kind of changeable ambivalence—seemingly playful, but no less threatening. (p. 37)

The Blood Knot showed how much Fugard had learned from reading Beckett's spare dialogue and how he had absorbed Beckett's feeling for two characters isolated on an empty stage. But Fugard had not abandoned what he calls, with no apology, his ''regional'' art. For him even the starkest absurdity must be rooted in a specific place. . . . Like much of Fugard's other work, *The Blood Knot* has been foolishly criticized for not being more specific about political problems in South Africa. But the starkly metaphoric style of the play makes one see in the antagonism between black and white man a complicity between master and servant that has little to do with legal restrictions. . . .

By the late Sixties Fugard had begun to retreat from the emphasis on the ''absurd'' one finds in *Boesman and Lena* and also from what he has called ''the inquisition of blank paper''; he worked out plays not at his writing table but through improvisations with actors, which he later rewrote. What are perhaps his best-known plays, *Sizwe Bansi Is Dead* and *The Island* . . . , were devised in collaboration with two black actors, John Kani and Winston Ntshona. Like many other members of Serpent Players, a group that Fugard had been directing since the early Sixties, they were untrained amateurs who worked during the day in menial factory jobs. They brought to Fugard's improvisation sessions their own direct concerns as black South Africans: for the passbook laws which provide the plot of *Sizwe Bansi* and the treatment of political prisoners on Robben Island. They used a hard sarcasm that was new to Fugard's work—a kind of ruthless banter that is never simple about politics and cuts even deeper than the humor of *The Blood Knot*. . . .

[*The Island* is] savage in tone. When John learns that he will soon be released from prison, Winston goads him with a description of the freedom that awaits him. John is simply reluctant to ruin the pleasure by anticipating it. But for Winston the vision of John drinking among their friends is an almost unbearable torment. . . . In the last scene of the play, when the two men perform *Antigone* for the other prisoners on the island, their thinly veiled comment on the injustice of the South African regime comes as little more than a bitter ironic coda to Winston's devastating outburst.

There is something of this deliberately unresolved ambivalence in *A Lesson From Aloes*: Piet's political activity is at once honorable and futile. . . .

[In this] new play, as before, Fugard's central concern is the snarled relation between two characters: the tenderness and loyalty that pass between Piet and Gladys, but also his feelings of guilt and her resentment of his strength. Piet is determined not to give in to the sense of futility that has troubled Gladys and Steve since they were humiliated by the police. (p. 38)

As long as the characters remain on stage together their efforts to be in touch with each other seem to match the threat of isolation and purposelessness—after all, without others around him, even Piet would have no sense of purpose. As long as they go on talking there is some hope that they may be able to sustain the illusion of their intimacy. But worse even than Gladys's perverse attempt to persuade Steve that it was Piet who betrayed him to the police is Piet's reply that he has ''nothing to say'' to the accusation. Piet has lost the will even to make a gesture to the other man. In the end, Steve goes home to continue packing and Gladys decides she must return to the asylum. Piet is left alone in the garden with his aloes. This resilient desert plant, which at times risks being an obvious symbol, now takes on yet another meaning. Throughout the evening, as Piet tends and boasts about the aloes, filling the awkward silences with talk about the varieties of the species, he seems at first funny, then pitiable, then courageous in his steadfast way. But his determined good humor will mean little if there is no one to listen. Fugard no longer sees much scope for heroes in South Africa.

A Lesson From Aloes takes place in a milieu very different from the ones in Fugard's earlier plays. The characters are not vagrants or hoods, but include an Afrikaner like himself and an English South African woman, all of them educated and politically aware. They face the real growing tension in South Africa and the question, which also troubles Fugard, of whether to leave the country. It is not Fugard's old preoccupation with the bitterness that can be part of intimacy and the courage of survivors but the texture of his work that has changed as he moves away from the symbolic style of his early plays. The new play is even bolder than the others in its direct use of South African experience. The author of *Tsotsi* is still determined to watch what is happening around him, no matter how ugly. (pp. 38-9)

Tamar Jacoby, *''No Place for Heroes,'' in* The New York Review of Books *(reprinted with permission from* The New York Review of Books; *copyright © 1981 Nyrev, Inc.),* Vol. XXVIII, No. 2, February 19, 1981, pp. 37-9.

ROBERT ASAHINA

There is little sentimentality to be found in Athol Fugard's *A Lesson from Aloes,* a searing three-character drama that has been receiving rave reviews—to my mind underserved. (p. 102)

There can be no doubt that Fugard means us to be as deeply involved as he is with his characters' fates; for years he has been heroically exposing the cost of *apartheid* in human suffering. Yet it is not his sincerity but his art that I question; for all its deep wells of feeling, which Fugard is not afraid to tap unembarrassedly, *A Lesson from Aloes* is a confused and ultimately artificial drama.

Too much of the characters' behavior is ill-motivated. Why should the Special Branch's confiscation of her diaries drive Gladys to a mental hospital? How can she possibly compare the ''violation'' of her privacy to literal rape . . . ? And why does Piet go into seclusion and allow his former comrades to blame him for Steve's arrest?

If he hadn't, of course, there would be no dramatic mainspring to propel us into Act II. Yet I can't help thinking that Fugard has simply fallen back on what might be called the Arthur Miller ploy. Just as John Proctor allowed himself to be executed in *The Crucible* for something he was not (a witch) because of his remorse over something he was (an adulterer), Piet permits the others to think him guilty of betrayal because he feels responsible for his wife's condition. But this is the kind of implausible behavior that occurs only on stage. Why should Piet accept Gladys' blame for the consequences of the raid, when he clearly was in no position to do anything about it—and when she must have been unstable in the first place to allow it to affect her so?

What all the furious denunciation and counter-denunciation in *A Lesson From Aloes* adds up to is little more than the familiar dramatic strategy of recriminations leading to revelations—a scheme that effectively bares a past obscured by the present, but does little to move the play into the future. Perhaps this was Fugard's intention, to show the absence of any future; the bitter irony of his setting such a hopeless situation in 1963, knowing full well that things have not improved in the intervening 17 years, is all too obvious.

Yet the clunky symbolism of the play seems to argue in the opposite direction. On the one hand, Gladys denounces Piet's aloes as "turgid with violence—like everything else in this country." "Is that the price of survival—thorns and bitterness?" she asks. Yet it is Piet who is surviving and persisting, after all; Gladys seems to be heading back to the institution at the end of the play, and Steve is off for England. Are we supposed to deplore or admire Piet's stolid enduring of his wife's abuse, his comrades' unjustified accusations, and even his best friend's suspicion—not to mention his continuing to live as an exile in his own home, a nation whose policies he abhors? (p. 103)

Robert Asahina, "Theatre Chronicle," in The Hudson Review *(copyright © 1981 by The Hudson Review, Inc.; reprinted by permission), Vol. XXXIV, No. 1, Spring, 1981, pp. 99-104.**

SHEILA ROBERTS

What is particularly fascinating about *Tsotsi* for the student of Fugard's drama is the discovery of so many scenes, ideas and conversations that Fugard was later to use expanded and elaborated in his plays. . . .

Tsotsi is evidence that had Fugard chosen a career as a novelist instead of being a playwright, he would have done important work. Here he develops at least three major characters and even more secondary ones. Tsotsi himself is a disturbing, haunting creation who remains in the reader's consciousness long after the book has been put down. The narrative strands . . . are cleverly interwoven. . . . The reader is moved by the depth of emotion with which Fugard constructs, piece by piece, the memories of childhood that return gradually to Tsotsi. . . . Tsotsi's unsuspected humanity and instinctive protectiveness have no tinge of that sudden, unconvincing character reversal dear to the pen of the amateur, and these scenes never degenerate into sentimentality.

But Fugard's greatest skill, it seems to me, is his use of language, his images, his rhythms and his ability to alter his style, pace and diction to suit the personality of each character. This is certainly a skill that was to prove useful to him in his development as a playwright. In *Tsotsi* it creates a rich, subtle, human world out of the poor, outward uniformity of the township.

Sheila Roberts, "South Africa: 'Tsotsi'," in World Literature Today *(copyright 1981 by the University*

of Oklahoma Press), Vol. 55, No. 2, Spring, 1981, p. 366.

GEORGE KEARNS

[*Tsotsi*] is an intense work set in a South African slum. The protagonist, a *tsotsi* ("thug" or "hoodlum")—he knows no other name—is a brutal leader of a small-time gang of murdering thieves; he has no past he can remember, no feelings, no conscience; his vision reaches no farther than the planning of each day's crime. Fugard attempts to convey the workings of this *tsotsi*'s mind as it moves from a brutish, atemporal condition toward the beginnings of "human" instincts, sympathies and conscience. . . . Fugard can hypnotize with his sense of place, and the condemnation of policies that have created such a place is stronger for being left implied rather than lectured on. Yet his confining the action of the novel to six days presents me with something of the problem I have in reading classical French or Restoration tragedy—knowing that "unity of time" is a convention doesn't help. Fugard's attempt to bring his *tsotsi* from near-animal to man within so constricted a time seems unnecessarily artificial. For all its earnestness, *Tsotsi* is too realistic to work as fable, and too fabular to convince as psychology or tragedy. (pp. 309-10)

George Kearns, "Fiction Chronicle," in The Hudson Review *(copyright © 1981 by The Hudson Review, Inc.; reprinted by permission), Vol. XXXIV, No. 2, Summer, 1981, pp. 299-313.**

CLIVE BARNES

[*Master Harold . . . and the Boys*] is a molotov-cocktail kind of a play. At first, as it almost creakingly gets going, it seems a homemade, almost ramshackle kind of play, but when it explodes, like an unexpected thunderclap, it doesn't make the rafters ring, it leaves them blackened.

And this intensely, but subtly political play, leaves the audience drained by the barely simulated intensity of its experience. It is a play that grabs you to its own heart with bands of steel.

It is a political play about South Africa. It is about the South African policy of apartheid—racial segregation—but it is about much more. To Fugard—South Africa's best-known artist—life is not a simplistic matter of black and white.

Thus, in the most general terms, *Master Harold* is a tragicomedy concerned with growing up and living together. . . .

Eventually, the play's texture becomes thrillingly complex. We are watching the emotional death of a young boy, but although Fugard is anything but nihilistic, also, the emotional death of a nation. Yet Fugard interweaves his themes with consummate skill. And the play's delayed explosion—it is as if, to change the metaphor, the play shifted the gears of its intention midway—casts, by the end, an ashladen retrospective glow on the beginning.

Fugard has directed the play himself with the utmost certainty—knowing precisely the effects he needs, the lines he can waste, the tension he can spare. He has the nerve to wait longer than most directors would to wind up that tension, to change that gear. And when he does, all frozen hell crashes loose. . . .

This is an exhilarating play. It sends you out into the world's cold air, shattered but uplifted, even cleansed. It is a triumph of playmaking, and unforgettable.

Clive Barnes, "'Master Harold' is Masterful Look at South African Life," in New York Post (reprinted by permission of the New York Post; © 1982, News Group Publications, Inc.), May 5, 1982 (and reprinted in New York Theatre Critics' Reviews, Vol. XXXXIII, No. 6, May 3-10, 1982, p. 307).

FRANK RICH

There may be two or three living playwrights in the world who can write as well as Athol Fugard, but I'm not sure that any of them has written a recent play that can match "'**Master Harold**' . . . **and the Boys.**" Mr. Fugard's drama—lyrical in design, shattering in impact—is likely to be an enduring part of the theater long after most of this Broadway season has turned to dust.

"**Master Harold**" . . . may even outlast the society that spawned it—the racially divided South Africa of apartheid. Though Mr. Fugard's play is set there in 1950, it could take place nearly anywhere at any time. The word "apartheid" is never mentioned; the South African references are minimal. The question that Mr. Fugard raises—how can men of all kinds find the courage to love one another?—is dealt with at such a profound level that "**Master Harold**" sweeps quickly beyond the transitory specifics of any one nation. . . .

What's more, the author deals with his issue without attitudinizing, without sentimentality, without lecturing the audience. "**Master Harold**" isn't another problem play in which people stand for ideological positions. By turns funny and tragic, it uncovers its moral imperatives by burrowing deeply into the small, intimately observed details of its three characters' lives.

We meet those characters on a rainy afternoon, as they josh and chat in a fading tea room. Two of them [Sam and Willie] . . . are black waiters who rehearse for a coming ballroom dancing contest while tidying up the restaurant. . . . Eventually they are joined by Hally . . . who is the son of the tea room's owner. . . .

The black servants are the boy's second family: they have been employed by his parents since Hally was in short trousers. But, for all the easy camaraderie and tender memories that unite master and servants, there's a slight distance in their relationship, too. . . .

The drama is catalyzed by a series of phone calls Hally receives from his real-life family offstage. Hally's father, we learn, is a drunk, a cripple and a racist; his mother is his long-suffering victim. Hally is caught between them, and, as old wounds are ripped open, the bitterness of his entire childhood comes raging to the surface. The boy is soon awash in tearful self-pity and, in the absence of his real father, takes out his anger on his surrogate father, Sam. What follows is an unstoppable, almost unwatchable outpouring of ugliness, in which Hally humiliates the black man he loves by insisting that he call him "Master Harold," by mocking their years of shared secrets, by spitting in his face.

Mr. Fugard's point is simple enough: Before we can practice compassion—before we can, as Sam says, "dance life like champions"—we must learn to respect ourselves. It is Hally's self-hatred that leads him to strike at the black man and his

crippled Dad and, in this sense, the boy is typical of anyone who attacks the defenseless to bolster his own self-esteem.

But "**Master Harold**" unlike many works that deal with the genesis of hatred, forces us to identify with the character who inflicts the cruelty. We like Hally so much in the play's early stages, and empathize with his familiar sorrow so keenly later on, that it's impossible to pull back once he lashes out. And because we can't sever ourselves from Hally, we're forced to confront our own capacity for cruelty—and to see all too clearly just who it is we really hurt when we give in to it.

Mr. Fugard can achieve this effect because he has the guts to face his own shame: Hally, a fledgling artist who believes in social reform, is too richly drawn not to be a ruthlessly honest portrait of the playwright as a young man. But if Mr. Fugard's relentless conscience gives "**Master Harold**" its remarkable moral center, his brilliance as an artist gives the play its classic esthetic simplicity. (p. 305)

The author doesn't provide [a] . . . happy ending, of course—it's not his to confer. But if "**Master Harold**" finally lifts us all the way from pain to hope, it's because Mr. Fugard insists that that ending can be—must be—ours to write. (p. 306)

Frank Rich, "Stage: 'Master Harold', Fugard's Drama on Origin of Hate," in The New York Times (© 1982 by The New York Times Company; reprinted by permission), May 5, 1982 (and reprinted in New York Theatre Critics' Reviews, Vol. XXXXIII, No. 6, May 3-10, 1982, pp. 305-06).

JOHN SIMON

Except for the overexplicit title, all is well with Athol Fugard's "**Master Harold**" . . . **and the boys.** Fugard has now perfected his way of writing plays about the tragedy of apartheid; he avoids the spectacular horrors and concentrates instead on the subtle corrosion and corruption, on the crumbling of the spirit for which the cure would be heroic action that may not be forthcoming, and which the blacks try to assuage with the salve of dreams, the whites with the cautery of oppression. For Fugard, the ultimate evil is the weakness, the cowardice, that is one of the constituents of so much human nature. When, rarely, unalloyed nobility does occur, its chances of prevailing are slim. Yet it exists, and its mere existence is reason enough for not wiping the name of mankind off the slate. The play springs two wonders on us: It is devastating without being depressing, and it is pungently specific without any loss in universality. . . .

"Master" Harold has a tricky, touchy relationship with Sam and Willie, the two black employees. . . . Not only are the relations between the white boy and the black men who helped him grow up an intricate network of generosities and withholdings, of frustrations and humiliations (not entirely one-sided, though the boy is selfish and the men are a trifle, just a trifle, too good), but even the interaction between Sam and Willie has its curious yet credible complexities. The psychological sharpness, dramatic scope, and existential suggestivity that Fugard wrests from humble but never trite ingredients are a precious, precarious compensation for the ills of being. The author cannot legislate justice for South Africa or the rest of the world, but his plays are among the few small, doughty justifications for carrying on. . . .

And Mr. Fugard directs with the same insight and control with which he writes. There is, despite the noble metaphor of life as ballroom dancing, a certain dearth of language here: These characters, almost by definition, cannot talk poetry, which only a few masters, such as Beckett, have been able to extract from rock-bottom prose. O'Neill, for instance, never quite could, yet it did not finally keep him from greatness. What Fugard offers is wave upon wave of comprehension, compassion, and achingly autobiographical honesty that create a poetry of their own. (p. 76)

John Simon, "Two Harolds and No Medea," in New York Magazine (copyright © 1982 by News Group Publications, Inc.; reprinted with the permission of New York Magazine), Vol. 15, No. 20, May 17, 1982, pp. 76, 79.*

BRENDAN GILL

["'**Master Harold**' . . . **and the Boys**"] has been almost universally hailed as a masterpiece, perhaps in part because its subject is a meritorious one—the turpitude of South Africa's continued policy of apartheid and, on a deeper level, the heartbreak implicit in every failure of respect and affection that takes place between human beings of whatever color, gender, age, and social position. To my mind, the play has a tendentious neatness of design that we often see and distrust in an overly literary short story. Mr. Fugard's Harold is a schoolboy who, like young Stephen Dedalus, is going to grow up to be a writer; at present, he is a miserable loner with a drunken father, an inattentive mother, and but two friends in the world—the black "boys" of the title, who make up the staff of his mother's not very properous-seeming tearoom. The play is short, and could have been shorter; the opening dialogue between the two blacks, which has to do with a forthcoming dance contest (and which also provides the means for a pleasantly sentimental final curtain), covers more time than ground, though it is amusing enough, and the climax of the plot, which amounts to a truly shocking coup de théâtre, is so thoroughly prepared for that one anticipates it rather as if it were an automobile accident that one observes approaching and yet can do nothing to prevent. (pp. 110, 112)

Brendan Gill, "B.C. to A.D." (© 1982 by Brendan Gill), in The New Yorker, Vol. LVIII, No. 13, May 17, 1982, pp. 110, 112, 114-15.*

ROBERT BRUSTEIN

[Athol Fugard's *Master Harold . . . and the boys*] like this South African playwright's other works, is distinguished more by his majestic spirit than by his artistic gifts. Fugard is not a dramatist of the first rank in a class with Beckett, Brecht, or even the late O'Neill—he makes no deep metaphysical probes, he fashions no striking poetic images, he doesn't change our way of looking at the world. His theatrical impulses are similar to those of Jean-Paul Sartre, Arthur Miller, Arnold Wesker—writers who put their craft at the service of an idea. Like them, Fugard is more interested in identifying social injustices and inequities than in transforming consciousness, which is to say that he is less a visionary poet than a man of great liberal conscience. Fugard's conscience, however, is a judicious instrument—scrupulous without being paralyzed, partial without being simplified. He avoids self-righteousness—the customary pitfall of such writing—by acknowledging that he may be implicated in his own indictments. If not the most inspired of contemporary playwrights, he certainly has the greatest heart, which makes him the most attractive character in his plays.

Fugard's compelling subject is the corrosive effect of apartheid on the spirit of South Africa; in *Master Harold,* he may have found his quintessential racial anecdote. . . . In the scorching concluding moments of the play, [Hally] insists that "the boys" call him "Master Harold," then tells a brutal racist joke and spits in Sam's face. . . .

Sam tries to turn the occasion into a positive learning experience about how one becomes a man; Hally is too ashamed to accept instruction. Sam offers reconciliation; Hally equivocates. The two part with a shared sense of failure and a shared conviction that the dream of racial brotherhood has suffered a damaging, perhaps irreparable blow. . . .

Fugard arranges his anecdote as if he were placing tiles in a mosaic. This sometimes creates an impression of contrivance—twice the phone rings, for example, with information that turns Hally vicious right after he has made fervent humanitarian affirmations. Then, perhaps because Sam's insights into the self-hatred motivating Hally's behavior are so cogent, you are left with a sense that everything has been said, that there is nothing more to be revealed, which robs the evening of ambiguity and suggestiveness. Still, there is no denying the explosive impact of that ending, and Fugard has directed a performance from the three players that is muscular and powerful. (p. 30)

The real spiritual beauty of the play comes from Fugard. *Master Harold* seems to be a much more personal statement than his other works; it also suggests that his obsession with the theme of racial injustice may be an expression of his own guilt, an act of expiation. Whatever the case, his writing continues to exude a sweetness and sanctity that more than compensates for what might be prosaic, rhetorical, or contrived about it. At this rate, Athol Fugard may become the first playwright in history to be a candidate for canonization. (pp. 30-1)

Robert Brustein, "Coming at History from Two Sides" (reprinted by permission of the author; © 1982 by Robert Brustein), in The New Republic, Vol. 186, No. 25, June 23, 1982, pp. 30-1.

Charles (H.) Fuller (Jr.)

1939-

Black American playwright.

Fuller explores racism as it relates to a small group of people and to society at large. Honestly and intelligently created, his black and white characters are whole people, not stereotypes. The racial conflict in which they are involved is therefore deeply disturbing—one recognizes Fuller's characters as profoundly human and the racism they face as tragically true.

The Brownsville Raid, **Fuller's first major success, is based on a true historical incident. In an almost documentary form and in a restrained style, Fuller artistically constructs the story of the dishonorable discharge of an entire black regiment from the U.S. Army. His portrayal of the black sergeant's subsequent crisis of faith is particularly moving.**

In 1982, Fuller won the Pulitzer Prize in drama for *A Soldier's Play,* **also a drama with a military setting. Though developed as a murder mystery, the real mystery studied is human behavior, in particular, black and white relations. As with** *The Brownsville Raid,* **critics of** *A Soldier's Play* **acclaim its authenticity and depth. Frank Rich describes the latter work as refracting "the effects of racism through people, without having us watch a fire-breathing white racist slap someone around."**

(See also *Contemporary Authors,* **Vol. 108 [brief entry].)**

Photograph by Arthur W. Wang

DAN SULLIVAN

["**The Village: A Party**"] leaves you thinking. Mr. Fuller has written a not-too-fanciful fantasy about racial integration that somberly concludes that it will not at present solve anybody's racial problems.

A charismatic black man, married to a white girl, has founded a community for other racially mixed couples. Superficially, the community has been a success, both in terms of the personal happiness of its members and the edification of the world at large; but now its leader has found another woman, and she is black.

Fearing for the community's "image" if their leader is allowed to defect from his dream, the group strikes him down at a birthday party. His widow it is decided, must marry a black man. Utopia has become not just a ghetto but a cell-block.

Mr. Fuller's initial situation is so intellectually provocative that his resolution seems disappointingly melodramatic. Even in a symbolic context, it is as hard to believe that these suburban types would automatically devour their leader as it was to believe a similar situation in Edward Albee's "Everything in the Garden"; in such well-appointed living rooms, discussion always precedes—and generally replaces—action.

However, "**The Village**" has enough things right with it to make you want to watch Mr. Fuller. His dialogue can crackle—"I knew you before you were black, Nick," the leader's wife tells him bitterly—and he knows how to make a point without words, as when the partygoers are shocked to find themselves pairing off for cards according to race, blacks with blacks, whites with whites.

The argument of Mr. Fuller's play—that integration exacerbates rather than relieves racial tensions—is too important to be treated in the brief fashion allowed here. The play's originality and urgency are unquestionable and so is the talent of the playwright.

> Dan Sullivan, "In Switch, Princeton Offers New Plays and Club Here an Old One," in The New York Times (© 1968 by The New York Times Company; reprinted by permission), November 13, 1968, p. 39.*

LAWRENCE VAN GELDER

[While] racial strife sunders the world outside, five husbands and wives who founded a village for integrated couples like themselves, meet for a birthday party.

With that as a beginning, "**The Perfect Party**" [or "**The Village: A Party**"] . . . proceeds to raise a number of questions and to answer some.

How are the marriages faring and why? Is the village a success? Is integration a realistic solution to the problems of blacks and whites in American society? . . .

As the couples—drinking, dancing, dining—circulate . . . Mr. Fuller examines them as individuals, as husbands and wives and as members of society. . . .

As individuals, the 10 characters appear little better or worse than any others. As partners in integrated marriages, they seem unable to surmount their own self-consciousness, ever ready to assume that their problems are soley the product of differences in race. Could there be no other reasons? Mr. Fuller appears to think not.

Given the caliber of the people concerned and their pervasive inability to confront their marriages in other than racial terms, the fate of the community is obvious. . . .

Mr. Fuller's smooth, natural dialogue and deft characterizations . . . keep **"The Perfect Party"** at a high level of interest until it falls victim to a quick, weak ending.

Mr. Fuller has permitted his blacks and whites to integrate but has barred them an opportunity to blend. The question of what might have been, or yet may be, remains open.

> Lawrence Van Gelder, *"Intermarriage under a Microscope,"* in The New York Times (© 1969 by The New York Times Company; reprinted by permission), March 21, 1969, p. 42.

MEL GUSSOW

["**In the Deepest Part of Sleep"**] is about the debilitating effect of a mentally disturbed mother on a Philadelphia family in the mid-nineteen-fifties.

As seen through the eyes of a young black adolescent on the brink of manhood, this may be a true experience, at least for the playwright, but it does not hold much interest as theatre.

As was also evident in Mr. Fuller's **"Candidate!"**, . . . the author has a tendency to overdraw his characters and his situations. . . .

In **"In the Deepest Part of Sleep,"** the mother, released from the hospital after a breakdown, makes obsessive demands on her son, his step-father and her nurse, who is decidedly provocative to both males in the family.

The situation is an obvious one, but it still might be dramatically viable if it were written with insight or at least if it were played in a natural, straightforward manner.

In the opening minutes the play is stricken by bathos and never fully recovers. . . . [The mother] cries and moans so much that she loses all of our sympathy (and we wonder how the other characters are able to endure her). The play continues, predictably, even, in the end, to a suggestion of an incestuous relationship. . . .

There are several moments in **"Deepest Sleep"**—just as there were in **"Candidate!"** (which was about the election of a black mayor in a northern city)—that make it clear that Mr. Fuller is a playwright who should be heard from.

In one touching encounter . . . the mother confesses her sexual craving to her husband, and when rebuffed, switches immediately to verbal attack. In another, the nurse tries to seduce the son, and the playwright is shrewdly observant about the ineptness of adolescence.

Unfortunately these are only flashes of reality in a play that asks for too much indulgence.

> Mel Gussow, *"Negro Ensemble Stages Fuller's 'Deepest Sleep',"* in The New York Times (© 1974 by The New York Times Company; reprinted by permission), June 5, 1974, p. 54.

MARTIN GOTTFRIED

[**"The Brownsville Raid"**] is based on a true incident. In 1906 the small southern town of Brownsville, Texas was shot up, with one fatality. The townspeople agreed that the rioters were soldiers from the nearby Army base, where the all-black 25th Infantry was stationed. Though there was neither consistency nor evidence from these witnesses, when none of the soldiers confessed the entire regiment of 167 men was dishonorably discharged. No formal charges were ever presented, no trial was ever conducted.

Though it is Fuller's intention to condemn this incident for the disgrace it was, his play is no mere tract. His white characters are not caricatures, his black soldiers are not made to be aware ahead of their times.

They are ordinary men, products of their era. They don't know they should resent their segregation in an all-black regiment. They are too acustomed to being ineligible for commissions to be angry about it. Treatment of them as inferiors was the American way and, in fact, they are proud to be soldiers, proud of the Army.

Such keeping of faith with social history was disciplined of Fuller and the discipline paid off. The power of his play lies in the realization of his characters that they have placed their faith in an Army, an America that would betray them the first chance it got. By staying his anger until it could pay off dramatically, Fuller reaped a more telling harvest of theatrical and thematic power.

His characters are members of a platoon in the doomed regiment. Several are shown, early on, sneaking into the barracks during the shoot-up. For a long stretch of the play they are very possibly guilty and their white captain is not painted as a bigot pure and simple. Quite the contrary, he isn't even a hypocritical liberal. He assumes his men to be honest and knows the locals for the rednecks they are. Only a threat to his career brings out his bigotry. (pp. 77-8)

Booker T. Washington doesn't appear in the play, his representative does, but Fuller is a playwright, not a ratifier of slogans. Washington is treated these days as the ultimate Uncle Tom and though Fuller suggests the man's compromises, they are far from unbitter.

So the play has control over its tone as well as an artistry to its construction. It also has its flaws. There are unnecessary domestic scenes between the platoon sergeant and his wife. There are romantic plot complications that are pure mechanics. The ending tries for irony in an overly familiar way, with the calling off of the soldiers' ultimate fates. . . .

By and large, though, the play is engrossing, unusual and strong. (p. 78)

> Martin Gottfried, *"A Powerful Play in 'Brownsville',"* in New York Post (reprinted by permission of the New York Post; © 1976, New York Post Corporation), December 6, 1976 (and reprinted in New York Theatre Critics' Reviews, Vol. XXXVII, No. 25, December 6, 1976, pp. 77-8).

EDITH OLIVER

Most of the action of **"The Brownsville Raid"** takes place in the barracks of one company, with additional scenes in the quarters of its black sergeant, Mingo Saunders; in the office of its white captain; and in Roosevelt's office in Washington. The script, although documentary in form, escapes most of the pitfalls of fact-as-fiction. . . . The vitality of the play is in the barracks, and so little is known today about the enlisted men that they are, to all intents, madeup characters. At first, as they go about their military routines, they seem almost anonymous, but so skillfully has Mr. Fuller delineated them that at the end, when each soldier is stripped of his rifle and insignia, while drums are ruffled and an orderly at attention reads to the audience a résumé of what happened to the man in later life, we know all of them pretty well.

The small personal dramas within the large one provide the conflicts and the mystery. . . . With one exception, Mr. Fuller's white characters are as interesting and as free of stereotype as his black ones. The exception is Theodore Roosevelt, who . . . is a cardboard figure out of a historical pageant. But **"The Brownsville Raid"** is no pageant; it is a tragedy, and its pivot is Sergeant Mingo Saunders, whose faith in the Army, after twenty-six years of service, and in the Army's obligation to protect its men, as he protects and rallies and bosses the handful of soldiers under him, is betrayed and totally shattered.

Edith Oliver, "Off Broadway," in The New Yorker *(© 1976 by The New Yorker Magazine, Inc.), Vol. LII, No. 44, December 20, 1976, p. 84.*

JULIUS NOVICK

The moral [of *The Brownsville Raid*] seems to be that black people had better beware of trusting white institutions, and the play carries all the more conviction for being written without hysteria or undue whitey-baiting. All I know about the Brownsville raid I know from Mr. Fuller's play; yet I had no hesitation in accepting his account as essentially factual.

The Brownsville Raid is scrupulous dramatically as well as ideologically: clear, methodical—and a bit dull. It feels as though it had been written according to a manual of playwriting: Everything is planted, prepared for, cemented carefully into place. The characters are plausible enough, but there is not much life to them. The dialogue is stiff and, in a bad sense, rhetorical. "There is just one thing we can do," the sergeant tells his troops, "and that is to stand together like men." Somebody even gets to say, "You forget yourself."

On the sidewalk during an intermission, I spoke up for the play. "It's not sloppy for a minute," I said. "And it's not imaginative for a second," said my friend. Well, at the very end it does become imaginative, for several seconds. As the men are discharged and have their stripes torn off their uniforms, the orderly who reads their names goes on to state what is known about what happened to each man after his discharge, suggesting with understated power how the discharge wrecked the lives of a number of men who had believed in the army. It is a telling stroke, but a small one—scarcely enough to redeem an entire evening. I do not blame Mr. Fuller for having written a realistic play—my continued faith in the possibilities of realism is a source of embarrassment to many of my friends—but for writing the kind of ploddingly conventional play that the enemies of realism have in mind when they attack. (p. 112)

Julius Novick, "How to Write a Play, Dully" (reprinted by permission of The Village Voice *and the author; copyright © The Village Voice, Inc., 1976), in* The Village Voice, *Vol. XXI, No. 51, December 20, 1976, pp. 111-12.*

GERALD WEALES

[*Zooman and the Sign* shows Charles Fuller] as an obviously talented playwright, ambitious in his attempt to deal with difficult and complex themes. Set in Philadelphia—suggested by an actual killing that occurred in that city—*Zooman* is concerned with the killer, the grieving family of the victim, and the presumably disintegrating society of which they are products and symptoms. The victim, who is dead when the play begins, is a little girl, killed accidentally as she played jacks on her front stoop. While her family acts out its grief, its need for vengeance or for justice, the teen-age killer is presented to the audience, a jittering, swaggering, self-justifying creature, constantly talking in a fragmented monologue that tells everything to the audience without ever explaining anything. We get the conventional biography—the missing family, the doubtful comradeship of fellow street hustlers, the piddling triumphs of a pointless existence—but the strength of Fuller's Zooman is that his strut and clamor define an imaginary reality in which his every act of violence is a righteous response to the aggression of women who will not let go of their purses, of little girls who persist in being in the line of stray bullets. Without excusing Zooman with the once fashionable assumptions about society as the real criminal, Fuller presents a character who has found his own unhappy, insufficient response to a world that he has known only in the physical and spiritual ruins around him.

The dead girl's family and the neighborhood in which they live are evidence of that decline. The family was coming apart before the murder, the husband and wife living separately. The girl's brother responds to her death by getting a gun, an impulse toward violence which is echoed in the angry speeches of his great uncle. The neighborhood, each family closed in on itself protectively, refuses to give evidence, not to cause trouble, not to become visible. No family, no community, this is a world that Zooman understands and can deal with, but, when the father hangs up the sign on the front porch, calling for witnesses, calling attention to the crime, the house, the street, the bewildered Zooman (in anger and disbelief) comes to tear it down and dies at the uncle's hand. His death becomes part of a larger loss, the loss of the victim and the values which her father somehow hopes to reinvigorate with his sign. The difficulty with the play is that Zooman is so completely realized . . . that the rest of the characters, however individualized, tend to become representative figures rather than fully formed people. Then, too, the second important theme, the one embedded in the neighborhood's angry response to the sign, is never fully realized, that important confrontation dying with Zooman. The play never quite succeeds in the ambitious terms in which it is conceived, but its aspirations and its incidental strengths make it far more fascinating than many a neater, smaller play. (pp. 600-01)

Gerald Weales, "American Theater Watch 1980-1981: 'Zooman and the Sign'," in The Georgia Review *(copyright, 1981, by the University of Georgia), Vol. XXXV, No. 3, Fall, 1981, pp. 600-01.*

FRANK RICH

"A Soldier's Play" is, to put it simply, a major breakthrough for the promising author of **"The Brownsville Raid"** and last season's **"Zooman and the Sign."** This is, in every way, a mature and accomplished work—from its inspired opening up of a conventional theatrical form to its skillful portraiture of a dozen characters to its remarkable breadth of social and historical vision. It's also a play that speaks to both blacks and whites without ever patronizing either group. Mr. Fuller writes characters of both races well—and he implicates both in the murder of Sergeant Waters. . . .

Waters isn't as simple as he seems in the play's early flashbacks. For all his venom and cruelty, he was also a prideful man who refused to toady to whites and who often wanted the best for his fellow blacks. "Who the hell was he?" asks the prosecutor in frustration as the evidence comes in—and it soon becomes apparent that the case can't be solved until that question is resolved.

As the answer comes, Mr. Fuller uses it to illuminate the behavior of every black character in the play, as well as the white society they inhabit. Waters is psychotic, all right, but the basis of his warped, cruel behavior is self-hatred, not hatred—and the cause of that self-hatred is his own recognition of the bankruptcy of his efforts to please whites. Much as he's tried to bury his black roots and as far as he's gone in the Army, Waters just can't escape the demon of racism—that sinking feeling that, for all his achievements, *they still hate you*. And in Waters's distorted personality, his men see a magnified, mirror image of what they most fear and hate in themselves—the fear of being destroyed by allowing white racism to define the ambitions of one's life.

While we can see why the men might have been tempted to murder Waters, Mr. Fuller recognizes such an act for what it is—both a symbolic and literal form of self-destruction. The playwright took this same moral position in **"Zooman,"** which told the story of a contemporary black community that was too cowardly to identify a murderer in its midst. Here, as before, the playwright has compassion for blacks who might be driven to murder their brothers—because he sees them as victims of a world they haven't made. Yet he doesn't let anyone off the hook. Mr. Fuller demands that his black characters find the courage to break out of their suicidal, fratricidal cycle—just as he demands that whites end the injustices that have locked his black characters into the nightmare.

At the same time, Mr. Fuller places his new play in a historical context that gives it a resonance beyond its specific details. As the investigation proceeds, another, larger drama is played out; the soldiers, who have not seen any wartime action, wait in desperate hope that they may get orders for overseas, so that they can prove that "colored boys can fight" Hitler as well as white boys. But in the playwright's view, this aspiration is just another version of Waters's misplaced ambition to deny his blackness by emulating whites—and just as likely to end in tragic, self-annihilating doom.

> Frank Rich, "Negro Ensemble Presents 'Soldier's Play'," in The New York Times, Section II (© 1981 by The New York Times Company; reprinted by permission), November 27, 1981, p. 3.

WALTER KERR

Charles Fuller's **"A Soldier's Play"** begins with a killing and ends with a kind of confession. Its particular excitement, however, doesn't really stem from the traditional business of tracking down the identity of the criminal. It comes instead from

tracking down the identity of the victim. Suddenly you realize that things just might work out that way. Figure out who the dead man is, or who he thought he was, and you're on your way to nailing the culprit. It's a startling process, and a satisfying one. . . .

[But the author] doesn't mean to settle for the mere cat-and-mouse pleasures of turning suspense-story conventions back to front. He wants to turn *everything* back to front. I don't think there's an assumption made or a posture adopted—noble or otherwise—that isn't instantly, and properly, stood on its ear. We learn in a hurry to take nothing for granted. . . .

Instead of piecing together a fact out of circumstantial fragments, we find ourselves putting together a face. Focusing and refocusing until definition becomes disturbingly sharp, we arrive at the image of a person, a portrait with a remembered voice and the terrible contrariness of flesh and blood. . . .

[Fuller] must by this time be recognized as one of the contemporary American theater's most forceful and original voices. He's not tendentious; the work isn't agitprop or anything near it. Mr. Fuller isn't really interested in special pleading, but in simply and directly—and cuttingly—observing what really does go on in this world of ours after you've brushed the stereotypes away.

It's fun, for instance, to catch Mr. Friedman, the white captain, in an impulsive compliment to blacks that just happens to be racist. . . . Then again, it's no fun at all—it's a distressing irony—to hear black troops instantly joyful at the news that they're to be shipped overseas and permitted to fight. The irony, and our distress, is compounded instantly of many things: the men's eagerness to prove themselves, their almost equal eagerness to be relieved of present boredom, the echo of [the sergeant's] disastrous ideals, the simple fact that breaking up camp at this moment may cut off the troubled investigation before its meaning can come plain. (It does come plain, just in time. But it's right that we should first feel alarm at the thought that a unit could be sent into action in order to sidestep a thorny issue.) The author handles every kind of complexity with a sure hand.

> Walter Kerr, "A Fine New Work from a Forceful Playwright," in The New York Times (© 1981 by The New York Times Company; reprinted by permission), December 6, 1981, p. 3.

LEO SAUVAGE

Few works this year, on or off Broadway, have been as powerful as Charles Fuller's *A Soldier's Play*. . . .

[It is a well-made mystery], complete with a wholly unexpected solution. True, Captain Davenport's detection is not always fed by satisfyingly hidden, brilliantly uncovered clues. He relies more on guessing than deduction, a shortcoming that, strictly speaking, makes him only third best after Nero Wolfe and Hercule Poirot. The mystery here ultimately concerns variations in human behavior, however, not methods of crime. Interesting people studied in depth offer highly dramatic compensation; we come to know Sergeant Waters, for instance, through what are for once coherent and gracefully introduced flashbacks. (p. 21)

> Leo Sauvage, "Plays That Got Away," in The New Leader (© 1982 by the American Labor Conference on International Affairs, Inc.), Vol. LXV, No. 14, July 12-26, 1982, pp. 21-22.*

Romain Gary

1914-1980

(Pseudonym of Romain Kacew; also transliterated as Kassef and Kacewgary; also wrote under pseudonym of Emile Ajar) Russian-born French novelist, autobiographer, short story writer, and dramatist.

Although Gary never attained the status of a major writer, he produced several best-selling novels and managed, with his Emile Ajar pseudonym, a literary hoax of surprising ingenuity. *Education européenne (A European Education)*, his first novel, was praised for its skillful evocation of the resistance movement in war-time France. Few of his later works were as highly acclaimed—notable exceptions being his symbolic novel, *Les racines du ciel (The Roots of Heaven)*, and his fictional autobiography, *La promesse de l'aube (Promise at Dawn)*, a poignant portrayal of his unusual mother.

It was not until the planned publication in 1981 of *Life and Death of Emile Ajar* by Gary that the literary world learned the true identity of Ajar, a pseudonym Gary had used for several novels, including *La vie devant soi (Momo)* and *Pseudo*. *La vie devant soi* received notoriety when its author (Ajar) refused the Prix Goncourt, a prize Gary had previously won for *The Roots of Heaven* and a prize which an author may only win once. Adding to the confusion was a signed statement by Gary that he was not Ajar and a later acknowledgement in *Pseudo* that Ajar was Gary's distant cousin, Paul Pavlowitch.

Gary was a passionate spokesman against various social injustices but the humanitarianism evident in his writings was often marred by sentimentality. His unexplained suicide ended his enigmatic career.

(See also *Contemporary Authors*, Vol. 102 [obituary] and *Contemporary Authors*, Vol. 108.)

© Jerry Bauer

JEAN GARRIGUE

[*The Company of Men* deals with the] wake of wild boys—"orphans of the state"—in France, during that postwar interim when living conditions had arrived at a kind of classic hopelessness. There have been other French novels on the same theme, but *The Company of Men,* taking off from the hardboiled American novel, arrives at a kind of brilliant freedom and boldness, combining realism with a delicacy of fantasy and imagination that makes for an exhilarating effect. Certain techniques, too—the way the short scene is focused upon, given a wring or twist, and then dropped, its barbed point still quivering—bring to mind the movie technique at its brightest—Chaplin here, Jean Vigo in France.

The first-person narration gives it another kind of leeway. Told by a young kid, twelve when his record begins, seventeen at the end when he is ready to join the company of men, the style is appropriately direct, slangy and bold. Getting around as he does, in stolen cars, acquainted with all the better people of the new underground, his ''book'' is a report on a society temporarily split down so many centers that a kind of totality of nihilism is about the most honest and realistic viewpoint that can be taken. . . . Everybody, at least, talks that way. . . .

Their theme is: Well, what has become of us; what has become of the concept of man? And who are we? Escape artists? Has living betrayed us? Gary answers in part by creating a very terrible ghost, a real specter of all modern indifferences and self-interest, the typical scarecrow of any slum garden, in the character of Vanderputte, weakened so thoroughly by his long life of moral isolation that to live, at any price, is the only answer left to him. He is pitiable, loathsome, a real monster; but any real monster must be understood. It is the kid's duty to understand this old man who says once: ''I'm not at all religious, but don't you think that God picked me out to teach men about themselves, to make them ashamed?''

How desperate all this sounds! And so it is—but told with what high spirits! When moral intent is delivered with such esthetic tang, art and meaning enjoy a happy life together.

> Jean Garrigue, ''Books in Review: 'The Company of Men''' (reprinted by permission of the Literary Estate of Jean Garrigue), in The New Republic, *Vol. 123, No. 6, August 7, 1950, p. 22.*

EARL W. FOELL

It seems strange that the publicists escorting [**''The Roots of Heaven''**] to its American debut have not compared it to ''Moby

Dick.'' M. Gary is not an imitator of Melville, but this latest, deep-searching work of his has many points of similarity to the American classic.

Elephants, rather than whales, are the subject. But they are treated, a la Melville, on two levels—both as symbols and as straightforward noble mammals. M. Gary's hero, Morel, is, like Ahab, a man possessed. What's more, following Morel in his pachyderm-obsessed mission is as motley a collection of adventurers, misanthropes, idealists, and mixed nationalities as ever sailed on the Pequod. Morel's expedition, like Ahab's, is punitive in nature. And both books are a complex mixture of gripping physical action and rather prolix metaphysical search. . . .

M. Gary manages to say a lot about the march of civilization in Africa, about man's extinction of the other species, about freedom, about idealism, about African nationalism, about race, about communism, about almost every crucial point of contemporary life. And, yes, about elephants. . . .

As writing, **''The Roots of Heaven''** is inexplicably up and down. Its opening pages are almost opaque with prolixity. Dialogue between characters runs more to monologue lasting for pages. Sentences are peculiarly convoluted. The story is recounted by a narrator speaking to a Jesuit missionary friend— a device that leads to confusing subquotes and mistaken identity.

Once beyond this frame into the picture proper, M. Gary . . . [is] all succinctness. The style is graphic, sardonically brilliant, and clear.

As to content, the novel . . . is an intellectual challenge in many directions. Its blunt ironies probe many of the weaknesses of East and West, of colonial and nationalist. But in exploring the moral worth of man, and his spiritual growth, it appears to be content to grasp not the main ''roots of heaven'' but merely a handful of the nearer capillaries.

Earl W. Foell, ''On Elephants and Other Matters,'' in The Christian Science Monitor *(reprinted by permission from* The Christian Science Monitor; © 1958 *The Christian Science Publishing Society; all rights reserved), January 23, 1958, p. 11.*

HENRI PEYRE

[**''The Roots of Heaven''**] should delight those readers who have lately assailed the French novel as over-introspective, pessimistic, and morbid. Romain Gary is a believer in life, action, freedom, an idealistic lover of exotic nature and of beasts. His heroes are the elephants of Equatorial Africa.

Morel, a Frenchman who endured the horrors of German concentration camps, emerged from his nightmarish experience as a crusader for all that mechanically enslaves or crushes men, animals, and nature in the modern age. He undertook a campaign to preserve the roots of heaven, as they are called in the Islamic world, planted by God in the depths of the human soul. (p. 15)

The complex story is told through a series of monologues by half a dozen characters, the chief ones being a kindly skeptic, Saint-Denis, who sympathizes with Morel's idealism, and a priest, who stands clearly for the late anthropologist and philosopher, Father Teilhard de Chardin. (pp. 15-16)

Faulkner's technique must have been studied and has indeed been mastered by Romain Gary. . . .

''The Roots of Heaven'' is often involved in its sentence structure, unshapely in construction, only half credible in its characterization. Yet it achieves dramatic power. The hero imposes himself less vividly upon the reader than the secondary characters and the splendid descriptions of equatorial scenery. The message of the novel is obvious in its allegorical form. ''Moby Dick'' and other allegories such as Camus' ''The Plague'' are called to mind. Good and evil are not clearly differentiated as in a Sunday-school story. But the Russian-born, French diplomat Gary, whose **''European Education''** was one of the most moving books on the Resistance, asserts here his impassioned plea for the salvation of a world threatened by cruelty and injustice, of which man is a victim or an accomplice. (p. 16)

Henri Peyre, ''Allegory of Cruelty,'' in The Saturday Review, *New York (© 1958 Saturday Review Magazine Co.; reprinted by permission), Vol. XLI, No. 5, February 1, 1958, pp. 15-16.*

THE TIMES LITERARY SUPPLEMENT

[M. Romain Gary's] *The Colours of the Day* was set in the highly civilized, sophisticated jungle of the South of France. Now looking for bigger game he has turned to elephants and made them the pretext for an unusual work [*The Roots of Heaven*] that is part adventure story, part fable and part the record of a philosophical search for an answer to the increasing materialism of the world. . . .

From the start M. Gary treats Morel as a legendary figure and as a result he remains rather indistinct as a person while being fully appreciable as a force. . . .

In his own attitude, which sets the tone of the book, M. Gary might possibly be described as a realistic romantic, since he has a journalistic eye for, and knowledge of, the sufferings and problems of the contemporary world, and yet remains an invincible optimist and believer in mankind. He has also a welcome sense of humour which several times rescues him when he is in danger of becoming pretentious. Sometimes he does in fact step over the border of absurdity, as when he imagines a conversation on the subject of the elephants in the shadow of the Kremlin; at others his piecemeal method of presenting his story makes it in places unnecessarily obscure, and he might well have condensed it without loss. But while one is not quite prepared to endorse his publisher's claim that he has written a ''truly great book,'' M. Gary has undoubtedly written a highly original, stimulating and on the whole heartening novel.

''Elephants and Men,'' in The Times Literary Supplement *(© Times Newspapers Ltd. (London) 1958; reproduced from* The Times Literary Supplement *by permission), No. 2914, March 7, 1958, p. 125.*

FREDERIC MORTON

[Romain Gary's] themes, being huge, demand huge stories. In **''Lady L,''** he indulged in melodramatic fluff lesser writers can do better. His **''The Colors of the Day''** suffered from its own overly glamorous background. But given a truly heroic setting, Gary proves himself one of the rare writers left who are capable of true heroes. This he demonstrated in **''The Roots of Heaven''** and in his undeservedly obscure **''The Company of Men.''** . . .

"The Company of Men" described Luc Martin's emergence at 14 from the anti-Nazi underground into the post-war underworld. Luc knows that his father, a Resistance fighter, was killed for some great good cause; and as the book builds poignantly, as Luc cuts and jabs his way through the blackmarket jungle, he is haunted by that unknown goodness the way good men are haunted by evil.

In **"A European Education"** the story is similar, though transposed a few years earlier and morally reversed. Again we have a teen-age boy who becomes an anvil to history. His name is Janek Twardowski; his father, too, has been killed fighting the Germans. He himself dwells among the partisans in the icy forests of occupied Poland. . . . His body withstands the stress. But his mind finds scant shelter against the rigor of certain thoughts: Is it really worth all the suffering? How much real freedom was there before the Germans came? How much will there be once they are driven off? How much culture is worth a million deaths? (p. 4)

The dramatization of this formidable doubt is the burden of the novel. Somehow Gary manages to make every crushed snowflake, every torn body, every numb dawn participate in the great debate. He deploys toward the same purpose his flair for flamboyant characterization. . . .

To some, Romain Gary will have written an old-fashioned novel. Old-fashioned because, on first blush, he seems to tell no more than an oft-told Resistance thriller. And old-fashioned because, on second blush, he dares dig into such un-hip words as freedom, truth and justice. To me **"A European Education"** confirms the author's peculiar genius. He can forge a great conception with all the incandescence of a romantic novelist—then give it final definition by tempering it in sad irony. He can, in other words, see through a human ideal without diminishing its necessity or demeaning its beauty. (p. 24)

> *Frederic Morton, "But Is the Game Worth the Candle?" in* The New York Times Book Review *(© 1960 by The New York Times Company; reprinted by permission), March 13, 1960, pp. 4, 24.*

CHARLES ROLO

It is, I submit, unsettling if not wicked for the author of a personal history to leave one guessing as to where fact ends and semifiction begins. This is my one complaint about Romain Gary's splendid book *Promise at Dawn*. . . . It is labeled nonfiction; the narrator is named Romain Gary; and he refers to his story, which coincides with the known facts of Gary's life, as "an autobiography." However, M. Gary has said: "This book is autobiographical in inspiration, but it is not an autobiography . . . truth has been reduced to artistic truth alone." Thus one is doomed not to know how much art has doctored life. . . . What is certain is that Gary, whether he has reproduced, retouched, or departed from reality, has done so with inspired results. His book is packed with memorable incidents—comic, touching, bizarre, fantastic. (p. 122)

Ludicrous, pathetic, cagey, magnificently heroic, Madame Kacew [Gary's mother] comes brilliantly to life as a fusion of lunatic romanticism and indomitable resourcefulness. Romain was taught, like a son of royalty, every accomplishment, while his mother struggled and slaved to provide. (pp. 122, 124)

Promise at Dawn is in turn extravagant, humorous, poignant, and reflective. Artfully combining the tragic and the comic,

Gary has written an altogether original and captivating memoir. (p. 124)

> *Charles Rolo, "Reader's Choice: 'Promise at Dawn'," in* The Atlantic Monthly *(copyright © 1961, by The Atlantic Monthly Company, Boston, Mass.; reprinted with permission), Vol. 208, No. 4, October, 1961, pp. 122, 124.*

CURTIS CATE

[Romain Gary's] books ring with the echo of a profoundly Russian, if not Manichean, bafflement before the spectacle of a world bristling with new satanic inventions—atomic bombs, brain washing, concentration camps.

This deep sense of protest is as evident as ever in his latest book, **"Promise at Dawn,"** which opens with an imaginary evocation of the grinning gods of stupidity, dogmatic truth, mediocrity and servility. Its original title was to have been "La Lutte Pour l'Honneur"—"the struggle for honor"—but no one needs to know it to realize that this romanticized autobiography is something more than a "life with mother" story. It is the story of a young boy's endeavor to achieve manhood in an age of crumbling values and revolutionary upheaval, and it explains, more explicitly and movingly than Gary has ever done before, why his books are so haunted by a sense of solitude, of bereavement, of a paradise irretrievably lost. (p. 1)

The narrative moves, with the irresistible momentum of a novel, toward . . . [a] climactic post-war rendezvous that was once again to reunite a doting mother with her battle-scarred and bemedaled son. . . .

"Promise at Dawn" is a deliberately picaresque autobiography. To some this may seem an offense against what is presumed to be historical veracity. Yet life being so often stranger than fiction, I incline to think that only a style in keeping with the mustache-twirling flourishes and languorous, heavy-lidded gestures of the Rudolf Valentino and Lillian Gish era could do justice to these extravagant interwar events and the marvelously extravagant woman who strides invincibly through them.

The one flaw in this book is an occasional weakness for baroque overemphasis, particularly in the reiteration of the author's sense of solitude. . . . Yet the occasional stammerings of speech and rococo lapses of taste . . . are too slight to mar the beauty of a memoir which is as lovely a posthumous bouquet as any loving mother could ever hope to receive. (p. 40)

> *Curtis Cate, "Growing Up in a Crumbling World," in* The New York Times Book Review *(© 1961 by The New York Times Company; reprinted by permission), October 15, 1961, pp. 1, 40.*

CHARLES C. LEHRMANN

In the autobiographical work, *La Promesse de l'aube,* Romain Gary tells us . . . about the factors that have determined his personal position and his humanitarian philosophy. First of all, this book is a moving tribute to his Jewish mother, a Russian woman, eccentric and mad in the eyes of her new French compatriots, who molds her son in her fashion and prepares him for an extraordinary career.

And he has . . . fulfilled the promise tacitly made to that mother to accomplish everything she expected from him in the sphere of heroism and self-realization. Rarely has filial piety expressed itself with greater affection, sensitivity, insight, gratitude. (p. 279)

There is no reference to the father where "Tartar and Jewish ancestors" are mentioned without indicating whether they are on the father's or the mother's side. But without having known his father and without having felt his direct influence, Romain Gary feels that he has toward him an incalculable spiritual debt, an atavistic consanguinity, accentuated by the tragedy of six million of his fellow Jews. . . .

Thus, it is through the heritage of his parents that Gary recognizes himself always and instantly in all those who suffer, man or even beast. . . .

These atavistic or conscious influences have favored in Romain Gary the decision to struggle against backward forces, or even against the limitations that nature herself seems to impose on man, on what is known as the human condition. (p. 280)

Here is a writer eminently successful in every aspect of his career, and whose services to his adopted country have been generously recognized and rewarded, but, who, at the pinnacle of fame, makes a proud confession of Jewish faith. Not a dogmatic confession, but in the form of a moving homage to the deepest roots of his person and his thinking. When a French education, that is to say humanistic, has been grafted on traditions going back to the dawn of civilization, we have a modern knight wielding a sword and a pen, hungry for justice, for liberty, for love, "these roots of heaven so deeply sunk in his breast." Is there a better illustration of the stimulating influence of the Jewish element on French literature? (pp. 282-83)

> Charles C. Lehrmann, "Three Goncourt Prizes: Romain Gary, Roger Ikor, André Schwarz-Bart," in his The Jewish Element in French Literature, translated by George Klin (translation copyright © 1971 by Associated University Presses, Inc.; originally published as L'élément juif dans la littérature française, deuxieme edition, Editions Albin Michel, 1961), Fairleigh Dickinson University Press, 1971, pp. 267-83.*

WILLIAM BARRETT

Hissing Tales . . . is a good illustration of [Romain Gary's] copious and lively imagination; and though his facility does not always serve him equally well, since the stories are quite uneven, the collection as a whole is remarkably provocative and enjoyable.

Most of the stories provide us with some melodramatic villain to hiss at. M. Gary revives successfully the old-fashioned story—like those of O. Henry, Frank Stockton, or some of Robert Louis Stevenson—that has a definite anecdotal point, perhaps even some twist at the end, rather than merely presenting a slice of life in the style of flat realism.

In "A Craving for Innocence" a Frenchman, aspiring to escape the sordid materialism of civilization, goes to Tahiti. But when he discovers some unknown paintings of Gauguin, all his commercial lusts return, and he can think only of getting back to France to make a killing. On the way home he finds out that the paintings are fakes. Corruption has spread even into the South Seas, and he, the idealist in search of innocence, has been betrayed once again. Of course, he is both corrupt and preposterous; and most of M. Gary's characters combine these two qualities.

Elsewhere it is M. Gary himself who seems to be hissing at the world and its monstrosities. . . .

In the grimmest of M. Gary's jokes, "The New Frontier," a crowd of people are awaiting the president's arrival for a speech. Slowly, bit by bit, we become aware that there is something different about these people. Survivors of an atomic war, they are undergoing mutations that are turning them into varieties of sea creatures. . . . After the president's stirring speech, they migrate into the water, from which life once arose, there to continue the resolute struggle against the Communists. Artistically, the story is not altogether successful, but no reader will be able to forget its point.

> William Barrett, "Tall Tales," in The Atlantic Monthly (copyright © 1964, by The Atlantic Monthly Company, Boston, Mass.; reprinted with permission), Vol. 213, No. 4, April, 1964, p. 148.

HENRI PEYRE

The wish to recover in fiction something of the boisterous illogic and of the impetuous action which had once entertained our ancestors in the Spanish, French, and English picaresque novels has spurred several Englishmen and a few Frenchmen to attempt a revival of the genre among us. . . . Romain Gary, soon after he made a startling entry into literature with one of the most moving books written about the underground in eastern Europe, Education européenne (1945) [A European Education], declared to a literary weekly, La Gazette des lettres, on October 12, 1946: the 'modern novel will be picaresque or it will not be at all. Picaresque, like a fresco teeming with adventures, motion and swarming characters, and also with optimism.' . . . He was determined to reintegrate laughter into fiction. Even more than his plea for the preservation of African elephants, Les Racines du ciel [(1956) The Roots of Heaven], which blended some symbolic didacticism with a vitality not unworthy of Alexandre Dumas, he succeeded as a humorous writer of fiction in his imaginative autobiography, La Promesse de l'aube (1960) [Promise of Dawn], one of the few entertaining and vigorously healthy books written in France since World War II. Romain Gary apparently altered the course of his talent after his reaching the perilous 'mezzo del camin' of his life (he was fifty in 1964) and his later books have failed to evince a deepening or an enrichment of his talent. (pp. 354-55)

> Henri Peyre, "Main Trends since World War II: The 'New Novel'," in his French Novelists of Today (copyright © 1967 by Oxford University Press, Inc.; reprinted by permission), revised edition, Oxford University Press, New York, 1967, pp. 337-97.*

PAMELA MARSH

[In Romain Gary's novel], treating the concentration camps as one huge joke hardly grates at all, especially when the joke is told by Genghis Cohn, who has seen it all from inside the barbed wire and now narrates "The Dance of Genghis Cohn." As Cohn says, "If you are the holder of a historical world record for sadness, all that is left for you to hang onto is your sense of humor."

But if the humor is not too black to swallow, most readers will find it blue enough, blasphemous enough, to leave a nasty taste in the mouth.

The tale begins with an irresistible fancy.

Cohn was once a Jewish comedian, known for his bawdy jokes. Even in the concentration camp, making ready for his own execution, he cannot resist playing for laughs and in his last moment fights back with the only weapon left to the Jews. He makes a comic, lewd gesture at his executioners and so impresses himself on the German officer, Schatz, in charge of the firing squad, that his spirit takes up residence with Schatz.

But **"The Dance of Genghis Cohn"** goes a step deeper—from fantasy into allegory with murder, nymphomania, Christ Jesus, and an interchangeable Cohn and Schatz involved in scenes that suggest a Chagall turned into obscene nightmare. A reader can clutch at straws that have meaning for him and make what bricks he can. But perhaps what comes nearest to Romain Gary's purpose in writing this novel is hinted in another interchange, this time between Cohn and a writer.

"'Sorry Cohn. Very sorry but you are through. You are no longer good material. We writers have to keep up with things, you know. Let's face it: Jewish suffering is rapidly becoming a bit of a bore. . . . You've been pretty valuable to us writers, but now we have the Blacks and Vietnam . . . so . . . next, please.'"

Romain Gary intends to keep the Jewish question an open one, a live issue for writers.

Pamela Marsh, "The Nazis As a Black Joke," in The Christian Science Monitor *(reprinted by permission from* The Christian Science Monitor; © *1968 The Christian Science Publishing Society; all rights reserved), October 3, 1968, p. 17.*

AUBERON WAUGH

[*White Dog*] is so boring and so disgusting that I would not review it at all if it did not demonstrate one reaction to the foreigners' predicament most vividly. Briefly, the foreigners' predicament is that they have no money and nobody is interested in what they think. Gary reckons to make a fortune by insulting the Americans, and I dare say he will succeed. Many of the things he says about black racists, professional Negroes and white liberals are perfectly valid, even if a trifle obvious. It is his repulsive way of saying it—spattering his narrative with he-man obscenities and unnecessary references to pus—which reveals the full depth of his intellectual dishonesty. Instead of telling intelligent, enlightened people what he feels wrong about race relations, he stages a one-man anti-American demonstration, which is doubly unsuccessful because the demonstrator is covered with warts, pus etc.

Although written in the form of a novel, the story features Gary as hero (whipping himself for making so much money from his compassion over the Negro problem) and his ex-wife, Jean Seberg, who loves the human race uncritically. The story itself is quite a good one, about a dog trained to attack Negroes which is taken by a Black Muslim and trained to attack whites. It would make an excellent novel, written by someone else. Even Gary could have improved it if he had taken out the repulsive face of the fictional Gary, although this would deprive us of the highly enjoyable ending when the fictional Gary is mauled by his own dog.

But what the real Gary fails to realize is that his fictional ex-wife, Jean Seberg, is an entirely comic character—sympathetic and charming, of course, but essentially comical—and so is the whole goodwill movement among middle-class Americans in relation to black militancy. Instead of which, Gary broods

darkly about pus and excrement, hoping to replace idiotic excesses of radical chic with a new idiocy, that of anti-radical-chic. This is a most bogus and unpleasant book, but worth reading to discover what some Frenchmen think they can get away with. (pp. 248-49)

Auberon Waugh, "Auberon Waugh on Foreign Novels," in The Spectator *(© 1971 by* The Spectator; *reprinted by permission of* The Spectator), *Vol. 227, No. 7468, August 14, 1971, pp. 248-49.*

DAVID LEITCH

Emile Ajar—whoever he is—has lately become a household name in France. His fame stems from having declined a literary prize, the Goncourt [for *La Vie devant Soi*].

There were several other bull points for news editors in the '*affaire Ajar*', not least the fact that his name is a pseudonym. . . . Naturally this began guessing games about his true identity: was he an already famous writer—Romain Gary, for instance—or a relation of his? . . .

In any case the novel became an immediate bestseller, even without the Goncourt *imprimatur*, while publishers and *littérateurs* savaged each other with a spite and gusto that would have made the appalling Goncourt brothers themselves feel thoroughly at home. All this quasi-literary passion is peculiarly Parisian and it makes it hard to read and assess the novel on its own merits.

Madame Rosa, the book's heroine, is a retired prostitute in her late sixties. . . . When the novel opens she is running a kind of freelance crèche and boardinghouse for the unwanted kids of younger comrades still on the game. . . . Among her charges is 'Momo', short for Mohammed, a precocious Arab boy who thinks he is about ten. (p. 43)

We are invited to look at the world through the eyes of [this] wise child, who sometimes sees more clearly than the adult reader, and sometimes makes mistakes which we with our superior wisdom can easily identify. He also makes errors in vocabulary from time to time; in conjunction with his quaint and formal manner of expressing himself, plus some excursions into the *argot* of Belleville, they add to the verbal fun. Momo is part of a literary tradition which includes Holden Caulfield and the ducks in Central Park as well as Zazie and her *argotic* subterranean Paris, although it would be wrong to imply that Ajar is capable of Salinger's bleak yet whimsical vision or Queneau's verbal pyrotechnics.

La Vie devant Soi is, in the last analysis, a cosy and cosmetic performance, fulfilling the role of sentimental literature, which is to smooth the jagged edges of uncomfortable reality, and make brimstone taste like treacle. It is, I think, a truly awful book, and its awfulness has a certain unexpected irony about it. Ajar may have nobly declined the Goncourt but in a sense his gesture was otiose: for his achievement has been to write the perfect Goncourt book, a bland novel which fits exactly into the wire basket, along with the frozen peas and the *marrons glacés* of the *supermarché*. (pp. 43-4)

David Leitch, "Prix Spécial," in New Statesman *(© 1976 The Statesman & Nation Publishing Co. Ltd.), Vol. 91, No. 2338, January 9, 1976, pp. 43-4.*

ROLAND A. CHAMPAGNE

[Momo, the narrator of *La Vie devant soi*,] is one of a group of children abandoned by Parisian prostitutes and brought up by a former Jewish streetwalker, Madame Rosa. . . . In trying to discover what it means to be a fourteen-year-old Arab in this ghetto, Momo provides an intriguing autobiography of French subcultures as well as of his own confrontations with them.

Momo's street idiom portrays the life-styles of the Jews, Arabs, Africans, Algerians, and other French immigrants of this unique ghetto in the stark reality of their shabby existence. But he does not give us stereotypes. Momo observes the mutual co-operation and cohabitation of this community of heterogeneous pimps, transvestites, prostitutes, and other pariahs of French society with a sensitivity to the individuality of the people involved. His witness to the genuine warmth and bitterness among marginal social types suggests this text as a twentieth-century version of Hugo's *Les Misérables*.

> Roland A. Champagne, "Reviews: 'La Vie devant soi'," in The Modern Language Journal, *Vol. LXI, Nos. 1 & 2, January-February, 1977, p. 65.*

BARBARA WRIGHT

"Le cas Ajar" became headline news in France with the publication of Ajar's first book, *Gros-Câlin*, in 1974; a year later he refused the Prix Goncourt for his second, *La Vie devant soi*. Both books were almost unanimously praised by the critics, but most reviews began: Who is Emile Ajar? . . .

[His third book, *Pseudo,* later attributed to Romain Gary], on one level, is the result of the author's finally agreeing to reveal at least some "facts" about himself. He writes it in the first person, as Paul Pavlowitch, one of the names he answers to in private life. . . . He describes, from the point of view of the quarry, the manhunt he was subjected to; he tells what it is like to be told that you don't exist, that you are "pseudo". He gives what is ostensibly an account of his love-hate relationship with his ever helpful cousin/uncle Romain Gary (here always referred to by the unkind sobriquet of "Tonton Macoute"), and he invents a version of how he came to write the present book. . . .

In all his books, however fantastic, Ajar paints an acute, anguished, and often very funny picture of the modern world. In *Pseudo,* Paul Pavlowitch is judged to be unbalanced because he takes the sins of that world upon himself; he identifies, for instance, with the leaders of states where terror and torture are practised. . . .

One of Ajar's basic themes is freedom of thought—and not merely its suppression in the countries generally recognized as being dictatorships. In the apparently desultory stream of observations, images and non-sequiturs of *Pseudo,* he frighteningly illustrates the pressures exerted on "one-off" citizens in "free" societies. Paul Pavlowitch stands for those who by temperament or philosophy wish to live their own lives in their own way. . . . *Pseudo* is written in the same fresh, inimitable and unimitative style as Ajar's previous books: casual, fluent, graphic, and funny with a kind of Marx Brothers or *Hellzapoppin cocasserie*. You have to have read *Gros-Câlin* and *La Vie devant soi* in order to savour *Pseudo* to the full—but these are two of the best and most moving books to have come out of France in recent years. . . . The last words of *Pseudo* are:

"Ceci est mon dernier livre." It would be a real loss if Ajar were to keep to this decision.

> Barbara Wright, "Count Me Out," in The Times Literary Supplement (© *Times Newspapers Ltd. (London) 1977; reproduced from* The Times Literary Supplement *by permission), No. 3912, March 4, 1977, p. 233.*

DAPHNE MERKIN

Momo is so strenuously, so determinedly heartwarming, that it seems in constant danger of blowing a fuse. As for the orphan boy Momo, he's a winsome tyke if ever there was one, a veritable Little Lord Fauntleroy of the gutter, and yet I must admit I managed to remain completely inured to his charms. In fact, with each new ingenuous pronouncement upon the human condition that the young *philosophe* made—"I believe that if you want to live, you should start very young because later on you're sure to depreciate and no one will make you any presents"—I found myself growling in belatedly-recognized sympathy with that childophobe, W. C. Fields.

Momo inverses the usual literary relationship: it is a novel by a "child" written for "adults." (p. 34)

Ajar can't seem to decide whether he wants Momo to talk like an illiterate or a college professor. His confusion is mirrored in the translation, which veers wildly between the vernacular—"far out"—and the literary—"flummoxed"—and occasionally careens into undisguised garble: "For somebody so alone it was amazing how much of her there was, and there in that can I think she must have felt more alone than ever." When Momo refers to his tattered clothes he points out that he has to "snatch garmentry," which is the most unusual and unchildlike description of shoplifting I've ever come across. Since Ralph Manheim is an able translator of long practice it is to be assumed that the crazy-quilt effect is intentional. Still one wonders: is this, perhaps, less strained in the original? Does all this smart-assed precocity sound more natural-voiced, or could it be that the French simply have a high tolerance for deadly coyness?

Momo tugs unabashedly at one's heart—or is it ham?—strings. I chuckled faintly once or twice and at no moment felt the urge to dab at what were after all perfectly dry eyes. In conception *Momo* is something of a throwback—much like the hugely successful musical *Annie*—to the raffish-spirited movies of the '40s, where the baby left on the door-step turns out to be a long-lost darling. It is, to be quite judicious, nothing worse than the equivalent of peasant's fare—hearty with plot, thick with good intentions, and heavily seasoned with slices of "reality." (pp. 35-6)

> Daphne Merkin, "Books Considered: 'Momo'," in The New Republic (reprinted by permission of The New Republic; © *1978 The New Republic, Inc.), Vol. 178, No. 16, April 22, 1978, pp. 34-6.*

JOHN NAUGHTON

So . . . what have we here? [Is *Momo* a] crateload of *schmaltz* about there being honour even among whores (and their children)? At one level, yes. At another, we have one of the funniest, saddest, most humane, most readable novels for years. The detachment of the child, his kerbside cynicism, the immediacy of the narrative style, the hilarious misuse of language ('dramatic' for 'traumatic', 'artistic' for 'autistic')—these are the features which lift *Momo* far above the level of mere corn and into the stratosphere whence it was discerningly plucked by the jury of the Prix Goncourt. (p. 851)

> *John Naughton, "Rosa's Children" (© British Broadcasting Corp. 1978; reprinted by permission of John Naughton), in* The Listener, *Vol. 99, No. 2566, June 29, 1978, pp. 850-51.**

PATRICK BRESLIN

Romain Gary, author of a score of books, is obsessed in this new novel [*Europa*] with the chasm between Europe's great cultural achievements and its great crimes—Nazi barbarism the best, but not the only, example. Gary pursues that obsession through the tale of the slide into schizophrenia of Jean Danthes, French ambassador to Rome, and produces a novel that is portentous and obsessive.

Danthes is "a man of immense culture" to whom Europe's cultural warehouse is as familiar as his own office, and more on his mind. Yet Danthes was two years in Dachau, and so has experienced Europe at its most barbarous. The two sides of Europe are pulling him apart.

So too is his complex relationship with two women (or are they the same?). . . . The two women represent the two sides of Europe and Danthes' relationship with them leads to his final crisis.

Much of what happens in the book turns out to be illusion— or does it? There's a lot of playing with mirrors here, excursions into witchery and into past centuries, convoluted schemes of revenge, maneuvers for position on the chessboard of fate. But the plot is overwhelmed by pages laden, leaden rather, with cultural references.

> *Patrick Breslin, "'Europa'," in* Book World—The Washington Post *(© 1978, The Washington Post), July 9, 1978, p. E6.*

G. MERMIER and F. COHEN

Romain Gary's *La bonne moitié* is a dramatic comedy in two acts; it is a play of the absurd, subtle, tragic and amusing, very much in the vein of Emile Ajar's *La vie devant soi,* linguistically speaking. The author plays with his culture, with his language and with the syntax, and that precisely because he is in full possession of each.

This is a perfectly balanced work, light and serious, deep and absurd and written with remarkable finesse. Children of executed World War II French Résistance fighters are taken care of by Theo Vanderputte, himself a former member of the Résistance turned informer for the Gestapo. Is this turncoat a traitor or a martyr? How is this half-buffoon and half-tragic hero going to be judged by his peers? According to the number of Germans he killed or to the number of Résistance figures he betrayed? The four adolescent children, next to Theo's duplicity, represent, on the contrary, objectivity, realism and adaptation to the shifting values of a constantly changing world. If they become judges of Theo, they remain lucid; their judgment is without malice or fanaticism. Theo Vanderputte's death is a mixture of justice and pity, and the four children face the future with the dignity and ideals which Luc Martin's father, a companion of the Liberation, has imparted to them.

La bonne moitié is an excellent play, light, mature and well written. The language is particularly interesting and full of surprises.

> *G. Mermier and F. Cohen, "French: 'La bonne moitié'," in* World Literature Today *(copyright 1980 by the University of Oklahoma Press), Vol. 54, No. 3, Summer, 1980, p. 406.*

TED R. SPIVEY

[Gary] has a visionary sweep that allows him to show how romantic idealism plays a role in modern life. Gary projects man into a new age that lies beyond modern tragedy; at the same time, *The Roots of Heaven* evokes the hell of the Hitlerian domination of Europe and contains one of the deepest contemporary views of the sufferings of man in modern times. . . . Gary's ontology is based on the idealism of both romanticism and neoromanticism, and it is bolstered by a strong sense of the freedom of the will. The idea, so strong in *The Roots of Heaven,* of man's being able to achieve his freedom by exercising free choice can be attributed in part to the existentialism of Sartre and Camus. Yet Gary has also found this idea in the mainstream of modern fiction, which includes writers like Conrad and Hemingway, whom he often resembles. Also he must have found it in the literature that sprang from the Nazi concentration camps, which he so often invokes. . . . (p. 127)

The Roots of Heaven stands at the end of the modern tradition and points toward the beginning of another. It contains visionary insights found in only a few books of this century. These insights and their relationship to modernism as well as to romanticism and to those vague stirrings of some new movement form the basis of a great novel.

The story in *The Roots of Heaven* is about a Frenchman named Morel who loves elephants and who believes that they should be preserved. . . . While imprisoned in a German concentration camp during World War II, Morel learns to bear suffering by imagining herds of elephants charging across African plains. After his release he goes to Africa to be near the great animals, and soon he finds himself working to protect them from slaughter. . . . This is a story that is interesting in itself; at the same time it is a work of extreme technical subtlety, reminiscent of Joseph Conrad's novels. The philosophy of the book, however, makes it far more than a well-told story.

Morel bears the chief burden of Gary's ideas. He is a new kind of idealist. . . . Morel's idealism is in some ways like that of humanists and humanitarians who bear the vague title of "liberal." Like Morel, these people have strong feelings about certain injustices, but they differ from him in that they have political and social aims. Morel, on the other hand, believes that as a new kind of idealist he must work to give meaning to new *symbols:* for without the symbols which man has lost, his social and political action is meaningless. But the idea behind the phrase "roots of heaven" is more than just a matter of symbols in the usual sense. The flora and fauna of nature can actually place a person in a relationship with a power whose source must be called heaven. Morel is advocating a return to a feeling for the tree of life, a motif central to mythology and religion. . . . Morel and his followers propose to bring man back to the basic roots of life. This return, they proclaim, will renew man's feeling for justice, freedom, and other abstract values. (pp. 127-29)

[Morel] is a novelist's image of what the new idealist will be.

The ways in which he is not like the old idealists, even a Gandhi or a Schweitzer, are made quite clear by Gary. For one thing, he has to fight practically alone against great forces of cynicism and materialism, as any new idealist would have to do. His very words appear strange to most people. For another thing, Morel concentrates his efforts on building a spiritual kingdom of a few followers who believe in the roots of heaven; he cares nothing for the political kingdom with its social and economic ideals. Morel leaves behind much of the Western past, but he keeps certain essentials; for instance, he always remembers that he is a Frenchman. Like any true spiritual revolutionary, he does not disown the past but takes what he needs from it in order to accomplish a mission for the good of the future. (pp. 129-30)

What has driven Morel to seek intimate knowledge of, as well as protection for, the roots of heaven (specifically, the elephants), is a suffering so extreme that only an unworn image could save him. In a Nazi concentration camp, where a systematic attempt to destroy the spirit was made, Morel knew an attack on the soul that no idealist like Gandhi or Schweitzer ever encountered. The way he survived was to keep in his mind the picture of wide-ranging elephants as an image of freedom. This ordeal was the beginning of his career as a new idealist. His real work from then on would be to bring himself and others into an emotional as well as a mental relationship with an image, and at the same time to establish once again a vital contact with nature. To do this work, he had to shed completely the materialistic philosophy of the West. Morel is Western man, voluntarily dispossessed, beginning a new religious life on the frontier of the world. (p. 130)

Morel's career illustrates one solution to a problem that has harassed thinkers and artists since the early days of romanticism: how to maintain idealism in the face of civilization's decay. In Morel's vision, true optimism and a complete acceptance of modern corruption are held in tension. This vision is only possible to one who believes in new creation and a new spiritual beginning. If this book can be written in the fifties, one can imagine new religious beginnings in the latter part of the twentieth century. Gary's contribution to a worldwide awakening is a clear, existential statement of several of the most important truths of a new beginning: that symbols must be found; that they must be believed in fervently; that true belief must come slowly, and it must develop by being tested in the fires of hardship and suffering; and, finally, that new beginnings are often made in remote places, sometimes on the very edge of civilization. These truths are stated as a part of a myth of our time, the essence of which is: the rejection of materialism by a new spiritual man, the search for new images of heaven, the reunion with the people of nature—provincial woman and man—and after that the continuing search for a greater understanding of heaven through closer union with its roots. (pp. 135-36)

Today, at the end of modernism, our art and institutions have become stale because we are out of touch with the "inexhaustible energies of the cosmos." A novel like *The Roots of Heaven* is one sign, however, that men are once again seeking to realize in their lives the ancient truths of myth and religion. At its deepest, *The Roots of Heaven* is about the return of modern man to basic human doctrines of the freedom of the will and the ontological basis of creation. (p. 138)

Ted R. Spivey, "Man's Divine Rootedness in the Earth: Romain Gary's Major Fiction," in his The Journey beyond Tragedy: A Study of Myth and Modern Fiction *(copyright © 1980 by the Board of Regents of the State of Florida), University Presses of Florida, 1980, pp. 126-38.*

SERGIO VILLANI

[The title of Romain Gary's novel, **Les clowns lyriques**], a phrase from Gorky, is an image of the despair which, according to Gary, tortures Western societies—the tragic despair of the bourgeois who constantly seeks distraction in order to escape the realities of his condition. In his pursuit of the impossible, he misses the few fleeting moments of happiness the present could offer.

This social ill is represented by a group of characters who have devised various escape mechanisms. . . .

The background of the action gives a social and historical perspective to the thesis. The references to Hollywood create the image of a factory of artificiality which nurtures and amuses Western escapist tendencies. The carnival in Nice, the setting of the novel, is presented as a grand celebration of disguise and buffoonery. Gary also suggests that historically it is the histrionics of leaders like Hitler and Stalin that create the idealism and illusions which detonate holocausts.

In his preface Gary warns the reader that he remains faithful to the values he attacks with his irony. Irony is a means of testing and strengthening these values. Gary's narrative style is constantly putting this irony into relief. The reader is drawn into the webs of illusion spun by the characters and then plunged again into the midst of the reality of things. The language is memorable for its figurative, suggestive power, but especially for several aphoristic, ironic statements which punctuate the text. The reader is rewarded by the linguistic beauty of this novel and the pleasures of its thought-provoking thesis. . . .

Sergio Villani, "French: 'Les clowns lyriques'," in World Literature Today *(copyright 1981 by the University of Oklahoma Press), Vol. 55, No. 1, Winter, 1981, p. 62.*

G. MERMIER

[In **Les cerfs-volants**] Ambroise Fleury is a postman for the French PTT, an unusual postman who plays with kites, who gives them familiar or funny names. . . . [He] and his family carry the love of France in their hearts; as true patriots, they know its history by heart. With his kite games the postman enjoys a reputation almost equal to the cuisine of Marcellin Duprat, master cook and *patron* of the Clos Joli restaurant: this is France, its little eccentricities and its love of good food! Page after page, the novel's narrator Ludo tells us about the people of Clery. . . .

But there is more, much more, in this admirable novel, so real with its vignettes of the war, of 1940, of the Resistance, but also so tender and so fervently human and poetic. For Romain Gary, the kites must seek the blue of heaven, no matter how many times they fall, but they need us, men, to keep them aloft. . . . *Les cerfs-volants,* no doubt a masterpiece of a novel, a masterpiece of fiction set in a contemporary historical framework, may well be Romain Gary's true last will. As such, the book deserves our admiration and respect.

G. Mermier, "French: 'Les cerfs-volants'," in World Literature Today *(copyright 1981 by the University of Oklahoma Press), Vol. 55, No. 3, Summer, 1981, p. 433.*

JOHN WEIGHTMAN

When the novelist, Romain Gary, committed suicide some months ago, he left behind [*Vie et Mort d'Émile Ajar,* a] small time-bomb to explode after his death and cause red faces among the members of the French literary establishment. It is an account of how, from the early 1970s onwards, he wrote four successful novels under the pseudonym of Émile Ajar, while continuing to publish other works under the name he had already long made famous. . . . His motive, he says, was a desire to renew himself, to escape from the persona in which the critics had imprisoned him. . . .

Sad to say, apart from discomforting some critics who no doubt deserve to be pilloried, the book falls a little flat. . . . Gary, as a mature writer, simply played a prank on the Parisian literary world by using a pseudonym, but there is no fundamental difference between the Ajar books and the novels he wrote under his original name. Contrary to what he implies, he did not renew himself from the creative point of view. There is, in any case, a contradiction in his argument; he points out that the critics ought to have guessed the truth, because of the many resemblances in style and incident between the Gary and the Ajar novels; if so, where is the renewal?

On reading some of the books of the two series side by side for the first time, I began by thinking that he perhaps gives freer rein to his characteristic emotionalism as Ajar than as Gary, but on reflection even this is not so; *Clair de femme,* which he published as Gary, is on the same level of feverish anguish as the Ajar-novel, *L'Angoisse du Roi Salomon.* All these later works, in fact, seem to be frantic variations on the impossibility of living by someone who is overwhelmed by the mystery of time and organic decay and the absence of an ultimate meaning. But it is one of the ironies of literature that even a genuine feeling, when it is given overheated expression, does not result in the best kind of art.

John Weightman, "Binominal Theorem," in The Times Literary Supplement *(© Times Newspapers Ltd. (London) 1981; reproduced from* The Times Literary Supplement *by permission), No. 4090, August 21, 1981, p. 953.*

DANIEL E. RIVAS

In spite of some biographical overtones, *Les Cerfs-Volants* is a piece of fiction, not a political or sociological tract, although some critics will inevitably search here for hidden meanings and obscure references that may provide clues to the author's state of mind and whatever motives may have compelled him to end his life.

Les Cerfs-Volants is inscribed into the tradition of the *Bildungsroman,* which has produced notable examples in French letters. From the point of view of technique, there is nothing revolutionary about this first-person narrative, which recounts the childhood, adolescence, and early adult years of Ludo Fléury. . . . The story is one of survival and perseverance during the Second World War years, as seen and experienced in a small French rural community.

Within the relatively uncomplicated and linear plot scheme of encounter, separation, and final reunion of the two main protagonists are woven a number of themes that support the broad structure of the novel. Of these, the conflict between reality and imagination figures most prominently. It allows Gary to explore the often complex psychology of his characters and to expose them in their relationship with their own selves, other people, and events. This is where Gary is definitely at his best. . . . (p. 156)

Daniel E. Rivas, "Reviews: 'Les cerfs-volants'," in The French Review *(copyright 1981 by the American Association of Teachers of French), Vol. LV, No. 1, October, 1981, pp. 156-57.*

Paul (Eliot) Green
1894-1981

American dramatist, novelist, and short story writer.

Throughout his career, Green's best work incorporated a respect for American tradition and folklore, along with a realistic and sensitive portrayal of the dignity of the oppressed individual.

Green's first full-length play, *In Abraham's Bosom*, won the 1927 Pulitzer Prize for drama. The play concerns the plight of an ambitious young black man whose attempts to improve his life end in tragic failure.

The Lost Colony, a depiction of the first British settlement in America, was performed at an outdoor theater and began a series of historical regional plays written by Green. As Green saw it, the restrictions of the Broadway theater could not "contain the richness of [the American] tradition." He called his plays "symphonic dramas," a mixture of dialogue, music, and dance.

(See also *Contemporary Authors*, Vols. 5-8, rev. ed., Vol. 103 [obituary]; *Contemporary Authors New Revision Series*, Vol. 3; *Dictionary of Literary Biography*, Vols. 7, 9; and *Dictionary of Literary Biography Yearbook: 1981*.)

Photograph by Lance Richardson; courtesy of The Paul Green Foundation, Inc.

BARRETT H. CLARK

[Paul Green has] evolved a type of lyrical folk drama unlike anything that has so far been written in this country. Such plays as *The End of the Row* and *In Abraham's Bosom* are as firmly rooted in the soil of the South as *Deep River* or *Swing Low, Sweet Chariot*. The more I read of his most significant work, the more firmly am I convinced that Mr. Green is doing for our drama what the writers of the spirituals have done for Negro music. I think our theater has found here an artist of rare gifts. I must qualify this statement, not because I hesitate to speak out what I feel or because I want to wait for Mr. Green's later plays to justify my first enthusiasm; I am just a little skeptical as to whether our theater, as it is now organized and run, is ready to give Mr. Green's plays the chance they ought to have. (pp. vii-viii)

[*White Dresses* marks the first time], so far as I am aware, a dramatist has taken a Negro theme almost as old as our literature, and made it live in dramatic form. Mr. Green knows his Negroes, and like John Synge, that other artist who created literature as well as drama out of the folk idiom, he has made use of the commonest words and phrases, giving them new and surprising turns, and making of them a living speech. (p. xi)

The second of his characteristic Negro plays is *The Prayer Meeting*. It seems strange that this is the first successful attempt to introduce into our theater the full-blooded Negro, the healthy animal, neither a downright villain nor a dreamy Uncle Tom's Cabin sort of sentimentalist. Mr. Green has learned from observation and experience that the Negro, living under the white man's civilization, has not had a pleasant time of it. The white man has given him religion, under the influence of which he often becomes a savage again; he has given him liquor, business methods, the vote, ambition, education; yet the Negro, only half assimilating what is theoretically his rightful heritage, finds himself up against the white man's prohibitions and prejudices.

But *The Prayer Meeting* is primarily a work of art, a human and not a sociological document. Mr. Green may care a good deal about the plight of the Negro, but his concern is primarily with human beings as individuals. This play is a marvelous exhibition of the vast fund of devilry in the soul of the Negro; it is a revelation of unsounded depths in the soul of the black man. With the instinct of a true dramatist, Mr. Green has taken a situation which is ready to hand. The Negro prayer meeting is a drama in itself, and I cannot understand why it has not been used before in a play. In this ready-made plot, the dramatist has simply set in motion a group of well-realized characters. He really needs no story at all, in the usual sense of the term, and no theatrical trickery.

The Prayer Meeting is a study in Negro psychology, with none of the disturbing elements introduced by white civilization. *Sam Tucker* skillfully introduces the tragic theme of the Negro in relation to the white man. The same theme is more tragically developed in the one-act version of *In Abraham's Bosom*. The Negro's effort to better himself by means of education is the basis of this tragic episode. It would be so easy to sentimentalize over Abraham's plight, to regard the play as a document; but there is nothing in it besides the human struggle. In treating the problems of the American Negro Mr. Green knows instinctively that the greatest problems are those that the human being must face as an individual.

What he scarcely more than touched upon in the one-act play, he has recently developed in an epic tragedy. The full-length work, also known as *In Abraham's Bosom*, . . . is one of the most beautiful and tragic modern plays I have ever read. The character of Abraham is developed through six scenes, each depicting a crisis in the hero's heartbreaking struggle to develop his limited mental powers. With the aid of a white man he is at first enabled to do some studying, and even succeeds in opening a small school for Negroes. But every time he seems on the point of success, he finds himself thwarted. Now, his tragedy is not altogether that of the Negro in a white man's world; as a matter of fact, his failure lies ultimately within himself, attributable to his racial and individual shortcomings.

In this play there is no effort to solve the problem: it is Mr. Green's business simply to state it in terms of humanity. Abraham remains a pitiful figure, held down by the limitations imposed upon him by nature and by man. (pp. xii-xiv)

The Hot Iron is one of the most affecting one-act plays I know. With the simplest imaginable dramatic elements and scarcely an episode by way of plot, the dramatist has animated his characters with the breath of life. By the intensity of his art Mr. Green has endowed the man and the woman with the sufferings and longings of mankind. I forget in reading it that the characters are Negroes from a part of the world I know little about, but it makes no difference: I am made to understand the people.

Mr. Green stands alone among our younger playwrights as a man who can touch with equal skill the lighter and more sentimental side of life, and the tragedy of it. There are two plays, not in *Lonesome Road* or *The Lord's Will*, quite as good in their way, though not so somber in mood, as the best in *Lonesome Road*. *The Man Who Died at Twelve O'Clock* is a delicious bit of grotesque horseplay, genuine, imaginative, poetic. (pp. xv-xvi)

In Aunt Mahaly's Cabin is described as a Negro melodrama. Two Negroes have killed a white man, and seek refuge in a deserted cabin once occupied by the witch woman Aunt Mahaly. The scene is reminiscent of *The Emperor Jones*, but it is elaborated by the introduction of a world of demonology in the shape of ghostly apparitions. One of the murderers kills the other, but not until he is himself mortally wounded in the fight. In his dying moments there passes before his over-wrought brain a panorama of all the mysterious practices of Aunt Mahaly. *In Aunt Mahaly's Cabin* is not so much a study of panic fear as a grotesque fantasy on Negro themes. There is far less conscious art in it than there is in O'Neill's play and more of the folk element. It is an elaborate pageant of dramatized folklore.

The last of the Negro plays is probably the best-known of all Mr. Green's work, *The No 'Count Boy*. Different from anything else he has done, this idyl is a most appealing and delightful poetic play. To say that it is somewhat reminiscent of Synge means little, for the characters and the language are altogether Mr. Green's own. This is the story of a dreamy boy who nearly succeeds in carrying off the fiancée of a practical-minded young Negro, simply by playing the mouth-organ and telling her of his (wholly imaginary) travels in distant cities. There is a wealth of poetry in the little scene, and rich characterization. (pp. xvi-xvii)

So far Mr. Green has shown an extraordinary adaptability in form and style; he can write tragedy and comedy, drab realism and highly imaginative fantasy. Like all young writers, he has his literary preferences, authors who have influenced him, for better or for worse. Hardy and Synge and O'Neill seem to predominate, but since Mr. Green knows this, there is perhaps less danger of conscious imitation than there would be in a less original artist.

I feel that his greatest gifts are his instinctive talent for seizing upon a dramatic situation, his poetic imagination, and his intuitive knowledge of character. I believe that poetic imagination is what our theater stands most in need of. We have skilled technicians a-plenty, and in O'Neill a great artist of many aspects. But as yet we have no genuine folk dramatist besides Paul Green. If he were at this moment to cease writing he would be entitled to a place of honor in the development of the American drama. But he is only beginning. Was any beginner ever better equipped? (p. xviii)

> *Barrett H. Clark, "Introduction" (reprinted with permission of The Estate of Barrett H. Clark), in* Lonesome Road: Six Plays for the Negro Theatre *by Paul Green, Robert M. McBride & Company, 1926, pp. vii-xviii.*

JOHN MASON BROWN

Ever since such fine and gripping one-acts as **"The No 'Count Boy"** and **"Lonesome Road"** [Paul Green] has been winning a wide and enthusiastic public for himself, achieving the rare prestige of being constantly compared to and mentioned with Eugene O'Neill. . . . He was hailed as a white hope, and had justified the faith of his admirers by his relentless, often beautiful, and almost always powerful one-act dramas of folk and Negro life in the Carolinas. Unfortunately, the step from the one-act form to the long play is not an easy one. Nor does the one-act gift in a dramatist any more imply that he is also possessor of a talent for the three-act form, than that a painter who is able to paint miniatures should have a like skill in murals, or that a short-story writer should also be adept as a novelist. **"The Field God"** and **"In Abraham's Bosom"** make this point only too clear. They reveal Mr. Green, with all of his considerable and very persuasive gifts, stumbling through a period of transition rather than mastering a new form. Both of them are plays of greater promise than accomplishment, and both of them expose certain serious faults which Mr. Green must conquer if his future work is to realize its expectations. Like O'Neill, he seems unable to edit himself. And, consequently, he often stands in the way of his own aim, permitting flaws to remain in his plays which should have disappeared in the second writing. **"In Abraham's Bosom,"** in particular, falls short of its goal. It is, even when its seventh scene is reached, only a series of one-act plays which are never quite whipped into final unity. Its story of a Negro Abraham who seeks to be a prophet among his own people only to invite misery on himself and his family is told with a fine fervor, but its repetitions show a careless hand. Its race problem is handled with a clumsiness which is only matched by its sincerity. But while its raw, chunky moments obstruct its flow they do not hide the vehement sympathy from which the play springs and the intermittent brilliance of the writing. Considered as a Pulitzer Prize winner, however, it cannot but seem that the judges of the Flower Show have given their award to a seed envelope rather than a full-grown plant. **"The Field God"** is, in many respects, a better play than **"In Abraham's Bosom."** In it Mr. Green has no problem to present and hence is freer to present both his characters and his plot. Of the two it must be admitted it is his characters which come off the better. His idiot boy, his gossiping neighbors, and his old washerwoman, who are the Gobbos of his tragedy, are sketched with an admirable skill and endowed with a humor that is rare among tragic writers. They form the chorus to the bleak, domestic tragedy Mr. Green narrates concerning the return of a city girl to a farm, where her married uncle and his younger friend both fall in love with her. Death follows death and evil piles on evil at such a breakneck rate that they strain credulity and numb the over-taxed emotions of both reader and spectator alike. The first two-thirds of the play, however, does give concrete evidence of Mr. Green's very real and remarkable earth-sprung talents. It shimmers with speeches which, while they are rich in a poetic imagery, are so burning with emotion and so faithful to character that they are beautifully adapted to the theatre's needs. But in the last two scenes, when Gilchrist, the rugged farmer who has defied God, finds him within his own breast, the writing takes on a maudlin and uncontrolled ecstasy which is, unfortunately, not written in dramatic terms. Then Mr. Green, the literary man, gets the better of Mr. Green, the dramatist, and the play slides steadily down hill, slipping from one transcendental frenzy to another and roaring passionately but ineffectually to its conclusion. (pp. 940-41)

John Mason Brown, *"Plays and Works," in* The Saturday Review of Literature *(copyright © 1927 by Saturday Review; all rights reserved; reprinted by permission), Vol. III, No. 49, July 2, 1927, pp. 939-41.*

JULIA PETERKIN

So much of Paul Green's work has concerned Negroes that his name is identified with his powerful ability to portray the experiences of black people. We who have spent our lives with them thick around us, seeing them constantly, hearing what they say day after day, have had our ears sharpened to their speech and our eyes guided to see deeper into the secret places of their hearts by what Paul Green has written about them.

A few Negroes, part white, part black, have places in his **"Wide Fields,"** but most of the book is given up to poor white farmers of the Carolina cotton belt, people who belong to that pathetic class situated between the descendants of former slave owners and those of former slaves. . . .

Paul Green knows them. In **"Wide Fields,"** he not only tells us about them, but he contrives to put us into their skins and make us suffer with them. Reading the book is not a pleasant experience, for while it holds comedy and humor, it is packed with stark, bitter tragedy.

A young wife who craves beauty and cleanliness gets choked to death because a high-collared dude tempts her to leave her sweaty, smelly, hard-working husband; a middle-aged virgin's birthday brings her day-dreams, then a pitiful sinful night-dream threatens her soul's salvation; the queer ways of a woods-colt and a gypsy woman and other humble people are put into words flavored all the way through with Elizabethan idiom, so they stand out in clear, sharp, heart-breaking lines. Surely, Paul Green's deep sincerity, his sense of pity, the dignity of his work, give him a high place in contemporary American literature.

Julia Peterkin, *"Poor White Trash," in* The Saturday Review of Literature *(copyright © 1928 by Saturday Review; all rights reserved; reprinted by permission), Vol. IV, No. 39, April 21, 1928, p. 780.*

JOSEPH WOOD KRUTCH

Mr. Green is coming of age at last, and to say that his play [**"The House of Connelly"**] is by far the most interesting presented this season on Broadway would be to say much too little. As a whole it is very, very good; in places it reveals writing as fine as it has ever been my privilege to admire in an American drama, and today we may safely speak not of "promise" but of accomplishment.

Hitherto Mr. Green has never sufficiently emerged as an individual from the group of which he was a part. Assiduous cultivator of the "folk drama" and savior of the Little Theater movement, his plays seemed so much what they were expected to be that the curse of an all-too-obvious worthiness was upon them, and they were made for the approval of a cult. But in **"The House of Connelly"** he achieves a fully developed individuality of method and of flavor; he speaks with a voice unmistakably his own; and he proves that he has something really valuable to give. Moreover, his tone seems doubly original for the reason that it is so little related to that of the best of our other playwrights. Howard, Stallings, Rice, and, to some extent, also O'Neill resemble one another at least to the extent that they are harsh and violent, that they have made art out of crassness and brutality. But Paul Green introduces a fresh note of poetry of a different kind. He is gentle, elegiac, and melancholy. His play, despite its elements of violence, is tender without sentimentality and almost wholly beautiful.

Superficially, to be sure, the story which he tells is one which any other folk dramatist might have chosen. . . . But what raises it to its present high level is the fact that its author has discovered how to exploit in his own sensitive way the poetry of its implications. In his hands it becomes not so much a story as a quasi-musical "arrangement," in which we see and hear and feel a situation rich not only in conflicts but in pathos and charm and loveliness as well. Here is a civilization which is dying and which should die; a civilization which was founded upon arrogant privilege and which revealed its rottenness through the shameful, illegitimate misalliances which it commonly tolerated. But it was a civilization which had its elements of beauty as well as its pride and its fortitude, and Mr. Green makes us feel all these things. . . .

The effect which Mr. Green achieves is one which irresistibly suggests one of the miracles of Chekhov, and it is accomplished in somewhat the same way—by the employment, that is to say, of scenes and dialogues which are almost magically suggestive. It is, perhaps, chiefly on those few occasions when the author strikes a false note that one realizes how frequently he has succeeded in suggesting what could never be effectively said. . . . Atmosphere is generated one hardly knows how, and emotion steals out over the footlights like some at first imperceptible perfume. One is relatively indifferent as to what finally happens and Mr. Green is certainly best when he is merely exhibiting his characters, but certain personages and certain scenes—like the Christmas dinner—will not easily be forgotten. They have a power without violence which is rare and memorable.

Joseph Wood Krutch, *"A Promise Fulfilled," in* The Nation *(copyright 1931 The Nation magazine, The*

Nation Associates, Inc.), Vol. CXXXIII, No. 3458, October 14, 1931, p. 408.

HAMILTON BASSO

In spite of the structural defects that result from Mr. Green's attempt to impose the technique of the theatre upon the technique of the novel, ["**This Body the Earth**"] is an outstanding addition to the literature of social protest that is being written by Southern writers.

The story of "**This Body the Earth**" is simple enough. Alvin Barnes is the son of a trifling, shiftless, holy-rolling cropper. He realizes, as a young boy, that there can be a decency and dignity to human life and determines to rise above his class. He scrimps, works like a mule, tries to educate himself. Finally, a grown man, he acquires (on paper) a few acres of his own. He marries the prettiest girl he knows. All his dreams seem to be coming true. . . . Then, suddenly, everything goes to pieces. . . .

Alvin Barnes will probably be compared, reasonably enough, with that other cropper who came out of the South to become a Broadway tradition: Mr. Erskine Caldwell's eloquent and profane Jeeter Lester. Mr. Green's hero will be used, especially in the South, to prove that the subhuman Jeeter is an extreme case; that there are tenant farmers with deep wells of ambition and pride. Such contentions, of course, are true . . . and because they are true, the tragedy of Alvin Barnes becomes even more heart-breaking. He is defeated, not by himself, but by the agricultural economy of the South. This economy, in Mr. Green's novel, becomes the Nemesis of the old Greek tragedies—merciless, vindictive, hounding a man to his death. The implicit moral is that the individual, no matter how rugged, cannot combat a system that makes individuals its prey.

The chapters of this book that are likely to receive most attention are those exposing the penal system of North Carolina—the whippings, the chain gang, the "sweat box." The description of a Negro prisoner's being whipped until his rump is lacerated and bleeding is not pretty to read and not pretty to remember. But it had to be written and it is sincerely to be hoped that these sections of "**This Body the Earth**" will serve the purpose for which they were obviously intended—the reformation of one of the most brutal and inhuman prison systems in the United States. Paul Green has written a brave, honest, eloquent book—his most important performance since "**In Abraham's Bosom.**"

Hamilton Basso, "Nemesis in the Cotton Belt" (reprinted by permission of the Literary Estate of Hamilton Basso), in The New Republic, *Vol. LXXXV, No. 1093, November 13, 1935, p. 24.*

JOSEPH WOOD KRUTCH

According to the Group, which is producing "**Johnny Johnson**" . . . , the piece in question is a "legend." That phrase will serve well enough in its place on the program, but it will hardly do to describe the curious fantasy, half musical and half dramatic, which Paul Green and Kurt Weill have concocted between them. The matter is as serious as possible, the manner often so broad as almost to suggest vaudeville or a revue, and yet the whole is somehow strangely effective. I am, in general, no great partisan of the experimental techniques, but "**Johnny Johnson**" is both amusing enough and moving enough to justify itself very handsomely indeed. (p. 675)

Everyone will, I fancy, agree that the piece is at times ragged and uncertain. Every now and then the mood is broken, every now and then the author of the text seems to lose his sense of style, and to write a speech or a scene too realistic on the one hand or too near burlesque on the other really to harmonize with the dominant manner, which is poised at some definite point between the two. But however far short it may fall of perfection, its success in general is never in doubt, and the thing is held together by Kurt Weill's score, which seems to me not only ideal for the purpose but consistent in a way that the text is not. (p. 676)

Joseph Wood Krutch, "Fool of God," in The Nation *(copyright 1936 The Nation magazine, The Nation Associates, Inc.), Vol. 143, No. 23, December 5, 1936, pp. 675-76.*

BROOKS ATKINSON

[The performance of a commemorative pageant entitled "**The Lost Colony**"] is a particularly inspiring event to the citizens of North Carolina and Virginia, who have been attending in increasing numbers. To others, less familiar with the details of Sir Walter Raleigh's valorous and tragic attempt to carry the English spirit into the wild new world it is an uncommonly impressive evocation of the daring that seeped into this country from the wave-beaten beaches just north of Hatteras. For Paul Green, author of "**The Lost Colony**," and the others who have contributed to a community celebration have approached their work in a reverent mood. (p. 1)

[In writing "**The Lost Colony**"], Mr. Green has infused history with a religious reverence for the men and women who laid down their lives to make Sir Walter's dream come true. Although the form of pageantry makes the description of character difficult and loosens the texture of narrative, Mr. Green has written history with a compassion that turns his characters into unconscious symbols of a brave new world. He has communicated their earnestness by contrasting the egotistical court of Queen Elizabeth with the rude austerity of life inside the embattled log fort amid hostile savages. The dances translate the freshness and wildness of the new world more eloquently than words or scenery could. The glory of the ancient English hymns, carols and ballads, sung to an organ accompaniment, pulls the lost colonists into the great stream of human nobility. Part pageant, part masque, "**The Lost Colony**" is a simply stated idealization of the adventurous impulse that founded this nation in the restless image of Shakespeare's England. We can be wise 350 years after the event. Mr. Green's wisdom is rooted in a poet's love of a fair land.

Apart from its function as a commemorative pageant, "**The Lost Colony**" also represents Mr. Green's old ambition to write what he sheepishly describes as "symphonic drama." He has been moving in that direction with "**Roll Sweet Chariot**" of 1934 and "**Johnny Johnson**," which he wrote with Kurt Weill last season. For he has the Wagnerian hope of composing dramas that employ the myriad arts of the theatre and that give themes a grand spiritual fervor by orchestrating the dance, song and acting. . . . "**The Lost Colony**" is a step toward [the fulfillment of that hope], although the nature of the current occasion confines the freedom of an author's imagination. He cannot master a scene in history as passionately as he can master the spirit of the individual man. At best pageantry is a horizontal art; drama is vertical, ranging from the inner life of the private man to the emptyrean of human aspiration. Drama is also more compact in structure and fiercer in spirit. Drama discloses in burning action the secretive tumult of the heart. What a pageant maker is compelled to describe externally the dramatic poet can show in the being. He can dissect first causes; he is there before the reporter has arrived. It is a heroic job, especially according to the dimensions Mr. Green has in mind; and it will require more practical craftsmanship than he has put into any of his previous plays and all the poetic vitality that lives within him. From the theatrical point of view, **"The Lost Colony"** is another trial-script for his great project of symphonic drama. (pp. 1-2)

Brooks Atkinson, "Founding Fathers," in The New York Times, *Section 10 (© 1937 by The New York Times Company; reprinted by permission), August 15, 1937, pp. 1-2.*

ANTHONY F. MERRILL

As a dramatic production, **The Lost Colony** more than justifies the growing acclaim which its audiences accord it. Paul Green, with his fine understanding and his ability to interpret that which is at his doorstep, has created something which seems to have grown right out of the very ground on which it takes place. Laid in the sixteenth century, the play-pageant tells first of the discovery of the island and Raleigh's success in founding a colony upon it. The second half deals with the struggles of the colonists to survive and their eventual disappearance.

The events in the tragic history of Fort Raleigh lend themselves admirably to dramatization. The period being Elizabethan, Green is able to take much from Shakespeare's book. Life and death contribute their share of humor and pathos, while throughout the tale runs a thread of romance evolving between John Borden, the colonists' leader, and Eleanor Dare, widowed mother of the first English child born in the New World. For color and suspense there are the Indians and their war dances, the fear of the roving Spanish galleons and the fight against starvation which finally forces the migration.

And through it all, one feels a sense of absolute reality in what transpires on the stage. Perhaps a great deal of this is due to the setting. Nothing could seem more tangible than the dramatic climax in which young Borden and Eleanor Dare agree that they must give up the security of their little fort for the uncertainty of more remote lands. From its height, the audience sees far beyond the two figures standing alone on the stage, beyond to the wide, empty expanse of bay, glistening in the moonlight. In the hush of the moment, Borden gives tongue to the full emotion of their silent departure from recorded history with a line that stirs the depths of imagination—' We two, standing here tonight upon the outpost of the world, the last survivors—keepers of a dream.'

And then to the onlooker comes the realization that for an hour or more, he too has stood with young John Borden and brave Eleanor Dare upon 'the outpost of the world,' keeping a dream. (pp. 521-22)

Anthony F. Merrill, "The Town That Is a Theatre" (copyright, 1939, by Theatre Arts, Inc.; reprinted by permission of the author), in Theatre Arts Monthly, Vol. XXIII, No. 7, July, 1939, pp. 518-22.

STARK YOUNG

As I ponder [the performance of **In Abraham's Bosom**] it seems moving and profound. Certainly the course of its struggle is full of tragic despair. . . . There is, too, a certain wise balance of parts in the dramatic elements; the white people mean to be kind, but they are as lost in the midst of a race situation as the Negro is; they are moved now by human or affectionate impulse and now by a blind racial instinct and an arbitrary, desperate sense of self-preservation. The climaxes in the play are strong and bold. I seem, as I think of it, to have been present at a full, passionate story, told by a poet. Certainly this material that Mr. Green attempts is ambitious of power and devastation and beauty; we are in very deep waters with such subject matter as he employs.

But what I remember last is that for three-fifths of the time I was dissatisfied and often more than bored. The first act, up to that really inventive moment at the very last when the three Negroes dance about at the sight of the love between Abe and Goldie, was very nearly unbearable. (p. 89)

The dialogue of this play, apart from some of the curtain climaxes, is flat and seems hastily written. Considering the bold, O'Neill sort of line that the treatment essays, the speeches are sometimes surprisingly false, borrowed, conventional. One of the best signs of promise in such a play as **In Abraham's Bosom** would lie in the ear; for nowhere in America is there better material for dialogue than in this world of Mr. Green's; nowhere is there a more special rhythm and flavor of speech than in the South, or more warmth and naïveté of words than in Negro speech. That Mr. Green made so little of this living stuff, that his lines have so little care and so little passion for the quivering beat of life that the words might carry, is a discouraging sign in what is obviously a marked theatre talent working with material that is wholly vibrant and freshly taken out of our American life.

The best places in this play of Negro life are those like that orgiastic end of the first act. . . . In these there is an essence that is racial, dramatic and moving. These moments take themselves out of the hands of the actors, the pulse quickens, the glow of strangeness and beauty comes over the scene; and for a little we have the sense of a soul working and of poetic truth.

But it is between these moments that the trouble lies with Mr. Green's play. Between these high moments we cannot ask an equal tension and imagination; but we can ask more pains, more reduction of the play's progress to firm outlines that would go better with its bold technical aim. The tenderness of feeling in this work, the love of the country and soil in which this history occurs, the courage of the character delineation and the range of sentiment, all deserve more care and choice on the author's part. The glow that is in these special passages could appear, though in smaller terms of course, in the speeches that lie between them. This play is of the kind that makes you wish it well; and you resent all the more the fact that the gloom that some of its spreads over you is not the gloom of tragedy, for that might be rich and stirring, but of casual form and bad writing. (p. 90)

. . . . .

The characters in [**The House of Connelly**] are clearly defined; their words—all but the heroine's—are profoundly Southern and have been well heard by the dramatist out of his own life in the South. Sometimes a detail though tiny is so startlingly Southern that none but a Southerner could savor its exactness. (p. 128)

The weakness of **The House of Connelly** lies in the girl's motive. There is tied up in [the] tenant's daughter the theme of the new life blending with the old, the new conditions, the strengthened blood turning back to the land, and so on. But this, though it is so large a motive in the drama, never gets quite expressed. Throughout the play, time is lost in other talk and other scenes when what we need is to get the main theme established. What has seemed to us the old love story of a beggar maid and prince turns out eventually to be the deep-laid scheme of a young woman who, with her eye on possessing the land, has seduced a weak, intense young man, and at last grown to love him. All this crucial matter is poured out in an explanatory speech, delivered at the very crisis of their emotional relations, and written like some college girl's explanation, arid and without the engaging passion or reality that so many of the other characters' lines have had. And the upshot is that thereupon the play's back is broken. On the whole, obviously, the trouble is that at bottom no dramatic image is ever discovered, no action or moment that would create for us the girl's meaning and point in the play.

The uncle's rôle, rather too long for the sting and pathos intended by it, runs somewhat too far toward the Russian flavor; and his suicide seems to me unconvincing, as well as being both untrue to this Southern type or temperament and harmful to the play's total impression on the memory. *The House of Connelly* remains, notwithstanding, well worth a dozen more facile works. Uncle, girl, problem or not, it is at its source poetic, by which I mean the richness, quiver and dilation that it often gives to the material presented. (pp. 128-29)

> Stark Young, "'In Abraham's Bosom'" and "The Shadow of Wings," in his Immortal Shadows: A Book of Dramatic Criticism *(copyright 1948 Charles Scribner's Sons; copyright renewed 1976 Lewis M. Isaacs, Jr., Executor of the Estate of Stark Young; reprinted with the permission of Charles Scribner's Sons), Charles Scribner's Sons, 1948, pp. 88-90, 127-31.*

AGATHA BOYD ADAMS

Paul Green's work is still very much in progress. A man of abundant energy and vitality, he has a rich store of as yet unrealized dreams and ideas. His work has shown both consistency and the power to expand: consistency in the underlying theme of compassion for and championship of those who are denied basic human rights; expansion in enlarging these themes to an application beyond the bounds of locality.

From a point of view so near to a living writer, it is impossible to say whether or not his books will supply that lack which Paul Green himself deplored in 1928 when he said: "North Carolina has made no lasting contribution to the art of the world." Even with a consideration of the towering figure of Thomas Wolfe, who burst upon the scene in 1929, it is possible, looking back on the body of Green's work, to say that Green has "with high-minded and intelligent devotion" recorded the lives of his fellow countrymen. He has been one of the most faithful and the most illuminating interpreters of the rural life of North Carolina, and through his intimate knowledge and understanding of one locality has been able to interpret also the South. Good sense and good judgment have made him willing to confine his writing to the area of his own observation and knowledge; imagination of heart and brain has enabled him to progress from that simple area to larger concern with the fundamental problems of mankind. Passion for justice for the Negro and the sharecropper led in his thinking to a passion for justice for all humanity, a belief in democracy as a way of human righteousness. The social and economic problems of Harnett County grew, in the historical plays, into the problems of the young United States, and by implication, of all human kind. (pp. 112-13)

As an interpreter of the South, Green has followed an individual as well as a thoroughly sincere course. He has avoided the romanticism and sentimentality which he so vigorously condemned in his first manifesto as editor of *The Reviewer*. He has also to a large extent avoided that Gothic quality in Southern writing which appears in the gargoyles and grotesques of realists such as Caldwell and Faulkner. . . . In the steadiness and balance with which he has regarded [the South] from his own angle of vision, he is not unlike that otherwise so different novelist, Ellen Glasgow. He lacks her irony, and the scenes which he depicts are farther from Richmond in spiritual climate than in actual geography; but the temper of observation, the sure knowledge of the familiar, the compassionate understanding, the lack of distortion, are similar in tone. For the most part, Green has been able to describe his section of the South without getting too excited about it, without creating angels and devils in a realm of fantasy. Perhaps in some plays, notably **Tread the Green Grass** and **Shroud My Body Down,** he has succumbed to the Southern impulse toward the ornate and the strange; but the main body of his published work concerns a very real segment of the rural South, described with honesty and sanity. His South is one of potential abundance of wasted and eroded land, of cruel injustice and of true neighborliness, of laughter and music and tragedy and courage and futility and aspiration; in short, a region peopled by human beings instead of by social and economic charts and ciphers and statistics, or by unrecognizable grotesques.

The mood of his generation, and his own intrinsic sincerity, determined that Green should write realistically. The poet that he naturally is, however, has almost always been dominant. This combination of poetry and realism forms part of the individual quality not only of his interpretation of the South, but of his work as a whole. Abraham McCranie inhabits a harshly realistic world of denial and deprivation and crime; yet his dreams and aspiration, his passion and his torture, are illuminated with poetry. In **The Common Glory,** the American Revolution moves forward in all the reality of human pain, but beyond this reality the author's deep understanding of heroic idealism lifts and shapes the play into a poetic whole. It is a matter for speculation whether or not in a different literary climate from the realistic one of the United States in the 1920's and 1930's Paul Green might have written only poetry and poetic drama; it is a matter for gratitude that the pull toward realism never overwhelmed the poet.

Poetry inheres not only in the lyrics of his plays, not only in the quick response to beauty of all sorts, but most essentially in his concern with noble issues and basic truths. He has never let himself be drawn into writing meretriciously; he has never denied his dedication to man's long climb toward righteousness, his profound convictions of justice and injustice, right and wrong. (pp. 113-15)

Unlike most writers, Paul Green has written no book which can be interpreted as autobiographical, although there are such passages, notably in **This Body The Earth.** In spite of the fact that he is introspective to a degree, his creative energies have been turned outward; he has used his own experiences, obviously, but always to create characters other than himself. (p. 115)

From the early folk plays of his Playmaker days, to the developing and expanding regional dramatic productions typified by the symphonic dramas, Paul Green has remained true to his purpose and his ambition to write plays about the people and for the people, to be produced not by commercial backing, but with the design of bringing music and poetry and color and drama within easy reach of people in communities far from Broadway. In this movement he has been an innovator. He has also pioneered in the combination of music and drama in a closely interwoven form. He has always suggested and pointed the way toward greater harmonies of interpretation. (pp. 115-16)

> Agatha Boyd Adams, in her Paul Green of Chapel Hill, *edited by Richard Walser (copyright, 1951, by The University of North Carolina Press; reprinted by permission of Alice Adams), The University of North Carolina Library, 1951, 116 p.*

GERALD RABKIN

The fact of "class" was one that few American dramatists escaped in the thirties; man was primarily a social, not a psychological, animal. Thus Paul Green in his drama of southern decadence, *The House of Connelly* (1931), is less concerned with the forms of this decadence than with the juxtaposition of a healthy alternative. (p. 84)

We might profitably contrast the south of *House of Connelly* with the south of Tennessee Williams. As Green paints the decay of the old order it seems to be, at first, in the manner of Williams: "Now the grace of hospitality is gone, the jovial host is gone, gone is the slave. The furniture is falling to pieces. . . . The dead Connellys in their frames wait for the end." The living Connellys exist in a past world of Belle Reves and Blue Mountains; the old order is crumbling before the onslaughts of new social forces, and the Connelly clan, like the Sartoris, can only rail against the powerful upstarts who have perverted the values of the Old South.

So far so good. Now were Tennessee Williams proceeding with the play, the old aristocracy, however decadent, would still be preferable to the new forces of change. After all, is there not virtue in the posture of gallantry? Surely there could be no rapprochement between the old order and the new. And yet this is Green's theme: "Out of this death and darkness—into the light!" . . . Will Connelly, the scion of the clan, recognizes that he cannot resuscitate a dead past, that the old, aristocratic order is gone forever. He finds in Patsy, the daughter of a tenant farmer, hope for the creation of a new future, and despite the cruelty of the choice (Patsy is bitterly resented by the older Connellys) he is convinced by her that it must be made. (pp. 84-5)

The premise that resides at the heart of *House of Connelly* is that decadence is a fact of institutions and classes; in the work of Tennessee Williams corruption is existential. The first premise makes the concept of social action meaningful, the second declares all social gestures essentially irrelevant.

Green, in his second play for the [Group Theatre] *Johnny Johnson* (1936), departs from his familiar regional environment, but he is again concerned with asserting a social thesis: in this case, the insanity of war. The method he employs—the juxtaposition of a supremely sane man against the organized absurdity of conventional institutions—has been employed more recently for purely comic effect in such military comedies as *No Time for Sergeants* and *At War with the Army*. But Green's purpose in *Johnny Johnson* is completely serious. As the play proceeds it becomes increasingly bitter in tone, until at last the

laws of sanity apply only within the confines of an insane asylum. Why had Johnny been committed? Merely because he had acted upon the "mad" conviction that human beings were reasonable creatures, that mankind would not willfully destroy itself.

Green's ironic fable . . . is not primarily concerned, as is *Peace on Earth,* with the causes of war; it is rather concerned with its ultimate absurdity and its devastating horror. In the name of country, religion, family, mankind forgets its common humanity and acts more viciously—because its actions are gratuitous—than the most vicious animal. Johnny's crime is that he demands a *reason* for fighting. (pp. 85-6)

Johnny Johnson is a protest against the final absurdity of war; the paradox of Green's play resides in the question of whether, in a world governed by insanity, the forces of sanity must be eternally suspect. The leaders of the "civilized" world reject Johnny's pacifism as madness; the inmates of the asylum accept his leadership and unanimously create a League of World Republics. But Green does not end the play on a note of despair; Johnny, when released from the asylum, again sees the war-clouds gathering, and again hears the familiar jingoism. Even when faced with the recurrence of mankind's perennial blight, Johnny does not lose his unconquerable optimism, his faith that sanity shall ultimately prevail. . . . (pp. 86-7)

Paul Green's dramatic contribution to the . . . [Group Theatre, a New York-based drama collective which was dedicated to plays reflecting contemporary social problems,] raises wistful considerations of the dramatist he once was. As his career progressed the intense regionalism, which in the twenties and thirties was illumined by social and psychological insight, degenerated into the hollow formalities of spectacle. The playwright who has shown himself capable of *In Abraham's Bosom, House of Connelly, Hymn to the Rising Sun* and *Johnny Johnson* abdicated in favor of the scenarist for such confederate flag-waving extravaganzas as *Wilderness Road, The Founders,* and *The Confederacy.* Surely this record does not indicate that social concerns distorted Green's accomplishment; his recent total dedication to patriotic spectacle of the most obvious banality ("The Confederacy is now our Lost Cause, but the ideals we served are not lost." "Yes. Yes.") raises the unfortunate apprehension that, like the Confederacy, Paul Green's dramatic seriousness will not rise again. (p. 87)

> Gerald Rabkin, "The Group Theatre: Theatre is Collective Art," *in his* Drama and Commitment: Politics in the American Theatre of the Thirties *(copyright © 1964 by Indiana University Press), Indiana University Press, 1964, pp. 71-94.*

HOWARD D. PEARCE

Recognized as a present writer of the outdoor pageant play (in his words, "symphonic drama") and a past writer of regional, "folk," and experimental drama, Paul Green is another of those dramatists such as T. S. Eliot and Tennessee Williams who have turned to myth in search of universal meanings. . . . Green's plays written between 1920 (*The Last of the Lowries*) and 1934 (*Roll Sweet Chariot*) show a progress from folk materials and realistic manner toward a blend of folk-mythic matter and symbolic, anti-realistic technique. Green recapitulates, then, an historical development from the superficial American regionalism of the late nineteenth century to the search for deeper reality through myth, symbol and experimental form. (p. 62)

[It] is impossible not to see that from the very beginning Green was a most literary writer, both in exploring the areas of dramatic technique and in turning to literature as a source for idea and image. (p. 64)

[Green] is not an unsophisticated provincial. He is highly conscious of various traditions of thought and literary modes. His methodical search of folklore likewise reveals a conscious craftsman. Assiduously he combed the materials of his region and his nation's history for inspiration and subject matter. (p. 65)

All Green's intense endeavor led him in a search toward the highest fulfillment of his art. Not a man of easy faith, he was yet eager to explore any path which might lead to the ultimate enrichment or perfection of his craft. (p. 66)

It was during the late 1920's and early 1930's that Green's individual plays became most heterogeneous as a result of his febrile quest for new forms. *Blue Thunder,* written in 1928, remains an enigmatic and provocative play. *Tread the Green Grass* was written in the same year, and *Shroud My Body Down* was written in the early 1930's. *Potter's Field* was begun in 1929 and *Roll Sweet Chariot,* its ultimate form, completed in 1934. *The Lost Colony* in 1937 marked the end of his quest for new form, for with it he had arrived at a plateau. He had taken the drama outdoors, had placed it on a panoramic stage, and had integrated pantomime, song, and dance, in an elevated and ceremonial style, with the materials of American history, achieving the noble ends of art.

Unfortunately, like the Marxian Utopia, this ultimate achievement of a dialectical progress, which must be produced through the thrust and counterthrust of forces, is as static and as dull as any paradise would be. I do not mean to condemn the symphonic plays outright. There is much that is good in them. But one feels in reading them (and they are not meant to be read, but seen in all their embellishments) that the old challenge for Green, the fire of discovery, has been lost. And that burning quest suffuses the plays of discovery, those experimental plays of the years between the mid-1920's and the mid-1930's, those plays which may often fail but do so with intensity and flourish, with power and sensitivity. (p. 67)

This quest for a higher art led Green through territories which lay in opposite directions. The continued refinement of dramatic technique which led him ultimately to a symphonic drama is actually opposite to that of a folk drama, which is by nature elemental, simple, and limited. His journey through the fields of conscious art, through sophistication of form and technique, through a refined and international exchange of ideas, led him away from the simplicity of folk style. He ultimately found in the stylization of the Japanese theater the closest approach to the ideal that he had ever seen: "The Kabuki theatre is the true representational [sic] theatre art as I've yearned to see it." . . . Here is a Green talking for whom direct message, didacticism, is a step below the etherealized pure art of the Japanese theatre. By such a criterion, it would seem that a few of the plays from the period of greatest experiment rose higher than both the thesis-studded earlier plays and the overtly nationalistic drama of the symphonic period.

There is implicit, however, a single goal in the opposite extremes through which Green worked. Both his sophisticated drama and his folk drama are aimed at baring the essential rhythms of life, the ceremonies by which all men live a common existence, the very essence of human nature which is the same whether abstracted through the refinement of art or perceived directly in the naked, unaccommodated form of elemental man.

It would seem then that Green, by the clarity of his vision of man's soul, worked toward the center of human experience, no matter on what diverging paths his travels seemed to take him.

Although firmly rooted in a more realistic world and peopled with characters of a more fully realized individuality than those of *Blue Thunder, Shroud My Body Down,* and *Tread the Green Grass, Roll Sweet Chariot* like those plays grows upward into an atmosphere of poetic rarefaction. It ostensibly moves from a Chekhovian flux of isolated souls touching and withdrawing from one another to a last-scene fusion of the individuals into a communal spirit. The resultant shift in style from the apparent slice of reality in Scene One to the ode on suffering and salvation in the final scene has been considered one of the play's major weaknesses. Similarly, the transformation of the folk hero John Henry from a confidence man into a spiritual leader has distressed those who require a conventional, realistic treatment of character. Yet, taken in the play's own terms, such seeming shifts result in the total harmony for which Green reached. The atmosphere of *Roll Sweet Chariot,* from beginning to end, is imbued with a poetic intensity which boils from the passionate love, fear, and hate; the reckless joy and impertinence; and the instinctive malice and selfishness of the folk themselves. Musical pattern and poetic image hold together what might indeed be, without them, unassimilated and drifting fragments. (pp. 68-9)

[From statements Green has made about *Roll Sweet Chariot,* it seems evident] that, although the ostensible theme of the play is justice, the conclusion does not result in an establishment of justice. If such is the case, so is it in Green's other major plays: *In Abraham's Bosom, The Field God, Tread the Green Grass, The House of Connelly.* Each of these plays contains as an important theme the problem of justice, but in none of them is justice precisely worked out in the end. In the last two mentioned there is an explicit denial of simple, earthly justice in the ritual sacrifices of the Young Reverend (or Tina) and Patsy Tate.

Roll Sweet Chariot, too, is about justice, but it concludes with the assurance that man can endure in spite of its earthly perversion, that he can grow toward a fulfillment of his potential regardless of a prevailing power of vengeance. The community, like the individual, is both innocent and guilty. (p. 76)

Although *Roll Sweet Chariot,* like the other plays of Green's experimental period, does not conform to a single tradition, it stands as one of Green's most exalted efforts, perhaps his best, to make a dramatic form carry his vision of mankind. In these plays his experiment in dramatic traditions and his synthesis of adopted ideas and images, patterns and language, found completion. Regardless of imperfections, plays like *Tread the Green Grass* and *Roll Sweet Chariot* deserve greater recognition than they have generally received. (p. 78)

Howard D. Pearce, "From Folklore to Mythology: Paul Green's 'Roll Sweet Chariot'," in The Southern Literary Journal *(copyright 1971 by the Department of English, University of North Carolina at Chapel Hill), Vol. III, No. 2, Spring, 1971, pp. 62-78.*

HOWARD D. PEARCE

America's "folk-drama" of the 1920's and 1930's appears a last stand of nineteenth-century regionalism. . . . [It] was a brief movement which capitalized on the quaintness and charm, the eccentricity and even grotesqueness, of character, dialect, and setting. There was some necessary superficiality in a tradition that relied too much on entertaining a sophisticated cosmopolitan audience with a parade of characters—or caricatures—from a province. Another rather superficial motive shows in this drama when it was locally produced: the region's own pride in its individuality. But the folk drama did often strive toward the expression of universal human problems and lasting values.

In both aspiration and achievement, the outstanding playwright produced by this movement in the United States was Paul Green. . . . Green knew intuitively the struggles of an unsophisticated people against the forces of both nature and society. These were the "folk" in whom Green found universal human values laid bare. When he began writing plays in the 1920's, he was immediately attracted to the so-called "folk" drama of the Irish playwright John Millington Synge, to such plays as *Riders to the Sea* and *Playboy of the Western World*. In his own region Green saw a native character parallel to that dramatized by Synge, and his natural impulse was, like Synge's, poetic: he converted folk idiom to poetry and drew the regional character in terms of eternal conflicts. (pp. 91-2)

The regional folk beliefs and customs . . . are part and parcel of the body of materials from which Green draws both incident and idea. Through these ideas and practices he expresses the personality of the folk who are at once individualized in their peculiarities and universalized in that those peculiarities express fundamental purposes and forces in human nature. He is striving to express the uniqueness of the folk but, paradoxically, the spiritual One that resides in the separate instances of the Many.

Whereas Green's exploration in folk beliefs and customs, even when he turned to written sources, provided him with a knowledge of the people themselves, his use of folktale and legend extended into another dimension, imaginative literature, characters and plots created by the folk. (pp. 94-5)

[Qualities] of folk literature inhere to a sometimes greater, sometimes lesser, degree in Green's entire body of plays. If the influence of folk literature bent Green toward stylization, formalization, and a heightened and romantic view, the folk themselves, being men in a natural state, inclined him toward a naturalistic treatment of his subjects. On the one hand, there exists a romanticizing, an ennoblement of humanity not unlike the vision by which the primitive sayer or seer transmutes the everyday into the miraculous, transfigures man through myth. On the other hand lies the realistic or naturalistic view of the folk, one which though sympathetic is inclined to see them as no better than they actually are. If his plays contain these seemingly contradictory views of the folk, they are part and parcel of the sources from which he drew.

Folk characters created in the plays are no homogeneous lot, for they grow out of this dualistic view. One character may appear to be drawn from Green's direct knowledge of people; another may retain strong suggestions of his literary prototype; and still another may show close kinship to a type in folklore. A figure who retains the earthy character of the folk may in his similarity to some literary mold suggest that he is drawn from types of both life and literature. (p. 97)

Green's quest for a folk hero . . . draws from folk and literary tradition, moving ever toward the vision of some prototypal hero. In so far as one is concerned with a literary man's use of heroic types to elevate his characters, there is little to be gained by making scholarly distinctions between myth, saga,

and folk tale, or between mythical, legendary, and historical heroes. . . . Whether a writer like Green implies that one of his characters is like Christ, Oedipus, King Arthur, or Paul Bunyan, his endeavor is to suggest the uncommon or even superhuman nature of that character, repeating once more the romantic idealization by which men in all ages have created heroes. Green himself suggests that, to counteract the rationalism and sterility, the categorizing and fact-finding of modern education, which hinder an appreciation of the truth and life to be found in literature, one should discover the power and beauty of literature itself, turning to the heroes of life for inspiration: Paul Bunyan, Davy Crockett, John Henry, Mike Fink, Roy Bean, Casey Jones, Johnny Appleseed, Br'er Rabbit, Thomas Jefferson, George Washington, and Abraham Lincoln. (As this partial list shows, Green would have no objection to fusing mythical, legendary, and historical heroes under one rubric: heroes of *life*.)

Although Green's short plays and tales seem to have offered him little room for developing a true folk hero, his interest in creating the type can be seen in the short works. (pp. 99-100)

[However, it is] in the long plays that Green most fully develops his folk heroes. Abe McCranie becomes noble in his compulsion to lift his people out of degradation, but the heroic figures of *The Field God* and *Roll Sweet Chariot* even more so than Abe have their heroic stature elevated to truly epic dimensions. It was in the symphonic outdoor plays that Green finally fulfilled his desire to dramatize the American hero, painting heroic portraits of such national figures as Jefferson and Washington.

Green's striding toward a timeless world of symbol, then, like his tireless search for new and more nearly perfect forms of drama, led him toward basal figures and patterns which underpin the plays. His search for a hero has been evidenced by his transmutation of the common man of his region into the precious metal of a folk hero. As this search led him in widening circles, one may with assurance follow him into the limits of folklore and literature from which he drew inspiration. . . .

[*Blue Thunder*] provides a most interesting study of Green's use of legendary and folk materials in a highly unrealistic and experimental manner. The play seems as uprooted from reality as do some of the short poetic dramas of William Butler Yeats such as *At the Hawk's Well* or *The Shadowy Waters*. Like these plays, it seems constantly to allude to some mythical, or at least distant and shadowy, referent. The language is stylized, the action ritualized, and, as in some of Yeats' plays, the distinctions between man and god blurred. (p. 100)

Briefly, the play concerns Blue Thunder, "the man who married a snake," who on a realistic level is a Negro ladies' man caught in the act of deserting his three mistresses. The women sing, like conventional mourners, songs of lamentation for the loss of their man, waiting patiently, while he boasts and demonstrates his supernatural powers, for the loss of power which they are certain will descend upon him. Greedily attacking his body after his own supernatural weapons have turned and killed him, they are surprised by the appearance of a little black man, who is death come to take them. (p. 101)

An explanation of this play's action on an entirely realistic basis is, then, almost valueless. The women are not merely mistresses who take revenge on a lover for his attempt to desert them. Read in terms of mythic action, *Blue Thunder* must be seen as a travesty, for the ultimate purpose of ritual, the reinstatement of positive spiritual powers in a new king, the resurrection of a god or the rebirth of nature, is not fulfilled. Blue

Thunder's mention of the cycle of nature emphasizes death as an end: "Farewell. I come in the spring and find you full in the flower, I leave you in the fall with the sap and bloom all gone.". . . He represents a perversion, a curtailment of the promise, of the dying god whose death, though lamented in the fall, promises the return of life in the spring.

In *Blue Thunder,* finally, folk, biblical, and mythic referents cast the entire action in an ironic light, for such allusions point to spiritual values which are subverted by the characters.

This review of Green's use of folk materials reveals a playwright bent on transforming them into poetic, symbolic drama. Rather than merely explicating the character and legend of his region, he is exploiting them. And this impulse to transcend the folk, to the degree that it informs Green's drama and fiction, makes Green's work viable and interesting today. (pp. 105-06)

Howard D. Pearce, "Transcending the Folk: Paul Green's Utilization of Folk Materials," in MOSAIC: A Journal for the Comparative Study of Literature and Ideas *(copyright ©1971 by the University of Manitoba; acknowledgement of previous publication is herewith made), Vol. IV, No. 4 (Summer, 1971), pp. 91-106.*

(Theodore) Wilson Harris

1921-

Guyanese novelist, short story writer, essayist, and poet.

Harris's "novels of expedition" are physical as well as spiritual journeys through the multicultural landscape of Guyana. Harris worked for more than fifteen years as a land surveyor and came to know the complexities of the Guyanese environment and culture. His novels are described as works of discovery and renewal because of Harris's attempts to rediscover the primitive foundation of his culture before it had become polarized by European colonizers.

From his first four novels, known collectively as the "Guiana Quartet" to *Tumatumari* and *Ascent to Omai*, Harris uses the landscape of his birthplace as a metaphor for the Guyanese psyche. In these complex and highly imaginative novels, Harris's characters often find a rich, unlimited potential in a life that contrasts sharply with what Harris perceives as a static Western culture. With *Black Marsden*, Harris began to shift the settings of his novels but he continued to include mystical experiences in order to expand views of existence and personality. In his recent work, Harris points to painting and the role of the artist as a further means of regenerating creative energy. Because of this desire to free the imagination from static values that nullify creativity and his deliberate inversion of literary conventions, Harris is often compared with William Blake.

To achieve a surrealistic and visionary quality in his writings, Harris employs exotic settings of the past and present, dream states, and death and resurrection symbolism. In addition, his writing fuses Christian allegory, Amerindian legend, and mythology from various civilizations. Harris's fiction has been praised for its depth but has also been criticized as difficult and over-ambitious.

(See also *Contemporary Authors*, Vols. 65-68.)

© Jerry Bauer

PAUL WEST

Mr Harris makes me feel cloddish and insensitive. [In *Palace of the Peacock* he's] taken a Christian-Creation sequence of seven days and piled it round with enough complex archetypes to keep a myth-critic busy for life. On one level the setting is the savannahs and forests of British Guiana; on another the inscape of Donne, an educated atavist leading an expedition to the interior. . . . I never quite know what's going on in this novel. . . . Its claustrophobic density reminds me of *The Emperor Jones;* but Mr Harris has an abstract rhetoric all of his own, and he wraps it like glass wool round the often vigorous talk of the characters. He also works to death the words 'dreaming' and 'musing'; but no repeated motif could guide us through a texture so muddy and a structure so daedal.

And yet, having confessed that this short fable maddens and baffles me, I must applaud stretches of pared, articulate narrative, the lilt of many rhetorically oblique conversations, and the authentic portrayal of a forest people who use surnames only—no frills in the lush mazes of vegetation. This is a religious, violent, often private piece of writing, in places appallingly turgid but in others virile, disciplined and vivid. Mr Harris is a fertile writer; having got this farrago out of his system he should now aim at steadiness, and learn to apply the knife.

Paul West, "New Novels: 'Palace of the Peacock'," in New Statesman (© 1960 The Statesman & Nation Publishing Co. Ltd.), Vol. LX, No. 1537, August 27, 1960, p. 282.

THE TIMES LITERARY SUPPLEMENT

Palace of the Peacock is a 150-page definition of mystical experience given in the guise of a novel. It is a difficult book to read, yet it is the very concreteness of Mr. Harris's imagery that makes its denseness so hard to penetrate. . . .

[Although] Mr. Harris's book gives the illusion of moving forward like an ordinary novel, its real movement is downward: it is an exploration in depth. By its end nothing is changed—not even those members of the crew drowned a second time; it is simply that the inner eye is opened.

Told in "a mixed futuristic order of memory and event" (the phrase is the narrator's), this work is in many ways startlingly like Rimbaud's *Le Bateau Ivre*, even down to the symbol of the boat. And it can stand the comparison. Like that poem, it slides away before any attempt to catch it in a net of paraphrase. No description can get its essence: it is what it is. Mr. Harris has certain peculiarities of style that are mild irritants: words come in pairs as regularly as phrases do in the Psalms (''a haze and a dream''; ''a climb and clamber''). But even this is not mere tricksiness—which anyway might be excusable in a first novel: between the two words with their hard-and-fast meaning falls the shadow of what the author wants to say. The near-repetition intensifies the air of incantation that permeates the whole book.

However *déréglé* he may be, Mr. Harris is never woolly. . . . And this concern with the concrete makes this the best of books for communicating the feel of British Guiana: better than a dozen laborious travel-books, or adventure-stories for ever getting caught up in their own machinery.

> *''Exploring in Depth,'' in* The Times Literary Supplement *(© Times Newspapers Ltd. (London) 1960; reproduced from* The Times Literary Supplement *by permission), No. 3057, September 30, 1960, p. 625.*

THE TIMES LITERARY SUPPLEMENT

With **Palace of the Peacock** Wilson Harris staked out a corner of his own in the rich new field of Caribbean writing, and his third novel, **The Whole Armour,** shows him still digging in the same spot. What he brings up is a mixture of local legend . . . and Christian allegory. . . . Other key influences are Hopkins and Blake. . . .

Mr. Harris does hint towards the end that roots must be understood and accepted before the past can be buried, and his characters certainly typify different degrees of this understanding—which does not automatically come, we gather, with education. . . . But it is hard work to extract a precise moral [from **The Whole Armour**] since the story is told in a highly personal way: reality, dream, and psychic experience are indistinguishably vivid, and the regional collective unconsciousness is never far below the surface.

What justifies this difficult approach is the imaginative power behind it; each scene has been genuinely visualized and retains a physical clarity to haunt the memory. Mr. Harris handles his complex imagery with the daring of a born poet.

> *''A Sense of Place,'' in* The Times Literary Supplement *(© Times Newspapers Ltd. (London) 1962; reproduced from* The Times Literary Supplement *by permission), No. 3158, September 7, 1962, p. 669.**

THE TIMES LITERARY SUPPLEMENT

In the first novel [of the **"Guiana Quartet"**], **Palace of the Peacock,** a man called Donne is going up-river to collect labour for his estate, but the reader must soon relinquish his grasp on such a workaday circumstance and commit himself, as it were, to the poetry of motion through a dark interior where words like *death* and *dream* are almost synonymous, where Donne and his crew exist in a limbo compounded of myth and reality. The disastrous journey becomes a struggle not so much to survive, one feels, as actually to re-create a world, ''a window on to the universe''—by which perhaps is meant a vantage point from which to watch the rest of the quartet unfold. Or, the reader may wonder, perhaps there has simply been laid the first of the four biblical cornerstones of Creation, Fall, Flood and Messiah? If so, to what particular Guianan purpose? Is

one in the end to come to nothing more enlivening than a parable of political emergence?

The task that faces the reader who is unfamiliar with West Indian myth and symbol is enormous, but for a time the biblical connotation seems to hold out promise of guidance on the journey through savannah and jungle, through ''the doom of the river and the waterfall''. In the second novel, **Far Journey of Oudin,** part-titles like The Covenant, and The Second Birth, are made to the expected measure, and the title of the third novel, **The Whole Armour** (a quotation from Ephesians, vi,13: ''Wherefore take unto you the whole armour of God''), suggests a point of total comprehension not far ahead. But in spite of these signposts, and others within the novels themselves, it is upon a growing sense of being borne up by forces no longer alien in a landscape increasingly imaginable that the reader eventually depends. . . .

If a first reading of the quartet does not uncover anything like the whole of the relationship the two middle novels need to bear to the first and last to rank as *structurally* indispensable, it does show them as indispensable in the business of conditioning the mind to immediate recognition of the fact that in the end of the quartet is its beginning.

The story in **The Secret Ladder** which we might have taken at its face value—of Fenwick, the young West Indian land-surveyor, charting the upper reaches of the Canje river and falling foul of a settlement ruled by an old African—we take instead in a mood, corresponding to Fenwick's, of ''inner rhapsody and grotesque meditation''. We have an understanding, if not exactly the measure, of what is really at stake: not the destruction of the settlement by flooding as a result of a new irrigation scheme but the destruction of a ''perception of depth more lasting than time'', and of the moral privilege and right of a place that has acquired ''the stamp of a multiple tradition and heritage''.

But what does this *mean*? Fenwick, in whom there is African, English, French, and Amerindian blood, says of his confrontation with the old African (Poseidon): ''I wish I could truly grasp the importance of this meeting. If I do not—if my generation do not—leviathan will swallow us.'' Is this a plea for the preservation of something that is being lost in Guiana, something purely African? If so, is it a political or a cultural loss? Or is Poseidon, this descendant of a runaway slave whose lips do not seem to Fenwick to move in unison with his speech, to be seen as the repository of an ''emotional dynamic of liberation'' that no longer guides a nation's conscience or consciousness?

In a final paragraph epitomizing the quartet Mr. Harris leaves Fenwick in a doubt we no longer really feel ourselves because the concept of that lost dynamic reaches beyond poetic Guianan imagery into our own human and national awareness. . . .

Quartet or no, the four novels culminating in **The Secret Ladder** are clearly the work of a man who should not be described as a West Indian writer in the narrow, restrictive sense of the words. He is a novelist of already distinguished talent writing in English out of a common perception, a particular experience, and a unique vision.

> *''Journey's End,'' in* The Times Literary Supplement *(© Times Newspapers Ltd. (London) 1963; reproduced from* The Times Literary Supplement *by permission), No. 3181, February 15, 1963, p. 105.*

THE TIMES LITERARY SUPPLEMENT

The territory [in *Heartland*] is remote, but not quite remote enough for Mr. Harris's purposes, which are not naturalistic; the jungle becomes a barely adequate backdrop for Stevenson's more exotic awareness of guilt and terror and his inexpressible spiritual aspirations. . . .

Although it is a very short novel it seems to contain a lot of words. Mr. Harris's gifts are clear; they are perhaps too abundant. He writes with an almost uncontrollable fluency. We wait for him to draw breath, to relax, to start again. But he rushes on in bursts of nervous energy, never quite catching up with what he has to say, which is perhaps not as complicated as he fears. The magic quality of words seduces him until he is within a short step of meaninglessness. He is always struggling back to the shores of lucidity and reason. Usually he does get back, and creates something haunting—haunting perhaps because it is unfinished.

"We, the Dismemberers," in The Times Literary Supplement *(©Times Newspapers Ltd. (London) 1964; reproduced from* The Times Literary Supplement *by permission), No. 3264, September 17, 1964, p. 864.**

THE TIMES LITERARY SUPPLEMENT

The novelist, unlike the poet, uses words which must remain for him merely a vehicle of expression, a means to a greater end. The problems of the modern novel spring from the dilemma of deciding what these ends are, or ought to be.

Mr. Harris, sadly, seems to have no clear conception of the fundamental differences between these two sets of problems. First it is clear that he is obsessed with the poetic dilemma. It is sufficient to read one paragraph of [*The Eye of the Scarecrow*], or indeed any of his previous works, to realize that he does not find it possible to relate words to each other in the conventional manner required by the grammar of the language. Indeed, the problem of the meaning which words symbolize seems, if not irrelevant, at least postponed, in his preoccupation with solving what is for him the primary problem of getting inside the structure of the language, of feeling and weighing it as a thing in itself.

The trouble with this kind of exercise is that success depends either on the possession of some measure of genius whereby the problem is grasped and resolved in a purely intuitive manner, or on the combination of talent and a great deal of luck. Mr. Harris, on the basis of this novel, lacks both genius and luck. . . .

Secondly, in so far as [*The Eye of the Scarecrow*] seeks to be a novel, all that can be said is that an attempt has been made to recapture certain traumatic experiences from childhood and early adulthood. . . .

What seems important is not so much the impact of these incidents on the central character at the time they happened but the effects their recollection produce on him in the present as he writes his diary. These effects are then supposed to lead to a transformation of the imagination which is fed back into the past and in the process of re-conceptualizing the past elevates it to a universal plane of rejuvenated innocence and beauty.

It is at this point that Mr. Harris unsuccessfully grapples with one of the central themes of the modern novel; a theme which is best illustrated in Joyce's *Ulysses* and Mann's *Joseph and His Brothers:* the transformation of individual, concrete characters into archetypal figures; the metamorphosis of unique reality into the universe of myth. The problem, in short, of relieving man of his material and temporal restrictions and placing him within some transcendental cosmic environment.

The main source of Mr. Harris's failure is that he is too ambitious. Certainly, it is inconceivable that any serious resolution of the issues posed could have been possible in as slim a volume as this. It is even doubtful whether Mr. Harris is fully aware of all the dimensions of the issues he concerns himself with. That he possesses considerable literary talent there can be no doubt, but until he realizes that more than half the effort needed to overcome the problems he is concerned with lies in asking the right questions, and in being fully aware of their assumptions and implications, and until he is able to discipline his rather flamboyant style and passion for words, his talents as a novelist will remain latent.

"Confusion in Words," in The Times Literary Supplement *(© Times Newspapers Ltd. (London) 1965; reproduced from* The Times Literary Supplement *by permission), No. 3328, December 9, 1965, p. 1121.*

THE TIMES LITERARY SUPPLEMENT

[A study of Wilson Harris's early poems in *Eternity to Season*] reveals that his preoccupation throughout his career as a writer has been to reveal man's dual role as a finite being inhabiting a defined "season" of time, and as an infinite extension of certain human attributes (modified by landscape, climate and historical experience) which exist in eternity. Now Mr. Harris has published an essay, **"Tradition and the West Indian Novel"** [in his *Tradition, the Writer and Society: Critical Essays*], which unveils the theory on which all his fiction has been based.

In essence, his argument is that the traditional Western novel has based its treatment of character upon the assumption that man plays only the first of these two roles. It has largely ignored the second. This has led to the elaboration of a technique which Mr. Harris calls "the consolidation of character"; the building up of finite individual character through the enumeration of attributes. . . .

Mr. Harris's experience of the West Indies, which have been subjected to waves of wildly differing conquest, to a succession of polyglot invaders, enslavers, colonizers, and liberators, has convinced him that character needs to be defined by other methods. Character needs to be set free in time and in space. . . . This method he calls the fulfilment of character, as opposed to its consolidation. . . . Looking again at the treatment of character in Mr. Harris's novels we can see how his people are mysteriously and incestuously linked with one another; linked not only with their many-hued ancestors but also with their collaterals and their unborn descendants. We can see why the linked characters in *Palace of the Peacock* . . . or *The Whole Armour* . . . continually reflect, inhabit and even become one another according to the dictates of their state of being. For such interfusions of character take place *within* the plane of time but *along* the plane of eternity. Caribbean man must be conceived of in both planes if the nature of his existence in a particular place and time is to be understood.

Yet the theory does not illuminate Mr. Harris's novels alone. Other modern novelists since Joyce (whose use of the *Odyssey* enabled him to establish the deepest possible temporal and mythic perspective) have often been concerned with freeing their characters in space and time in very much the way envisaged by Harris, though few have been as radical as he in the means they employ. Few, for instance, have exhibited a free interflow not only between character and character but between man and landscape, as Vigilance and the Arawak Woman in *Palace of the Peacock* become one with the rockface and the boiling stream.

West Indian literature itself, however, offers the example of George Lamming, whose *Of Age and Innocence* seems to be moving towards a theory of character akin to Mr. Harris's. . . .

Mr. Harris's essay, then, has the dual importance of illuminating his own practice and casting a searching light upon the evolution of the contemporary novel in general. It is improbable that anyone will be content much longer with sequential order and finite character or event, which the film alone has done so much to question. . . . In another essay Wilson Harris compares the evocation of primordial character to the consciousness of a *vodun* dancer, who starts out with a complete body imprisoned in temporality but dances until "one leg is drawn up into the womb of space". In this state conventional memory is erased, but it is replaced by a kind of primordial memory, born of overlapping spheres of reflection, "like a one-legged bird which joins itself to its sleeping reflection in a pool". As Yeats was concerned with the moment when dancer and dance become one, so Wilson Harris sees the trance as a state experienced subjectively by the dancer, but also exteriorized as "an intense drama of images in space". This perfect equipoise of the inner and the outer life is that which the novelist should now seek to evoke.

"Along the Plane of Eternity," in The Times Literary Supplement (© *Times Newspapers Ltd. (London) 1968; reproduced from* The Times Literary Supplement *by permission), No. 3462, July 4, 1968, p. 706.*

JOHN HEARNE

It is from Yeats's great phrase about "the unity from a mythology that marries us to rock and hill" that we may, justifiably, begin an examination of Wilson Harris's singular exploration of his corner of the West Indian experience. To Harris, this sacramental union of man and landscape remains the lost, or never established, factor in our lives. We enjoy, we exploit, we are coarsely nourished by our respective Caribbean territories—but illegitimately. We have yet to put our signatures to that great contract of the imagination by which a people and a place enter into a domestic relationship rather than drift into the uncertainties of liaison. No other British Caribbean novelist has made quite such an explicit and conscious effort as Harris to reduce the material reckonings of everyday life to the significance of myth. It is useful to consider first the geographical matrix in which his imagination was fashioned. (p. 177)

[The Guyanese landscape is] one of the great primary landscapes of the world, and it can crush the mind like sleep. Like sleep, it inspires the dreams by which we record the progress of our waking life.

It is important to remember this element of the dream, and of the dream's sister, death, if we are to come to any understanding of these four Wilson Harris novels—[*Palace of the Peacock, The Far Journey of Oudin, The Whole Armour,* and *The Secret Ladder*]. . . . For the quartet opens with one dream of death, and closes with another dream of creation. Between these two dreams lies an evocation of being not accessible to any reviewer's summary. If we are to share the writer's experience, we must accept possession of the living by the dead; we must accept the resurrected man and the fact that "the end precedes the beginning" and that "the end and beginning were always there." Harris's world is not only one of prosaic action, but one of rite and mythical formation. "The first condition for understanding the Greek myth, " said Gide, "is to believe in it." And it is not improper that Harris makes belief the condition for entry into his Guyanese world.

In *Palace of the Peacock,* the first of the quartet and Harris's first novel, we are immediately presented with this pattern of interwoven dream and waking. It opens with a horseman shot from his saddle as he gallops, the discovery of the corpse by the elusive figure who is to become the narrator, and the narrator's dreaming conviction after the discovery that, somehow, he the living has lost his sight and can see only with a dead man's "open and obstinate" eye. This symbol of the eye recurs frequently in the four stories of the quartet. It is, I think, the clearest hint that Harris gives us of the structure and methods we must expect to find throughout his work. The human eye, living and dead, serves something of the same purpose as the mirror on the wall in a Dutch interior painting. Both reflector and captor, it enhances the material vividness of the foreground figures, yet its troubling duplication reminds us of the other life it holds captive in an infinite and shrinking series. Nor are the diminished figures in the glass—or in the eye—any less real for being reduced. What disturbs us is their jewel brightness, their sense of independent life, their possession of a separate but complementary world. (pp. 178-79)

If I have given priority to this analysis of Harris's reflecting and imprisoning "eye," it is because his use of it does serve to introduce us to the fictive world his persons inhabit. The passages in which he assembles, in our nerves, the power and meaning of the eye are intricate and compelling; we are sensuously convinced before we cerebrally grasp. And if, as I have suggested, he sees his mandate as one of creating a mythical framework, then his use of the "eye" is legitimate. For the imperceptible shuttle system from dream to waking and death to life, the dogmatic *possibility* of causal relationships between these states, give the essences of much of myth. Harris does not, like the naturalistic novelist, offer us the demonstrable proofs of observation; he simply throws himself on our willing agreement. And this, for Harris, is the only way for the artist in the modern world where he is deprived of his traditional assurances. "The creative human consolation," he wrote in *Tradition and the West Indian Novel* . . . , "—if one dwells upon it meaningfully today—lies in the search for a kind of *inward* dialogue and space when one is *deprived* of a ready conversational tongue and hackneyed comfortable approach." [My italics.]

This is one of the most fruitful obsessions any novelist can carry into his study of the human heart today; it is also an extremely dangerous one. For in so doing, he offers his artistic throat to the knives of ridicule, inattention and misunderstanding. Obversely, his mendicant's role imposes a certain limitation on his own freedom of aesthetic venture. He must work, in short, within an extremely limited frame and convince us by his intensity rather than by his generous scope. C.L.R. James and other critics have made much of Wilson Harris's relation to the existentialists, but his technique seems to me to lie in the symbolist tradition. (pp. 179-80)

On the surface, the plot of *Palace of the Peacock* seems simple enough. It describes the struggles of a boat's crew as they forge a passage up a nameless Guyanese river, through rapids, between walls of forests and under towering battlements of cliff face, to the great falls at the head of the stream. . . . They hope to make contact with a fugitive and sensibly suspicious "folk," who, while accompanying their passage along the banks of the river, never appear, but send them only the shy and enigmatic missives of the forest; a wounded tapir or a parrot with a silver ring around its leg. At the end all are dead. The last is transfixed, or translated, at the moment of his death by a knowledge of a loving communion between the living and the dead that completely obliterates the hope of the treasure he had come to seize for the purchase of vulgar consolations he can now barely remember.

On this level it is a mere morality and, to borrow Harris's adjective, a rather "hackneyed" one at that. But we are early relieved of this possible banality by the realization that the crew's names match, man for man, those of another legendary crew who had all perished many years before in the rapids near the beginning of a similar venture into the interior. At this point, it becomes the reader's pleasure, as it must have become the writer's excitement, to determine the extent to which each crew possesses the other; to decide at what moment the anguish of one group is simply that of commonplace muscle and endurance pitted against the immediate pressures of a river's current, or is the accumulated reflections of the greed and love, cruelty and faithfulness which another body of men had once imposed on those among whom they had lived, on the land they had once tried to dominate. (p. 180)

Harris is not an "easy" writer. . . . The contending experiences he is attempting to resolve in a finished, persuasive work of art do not really yield to the methods and syntax of, say, Naipaul. But it is worth joining battle with him, even when he fails to carry off his attack. His effects are cumulative. Images, metaphors, incidents and assertions which, at the beginning of any of his stories, may at first seem examples only of a wilful and unrelated vividness will suddenly, by a process of duplication in a new setting, become clear and powerful factors in an orderly poetic statement. He is very seldom self-indulgent.

So, the nameless boat, with its twice-named crew, continues to beat up the nameless river towards the Palace of the Peacock. With a quite astonishing coolness of nerve, almost, one might say, with arrogance, Harris continues to shift his characters from phase to phase of reality and of Time. His transitions are often so abrupt, so arbitrary, that we are, momentarily, confused, until we learn to accept the use to which our sensations are being put. This is a world of hallucination, or rather, a world in which hallucinatory apprehensions of Time's circular and organic wholeness is a commonplace of existence. Quarrels between the crew occur, and they die by accident, exhaustion or murder. Sometimes the dead ones are replaced, for a second or for a day, by counterparts from the other crew who were swallowed by the river at the beginning of *their* venture. But even those who die in the present follow the progress of the boat along the enormous heights of cliff face above the river, for they too are forever reflected in the undying eye; they too survive on what Harris terms "the elastic frontier" which stretches to and fro to enclose whole provinces of the territory of death and the territory of life. The "folk," the indigenes, remain unapproachable. They live, unconsciously, in harmonious relationship with the organic body of a land through which Time moves like blood, carrying action, dream and death on an unending circulatory voyage of nourishment, salvage and renewal. (pp. 181-82)

The expedition which had begun as a pedestrian, rather sordid, gold rush has ended as an argosy, because of the suffering, and because of the surrender of the primal solitude of the landscape and to the implacable occupation of their dreams. They are dead men, to be sure, but by their deaths they have won admittance to the antique, beautiful and imperishable palace that, in each year of our obsessive enslavement of the earth, is moved beyond yet another horizon. The Golden Palace that they can bring back to us in our dreams is the knowledge that all the territories "overwhelmed and abandoned [have] always been ours to rule and take."

Inevitably, such a brief critical reduction of so dense, intricate and active a work as *Palace of the Peacock* must do the book a disservice. Harris's vision is too subtle, and his technique too sculptural, for us to do other than to enter his work and try to join the highly idiosyncratic celebration he is conducting. Once we accept the ritual stages, without necessarily committing ourselves, we begin to understand what he is trying to communicate. This is straightforward enough. It is the conviction that, in his time, in his corner of the world, a people must learn not only the gross and monotonous facts of their immediate history but must assemble, from the exchanges of their daily lives, the assurances and inspiring reverberations of myth. It is a uniquely difficult commission to execute. For they must do this in a self-conscious age of technology in which there are fewer and fewer effective symbols—a multiple furrow tractor, for instance, can never become the key to that door of perception which we can make out of a horse, a plough, and a man behind the plough. They must do it at a time when they are living at the beginning of a history. *Palace of the Peacock* is one of the few pieces of evidence we have that success in this task is possible.

If I have given to *Palace of the Peacock* a great deal of the space allowed me in this essay, it is because this first book in the quartet seems to state most of the themes which are later developed in the others. Like many other novelists who rely heavily on the use of symbol to give resonance to their work, Harris tends to find a symphonic design best suited to his purpose. The images employed in the several stories depend for their final "proof" on the manner in which they are later reworked and given new moulded structures by the author.

It is therefore a pity that limitation of space prevents a detailed study of *The Far Journey of Oudin*. In this story, we are returned to the crafty, suspicious and greedy peasant world of the coastal savannahs. The basic theme is one of Harris's constant preoccupations, that of dominion, of tyrannical and thus sterile authority which is hardly distinguishable from rape. (pp. 182-83)

This book, the most complex of the quartet, is also the least satisfactory. The main fault lies in failure of nerve on the author's part. Faced with the drab and mercenary domestic exchanges of a *khulak* community, the author panics, becomes rhetorical, pretentious and sometimes nearly bombastic. He robes his innocent and uncaring people in philosophical vestments which they wear about as comfortably as would a navvy dressed in a duke's full coronation regalia. Unlike any other stories in the quartet, this one also seems to preach a message, and the message is in the end platitudinous: "all that glitters is not gold," "you can't take it with you," and so on.

With *The Whole Armour,* we see Harris restored to the heights of his impressive powers. It is perhaps the most accomplished work of the series. Plot, image, character, architecture and language all fuse into a whole that is as compact, shapely and penetrative as a bullet. In it, he returns to that ideal frontier which is as much a spiritual as a geographical boundary—the line between the challenging wilderness and the cultivated sensibility—and which is the setting in which he always moves most confidently. Once more the plot is austere; an undecorated stage on which the principals are the foci of our total attention. In this story, too, Harris undertakes the portrayal of a relationship which seems to be beyond the powers or outside the interest of most West Indian novelists; the complexities of love between a man and a woman who is a *person* in whom the subtleties of erotic response can be kindled or who is approached, as a new-found land, with awe, delight and a careful sounding of the shoals. Sharon, the young girl in *The Whole Armour,* is such a one, and the relationship between her and Cristo, the fugitive accused of murder, gives a lyric immediacy and profane disturbance that is very rare indeed in West Indian fiction. (p. 184)

[Here], for the first time in British West Indian fiction, we are faced with a serenely confident charter of liberation from the immediate past. Cristo not only thinks what he says but lives it. He is freed from the squalid commercial transaction between white and black, aborigines and conquistadors, which is most of West Indian history. . . . His proximate responsibility for the death of his putative father Abram, his assumption of the skin of "Christ, the tiger," his return to the coastlands, his fathering of a child, his legacy to that child of a more audacious understanding and use of the land, are all part of a carefully fashioned, artistic criticism of a system that for too long nourished itself on the cycle of parturition, forced labour and the flesh's surrender, but which never acknowledged the reality of holy dying.

The Secret Ladder confirms the sense one had in reading *The Whole Armour* that Harris was developing a new assurance in handling the techniques of fiction. The story is perhaps the most interesting of any in the quartet. (pp. 185-86)

Simply on the level of a drama played out between the invading, often impatient forces of material progress and the dispossession of a timid, uncomprehending folk, this would be a fine story. The characters of the crew are distinct; the tension of wills (between Fenwick and his men) in the heavy atmosphere of a jungle just before the rains, the lack of communication between the tough, Faustian surveyors and the frightened, dream-burdened people of the river are both sustained with great skill. So is Fenwick's mingled guilt and exasperation over his failure to convince Poseidon of their good intentions; his recognition that the magnificent and inconsolable old man has a part of the truth that the planners must recognize if their future of material plenty is to give them nourishment.

But there is another exploration of meaning carried in the current of the social conflict for, in *The Secret Ladder,* Harris returns to many of the themes and symbols of the first book. The action takes place over seven days. Fenwick's boat is named *Palace of the Peacock.* To him, the rivers of Guyana are "the curious rungs in a ladder on which one sets one's musing foot again and again, to climb into both the past and the future of the continent of mystery." The crew, although more substantial and prosaic than the first crew, are yet seen, through Fenwick's eyes, as actors in an inward drama of his dreams. And these dreams are inspired by—or, if you prefer, are the other side of—what Harris once called "the material structural witnesses" of history. For Fenwick, as for Wilson Harris, the experiences of the day must be revised in the lan-

guage of dreams, of free association, so that in the end, by the potent magic of image, all the fragments of our strange, broken heritage may begin to act one upon the other, become whole within our instinctive grasp. It is only when this has been achieved that we will enter into an active, conscious possession and use of the West Indian inheritance. (pp. 186-87)

> *John Hearne, "The Fugitive in the Forest: Four Novels by Wilson Harris," in* The Islands in Between: Essays on West Indian Literature, *edited by Louis James (© Oxford University Press 1968; reprinted by permission of Oxford University Press), Oxford University Press, London, 1968 (and reprinted in* Modern Black Novelists: A Collection of Critical Essays, *edited by M. G. Cooke, Prentice-Hall, Inc., 1971, pp. 177-87).*

JOYCE ADLER

It is implicit in *Tumatumari* that man, if he is to survive the imminent danger of self-annihilation, will have to free and transform his imagination so that it will be able to work in harmony with the fundamental laws of change and re-creation, rather than, catastrophically, to resist them.

Imagination is embodied in *Tumatumari* in the 'heroine' Prudence, this novel's representative of Man. She is the 'soul of man' awakening in a transitional age that may have already begun, feeling at last the need to develop and transform itself if the family of Man is to continue. To understand herself and her needs and desires, she reaches into memory, the well of the past. The search for the significance of the history of her own family, a middle-class 'mixed' family in Guyana, leads to an exploration of twentieth-century civilization generally, as symbolized by the life of this single 'civilized' family, and expands further into an exploration of the relationship between the twentieth century in Guyana (the land of Harris's birth and development) and other times and other places. Only in this broader search can Prudence find her own real identity, her identity with the whole human family, its evolutionary past, its complex present, and its two possible futures, not yet determined in this 'moment' of history. The implications of Prudence's search reach out without limit backward in time, outward without limit into space, and inward from one horizon of imagination to the next.

The implication is that in *Tumatumari* Harris, too, set out to put the history of his own family and country together, and that out of the immersion of his imagination in this material, *Tumatumari,* with its constantly widening implications, developed. For to Harris, the story of Guyana and its different peoples is charged with the deepest meanings and the largest questions. Out of his continuously widening exploration as he created *Tumatumari* came the questions: Of what contradictory elements is the civilization of our age composed? Out of what womb did it come? Is it capable or incapable of giving birth in its turn? Is civilization now a totally barren thing truly lusting for self-destruction? If not, is it capable of a new kind of conception, a conception of something new, capable of surviving after its birth . . .? Will the breakdown of life in this century and the consequent sense of the imminence of danger give mankind the necessary humility to surrender long-cherished but long-outworn and now barren concepts and idolatries? Can so-called 'modern Man' bear to face himself as still no more than primitive, living by primitive concepts, still offering living sacrifices to his gods, still sacrificing himself and others in the name of separate 'incestuous' family or nation, tribe or race? . . . Can concern for the individual family and concern for the whole human family be fused by imagination, giving birth to an entirely new conception—that of an integrated, unalienated, creative and truly human Man? And, to return to Guyana in a broader, non-national sense, does the Central and South American 'new world', the melting pot of ancient and new, and of many races and cultures, have, perhaps, the best potential for being the crucible of change in the world today?

The interaction of this rich mass of questions and material with Harris's highly-cultivated and informed twentieth-century mind and fluid imagination results in what is undoubtedly one of the most complex novels ever written. Reading and re-reading *Tumatumari* is a gruelling as well as a rewarding experience; it is a rigorous challenge to the reading ability and imagination of the reader.

One sign of the complexity of *Tumatumari* is that, in comparison with it, Harris's previous novel, *The Waiting Room*, can be described as relatively straightforward! A few comparisons with the earlier novel may help to put *Tumatumari* in perspective (in so far as its 'method' is concerned). . . . (p. 22)

In the earlier novel it was possible for the reader, once he saw the main thread, to follow it through the labyrinth of the book. But *Tumatumari* has innumerable intertwining threads, moving up and down as well as across; it is densely-matted, very much like the mat of half-submerged vegetation which Prudence lifts out of the river at the beginning of the book. In its density and complexity it is a counterpart of the material under consideration, the complex fabric of twentieth-century civilization in which are caught up innumerable strands of the past, even the ancient past before man was man.

In *The Waiting Room* there are only two characters and their role is soon seen as symbolic and complementary; they represent all dynamic and fulfilling 'opposites'. But *Tumatumari* has a dozen characters, no two exactly complementary, or contrasting, or simply 'individual' but all in *some* respect 'equivalent' to each other, so that all their significances are interwoven, until finally all the other characters merge into Prudence as she takes on the significance of humanity as a whole, on the hairline of transition to a new age—whatever that age will prove to be. Incorporating them all, she may, like the phoenix, be capable of being reborn, because she becomes capable of entering into the others (of past and present) and of letting them enter into and become part of her.

Tumatumari is different from *The Waiting Room* also in its imagery. Whereas *The Waiting Room* was made up of a set of related images, *Tumatumari* contains a myriad of images which do not resemble each other—images deriving from physics and microphysics, mathematics, chemistry, anthropology, economics, genetics and the study of evolution, and much more: images which are only slowly seen as related or 'equivalent' to others in *some* respect, and then only in a philosophical sense; these relationships are not 'visualizable', as were the waves and echoes of *The Waiting Room*, but are extremely abstract, involving such concepts as 'reciprocity' or 'interpenetration' of elements. Only near the end of the novel (in the section on the Canje River area) are the abstract relationships envisioned in a stunning artistic synthesis of almost all the novel's themes and concepts to that point.

With *The Waiting Room* it is possible to speak of the basic shape of the novel, as epitomized by the spiral seashell near the end. *Tumatumari*, however, has rather a *shaping* than a shape, a continuous growth and retaking of shape much like

the gestation and evolutionary processes taking place in the various wombs in the novel: the physical wombs, the womb of history, and the wall-less wombs of space and imagination. All the developments come to be seen as part of 'chains' of development, one thing growing within and then out of another which then disintegrates and yet lives on in the new, part of a continuity of overlapping rings or clasps. (pp. 22-3)

Gestation and evolutionary processes take place also in history as it is viewed in *Tumatumari,* and the images of wombs, gateways, doors, passages of entry and passages of exodus have many variations in the work. Guyana (in its larger geographical, not national, sense) is seen as being like the Mediterranean of the past, a gateway between the past and the future. The history of the country of Guyana (that was British Guiana), which has been one of *de facto* racial separation and discrimination, is also conceived of in these images. (p. 23)

This kind of conception of the world, with its emphasis on dynamic change and evolutionary processes, expresses Wilson Harris's pervading scientific view of all aspects of human life, biological, psychological and social. The result, in *Tumatumari,* is a rare synthesis of scientific outlook, philosophy and art. Harris seems to share the belief of the physicist de Broglie, that modern scientific approaches have enormous philosophical implications, illuminating realities of all kinds. (pp. 23-4)

There is in *Tumatumari* a thorough 'interpenetration' and interaction of the philosophical, scientific and artistic conceptions. This is one of the book's strengths, but it is at the same time one of the things that makes the reading so difficult. For example, because the content and form are so completely one, the development of *Tumatumari* is not novelistic or even literary in any usual sense, unless we are to conceive of the work as a long poem, which in a way it is. Its development is more musical than anything else: a prelude states the theme, but in disguise; then comes the appearance in a kind of hide-and-seek, of the various elements of the story that Prudence raises up from the well of memory; this is followed by the coming together of the significances of these memories and the emergence of the underlying themes and rhythms, which brings the work to a climax; then in the last section there is a restatement on a new level of the question implied in the prelude, and the work closes with a series of chords that are left suspended, suggesting a further development in the silence that follows. Eventually the reader who has come so far returns to the prelude which is now seen not only as an introduction to the work but as a kind of allegorical summary of it. Until this process of the development of the novel is perceived, the difficulties of following the 'story' are great. (p. 24)

In the main body of the work, in the search for her own significance and real desires, Prudence searches the paths which have led to her. The principal figure in her past is her father, Henry Tenby, head of a Guyanese middle-class family until his death in 1957. He is the novel's symbol of the dominant outlook and way of life of the first half of the twentieth century. (p. 25)

Prudence comes to understand him as representative of Man in the age of individualism and free enterprise, who is in truth as unfree as possible. Placarded by history as being the soul of freedom, he wears chains of gold upon his heart and wrist. Prudence's feeling for him years later is a feeling of compassion. She sees him as unable to advance far beyond the limits of the past out of which he came. She sees both him and her husband Roi as manifestations of Man in the two major periods of this century, the periods following each of the world wars. . . . (p. 27)

[Roi] is shown to be like the ancient 'divine king' whose life, it was believed, had to be sacrificed when there came a breakdown in the life of the people. But Harris implies that no such outworn primitive rituals and idolatries can save twentieth-century Man, who must himself accept the responsibility for his fate, not shift it to any god or gods. No sacrifices will help except the sacrifice of outworn conceptions, such as the idea that the world is inevitably made up of hunter and hunted. The only hope of survival lies in more deeply scientific knowledge of nature and its processes and in the renewal of man's own creative power. Man himself must be the creator of the new Man. His future depends on himself. (p. 28)

In *Tumatumari,* then, the central figure or symbol is Man himself, in his manifestations in various periods in his whole history, during which he has lived in many different societies and within the wider environment of nature—within the womb of space and time. The title of *Tumatumari* derives from the idea of nature and its processes in time ('Tumatumari' is said to mean 'sleeping rocks'). The scene of Tumatumari suggests that in time even rocks crack, and imaginations awaken, and sudden leaps in development take place.

In contrast, the titles of the five sub-divisions of the book derive from social forms and concepts, those that have lasted beyond their time, that once were meaningful, perhaps, but which now are death-dealing. They represent old ideas that can have meaning now not as binding, rock-like traditions and idolatries, but only as 'transformed and transforming' tradition, meaningful for this age. . . . It is the originality and independence of spirit that is still valid and not the long outworn interpretations of life and nature. (p. 29)

In spite of the almost indescribable difficulty of *Tumatumari* as a whole, large sections of it read along smoothly enough, and many passages can be enjoyed for their sheer sensuous beauty (while others read like the output of a computer). The novel can be read simply as 'experience'; in fact this novel, like all of Harris's novels, should be read for the first time in just this way and not primarily for the intellectual pleasure of it. What will happen with this kind of relaxed approach to it is that some of the underlying philosophical significance will gradually come through to provide illumination for subsequent readings in which intellectual perceptions and sense perceptions will be united.

Many aspects of the novel that seemed to stand out as flaws in early readings of *Tumatumari* took on an essential logic and authority of their own in subsequent readings, although this reader continues to find unsatisfying Harris's way of handling, in a kind of lecture exposition, the 'moment of articulation' by the character who has plumbed his own depths and arrived at a new conception of himself and the world (Christo in *The Whole Armour,* the lover in *The Waiting Room,* and to a lesser extent Prudence in *Tumatumari*). In his essays Harris speaks of the need for writers to discover new, fresh potentialities of language. Harris, himself, in all his works, shows that he is capable of making such discoveries. (p. 30)

Joyce Adler, "'Tumatumari' and the Imagination of Wilson Harris" (copyright Joyce Adler; by permission of Hans Zell Publishers, an imprint of K. G. Saur Verlag), in Journal of Commonwealth Literature, *No. 7, July, 1969, pp. 20-31.*

STANLEY REYNOLDS

The West Indies is surely one of the places the English novel may look to for plasma: to Andrew Salkey, Garth St Omer, Peter Marshall, and the wildly poetic Wilson Harris, who writes in *Ascent to Omai* like an academic on an acid trip. Europe, Africa, the East, and the new world; a reference to Odin's ravens followed by one about Julius Reuter's pigeons—here is a writer from Guyana, a culture that is part old Europe, part the mysterious Zen East, and part slave-dark Africa, and somehow he is able to encompass it all, be aware of it all and use it. But he is difficult. The reader can't keep up, catch the wild use of language, the dreamy slides and slips of plot from present to past, the use of omens (what are omens to us but a cliché word of political reporters?), omens used as practical devices of plot. But the language is hypnotic. I read some parts out loud and doing that caught the marvellous repetitions, the poetry of it, without understanding the meaning. At its worst—and this could be a recommendation to many—the style is like one of those obscure pop songs. . . . Wilson Harris, towards the end of the novel explains his style:

> My intention, in part, is to repudiate the vicarious novel—vicarious sex-mask, death-mask—where the writer, following a certain canon of clarity, claims to enter the most obscure and difficult terrain of experience without incurring a necessary burden of authenticity, obscurity or difficulty at the same time.

This is one of the simplest, most straightforward sentences in the book, but Mr Harris is quite right and the lazy reader is wrong; the novel is dying because the trick of the vicarious thrill has been tumbled and Mr Harris's poetic voodoo is one way back to health.

Stanley Reynolds, "Quipped the Raven," in New Statesman *(© 1970 The Statesman & Nation Publishing Co. Ltd.), Vol. 79, No. 2033, February 27, 1970, p. 300.*

THE TIMES LITERARY SUPPLEMENT

[Wilson Harris] has argued against the common belief that there is no such thing as a West Indian personality: he would rather claim that study of "the West Indian in depth" reveals a series of "subtle and nebulous links, the latent ground of old and new personalities". These links are the subject matter for his difficult, imagist and metaphysical novels, *Ascent to Omai* being the ninth. The reader is required to have a little Latin and less Greek, also to be familiar with Rimbaud and Donne, and with the regions, customs and patois of Guyana. *Hubris* and *opus contra naturam* are jammed up tight against Guyanese words and concepts. . . .

No reader should attempt Mr. Harris's novels unless he is willing to work at them. . . .

[*Ascent to Omai*] contains an illustrative diagram consisting of eight concentric circles, each one labelled "Epitaph One", "Epitaph Two", and so on, to "Epitaph Nine". Opposite this column of labels is another, consisting of nine words—"Rose", "Madonna", "Petticoat", &c.—all of them recurring images in the novel. The diagram is like the ripples caused by a stone thrown into a pool, and the novel begins with Victor being hit by a stone as he ascends a mountain: the novel perhaps consists of ripples caused by that stone, kicked down accidentally by . . . a ruined porknocker walking ahead of Victor, a man with a black *tabula rasa* for a face. But the diagram also looks like the cross-section of a tree trunk, thought of as growing thicker rather than taller as it grows older. The past remains contemporary, each ring of the tree's trunk acting as an "epitaph" to an era that is not wholly dead. . . .

Readers must judge for themselves whether they wish to enter this hermetic world. There *is* a story to *Ascent to Omai*—about a clever Guyanese boy thinking about his ill-educated and militant father—but it needs a line-by-line commentary rather than a review.

> "Reading the Ripples," *in* The Times Literary Supplement *(© Times Newspapers Ltd. (London) 1970; reproduced from* The Times Literary Supplement *by permission), No. 3560, May 21, 1970, p. 555.*

LOUIS JAMES

The novels of Wilson Harris . . . form one ongoing whole. Each work is individual; yet the whole sequence can be seen as a continuous, ever-widening exploration of civilization and creative art. *The Ascent to Omai* . . . , for instance, took subjective consciousness to a point beyond which further communication seemed impossible. This was answered, after two excursions into the realm of folklore, with *Black Marsden* . . . , in which the creative imagination is Marsden, a trickster/illusionist whom the artist hero finally throws into the street. In *Companions of the Day and Night* the hero of *Black Marsden* is sent manuscripts by Marsden himself which he orders into an assertion of the creative interpenetration of history and imagination. . . .

Wilson Harris [recently] explained his present preoccupation with moments in which a suppressed cultural pattern erupts through a decaying later one. In *Black Marsden*, it was Scottish history in Edinburgh. In [*Companions of the Day and Night*], it is Mexico City, where Christian and Western patterns overlie traditional cultures going back to pre-Conquest Toltec times. Recurrent archetypes are the focus for conflicting cultural strata; and the naked, creative, suffering human spirit is embodied in the Fool, Nameless, or Christ, with his answering image of spiritual love, Mary or Beatrice. In the ancient Mexican religion he was a human sacrifice; in the Catholic conquest, the figure of Christ; in the modern world, a political martyr.

The Fool is in Mexico City. It is a modern Easter, with the mingling of Christian and pagan rituals. He encounters a fire-eater performing in the waning light against a ruined building, and falls into a trance. As his consciousness expands, he becomes the Christ figure, seeking the virgin associated with the Easter rituals. He moves backwards and forwards through time, and outward towards the new world of North America. To reach understanding is to be crucified by a blind world. At the Easter weekend the Fool is found crushed below a sacrificial pyramid of the sun.

This summary bears little relation to the experience of reading the book, a surrealist and hallucinatory prose-poem. Time and place, even the logic of language, are violated to attempt a new alchemy of awareness. . . .

Companions of the Day and Night is not Wilson Harris's finest novel. It does not have the architectonic strength of *Tumatumari* or the better known *Palace of the Peacock*. The surrealist fantasy weakens the texture of the sacrificial drama. But never has the wily magician Black Marsden created more startling effects, or Mr Harris's extraordinary use of language been more assured.

> Louis James, "Easter Offering," *in* The Times Literary Supplement *(© Times Newspapers Ltd. (London) 1975; reproduced from* The Times Literary Supplement *by permission), No. 3839, October 10, 1975, p. 1217.*

MICHAEL GILKES

Companions of the Day and Night, his most recent novel, is another addition to the "infinite canvas" of Wilson Harris' work. There is a remarkable continuity of imagery, style and theme between his thirteen published books of fiction, which may be regarded not as separate works, but rather as several aspects of one continuing *oeuvre*. (p. 161)

In *Companions of the Day and Night,* a sequel to *Black Marsden,* Goodrich receives from Marsden a collection of manuscripts, sculptures and paintings—the "Idiot Nameless collection," the work of an unknown man, a tourist, whose dead body has been found at the base of the Pyramid of the Sun at Teotihuacán in Mexico. As Goodrich explains in the "Editor's Introduction," the collection reveals "doorways through which Idiot Nameless moved" . . . and as he edits and translates the writings into a novel, he is aware of "the mystery of companionship in those pages and of a frightening wisdom they embodied . . . ". . . . This is, of course, the continuous, creative process of psychic reconstruction implicit in all of Harris' work. (p. 163)

The novel's title comes from the motifs of the ancient Aztec calendar stone where they appear as components of a thirteen-day cycle ("companions of the day") and of a nine-day cycle ("companions of the night"). Days eight and nine are called "dateless days" which absorbs into the nine-day cycle the "missing" four days. Harris' novel also attempts to represent and embody a reality which *includes* and allows for the numinous or "magical" element of human experience; the missing component of historical, dead time.

By arguing for the reality of the creative imagination as a means of questioning monolithic attitudes, of creating a genuine dialogue between cultures, Harris in all his work seeks to address the problem of Twentieth-Century Man's lack of "authenticity," of wholeness. The anxiety of Modern Man . . . is hinted at and counterpointed in *Companions of the Day and Night* by reference, for example, to the Aztec's fear of loss of the sun and the consequent degeneration of their religion to the horror of automatic, mass human sacrifice to "feed" a dying sun. Their fear of "losing" the sun is related to our own equally "primitive" fear of loss of self; the *deisidaemonia* of modern psychology. In this "cross-referencing" between cultures we are being assisted towards an understanding of the ground of our present *angst*. And just as the gods and motifs of the Aztec calendrical cosmos—the "companions of the day and night"—reflect and are part of a complex spiritual progress, a cyclical movement towards self-integration (as in the Mayan *Chilam Balam*) in which one was assisted at various stages by the gods and spirits; so this *tabula rasa* novel hints at a reconstruction of the modern, divided psyche, a bridging of the gap between historical, factual time and the visionary or dream-time through which (as in the Black Holes of gravity in the universe) whole unsuspected new worlds may lie. (pp. 164-65)

Idiot Nameless' visit to Mexico is an imaginative re-creation of landscape in depth as it affects and is reflected by his own developing, heterogeneous sensibility. There is an interpenetration of self and situation, object and viewer, past and present, and the result is a brilliantly creative *bridging* of apparently opposed and static cultural, historical and emotional climates. An example of this is the Idiot's first experience; a sudden meeting at night with a fire-eater, (a pavement artist, entertainer and vendor) near the Avenida Reforma. . . . The fire-eater is an evocation of both the fire-god Huehueteotl ("a companion of the night" one of the chief deities in the Aztec pantheon: the fire-eater is a central symbol in the book) and the Aztec obsession with a "dying" sun, swallowed daily by the lake and requiring sacrifices in order to rise again. The Idiot feels as if he is falling downwards through space and time, back into history. . . . Yet the whole, dreamlike incident is perfectly credible, since Nameless suffers from epilepsy ("falling sickness"). . . . From [the] first remarkable chapter, subtitled *A Door into the Forge of Creation*, the Idiot moves, aided in his spiritual progress by the companions of day and night, through the stages of the nine-day cycle into which he has "fallen." The book ends on the "Dateless Days" during which Nameless visits Mrs. Black Marsden in New York and his fall from the pyramid is prefigured, or reenacted, since the time sequence, like character, is not fixed or solid, but fluid and shifting. (pp. 165-67)

> Michael Gilkes, "An Infinite Canvas," in World Literature Written in English (© copyright 1976 WLWE-World Literature Written in English), Vol. 15, No. 1, April, 1976, pp. 161-73.

MICHAEL GILKES

The present need for what Nicholas Mosley called an "intelligent language of crisis" capable, through paradox and allusion, of holding apparent opposites together, is a practical concern of Wilson Harris's writing. His novels, a continually deepening exploration of "the problem of opposite tendencies", use paradoxical, allusive language . . . to convey the interdependence of opposites: "strong", sovereign cultures, "weak" or vanished civilizations.

The hero of *Da Silva da Silva's Cultivated Wilderness* is married and lives in a Kensington flat. He is a composite man. Born in Brazil of Spanish, Portuguese and African stock, orphaned early, he survives cyclone and flood and is adopted by the British ambassador. He grows up in England with access to his rich benefactor's library and thrives on a varied cultural diet; an interest in painting develops and he gradually becomes convinced that his "parentless" condition obliges him to create, to "paint" himself and his world anew. Seeing everything in terms of his art, he discovers new "illuminations" and "unpredictable densities" within the most apparently solid and uniform people and places. As his "paintings" multiply, the range of his awareness widens, relationships deepen. . . .

Genesis of the Clowns emerges from the brooding recollections of Frank Wellington, who also lives in a London flat: Wellington, a government land surveyor in British Guiana in the 1940s, had settled in Britain in 1954. One morning in the 1970s he receives an anonymous letter telling him of the death of Hope, the black foreman of a survey team he had led thirty years ago in the interior. At the same time a letter from a solicitor in Hope Street, Dunfermline, brings news of a small inheritance through the death of a relative in Scotland. It is the first of a number of related coincidences. His now receptive mind drifts back into the past where he is, once again, leader and paymaster of a racially mixed crew. As the ghosts of the men again come forward to the paytable, Wellington finds that his relationship with each has been subtly altered.

These two novels [*Da Silva da Silva's Cultivated Wilderness* and *Genesis of the Clowns*] are complementary explorations of modern existence. The fallen blossoms swirling "in circles and counter-circles" along Holland Villas Road conjure up the contrary undercurrents of Wellington's river surveys as well as those of "revolutionary" Guyanese politics and society (and of societies in general). The tent-like Commonwealth Institute of *Da Silva etc* reappears as Wellington's fragile tent, the collapse of which, during a thunderstorm, forces him to question his role as father-figure and colonial "master" of all he surveys through the inverting eye of his theodolite. Both painter and surveyor, the complementary worlds of art and science, recognize the need for a revolution of sensibility, a new "circulation of the light".

> Michael Gilkes, "Hidden Densities," in The Times Literary Supplement (© Times Newspapers Ltd. (London) 1977; reproduced from The Times Literary Supplement by permission), No. 3915, March 25, 1977, p. 334.

SHIRLEY CHEW

In *The Tree of the Sun*, which is a sequel to *Da Silva da Silva's Cultivated Wilderness*, the central character attempts once again "to paint antecedents and unborn worlds". . . . While in the earlier novel [Da Silva] had set out to paint his own past, he is drawn in *The Tree of the Sun* into the unfulfilled lives of a childless couple, once tenants of the same flat in Holland Park Gardens and long since dead, and, through these people, into the shifting drama of a universal city, and into West Indian culture and history.

Da Silva finds Francis's unfinished book and Julia's large collection of letters hidden in a hole in the wall of the flat, and with the help of his wife, Jen, who is two months pregnant, he begins to edit the pages, and to sketch and paint these lovers. In this way he becomes involved in their resurrection.

One cannot deny that Wilson Harris's powers of invention are vigorous and fertile. . . . Nor can one deny that, bristling in the intricate criss-cross of "parallel and estranged expeditions" which form the structure of the novel, are important ideas and themes: the precarious progress of self-discovery, the elusive bond of community, the artist's relation to his subject, the limits of his access to the truth, the extent to which art is capable of enlarging our sympathy with other lives and our understanding of life.

If then, for all its cleverness and its serious intentions, *The Tree of the Sun* neither captivates nor moves, it must be because Wilson Harris has failed to rise to some of the more common expectations one brings to the reading of a novel. His story and situations are manifestly so many pegs upon which to hang his symbolic weights. His characters are first and foremost mythical presences and, as such, are less inclined to speak to one another than to expound their impenetrable views, rather in the manner of one addressing a symposium on the Sociology of Art, or the Anthropology of Myth.

Critics have frequently compared Wilson Harris with Conrad or Patrick White, because of their shared interest in the expedition both as a physical journey and as a metaphor of self-discovery. What is not usually stressed is their different approaches as novelists—and it is a difference which marks the distance between their achievements. Conrad aimed to bring "to light the truth, manifold and one" but was passionately concerned also with the need "to make you hear, to make you feel . . . above all, to make you *see*". Patrick White's characters have been said to cause "the world of substance to quake" but his world is solidly and unmistakably there. In comparison, despite the claims which are made for heterogeneous backgrounds and cultures, "all colours, all pigmentations, all illuminations, all creatures", Wilson Harris's latest novel seems at the same time deliquescent and opaque.

Shirley Chew, "Crisses and Crosses," in The Times Literary Supplement *(© Times Newspapers Ltd. (London) 1978; reproduced from* The Times Literary Supplement *by permission), No. 3972, May 19, 1978, p. 564.*

LLOYD W. BROWN

Wilson Harris has done most of his work in the novel form, but his second volume of poetry, *Eternity to Season,* published three years after the first [*Fetish*], demonstrates that he is also a poet of some substance. *Fetish* is pretentious rather than substantial, due largely to metaphoric excesses that make for a turgid, unreadable style. *Eternity to Season* is much better written on the whole, but it too suffers from the old excesses in spots. It seems that Harris himself is aware of this fault since in a recent reprint of the collection he has excised some of the troublesome verbiage. But a recurrent drawback is not simply verbiage as such but also a matter of feeling. There is a flood of carefully devised images which sometimes fail to communicate the kind of intellectual and emotional pressure that would justify such an abundance. In works like **"The Beggar Is King"** this lack of justification results in a pompous incongruity between subject (the impoverished Guyanese laborer) and the obvious, rather obtrusive convolutions of Harris' imagery. Curiously enough, Harris at his metaphoric worst is not distracting (in the tradition of most poets who suffer from the same affliction) but simply monotonous. In **"Rice,"** for example, the relentless succession of metaphoric elaborations and convoluted statements creates its own peculiar sameness. (pp. 93-4)

The dramatic poem **"Canje,"** set in a rural Guyanese village, is awkwardly executed throughout with a great deal of excessive writing. But Harris' general drift is always arresting. Anticipating Derek Walcott's *Another Life* by nearly twenty years, Harris' poem examines the lives of his folk through the archetypes of Greek myth—Ulysses, Tiresias, Achilles, and so forth. The objective conforms with the bicultural dimensions within which Harris and others perceive the West Indian experience. The Greco-Guyanese myth-heroes embody the duality of the Guyanese experience; and more specifically, the poet-seer Tiresias now represents the Guyanese poet as the essence and analyst of that duality: the bisexual image of Tiresias symbolizes the bicultural identity of the poet, his imagination, and his folk. (p. 94)

Harris is using [the] archetypal roots of Greco-Roman and Western culture as a means of exploring the cultural roots of the West Indies: the very concept and use of archetypes are based on a preoccupation with a sense of roots. Moreover, the archetypal mode is used to explore time-as-experience. The archetype is the creation of the past, a symbol and function of the links between past and present, and accordingly, the poet's perspective on the cultural history of his own world. Hence in

"Teiresias" the poet-as-seer represents the ability to perceive the future in the present, just as the **"Teiresias"** archetype himself embodies a continuity between the (Greco-Roman) past and the (Afro-West Indian) present. . . . (pp. 94-5)

"Teiresias" is one of those rare poems in which Harris sustains an ease and a directness of statement without lapsing into strangling verbiage. And this achievement may be of special significance since Tiresias as poet and seer represents the clarity of a fully aware perception of history and the role of the artist. (p. 95)

On the whole **"Achilles"** is another well written poem displaying the kind of discipline which allows Harris to blend his archetypal symbolism (mobility, power, creativity) into his central theme with economy and precision. This is also true of **"Creation"** in which the abstraction of Harris' theme (creation itself as freedom and infinite power) is developed without undue flourish in a succession of clearly defined and concrete images. First, that familiar Guyanese sense of an infinite landscape lends itself easily to the grasp of creation as an infinite, universal force. . . . Second, it is an "immensity of greatest power" that is symbolized by that ocean which links Harris' continent with the West Indian islander's perennial consciousness of the sea. Thirdly, it is represented by the "strips of coast" that are Guyana itself with its Afro-West Indian capacity to survive and transcend the Middle Passage past through a "celebration of spirit." And fourthly, to complete the pattern of increasingly specialized, or microcosmic examples, creation is the individual spirit itself. . . . The pattern of the poem progresses inward from the perception of a universal macrocosm to the individual as microcosm. As such it represents a kind of focusing. It is therefore an aesthetic confirmation of Harris' emphasis on perception as movement and on creation as an endless, infinite movement. In poems like these Harris' craftsmanship is superb, and the clarity of vision is unsurpassed. After this volume of poetry he turns to prose fiction, producing a series of some of the most distinguished novels in West Indian literature. But even on its own and despite its undeniable shortcomings *Eternity to Season* represents a major contribution to the West Indian poet's exploration of time and history in the Caribbean experience. (pp. 95-6)

Lloyd W. Brown, "The Emergence of Modern West Indian Poetry: 1940-1960," in his West Indian Poetry *(copyright © 1978 by Twayne Publishers, Inc.; reprinted with the permission of Twayne Publishers, a Division of G. K. Hall & Co., Boston), Twayne, 1978, pp. 63-99.*

HENA MAES-JELINEK

Its constantly evolving character notwithstanding, a remarkable unity of thought informs [Wilson Harris's] considerable opus. Two major elements seem to have shaped Harris's approach to art and his philosophy of existence: the impressive contrasts of the Guyanese landscapes, with which his survey expeditions made him familiar, and the successive waves of conquest which gave Guyana its heterogeneous population polarised for centuries into oppressors and their victims. The two, landscape and history, merge in his work into single metaphors symbolising man's inner space saturated with the effects of historical—that is, temporal—experiences. The jungle, for example, is for Harris both outer and inner unreclaimed territory, the actual 'landscape of history' for those who only survived by disappearing into it and a metaphor for that inner psychological recess to which his characters relegate both their forgotten ancestors and the living whom they dominate. It contrasts with the savannahs and is itself full of contrasts. Though teeming with life, much of it is invisible to the ordinary 'material' eye, just as those who, willingly or not, lead an underground existence remain unseen save to the 'spiritual' (imaginative) eye. The jungle's extra-human dimensions suggest timelessness and offer a glimpse of eternity, while the constant renewal of the vegetation confirms its existence within a cyclical time pattern. In Harris's words the jungle 'travels eternity to season'; and the Amerindians, who move to and fro between that secret primeval world and the modern areas where they can find work, subsist, as he writes in *Tumatumari* . . . , 'on a dislocated scale of time'. They are an essential link between the modern Guyanese and the lost world of their undigested past, and must be retrieved from their buried existence in both real and symbolical *terra incognita* if Guyana (and the individual soul) is to absorb all its components into a harmonious community.

Already in his poetry Harris had dealt jointly with the contrasts and polarisations in nature and history, and presented spiritual freedom as a capacity to move between opposites. . . . The very form of his verse reflects the reconciliation of opposites by freely mixing concrete with symbolical or outer with inner planes of existence. . . . [His] substantial volume of poetry, *Eternity to Season* . . .—significantly subtitled 'Poems of separation and reunion'—is an epic in which the characters, called after Greek mythological heroes, turn out to be humble Guyanese labourers. Their mythological stature indicates perhaps where the Guyanese should look for their archetypes. Harris gives his own idiosyncratic interpretation of Homeric adventures just as he was later to fill Christian and Amerindian myths with new content. His free borrowing from various cultures is one of many ways in which he attempts to break down barriers between men and between civilisations. He does not deny the specific character and experience of each people, and his poems are meant to awaken the sensibility and imagination of the Guyanese to the real nature of their environment. But he rejects all static ways of being. Man cannot help being imprisoned within time and history; he can, however, achieve partial liberation and distance from even necessary orders by tending towards an 'other', provided this 'other' is not allowed to become another absolute. This dualistic and dynamic view of existence accounts for Harris's many-layered and paradoxical language, particularly his juxtaposition of contradictory terms which challenge our modes of perception and thought (as in 'blossoming coals of immortal imperfection'). Many of the basic metaphors Harris was to use in his fiction are already found with a potentially double meaning in his poetry. But while the vision is as boldly original in the one as in the other, it has achieved a greater impact by being embodied in the more concrete setting and highly individualised characters of his fiction. Harris is primarily a novelist even though his fictional language has the concentrated richness of poetry and, as has often been pointed out, demands the same minute reading and explication. True, the poet has always had greater licence than the novelist to deal with the transcendental, but Harris's way of dealing with it has introduced a new dimension into the novel.

Harris's fiction began to appear at a crucial time for both the nascent West Indian fiction and the novel in English since, in the fifties and early sixties, the trends in English and American fiction indicated that many inheritors of established traditions had ceased to believe in them. The dissolution of values and forms due to the combined action of history and science had left artists in a void similar in kind to that experienced with

more tragic intensity by West Indians throughout their history. With a few notable exceptions, English and American novelists reacted to this loss of certainty by either seeking refuge and renewing their faith in realism, or turning experimental fiction into an art of the absurd, technically brilliant and innovatory but often undermining the very purpose of art. Wilson Harris is among the few West Indian writers who pointed out the irrelevance of both trends to a 'native' art of fiction. While insisting that the disorientation of the 'diminished man' in formerly strong societies had been experienced for centuries by the conquered populations in the Caribbean and the Americas, he warned particularly against the influence on West Indian writers of the post-war European art of despair. His own 'art of compassion' does not involve, as has sometimes been suggested, a withdrawal from history in order to transcend it. It is, on the contrary, intensely concerned with the impact of history on the ordinary 'obscure human person' and expresses a passionate denial of what has been termed the 'historylessness' of the Caribbean: it shows that people exist by virtue of their silent suffering as much as by celebrated deeds or a materially recognisable civilisation, of which incidentally obscure men are the unacknowledged executors. My main purpose is to show how Harris's view of Caribbean history has shaped his art of the novel.

The major historical facts endured by the Caribbean peoples were dismemberment, exile, eclipse and, for many, slavery, with the result that for several centuries they lived destitute and inarticulate in a political, social and cultural void. In much of Harris's fiction these catastrophic experiences are recreated both as facts and as inner states to be digested by the individual consciousness. Most of his novels present an outer-world and an inner confrontation between a conqueror or oppressor and his victim, as well as the traumas that result from the violation of a people or of an individual soul. They all explore possibilities of rebirth and of genuine community between polarised people(s) and between antithetical ways of being. This basic and recurrent theme determines Harris's conception of character, the structure of his novels and their narrative texture as well as his style. Harris equates dominant and fixed forms in art with dominant and static social structures, local, national or international. Hence his attempt to find a fluid mode of expression to render the duality of life, the necessary movement between its opposite poles, and above all the mobility of consciousness.

Harris's fictional work to date can be divided into three major phases. In the first of these the *Guiana Quartet* creates a composite picture of the many facets of Guyanese life: the paradoxes and unpredictable manifestations of a nature that is not easily mastered, the historical vestiges, visible and invisible, that give each area a specific 'spirit of the place', and the activities of a multiracial population often self-divided and alienated from its 'lost' or unintegrated groups such as the Amerindians or the descendants of runaway slaves. There is a sense in which the first novel, *Palace of the Peacock,* contains in embryo all further developments. It recreates the main fact of Caribbean history, the endlessly renewed exploitation of land and people, from time immemorial through the Renaissance to the present day, by waves of invaders intent on winning the country's riches for themselves. 'Rule the land . . . and you rule the world,' says the skipper Donne, who pursues an invisible Amerindian tribe on a nameless river through the jungle, and shows the mixture of idealism and brutality that has characterised many an ambitious enterprise in modern times. (pp. 179-83)

The opening of the novel on the frontier between life and death establishes at the outset Harris's dual view of existence and his conception of death as eclipse rather than annihilation. The dead in his fiction are an essential part of a community of being and must be retrieved from oblivion by imagination. In *Palace* the narrator's reconstruction of the past is both an 'act of memory' and a 'dream', Harris's word to describe an intuitive, imaginative apprehension of reality, one that frees man from the limitations of exclusively rational and/or sensory perceptions and makes possible the reconciliation of apparently incompatible opposites. The double perspective due to the juxtaposition of material perception and spiritual vision in Donne and the Narrator is paralleled by a similar duality in the phenomenal world itself, which offers an insight into its immaterial counterpart. There is the 'skeleton footfall' on the river bank disclosing an invisible presence, or the tree that suddenly sheds all its leaves, revealing the simple inner structure that underlies its external profusion.

Donne and the crew must recognise their exploitation of both land and people (united by a similar 'namelessness'). As they travel upriver and re-enact their possessive or murderous deeds, the dangers they meet gradually decimate their ranks and turn them into pursued men longing for redemption through the muse they have all abused in one way or another. . . . The main effect of the trials they have gone through has been to shake them out of their fixed sense of identity, and although they are not aware of it until they come together in the manifold symbol of the peacock's tail at the very end, their dying to themselves (their 'Second Death') is a momentary surrender to 'otherness', the lifeblood of community. The final conversion, however, occurs in Donne and offers the first example in Harris's fiction of the necessary interdependence between the imaginative artist (for Donne is also that) and the ordinary folk.

A further illustration of duality is to be found in the shift from the concrete to the purely symbolical as the narrative draws to an end, suggesting that spiritual rebirth is a feat of the imagination, which is itself regenerated. . . . Donne's fall into the void is a symbolical re-enactment of the fate of the victims of conquest. Whether in *Palace, Tumatumari* (in which the severing of Roi's head in a collision with a rock in the waterfall symbolises the dismemberment of the Amerindians and the loss of their leadership) or in *Companions of the Day and Night* . . . , the fall down a natural escarpment in Guyana or from a Mexican pyramid stands for the collapse of a people and recreates the terrifying sense of void they experienced.

The fall in *Palace of the Peacock* is followed by a rebirth from what Harris sees as both the 'grave' and the 'womb' of history. It is Donne's spiritual self that is resurrected to apprehend the evanescent moment in which the members of his heterogeneous crew or community come together as stars and eyes in the peacock's tail, fragments of the splintered sun, which in the first part of the novel was a symbol of Donne's implacable tyranny. The metamorphosis of images corresponds to a similar transformation and displacement of formerly fixed attitudes within the characters. That is why the vision of the crew's reunion at the end is so brief. It actualises the Narrator's moments of intuitive perception of wholeness which have alternated with the crew's actions and physical progress throughout the narrative. Owing to this alternation the structure of the novel is informed by the ebb and flow movement that Harris sees in all forms of outer life and deems essential within man's consciousness.

The other novels of the *Quartet* also illustrate the frightening but necessary disorientation this regained fluidity of being entails in men confronted by violence and murder, the residues of slavery and the desire of former victims to become exploiters in their turn, 'as though the oppressed convention nurses identical expectations of achieving power', and the continuing exploitation of minority or eclipsed groups. *The Far Journey of Oudin* focuses on the master-servant relationship on the East Indian rice plantations between the savannahs and the coast. *The Whole Armour* takes place on the Pomeroon river and the precarious strip of land between bush and sea. Cristo, a young man wrongly accused of murder, agrees to sacrifice himself to redeem the community. In *The Secret Ladder* the land surveyor Fenwick and his crew stationed in the jungle gauge the river Canje prior to the building of a dam that would flood the territory from which the descendants of slaves refuse to move. None of these novels has the linear simplicity of *Palace of the Peacock;* the more commonplace experiences of the earthbound characters and the more complex plots give them a density and an immediacy further enhanced by a more extensive use of dialect. But the issues raised do not find a worldly resolution. The emphasis is on spiritual freedom, responsibility and a genuine authority which, like the sense of unity in *Palace,* are envisaged through the recognition of the alien and weak element in the community as its true roots and therefore springhead of change. The crux of each novel lies in the possibility of unlocking a fixed order of things and eroding the certainties and imperatives that imprison the protagonists within a one-sided and rigid sense of self. Hence the crumbling rather than 'consolidation' of personality, the disturbing resemblances between dead and living characters, or sometimes even the reappearance of the dead among the living, and the frequency of 'doubles' or twins to 'break through from patterns of implacable identities'. In keeping with Harris's concentration on process rather than achievement, the end of the *Quartet* is inconclusive. A central motif running through its four movements is the need for the Guyanese (as for Donne) 'to understand and transform [their] beginnings'. That is why each novel raises the question of who the characters' true parents are. What Harris calls 'the mystery of origins' can only be penetrated, though never completely, by 'dismantling a prison of appearance'. This course of action, initiated by Fenwick in *The Secret Ladder,* is the major theme and shaping factor of his next cycle of novels.

Harris's fifth novel, *Heartland* . . . , is an essential link between the *Guiana Quartet* and his next works. . . . At the end of the novel [the protagonist] Stevenson . . . disappears into the heartland, leaving in his half-burnt resthouse fragments of letters and poems. The uncertainty of his fate in the intermediate life-and-death world of the jungle suggests that, like characters in the following novels, he has lost himself in the third nameless dimension Harris has now started to explore. This is the void once inherent in the Caribbean psyche, seen as a possible vessel of rebirth for all men and as a state to be experienced by the artist who shuns the tyranny of one dominant world-view and allows contradictory voices to speak through him. The novel tends towards the interiorisation of action that is wholly characteristic of Harris's second phase. At the same time the pattern of pursuit and flight specific to the *Quartet* gives way momentarily, through Stevenson's relationship with the Amerindian woman, Petra, to reciprocity between the exploring consciousness and the eclipsed 'other'. . . . 'Crumbling', 'retiring' and 'advancing' outline the course henceforth taken by Harris's characters, first an erosion of biased assumptions followed by a double movement of advance and retreat (for the self as for the other) which precludes total identification with another and therefore total loss or gain for one or the other. The 'vicarious hollow and original substance' towards which Stevenson moves, but is not known to have reached, sums up the simultaneous condition of nothingness and starting point of creation that Harris sees as the essence of Caribbean experience and art.

Without unduly schematising, one can discern in Harris's next four novels some common features which throw light on his purpose as a novelist. They all recreate the past of an individual Guyanese family, whose trials and present circumstances reflect the 'burden of history' that still weighs on the society they live in. The condition explored in each novel is one of void or loss. (pp. 184-88)

There is a double preoccupation in these novels, with the state of loss incurred in the past and the kind of fiction that the artist, his narrator or protagonist attempts to conceive. The two are closely linked together and it will be seen that these works are as much about the art of fiction as about the revival or 'art' of community. The Narrator in *The Eye* who re-lives his past again and again, Susan and her lover re-living their affair through the author's editorship, Prudence re-creating twentieth-century Guyanese history from her own memories and her father's papers, and Victor writing a novel about his father's trial, all are creators or characters in search of a 'primordial species of fiction'. The phrase implies that the stuff of fiction is to be found in what is both fundamental and primeval (in themselves and in the outer world) which the protagonists have long neglected, ignored or misrepresented to themselves. The primordial is shown to be a dynamic relationship between all forms of life but first and foremost between human beings. . . . As each explorer of the past discovers, however, the nothingness, deadness, stagnation or even inflexibility of those whom the Narrator in *The Eye* seeks beyond 'a dead masked frontier' is only an illusion. Their essential livingness and even capacity to reverse given situations and become tyrannical in turn is one of the protagonists' main discoveries. The basic rapport the protagonist achieves with the object of his exploration is one in which each moves towards the other without ever finally succumbing or identifying with that other. This is the bare outline of a process that must be traced through the complex structure and the rich metaphorical texture of the narrative; these vary greatly from one novel to another as Harris extends the limits of the reality he explores and approaches his material from different angles.

Nature and society (even when the latter is refined and abstracted, as in *The Waiting Room*) are the starting point of the characters' exploration, for in Harris's fiction it is always a keen sensitivity to the material world which leads to the perception of an immaterial perspective (or of those that are judged immaterial: 'the nameless sleeping living and the nameless forgotten dead'). The emphasis is no longer as in the early novels on the breakdown of the protagonists' personality: this is now their condition when the novels open. Their breakdown, however, turns out to be an asset: in their initial state of weakness or emptiness they no longer try to imprison within a given or final view the experience they re-live or the people they knew. Each becomes a medium ('vicarious hollow') in which the past re-enacts itself. In both *The Eye* and *The Waiting Room* the narrator's declared purpose is to allow a free and living 'construction of events' to emerge from the evocation of the past. What happens is that the 'broken' memory or the unsettled state of the characters yields a fragmented version of events;

these gradually reveal possibilities of interpretation different from their original one. In other words, the past, which is now the main substance of the novel, is subject to the same process of crumbling and reshaping as the character who re-lives it. Time and space (inner and outer) are not seen as rigid and divisive frames of existence; these barriers come apart too, disclosing, for example, the disregarded or unsuspected feelings of individuals and peoples whose behaviour had been represented in one light only. There is thus a dislocation of surface reality in all its forms—and therefore a fragmentation of the narrative structure—which makes the protagonists aware of 'the stranger animation one sees within the cycle of time'— in nature, that is; in the seemingly frozen past; in the retrenched and silent existence of the uninitiate and in the protagonists' own unconscious. This fragmentation alone opens the way into what is apparently dead within and beyond the perceptible world but is in fact alien, mysterious, 'opposite' life, sometimes fierce destructive force, sometimes frail, indistinct spirit. The protagonist himself is healed, his own memory and imagination regenerated, to the extent that he can *feel* that life by incurring its 'burden of authenticity, obscurity or difficulty'. It is what Harris means by 'revising contrasting spaces' in order to allow a 'new dimension of feeling' to emerge. It is brilliantly illustrated in *Tumatumari* in the symbolic vision of harmony between Prudence and her husband's despised Amerindian mistress, Rakka, revolving together and changing places in a whirlpool of death and rebirth.

The characters' transformation ('gestation of the soul') is rendered symbolically through serial metamorphoses of metaphors, which is wholly consistent with Harris's belief that the individual consciousness is saturated with 'given' images of the past, and with the fact that metaphors alone can convey the unity underlying the apparently disparate shapes of life. A good example of this is the scarecrow in the first novel of this cycle, a metaphor for the diminished state of man, for the disruptions that can be observed in nature, for disintegrating tenements in Georgetown and for the dying British Empire. This accumulation of various scarecrow images (like the many versions of the severed head perceived by Prudence in *Tumatumari*) renders the underlying unity or 'unfathomable wholeness' that belies the void or *tabula rasa*. Wholeness is also expressed in single metaphors as, for example, in the symbolic union of Prudence and Rakka mentioned above or (in *The Waiting Room*) in an image inspired by the myth of Ulysses; his dependence on an insensitive mast and deaf crew is used to convey the union between the lovers, each being for the other the deaf mast or crew which allows his or her companion to hear the otherworldly muse. Some single key metaphors, like the sun and the whirlpool, develop fresh contrasting meanings from one novel to another. Single words also frequently express one thing and its opposite. So the word 'silence' in the same novel is both Susan's injunction to her lover, which denies him, and the expression of her longing for the silence and potential fulfilment allied to the nameless dimension.

Although I have already suggested as much, it is necessary to insist that while wholeness is tentatively reconstructed or approached in the narrative through an accumulation of images, and perceived by the protagonist in visionary moments, it is never actually attained. The narratives trace the characters' oscillations between the finite world and their vision of the 'infinite' as they grope towards a metaphysical reality which both fascinates and terrifies them. They make some progress towards it as they move towards the nameless in probing into human history, into the mystery of eclipsed lives and of injustice. When they have shed their own identity, have become *in imagination* and temporarily 'Idiot Nameless' (the trickster without identity of Caribbean history), the metamorphosis of their vision, and therefore of themselves, takes place. Self-negation achieved, their consciousness becomes a vehicle for the transmutation of static images and is itself transformed metaphorically: the scarecrow, an image of unconsciousness when the novel opens, is released, like the Narrator, from the blindness of self-sufficiency and becomes the medium of an interplay of opposites, the foundation of true vision; the waiting room, at first a place where Susan broods over the past and suffers, becomes a 'womb' of rebirth (reconciliation and vision); the severed head in *Tumatumari* turns into a smiling and flowering Gorgon's head; in *Ascent to Omai* the stone in the pool, which sends out concentric rings or horizons of memory delimiting frustrating periods of Victor's life, initiates a dance (a series of harmonious movements) between these formerly blocked slices of life.

Namelessness, moreover, is not wholeness (the coincidence of opposites) but only the contrary and negative pole of a clearly defined identity. In *Black Marsden* . . . , which initiates the third cycle of his fiction, Harris warns against the danger of erecting former victims into the powerful instrument of a new tyranny in the name of a misconceived revolution. During his trip to Namless [sic]—at once his country of origin and an imaginary wasteland, modern man's ruined consciousness—Goodrich, the main character, realises that formerly exploited workers have been trapped into a spiral of self-destructive strikes by their employers and by obscure forces. The *tabula rasa* state of Victor's father in *Ascent to Omai* has developed into the *tabula rasa* theatre directed by Black Marsden, who stimulates Goodrich's generosity and spiritual liberation but threatens to engulf and 'deplete' him like all Marsden's other agents when they yield to him. Through Goodrich's association with Marsden it becomes clear that the material generosity of individuals (or nations) will not redeem them from their sense of guilt towards the poor. Goodrich possesses 'the eye of the scarecrow' which eventually helps him resist the hypnotic spell Marsden had cast over him. At the end of the novel he stands 'utterly alone', free from imposed thought yet still moved by 'the strange inner fire' that had first sent him on an expedition into 'infinity'.

This state of aloneness and the passion for infinity that Goodrich cannot wholly assuage if he wants to stay alive are further explored in *Companions of the Day and Night*, a sequel to *Black Marsden,* in which he becomes more deeply involved in the smouldering existence of the dead by editing Idiot Nameless's paintings and sculptures, the 'equation' of his exploration of Mexico. Through Nameless's 'descent' into Mexican historical vestiges, Harris brings together the theme of the enforced eclipse of civilisations and his belief in a possible 'treaty of sensibility between alien cultures'. Essentially, the novel is about the fall of man and his terror of extinction; it gives the experience of the void a universal and even a cosmic scale. Goodrich compares the pre-Columbians' dread that their world might come to an end unless they offered the sun human sacrifices with modern man's fear that his world might fall into a 'black hole of gravity'. The pre-Columbians fell under Cortez and the conquering, not humble and life-giving, Christ that followed in his wake; the Christian Church, however, was itself driven underground by a revolution early in the twentieth century that led to further repression. Nameless too suffers from a 'falling sickness' (a psychological equivalent to the possibility of cosmic

fall) which nevertheless enables him to confront and unravel the self-destructive models of pre-Columbian and Christian institutions, to retrieve also the original 'spark' or element of conscience, inherent in each civilisation, which was buried with these institutions when each in turn was sacrificed. Nameless lives at once through the days of the Mexican calendar and the pre-Easter period as the predicaments of the interchangeable conquerors and victims merge in his consciousness. It is indeed the contradictory aspects of his own condition as both victor and victim that Nameless explores and reconciles in himself. At the same time his transformation into a spark after his fall from the pyramid of the sun together with the impression he gives at the end that he is a frail Christ who is once more denied physical life suggest the possible emergence of a new centre of illumination from within the very deadlock of history.

A fundamental aspect of *Companions* is the way in which old forms (such as institutions or myths) prove susceptible of new content through the mediation of the individual consciousness. Together with Nameless's 'painting' this leads to yet another development in Harris's presentation of characters. The aspect of namelessness explored in *Black Marsden* is still there, symbolised by the coat of uniformity worn by post-revolutionary workers and by the destitute madonna in the next novel, *Da Silva da Silva's Cultivated Wilderness*. . . . But more importance is given to Nameless's own freedom from codified ways of thinking and the capacity it gives him to play many roles in life and suffer the predicament of different people. Already in *Ascent to Omai* the judge, not knowing what became of Victor, shuffles blank cards while recreating the trial, thus envisaging for him alternative existences, for this blankness is like 'a consciousness without content which nevertheless permitted all alien contents to exist'. While in *The Eye* Harris presented language as an equation of the arousal of vision from that blankness, in his latest novels he has added a term to the equation: painting as an art of grasping the 'inimitable'. The main character is now a painter whose works are so many partial versions of, yet also 'doorways' into, an inner reality or light that can be neither wholly unearthed nor trapped. The narrative itself is like a large canvas which corresponds to the painter's field of vision. The existences on this canvas reveal unpredictable resources that modify the relation between the two faces of tradition, the conqueror's and the victim's or, in a different form, the 'dying' tradition of perceptible achievements and its immortal counterpart growing out of unacknowledged sacrifice. The need for an imaginative, necessarily precarious balance between the two underlies the painter's ceaseless effort to create a 'middle ground' between the contrasting figures he 'paints' into existence, people whom he sees as resurrected selves moving in and out of his consciousness.

Since *Black Marsden* these 'painted' resurrected lives (resurrection leading to community is the major theme of the third cycle of novels) are evoked with increased sensuousness. Because the main concern in Harris's novels lies in the impact of the outside world (the apparently trivial as much as the more dramatic incidents of everyday life) on the individual's inner self, the recreated 'drama of consciousness' involves flesh-and-blood people. In the novels of Harris's second phase the possibility of reconciliation between the protagonist and those he revives is largely expressed metaphorically. Although the metaphors are borrowed from *living* nature, the reconstructed experience has a more abstract or structural character than in the earlier or later fiction. In the third phase, however, the revived figures are always solidly there; in the Da Silva novels they are significantly conceived, brought to life, through the tender physical relations between the creative artist and his earthly muse or madonna. (pp. 188-95)

Hena Maes-Jelinek, "Wilson Harris," in West Indian Literature, *edited by Bruce King (© Bruce King 1979; reprinted by permission of Archon Books, an imprint of The Shoe String Press, Inc.), Archon Books, Hamden, Connecticut, 1979, pp. 179-95.*

GARY CREW

In his companion collections of short stories, *The Sleepers of Roraima* and *The Age of the Rainmakers,* Wilson Harris reaches through time and presents to the contemporary reader legends of the Amerindian people. It is not his intention merely to record such legends as the superstitious mythopoetic rationalizing of a "primitive" people; rather, Harris uses these legends to explore and activate the original and timeless quality of the imagination, a quality which twentieth-century man has nullified by his obsession with totalities or fixed perspectives of time, history and race. Through his stories, Harris demonstrates the error of such limited perception, which may be overcome if the imagination is reactivated as the original and vital human force. It is the imagination which destroys the limiting concepts of past, present and future, unifying all that has been, is and will be, in the moment now, the eternal present. (p. 218)

An examination of **"Arawak Horizon,"** the final story of *The Age of the Rainmakers,* will serve as an introduction to the method employed by Harris in adapting Arawak legend to expand the limitations of contemporary man's imagination. Using the numerals 0 through 9 as a basis, he reveals that to the twentieth-century consciousness such numerals are no more than static symbols, capable only of mechanistic or economic interpretation. However, when he, or his narrator counterpart, allows himself to be taken back in time across the Arawak horizon, he views the numerals from a primal viewpoint: in this story, that of an Arawak child. This child sees in the numerals not mathematical codes, but abstract symbols "illuminated by consciousness." In this way the numeral 0 becomes the "first prisoner to creep through the walls of fire" . . ., and when freed from preconceived interpretation, appears to the Arawak child as as symbol of unlimited potential, . . .

The numerals serve the function of a concrete twentieth-century corelative to the working of the "primitive" mind, and because of their contemporary connotation as easily comprehended mathematical symbols, they provide a simpler starting point for an analysis of the companion stories than the ancient abstract rock paintings which evoke a similar imaginative metamorphosis in the first volume, *The Sleepers of Roraima.* (p. 219)

The stories of this first volume, *The Sleepers of Roraima,* **"Couvade," "I, Quiyumucon"** and **"Yurokon,"** each describe an attempt to preserve the pure bloodline of the Caribs as the tribe progresses through migration and invasion to its final assimilation into the multi-racial population of twentieth-century Guyana. In their obsession with preserving purity of race, the Caribs find themselves threatened; initially, in **"Couvade,"** by their own local tribesmen, in **"I, Quiyumucon"** by assimilation into the tribes of the Arawaks, and finally in **"Yurokon,"** by the infiltration of the Spanish and the Christian influence of Europe. (pp. 219-20)

[In] contrast to the dominant threat of human incursion found in *The Sleepers of Roraima,* in the second collection of legends natural phenomena, rain and drought, are the principal forces against which the Amerindian must struggle if he is to survive. Harris employs these physical elements to symbolize the barren psychic outlook of the contemporary Amerindian. The imaginative stasis of the people is revealed in their continued rebellion against invasion, real or imagined, which may be interpreted as a period of drought. In order to overcome this psychic and physical calamity, the Amerindian must reach back to the legendary age of the rainmakers, and rediscover, through legend, the fertile imagination.

The first story of *The Age of the Rainmakers,* **"The Age of Kaie,"** focusses on Paterson, a half-caste twentieth-century revolutionary who is also the reincarnation of Kaie, an ancestral figure of legend. Yet, as is typical of Harris, this ambivalent figure may separate to create a pair of contemporary/ancient freedom fighters. In this guise Paterson and Kaie lie wounded on a modern battlefield and "loss of blood gave them this sensation—as if they shared the same interior, the same echoing body of fragmentary particulars, and the elements were hallucinated within them and without." . . . There is, however, a fundamental difference in the two figures. Kaie, the older and wiser, is aware that Paterson fights because the Amerindians have always felt threatened by invasion and loss of identity; Paterson's fighting spirit is the "naiveté of revolutionary fatherhood," . . . an adherence to the principle of the "creation of the enemy" as demonstrated in **"Couvade,"** where such an enemy may in fact be his "own fierce nostalgic creation." . . . This concept is fundamentally static and therefore self-negating. In death, his voice rising and falling with flippancy, Paterson becomes aware of his error: "And Paterson had the curious ironic sensation that in the hollow pit of his body—ancestral Indian enemy—Kaie's breath had been caged for centuries instinctive to the residue of legend—betrothal of opposites." . . . The "hollow pit of his body" is symbolic of the drought which should be broken by the rainmakers. It has been an age of historical and imaginative stasis for Paterson's people, a period of empty rebellion signifying nothing, a time of reliance on the residue of legend left by the great age of Kaie. Thus Paterson, alias Kaie, relives the age of the rainmakers and finds a "new maiden architecture of place" and the "distances of history melt or multiply with each convertible echo." . . . (pp. 222-23)

The idea of cyclical regeneration takes a dramatic conceptual change in **"The Laughter of the Wapishanas."** Here, a legendary girl, Wapishana, sets out to find a means of diverting her tribe's attention from the rigours of drought. She searches for the source of laughter, which she is determined to restore to the lips of her people. Harris uses this search to develop the significance of the decoy in diverting mankind from reality. Wapishana finds that each landmark she gains is "less a question of marching time than of alterations of horizon—legs or scissors into decoy of space or reality of the game." . . . Each tribe or age has its own method of disguise to avoid extinction. Thus, on reaching the "pool of laughter" Wapishana finds the fish symbolizing the "ironic lifeline of Christ," . . . the decoy of Christianity. By this method Harris exposes the more abstract "decoy of space," the trickery of time which can alter historical derivations to a non-compassionate, static conception. Again the story stresses the significance of the eternal present; contemporary man may adopt physical or spiritual disguises (sunglasses or Christianity) to avoid "the true game of reality . . . down the arch of the road through and beyond the purchase of extinction." . . . (p. 225)

It is now possible to view in context the universal conception of the eternal present in the final story, **"Arawak Horizon,"** with a more compassionate sensibility. As the ancient Arawak child plays with and interprets static twentieth-century numerals, they become living things. With his original imagination, "milestone of Arawak survival across the seas of soul," . . . he can make what was doomed to mathematical or economic formulation span the decoy of space and recreate the age of the rainmakers. . . . There is, therefore, no Arawak horizon, only a decoy of space, which is as limitless as the creative imagination of all mankind. (p. 226)

> *Gary Crew, "The Eternal Present in Wilson Harris's 'The Sleepers of Roraima' and 'The Age of the Rainmakers'," in* World Literature Written in English *(© copyright 1980 WLWE-World Literature Written in English), Vol. 19, No. 2, Autumn, 1980, pp. 218-27.*

MICHAEL GILKES

Harris's work, because of its syncretic approach to language and to the symbolic meaning of experience, is notoriously "difficult." Concerned more with the symbolic and contradictory—rather than the literal—meaning of language, he has produced a highly innovative novel-form. . . . [His] approach to the novel-as-painting, where words are used to suggest—like the brush strokes of the artist—areas of color, light, and shade, and where the writer's purpose is "to break down things in order to sense a vision through things" boldly challenges the conventional narrative form of the novel. Like James Joyce or Virginia Woolf, Harris, in attempting to explore the deeper resources of language and experience, is in fact extending the boundaries of what we call fiction. One frequently gets the impression of an apparent "breakdown" of language in Harris's fiction. . . . [His writing] creates an impression similar to that of certain "surrealistic" paintings, and, to some extent, Harris intends to shock the reader. But the "controlled chaos" of the writing is really part of a desire (like that of the early French surrealist painters Andre Breton, Magritte, Chagall, and others) to *dislocate* the fixed, conventional habit of perception: it is a desire related to what Mircea Eliade calls "the destruction of the language of art" which, as he sees it, is a systematic and radical transformation. (pp. 147-48)

[Harris's] novels, from **Palace of the Peacock** onward, illustrate the development of a continually expanding sensibility which questions, fragments, and reassembles "reality" in its search for a genuinely new, all-embracing Art. . . . (p. 148)

> *Michael Gilkes, "New Directions: From W. Hudson's 'Green Mansions' to W. Harris's Cultivated Wilderness," in his* The West Indian Novel *(copyright © 1981 by Twayne Publishers, Inc.; reprinted with the permission of Twayne Publishers, a Division of G. K. Hall & Co., Boston), Twayne, 1981, pp. 132-58.* *

Václav Havel

1936-

Czechoslovakian dramatist, essayist, and poet.

Havel is associated with the respected Theater on the Balustrade, Prague's leading avant-garde theater of the 1960s. His work is "blackly" comic and often disturbing. It is also controversial among leaders of the Communist regime in Czechoslovakia, yet Havel is acclaimed by critics in his own country and abroad. Some describe him as the most important Czech dramatist since Karel Čapek.

Working from a broad interest in the absurd nature of human existence, Havel writes plays that have a universal appeal despite their Czechoslovakian settings. In general, his dramas depict the mechanization of the individual by society and the role of language in this dehumanization process. These works have an intriguing circular quality: their focus shifts rapidly and repeatedly from the psychological to the metaphysical, to the social, to the patently absurd. His most famous plays, *Zahradni Slavnost (The Garden Party)* and *Vyrozumeny (The Memorandum)*, are absurdist works, full of humorous social commentary, political parody, and bleak philosophical observations.

In 1979 Havel, who often and effectively satirizes bureaucracies, was arrested and sentenced to four and a half years in prison for allegedly subversive activities. His plays were also banned from the Czech stage. Havel, nonetheless, has strong supporters in and out of his country. He is a close friend and confidant of dramatist Tom Stoppard. Samuel Beckett's recent brief play, *Catastrophe for Václav Havel* is an antitotalitarian statement written to protest Havel's imprisonment.

(See also *Contemporary Authors*, Vol. 104.)

Photograph by Liba Taylor

JAN GROSSMAN

A great theatre reveals not only itself and its story; it also reveals the viewer's story, and with it his urgent need to confront his own experience with the theme presented on stage. Such a play does not end with the performance; the curtain is only the beginning.

In his plays, Vaclav Havel has shown this true dramatic ability as have few in contemporary Czech literature. His key concern is the mechanization of man. . . . At the beginning of *The Garden Party* or *The Memorandum,* the audience is not dazzled by dramatic skills which elaborate on the subject; instead, there is mechanization itself, experienced as well as mediated by a manner which is technical and theoretical rather than dramatic.

Havel's potential as a playwright was once doubted by people who, however much they praised his literary talent, his analytical ability, his cutting aphorisms, thought he was too rationalistic and precise to fulfill current ideas of dramatic narrative and psychology. . . . Havel the analyst produced Havel the playwright at the moment he found the courage to be only what he really was; he derived a theatrical method from his own view of reality as soon as he discovered in it the fundamental characteristics of dialogue, which is the most valuable trait of his plays and the source of their universal appeal. They create a specific dialogue between stage and audience, with ample room for complementary meanings and associations.

In both *The Garden Party* and *The Memorandum,* the protagonist is the mechanism which controls the human characters. The mechanism of cliché dominates the former play: man does not use cliché, cliché uses man. Cliché is the hero, it causes, advances, and complicates the plot, determines human action, and, deviating further and further from our given reality, creates its own.

In *The Memorandum,* the protagonist also comes from human speech: man makes an artificial language which is intended to render communication perfect and objective, but which actually leads to constantly deepening alienation and disturbance in human relations. *The Garden Party* demonstrated the process in a manner which—within the framework of the playwright's poetry—was humorously aggressive propaganda, but the characters in *The Memorandum* no longer serve primarily to carry a message; they grow organically from the concept, represent it, contain it; and the author disappears behind his story and his style.

The theme has become psychological, by which I mean not that it has been softened by "human" details but, on the contrary, that the entire technique is mechanized, the characters are mechanized, and the material is interpreted on many different levels. Abstract speech is the subject: it is projected onto the mechanism of cowardice, the mechanism of power, the mechanism of indifference, and each of these in itself—as well as all of them in harmony—creates a stratified, complex picture of human depersonalization.

I do not know whether Havel's theatre belongs to the "absurd"—surely any influence shows only on its widest concepts. His plays are invented, artificial; but this quality has nothing to do with romantic fantasies or the unbridled insanity in which, forced to proceed according to the "law" of fantasy, people walk on their heads rather than their feet. Havel's artificial structuring of the world is made up of real, even commonplace and banal, components, joined most reasonably into a whole. *The Memorandum*'s story of an artificial language never happened and probably never will, yet Havel convinces us that it *could,* at any time. His world is hypothetical; therefore, possible. And it is no sweet and rosy possibility, but somewhat cruel and definitely negative. The hero is not protagonist but antagonist: the ever negating spirit which, creating its own truth, forces us to face an always-possible doom. Yet it also expects us to rebel against the truth it "creates," it provokes a discussion, turns our point of view around, upsets our actions, our fantasies, and our ideas. (pp. 118-19)

> *Jan Grossman, "A Preface to Havel" (reprinted by permission of the author; an excerpt originally from his introduction to* Protokoly *by Václav Havel, Mladá fronta, 1966), in* Tulane Drama Review, *Vol. II, No. 3, Spring, 1967, pp. 117-20.*

PAUL I. TRENSKY

The work of Havel epitomizes the state of Czech literature in the middle 1960's, which is characterized by two main features: first, an orientation toward the West in general philosophical questions and literary techniques, and, secondly, an outspokenly critical attitude toward Stalinism and its contemporary vestiges. Havel's work would be unthinkable without the influence of the so-called theater of the absurd, but at the same time it is deeply involved in an examination of the social ills of Czechoslovakia. . . .

As is the case with most absurd dramas, there is no plot, intrigue, or conflict in the traditional sense of the word in *The Garden Party.* The principal character of the work is Hugo Pludek, and, in the stratum of the action, the play deals with his overnight success. (p. 42)

His swift career is, however, realized at the expense of his personality. The most outstanding feature of Hugo is his ability to adapt to his surroundings, through which alone he is able to succeed in the world of bureaucracy. As he is constantly forced to assimilate to the new milieu, he gradually destroys his own self to such a degree that he ceases to be aware of his original identity. At the end of the drama Hugo does not even recognize his parents, nor do they recognize him. He has become a different, faceless being.

On the psychological level one could regard the play as being based on the traditional theme of the degradation of man by his lack of principles. . . . The techniques of *The Garden Party,* however, have little in common with the traditional drama or novel. Hugo, while trying to adapt himself, mutates directly into other personalities. The decomposition of his ego is realized not merely on the psychological level, but in the very structure of the drama. The essential dramaturgical device of the play rests in a direct character metamorphosis, which is,

in general, widely used by the absurd dramatists. . . . Havel shares with other absurd dramatists the conception of modern man's identity as a vacuum; consequently, man can become anything at any time, depending largely on the influences to which he is exposed. All his characters are soulless, mechanical creatures who are formed and defined only by their environment. The human world is an impersonal world in which individuals are exchangeable.

An analysis of *The Garden Party* must of necessity focus primarily upon its language. Lacking a real plot, conflict, and set of characters, the play rests on a highly complex verbal structure, and it is actually the language which is its primary moving force. This aspect of Havel's play is also identifiable with the absurd theater in the West, which has substantially changed the role of language in the structure of the dramatic genre. . . . In the traditional theater the role of language was largely secondary. It served merely as a vehicle for expressing the ideas and emotions of the characters, for the elaboration of the theme and conflict, and as a necessary link between the stage and the audience. In a theater which accredits to characters no inner life, however, words cannot be used just as projections to the outer world. Language not only ceases to serve character development, but the opposite becomes the fact, characters being made the vehicle of language. Words form people by filling their inner void until human speech stops functioning as a means of communication and becomes a form of social behavior. And since language no longer serves to express ideas, it also has to be contentless. Indeed, long dialogues in *The Garden Party* are nothing but a collection of prefabricated clichés which the characters repeat over and over, or the more creative ones intertwine and twist, but seldom does the human mind exhibit any more originality than a perfectly functioning linguistic computer. Language is the symptom of the alienation of man, but in a much more intense way than, for instance, in Čexov's plays. It points up not only the impossibility of communication between people, but the very corruption of intellect by language. People cannot understand each other because they simply do not say anything. The play presents language as a proliferating object of a monstrous energy. Words constantly threaten to take over and play with their victims at their whim.

The first act of *The Garden Party* is a parody of the family drama in a sense similar to the well-known one-act comedies of Ionesco. The stock situation and the cliché language of the soap opera are studiously burlesqued in order to unmask the bizarre nature of the petty bourgeois world which this genre glorifies. Both playwrights' conceptions of the bourgeois seem to be quite similar, based not on political factors, but on moral ones. The petty bourgeois is for them the incarnation of opportunism, mediocrity, and especially of conformity. . . . In Havel's play the spokesman for the bourgeois morality is Pludek-father, who is appalled by the nonconformist appearance of his elder son, Peter, and puts all his hope in his more ordinary yet apathetic younger son, Hugo. Pludek's complacent sense of purpose and propriety is, however, only a thin layer masking his inner void, which betrays itself in his hopelessly futile attempts to verbalize his creed concerning the messianic role of the middle class. (pp. 43-5)

The humorous effect of Pludek's speeches (and basically of all the characters' speeches in the play) is based upon the discrepancy between the form and the content. Pludek's posture is completely self-assured, showing great faith in his ideals, and at superficial reading the statements even give the impression of having been carefully chosen; yet he says precisely nothing. The sentences nullify themselves as they originate. From the dramaturgical viewpoint, the function of the phrases lies precisely in their meaninglessness. The abject way in which people speak is hyperbolized here to such an extreme that its absurdity comes fully to the fore. Circular logic and false syllogisms are constantly present in the dialogue. (p. 45)

The most conspicuous feature of the first act is the nonsense proverbs. Ionesco's use of this device, especially in *La Cantatrice chauve*, was probably the main source for the Czech author, who, however, extends its symbolic significance.

Proverbs are considered the deepest emanation of popular wisdom. Concentrated in their phrasing, vivid in their imagination, and compelling in logic, they are among the most distinguished verbal accomplishments of man. If their use becomes automatic, however, the speaker often ceases to perceive their content and easily distorts them. In *The Garden Party* the distortion of proverbs is symbolic of the downfall of traditional values. (p. 46)

The great originality of Havel's talent finds its full expression especially in the subsequent acts, when the play acquires the character of a political satire. All the features of the avant-garde dramaturgy are retained, but, while continuing to be a general critique of modern mechanized society, the play goes on to expose the absurdities of the socialist system in particular. The second act is an easily recognized allegory on the institutionalization of private life in present-day Czechoslovakia, while the third act lampoons the monstrous bureaucratic machinery of the country. The connection between the first act and the succeeding ones is made not only in the stratum of the action (Hugo's adventures), but in the ideological stratum as well. There are unmistakable parallels between the home of the Pludeks and the outside world. Life guided by the socialist ideal turns out to be as soulless and degenerate as that of the petty bourgeois. It is governed to an even larger degree by opportunism and conformity, with people acting and speaking as senselessly; the only difference actually is in the replacing of one type of verbal gesture by another. The ''conservative'' maxims of Pludek-father are superseded by the mechanical repetition of official statements, slogans, and ideological clichés. (p. 47)

The last act of the play (Hugo's homecoming) contains some of the best examples of absurd dialogue, one being the dispute that develops among the Pludeks over their son's accepting the assignment concerning the liquidation of the Liquidation Office. Most important, however, is Hugo's lengthy tirade, which can be regarded as a clue to the symbolic meaning of the play. In answer to his parents' question as to who he is, Hugo defines his ultimate alienation: . . .

> There is nothing permanent, eternal, absolute in man, he is perpetual change, proudly ringing change, of course! Nowadays, the time of static, unchangeable categories is over; nowadays, A is not just A, and B just B; today we know that A can often be also B, and B at the same time A; that B can be B, as well as A and C; by the same token, C can be not only C, but also A, B, and D, and under certain circumstances, F can be Q or even Y or R!

There can be little doubt that this passage contains a parody of Marxian dialectics, referring to the thesis of permanent change. . . . In a world without absolutes, the thesis of permanent change became a method of proving everything as well as denying everything. The idea which was meant to be a

weapon against the dogmatism of stilted values developed into a convenient tool for the justification of moral nihilism. In Hugo's mouth, dialectics serve as a theoretical justification of his opportunism. He applied the principle to himself so thoroughly that he changed from situation to situation virtually in front of our eyes.

The Garden Party offers wider possibilities for interpreting it as a parody of dialectics. Besides the thesis of permanent change, the work also seems to burlesque an equally important part of Marxian dialectics, the struggle of opposites, derived from the Hegelian triad. The opposite forces (thesis and antithesis) lead to a synthesis which is qualitatively superior to both, not just their mechanical agglomeration. We have a number of syntheses in the work. The competing Liquidation and Inauguration Offices are fused into one big institution. The old bourgeois world of the Pludeks and the new system are synthesized in the very personality of Hugo, who is also a curious fusion of both Plzák and the Director. The syntheses by no means lead to a qualitative improvement, however, but only to magnified absurdity. (pp. 54-6)

[*The Memorandum*] exhibits an easily recognizable affinity with the basic theme of *The Garden Party:* the subjugation of man by language. Language is again the main ''hero,'' but the techniques employed in the work are different. The theme is externalized in a distinct plot, and character development is more psychological. *The Memorandum* is based upon more traditional standards, differing from *The Garden Party* very much in the way Ionesco's early plays differ from his later ones. This does not mean that diction has lost its significance, but it is no longer the sole stratum in which the drama is realized.

The role of Ptydepe [a new language] (and later Chorukor) in the structure of the drama is central. It creates the conflict between characters, influences their fate, and reveals, through their attitude toward it, their true nature. . . . [Ptydepe] has become a fetish to which everything is sacrificed—time, common sense, conscience, and people. Ptydepe symbolizes man's obsession with the idea of a rationally organized world. Language, the most ancient attribute of humanity, is found to be too spontaneous a product to satisfy modern man. (pp. 57-8)

The dehumanization in the play is complete. The intellectual content of man is narrowed to the problem of Ptydepe, and we never even find out what the actual business of the big office is. No other spiritual ambitions seem to be necessary, and once Ptydepe is not discussed, the dialogue turns to the most trivial matters imaginable. People vegetate in a vacuum limited by Ptydepe on the one side, and by physiological needs on the other. Havel uses some specific devices to emphasize the grotesque polarity. Physical details are given unusual prominence in the dialogue as well as in stage directions. The secretary of the Director, for example, is to sit throughout the play at her desk engaging in no other activity than teasing her hair. The only times she shows other initiative is when she asks permission to run errands for milk, rolls, and peanuts. (p. 58)

Lengthy dialogues consist of nothing but the evaluation of meals and drinks just consumed, cigars smoked, etc., in vivid detail. Sounds of drunken parties held in neighboring offices repeatedly reach the stage from behind the scene. Even more naturalistic details concerning man's physical needs are present. The scene involving Gross and Mašát is abruptly interrupted by the latter's departure, and the stage directions stress that Mašát is still zipping up his trousers when he returns so that the purpose of his absence is evident. (pp. 58-9)

The scenes with the greatest force of absurd comedy are those in which Ptydepe is given voice directly. The use of the synthetic language on the stage creates complex problems, since the non-representational linguistic material has to be used in such a way that it acquires dramatic significance. Havel's experimentation with abstract language goes back to the time of his preoccupation with the so-called "evident" and "concrete" poetry of which he is a distinguished practitioner in Czechoslovakia. From the dramatic viewpoint, the use of Ptydepe in the play is a most important device for creating Gross's comical frustration. Starting with the opening scene in which he reads the incomprehensible text, it is constantly a force precluding him from communicating with others. His frustrations are especially strong when he attempts to discuss the idea with its followers, but the dialogue constantly slips from the existing language into Ptydepe. . . . (p. 59)

The Memorandum has, of course, much wider satirical implications concerning contemporary Czechoslovak society. A critique of the monstrous bureaucratic machinery is the most apparent, but not the most important symbolic meaning of the work. Of greater importance is the obvious disdain for the reforms introduced in the post-Stalin era that is clearly implied in the play. Ptydepe has been condemned, its failure recognized, its scapegoats sacrificed, but the system, breeding monstrosities of this kind, remains intact. The play ends as it began, one circle has been closed after which others will follow. There is a deeply pessimistic undertone in the play, despite the fact that it often radiates quite open satisfaction with the plights of the system which it portrays and which seemingly do not meet with the author's approval.

Havel's work represents a rare unity of a satirical, "committed" art with art of wide philosophical implications, at which Ionesco was striving in some of his latest plays, but never achieved to such a degree. From this viewpoint, Havel's plays have a unique position in world dramaturgy and the further course of the young playwright deserves to be watched with the greatest of interest. (pp. 64-5)

> *Paul I. Trensky, "Václav Havel and the Language of the Absurd," in* Slavic and East European Journal *(© 1969 by AATSEEL of the U.S., Inc.), Vol. XIII, No. 1, Spring, 1969, pp. 42-65.*

MARTIN ESSLIN

Havel's cheerfully beaming appearance is deceptive. His plays are very funny, certainly, but there is a core of deep pessimism, even despair in them. They are a mixture of political satire, absurdist images of the human condition, philosophical parables, and zany, black humor. Kafka and Hašek, the twin tutelary spirits of Prague, are equally present in them. (p. 139)

Kafka built up a picture of human anguish in the face of the mysteries of existence that was both dreamlike and concrete, fantastic and real. Kafka's subject matter is the most universal, his imagery the most local; it owes everything to Prague, its atmosphere and history.

Hašek's *Good Soldier Schweik* is also both local and universal. Here too we have the Czech's reaction against the incomprehensible, the blatantly idiotic rule of an alien and stupid militarist caste: Schweik reacts against the stupidity of his oppressors by taking their stupid orders at their face value and stupidly carrying them out to the last detail. He too, like Kafka's anguished and tormented heroes, finds himself in an absurd world, but he strives to end its absurdity by carrying it, *ad*

absurdum, to the point where it must collapse because, at the back of his mind, he has a faint hope that the crash of the absurd order will leave room for a more rational one. (p. 140)

[In] a wildly absurd world [Havel's] characters conform to the apparent logic of absurdity by behaving in a wildly absurd yet logical manner. In *The Garden Party* they surrender to the logical dilemma that a government that asks the Office of Inauguration to abolish the Office of Liquidation cannot really abolish the Office of Liquidation because only the Office of Liquidation can carry out a liquidation, and therefore to carry out the liquidation of the Office of Liquidation you have to keep the Office of Liquidation unliquidated. In *The Memorandum* we find the similar dilemma that the order for the introduction of a new official language, being written in that new official language, cannot be correctly interpreted because it is written in a language that the official charged with implementing the order cannot understand. These are Schweikian situations, but their implications on a deeper level of significance are truly Kafkaesque. It would be wrong to interpret Havel's Schweikian dilemmas as mere satire against the idiocy of a local bureaucracy. The bureaucracy depicted by Havel has profound metaphysical features; it also represents the inner, logical contradictions of existence itself, the dilemma inherent in the use of all language (and Havel's logico-linguistic antinomies have much in common with Wittgenstein's critique of language as a vehicle for logic), the antinomies inherent in all rules of conduct. (p. 141)

> *Martin Esslin, "A Czech Absurdist: Vaclav Havel," in his* Reflections: Essays on Modern Theatre *(copyright © 1961, 1962, 1963, 1966, 1967, 1968, 1969 by Martin Esslin; reprinted by permission of Doubleday & Company, Inc.), Doubleday, 1969, pp. 139-42.*

MARTIN ESSLIN

[*The Garden Party*] displays a mixture of hard-hitting political satire, Schweikian humour and Kafkaesque depths which are highly characteristic of Havel's work. (p. 278)

[*The Memorandum*] delves into the tortuous world of bureaucracy. It shows an organization of uncertain purpose but vast complexity which suddenly finds itself confronted with the fact that someone has introduced a new official language in which all business must henceforth be transacted. (pp. 278-79)

The theory of the new languages discussed in the play is brilliantly worked out (Prague after all is the home of modern structural linguistics and Havel uses the terminology of redundancy and information theory to great effect) and their value as a metaphor of the situation in a country where life and death have in the past depended on the exact interpretation given by the individual to sacred Marxist texts, is clearly immense. The construction of the action is completely symmetrical, each scene on Gross's downward path exactly corresponding to one on his renewed rise to power. Havel is a master of the ironical, inverted repetition, of almost identical phrases in different contexts. And behind the mockery of bureaucratic procedure, behind the Wittgensteinian language game, there is a third level of significance: for Gross is a kind of Everyman enmeshed in an endless and futile struggle for status, power and recognition. (pp. 279-80)

> *Martin Esslin, "Parallels and Proselytes," in his* The Theatre of the Absurd *(copyright © 1961, 1968, 1969 by Martin Esslin; reprinted by permission of*

Doubleday & Company, Inc.), revised edition, Doubleday, 1969, pp. 198-280.*

THE TIMES LITERARY SUPPLEMENT

[The] controlling idea [of *The Increased Difficulty of Concentration*] could be best summed up by such fashionable sociological terms as "alienation", "frustration", "lack of communication", "loss of identity". The trouble is that the author evidently mistrusts such "scientific" interpretations of human behaviour, or at least does not believe that they can be of any help in themselves. He reminds one of a man treating lack of feeling in purely rationalist terms; however analytical his play may seem to be, this approach, too, is exposed as part of the general decay.

Thus the essay on human values which the main character, a social scientist, is dictating throughout the play may impress as quite reasonable and acceptable in its premises: seen against the utter confusion of its author's personal life and his obvious inability to establish any genuine relationship with his wife or his mistress or anyone else for that matter, it becomes a sham. The point is emphasized by the pathetic little machine which a quasi-sociological team brings to the hero's home in order to compute his identity; it fails as miserably as he does.

In such a centre-less, spiritually mechanized life concentration is difficult if not impossible, and all experience equally worthless. This is made plain by Havel's ingenious rearrangement of the chronological sequence, very much like the cutting up and splicing of a recording tape; the play hardly has a beginning or an end; the seams have been made invisible. The dramatic effect is remarkable and the message even clearer.

"Mechanized Minds," in The Times Literary Supplement *(© Times Newspapers Ltd. (London) 1972; reproduced from* The Times Literary Supplement *by permission), No. 3653, March 10, 1972, p. 267.*

JARKA M. BURIAN

[*The Increased Difficulty of Concentration*] is a more humanly oriented work [than *The Memorandum*]. The satire is less sharp for its only object is the absurdity of scientific attempts to analyze man in the name of humanistic goals. Here the central dramatic device is *Puzuk*, a sensitive, childish machine designed to interview people. Whimsically, the machine seems more delicate and temperamental than the humans that use it. The general theme is frustrated humanness in the context of domesticity become routine. The central character is a writer, given to philosophical speculations about human values and needs, who finally stresses the need to have needs.

[The] play's action approaches that of a conventional comedy much more closely than [either *The Memorandum* or *The Garden Party*]. What reveals Havel's signature, however, is its structure. Havel presents the action in cubistic fashion, to convey the fragmented consciousness of man. As scene follows scene, we realize that Havel is juggling with time to parallel scenes with the wife and with the mistress. Although we seem to be progressing normally, we are actually witnessing deliberately repeated scenes with different characters, and jumping back and forth in time. . . . At the end of the play we have once again arrived at the very beginning, with the repetition of the opening lines. (pp. 311-12)

Jarka M. Burian, "Post-War Drama in Czechoslovakia: 'The Increased Difficulty of Concentration',"

in Educational Theatre Journal *(© 1973 University College Theatre Association of the American Theatre Association), Vol. 25, No. 3, October, 1973, pp. 311-12.*

WALTER SCHAMSCHULA

The theater of the absurd, in my view, has two genetic components which determine its life as long as it persists in the way we know it from Beckett and Ionesco. One is its innovative dynamism which opposes it to the theater of the naturalist tradition. The other component is its indebtedness to the philosophy of existentialism which itself is based upon the collective experience of World Wars I and II. Hence, there is a component inherent to the dynamism of the drama itself, and a component imported from outside literature into the world of art.

As to the first, there is evidence in Ionesco's theoretical writings that the drive for innovation is one of the major forces in the genesis of the theater of the absurd. Our century has eradicated taboos and traditional concepts in the arts more thoroughly than have previous millennia. . . . [Drama] has done away with motivated action, the element without which playing theater earlier would have appeared senseless. The motivation (be it psychological, ethical or sociological) has been destroyed either entirely or in part, so that the remaining fragments of a "meaningful" action have lost their logic. Ionesco and Beckett criticism have used the terms "non-action" or "anti-action," that is to say that the audience is no more involved in the *déroulement* of changing human interrelations, but that it is now increasingly fascinated by the way the familiar item called action is being torn apart. The process of destruction is now being focused upon. The defamiliarizing device has become fully autonomous, whereas in the traditional theater the device had merely a subsidiary function.

Let us now return to the just mentioned way of destroying the action. Both types, the total destruction and the partial one, are represented in Havel's plays. In some of the plays the annihilation of anything that seemed vital to the theater is brought to perfection, and the very identity of the acting persons is at stake, e.g. in *The Mountain Hotel*. But he also offers examples of a partial destruction of the motivation with the result that the remaining fragments of an action have turned into nonsense. Such a partial abolition of logic may be found in *The Increased Difficulty of Concentration*. . . . (pp. 338-39)

Let me . . . briefly discuss the other component of the theater of the absurd: the impact of existentialist thought (it may be too pretentious to speak of existentialist philosophy). The symbolism of human abandonment in a hostile world, man's being unsheltered ("unbehaust") and left prey to the malice of this world, enters, in some plays of the French theater of the absurd, into the idea of some prison or cage, or of a trash can in which the acting persons find themselves trapped and from which there is no escape. The existentialist background of this type of theater has turned all attention to questions of existence, such as physical survival, identity, physical desires, freedom versus captivity, etc. The moral issue has lost its significance where the individual is exposed to a system of madness which is beyond human control. (p. 339)

Since the world is conceived of as a huge madhouse, a system of defunctionalized interrelations, it is obvious that the easiest access which satire could find in this type of drama is in an area where not single phenomena but entire social systems or systems of communication are satirized. In Havel's work, the mentioned destruction of motivation of action undoubtedly also reflects a perversion of the social order. But this does not fully answer the question, which of the two components is more essential to his drama: the existentialist experience of the individual or the satiric defamiliarization of social structures with at least a glimmer of hope that some of these structures could be repaired.

Let us now analyze Havel's major techniques in order to provide a broader basis for answering the central question. While discussing *The Garden Party,* [critic Miroslav] Kačer introduced the notion ''absurdní ozvláštnění'' (the absurd defamiliarization) which seems workable. Taking this notion as point of departure, I will now discuss the most prominent types of ''absurd defamiliarization'' in Havel's work. As far as *The Garden Party* is concerned, some of them have already been described by Kačer. The list, however, has to be completed in view of the more recent plays.

One of [the devices that Havel uses to gain an absurd defamiliarization] is called the GAG by Havel himself. The gag, in his definition, is a sequence of two phases which, taken by themselves, do not cause any particular effect. Only in their close succession do they become efficient as a comical device. The gag has the most immediate effect, being the most concise form of defamiliarization and resembling the joke as described by Freud. ''The inauguration of a monument to prosperity is not a gag. A sleeping Chaplin is not a gag. When, however, the monument to prosperity is inaugurated and, while the cloth falls, it becomes apparent that the beggar Chaplin sleeps in the arms of the statue, then this is a gag.''

There are, according to Kačer, several type of gags in *The Garden Party* such as the VERBAL GAG with a great variety of possibilities. There is e.g., the word game which adds a grotesque element to the language as a communication system that has lost all meaning. . . . (p. 340)

Another type of gag is the sudden, seemingly unmotivated transition from one language to the other, a burlesque element widely utilized in a different context, in the medieval macaronic poetry of the vagrants. In *The Garden Party,* the alternating language is sometimes Slovak. This reflects a certain everyday experience in contemporary Czechoslovakia, where Slovak has been increasingly upgraded since the end of the war. In radio and TV, Czech and Slovak broadcasts alternate without being translated. The way this bilingualism is introduced in *The Garden Party,* however, is a particular effect which cannot be translated into any foreign language. . . .

[In addition to gags, two] more structural elements should be mentioned. One of them has been identified by Kačer as a parody of the proverb. It could also be called a PSEUDO-PROVERB. The other one is a PARODY OF THE RHETORICAL STYLE of official propaganda machineries. . . . (p. 341)

The essence of Havel's pseudoproverbs is that while their structure promises profound wisdom, the promise, however, remains unfulfilled. (p. 342)

Besides the verbal gag, the author also works with MIMETIC DEVICES. Wordless action, a traditional element of the burlesque, farcical theater, with a climax in the silent film and contemporary pantomime, has also been utilized in the theater of the absurd. . . . In Havel's plays, pantomimic action is sometimes the continuation of the spoken theatrical dialogue. In Act III of *The Garden Party,* the secretary performs her act of liquidation first by registering, then by putting the registered

documents into the wastepaper basket, thereafter by undressing the director and throwing his articles into the basket until he remains in his underwear. In *The Audience,* drinking beer is an important means of characterizing the two *dramatis personae.* The brewer drinks beer at short intervals and urges the writer Vaněk to join him who, as an intellectual, does not like beer and only sips at the glass. Repeatedly—this is one of the recurrent elements—the brewer goes to the men's room and returns, buttoning his fly. At the time of his absence, Vaněk pours the contents of his glass into the glass of the brewer. Mimetic action has thus become a substantial part of the play and underlies the principles of defamiliarization.

The devices listed above are also procedures of the traditional burlesque theater and not necessarily an innovation of the theater of the absurd or of Václav Havel. What is new about them is that they are employed within the context of the absurd, adding to the overall idea of a world absorbed in senselessness. This context, however, is created by components of greater capacity than the listed burlesque devices: by the arrangements of larger units of the dialogue and the abolition of a semantic continuum. In this respect Havel appears to be very innovative and original.

Perhaps the most unmistakable trademark of the theater of the absurd is the abolition of those components that seemed to be essential to the theater: identity of characters, integrity and dramatism of action, and everything that comes with it.

Perhaps the most complex topic for an analyst of Havel's plays will be the question of identity of characters. There is no guarantee in his dramatic work that a person stays what he is throughout the entire play. Roles are interchangeable. A dialogue may be reversed in the sense that what had been said by person A and answered by person B is later said by person B and answered by person A. This already occurs in *The Garden Party* and becomes one of the prominent techniques in *The Mountain Hotel.* (pp. 342-43)

[In *The Mountain Hotel*] which contains the most consistent use of this technique, a stereotyped set of absurd actions is passed on from one person to the other. It is, however, quite sizable in two other pieces also, *The Beggar's Opera* and *The Conspirators,* plays with a relatively traditional structure of action. (p. 343)

Havel [also] likes to make use of a CYCLICAL STRUCTURE of his theatrical pieces. In some of his plays, furthermore, a decisive breakthrough or solution is avoided by a reentry into the action from the very beginning. This is the case in *The Memorandum, The Conspirators, The Audience* and *The Varnishing Day* [*Vernissage*] where the end marks a new start from the very beginning, which produces an impression of relativity and futility. Everything appears useless like the actions of Sisyphus who never reaches the top of the hill with his rock. The cyclical order of many of Havel's plays, of course, speaks much in favor of a more profound involvement of the philosophy of existentialism in his work.

There are, on the other hand, instances when Havel's plays result in a genuinely dramatic outcome, like in *The Guardian Angel,* where Machoň succeeds in cutting Vavák's ears. This type of a climaxing end of a drama is the alternative offered by some pieces of the theater of the absurd: a cruelty which is neither psychologically nor logically motivated and appears as senseless as the cyclical replay of the action. It therefore misses . . . the effect of the classical tragedy: identification of the audience with the heroes and shared grief. (p. 344)

In connection with the recurrence of elements of the dialogue, we should also mention a particular effect which has been recognized and named by Jiří Voskovec in his preface to the 1977 edition of Havel's plays. He calls this device havlovská spirála, the HAVEL SPIRAL. . . . The best example of a Havel spiral may be found in *The Increased Difficulty of Concentration:* certain recurrent replicas tend to be repeated more often and at an increased pace until all of them, like an avalanche, burst upon the scene. Nonsense turns into madness, the nightmare has become a menacing reality, and the listener as the addressee of the performance has joined the author in this existential tarantella.

Let us now raise the question whether Havel has shown a development in the sense that, as a result of changes in the political situation in his country and in his personal life, some of his positions have been abandoned or modified. This is a legitimate question since the author himself has declared that the year 1968 marks a turning point in his career as a writer. After that year he found himself deprived of the possibility of being staged or printed in Czechoslovakia. Performances abroad could not be of any help since Havel was used to writing for a very specific public, the audience of the Theater at the Balustrade. So he had to rethink and reconsider his way of writing plays, and he underwent a crisis of creativity. . . . (pp. 344-45)

Havel tried to overcome the crisis by experimenting and searching for new means of expression. The question is, however, whether there is a fundamental shift from one position to another, from the critical period of his early plays to a more or less didactic or satiric drama. The first effect of the political changes was the creation of *The Conspirators,* where he translates the history of the communist road to power in Czechoslovakia into a permanent non-action. The form is cyclical, there is a constant exchange of characters and roles, complete promiscuity of sexes (which is one of the expressions of the loss of action). At the end, the revolution stands where it stood at the beginning. (p. 345)

[*The Mountain Hotel*] is the piece where the experiment has become the subject, where the exchange of characters and roles is made a system. . . . The mountain hotel, where the play is located, is one of the "windowless cages," Thomas Mann's Magic Mountain turned into a madhouse with no escape.

After *The Mountain Hotel,* the two one-act plays *The Audience* and *The Varnishing Day,* the most successful pieces of the second period of Havel's creativity, show a return to a reproduction of real circumstances, and this reproduction is more realistic than anything in Havel's work. There is no "exorcism of history" as in *The Mountain Hotel,* but the historical—for the most part autobiographical—details do not create a system of logical motivations of action. The cyclical structure of the plays prevents them from becoming semantically valid in an unequivocal way. On the surface, these plays are satires of certain aspects of contemporary Czech society. Underneath, however, the secret police in *The Audience* and the conformist couple in *The Varnishing Day* are becoming symbols of the uncontrollable menace of absurdity.

In terms of the employment of certain techniques and procedures, the second part of Havel's creative career shows more of an evolution than the first. He is indeed experimenting; his experiments, however, do not aim in one specific direction. But still, there is a common denominator: Havel has concentrated his devices, limited himself to a handful of tricks. While *The Garden Party* was a firework of gags and punch-lines, the reduction of devices in the later period has created a more somber and depressing atmosphere. *The Mountain Hotel* is no exception from this rule: there is an expression of anguish in the piece, of erosion of human values, a destructive force which is translucent through the entire mechanism of the experimental theater. It is not by accident that the most threatening image of anxiety, the Havel spiral occurs in the last three pieces.

As to the intensity of disintegrating action, the plays of the second period show a variety of possibilities. *The Mountain Hotel* offers a maximum, the two one-act plays a minimum, of destructive techniques. Yet the destructive elements are there and forceful enough to short-circuit the fragments of an action which reflect the social reality around the author.

Since Havel's entire work shows consistency in its subordination under the principles of the theater of the absurd, the question remains to be answered whether this theater employs the model of the absurd in order to satirize the society in which the author lives or whether the defamiliarization of concrete circumstances of that social life serves to unveil something more profound and essential: the helplessness of a thinking individual in face of a mechanism of power which is universal. By formulating this question, I suppose I have already answered it: Havel's plays increasingly reflect a universal nightmare. An unfulfilled dream has turned into an evil one. (pp. 345-46)

Walter Schamschula, "Václav Havel: Between the Theatre of the Absurd and Engaged Theatre" (originally a paper presented at the University of California between March 30 and April 2, 1978; copyright © 1980 by Walter Schamschula; reprinted by permission of the author), in Fiction and Drama in Eastern and Southeastern Europe: Evolution and Experiment in the Postwar Period, *edited by Henrik Birnbaum and Thomas Eekman, Slavica Publishers, Inc., 1980, pp. 337-48.*

MARKETA GOETZ-STANKIEWICZ

In approaching Havel's brilliant and startling plays it might be useful to become aware of how the main theme of his work, which had been formulated as 'the relationship between man and the system' in 1968, expanded and deepened to what the author himself calls the 'existential dimension of the world.' Perhaps the development Havel has undergone in his relatively brief career as a dramatist can be followed best by starting with a simple proposition: that social systems make their—more or less pronounced—demands to organize individual man into a system, in order to achieve certain—more or less laudable—aims which in turn are to serve the interests of man. Already we see a suggestion of a vicious circle in the argument: man is an organism, the system functions as a mechanism; one must subdue the other or be subdued. Around these tensions Václav Havel builds his unique, grimly comic theatre. (p. 45)

Havel's theatre explores language as the primary agent in man's absurd situation. The real hero of his plays is the mechanistic phrase, uttered from habit, repeated with parrot-like readiness, which decides people's actions, composes events, and creates its own absurd reality. . . . [His theatre is made up of] an exploration of the tremendous power of the word or phrase which becomes the unquestioned property of all, prevents anyone from thinking, and is the prime enemy of common sense and reason. (p. 46)

Regarded on the surface the absurd has no place at all in Havel's work. But then, in the fashion of some Surrealist painters, he injects into this perfectly sane situation one absurd element which inverts the whole meaning and stands it on its head. . . . [Human reasoning is] proved irrational. However, with Havel the point at which the 'reversal into absurdity' takes place is identifiable: it is the moment when the project in a man's mind—an idea, let us say—can create a mechanism which, once it begins to function, adapts everything to its function and makes it part of the mechanism. The theme of mechanization in Havel's plays is the search for that concealed point at which reasoning becomes absurd. The same theme in the Western branch of absurd theatre revolves around the claim that this point can never be found. (p. 48)

A Czech critic said of Havel that when watching his plays one has the impression of listening to conversations between two rather primitive cybernetic machines which have at their disposal only a very limited range of answers to a very limited range of questions. In Havel's first full-length play, *The Garden Party,* we are even made the witnesses of the schooling process of such a machine, a young man named Hugo Pludek. In the course of the action he rises from being a monosyllabic, chess-playing son of an obscure middle-class family to the honourable position of heading a newly established ministerial commission which is to solve the political impasse in society (we never find out which society nor which political system—and it does not matter in the least). On closer inspection it appears that the impasse is a strange one indeed: the difficulty turns out to be a linguistic one; it is language that has created an acute political problem. How does Havel go about putting such intangible and undramatic material on the stage? He builds his play quite logically around one point of language and leads his audience on an extremely comic four-act exploration of the power of language itself. At one moment words seem to provide the only logical element on stage, at the next moment they create complete confusion. The audience, unable to stop laughing, is taken through bounds and leaps of reasoning, across swamps of phraseology, as it watches sense turn into nonsense and nonsense into sense. (pp. 50-1)

[In *The Garden Party,* Havel's main concern is] the power of language as a perpetuator of systems, a tool to influence man's mind and therefore one of the strongest (though secret) weapons of any system that wants to mould him to become a well-functioning part of a system rather than a free spirit—unpredictable, erring, imaginative, mysterious in his tireless search for the truth.

The Memorandum, although again highly amusing, is an even more relentless exploration of language as a tool of power. The subject is grimmer than that of *The Garden Party,* not only because the hero's absorption into the system is represented not as a career but as a matter of survival, but also because Havel has by now mastered the art of placing the action against a background of 'real' life in an office hardly distinguishable, as a Czech critic says, 'from the office where we were yesterday.' The setting is deceptively naturalistic and only some time after the opening of the curtain does the audience begin to adjust to the fact that only the surface looks normal, everything else is absurd! Or does this realization itself make it realistic in the deeper sense of the word? It seems that this secret tie—almost complicity—between the absurd and real emerges in the works of many of the best modern writers. (p. 53)

By the half-way mark of the play the hero's fortunes have reached their lowest point. In the second half we are shown his gradual recovery and renewed rise to the position of di-

rector. Just as his downfall had been paralleled by the relentless rise of Ptydepe, his ascent now takes place against the background of Ptydepe's dwindling fortunes. (p. 55)

[Near the end of the play], Gross is given the opportunity he had yearned for when his fortunes were low: to be able to start all over again and do things differently. But in the last moment Havel crushes our hopes. The symmetry of the play suddenly reveals itself not as reflecting the rise of goodness and fall of evil, as it had seemed to, but rather as a constant, rigidly mechanized process. The theme of mechanical adjustment which was treated with bright exuberance in *The Garden Party* is struck here on a more sinister level. Against his better convictions and allegedly humanistic ideals, Gross succumbs in turn to the absurd order of the Ptydepe movement, to the empty slogans, promises, and flattery of the opportunists, and finally to the new but equally absurd order of a new synthetic language, Chorukor, introduced at the end of the play. . . .

In his next play, *The Increased Difficulty of Concentration,* Havel again manages to amuse us while he unfolds before our eyes one of the grave problems of our century. (p. 56)

Again, as in Havel's earlier plays, language reveals its mechanizing power with frightening obviousness. Each thought and each emotion that is expressed is dictated by stereotyped language. The hollow ring of duplicated words pervades the whole play.

It is in this play that Havel has mastered the task of revealing language as a killer of intellect and feeling. Man is no longer the victim of the system as shown implicitly in *The Garden Party* and explicitly in *The Memorandum.* Rather man perpetuates the system by modelling his own life on it, and he depends on it as his stronghold. At first he fails to recognize that it is also his prison and tries to escape from this anonymous monster that schematizes his daily life and mechanizes his emotions. But the way he goes about escaping shows that the harm has been done: Huml wants to escape not by breaking but by doubling the system, and he thus creates a new mechanism which, far from destroying the old one, neatly fits into the spinning cogs. By necessity Huml himself becomes doubly mechanical and begins to repeat his own responses with machine-like exactitude. The events on stage appear as in a broken and endlessly repeated mirror-reflection and as the play proceeds, we feel an increasing certainty about being able to predict with machine-like precision the actions and reactions of the individual characters. (p. 59)

Havel has achieved a surprising tour de force. By making the audience adopt an almost automatic reaction to the characters on stage, he has shown that the tendency to mechanize the process of living resides secretly within the individual character and is therefore both more intangible and more dangerous than we take it to be.

If *The Increased Difficulty of Concentration* explores man's notorious tendency to mechanize his life and thus reduce it to the primitive level of adapting to and functioning in a certain environment, Havel's next play, *The Conspirators,* is a test of what happens when this idea is applied to a political situation. *The Conspirators* . . . is a merry-go-round of political power. The play is constructed with mathematical precision. In fifteen scenes which follow one another like hammer blows, the struggle for political power unfolds with the inevitability of a mechanism set in motion. What sets it in motion is man's greed for power which, when rigidified and mechanized by a social system, becomes a sine qua non of his life. He tries to attain it by any means and his claims about high ideals—the common good, the nation's welfare, freedom from oppression—are merely coverups for his ruthless struggle to get where he wants to be. All in all this is not a highly original theme: from *Macbeth* to Büchner's *Danton's Death* and Brecht's *The Rise of Arturo Ui* man's craving for political power has proved to be among playwrights' main sources of inspiration.

However, Havel's signature on the play is unmistakable. Reduced to the bare essentials, the struggle for power of four 'public figures' (the chief prosecutor and the heads of the police, the military, and culture) is stylized into a grotesque circular dance of greed and deceit in which moves are as predictable as the periodical return of, say, the fiery white horse or the leaping lion on a moving merry-go-round. The central mechanism (provided in this case by the system) has taken over and the characters seized by its rhythm not only succumb to it but, as it were, propel its motion into greater smoothness by their own weight (the make-up of their characters—in turn formed by the system).

By saying that *The Conspirators* is about the struggle for power, we have indicated the inner meaning of the play. On the surface—as far as the characters themselves are concerned—it is a play about revolution. Again, as in Havel's other plays, it is revolution studied in a test tube. Not for one instant does the action even remotely approach a concrete problem. It remains suspended in the thin air of theoretical abstractions, and in the lengthy discussions 'freedom' and 'political oppression,' 'democracy' and the 'evils of anarchy,' 'unifying action' and 'reactionary groups' remain linguistic labels which have never been exposed to a real situation. The revolution never gets beyond the language lab. Havel's pen is getting sharper, his wit is getting more sinister. The mood of *The Conspirators* is dark indeed. (pp. 59-60)

[*The Mountain Resort*] is a logical outcome of the author's earlier work. Throughout his earlier plays Havel had explored the impact of mechanization on thought and behaviour. In *The Mountain Resort* he takes this approach to its 'absurd' conclusion by allowing it to take over the entire action. It is as if he had fed a number of attitudes, actions, gestures, and dialogues into a computer and let the computer rearrange them until they represent an organized, geometrical structure. The result is a seemingly well-constructed five-act play, in which, however, phrases, movements, and gestures have become autonomous, and the characters entirely inter-changeable.

The action takes place on the terrace of a mountain resort; the characters are a group of holiday-makers. . . . [They] speak each other's words, remember each other's pasts, go through each other's movements. To put it in another way, the gesture or word is there, but the character who carries it out or speaks it changes from act to act; the memory of Paris is there but in each act someone else remembers and someone else forgets. Havel tried to make these occurrences the subject matter of the play, in order to find out 'to what extent they are capable—all on their own—to create meaning.' The themes of the disintegration of human identity and existential schizophrenia which Havel has repeatedly called his main concerns, are obviously apparent again insofar as they can be expressed solely by these 'automatized occurrences.' (pp. 68-9)

Havel has revealed to us this realization: the closer his writing reflects a situation he knows personally, the better he writes and the broader his appeal will be. *Vernissage* is a parable on the hollowness of a successful life. All the clichés of 'Happiness' which have moulded the imagination of the average man from Prague to New York, from Sydney to Stockholm,

are juggled throughout the play, and produce a terrible, hollow sound. It is a happiness which depends on an audience, for it is meaningless in itself; with an audience it loses its reason for being. It is remarkable that this play emerged from a 'Socialist' society and was written by an author who felt he 'had to lean on what [he] knew.' As a comment on contemporary Czechoslovakia it is certainly a fascinating document about a society, the official, constantly reiterated ideals, aims, and evaluations of which bear no relation whatsoever to the values of an individual who thrives under this regime. However, from a Western point of view *Vernissage* can plainly also be regarded as a critical comment on the materialistic values of an affluent society. Although Havel, with typical modesty, calls his two one-act plays [*Vernissage* and *Audience*] 'miniatures, written on the side,' both succeed in communicating strong meaning on an international scale.

Havel's most recent one-act play, *Protest,* draws even more openly on the author's basic experience as a 'dissident' writer. . . . In *Protest* Havel takes the bull by the horns and writes about the most acute problem not only of Czech writers and intellectuals but also of creative men anywhere in the world where freedom of expression has been harnessed by a stultifying ideology. *Protest* is a brilliant dialogue during an encounter between two writers. There is Staněk who has managed to swim with political currents, who is on good terms with the authorities, and whose works are still produced on television and in film studios. (p. 71)

The other writer, Vaněk (a partly autobiographical figure who also appears in *Audience*), is a playwright whose works used to be staged successfully in Czech theatres but who, after a drastic change in the political climate, has become ostracized and persecuted by the regime, writing for underground circulation only, and spending most of his time and energy in composing petitions and letters of protest which find their way into the press abroad but which have little effect on circumstances in his own country.

The play consists of a visit Vaněk pays to Staněk, whose success with things in general is reflected in the superbly blossoming magnolia tree outside his window, his recently acquired villa, and the surrealist painting in his elegant study. In the course of the conversation between the two—Vaněk shy, clutching a briefacse, in stocking feet; Staněk effusive, pouring cognacs, offering cigars and his own slippers—we discover that after years of non-communication Staněk had asked Vaněk to visit him. . . . Finally, as his motivations become increasingly puzzling, he steers the conversation to its inevitable aim: he would like to ask Vaněk to initiate 'some kind of protest or petition' on behalf of composer-singer Javůrek who has recently been imprisoned.

However, as Vaněk (and the audience) are trying to cope with this extraordinary request, it becomes clear that Staněk's motivation is not indignation about the persecution of innocent people but that he has a personal axe to grind—his daughter is expecting a child by Javůrek. For once Vaněk responds with assurance and efficiency. Rummaging in his brief-case he produces a petition of the kind Staněk had had in mind. (pp. 71-2)

[When Vaněk] ventures the hesitant question whether he, Staněk, would not like to add his signature to the petition, the benevolent host embarks slowly but with increasing rhetorical power on an argument which proves, with irresistible logic, that he would do great harm to the cause of the dissidents if he did sign the document and that, due to his solidarity with those who tried to preserve the moral fibre of the nation, he would have to abstain from what he basically would like to do. (pp. 72-3)

In addition to its weighty political meaning *Protest* is an incontestable proof of Havel having grasped a basic ailment of our age. Psychology, ideology, and scientific objectivity have taught modern man to rationalize his moves. His knowledge of set patterns of behavior make him act consciously in relation to such patterns. This can be inocuous or sinister. It can spell mediocrity or evil. In his three one-act plays Václav Havel expresses what he is striving to portray, namely 'the existential dimension of the world.'

In a way all Havel's writings are a critique of the reassuring first line of the Gospel according to St John: 'In the beginning was the Word.' That does not mean that he has created characters who indulge in the language of silence (like some of the characters of Beckett or Peter Handke). On the contrary, language is 'the primary moving force' in Havel's plays and his characters talk a lot, too much in fact. But the more they talk, the less they say. Their conversations read like parodies of elementary phrase-books with sections like 'How to converse about world affairs with a sixty-word vocabulary'. . . . It would take a volume in itself to define and order the great and resourceful variety of stock phrases in Havel's plays. . . . [They] consist of words which no longer express reality but obscure it. Isolated from the real world, they create a solipsistic universe of abstractions which obliterates both rational thought and common sense. (p. 73)

Our primitive ancestors believed that once a force was named, its power-spell was broken. Contemporary man, by constantly repeating the great cliché nightmares of his age, somehow believes he is dealing with them. Modern psychology has frequently used this ancient insight: formulating your fears and doubts will help you to overcome them. Havel shows us again and again that this act of the recognition of a problem can be useless if it takes place in language only. (pp. 74-5)

In this instance the meaning of Havel's works for our Western society becomes particularly obvious. Although certain forms of standardization and mechanical conformism have for some time been the targets of attacks by some of those believing in 'individualism,' another form of standardization has developed among them. The 'non conformists' have formed another standardized group, whose reactions and type of language (not to mention clothes or haircuts) have become as predictable as those of the 'conformists.' Havel's comment on this kind of phenomenon has not been matched by a Western playwright.

Another target of Havel's is folksy wisdom mechanized by habitual thoughtless usage. In *The Garden Party* the hero's father, Pludek senior, reacts to most things with comments that have the ring of proverbs but are sheer nonsense. The form is empty, the content has gone: leather-bound volumes of Shakespeare and Milton contain whisky bottles, the opening line of an ancient song is used to sell shaving lotion. (p. 75)

The patterns of repetition in Havel's plays seem at first arbitrary, even chaotic, but on closer inspection one discovers highly structured, almost geometric forms. Scenes are re-enacted with reversed characters; identical situations have opposite meanings because the context is different. Like a hall of mirrors Havel's work reflects itself. (p. 76)

[In *The Increased Difficulty of Concentration*] Havel explores the most disturbing aspect of the destruction of man by language. When Renata wants to know whether he is still in love with his wife, we hear the voice of Huml (who is busy hanging up her coat back-stage) 'You know very well I stopped loving her long ago! I just like her as a friend, a housewife, a companion of my life—.' In this brief scene Havel shows us how the cliché can be used to prove or disprove anything. A clichéd image of 'love' has taken over the form of the word like a parasite and pushed out its real content. Here this process of forcing out the true meaning of a word is demonstrated before our very eyes. The word we are left with becomes an empty shell.

Toward the end of most of Havel's plays the protagonist gives a lengthy speech in which he summarizes his outlook on man, society, and life in general. The speeches are highly amusing conglomerations of logical fallacies, pseudo-dialectics, and false analogies. With his acute sense for the mechanizing power of the word, Havel explores man as the victim of the language he has created. He does so by exploring the area where the system and the individual meet, where standardization penetrates into every fold of life. It has been pointed out repeatedly that this is obviously the work of a man who has grasped the enormous effect of a centralized political system on the life of the average man.

But it would do injustice to Havel's dramatic genius if his work were to be interpreted merely from a political point of view. The playwright himself has told us that 'the theatre shows the truth about politics not because it has a political aim. The theatre can depict politics precisely because it has no political aim. For this reason it seems to me that all ideas of the so-called ''political theatre'' are mistaken . . .' By trying to give expression to the tensions between the individual and the social system in his own society—and there is no question as to who remains the victor there—Havel has also made one of the most intelligent artistic comments on man in modern mass society in general—applicable in New York as well as Prague, Stockholm, Rome, or Warsaw.

He does this by taking to task the nature of language itself, particularly the catch-phrase or slogan whose power, well known to dictators of all kinds, is mostly misjudged by well-meaning defenders of the humanistic values of a free society. It is here that Havel's main contribution to the Theatre of the Absurd is to be found. (pp. 78-9)

Havel has forced us into literal logic. Beginning with a sort of Kantian proposition that man cannot perceive or express truth in its entirety, he then reverses the argument by reducing the possibilities of expression to *one* word. He therefore implies that, under certain circumstances, one word *could* express a complex phenomenon. In other words, . . . one single word can wield great intellectual weight—which is, of course, a fallacy, but is also an astute observation of the power of slogans which carry a built-in, incontrovertible evaluation. This is explosive material in quite different types of modern society where slogans—whether they be 'enemies of the people' or 'women's liberation'—with their absolute evaluations are part and parcel of the daily life of the average citizen. (p. 79)

Havel's most recent play *Protest* takes his exploration of language as a vehicle for a certain mode of thought still another significant step further. In a long speech, Staněk, faced with the request to sign a petition on human rights, explains to Vaněk (who has handed him the petition) that, if he wants to act 'truly ethically,' he must abstain from signing the document. The arguments which lead to this conclusion seem to me to contain the most brilliant tour de force of logic which Havel has written to this point. (p. 84)

Staněk in *Protest,* assessing the consequences of certain political moves in a totalitarian country which tries to cope with a small number of people who try to show that they do not agree with the regime, does so with the foresight of a brilliant chess player. (p. 85)

Staněk's weighing of pros and cons corresponds to reality but only to a reality within the patterns of thought which permeate a society which has been forced to think in these patterns. Staněk has applied the reasoning process of a closed system of thought to a simple ethical question: Should I lend my voice to try to help an innocent man who is in trouble? The whole intricate net of reasoning which he unfurls before our eyes is the type of reasoning he has been taught by the system he lives in. It is pseudo-reasoning, and totally false in absolute terms. It is, in a nut-shell, perhaps the best portrayal of perverted 'rational' thinking that has ever been put on stage in modern theatre. As such, Staněk's arguments are also more important than might appear at first sight for a Western democratic society where moral norms are questioned and relativistic points of view have often become ethical guide-posts. A Polish cartoon sums up the issue in a humourous way: Two men are having a discussion. One has just finished his argument. The other scratches his head thoughtfully: 'Clearly you are right . . . But . . . from which point of view?'

There is no question that Havel's plays deal with the burning issues in his own society. However, they not only turn out to contain surprisingly apt comments on another society that wrestles with different kinds of problems, but they also reveal themselves in their timeless aspects—wisdom expressed in terms of excellent theatre. Havel himself seems to know how these things work: 'Drama's success in transcending the limits of its age and country depends entirely on how far it succeeds in finding a way to its own place and time . . . If Shakespeare is played all over the world in the twentieth century it is not because in the seventeenth century he wrote plays for the twentieth century and for the whole world but because he wrote plays for seventeeth-century England as best he could. Without wanting to compare Havel with Shakespeare we can nevertheless see that the principle is the same. Havel writes for Czechoslovakia as best he can, *therefore* (as he would say) his work carries so strong a message outside its borders. (pp. 86-7)

> *Marketa Goetz-Stankiewicz, "Václav Havel," in her* The Silenced Theatre: Czech Playwrights without a Stage *(© University of Toronto Press 1979), University of Toronto Press, 1979, pp. 43-88.*

MARKETA GOETZ-STANKIEWICZ

[Under their present regime, the Czechs are] faced daily with an official language. . . . With the "official" language there goes an "official" consciousness which is outside the daily life of an average person. The process of constant pigeonholing of everything as either good or bad, the unshakable value judgments which go with these words (examples like "enemy of the people," "subversive bourgeois revisionists" or "lackeys of Imperialism" will suffice) have created a chasm between everyday language and the official language; and this has resulted in a sort of linguistic schizophrenia of every person who has some sort of official post. In this connection one is bound to remember Orwell's concept of "Newspeak," which was intended to subjugate the mind by linguistic means.

Havel has brought this phenomenon to the stage for the first time and in an inimitable way. The three plays [*The Garden Party, The Memorandum,* and *The Mountain Hotel*] . . . are examples of this. The first play is about a young man, Hugo Pludek, who acquires a new consciousness through learning the official language. . . . This learning process makes for entertaining theatre: the audience watches Hugo's rise to power as he begins to declaim snappy proverbs which are rhythmically perfect but make no logical sense, as his self-assurance grows when he spoons out arguments in circular logic, as he achieves agility in balancing false syllogisms and prefabricated phrases like a sword-juggler. Thought is no longer needed—and indeed, in true "Newspeak" style, to be avoided—if the acrobatics of linguistic devices hold the floor. (p. 390)

[At the end of the play] Hugo has become a talking machine, a robot, repeating language which has become independent of its user. He has become a well-functioning particle in a system.

Havel's next and possibly best-known play, *The Memorandum* . . . , takes up the same theme; but by now language (or "Newspeak") has become, as it were, the central character, and the human figures around it seem to exist only in relationship to that center, which is both the most explicit as well as the most alienating aspect of the play, because the author has performed the dramatic feat of having literally created a new synthetic language. Despite the humor of the play, however, the tone is a shade grimmer than that of *The Garden Party.* The learning of a new language is no longer seen as a tool for a career but has become a necessity for survival. The setting is a huge bureaucratic establishment. . . . Everything is predictable; any particle of the set pattern of events (be it another figure or another synthetic language) could easily be substituted.

The Mountain Hotel . . . takes this notion to its dramatic as well as philosophical conclusion. . . . The mechanizing of communication has become the very subject of the play. A number of phrases pertaining to food, joy, the weather, memory, sex, hope, disappointment, et cetera have been distributed regularly throughout the play, as if a computer had ordered input data in a certain way. Then certain characters are attached to the phrases and made to speak them at various times. Of course, since the regular reappearance of the phrases is the first concern of the play, the characters are secondary and are shuffled around so that each of them gets to say a certain phrase at a certain time. The result is a perfectly constructed "well-made play," except that its form is inverted. Phrases and movements have become autonomous, and the characters have become interchangeable. The play is perhaps the only literary work setting up one consistent portrayal of what we call modern man's disintegration of personality.

Another aspect of Havel's work in which he touches an essential fiber of contemporary consciousness is his startling treatment of a theme which has become the trusty war-horse of academic research projects—the dynamics of man's life in groups, namely the "tension between the individual and society." (pp. 390-91)

[*The Conspirators* is a stark] version of the self-propelled circuit of social endeavor. The play could be called a computerized study of revolution. In their systematic struggle for power the four main figures, representatives of public guidance and safety (the Heads of the Police, the Military, the Law and Culture), are choreographed through a series of steps of a dance of power, nourished by greed and triggered by deceit, the movements of which become entirely foreseeable by the second act and inevitably lead back to the initial constellation. (p. 391)

[Havel's three short plays, *Audience, Vernissage,* and *Protest*] have one remarkable feature in common. They are all built around one and the same character: a semi-autobiographical figure, a quiet, thoughtful, shy man named Vaněk who is faced with different situations to which he responds in his own particular way; his figure takes on a reality which goes far beyond the time and place of the actual stage play. If the character itself is semi-autobiographical, the situations he gets into are entirely realistic in that they deal with various facets of what the West has come to call a "dissident" writer under a totalitarian regime. (pp. 391-92)

[In *Protest* Havel] takes up the complex, burning issue of freedom of speech and molds it into a remarkable one-act play with two characters and a briefcase, some brandy glasses, a pair of slippers and a magnolia tree as the only props. The content of the play revolves around the signing of a petition which lands in the furnace at the end of the play. Vaněk comes with the document in his briefcase to another writer who is getting along well and whose plays are performed all over the country because he is accommodating to the rules of the regime and writes only what is "allowed." The intellectual and dramatic highlight lies in the final speech with which the successful writer explains to Vaněk why—in the interests of the common good and "relentless objective reflection" on the issue rather than "subjective inner feeling"—he could not possibly sign the human rights petition to free a recently imprisoned composer-singer. The singer is freed for other reasons before the end of the play, and the tangible value of the petition is nullified. However, we have witnessed an argument on social ethics which Havel has left as a sort of interim legacy for the theatres of the world. It is food for thought for directors and actors just as much as for philosophers and social scientists—and above all, perhaps, for thinking human beings under any regime. . . .

Havel's work, though reflecting in a unique way the features of his own society, contains startling resources for the Western consciousness and emerges in all its artistic and philosophical importance, if considered in the context of contemporary international literature. His figure Vaněk (which has already been taken up by two other Czech playwrights, Pavel Kohout and Pavel Landovský, who have used the character in two of their own plays and have thus given it continuum and an additional realistic dimension) is a sort of ethical, incorruptible Alice in a dubious land where reasoning and actions are based on the attempt to survive within a system whose nature is accepted without question. As to the issue of the Individual versus Society, Havel's work reveals the relativism of ethical standpoints in Western literature (examples from Pinter to Robbe-Grillet from Beckett to Pynchon abound). . . . Havel's explorations of language as a tool of power relates as much to the West German playwright Peter Handke's angry study of a man molded linguistically into a social system, as it illuminates a burning problem of Central-Eastern European writers and cultures: namely, that the struggle for a free language is in fact a struggle for political and social independence. (p. 392)

[Havel] is not only a playwright who gives shape to some of the most important issues of our time but also a thinker who from his small place in a small country in the heart of Europe sends forth an eloquent artistic diagnosis of men living in social groups East or West. More than that. While imparting his diagnosis of our ills, he makes us laugh—which, they tell me, is half the cure. (pp. 392-93)

Marketa Goetz-Stankiewicz, "Václav Havel: A Writer of Today's Season," in World Literature Today

(copyright 1981 by the University of Oklahoma Press), Vol. 55, No. 3, Summer, 1981, pp. 388-93.

SAMUEL BECKETT

DIRECTOR (D)
HIS FEMALE ASSISTANT (A)
PROTAGONIST (P)
LUKE, IN CHARGE OF THE
   LIGHTING, OFFSTAGE (L)

Rehearsal. Final touches to the last scene. Bare stage. A and L have just set the lighting. D has just arrived.

D in an armchair downstage audience left. Fur coat. Fur toque to match. Age and physique unimportant.

A standing beside him. White coverall. Bare head. Pencil on ear. Age and physique unimportant.

P midstage standing on a black block 18" high. Black wide-brimmed hat. Black dressing gown to ankles. Barefoot. Head bowed. Hands in pockets. Age and physique unimportant.

D and A contemplate P.

Long pause.

A (*finally*): Like the look of him?
D: So-so. (*Pause.*) Why the plinth?
A: To let the stalls see the feet.
(*Pause.*)
D: Why the hat?
A: To help hide the face.
(*Pause.*)
D: Why the gown?
A: To have him all black.
(*Pause.*)
D: What has he on underneath? (*A moves toward P.*) Say it.
(*A halts.*)
A: His night attire.
D: Color?
A: Ash.
(*D takes out a cigar.*)
D: Light.
(*A returns, lights the cigar, stands still. D smokes.*)
D: How's the skull?
A: You've seen it.
D: I forget. (*A moves toward P.*) Say it.
(*A halts.*)
A: Molting. A few tufts.
D: Color?
A: Ash.
(*Pause.*)
D: Why hands in pockets?
A: To help have him all black.
D: They mustn't.
A: I make a note. (*She takes out a pad, takes pencil, notes.*) Hands exposed. (*She puts back pad and pencil.*)
D: How are they?
(*A at a loss.*)
D (*irritably*): The hands, how are the hands?
A: You've seen them.
D: I forget.
A: Crippled. Fibrous degeneration.

D: Clawlike?

A: If you like.

D: Two claws?

A: Unless he clench his fists.

D: He mustn't.

A: I make a note. (*She takes out pad, takes pencil, notes.*) Hands limp. (*She puts back pad and pencil.*)

D: Light.

(*A returns, relights the cigar, stands still. D smokes.*)

D: Good. Now let's have a look.

(*A at a loss.*)

D (*irritably*): Get going. Lose that gown. (*He consults his chronometer.*) Step on it. I have a caucus.

(*A goes to P, takes off the gown. P submits, inert. A steps back, the gown over her arm. P in old gray pajamas, head bowed, fists clenched. Pause.*)

A: Like him better without? (*Pause.*) He's shivering.

D: Not all that. Hat.

(*A advances, takes off hat, steps back, hat in hand. Pause.*)

A: Like that cranium?

D: Needs whitening.

A: I make a note. (*She drops hat and gown, takes out pad, takes pencil, notes.*) Whiten cranium. (*She puts back pad and pencil.*)

D: The hands.

(*A at a loss.*)

D (*irritably*): The fists. Get going.

(*A advances, unclenches fists, steps back.*)

D: And whiten.

A: I make a note. (*She takes out pad, takes pencil, notes.*) Whiten hands. (*She puts back pad and pencil. They contemplate P.*)

D (*finally*): Something wrong. (*Distraught*) What is it?

A (*timidly*): What if we were to . . . were to . . . join them?

D: No harm trying. (*A advances, joins the hands, steps back.*) Higher. (*A advances, raises waist-high the joined hands, steps back.*) A touch more. (*A advances, raises breast-high the joined hands.*) Stop! (*A steps back.*) Better. It's coming. Light.

(*A returns, relights the cigar, stands still. D smokes.*)

A: He's shivering.

D: Bless his heart.

(*Pause.*)

A (*timidly*): What about a little . . . a little . . . gag?

D: For God's sake! This craze for explicitation! Every *i* dotted to death! Little gag! For God's sake!

A: Sure he won't utter?

D: Not a squeak. (*He consults his chronometer.*) Just time. I'll go and see how it looks from the house.

(*Exit D, not to appear again. A subsides in the armchair, springs to her feet no sooner seated, takes out a rag, wipes vigorously back and seat of chair, discards rag, sits again. Pause.*)

D (*off, plaintive*): I can't see the toes. (*Irritably*) I'm sitting in the front row of the stalls and can't see the toes.

A (*rising*): I make a note. (*She takes out pad, takes pencil, notes.*) Raise pedestal.

D: There's a trace of face.

A: I make a note. (*She takes out pad, takes pencil, makes to note.*)

D: Down the head.

(*A at a loss.*)

D (*irritably*): Get going. Down his head. (*A puts back pad and pencil, goes to P, bows his head further, steps back.*) A shade more. (*A advances, bows the head further.*) Stop! (*A steps back.*) Fine. It's coming. (*Pause.*) Could do with more nudity.

A: I make a note. (*She takes out pad, makes to take pencil.*)

D: Get going! Get going! (*A puts back the pad, goes to P, stands irresolute.*) Bare the neck. (*A undoes top buttons, parts the flaps, steps back.*) The legs. The shins. (*A advances, rolls up to below knee one trouser leg, steps back.*) The other. (*Same for other leg, steps back.*) Higher. The knees. (*A advances, rolls up to above knees both trouser legs, steps back.*) And whiten.

A: I make a note. (*She takes out pad, takes pencil, notes.*) Whiten all flesh.

D: It's coming. Is Luke around?

A (*calling*): Luke! (*Pause. Louder*) Luke!

L (*off, distant*): I hear you. (*Pause. Nearer*) What's the trouble now?

A: Luke's around.

D: Black out stage.

L: What?

(*A transmits in technical terms. Fadeout of general light. Light on P alone. A in shadow.*)

D: Just the head.

L: What?

(*A transmits in technical terms. Fadeout of light on P's body. Light on head alone. Long pause.*)

D: Lovely.

(*Pause.*)

A (*timidly*): What if he were to . . . were to . . . raise his head . . . an instant . . . show his face . . . just an instant?

D: For God's sake! What next? Raise his head! Where do you think we are? In Patagonia? Raise his head! For God's sake! (*Pause.*) Good. There's our catastrophe. In the bag. Once more and I'm off.

A (*to L*): Once more and he's off.

(*Fadeup of light on P's body. Pause. Fadeup of general light.*)

D: Stop! (*Pause.*) Now . . . let 'em have it. (*Fadeout of general light. Pause. Fadeout of light on body. Light on head alone. Long pause.*) Terrific! He'll have them on their feet. I can hear it from here.

(*Pause. Distant storm of applause. P raises his head, fixes the audience. The applause falters, dies.*

Long pause.

Fadeout of light on face.)

(pp. 26-7)

Samuel Beckett, " 'Catastrophe' " (a play written for Václav Havel; reprinted by permission of Grove Press, Inc.; © by Samuel Beckett), in The New Yorker, *Vol. LVIII, No. 47, January 10, 1983, pp. 26-7.*

Bessie Head

1937-

South African novelist, short story writer, and nonfiction writer.

Head's fiction explores the domination of racism in the lives of southern African peoples. As a person of mixed race, she has suffered from discrimination both in her birthplace, South Africa, and in her adopted land, Botswana. Her novels rise above the bitterness common to much protest literature in that Head strives to understand not only the effects of prejudice but also the causes. She demonstrates, too, a mastery of economic, social, and political realities that adds interest and authenticity to her work.

Each of Head's novels reveals a progression in her examination of the evils of racism. In *When Rain Clouds Gather*, Head portrays a black South African male victimized by apartheid in his country of birth and then treated unequally as a refugee in Botswana. With her second novel, *Maru*, Head depicts the racism within black society and shows that love between man and woman is a way of breaking through prejudice systems. *A Question of Power* is her most introspective and complex work. The struggle within the protagonist's psyche for freedom from inferiority, hatred, and madness may be seen as symbolic of the struggle against intolerance within Africa.

(See also *Contemporary Authors*, Vols. 29-32, rev. ed.)

Courtesy of Bessie Head

MARY BORG

[An] outcast is the central figure in Bessie Head's first novel [*When Rain Clouds Gather,* a] naked sociological commentary . . . .

There is too much undiluted sociological and agricultural textbook language, but the book is justified by loving and humorous descriptions of African land and people, by powerful, generous feeling and passionate analysis of the situation of the black African. She is especially moving on the position of women, emerging painfully from the chrysalis of tribalist attitudes into a new evaluation of their relationship to men and their position in society; and she is coolly humorous about British colonial administrators, reserving rancorous irony for the newly-emergent twopenny-halfpenny revolutionaries. Bessie Head is herself an African refugee from South Africa: she has opted for understanding, generosity and gradual progress, and her book is a splendid argument for this stand.

> Mary Borg, "Victims," in New Statesman (© 1969
> The Statesman & Nation Publishing Co. Ltd.), Vol.
> 77, No. 1992, May 16, 1969, p. 696.*

THE TIMES LITERARY SUPPLEMENT

Maru is set in similar territory [as *When Rain Clouds Gather*], and this time Mrs. Head concentrates on the relationships of a handful of educated Africans. Two young chiefs fall in love with a schoolteacher who, though brought up and educated by a missionary's wife (a character so well drawn that it is a pity she disappears so soon from the story), belongs to the despised Bushman tribe. The story depends on the belief—much insisted

on but never quite realized in terms of character—that the two men, though friends, approach life, love and their own destinies in quite opposite ways. For both of them love for the girl involves the end of their friendship and a rethinking of their attitudes to the Bushmen, whom they have always used as slaves. . . . Margaret, the object of all this, is a remarkably passive, shadowy character, represented as intelligent and talented, yet hardly possessed of the hypnotic qualities attributed to her.

There are delightful touches in Mrs. Head's account of the village and its institutions, a comical showdown with the headmaster, glimpses of the benevolent tyranny exercised by the two heroes; but the friendship of the two men and their different responses to love are too often obscured by a wilful invocation of the arcane.

> "Other New Novels: 'Maru'," in The Times Literary
> Supplement (© Times Newspapers Ltd. (London)
> 1971; reproduced from The Times Literary Supplement by permission), No. 3597, February 5, 1971,
> p. 145.*

ROBERTA RUBENSTEIN

If one unconsciously thinks of schizophrenia as a unique product of Western culture, it is startling to discover in *A Question of Power,* by the South African novelist Bessie Head, a profound enlargement of the geographical as well as the symbolic regions of madness. (p. 30)

The "question of power" is the many-leveled issue of the novel, expanded to include both internal and external dimensions. Elizabeth's dissociated personality first reveals the idea of "soul power"—in which specters of her own psyche dramatize her lack of personal identity, as well as her spiritual and emotional paralysis. That powerlessness in turn symbolizes the non-white South African's political and social situation. . . .

The most important kind of power implied in the novel is, finally, the power of the human spirit to overcome its own movement toward annihilation. . . . [Elizabeth's] internal battle ceases when she at last exorcises the negative "powers" within, and finds in their place that "There is only one God and his name is Man."

Extending the landscape of madness, then, Bessie Head has imaginatively shown its central relationship to powerlessness. . . .

A Question of Power succeeds as an intense, even mythic, dramatization of the mind's struggle for autonomy and as a symbolic protest against the political realities of South Africa. Bessie Head skillfully involves the reader in the immediacy and terror of Elizabeth's confrontations with her demons. Yet the rhythmic alternation with her progress in the village provides an almost pastoral balance to the Dostoevskian intensity of the mad episodes. The result is a work of striking virtuosity—an artistically shaped descent into the linked hells of madness and oppression, and a resolution that provides the hope of both internal and external reconciliation. (p. 31)

Roberta Rubenstein, "Recent Notable Fiction: 'A Question of Power'," in The New Republic (reprinted by permission of The New Republic; ©1974 The New Republic, Inc.), Vol. 170, No. 17, April 27, 1974, pp. 30-1.

ROBERT L. BERNER

Bessie Head's third novel [*A Question of Power*] is a remarkable attempt to escape from the limitations of mere "protest" literature in which Black South African writers so often find themselves. It would have been natural for her, and easier, to have written an attack on the indignities of apartheid which have driven her into exile in Botswana. Certainly South African racism is the ultimate source of the difficulties besetting Elizabeth, her "coloured" protagonist. But Head chooses to make her novel out of Elizabeth's response to injustice—first in madness and finally in a heroic struggle out of that madness into wholeness and wisdom. The novel's subject is power in all its physical and moral ramifications, and Elizabeth's final wisdom is understood in terms of her achievement of the power of love and human understanding. (p. 176)

Because of the essential wisdom of the novel it is unfortunate that the nightmare passages, though imaginative and remarkable in their way, are not more successful. Regrettably they too often seem to be out of the writer's control. Still, the novel is significant as a talented writer's attempt to avoid the didactic pitfalls which so often endanger spokesmen for oppressed peoples. (pp. 176-77)

Robert L. Berner, "South Africa: 'A Question of Power'," in Books Abroad (copyright 1975 by the

University of Oklahoma Press), Vol. 49, No. 1, Winter, 1975, pp. 176-77.

ARTHUR RAVENSCROFT

[Bessie Head's novels] are strange, ambiguous, deeply personal books which initially do not seem to be 'political' in any ordinary sense of the word. On the contrary, any reader with either Marxist or Pan-Africanist political affinities is likely to be irritated by the seeming emphasis on the quest for personal contentment, the abdication of political kingship—metaphorically in *When Rain Clouds Gather,* literally in *Maru,* and one might say wholesale in *A Question of Power.* The novelist's preoccupations would seem to suggest a steady progression from the first novel to the third into ever murkier depths of alienation from the currents of South African, and African, matters of politics and power—indeed in *A Question of Power* we are taken nightmarishly into the central character's process of mental breakdown, through lurid cascades of hallucination and a pathological blurring of the frontiers between insanity and any kind of normalcy. It is precisely this journeying into the various characters' most secret interior recesses of mind and (we must not fight shy of the word) of soul, that gives the three novels a quite remarkable cohesion and makes them a sort of trilogy. . . . It seems to me that with Bessie Head . . . each novel both strikes out anew, and also re-shoulders the same burden. It is as if one were observing a process that involves simultaneously progression, introgression, and circumgression; but also (and here I believe lies her particular creative power) organic growth in both her art and her central concerns. For all our being lured as readers into the labyrinth of Elizabeth's tortured mind in *A Question of Power,* and then, as it were, left there to face with her the phantasmagoric riot of nightmare and horror, one nevertheless senses throughout that the imagination which unleashes this fevered torrent resides in a creative mind that is exceedingly tough. It is not just that the fictional character emerges worn down yet regenerated and incredibly alive still after her long ordeal, but that her experience at the narrative level is also a figuring of the creative imagination in our time—that that process is both part of the multi-layered theme *and* the method of its communication. And that process as an embodiment of the novelist's art is a tough, demanding labour. (p. 175)

There are two major clues to the overall homogeneity of Bessie Head's novels. It is impossible to avoid noticing how frequently the words 'control' and 'prison' (and phrases and images of equivalent value) occur in all three novels, in many different ways certainly, and probably not as an altogether conscious patterning. 'Control' occurs in contexts tending towards the idea of control over appetites felt as detonators that set off the explosions in individual lives, no less than in the affairs of mankind, which leave those broken trails of blasted humanity that are a peculiar mark of our times. 'Prison' occurs in more varied uses, but most often related to a voluntary shutting of oneself away from what goes on around one. Sometimes it may be straight escapism or alienation, but more often it suggests a willed control over a naturally outgoing personality, an imprisonment not for stagnation but for recollection and renewal—a severely practical self-imposed isolation which is part of natural growth. Like the silk-worm's cocoon, it is made for shelter, while strengths are gathered for outbreak and a fresh continuance. (p. 176)

To the characters [in *When Rain Clouds Gather*], Golema Mmidi may be a kind of pastoral retreat after their earlier rough encounters with life, but the haven is a place of tough, demanding labour, of recurrent crises, of improvisation and ingenuity, of the constant threat of disruption from a power-hungry, resentful local chief. Their co-operative efforts constitute an image of creativity in which sweat and imagination, harsh reality and an ultimate dream to be fulfilled are mixed in just about equal proportions. Out of this creative, co-operative enterprise of constructive energy Bessie Head generates a powerful sense of potential fulfilment for characters who have jealously guarded, enclosed, shut up tightly their private individualities. Against a political background of self-indulgent, serf-owning traditional chiefs and self-seeking, new politicians more interested in power than people, the village of Golema Mmidi is offered as a difficult alternative: not so much a rural utopia for the Africa of the future to aim at, as a means of personal and economic independence and interdependence, where the qualities that count are benign austerity, reverence for the lives of ordinary people (whether university-educated experts or illiterate villagers), and, above all, the ability to break out of the prison of selfhood without destroying individual privacy and integrity.

Makhaya's quest for personal freedom was a flight not only from South Africa's police-van sirens and the burden of oppression, but also from the personal demands upon him of his immediate relations. The last thing he is looking for when he enters Botswana is a new network of intimate relationships or a new struggle against a different oppression. And of course he finds both. That is why the 'peaceful haven' idea in the book is really very deceptive. Golema Mmidi is no Garden of Eden, even if its potentialities are indeed richer than the South African life Makhaya left behind could offer him. (p. 177)

Makhaya does find innocence, trust, and respect, though not as unqualified absolutes. He has to give of himself both in physical labour and in the opening of the cell door to his private sanctum. His marriage to Paulina Sebeso near the end of the novel is, of course, also a finding of himself, with the ghosts of his former 'gray graveyard' life no longer visible, now, in the merciful darkness of Paulina's hut. . . . (p. 178)

The precise relationship between individual freedom and political independence, and between a guarded core of privacy and an unbudding towards others, may seem rather elusive, perhaps even mystical, in my reading of the novel, and I see it as one of the weaknesses of **When Rain Clouds Gather**. It is a straightforward narrative with no unexpected tricks of technique and very down-to-earth in the minutiae of an agricultural hard grind of a way of life. . . . There are moments of melodrama and excessive romanticism, but the real life of the novel is of creativity, resilience, reconstruction, fulfilment. Of the six major characters, four are themselves Batswana but all are in one sense or another handicapped exiles, learning how to mend their lives in the exacting but ultimately viable sands of Golema Mmidi. It is the vision behind their effortful embracing of exile that gives Bessie Head's first novel an unusual maturity. (pp. 178-79)

[*Maru*] immediately proclaims itself as technically a very different sort of book. The first six pages present the outcome of the events narrated in the rest of the novel, and, though they are essential for our adequate grasp of how those events unfold, they don't make sense at first, not until one has read to the end. The opening is thus both a species of sealed orders for the reader and an epilogue. And are we sure, at the end, that the two chief male characters, Maru and Moleka, who are close, intimate friends until they become bitter antagonists, are indeed two separate fictional characters, or that they are symbolic extensions of contending character-traits within the same man? (p. 179)

Maru's methods, 'cold, calculating and ruthless', are the normal methods of those who seek and wield power, and yet Maru's role in the novel is the very antithesis of power-wielding. He renounces the kingdom of political power in favour of the kingdom of love. But before he does so, he manipulates, engineers, 'fixes' the delicate relationships among himself, his sister Dikeledi, his friend Moleka, and Margaret the Masarwa woman, with whom both he and Moleka are in love. With the help of his three spies, Maru is able to manoeuvre Moleka against his real will to marry Dikeledi, who loves him; Maru is then able to marry Margaret, whom Moleka really loves. And Maru can exert such a persuasive influence upon Margaret that she begins to learn to love him, though it is Moleka with whom she has been secretly in love since her arrival in the village. (p. 180)

Maru's almost god-like perspicacity justifies his seemingly devious methods of preventing Moleka from obtaining Margaret's love. Maru knows that because his kingdom is of love, he has the strength to marry Margaret and live by all the consequences. (pp. 181-82)

Maru is no god. He remains a man with doubts. We know from the beginning that he and Margaret have not got away to another Garden of Eden. Rich and fulfilled and symbolically healthful as their life together is, it nevertheless has shadows and questions over it. Though Maru has obeyed the voices of the gods in his heart and trusts them, the closed door in Moleka's heart still hides an uncertainty. . . .

This doubt and with it his willingness to give up Margaret, despite his deep love for her, if he should one day be proved wrong about Moleka, comes in those pages of introductory epilogue that I mentioned earlier, and throughout the novel influences our view of Maru and his actions.

On the one hand Maru's marriage is a deeply personal thing. He knows he 'could not marry a tribe or race.' . . . On the other hand the marriage also carries a considerable political symbolism. (p. 182)

Much more than **When Rain Clouds Gather**, **Maru** is a novel about interior experience, about thinking, feeling, sensing, about control over rebellious lusts of the spirit; and, ironically, ambiguously, in Bessie Head's comprehending vision, it is also a more 'political' novel than **When Rain Clouds Gather**. I am not sure that the two things are satisfyingly fused, even whether it is the sort of novel in which they *should* be so fused, but I am much impressed and moved by the power with which they are conveyed. That power resides in the vitality of the enterprise, which projects the personal and the political implications in such vivid, authentic parallels that one feels they are being closely held together, like the lengths of steel on a railway track, which fuse only in optical illusion and are indeed useless if they don't maintain their divided parallelism. . . .

Bessie Head's most recent novel, **A Question of Power,** is clearly more ambitious than its two predecessors, and less immediately accessible, and altogether a more risky undertaking. The movement here is even deeper (and more disturbingly so) into the vast caverns of interior personal experience. (p. 183)

Bessie Head's common-sensical rootedness in the earthy level of everyday reality is still there to anchor for the reader the terrifying world of Elizabeth's hallucinations, but it is the events of that world that dominate the book. Even more than in the two earlier novels, one finds an intimate relationship between an individual character's private odyssey of the soul and public convulsions that range across the world and from one civilization to another. To see Bessie Head's handling of Elizabeth's mental instability as a clever literary device to make possible an epic confrontation between Good and Evil within the confines of a realist novel, is to underestimate the achievement. One wonders again and again whether the phantom world that comes to life whenever Elizabeth is alone in her hut could have been invented by a novelist who had not herself gone through similar experiences, so frighteningly and authentically does it all pass before one's eyes. But there is no confusion of identity between the novelist and the character, and Bessie Head makes one realize often how close is the similarity between the most fevered creations of a deranged mind and the insanities of deranged societies. (pp. 183-84)

The characteristic Bessie Head irony comes out in the fact that even as Elizabeth, the South African coloured refugee among the Batswana, finds herself screaming in her nightmares that she hates black Africans, she is none the less in what appears to her the almost dream-like world of her workaday activities in the co-operative vegetable garden, forging, steadily and genuinely, links of personal regard and affection with the Batswana villagers and with the foreign helpers. The last words of the novel are 'a gesture of belonging' . . . as Elizabeth settles herself for her first untortured night's sleep in three years, annealed both spiritually and socially, as in imagination she places one soft hand over her land.

I do not believe that Bessie Head's novels are offering anything as facile as universal brotherhood and love for a political blueprint for either South Africa or all of Africa. In *Maru* common sense is described as the next best thing to changing the world on the basis of love of mankind. What the three novels do say very clearly is that whoever exercises political power, however laudable his aims, will trample upon the faces and limbs of ordinary people, and will lust in that trampling. That horrible obscenity mankind must recognize in its collective interior soul. The corollary is not liberal abstention from action, but rather modest action in very practical terms, and with individual hearts flushed and cleansed for collective purpose. The divinity that she acknowledges is a new, less arrogant kind of humanism, a remorseless God who demands that iron integrity in personal conduct should inform political action too. Of course the novels don't sermonize like this, but grow out of a moral basis of this kind of order. (p. 185)

In the development of the South African novel, this disturbing toughness of Bessie Head's creative imagination returns to us that gesture of belonging with which *A Question of Power* ends. All three novels are fraught with the loneliness and despair of exile, but the resilience of the exiled characters is even more remarkable. Bessie Head refuses to look for the deceiving gleam that draws one to expect the dawn of liberation in the South, but accepts what the meagre, even parched, present offers. (p. 186)

*Arthur Ravenscroft, "The Novels of Bessie Head,"
in* Aspects of South African Literature, *edited by
Christopher Heywood (copyright © 1976 by Christopher Heywood; reprinted by permission of Africana
Publishing Company, a division of Holmes & Meier
Publishers, Inc.; IUB Building, 30 Irving Place, New
York, NY 10003), Africana, 1976, pp. 174-86.*

CHARLES R. LARSON

Bessie Head's *A Question of Power* is important not solely because it is an introspective novel by an African woman but because the topics of her concern are also, for the most part, foreign to African fiction as a sub-division of the novel in the Third World: madness, sexuality, guilt. In its concern with these ideas, *A Question of Power* bears closer affinity to the works by two Caucasian writers from southern Africa—Doris Lessing and Nadine Gordimer—than to those of Ms. Head's African contemporaries.

Although *A Question of Power* is told in the third person, the point of view is always Elizabeth's. The reader understands the events in the story the same way that Elizabeth does, which is to say that when she is confused (which is often) he is confused. The extended passages of introspection are depicted primarily through the use of the internal monologue; the chronology of the narrative is often associative. (p. 165)

Most of the guilt that Elizabeth develops originates from . . . early events in her life: her Coloured classification, her orphan status at the mission, and her short-lived marriage. All of these factors are direct results of the South African policy of apartheid which treats people as something other than human beings. (p. 166)

At its very base, then, *A Question of Power* . . . is concerned with the power play between the West (the white South Africans) and the Third World. There are the ubiquitous problems of racism that we have already seen in many novels—the relationship between subjugators and the subjugated. . . . The basis of the story, then, is racial; it is the development of the narrative that is so unusual, though there are novels of South African life in which neuroses abound. . . .

The layers of guilt that develop out of the early situations of Elizabeth's life are often embellished with her sexual fantasies. . . .

The failure of her marriage also contributes to her guilt, for Elizabeth feels that if she were more attractive, her husband would not have turned to other women (and men) to fulfill his sexual desires. As her guilt intensifies, she wonders if she is not responsible for turning the men around her into homosexuals. (p. 167)

All of these aspects of sexual guilt are related to Elizabeth's racial origins and the issues of exile and alienation. (p. 168)

As these feelings of exile and alienation become intensified, Elizabeth comes to realize that almost every aspect of the life around her reminds her of her guilt. . . . She has developed a love/hate relationship with the Africans around her. On the one hand she wants to be one of them; on the other, she hates them, believing they are inferior. To that extent the apartheid indoctrination she has undergone has been successful. (pp. 168-69)

Elizabeth's "recovery" in the insane asylum is intended to be more than ironic; it is hardly the result of the medicine or the treatment she receives. Rather, the asylum brings out the strongest of her aversions, and she is forced to acknowledge them for the first time. . . . It is the European psychiatrist—the only one in the country—who makes her fully cognizant of her racial feelings. . . .

Besides her race prejudice, the European doctor helps Elizabeth discover an equally destructive prejudice she has harbored during her years in Botswana: intellectual superiority, pride. She has, in fact, willingly isolated herself from the people around her, because she has always considered herself above them. (p. 170)

Eventually Elizabeth seeks solace in the land, returning to the garden, and the village co-operative of which she had earlier been a part. From Kenosi, an African woman, she learns to respect the soil and the people of Botswana. Her error has been her inability to comprehend the African sense of humanity—she fled those people who would harbor her. . . . The journey of the singular consciousness has once again ended in the collective consciousness, the brotherhood of man.

The question of power in the title of Bessie Head's novel is as many-layered as the multiple fears and guilts from which Elizabeth has been fleeing for much of her adult life. Initially, Ms. Head speaks of this as one's personal power and the way it operates in relationships with others. . . . To this Ms. Head adds a whole list of extraterrestrial powers: "energies, stars, planets, universes and all kinds of swirling magic and mystery . . ." . . .—forces over which the individual has little control. (p. 171)

As these ideas embellish the narrative of Elizabeth's own struggles for personal power to pull her life together, they take on a quasi-religious framework of spiritual power—the struggle between God and man. . . . Finally, then, spiritual power becomes personal power—the power of the individual to resist evil, to pull his life together. . . .

[Political power is] a given throughout the entire work: the South African apartheid policies start Elizabeth on her road to madness. If she had remained in South Africa, her life would always have been politically controlled by the Europeans. As a Coloured, she will be a kind of outsider no matter where she goes in Africa—though Botswana, an enclave dependent on South Africa in so many ways, is a particularly ironic choice to flee to. (p. 172)

In the final analysis, Bessie Head wants us to consider all of these variations of power as the evils that thwart each individual's desire to be part of the human race, part of the brotherhood of man. The facts of one's race, color, religion, education—these should not be considered prerequisites for membership in the human race. This is the supreme reality of *A Question of Power*. . . . (pp. 172-73)

> *Charles R. Larson, "The Singular Consciousness," in his* The Novel in the Third World *(copyright © 1976 by Charles R. Larson; reprinted by permission of the author), Inscape Publishers, 1976, pp. 153-74.**

CECIL A. ABRAHAMS

Even though in a narrow sense the context of Bessie Head's fiction is Botswana, her novels, preoccupied with themes of political and spiritual exile, racial hatred and the source of corrupting power and authority, reflect in an important and deep way the bitter world of inhumanity and racism which exists throughout South Africa. The physical landscape of Botswana is colored with her own history of exile, race confusion and her search for what she labels in her first novel, *When Rain Clouds Gather*, an "illusion of freedom." . . . Head is concerned particularly with the racial question as it pertains to her mixed-blood status. In her novels, *When Rain Clouds Gather*, *Maru*, and *A Question of Power*, Bessie Head seeks to examine

the causes of the evil of race prejudice and, concomitantly, to explore potential sources of generosity and goodness.

In trying to unearth the root of racial prejudice, Bessie Head differs from other South African writers in her approach to and understanding of the problem. Being exiled and long suffering products of a white supremacist society, black South African writers characteristically confront their cruel tormentors in a direct manner. They see the root of evil as being firmly and solely embedded in the obdurate heart of the white person and dismiss the corruption of blacks as being the natural consequence of an evil which has been manufactured by whites. *When Rain Clouds Gather,* seems at first to repeat this pattern of blame and confrontation. . . . But ultimately the transplanted Makhaya, and therefore the reader, cannot escape the realities of either the often cruel desert environment where the rain clouds gather hopefully but fail to burst into fruitful rain, or the social milieu where many white men and women of a generous nature assist the eager peasants to develop the land.

In her second novel, *Maru*, which is the study of racial prejudice against the ancient Masarwa or Bushmen people, Head rejoins the tradition of other South African writers as she looks at the cruel results of blatant racial discrimination and suggests that open challenge is the only solution to the problem. She does not lead the question outside the familiar orbit of victim and victimizer; the result is that *Maru* is a rather weak, vapoury study on the theme of racial prejudice. The plot, which deals with the prejudice that Margaret, the Masarwa girl, experiences in the narrowminded Botswana society, culminates in a fairy tale marriage and seems somewhat contrived.

One reason why *Maru* may be usefully studied, however, is that it is a necessary step in Head's continuing study of evil. The strength and perception of Head's study of evil in her third novel, *A Question of Power*, might not have materialized without the lessons that are learned about evil in *Maru*. Head recognizes in both these novels that racism is not limited to the whites of the South African soil. As a coloured South African who had received her fair share of racial criticism from blacks, she is sensitive to the fact that, because of their particular racial colour and physical features, the Masarwa, though a black race, are regarded as the "low man" on the totem pole and suffer all the injustices of that position. (pp. 22-3)

In *A Question of Power* . . . the main character, Elizabeth, is a coloured South African woman; this, of course, is the race of Head herself. Since coloured people are the product of mixed procreative relationships between whites and blacks, in a racist South African society where sexual relationships between whites and blacks are outlawed, the progeny of such sexual encounters carry with them a life-long stigma of illegitimacy. (p. 24)

Like all other coloured South Africans, Elizabeth is regarded as a queer specimen of humanity who does not belong to either the white or black race. (p. 25)

Although *When Rain Clouds Gather* and *A Question of Power* clearly distinguish between their protagonists' understanding of racism, the two novels, together with *Maru*, show that Head's novels are progressive in their philosophical conclusion about the nature and source of racism. Ultimately, Head examines three sources of evil and, conversely, of potential goodness. The most obvious source is the sphere of political power and authority; it is clear that if the political institutions which decree and regulate the lives of the society are reformed or abolished a better or new society can be established. Makhaya in *When Rain Clouds Gather* and Elizabeth in *A Question of Power*, having been victims of the political authority of South Africa, escape to Botswana; both imagine that in a newly independent and seemingly simple society like Botswana's, they will be able to find peace and harmony. Makhaya discovers, however, that his refugee status is not acceptable to the authorities and, furthermore, that even in a black-dominated political structure, his position is somewhat precarious. Hence, he has to endure the hateful insults of Chief Matenge. . . . Elizabeth experiences similar insults at the hands of Dan or Medusa in *A Question of Power.* In both instances it is the power of the elite, be it white or black, which creates prejudice against them. Head concludes in *Maru* that evil is not the domain solely of the white racist, that in fact evil permeates all races. (pp. 26-7)

Bessie Head's fiction leads back, again and again, to the corrupt, greedy and power hungry elite of politicians, tribal chiefs and teachers. She singles out the African politician in *When Rain Clouds Gather,* focusing on Makhaya who had in South Africa regarded the African politician as the saviour of the oppressed. . . .

Head also examines whether the transformation of economic institutions to ensure a better standard of living for the African people leads to freedom from prejudice and narrowness. This is the solution that is suggested by Gilbert Balfour, Eugene and Gunner in *When Rain Clouds Gather.* These men are foreigners who are searching for a more humane world. (p. 27)

[But] Makhaya and Elizabeth both know that Africa needs more than an economic revolution to confront the problems of race prejudice. So even though Bessie Head treats the motives of Gilbert, Eugene and Tom with respect, she recognizes that their solution is an inadequate answer for Botswana's main questions.

In *A Question of Power* Head finds an answer to her search for man's evil and his good. And it is here that she realizes that political and economic institutions can be truly transformed for the betterment of man after man has analyzed and resolved the questions of good and evil embedded in his soul. Hence, Botswana, the place of escape, becomes the area where there is a "total demystifying of all illusions." . . . In thinking that she has escaped the "filth" of South Africa, Elizabeth, like Makhaya, is challenged to understand the causes for the South African deadness and to create a living hope. . . . The world of the future must be freed of the Medusa-like power-seekers and elitists in authority. And to accomplish this task Elizabeth, like Makhaya, must dedicate herself to eradicating evil in all its forms. (p. 28)

Bessie Head's solution to the South African problem is, then, spiritual, from within the soul of man. It is pointless, says Sello, to hate the racist whites for what oppression they have inflicted and continue to inflict on the black people of South Africa. As racists, they are not free, they simply imprison their souls in their own cobweb of hatred. Their racism must be overcome through love and not violence, nor through the deceptive power-seeking black elite of Africa. . . . While proposing a spiritual solution to the South African question, she has chosen an angle which, although frustrating to the more militant oppressed, is new in its context. (p. 29)

> Cecil A. Abrahams, "The Tyranny of Place: The Context of Bessie Head's Fiction," in World Literature Written in English (© copyright 1978 WLWE-World Literature Written in English), Vol. 17, No. 1, April, 1978, pp. 22-9.

JOHN MELLORS

In a footnote to the first of her 'Botswana village tales' in *The Collector of Treasures,* Bessie Head says that she has 'romanticised and fictionalised' data provided by old men of the tribe whose memories are unreliable. The farther she goes into history and tradition, the less convincing the results, but the stories come wonderfully alive when she deals with Botswana just before and after independence. The clash between old tribal ways and the temptations of modern society plays havoc with family life, and leads to prostitution, desertion and murder. Bessie Head blames most of this on the animal behaviour of men towards women; however, she tempers this feminist standpoint by ascribing the men's insensitivity not to an inherent brutishness but to the effects of a colonialism which has left the male 'a broken wreck with no inner resources' with which to adapt to his new-found liberty.

> John Mellors, "Exuberant Lies" (© British Broadcasting Corp. 1978; reprinted by permission of John Mellors), in The Listener, Vol. 99, No. 2556, April 20, 1978, p. 510.*

JEAN MARQUARD

[Bessie Head's three novels] deal in different ways with exile and oppression. The protagonists are outsiders, new arrivals who try to forge a life for themselves in a poor, under-populated third world country, where traditional and modern attitudes to soil and society are in conflict. These are familiar themes in African writing but Bessie Head may be distinguished from other African writers in at least two respects. In the first place she does not idealize the African past and in the second she resists facile polarities, emphasizing personal rather than political motives for tensions between victim and oppressor. She moves beyond the stereotype of white oppressing black to show, particularly in *Maru,* systems of privilege and discrimination working solely within black society.

Makhaya, the hero of *When Rain Clouds Gather* is an exile from South Africa who has fled across the border to Botswana, having served a prison sentence for alleged political activities with banned organizations. He seeks, we are told in the opening paragraph, 'whatever illusion of freedom lay ahead'. Thus it is clear from the outset that independent Africa will not necessarily offer the victim of apartheid an easier life than the one he has left behind. . . . Makhaya, himself an exponent of modern, Western ideas, rejects tribalism as a barbarous system in which women are discriminated against and in which the village witchdoctors perpetuate their power over the community by encouraging superstition and ignorance. (pp. 54-5)

Makhaya settles in Golema Mmidi, a village distinguished from others in Botswana by its system of permanent settlement. . . . (p. 55)

In the creation of Golema Mmidi Bessie Head combines fictive metaphor—the village as Eden—with realistic social detail. The Utopian qualities of the village are balanced by hard realities. Thus the dream of creating a garden in the desert is constantly eroded by poverty, the lack of rain, (staple currency in Botswana is the *pula,* a Tswana word meaning rain) and by prejudice and corruption in local government.

In Golema Mmidi Makhaya meets Gilbert, an idealistic Englishman. . . . (p. 56)

Makhaya and Gilbert are spokesmen for reason, hard work and the abolition of tribal habits in favour of science and progress.

Under the influence of Gilbert, Makhaya abandons 'hate-making political ideologies' as ultimately retrogressive and turns instead to agriculture 'for his salvation'. (pp. 56-7)

Factual social detail is closely integrated into the movement of the plot and is seldom merely digressive or episodic. At the same time a good deal of writing is devoted to accurate analysis of climate, crops, cattle diseases and the problems of land enclosure. This concern for practical bread-and-butter issues is a striking feature of all [Bessie Head's] work and even in the short stories the reader is supplied with accurate social, domestic and economic detail. (p. 57)

In *Maru* Bessie Head continues to explore the conflict between change and tradition in rural Southern Africa. The heroine of this novel is Margaret Cadmore. . . . Margaret's actual superiority over those who regard her as socially inferior [because she is a Masarwa or Bushman by birth] is given repeated emphasis. She has had a better education than anyone else in the village, she is more beautiful and more refined, she is a talented artist with visionary powers, she is affectionate and patient, animals love her, people are drawn to her in spite of their prejudices. Not surprisingly therefore, the two most powerful men in the village, Maru and Moleka, both fall in love with her. Moleka suppresses his love in conformity with social decorum, but Maru, who is paramount chief elect, abdicates his position in order to marry Margaret. Thus in *Maru* the conflict between freedom and the closed system is explored in the context of love and marriage rather than agriculture. (p. 58)

The idea that social change is brought about by the action of powerful individuals rather than gradual temporal evolution (the winds of change are not seen as 'natural' or arbitrary forces) motivates much of the action of *When Rain Clouds Gather.* In her second novel Bessie Head explores this idea in more subtle ways. Maru, to all appearances, decides to renounce the world for love. But his choice is equally the enactment of the individualist principles by which he lives. . . . Maru obeys his gods even when they tell him to deceive his rival. (pp. 58-9)

The sources of power are more fully explored in Bessie Head's third novel, as the title suggests. The semi-autobiographical tone of *Maru* becomes more explicit in *A Question of Power* where parallels between the protagonist and the writer include their mutual South African 'coloured' origins, their attempts to form new beginnings in Botswana and, more significantly, their temporary break-down as a result of the mental stresses of exile and loneliness. Although these correspondences are frankly outlined Bessie Head does not allow the subjective involvement which gives a particularly vivid sense of authenticity to Elizabeth's interior life to diminish the broader theme this life exemplifies. Elizabeth's private sufferings are assimilated to the historical sufferings of mankind through a network of wide-ranging images, the seemingly random nature of which points to their inclusiveness.

This universalizing expression, with its attendant extravagance, is balanced by a steady concentration in the novel on Elizabeth's inner life which ranges from 'the elegant pathway of private thought' to the agony of madness. Thematic development in Bessie Head's three novels reveals a consistent movement inwards from a social to a metaphysical treatment of human insecurities and in the last novel the problem of adaptation to a new world, or new schemes of values, is located in the mind of a single character. It is still Africa's problem however and the ideal garden is once again cultivated on a co-

operative basis. Once more the dream of prosperity is in close touch with the necessity for hard work. As in *When Rain Clouds Gather,* the pioneer of the new schemes for Africa is a white immigrant, this time a South African. The heroine's task is to integrate the external world of innocent productivity, burgeoning growth and friendship in a mini-international community (Golema Mmidi reappears in this novel as Motabeng) with her chaotic inner experience. For Elizabeth, as for Makhaya, sanity means making friends. Those sections of the novel that deal with Elizabeth's madness dramatize her struggle to exorcise feelings of inferiority and resentment which breed estrangement. Each of her two nervous breakdowns is preceded by racial aggression, first against the indigenous population and then against one of the European volunteers. In the creation of two shadowy male figures called Dan and Sello who plague Elizabeth's dreams, forms of oppression, or power are depoliticized, identified as the desire for either spiritual or sexual domination over others. . . . The lesson to be learnt thus, in all three novels, is that love and humility lead the exiled consciousness from estrangement, 'pride and arrogance and egoism of the soul' to 'an identification with mankind' or, as the author expresses it in the novel's last sentence, 'the warm embrace of the brotherhood of man'. These phrases . . . are condemned when used as slogans by political opportunists. In *A Question of Power,* however, where the writing is spare, concentrated and tough, they are invested with the meaning of Elizabeth's painful quest for peace of mind. Throughout the novel the process of 'becoming' African is double edged, involving not only the assumption of social identity but also purification of the spirit. Bessie Head's treatment of Africa is both realistic and symbolic. In one sense the large, empty, barren desert that is repeatedly invoked is a mind landscape too, the storm clouds gather in the individual psyche, Africa becomes a way of being. In the concluding sentence of *A Question of Power,* Elizabeth is described as placing 'one soft hand over her land'. And finally, we are told, 'It was a gesture of belonging.'

It is also a private gesture, with a deeply personal meaning and it exemplifies Bessie Head's achievement in fusing the ideal of community and brotherhood with a belief in the value of the one over the many. *A Question of Power* is the first metaphysical novel on the subject of nation and a national identity to come out of Southern Africa. (pp. 59-61)

Jean Marquard, "Bessie Head: Exile and Community in Southern Africa," in London Magazine *(© London Magazine 1979), Vol. 18, Nos. 9 & 10, December-January, 1978-79, pp. 48-61.*

PADDY KITCHEN

In *Serowe: Village of the Rain Wind,* [Bessie Head] has written a chronicle that makes her adopted home . . . accessible to the imagination of outsiders. . . . Her task was almost intractably complex, given that she could assume no shared background knowledge among the majority of her readers. It was no doubt the novelist in her that extracted a structure for the book from the characters of Serowe's three most beneficial leaders. (p. 23)

Within this tripartite framework, the words of nearly 100 inhabitants provide the flesh of the book. One of Bessie Head's intentions has been to collect a verbal record of the old craft methods such as ploughing, potting, basket-making, tanning, thatching and building in mud. Serowe is primarily a village of mud and thatch, and by English standards it is huge, with a shifting population of up to 35,000. Its citizens give their testimonies, both personal and practical, in an unselfconscious way, and Bessie Head—in true African style—orders the information so that, above all, it tells a story. I believe it is a story which readers will find themselves using as a text from which to meditate on many aspects of society. As a refugee, she found in Serowe the peace that can come from 'just living'. (p. 24)

Paddy Kitchen, "Peace in Serowe" (© British Broadcasting Corp. 1981; reprinted by permission of Paddy Kitchen), in The Listener, *Vol. 106, No. 2718, July 2, 1981, pp. 23-4.*

CHARLES R. LARSON

Reading any book by Bessie Head is always a pleasure, though this talented South African writer's newest work, *Serowe: Village of the Rain Wind,* . . . falls in a special category. What Head has so effectively done is to take all her gifts as a novelist and use these talents in shaping a quasi-sociological account of the village in Botswana where she has lived for most of the past ten years. Part history, part anthropology and folklore, *Serowe* conjured up for me memories of Studs Terkel's *Hard Times.* As the author states in her introduction, "Serowe is an historic village but not spectacularly so, its history is precariously oral." Thus Head has interviewed dozens of people who live in Serowe today and has orchestrated their stories into the wider perspective of village life. The results are often astonishingly beautiful. What this book so strongly demonstrates is the possibility for harmony within a multi-racial community. (p. 66)

Charles R. Larson, "Third World Writing in English," in World Literature Today *(copyright 1982 by the University of Oklahoma Press), Vol. 56, No. 1, Winter, 1982, pp. 64-6.**

Seamus (Justin) Heaney

1939-

Irish poet and essayist.

Critics are divided over Heaney's position in Irish poetry, some even casting him as the greatest Irish poet since W. B. Yeats. Most would agree, however, that he is a poet of "sustained achievement," who has become a spokesperson for Ireland. Heaney provides in his poetry a remarkable balance of the personal, the topical, and the universal which has made his work read and respected by a large audience in Great Britain and America. His search for continuity, as he "digs with his pen" through Irish history and culture and into the "troubles" in contemporary Northern Ireland is described in a concrete, sensuous language that has developed in resonance, density, and fineness of tone. Images of the Irish land and the Irish bog, prominent in his work, serve as important symbols: the land as the subject of the historical-contemporary struggle for possession and the bog as the metaphor for the dark unconscious of Ireland and the self.

***Death of a Naturalist*, *Door into the Dark*, and *Wintering Out*, his earlier works, are in the pastoral tradition, evoking the atmosphere of rural life. His later works, *North* and *Field Work*, are called his major accomplishments. In *North*, his most political poetry, the pastoral element is diminished. Here, Heaney links the grim Irish past with the Irish present, suggesting that love is the redeeming quality—the quality of survival. *Field Work* is a restrained balance between poetry and politics, Heaney having personally left the violent north to settle in Dublin. His recent *Preoccupations* is a collection of lectures and reviews in which Heaney examines the history of language, the poetic tradition, and the work of other poets.**

(See also *CLC*, Vols. 5, 7, 14 and *Contemporary Authors*, Vols. 85-88.)

© Kelly Wise

TERENCE BROWN

It is a mistake . . . to think of Heaney as merely a descriptive poet, endowed with unusual powers of observation. From the first his involvement with landscape and locale, with the physical world, has been both more personal and more remarkable in its implications than any mere act of observation and record could be. (p. 173)

For Heaney, the natural world must be accepted for what it is—heavy, palpable in its irrefutable bulk, in its almost intractable forms. He paints it in thick oils, rarely allowing (except in the delightful '**Lovers on Aran**') for light, fire, air, for what the poet has himself called 'the sideral beauty' of things. (p. 174)

Heaney's sense of landscape combines erotic and religious impulses. He responds with a deep sense of the numinous in the natural world, and reads a scene as if it were governed by feminine, sexual principles. (pp. 174-75)

In Heaney's imagination, which is synthetic and osmotic (in the sense that ideas and intuitions seep across thin membranes to blend with each other), this sense of landscape and the natural world extends in its implications into his treatment of another

major obsession—Irish history and mythology. The implications of his vision of landscape are that nature, for all its processes, is a static form shaped by feminine forces, worked on by energetic, crafty makers, diggers, ploughmen. Irish history too reveals itself in his poetry as a landscape, feminine, protective, preservative, in which man's artifacts and deeds are received in an embracing comprehension. Love for this deity induces dark fantasy and nightmare, drives to deeds of desperation. A more strictly historical intelligence than Heaney's moves to distinguish nature and history. Heaney, dominated by a sense of nature's powers, reads history, language and myth as bound up with nature, with territory and with landscape. (p. 175)

Heaney's sense of the self and of the poetic imagination is markedly similar to his apprehension of nature and history. He himself has remarked, indeed, that in Ireland 'our sense of the past, our sense of the land and perhaps even our sense of identity are inextricably interwoven'. So the imagination has its dark bog-like depths, its sediments and strata from which images and metaphors emerge unbidden into the light of consciousness. . . . Such a sense of self as bound up with, and almost indistinguishable from, the dense complex of Irish natural and historical experience, obviously allows Heaney to explore Ulster's contemporary social and political crisis through attending to his own memories and obsessions. Ireland and her goddess of territory shaped unchangeable patterns in the pre-histories of landscape and of the self. History and experience lay strata upon strata, and the poet takes his soundings. So poems such as **'The Other Side'** and **'A Northern Hoard'** consider the poet's personal life, his recollections and nightmares, as moments when Irish reality becomes explicit in himself. (pp. 180-81)

The formal development of Heaney's poetry relates to [his] passive sense of life. His first poems, rich in texture and heavy with the weight of language and rhythm, established a vision of reality as a palpable intractable absolute from which the poet, the conscious self, must accept what gifts may come. His recent poetry is more spare, the line less loaded with poetic and linguistic ore; these poems are moments of revelation when the past, the land and the imagination permit insight into their packed depths. Where Heaney's early poems attempted to comprehend the whole of their experiences in crowded, apparently unselective, sensuously inclusive poetic organisms, his recent poems seem the minimal revelations of a reality that exists at the beck and call of no man—not even of the poet.

An impression of poetic and imaginative humility is one of these poems' initially attractive features. Yet it is this very humility, which one suspects in fact may be a quietist acquiescence, a passivity before the goddess, that this reader finds unsatisfying in Heaney's work, confining its emotional and dramatic possibilities. Heaney has in a singularly beautiful phrase defined a poem as 'a completely successful love act between the craft and the gift'. He clearly thinks that a poem comes up out of the dark, almost unbidden, organically oozing up through capillary channels pressured by incomprehensible forces. He contrasts this to what he considers a 'more Yeatsian view of poetry':

> When he talked about poetry, Yeats never talked about the 'ooze' or 'nurture'. He always talked about the 'labour' and the 'making' and 'the fascination of what's difficult'.
>
> (pp. 181-82)

But for Yeats 'labour' was as much the arduous task, between poems, of remaking over and over again his poetic, imaginative self, as it was concern with rhyme and rhythms. For Yeats the self was not an intractable absolute, but a field of possibilities among which the poet is forced to choose, the drama of the choice itself being charged with poetic opportunity.

There is evidence in Heaney's work that such knowledge of the poetic self has not yet been achieved. The poems often give the impression that Heaney has not decided fully what his feelings about the matter of his poetry could be. Choice of either a consistent or a dramatically inconsistent stance within a poem is avoided in an indirection which, however admirable it may be with regard to journalistic exploitation of Ulster's present troubles, renders much of his recent work gnomic and, in some instances, emotionally ambiguous to the point where feeling itself drains from the poems. At moments Heaney himself seems aware that his poetry avoids choices, since he occasionally dramatises himself in positions of hesitating indecision. **'The Forge'**, for example, ends with the poet still at the door of the forge. (pp. 182-83)

His recent poetry has therefore seemed at times a remarkably skilled, compelling poetic organisation of his indecision, lacking emotional range and drama.

The emotions that I detect running underground through Heaney's work, emotions that have surfaced only once or twice as the subjects of poems, are feelings of revulsion and attraction to violence, pain and death. These are often implicit in the poet's images where empathetic identifications with victims' shame or with oppressors' sadistic sensations are persistent features. (p. 183)

In one poem, **'Summer Home'**, Heaney allows such feelings as sadistic cruelty and masochistic ambivalence about pain to serve as the explicit matter of his work. The poem is one of his finest so far. Here the poet knows what his feelings are, recognises they are bitter and dark, yet risks making a poem of them. . . . Such a poem emerges not from the impersonal unconscious but from the pain and complexity of experience which the poet has accepted as his proper territory. This poem is no corpse from the bog, no gift from a dark goddess passively accepted by a craft-conscious artist. (p. 185)

Terence Brown, "Four New Voices: Poets of the Present," in his Northern Voices: Poets from Ulster *(© Terence Brown, 1975), Rowman and Littlefield, 1975, pp. 171-213.**

ROBERT BUTTEL

Sculptural incisiveness is just one of the characteristics of style in *Death of a Naturalist*.

What chiefly makes these early poems Heaney's own is another, complementary quality. Put briefly, it is a sensuous, vital energy which determines their diction, imagery, and prosody. To an unusual degree details register with an immediacy on the reader's senses. Note for example this image in **"Death of a Naturalist"**: "the warm thick slobber / of frogspawn that grew like clotted water." Much of the effect derives from the gross, labial "slobber," but in "clotted water" the substance verbally thickens into tangible density. (p. 37)

Augmenting the physical authenticity and the clean, decisive art of the best of the early poems, mainly the ones concerned with the impact of the recollected initiatory experiences of childhood and youth, is the human voice that speaks in them. At its most distinctive it is unpretentious, open, modest, and yet poised, aware, fundamentally serious despite its occasional humorous or ironic turn. Within an anecdotal, sometimes colloquial, or matter-of-fact context it can be terse, suddenly dramatic, charged with emotion, shock or wonder breaking through understatement. It is flexible, open to modulations and complexities of tone. Generally the rhythms are natural though in accord with the predominant pattern and metrics of a given poem. . . .

Nor would I begin to claim for it the mastery of Yeats or Frost, but it does show that he had learned something of their skill in crossing natural speech with traditional verse structure: form and a living speech working together. (p. 40)

In **"Death of a Naturalist"** . . . Heaney most successfully exploited the qualities I have described so far. The poem begins with seemingly matter-of-fact description. . . . But the description prepares for the grotesque initiation [the young boy] would undergo on a later occasion. . . . The poem is uniquely Heaney's, the high point of his achievement at this stage of his development. The details at the end are at once true to the nauseating reality of the frogs and to their surreal psychological implications—all the obscure but immediate sexual turmoil of puberty and adolescence nightmarishly concentrated, erupting in the repulsive images.

To consider the volume [*Death of a Naturalist*] as a whole, however, is to become aware of its unevenness; we should not expect every poem to reach the level of [the title poem]. As the poet tested his new-found skills with a variety of subjects and modes, he wrote some poems in which technique turns into manner. Now and then, for example, the attempt to infuse the poems with energy degenerates into forced metaphor. (pp. 41-3)

[The impact of **"Waterfall,"** for example,] is reduced by the excess of imagistic ingenuity. Ordinance and military terms in this poem and others threaten to become a metaphorical tic. (p. 44)

The love poems in *Death of a Naturalist* are unpretentious and direct in their feelings yet undistinguished. (p. 47)

But about a third of the poems in this first book . . . established Heaney's as a voice to be reckoned with. The successes arose from his risktaking, the virtuoso prosody, the bold word choices, the delving into. the potentially sentimental subject matter of recollected childhood and adolescent experience on a farm. Dangers lay in the method. The words, for instance, that so characterize his style, Heaney words such as slobber, soused, plumped, knobbed, and clotted, are susceptible to overuse, to the possibility of eventual self-parody, though it was by running this danger that he gained an earthy concreteness; also his diction would undergo a continuing evolution in the succeeding two volumes. He would extend and deepen his subject matter, too, and one means of advance would be to explore more fully those forces underlying plain sense and observation. (p. 48)

> *Robert Buttel, in his* Seamus Heaney *(© 1975 by Associated University Presses, Inc.), Bucknell University Press, 1975, 88 p.*

ANNE STEVENSON

[Heaney] seems to do effortlessly what poets in Britain have been trying to do for a long time; that is, to write a profound and important poetry which is at once topical and private, and which is at the same time classically elegant, rich with language, and beautiful to the ear.

Heaney is the most loved and envied of poets, both profound and accessible. Undisturbed in his development into the finest Irish poet since Yeats, he seems able to write of the anguish of Northern Ireland without panic or obscurity. (p. 320)

> *Anne Stevenson, "The Recognition of the Savage God: Poetry in Britain Today," in* New England Review *(copyright © 1979 by Kenyon Hill Publications, Inc.; reprinted by permission of* New England Review*), Vol. II, No. 2, Winter, 1979, pp. 315-26.**

CALVIN BEDIENT

Seamus Heaney's reputation for power, resonance, consummate phrasing, striking talent, uncanniness, etc.—which sprang up like a genie with his very first book, *Death of a Naturalist* . . . , and which, as the early reviews come in, still looms with tweedy arms crossed above his fifth, *Field Work*—is astonishing in view of his modest ambition and tone. The Irish, British, and Americans alike have taken turns rubbing the lamp, as if it were indeed Wonderful, and pure gold. But Heaney himself, it is clear from almost every line, knows what it really is: a very respectable pewter.

Heaney's strength, such as it is, lies in making the most of his real if limited advantages—his rural North Ireland childhood, with its blackberrying, its hunting and fishing, its "Cows cudding, watching, and knowing"; his sense of language, which (*pace* A. Alvarez) is not really for the pretty or grand, despite lapses, but a squatting farmer's feel for the richest mold; and his nature, which toils not neither does it spin, but keeps a steady repose, *being* one for whatever it mirrors and finding one in the measures of the poem.

Of these, the most remarkable and restricting is, almost paradoxically, the last. How dormant in Heaney is what Hegel, admittedly Romantic, deemed the very nature of Spirit, which is to be self-determining. Difficult to know this unassuming personality is around, you might think, except as you take notice of a pond because, without any suddenness that you are aware of, it has gathered a full freight of reflection. We are so used to the restless romantic ego in our own poetry that Heaney seems both a rebuke and a reduction—seems more English than Irish, even, in his modesty. (p. 109)

Heaney scarcely projects a point of view. Most of what he writes is no more, if no less, than potato deep—earth-bound if earth-enriched, placidly rooted in top soil, far from unfathomable. Often he turns to the past, especially the personal past, but it's not a great subject with him as it is with Philip Levine or Geoffrey Hill—not a quest for wholeness or a flagellant's discipline. Lacking identifying conceptions, or the desire to press to the edge of what he already knows, or the leadings-on of passion, or struggles (even secret struggles) of personality, Heaney writes poems only of memory or occasion, gently given responses. . . .

At most, excepting a few of the very earliest and very latest poems, Heaney has been a poet merely of the desire for profundity—of its tease and glamour. His good nature feels, at moments, the tug of the primeval, but it's not set going like the well-witching wand that agonizes as if it would root at once in the secreted water. . . . [For example, **"The Grauballe Man"**] is deliberate myth-making, not the stab of astonishment—an ornamental superposition of natural images (river, grain, egg, etc.) on a man already fused with a bog. (p. 110)

An arguable exception: **"The Skunk,"** one of the two or three best poems in *Field Work*. This poem disturbs propriety at least enough to liken the poet's wife to a skunk, and on no less a point than sexual glamour. . . .

"The Skunk" is the more valid for finding the mysterious in the ordinary, indeed in accidental patterns lighting up totemic necessities. This reliance on the contingent is Heaney's chief way of being modern. (p. 112)

The up-beat, slightly syncopated, adjectival beginning of **"The Skunk"** flags an enlivening accession to actuality and what Heaney himself learned as a college student to call "concrete realization"—the staple of the new candid poem. It exemplifies the way the series approaches autonomy in this mode, poetry having fallen on reality in a distraction of naming. (p. 114)

How important, how profound, is **"The Skunk"**? As we read it, crows wake on the brow; but, delightful though it is, we can tell from it that this poet's work as a whole is not apt to be greater than the sum of its parts. Neither the mind nor the personality evident in it promises a significant unity in the whole work; neither greatly detains. (p. 116)

[Up to the publication of *Field Work*], Heaney's interest, for me at least, has lain in his Irish subjects—rural life particularly—and his language. An urban American cannot but take at least a tourist's interest in the first, and the second has approached a perfection of unassumingness with little or no sacrifice of density. How natural his language is . . . , how refreshingly free from facility. Heaney has the Jacobean and modern trick of thick texture: "Outside the kitchen window a black rat / Sways on the briar like infected fruit." . . . He constantly holds the ear, his language seldom racing past itself, especially now that his sense of the line finally serves it. The secret perhaps lies in clearly spaced emphases, closely played consonance and assonance, the select but simple word, and unfussy specificity—all of which he employs with rare unobtrusiveness.

But in the light of . . . [certain poems in *Field Work*], Heaney may become equally notable for his way with a poem, his "slipstream" approaches to the centerless truth of things. In the first and fourth Glanmore sonnets and in **"The Skunk,"** **"The Harvest Bow,"** and **"Homecomings,"** human universals (art, sexual attraction, disillusionment, etc.) and natural particulars mix with and modify one another beyond paraphrase. For the most part, the universals are not expressed in the abstract language of the understanding at all. . . . It is, instead, an implication of the images, whether natural or human. By this strategy—though in the poems it feels like nothing so cold as "strategy"—Heaney cancels the defect of his lack of ideation. He exploits his gravitation toward the actual without falling down plumb upon it. His interest in the accidental is tasked as a way into the tangled core of experience.

In particular, he gets around his self-conscious identification of himself as a poet—a narrowly conceived role standing a kind of scarecrow's sentry over so many of his poems, keeping off the far more interesting crows. So restricted a poet cannot afford so restricting an identity. (Thus the first Glanmore sonnet does not soar until he leaves off thinking about it.) Heaney is the opposite of the astonishing Ashbery, who somehow makes the idea of poetry an elastic that binds and snaps at everything. Since as a poet he does not much care to think, he has nothing of particular interest to say about poetry or being a poet—while over and over choosing it as his subject. A sentimental association of words with soil and of a pen with a potato digger's spade and his store of things to say is more or less exhausted.

So by all means let him dodge universals, if he has a mind to. Let him cry, "Wait then . . ." and, taking a breath, proceed by inspired immediacies to his goals. (pp. 121-22)

Calvin Bedient, "The Music of What Happens," in Parnassus: Poetry in Review *(copyright © Poetry in Review Foundation), Vol. 8, No. 1, Fall-Winter, 1979, pp. 109-22.*

GREGORY A. SCHIRMER

The difficulty that poets face in negotiating between the local and the universal, between a wish to be true to one's place and cultural heritage and a desire to create an art that will reach beyond the confines of locality, particularly troubles Irish poets, writing, as they do, out of an especially singular culture and writing for an audience largely estranged from that culture. Yeats, of course, provides the most obvious example of an Irish poet able to reach from the particular to the transcendent, but in the decades following Yeats's death, no other Irish poet, with the questionable exception of Patrick Kavanagh, seemed able to fashion a poetic that was both rooted in its native soil

and, at the same time, of notable appeal beyond the shores of Ireland.

In the past few years, however, Ireland seems to have produced, in Seamus Heaney, a poet possessing this rather rare capacity. . . . [By the time that Heaney published *Field Work*], he was matter-of-factly being described in British and American journals as the most important contemporary voice in Irish poetry and being compared, even, to the great Yeats himself. The question, of course, is why? And, more important, what does Heaney's rather astonishing success among non-Irish readers say about the larger problem of how Irish poets—or poets in general, for that matter—create an art of universal import out of the sticks and stones of their own culture and locality?

Heaney's striking power of rendering experience concretely and sensuously—of creating, as his fellow poet Richard Murphy has said, "the feeling as you read his poems that you are actually doing what they describe"—surely accounts for some of Heaney's success outside his own country. Also, Heaney's immediate welcome among non-Irish readers may owe something to the image of Ireland that his first books tended to present: that of a pastoral world governed by rural values—precisely the kind of Ireland that many English and American readers nostalgically wanted to see. (pp. 139-40)

Heaney certainly, as a poet, has surrendered to his native land and culture: not only has he refused to turn his eyes toward the metropolis, but he also has, in the best of his poems, directed his poetic gaze as far into the depths of his cultural heritage as possible. Indeed, Heaney's poetry as a whole seems informed by the principle of excavation, of digging into his personal past, his language, and, perhaps most important, the cultural past of his country. (p. 141)

Of course, other poets—including other Irish poets: Austin Clarke being the most obvious—have trusted the feel of what they know best, have worked out of a deep commitment to their native culture, and, in terms of their reception outside their own country, have suffered because of it. What makes Heaney different is the archetypal dimension of his poetic involvement with Irish culture. Nowhere is this more evident—and nowhere is Heaney's art more transcendent—than in the poems that Heaney has written about the peat bogs of Ireland and Jutland and the treasures and horrors that they have preserved. (p. 142)

Starting with **"Bogland"** in *Door Into the Dark,* continuing with **"The Tollund Man"** in *Wintering Out,* and culminating in a series of poems about figures preserved by the bog in *North,* his fourth volume, Heaney has developed the image of the bog into a powerful symbol of the continuity of human experience that at once enables him to write about the particularities of his own parish, past and present, and to transcend, at the same time, those particularities.

Heaney has compared the bog in Irish culture to the frontier in American culture, and has described his use of the bog "as an answering Irish myth," but it serves as more than that. As the figures of bog queens, sacrificial victims, and adulteresses are raised from the bog by Heaney's poetry, they take on archetypal significance, calling to mind not just the specific values of an ancient northern culture, but also qualities of human experience that are timeless and not the exclusive property of one culture. Poems like **"Bog Queen," "The Grauballe Man," "Punishment," "Strange Fruit,"** and **"Kinship"**—all in *North*—are local in so far as they insist on the connection between the violence and terror of the Viking age and the violence and terror of contemporary Belfast and Derry. They have universality insofar as they insist, as they do, that the evidence found in these bogs of human cruelty—and, concurrently, of the human need for ritual and community—has something to say about human nature as it has always existed. In this sense, the bog functions in Heaney's poems much as the Homeric parallel functions in Joyce's *Ulysses* and much as the fertility myths and Arthurian legends function in Eliot's *The Waste Land*. (p. 143)

The kind of archetypal power found in Heaney's bog poems is not, of course, a required ingredient for poetry that seeks to transcend the confines of locality. One need only to turn to . . . [*Field Work*]—and especially to poems like **"The Guttural Muse,"** **"The Otter,"** **"The Skunk,"** **"Harvest Bow,"** and the Glanmore sonnet sequence—to verify this. For an Irish poet writing in the 20th century, and trying to remain true to his roots in a culture largely unfamiliar to most of his readers, the poetic that Heaney has fashioned out of the notion of excavation and, more specifically, out of the image of the bog, provides a means both of expressing a faith in "the social and artistic validity of his parish," and, at the same time, of creating an art that bears significantly on the "fundamentals" of human experience. (pp. 145-46)

> *Gregory A. Schirmer, "Seamus Heaney's: 'Salvation in Surrender'," in* Eire-Ireland *(copyright Irish American Cultural Institute), Vol. XV, No. 4, Winter, 1980, pp. 139-46.*

JAY PARINI

North is a major accomplishment, a book-length sequence of lyrics which exploits the metaphor of possession more fully than any other Irish poet has done. The poems are richly autobiographical, yet [Seamus Heaney] consistently weaves the particulars of his life into a mythic frame; he has evolved a unique species of political poetry which refers at once to the current Irish "troubles" and to the human situation generally. One would have to invoke Pablo Neruda's *Heights of Macchu Picchu* for a parallel. Consequently, I think Heaney is among the finest poets writing today in English, and I shall examine his work to date to support my large claim for him. His poetry has evolved with remarkable integrity from the beginning. He has drawn ever widening concentric rings around the first few themes he circled; his language has grown steadily more dense, more resonant, more singularly his own with each successive volume. And now, at the height of his powers, one awaits each new book with the same expectancy afforded Yeats and Eliot in their middle years.

Heaney comes from the north, from Derry, and his first book conjured the pastoral topography of his childhood on the farm. One should remember, of course, that even Theocritus and Virgil did not write for country folk, to put it mildly; rather, they evinced the atmosphere of rural life for the benefit of cultivated city dwellers who would appreciate the subtle texture of meaning embedded in their eclogues. This is the pastoral tradition, and Heaney's *Death of a Naturalist* . . . fits into it. He *was* in fact a farm boy, and he writes from immediate experience; but his craft was learned in the city, at Queens University, Belfast, where he enjoyed the tutelage of Philip Hobsbaum, the poet-critic, among others. Hobsbaum's bias toward lean, physical language wedded to intellectual toughness shows up in Heaney's early work, as in the first lines of **"Digging."** . . . Heaney furls us into his vision with lines

admitting no abstraction; his experience thrusts itself upon us directly, and we cannot doubt "the cold smell of potato mould, the squelch and slap / Of soggy peat, the curt cuts of an edge." . . . Like Wordsworth, who says in *The Prelude* that he was "fostered alike by beauty and by fear," this poet lays claim to a similar parentage. (pp. 100-01)

Death of a Naturalist is an apprentice volume, one in which a young poet tests the limits of his abilities, tries out various verse forms and metrical patterns. But if there are echoes in these poems, they are well assimilated. A major poet often steps into his own clearing from the start, and Heaney does this here. The controlled irony of **"The Early Purges,"** with its adumbration of things to come in later volumes, shows this young writer possessed of a maturity beyond his years. . . . None of the sentimental flurries characteristic of Yeats as a novice can be found in Heaney; he writes with a stern grip on reality. (pp. 102-03)

The boyhood evoked in these poems is tinged with violence . . . but not blotted out by it. (p. 103)

Family deaths, the persistence of old ghosts, hunting expeditions, potato diggings, and the normal preoccupations of a life in County Derry provide material for *Death of a Naturalist;* yet the loveliest poems in the book are those addressed to Marie Heaney, the poet's wife. **"Valediction"** sets the standard. . . . Not an ounce of fat detracts from the poem's swift statement and hard, clear edges. It is a minor classic. (pp. 103-04)

"Personal Helicon" concludes the book, and it is as good as anything Heaney has written since. It pulls into a single locus the varied themes of *Death of a Naturalist,* and it may be thought of as a poetic *credo,* a guide to this poet's personal iconography. Heaney's version of Helicon, the stream which ran from Parnassus and the source of inspiration to ancient poets, is the well on his farm. . . . The well of memory, with its slippery sides and musky odors, goes down "so deep you saw no reflection in it." Like a poem, it "gave back your own call / With a clean new music in it." This world of dangling roots and slime, of soft mulch and scary ferns, recalls the greenhouse poems of Theodore Roethke, with whom Heaney has much in common at this stage in his development. Here is concrete poetry with a vengeance, what Roethke called "that anguish of concreteness." (p. 105)

With *Door into the Dark* . . . , Heaney opens a new vein of subject matter and works his way slowly, at times painfully, toward the mature style fully realized in *North*. There is the expected carry-over from *Death of a Naturalist;* anything that good deserves carrying-over! The folksy, pastoral side begins to dwindle, although poems like **"The Outlaw"** . . . , **"The Thatcher,"** and **"The Wife's Tale"** are a fine addition to earlier poems like **"Churning Day"** and **"The Diviner."** Heaney's geniality, compassion, and impish wit run through these poems like a watermark. There is great precedence in British poetry for this kind of poem, of course, and this poet adds a few fresh lyrics to this tradition (which reaches back well beyond Wordsworth, who comes to mind as a master of this genre). Heaney is matched among his British/Irish contemporaries writing this kind of romantic-pastoral verse only by R. S. Thomas and George Mackay Brown. What interests me especially about *Door into the Dark* is Heaney's discovery of natural symbols in rural life—which gives his work a new resonance; also, I am intrigued by the sudden compression of style, the tough intellectual sinew flexed in phrase after phrase, and the laser-beam focus of his vision: the image is seared indelibly on the reader's mind.

Heaney pushes his style toward a spareness, an absence of rhetoric and normal syntactical connective tissue, which culminates in the granite style of *Wintering Out*. . . . The style [of *Door into the Dark*] recalls Hopkins, one of Heaney's dominant ancestors, with its heavy alliteration, "sprung" rhythm, and the tightly packed imagery. A tendency toward symbolism is also in evidence. . . . (pp. 105-06)

"Description is revelation"—a phrase from *North*—illumines the technique behind many of the poems in *Door into the Dark,* where each act of description becomes a repossession of experience. Often Heaney's tone, as in **"Girls Bathing, Galway 1965,"** is whimsical, using bathos as a common trope; but one finds a seriousness underlying even this light poem. (p. 107)

The remaining poems of *Door into the Dark* are closely autobiographical and anecdotal. . . . **"Elegy for a Stillborn Child"** stands out among these more personal poems for its startling analogies. . . . (p. 108)

The most important poem in the book, I believe, comes last. **"Bogland"** concludes *Door into the Dark* and lends additional meaning to the title, for the Irish bogs (which preserve generations of Irish civilization intact) may be thought of as openings into the dark of history. The theme of this poem is the literal repossession of the ground, a theme which becomes central in Heaney's next two books. . . . The suggestive possibilities of bogland seem unbounded, and Heaney knows this; but he refuses to go much beyond a literal representation until the last line: "The wet centre is bottomless." As a symbol of the unconscious past which must be unfolded, layer by layer, the bog image will prove indispensable. For this reason, **"Bogland"** is a watershed poem in the Heaney corpus. After it, one rereads all the poems coming before it with a new lens, realizing that this poet's vision of historical sequence reaches beyond the pastoral-folk tradition. The theme of digging, registered twice in *Death of a Naturalist* (potato digging, then), moves into a rich light now, acquiring new potency from the symbolic force of the bogland metaphor.

In *Wintering Out* . . . Heaney was quick to pick up the end note of *Door into the Dark* to mine the ore still locked inside this vein. Ireland's archaelogical sites yield poems like **"Bog Oak," "Anahorish,"** and **"Toome,"** and Heaney's research into Danish excavations results in **"The Tollund Man"** and **"Nerthus."** These poems exploit the metaphoric plunge backward through time tenaciously. As one delves in bogland, history peels away like the layers of an onion; one falls through shelves of civilizations often represented by odds and ends. . . . (pp. 109-10)

The poems in part 1 of this collection all reconstruct historical instances or offer a meditation on some fact of the lost past. **"Servant Boy,"** for example, draws a simple portrait of a lower-class child. . . . The poet clearly identifies with this "jobber among shadows." Placed where it is, in the sequence of bog poems, **"Servant Boy"** stands out as a reminder of Heaney's breadth of vision, his empathetic range. The poem recollects the old feud between invading noblemen and the indigenous servant classes; it helps to explain the present Irish conflict by pointing to centuries of accrued resentment. There is nothing overtly political about **"Servant Boy,"** of course. Heaney stays rather far away from engagement of this sort until *North;* but one senses the gathering storm. (p. 110)

Part 2 of *Wintering Out* moves away from the wide historical rummage of part 1 into the private arena of one man's life; I prefer the poems in this section on the whole, no doubt because they are less dense, less tortuously argued. (p. 112)

[*North*] represents this poet's latest repossession of history, of his tongue, of himself. There is a new directness here, indicated by the title; but Heaney loses none of the suggestive power of controlled ambiguity seen in earlier volumes. His "north" is not just Northern Ireland. The tone of the book rings like a struck anvil; it is stark, cold, brisk as the northerly themes and diction which suffuse these poems. The poet-as-*scop* (Old English minstrel) entertains us with our foibles, with the past (we identify with *his* past) reenacting itself on the native ground. The setting is specifically Irish, of course, but the subject matter obtains for all of us, in any country of the present. His theme, that love is what redeems the past and makes living possible in today's violent world, is set out in the two dedicatory poems, **"Sunlight"** and **"The Seed Cutters,"** both of which evoke the idyll of remembrance.

Once again, Heaney uses a two-part division, working in the same overall pattern used so effectively in *Wintering Out*. In the first part, beginning and ending with poems referring to Antaeus, the mythical giant whose strength derived from contact with the ground, Heaney investigates the burden of Irish history once more: the history of possession and repossession of the island by various tribes. The magnificent **"Belderg"** begins with another of the poet's bog poems. . . . I find these bog poems much more easily comprehensible, but not less dense or complex, than similar poems in *Wintering Out*. (pp. 116-17)

The majestic title poem **"North"** itself focuses on Viking invasions. . . . Here, the "ocean-deafened voices" of the past speak to him, explaining how "Thor's hammer swung / to geography and trade, / thick-witted couplings and revenges." The violence foisted upon man by man is rooted in economic necessity and irrational desires. The "longship's swimming tongue" says, "Lie down / in the word-hoard . . . compose in darkness." This Heaney does, consummately. (p. 117)

"Ocean's Love to Ireland" shifts to the Elizabethan colonial possession of Heaney's island, and its theme is summed up in the last line—my principal theme in this essay—"The ground possessed and repossessed." Heaney envisions the English-Irish relation in explicit sexual terms, making literal the metaphor of "possession." **"Act of Union,"** which follows shortly, pursues the analogy further, making the poet's beloved into "the heaving province where our past has grown." . . . A deeply plunging terror underlies this poem, one of Heaney's memorable achievements. The political implications suggest that no treaty will salve the wound inflicted by England on this "ruined maid" of Ireland. To quote William Empson, "It is the pain, it is the pain endures."

Pain, in all its sinister permutations, obsesses Heaney in part 2 of *North*. . . . [These poems] must be read *qua* poems, not political tracts. They register one sensitive man's response to an impossible historical situation, a country "where bad news is no longer news." . . . The pastoral element has disappeared; the pastoral whimsicality of some of the earlier work fades as the poet offers a stinging new version of reality, almost without comment save in the implicit irony of such lines as "Whatever you say, say nothing."

The last sequence of seven poems is called **"Singing School,"** a title summoning the ghost of Yeats; it's theme may be called the growth of the poet, "fostered alike by beauty and by fear." (pp. 119-20)

"Fosterage," the penultimate poem of this final sequence, pictures Heaney "with words / Imposing on my tongue like obols" (silver coins). Its grand first line, "Description is revelation," a quotation, could easily serve as an epigraph to Heaney's *oeuvre*. In his poems description gives way, continually, to evaluation, to revelation. The poet becomes seer, "a transparent eyeball" in Emerson's great phrase. He becomes everything and nothing, fixing his eye on the object, transforming it. "Fosterage" ends with a tribute to Hopkins, who sought the *inscape* of each object, who "discerned / The lineaments of patience everywhere." Hopkins, of course, continues as the dominant ancestor for Heaney, the source, the starting point of his own angle of vision. But "Fosterage" remains a preface to poetry, not the thing itself, a prelude to "Exposure," the last poem of "Singing School" and *North* as a whole.

"Exposure" is, again, a meditation of the poet's responsibility in a desperate historical moment. It is a poem about withdrawal, deeply autobiographical; for Heaney has himself in a sense withdrawn into Eire, the south. He lives, now, with his wife, Marie, and children in a stone house in Dublin, looking out to Joyce's fabled Martello tower from *Ulysses*. He is in his own tower of imagining there. "Exposure," being the last poem in a sequence tracing the growth of a poet, should be triumphal. That it lacks this note, for the most part, points not to the poet's failure but to a particular kind of success. Heaney's tower is not Yeats's. His escape is not into the artifice of eternity but into the recesses of his own solitude. . . . "How did I end up like this?" he wonders, thinking of "the anvil brains of some who hate me / As I sit weighing and weighing / My responsible *tristia*." A wonderful self-irony permeates "responsible" here as Heaney acknowledges the need for detachment and engagement at the same time. Yeats could manage this combination, of course; indeed, the cutting edge of his best poems can be described as the point where these seemingly incompatible realms touch. And Heaney's greatness in "Exposure" derives from a similar balance of conflicting needs. . . . Without independence and withdrawal, a poet's work becomes infected with the langauge of propaganda; but this independence depends, paradoxically, on an intimacy with his environment that has made Heaney Ireland's successor to Yeats.

"Ulster was British," Heaney writes in "Singing School," "but with no rights on / The English lyric." He claims for himself, now, the rights denied to his countrymen at an earlier date. He has turned aggressor, repossessing the ancient role of *scop*, and his poems have become, progressively, a private *reclamatio*—a protest—and a personal reclamation of a heritage buried under layers of earth and language. Heaney digs with his pen, exhuming a past which informs and enriches the present and which has designs upon the future. His delving in the philological soil has yielded a poetry of the first order already; indeed, Seamus Heaney is a major poet writing today at the height of his powers. (pp. 121-23)

> *Jay Parini, "Seamus Heaney: The Ground Possessed" (copyright, 1980, by Jay Parini), in* The Southern Review, *Vol. 16, No. 1, January, 1980, pp. 100-23.*

HAROLD BLOOM

I would not say that the Northern Ireland poet Seamus Heaney, at forty, has printed any single poem necessarily as fine as [Yeats's] "Adam's Curse", but the lyric called "**The Harvest Bow**" in *Field Work* may yet seem that strong against all of time's revenges. There are other poems in *Field Work* worthy of comparison to the Yeats of *In the Seven Woods* (1904), and it begins to seem not far-fetched to wonder how remarkable a poet Heaney may yet become, if he can continue the steady growth of an art as deliberate, as restrained, and yet as authoritative and universal as the poems of *Field Work*—his fifth and much his best volume in the thirteen years since his first book, *Death of a Naturalist*. . . .

That book, praised for its countryman's veracity and vividness of soil-sense, reads in retrospect as a kind of dark hymn of poetic incarnation, a sombre record of the transgression of having been a Clare-like changeling. Heaney's first poems hold implicit his central trope, *the vowel of earth,* and move in a cycle between the guilt of having forsaken spade for pen, and the redemption of poetic work: "I rhyme / To see myself, to set the darkness echoing". *Door into the Dark* . . . seems now, as it did to me a decade ago, mostly a repetition, albeit in a finer tone, and I remember putting the book aside with the sad reflection that Heaney was fixated in a rugged but minimalist lyrical art. I was mistaken, and should have read more carefully the book's last poem, "**Bogland**", where Heaney began to open both to the Irish, and to his own, abyss. . . .

Heaney was poised upon the verge of becoming a poet of the Northern Ireland Troubles, a role he now wisely seeks to evade, but in a morally rich sense of "evade". . . . [*Wintering Out*] seems stronger than it did seven years ago, when it began to change my mind about Heaney's importance. It is a book about nearing the journey's centre, and takes as its concern the poet's severe questioning of his own language, the English at once his own and not his own, since Heaney is of the Catholic Irish of Derry. Few books of poems brood so hard upon names, or touch so overtly upon particular words *as* words. No single poem stands out, even upon re-reading, for this is the last volume of Heaney's careful apprenticeship, as he works towards his deferred glory. *North* . . . begins that glory, a vital achievement by any standards. . . .

What emerges in *North*, and stands clear in *Field Work*, is the precursor proper, the middle Yeats, with whom the agon of the strong Irish poet must be fought, as much by Heaney in his maturity as it is by Kinsella, with the agony itself guaranteeing why Heaney and Kinsella are likely to become more memorable than Kavanagh and Clarke, among the Irish poets following Yeats. . . .

The enduring poems in *North* include the majestic title-piece, as well as "**Funeral Rites**", "**Kinship**", "**Whatever You Say Say Nothing**" and, best of all, the sequence of poetic incarnation with the Yeatsian title, "**Singing School**". . . .

The problem for Heaney as a poet henceforward is how not to drown in [the] blood-dimmed tide. His great precedent is the Yeats of "Meditations in Time of Civil War" and "Nineteen Hundred and Nineteen" and it cannot be said in *North* that this precedent is met, even in "**Whatever You Say Say Nothing**", where the exuberance of the language achieves a genuine phantasmagoria. But "**Singing School**", with its queerly appropriate mix of Wordsworth and Yeats, does even better, ending poem and book with a finely rueful self-accepting portrait of the poet, still waiting for the word that is his alone. . . .

That is true eloquence, but fortunately not the whole truth, as *Field Work* richly shows. Heaney is the poet of the vowel of earth, and not of any portentous comet. In *Field Work*, he has gone south, away from the Belfast violence. . . .

Like Emerson, Heaney has learnt that he has imprisoned thoughts of his own which only he can set free. No poem in *Field Work* is without its clear distinction, but I exercise here the critic's privilege of . . . [naming] those poems that move me most: **"Casualty"**, **"The Badgers"**, **"The Singer's House"**, the lovely sequence of ten **"Glanmore Sonnets"**, **"The Harvest Bow"** (Heaney's masterpiece so far), and the beautiful elegy **"In Memoriam Francis Ledwidge"**, for the Irish poet killed on the Western Front in 1917. All of these lyrics and meditations practise a rich negation, an art of excluded meanings, vowels of earth almost lost between guttural consonants of history. (p. 137)

To this critic, on the other side of the Atlantic, Heaney is joined now with Geoffrey Hill as a poet so severe and urgent that he compels the same attention as his strongest American contemporaries, and indeed as only the very strongest among them. (p. 138)

> Harold Bloom, *"The Voice of Kinship,"* in The Times Literary Supplement (© *Times Newspapers Ltd.* (London) 1980; reproduced from The Times Literary Supplement *by permission), No. 4011, February 8, 1980, pp. 137-38.*

A. ALVAREZ

Heaney has in abundance a gift which the English distrust in one another but expect of the Irish: a fine way with the language. What in Brendan Behan, for instance, was a brilliant, boozy gift of the gab is transformed by Heaney into rich and sonorous rhetoric. He is a man besotted with words and, like all lovers, he wants to display the beauties and range and subtleties of his beloved. Unlike most, however, he disciplines his passion, reining it in for better effect. It is an admirable procedure, although there are times when the urge to make a nice noise gets the better of him. . . .

It is something of a miracle for a poet writing at the latter end of the twentieth century to sound . . . Victorian without, at the same time, sounding merely pompous and secondhand. Heaney's skill in bringing off this difficult balancing act is, I suspect, the clue to his extraordinary popularity. The British have never taken easily or willingly to Modernism. . . . So they are comfortable with Heaney because he himself is comfortably in a recognizable tradition.

He is also a rural poet, born and brought up in the country and now wisely retired to it from the hurly-burly of literary life. . . .

Heaney's position in it, however, is far from countrified. He is an intensely literary writer: his poems on the Irish troubles sound like Yeats, his elegy on Lowell sounds like Lowell; he brings in heroes and heroines with beautiful names from Irish myth, and quotes Wyatt and Dante, whom he also "imitates," Lowell-fashion. There are, in fact, moments when his literariness turns into downright pedantry. (p. 16)

Heaney is not rural and sturdy and domestic, with his feet planted firmly in the Irish mud, but is instead an ornamentalist, a word collector, a connoisseur of fine language for its own sake.

The exception is *North,* his fourth and best book, which opened with an imposing sequence of poems linking the grim Irish present with its even grimmer past of Norse invasions and ancient feuding. The tone was appropriately stern, but also distanced, the language spare, as though stripped back to its Anglo-Saxon skeleton. For the space of these dozen and a half

poems Heaney seemed to have found a theme so absorbing that charm and rhetoric were irrelevant. The poems were as simple, demanding, and irreducible as the archaic trophies from the bog which they celebrated. And like an archaeologist, he pared away the extraneous matter and kept himself decently in the background.

That reticence and self-containment have largely gone from *Field Work.* He is back with the seductions of fine language, the verbal showman's charming sleights of hand. Consider, for example, the first stanza of **"Oysters,"** the opening poem of the book. . . . First there is a verbal discovery, "clacked," the right and precise word to set the scene; then a precise evocation of the seawater taste of the creatures, "My tongue was a filling estuary''; after that, Heaney takes off into graceful, expanding variations on the same theme. In other words, the poem does not advance into unknown territory, it circles elegantly around and around on itself until it ends where it began, with language. . . . This is a twentieth-century expression of a nineteenth-century preoccupation, old aestheticism and new linguistics, Gautier filtered through Barthes.

Heaney's real strength and originality are not, I think, in his flashy rhetorical pieces, or in the poems where he takes on the big themes that are unavoidable for a serious poet living in Northern Ireland. They are, instead, in modest, perfect little poems like **"Homecomings,"** or the short sequence which gives this book its title, or the closing stanzas of **"The Skunk."** . . . Heaney's originality [in **"The Skunk"**] lies in his aroused, free-floating sensuality which pushes at the language, mingling the other senses—smell, sound, touch, taste—in visual images. . . . When Heaney is at his best he maintains a tender, fruitful muddle between the body of the natural world and the body of his wife. It is beautifully done in a way perfected most recently by poets like Snodgrass and Wilbur: pure and expert and deliberately low-key. (pp. 16-17)

[Heaney's work] challenges no presuppositions, does not upset or scare, is mellifluous, craftsmanly, and often perfect within its chosen limits. In other words, it is beautiful minor poetry, like Philip Larkin's, though replacing his tetchy, bachelor gloom with something sweeter, more sensual, more open to the world—more, in a word, married.

It is, however, precisely these reassuring qualities which have been seized on by his champions as proof of the fact that in Heaney Britain has, at last, another major poet. This seems to me grossly disproportionate both to the fragility of the verse and also to Heaney's own modest intentions. After all, he does not often come on like Yeats reincarnated and much of his excellence depends on his knowing his own range and keeping rigorously to it, no more, no less. . . .

If Heaney really is the best we can do, then the whole troubled, exploratory thrust of modern poetry has been a diversion from the right true way. Eliot and his contemporaries, Lowell and his, Plath and hers had it all wrong: to try to make clearings of sense and discipline and style in the untamed, unfenced darkness was to mistake morbidity for inspiration. It was, in the end, mere melodrama, understandable perhaps in the Americans who lack a tradition in these matters, but inexcusable in the British.

These, as I understand them, are the implications of Heaney's abrupt elevation into the pantheon of British poetry. (p. 17)

> A. Alvarez, *"A Fine Way with the Language,"* in The New York Review of Books *(reprinted with permission from* The New York Review of Books;

copyright © 1980 Nyrev, Inc.), Vol. XXVII, No. 3, March 6, 1980, pp. 16-17.

SHAUN O'CONNELL

[Since Seamus Heaney] is a poet of sustained achievement and since his life has touched so many sides of Ireland—North-South, rural-urban, violent-pacific—he is contended for, like a valuable piece of land, by squads of contrary critics. The intensity of these critical responses suggests how much his poetry, as well as the political situation he sometimes describes, *affects*. (p. 3)

From his first poem, **"Digging,"** in his first book, ***Death of a Naturalist,*** Heaney pulled away from poetry of overt political purpose. . . . This, though, may have been a resolution more easily arrived at in 1966, before the resurgence of violence in the North. In any case, since then Heaney has sought more elaborate and remote imagery in which to implant his oblique commentaries, though at times he is willing, outside his poems, to decode his imagery in order to point up his thematic purposes. In 1979, for example, he contributed a revealing preface to a handsomely-illustrated edition of his **"Ugolino,"** the savage poem which concludes *Field Work;* Heaney makes his political-poetical purposes unmistakable when he explains that he was drawn to the material

> because I sensed there was something intimate, almost carnal, about these feuds and sorrows of mediaeval Pisa, something that could perhaps mesh with and house the equivalent and destructive energies at work in, say, contemporary Belfast.

As Heaney digs through time for apt tropes to mesh with matters of great and immediate moment, it is not clear that he is not using his spade as something of a weapon.

For all that, it is clear too that Heaney also feels personal distress at any overt political purposes to which his poetry might be put. . . .

Heaney's ambivalent attitude—his poetry both consumed and nurtured by the Troubles—is beautifully caught in the implications of his epigraph, from Yeats, for *Preoccupations* . . . and his later reflections upon it. In *Explorations* Yeats argued that *Cathleen ni Houlihan* was not written to affect opinion. If he had written it with an audience in mind "all would be oratorical and insincere." The poet, Yeats argues, can only move others by reaching into himself "because all life has the same root." . . .

[Heaney's] poems bear oblique paradoxical relation to the crisis in Northern Ireland. . . . [He] has politicized his imagery, as he has put it, in **"The Tollund Man,"** from *Wintering Out,* a poem in which an unearthed corpse from a Jutland bog made him feel both "unhappy and at home," made him feel an essential identity between old and new "man-killing parishes." There and in **"Whatever You Say Say Nothing,"** from *North,* Heaney speaks directly of the killing grounds of conflict in political imagery, but without evident partisanship. He would, then, dance near the edge of direct statement, yet pull back into enlarging metaphors, particularly those associated with bogs. . . .

Part of Heaney, it seems, wishes to retreat from political responsibility into the personal, yet another part of him wishes to move through the personal into realms of larger signifi-cance. . . . Thus *Field Work* is well-balanced between personal, even confessional poems, particularly the stately **"Glanmore Sonnets,"** in which the acts of union are computed in the algebra of private calculation, and those poems that cast a wider net, particularly **"Triptych,"** filled as it is with the comfortless noises of gunshot and helicopter. In **"The Strand at Lough Beg,"** a poem of mourning for his assassinated cousin, Heaney appears as a character, at once grieving relative and celebrating poet, washing the body clean with dew. Death is noted, shock and rage are registered, then all is incorporated, perhaps too easily, into the cleansing ceremony of elegy. Poetry replaces terror. . . .

Heaney invokes paradox when he attempts to make the poems in *Field Work* at once less political and more public, both more personal and more direct. Yet it is in the midst of these tensions that Heaney's poetry gains its force. . . . [The] Troubles provide Heaney with a frame of reference, another level of allusion, a field of tropes, all of which make his poetry tensely relevant, about something that hovers between the personal and the universal. The Troubles become a network of metaphors that lie behind and beyond even those poems that do not invoke the political situation.

All of this is evident in **"Oysters,"** the first poem in *Field Work*. . . .

Though **"Oysters"** is not directly about the Irish Troubles, it takes little imagination to connect the men who violate "lower" orders of being for their taste with the fierce power politics of Ireland. Still, here it is best left unsaid by the poet, who dramatizes a perception only incidentally Irish. As in his bog poetry, Heaney here has dug beneath the particular politics of the moment and unearthed a larger pattern of violation. (p. 4)

Those who see Seamus Heaney as a symbol of hope in a troubled land are not, of course, wrong to do so, though they may be missing much of the undercutting complexities of his poetry, the backwash of ironies which make him as bleak as he is bright. Those who see him as the darling of the undemanding critical establishment are not talking about all that goes on in his poetry. Furthermore, it seems a dangerous game— . . . to move too freely across the boundary lines between poetry and politics, between pure verb and impure propaganda. Heaney's best poetry swings between, combining clarity of statement with poised paradox: the imagery of shock which reaches under the divisions of the moment and stretches beyond. . . .

In *Preoccupations* he speaks of poetry as divination, "as a restoration of the culture to itself," though he wisely adds a characteristic qualification: "to forge a poem is one thing, to forge the uncreated conscience of the race, as Stephen Dedalus put it, is quite another and places daunting pressures and responsibilities on anyone who would risk the name of poet." The problem, perhaps, resides with those who read Heaney, readers who should be quite cautious about asking this poet to stand as a symbol of national unity. Neither the problems of Ireland nor the possibilities of poetry are well served by fusing the two. . . .

Still, a poet remains interesting for the risks he chooses to run. Heaney bears watching in part because he is a poet who will sustain tension: write for himself before his audience, yet also, as he has said of Yeats, "pay into the public life." A neat trick, a delicate balance. (p. 5)

Shaun O'Connell, "Seamus Heaney: Poetry and Power," in New Boston Review *(copyright 1980 by*

Boston Critic, Inc.), Vol. V, Nos. V & VI, August-September, 1980, pp. 3-5.

ANTHONY THWAITE

The first six pieces in [*Preoccupations: Selected Prose 1968-1978*], all quite short, form an untitled section on their own, though three are headed "**Mossbawn**" and three "**Belfast**". They are all, in the best sense, self-centred—informal circumstantial sketches of [Heaney's] upbringing in Co Derry, his childhood reading and absorption of "rhymes", his literary apprenticeship as an undergraduate at Queen's . . . , and a laconic Christmas 1971 message from the battlefront. . . .

One of Heaney's considerable gifts in these prose pieces is that he keeps a proper—and not mock-modest—commonsensical balance, whether he is talking about himself or other poets. . . .

The refinement and extension of Heaney's art, which reached its striven-for level in *North* . . . , goes hand-in-glove with his strong but delicate handling of other men's flowers. In *Preoccupations,* lectures and reviews show a generosity of spirit, and an acuteness of mind, which can see the best in such different recent poets as Ted Hughes, Geoffrey Hill, Philip Larkin, Theodore Roethke, Hugh MacDiarmid, Stevie Smith, Robert Lowell; among the Irish, Patrick Kavanagh, John Hewitt, John Montague, Paul Muldoon—as well as, presidingly and almost forbiddingly, Yeats; which can find as much nourishment, unobviously, in Wordsworth as in, obviously, Hopkins. In all these plumbings in prose, what is felt for is the nerve of the rhythm, the energy of the word, which, together, reach what Eliot . . . called "the auditory imagination". . . .

Although, on the face of it, many of the preoccupations of Heaney's prose may seem to be personal and/or Irish (and perhaps there is no need for the "and/or"), the most impressive single piece in the book is a long lecture called "**Englands of the Mind**", which takes three poets who "treat England as a region—or rather treat their region as England—in different and complementary ways": Hughes, Hill, and Larkin. Heaney's sensitive and sympathetic discussion of these three concentrates on their speech, their special language, in a way that has eluded most of their explicators and standardbearers. . . . What Heaney establishes is the way in which "their three separate voices are guaranteed by three separate foundations which, when combined, represent almost the total resources of the English language itself", and how these draw on distinct landscapes. . . . This essay is an altogether masterly analysis, precise in its convictions, of a kind that only a poet could achieve and only a specially gifted poet could communicate so effortlessly and scrupulously. . . .

Taken together (and taking the unrepresented *Field Work* into account too), . . . *Selected Poems* and *Preoccupations* show Heaney as all of a piece, a man in whom technique and craft (he makes his distinction between them in "**Feelings into Words**") have made a happy marriage. If he was overpraised for his early poems, as I think he was, he is now in danger of being cut down to size by those repelled by the lumbering tread of the symbolic exegetes and the over-attention of the elephantine misreaders. But he seems to me a man who knows his own mind and will not easily be deflected.

Anthony Thwaite, "The Hiding Places of Power," in The Times Literary Supplement *(© Times Newspapers Ltd. (London) 1980; reproduced from* The Times Literary Supplement *by permission), No. 4048, October 31, 1980, p. 1222.*

DAVID WRIGHT

[*Selected Poems 1965-1975*] is an impressive little book in that the poems have an obsidian polish and are obviously made to last; that some will, there is no doubt. They are documentary, rural poems shaped out of spare packed words, as if written by a staccato Edward Thomas. The best are pure lyrics like "**Anahorish**", "**The Given Note**", and "**A New Song**"; the least compelling are the ones whose intentions impose on the reader—the well-known bog poems for example. . . .

What has opened my eyes to Mr Heaney's quality is his prose, backhanded though the compliment may seem. . . . [The calibre of *Preoccupations*] is such as to establish Mr Heaney as that rarest of rare birds, a serious critic in the class of Yeats, Pound and Eliot. Like them he has the advantage (I would say the *sine qua non*) of being a practitioner of the art he examines. . . .

The difference between craft and technique, the importance of the speaking voice, sense of place, origins, lines of communication with the past, are among Mr Heaney's persistent preoccupations: and what he has to say about them is of the greatest value and appositeness.

David Wright, "A Poet's Prose," in The Times Educational Supplement *(© Times Newspapers Ltd. (London) 1980; reproduced from* The Times Educational Supplement *by permission), No. 3360, November 14, 1980, p. 20.*

ROBERT PINSKY

The strengths and limitations of poet-critics, as a class, seem to come from intensity of focus: They need to think about writing, about poetic composition. And any insight or idea in their criticism grows somehow from the complex, subterranean roots of concern with composition, and with the circumstances of composition. These collected lectures and reviews ["**Preoccupations**"] by the gifted Irish poet Seamus Heaney often explore those roots in exciting ways, dealing intimately with composition as an act of mind more profound than mere rhetoric, and showing how the circumstances of composition extend to the most urgent, painful historical questions.

The moments of such penetration come primarily, I find, when Mr. Heaney meditates on his personal and national past—Irish speech, landscape, history, poetry, and hereditary blood-struggles—touching and testing the links between them. The most moving piece in the book, the lecture "**Feeling Into Words**," confirms the idea that Mr. Heaney's vitality and seriousness rely in large measure upon a particular soil and its past. . . .

As a prose writer, Mr. Heaney has a nimble, elegant charm and the ability to rise suddenly, at his best, from conventional ideas to home truths. He manages to keep a little of the charm of thought even in the journeyman reviews included in "**Preoccupations.**" . . .

On the subject of poets close to him—Wordsworth, Hopkins, Mandelstam, Lowell, his own opposed tutelary geniuses Yeats and Patrick Kavanagh—Mr. Heaney writes with authority, persuasive intensity and learning. His ability to go into the texture of poetic language and figures of sound, and his speculations about the way a life and times inform a life's work, remind one that there is a taste to be satisfied by literary criticism. . . .

If any mannerisms mar the book here and there, the offending ones to my taste would be the tones of the literary journalist, not the university instructor. In the service of a convenient orotundity, for instance, he sprinkles little allusive tags into his sentences now and then with an effect I find mechanical. . . .

Such coasting makes the moments when Mr. Heaney's underlying alertness and seriousness come all the way into the foreground that much more stirring by contrast. If the solemn tag lines indicate that he is allowing himself an easy moment, comic charm can sometimes indicate that he is about to deal with crucial matters.

> Robert Pinsky, ''The Prose of an Irish Poet,'' in The New York Times Book Review (© 1980 by The New York Times Company; reprinted by permission), December 21, 1980, p. 4.

MARJORIE PERLOFF

[Of] the 10 essays in **Preoccupations** (there are also 11 short reviews), only one stands out: the Berkeley lecture (1976) called **"Englands of the Mind,"** in which Heaney discusses the ways in which sense of place functions as ''a confirmation of an identity which is threatened'' in the poetic language of Ted Hughes, Geoffrey Hill, and Philip Larkin. The distinctions drawn between Hughes' Anglo-Saxon, Hill's ''Anglo-Romanesque,'' and Larkin's ''English language . . . turned humanist'' and ''besomed clean of its inkhornisms and its irrational magics by the eighteenth century'' are both interesting and convincing. But when Heaney writes about his own childhood or about the poets who have meant most to him—Wordsworth, Hopkins, Yeats—he is given to commonplaces. . . .

[And] Heaney's statements of poetics, whether his own or that of others, are curiously bland. . . .

There is not a statement here with which anyone would want to take issue for these are, after all, classroom pieties. What is missing is a particular point of view, an individual perspective, at least one if not 13 ways of looking at a blackbird. . . . [It] is hard to remember what Heaney says about Yeats, for his Yeats, the dreamer turned practical man turned visionary, is a familiar textbook figure. (p. 5)

It is [his] inclination to speechify rather than to engage his subject directly that makes even such celebrated Heaney poems as **"The Bog People"** and **"The Grauballe Man"** a case of what Calvin Bedient calls ''deliberate myth-making, not the stab of astonishment'' [see excerpt above]. Even **"The Harvest Knot,"** which Bloom praises so extravagantly, [see excerpt above] is almost spoiled by the reference to the love-knot made of straw as a ''knowable corona,'' an epithet that almost gives the poet's game away. Perhaps the problem is that, as the prose pieces suggest, Heaney doesn't really trust his emotions or his intellect, that he doubts repeatedly whether his own particular response to things is significant. Having been cast by friendly critics in the role of ''the greatest Irish poet since Yeats,'' as the spokesman of decency and good sense in a world torn by the violence of the Ulster war, Heaney seems to have withdrawn into a realm of easy solutions. (p. 11)

> Marjorie Perloff, ''Seamus Heaney: Peat, Politics and Poetry,'' in Book World—The Washington Post (© 1981, The Washington Post), January 25, 1981, pp. 5, 11.

RODNEY RYBUS

[The essays in **Preoccupations**] are freely admitted to be occasional pieces brought about by the life of a freelance writer rather than an academic critic, and none at all the worse for that, though I think that on balance they do throw more light on Heaney's own poetry than others'. Sometimes the writing wears its public responsibility too heavily, the language becoming orotund or tortuous. . . . Heaney must be as widely read and respected now as any living writer of poetry in English . . . in this country [England], perhaps because the detailed and sensuously vivid evocation of rural Ireland and childhood has appealed to urban poetry-readers on account of its 'distance': pastorally attractive but largely unchallenging. While Heaney is rightly cautious of turning Irish-English contentions and writing into a 'spectator sport', he has shown in **North** and **Field Work** . . . a desire to engage more directly with Ulster's contemporary pain. . . . What is clear from his verse and prose is that of all the Irish poets now writing [Heaney] has most actively and consistently worked to forge a new voice for Irish poetry, worked with a Yeatsian intensity for it. That doesn't mean that he is a similar kind of poet or that he is 'the best poet since W. B. Yeats': no poet at Heaney's time of life should be saddled with that kind of public approbation. . . . It undervalues the considerable virtues of poets like Montague, Murphy, Mahon and Longley, and makes it no easier, surely, for Heaney himself to find his 'befitting emblems of adversity'. (pp. 77-8)

> Rodney Rybus, ''Matters of Ireland: Recent Irish Poetry,'' in Stand (copyright © by Stand), Vol. 22, No. 3, (1981), pp. 72-8.*

W. S. DI PIERO

[Heaney's] work, poetry and prose alike, is rooted in the need to penetrate, claim, and express the rough exigencies of history. He seeks coherence and continuity. **"Digging,"** the opening poem in **Death of a Naturalist** . . . and the initial poem in [**Poems: 1965-1975**], announces the work that will follow. Writing by a window, the poet hears the ''clean rasping sound'' of his father digging turf, and in that sound hears his grandfather's work before him. Digging becomes at once a signal of origins and legacies and a sounding of Heaney's own poetic ambitions. He has ''no spade to follow men like them,'' so he will dig instead with his pen. . . . The metaphor is meant to articulate the method by which the poet will carry on, while at the same time departing from, the family tradition. Although the fancy may be somewhat strained and self-important, Heaney's intention is clear enough: he wants connections, continuities, and historical justification for his art.

In one essential particular the truth of the metaphor is redeemed, for in many of his poems Heaney does dig with his pen, excavating, unearthing histories of families, country, and self. But in the poem's opening lines, he also describes the feel of the pen in his hand as ''snug as a gun.'' The figure is at first glance rather impressive, and its apparent authority is boosted by the clicking backward rhyme; but what has this terrorist image to do with agriculture, archaeology, or intellectual exertion of any sort? I question the integrity of this core metaphor because it prefigures a larger problem in Heaney's work. . . . [It] must be said that his ambition, which is in almost every way admirable and pure, does on occasion lead him to will connections by virtue of overwrought metaphor, leading him into good writing which is not always good poetry.

The danger for someone of Heaney's abundant talent is that his aspiration will spiral his work away from integral metaphoric truth. But when the two, aspiration and metaphoric truth, are unified, the poetry is exact, deliberate, and natural, as in **"At a Potato Digging."** . . . This poem is an extraordinary meditation on natural dependencies, Irish sorrow, the body as bearer of history, the legacies of deprivation and blight. The language has the gritty sonority one hears in Dante. . . . (pp. 558-59)

A poet often writes prose to articulate an investigative technique or explanatory procedure, by which his intended discovery, probably initially intuited, may be claimed and justified. An exhibition of need and will, it's also an act of self-declaration. The essays in **Preoccupations** demonstrate Heaney's aspirations, his awareness of his own position in the larger poetic tradition, and an account of those patterns of exploration which comprise the nervous system of his verse. Heaney is almost obsessively concerned with what we might call the natural history of language, its origins, morphologies, homologies. Whatever the occasion—childhood, farm life, politics and culture in Northern Ireland, other poets past and present—Heaney strikes time and again at the taproot of language, examining its genetic structures, trying to discover how it has served, in all its changes, as a culture bearer, a world to contain imaginations, at once a rhetorical weapon and nutriment of spirit. He writes of these matters with rare discrimination and resourcefulness, and a winning impatience with the received wisdom. . . .

Heaney's essays are studded with reiterated phrases and notions, but such repetition is less a sign of indolence than of a coherent and strong-willed intellect testing, tuning, and revising its themes. (p. 560)

At every point, Heaney shows himself a discriminating and intense diagnostician of the poetic tradition. He brilliantly explains the way in which poetry issues from the roughly shaped, vaguely stirring beginnings in intuition and compulsion. He draws firm distinctions between his predecessors, clarifying that diversity (and divisiveness) which gives such quarrelsome vitality to poetic tradition. . . .

The most crucial distinction Heaney makes regarding the writing of poetry is that between craft [and technique]. . . . (p. 561)

North, the last volume collected in **Poems: 1965-1975,** suffers from the dominion of craft over technique. The territory, as in all of Heaney's books, is clearly demarcated. **North** is in large part an anthology of death chants, songs of bones and boglands, anatomizations of the body of language and history, another dig into the geological strata of culture, its residues, seepages, signs. A number of the poems, however, like the early **"Digging,"** demonstrate the triumph of rhetoric over theme, of mere good writing over investigative vision. . . . Poems like **"Bog Queen," "The Grauballe Man,"** and **"Kinship,"** which at first shine forth with the sort of writing that one might praise for its ingenuity and intensity, are finally so clenched, or so overwrought in metaphor, that they inevitably become little more than a stage on which the poet performs. When style comes unstuck from feeling, subject matter dissociated from thematic explorations, the result is the kind of poem that bullies the reader into admiration. (pp. 561-62)

I'm not suggesting that Seamus Heaney is going stale, or that his inspiration is failing, or that he is writing too much. I do, however, feel obliged to say that at this point in his work, now that the public office has imposed itself upon the private, and now that **Field Work** has shown that he still has not resolved what seem to me major questions of craft and vision (questions appropriately asked only of a poet of unmistakably major talent), he may now need to be more vigilant than ever. (p. 562)

W. S. Di Piero, "Digs," in The American Scholar *(copyright © 1981 by the United Chapters of Phi Beta Kappa; reprinted by permission of the publishers), Vol. 50, No. 4, Autumn, 1981, pp. 558-62.*

Carolyn G(old) Heilbrun

1926-

(Also writes under the pseudonym Amanda Cross) American novelist, critic, and biographer.

Heilbrun has a double identity as an author. She is a professor of English who examines feminist issues, often relating them to literature in her scholarly works and she is Amanda Cross, a creator of detective stories that also show her awareness of literary matters and sexual politics.

In her scholarly *Towards a Recognition of Androgyny* and *Reinventing Womanhood*, Heilbrun argues against sexual polarization, questions theories of criticism that she feels were influenced by cultural bias, and offers inspiration to women struggling for success in the modern world.

The action of her mystery novels is usually built around literature such as the seminar on Antigone featured in *Theban Mysteries* and the James Joyce correspondence of *The James Joyce Murder*. Kate Fansler, the amateur sleuth in these stories is a professor like Heilbrun herself.

(See also *Contemporary Authors*, Vols. 45-48 and *Contemporary Authors New Revision Series*, Vol. 1.)

RICHARD HOGGART

[*The Garnett Family*] has some respectable qualities: it is clearly written and commonsensically planned; it is almost entirely free from those intrusions of the author's personality which mar many social biographies; it is not wrested into a strange shape so as to body out a proud thesis. Miss Heilbrun has pursued her facts patiently and, so far as I can judge, scrupulously; her book can hardly help being very interesting.

For all that, it is a slight book and lacks the texture its subject demands. It is difficult to understand how anyone could have gathered so many interesting details without being driven to attempt wider, deeper and more intricate connections. . . .

The individualist aesthetic, the intense personal responsibility, the sometimes arrogant anti-vulgarity, the reaction from bourgeois conventionalism—all are parts of that complex of attitudes which a book about the Garnetts should not fail to examine. Unfortunately, Miss Heilbrun does little more than make us realise that this is indeed what *should* be done.

> *Richard Hoggart, "Chosen Tasks," in* New Statesman *(©1961 The Statesman & Nation Publishing Co. Ltd.), Vol. LXII, No. 1582, July 7, 1961, p. 22.*

MELVIN J. FRIEDMAN

Amanda Cross, a skilled detective story writer, has given us a lighter side of ["Joyceana"] in her *The James Joyce Murder*. She has kept pace with the Joyce "industry" and has given us a series of quite plausible events leading to a murder and its curious aftermath. . . .

Each chapter is ingeniously titled after a story from *Dubliners*. Amanda Cross manages this with a minimum of awkwardness. She must stretch a bit to call a Berkshire town "Araby" and

to arrange for a full-scale discussion of "Ivy Day in the Committee Room" to justify the titles of two chapters. Yet she is so at home with Joyce lore and scholarship that everything proceeds with great fluency and ease.

I suspect that Amanda Cross is intimately in touch with the latest developments in fiction, especially with the post-Joycean antics of the *nouveau roman*. *The James Joyce Murder* strikes me as being very close at times to certain procedures of Alain Robbe-Grillet, Nathalie Sarraute, and Michel Butor. There is something gently mock-detective about it, in the best tradition of these French contemporaries and also of the Truman Capote of *In Cold Blood*, the William Styron of *Set This House on Fire*, and the Colin Wilson of *Ritual in the Dark*. Even though Amanda Cross' murderer is apprehended in the end, there are many false starts and stops, there are detectives who are more expert at literary criticism than solving crimes, and other mock-ingredients. . . .

Amanda Cross has a fine ear for academic conversation. She does occasionally overdo it. There is too much "hash-joint-cum-bar," "buddy-cum-tutor," and "cleaning woman-cum-cook;" even academics do not talk this way. But generally the dialogue is convincing.

The James Joyce Murder is a very intriguing book. It is a superior mystery and at the same time manages to say interesting things about the literary mentality. It is, furthermore, a tribute to the importance of Joyce study in this country and deserves a position among a select list of Joyce criticism—despite its fictional nature.

> *Melvin J. Friedman, "Book Reviews: 'The James Joyce Murder'," in* The Modern Language Journal, *Vol. LI, No. 6, October, 1967, p. 373.*

NEWGATE CALLENDAR

Amanda Cross in recent years has been attracting attention with her Kate Fansler stories and the latest is **"The Theban Mysteries."** . . . Again the action is built around literature, in this case a seminar on "Antigone." There is something of the Elizabeth Daly quality about the literate, low-keyed, sophisticated writing. There is no great drama in this story of an expensive girls' school in New York. But we get a study of rebellious youth, and even a few insights into the relevance of Sophocles to our time.

As novels go, **"The Theban Mysteries"** is gentle. And it is thoughtful.

> *Newgate Callendar, "Criminals at Large: 'The Theban Mysteries'," in* The New York Times Book Review *(© 1971 by The New York Times Company; reprinted by permission), October 31, 1971, p. 30.*

JOYCE CAROL OATES

To Carolyn Heilbrun . . . the very salvation of our species depends upon our "recognition of androgyny" as a conscious ideal; her book [*Toward a Recognition of Androgyny*] is a frank, passionate plea for us to move "away from sexual polarization and the prison of gender toward a world in which individual roles and modes of personal behavior can be freely chosen." Though she has constructed a critical-scholarly study to support her argument—she moves with dizzying rapidity from Homer to Joan Didion in 189 pages—the essence of her book is this imperative. . . .

Heilbrun's is an interesting, lively, and valuable general introduction to a new way of perceiving our Western cultural tradition, with emphasis upon English literature from Clarissa Harlowe to Clarissa Dalloway. Fired by a passionate need to express her belief in the imminent doom of our species *unless* we move toward an androgynous ideal, she has done a fantastic amount of reading: She attempts a re-evaluation of the role of woman in practically everything ever written, Greek literature, the Bible, the epic, the romance, the plays of Shakespeare ("a genius as devoted to the androgynous ideal as anyone who has ever written"), and, of course, Richardson, Ibsen, James, Austen, Dickens, the Brontës, George Eliot, Lawrence.

It was a heroic undertaking and, having herself admitted that she was not entirely suited for the task, lacking much knowledge of history or language, she is certainly not to be blamed for having produced a sketchy book. The section on the Bloomsbury Group is most rewarding, because Heilbrun is convinced that Woolf and her friends were the first people to actually attempt, in daily life, the androgynous ideal.

We keep returning to that word, and we never know exactly what it means. Sometimes it means simply sexless, sometimes bisexual; sometimes it means (in the case of the novel) a work in which "the reader identifies with the male and female characters equally; in feminist novels only with the female hero." Sometimes it means simply a synthesis of Taoist opposites of activity/passivity, Yin/Yang, rationality, intuitions—which no sane person would quarrel with. Who is the admitted enemy of equilibrium in individual and society?

Unfortunately, when sexual politics enter literary criticism, and when unique works of art—"Women in Love," for instance—are to be put on trial, ransacked for stray sentences that appear to be chauvinistic, it is easy to lose one's equilibrium. Heilbrun has done an excellent job in avoiding the excesses of anti-Lawrentian feminist criticism, and her detailed analysis of "The Rainbow" is a sympathetic one, since Ursula answers the demands of a currently fashionable ethic (that a woman be "emancipated"—and that the esthetic beauty of the novel she happens to be portrayed in is simply a secondary consideration). Yet even Heilbrun is so biased against Lawrence generally as to fail to recognize that "Women in Love" is exactly the androgynous-ideal novel she might have praised. (p. 7)

It is puzzling that Heilbrun totally neglects a number of very important contemporary novelists who would have supported her thesis and who have written near-masterpieces. What of Sarah in John Fowles's "The French Lieutenant's Woman," what of Martha Quest in Doris Lessing's "Children of Violence" series? What about Iris Murdoch, who has attempted to deal with androgyny in book after book? The young English novelist, Margaret Drabble, has written a number of important novels of this type, but she is not even mentioned. Heilbrun spends far too much time with Clarissa and Lovelace at the expense of Mary McCarthy, Katherine Anne Porter, Eudora Welty, Carson McCullers, Flannery O'Connor (*there* was a fierce imagination) and others. Malamud's "Pictures of Fi-

delman" attempts a bisexual-androgynous ideal but it is not mentioned either. Heilbrun concludes her study by saying that she is confident that "great androgynous works will soon be written"; she might more accurately have said *greater*. (pp. 7, 10)

Joyce Carol Oates, "An Imperative to Escape the Prison of Gender," in The New York Times Book Review *(© 1973 by The New York Times Company; reprinted by permission), April 15, 1973, pp. 7, 10, 12.**

THE YALE REVIEW

[*Toward a Recognition of Androgyny*] has three parts: the first, "The Hidden River of Androgyny," catalogues random appearances of androgyny in literature from Homer onward; the second examines the emergence of female central characters in the novel; the third presents Bloomsbury as real-life exemplar of "an androgynous world." (p. viii)

Unfortunately, Heilbrun's book is so poorly researched that it may disgrace the subject in the eyes of serious scholars. . . . . "The hidden river of androgyny" is a mistaken metaphor: there is no determining link between earlier and later literary appearances of the androgyne, not in the sense that one could, for example, rightly speak of a "hidden river" of astrological and alchemical lore passing from antiquity to the present. The history of the androgyne is instead one of continually rediscovered perceptions originating in the psyche.

From the work of Jane Harrison, Heilbrun selects that great scholar's one error: her belief in a primeval Mediterranean matriarchy. . . . [This] myth, for which there is not a shred of evidence, is fast becoming the new barbarism of the women's movement. Heilbrun therefore pointlessly belabors male-centered, nastily warmongering Western civilization for its departure from "the lost androgynous ideal" of a nonexistent matriarchal age.

Her definition of androgyny is so idiosyncratic as to be nearly useless. Indeed, her terminology shifts fuzzily from page to page: sometimes androgyny is "the equality of the masculine and feminine impulses"; more often it is "the recognition of the feminine principle as central." In order to exalt the feminine principle over the masculine, she is determined to make the androgyne an anti-war symbol, all love, peace, and brotherhood, thus obfuscating the way literature has, in the overwhelming majority of cases, actually used the image. More importantly, this tiresome perpetual talk of "forgiveness and redemption" is post-Christian platitudinizing, grotesquely inappropriate to the Greek sensibility, which is closer to the Mafia code than to the New Testament. Heilbrun's theory can do nothing with the savage Artemis—or, for that matter, with Shakespeare's Cleopatra, whom she does not even mention, occupied as she is with patching together a trivial *Hamlet*.

One would never know from this book that the androgyne is far more often perversely diabolical than sunnily utopian. Heilbrun does not dare mention the decadent androgynes of the Roman Empire or late nineteenth century (or even negative examples from the Renaissance), because they seem to support the conventional view of a fusion of the sexes as neurotic. Having applied no powers of analysis to her subject, she sees only one androgynous type. In point of fact, there are at least ten major categories of the androgyne; cutting across in another direction there is a further division into two primary formal modes. Of all this abundance, Heilbrun's peaceable androgyne is a minuscule, and banal, minority.

She shrinks from pushing her theory to its necessary conclusion: surely if men may elect passivity, women may elect bloody-mindedness. But this is a book with a muddled, naively sentimental view of human nature: for Heilbrun "the hideous strictures" of society keep us from doing our own thing. There is not the slightest consideration of the rival claims of order, stability, and social coherence; no sense that multiplicity of role might be anarchic; no allusion to aggression or to the hormonal basis of behavior. In extending Bloomsbury as an androgynous model, she fails to weigh whether absolute fluidity of sexual identity might not be the prerogative of a moneyed elite, at the expense of a vast laboring middle class. Everywhere, her error lies in making facile projections into actual life of a symbol that is principally an imaginative construction. (pp. viii, x)

> *"Reader's Guide: 'Toward a Recognition of Androgyny'," in* The Yale Review *(© 1973 by Yale University; reprinted by permission of the editors), Vol. LXII, No. 4, Summer, 1973, pp. viii, x.*

NEWGATE CALLENDAR

Amanda Cross writes mystery stories featuring a college professor (of English) named Kate Fansler. The dialogue in her books is supercivilized, in the drawing-room tradition, with long, resounding periods. . . .

Amanda Cross knows her Wilde and Shaw, and fine models they are for any writer. But the trouble with **"The Question of Max"** is that it wears this kind of Beautiful Writing like a great purple badge. Most of the Cross characters tend to talk this way; and since the author, after all, is not up to Wildean or Shavian flights, the result can be interminably dull, not to say pretentious.

Like most of the Cross books, **"The Question of Max"** takes plenty of time in its presentation. It is about lady authors, a quiet murder, a quiet solution and a traditional final confrontation in which the killer faces Professor Fansler with evil intent. And she is all alone. There is a subsidiary plot about cheating on college boards; but this, of course, is tied up with the main mystery. This book is for specialized tastes.

> *Newgate Callendar, "Criminals at Large: 'The Question of Max'," in* The New York Times Book Review *(© 1976 by The New York Times Company; reprinted by permission), October 3, 1976, p. 36.*

MARGO JEFFERSON

[Carolyn Heilbrun] is no different from any number of women who became feminists by joining private feelings to a set of political and philosophical principles that have been extant and evolving for—well, let us take Mary Wollstonecraft as a starting point—nearly two centuries. [The] unsettling practice of draping an oft-stated notion or simple observation in the garments of radical originality pervades [**"Reinventing Womanhood"**].

Mrs. Heilbrun . . . believes that few women imagine themselves powerful or independent; those who do (succeeding thereby in male-dominated professions) sacrifice their female identity. . . . [Mrs. Heilbrun writes: "Women must learn to appropriate for their own use the examples of human autonomy

and self-fulfillment displayed to us by the male world."] This is close to what she called the androgynous ideal in her last book, **"Toward a Recognition of Androgyny."** There, she used literature to illustrate her point; here she travels "a winding path between life and literature, refusing to separate them, to confine myself, as a woman, to one or the other."

Life and literature are shortchanged, whether Mrs. Heilbrun is considering the social forces that shape achieving women, the need for female bonding or the case for restructuring the family. Take the complexities raised in the chapter "Woman as Outsider." Feminism, she says, cannot be sustained unless a woman has some other consciousness of being an outsider—based, for example, on religion, race or class. But though she describes the contradictions of her own Jewish heritage—the feeling of being oppressed by the culture's anti-Semitism and by Judaism's partiarchy—the ground between autobiography and theory remains uncharted. She explains that she has this consciousness; regrets that many others, Jewish and gentile, have not; and there the matter rather smugly rests.

A discussion of Lionel Trilling, with whom Professor Heilbrun taught at Columbia, proposes to "question the masculine values" of his work, then settles for advocating that these values be considered feminine as well and left intact. Surely, if "women were beyond consideration of his general statements about moral ideas," then it is the substance of these statements, not merely their application, that should be questioned. By contrast, the substance of the *Oresteia* is virtually discarded in her dubious reinterpretation: large portions of the text must be ignored to see Orestes as a symbolic daughter who, in killing Clytemnestra, destroys institutionalized motherhood and establishes "a political situation in which power is vested in neither sex."

Mrs. Heilbrun chastises women novelists severely for failing to create "autonomous" women characters, while ignoring Colette, Dorothy Richardson, Virginia Woolf, Christina Stead and Doris Lessing among others. It is women poets, she claims, who have found the "lyrical voice for their own sense of themselves, for their anger, their particular isolation"; George Eliot, the Brontës and Jane Austen are accused of having written novels to avoid confronting this sense. No, Professor Heilbrun does not reinvent; she falsifies and reduces. (pp. 7, 31)

> *Margo Jefferson, "The Lives of Women," in* The New York Times Book Review *(© 1979 by The New York Times Company; reprinted by permission), May 13, 1979, pp. 7, 31.**

SARA RUDDICK

[In *Reinventing Womanhood*] Heilbrun is angry at her colleagues' refusal to help those women who struggle to change male thought and institutions in a serious way. Recognizing their pain and anxiety, she nonetheless urges them to remain outsiders rather than scurrying for a safe place at the male center, to "bond with the powerless against those in power." . . . Yet angry as she is, Heilbrun respects the sheer fact of female achievement and studies the lives of distinguished women in order to identify the conditions of their success. . . .

Heilbrun urges all women, whether or not they count themselves achievers, to admit their own and other women's pain. A woman-identified, raised consciousness is necessary for the "reinvention of womanhood" that Heilbrun envisions. The courage to seek this consciousness without self-deception or denial is a necessary step to independent strength and collective action. But this first step leads only to despair unless we imagine ourselves as protagonists, adventurers in our own life stories. . . .

Heilbrun recognizes a new kind of heroine, independent and brave, in the work of some contemporary feminist novelists and poets, especially Adrienne Rich, the central moral presence in this book. However, Heilbrun's examination of literature and biography concludes that female protagonists and heroines, past and present, are not enough. We women must claim men's inspiration, adopt for ourselves male models of achievement, take upon ourselves male quests and desires, for the male past "is the only past we have." . . . (p. 550)

Summarizing Heilbrun's arguments does not do justice to her wide-ranging literary erudition, to the wit of her examples, or to her compelling personal style. Her choice of writing autobiographically, she tells us, was a difficult and deliberate one. By refusing to separate personal history from impersonal truth she engages us fully in her work, and we understand its particular origins in her life.

Heilbrun's account of her relationship with Lionel Trilling, whose work she honors, is harrowing. . . . Though Heilbrun imagined that she might some day "engage in dialogue" with him—"the ponderous phrase explains exactly what I aspired to" . . .—in reality they barely spoke. Such brave and personal accounts of psychological abuse are worth chapters of impersonal analysis of women's difficulties with mentors. Only Trilling's death freed Heilbrun to adapt his work as best she could for herself and other women.

As Heilbrun knows, she is often at odds with feminists and their recent work. At several points I include myself among them. . . . Our difference lies in our relative evaluation of male and female as those terms are conventionally understood. Heilbrun tends to undervalue women's past and present endeavors. At the same time, she accepts too uncritically concepts of achievement and adventure which are both male and privileged.

Heilbrun seems to me to underestimate the intellectual, emotional, and sexual support women give each other. In her search through the lives of achievers, she fails to note the importance of female love to the development of autonomous strength, even when, as in the case of Gertrude Stein, the omission is striking. She rightly decries the failure of many women to ally with each other, but does not say that throughout history, and especially now, women are engaging in intense emotional and sometimes sexual comradeship. (pp. 551-52)

The reinvention of womanhood is a cooperative endeavor. The issues of feminism are complex and profound, they cut to the bone of our sexual, domestic, and public lives. We cannot afford narrow partisanship or the luxury of magnifying small differences. Heilbrun's book has neither of these defects. It is written with an openness and generosity that invites disagreement as well as assent. *Reinventing Womanhood* is a challenging gift: Heilbrun's questions are central, her answers sensitive and intelligent. She writes out of a commitment to *women* with a compassion and courage we would do well to emulate. (p. 553)

> *Sara Ruddick, in her review of "Reinventing Womanhood," in* Harvard Educational Review *(copyright © 1979 by President and Fellows of Harvard College), Vol. 49, No. 4, November, 1979, pp. 549-53.*

J. M. PURCELL

[There are a few] structural limitations or "faults" which amateurize the Cross books a little. . . . (p. 37)

To begin with her dialogue, which is more important in Cross than for another style of writer: Cross adopts the technical convention that each important *speaker*—as opposed to "character"—shares the same conversational style; by implication, the same background. . . .

This dialogue convention is adopted unconsciously by very bad writers because of course bad writers are tone deaf, employ limited vocabularies, etc.: these are all weaknesses not applying to Amanda Cross. On the other hand, one reason bad writers, including bad mystery writers, are bad, is that they are morally stupid and therefore assume that everybody else "really" agrees with them except those who "pretend" to disagree. To this last vice, I think Cross becomes a little more susceptible.

Her dialogue convention—which is also used by Henry James, "witty" playwrights, and nearly all narrative poets—receives its most interesting modern use in the William Haggard spy thrillers. . . . This conversational device is artistically more successful with Haggard than with Cross, because any reader of a book is grateful and noncritical when the minor characters are able and willing to communicate in shorthand.

By contrast, Cross's characters (and those of her main influence, Sayers) labor to convince us that they are educated, while at the same time not quite concealing the fact that they don't really trust us, the readers, to catch too elliptic allusions or references. . . .

Complaint No. 2 about Cross is more seriously derogatory of her novels as purist mysteries than my technical point about dialogue. . . . This is the complaint that, beneath a veneer of educated allusion, the Cross mysteries are fairly simpleminded, considered as mysteries. The special technical characteristic of the purist detective story is, after all, the play of appearance and of illusion in social relationships. . . .

[However] "sophisticated" her admirers and reviewers find Cross, her books are *naif* in the sense that the seemingly "bad" (disapproved) characters stay "bad" and the seemingly "good" (approved) people stay "good"—just like with Mickey Spillane or Nancy Drew. Cross is so simplistic with this important matter of mystery-characterization that the first-time reader of one of her books must often be double-bluffed, the way Christie did it deliberately in her *Mysterious Affair at Styles*. Perhaps Cross's most incredible gaffe, by purist-mystery rules, occurs in her debut: *In the Last Analysis*. . . . Herein a nightmare identifies one particular character as a serious suspect, and by God he turns out the murderer!

Another technical difficulty concerns Cross not individually but representatively, in terms of the closed-society, upper-crust; comfortable-people style of book she and Sayers-Innes-Christie all write. (p. 38)

[One] cannot pretend Cross is an isolated offender, though *Poetic Justice* could, both in mainstream and in mystery terms, have been her best book because she had the fascinating idea of attempting herein to turn her distinguished colleague and apparent friend, Lionel Trilling, into a mystery villain.

Not only, as readers of *Justice* know, does Cross "cheat" by making the homicide in *Justice* accidental, the result of a stupid practical joke: not only does she back away from turning "Trilling" into a killer but, more seriously (and unlike C. P. Snow) she also fails to invent for her fictional "Trilling" a criminal act or moral offense that will articulate whatever serious criticism she is making of him. (The question is not whether the real-life Trilling, contrary to his public image, played practical jokes.) The point is that, under the sophisticated Cross veneer, we once again find some taint of amateurism in bread-and-butter matters of plot and theme. (pp. 38-9)

Cross is generally treated by the reviewers as a "satiric" comic writer. However, she never satirizes the characteristic most commonly observed by educated writers who study our intellectual community: its tendency to indulge in cant, or to think, speak and write in a truistic terminology borrowed from each other. Indeed, most imaginative writers with talent who do books about the American intellectual find themselves *obliged* to write parodies. Already in the 1930's, Sig Perelman was a more accurate observer than Dos Passos or the early O'Hara because of his parodic talents. And later students of our clerisy—from Mary McCarthy to Tom Wolfe—have made careers out of quoting and citing intellectual cant. (p. 39)

"Amanda Cross"—created Michelangelically by Professor Heilbrun and given leave to produce Kate Fansler and Kate's whole "secondary" world—enjoys herself by putting her view of the U.S. into print, writing off the top of her head to some extent, faking at times on matters of theme and structure, and never seriously attempting the more disturbing world of illusion and betrayal that we find in the structurally skilled mystery novel. (p. 40)

> J. M. Purcell, "The 'Amanda Cross' Case: Sociologizing the U.S. Academic Mystery," in The Armchair Detective (copyright © 1980 by The Armchair Detective), Vol. 13, No. 1, Winter, 1980, pp. 36-40.

JEAN M. WHITE

Murder doesn't have to be a dreadful, dreary business, at least when it occurs in the pages of fiction. It can be told in a civilized, witty, and learned fashion with an observant eye on society's pretensions and pomposities. And no one has a sharper eye than Amanda Cross, whose delightful Kate Fansler, professor-cum-sleuth, returns to find *Death in a Tenured Position*. . . .

One of Kate's former classmates has been appointed to the Harvard University faculty as its first woman English professor in a tenured post. Janet Mandelbaum, a dour, earnest scholar, has never been one of Kate's favorite people. But when Janet becomes the victim of a vicious prank linking her to radical lesbians, Kate goes to the rescue. She finds she can give little comfort to Janet, who soon is found dead of cyanide poisoning in a men's washroom.

If Cross has wicked fun with Harvard's entrenched male establishment, so determined to save the university from female encroachment, she is not espousing militant feminism. Kate is an independent woman who can see the absurdities of over-ardent feminists. . . .

Cross wears the mantle of learning jauntily. *Death in a Tenured Position* is sprinkled with literary allusions that provide pungent commentary without becoming an exhibition of stuffy erudition. In the end, it is a quote from a 17th-century poet that provides Kate with the clue to the truth of Janet's death. . . .

[Cross] recently confessed in a newspaper column that she has been flirting with the idea of writing a modern comedy of manners, which requires that women be equal to men in intelligence and wit. She has done just that in *Death in a Tenured Position*.

> Jean M. White, "Mysteries: 'Death in a Tenured Position'," in Book World—The Washington Post (© 1981, The Washington Post), March 15, 1981, p. 6.

JOHN LEONARD

"Death in a Tenured Position" is set at Harvard. (p. 253)

Miss Cross, in the person of Kate, hates Harvard and quotes Henry James. She quotes Henry James because Kate always quotes somebody in every Amanda Cross mystery—as if she were trying to be Harriet Vale in a novel by Dorothy Sayers—and she hates Harvard because of sexism.

"Death in a Tenured Position" is a good mystery and a very angry book. The dead professor, Janet Mandelbaum, was not a feminist; otherwise, she would never have been offered her job. Kate, however, is a feminist, and since her husband, Reed, the assistant district attorney, has been exiled to Africa for the duration of this novel, she has the leisure to investigate and fulminate. The fulminations are acidulous; the situation may even be worse. How many females at Harvard with tenure can you name?

Janet dies because she is a woman in a place where they don't want women. Miss Cross, who has in the past suffered from fits of coyness, is so mad this time that her mystery moves into a higher gear. We sit in on department meetings, go to wretched parties, listen to insufferable people and emerge hurting. To be sure, there are dogs named Jocasta and Virginia Woolf T-shirts, and references to Simone Weil and George Herbert. And a man tells Kate: "I love it when you use words like beastly." But the mood is generally bitter; Miss Cross seeks less to entertain than to revile.

She not only makes her point, she also hammers on it, leaving a nail in our skulls. That we, and Harvard, deserve that nail, is incontestable. Miss Cross may go too far, in her disdain of Cambridge, by suggesting that there's no place to walk except around the Mount Auburn cemetery, and she is surely wrong in permitting someone to say that no one at Harvard bothers with the Red Sox. She arrives, though, at a nasty truth. (pp. 253-54)

> John Leonard, "'Reflex' and 'Death in a Tenured Position'," in The New York Times, Section III (© 1981 by The New York Times Company; reprinted by permission), March 20, 1981 (and reprinted in Books of the Times, Vol. IV, No. 6, June, 1981, pp. 252-54).*

JEFFREY BURKE

Amanda Cross's *Death in a Tenured Position* features her recurring amateur detective and professor of English, Kate Fansler. She is witty, attractive, well-bred, and independent though married. These qualities make for excellent verbal fencing with the lesbians who need her help to remove suspicion from them. . . . Cross pokes a good deal of pointed fun at a crusty institution, and a little at feminist extremism. When she is not tied down by exposition, her prose is abundantly witty, but several times I found myself wishing that someone would just walk in, order a sandwich, eat it, pay for it, and leave. Still, she writes well, and though I found the solution disappointing, I thought the solving, which depends on psychological insight and sly literary clues, top-notch. (p. 74)

Jeffrey Burke, "Mysteries for the Misbegotten," in Harper's *(copyright © 1981 by* Harper's Magazine; *all rights reserved; reprinted from the July, 1981 issue by special permission), Vol. 263, No. 1574, July, 1981, pp. 72, 74.**

PATRICIA CRAIG

Readers of Amanda Cross's earlier books will know that Kate's own manner is thoroughly agreeable, her observations witty and her erudition lightly displayed. All the qualities that make her so engaging a heroine are still apparent—but somehow her detecting has become a little perfunctory [in *A Death in the Faculty,* published in the United States as *Death in a Tenured Position*]. "Not exactly a full roster of suspects, Kate sadly thought"; certainly this novel has neither the density of plot that distinguished *The Question of Max* . . . nor the scholarly ebullience that made, say, *Poetic Justice* . . . so entertaining. If, like Sayers's *Gaudy Night,* . . . *A Death in the Faculty* links its mystery with a topical question (interestingly, the same one: feminism, and the varieties of dogma it can accommodate), it is less satisfactory than the Sayers novel in its resolution and in the intricacy of its puzzle-making. Narrative delicacy and cogency, however: these remain undiminished.

Patricia Craig, "In the Men's Room," in The Times Literary Supplement *(© Times Newspapers Ltd.*

(London) 1981; reproduced from The Times Literary Supplement *by permission), No. 4083, July 3, 1981, p. 758.*

KATHA POLLITT

What better locale for a feminist murder mystery than Harvard, where women make up a minuscule three percent of the tenured faculty and sexism-and-sherry in the senior common room is still an honored tradition? . . .

As it happens, I went to Harvard, and was prepared from page 1 [of *Death in a Tenured Position*] to cheer Cross' spirited dishing of my lamentably sexist alma mater. Said dishing is easily the book's best feature. This time out, Cross . . . is a better feminist than mystery novelist. A paucity of plausible suspects is one problem. Kate Fansler is another. Americans—even rich, WASP, elegant, tenured Americans—just don't say "beastly," call their nieces "my dear" and complain pedantically about the perfectly acceptable phrase "as such." Fansler is supposed to be ultracivilized; to my ear, she just sounds arch.

Katha Pollitt, "Books in Brief: 'Death in a Tenured Position' " (copyright © 1981 by the Foundation for National Progress; reprinted by permission of the author), in Mother Jones, *Vol. VI, No. VII, August, 1981, p. 65.*

Hermann Hesse

1877-1962

German-born Swiss novelist, poet, short story writer, editor, and critic.

All of Hesse's major novels are autobiographical in some way. *Demian* reflects Hesse's experience with psychoanalysis and his abhorrence of war. *Siddhartha* is the result of an extended visit to India where Hesse sought the peace of mind that he believed could be found in oriental religions. His school novel *Unterm Rad (The Prodigy)* depicts the educational institution as being fatal to the human spirit that does not conform. Within many of Hesse's works there is a theme of the conflict of spirit and flesh. *Der Steppenwolf* is perhaps the best example of this struggle, in which the animalistic urges of the intellectual Harry Haller strive for release. In *Das Glasperlenspiel (The Glass Bead Game* or *Magister Ludi)* Hesse treats nearly all of the themes present in his previous works. He contrasts the active world with the contemplative world and this time finds the world of the spirit lacking. There are critics who feel, however, that *Das Glasperlenspiel* is Hesse's slightest work, for here he deviates from his earlier effective portrayals of passionate youth.

Hesse's continued popularity among the youth of several countries has prompted posthumous publications of his poems, letters, and short stories. Although he wrote poetry throughout his life, only Hesse's earliest poems have been published. The confessional mode of his best-known fiction, however, can be seen in them. The letters offer revealing insights into the man and the motivations behind the writer. Perhaps the most interesting of these works is the collection of short stories, *Pictor's Metamorphoses and Other Fantasies.* As the title indicates, the stories are written in the genre of fantasy, which many critics consider the logical product of a mind which persisted in rejecting reality. Consequently, critics find in the stories a definite link to Hesse's other fiction. Hesse was awarded the Nobel Prize for Literature in 1946.

(See also *CLC*, Vols. 1, 2, 3, 6, 11, 17; *Contemporary Authors,* Vols. 16-20, rev. ed.; and *Contemporary Authors Permanent Series,* Vol. 2.)

CHRISTOPHER MIDDLETON

[In] spite of his 1946 Nobel Prize [Hesse's] work is somehow not admitted into the canon of "great" twentieth-century German authors. Germans, at least, would be amused nowadays, or mildly astonished, if a foreigner were to mention him along with Thomas Mann, Hofmannsthal, Rilke, Kafka, or Brecht. . . .

It is partly because the canon has no place for a writer whose work, though a coherent whole, is so curiously mixed. It is sometimes cloying, sometimes profound, then quixotically unironic, then at once brisk, mysterious, and topical, and at other times, if not in his last two fictions, what Germans patronizingly call *pubertär*—and most of this in a prose that has a mercurial texture all its own. . . .

[The years Hesse spent with his first wife at Gaienfofen, on Lake Constance, shaped him] as a mildly disturbed but polite author of Swabian small-town tales and of two novels about desperate but rather dreary artists. He was successful, second-rate, and trapped. The change came in the middle of the First World War. . . .

Yet Hesse does not quite belong among those writers who extracted from the war, besides horror, disgust, and irony, a distinctly altered outlook, a vocabulary purged of cant, and a new approach to poetry. Doubt toward any pretension to dignity and nobility—that is one attitude Hesse confessed he drew from the war. Also a heightening of the color, tempo, urgency of his prose could be taken for a sign that he too now believed all the idylls were over. But this is not quite the case. Hesse's utopian fantastic impulse was not subdued but quickened, and its shattering against the historical world was recorded now with just that much more intensity. What did change Hesse, or what he came to create, was a new narrative form, in which his polymorphous interior life could be reflected. This was the fictionalized monologue, with a figured bass of images (later he called this his "private mythology") that recur in modulations and, from book to book, explicitly or tacitly organize the events. . . .

Hesse was one of the first European writers to be psychoanalyzed, but his analysis was never purely clinical and always broken off. He duly became . . . a self-analytical novelist whose fictions orchestrated psychic crises of his own, and, rather mysteriously, thousands of readers could find their own troubles reflected in those of his protagonists. (p. 31)

Although he was basically a confessional writer, his self-revelations are (to us now, it must be said) mostly moderated by a discretion which used to be the mark of civilized persons. Hesse never was the sort of untamed self-eviscerator whom Henry Miller and Timothy Leary thought they were shepherding into the scene when they praised him. . . .

Hesse's sentimentality and solipsism often tiresomely overshadow the more incandescent aspects of his personality and work, manifesting themselves in limp stereotypes, clichés, and other forms of low-energy escapism. . . .

[Non-German] readers could not see how Hesse's sentimental and solipsistic aspects connect the writer Hesse with all kinds of German psychosocial malaise—with morose philistine paltriness, self-pity, and self-aggrandizement. His other-worldly utopianism, whether or not accompanied by deep Indian equations between the self and the world, was eccentrically part of a broader tendency to wishful thinking that inched the German middle class via hero-worship and "inwardness" into hideous self-deception and eventually Nazism. The "floating irrationality" which American fans adored in Hesse was, as a matter of historical fact, a major impulse in German middle-class psychology. . . .

I am not saying that Hesse was a deliberate irrationalist like D. H. Lawrence or Knut Hamsun. . . . In fact, for all his quasi-mystical proclivity, Hesse never did espouse irrationalism, least of all its terrorist fringe. Quite the reverse: he thought his task in the 1930s was to wrest the utopian impulse from its manipulators, and to enshrine it in an unassailable imaginative form (*The Glass Bead Game*). (p. 32)

For me . . . there is a durable but *abstruse* Hesse to be disengaged from the defenses he built into his writings and around them. All the seraphic talk of his being a pilgrim, wayfarer, a magician, a sage, and so forth tends to reflect only the sedentary and cerebral habits of readers who fancy Hesse so.

Yet he certainly was what Germans call a "seeker." In his thirties he used to advertise himself as a "quiet" or "secret" lyricist. If only his poems were not so insipid, this might offer a clue to his abstruse side. . . . His naïveté is perhaps what deserves to be noticed now, and understood. (p. 34)

There was, in and under everything, something wild about Hesse, something of the ungovernable child of Pietist missionaries. He kept it alive, sometimes in grotesque forms, sometimes in luminous ones. And there was in him, too, something of his Swabian intellectual ancestors, whom he came upon quite late in life: great God-hounded deviants, dreamers, and delinquents, from Albertus Magnus to Hölderlin and Mörike, each peculiarly rapt in his vision of the One in the Many, the Many in the One, and some of them coming apart in pursuit of that vision. What is it, after all, that Hesse's protagonists seek, if not naïveté reborn as illumination through grace? And something more: not the subjugation of reason to any system, but a just peace between the naïf and intellectual claims of consciousness. Just you listen, he says, listen actively, there it is, "the wooden horse is neighing in the wind." (p. 35)

Christopher Middleton, "Neighing in the Wind," in The New York Review of Books *(reprinted with permission from* The New York Review of Books; *copyright © 1979 Nyrev, Inc.), Vol. XXVI, No. 3, March 8, 1979, pp. 31-5.*

PUBLISHERS WEEKLY

The theme of fantasy runs strong in all Hesse's work; in this selection of 19 stories [*Pictor's Metamorphoses and Other Fantasies*], which span his entire writing career and embody many literary forms, he gives it its head. The title story, an allegorical account of a love affair of his own, is a charming but watercolor fable about the search for true happiness. "**Lulu**," the longest story and also the first written (1900), is a lushly romantic fairy tale, mingling fantasy and realism. . . . "**Among the Massagetae**" and "**King Yu**," written much later, skillfully turn fable to the uses of social satire. "**The Jackdaw**" (1951), one of the simplest but most effective pieces, is a rumination on an eccentric jackdaw, a solitary like Hesse himself (whose third wife nicknamed him "Bird"). For all their limpidity of style, ingenuity of fancy and attempts to portray the eternal verities of the human soul in the guise of magic, these stories do not have the power of a tale by the Brothers Grimm (who influenced Hesse greatly). Nor are they likely to disarm those critics who, not in the way of flattery, regard Hesse as the writer *par excellence* of adolescence.

"Fiction: 'Pictor's Metamorphoses and Other Fantasies'," in Publishers Weekly *(reprinted from the November 20, 1981 issue of* Publishers Weekly, *published by R. R. Bowker Company, a Xerox company; copyright © 1981 by Xerox Corporation), Vol. 220, No. 21, November 20, 1981, p. 44.*

THOMAS A. KAMLA

[The stories in *Pictor's Metamorphoses and Other Fantasies* are] generically linked to a specific narrative medium, namely the fantastic. This rubric ought not disarm the reader; for Hesse, the fantastic is not an escapist mode for solipsistic flights of the imagination. Rather, many of the themes that problematize his other works surface here just as compellingly. The conflict between life and mind in modern man's soul, the situation of the intellectual and artist in a highly restrictive and hostile environment, man's union with nature, rebellion against bourgeois philistinism—these are characteristic themes in Hesse's writings that also impact on the fantastic mode. The form he adopts in *Pictor's Metamorphoses,* the fairy tale and the legend, simply constitutes an extended metaphor of the way he envisions and confronts these themes.

The nineteen stories presented in this volume vary vastly in their individual plots, e.g., the artist and the objective world, religious hypocrisy, nature contra technology, the individual and the political state, psychology and dream; still, they are held together by a recurrent leitmotif, the alienation of man from his true self, a theme typical of Hesse depicting man's loss of an original state of primitive innocence through the process of civilization. By turning to the idealized realm of fairy tale and legend, Hesse is able to exercise greater aesthetic freedom in creating an ethical and spiritual goal to which man, denatured by the ravages that a disjointed reality has made on his soul, may aspire.

The selections span most of Hesse's writing career . . . and extend from the simple message of parable ("**Three Lindens**") to the more abstract level of allegory ("**Bird**"); thus they should appeal to a wide readership. (pp. 325-26)

Thomas A. Kamla, "Fiction: 'Pictor's Metamorphoses and Other Fantasies," in Best Sellers (copyright © 1981 Helen Dwight Reid Educational Foundation), Vol. 41, No. 9, December, 1981, pp. 325-26.

THEODORE ZIOLKOWSKI

[The] distrust of everyday "reality"—it is characteristic that [Hesse] customarily bracketed the term with quotation marks to indicate what he regarded as its tentative, problematic nature—remained a conspicuous theme in Hesse's thought throughout his life. (p. vii)

At the same time, Hesse inevitably coupled his rejection of present "reality" with an assertion of his faith in a higher truth. . . . In 1940 his denial of "so-called reality" concluded with the claim that "all spiritual reality, all truth, all beauty, all longing for these things, appears today to be more essential than ever."

This perceived dichotomy between contemporary "reality" and eternal values produces the tension that is characteristic of Hesse's entire literary oeuvre. The heroes of his best-known novels . . . are men driven by their longing for a higher reality that they have glimpsed in their dreams, their visions, their epiphanies, but tied by history and destiny to a "reality" that they cannot escape. At times, however, Hesse sought to depict that other world outright, and not simply as the vision of a figure otherwise rooted in this world.

Northrop Frye has observed that "fantasy is the normal technique for fiction writers who do not believe in the permanence or continuity of the society they belong to." Accordingly, fantasy is the appropriate generic term for Hesse's attempts—both in his fiction and . . . in his painting—to render the world of which his fictional surrogates can only dream. In his classic essay "On Fairy-Stories" . . . , Tolkien defined fantasy as "the making or glimpsing of Other-worlds," and many of Hesse's works display precisely the "arresting strangeness," the "freedom from the domination of observed fact," that Tolkien has elsewhere called the essential qualities of fantasy. But fantasy, as the tension between an unsatisfactory "reality" and an ideal reality suggests, is more than the creation of other-worlds *per se*. A more precise definition might specify that fantasy is a literary genre whose effect is an ethical insight stemming from the contemplation of an other-world governed by supernatural laws.

By far the most common form of fantasy practiced by Hesse was the fairy tale or, to use the somewhat broader German term, the *Märchen*. Symptomatically, his earliest extant prose composition was a fairy tale entitled "The Two Brothers" (included [in *Pictor's Metamorphoses and Other Fantasies*] in the piece called "Christmas with Two Children's Stories" [one tale written by the ten-year-old Hesse and one tale written by his grandson]). (pp. viii-ix)

When he compared his early story "The Two Brothers" with a similar tale written some sixty years later by his grandson, Hesse observed that in both cases a wish is magically fulfilled, and in both cases the narrator has constructed for his hero a role of moral glory, a "crown of virtue." In short, both tales are characterized by elements of the supernatural (magical wish fulfillment) and by an explicit ethical dimension. (p. xii)

In every case, . . . from the fairy tale of the ten-year-old Hesse to the ironic fable of the sixty-year-old, the narratives that

Hesse specifically labeled as *Märchen* display two characteristics that distinguish them from his other prose narratives. There is an element of magic that is taken for granted: wish fulfillment, metamorphosis, animation of natural objects, and the like. And this magic incident produces in the hero a new dimension of ethical awareness: the necessity of love in life, the inappropriateness of ambition, and so forth. To be sure, wonders and miracles occur in other forms of fantasy employed by Hesse: but elsewhere the miracle is regarded as an interruption or suspension of normal laws. In the legends, for instance, the miracle represents an intervention by some higher power (e.g., "The Merman" or "Three Lindens") that underscores the special nature of the occurrence. The figures in the fairy tales, in contrast, accept the wonders as self-evident: they do not represent any intrusion of the supernatural into the rational world, because the entire world of the *Märchen* operates according to supernatural laws. Little Red Riding Hood takes it for granted that the wolf can talk; the wicked stepmother in "Snow White" consults her magic mirror just as routinely as a modern woman might switch on her television set; and the tailor's son is not astonished at a table that sets itself with a feast when the proper formula is uttered. Hesse's *Märchen* share this quality of self-evident magic. Pictor [in the title story] does not question the powers of the magic stone; the aspiring young artist [in "Tale of the Wicker Chair"] is not astonished when the wicker chair talks back to him.

However, a world in which magic is taken for granted does not in itself suffice to make a fairy tale: it must also be a world with an explicit ethical dimension. . . . As Bruno Bettelheim points out in *The Uses of Enchantment*, "the child can find meaning through fairy tales," which offer an experience in moral education through which he brings order into the turmoil of his feelings. This is precisely the message of Hesse's *Märchen*: the characters are brought to an awareness of some principle of meaning that they had previously misunderstood. (pp. xiv-xv)

The impulse toward fantasy remained powerful in Hesse's temperament throughout his life. (p. xvi)

[As an outlet for his fantasy], Hesse chose a form consistent with his current realism—the legend, a genre in which the supernatural was not entirely implausible because it could be attributed to the mythic consciousness that existed in remote times and places. . . . As we noted, however, the supernatural occurrences in the legends are regarded as an interruption of normal "reality" and not, as in the fairy tales, as self-evident. But Hesse soon found other ways of dealing with fantasy.

Dreams always played a lively role in Hesse's psychic life, as he tells us in the late essay "Nocturnal Games." The ominous precognitive dream of war related in "The Dream of the Gods" . . . is significant because it signaled the unleashing of the powers of fantasy that Hesse had sought for more than a decade to suppress. During World War I, a variety of pressures . . . produced in Hesse an emotional crisis so severe that, in 1916 and 1917, he sought help in psychoanalysis. It was Jungian analysis, with its emphasis on dreams and their interpretation, that enabled Hesse to recover the childlike contact with the world of fantasy that he had attempted so long to repress. . . . [Several] of the fairy tales that he wrote during the war are barely disguised metaphors for the recovery of the past through psychoanalysis. . . . (pp. xvii-xviii)

Hesse was fully aware of the significance of the wartime *Märchen* and dreams in his personal development. In August of 1919 he wrote his publisher that **Demian** along with the *Märchen* that he composed from 1913 to 1918 were "tentative efforts toward a liberation, which I now regard as virtually complete." By means of the fairy tale, he had succeeded in reestablishing the link with the unconscious that had been ruptured. . . . However, the tone begins to change from the high seriousness of the wartime fables to the irony of **"The Painter"** and **"Tale of the Wicker Chair,"** which anticipate Hesse's movement toward social satire in the twenties. (p. xix)

Hesse's late stories, while they bring no new variations in form, nevertheless display his continuing experimentation with the forms of fantasy. Indeed, the narrative is often encapsulated within a speculative framework in which the writer reflects on the nature of fantasy. **"Nocturnal Games"** embeds the account of several dreams in a rumination on the meaning of dreams in Hesse's life. **"Report from Normalia,"** the fragment of an unfinished novel that might well have grown into a satirical counterpart to the utopian vision of **The Glass Bead Game,** depicts a Central European country "in the north of Aquitaine." "Normalia," we are told, emerged by expansion from the parklike grounds of a onetime insane asylum to become the most rational nation in Europe. But Hesse, making use of a fictional device that has recently appealed to writers of the absurd, casts doubt on all our assumptions concerning "normality." The narrator, it turns out, is ultimately unsure whether the former madhouse he inhabits has indeed become the seat of sanity in a mad world or whether it is not in fact still a madhouse. In **"Christmas with Two Children's Stories"** the two fairy tales—Hesse's own and the tale written by his grandson—generate a theoretical digression on the function and nature of fantasy. And in **"The Jackdaw"** . . . Hesse shares with us the manner in which his imagination plays with reality to generate stories about an unusually tame bird that he encounters at the spa in Baden. (pp. xxii-xxiii)

While fantasy in the unadulterated form that it displays in **"Pictor's Metamorphoses"** (where we are dealing literally with an "other-world" in Tolkien's sense) occurs infrequently in Hesse's mature works, it is fair to say that the tendency toward fantasy is evident in his writing from childhood to old age. Indeed, fantasy can be called the hallmark of Hesse's major novels of the twenties and thirties, the surreal quality that disturbs critics of a more realistic persuasion: for instance, the Magic Theater in **Steppenwolf** or the fanciful scenes in **The Journey to the East,** where reality blends into myth and fantasy. Indeed, fantasy is a state of mind into which Hesse and his literary surrogates enter with remarkable ease. (p. xxiii)

It would be a mistake to regard the tendency toward fantasy, in Hesse or other writers, as mere escapism. . . . [Fantasy], with its explicitly didactic tendency, represents not so much a flight from confrontation as, rather, a mode in which the confrontation can be enacted in a realm of esthetic detachment, where clear ethical judgments are possible. Indeed, fantasy often reveals the values of a given epoch more vividly than the so-called realisms it may bring forth. In any case, a generation that decorates its walls with the calendars of the Brothers Hildebrandt while perusing Tolkien's *Lord of the Rings,* that hastens from meetings of the C. S. Lewis Society to performances of space fantasies like *Star Wars,* has mastered the semiotics necessary to decode the hidden signs of **"Pictor's Metamorphoses"** and Hesse's other fantasies. (pp. xxiv-xxv)

Theodore Ziolkowski, "Introduction" (reprinted by permission of Farrar, Straus and Giroux, Inc.; copyright © 1981, 1982 by Farrar, Straus and Giroux, Inc.), in Pictor's Metamorphoses and Other Fantasies *by Hermann Hesse, edited by Theodore Ziolkowski, translated by Rika Lesser, Farrar, Straus and Giroux, 1982, pp. vii-xxv.*

SALLY EMERSON

Hermann Hesse's fairy tales in **Pictor's Metamorphoses and Other Fantasies** are nowhere near the standard of his great work. Hesse thrives on the shifting, blurring, dangerous balance between fantasy and what we call reality: it is this balance between real and imagined worlds which characterizes his masterpieces **Steppenwolf** or the magnificent and sustained **The Glass Bead Game.** Only one story stands out from this collection, published in an authorized translation in Britain for the first time, **Pictor's Metamorphoses** itself, which tells in allegorical form his love for his second wife, the singer Ruth Winger whom he married briefly after living in an isolation he found unconducive to happiness or creation. . . .

In these fairy tales full of stock characters—the merman, the simple wise boy, the virgin, the three brothers— Hesse limbers up for his major work, establishing links between his conscious and the deeper, unconscious world of myth and legend. Hesse was a connoisseur of fairy tales and anyone who is a fan of his would do well to read this varied collection of the master storyteller, who was on talking terms with the moon and the devil.

Sally Emerson, "Recent Fiction: 'Pictor's Metamorphoses and Other Fantasies'," in The Illustrated London News (© *1982 The Illustrated London News & Sketch Ltd.), Vol. 270, No. 7010, September, 1982, p. 59.*

IDRIS PARRY

All nineteen pieces in [**Pictor's Metamorphoses and Other Fantasies**] are fantasies, chosen by Theodore Ziolkowski from a half century of Hesse's writings. Some are tales of magic in the style of the Brothers Grimm or *The Arabian Nights;* at the other extreme we find social satires in which prevalent and objectionable trends are exaggerated to appear fantastical. All are perfectly representative of an author whose fictional heroes, from Demian to Harry Haller in **Steppenwolf** and Josef Knecht in **The Glass Bead Game,** are aware of the plausible explanation and reject it in favour of dream.

Hesse includes in one of his later stories published here a fairy-tale written when he was ten. It is his first known piece of prose composition, and it sets the tone for the "soul biographies" (his term) which are his collected works. In every case the illogical starts from known life. . . . Incidents from the remote past surface in the present, myth takes its place as a familiar component of life. This author wants to tell us that there is always a bridge between the visible and invisible. The admirable thing about Hesse is that he elaborates the obvious with such affecting sincerity. For him originality means simply going back to the origins. He does not suprrise, but he satisfies.

When he describes dreams in one of these stories as "nocturnal games" he connects with a constant theme of his work, the dream or fantasy as a gambit, a new throw which shakes up and rearranges what is already there. Every *Märchen* owes its existence to the belief that at each moment there is a fresh arrangement of pieces, always in the process of transformation, and that each moment and each piece contains the possibility of every other. The many transformations of this book's title story (bird becomes flower becomes butterfly becomes gemstone) signify the effortless intimacy with all life, embracing all connections, which the author hopes for himself. As his first metamorphosis Pictor becomes a tree, which must be the most common poetic symbol for receptivity.

The outsider is a persistent figure in these tales. The hero of the story **"Hannes"** is reputedly stupid because he will take no part in the activities of his fellows. Eventually they come to regard him, because of his deep familiarity with nature, as an intermediary between men and the gods, another divine fool with insight into the other world. . . .

"The Jackdaw" is a perfect example of how the writer can transform fact into legend. The tale starts normally enough. Hesse walks in the everyday world of his favourite resort, Baden. He observes a tame jackdaw hopping on a bridge. This bird, familiar with humanity, exhibits an abnormal degree of individuality and so becomes an outsider. Hesse speculates that the jackdaw may have been separated from his fellows because he was a mischief-maker, "which in no way rules out his being a genius." Perhaps he was such a nuisance to his family and society that he was "solemnly excommunicated and, like the scapegoat, driven out into the wilderness". From the familiar bridge at Baden Hesse projects his story into the mystery of the sacrificed king, connects with magic and religion, and links with the first fantasy in this book, written fifty years earlier, where he says he wants "to go back to where all things begin". He does all this by means of the less plausible explanation.

Idris Parry, "A New Throw at the Old Game," in The Times Literary Supplement (© *Times Newspapers Ltd. (London) 1982; reproduced from* The Times Literary Supplement *by permission), No. 4145, September 10, 1982, p. 965.*

Russell C(onwell) Hoban

1925-

American novelist.

Hoban has had a successful career as a writer and illustrator of children's stories, often employing animals as his protagonists. With *The Lion of Boaz-Jachin and Jachin-Boaz* and *Kleinzeit* Hoban began to write allegorical novels for adult readers, but he retained the magical and bizarre worlds of his children's stories. Consistent throughout his adult novels is Hoban's search for the patterns that make life significant— and this often in the face of a threatening, desolate, or near mad world. For example, in *Turtle Diary*, his third novel, his adult protagonists seek meaning for their own lives by freeing sea turtles from a zoo. Hoban's prose style, markedly individual, fresh, and often funny, is a linguistic match for his metaphysical themes.

***Riddley Walker*, Hoban's recent novel, has been hailed as his finest achievement to date. Some critics predict that it will become a cult novel, similar to Tolkien's *Hobbit* stories. Set in the distant future after a twentieth-century atomic holocaust, *Riddley Walker* has received special acclaim for Hoban's use of a barely recognizable but phonetically decipherable English language that reflects the outcome of disrupted civilization.**

(See also *CLC*, Vol. 7; *Children's Literature Review*, Vol. 3; *Contemporary Authors*, Vols. 5-8, rev. ed.; and *Somthing about the Author*, Vol. 1.)

© Jerry Bauer

THE TIMES LITERARY SUPPLEMENT

There are moments in this strange novel [*The Lion of Boaz-Jachin and Jachin-Boaz*] when the full meaning is almost within grasp; but the moment passes and the reader is left hanging on to the present pleasures of comic, heroic and romantic episodes.

Russell Hoban extended his reputation beyond the small enclosed world of children's books in 1969 when *The Mouse and His Child*, which came out with a children's book imprint in the way that *The Hobbit* did, found devoted readers of all ages. . . . Mr Hoban has something very important to say. But it is not quite clear that he has yet found the right way of saying it.

Jachin-Boaz lives in a world without lions. The last wild lions were destroyed by hunting; the tamed specimens in zoos died in an epidemic. Jachin-Boaz is a map-maker. He makes very useful maps. . . . His leisure hours are devoted to a map for his son Boaz-Jachin, containing everything that he could wish for. But it does not show where Boaz-Jachin could find a lion.

Then Jachin-Boaz goes away, deserting his wife and son. His farewell note reads: "I have gone to look for a lion", but what he finds is a mistress and a job in a bookshop. His son goes lion-seeking too, and finds what he is looking for in the ruins of a dead civilization. . . . The narrative thereafter follows successively the fortunes of father and son in a world in which a phantom lion—but one with effective claws and teeth—stalks the streets by day and night. . . . The two are reunited in a strong climax in which both challenge the lion simultaneously; it vanishes and father and son go home together for breakfast.

The underlying allegory, put into plain words, would, like most poetic allegories, appear trivial and insufficient justification for a novel of nearly 200 pages. What matters is that the theme is dressed in intriguing clothes, now fantastic, now hilarious, now sombre. The fantasy is set against the real world of telephone kiosks and cops, the underground and sex. Jachin-Boaz, thumbing his way around the world, has some memorable encounters, notably with a homosexual lorry-driver who represents "the triumph of whoring over pimping", and with a coasting trader who navigates by memory but can't tell the time. . . . Mr. Hoban excels in the clash of the physical and metaphysical. He is a master of the calculated use of bathos. Even in the climax of his story he allows himself, most effectively, a sudden switch to broad comedy. It is some measure of his success that, remembering with gratitude these gay and wry touches, the reader does not forget the lion who answered the call of a distant world and for whom "there were no maps, no places, no time".

"Father and Son," in The Times Literary Supplement *(© Times Newspapers Ltd. (London) 1973; reproduced from* The Times Literary Supplement *by permission), No. 3706, March 16, 1973, p. 285.*

THE TIMES LITERARY SUPPLEMENT

Once one is acclimatized to [Hoban's] mannerisms—a blend of conscious advertising and journalistic jargon and highly quirky use of words, and to his personification of inanimate objects—[*Kleinzeit*] flows freely. . . .

It will be noted that Mr. Hoban has solved the problem facing all "medical" novelists. Instead of cluttering up his pages with baffling technical terms, he invents his own as he goes along. . . .

It is a measure of Mr. Hoban's talent that [the frolics he depicts], some of them childish and not to all tastes, contribute to the serious impact of his novel. He is a master of the significantly trivial. . . . The action is worked out by Kleinzeit, Sister and the doctors, but also by personifications: Hospital, who welcomes Kleinzeit not only as a patient but as a lover, Death with dirty finger-nails, Word whose proud boast is that he "employs God", Pain, not a single being but a whole Company roaring on motorcycles in pursuit of Kleinzeit, and God, a modest and considerate soul—"Don't expect me to be human, said God." . . .

This strange novel, seeming at first diffuse and confusing, reveals itself as a masterly piece of economy, a mosaic in which each tiny fragment of wit or dirt or profundity has its appointed place.

"In Jugular Vein," in The Times Literary Supplement *(© Times Newspapers Ltd. (London) 1974; reproduced from* The Times Literary Supplement *by permission), No. 3760, March 29, 1974, p. 345.*

VICTORIA GLENDINNING

[*Riddley Walker*] is extraordinary. It is not 'like' anything, though John Gardner in *Grendel* and William Golding in *The Inheritors* ventured tentatively down Riddley Walker's road—but backwards. For this story is about the distant future, several centuries after England has suffered a major nuclear attack. Reading and writing skills have been lost for hundreds of years and are only now beginning again; the story is written by Riddley, who is only 12 but a 'connection man', a seer who interprets the government puppet show. Language survived only orally and has mutated in strange ways; the new English in which the book is written is a shock. . . .

At first, one seems to be reading gibberish, but having suddenly grasped that the 'Ardship of Cambry' is the Archbishop of Canterbury, one goes on to deduce the derivation of 'Pry Mincer', and of those long-ago technocrats, the 'Puter Leat' [computer elite]; one can interpret, as the singers cannot, their magic nonsense rhymes about 'Galack Seas', the 'nebyul eye' and 'party cools'. This makes one feel mighty clever, which is not really to be clever at all, since 'clevver' is the word they use for our own era of destructive technology. Riddley knows that before that, in primitive times, men had another, instinctual wisdom. . . .

There are some quite arbitrary cultural survivals which become sacred—a Punch and Judy fit-up with the traditional patter, an image of the Green Man (the inexplicable foliate head of mediaeval sculpture), and the legend of St Eustace and the stag. . . . [After] 100 pages or so of Riddley's English, our own looks baroque and exotic, and one feels daftly clever at being able to read it so fluently. Riddley's wise friend gives a dottily surreal interpretation of this text, with the bluffing pedantry of a modern biblical scholar. But from it the formula for causing an explosion is deduced, since 'Theres all ways some kynd of

clevverness waiting somers near or far its all ways waiting to happen its all ways waiting for some 1 to bring it down on the res of us.'

There is a lot more in this book—a search for a meaning to existence ('the idea of us'), and much to be deduced by us doomed clevvers about perception and innate knowledge. There are in *Riddley Walker*, too, a lot of clevver linguistic jokes, and whimsicality, theology, true originality, and a terrifying imaginative projection. It will be a cult book, and not a mere nine days' wonder. It's here to stay.

Victoria Glendinning, "The 1 Big 1" (© British Broadcasting Corp., 1980; reprinted by permission of Victoria Glendinning), in The Listener, *Vol. 104, No. 2685, October 30, 1980, p. 589.*

MARION GLASTONBURY

[The sub-literate narration in *Riddley Walker*] is initially painful for us fast readers and good spellers. But the heavy head-work required to decipher it is justified, in the long run by the unexpected meanings that seep through the cracks when conventional orthography is fractured. Hoban the master wordsmith has fun with the remnants of our administrative system . . . and with the terminology of science. . . .

While engaged on this elaborate invention, Hoban wrote an introduction to Grimms Tales in which he expounded the ideas that [*Riddley Walker*] seeks to embody. Thus, domestic unity encompasses human existence. The myths that are in us prove our affinity with the cycle of the collective mind, illustrate the cosmic pattern, the infinite rhythm, of which our destinies are a part. "All of us have been, all of us are, everything."

Unfortunately, when a metaphysican casts his net over the whole of human consciousness, as it was in the beginning, is now and ever shall be, and returns in triumph to share what he has caught, he appears to everyone but himself to be empty handed. The secret is incommunicable; the revelation void. So, in this creation, despite wonderful energy, an intricate structure, poignant characters, and a compelling landscape the message, of survival through renunciation . . . , cannot escape bathos.

Marion Glastonbury, "Incommunicable Secrets," in The Times Educational Supplement *(© Times Newspapers Ltd. (London) 1980; reproduced from* The Times Educational Supplement *by permission), No. 3358, October 31, 1980, p. 22.*

JENNIFER UGLOW

Riddley Walker, as the name suggests, is a novel which courts obscurity. Perhaps twenty years as a successful children's writer has taught Russell Hoban that our capacity to respond to the bizarre does not atrophy with age. Here he tells the story of a twelve-year-old "connexion man" interpreting puppet shows in the year 2347 o.c. ("Our Count") while the topography remains (just) recognizably that of East Kent.

Hoban's confidence in our ability to accept the strange allows him to tackle a problem which most futuristic writers evade. This is the recognition that total change, whether it be to post-holocaust desolation, as here, or to Utopian socialism, must involve a modification of consciousness which will be reflected in, and then structured by, our use of language. His solution is to imagine how language would evolve—or rather decay—

book is an artistic *tour de force* in every possible way and the language he has invented for it reflects with extraordinary precision both the narrator's understanding and the desolate landscape he moves through. . . . (p. 16)

Russell Hoban has transformed what might have been just another fantasy of the future into a novel of exceptional depth and originality. He has created a hero who, deprived of all other references, reads the world through his instincts, his imagination, his unconscious, without losing touch with his own reality or becoming either more or less than he is: a twelve-year-old who has become a man and is fighting to maintain his clarity and independence in a devastated land. He is also an orphan haunted by an unspecified sense of grief; the Iron Age he lives in is made even more desolate by the vague memory of what has been lost and will never be recovered, a civilization that had "boats in the air and picters on the wind."
. . . Again and again, Hoban transforms Riddley's broken dialect into prose which reflects every tremor of his fierce and unanswerable world. It is an extraordinary achievement, comparable, in its way, to *Huckleberry Finn* itself. (p. 17)

A. Alvarez, "Past, Present & Future," in The New York Review of Books *(reprinted with permission from* The New York Review of Books; *copyright ©
1981 Nyrev, Inc.), Vol. XXVIII, No. 18, November 19, 1981, pp. 16-18.**

PENELOPE MESIC

Russell Hoban has made the unthinkable familiar ground. *Riddley Walker* concerns itself with a young hero, newly initiated as a soothsayer or "connection man" of his tribe, who dimly senses the greatness of past civilization, fears the spreading mania for tinkering pointlessly with explosive, mysterious compounds of charcoal, saltpeter and sulphur, and feels the tension of his times as tribes or "crowds" shift from a hunter-gatherer society to an agricultural one. . . .

Hoban has used his considerable art to insure that we find his image of the future a cause for thought rather than incredulity. The logic of his world is such that, sad as it is, there is a pleasure in the invention of it, a wish to peep at different aspects never shown. . . .

The force and beauty and awfulness of Hoban's creation is shattering. His cleverness in fabricating Riddley Walker's poor broken language as if believably descended from our own and giving it the crudeness and strength and fresh comeliness of Chaucerian English is equal to his courage in using that language to describe a time of bleakness unbearable to anyone who ever loved a book or happened on a formula with delight, glorified in the Earth's diversity of life (we notice all that are left are pigs, dogs, humans, chickens, crows: only unfastidious creatures have the run of this burnt planet). . . .

Hoban's novel restores the freshness of delight to language and the freshness of horror to the Earth's ruin. For both he should be congratulated and more to the point should be read. (p. 50)

Penelope Mesic, "Reviews: 'Riddley Walker'," in Bulletin of the Atomic Scientists: a magazine of science and public affairs *(reprinted by permission of The Bulletin of the Atomic Scientists: a magazine of science and public affairs; copyright © 1982 by the Educational Foundation for Nuclear Science, Chicago, Il, 60637), Vol. 38, No. 6, June, 1982, pp. 49-50.*

Laura Z(ametkin) Hobson

1900-

American novelist.

Hobson's novels center on such controversial social issues as anti-Semitism, homosexuality, and the plight of refugees. Her concern is to uncover prejudice and intolerance. She is best known for *Gentleman's Agreement*, an exposé of blatant and subtle anti-Semitism.

Although some critics praise the depth of her exploration of a given problem, others feel her polemics and editorial asides detract from character and plot development.

(See also *CLC*, Vol. 7; and *Contemporary Authors*, Vols. 17-20, rev. ed.)

Photograph by Alex Gotfryd

GLADYS GRAHAM BATES

It is strange, but desperately appropriate in these bitter days, to open a novel upon no heroine, no hero, and no peculiar personal problem. To find rather upon the beginning pages the sweep of continental movement, peoples—not people—on the march—a march not made voluntarily towards some desired goal but forced on before brutality, disaster, and extinction. ["**The Trespassers**"] starts clearly with the broader theme. The story, intense, embattled, and sharply individualized, is swept forward on the implacable wave of the present. . . .

[Vera Marriner] is lovely to look at, smart, and finished with gloss of the cover girl but with personality and character to take the curse off that; she is shrewd and firm in business but generous, extravagant, and altruistic outside it. She illogically demands a logical righting of wrongs in a world given over to irrationality.

And Jasper Crown! Here is a character destined for discussion, dissension, and disbelief. No sooner will A contend that a man of such vehemence, contradiction, power, and weakness could never actually exist, than B will retort that he knows Jasper Crown in real life,—he is so-and-so. Two or three men in public life are sure to be taken as the prototypes of this radio tycoon who succeeds in bringing the arc of the world within his influence in a vain effort to forget that whatever else he can do the simple, natural desire for a son, for a continuance of himself in this tangible form cannot be realized.

This portrait of a present-day, up-to-the-very minute, business man, is one of the most interesting aspects of the novel. Compare him with Dreiser's Titan, with Lewis's Babbitt. How much of the differences are accounted for by Mrs. Hobson's dexterous psychoanalyzing? How much by the woman's point of view? And how much by the strange commodity which Jasper handles (opinion and propaganda)? The driving power which carries him so precariously far derives from his neurotic urge to compensate for his sterility. . . .

[Mrs. Hobson] has not been able to merge her two themes entirely smoothly. The story of the individuals and the saga of the migrant exiles,—the two do not quite meet in the end. But the experiment is interesting in itself and gratifying in bringing to the novel a breadth and depth so often lacking in entertain-

ment fiction. And "**The Trespassers**" is entertaining. One criticism might be that it is occasionally a little too facile in its event-packed unfolding, its slick dialogue, its smart magazine type of detail. But if readers, like flies, are more addicted to honey than vinegar then Laura Hobson is justified in her use of enticement, for hers is a novel that deserves readers. It has something to say and says it with both sincerity and vigor.

Gladys Graham Bates, "Modern Mixture," in The Saturday Review of Literature *(© 1943, copyright renewed © 1970, Saturday Review Magazine Co.; Saturday Review; all rights reserved; reprinted by permission), Vol. XXVI, No. 38, September 18, 1943, p. 18.*

FLORENCE HAXTON BULLOCK

[The] dominant theme of "**The Trespassers**" is not Vera's and Jasper's affair—though that, sometimes piercingly sweet, sometimes painfully, jarringly troubled and tragic, generally carried the melody and provides the emotional suspense—but rather the unique and greatest tragedy of our times: the huge migrations of the '30s and '40s [by] . . . millions of pitiful ones, whose chief crime has been that, for reasons of faith or race or political belief, they have been counted out in the ridiculous eeney-meaney-miney-moe of totalitarian ambitions. . . .

It is a tribute to Miss Hobson's gifts as a novelist that she is able to carry with a high hand into her story, and yet sustain its suspense, the kind of complicated detail and repeated deferment that make the heart sick and—all too often—kill the gentle reader's interest. Part of her success arises from the fact that she very convincingly and fundamentally relates the elements of her story. The great migrations of the unwanted and Vera's own unborn baby, unwanted by the man who deliberately begot him, are in their meanings closely akin. The whole exposition of Crown's attitude introduces fresh, new material and motives into this vivid account of the old, old battle of the sexes.

So good a job is this first novel of Miss Hobson's that I believe it is not out of order to suggest that she has invaded Nancy Hale's and Clare Boothe's field, "the women," and, in one respect at least, beaten both at their own game—chiefly, perhaps, because Miss Hobson imparts more meaning, more significant character-in-the-making, into the people she creates and the story she tells about them. She is, in fact, a writer of large ideas.

> *Florence Haxton Bullock, "Themes Deftly Intermingled," in* New York Herald Tribune Weekly Book Review *(© I.H.T. Corporation; reprinted by permission), September 19, 1943, p. 6.*

MARJORIE FARBER

Not all the mistakes of America can be blamed on the State Department. Some are collective immoralities, such as the discrepancy between our pretensions as a land of refuge and our actual, eyedropper admission of refugees. Our quotas have been steadily reduced ever since Hitler came to power, in exact proportion as the need grew. . . .

This, oddly enough, is the main theme of a first novel ["**The Trespassers**"] which includes a love story, a description of Freud's farewell meeting with the Vienna Psychoanalytic Society, and the case history of Jasper Crown, high-powered owner of a radio network, whose brutal drive toward success is motivated by fear of his own sexual sterility.

The novel, overburdened with symbolism, rocks between two parallel themes of rejection. "**The Trespassers**" on the earth, rejected by their own country and unwanted, apparently, by any other, are here represented by a Viennese psychoanalyst and his family, stranded in Switzerland. Their unknown benefactress in America, moving heaven, earth and the State Department to get them out, is involved in a destructive love affair with Jasper Crown. Although he has been passionately interested in disproving a diagnosis of sterility, he rejects her when she becomes pregnant. Under the circumstances this is a treacherous refusal of paternity, but I found the parallel—unborn child rejected by its fatherland—a little far-fetched. This is the kind of symbolism without emotional meaning which always runs the risk of being intellectually absurd. The motivation of Crown's fear of marriage and his drive toward power seems convincing. But as a character he remains pretty much the standard Ruthless Tycoon of fiction.

In fact, this half of the book seems to have been written in an emotional vacuum; all the warmth and directness of feeling are devoted to the refugee problem. This unevenness is reflected in the style. . . .

What emerges from [Mrs. Hobson's] first novel is an honest anger at America's treatment of refugees, conveyed less by fictional means than by the reporting of facts and statistics. It would have been a good novel if this emotion had been conveyed by the story itself. For instance, the climax of the refugee theme is supposed to be the death of the doctor's wife, following a year of homelessness, dwindling hope and the hundred daily humiliations which the word "refugee" entails. Instead, she dies just in time to clear the field for a therapeutic romance between the doctor and the American woman.

"**The Trespassers**" does succeed in being a shocking book, but not because of its fearless revelations about sexual sterility. Mrs. Hobson has compiled a fairly complete record of another kind of sterility, including a world-wide and almost total failure of the imagination.

> *Marjorie Farber, "Refugees' Dilemma," in* The New York Times Book Review *(© 1943 by The New York Times Company; reprinted by permission), September 19, 1943, p. 5.*

WILLIAM Du BOIS

Schuyler Green (the hero of this Grade-A tract ["**Gentleman's Agreement**"], which Mrs. Hobson has cleverly camouflaged as a novel) is a crusading writer for Smith's Magazine. . . . Schuyler, after he has reluctantly taken over the assignment [of writing a series of articles on anti-Semitism], leaps into harness with all his heart and soul. . . . [Since] he is unknown in New York, he prepares for the present series by taking a flat in walk-up Bohemia, and pretending to be Jewish—the only way to encompass his problem at first hand. . . .

When he turns in the last article (and signs a book contract with an enterprising publisher) he has run the familiar gamut, discovered a great deal about the innate savagery of his fellow-man and a great deal about himself as well. It begins with his fiancée, a lip-service liberal who applauds his approach to his material—but who can't quite refrain from checking on that Episcopalian background once again. (p. 5)

There's more in the same vein, and Mrs. Hobson manages it all with brilliance and dispatch: a taut description of a contretemps in a night club; a slick evasion of fundamentals at a Connecticut week-end, which the author identifies far too precisely for comfort; the inevitable howls of the wolf-cubs as they close in on Schuyler's son. In the end, of course, the series is a slam-bang success and the hero's fiancée redeems herself—in a way that seemed particularly unfortunate to this reviewer.

But this dénouement, like the whole book, is something that each reader should sample for himself. "**Gentleman's Agreement**" is honest—even when its plot is most flagrantly thimble-rigged. Its polemics are far better than its probing of the verities; but it is still required reading for every thoughtful citizen in this parlous century. "It might not be the American century after all," says Mrs. Hobson, in one of those editorial asides that somehow seem to crowd out most of the narrative, "or the Russian century, or the atomic century. Perhaps it would be the century that broadened and implemented the idea of freedom, all the freedoms. Of all men." Current headlines hardly seem to bear her out, but she has every right to hope. (pp. 5, 36)

> *William Du Bois, "Schuyler Green's Metamorphosis," in* The New York Times Book Review *(© 1947*

by The New York Times Company; reprinted by permission), March 2, 1947, pp. 5, 36.

REX STOUT

Most of the reviews and nearly all the talk of this novel [**"Gentleman's Agreement"**] by Laura Hobson will treat it as a book about anti-Semitism. That is too bad, for first of all it is a good job of story telling. Mrs. Hobson had to choose her characters by types—that is inevitable in a propaganda novel—but, having picked them and named them, she put something much more human than synthetic sawdust inside their skins and pumped in real blood. The theme of the tale is anti-Semitism, there's no question about that, but it would have been a first-rate story about people no matter what the theme. . . .

But while Mrs. Hobson undertook to make up and tell a story, and succeeded, she is probably willing to have her novel judged not only as a story but as a book about anti-Semitism. What about that?

It is overwhelming.

Probably a reviewer should let it go at that and merely add, read the book. Read a good story, get, along with it, a tough, acute and comprehensive portrait of one of the ugliest of the demons that live and work inside of men. But while it would be no service to Mrs. Hobson's book, and futile as demonocide, to list the points she makes and say "me, too," she may at least be saluted and applauded for her recognition of the spots on the demon's anatomy where its ugliness is most intolerable and most cunningly concealed.

Mrs. Hobson, of course, knows all about the mean little Jew-haters, the neurotic crackpots, the Christian Fronters and the diseased ambitions of men in public life who use anti-Semitism as poison bait for votes; she does not minimize their destructive effect on the hope of decent Americans to make their country a decent place to live. But she knows, too, that while those are the demon's most visible and grotesque deformities, a majority of us do recognize them as deformities. Mrs. Hobson goes closer and deeper. She looks behind the demon's ears and down its throat, and tells what she sees. She makes it all part of the story.

Rex Stout, "A Jew for Two Months—What He Learned," in New York Herald Tribune Weekly Book Review (© I.H.T. Corporation; reprinted by permission), March 9, 1947, p. 5.

BUDD SCHULBERG

The military victory against the world's most efficient anti-Semites has been won. And yet millions of Americans who take their democracy seriously are asking themselves whether the war which was won on the Rhine and the Elbe will be lost on the Mississippi and the Hudson.

It is this vital question which Laura Z. Hobson tackles with great clarity and missionary persuasiveness in this slick, readable and valuable novel on anti-Semitism [*Gentleman's Agreement*]. . . .

This decisive theme—in the knowledge of this reviewer—has never been developed in American fiction before. For rushing in where more gifted novelists have feared or neglected to tread, Mrs. Hobson deserves whatever prizes a push-me-pull-you de-

mocracy can bestow on one of its more responsible and aroused citizens. . . .

Kathy Lacey—Mrs. Hobson's somewhat too convenient heroine—while able to suggest [that her fiance, Phil Green, do a series of articles on anti-Semitism] . . . , begins shedding her convictions when her idealistic chickens come home to roost. . . . Thus Green makes a profound discovery—that in his search for anti-Semitism he need look no further than his "enlightened" fiancée, whose idea it had been to do the articles in the first place.

This sharply observed irony is developed with a wealth of wise and pointed documentation. . . .

Even a happy ending in the best women's-magazine tradition, and sentences like, "Again her heart hammered once against his ribs," don't blunt the sharp, hard point of this welcome, timely, able tract. . . . Mrs. Hobson's novel is a Stop-Look-Listen-and-Do-Something warning for every American who may be in danger of slipping, no matter how "innocently," into a Gentleman's Agreement.

Budd Schulberg, "Kid-Glove Cruelty" (reprinted by permission of the author), in The New Republic, Vol. 116, No. 11, March 17, 1947, p. 36.

JOHN MASON BROWN

[*Gentleman's Agreement* represents a large undertaking] both in its difficulties and ambitions. It may have its scattered interludes written for the sake of amusement. It may tell in unconventional terms a conventional love story about a boy who meets, loses, and gets a girl. Yet it remains so faithful to its theme that it takes few recesses from it. Anti-Semitism is its plot; ideas are its concern; and instances of prejudice supply its action. This is at once its audacity and significance. Yes, and why it must be welcomed as innovational. (p. 53)

I read Mrs. Hobson's book with mixed emotions. It is a healthy book to have in circulation. My sympathy with its theme is complete. My admiration is also genuine for the way in which Mrs. Hobson scores her truest triumph by demonstrating the racial intolerance which haunts the hearts and minds of nice people who think of themselves as liberals. I grant, too, that Mrs. Hobson can tell a story adroitly in popular terms. I, however, must confess that I regret the slick magazine quality in much of her writing. . . .

What really bothers me in Mrs. Hobson's book . . . [is that] I am conscious of having been presented with no more than a laundry list of indignities to which Jews are submitted in this country. Although happy to have such dirty linen aired, I wish Mrs. Hobson had also shown us the many sources of rightful pride special to the Jews, no less than the humiliations to which they are exposed by Gentiles who fancy themselves democrats. (p. 54)

I distrust Mrs. Hobson's plot device of having her hero a Gentile who pretends to be a Jew for eight weeks in order to understand the sufferings of the Jewish people. A device is at best a stunt for display, a trick to capture the attention, a deliberately false approach to the truth. However serviceable for storytelling Mrs. Hobson may have found such a contrived situation, it seems to me to condemn her novel to do no more than scratch the surface of her subject. The inner anxieties of persecuted races cannot be explored by tourists. They are known only to those who dwell as natives among such slights, apprehensions, and shameful humiliations.

I find myself disturbed by another aspect of Mrs. Hobson's central character. He is supposed to be a brilliant journalist, thoroughly conversant with the world as it is. Yet he must not have got around as much as his editor thought or Mrs. Hobson would have us believe. The surprise of this alert journalist at his discovery of how real and shocking are the meannesses directed against the Jews even by enlightened people in this country is naïve, to say the least. He must have gone through life with cotton in his ears and blinders on his eyes. If his ignorance is comfortable for him, it can claim its values for us. . . . It may snatch the blinders off countless unseeing eyes in America, and force millions to listen to what cries for the widest public statement.

It is because it dares to call real abuses by their proper names and to skywrite some of the ugly, underground truths of racial intolerance in this country that *Gentleman's Agreement* . . . can claim importance. (pp. 54-5)

> *John Mason Brown, "If You Prick Us," in The Saturday Review of Literature (© 1947, copyright renewed © 1975, Saturday Review Magazine Co.; reprinted by permission), Vol. XXX, No. 49, December 6, 1947 (and reprinted in his Seeing More Things, McGraw-Hill, 1948, pp. 49-56).*

CHARLES LEE

Laura Hobson likes to throw light into dark places. In her celebrated novel, **"Gentleman's Agreement,"** she explored the social disease of anti-Semitism. In [**"The Other Father"**] she explores the personal disease of excessive and misdirected love.

At the center of a story rich in psychological analysis stands Andrew Dynes, to all outward appearances an exemplary, middle-class family man. . . .

However, the soul of Andrew Dynes is afflicted with the "pale disease of emptying time." He is bored by his wife, and he despises his work. By a freak of circumstance he has fallen in love with a young girl. . . .

[One night he learns] that his daughter Peg is engaged in an illicit love affair with a married man.

Miss Hobson handles the complex counterpoint of this situation with dramatic skill and emotional conviction. Peg's lover is no fickle bee. He has money, stability, determination; however, it is not only these ironic differences between lover and father that agitate Andrew almost to the point of self-destruction. It is their similarity in age, the reverse parallelism of passion between himself and his daughter, and the terrifying command, placed upon him not by coincidence but by the "dark logic of cause and effect," to discover and destroy "the other father" within himself.

There's more than psychoanalytical melodrama here. Miss Hobson may not have all the answers, but she raises the right questions about fatherhood. In a story shot through with melancholy and burdened by analysis, she has achieved a dramatic revelation of the complex meshing of human lives. **"The Other Father"** deserves the attention of intelligent readers.

> *Charles Lee, "The Father of a Family," in The New York Times Book Review (© 1950 by The New York Times Company; reprinted by permission), May 14, 1950, p. 5.*

THE CHRISTIAN SCIENCE MONITOR

[In **"The Other Father,"** Laura Hobson] has written another study in human relationships. But the implications this time are less social and more exclusively personal. . . .

The mother-son and father-daughter relationships, both of which are examined here, have been explored in literature since the time of the Greeks. Mrs. Hobson adds very little that is fresh or that goes beyond narrow psychological interpretation. What is needed in this type of book is a frame of reference, a basic morality against which the struggles and actions of the characters achieve significance. In **"The Other Father"** this is entirely missing. Under a veneer of family affection the behavior of the Dyneses appeared to this reader as superficial, selfish, and cheap. But Mrs. Hobson presents most of it as quite admirable. Conceivably, she has her tongue in cheek. In any event, by not making her position clear—by establishing no base in even the most conventional standards of decent, fair behavior—she has sacrificed much of the dramatic potentiality and moral validity of her book.

> *"The Bookshelf: 'The Other Father'," in The Christian Science Monitor (reprinted by permission from The Christian Science Monitor; © 1950 The Christian Science Publishing Society; all rights reserved), June 10, 1950, p. 8.*

DON M. MANKIEWICZ

Though Laura Hobson, who wrote **"Gentleman's Agreement,"** is undoubtedly a celebrity in her own right, there is nothing autobiographical in [**"The Celebrity"**], her fourth—and perhaps her best—novel. The story centers on the selection of "The Good World," a novel by the brother of her title character, by a book club "bigger than the Literary Guild and the Book-of-the-Month Club," and of what follows the bestowal of such an honor. . . . [We are] given a detailed and intriguing account of the effect of the work's sudden success on Gregory Johns, who wrote it, on his brother Thornton, on their wives, on the book's publishers and their employees, and on a number of others of varying consanguinity.

Gregory, though momentarily shaken by the brouhaha attendant on the production of a best seller, is the only one to emerge from the experience substantially unchanged. The others are scarred beyond repair by association, however tenuous, with "a runaway best seller."

The story of these changes—and of Gregory's resistance thereto—is told with a meticulous calm, a careful understatement which makes it possible for the book to tread close to caricature without losing touch with reality. Mrs. Hobson has not misplaced the ability—so admirably revealed in **"Gentleman's Agreement"**—to share with the reader her rage at human idiocy without permitting him to take his eye or his mind from a vitally exciting story.

The special idiocy with which we are here confronted is the creation, in our century, of a new and meritless aristocracy, the celebrities who have become such not by any notable accomplishment, but merely by working hard at *being* celebrities.

Thornton Johns, brother of the author of "The Good World," becomes a member of this aristocracy. . . .

With the development of mass media of communication, almost anyone can become a celebrity, except a man who tells the sort of jokes in which Thornton delights.

This is, however, an extremely small flaw in a compelling and revealing novel. **"The Celebrity"** offers satisfying support to those who hold that there is as valid Americana to be found on Madison Avenue as on Main Street.

> *Don M. Mankiewicz, "Fame Is a Crowded Room,"
> in* The New York Times Book Review *(© 1951 by
> The New York Times Company; reprinted by per-
> mission), October 26, 1951, p. 4.*

THOMAS CURLEY

["**First Papers**"] is a long book in the midst of which the neurotic reviewer is apt to mutter, "Still so much to go?" But the reader who does not suffer from anxiety, and can afford to relax, will find that Alexandra Ivarin's reflections as she gazes at her husband are true of **"First Papers"** as a whole. Full of life and change, chaotic, undisciplined, this book throbs with genial emotions that give it an appeal rather like that of "One Man's Family." . . .

Stefan Ivarin is the center of this novel, but Mrs. Hobson changes her focus often. Writing from within first one of her characters and then another, she presents so many and such varied incidents that it is hard to see the trees for the forest. The impression one gets is that no single action, or set of actions, is as important as the life process itself. As in "One Man's Family," life goes on.

There is tragedy in Stefan Ivarin's life—but in these many pages what is tragic becomes sentimental, or at most, quixotic. It is as if God himself were not a capitalist—but a purblind doomster, made in the image of Thomas Hardy.

> *Thomas Curley, "Careworn Crusader," in* The New
> York Times Book Review *(© 1964 by The New York
> Times Company; reprinted by permission), Novem-
> ber 1, 1964, p. 28.*

FELICIA LAMPORT

[*First Papers* is a] leisurely, warm-hearted novel. . . .

[Laura Hobson] writes with sympathy and affection of Stefan Ivarin, an intelligent, idealistic Russian immigrant who became an American not only "by choice, by law, by document," but more profoundly by the conviction that came to him with his first naturalization papers that "a lifetime might go toward validating those papers and being worthy of them." . . .

His wife, Alexandra, is devoted and worshipful—up to a point; she is herself a woman of energy, passionate convictions, warmth, and an originality that often strikes her conventional children as eccentricity. She mortifies them by such things as her habit of standing on the porch in her old grey bathrobe, lecturing on socialism to the milkman, the garbage man, the delivery man. . . .

Mrs. Hobson succeeds in making Stefan and Alexandra lively, sympathetic people, but she is less successful with her other characters. Eli and Fran serve as little more than pasteboard foils for their idealistic parents; the Ivarins' best friends, the Paiges, move through the novel exuding only a calm, classic New England virtue.

First Papers is rich in details that evoke the early years of this century, but the movement of the story is hobbled by a kind of pleated technique that consists of describing an episode from one point of view and then doubling back to recapitulate it from another. The pace is slowed further by taking the reader into the thoughts of each character in turn, and by the almost flat-footed simplicity of a style in which every detail is spelled out, every nuance explored, explained, and occasionally even reiterated. This is a pity because so much of the material speaks beautifully for itself.

> *Felicia Lamport, "Two Square Pegs Who Really Fit,"
> in* Book Week—The Sunday Herald Tribune *(© 1964,
> The Washington Post), November 8, 1964, p. 5.*

PUBLISHERS WEEKLY

[In Hobson's *Over and Above*] theme is writ large, almost obscuring the characterizations designed to bring it to life. She examines the dilemmas and complexities of being Jewish in America, creating a character-spectrum of middle-class, educated Jewish-Americans ranging from those who enjoy their heritage to those who deny it. The focus is on three generations of one family, who, although Jewish by birth, have been assimilated for many years. . . . To some, Hobson's narrative may read like a propaganda tract for Israel and against international terrorism. To others, however, including those who are engaged in the generational tug-of-war between mother and daughter, it will strike a responsive chord.

> *"PW Forecasts, Fiction: 'Over and Above'," in*
> Publishers Weekly *(reprinted from the July 2, 1979,
> issue of* Publishers Weekly, *published by R. R. Bowker
> Company, a Xerox company; copyright © 1979 by
> Xerox Corporation), Vol. 216, No. 1, July 2, 1979,
> p. 95.*

JOAN P. LEB

Three generations of Maxe women interact in this novel [*Over and Above*] set in New York from the time of the UN resolution on Zionism to the events of Entebbe. . . . Hobson touches on many provocative topics—the Jewish identity remaining after generations of assimilation; the difference between terrorists and freedom-fighters; the difficulties of parent-child relationships; the concerns of the aged. The story is too slim to carry all this provocation and one never gets close enough to the characters to care about their solutions, but the contemporary scene and the strong women protagonists will appeal to many readers. (pp. 1718-19)

> *Joan P. Leb, "Fiction: 'Over and Above'," in* Li-
> brary Journal *(reprinted from* Library Journal, *Sep-
> tember 1, 1979; published by R. R. Bowker Co. (a
> Xerox company); copyright ©1979 by Xerox Cor-
> poration), Vol. 104, No. 15, September 1, 1979, pp.
> 1718-19.*

NORA JOHNSON

That money corrupts is a cliché dear to our hearts, and the [heroine of Laura Hobson's **"Untold Millions"** opposes] . . . that corruption in varying ways.

In **"Untold Millions,"** Jossie Stone's lover, Rick Baird, can't resist the trappings of success even though he usually can't afford them. . . .

This is Laura Hobson's ninth novel, and it's a pleasure to be in the hands of a pro. The narrative line is tight and steady, and Miss Hobson always tells us what we want to know just before we become aware that we want to know it. There is a sort of counterpoint of numbers—the $10 raise, the debt that dwindles from $70 to $60—which carries the theme on another level, and reminds us how tied our lives are to such music. . . .

As Rick puts one book aside and begins another, amasses more debts and starts having affairs with other women (which he justifies with a Havelock Ellis-inspired philosophy), Jossie's blindness to Rick's faults becomes steadily more annoying. Finally she sees that she has collaborated in her own exploitation. If her realization comes in a rather obvious way, rather like the moral at the end of an Aesop's fable, it hardly detracts from an otherwise absorbing story. (p. 14)

> *Nora Johnson, "Money Problems," in* The New York Times Book Review *(© 1982 by The New York Times Company; reprinted by permission), March 28, 1982, pp. 14, 29.**

ELEANOR P. DENUEL

Veteran author Laura Hobson has [in *Untold Millions*] another novel with a message: sometimes we must pay a great price for something. The particular thing this time is maturity. . . .

Laura Hobson paints a multi-dimensional word-portrait of one child helping another child, one who learns a great deal from the experience, and one who is left behind. She leaps with ease from Jossie's thoughts to those of Rick, either by allowing us to peek into their innermost selves, or through Jossie's journal, in which we see her gradual rise to emotional adulthood. Indeed, the truth can make you free, she learns.

The book imparts the flavor of the Twenties, the days of Gershwin and Whiteman, of Lunt and Fontanne, without overdoing it; the book is not a "period piece." There have always been, and there will always be, those who grow, and those who merely grow older.

> *Eleanor P. Denuel, "Fiction: 'Untold Millions'," in* Best Sellers *(copyright © 1982 Helen Dwight Reid Educational Foundation), Vol. 42, No. 1, April, 1982, p. 7.*

William X(avier) Kienzle

1928-

American mystery writer.

Kienzle draws upon his experiences as a former Roman Catholic priest in the writing of his murder mysteries. His works center on a character named Father Koesler, a priest-sleuth who is called in to investigate mysterious deaths in his diocese in Detroit. As these mysteries are solved, Kienzle offers the reader glimpses of life in the priesthood and comments on controversial issues within the Catholic church.

(See also *Contemporary Authors*, Vols. 93-96 and *Contemporary Authors New Revision Series*, Vol. 9.)

JOSEPH A. TETLOW

[In his *The Rosary Murders*, William Kienzle] has rounded up a great crowd of current church types and brought them vividly alive in a zippy, church-wise whodunit. His is a gently bemused but dry-eyed picture of the church in the postmodern world, a.k.a. the Archdiocese of Detroit in Murder City. But Kienzle *likes* his people. How often do murder mystery readers feel as though they've lost a friend in the murder victims? Of course, the church has changed: Chesterton's Father Brown emerged a mystery wrapped in an enigma; Kienzle's hero-priest emerges merely a puzzle. There it is. But Kienzle seems to intend the priest and nun victims as metaphors for religious servants' dedicated availability in today's frantic world, and their relatively easy destruction. Maybe that's a *Weltanschauung*. If it's humbug, it's very high-grade.

> Joseph A. Tetlow, "Benedicamus Domino," in America *(reprinted with permission of America Press, Inc.; © 1979; all rights reserved)*, Vol. 140, No. 17, May 5, 1979, p. 375.*

WINSLOW DIX

The Rosary Murders, a first novel by William X. Kienzle, is an old-fashioned thriller that doesn't unclench its grip on the reader until the final pages. A psychotic killer, loose in Detroit, brutally murders the most accessible people in the world: Catholic nuns and priests. His calling card: a black rosary wrapped around each victim's wrist.

Kienzle's meticulous description of each murder is chillingly graphic. The prose suddenly halts, and the slow-motion camera assumes control, as in the final scene of "Bonnie and Clyde" when the anti-heroes are gunned to smithereens. . . .

Full of clichés, it is, nonetheless, compelling reading. When not lavishly depicting the slaughter of individual innocents, Kienzle vividly dramatizes American clerical life: the stale jokes, boredom, and over-indulgence in food, drink, and tobacco. The very names of the characters—Archbishop Mark Boyle, Monsignor O'Brien, Mother Mary Honora—nostalgically evoke a chapter in American Catholicism.

Father Robert Koesler, Kienzle's amateur sleuth, pores over mysteries "like some priests read the Bible." His wit, honed by years of Agatha Christie, solves a puzzle that is worthy of

his mentor at her most deceptive. Lieutenant Koznicki, Polish Catholic and exemplary family man, is the perceptive, relentless professional detective.

The Rosary Murders has its flaws—the plot meanders far too frequently into the sexual escapades of newspaper reporter Joe Cox; the priests and nuns are mere types; and the final three pages, after the mystery has been solved, should have been excised. But the book does not commit the unpardonable sin: boredom. All its sins are venial, quickly forgiven every time the rosary-murderer ritualistically drapes another string of beads around a victim's wrist.

> Winslow Dix, "From Massacre in Maine to Murder in Miami: Investigating a Lethal Fictional Foursome," in The Chronicle Review *(copyright © 1979 by The Chronicle of Higher Education, Inc.)*, May 29, 1979, p. R-15.*

TONY BEDNARCZYK

Mystery lovers can rejoice as a new star appears in the heavens of whodunits! That new star is William X. Kienzle, whose first work [*The Rosary Murders*] is an engrossing thriller that will satisfy the most demanding armchair detectives.

On Ash Wednesday, someone pulls the plug on an aging priest's respirator. The following Friday, a nun is murdered in an inner city convent. On each of the next six Fridays, some brutal madman claims a victim from the ranks of the Detroit archdiocese. . . .

Kienzle, a former priest and news editor, knows the rectory and the city room to the smallest detail and that knowledge shows in the various locales that arise during the course of this well paced, tightly written novel. More importantly, Kienzle creates well defined characters that inhabit his story rather than decorate it. The reader is shown, in a premonition, the victims at their daily lives and these personal introductions heighten the horror of their deaths.

With *The Rosary Murders,* one gets the distinctly satisfying impression that Kienzle, a most talented newcomer to the genre, will again delight readers with a second superbly crafted mystery and that Father Koesler may very likely become the successful Catholic answer to Rabbi Small. One sincerely hopes the wait will not be long.

> Tony Bednarczyk, "Fiction: 'The Rosary Murders'," in Best Sellers (copyright © 1979 Helen Dwight Reid Educational Foundation), Vol. 39, No. 4, July, 1979, p. 125.

PUBLISHER'S WEEKLY

Kienzle's second thriller ["**Death Wears a Red Hat**"] matches "**The Rosary Murders**" as a dazzling fusion of acid comedy and grisly doings connected to Roman Catholic traditions. Father Koesler, the detectives and newspaper reporters—familiar from the first novel—work hard to solve another wave of murders in Detroit. The shocks begin with the discovery of a mobster's severed head, tied to a Cardinal's hat in the cathedral. Then more heads of notorious criminals who have escaped justice turn up, replacing the tops of statues in churches and the seminary. The gruesome "capital" punishments give Father Koesler solid clues; so does his knowledge of voodoo rites, leading to the killers' unmasking. But the priest then has to wrestle with the dilemma of whether to report his secret. The story is a rouser in more ways than one; it could make any reader with a guilty conscience a bit uneasy.

> "Mysteries: 'Death Wears a Red Hat'," in Publishers Weekly (reprinted from the February 22, 1980, issue of Publisher's Weekly, published by R. R. Bowker Company, a Xerox company; copyright © 1980 by Xerox Corporation), Vol. 217, No. 7, February 22, 1980, p. 93.

NEWGATE CALLENDAR

Of the writers who deal with mystery and murder as seen through the eyes of a priest, Ralph McInerny and William X. Kienzle are probably the two leading American practitioners. . . . Mr. Kienzle's man is Father Robert Koesler in Detroit. He first appeared in "**The Rosary Murders**," which attracted a good deal of attention. Now Father Koesler is back, in ["**Death Wears a Red Hat**"]. . . .

Basically the book is a procedural. Father Koesler works with the police. But the thrust of the book is religious, with many observations about Catholicism in the modern world. The murders can be solved only by someone with a Catholic background. And very perplexing murders they are. Somebody is hacking the heads off victims and putting them on statues in churches. It so happens that all of the victims are villains, and there are those in Detroit who want to give the murderer the keys to the city. . . .

The situation is highly contrived. "**Death Wears a Red Hat**" is in some respects a throwback to the Ellery Queen mysteries—ingenious but improbable. Also improbable is the modus operandi that the author asks the reader to accept. But the ending is interesting, and contains a moral problem that confuses the law enforcement people. When is a murder not a murder? "**Death Wears a Red Hat**" will not bore you. The book is well written and has some well-drawn characters, including a pair of competing reporters and some believable cops. And priests, all over the place, who play golf, specialize in arcane church lore, pass themselves off as restaurant critics (at least, one of them does), argue and complain.

> Newgate Callendar, "Crime: 'Death Wears a Red Hat'," in The New York Times Book Review (© 1980 by The New York Times Company; reprinted by permission), June 15, 1980, p. 17.

NEWGATE CALLENDAR

In "**Mind Over Murder**," Mr. Kienzle has set out to write a murder mystery, but for a long time, nothing much happens. Drawing on his own experiences as a priest, the author must have his say about the bureaucracy of the Roman Catholic Church. He reflects a liberal viewpoint: The way both evil and good men can subvert the essential meaning of the church clearly disturbs him. The result is writing that bogs down into didacticism.

When things do happen, the plotting suddenly gets very tricky. About halfway through, the killer is revealed. But soon afterwards, the same priest who was murdered once is again murdered—by another killer. And by a third, a fourth, a fifth. Eventually the "mystery" has to end in a rational explanation, but Mr. Kienzle comes up with a fairly lame one. He is a good writer, but here he is too clever for his own good, and some readers may feel cheated.

> Newgate Callendar, "Crime: 'Mind over Murder'," in The New York Times Book Review (© 1981 by The New York Times Company; reprinted by permission), June 21, 1981, p. 29.

KATHA POLLITT

Remember Father Brown? G. K. Chesterton's Edwardian Catholic priest-detective solved the most ingenious murders effortlessly, thanks to a childlike simplicity and an unshakable trust in the doctrines of the Church—which often had an uncanny bearing on his cases. The years have not been kind to Catholic certainties, and that may be why Father Koesler of Detroit needs almost 300 pages [in *Mind Over Murder*] to solve a crime that Father Brown would have wrapped up in 20. Unlike Father Brown, poor Koesler has to contend with loneliness, doubt, Church bureaucracy, declining attendance at Mass and his fellow priests. His resultant air of detachment and faint depression slow him down a bit as a detective—even I solved this mystery before he did—but it makes him believable, and far more likeable than our other contemporary ecclesiastical sleuth, Harry Kemelman's egocentric and complacent Rabbi Small. . . .

Kienzle is no stylist—he favors the sort of tough-guy writing in which drinks are "built," not mixed—but he is an ex-priest, and his satirical vignettes of the religious life ring dismally true. Squabbling around the rectory dining table, trading dirty jokes, goofing off on the golf course, Koesler's colleagues are, with few exceptions, about as spiritual as traveling salesmen, and a lot less grown-up.

> *Katha Pollitt, "Books in Brief: 'Mind over Murder'" (copyright © 1981 by the Foundation for National Progress; reprinted by permission of the author), in* Mother Jones, *Vol VI, No. VII, August, 1981, p. 65.*

ANDREW M. GREELEY

William Kienzle is the Harry Kemelman of Catholicism, and his priest detective, Robert Koesler (like Kienzle, sometimes editor of the Michigan Catholic), is the Detroit response to Rabbi Small. . . .

Like Kemelman, Kienzle has an eye and an ear for mystery stories. Kienzle's sensitivity to pathos and foolishness, shallow fads and rigid ideologies, mindless nonsense and deep faith of the contemporary Catholic scene compares favorably with Kemelman's vivid description of suburban Jewish life.

Both men are superb sociologists of ethnicity.

"Assault With Intent" is about six attempted murders in a declining Roman Catholic seminary—and one real murder—which may be connected to an ultra-right Catholic religious group opposed to change in the church.

Like Kienzle's previous works, the story is a puzzle rather than a mystery. The reader is not provided either with the clues or background information necessary to solve the crimes. Rather, he is entertained by an elegant puzzle and by the detective's ability to unwrap the puzzle. If a mystery buff demands intriguing mind benders, he will find them in Father Koesler stories. If he wants a chance to solve the crime, he will be disappointed.

"Assault With Intent" is in some respects an improvement over Kienzle's previous books, where characters were dispatched with great dispassion and little sense of horror. Moreover, the frequent and also dispassionate couplings of his love interests (two Detroit reporters) are less frequent, though the aging lovers are now quite irrelevant to the story.

On the negative side, Kienzle is at least as good a sociologist and puzzle constructor as Kemelman, but not as deft a storyteller. His characters still tend to be without the warmth or attractiveness of Rabbi Small's congregants, And, there is too much dialogue, not enough suspense-building narration.

"Assault With Intent," then, will appeal to the very substantial audience that likes literary equivalents to crossword puzzles. It will not appeal to the audience that demands more in a mystery story.

If anything, the Catholic atmosphere in "Assault With Intent" is better than in previous books, though, for whatever one reviewer's opinion is worth, the puzzles may be wearing a little thin around the edges.

> *Andrew M. Greeley, "Murder Mystery in Catholic Seminary," in* Los Angeles Times Book Review *(copyright, 1982, Los Angeles Times; reprinted by permission), May 23, 1982, p. 18.*

NEWGATE CALLENDAR

[*Assault with Intent*] is the latest in the series featuring Father Koesler, the Catholic priest who operates out of a parish in the Detroit area. In this case, is there a homicidal maniac on the loose, who intends to decimate the Detroit priesthood? Someone makes several murder attempts, and the newspapers (and then the media in general) get into the act. The two Detroit newspapers' star reporters, Patricia Lennon and Joe Cox (who happen to be living together), are on the story. (They have appeared previously in this series.) But when an attempt is made on his life, everything becomes very personal to Father Koesler. Of course he finally figures everything out.

But Mr. Kienzle has set up straw men. The far-right plotters are too ridiculous to be taken seriously, all the more so because they are depicted in a farcical rather than a serious manner. They are too blundering, too stupid, too bigoted, too unlovely to have any real contact with life. In addition, the book is hampered, as the three previous ones have been, by the author's insistence on dragging in elements of Catholic liturgy, extraneous details about the way priests think and operate.

Mr. Kienzle seems to be something of a liberal, but his excursions outside the main plot lines only result in didacticism while not furthering the plot.

> *Newgate Callendar, "Crime: 'Assault with Intent'," in* The New York Times Book Review *(© 1982 by The New York Times Company; reprinted by permission), May 23, 1982, p. 41.*

MARC HART

[*Assault with Intent*] is mildly entertaining and gives a rather interesting view of modern Catholics, from the old priests in the seminary who find the new ways of the Church difficult to understand to the conservative group called the Tridentines, who are pretty much a caricature of people on the lunatic fringe of conservatism. In addition, the author describes the actions of a group of inept people in great detail. The net effect is a great many comic situations. Because of the large number of sight gags, under proper direction this book could well be made into a good comedy-mystery movie. (It even has the required nude female scene.) In fact the movie would probably be better than the book. Father Koesler is all right as a detective, "but he is not Father Brown."

> *Marc Hart, "Sleuths and Spies: 'Assault with Intent'," in* Best Sellers *(copyright © 1982 Helen Dwight Reid Educational Foundation), Vol. 42, No. 4, July, 1982, p. 137.*

Louis L'Amour

1908?-

(Born Louis Dearborn LaMoore; also writes under the pseudonyms of Tex Burns and Jim Mayo) American novelist.

L'Amour is a prolific and popular writer who has written over eighty frontier novels that have sold in excess of one-hundred million copies. His style of storytelling is suggestive of a campfire raconteur with an endless string of tales about life in the Old West. All of L'Amour's frontier fiction reinforces a traditional value system—a respect for the land, a protective attitude towards women, a dedication to the family unit, and a life and death with honor—which, along with L'Amour's entertaining style, makes his novels appealing to a large audience. Many of L'Amour's works have been turned into cinema and television movies, including *Hondo* and *How the West Was Won.*

L'Amour's works may be divided into two subjects. His earliest stories, and many others throughout his career, portray the wandering, tough frontier hero who is embroiled in many fights for justice, and finally becomes domesticated. *Hondo* is considered the best story of this type. L'Amour's second and most ambitious project is his continuing saga of three families (the Sacketts, the Chantrys, and the Talons), which parallels the historical settlement of the frontier.

(See also *Contemporary Authors,* Vols. 1-4, rev. ed.; *Contemporary Authors New Revision Series,* Vol. 3; and *Dictionary of Literary Biography Yearbook: 1980.*)

© Jerry Bauer

MICHAEL T. MARSDEN

Louis L'Amour is the best selling Western writer of all-time. The reasons for his remarkable success in the marketplace are many, but none seems as pervasive or as consistently developed in his fiction as the concept of the family in the West.

The families in L'Amour's fiction, for example, his famous Sacketts, are often uprooted and transplanted from Eastern Soil to the Western landscape with their civilized virtues intact. Their romantic, idealistic, familiar attitudes serve them well on the Western frontier where they work to establish a new world in which civilization can thrive. While on the one hand presenting us with the formal familial triad of the Sacketts (the pioneers), the Talons (the builders) and the Chantrys (the thinkers), he also presents us with the more general family unit as a measure by which all other values in his novels are defined. (p. 12)

While his novels have most of the traditional, or conventional, elements that characterize popular Western fiction, they also contain a number of inventional elements that separate his fiction from the efforts of his less popular colleagues. For example, while the L'Amour hero is a tough, silent, and virile force protecting the interests of civilization that are constantly being threatened by the forces of the wilderness, he is also . . . in search of domesticity, of the family. (p. 13)

His development of a triad of families as a frame for viewing the settling of the West is a highly innovative element in his fiction. (p. 15)

[The] formal family groupings may well constitute the most ambitious and complex attempt to date to create a Faulknerian series of interrelated characters and events in the popular Western tradition. L'Amour seems to be able to create in his readers a feeling of belonging to a tradition; this in turn provides L'Amour with the basis for a popular, organic fiction that creates a familiar yet ever unfolding world within the formulaic Western world.

While this triad of families provides a formal structure within which the characters and events exist and to which the readers relate and refer throughout his fiction, there are also less formal family structures and images in L'Amour's works which provide the overall framework for an entire set of beliefs, attitudes, and values which characterize his fiction. The concept of the family is the thread that becomes the texture of his most successful fiction. (p. 16)

Whether the particular L'Amour hero is a pioneer, a gunfighter, a builder, or an intellectual, his value system is the same. For his qualities are those that built the West of the American imagination and qualities that define the fiction of Louis L'Amour.

The Female Principle receives significant attention in L'Amour's fiction because it is an essential element of his formulaic innovation of the concept of the family. A particular theme that receives repeated emphasis is the scarcity and consequent sanctity of womanhood in the West. In L'Amour's fiction there is no greater Western sin than molesting a woman. . . . (p. 17)

L'Amour's fiction moves towards the hearth and the implied social institutions with the same certainty evidenced by the lone cowboy in the well-known Christmas season advertisement for Marlboro cigarettes who drags his Christmas tree behind his horse as they move slowly, gracefully, yet surely towards the cabin marked in the snow by the warm, hearth-centered smoke pouring from its humble yet solid chimney. (p. 18)

While they embrace the hearth, the characters in L'Amour's fiction are at the same time quite conscious of their ties to the land, a conventional aspect of popular Western fiction that L'Amour enlarges by suggesting that the hearth is a second stage of development. . . . This hearth-modified view of the landscape adds the dimension of holding the land in trust for future generations to L'Amour's fiction. (p. 19)

The family is the protector of the law, moral standards, and social order. Without the family there is only the wilderness and its counterpart, savagery, a truth of which the Indians in L'Amour's fiction are keenly aware. For they, unlike the white man they often had to fight, would return to their lodges and their families after a battle. They considered their white enemies savages who wanted to fight family-less wars instead of family-centered battles.

L'Amour considers himself and his novels to be in the tradition of the oral story teller and his tales; he uses fiction as the vehicle of communicating with his ever increasing audience. But he considers his fiction a continuing epic of the American West that is a romance which combines elements of the West as it was with qualities of the West as it ought to have been. Despite the fact that he has sixty-seven titles in print, Louis L'Amour is writing one long tale with many parts, focusing on three families in particular and on the concept of the family in general as he unfolds the saga of the settling of the West. (p. 21)

> *Michael T. Marsden, "The Concept of the Family in the Fiction of Louis L'Amour" (originally a paper presented at the Popular Culture Association convention in April, 1977), in* North Dakota Quarterly *(copyright 1978 by The University of North Dakota), Vol. 46, No. 3, Summer, 1978, pp. 12-21.*

PAUL BAILEY

[In *The Burning Hills* Louis L'Amour] made his one and only attempt at Literature—but Literature lost, and Louis L'Amour became famous. Twenty years ago, L'Amour was obviously under the influence of T. S. Eliot: *The Burning Hills* contains dozens of references to "The Hollow Men" and the final section of *The Waste Land*. Early in the narrative, the hero, Trace Jordan, scoops up "a handful of dust" from the "red rock" in the shadow of which he is hiding, and in the book's closing pages thunder and lightning contribute much lively dialogue to scenes otherwise half-dead from exhaustion. . . .

The women who feature in the L'Amour oeuvre are firebrands more often than not, as the philosophical Mabry in *Where the Long Grass Blows* has found to his cost. . . . Or they are like Maria Christina in *The Burning Hills*—part firebrand, part spit-fire, part saint, but All Woman. . . .

There is no sex to speak of in his fifty-odd novels. The only beds mentioned are at the bottom of rivers. L'Amour always fades out discreetly, . . . when passion looms. What rape there is is of the English language. L'Amour once said . . . that he was sick of writers who purveyed nothing but clichés about the old West. His self-loathing must have risen to immense proportions, in that case—stuck between the three stops of which he is so enamoured are nothing but well-tried, well-worn, well . . . clichés about the old West. And other clichés, too; "His eyes narrowed with thought" is a good example. Try it. In all fairness, though, it has to be conceded that there are some fine moments, as the following exchange indicates:

> "Mort?"
> "He's dead. . . ."

Temperamental as he is not, L'Amour is not exactly adept at ringing the changes of his plots either. . . . For all that, **High Lonesome** is not radically different from **The Burning Hills**. The good man triumphs over the villains, who are in hot pursuit, and ends up in the arms of the tamed tigress.

> *Paul Bailey, "A Man Is a Man . . .," in* The Times Literary Supplement *(© Times Newspapers Ltd. (London) 1977; reproduced from* The Times Literary Supplement *by permission), No. 3937, August 26, 1977, p. 1037.*

MICHAEL T. MARSDEN

Popular Western fiction has strong ties to the oral tradition in American culture. In his works, L'Amour clearly considers himself to be in the tradition of the oral storyteller. . . . (p. 206)

[In] the case of the oral storyteller, the writer is expected to be the spokesperson for the "community." This role is especially clear in the fiction of Louis L'Amour which reveals how a writer can function as a cultural filter, creating what become artifacts of immense significance for understanding the complex nature of American culture. (p. 209)

In L'Amour's fiction, the past is of major significance, for nothing is ever really new or being done for the first time. The present is closely linked to the immediate as well as to the distant past, especially in his more recent works, and the characters in his novels are quite conscious of their place in history. His readers are encouraged to share with the characters a sense of the past and are made to feel a part of it through the continuing development of the central families in his fiction. (p. 210)

[L'Amour] provides his readers with popular historical treatments of everything from the Custer disaster to the Westward migration. . . . In a single novel (**Lando** . . .), L'Amour instructs his readers on the historical and cultural importance of Madeira wine, the nature of longhorn cattle, the Great Hurricane of 1844, and the several cultural functions of a Western saloon, all the while providing them with an entertaining romance. This approach to writing popular fiction is what Irving Wallace refers to as "faction," or the careful and skillful combination of real details with a fictional story. L'Amour takes the classical mandate for the writer/storyteller quite seriously: he writes to instruct as well as to entertain. (p. 211)

L'Amour's treatment of the American Indian is worthy of special note as a cultural indicator. His fiction early deviated from the purely formulaic treatment of the Indian and developed an interesting balanced view. (p. 212)

L'Amour's success as a writer has provided him the freedom to delineate his views on the Indian—who has been both maligned and beatified but not understood—in an extended number of novels.

L'Amour's treatment of women, however, has been inconsistent, suggesting that various social and cultural pressures, some contemporary and some historical, have influenced his work. . . . [Emily Talon in **Ride the Dark Trail**] defends the Talon empire against the villains who would destroy what she and her husband had built for future generations. She is quick and deadly, and by the end of the novel has not only shot out both kneecaps of a particular villain, but has also littered her homestead with a large number of corpses. Yet, at the same time, L'Amour stresses the stereotyped attitudes towards women, such as their being graceful creatures in need of zealous protection. He reflects a generally protective attitude toward women (evident in plots that emphasize that the quickest way to get hanged was to molest a woman), but invariably he has his protagonist indicate that he is looking for a woman who "will walk beside him and not behind him."

A possible explanation for this inconsistency is that L'Amour himself does not have a clear image of American womanhood. An even more probable explanation is that his fiction, like that of other popular writers who enjoy large audiences, reflects the pluralism of his society. To be successful, popular fiction must come to terms with a multiplicity of roles, sexual and other, which exist in the larger society. (p. 213)

> *Michael T. Marsden, "The Popular Western Novel As a Cultural Artifact" (reprinted by permission of the author; a revision of a lecture read at the American Historical Association on August 18, 1978), in* Arizona and the West, *Vol. 20, No. 3, Autumn, 1978, pp. 203-14.**

JON TUSKA

[**Hondo**] remains a fine book unlike those which profligacy have recently made tediously repetitious. Hondo Lane is one of L'Amour's most engaging and interesting characters, rivaling in another genre Dashiell Hammett's creation of Ned Beaumont in *The Glass Key* in 1931 or Raymond Chandler's Philip Marlowe before Marlowe became sentimental. Hondo is self-reliant, capable without being excessively aggressive, sufficient unto himself without surrendering to greed. . . . Hondo is able to bridge the white and red cultures because he has lived five years among the Apaches and he possesses independence of perspective as well as of character. . . . L'Amour's conception of sexual relationships between men and women, such an important theme throughout his fiction, is a variation of [his belief] . . . that every man and every woman is a separate individual, best together when they are heading in the same direction. (p. 77)

> *Jon Tuska, "The Westerner Returns," in* West Coast Review of Books *(copyright 1978 by Rapport Publishing Co., Inc.), Vol. 4, No. 6, November, 1978, pp. 73-9.**

JOHN D. NESBITT

To the person who reads with a slightly less abandoned mind, and to the critic who does not dismiss L'Amour with ridicule and contempt, L'Amour's novels are not just the same old story with the hero of each new volume given a different name

and a different colored horse. His books have changed over the years, independently of story lines or plot formulas, according to an apparent change in moral and historical purpose. L'Amour's career can be divided into three phases—early, middle, and recent—and the novels from each phase reflect a change in his use of historical detail accompanied by a change in moral focus. (p. 150)

The novels of [the] early phase are entertaining in their unbridled violence, their directness of moral utterance, and their frequent (if pedantic) tidbits of Western lore and trivia. . . . Two of the novels from this period, *Utah Blaine* . . . and *Showdown at Yellow Butte* . . . , reflect L'Amour's simplest use of history and his most direct statement of morality. . . . In both of these books, history is the setting but not the subject. Historical range wars such as the Lincoln County War and the Mason County War, and mention of contemporary gunfighters such as Clay Allison and Wild Bill Hickok, constitute the backdrop of the land wars of these two novels. In addition, we are treated to details about pistols, rifles, and shotguns that were used during that period of time. But neither of these books attempts to articulate or depict history itself; they are, as Henry James said of romantic fiction, "at large and unrelated," isolated excursions into a fictional and stylized Wild West. Out of these two conventional stories of the struggle for land come the expected moral conclusions: it is wrong to defraud the government of land, it is wrong to grab land from honest homesteaders, and it is wrong to settle the land without having reverence for it. It is right to love the land, to care for one's horse, and to give up the driftin' life in favor of settling down to married life and ranching. And along the way we learn a little lore as well, such as "Man freezes mightly quick, drinkin' whisky," and that a man can boil water in a cup made of birch bark. All in all, the lore, the trivia, the historical detail, and the morality, along with the numerous shootings and fistfights, add up to pretty light material—even for L'Amour.

In his other novels of this period, L'Amour's fiction takes on more purpose in depicting time and place and in expressing morality. *Hondo* is his best-known novel of the early phase, and one of his best-known overall. . . . The setting is more than functional . . . in the dimensions that it takes on. The desert, with its historical endowment of hostile Apaches, pervades all that takes place in the actions and thoughts of the main characters. Hondo Lane's guiding principle is to understand the desert, to know it, and to survive wisely in it. . . . Hondo's outlook, then, is a moral framework for information that would otherwise be gratuitous. In *Hondo* we learn, as we often do in L'Amour's novels, how to build a fire that won't be seen. We also learn, as we do elsewhere, that Apaches eat mule and horse meat, but not pork or fish. Where in other contexts this information is thrust in irrelevantly, here it sustains the prevailing sense of the desert and the need to live thoughtfully in it. (pp. 151-52)

In this novel the highest values are to survive with honor, to pass on what one has learned, and to die well. Like the characteristic L'Amour hero, Hondo doesn't die, but he does prepare to die well when he is faced with what seems to be certain death.

The values embodied and enacted by early L'Amour heroes are essentially those of the individual on the borderline of civilization. The hero is neither alienated nor isolated, since nearly every L'Amour plot involves the hero in someone else's complications. The opening up of the West nourishes the bullies, landgrabbers, and robbers, while the dangers of the frontier bring out the weaknesses of men who cannot cope and who expose virtuous women to the threat of hostile Indians and unscrupulous white men. (p. 152)

[The] novels of the early phase still share a broad central characteristic. In the context of historical conditions and touchstones, the footloose hero becomes civilized into a settler. Although L'Amour reiterates his American myth of domesticating the wandering fighting man, these early novels do not constitute—individually or collectively—an *apologia* for Westward settlement. That ambition would come later. For the present, he satisfied his reader with conventional plots, each cut loose and detached from the other, and "at large and unrelated" to any historical vision.

L'Amour's middle phase reaches from the late 1950's to the early 1970's and includes over half of his sixty-odd novels. This phase continues some of his established patterns, and lays the foundation for his later ambitions and purposes. Accordingly, the novels divide mainly into two groups. There is the continuing march of stories about the wandering hero who gets involved in other people's scrapes, and who meets a woman who will walk beside him and not behind him. Except for an occasional exception such as *Kiowa Trail* and *The First Fast Draw*, these novels are narrated in the third person as the early novels are. Also like the early novels, these novels have a different name for each new hero, as if to offer up an eligible bachelor for each new plot. From a survey of these books it would seem that nothing could shake L'Amour's fell purpose of domesticating tall, tough, broad-shouldered, fast-drawing men over thirty years old. But then there is the other group of novels, the ones with the same family names and the same men cropping up time and again. These books are almost all narrated in the first person, and refer to incidents . . . that take place in other novels in the group. While L'Amour continues producing the good old standbys in the middle phase of his career, he is apparently working, simultaneously, on a sort of interlocking family mythology. For what purposes, his later phase will tell.

In the good old standbys of this period we are treated to the L'Amour fare of variation and repetition in plot structure that we have come to expect and enjoy. In addition, a new dimension appears in several of the heroes in this group of novels. The hero is often a gentleman, and has been to Europe prior to knocking around on the frontier. The continental finish offers a less rough-hewn morality to be expressed through the hero, and it adds a new set of historical details that place L'Amour's stories in a broader historical context. (p. 153)

While L'Amour was working his way towards new moral vistas, he was creating a new race of heroes as well. The Sacketts are, we are told time and again, "fierce fighting men" from the hills of Tennessee. Being a fighting man is central to all L'Amour heroes, but the Sacketts are of a breed all to themselves. For one thing, even though one of them may get married and settle down, there is every possibility that he will re-appear in another Sackett novel. (p. 155)

L'Amour is not merely writing several stories about the same character as he did in his salad days with Hopalong Cassidy; he is putting together an assembly of interlocking stories about an extensive and ever-extending family. No longer is the reader set free with each new novel, to be entertained with a story "at large and unrelated" to all others. Each Sackett novel carries with it the burden of attachment to all other Sackett novels, and sooner or later the reader is obliged to feel that he is piecing in a larger story.

At about the time the reader is getting into more than he bargained for, he is also being treated to some of L'Amour's least successful narration. These novels are narrated in two ways: entirely first person, and alternating between first and third person. *The Daybreakers* is characteristic of L'Amour's first-person narration. . . . [We] don't always know whether L'Amour or Sackett should be the object of our smile. . . . (pp. 155-56)

The alternating narration of *The Lonely Men* has its drawbacks as well. One would think that L'Amour alternates his narration in order to have Tell Sackett narrate tersely and inarticulately, and leave the more garrulous business to the usual third-person narrator. But the separation of narrative effect is not maintained. . . . It seems that L'Amour merely follows a personal convention in having the Sacketts tell their own stories. Since the narrative texture is not at stake, he goes outside their point of view for expediency in giving the circumstances of the plot. . . . Writers like John Seelye and Jack Schaefer create narrators who tell much more than they understand at the time, but L'Amour doesn't try for that effect. Nor is he concerned with the sophisticated use of alternating narration that Dickens achieves in *Bleak House*. Rather than attempt narrative integrity· or complexity, he follows the easiest trail in order to tell the story. As a consequence, the reader may become impatient, and his impatience may well vitiate the entertainment that is sought so expediently and that is usually the reward of a L'Amour novel.

The obscure motives behind the family web of the Sackett stories and the dawning morality of *Under the Sweetwater Rim* come to light in *Sackett's Land*. In the "Preface" to this book, L'Amour reveals the purpose (and status) he claims for himself . . . .

> Story by story, generation by generation, these families are moving westward. When the journeys are ended and the forty-odd books are completed, the reader should have a fairly true sense of what happened on the American frontier. . . .

Apparently, then, the first-person narration of the Sackett stories is not an arbitrary choice. Telling "the story of the American frontier through the eyes of three families" is meant to give conviction and immediacy to L'Amour's version and vision of the American frontier. (pp. 156-57)

[L'Amour has become] a self-appointed chronicler of the Western movement. Consequently, his recent books are less autonomous than even the early Sackett sagas, and in no way as unfettered as the earlier stories about the tough man of the frontier. In the later phase, where characters and plots are spun for a grander web, L'Amour is a self-styled historian and apologist for Western settlement.

[*Sackett's Land* and *Rivers West*] were obviously written to fit into the overall design. The former tells the story of the first Sackett to come to America from Wales in 1599, and the latter tells of the first Talon to come from Canada in 1821. . . . By producing these two immigrant heroes, heroes who saw that their destinies were to help build and settle America, L'Amour coordinated his ethnic appeal with a larger trend in popular sentiment: the bicentennial fever. In his three bicentennial families [the Sacketts, the Talons, and the Chantrys] he established a fairly comprehensive ethnic and occupational range for his chronicles.

L'Amour's new mode could be maintained by his established conventions of plot and character, which could be modified with bicentennial history and morality. . . . What is new about the Sackett narrator is that he is now a mouthpiece for his author's moral version of history. (pp. 157-58)

Details that formerly might have offered a bit of historical verisimilitude (or at least momentary diversion) now cumulatively assert the veracity of L'Amour's historical overview. Where we used to smile at being informed, as in a passage on the culinary preferences of the Apaches, we now grimace at history being filled in for us pedantically, detail by detail, as part of an overbearing design. L'Amour the historian goes too far in these two novels, in that the narrative is constantly cloyed with historical detail and circumstance; and L'Amour the moral historian simply overdoes it in justifying American settlement as justice and democracy in action.

Following these two grandaddy novels, L'Amour's later phase has continued to produce stories about his bicentennial families, and about unrelated heroes. **The Man from the Broken Hills** and **Over on the Dry Side** . . . advance the family sagas and blend the ethnic and vocational elements of the original families into new characters. As he did in his middle phase, L'Amour lards his family stories with references to events and family members that the reader is likely to read of elsewhere. (pp. 159-60)

As extensions of L'Amour's family plan . . . , both of these novels fit into his monomythic rendition of American settlement. They also display the extremes in narrative quality that emerge from the master plan. **The Man from the Broken Hills** has a successfully created narrator. The speaking voice lapses occasionally, but for the most part Milo Talon's narration is evenly textured with humor and vernacular. . . . L'Amour achieves a narrator who is also an engaging character and who, unlike previous Sacketts and Talons, can tell a complimentary story about himself without boasting or apologizing. And since Milo is a tolerable narrator, L'Amour's stream of cowhand lore arises comfortably out of the narration. (p. 160)

While he achieves enjoyable narration in **The Man from the Broken Hills,** he does the opposite in **Over on the Dry Side.** As in **The Lonely Men,** the narration alternates between first person and third person, with many of the same flaws. . . . [What] results is a tedious story that serves as a vehicle for L'Amour's characteristic lectures. Entertaining narrative effect is lost in favor of flat introduction of historical details and moral speeches. The reader is left with the impression that L'Amour's fiction sometimes rises above and sometimes sinks below his avowed purposes.

For the reader who is not entirely in sympathy with the new demands placed on him—the demands of piecing together family chronicles and American history, all fraught with significance—L'Amour continues to produce the good old standby stories. . . . In **Where the Long Grass Blows,** L'Amour portrays an historically interesting West without presenting urgent messages that would get in the way of his perenially most successful work. In this novel the story of the range war is revived. Like **The Man from the Broken Hills,** the novel introduces information on how cattlemen used the range, how they discreetly stole from one another, how they conducted their roundups, and so forth. The information is more appropriate and interesting than the rundown on Elizabethan décor in **Sackett's Land,** and L'Amour succeeds at presenting material that bears upon the story line and is not inserted simply for the reader's edi-

fication. . . . This is not to say that in these books L'Amour achieves realistic fiction and the texture of historical reality, while in the Sackett-Talon-Chantry volumes he doesn't. L'Amour's strong suit has always been entertainment and his fiction entertains the reader with action, dialogue, description, *and* information. When the information advances rather than impedes the entertainment, the book is more successful and less pretentious. (pp. 161-62)

[From L'Amour] we can expect many more productions within his established range of fiction. Inelegancies of grammar and punctuation may well continue, accompanied by a not-so-rigorous control of narrative point of view. We will be wrong to expect high art or exquisitely crafted fiction. But we will not be disappointed if we expect a continuing variety of entertainment from an author who has regaled us with "stories that take off like a bullet" for a quarter of a century. (p. 163)

> *John D. Nesbitt, "Change of Purpose in the Novels of Louis L'Amour," in* Western American Literature *(copyright, 1978, by the Western Literature Association), Vol. XIII, No. 1, May, 1978 (and reprinted in* Critical Essays on the Western American Novel, *edited by William T. Pilkington, G. K. Hall & Co., 1980, pp. 150-63).*

STEVE BERNER

In **Comstock Lode** L'Amour tells, obviously, the story of people caught up in the great silver rush that played such an important part in this nation's history. If some of the writing is flat, and some of the characters incomplete or contradictory, well much the same can be said of life itself.

It is, in fact, pointless to discuss either the merits or weaknesses of L'Amour's writings, both of which abound, since it will have little or no effect on either the author or his public, which covers all ages, sexes, and intellectual areas. Suffice to say that the books do exactly what their creator intends. They present a historically accurate picture in an entertaining and informative manner of people facing a great challenge. Thus, while he may never be the subject of learned discourse in a creative writing class, it is not inconceivable that future generations may look to Louis L'Amour for guidance to the pathways of the past in history and sociology. Certainly he provides these lessons in a more energetic and painless way than, say, James Michener, to whom the comparison is more apt than many might think.

> *Steve Berner, "Tales of L'Amour," in* Lone Star Review *(copyright © 1981 Lone Star Review, Inc.), Vol. 3, No. 3, May, 1981, p. 10.*

JOHN D. NESBITT

Readers who wish to get a full sense of Louis L'Amour's productions, for whatever purposes, must inevitably take on his two blockbusters, **Bendigo Shafter** and **Comstock Lode.** These two novels, in their separate ways, continue the historical mode that L'Amour launched into with **Sackett's Land, Rivers West,** and **Fair Blows the Wind,** with the exception that the main characters of the later two novels are not members of the Sackett, Talon, or Chantry families. Both are marketed as historical novels rather than as Westerns. . . .

In their broader features they perpetuate the pattern of all of L'Amour's fiction: there is a superlative hero who fights through adversity to ensure that the country will be settled and developed properly. Good and evil are clearly distinguishable from one another, and the conflict is resolved unequivocally through violence. The plot resolution, along with a steady stream of narrative comments, affirms the broadly held values of the mass audience. And in these novels, as in all of L'Amour's fiction, there is a sprinkling of errors in grammar, sentence structure, and word usage—errors that are overshadowed by a profusion of corpses and a liberal fare of "authentic" historical and geographical detail.

In **Bendigo Shafter,** the titular hero tells his own story of coming to manhood. Wise beyond his tender years, he lavishes upon his reader many mini-sermons about the building of a country; almost innumerable lectures on frontier lore; occasional analogies between the Plains Indians and Arthurian Knights, Bantus, and Europeans; and prophecies about the passing of the Indians and the buffaloes, and about the probability of stellar travel. (p. 315)

All of this would be more tolerable if it were not narrated in the first person, a point of view that L'Amour has labored with frequently and without much success. It seems that when the narrator is not serving as the author's mouthpiece for lectures in history and civilization, he is telling the reader of the many compliments he receives for his strength, good looks, and acute mind. As a youthful narrator, Bendigo Shafter dwindles in comparison with Dickens' Pip, Twain's Huck, or Schaefer's Bob Starrett, even though he is not quite as risible as the narrators of L'Amour's **Rivers West** and **The Proving Trail.**

Comstock Lode is a less comprehensive, less visionary book than **Bendigo Shafter;** perhaps also because it is written in the third person, it is more readable. In **Comstock Lode** L'Amour introduces a new set of authentic details, the fruits of L'Amour's renewed research, as he reworks the melodramatic plot of such novels as **Reilly's Luck** and **The Proving Trail**—the story of a young man who avenges his parents' death (the two earlier novels had a father and a father figure killed, while in this one L'Amour sets the wheels rolling with two murdered fathers and two violated, murdered mothers). Val Trevallion, like some of L'Amour's other recent heroes, is an immigrant who soon becomes whole-heartedly American in his devotion to developing the country. (p. 316)

Like Bendigo Shafter and L'Amour himself, Trevallion marries an actress. Grita Redaway, as she has earlier told the villain, will leave the theater only for love of the right man. To complete the melodramatic scheme, L'Amour has a villain who is as despicable as the hero and heroine are virtuous. He commits arson, rape, robbery, burglary, embezzlement, and murder. He bludgeons, stabs, and smothers his victims, and hires out his shooting. Moreover, he doesn't believe that women can be intelligent. But even though **Comstock Lode** is excessive in its melodrama, it is well plotted and well paced, and the lectures on history and mining are less gratuitous than the disquisitions in **Bendigo Shafter.** (pp. 316-17)

These two novels are thus far the pinnacle of L'Amour's craft, and they demonstrate how the conventional Western can be expanded without having its basic form altered. They will gratify the reader who likes historical and moral lessons as part of his or her entertainment, but they will not buoy up the reader who is looking for improvement or artistic innovation in the craft of popular fiction. (p. 317)

John D. Nesbitt, "Reviews: 'Bendigo Shafter' and 'Comstock Lode'," in Western American Literature *(copyright, 1982, by the Western Literature Association), Vol. XVI, No. 4, February, 1982, pp. 315-17.*

JOHN PIVOVARNICK

Louis L'Amour's [*The Cherokee Trail*] is both a little more and a little less than what I expected of the famed King of the Oat Epic.

It was more than I expected simply in the fact that I enjoyed it. . . .

The story is mildly complicated in that many of the characters are thrust at the reader early in the story, and you have to keep them straight. Mr. L'Amour's simple, point-to-point prose is deceptively charming, and the unwary will find themselves swept up quite quickly in his tale-spinning.

In short, **The Cherokee Trail** is light, fast, and fun reading. It is ideal for the person who doesn't have much time to read, because you can put it down for a while, and still get right back into it. Mr. L'Amour recaps his action frequently. . . .

Oh—*Cherokee Trail* was something less than I expected, because I thought there'd be more gunfights.

John Pivovarnick, "Fiction: 'The Cherokee Trail'," in Best Sellers *(copyright © 1982 Helen Dwight Reid Educational Foundation), Vol. 42, No. 7, October, 1982, p. 260.*

Patrick Lane

1939-

Canadian poet.

Lane has been called a "maverick poet" for his often brusque and unflinchingly rough portrayals of life in British Columbia. Though he has written some lyric and introspective poetry, Lane's narrative poems have been most successful. As the poet-observer, he records the stories of hard-working people, failures, and outcasts with dramatic images rendered through a disturbing voice. Some critics find Lane's visceral style sensational in its emphasis on violence. Others praise him for combining "the grotesque with the deeply human" to achieve a harsh but true realism.

Lane's early poetry was marked by experiments in language and form through which he gradually developed a unique, documentary style. Most critics feel his poetry matured with the volumes *Beware the Months of Fire* and *Unborn Things;* the latter recounts his experiences while traveling in South America. For *Poems New and Selected* Lane received the Governor General's Award in 1978. His recent collection, *The Measure,* has further expanded Lane's reputation as one of Canada's most distinctive poets.

(See also *Contemporary Authors*, Vols. 97-100.)

Photograph by William Toye, Editorial Director, Oxford University Press, Canada

PETER STEVENS

[In *Letters From the Savage Mind* Patrick Lane] allows his persona to stand at the centre of the majority of his poems, which are especially good when he deals with the ordinary affairs of himself and his family. Just under the surface of these poems lie enormous fears and questions but they never assume moral proportions. The encroachments of age, the madness of political situations, childlessness, loneliness and anonymity in the big city, outbursts of violence are all fixed within the circle of himself and the environments he lives in, visits or remembers. Ordinary things take on aspects of seriousness; they belong to individuals, and individuals are what matter in this terrifying world. Thus, the poetry focuses on seemingly small and unimportant things: cats, dogs—alive or dead, an ant, children and children's games, an orange lawnmower, a carved wooden fish. He remembers the outer world by things immediate and personal to him: the Cuban crisis by cougar tracks and Pope Paul's visit to the U.N. by the first hard rain of winter. Lights on ships create myths for him—there are several poems about the sea and the mountains, making an overwhelming environment for man. But somehow man survives by means of his ordinary everyday affairs and relationships.

Sometimes these ordinary things reduce the poems to ordinariness. Sometimes Patrick Lane becomes strangely pretentious: I find the two long poems in the book, particularly **"The Carnival Man"** (however important it may be to the poet himself), too overwrought. He is best in dealing with immediacies and there are many poems in *Letters From The Savage Mind* of this kind. The cumulative effect of these poems is to make the reader feel that this poet is an individual keenly observant about himself and the world around him, sensitive without being over-emotional, realistic without milking the realism too often. This is a very good collection. (p. 283)

Peter Stevens, "Stones' Throw from the West," in The Canadian Forum, *Vol. XLVII, No. 566, March,* 1968, pp. 282-83.*

DOUG FETHERLING

Lane's poems are more visceral than cerebral and are not abstract at all. At their most representative they focus on a specific person or place in his life, such as a whore or a lumberjack, a jail cell or a highway, and they are characterized by a general surefootedness and realism through which he sprinkles the occasional brilliant image, the odd burst of poetry so pure it makes you squirm. This places him in direct contrast with those who favour the halting and the indirect, who esteem the distillation of experience to the point where the poem is the residue of the moment and the thought. Likewise it removes him from those of the other popular extreme for whom the poem is a topical thing dashed off to preserve the moment of its birth; who do not eliminate, rework and reshape but who believe in the blanket method of trying to isolate truths. In the age of extremists, then, Lane is a moderate who does not see a potential poem in every experience and who does not too much belabour, according to fashion, those things he does undertake. He goes his own way, without followers but with at least one teacher.

For many years associated with West Coast writing, he seems in this retrospective collection [*The Sun Has Begun to Eat the Mountain*] to be at his best in several cases when dealing with British Columbia. The best instance is a longer poem called **"Sam Sam the Candy Man."** . . . It is a childhood memory of the town simpleton and his death in the local pool room. It is violent in its nostalgia and in technique is an extension of such poems as **"Bunkhouse North,"** in which one man's senseless toying with his well-oiled rifle brings sad and vicious responses from his fellow workers. . . . (p. 35)

As a troubadour, as a *Minnesinger*, as one who—in the tradition of Vachel Lindsay, W. H. Davies and scores of other poets of even less acclaim—has given his poems away in exchange for bread, [Lane] has gone back in a way to an earlier time's idea of what the poet should be and has had little to do with the modern notion of the poet as academic or academic-without-portfolio or of the professional experimenter moving in his or her own circle. The consequences have been freedom from misrepresentation, freedom from classification and . . . a near-complete denial of his rightful place as a solid, substantial Canadian poet of the generation now in full flower. This collection . . . should be read with a view toward rediscovery. (p. 37)

> Doug Fetherling, "Surefooted Poetry from the West Coast" (copyright © 1972 by Saturday Night; reprinted by permission of the author), in Saturday Night, Vol. 87, No. 8, August, 1972, pp. 35, 37.*

LORNE HICKS

Beware the Months of Fire is a book which is sometimes brutal, often morbid, usually disturbing. Like Yeats, Lane finds his muse "In the foul rag-and-bone shop of the heart", but what a foul shop this is, leading to darkness rather than Byzantium. These poems explore an intensely black vision, remindful both in grotesque point of view and morbid tone of Sylvia Plath's work. Just as Plath once confided that she enjoyed watching "cadavers cut open", Lane's poetry reveals a similar grisly fascination with bodies, both dead and dying. . . . Although death is treated graphically by Lane, rather than as an abstraction, there is an underlying sense of purpose in his poetry, summarized by the epigraph: "The greatest defeat, in anything, is to forget, and above all to forget what it is that has smashed you, and to let yourself be smashed without ever realizing how thoroughly devilish men can be." (Céline, *Journey To The End of Night*). This collection is autobiographical, and its characters—all either failures or outcasts—never allow Lane "to forget"; each of them has been cruelly "smashed"; death is degrading rather than ennobling. (p. 22)

The central concern of Lane's poetry is to gain a gut response to the grotesque *action* of his work, rather than leading the reader to a sympathetic understanding of character or motive. It's tough, but effective. While a picture may be worth a thousand words, a poem such as **"There was a Woman Bending"** carries more impact than a long polemic dealing with abortion. . . . This is a stunning, moving poem which carries an immense feeling of emptiness and waste, even though it doesn't proselytize. . . . In **"July"**, Pat Lane writes that "compassion is only the beginning of suffering." In the end, however, the poet describes what has smashed him through the symbolic act of remembering. Although pain and death are central here,

Beware the Months of Fire is a collection provoked by love and understanding rather than hate and bitterness. (pp. 22-3)

> Lorne Hicks, "Literature: 'Beware the Months of Fire'," in The Canadian Forum, Vol. LIV, Nos. 640 & 641, May-June, 1974, pp. 20-3.*

LEN GASPARINI

Lane's poems tell us about things we would like to forget. They are the acerbic documents of an imagination turned inside out. Lane records his impressions of reality with guts. There is no jive circumlocution in his style—an unschooled, street-cool one that serves the purpose of his perception. Neither does he run at the mouth for the sake of vocabulary. . . .

Beware the Months of Fire is Lane's ninth collection, and it contains many poems from earlier, now out-of-print editions. The new poems complement the range of Lane's voice. They also touch upon familiar and poignant subjects: from the almost scatological view of **"What Does Not Change"** to the brutality of **"Gerald"**; from big city streets to country jails to the haunting isolation of the B.C. interior, and from the malaise called South America to Canada's own spectral Indian Reservations. Lane has covered them all. His poems are mirrors with the spidery cracks of truth in them. He doesn't flinch from the ugliness and cruelty of life, but observes it with ironic compassion. Like Layton and Jeffers, he knows the grimace behind the grin. (p. 92)

Lane's vision encompasses the surfeit of experience pushed to its extremity. Whether he writes about wild dogs or lovemaking, **"Toronto the Ugly"** or the "shredded" walls in a tenement house, he is right there, gripping the essential, inducing us to look. He feeds us raw chunks of life.

Because of his seeming obsession with the seamier aspects of life, the lyrical and reflective moments in his poetry (And they do happen!) hit us unexpectedly. **"The Bird"**, **"Saskatchewan"**, **"October"**, **"Cariboo Winter"**, and **"Similkameen Deer"** are evocative of nature and the tender ceremonies of love. In these pieces Lane transforms the "I" and gives it an objective dignity. Metaphor and meaning create a kind of magnetic field, and the poet places the "I" within that space. . . . [*Beware the Months of Fire*] is easily the best book of poems to come out of Canada this year. (p. 93)

> Len Gasparini, "One Plus Three" (reprinted by permission of the author), in Canadian Literature, No. 63, Winter, 1975, pp. 92-5.*

GEORGE WOODCOCK

[*Unborn Things: South American Poems* is Patrick Lane's] threnodies of the Inca past and his appalled presentations of the here-and-now in which the descendants of those who created the Andean civilizations survive. Patrick Lane's earlier poems have already shown his exceptional quality as a poet recording with mingled delight and anger the splendour of the world and the shame of what man has done to it and to his fellow inhabitants. . . . [The main suite of *Unborn Things*, **"Macchu Picchu"**,] evokes the past of that lost final fortress of the Inca realm, perched on its splendid crags above the jungle and the river: the departure of Manco Capac, the last Inca, to die in a Spanish ambush; the dying out of the deserted Virgins of the Sun; and the fate their refuge now shares with other tragic loci of history, with Mycenae and Elsinore, with Taxila and Persepolis. . . . (p. 87)

The kind of transference that equates modern man's brutality to a snake with the Spaniards' destruction of a civilization they could not understand, is extended to other poems in *Unborn Things,* which is not unexpected when one remembers the indictments of man's abuse of his will and power over other beings in earlier Lane poems like **"Mountain Oysters"** and **"The Black Filly"**. **"At the Edge of the Jungle"** is a poem about disillusionment with a place romantically anticipated, and the narrative of horror begins with a dog burying its head in the Amazon mud to evade the flies that swarm on his sore eyes; it ends with a tethered rooster whose beak children have cut away so that he cannot eat. It is a fine, appalling poem, whose truth I recognize from having made that journey myself, over the Andean sierra and down to the Amazonian headwaters. . . .

South America has provoked Canadian poets to remarkable work. It gave Earle Birney the hints for some of his best poems, and the same is true of Patrick Lane, whose recent work—this volume and *Beware the Months of Fire,* establish him clearly as a poet unusual in his direct and telling response to experience, whether that experience is a memory of the collective mind or an episode individually lived. (p. 88)

> George Woodcock, *"Playing with Freezing Fire"*
> *(reprinted by permission of the author), in* Canadian
> Literature, *No. 70, Autumn, 1976, pp. 84-91.**

MARILYN BOWERING

Lane's early work struggles to find a sincere language. He tries out modes of speech, tones, roles. There is a hostile/aggressive/macho touch even where he tries for the lyric—bravado substituting for feeling—and an occasional line or poem which learns, under the impetus of betrayal/anger, to say what it means. (p. 26)

His devices, clumsy at first, are sound. They teach him structure, how a change in syntax, the substitution of a word in a familiar phrase, or the reversal of normal perspective, can make something new. . . . The language gains independence. It has its own drive apart from anything the poet knows he knows. Lane discovers how to elicit meaningful connections (rather than the strained, as in **"Krestova Solitaire"** or **"Bottle Pickers"**) between animate and inanimate, internal and external. He does so accurately first in a very early poem (from *Letters From The Savage Mind* . . .), **"The Myth Makers"**. (p. 27)

Much [in this particular poem] parallels the development of any young poet, but the difference with Lane was his refusal to imitate anything he didn't know firsthand (family, job, no-job), an anti-intellectual/anti-ivory tower stand risking a literature of surfaces, but allowing him to develop slowly, a poetry that is justifiably self-confident. The other factor of interest in the early Lane is his continuing concern to give voice to a community; to be a poet with justification—thus his narrative poems, the looking for something to share poems. He begins with the only sane response there is to being somewhere uncharted. He records placing himself, drawing attention to the details of *here*. He makes ceremony in everyday life, the ceremony beaten, often, by the banality of its concerns, but he continues. Gradually these poems become less anecdotal, more fully narrative. The fault of the anecdote is voyeurism (as in **"Mountain Oysters"** or **"Sam Sam The Candy Man"**), detachment. Its antidote is not identification, but imagination, compassion. **"Grey John"** is a fine anecdote/narrative written this way.

The ability to be part rather than watcher is the most significant advance in Lane's poetry. The clean break is at *Unborn Things* . . . , though a number of poems in the collection *Beware the Months of Fire* . . . show he is capable of doing this. With *Unborn Things,* confirmed by *Albino Pheasants* . . . , he is consistent.

If a narrative is to have a community function, it must have a point, often a moral. The abuse of this form in British Columbia is legion. The purpose of giving "voice" to people by using the material of their working lives is surely to reveal (or discover as is more often necessary) the meaning inherent in such lives, not to perpetuate its technology. It is not the work ethic . . . that needs elaboration but the connection of living things to living things. . . . The enshrinement of unintegrated, unconsidered incident may provide brief local excitement, but it is one more warp in the cloth of isolation and exile that we've been busily working these past hundred odd years. Lane understands this, and his imitators should take note. (pp. 28-9)

"Slash Burning on Silver Star", from *Albino Pheasants* is a remarkable poem, a pivotal poem. With its anger born of difference, of not being one with things, it is an explication, nearly, of the combination narrative/violent/impetus of West Coast poetry. . . . The hostility is between subject and object, between the place and self. The bond is fear and necessity: the fear—of defeat and of the inevitablity of defeat. . . . It is self-mutilation with the objective change. It is knowledge of impermanence and ineffectuality, it is inability to do/be anything else. Survival of the self depends on separation from the place; survival depends on the place, whatever self-identity there is depends on the place. There is no Coleridgian "blessing unawares" to heal: no panacea: no apples.

In *Unborn Things* (both the poem and the book) the separation between self and object is blurred. The earth is not "other". (If you become one with place, you need not fear it.) The myth of the dying/resurrected god emerges as solution. With resurrection, fear and separation lose power. . . . When Lane takes on this myth, he becomes capable of giving accurate voice to the reference community. He can do so because he is *no longer* identical with it (and with its concomitant fears). All possibilities, because of regeneration, are available. The transforming poem can be itself and other; its wounds and its healing are one and the same. The place is internal; internalizes.

In the Lane of *Albino Pheasants* and *Unborn Things,* there are no more questions and answers (the early Lane providing both), but cycles, seasons, elements. . . . The poems of *Unborn Things* are sun poems, or more exactly, of the loss of Sun, of knowledge. They are sensuous, rich and certain, exchanging that knowledge for the irrational, dark-natured Moon knowledge . . . which develops in *Albino Pheasants.* The narratives no longer close off . . . , but widen. . . . The images are circular: sun, flower, cup. Released from ego totalitarianism, the poems speak with new voices. Lane does with the South American poems what he hasn't yet or can't quite do with Canada. He makes the place timeless, developing a language that suits.

The poems of *Albino Pheasants* are less lush, simpler, better formed than *Unborn Things;* reducing to light and dark and to circles bounded and unbounded. Lane recreates a primitive landscape in the classic tradition. . . . His vocabulary is plainer, strong, life forms simplify—crab/womb/tree/seed. The poems are evocative, and drop into the quietness of mind like stones in a pool. A poem, **"Still Hunting"**, is resonant of a hero's quest, of Japanese painting, even of Tolstoi's "Pilgrim Song." Lane has worked through to certainties—the same he began with—fear and death, but with new names: sameness and change.

What makes these "Lane" poems is an undercutting of the traditionalism which occurs, in most of the poems, with a line or several phrases which "ground" the central mystery to a specific locale. There is an interruption of local colour/dialect/diction to the body of the poem to "place" it. Where this works, as in **"And Say of What You See In The Dark"**, **"Albino Pheasants"**, and Lane's best poem, **"When"**, the result is a balanced, delicate, skillful dance of "interaction of the within and the without". Where it doesn't work, as in **"Exile"**, **"Quitting Time"**, **"That Quick and Instant Flight"**, it often comes close; though at its worst, the result is bathetic. (pp. 29-32)

At the end of eleven years of published poetry, place and placing remain as essential to Lane as at the beginning. He has succeeded in unearthing and voicing some few truths about the meaning of place in terms of the people living there—no small feat. He writes with clarity, with sureness of craft and continues risks with his art. He has maimed if not disabled the habit of self-deceit. His poetry is self-made, self-justified. (p. 33)

> *Marilyn Bowering, "Pine Boughs and Apple Trees; The Poetry of Patrick Lane," in* The Malahat Review *(© The Malahat Review, 1978), No. 45, January, 1978, pp. 24-34.*

LEN GASPARINI

I have always had the utmost respect for Lane's work in books and magazines, and this new volume [*Poems New & Selected*] is an ostensible culmination of his poetic talent. His themes are earthy, steeped in raw experience, the sweat of working and loving, and his language rages with pain, a violent beauty, and Neruda's "confused impurity of the human condition." His imagery is seldom bland; in fact, it often relies on a shock effect. . . .

Lane's poems are poignantly impressionistic observations on the menacing aspects of man and nature. He writes about his native British Columbia with passion and irony, like a man who knows its moods inside out. He can soar into the lyricism of **"Macchu Picchu,"** or dive into himself with **"The Trace of Being."** The feeling is always there, taut with emotion, every word a muscle expressing the imagination of a true poet whose sensibilities thrum like guitar strings. Patrick Lane speaks first and last for himself, and his *Poems New & Selected* is a testament toward that end. . . .

> *Len Gasparini, "Pain, Thunder, and Rainbows" (reprinted by permission of the author), in* Books in Canada, *Vol. 8, No. 2, February, 1979, p. 24.**

ROSEMARY SULLIVAN

Pat Lane is from the BC interior and in his poetry [recently collected in *Poems New & Selected*] you find the West Coast landscape and temperament. He writes of logging camps and forests, the native people, hunting and bush farming, but you don't feel the poet has turned to these subjects as the compulsory material of his region. This is Lane's natural world. He writes a tough-minded, anecdotal poetry full of narratives

of the hard lives of ordinary people. The voice he chooses is often raw and violent, and his best quality is a remarkable and moving empathy for all of life that is vulnerable and pained: the woman who aborts herself in a dingy hotel, the boy who blows his mother's arms off with a bomb, the pregnant cat dipped in gas and set alight. Lane has a fine gift for image, and writes of the tragic not histrionically but in understatement, deflecting attention to some small detail that is made to carry the full horror of the situation. A great deal of the poetic energy comes from a real understanding of violence that challenges our complacency. . . . I like to think of poets in terms of emblems, and Lane's self-image is of a mutilated bird—its beak broken by sadistic children—that is forced to look but unable to eat. This is not posturing. Whatever the private complex out of which he writes, Lane does understand pain.

Most of the time he looks outward; he is the observer, the recording eye. Some of his best poems come from his wanderings as a tourist in South America. In fact, one has the sense that Lane came of age as a writer there; that like many Canadian poets, he needed another culture to catalyze the deepest impulses in his work. South America's brooding violence and intensity, which turn so readily towards the mythic, gave Lane wonderful poems like **"Unborn Things,"** **"The Hustler,"** and **"Chile,"** where he is at his best because the mode is dramatic.

Lane also writes an introspective poetry, particularly as a son and a lover. But in the former role his ground is less sure. He writes often of his father, but obliquely, as if the subject were too powerful. The point is not confessionalism but emotional clarity, and one senses that when Lane is really ready to meet this subject, it may prove the most powerful he has attempted.

Meanwhile he is preparing himself by a careful study of poetics. I have noted a similar commitment to craft in other West Coast writers. The best combine a raw exuberance with a reverence for formal structure. One can admire Lane's experimentations in language and form even when there are real problems. In moments when he is off, there can be a sententiousness of tone and a reaching after philosophical statement that is annoying. . . . Yet one allows him these misses for the elegance of such lines as "the green perfection of the space / A leaf includes in its growing." Lane's greatest weakness is posturing; he falls too easily into a highly rhetorical despair. . . . And there is a predictability of form he will want to watch: the first stanza of a poem as a single sentence with the verb buried deep in the centre under a string of participles. But this is a poet with staying power. There is a fine sensual energy in his work, as well as humour, and at moments a depth of vision that make him the best of his generation of poets.

> *Rosemary Sullivan, "Staying Power," in* The Canadian Forum, *Vol. LVIII, No. 687, March, 1979, p. 34.*

JOHN COOK

[Patrick Lane] continues to produce sharp and crafty verse. In [*No Longer Two People*] he has entangled his imagination with Lorna Uher's to produce a duet of violent, but ultimately gentle, love poems. . . .

No Longer Two People takes the form of a poetic dialogue with alternating statements, Uher's under the emblem of a spreading tree, and Lane's under what I take to be a rising sun although his poems themselves speak often of death and the approach of winter. Each poet reacts to and develops the imagery and themes of the other producing a blending of visions that parallels the theme of personal union explored in the poems. It is a unity born of the violence of love with its conflict of desire and fear and its surrender of selves. Against a background of seasonal change this cycle of love poems develops a metaphor drawn from the hunt and makes mythic what might be mere kissing and telling. . . .

The book at times suffers from a lack of freshness of diction. There is, for instance, more than a passing resemblance to Atwood's gothic vision with its occasional grotesque images and its use of metaphor drawn from Susanna Moodie and the pioneer experience. One wonders what might have transpired if the authors had taken the time to seek out the fresh image. For in spite of these lapses, the openness, the brutal frankness makes for compelling reading. (p. 39)

> John Cook, "New Directions and Old," in The Canadian Forum, Vol. LIX, No. 697, March, 1980, pp. 38-9.*

CHRISTOPHER LEVENSON

Usually what attracts or repels one in poetry is the way something is said, the striking perspective, rather than the subject matter as such. Let me start, then, by saying that, purely in terms of linguistic control, mastery of cadence and verse movement, and command of imagery, Patrick Lane, winner of the 1978 Governor-General's award for poetry, has to be classed along with John Newlove and Margaret Atwood as among Canada's most accomplished contemporary poets.

However, *what* a poem is saying cannot be ignored, especially if, as is the case with Lane, there is such a consistent, indeed obsessive pattern to his work. His main concerns are with violence and squalor. Any writer may choose to see certain aspects of life and to ignore others, but to concentrate on brutality and ugliness may be as partial and as sentimental (because excessive) as to exclude such aspects entirely. Moreover, in Lane's case, what we are given is no dispassionate reportage: the poet frequently seems intoxicated by the violence and cruelty that he evokes. And when cruelty not only informs the subject matter but also, via imagery, permeates the manner of the poetry, we are entitled to regret the absence of any controlling moral stance, just as we are entitled to ask whether a talent, no matter how remarkable, that indulges in gratuitous descriptions of cruelty can ever attain to greatness.

This is not an issue peculiar to Patrick Lane's work. . . . There is in Canada today a mystique of cruelty that makes it far too easy to equate power—which in discussing poetry can only mean power over the resources of language—with the description of violence and cruelty, and while Patrick Lane is not its initiator he is among its most distinguished representatives.

Much of the cruelty that Lane celebrates is the cruelty, deliberate or accidental, of men towards nature. Thus in the first thirty pages [of *Poems New and Selected*] we find a blue-jay that "has broken its fingernail skull / on the wall of the boxcar" (**"Loading Boxcars"**), the castrating of rams in **"Mountain Oysters,"** someone's setting the poet's pregnant cat alight in **"Last night in darkness,"** the apparently random shooting of six wild horses in **"Wild Horses,"** and putting a crushed kitten out of its misery by stepping on its head in **"Because I never learned."** (pp. 279-80)

Certainly where man is not being cruel to animals he is shown brutalizing his fellow man or, more often, his fellow woman.

Thus in **"There was a woman bending"** we are shown a botched abortion. . . . At the end of this poem the woman has died and the poet comments: "It was the walls her eyelids made / that I remember. The silences they bred. / And her eyes, / eyes I will never know the colours of." One wonders, does it really matter? Isn't this akin to the sentimentality of those anti-Vietnam War poets who lamented the napalming of the "beautiful brown people"? The agony is the same whatever the complexion or color of eyes. (p. 280)

Indeed [in Lane's poetry] there is much of what [he] elsewhere terms "the brutal anger that cannot be relieved / except on things"—and, one might add, on people, especially women. Is it significant that in the poem **"Albino Pheasants"** and elsewhere he writes "no man" and "men" rather than "no one" and "people"? Both in terms of settings and of attitudes most of what Lane writes about is masculine in the most restricted, traditional sense, and his selected cruelties come across as part of a more pervasive *machismo*. . . . In fact, **"Thinking of that contest,"** which evokes the ritual of women hanging up clothes on a line in the freezing cold, is one of very few poems where Lane portrays a woman as an active participant rather than as victim or object. More usual for the relationships between men and women are the tough, hard-bitten epigrammatic endings (as in **"Surcease"**: "Play with me gently woman / I'm made of glass") or the "lesson" that nature provides in **"Poem for a gone woman,"** where the lovers watch as a snake vainly tries to swallow a live frog. . . . (pp. 280-81)

When situations that do not otherwise involve sexual violence have it thrust upon them one begins to find Lane's imagery exploitative. Thus in **"At the edge of the jungle,"** "I turn to where orchids gape / like the vulvas of hanged women." This may or may not be visually accurate—I don't know and I wonder how many naked hanged women the poet has actually inspected—but its effect is gratuitously violent and degrading for, unlike, say, Ted Hughes, Lane does not himself embody nature, he does not become crow or pike or otter, but instead remains an observer, sometimes, one feels, a voyeur.

Much the same may be said of the non-sexual violence of, say, **"A Murder of Crows"** which shows the crow's "body hanging down from its tripod. / My knife slid up and steaming ribbons of gut / fell to the ground." . . . Isn't this overkill? How much do we really need to see every time? What is the poet trying to prove about himself? . . . Wounds and knives come too easily to Lane's imagination.

Such indulgence in violence and corruption might, however, be tolerable if subordinated to some over-riding vision or philosophy. But is it? There are attempts, certainly. (pp. 281-82)

[But] except perhaps in a poem such as **"Pissaro's Tomb,"** where, with historical imagination, Lane works up to a rhetoric of negation, a grandeur that is past, we are given few realized positives. Instead we are constantly presented with findings that I at least find *not* inevitable, *not* justified, mere assertions unbacked by anything worked through in the poem, such as we find here in **"A murder of crows"**: "What can be said? words are dark rainbows / Without roots, a murder of crows, / a memory of music reduced to guile." Yet that last line is excellently cadenced and creates the illusion of profundity. Lane is, in fact, an accomplished illusionist with a gift for the lapidary statement that at times even approaches a kind of Yeatsian eloquence (see "The Trace of being"). Nor does he shrink from the big, often romantic gestures and the unearned resonance of lines like: "Ah, heart, I cannot scorn the armies of your pain,'' or from the pseudo-heroic afflatus at the end of **''In every world.''** . . . (p. 282)

Having said all this, one must add that there are also many poems where Lane evokes a scene with exciting economy and where the harshness or cruelty is wholly appropriate. . . . In the anecdotal **''After,''** the poet lets us see and feel the pathos of a man who had lost all the nerves in one arm that had been caught in a machine and would sit in a bar ''telling stories for drinks.'' But perhaps the most impressive of such poems is **''Sleep is the silence darkness takes,''** which is dedicated to the poet's father and speaks through his persona of a hard childhood and adolescence, marriage, war service and [death]. . . . This poem, it seems to me, exhibits a sustained power that is tactile and meditative but not sensational, and successfully explores beyond the poet's own experience.

There are a number of other such poems in the short earlier volume, *Albino Pheasants* . . . and interestingly they are mostly concerned with people at work, whom he evokes, admiringly and sympathetically, with the same kind of realism about work situations that one finds in Al Purdy, Milton Acorn, Tom Wayman, and Sid Marty. In **''Mill Cry,'' ''The Carpenter,'' ''In railroad yards,'' ''Quitting time,''** and **''From the hot hills''**—the last telling of Sikh workers at a logging camp who are ridiculed and beaten up. Here for once Lane is content to let the facts speak for themselves. . . . Here and in **''Farmers,''** which documents the harsh life of Andean peasants ''scraping their lives from stone,'' Lane achieves the same kind of controlled compassion for the stranger and for the impoverished that we find in Newlove's ''Doukhobor.'' The poetry arises from the selection and juxtaposition of the details. Lane is at his best simply observing, directly and without rhetoric, without drawing conclusions for us, ordinary lives.

Unfortunately these qualities are all but lost in his latest work, *No Longer Two People,* a beautifully produced book that consists of a poetic dialogue with Lorna Uher. To the co-authors such a dialogue of love poems obviously seemed a very good idea. ''It is rare,'' they tell us in their introduction, ''for two poets to exist in love and even rarer that they risk themselves by speaking through their art to each other. These poems were torn from us in our need. There was no time in the writing to question, consider or judge what we were doing. There is a nakedness here, a vulnerability, and more than that, a discovery. Our trust allowed us these poems, that, and our desire to praise.'' Unfortunately, a desire to wound is at least as evident as vulnerability, while the tactile context of the relationship is largely missing. Inevitably, then, much remains at the level of sheer assertion, as in Uher's ''I want / to feel my fist / push through / to the cries that were / before words.'' Because so much of the action is present only symbolically, the favorite recurrent symbols—of fists, breaking, starvation, the cold, nakedness, and the inevitable wounds and scars—seem to inhabit a separate world. (pp. 283-84)

The way certain motifs, such as seasonal changes, fish ribs, or feathers are introduced first by the one and then taken up by the other is attractive and often ingenious, but the overall view of love that emerges is unrelentingly grim and is not palliated by the fact that both writers are engaged primarily in mutual exploitation for copy for their poems. . . .

No one will deny that both the kind of world that Lane evokes in most of his poetry and the kind of love that Uher and Lane project do exist. Whether they have been made poetically significant is another matter. The sensationalism in which Patrick

Lane still seems caught is surely a *cul de sac*. To me he appears to have many of the attributes of a major poet without yet having achieved indisputably major poetry. It will be fascinating to see where his next collection takes him, and us. (p. 285)

Christopher Levenson, ''Patrick Lane's Violent Poetry,'' in Queen's Quarterly, *Vol. 87, No. 2, Summer, 1980, pp. 279-85.*

IAN SOWTON

It seems to me that Patrick Lane is one of our better contemporary poets when it comes to telling us about the place they inhabit with us. *The Measure* is a recent milestone/signpost of his being there—particularly West and Northwest. A controlling pattern of his earlier books like *Beware the Months of Fire* . . . and *Poems New and Selected* . . . is even clearer here: short sojourns, many journeys. He is but a little mad north-northwest; but whichever direction the wind sits that blows through so many of his poems, he has a bracing body of work and calloused hands to show for his and his persona's travels. (p. 102)

As in a lot of our poetry, outer topography of *The Measure*'s place is mountains, the edge between prairie and mountain, trees, stones, and the lineaments of winter. So what's new? Well, in most of these poems the sense is of a looker really seeing, a hearer who really listens (especially to stories or to what asks to be turned into a story), a toucher who actually feels and is touched. That is always new. As for the human figure—inner map and all—who completes any topography if only in the sense of giving it a fragile, temporary voice, the teller of these poems is in full touch with those mountains, edges, trees, and stones. Especially with the stones. Metaphor and symbol are noble, serviceable creations but we're so apt at conjuring them into often trivialized, merely psychological states. Lane doesn't do this. . . . He tries to stay on the edge between inner and outer landscapes. The magus wordmaker inside remains in difficult commerce with what's out there, which includes other people and other forms of life wild and domestic. . . . He is not interested in transmogrifying this intractable outside into humid privacies of the confessional. (pp. 102-03)

In *The Measure* the predicament, strongly sounded in its title page, is to find the measure, take the measure of being in this place. (p. 103)

The Measure ends on a discouraged note. To other perplexities have been added deeper ones: the dark suspicion that it may not be worth going on telling, or even living, is compounded by the compulsion to go on nevertheless in spite of all the waste, violence, trivia, and zombyism. . . . I find Lane's rendition of being in this place a moving one. I hope he is not too tired. I hope he goes on journeying and telling us. (p. 104)

Ian Sowton, ''North-Northwest'' (reprinted by permission of the author), in Canadian Literature, *No. 91, Winter, 1981, pp. 102-04.*

ROSEMARY AUBERT

The poems [in *The Measure*] fall roughly into three categories.

A few poems like **''Temenos''** are basically philosophical in nature. While they certainly cannot be dismissed as merely abstract, they are ponderous and occasionally fall victim to a too-frequent use of rhetorical questions. A second class of poem encompasses works such as "**The Long Coyote Line.**" These are enriched nature poems, descriptive, but also offering comment on what is described. These poems are both strong and delicate, reminiscent of fine Oriental poetry.

But the third type of poem shows the real strength of this collection: the narratives. Every one of them is vigorous, gripping and nearly unforgettable. "**Just Living,**" a truly striking poem, manages to combine the grotesque and the deeply human without ever straining credulity or forcing emotion. Its language is purely natural, its effect pure art. And it is a diamond among other precious stones. "**Annie She,**" "**Something Other Than Our Own,**" and the marvellous closing poem, "**Certs,**" prove that Lane is a master of narrative. These poems grab the reader and hang on to him, the way a well-told tale does.

> *Rosemary Aubert, "Poetry: 'The Measure',"* in Quill and Quire *(reprinted by permission of* Quill and Quire*), Vol. 47, No. 2, February, 1981, p. 48.*

JOHN CRUICKSHANK

The title poem of [*The Measure*] should quickly find its way into the anthologies, not because it is the best of the 25 poems brought together in this volume, but because it is the most striking. "**The Measure**" depicts a dead dog in a field being watched over by a magpie; it is a small, almost perfect song in a minor key. The metaphor is precise and compelling, drawing the reader into a slightly claustrophobic but richly furnished poetic world. And, like much of the best anthology poetry—though not always the best verse—"**The Measure**" feels authorless and timeless. . . . Such words as "bone" and "stark," and such images as wind whipping away sound, seem to suspend the poem in time and place, giving it a universal quality.

In fact, I'd advise readers to make their way through the title poem before grappling with Lane's rather bathetic screed for himself on the back cover: "I sometimes think I was born old," he writes. "If that is true then these poems are a way of return to an innocence I never knew." Unfortunately, this triumph of grammar and logic intrudes into some of Lane's poems. A poet's reflections on life and community are often valuable—perhaps when recounted in memoirs or magazine articles—but when in poems they force the reader to stop in mid-stanza to ask why he is being subjected to this or that opinion, the coherence of the reading experience suffers.

Many of the poems are of the "Most Unforgettable Character I Have Known" variety, which now seems so much in vogue. They are entertaining, cleanly written, and though at times they are little more than loosely punctuated short stories, they are at least free of the preciousness that creeps into some of Lane's lyrical work.

> *John Cruickshank, "Precious Little,"* in Books in Canada, *Vol. 10, No. 7, August-September, 1981, p. 18.*

DON GUTTERIDGE

Old Mother contains three quite distinct sections. First there is a long sequence called "**Prairie Poems,**" which confirms Lane's reputation as one of our best poets. Read individually, these poems afford the pleasure we have come to expect from his verse: a sense of immediacy, of living through powerful emotional and sensuous experiences expressed in stark, occasionally bizarre, imagery and controlled by a constant voice whose rhythms are as sure as they are haunting. Lane's has always been the voice of the outsider, the alienated, the man with the crooked eye—a voice tempered always by compassion and the anguish it brings. In "**Prairie Poems**" these concerns are vividly focussed on the everyday world of rural life where seemingly callous rituals are routinely acted out: a pair of country lovers toss a couple of exotic birds . . . into a mob of local cockerels where they are torn to pieces. . . . Other brutal and random violence recurs: the mandatory "geek" lunching on live chicken, a girl accidentally crushing eggs full of rotting foetuses, etc. What saves these poems from (black) sentimentality is Lane's fierce desire to see and understand. In many of them, a young hired hand is directly involved as watcher or participant—setting up a tension between the horror of the action and the innocence of the persona. Even in poems without the observing "I," Lane creates a sense of its presence, largely through the candour and empathy of the language through which he enters into and renders the spirit of his trapped and bewildered dream-creatures. . . .

On another level "**Prairie Poems**" is a sequence in which the immediate experience poems . . . are interwoven with pieces that explore the history and landscape in which the action takes place. The masculine rituals of aggression, dominance, lust, and undirected violence are beautifully counterpointed by the feminine principles of endurance, suffering, forebearance, remembrance, continuity and the pure poetry of being-in-time. No brief review can do justice to the subtle ironies and tensions set up by the complex web of symbols surrounding the old mother (hawk, brooding hen, provider, prairie herself with her ancient winds and sacred boneyards) that frame, balance and render sanity to Lane's nightmarish vision of the dislocated present. That such a framing is intentional is indicated by the first and last poems of this section, which clearly signal the role this poet has chosen for himself and reveal the significance of the brooding mother for our understanding of a society temporarily out of touch with its roots. . . .

In the book's second part, in a long poem called "**The Weight,**" Lane takes his own advice and goes searching for family roots in North America, blending personal history with political in a somewhat macabre and surreal dance of events. While interesting, especially in light of "**Prairie Poems,**" the open forms and ambitious collaging effects here are not as surely handled as the tight weave of luminous graphics in the latter. The book concludes with a series of "**China Poems,**" where Lane's eye for on-site detail and his sure voice give us a set of finely crafted lyrics echoing in softer tones the earlier themes of an ancient people on the verge of forgetting the past.

> *Don Gutteridge, "A Sure Voice,"* in The Canadian Forum, *Vol. LXII, No. 726, March, 1983, p. 34.*

Halldór (Kiljan) Laxness

1902-

(Born Halldór Kiljan Guðjonsson) Icelandic novelist, essayist, dramatist, short story writer, travel writer, translator, autobiographer, historian, and poet.

Laxness won the Nobel Prize for Literature in 1955 for his success at invigorating the staid literature of Iceland and for his adept portrayal of the problems that modernization had brought to that isolated and ancient culture. Unfortunately, his innovations, symbolism, and lyricism cannot be fully appreciated in translation. Thus, though Laxness's work is monumental in Icelandic literature, he is not well known outside Scandinavia.

Laxness travelled extensively through post-World War I Europe and was influenced by literary trends there. *Vefarinn mikli frá Kasmír (The Great Weaver from Kashmir)* is a notable work from this period of his career. It shows Laxness to have been under the sway of expressionism and deeply interested in religious questions. Written while Laxness was living in a monastery in Luxembourg, *Vefarinn mikli frá Kasmír* is a novel of ideas, full of general philosophical speculation and explorations of Catholic theology.

In 1929, Laxness published a collection of radical essays entitled *Alþýðubókin (The Book of the People)*. Clearly socialist in many of its stances, this book marks the beginning of a long period in which Laxness's political beliefs were quite obviously integrated into his fiction. *Salka Valka* epitomizes the type of fiction produced by Laxness during this stage of his career. Set in an economically depressed fishing village in Iceland and written in an epic style, the novel contains a good deal of social criticism. Its world view is bleak, as is its view of human nature.

Laxness published the novel *Brekkukotsannáll (The Fish Can Sing)* in 1957, a work that is said to mark a third period in Laxness's writing. This novel and those that follow it contain less social and political criticism than the earlier works. They are more lyrical and introspective. Beginning with *Brekkukotsannáll*, Laxness seems to find solace in the human capacity for dignity and goodness.

(See also *Contemporary Authors*, Vol. 103.)

PHILLIPS D. CARLETON

[In *Salka Valka*] Halldor Laxness has portrayed a world without hope, without gentleness, without even the concept of progress. . . .

In [a] fishing village on the coast of Iceland, the common people live in such misery that the birth of a child is a misfortune, and death a wretched commonplace. . . . The civil and state officials are either corrupt or indifferent to the poverty of their charges. . . . (p. 12)

One group of the populace—the seamen—start to benefit themselves at the cost of the shore workers; the town is divided by snarling hate. Then communism comes to town and there begin the long privations of a strike and port blockade. Even now

© Lütfi Özkök

the author allows no amelioration of the grim scene. . . . The long strike ends by giving new masters to the village; the new coöperative is quietly absorbed; the dreams, feeble as they were, fade and the village sinks back into a lethargy more confirmed than ever. Mr. Laxness does not believe for a minute that these villagers have learned the most elementary lessons of union or coöperation.

Salka Valka, the daughter of a woman marooned in this town, is the one through whom we see these happenings; she is a member of the seamen's union; she first fights and then falls in love with the communistic leader. He deserts her and his cause; she stands in the end momentarily at peace in a false glow of martyrdom.

The vision that Halldor Laxness holds of the world—or at least of the Icelandic world—is wholly dark: the forces of nature are harsh and terrifying; the people themselves are sunk in a misery from which there is no redemption; the brief flame of the spirit is quenched soon by hard economic circumstance. The only hope of the average inhabitant is that he may have bright moments which can never be rooted out of memory. This vision of the world must have been reached after profound disillusion; it has the great virtue of being of necessity a point of departure toward some affirmative level. Logically Mr. Laxness must seize on some point of light in this abyss of despair if he is to continue to deal in literary values and not direct action. Meanwhile this book bears witness to a fairly unrelenting stare on the gross realities of existence. (pp. 12-13)

Phillips D. Carleton, "World without Hope," in The Saturday Review of Literature *(© 1936 Saturday Review Magazine Co.; reprinted by permission), Vol. XIV, No. 4, May 23, 1936, pp. 12-13.*

STEFÁN EINARSSON

Halldór Kiljan Laxness is [the] most original [of all the Icelandic writers who began to write after World War I]. Like nobody else he represents the young urban population of Reykjavík, cut loose from the secure moorings of the thousand year old farm-culture, searching vigorously for a new mode of living among the possibilities of the post-war world. . . . A monument to his Catholic days *Vefarinn Mikli frá Kasmir* . . . looms as a milestone of a new age in Icelandic novelistics; it is expressionistic and autobiographic, a true picture of the turmoil of the author's mind. After 1930 Laxness has described Icelandic land and people from his communistic point of view. . . . Laxness novels are conceived on the grand scale; the poor village girl and the independent cottage farmer emerging as heroes of monumental stature, individuals and symbols of their class at the same time. The poet, though no hero, but rather the lowly subject and scapegoat of a cruel world, is no less grandly conceived as a symbol of the suffering spirit that will survive and spread light even under the most terrible circumstances. In his novels Laxness has created a new style, whose storms and stresses contrast vividly to the classic saga-like style of his predecessors and has left its mark on contemporary novelists after 1930. A fierce social criticism runs through all his novels; this has alienated readers both at home and abroad. But more discriminating readers have admired the brilliance of his style, his vigorous symbolism, and the art with which he fuses his characters and his scenery into one vast and drab panorama of intensified reality. (pp. 257-58)

Stefán Einarsson, "Five Icelandic Novelists," in Books Abroad *(copyright 1942 by the University of Oklahoma Press), Vol. 16, No. 3, Summer, 1942, pp. 254-59.**

ROBERT GORHAM DAVIS

The man Bjartur [protagonist of **"Independent People"** (**"Sjálfstaett fólk"**)] is a magnificent and complex symbol of peasant independence, and this whole great novel might be considered a profoundly imaginative projection of Hardy's poem, "In Time of 'The Breaking of Nations'." Bjartur is the modern Icelandic counterpart of the figure Hardy saw harrowing clods, hidden in "thin smoke without flame from heaps of couchgrass," working without change though dynasties rise and fall. . . .

Bjartur is a magnificent symbol because he is at once and so completely Icelander, peasant, man. . . .

And in the Western world the culture of Icelandic peasants is uniquely high and pure. These are the descendants of Vikings who established in Iceland an independent, democratic republic, a government of laws under the Althing, long before the English Magna Carta. And they still speak the uncorrupted language of the great eddas and sagas of the North which only highly literate Iceland preserved for the rest of the world. Bjartur could recite the exploits of the poet-heroes of the sagas,

and of Grettis and Burnt Njal. He constantly made poems for his own delight, poems in the measures of the eighteenth century with all the metrical ingenuity of the ancient scalds. . . . Contemptuous of clergymen and state schools, he taught his beloved Asta Sollilja the Orvar-Odds Saga and the difficult kennings of the Jomsviking poems. This was the culture, the literature of freedom, that "preserved the nation's life. . . . "

The author is a sociologist writing in the naturalist tradition. He knows exactly how Bjartur's way of life is conditioned by developments in scientific sheep breeding, farmers cooperatives, world markets, international loans. He knows that peasant individualism is not eternal, that it is disappearing fast in Russia, and may in many other parts of the world within this century. But as many of our American social novelists do not have, Laxness has also a poet's imagination and a poet's gift for phrase and symbol. When he moves into the minds of his characters, life takes on the shape and color and meaning it has for them. . . . (p. 25)

Robert Gorham Davis, "History of an 'Independent Man'," in The New York Times Book Review *(© 1946 by The New York Times Company; reprinted by permission), July 28, 1946, pp. 1, 25.*

HAMILTON BASSO

["**Independent People**"], laid in Iceland, tells about a man who struggles for eighteen years to get hold of enough money to buy a sheep farm and then has to struggle just as hard to keep hold of it. Since such epical efforts cannot be confined within the dimensions of the ordinary novel and since Mr. Laxness's theme is that of man against the universe, he lets himself go for four hundred and seventy pages of just about solid type. His book consequently moves at the pace of one of the livelier glaciers. I can't say that it is altogether enjoyable, particularly those long passages of somewhat murky philosophy that are as essential to an epic as the theme of man against the universe, but it's not altogether unreadable, either. Mr. Laxness's hero, it might be added, is as disagreeable a character as ever an epic was built around—hard, bigoted, and mean— and there are times when, despite his motto, "This land will not betray its flocks," he clearly hates the hell out of everything. The book has a certain impressiveness, but I can't get rid of the notion that much of what looks like impressiveness is simply bulk. There must be a few writers in the cold countries who are not epic. . . . (pp. 88-9)

Hamilton Basso, "Shakespeare, Another Epic, and Nehru," in The New Yorker *(© 1946 by The New Yorker Magazine, Inc.), Vol. XXII, No. 27, August 17, 1946, pp. 88-9.**

BRUCE LANCASTER

There is a strange quality that seems inseparable from Scandinavian writings—somber, pitched in a minor key, harsh, and, at first glance, cold and colorless as the light of an Arctic false dawn. . . . Yet this seeming drabness is deceptive. The lowering tones of false dawn slowly vanish to reveal a rich, warm life that is none the less real for all its neutral tints.

Now out of Iceland comes a strange story, vibrant and alive under its sinister overtones. . . . [*Independent People*] tells of the struggle of an Iceland crofter to achieve self-sufficiency, of his obsession for independence, a craving so deep that in his pursuit of it he becomes a slave to his ideal. . . .

Every step of [Bjartur's] long fight, every success, every failure, flows through these pages with bitter relentlessness, a dour inevitability. It is the age-old story of the peasant against the world, and through the author's skill, it achieves a rare timelessness and universality. . . .

Bitter and somber as the story is, there is a rare beauty in its telling, a beauty as surprising as the authentic strain of poetry that lies in the shoving, battering Icelander, the master of "Summerhouses."

> *Bruce Lancaster, "'Independent People'," in* The Atlantic Monthly *(copyright © 1946, by The Atlantic Monthly Company, Boston, Mass.; reprinted with permission), Vol. 178, No. 3, September, 1946, p. 150.*

WILLIAM BARRETT

[Halldor Laxness] never acquired the audience in the United States that his unusual and fine talent deserved. The life in Iceland that he portrayed may have been too stark and remote for American tastes. Now that in *Paradise Reclaimed* [*Paradísarheimt*] . . . his story moves from Iceland to Utah, he ought to be able to capture a few more readers.

Mist-shrouded Iceland and the desert flats of Utah seem to be spots as unrelated as any two you could pick on this globe; Mr. Laxness ties them together by the common dream of a real earthly paradise that circulated among Icelanders and Mormons in the nineteenth century. His hero, a small farmer named Steinar Steinsson, is persuaded by a Mormon missionary in Iceland to make the long pilgrimage to the land of the Latter-Day Saints. . . . At the end we see him revisiting Iceland, gazing at the ruins of his farm and wondering whether paradise might not be found in Iceland as much, or as little, as in Utah— the eternal query of the returning immigrant. (pp. 172, 174)

The qualities of the sagas pervade [Laxness's] writing, and particularly a kind of humor—oblique, stylized, and childlike—that can be found in no other contemporary writer. Steinar himself, the unpredictable dreamer, is a very beguiling figure, a humble man who nevertheless carries the unquenchable spark of the old Vikings. (p. 174)

> *William Barrett, "Forgotten Novelist," in* The Atlantic Monthly *(copyright © 1962, by The Atlantic Monthly Company, Boston, Mass.; reprinted with permission), Vol. 210, No. 6, December, 1962, pp. 172, 174.*

EDWIN MORGAN

Though much in [*The Fish Can Sing*] is ironic and ambiguous, in form it is a straightforward account of an orphan boy growing up in an old fisherman's cottage near Reykjavik, early this century. But of course the theme is Iceland itself, its emergence into the international modern world, an extreme and often philistine yet not unimpressive provincialism being teased out of itself year by year. A native son returns—Gardar Holm, apparently a singer who has won world-wide acclaim but who never proves this claim in public in Reykjavik. The town wants to believe it, for Iceland's sake: 'We want to prove to the rest of the world that "the fish can sing just like a bird".' But it is the young hero of the book who has to sing at Holm's funeral, and at the end he leaves Iceland, another Stephen Dedalus. (p. 486)

> *Edwin Morgan, "Predestination," in* New Statesman *(© 1966 The Statesman & Nation Publishing Co. Ltd.), Vol. 73, No. 1855, September 30, 1966, pp. 485-86.**

PHOEBE-LOU ADAMS

When an author has won a Nobel Prize, it is not unsafe to assume that his work is imbued with high seriousness and earnest purpose, for the Nobel committee has never shown much affection for comedians. The Icelander Halldor Laxness comes, therefore, as a delightful lapse from tradition. His novel *The Fish Can Sing* . . . simmers with an ironic, disrespectful mirth which gives unexpected dimensions to the themes of lost innocence and the nature of art. These themes are sober enough, but as Mr. Laxness develops them through the experiences of young Alfgrim in Reykjavik at the start of the century, they lead to . . . memorable absurdities. . . .

Iceland was a Danish colony in those days, and Mr. Laxness has a great deal of fun with provincial imitations of Copenhagen manners. . . . The basis of Mr. Laxness' style is . . . Icelandic bluntness, which is not bluntness at all but a literary technique that goes right back to the sagas. It involves an artful, calculated, and even devious arrangement of what appear to be mere surface details, which by their juxtaposition produce meanings and emotional responses that are never mentioned in the understated text. . . . How things looked, what was done, and what was said are almost the entire substance of *The Fish Can Sing*. Toward the end, when discussion of the position and reward of the artist becomes too complicated for Alfgrim's wide-eyed bumpkin pitch, Mr. Laxness emerges briefly and warily from behind the mask, but until that point, reflection, explanation, and analysis are rigorously avoided. Nor are they missed.

> *Phoebe-Lou Adams, "Potpourri," in* The Atlantic Monthly *(copyright © 1967, by The Atlantic Monthly Company, Boston, Mass.; reprinted with permission), Vol. 219, No. 4, April, 1967, p. 150.**

BARRY JACOBS

Perhaps no Western country has been so deeply absorbed in its own past as Iceland, where the sagas are still popular literature. A number of nineteenth- and twentieth-century writers, particularly the Scandinavian Naturalists, have been attracted by the narrative power and the complete objectivity of these family sagas. But whereas a few writers—Selma Lagerlöf, Knut Hamsun, and Sigrid Undset among them—have successfully extracted certain stylistic features from the sagas and incorporated them into modern novels, most attempts to imitate the sagas have only resulted in slightly comic pastiches. Nobel Prize-winner Halldor Laxness is the one writer who has been able to resurrect the saga and make it into a viable narrative form. *The Fish Can Sing* . . . is a perfect illustration of the stylistic synthesis he has achieved. . . .

Alfgrim Hansson, the narrator of *The Fish Can Sing,* begins to unfold the story of his childhood and youth at Brekkukot, a cottage near Reykjavik, with the strict impersonality and methodical objectivity of the sagas. His childhood is dominated by his foster grandparents, two silent, self-sufficient figures who seem to have stepped directly from the saga-world into the twentieth century. The Icelandic title of the novel, **"The Annals of Brekkukot,"** emphasizes the importance of this humble farm, which represents the traditional culture of Iceland. . . . Alfgrim's grandfather, Bjorn of Brekkukot, is a poor fisherman, but his actions are governed by the same code of honor that prevailed in the heroic age. Old Bjorn is the ethical center of this novel, and from his example Aflgrim learns how a man should react to life. Viewed from the inside, this laconic world of Brekkukot is noble and dignified.

We do not, however, always see Brekkukot entirely from within, and Bjorn sometimes appears to be ridiculous, as he does in the chapter entitled "What Is the Value of the Bible?" When it was translated into Icelandic in the sixteenth century, the Bible cost the equivalent of one cow. As far as Bjorn is concerned, values are immutable; thus when a Baptist missionary offers him a copy of the Bible, he feels compelled to accept it and resigns himself to parting with his only cow. The astonished missionary takes to his heels, and the Bible is returned. Because of Laxness's masterful synthesis of styles, he can create richly comic scenes like this one, which simultaneously ridicules and affirms the values of Brekkukot. The irony that results from this double point of view informs the entire novel.

Opposed to the Brekkukot way of life is that of Gudmund Gudmundsen. . . . [The] Gudmundsens control the economic life of the town and own the newspaper. They represent the corrupt business morality of the modern world. To them Bjorn of Brekkukot is a crude peasant with no ambition; what the Gudmundsens value is European culture. By far the cruellest satire in the book is aimed at merchant Gudmundsen, who attempts to appear cultivated by lacing his after-dinner speech with phrases from a German primer. This time there is no redeeming irony. . . .

The real plot of this novel, however, concerns the way in which Alfgrim's development is influenced by a mysterious relative, Gardar Holm. According to the newspaper, Holm is a world-famous singer, but at Brekkukot no one ever mentions his name. He seems to regard Alfgrim as his own true self, before he was corrupted by fame; consequently, he takes great interest in the boy. . . .

The trouble is that Holm is a kind of ghost. . . . He is a fraud and a failure; his triumphant career is nothing but fantasy. In love with that dream, Gudmundsen's daughter allows herself to be seduced by Holm, who is really a sort of Icelandic Peer Gynt. The whole complexity of his character is contained in the paradox of the singing fish, which merchant Gudmundsen introduces into his ridiculous speech. He means that fish cannot sing, and neither can Gardar Holm, who has returned to Iceland to face himself and become reconciled to his heritage, as Laxness once did.

Nevertheless, for all his faults, Holm has understood that art must embody the dream of a better life. Thus, the fish *can* sing.

Barry Jacobs, "Back Home to a Stern Heritage," in Saturday Review (© 1967 Saturday Review Magazine Co.; reprinted by permission), Vol. L, No. 21, May 27, 1967, p. 31.

ROBERT D. SPECTOR

Bitter and hopeful, realistic and bizarre, **World Light** [*Heimsljós*] . . . captures the contradictions and ambiguities that have characterized not only the literary achievement but even the Icelandic reputation of Halldór Laxness. . . . To his Icelandic countrymen Laxness is a source of pride for his masterful writing and yet a constant irritant because of his relentlessly honest portrayal of the meanest, along with the noblest, qualities of his Icelandic characters.

World Light was hardly designed to meet the demands of chauvinistic critics. Its village and peasant characters range from narrowminded superstitiousness to parochial foolishness in their conduct. (pp. 420-21)

Laxness portrays these characteristics through his narrative of Olaf Karason, a folk poet of less talent than desire. Olaf's adventures, by turn grimly realistic and wildly incredible, mark him as an outsider to be buffeted and abused by his society, a society that admires poetry, at least nominally, but scorns poets. In great detail Laxness provides the necessary sense of place, the idea of community, and the prevailing values. In oddly Dickensian or Kafkaesque dialogue and episodes, he sends Olaf through an endless quest for the secret of life, a search for beauty. In Laxness' story the miraculous mingles with the brutally realistic to somehow make the latter bearable.

Yet, if superficially the portrait of Iceland appears unappealing, the final effect proves otherwise. For all of their weaknesses and meanness, Laxness' Icelanders are a rugged and fearless people, confronting a difficult existence with determination and poetically aware of the awesome beauty of their environment. Behind his anger Laxness hides an enormous love for his country and its people. (p. 421)

Robert D. Spector, "Books: 'World Light'," in The American Scandinavian Review (copyright 1969 by The American-Scandinavian Foundation), Vol. LVII, No. 4, Winter, 1969-70, pp. 420-21.

PETER HALLBERG

As an Icelander and a member of a very small Scandinavian nation with an ancient and unique literary culture, Halldór Laxness has rather special qualifications as a writer. Throughout the period of his literary achievement, which has now continued for almost half a century, the Icelandic heritage has constantly been a living force in his work, contrasting or combining in various ways with his modernism and preoccupation with the problems of his time. The tension between the native and the foreign, the national and the cosmopolitan, has formed one of the fruitful contrasts which run through all his writing. (p. 5)

Three stages in his development may be fairly clearly distinguished. The first is characterized by his attempts as a young man to find his way among conceptions of life and literary trends in Europe after the First World War. It is a period of vehement and restless searching, which finds its artistic liberation in the cosmopolitan novel of ideas *Vefarinn mikli frá Kasmír*. . . . After a few years stay in America . . . , Laxness began his long succession of novels with subjects drawn from the social life of Iceland, past and present. This stage, with *Gerpla* (*The Happy Warriors* . . .), as its last great literary manifestation, is in part quite strongly colored by the writer's involvement in political and social life, and by his socialistic criticism of society. In his present phase, finally, which began around the time of the Nobel Prize award, his creative powers have . . . been directed in no small measure towards the drama. But the novels and short stories written in these later years also differ in tone and spirit from his earlier epic works. They have become "de-ideologized" and have, on the whole, a more calmly retrospective and chronicle-like character; their relation to Icelandic tradition seems to be more free of tension, more conservative. (p. 6)

[The] great literary document of the Catholic episode in Laxness' development is the novel *Vefarinn mikli frá Kasmír*. . . . (p. 36)

The main character, Steinn Elliði, on whom the whole novel turns, belongs to the merchant aristocracy of Reykjavík. . . . A strong feeling of restlessness pervades his whole character, a violent feeling of protest against the family circle with its solid middle-class respectability and plodding business mentality.

As a young man Steinn roams about in postwar Europe, desperately searching for footholds in life. He wins a certain reputation as a poet in English. In the course of time he has grown to feel alien and misunderstood among his countrymen, too big for the limiting conditions of his native land. Crushed and anguished, he at last finds a haven of refuge in a Central European monastery, and decides to give his life entirely to the service of the Catholic Church. Before doing so, however, he decides to spend a last summer in Iceland. There he meets again his former love, Diljá. . . . [The book] ends with Diljá visiting Steinn at the seminary in Rome where he is going to complete his education as a Catholic theologian. . . . But he rejects her. . . . (pp. 37-8)

The actual outlines of the story, the framework of fiction in which it is set, are nonetheless of relatively minor importance. The essential feature of *Vefarinn mikli* is the witches' brew of ideas presented in a *furioso* of style. With his bitterly revealing analysis the author steers his ruthless course through current expressions and ideals. Diametrically opposed attitudes are confronted with each other, driven to their extreme limits, and rejected. As far as we can judge, Laxness sees this radical skepticism, this revaluation of all values, as one of the characteristics of the time. Steinn Elliði finds himself to be a completely new kind of human being, having nothing at all in common with earlier generations. The First World War marks a landslide in man's historical development. (p. 38)

The chief preoccupation here is the profound change which man's living conditions, and hence man himself, have undergone in the melting-pot of contemporary events. (p. 39)

One of the many values and concepts which are subjected to ruthless analysis in *Vefarinn mikli* is creative writing itself. . . . [Steinn] formulates his misgivings on the subject of poetry and the poet in . . . violent terms. He denies that he or anyone else writes his masterpieces to the honor of God or in the service of humanity. . . . (p. 41)

[It] is the element of exhibitionism, selfishness, and amoralism in the life and work of the artist which arouses disgust in the disillusioned young poet. But Steinn has yet another accusation to throw in the face of the poets, in that he gives a gross physiological interpretation of their whole endeavor: "They are all love-sick men; they never think a thought so high that it is not a dream of conquered women and quivering wombs. . . ."

The artist is . . . described as being among other things a slave to woman. On the whole, Woman plays a remarkable role in the novel about the Great Weaver. The book contains a strong element of misogyny, with impulses drawn from many sources. (p. 42)

Woman, of course, has for centuries often been regarded, in the Christian world, as the embodiment of temptation and sin. It is natural that such notions as this should have become actualized and intensified both for Laxness himself and for his alter ego, Steinn Elliði, in view of their time spent in monasteries. In *Vefarinn mikli* God and woman are placed in direct contrast to each other. The struggle for Steinn's soul takes place between God on the one hand, and woman, who represents the world, on the other. Woman appears as God's only really dangerous competitor for man, the incarnation of everything that man must overcome in order to accomplish his mission in life. Steinn says that he early discovered that woman appealed only to the evil side of his nature. . . . (pp. 42-3)

If we remember that in Steinn's eyes woman represents man's earthly existence in general, this outburst of his provides in a nutshell the problems with which the whole work deals, as well as the key to Laxness' own continued development. The struggle within Steinn between God and Woman-world, conceived as two irreconcilable principles, is balanced so precariously, that in spite of an intense mustering of the will God's victory is every moment threatened. (p. 44)

Among the more sophisticated stylistic models for *Vefarinn mikli* should first of all be mentioned the works of August Strindberg. (p. 47)

In this connection Laxness describes *Vefarinn mikli* as "a pure Strindbergiad." This, of course, is a spirited exaggeration, but it points in the right direction. It is in this work of his "breakthrough" that his knowledge of Strindberg's works has first borne real fruit in his own. It is true that the direct references to Strindberg are not particularly striking in *Vefarinn mikli*— a book which otherwise contains such a large number of literary allusions. Strindberg and Laxness have obvious points in common—above all, perhaps, their criticism of woman and of marriage. But these are of secondary importance beside a more general and at the same time more essential similarity—the tremendous appetite for the problems of life, the inexhaustible debate, in which the arguments pile up on each other or collide with each other in a never-ending stream, and the very intensity of the discussion, the fierce pulse of the style, the rich and often shocking choice of words. (pp. 47-8)

As a young writer conscious of the age in which he lived, Laxness naturally lost no time in making himself familiar with the most recent movements in literature. Among them was the one initiated by André Breton's first *Manifeste du surréalisme*. . . . (p. 49)

Laxness has himself employed surrealism in *Vefarinn mikli* as—to use his own ingenious image—a kind of *spiritus concentratus,* suitably diluted. This, moreover, is characteristic of his way of assimilating literary impressions generally. Artistically speaking, he has never committed himself to any fixed doctrine or technique. The impulses from without have purposefully been subordinated to the demands of the creative and formative impulse within himself.

When discussing a work like *Vefarinn mikli,* we naturally look first for points of connection in literary history outside Iceland. Laxness himself was very conscious of the fact that his work implied a sharp break with the native Icelandic tradition. On the other hand, it is quite clear that not even an iconoclast like this young Icelander could disclaim all interest in his literary inheritance. . . . Naturally enough, the work met with the greatest understanding and enthusiasm among Laxness' contemporaries in age. They saw in Laxness the first "postwar writer," and in Steinn Elliði the first "postwar man" ever to be presented to Icelandic readers. (p. 51)

Vefarinn mikli frá kasmír brought with it no resolution of life's problems—or not, at least, for its author. In a letter written just before he began his work on the book he had said that he wished to write a "Catholic novel." The actual outcome of the novel's events might indeed lead us to believe that this end had been achieved, for the writer's alter ego finally turns his back on the World and on Woman, in order to dedicate himself to the service of God. But this was no unraveling of the Gordian knot, it was a desperate severance of it. The loud-voiced argumentation can by no means smother the doubt. Many of the arguments in the book show a rebellious and even blasphemous spirit and seriously threaten the Christian view of life, to which Steinn Elliði clings. The reader fancies that all the time he is treading on volcanic ground where a slight earthquake is all that is needed for the ground beneath his feet to collapse. In this intellectual atmosphere the paradoxes flourish; and we have the feeling that the one extreme can pass over into the other at any moment. (p. 52)

A work of another kind stands out as the central literary document from this period of the author's life—the collection of essays entitled *Alþýðubókin.* . . . *Vefarinn mikli*, the novel of ideas, may be regarded as a summing up of his youth, with the sojourn in the monastery as its crucial experience, while *Alþýðubókin* collects and resolves the experiences of his years in America. Laxness has himself hinted, moreover, that he regarded the two books as each other's counterparts and polar opposites. The new work appears as an important milestone, especially in the light of his later development: for during the thirties and the forties, his most productive period, he adopts in all essentials the same theoretical attitude, and embraces the same view of life that he recorded in *Alþýðubókin.*

This collection of essays covers a wide range of subjects taken from both material and spiritual culture. . . . What binds these diverse elements together into a whole is the fundamental socialist attitude which permeates them all in greater or lesser degree. *Alþýðubókin* may be regarded as the author's confession of loyalty to socialism—though it is socialism of a kind more fresh and enthusiastic than dogmatic. (pp. 55-6)

Laxness' ideological reorientation also involved a reconsideration of his view of literature and its purpose. The first chapter of *Alþýðubókin* is entitled "Bækur" (Books), but begins, curiously enough, with a warning *against* books. For the truth lies "not in books, not even in good books, but in people of good heart." . . .

Laxness gives a controversial review of contemporary literature and casts his critical eye in two directions: mainly at the fashionably superficial and artistically worthless novels which are currently turned out, but in some measure also at novels of a more unconventional and exclusive nature. In both cases he finds that the authors have little or no fruitful contact with ordinary people and their problems. (p. 63)

It is of course quite natural that a socialist "manifesto" like *Alþýðubókin* should dissociate itself not only from everything that carries a hint of Art for Art's sake, but also from exclusively esthetic points of view in general. If you have something on your mind which you want to communicate to the public, you should acquire "the knowledge necessary for saying the thing plainly instead of wrapping it in some disguise." . . . (p. 65)

We are left with the strong impression that artistic resources were released within Laxness by the ideological decision he made after the completion of *Vefarinn mikli.* Like Steinn Elliði he had searched for God with an egocentric and fanatical desire for perfection. This had led him into a "blind alley" as a writer. It is as if his resolve to concentrate on the world and ordinary people had supplied him with unsuspected powers as an objective literary creator. In his great novels of the thirties, which deal in turn with the fisher girl Salka Valka, with the small farmer Bjartur í Sumarhúsum, and with Ólafur Kárason, the parish pauper and folk poet, he develops a masterly strength as an epic writer. . . . The new dynamic quality in Laxness' art is undoubtedly linked with the fact that after his cosmopolitan years of wandering, his period of restless searching, he found his proper role as a portrayer of the Icelandic people. The certainty of this must have filled him with exultation and strength. And in the socialist view of society, in the socialist dream of a new state for the people, he found nourishment for his own visions. It became the myth which gave wings to his imaginative work, and which gave it passionate vehemence, dramatic intensity, and a sweeping perspective. (pp. 66-7)

Laxness' first literary work after his return to Iceland from America was a book of poems, *Kvaeðakver* (**Poems** . . .), his only collection of poems to date. Their style is highly experimental. In the foreword the poet refers to his poems as being among other things "efforts in the technique of the lyric, researches into the elasticity of the lyrical style." Traces of surrealistic influence show themselves in the fitful flow of the associations, in the occasionally bizarre imagery. The break with traditional Icelandic poetry, with its form and choice of subjects, is as sharp as it could possibly be. (p. 68)

[In *Salka Valka*] the writer has placed himself in the midst of a God-forsaken Icelandic fishing village where the people are engaged in a daily struggle for existence in a barren and seldom attractive natural setting. (pp. 72-3)

What is stressed above all in the author's comments is nature's indifference to the fate of these people. . . .

Steinþór Steinsson has been made to embody the village of Óseyri in a manner almost overemphatic. He is a brutal figure who is nonetheless able to suffuse his existence with a certain kind of primitive poetry. (p. 73)

All ethical standards and all sense of social responsibility are totally foreign to Steinþór. His only guiding principle is his own ego, with its greedy appetite for life. Of course he cares nothing for religious sentiments and ideas. . . . (p. 74)

It often seems as if the writer himself has imagined Steinþór as an incarnation of the soul of the fishing village: a raw, amoral life force, which must be tamed and must submit to the laws of social coexistence, before one can speak of humanity. Hence a kind of grandeur and rugged lyricism plays around this otherwise repellent figure. Steinþór is given, at times, some measure of the dimensions of saga or myth. (pp. 74-5)

At the same time, however, the author may rather abruptly deprive the reader of this illusion about Steinþór and give a quite sober account of the man's character and behavior. . . .

The portrait of Steinþór thus illustrates the writer's twofold vision; it shows a combination of attraction and repulsion, of empathy and cold observation. It may thus seem difficult, both for writer and reader, to retain a harmonious impression of a character such as Steinþór. . . . He is at once a realistically drawn character and something of a symbol. (p. 75)

Laxness generally works with strong contrasts; and in this respect his characterization is no exception. Steinþór has a female counterpart and polar opposite in Sigurlína. The primitive streak in both of them is strongly emphasized. But while the man may be said to embody brutal strength and activity, the woman's nature may be marked down as harmlessly submissive and passive. While Steinþór shapes his life according to his own primitive nature, Sigurlína is carried unresistingly along by the wayward vicissitudes of fortune. (p. 76)

Salka Valka is of course the dominating figure of the book, and perhaps the most living portrait of a woman that Laxness has ever created. The portrait stands out in sharp relief, and is seen most fully in her relations with the three other main characters—her mother, Steinþór, and Arnaldur. (p. 81)

If Steinþór represents primitive nature, and the life force which in itself is amoral, Arnaldur represents culture, and the struggle fought in the service of an ideal. . . .

On the other hand, Salka Valka with her manifestly earthbound existence is the sure foundation, the one absolute foothold in life for Arnaldur, the uneasy dreamer. (p. 82)

We may, if we so wish, see the reunion of Arnaldur and Salka Valka as symbolizing the new relationship between the writer himself and his native country. Like Arnaldur, he returned from abroad, full of "the pros and cons of the world." In *Alþýðubókin* the young author had come forward as the educator of his people, as the prophet of modern civilization in all its aspects. Arnaldur teaching Salka Valka to brush her teeth and not to stick the table knife in her mouth is very much in the spirit of *Alþýðubókin*. But his influence on her way of living and thinking is not limited to trivial details of this kind. When Arnaldur returns to Óseyri as a grown man, he comes, like Laxness in *Alþýðubókin,* bearing the message of socialism; he has the exultation and the passionate zeal of the social reformer. And Salka Valka joins his side. Arnaldur's dream of a new world can, just as much as Steinþór's animal nature, exercise a strange fascination upon her.

Yet Salka Valka, with her warmly spontaneous reactions to the hardships of those around her, can grow skeptical of the abstract element in Arnaldur's idealism; she often sees this idealism as something coldly foreign to the immediate needs of the individual. (p. 83)

In *Vefarinn mikli frá Kasmír* woman had for the most part been negatively judged as a serious obstacle on man's road towards perfection. Now, in the figure of Salka Valka, woman is positively valued as an incarnation of uncorrupted life itself. (p. 86)

As is usually the case in Laxness' novels, the satire in *Salka Valka* strikes first and foremost at social conditions and political life. An Icelandic reader could easily recognize in the novel a good deal of topical material taken from the contemporary history of Iceland. (p. 87)

With *Salka Valka* Laxness' interests as a writer had become firmly rooted in the soil of his native country. In one work after another during the thirties he adopts typically Icelandic subjects and gives them broad epic form. The book dealing with the fishing community of Óseyri was followed by the story of the Icelandic small farmer—the novel *Sjálfstaett fólk*. . . .

[The main character, Bjartur,] has managed to scrape together enough money to buy his own little farm. . . .

Yet his life as an independent farmer, the life he has so passionately desired [is characterized by one tragedy after another]. (p. 93)

In *Sjálfstaett fólk* economic policy and trade conditions are made to shape the course of the farmer's life both perceptibly and irrevocably. (p. 98)

Sjálfstaett fólk confronts the reader with the question of how it can happen that a man like Bjartur, with his cunning, his strength of will, his physical endurance and toughness and the endless anxiety he suffers on behalf of man and beast, must nonetheless see himself defeated in the struggle for his own and his family's livelihood. (p. 101)

In the eyes of their describer, the activities of Bjartur and his like are hopeless as a solution to the practical problems of life. Their independence, which they uphold with tooth and claw, is an illusion . . . ; we ought, indeed, to imagine ironic quotation marks on either side of the book's title. . . . For his own part Bjartur cannot, or will not, revise his opinions. But he leaves his son behind among the strikers in the coastal village, where the exploited workers who have begun to grow aware of the mechanism of society glimpse a solution to the problem in the idea of joining forces and working together in the struggle for a better existence.

But once it has been pointed out and established that this social attitude is adopted in the book, we see at once how inadequate it is as an expression of the work's individual character. Considering the great extent to which socially critical viewpoints contributed towards the origin of *Sjálfstaett fólk*, it is surprising indeed that this social slant does not thrust itself more directly forward in the finished work. The chief reason for this is probably that the social motif has expanded to mythical proportions of universal applicability. (p. 102)

Despite the fact that we have the First World War as a landmark in the chronology of the narrative, the story of Bjartur leaves an impression of bewildering timelessness. According to the Marxist pattern, and perhaps in accordance with the writer's earlier intentions, the poor farmer, who is forced to leave his farm, ought surely to have been made to join up with "the crowd of unemployed in the towns." But the final scene in *Sjálfstaett fólk* shows the aging Bjartur, still unbroken, leaving Sumarhús to start life all over again in a new dwelling place. As a character in the book he has grown away from the pattern and acts according to his own inherent logic.

Bjartur himself has been given some measure of the Icelandic sagas' dimensions, of their heroes' superhuman toughness and strength of will. (p. 104)

With *Salka Valka* and *Sjálfstaett fólk* Laxness had become indisputably the leading novelist in Icelandic, and was also well on the way to becoming internationally known. But he did not rest on his laurels, for during the following years the four volumes of his novel [collectively entitled *Heimsljós*] about Ólafur Kárason, the parish pauper and folk poet, appeared in rapid succession. (p. 117)

In [*Heimsljós*] we find a rich abundance of symbolically concentrated characterization alternating between, on the one hand, gay humor and biting satire, and on the other incurable melancholy and trembling pathos. And the undulating movement of the narrative, with its sudden turns and changes, is accompanied by a personal style in which the Icelandic language has gained a more flexible fullness of expression that perhaps ever before.

For all its varying components, the work is far from giving an impression of looseness and disunity. The component elements are held together in a purposeful and well-balanced structure. . . . (p. 124)

This time, in fact, Laxness has had unusually diverse materials to fuse together in the crucible of the imagination. At the same time, the conditions for following the process of artistic assimilation are in this case particularly favorable. For the description of Ólafur Kárason's destiny is based on a real and well documented life history [that of Magnús Hjaltason who kept a diary from 1892-1916]. (p. 125)

While Magnús Hjaltason's diaries must have been fascinating material for Laxness to work with, it is nonetheless wisest not to emphasize too strongly the numerous points which fiction and reality have in common. All these elements have provided Laxness with hints and glimpses, and footholds for the literary imagination. But without a powerful vision of his own he would never have been able to fuse them into a new and great work of art; many of them, in any case, are displayed to much greater advantage in the framework he provides. To a large extent, and perhaps for the most part, the diaries make rather colorless reading; and the many poems are seldom more inspired than those of any Icelandic rustic poet of average quality. Laxness has freed Magnús Hjaltason's destiny from its national limitations; he has broadened its scope, and given it universality; from the house of the poet he has opened a view over the world. . . .

[The] social slant in the novel about Ólafur Kárason must be attributed to the author himself. And here Laxness has drawn copiously from his personal experience of Iceland as it was in the thirties. (p. 127)

The elements of social satire in the novel thus really belong to the thirties, while Magnús Hjaltason's life ran its course about one generation earlier. The fusing together of these two periods may seem a hazardous undertaking; for it would surely be difficult to avoid offending against verisimilitude in a manner fatal to the element of artistic suggestion. But in this respect Laxness has been greatly helped by the very structure of Icelandic society, by its sometimes paradoxical points of contact between old and new. The contrast between ancient and modern is hardly more striking in his literary work than in Magnús Hjaltason's diaries. Thanks, perhaps, to a certain distancing or chiaroscuro effect, he has actually made the world of the novel seem more homogeneous than that of reality. (p. 128)

It is . . . clear that in his description of the poet Ólafur Kárason's position in society Laxness has made full use of elements both old and new: of the Icelandic tradition as well as his own experiences as a writer in the Europe of the nineteen-thirties. This living contact with contemporary problems is perhaps not the least important of the factors contributing to the universality of his fiction—the universal appeal of a setting and dramatis personae which are characteristically and inimitably Icelandic. (p. 131)

[*Heimsljós*] may be read, not least of all, as a memorial to the Icelandic folk poet through the ages. Ólafur Kárason is himself such a poet. . . .

In this folk poet Laxness has above all given a portrait of the Poet, in a general sense. As a description of the problems posed by creative writing the work certainly has no equal in the Scandinavian countries, and may even be unequaled in world literature. (p. 136)

For all the distress which assails him, Ólafur is one of the elect; he is a vocational and compulsive poet. Through the whole of his life he is accompanied by a wonderful voice which at any moment can be made to sound within him. (p. 137)

[His] blissfully intoxicating awareness, [his] sense of a mystical expansion and ascension of the individual self into the cosmos, is released first and foremost in the heart of the Icelandic countryside. In this work it is striking, too, how often nature is animated, and appears to merge together with the nature of man in a pantheistic and monistic experience of total oneness. (pp. 137-38)

In the figure of Ólafur Kárason, the poet's ineptitude in worldly matters has been strongly underlined. But although the poet, viewed from without, perhaps seems more vulnerable and defenseless than his fellow creatures, his spiritual experiences, on the other hand, and his status as one of the elect render him unassailable in his innermost being. (p. 138)

We can surely see a [deep] symbolism in the fact that the poet is personified as a parish pauper. For in spite of his feeling of being a complete outsider, he is utterly loyal to the outcasts and oppressed members of society. . . . [But] unlike his creator, Ólafur is no socialist. His idealistic longing is expressed in more general—even vaguer—terms. It reaches towards an existence in which goodness has been realized in human cohabitation. The poet does not talk of economic systems or practical politics. He only knows what the "better world" of his dreams should be like. . . .

All attempts at fixing in unequivocal formulae the world of Laxness' literary creation are frustrated, not least of all, by the markedly dialectical slant which pervades it—which penetrates the ideational content, the characterization, the design of the work, and the smallest details of the style. A thesis may suddenly turn into its own antithesis; and a reserve of irony lurks beneath the surface of even the most wholehearted pathos. The reader is never given the opportunity to settle down in safe possession of an insight or a final judgment. The writer carries the reader along with him in a continuous discussion of problems to which form is given in the characters and situations of the narrative. (p. 140)

In the throes of the Second World War, Scandinavian writers often harked back to earlier periods in the lives of their nations. This must have been partly due to the current necessity of disguising certain aims of dangerously topical relevance; it was partly due also, however, to the fact that temporal distance could throw into relief the national and universally human values for which the struggle was being waged. In *Íslandsklukkan* Laxness also turned to his country's past. The action of the novel takes place in the late seventeenth and early eighteenth centuries. It is true that the author avoids any direct dating of its events; indeed, he has prefaced all three parts of the work with the comment that it is not a "historical novel" inasmuch as its "characters, action, and style conform exclusively to the work's own laws." . . . Laxness has, in fact, made himself thoroughly familiar with the history of the time and has very skillfully recreated the atmosphere of the past from historical and legal records. . . . (p. 145)

[We] should not stress the element of saga style in *Íslandsklukkan* too onesidedly. It is true that it provides the work with its actual keynote of coolness and purity. But this is made to conflict with certain other stylistic elements. The coldly matter-of-fact mode of expression alternates with a Danicized "officialese" and a religious rhetoric which have borrowed their coloring from contemporary documents. This archaizing dress of language never runs the risk, however, of leaving an impression of patchwork or of a laboriously handled apparatus of learning. It is carried off with sovereign facility and seems to blend quite naturally with the narrative's own rhythm. (p. 155)

The hotly debated subject of yielding up the military bases in Iceland [to the United States] plays a prominent part in [the short novel *Atómstöðin (The Atom Station)* . . .] . . . [Laxness] takes the question of high politics connected with the base and couples it together with the grotesque complications surrounding the bringing home and burial of the body of Jónas Hall-grímsson, the national poet, which had lain at rest for a century in Copenhagen; for this memorable event happened to coincide with the hectic final stages in the . . . handling of the base question. (p. 158)

Atómstöðin is presented in a rather unusual way. The entire narrative is placed in the mouth of Ugla Falsdóttir, a young country girl from northern Iceland, who comes to Reykjavík to learn to play the organ. This fictitious narrator can hardly be regarded as thoroughly true to life. Ugla's thoughts sometimes seem improbably mature and artistically formulated. As a type, however, the girl from the north is realistically drawn. The Icelandic country people's traditional book knowledge and thirst for education are not mythical; and among the young people of the present day intellectual curiosity has found new aims and pursuits. When Ugla of Eystridalur reflects on modern music and sculpture, she represents Iceland as it really is, albeit in a stylized way.

In order to earn her living in Reykjavík the girl from the north takes the post of domestic help in the house of Búi Árland, political economist, wholesale merchant, and member of Parliament. In his house she gains an insight into the life and mentality of the country's leading circles. But she also comes into contact with other aspects of life in the capital. At the house of her eccentric organ teacher, whom she visits in the evenings after her working hours, she is introduced to an environment in which thieves, harlots, police constables, and country parsons can meet together in an atmosphere of mutual tolerance. This new and strange world stands out in bold relief against the background of Ugla's isolated home valley.

Búi Árland is described as an intelligent and kindly representative of the upper middle class. He seems to be endowed with everything a human being can desire: good looks, the power to charm, education, and wealth. But his character is marked by a tired skepticism; he lacks faith in life. He awaits with equanimity the collapse of his social class and of its capitalistic culture. . . . [His fantasies of starting a new life] basically serve merely to underline his sense of rootlessness. And indeed, when it really comes to the point he continues to play the part imposed on him by his environment and position. In the last pages of the book we find him at the wretchedly attended funeral of the Beloved Son of the Nation, helping a few high-ranking mourners to carry the coffin containing the great poet's mortal remains, recently exhumed in Denmark. The procession is followed by jeering cries from the onlookers in the street about selling the country, digging up bones. (pp. 158-59)

Ugla Falsdóttir acts as Búi Árland's foil; her natural anchorage in the real life of the people, and her uncorrupted sense of what is right stand in contrast to his melancholic nihilism. She is a sister to Salka Valka; these two country girls both embody the indestructible powers of the nation. (p. 161)

Atómstöðin was undoubtedly a spear thrown with the warrior's intention of wounding and killing—if indeed we should not rather compare it with a bomb. Certain circles within Icelandic society were deeply offended by it, for all their attempts to see it as nothing but an uncontrolled outburst of fury, a *roman à clef*, and a political lampoon.

In spite of this, however, *Atómstöðin* in no way betrays any prejudiced kind of political inspiration or purpose. As far as we can judge, the atom station is, broadly speaking, the symbol of a certain disintegration or explosion of accustomed ideas and associations. The Reykjavík of the war years, with its trade boom and its hectic life of business and pleasure, offered a background favorable to all kinds of picturesque types and eccentricities. And indeed, *Atómstöðin* has a rich array of characters, some of which are exceedingly bizarre. . . . The very action of the book also has elements of fantasy—even though the author, as we have already indicated, perhaps keeps closer to real life in Iceland than may seem apparent to an outsider.

But photographic realism has certainly never been Laxness' main concern, and in spite of all its reminiscences of real people and events it would be absurd to regard *Atómstöðin* as a kind of *roman à clef*. The author is bent on presenting a synthesis, an artistically intensified experience of things. His tendency towards bold stylization culminates sharply in this book, which thus acquires a fiercer rhythm than the broader narrative flow of the epic in *Sjálfstaett fólk* or *Íslandsklukkan,* for example. But this is exactly the way in which Laxness, with brilliant intuition, has captured the scattered and hectic features of the environment he wishes to describe. (pp. 163-64)

With *Atómstöðin* Laxness had plunged directly into the Icelandic world of his own times. His next novel, *Gerpla* . . . , which was published in 1952, deals with Vikings of around the year 1000. It testifies in its own way to the contrasts and vigorous oscillations in his art; although in Iceland it is not unusual to find the old and the new in close and direct proximity to each other. (p. 165)

[In *Gerpla*] Laxness has allied himself with the native Icelandic tradition both ambitiously and consistently. . . . Laxness has actually wished to write his saga on the same basis as the ancient writers, and for this reason he records meticulously, in the very beginning of the book, the sources from which he has drawn his knowledge. . . . [He] does, of course, work as a novelist and not as a historian, and his opening section is primarily an artistic stroke made with the purpose of arousing the reader's confidence in the narrative to follow. (pp. 166-67)

It is also clear that in spite of everything Laxness is not writing this Icelandic saga from the same angle of approach as his fellow writers of the Middle Ages. Had this been the case his own work would merely have become a pastiche, a rehashing of traditional material, and not a new saga, with its own set of problems. The author's own times show through in his work in many different ways. . . .

The author has got the actual idea for his work from *Fóst-braeðra saga,* which describes the fortunes of the two foster brothers Þorgeir Hávarsson and Þormóður Kolbrúnarskáld, including their relations with Ólafur Haraldsson, king of Norway. . . . (p. 167)

A richly humorous contrast develops when the [first] young man is supposed to start putting into practice the words of wisdom he has earlier imbibed on the subject of kings, gold, heroes, norns, and valkyries in the guise of swans. When he and his foster brother Þormóður establish themselves as Vikings in their own home district and make coastal raids in the fjords in a barely seaworthy vessel, their story turns into a parody of the Viking life. (p. 169)

Ironically enough, the mighty warrior is given, in his new saga, the most ignominious end that could possibly befall him. He is decapitated in his sleep by people of such insignificance that it is hardly worth the trouble to take revenge on them. . . .

Laxness has himself called *Gerpla* a book about war and peace, and has thus touched upon what could be called the purpose of the work, and the pathos which trembles beneath its severe and cold external form. In his view the remote period which he describes is not so homogeneous as it may seem to be in the ancient sagas. Deep within itself the society of the *söguöld* contains powerful tensions between different interests and ideals—not least between the ruler and his subjects, where a remorseless antagonism may prevail. (p. 170)

[*Gerpla* ends with Þormóður refusing to recite his poem to the king.] The atmosphere of this meeting between king and skald in the night of late summer is charged with fate. We know from other sources what happened to them—both of them were slain the following day in the battle against the peasant army of Norway. . . . The reason why the figure of Þormóður has become so very much alive may be that Laxness the writer has in some way felt himself to be sharing in the fate of the skald, has felt himself disillusioned by his own commitments and his own idols. This conjecture seems to find gradual confirmation in a close study of Laxness' life and work. (pp. 177-78)

As a work of art *Gerpla* itself is an unusually powerful achievement. Laxness has not transposed his subject into a modern key; he has chosen to preserve a close link with the style of the ancient sagas. . . . Of course, Laxness has also allowed himself some obvious and conscious deviations from the form of the classical sagas. Yet in spite of this, it is surprising indeed how closely he has managed to follow it. The saga style of *Gerpla*, while having its own highly individual character, is not seriously at variance with that of the ancient sagas. The writer has managed to give the impression that the tradition of saga writing is quite unbroken. (p. 179)

> *Peter Hallberg, in his* Halldór Laxness, *translated by Rory McTurk (copyright © 1971 by Twayne Publishers, Inc.; reprinted with the permission of Twayne Publishers, a Division of G. K. Hall & Co., Boston), Twayne, 1971, 220 p.*

GEORGE S. TATE

[Certain difficulties confront the Mormon reader of *Paradise Reclaimed* who is] unaware of the background of the novel and its position in Laxness' literary output, and it is in an effort to overcome these that I would like, by way of apologia for the novel, to make four points. The first is that Laxness' humor is an enigmatic and puzzling feature of virtually all his fiction. His creative energy thrives on tension between humor and satire on the one hand and melancholy pathos on the other. (p. 30)

An ironist with a keen eye for incongruities, Laxness lets nothing, however sacred—not the sagas, not Christianity, not socialism, certainly not himself—escape this "twofold vision" of sympathy and satire. (pp. 30-1)

Secondly, in several of his novels Laxness draws heavily but imaginatively on the writings of obscure figures whose lives are nevertheless well-documented. Thus the overall plot of the tetralogy *World Light* and many features of its hero Oláfur

Kárason are adapted from the unpublished autobiography and diaries of the Icelandic folk-poet Magnús Hjaltason. The same is true of *Paradise Reclaimed*. The Mormon reader should realize that the larger outline of the plot and many details are drawn from the writings of Eiríkur á Brúnum (1832-1900), a colorful figure and rather well-known writer of naive travel books and other autobiographical pieces. (pp. 31-2)

Thirdly, if Laxness had intended, as he assures us he did not, to satirize Mormon beliefs or society, Eiríkur's writings could have provided him much ammunition. Although Eiríkur does not make a point of slandering the society with which he has become disillusioned, he does mention such things as the occasional rejection of an older wife upon the arrival of a younger one. He tells of a Danish convert whom he knew to be a "well-behaved and sensible man" who was so appalled at his first visit to the temple (Eiríkur never went) that he not only walked out of the building but out of the Church as well. Perhaps the best of this ammunition would have been Eiríkur's account of his reasons for breaking with the Mormons. (p. 32)

While Eiríkur is vocal both about his conversion and his renunciation of the Church, Steinar says nothing. Indeed, one senses that his disillusionment runs too deep and is too dimly perceived to be articulated. But it is not disillusionment with the doctrine or even with the society.

The final and most important point of this apologia has to do with the relationship of the novel to Laxness himself. Peter Hallberg finds it tempting to interpret Steinar's journey to Copenhagen . . . as corresponding to Laxness' early immersion in Catholicism, Steinar's quest for a material paradise for his family in Utah as representing Laxness' socialist stage, and the final resignation as characterizing his own present refusal to be identified with any ideology.

Hallberg rightly cautions that such topical equation would be too pat, but it does seem important that the Mormon reader understand that Laxness is not writing a biography of Eiríkur á Brúnum or a story specifically about the Mormons. *Paradise Reclaimed* is at once personal and universal. There is something of Laxness in Steinar, something of his own spiritual or ideological odyssey that has taken him from monasticism, to socialism, to his present renunciation and mistrust of ideologies and dogmas. From the standpoint of its overall treatment of a quest for truth and utopia, *Paradise Reclaimed* is perhaps Laxness' most nearly autobiographical novel. (p. 33.)

> *George S. Tate, "Halldór Laxness, the Mormons and the Promised Land," in* Dialogue: A Journal of Mormon Thought *(copyright © 1978 by the Dialogue Foundation), Vol. XI, No. 2, Summer, 1978, pp. 25-37.*

SIGURÐUR A. MAGNÚSSON

With his narrative skill and vivid style [Halldór Laxness] has done more than any modern novelist to renew Icelandic prose. Indeed, he dominated the literary scene in Iceland from the mid-1920s to the mid-1960s. In his heyday he was an odd mixture of a universal creative genius and a partisan essayist propagating radical socialism and revolution. However, he made a point of separating his art and his social and political preaching, with the result that his novels are largely free from those tendencies which often mar the works of socially conscious writers. He has a surprisingly large range of styles and subjects, so that no two of his novels resemble one another in anything but their felicity of expression and power of character portrayal.

A large number of his characters have become as much house-hold figures in Iceland as the old saga heroes or, say, Babbitt and Gatsby in America.

After completing four monumental novels between 1931 and 1946 which capture the Icelandic scene more thoroughly than do any works written in Iceland since the thirteenth century, Laxness in 1948 published a brilliantly executed and consciously tendentious satirical fantasy on contemporary Iceland, *Atómstöðin* . . . , which prompted some older patriots to demand that its translation into foreign languages be forbidden. In 1952 came *Gerpla* . . . , based on certain classical sagas and written with unfaltering skill in the idiom of the thirteenth century, a feat which most experts would have considered impossible. The novel is a thorough deflation of the ancient heroic spirit and understandably upset some classical scholars in Scandinavia. In 1957 Laxness again surprised his compatriots with a finely wrought, almost lyrical novel about life in Reykjavík at the turn of the century, *Brekkukotsannáll*. . . . This was the least socially critical of his novels and inaugurated a new phase in his writing. The picaresque novel *Paradísarheimt* (. . . 1960) was a further departure from his earlier works; it is essentially a philosophical fable about man's quest for the infinite, partly set in the Icelandic Mormon settlement in Utah.

At that point Laxness suddenly turned to the theatre and wrote several plays with moderate success. This detour was misguided, since his peculiar talent is above all epic and only dramatic in the non-theatrical sense. The upshot was that he returned to the novel and published in 1969 *Kristnihald undir jökli* . . . , a quasi-fable on the theme of the self-effacing, saintly man of inner peace and natural charity pitted against a man of the world with all the trappings of power and financial success. This is also the theme of his best play, *Dúfnaveislan* . . . and of most of his later work, including *Innansveitarkrónika* [1970]. . . . [His] book of autobiographical sketches, *Skáldatími* (. . . 1963), aroused international attention owing to the author's scathing revelation of his own gullibility while under the spell of Stalin and communism. (pp. 21-2)

Sigurður A. Magnússon, "Postwar Literature in Iceland," in World Literature Today *(copyright 1982 by the University of Oklahoma Press), Vol. 56, No. 1, Winter, 1982, pp. 18-23.**

PUBLISHERS WEEKLY

[*The Atom Station*] deals with Iceland's entry into the atomic age and its introduction to the accompanying anxiety and despair, as Parliament debates whether or not to sell the country to other nations for use as an "atom station." Ugla, a strapping, honest-minded girl from the north, comes to Reykjavik to study organ, working as a maid in a Parliament member's home. Symbolizing the heathenish, uncorrupted Iceland of the Sagas, Ugla is appalled by and pitying of the spiritual poverty and boredom of her employers and their kids. . . . Sometimes the symbolism is full of clichés, but Laxness nevertheless offers insight into a culture that is both isolated from and inexorably tied to the world as a whole. A serious novel in which black humor and shy humanism relieve some of the mordancy.

"Fiction: 'The Atom Station','" in Publishers Weekly *(reprinted from the May 28, 1982, issue of* Publishers Weekly, *published by R. R. Bowker Company, a Xerox company; copyright © 1982 by Xerox Corporation), Vol. 221, No. 22, May 28, 1982, p. 67.*

PHOEBE-LOU ADAMS

[*The Atom Station*] has never before been issued in the United States, possibly because it was considered pro-Communist, possibly because Mr. Laxness's sardonic, deadpan style of comedy has never attracted much interest in this country. Such neglect is regrettable, for his plague-on-all-your-houses view of government is wickedly attractive, his absurd political and artistic characters are internationally recognizable, and his dim view of atomic enterprise is no longer either exotic or unreasonable.

Phoebe-Lou Adams, "Short Reviews: 'The Atom Station'," in The Atlantic Monthly *(copyright © 1982, by The Atlantic Monthly Company, Boston, Mass.; reprinted with permission), Vol. 250, No. 2, August, 1982, p. 97.*

Fritz (Reuter) Leiber (Jr.)

1910-

American fantasy and science fiction writer.

A writer of speculative fiction since the 1930s, Fritz Leiber received his first Hugo award in 1958 for *The Big Time*, a part of his acclaimed *Change War* series. He is noted for his skillful portrayals of the human condition within possible futures. Leiber has also been consistently praised for his strong characterizations, vivid, almost tactile imagery, and the ability to create dark atmospheres of terror and superstition in the midst of rational, modern settings. His theatrical background is evident in his use of settings which serve as imaginary stages upon which psychological dramas are enacted with precise, unpretentious dialogue. Nowhere is this sense of dramatic unity better demonstrated than in *The Big Time*, in which, for most of the action, a single room is used as the backdrop for a war waged through time.

Another important novel in Leiber's career is the earlier *Gather, Darkness!* It is typical in its posing of social commentary—in this case, the responsibility inherent in technological advancement—within an entertaining framework. His other Hugo winner, *The Wanderer*, again shows his concern for the individual within society. In allowing readers to anticipate imminent disaster through the eyes of ordinary people, he persuades them to care about the characters and their plight.

Leiber's fantasy chronicles, notably the *Grey Mouser/Fafhrd* stories, are among the most literate and realistic in the heroic-adventure form. Unlike many earlier varieties of hero tale, Leiber's stories have believable protagonists who owe their fortunes to resourcefulness and luck, rather than brawn and violence.

Because of the enduring quality and distinctive style of Leiber's work, many critics have decried the lack of recognition which he has received outside the community of fantasy and science fiction writers.

(See also *Contemporary Authors*, Vols. 45-48; *Contemporary Authors New Revision Series*, Vol. 2; and *Dictionary of Literary Biography*, Vol. 8.)

Photograph by Jay Kay Klein

H. H. HOLMES

Ever since its magazine appearance ten years ago, Fritz Leiber's "Conjure Wife" has been esteemed as the definitive novelistic treatment of witchcraft in the modern world. A precisely balanced blend of fantasy and science fiction, of psychological novel and suspense melodrama, it stands on a plane with Leiber's own "Gather, Darkness!" or "Destiny Times Three"—which means all of the impact and excitement of the best pulp story-telling, with a literacy and subtlety advanced well beyond most of Mr. Leiber's colleagues.

H. H. Holmes, "Science and Fantasy," in New York Herald Tribune Book Review (© I.H.T. Corporation; reprinted by permission), December 21, 1952, p. 9.*

H. H. HOLMES

You will recall from anthologies such brilliant Leiber stories as "Coming Attraction" and "A Bad Day for Sales" bitterly depicting a near-future American society in which present trends of sadism, exploitation and hypocrisy have reached their nadir of decadence. ["The Green Millennium"] is a full-scale novel of that society, evoked with Heinleinesque skill at detailed indirect exposition—and of how men rose from that nadir because a technologically unemployed young man happened to adopt a green cat and to glimpse a female satyr. It's a story as imaginative, unexpected, even surrealist as that odd but accurate synopsis indicates; and it's also a thundering action-melodrama, as it becomes apparent that the fate of the world hinges incredibly upon the green cat and every force in society, from the underworld to the Federal Bureau of Loyalty, concentrates on its capture. You may read this as an extraordinarily good suspense-thriller, or as the Writing on the Wall of a funhouse, reflecting in distorting mirrors the message that we are weighed in the balance; in either fashion, read it you must.

H. H. Holmes, "Science and Fantasy," in New York Herald Tribune (© I.H.T. Corporation; reprinted by permission), November 15, 1953, p. 14.*

SAM MOSKOWITZ

[*Adept's Gambit*], built around the characters of The Grey Mouser

301

(personifying Harry Fischer) and the seven-foot sword-wielding giant Fafhrd (the romantic incarnation of Fritz Leiber, Jr.), is beyond question not only the first but the best of the entire series Leiber was to write about these characters. . . . From the moment that the spell is cast upon Fafhrd that temporarily changes every woman into a pig the instant he kisses her; on to the Grey Mouser's consultation with the seven-eyed Ningauble, gossiper with the Gods, about what to do about it; through the supernatural sword battle with Anara; to the finale, in which the adept turned to a mouse contemplatively evaluates its chances of killing a bear cub, the story is a delight to read.

Leiber's sense of pace, rich background detail, taut battle scenes, fine characterization, fascinating supernatural elements, together with his extraordinary talent for weaving tasteful humor throughout the entire fabric of his story—a talent unsurpassed by any living fantasy writer today—make this a classic fantasy. (p. 290)

In the outline for *Gather, Darkness!* Leiber suggested an underground using witchcraft and holding up Satan as its idol to overthrow the despotic scientific religion. (p. 293)

Perhaps Leiber was the better merchandiser of such ideas, possibly he was convincing where the others were not, but whatever the reason, and erroneously or not, in the minds of readers he came to be regarded as *the* transitional author who tied well-known elements of superstition to science in fiction.

Before the appearance of *Gather, Darkness!* Leiber was regarded as an important writer. That one story placed him among the "big names." Yet, its techniques and stylistic flow are clearly devices taken from Edgar Rice Burroughs; the author keeps two or more situations going simultaneously, carrying them along in alternating chapters. The chase scene in which the hero, Jarles, is rescued from the mob by the old "witch" Mother Jujy is obviously indebted to A. E. van Vogt's treatment in *Slan*, where Jommy Cross is saved from the mob by Granny. The personality changer used on Jarles is reminiscent of Stanley G. Weinbaum's "attitudinizer" in *Point of View*. From Leiber's own acrobatic tower in *Two Sought Adventure* comes the notion of the flexible "haunted" house. But these were merely ingredients that Leiber obtained for the literary stew; the spice he added to flavor it no one could lend him. There is the satire, pitiless in its excoriation of religion, satire deriving from Leiber's own personal observations. There is the cynicism regarding the scientists' ability to do any better than the politicians. There is the humor, mature, not light, not raucous, blending into the story. And there is the gift for characterization, effectively evidenced in Brother Chulian, Jarles, Mother Jujy, and the Familiar. (pp. 293-94)

Only slightly less successful than *Gather, Darkness!* was *Destiny Times Three* . . . to which *Business of Killing* . . . , a short story of the contemplated exploitation of simultaneous worlds, was a prelude. A machine built by an Olaf Stapledonian intelligence accidentally fragments the time stream of our planet into a number of "worlds of if," three of which, at least, have duplicated individuals on them leading different lives. One, an Orwellian world, decides to take over the original earth. The interplay of three alternate situations is again handled in the Edgar Rice Burroughs technique. Nightmares are explained as contacts with our duplicates on alternate worlds, as are many of our superstitions. Influences of H. P. Lovecraft are stronger here than in any other major Leiber story. Fundamentally, the novel is a fantastic allegory, splendidly readable, with fast-moving action, and thoroughly polished. (pp. 295-96)

Leiber had felt a lifelong dissatisfaction with the sexual patterns of Western culture, holding that unhealthy frustrations contributed to the "sick" aspects of our culture. His personal preference rested with the social mores of The Last Men in Olaf Stapledon's *Last and First Men* . . . , in which men and women live in groups ". . . but in most groups all the members of the male sexes have intercourse with all the members of the female sexes. Thus sex with us is essentially social." . . .

Leiber's ideas on sex were presented in such impeccable good taste that there was little reaction to them. The opposite was true of *Coming Attraction* . . . , which in every sense epitomized his second big successful period as a science-fiction writer. *Coming Attraction* introduces a British visitor to post-atomic-war life in New York City, where it is stylish for women to wear masks (since many of their faces were seared by atomic blasts) and where a warped culture has arisen which Leiber artistically unveils with magnificent indirection and almost psychiatric insight to produce one of the masterpieces of short science fiction. (p. 297)

[Leiber's award-winning novel *The Big Time* is a tale] of a war fought by changing the past and the future, and it is told in the vernacular of a party girl who is a hostess of The Place, a timeless night club suspended outside the cosmos. The philosophical upshot is the comprehension by mankind of a higher state of consciousness, and its evolution from time-binding (the unification of events through memory) to possibility binding (making all of what might be part of what is). (pp. 298-99)

[*The Wanderer* is about] a lacquered planet which abruptly appears in space alongside the moon, causing earthquakes and tidal disasters on Earth. This was intended to be the definitive world-doom story, told in alternating vignettes of various stratas of society.

Sticking close to grim "realism" has paid off richly in science fiction for Robert A. Heinlein, Arthur C. Clarke, John Wyndham, John Christopher, and various others, and it might have for Leiber, too, but he wouldn't follow the rules. Instead of settling for a single departure from the norm and then throwing the spotlight on human reaction, Leiber has connected the actions of his characters with bizarre extraterrestrial happenings.

The story builds with increasing fascination into a highly advanced epic, conceptually in the vanguard of modern science fiction and to that degree gratifying to the seasoned reader sated with predigested pabulum marketable to the masses by virtue of a self-imposed limit on imagination. The world-doom story, with the focus entirely on the fate and reactions of the "man in the street," has been told with high skill and extraordinary effectiveness for over 150 years. . . . Yet, it is quite possible that in *The Wanderer*, Fritz Leiber has shown that there are ways of writing science fiction so that it can hold both the basic and the advanced audience. In attempting to show the effect of the catastrophe on a dozen or more people concurrently, Leiber's effect becomes unartfully choppy. Nevertheless, though the reader moves bumpily along, he remains interested, never losing track of the disparate variety of characters and situations. As the invading planet is discovered to be a propelled world, inhabited by multitudinous diverse creatures working in harmony; with their revelation of the state of galactic civilization and travel through hyperspace, the story moves into superscience, but this is balanced and even made more acceptable by contrast with more ordinary events on earth and the reactions of the earthmen. (pp. 300-01)

The Wanderer is flawed but far from a failure. (p. 301)

While Fritz Leiber has made his mark, his story is in every sense an unfinished one. The Grey Mouser series has established him as the greatest living writer in the sword and sorcery tradition. A pioneer in the attempt to modernize the ancient symbols of terror, he has also gained recognition for spearheading a movement to the lore of fantasy and witchcraft in the body of science fiction. As a stylist he ranks among the finest writers of fantasy today, one possessing rare gifts of characterization and humor. Even as an entertainer he has something to say, taking definite stands on social questions.

Throughout his writing career the "branches of time" theme has fascinated him. In three of his biggest novels, *Destiny Times Three, The Big Time,* and *The Wanderer,* as well as in many shorter works, he has speculated on what might happen if the reel of life could be rewound and played out again. (p. 302)

> Sam Moskowitz, *"Fritz Leiber,"* in his Seekers of Tomorrow: Masters of Modern Science Fiction *(copyright © 1966, 1964, 1963, 1962, 1961 by Sam Moskowitz; reprinted by permission of the author, World Publishing Co., 1966, pp. 283-302.*

THE TIMES LITERARY SUPPLEMENT

Imagined monsters are generally more successful than manufactured ones where nasty tales are concerned, and Fritz Leiber demonstrates this effortlessly with [*Night Monsters*]. One or two of the early stories tend towards the weak and garrulous, and "The Girl with the Hungry Eyes"—which is about the devouring She rather than vampirism proper—would surely have been impossible at a later stage of Mr. Leiber's psychosexual knowingness. But the more recent tales such as "Midnight in the Mirror World" are sincerely horrid, this particular one being an extension of Charles Addams's cartoon about the man in a washroom standing between double mirrors and seeing a dozen dwindling versions of himself of which the third or fourth version is emphatically not him at all. Mr. Leiber intuitively knows . . . that correct atmosphere can overcome most deficiencies of plot. His imagined fragments of dark have a tactile quality about them such as only the best writers in the genre achieve.

> *"Science Fiction in Short,"* in The Times Literary Supplement (© *Times Newspapers Ltd. (London) 1974; reproduced from* The Times Literary Supplement *by permission), No. 3769, May 31, 1974, p. 591.*

POUL ANDERSON

It's too bad that we have no tale of Fafhrd and the Gray Mouser [in *The Best of Fritz Leiber*]. Not only did that charming pair of rogues—the tall Northern barbarian and the small city-bred trickster—launch the author's career; they are still going strong, to the joy of everybody who appreciates a rattling good fantasy adventure. But by no means are these stories conventional "sword and sorcery." The world of Nehwon is made real in wondrously imaginative detail, its human aspects as true as in any conscientious job of reporting. To visit the city of Lankhmar is to learn what decadence in fact means; to roam with our vulnerable vagabonds is to experience pity and terror as well as suspense, wry humor, and uproarious hilarity. Here Leiber in his way—like the late J.R.R. Tolkien in his, and not vastly different—has done, and is doing, for the heroic fantasy what Robert Louis Stevenson did for the pirate yarn: by orig-

inality and sheer writing genius, he revived an ossified genre and started it off on a fresh path.

I could likewise wish that this book held a sample or two of Leiber's horror stories. In my opinion, which Fritz modestly does not share, Lovecraft and Poe himself never dealt out comparable chills. The typical Leiber frightener gains tremendous power by its economy, its evocative contemporary setting, and its bleak brilliance of concept—like "Smoke Ghost," to name a single tale, whose phantom is in and of the corrupted air pervading a modern industrial city. (pp. x-xi)

The novels were inevitably excluded. But any discussion of Leiber's work, or of science fantasy as a whole, must consider them. They are few in number, but each is unique and, with two exceptions, of major significance in the development of present-day imaginative literature.

The first exception is *Tarzan and the City of Gold,* "only" a delightful continuation of Burroughs. Come to think of it, though, a scholar of English letters would find it most interesting to trace out how Leiber managed to convey the flavor of his model while avoiding all its crudities, outdoing Burroughs in every way that counts, and throwing occasional philosophical and moral issues into the bargain. . . .

Doubtless many will argue with my assertion that *The Green Millennium* is not a landmark. It is, in the sense of being a fine book, highly recommended. But it carries further the world of "Coming Attraction" and "Poor Superman," . . . and thus does not break new ground—by Leiber's standards—however inventive and often astoundingly witty it is. (p. xi)

[Several] of Leiber's stories are part of a series incorporating the many-branched time-lines whose origins were described in the short novel *Destiny Times Three*. Ranging from a placid utopia through a cruel dictatorship to a freezing ruin of an Earth—and beyond—this novel is more than a fast-paced chase story; it is a vatic study of power over nature and over man, so easy to misuse and so nearly impossible to use rightly.

Similarly, Leiber wrote a number of stories in what has come to be known as the Change-War cycles. . . . The heart of the cycle is in another novel, *The Big Time*. Few comparable tours de force exist anywhere in literature. The action takes place continuously in a single setting, a station outside the cosmos to which half-crazed soldiers from all time and space are sent for a little rest and recreation. Beneath the flamboyancies, tension racks up notch by notch toward a breaking-point climax followed by an ironic dénouement. It's fantastically good theater—literally. How I wish to see it staged!

Being such a virtuoso performance, *The Big Time* doesn't seem to have had any followers. I admit to keeping it in mind while writing my own *A Midsummer Tempest,* but cannot claim that that employs the dramatic unities as the former book did. Evidently nobody in our field can match Fritz Leiber here.

He went on to a different technique, the out-and-out satirical, in *The Silver Eggheads*. This account of an ultra-mechanized future lacks the misanthropy of a Swift but bites just as hard. I really think its blend of sardonicism, earthy (even slapstick) mirth, and underlying compassion is best likened to Aristophanes. (pp. xii-xiii)

[*The Wanderer*] concerns the effects on a large and varied cast of characters of a mobile planet coming near Earth. All kinds of things happen, all fascinating. But I have a reason for singling out the relationship, which eventually becomes erotic, between the human Paul and the highly evolved, feline-like Tigerishka. Leiber flinches no more from the fact that we are sexual beings than he does from the fact that we are limited, usually ridiculous, and ultimately mortal. (pp. xiii-xiv)

To be thus aware of mortality, and of the ancient deeps within us while we live, is not morbid but mature. Leiber can even laugh with them—not at them, which is an evasion, but with them. He does so in *A Specter Is Haunting Texas*. The satire there is more stark than in *The Silver Eggheads*, more reminiscent of Huxley or Heine though with a strong dash of . . . shall we say Buster Keaton? The hero, born and reared on the Moon, has in its low gravity grown up excessively tall and thin. Forced to visit Earth, he must wear a skeleton-like supportive framework which, with his black garb, makes him Death discarnate to the inhabitants of a crazy-quilt of nations formed after a nuclear war. One of his loves is equally a Death figure, the other Flesh itself. Needless to say, the author never puts it this crudely or obviously, and the overtones are infinite. Perhaps no other modern writers except James Branch Cabell and Vladimir Nabokov have gotten such fun out of the human tragicomedy; and they, for all their wit, have never had Leiber's uninhibited gusto. (pp. xiv-xv)

> *Poul Anderson, "The Wizard of Newhon" (copyright © 1974 by Poul Anderson; reprinted by permission of Ballantine Books, a Division of Random House, Inc.), in* The Best of Fritz Leiber *by Fritz Leiber, Ballantine Books, 1974 (and reprinted by Doubleday, 1974, pp. vii-xv).*

FRITZ LEIBER

All I ever try to write is a good story with a good measure of strangeness in it. The supreme goddess of the universe is Mystery, and being well entertained is the highest joy.

I write my stories against backgrounds of science, history and fantasy worlds of swords and sorcery. I write about the intensely strange everyday human mind and the weird and occult—about which I am a skeptic yet which interest me vastly. I always try to be meticulously accurate in handling these backgrounds, to be sure of my facts no matter what fantastic stories I build from them.

The tales in [*The Best of Fritz Leiber*] are predominantly science fantasy. They are arranged in the order in which they were first published, all except **"Gonna Roll the Bones."** It seemed best to lead off with a story that displayed to advantage all my talents, such as they are. It was actually written next to the last of the twenty-two stories in this book. (p. 298)

["Sanity" and "Wanted—An Enemy"] reflect my wry worries about war, pacifism, and world government. . . .

"The Ship Sails at Midnight" is the romantic tale of a love that was unconventional, at least then. The goddess Mystery makes an appearance, perhaps. I picked it as my best single story for an [August] Derleth anthology. . . .

["Coming Attraction"] was denounced by a minority of its first readers as Unamerican (I don't know why—it's Unrussian too) and praised by quite a few fellow writers. . . . It and the novelette **"Poor Superman"** mirror the intense concern of 1950 with McCarthyism, computerization and, above all, the bomb. (p. 299)

I wrote **"The Night He Cried"** because I was distantly angry at Mickey Spillane for the self-satisfied violence and loveless sex and anti-feminism he was introducing into detective fiction *and* because he had the temerity to publish a couple of stories in the fantasy field, about which I have a parental concern. My rage seems remote now, yet the point was valid. (p. 300)

"Little Old Miss Macbeth" caused Robert P. Mills, then editor of *Fantasy and Science Fiction*, to observe, "Surely Fritz Leiber is the most vividly *visual* of all science-fantasy writers." This seems extreme, yet for me vision *is* "worth all the rest" of the senses, as Macbeth put it. It may be due to my youth as an actor and the child of actors. I visualize most of my stories and set many of them on an imaginary stage. Some, like *The Big Time*, have only one set. (pp. 300-01)

"The Good New Days" looks at the Beat Generation and our slum planet, but aims at entertainment first.

"America the Beautiful" might be thought of as **"Coming Attraction"** revisited. Another Britisher encounters a different, but equally disturbing future America. Low-key and heavy on the atmosphere, but as always I've tried to make the story the thing. . . .

I seem to have had four chief bursts of creativity, triggered off by the Second World War, the nuclear bomb, the sputniks, and the war in Vietnam. I'm glad I've been able to react to those dreadful stimuli with laughter as well as fears. . . .

So, as I say, there you have them, the best of my science-fantasy stories. But I hope to write better ones. I'll never stop writing. It's one occupation in which being crazy, even senile, *might* help. (p. 301)

> *Fritz Leiber, in his afterword to his* The Best of Fritz Leiber *(copyright © 1974 by Fritz Leiber; reprinted by permission of Doubleday & Company, Inc.), Doubleday, 1974, pp. 298-301.*

ROBERT THURSTON

For more than thirty years, Fritz Leiber has been giving his readers glimpses of Heaven and Hell in his own special time machine/spaceship theater. One might describe it, if the metaphor is not too conventional, as the theater of his imagination. Such a metaphor is more accurate than usual in the case of Leiber, since he often designs his stories according to theatrical conceptions. (p. v)

The influence of theater upon his work is more than just a simple costuming of his fantasy and science-fiction stories in the paraphernalia of the stage, more than just the fact that his characters often perform plays or put on little shows or gather together for poetry and song recitals in the course of their adventures. The ideas, structures, and machinery of the drama, as practiced from the time of the ancient Greeks right up to the present, are such basic elements in his fiction that it is difficult to find a Leiber story or novel that does not, in some way, suggest his ties to the theater. (pp. v-vi)

Leiber's work has been distinguished for his ability to create mood, especially the dark mood of the occult and supernatural, and to tell stories complex in plot and theme at a fast pace. He is perhaps better than any other fantasy-sf author at creating good dialogue (although in some science fiction circles, that observation might be classified as faint praise). He has the knack of writing emotionally-charged dialogue that is believable and effective, without resorting to the kinds of melodramatic formulae so common to the *genre*. And he portrays character vividly, whether the character is human or alien. In a literature often accused of male chauvinist leanings, he has consistently etched effective characterizations of women and, in advance of the current women's lib concerns, shown understanding of and sympathy for the role of women in a male-dominated society. In fact, many of Leiber's themes, derived perhaps from his continuing interest in liberal beliefs and causes, are underlain with politically-radical ideas, especially when viewed in light of the generally reactionary themes of many of his contemporaries in the field. In addition to his work in fantasy and science fiction, he has made his mark in the related sword-and-sorcery subgenre with his memorable tales of Fafhrd and the Gray Mouser.

Looking back on Leiber's work, I came to the conclusion that its best features derived from his concern with, and interest in, theater. Most of these are to be found in the Hugo Award winning novel, *The Big Time,* as well as in some of the other stories in the Change-War cycle. (pp. vii-viii)

The Change War is one of those intriguing science-fiction concepts that makes other sf writers envious and leaves readers breathless. Still, the depiction of soldiers fighting a war across time, rearranging history as a part of the overall battle, would be just a clever one if Leiber had chosen to treat it in a conventional sf way. Instead, his selection of setting (a rest and recuperation center outside of the war and, for that matter, time) is a shrewd device, particularly in the way he is able to suggest the range and character of the time-war through the statements and thoughts of the people in The Place. Also, his treatment of his major themes (time and change especially) gives the narrative a solid philosophical framework that makes the plight of these minor warriors and entertainers all the more poignant and mysterious, almost in a Shakespearian way. . . . Much of [*The Big Time*] is concerned with the ideological frustrations of Greta and the others, trapped not only for a few hours in The Place but for always in a war whose meaning they can only theorize about. . . . Each of the individual thematic speculations could become the basis of single novels. Leiber, on the other hand, packs them securely and effectively into this relatively short novel.

Leiber's mastery of divergent styles, a praiseworthy characteristic of all his work, is especially evident in *The Big Time,* with its rich mixture of poetic language and slang. Much of this richness comes from the influence of his dramatic background on the writing. (pp. viii-ix)

Perhaps the finest achievement in this novel is the character of Greta, who starts out appearing to be what she says she is, an ordinary Entertainer plucked out of her ordinary lifeline, but who, by the end of the story, has become a kind of Everywoman who perceives events and people more clearly and more eloquently than any of the other characters. . . . After choosing Greta as the tale-teller, [Leiber] strived to make it seem as if she were talking to somebody rather than writing the story down. The audience he envisions for her is one or more new recruit-entertainers on the verge of entering the Change World. The fact that Greta is such a fascinating character attests to the success of his method. Again the approach is essentially theatrical, deriving chiefly from the dramatic monologue. (p. x)

The most striking similarity to theater is Leiber's use of dialogue. The men and women who are his players often talk as if on a stage. . . . Conflicts between characters are structured according to dialogue exchanges which are "built" in intensity, according to theatrical custom. Most important of all, it is well-written dialogue. . . . (p. xi)

Of all the narratives in the Change-War Cycle, *The Big Time* is the most daring, the most flamboyant, and the most significant as a contribution to science fiction. In it Leiber shows how a concept that has seemingly been done to death can be resurrected by taking a new slant on the subject. Time travel has been again and again declared a dead science-fiction theme by readers and writers alike, yet Leiber and others keep returning to it and discovering that there are still areas of the subject that have possibilities. (p. xiv)

> Robert Thurston, "Introduction" (copyright © 1976 by G. K. Hall & Co.; reprinted by permission of the author), in The Big Time by Fritz Leiber, Gregg Press, 1976, pp. v-xv.

ALEXEI PANSHIN and CORY PANSHIN

A Specter Is Haunting Texas resembles Fritz Leiber's very first science fiction novel—*Gather, Darkness!* . . .—in being an intermittently satirical melodrama about revolution. The target of both satire and revolution in *Gather, Darkness!* was organized religion. The target in *A Specter Is Haunting Texas* is Texas—which is to say the American impulse toward gigantism. (p. 15)

The differences that twenty-five years have made are that the satire in *Specter*—while it lasts—is painted in broader strokes than the satire in *Gather, Darkness!* and that the revolution in the newer book is a temporary failure rather than a success. Otherwise, the books are much of a piece.

At its best, *Specter* is not particularly original. It covers ground covered better in the Fifties by H. Beam Piper and John J. McGuire. . . . [Its] greatest strength, in fact, is in conceits and occasional lines. And two-thirds of the way through it falls apart, its satire forgotten in favor of the melodramatic requirement of movement at any cost. (pp. 15-16)

A Specter Is Haunting Texas, like *Gather, Darkness!* before it, is without the same claims to stature, similarly spoiled. (p. 16)

> Alexei Panshin and Cory Panshin, "The Elizabethan Theatre in 1590" (copyright © 1969 by Mercury Press, Inc.; reprinted by courtesy of Advent Publishers, Inc.), in their SF in Dimension: A Book of Explorations, Advent, 1976, pp. 11-18.*

TOM SHIPPEY

[In *The Golden Bough* Sir James Frazer deduced] that in essence primitive magic was not like primitive religion, as most observers had assumed, but was instead *similar to science,* in its belief that the universe was subject to "immutable laws, the operation of which can be foreseen and calculated precisely". *The Golden Bough* makes this claim overtly. . . . [And] it is a relatively short step from saying that magic is *very like* science to saying that it is actually *a form of* science. It is this further step which many science fiction authors have, with varying levels of seriousness, been happy to take. (pp. 121-22)

[The] real potentials of the "Frazerian" story were exposed as well as anywhere . . . by Fritz Leiber's unduly-neglected novel, *Conjure Wife.* . . . (p. 122)

Leiber's hero, Professor Saylor, discovers suddenly and by accident that his wife has constructed round him a great web of magic defences to cover him from the malice of the other faculty wives, all of whom, like her, are witches by instinct and tradition. Dismissing it as superstition, he makes her burn her charms; and then, of course, his life turns into a paranoid's nightmare, with student accusations, missed promotions, charges of academic plagiarism, and so on. In the end his wife, left magically defenceless, is turned into a soulless zombie by her female enemies. . . . [While Leiber's] images of the powers of witches are at least as gruesome as ancient ones, he nevertheless accepts magic as ethically neutral, usable protectively as well as aggressively. Nor does the place of magic against religion concern him at all, however vital it was for the witchhunters. . . . Further, at the moment of crisis *The Golden Bough* appears, as talisman-cum-guidebook. For Saylor is a professor of *sociology* (which we would now call social anthropology) and, faced by a zombie wife, he falls back on his academic speciality. He accepts the assumption that the superstitions he has studied detachedly for so long are all garbled reflections of a real truth; takes down his textbooks (*The Golden Bough* is the only one mentioned); finds some seventeen formulas for calling back the soul recorded by primitive peoples, and reduces them all to a master formula. This combination of superstition and scientific method proves unconquerable, and the story ends . . . with triumph and reunion.

The surprise in all this, for an unprepared reader, lies in the direction of Professor Saylor's progress. When we hear the word "magic" we inevitably think of reversion, savagery, effortless absence of ratiocination; to find magic then put into an academic context and sharpened by mathematical rigour is inevitably arresting. The juxtaposition becomes part of the stock-in-trade of all "magical" authors, who have a particular penchant for setting stories in and around learned conferences; there is an especially close resemblance to *Conjure Wife* thirty years later in Roger Zelazny's *Jack of Shadows* . . . , where a computer is even dragged in to replace Professor Saylor's symbolic logic. But it is obvious, too, that Leiber enjoys the process of academic argument for its own sake. After all, if his hypothesis is true, it throws up one major question straight away: why has magic never been reduced to order *before* (given the amount of research dedicated to it the world over)? The question is in a way the reverse of one asked by Frazer, which was why magic had not been *exposed* before: and the answers to both are curiously similar. . . . "Magic is a practical science", Saylor theorises, because it is inevitably concerned with "getting or accomplishing something". This means that the personality of the operator is a part of the magical operation; and *this* means that experiments are inherently non-repeatable. One of the bases of scientific method is accordingly removed, helping on the one hand to explain the absence of any "general theory" of magic, and on the other administering a check to modern assumptions about the universal scope of experimental science. A second point returns one to the definition of magic in the [*Oxford English Dictionary*], "the power of compelling the intervention of spiritual *beings*". Obviously, if personalities rather than forces are the object of experimentation, further irregularities are likely to enter, making the whole thing more difficult. And finally Saylor notes that "Magic appears to be a science which markedly depends on its environment"—in other words, it is subject to rapid change. The constants of physics may perhaps change as well (so Leiber suggests), but if they do, they do so slowly. Magic, however, needs to be continuously updated by trial-and-error, and is as a result likely every now and then to fail and be discredited. (pp. 122-23)

Conjure Wife draws power from its cool and rational tone, its everyday setting, while its central images—the cement dragon, the Prince Rupert drop, the shattering mirror—all carry a phys-

ical as well as a magical explanation. The book's penultimate paragraph, indeed, offers a rational explanation (that all the women involved are psychotic) as an alternative to the fantastic one (that they are all witches), while the last words of all are Professor Saylor saying evasively "I don't really know". All this makes *Conjure Wife* fit one rather strict definition of fantasy, that it takes place just as long as one is uncertain about how to explain events. However, it also points out one way in which *Conjure Wife* does *not* fit the normal development of 'Frazerian' science fiction, for all its pioneering motifs and explanations.

This is, that most 'worlds where magic works' are alternate worlds, parallel worlds, future worlds, far-past worlds. *Conjure Wife* is one of very few to be set in a recognisable present. It gains from this, of course, in realism; but loses inevitably a quality of romance. It has witches, and spells, and even the glimpsed presence of He Who Walks Behind; but there are no centaurs, or werewolves, or mermaids, or basilisks, or any of the other ancient images of fantasy. The only dragon in *Conjure Wife* is a cement one. Yet there is clearly an urge in many writers and readers to resurrect these images and use them again, partly no doubt as a result of 'escapism', but at least as much out of a kind of intellectual thrift: ideas compulsively attractive to mankind for so long, it is felt, are too good to throw away. Nevertheless this urge, powerful though it is, is met by an equally powerful current of scepticism. Twentieth-century readers, especially those with some scientific training or inclination, cannot even *pretend* to believe in anything that makes no sense, i.e. anything that has no rationalistic theory to cover it. Frazer and *The Golden Bough* provided a rationale for magic, as exploited by Leiber in *Conjure Wife*. (pp. 123-24)

> Tom Shippey, " 'The Golden Bough' and the Incorporations of Magic in Science Fiction" (a revision of a talk originally delivered at Novacon 4 in November, 1974), in Foundation (copyright © 1977 by the Science Fiction Foundation), Nos. 11 & 12, March, 1977, pp. 119-34.*

RICHARD DELAP

[*Our Lady of Darkness* is] an absolutely superb book, Leiber's first novel of the supernatural since the incredible *Conjure Wife*. . . . (p. 4)

While the novel is easy to read and follow, almost every page is filled with little sub-plots and commentaries that shift and slide with ambiguous purpose. The reader who is familiar with Leiber's own background may be convinced the book is only a thinly disguised autobiography embellished with interludes of supernatural horror. And those with a solid grounding in supernatural literature and the histories of its practitioners (especially H. P. Lovecraft) will understand how Leiber is creating a fantastically successful tour de force of the entire genre. The whole performance is a sophisticated sleight-of-hand creation that may seem perilous to "mainstream" readers . . . but is not so esoteric that it cannot be enjoyed simply as a witty, amusing and, finally, terrifying tale of occult forces at work in the modern world.

What is especially remarkable about the book is Leiber's cast of characters, the most engaging ensemble to appear in many years.

Franz Westen is recovering from a long bout with alcoholism and the death of his beloved wife, Daisy. His private quirks

. . . become not only a revelation of character but an important aspect of the half-century curse and how it will seek to destroy Franz by taking advantage of his own psychological weaknesses. Leiber could have given us lengthy interior monologues to familiarize us with Franz's obsessions, but he realizes the danger of boredom in this technique and so wisely lets Franz react to a splendid menagerie of supporting characters, each of whom serves a revelatory purpose yet remains a full-bodied creation and not a stereotype. . . .

None of [the] characters are introduced merely for the color they add, although all are extremely colorful and manage to even get away with some quite complicated dialogue ("bookish," as it is often called); but rather each has a definite and telling part to play as the web of horror draws tighter and tighter around the threatened Franz. Their characterizations are developed so that when they must do something vital to the plot, their actions are totally believable and in character.

Finally, there is Leiber's writing itself. Already acknowledged as one of the finest stylists in the field, versatile, sophisticated and armed with a perceptive wit that continually astounds and surprises with its offtrail directions, Leiber has here produced some of the best writing in his long and distinguished career. . . .

The novel is quite obviously an homage to the Lovecraft oeuvre—the slow, steady build to a moment of supreme terror—but deliciously cut with worldly-wise humor and sprightly sexual innuendo that make it palatable for today's less shockable readers. Along with the important and pervasive elements of pathos and kindness, this gives the book a distinctive taste of its own that should delight readers of every persuasion. Moreover, there are recurring images (the "spider" in the elevator, for example) that personify with exactitude Leiber's unique cross of modern and primeval fears. (p. 5)

> Richard Delap, "Fiction: 'Our Lady of Darkness'," in Delap's Fantasy & Science Fiction Review (copyright ©1977 by Richard Delap), Vol. 3, No. 4, April, 1977, pp. 4-5.

MARY S. WEINKAUF

The Book of Fritz Leiber includes ten stories and nine essays illustrating his range. . . . Leiber's imaginative and playful range of thought brightens up the topics he chooses, though his reviews and the essays on foreign words and *King Lear* are not particularly stimulating or new. Very few of the stories other than **"The Spider"** and **"Cat's Cradle"** match the quality of his commonly anthologized fiction or of those which have won awards, giving the suspicion that this is a way to collect the also-rans in permanent form. . . .

Although Leiber comes right out and says what made him write these pieces and that Lovecraft and Shakespeare are his chief literary influences, the book also shows his enjoyment of language, his appreciation for Renaissance and Jacobean drama, and his interest in the way the human mind solves everyday problems and how that carries over to the way it handles paranormal ones. Leiber's best work gets inside the human mind and down to the layers where myth waits to unite individual experience to the pattern we call humanity. In short, this book gives only a very limited sampling of a respected writer's great skill. . . .

> Mary S. Weinkauf, "Paperbacks: 'The Book of Fritz Leiber'," in Delap's Fantasy & Science Fiction Review (copyright ©1977 by Richard Delap), Vol. 3, No. 4, April, 1977, p. 29.

MICHAEL BISHOP

[Many of the pieces in *The Worlds of Fritz Leiber*] are either overwritten or unimaginatively resolved, if not both together. . . . [To] Leiber's credit is the fact that none of these stories pretends to be anything more than an entertainment—even though he manages to touch on such weighty subjects as political witch-hunting, cold-war politics, the Bomb, father-and-son relationships, bungling bureaucracy, growing old, cats, and (obsessively but chastely, as if afraid to confront a healthy lust in anything but the most decorous or tangential terms) nubile and pre-nubile young women. Fine. The problem is that too many of these entertainments are so trivial as to be irritating or so facile in their resolutions as to border on cliches. Many would benefit from cutting. (pp. 29-30)

[**"Catch That Zeppelin!"** is fascinating] and believable historical speculation, and Leiber's erudition shows to good advantage.

Structurally and stylistically, however, the story is a failure. Leiber resorts to the expedient of making one of his characters a "social historian" who lectures his father, the narrator, about all his most recent findings. And, at the story's end, when the narrator is finally cornered by an enigmatic Jew who has been following him, two puzzling but disgracefully convenient shifts of the temporal continuum return him safely to the present. That, friends—unless your name is Euripedes, and maybe even then—is known as a cop-out. . . .

But the collection's greatest disappointments, because they initially promise so much, are two fairly recent stories, [**"Waif"** and **"Night Passage"**]. . . . Each declines so rapidly into cliche that one is amazed to find them under Leiber's byline. And the latter is the worse offender. Set in a Las Vegas casino, **"Night Passage"** seems at first to promise the phantasmagoric fireworks of the author's award-winning **"Gonna Roll The Bones."** Instead, it explains away its briefly intriguing "mystery lady" and its sinister casino operators with their diamond-pupiled eyes as aliens engaged in a deadly game right under our unsuspecting noses. (p. 30)

As a partial antidote to the foregoing crankiness, I'd like to end this overview of *The Worlds of Fritz Leiber* on a note of unqualified praise. In the apparently little-known **"Endfray of the Ofay,"** . . . Leiber altogether successfully combines plot, character, speculation, and style, serving up an entertainment that so wackily glosses contemporary world affairs that one's laughter has a nervous edge. . . . Here Leiber's wit, humor, and stylistic gymnastics are perfectly in tune with his subject matter . . . ; and the Endfray of the title, while being distinctly himself, reminds me of Harlan Ellison's non-conformist protagonist in "'Repent, Harlequin!' Said the Ticktockman." This is the one story in *The Worlds of Fritz Leiber* that I believe I could read again with unfeigned eagerness. (pp. 30-1)

> Michael Bishop, "Paperbacks: 'The Worlds of Fritz Leiber'," in Delap's Fantasy & Science Fiction Review (copyright © 1977 by Richard Delap), Vol. 3, No. 4, April, 1977, pp. 29-31.

ALGIS BUDRYS

Night's Black Agents, a collection of Fritz Leiber short work, is an outstanding bargain. Leiber is famous for being neglected.

That is to say, periodically a critic discovers that this still-active master storyteller has been consistently ahead of his time over a very long career in SF. What matters truly is that, whether as a traditional fantasist, or a sword-and-sorcery writer, or an artist of "straight" science fiction, Leiber is unfailingly entertaining on a very high level. . . . *Night's Black Agents* is a sampler of Leiber at his best, and of the best that SF can attain in many of its modes. (p. F2)

Algis Budrys, "Tales of Time and Space," in Book World—The Washington Post (© 1978, The Washington Post), March 5, 1978, pp. F1-F2.*

JOHN CLUTE

Here is a mistake from Fritz Leiber, though it warms the heart. *Our Lady of Darkness* is a mistake of displacement. Whatever one reads of Leiber, in whatever genre he presents to us his skill and touch, the implied author (the author visible in the text, all we have a right to know) who speaks to one seems to exhale a kind of shy sacrificial gravitas, however garish or commercial the story he's telling happens to be. It somehow seems *brave* for an adult person like Fritz Leiber to expose himself without condescension or disguise to a readership comprised of people like us—young, claquish, aggressive, intrusive, we tend to demand complicity of our authors, and to punish those who turn a blank face, or (like Silverberg) a mask of anguish. Perhaps anguish comes too close to the foul rag and bone shop to be amenable to claims of complicity. And perhaps Leiber was after all right, in *Our Lady of Darkness,* to avoid telling the tale of anguish and mourning that lies palpably at the heart of its inspiration, and instead to displace that story into a routine tale of externalized haunting, even though injected with elements of an sf rationale, a good deal of social realism scarifyingly illuminating about life in California now (and in our future soon enough), and some interesting speculative musing about what the modern world-city may be beginning to do to us. (p. 64)

[The] implied author of *Our Lady of Darkness* sounds singularly ill-at-ease in his efforts to present to us the story he does as though it were the real story. Thin ice does seem to bring out the jocosity in the best of us . . . And matters are not made any better when one realizes that the protagonist of the novel, whose name is Franz Westen, patently stands in as a kind of pun, whether or not a lying one, for the author himself. . . . As the novel opens, he has apparently been comfortably reinstated in human society for some months after a three year period of drunkenness that followed the gruesome death of his wife by brain cancer. Franz Westen is all right now, you bet, as he seems to tell us, and as the implied author of the book insists in words that grin. But what reader is going to believe that? It sounds like a classic opening to a novel whose subject lies in the examination of forms of intolerable suffering. After ten pages, the reader is bracing himself for a descent into the Hell indoors, and each time the text protests that Hell is somewhere in the past the reader recognizes a conventional ploy. (pp. 64-5)

[Leiber makes] some attempt to relate the external haunting that comprises the ostensible subject of the book (and most of its bulk) to an interior story of insecurely managed grief; the connection of wife to Scholar's Mistress to Noseless Whatsit, though made little of, comprises the real line of power and esemplasy in the novel. But what Leiber has done with this line of potency, however, is to reverse its thrust; the dead wife

serves to illustrate and add resonance to the tale of a haunting, not the reverse, and it is precisely here that the displacement can be identified as having taken place. Reverse the thrust at this point, and the emotional force, the edgy sombreness, the sense of walking on eggshells that permeates the novel begins to come clear, and the discursive yakking about the fatuous de Castries and crew comes to read as a sequence of desperate manoeuvrings away from the real trauma, the real horror. But one can only reverse the thrust abstractly, like this, after a selective synopsis: the novel itself resists this reversal strenuously and, to our loss, successfully.

So one reads Fritz Leiber—exuding the decency and gravitas he does exude in his texts—as telling a kind of fib, grimacing a little, dragging in Lovecraft Sauce and C. A. Smith and Lord help us Ambrose Bierce to protest too much along beside him, and one wonders what it was, what caused this forgivable treason. Perhaps it was only a marketing decision. Crap about paramental dingbats fits genre expectations; the dark night of the soul, on the other hand, is death on the stalls. And Fritz Leiber has to live. In some ways he's produced a pretty effective tale. But the face of the implied author stares at one from within the text, and I'm afraid I read that face as confessing all, and I thanked it. (pp. 65-6)

John Clute, "Reviews: 'Our Lady of Darkness'," in Foundation (copyright © 1978 by the Science Fiction Foundation), No. 14, September, 1978, pp. 64-6.

JOHN SILBERSACK

[*The Change War*] stories reflect Leiber's fascination with the instability of much of modern American life. In Leiber's best fictions he is able to endow this instability, this American capacity for change, with a profound supernaturalism that can turn the most freakish accidents of urban chance into nightmares of paranoic intensity.

The Changewar plots are created around the premise that there are two forces in the universe battling for supremacy in the greatest war ever—a war conducted in all places and over all time. The war's object is to alter the course of past and present history in favor of one or the other of the two forces, known as Snakes or Spiders. At the end of time one side will have ultimately won by actually channeling history to its advantage. (pp. vii-viii)

The Changewar is an exercise in thought that can be carried in many directions, and most other writers would have taken it elsewhere. By choosing as he has, Leiber scorns some easy crowd-pleasing effects in order to test the boundaries of science fiction and gothic horror as they apply to modern life. In this he is foregoing the traditions of both fields and attempting something new, exciting, and quite valuable. Leiber writes in the tradition of the English, French and German gothic writers of the early 19th century who reacted to their revolutionary age by acknowledging the vastness of human ignorance. But Leiber also stands with the early optimistic science fiction writers, with Jules Verne and H. G. Wells, because of his faith in man's innate ability to adapt and equip himself for the future whatever it may hold. In this conjunction of praise and disparise he follows only one gothic writer of real power, Mary Shelley. He simultaneously challenges the dark fearful past and the uncertain but possibly bright future. (p. viii)

It is no coincidence that Leiber chooses the early 20th century, instead of any other historical or future era, as the Greenwich

Standard Time of the Changewar. The 20th century is like no other for complexity and confusion on a worldwide scale—or within the individual mind. The Changewar is a rationalizing metaphor for the inexplicable in modern life, a fantastic model for an even more fantastical universe in which nothing is just exactly as it appears. . . . We are all part of the Changewar in our secret fear that our private worlds will come tumbling down around us.

This personal horror is the source of many of Leiber's best fictions. It is at its most intense and provocative when he deals with modern, particularly urban life. . . . This is the fabric of a modern peculiarly urban gothic mode—a transformation of a traditional horror form to the 20th century cityscape—a transformation that takes its most complete and satisfying shape in the Changewar saga.

The Changewar stories proved to be particularly apt vehicles for the reworking of old forms. Their basic premise is the theory of change, a theory which Leiber has equipped with a science-fictional apparatus as fascinating and telling as Isaac Asimov's Laws of Robotics. The basic theme of these stories is the consequences of change, particularly on the individual. Leiber seems to be telling us that we cannot live in an increasingly complex and manifold world without feeling some ill effects. His Changewar stories emphasize the complected nature of modern life by mixing science fiction with gothically conceived descriptive elements (his spiders and snakes, wolves and ghosts) thereby attempting to reconcile technology with the supernatural mind with matter in the modern world. (pp. ix-x)

Robert Thurston in his introduction to . . . *The Big Time* [see excerpt above], makes a good case for theatre as a device and metaphor in Leiber's fictions. With Leiber's theatrical and film background it comes as no surprise that he is adept at setting a stage and bringing players to life. Leiber's stories are in a very real sense psychological dramas, the action taking place in the character's minds. The settings, the science-fictional and gothic props, serve the same staging purpose as, say, Yorick's skull—a point of departure for the real meat of the story, an individual's self-discovery. (pp. x-xi)

[Leiber's] is a fiction of paradoxes if not opposites. Good and evil, ignorance and knowledge, inside and outside, praise and dispraise, past and future: all play their part in Leiber's world. Science fiction and gothic horror, too, are opposites which Leiber has successfully wedded in the Changewar saga in order to better probe the scienti-supernaturalism of modern life. Fritz Leiber is one of the first to make this connection between the dark recesses of man's psyche and the swiftly eddying future. (p. xvi)

> *John Silbersack, "Introduction" (copyright © 1978 by John Silbersack; reprinted by permission of the author), in* The Change War *by Fritz Leiber, Gregg Press, 1978, pp. vii-xvi.*

JUSTIN LEIBER

The Big Time introduces the "Change War" world in which a vast war is conducted through space and time by "Spiders" and "Snakes," and by humans and extra-terrestrials who have the rare quality of flexibility and alienatedness that allows them to be recruited out of their ordinary life and time into the big time, the world of all times and possibilities. Many time travel stories suggest that one might travel to the Ice Age, mash a blade of grass, and change all history. . . . But if you think

about it, *if time travel is possible*, then all of time must exist at once in some sense—the past cannot have wholly disappeared if you can get to it, nor can the future be wholly unmade if you can go there and back. This raises the question as to how one can change the future or the past. This also raises the question: what is "the present"? If you can travel the big time continuum of space-time-history from ancient Egypt to the distant future, who is to say what slice is the present? Strikingly, Fritz has an elegant answer to these questions: the "law of the conservation of reality."

The idea is to extend the conservation laws of physics once more, into the psychological, historical, and higher physical sciences. (p. 12)

The law of the conservation of reality, like the other conservation laws, suggests that nothing is really lost, nothing spontaneously evaporates or appears: you can, with a great expenditure of reality through time-travel agents, transform something in the space-time-history continuum (replace Julius Caesar with a secret spider agent, throw a tactical A-bomb into the Peloponnesian War), *but the rest of the historical continuum will conserve reality*, it will change the absolute minimum needed to accommodate this intervention. . . . Time travel in ordinary time violates reality: reality reshapes the pattern of events so that the violation fits right in with a new reality of ordinary time.

What has to be the "present" in the continuum of ordinary time? The "present" is simply the slice of history that is most conserved, least changeable, most influential.

Formally, *The Big Time* maintains the most strict unities of classical drama. *All* the story takes place within a few hours and in one large room, a rest and recreation station outside of time. The cast—the Place is obviously a theater and the action dramatic—of entertainers and agents come from choice points in history, or slight-altered, "change-war torn" history. This provides the challenge of displaying very different accents and ways of thought together. The Place is like a ghostly theater in which characters from different plays meet. (pp. 12-13)

The mind is the big time. For we find there a constructed reality, a panorama of space-time-history that flexes and readjusts as one reconstructs the past and repredicts the future, reintegrates the macrocosm and microcosm: at the same time, in the mind's big time, there is the continual play of possibilities, of alternate histories and worlds. The cast of the Place worry that the Snakes and Spiders may have messed so much with the fabric of historical reality that it may fission, smashing the conservation of reality as an atomic bomb explodes the conservation of matter. But that's what madness is, isn't it? The Ego can put it together no longer.

You will also notice a view of the mind that is as old as Plato and as new as Hermann Hesse's *Steppenwolf*: the mind is composed of many persons, forged in fear and love, from experience, history, and imagination, and when the mind acts or receives reports, it does so through one or another of these characters and must take account of that character's weaknesses. (p. 14)

[It] is part of my thesis that Fritz started with escapist, and deliberately unpretentious, genres—Id demanded gross meals, and shyness (murderous Superego) insisted on concealment in pulp genre—but, as Fritz improved his art and grasp of form, his artistic daemon, reflecting on past work and planning new, simply forced him to realize various pathologies in himself, forced him into better self-understanding. . . .

Fritz soon grew unchallenged by the supernatural horror and sword & sorcery forms with which he began: once one gives oneself to art it may become discontent with simple tasks and low dreams. The first substantial works he made are rich in ideas and technologies, though retaining much of the atmosphere of the earlier tales. The unpretentious pose of professional pulp writer is maintained. The ideas and characters are there to wring the maximum punch from the dramatic, swift-moving action that clever plotting affords; style and narrative structure are unobtrusive. The protagonist is invariably an attractive and uncomplicated character with whom the reader may easily identify, both innocently awaiting the tricks that are in store. Though the protagonist often shares a couple of skills or experiences with the real Fritz—the writer has to know something about the settings he puts his characters into, surely—the protagonist is no confession of the real Fritz, nor is there any tricky interplay between protagonist and artist. All this begins to turn about in the later works. *You're All Alone, Gather, Darkness!,* and *Conjure Wife* of the 1940s are followed by *The Big Time,* [*A Specter is Haunting Texas*] and *Our Lady of Darkness.*

In *You're All Alone* . . . is one of the narrowest and most dramatic expressions of paranoia that I know. . . . It's a scary story, and should one stand back and think about it, suggests something about the writer (about a grim Chicago downtown business-and-bar world), but everything is done to lead the reader away from that issue, and the author has no place in the story. It's ''you're all alone,'' not ''I'm all alone,'' or even ''we're all alone.''

On the other hand, in *The Big Time* . . . we have not the simple paranoiac punch, but the gay, giddy, multileveled fabric of high art, of the ''everybody and nobody,'' in which the Place, dancing with drama and history, is of course also revealed as the mind of Fritz Leiber and his Art. . . .

[*Gather, Darkness!*] is one of the first and perhaps *the* classical novel of a future, post-WWIII world dominated by an authoritarian, medieval-modeled church hierarchy whose inner-circle employs a secret scientific technology to keep the superstitious public and lower priesthood under control. The action is dramatic and colorful, the technology cunning and charming, the plot stunningly well-constructed. One idea that gives the work its classical balance is the logic of a revolution against such a hierarchy of white magic: the revolutionaries will play satanists, a hierarchy of *black* magic which will dismay, frighten, or win over people who are adjusted to think in magical, not scientific, ways. (p. 15)

[But] when we get to *A Specter is Haunting Texas* . . . , we have a more multi-leveled, more comic and more realistic story of our post-WWIII future. Scully (Fritz, narrator, Death, Dark Art), actor from Circumluna, is dragged into the bent-back revolution against hormone-hiked, conquering Texans, who identify with LBJ and (no doubt) a certain war . . . And Scully knows that history is hardly ever a tale of technologically-inventive elites, coldly manipulating the credulous masses. You don't reason its craziness out, you sing it, chant it, farce it out. (pp. 15-16)

As Fritz' art has developed it becomes ever more willing to play and joke, to fool with words and themes, to inject comic gaiety into the midst of tragedy. (My favorite in the pure comic vein is ''**Mysterious Doings in the Metropolitan Museum,**'' . . . a tale of insect political conventioneering.)

I have suggested that as Fritz' art developed he came to employ richer and more complicated forms, came to use himself and his artistic self-image in his art, came to play the mirror tricks of high art. But one might argue that this doesn't fit the Fafhrd-Gray Mouser stories with which Fritz began and which he has continued through his career. Surely, Fafhrd is a vision of Fritz himself, or so someone might object. . . .

I am inclined to think that Fritz wasn't Fafhrd from the beginning. Though Fafhrd eventually becomes more Fritz-like. Certainly, there are some revealing and confessional changes as the saga develops. The first tales are quest stories in which the twain are lured into some doomful quest, drawn and nearly overwhelmed by some distant and lonely horror. The atmosphere strives for a relatively uniform feeling of somber eeriness mounting to arcane and chilling climax. As the latter stories appear, Fritz has a much surer and broader sense of language and plot. Comedy and gaiety invade the saga, romance and drunken silliness appear, and grand Lankhmar becomes central with its motley of religions, beggars and thieves guilds, necromancers and decadent aristocrats, gates and streets, mysterious houses and musty passages, shops and taverns, gods and human-like animals. My favorite is ''**Lean Times in Lankhmar,**'' in which the penniless and disaffected twain separate, Mouser hiring himself out to a protection racket enforcer covering the religions that move up the Street of the Gods as they attract a following and down as they lose it, and Fafhrd becoming an acolyte of Issek of the Jug, swearing off booze and swords. The confrontation that must occur as Issek of the Jug moves up to the successful part of the street is managed with such astonishing deftness, twist upon twist, that one finds oneself laughing ''too much, too much,'' only to have yet another carefully-prepared rabbit pop out of the hat, and yet another after that. The story plays effortlessly with the inversions of high art.

Fritz (and reality) seep into the saga world. Fritz has some fairly somber morals to point out about hard drinking that point much more to Fritz than to the Fafhrd of the very first stories. (p. 17)

Fritz combines an awesome and precise command of language with a joyous willingness to measure it against every sort of verbal challenge. Fritz' tendency to distinguish the smallest literary favor with precision and imagination is par with his tendency to treat even the most fetid and undistinguished humans with a respectful and friendly manner. (p. 18)

Justin Leiber, ''Fritz Leiber & Eyes,'' in Starship, *Vol. 16, No. 35, Summer, 1979, pp. 9-18.*

JEFF FRANE

The element of *change* and the effect it has on human society is a persistent theme in Leiber's fiction, and he is one of the few science-fiction writers of his generation to consistently stay abreast of the cultural changes around him. Leiber, above all, has been aware that change—or evolution—is not only inevitable, but necessary to human growth. It is a theme that is most obvious in his Change War stories, but it can be found in subtler forms throughout his fiction. (pp. 13-14)

Gather, Darkness takes place in the far future on Earth, with a group called the Hierarchy holding sway over the commoners. The religion they have formed is a corrupted form of Roman

Catholicism, with a structure reminiscent of Dante's Inferno. The priesthood is defined by a series of circles, with the outermost circle being the first, and the whole governed by the Apex Council, within the seventh circle. The Hierarchy has sole control over the highly advanced technology which makes the priests' lives so comfortable; the commoners are reduced to a state of physical and intellectual poverty comparable to the peasants of Europe's Dark Ages. As priests advance inward, they receive more and more information about the real activities of the Hierarchy. Those in the Apex Council have achieved the peak of cynicism and available knowledge. (p. 20)

[Brother Goniface, one of the archpriests of the Apex Council,] faced with the realization that the Witchcraft has begun to create a real threat to the Hierarchy, has decided to foment a minor crisis in an attempt to draw out his opponents. (pp. 20-1)

The members of the Witchcraft have developed all the "mummeries" of Black Magic in the same manner that the Hierarchy has adopted the trappings of the Christian church. They have "familiars," attendant beings grown from their own tissue (a concept considerably predating research into DNA and cloning); the rocket-powered "angels" of the Hierarchy are fought by similar missiles disguised with batwings and leering faces; and they haunt the countryside, frightening commoners and priests alike. (p. 21)

The obvious decadence of the Hierarchy . . . provides a more realistic venue for a successful revolt than that of many science-fiction stories. The concept of a small group, or a single individual, leading the liberation of society from an all-powerful, oppressive elite is a common theme in science fiction. In *Gather, Darkness,* the Witchcraft ultimately succeeds, but it does so because it has arisen at a time when the Hierarchy is already crumbling from within; Goniface has seen that his own rapid rise, virtually unopposed, is not the sign of a vigorous state.

Gather, Darkness, although couched as an adventure tale, posits some questions about the functions and responsibilities of scientists that are particularly relevant to today's society. At the conclusion of the book, it is clear that no simplistic answers are offered, even within the context of a "happy ending." (p. 22)

While acknowledging the real benefits of technology, Leiber is offering cautions. Scientists have no reason to assume a godlike status, and equally, this status should not be conferred upon them by others. There also seems to be a message to the "commoners"—the non-scientists—that it is their responsibility to gain as much knowledge about what scientists are working on, and the manner in which the world is constructed, as is needed to make informed decisions within society. Considering the fact that this novel was written several years before the revelations about the Manhattan project and decades before such volatile subjects as research into recombinant DNA, it is a message that seems prophetic indeed. (p. 23)

The Big Time is a highly compact book, only 129 pages long; yet within it Leiber has created what may be structurally and emotionally his best novel. It is very deliberately modeled on the dramatic form. . . . Following the demands of the dramatic form, much of the information and significance is carried through the dialogue, and the prose is impressively lean.

The novel opens with a narrative introduction. Greta Forzane, the point-of-view character throughout, is a participant in the action to follow, but at the same time is a careful observer; her occasional failures to see things happening on stage are simply those failures that a playwright would rely on from a live audience. Greta herself is a fusion of audience and narrator. (p. 24)

Greta sets the stage, describing its location and physical appearance. Then each of the on-stage characters is introduced, each located physically and given a brief précis. We are actually being given only a little more information about each than would be offered in a theatrical presentation, and in fact, a good deal of what Greta says about them could be suggested by careful costuming and direction. . . .

The characters that fill the stage of *The Big Time* are from a wide variety of times and places, and only the dialogue (and costuming) is available to communicate this to the audience. At times, the speech patterns seem to verge on the stereotypic, but some such device as this is necessary to communicate information in theatrical terms.

The New Boy (Bruce Marchant) is clearly British with his first line: "Why'd you pull out so bloody fast?" Erich is clearly German: "Didn't you feel their stun guns, *Dumpkopf,* when they sprung the trap—too soon, *Gott sei Dank?*"

We are thus immediately presented with the conflict that will gather throughout the story, not only the obvious falling-out between two war-companions, but the concern that Bruce has with his own fears of war and cowardice, and the enormous ego that drives Erich. (p. 25)

A great deal of the insecurity and internal conflict of all of the characters stems from the problem that Marchant outlines. . . . All of them are being manipulated by forces that they have no direct contact with or knowledge of, and they are sent out into a battle whose direction and purpose are equally unknown. They have been told that their enemy is "bent on perverting and enslaving the whole cosmos, past, present, and future," . . . but they have no real way of evaluating this assertion. . . .

We find that the opposing sides are involved in a conflict that ranges up and down the line of history and spans the galaxy. The Snake and Spider leaderships, whoever or whatever they might be, are attempting to create some final result by altering or eliminating entire cultural patterns and societies. The concept itself is not completely original within science fiction, but Leiber adds an element that resolves a number of paradoxes inherent in time travel as well as adding a certain scientific plausibility to the entire scheme. (p. 26)

[In the end], we learn that Bruce and Lili attempted to shut all of them off from the Change War, but it is clear that Leiber is saying that this is impossible; we cannot cut ourselves off from the real world and the changes that occur in it; we cannot escape to some place where there is no Change. (p. 29)

[*The Big Time* is] very likely Fritz Leiber's best novel. Rarely has his work—or any science-fiction novel—existed on so many levels and in such a compact form. (p. 30)

The Wanderer [is] a disaster story that, in some ways, became a formula for other writers to follow. . . .

In most disaster novels, a prevalent sub-genre within science fiction, a natural cataclysm destroys most of human civilization. The author frequently begins the story with the approach of the disaster—whether it be impending comet, flood, plague, or wind—and skips back and forth among a number of characters. After the cataclysm, the characters are drawn together in the struggle for survival, and the human element of interaction is used as a plot device.

In *The Wanderer* another level is added through Leiber's fertile imagination. It is also Leiber's first lengthy piece of what is commonly called "hard" science fiction, the type of story that requires a great deal of scientific research and extrapolation. . . .

Through alternating chapter sections, Leiber introduces the reader to a series of characters around the world. . . . Leiber deliberately chooses what he calls the "'little people,' avoiding scientists, engineers, public officials, etc. The story is told in terms of individual and small group efforts at facing up to a (for the Earth) cosmic catastrophe." In fact, the only scientist mentioned in the book, Morton Opperly, is on-stage only briefly, and that at the end of the book.

Leiber carefully constructs an air of expectation. We know that *something* is going to happen but not what or when. At the same time, he involves us in the lives of his characters, so that their subsequent disruption will have some meaning for us, rather than being an experience that is happening to someone else we do not care about.

The Wanderer [an alien planet] appears suddenly in the night sky, immediately following an eclipse of the moon. (p. 33)

The Wanderer destroys and "devours" the Moon, and the tidal disruption of the Earth causes widespread earthquakes, tsunamis, floods, and fires. Leiber's first-page parallel with the Earth and the human soul is very important, for the "deep fissures" are physical and emotional.

The added element of *The Wanderer* that so excites the imagination is the wandering planet itself. Unlike other stories, the causal agent in the disaster is *not* natural. The planet is an artificial construct; the inhabitants live throughout the interior of the sphere and move it around the galaxy. It is truly a wanderer. . . .

The people of the Wanderer are rebellious types, fleeing from an oppressive galactic civilization that is slowly drowning out the lights of the galaxy. The picture that is drawn of that civilization is in distinct contrast to most science-fiction images; it is highly pessimistic, even though it does acknowledge a "superior" civilization. In a great many science-fiction stories, the offer from such an advanced extraterrestrial culture affords the bright promise of high technology and sophistication. In *The Wanderer*, however, the promise is grim. . . . (p. 34)

It is an appalling picture of the Universe that Leiber presents, yet ultimately as believeable and likely as that of one dominated by benevolent super-cultures, or lying open to human exploration in a parallel to the Great Frontier (with aliens/Indians occasionally in the way of civilization's expansion). (p. 35)

At the conclusion of the novel, a second planet arrives and a cosmic battle between the two visitors is briefly featured. The Wanderer departs with the police planet in pursuit. Leiber leaves us, however, with a feeling of ambiguity. . . . Although this disaster has ended, there is nothing that humans can do to avert a later and more final one.

Leiber's next science-fiction novel, *A Specter Is Haunting Texas*, also has elements of a "hard" science-fiction book. Unlike *The Wanderer*, however, it is composed of broad satire and betrays Leiber's gift for black humor. In this post-World-War-III world, most of the United States has been destroyed, and Texas has spread its borders to encompass most of North America. The Texan obsession with bigness has been personified in its white rulers, hormonally grown to giant stature. The other inhabitants, the Mexes, have been deliberately stunted and enslaved to further magnify the egos of the white Texans. Throughout the novel, Leiber satirizes then-current political figures and the institutions that fostered them: "Ever since Lyndon ousted Jack in the Early Atomic Age, the term of a President of Texas has been from inauguration to assassination. Murder is merely the continuation of politics by other means." . . .

Into this world Leiber drops the intriguing character of Scully La Cruz from a free-fall community orbiting the Moon. (p. 36)

The story moves quickly, through the charm of Scully's character and Leiber's undeniable gift for evocative visual imagery. The novel includes what surely must be the most vivid and believable description of what it would be like to be trapped in gravity for the first time in one's life. . . .

In a somewhat atypical fashion, *A Specter Is Haunting Texas* has a "happy" ending. On the personal level at least, Scully's problems are solved. The revolution, in which he had little emotional investment, is less of a success. Leiber is not given to simplistic solutions. (p. 37)

[In the tales of Fafhrd and the Gray Mouser], Leiber has created what amounts to a saga, a heroic mythology built around two highly-developed characters. He has carried them from youth to near middle-age, and at the same time he has created a wholly fascinating secondary world, as complex and richly imagined as anything in "high" fantasy. (p. 38)

The earliest Fafhrd and Mouser stories were fairly simple adventures. Unlike the heroes of most sword-and-sorcery tales, Leiber's two characters rarely disengage themselves from a predicament through brawn (although Fafhrd is in many ways the physical stereotype of the hulking barbarian, and both are adept swordsmen) but rather through a combination of wit and luck. Leiber, to some extent under the influence of H. P. Lovecraft, succeeded in infusing the stories with an atmosphere of melancholy; Nehwon (read backwards: Nowhen) is a land under the hands of capricious gods, and chaos rather than order is the general rule.

Most important, though, are the characters of the two heroes. The interplay between the small, clever Mouser and the towering, complex Northerner Fafhrd is intriguing from the earliest stories, and becomes more so as Leiber gains better control over his writing and "learns" more about the two characters.

The relationship between the two is that of two men, loyal to each other, occasionally jealous of the other's perhaps better fortune. From time to time one grows tired of the companionship, and conceives the notion that he could do better alone. Always, though, they find their lives intertwined. (pp. 38-9)

In the later stories, Leiber seems more sure of himself and his characters. He allows each to occasionally play the fool. Leiber also begins infusing a little of the real world into his created Nehwon, sometimes successfully, sometimes with jarring notes of anachronism. . . .

In the most recent stories, however, this infusion from the outer world includes some of the author's reflections on the problems of hard drinking and finally introduces women characters who are more than complications or love interests in the lives of Fafhrd and the Mouser. (p. 39)

Taken as a whole, the saga of Fafhrd and the Gray Mouser can be considered "mere" adventure stories. There is a very real tendency among some critical schools to denigrate the adventure story as being of lesser value than other types of fiction. . . . It must be remembered that the form itself is not indicative of value. The tales of adventurers embroiled in warfare and magic derive from the epics of Homer, the Icelandic Eddas, and such ''adventure stories'' as Beowulf. These stories continue to be important, and continue to be written, because they tap some aspect of the human subconscious that other types cannot reach. There are archetypes in all good fantasy, as in these stories, that touch us at a profound level if we allow them to. (p. 41)

Although we have noted a number of consistent themes in Fritz Leiber's fiction, it should be clear that he is in no danger of being termed a ''one-story'' author. Perhaps more than any other writer in the field of speculative fiction, Leiber has written in a wide range of styles and forms, ranging from social commentary to horror (often interweaving the two), black comedy to whimsy. Whenever he has dealt with a traditional science-fiction element, he has invested it with a new approach (e.g., time travel in *The Big Time*). (p. 42)

While other science fiction writers were producing adventures that spanned the galaxies, Leiber dealt with *people,* not in the mass but as individuals. It is perhaps this, his concern with and empathy for people as thinking, feeling, *unique* entities— an empathy shared only by such rare writers as Theodore Sturgeon—that has made Fritz Leiber one of the best-loved creators of speculative fiction. (p. 47)

> *Jeff Frane, in his* Fritz Leiber *(copyright © 1980 by Starmont House), Starmont House, 1980, 64 p.*

Leonard Michaels

1933-

American short story writer and novelist.

Michaels's two collections of short stories, *Going Places* and *I Would Have Saved Them If I Could*, attain their impact by contrasting ordinary events in the lives of middle-class Americans with unsuspected, surrealistic violence. Michaels's bizarre humor, in which critics see various literary influences, balances the otherwise grim theme of his works: the lack of meaning in modern life.

His first novel, *The Men's Club*, is written in a format similar to *The Canterbury Tales;* the characters take turns telling the story of their lives. While some critics found *The Men's Club* too episodic, others lauded Michaels for his success in evoking the changing personality of a group from awkwardness, to intimacy, and then to something primitive—a *Lord of the Flies* transposed to California.

(See also *CLC*, Vol. 6 and *Contemporary Authors*, Vols. 61-64.)

© Jerry Bauer

JOYCE CAROL OATES

Going Places suffers from being unable to take itself seriously. . . .

The best story in the group, **"Going Places,"** leaves a man named Beckman on the brink of an ordeal he will overcome, and we are reminded of *Christ in Concrete* and other horrendous tales of physical suffering in which a man's wits and strength are reduced to nothing much, and only his will remains.

Other stories deal with a trio of pop characters or non-characters, Phillip, Henry, and the stuttering pathetic girl they share or seem to share, Margery. It is here that Michaels's talent fails him, for he simply cannot make us share a sustained interest in the wacky dialogue and the wackier activities of these three. And story after story resolves itself in comic violence, fights or orgies or self-annihilating tricks ("I started eating my face"). Charming though the bizarre antics may seem in the first few stories, they become largely tedious and unconvincing as the volume goes on and we realize that nothing, nothing is impossible because there is nothing on the page except words.

Michaels shows the influence of Malamud, but most obviously that of Donald Barthelme and Philip Roth. His own whimsical, antic style needs something harder behind it, something less arbitrary and less cartoon-like, if it is going to create fiction in proportion to his obvious intelligence.

Joyce Carol Oates, *"Please Tell Me It's Just a Story,"* in Book World—Chicago Tribune (© *1969 Postrib Corp.; reprinted by permission of* Chicago Tribune *and* The Washington Post), *March 30, 1969, p. 6.*

LAURENCE LIEBERMAN

The key events in [Leonard Michaels' first collection of short stories, *Going Places*]—usually holocausts in the lives of his protagonists—are indistinguishable from the settings in which they occur. Settings are felt to be a physical extension of the agonized victims who inhabit them. I am constantly reminded by Michaels' emblematic stage sets that no other time and no other place could have fostered precisely the form or quality of torture that strikes the persona dumb, dead, or fiercely awake—excruciatingly alive for the first time. . . . These are not simply locales, settings—traditional background—ever. Life does not merely occur in these machines, edifices; life transfigures the forms that enshrine its daily happening, the forms merging with the bodies they enclose, altering and entering into their life stream.

In **"Going Places,"** the title story, Michaels realizes a totally plastic, epidermal style. Every sentence is charged with a tactility of phrasing that suggests oddly that words are somehow being alchemized into skin. It is a style that gives new significance, a new literalness, to the expression, *he put a skin on everything he said.* . . .

In two of the stories, **"Crossbones"** and **"Intimations,"** Michaels is perhaps inventing a new genre, which may stand in the same relation to the conventional story as does the story, say, to the novella. The short-short form appropriates the compression and density of lyric poetry and brings them into fiction. Only a couple of pages in length, these stories need to be reread many times, and gradually, they leave the reader feeling the sense of totally apprehending complex human alliances—or misalliances—ordinarily possible only in the longer forms. One gets a marvelous grasp of the total life-network of the characters in Michaels' short-shorts, as though the essence of a whole novel has been successfully encapsulated in a couple of pages. Michaels' most impressive device in these stories is the elaboration of a long sinuous "crocodilian" sentence which manipulates syntax to catapult words across gulfs of experience; not unusually, seven or eight transitions—in thought or action—are scaled within a single synchromeshed sentence, a sentence that can shift instantly from high gear to low without friction.

The weaker stories in this volume are the wacky sexual fantasies. In some of them Michaels resorts overmuch to clever stunts. The characters display gimmicky dialogue and quirky personality trappings—nervous tics, limps, mutilations, all manner of Freudian and Reichian hangups—but the varieties of gaminess don't conceal the hollow characterization or the frayed seams in a story's overextended structure. These erotic stories are often wildly funny, but the humor is pitched to a scale of laughter that approximates—in its zany crudeness—the cartoons and jokes one finds in *Playboy*.

In the better stories of this type, **"City Boy"** and **"Fingers and Toes,"** Michaels succeeds in burlesquing the stock responses of slick pornography and achieves erotic satire of unmistakable originality. . . .

Michaels' language is a created, a freshly discovered, idiom revealing the remarkable plasticity of people who are at once trapped—and fantastically bursting alive—in their bodies. The body is always discovered shockingly anew to be the most grotesquely beautiful and delicate of machines; the body, acted upon by the crowded machinery in close quarters of the overpopulated Manhattan, can re-enact through exquisite sexuality—and thereby translate into personality and spirit—the numbingly complex physical intensities and can transform into a reordering synthesis countless and unrememberable daily physical contortions in autos, elevators, and phone booths. Sexuality in the stories assimilates monstrous mental and physical violations of the partner, but transcends them all in a wisdom of the body which can never be learned in any other way, and which must seem—in the world of these stories—to be worth any price that must be paid. (p. 132)

> *Laurence Lieberman, "Words into Skin," in* The Atlantic Monthly *(copyright © 1969, by The Atlantic Monthly Company, Boston, Mass.; reprinted with permission), Vol. 223, No. 4, April, 1969, pp. 131-32.*

WILLIAM C. HAMLIN

[Leonard Michaels] is a very funny man. Given a world where "no one feels anymore," where there is "no connection with elemental life," humor would appear out of place. On the contrary, [the stories in *Going Places*] remind us that humor is one of the few things that *does* have a place. Otherwise, as less resourceful fiction demonstrates, an overdose of anguish can become routine, even dull.

Mr. Michaels himself is never dull. His ability to set the commonplace alongside the unexpected and horrifying . . . demonstrates the maddening disorientation of modern man. Carefully controlled but always giving the impression of associative freedom, his prose drives from one fresh image to another. It

tells us again and again that in spite of the odds against it, something is being *said*, not completely to be sure, nothing final, but something natural and necessary.

Comparisons with the free-flowing style of Donleavy, with the raw nerve ends of Salinger, with the scenic horrors of Purdy and O'Connor, with the overall range of Malamud are obvious and to the credit of the writer.

> *William C. Hamlin, "On the Brink," in* The New York Times Book Review *(© 1969 by The New York Times Company; reprinted by permission), May 25, 1969, p. 49.*

RONALD CHRIST

[Leonard Michaels' stories in *Going Places*] present a weirdly heightened world where simple acts and feelings are translated into nightmarish reality by means of a distinctive style that gives substance to humorous, horrifying whimsy. "Only a dream, but so is life," remarks the narrator in **"Sticks and Stones."** . . . Just as in dreams, embarrassment, frustration, crazy violence and agony of mind expressed as torment of body are the stuff of these stories; but also as in dreams, everything is madly, pathetically funny—not to the dreamer of course, but to us who read the dream. . . . The balance between the plaintively humorous and the grotesquely sad is what gives full dimension to Michaels' fiction—that and a charged language in which every sentence surprises so vigorously that you will hold your breath just waiting to see if he can keep it up. He can.

Emily Dickinson said a good poem would blow off the top of your head; A. E. Housman said it would make your whiskers bristle; but one of Michaels' own characters offers the best norm for these stories: "I could say things about you that would make your nipples pucker." They do just that, and the shock of your visceral response will keep you coming back to *Going Places* to feast on a rare talent in perfect control of its power. The book's title tells you all you need to know about the career of this young writer. (p. 571)

> *Ronald Christ, "Books: 'Going Places'," in* Commonweal *(copyright © 1969 Commonweal Publishing Co., Inc.; reprinted by permission of Commonweal Publishing Co., Inc.), Vol. XC, No. 21, September 19, 1969, pp. 570-71.*

ELLIOT L. GILBERT

In *Going Places,* Leonard Michaels has given us what must surely be one of the longest 192-page books of short stories ever written. And since this remark, intended as a compliment, may be open to misinterpretation, let me quickly add that the apparent extraordinary length of the volume is the result not of any . . . *longueurs* in the work but of a narrative and stylistic density so marked that it causes whole worlds to form, pass through their cycles, and vanish away on a single page. Where, for example, most writers, dedicated to capturing the synaptic leap on paper—but worried, perhaps, about not being understood—work as hard to reproduce the nerve fibers as they do to depict the energy that passes between them, Michaels, in some sort of haunted hurry (going places?), concentrates entirely on rendering the electric charge as it jumps the gap. (p. 422)

Taken together, the pieces present a sometimes surrealistic, frequently very funny vision of that particular brand of New

York-Jewish hysteria about which one might have supposed very little new could be said. But Michaels brings to what is today familiar enough material (boy meets girl at a neighborhood orgy) a compression of language and an intensity of imagery which constitute the real excitement of this first book. (pp. 422-23)

Michaels' virtuoso style runs to dazzling cinematic jump cuts ("**Isaac**") and to flashbacks ("**Sticks and Stones**") so complex and intentionally confusing as to obliterate any sense the reader may desperately be trying to retain of "real" time. But these familiar devices for undercutting the illusion of process and causality in fiction are in these pieces entirely functional. That is, the writer is obviously committed on every level of his work to the vision of things which his structures imply: to a sense, for example, that the world is only to be experienced in discrete, timeless, essentially static moments of intense living, moments which owe little or nothing to past or future but which are, to insist on the metaphor, the veritable sparks in the act of jumping the gap.

The title story of the collection makes this point most directly. Beckman, its protagonist, has dropped out of conventional, middle-class life, has rejected his parents' ambitions for him, and has taken to taxi driving to satisfy some obscure desire for random motion. (p. 423)

The theme of the story, conveyed as much by its structure as by its clearly symbolic events, is every man's need to discover for himself the experience which will most infallibly embody his own particular fate. In this quest for the ultimately expressive experience, movement is a sure sign of unfulfillment, a sign that the goal has still to be reached. Thus, the story opens with a long, meandering, grammatically ambiguous sentence, detailing Beckman's equally random and unfocused career. (pp. 423-24)

In one way or another, nearly all the stories in this collection set out from the irony implicit in the title to show that, as D. H. Lawrence puts it, "the end cracks open with the beginning," and that therefore the notion of progress with which we customarily fill up the space between beginnings and ends is in large measure illusory. The point is made quite explicitly in "**City Boy**," a tale which begins and ends with the same scene—a passionate romp on a living-room rug—and in which the author suggests the absurdity of the protagonist's progress from the first seduction to the last by having him accomplish it stark naked and walking on his hands. But other of the stories circle around the same idea. . . . And in perhaps the most brilliant of the pieces in the collection, "**Sticks and Stones**," random, violent movement is gradually reduced to a fixed, timeless moment of pure motion just as the protagonist, a compulsive sprinter, gradually rarefies and *slows* to the fixed, timeless, Platonic pure form of the sprinter—"a head on legs. Running." (p. 424)

Perhaps *Going Places* is a remarkable first step in its author's quest for the ultimate page, the perfect paragraph which will somehow apocalyptically expand to occupy all time. Or perhaps Michaels will now turn to longer and more extensive fictional modes. In any case, in this brilliant first book he has surely fulfilled his own definition of success. He is not merely going places; he has already gotten there. (p. 425)

Elliot L. Gilbert, "Reviews: 'Going Places'," in The Kenyon Review *(copyright 1969 by Kenyon College), Vol. XXXI, No. 125, 1969, pp. 422-25.*

ANTHONY DeCURTIS

In his two collections of short stories [*Going Places* and *I Would Have Saved Them if I Could*], Leonard Michaels depicts the contemporary struggle to shape a sensibility sufficiently intelligent, flexible, detached, and controlled to negotiate the contemporary world. The characteristic setting for his stories is New York City—the modern urban landscape, violent, unpredictable, energetic, taxing—challenging and meaningful enough to be a "vale of soulmaking," dangerous and depersonalizing enough to be a hell. Michaels criticizes the modern tendency to perceive the problems of life in such an environment as intellectual puzzles, to be resolved by calling in reserves of greater and greater amounts of consciousness, but his criticism is not the silly, fashionable kind that derides all intellectual processes in the name of the emotional life betrayed. While some of his characters "suffer from too much consciousness . . . a sort of modern disease in which the operations of mind exceed the requirements of life," Michaels' positive characters are witty, smart individuals for whom thinking is an active, energetic process which culminates in actions in the world. By isolating the pitfall of being entrapped by mind to the point of emotional paralysis, of seeking in the mind for solutions which only action can bring, Michaels has defined a psychological dilemma central to contemporary American fiction.

The most pressing problem Michaels' characters face is maintaining their humanity in the brutalizing circumstances of contemporary life. Violence becomes the natural force in a world in which nothing is really natural. At once random and horrifyingly specific in its focus, violence represents a twofold threat. Its victims must resist turning themselves into unfeeling objects, able to cope because nothing can penetrate their guard, at the same time that they withstand the temptation to elevate themselves to the level of secular holy men, "seized" and purified by violence "as the spirit seizes the prophet." Similarly, the depersonalization of intimate relations poses a threat to anyone who wants to be more than another indistinct face in the mass: "it wasn't easy to think, to ignore the great pull of the worm bucket and pretend to individuation." More generally, Michaels is concerned about the forces working in the twentieth century to annihilate any meaningful notion about the significance of the individual life.

Michaels' stories evoke a sense of how tenuous the props are which provide some semblance of continuity to modern lives. . . . The kinds of relationships and work which provide more substantial links to one's days and weeks are difficult to locate and certainly to sustain. The tendency is to paste the fragments of one's life together and be like Beckman, the cabdriver in "**Going Places**," described as "waiting for change to come into his life as if it might hail him from a corner like another fare." . . . (pp. 101-02)

The disruptiveness of modern life is a crucial theme in Michaels' stories, but too great an awareness of the problem debilitates some of his characters as much as no awareness of it at all dehumanizes others. . . . Discussions about "the keystone of modernity," "what's modern," the loss of "connection with the elemental life" occur with some frequency in Michael's stories and are symptoms of the very problem they assume as their topic. That these conversations typically take place at parties, the inevitable setting in contemporary literature of interactions which are artificial and contrived with the pretense of being intimate and communal, further emphasizes their shallowness. (pp. 102-03)

The question of moral knowledge itself is not abstract nor philosophical for Michaels, but rather intuitive, emotional, and affective. . . . [But] one should not confuse this notion with a shallow primitivism in which the problems of life dissolve if one merely has one's guts in the right place. In the "pits" of the *mind*, intellect and emotion can fuse, producing energetic, appropriate action. Morality in Michaels' stories is passionate, intelligent engagement with the world, not the measurement of one's doings against one or another internalized, external standard. The complexities of life in the twentieth century do not allow for the latter.

The images Michaels uses to evoke the psychic underworld which can give us "pure, deep knowledge of right and wrong" are those of darkness and blackness. The light of reason and logic does not provide the means by which the situations of life can be comprehended and seen as subject to our control. Genuine insight is the product of emotion and intellect, and itself produces movement. (p. 103)

As a stylist, Michaels is most interested in condensed, compact expression. His desire for compression, which obviously does not allow for very much standard description, places rhetorical responsibility for communicating a story's meaning on its verbs. The emphasis on action and movement suggested by Michaels' striking verbs is reflected also in the title of some of his stories: **"Making Changes"** and **"Going Places."** While stagnation is deadening, motion makes us tap the sources for self-knowledge within the self. (p. 104)

[Many characters in contemporary fiction] are connoisseurs of the grotesque; they hunger for experience, to see and do it all and intensely, but are finally left jaded and unsatisfied; they are initially appalled by their violent, horrific world, but ultimately confused about how to come to terms with it. Does the notion of shock lose its currency when one is shocked at every moment and when shock is compromised by fascination? Indifference seems at times to be the necessary strategy of a survivor in an environment in which brutality is the stuff of everyday, but the lingering sense of guilt and shame it entails intimates that such indifference may be morally indistinguishable from cowardice. Finally, the combination of positive intentions and powerlessness is deadly, because the real presence of either raises suspicions about the authenticity of the other. The ungenuine life beckons like a desert mirage when reality is emotionally and morally undifferentiated. Leonard Michaels' stories effectively dramatize the ennobling power of resistance to that false appeal. (p. 110)

Anthony DeCurtis, "Self under Seige: The Stories of Leonard Michaels," in Critique: Studies in Modern Fiction (copyright © by James Dean Young 1979), Vol. XXI, No. 2, 1979, pp. 101-10.

ROBERT TOWERS

There is no need to overpraise **"The Men's Club."** It is more novella than "important" novel. Only three of its characters are developed enough to be in any way memorable; the narrator in particular remains ghostly, his profession and participation never made credible. Toward the end, the satire of California encounter-group jargon becomes too broad . . . and blunts the wittiness that elsewhere prevails. But such weaknesses inflict little damage. **"The Men's Club"** is excellent comedy with a mouth-puckering aftertaste, a book for head-shaking and long sighs of recognition as well as laughter. Its style is full of small verbal surprises that match the glancing quality of its insights.

Evidently the shifting of his fictional scene from New York to the Bay Area has been good for Mr. Michaels's art. There is a new expansiveness, an ease, in the writing of **"The Men's Club"** that distinguishes it from the rather twitchy and abrasive quality of the short stories. . . . The literary influences so evident in the stories have now been largely assimilated. Leonard Michaels has become his own man, with his own voice and a subject substantial enough to grant his talents the scope they have needed all along. (p. 29)

Robert Towers, "Men Talking about Women," in The New York Times Book Review (© 1981 by The New York Times Company; reprinted by permission), April 12, 1981, pp. 1, 28-9.

STEPHEN GOODWIN

[The] temptation to write a perfect novel is . . . natural, especially to a writer like Leonard Michaels, who comes to it by way of the short story. . . .

The novel is the great test for a fiction writer—but a test of what? Peter Taylor, surely one of our best short story writers, once said in an interview that he suspected that a talent for the shorter form was incompatible with a novelistic talent. The novel, alas, is much messier than the short story, and some short story writers—the impeccable Borges, for one—won't touch it. The difference between the two seems to have to do with perfectibility.

The Men's Club begins as if Michaels is willing to risk imperfection. "Women wanted to talk about anger, identity, politics, etc." says the narrator, a college professor who has just been invited to join a men's club. He balks. "I should have said yes immediately, but something in me resisted. The prospect of leaving my house after dinner to go to a meeting. Blood is heavy then. Brain is slow. Besides, wasn't this club idea corny? . . ."

Right away we hear the distinctive cadence of the narrator's voice and feel the strongly conflicting desires within him. He attends the meeting, of course. (p. 4)

Yet what takes place . . . is strangely, ruefully subdued. The seven men who've gathered there—a doctor, a therapist, an accountant, a once-famous basketball player, all "solid types"—cast about at first to define the purpose of their club. . . . They end up telling each other stories. (pp. 4-5)

The form of this novel owes something to Chaucer's *Canterbury Tales*, in which the pilgrims lighten their journey by telling stories. To make sure that we don't miss the connection, Michaels has named one of his characters Harold Canterbury. And to make sure that we don't miss the ironic nature of the comparison, he has made Canterbury the most silent and grudging member of the club, the most distrustful of the stories that are told.

Chaucer's stories are wonderfully artful and full of guile. They reflect the personality of the teller in a sly, singular way. The stories told at the men's club are artless and they don't reflect personality so much as they reflect a condition. . . .

The stories in ***The Men's Club*** may not apply to millions—the members are white, prosperous, and more or less monogamous—but almost any of the stories could be told by any member of the club. They all speak in a direct, muted voice like the narrator's (the only exception is Kramer, poor Kramer, who is, like, very Californian). And while the characters are very distinct from one another physically, Michaels calls attention to their similarities rather than their differences. He wants us to recognize that their stories are common property, ours as well as theirs.

He also wants us to recognize that the stories have no point. Several times during the evening, one of the men begins to speak with enthusiasm, only to realize that the story doesn't lead anywhere. . . .

That accounts for the dignity which these men acquire during their long evening together. They don't know what their stories mean, but they are willing, even driven, to tell them, to entrust them to the others, and that's enough. During their meeting, they move from awkwardness to intimacy to something deeper, more dangerous and more primitive than sympathy. . . . By the end of the night all seven men are howling together, literally howling, like a pack of wolves. . . .

That lament is the way this meeting has to end, the wail of loss and longing these men are doomed to raise. It is the perfect conclusion to the drift of their emotions—perfect, but the only thing eerie about that howl is that it is so dispassionate. It is represented as a metaphor, not an event. The howl cannot be said to *happen*. . . .

I don't think that it is too much to ask that a novel about passion be passionate itself. In *The Men's Club,* however, the passions are figurative, not felt. This funny, brilliant and, yes, perfect novel is oddly sedate, and that may be too great a price to pay for perfection. We get the meaning, but we miss the experience. (p. 5)

> Stephen Goodwin, "Talk Around the Clock," in Book World—The Washington Post (© 1981, The Washington Post), April 26, 1981, pp. 4-5.

JAMES WALCOTT

[*The Men's Club*] is a talky little novella about a group of men who troop into a vine-covered Berkeley home to rake over their pasts and give their consciousness a lift. Since Michaels is one of those fiction writers overfond of toning up their prose with homages to Kafka, I waited for the book's obligatory reference to the illustrious K., and I was swiftly rewarded. Chapter Three begins: "'I wait like an ox,' says Kafka." The novella itself is a piece of Kafkaesque slapstick. . . . Michaels has a flair for deadpan comedy and slightly askew lyricism, but he's also capable of show-offy coarseness (as when he describes a man sucking in marijuana smoke "against crackling sheets of snot").

As a pop allegory, *The Men's Club* lacks clarity, compactness; the spilling, sprawling secrets of these Berkeley clubbies soon leave the book awash in chatter and confusion. Brief as the book is, it's still a long-winded wheeze.

> James Walcott, "Books: 'The Men's Club'" (copyright © 1981, Esquire Associates; used by courtesy of the magazine), in Esquire, Vol. 95, No. 5, May, 1981, p. 19.

ANNE TYLER

[*The Men's Club*] seems more a short story writer's idea of a novel—a mistaken idea, though understandably so, and an oversimplified one, in which the novel is seen as merely a longer form of short story. This is not longer by much, either. . . . It takes more time to read, but delves no further in

that time; it features a larger cast of characters, but reveals no new layers within them as the story progresses. Even its considerable virtues are a short story's virtues: stunning efficiency, speedy flashes of description, and a breathtaking singleness of purpose. (p. 31)

[The] men seem poorly characterized. They can be distinguished from one another only by the grossest of quirks, a kind of shorthand method of identification. . . . Essentially, they do not differ; they are "talking heads," combining their voices to state the embattled male viewpoint. Least distinct of all is the narrator, who appears to have been plopped into the story solely to record and react—a faceless "I."

Certain lines in this book made me laugh; others went too far, and I flinched. . . . There's an underestimation of the reader here that's just short of insulting. Give us some credit! we want to tell the author. Don't you think we get the idea? Like many extended jokes, *The Men's Club* fosters a feeling of edginess; it teeters between understatement and overstatement. There's always the possibility that part of the joke has slipped past us undetected, while other parts are hammered in too forcefully. . . .

I am awed by Leonard Michaels's dash and verve, annoyed by his obtrusive cleverness, and hopeful that in the future he will loosen his control enough to allow us a deeper glimpse into a most ingenious and fertile mind. (p. 32)

> Anne Tyler, "Men Will Be Boys," in The New Republic (reprinted by permission of The New Republic; © 1981 The New Republic, Inc.), Vol. 184, No. 18, May 2, 1981, pp. 31-2.

DAVID REID

Yeats says that a civilization is a struggle for self-control. "The loss of control over thought comes toward the end; first a sinking in upon the moral being, then the last surrender, the irrational cry, revelation—the scream of Juno's peacock." If so, this particular civilization plainly is in deep trouble.

Cultural scouts may find suggestive evidence (if more is needed) in this remarkable, haunting, and very funny first novel by Leonard Michaels [*The Men's Club*]. . . . As the narrator, a Berkeley professor, concedes, "Men's groups. Women's groups. They suggest incurable disorders."

On the other hand, *The Men's Club* seems to be the kind of novel whose strategy is to invite you to understand it too quickly. It is not about the Decline of the West. Though wickedly knowing and accurately, even passionately observed, it is only incidentally a satire on California manners and mores. If Michaels brings back frontline reports from the war of the sexes, it is by way of conducting a tour of Yeats's old establishment, the foul rag-and-bone shop of the heart. . . .

Early notices of *The Men's Club* tend to agree that the characters are a baffled, desperate, dangerous, and probably empty-headed lot. And yet, as R. P. Blackmur says somewhere, "To find a way of seeing what has happened to us sometimes seems our highest legitimate aspiration." What else, really, is their club about?

On the other hand, one understands why *The Men's Club* has already reminded reviewers of Dostoyevsky, Chekhov, Chaucer. Let me add to the list Kafka, Kierkegaard, and Hegel on self-consciousness. Leonard Michaels' stories established him as a master phenomenologist of dread and desire. *The Men's Club* will confirm and enlarge that reputation.

David Reid, "Jolly Good Fellows," in The Three-penny Review (© copyright 1981 by The Threepenny Review), Vol. II, No. 2, Summer, 1981, p. 8.

DAVID EVANIER

One way to evaluate a new work is to place it against works of art from other times that deal with similar subjects and settings, and determine whether the insights and achievements of those earlier works have been enlarged and built upon—whether, in fact, the work under consideration makes contemporaneous an old tale. *The Iceman Cometh* and *That Championship Season* most readily come to mind as predecessors to *The Men's Club*.

The Men's Club also deals mainly with a group of men in a male domain. While it is not a play, its form (it is almost entirely in dialogue rather than narration), makes it seem akin to one. And Michaels's forte is the creation of some of the most piercing dialogue I have read recently.

In such a comparison, *The Men's Club* succeeds at a high level. It does take us further. It is no masterpiece, but on its own terms it is a considerable novel. Nothing in Michaels's two previous books of short stories (very short and stylized) prepared me for the relentlessly dark and brilliant strength of these pages. Here is a middle-aged predatory Berkeley inferno of loss and chaos. (pp. 1088-89)

[A group of men gather together] to "tell their life stories" to each other. What they relate is something else: sharp memories of other women that have stayed in their heads, marital fights, stories of givers and takers, pals unjustifiably worshipped and losers who prey on the storytellers' consciences. Stories triggered by other stories add up coherently and eloquently to a paradigm of human confusion.

These are the stories within the main story, which is the account of the evening with the men: the conflicts and the shifting moods among them as they become heavy with marijuana, alcohol, and the mountains of food they steal from the refrigerator. . . . They eat with Bacchanalian glee. . . . As the night progresses, the men fight, throw knives, destroy furniture, and howl together in unison. The message they are howling is that they do not understand themselves, their wives, their lives—that their lives are over.

They are ridiculous figures, but Michaels does not aim at ridicule. He is dealing with the absurd and the inexplicable. . . .

The men's monologues reveal people totally locked into themselves. Most of them are predatory. Those of them who admire others are losers who enjoy being taken advantage of. The women come off no better: they too are plunderers, fixated, chaotic, lost. If there is a central weakness in the novel, it may be that its characters uniformly serve the author's thesis: "Life is an unfair business, who ever said otherwise? It is a billion bad shows, low blows, and number one has more fun." And such a view of humanity may explain why the men all sound alike. . . .

A writer must achieve a high level of craft today to evoke unsentimental compassion for his characters. For we know too much, and we expect our writers to know even more. Hickey's confession in *Iceman* of murderous hatred for his wife (and the murder itself) would no longer strike us as the final truth of a work. Leonard Michaels breaks new ground, in the tradition of the artist who does not stand still. (p. 1089)

David Evanier, "A Man's World," in National Review (© National Review, Inc., 1981; 150 East 35th St., New York, NY 10016), Vol. XXXIII, No. 18, September 18, 1981, pp. 1088-89.

CAROL RUMENS

The Men's Club is a provocative title that seems to herald male chauvinism's answer to *The Women's Room* and novels of that genre; a firing of defensive salvoes, perhaps, or even a counter-attack claiming that the problems caused by negative discrimination are nothing to those engendered by the positive variety. But in fact, for all its surface liveliness, Michael's novel turns out to have little to add to the increasingly lacklustre debate on sexual politics; its effect is merely to corroborate traditional views of the male and female character (female = nuturing, male = aggressive), despite a hint of tables being turned (almost literally; a dresser is crashed to the floor by an irate wife) in the final pages.

Michaels writes a choppy, muscle-flexing prose, intending, perhaps, to express an ironical stance towards the Maileresque style of literary tough-talking. Having accustomed oneself to nouns lopped of their articles and full-stops like kicks in the shins, one must admit that such a style has the virtue of tightness and immediacy, and also that it modulates easily into dialogue, a useful facility in a novel whose action takes place in the context of a group discussion. . . .

The narrator's role as conscience of the group remains a shadowy one. Though a kind of catalyst who, despite his private reservations, encourages the others to keep talking, he too is shown to be at the mercy of the collective mind, allowing it to sweep him away in its headlong dive towards its worst instincts. Beer and marijuana peel off the first layer of inhibitions, helped by the heady sense of being "off the leash". . . .

It is a little as if Golding's *Lord of the Flies* had been transposed to middle-class, middle-aging California. . . .

The symbolism of food dominates the book. Even the most sustained and pivotal of the sexual confessions is about a man's desertion of the woman he loves because she steals a forkful of his pudding. It is not easy to sympathize with his chagrin, particularly as the dish in question is strawberries under flaming chocolate, a concoction that sounds more like a metaphor than a dessert. The novel falls short of its ambitions for a similar reason; at crucial moments the action seems to be dictated by the manipulation of symbols rather than the compulsions of character.

Carol Rumens, "Off the Leash," in The Times Literary Supplement (© Times Newspapers Ltd. (London) 1981; reproduced from The Times Literary Supplement by permission), No. 4098, October 16, 1981, p. 1219.

CORINNE ROBINS

The Men's Club is Leonard Michaels' version of a Walpurgis Night, of a Freudian male herd reborn in a group of California men, at least two of whom are aware in the hip, consciousness-raised Berkeley tradition of "feeling your own feelings." But despite the occasional use of such cliches, *The Men's Club* is not satire because there is more sadness than mockery in the author's treatment of such awareness, and because Michaels is too desperate and despairing a writer. . . .

Michaels uses the psychological jargon the way he uses different ways of eating and screwing to describe, to try and reach the raw edge of being human, to examine the emotions on which human behavior turns. . . .

Michaels is the opposite of the graceful, accomplished observer in the manner of the *New Yorker*'s John Updike. He is, rather, a precisionist of painful emotions. He aims, as his narrator says, for "definite matter. Truth pressed by flesh." Thus, Michaels is involved with revelation, with the kind of literature that Kafka, Herbert Huncke, Raymond Carver and Jean Rhys sometimes deliver. He belongs to that group of writers who are concerned with meaning as salvation, and with the extreme ends and purposes of life, writers whose lives in their books at least seem to become an unending tug of war of pleasure and pain. . . .

The Men's Club is structured more like a drama than a novel, a drama observing the classical unities of time and space. The men's individual stories are a kind of action, a play within a play for the men to react off of while responding to one another as audience. The personality of the group, the shifting control of individual men, what psychologists call interaction in *The Men's Club* becomes a raw experience. . . . All of the group's actions assume ceremonial proportions as part of Michaels' unfolding drama. *The Men's Club* does not have the rhythm of a novel: it is too time-structured. It is as if there is something about Michaels' orchestrating of the men's movements that is too controlled and too formal. . . .

The Men's Club is a short book, an easy read and, as a feminist, I felt it excluded me. Now I am aware that its easiness was an illusion, as the men's pain and urgency via the novel have become embedded in my life.

Corinne Robins, "'The Men's Club'," in The American Book Review *(© 1982 by* The American Book Review*), Vol. 4, No. 3, March-April, 1982, p. 8.*

W(illiam) O(rmond) Mitchell

1914-

Canadian novelist, scriptwriter, dramatist, and short story writer.

Mitchell first became known by his radio series of the 1950s, *Jake and the Kid,* a warmly humorous serial about a loveable old man, his young companion, and their adventures in a small town in western Canada. Mitchell's subsequent writing reflects his close association with the Canadian landscape, notably the Saskatchewan prairie, and his keen awareness of the sensibility of children and the pleasures of boyhood. *Who Has Seen the Wind* exemplifies these thematic concerns and is considered by many to be his best work.

Some critics feel that Mitchell's strongest point is his ability to probe deeply into human nature, while others feel that his attempts at seriousness detract from his true talent which is to reveal, humorously, the quirks and foibles of daily life.

(See also *Contemporary Authors,* Vols. 77-80.)

RICHARD SULLIVAN

["**Who Has Seen the Wind**"] is a piece of brilliantly sustained prose, a very beautiful, keen, perceptive rendering of human beings engaged in the ordinary yet profoundly—almost mysteriously—meaningful drama of every day.

A quiet, loose, free sort of book, this one is devoted primarily to the experience of its central character, the boy Brian O'Connal. From his fourth to his twelfth year Brian searches—quite unselfconsciously, quite naturally—for God, for purpose, for meaning in the absolute. . . .

But there is no fulfillment for him, no end to his search at the book's end. Indeed there, in a full and self-conscious way, his quest is only beginning. Through the passage of these early years the small child's often shocking directness has gradually turned into the boy's more penetrant awareness; . . . without the malice of Ahab hunting the whale, but with a fairly comparable urgency. . . .

But because it is a loose, quiet, free sort of book, not so much plotted as ingeniously composed, "**Who Has Seen the Wind**" ranges frequently away from Brian out over the life of the Canadian prairie town which he inhabits. . . .

And quite as real as any of the human characters, quite as directly a part of the whole effect, is the natural background . . . of Saskatchewan prairie. . . . [As] memorable as anything in a genuinely and thoroughly well-done book are some of the renderings of grass and storm and sky, and of the delicately symbolical wind that keeps blowing.

> Richard Sullivan, "*Canadian Boyhood,*" *in* The New York Times Book Review (© *1947 by The New York Times Company; reprinted by permission), February 23, 1947, p. 5.*

WALTER HAVIGHURST

This ardent but unsure first novel [*Who Has Seen the Wind*] portrays a number of people in [a town on a Saskatchewan

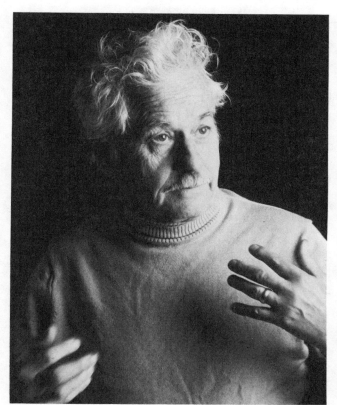

Photograph by Peter Patterson; courtesy of Macmillan of Canada

prairie]. . . . The story centers about Brian O'Connal and the growing years of his boyhood.

Brian had a curiosity about all sorts of things, from gophers to God. Though he couldn't put it into words, he was especially curious about the cycle of life. . . .

Every street in the town ended in the open prairie, and every moving experience in the boy's life led him to an elusive meaning that he longed to grasp. . . .

Where Brian is concerned this is a seeking book. Like many first novels, it describes the growing pains of youth and the enlarging claims that the mind and heart make on the world. . . .

Probably all the people in the town had some part in Brian's attempt to figure things out. Still, the novel suffers from diffusion. . . . Certain episodes, like the exploding of Old Ben's still in the church basement during the minister's sermon, are low farce, out of key with the theme of a novel in which the wind is "symbolic of Godhood."

Yet there is freshness and credibility in the O'Connal family. . . . There is undeniable human nature in some of the townspeople, and there is a haunting quality about gray-eyed young Ben gazing over the prairie. . . .

If this novel is not as good as its material, and as the author's feeling for his people, it may be because the narrative lacks

321

the long, sustained rhythms, the flowing lines, of the prairie itself. . . .

It seems as if the author had not quite decided whether to write a book about a boy's search for significance, or a prairie Winesburg.

Walter Havighurst, "Saskatchewan Prairie," in New York Herald Tribune Weekly Book Review (© I.H.T. Corporation; reprinted by permission), March 2, 1947, p. 10.

MARGARET LAURENCE

W. O. Mitchell's stories about Jake and the kid began appearing in *Maclean's* during the war. A great many Canadians must have found them then, as I did, extremely appealing. In the first place, the kid's father was overseas with the South Saskatchewans, and the kid, his mother and Jake, the elderly and loquacious hired man, were keeping the home fires burning. In the second place, these stories were among the first that many of us who lived on the prairies had ever read concerning our own people, our own place and our own time. . . . A prevalent feeling on the subject was, as I recall—*that's us; he's writing about us.*

Quite a few years have gone by. The image of the prairie people presented by Mitchell now [in the collected stories, *Jake and the Kid,*] seems like some blurred recollection of childhood, partially appealing because of its over-simplification, partially repellent for the same reason. I can no longer be convinced that even the genuinely ludicrous aspect of people anywhere was ever as unreservedly warm hearted as the author of *Jake and the Kid* would have us believe. Here is comedy with no bite of acid to cut the sweet taste. No good person ever comes to harm in Crocus, and the overwhelming majority of citizens are unquestionably good. The few villains such as Sam Bottom and Doc Toovey are truly villainous and are always defeated. (pp. 68-9)

The emotions expressed in these stories, especially in the wartime ones, now appear to contain a large measure of sentimentality. (p. 69)

A good deal of humour, however, comes across as freshly as ever. Jake is still inimitable as the man who made Looie Riel say uncle three times, in English, French and Cree. His version of history is a delight. . . .

Had Mitchell been content with unvarnished humour, his characters, however simple-minded or unequivocally well-intentioned, might still have emerged victorious, or at any rate emerged. But in addition to the thick coating of emotionalism, each tale has yet another layer in the form of a clearly indicated moral. Be kind to those less fortunate than yourself. Treat animals with care and affection and they will not let you down. . . . Such maxims may be perfectly worthy, as far as they go, but they can hardly be said to go far enough.

In one sense, I feel like a traitor in carping about these stories, because I am really fond of them. I cannot dismiss them, for they are a part of my life. But I can no longer read them. I can only conclude that they require a younger audience. (p. 70)

Margaret Laurence, "A Canadian Classic?" (reprinted by permission of the author), in Canadian Literature, No. 11, Winter, 1962, pp. 68-70.

WILLIAM H. NEW

In his two novels, *The Kite* and *Who Has Seen the Wind,* W. O. Mitchell makes use of [the transition from childhood to maturity] as a means to consider man's awareness of time and perception of reality during his life's span on earth. The two novels explore these questions, however, from different points of view. Though one is an artistic success while the other falls short of this, part of their interest lies in the extent to which they complement each other. . . . (p. 45)

Mitchell's first novel, *Who Has Seen the Wind,* is the success. It is a study of the development involved in a boy's increasing conscious awareness of abstraction, a study of Brian O'Connal's transition from the perfection of sensitive childhood, through conflict, to a balance that is achieved in early maturity. In *The Kite,* which fails largely because of technical difficulties, Keith Maclean is parallel to Brian in many respects, but the author is concerned less with the growth of a child than with the effect of continuing awareness of time on an old man, Daddy Sherry, and the late awareness of the truth of emotional abstractions that comes to the apparently mature David Lang.

Brian O'Connal's growth begins in perfection. He is a child, complete in his own environment, when *Who Has Seen the Wind* opens; he meets existence from an awareness of self and by sense perception of the material things around him. For the actual growth to take place, however, this state of harmonious innocence must be disrupted, and it is, by the conflict that is aroused in Brian as he is brought into contact with death. . . . [Each] of the six death scenes in the novel [demonstrates] . . . Brian's changing reactions—his growth—and the extent to which he transcends age in developing to maturity. (pp. 45-6)

In introducing characters such as the Young Ben or Saint Sammy, who are in some ways the most vividly drawn of all the people in [*Who Has Seen the Wind*], Mitchell runs the danger of letting his focus shift from the central development. Such a shift occurs in *The Kite* and weakens that book, but in *Who Has Seen the Wind* the focus is fortunately sustained, and because of this, the author achieves a remarkable insight into the operation of his central character's mind. Though much of this novel deals with characters other than Brian O'Connal, Brian's growth to responsibility always remains central, and the various successful and unsuccessful adaptations that the minor characters make in their respective situations of conflict, reflect upon this central growth. Svarich, for example, fails to accept his Ukrainian identity; Hislop fails to accept the existence of opposition in his church and merely resigns. Sean, Digby, and Miss Thompson, however, come to take responsible positions in their own spheres; they act positively to solve the conflict in which they find themselves, and yet they are able at the same time to accept what they cannot control. Brian, therefore, has both examples before him. Also before him are the vividly-drawn Saint Sammy and Young Ben with their strange adaptive abilities, but even they remain minor figures, because they, too, serve to contribute to an understanding of the emotional sensitivity of Brian himself. (pp. 48-9)

David's contact with [Daddy Sherry] is the central relationship in *The Kite,* and the growth that occurs through this relationship is David's, not Daddy's. The danger of shift of focus, however, that had been circumvented in the case of the Young Ben and Saint Sammy in *Who Has Seen the Wind,* recurs here with results that weaken this novel. Structurally and thematically, Daddy Sherry is a minor figure, but the vividness with which he is drawn and the frequency with which he appears in the novel combine to draw attention away from David Lang. Neither character is sufficiently created to take a central position therefore, and the novel suffers from the resultant lack of an insight into human behaviour comparable to that achieved in the depiction of Brian O'Connal.

To achieve in *The Kite* the focus he desires, Mitchell has set up reflector patterns in the subplots comparable to those in *Who Has Seen the Wind;* he depicts a series of relationships with Daddy on the part of the Shelby townspeople that should act as reflectors or commentaries on the central interaction. Unfortunately this device fails in operation. Because Daddy figures prominently in each case, and because David himself remains relatively passive during the recounted anecdotes, the focus shifts to Daddy, and David's centrality is concomitantly diminished. (p. 52)

Both David Lang and Brian O'Connal . . . undergo a process of growth and development that results in their increased awareness of realities beyond the physical. But though their situations are in a sense complementary—the sensitive boy balancing emotion with intellect and the man in limbo balancing intellect with emotion—the two novels that explore these situations differ markedly. (p. 58)

William H. New, "A Feeling of Completion: Aspects of W. O. Mitchell" (1963) in his Articulating West: Essays on Purpose and Form in Modern Canadian Literature *(copyright © 1972 W. H. New), New Press, 1972, pp. 45-59.*

W. H. NEW

In 1953, W. O. Mitchell published in serial form a novel called *The Alien.* It told the story of a part-Blood Indian named Carlyle Sinclair, a teacher at the Paradise Valley Reserve, who after alienating himself from both white and Indian cultures finally accommodates himself to his mixed heritage. In the twenty years since, Mitchell has refashioned that novel into a larger canvas of Alberta society. The Carlyle Sinclair of *The Vanishing Point* is still a teacher at Paradise Valley, which is now a Stony reserve, but he is also white, a widower, the Indian agent, and more frustrated by his contacts with the people around him than alienated from them.

The result is often very funny. Mitchell's skill at recording speech, demonstrated before now in the *Jake and the Kid* scripts and in *Who Has Seen The Wind,* proves itself here again. Laconic, excited, and bawdy voices intertwine, landing the characters in bizarre situations to which laughter, as Carlyle himself reflects, provides the only logical response. . . . But along the way, life often proves more vicious. Disease, prejudice, ignorance, hypocrisy, narrow-mindedness, prostitution, double standards: these are what face the Indians under Carlyle's tutelage. Their efforts to keep self-respect and his own to find it assert an insistent moral dilemma in the book. However entertaining many of the episodes are, the overall effect is one of moral disarray, against which Mitchell's quiet humanitarianism seems both idealistic and remarkably kind.

The plot is relatively simple. Sinclair alternately lives the present and relives the events of his past. . . . Despite all Mitchell's seriousness, such a plot simply doesn't sustain the social comment it is asked to.

The problem has partly to do with character, for Carlyle and Victoria are neither complex enough nor unpredictable enough to maintain interest for long. They live two-dimensional lives. . . . (pp. 26-7)

What Mitchell is doing is constructing a kind of Western equivalent of Hugh MacLennan's *Two Solitudes.* His two cultures are Indian and white, rather than English and French, but they are also balanced against each other in the same landscape and shown to be pursuing separate but parallel paths. Laconic Scots stubbornness is matched by laconic Indian stubbornness. Ritual in one culture is matched by ritual in the other. And like MacLennan, Mitchell shrewdly observes his society, evocatively draws upon the natural landscape, cleverly animates some minor characters, and completely fails with his major ones. Bringing them together, asserting a vanishing point despite the separateness they know to be real, reiterates a recurrent Canadian literary theme. But here it reads like a romantic cliché. The radical simplification which (as in Leacock, for example) works to invigorate a humour vignette—and works, here, in Mitchell's inveterate scene-making—weakens the book as a whole. What it comes to is that a novel full of warmth, wit, and precise observation is made to seem facile, which is disappointing. (p. 27)

W. H. New, "Books Reviewed: 'The Vanishing Point'," in The Canadian Forum, *Vol. LIV, May-June, 1974, pp. 26-7.*

HERBERT ROSENGARTEN

The title of W. O. Mitchell's new novel alludes to the pictorial device by which converging lines, meeting at a "vanishing point" on the horizon, create the illusion of depth; and the novel itself is concerned with the lines men draw for themselves and for others in their desire to impose order, purpose, direction, on human life. That this is at best an illusory goal is the conclusion reached by *The Vanishing Point,* which describes the uneasy relations between an Indian band and white administrators on a reserve in the Albertan foothills. The representative of white authority is Carlyle Sinclair, a thirty-six year old widower who acts as both schoolteacher and agent on the Paradise Valley reserve. . . . After nine frustrating years, his efforts to bring the Stonys into the twentieth century seem to have met with at least one success: one of his pupils has passed her examinations, and begun her training as a nurse at the city hospital. Early in the novel, Sinclair travels to the city to visit the girl, Victoria, only to find that she has disappeared from the hospital, and in all likelihood taken up the life of prostitution so often the fate of Indian girls in the city.

Mitchell deals sympathetically but unsentimentally with the problems which confront white administrators of Indian affairs. . . . Though Sinclair is himself an instrument of white government, he is not blind to its follies; he hates the Ottawa bureaucracy, "the slow and narcotizing routine—the impersonal red tape that formalized hunger and sickness and death." But the Indians anger him too, by their reluctance to abandon the old ways, and their refusal to adopt white standards. Yearning to reach them, Sinclair seeks a bridge like that which connects the reserve to the highway and the world outside. . . . Through his love for Victoria, he learns that a man must build such bridges himself by accepting his responsibility for his fellows, not by seeking to dominate them. At the end of the novel, Sinclair joins the reclaimed Victoria in a ritual Indian dance; he has ignored official advice not to become personally involved; and he has lost the desire to alter the Indians' self-image, learning instead to accept them for what they are.

The message of *The Vanishing Point,* that all men are brothers and thus accountable to each other, is one to which no reader will take exception. . . . The sentiments which Carlyle expresses, or which are expressed through him, do not lack conviction or appeal; but Carlyle himself, primarily a vehicle for the author's ideas, never really comes to life as a character. His creator endows him with a very active interior life, granting us frequent entry into his inner thoughts and fantasies, as well as his recurring childhood memories; but the insights we gain do little to explain why Carlyle feels or acts as he does. That his Aunt Pearl produced white stools, or that his best friend caught diphtheria from him and died, suggest possible sources of guilt and alienation, but these reminiscences seem at best tenuously associated with his adult motivation. . . . The problem arises in part from Mitchell's desire to work obliquely towards the creation of character, conveying personality in spurts of dialogue, fragments of memory or description, the meaning of which becomes clearer as the novel progresses; but the piecing-together process takes a long time, and in Carlyle's case doesn't seem complete—he remains flat and featureless. The object of his devotion, the "little lost lamb" Victoria, is even less clearly realized; although we learn something about her from Carlyle, and hear her speak on occasion, she is a colourless and indistinct figure throughout. It may have been the author's intention to show her only through Carlyle's eyes, first as a symbol of the teacher's mistaken beliefs about the future role of the native Indian, then as simply a young woman reaching out to him with her love. Either way, Victoria is little more to us than a name.

The reader may also be puzzled by the novel's fluctuations of tone, and the several shifts of narrative viewpoint. The serious and the comic are complementary moods, and may exist side by side without any sense of incongruity; but the comic elements of *The Vanishing Point* do not always contribute to the novel's essentially serious purposes. . . . A further diffusion of effect occurs when the novel leaves Carlyle Sinclair for lesser figures like the wily Indian Archie Nicotine, or the Reverend Healy Richards, a bush-league evangelist with an eye to the big time. These characters are amusing and well-drawn, but they assume a prominence in the story which is out of proportion to their rôles; lodging the point-of-view in Archie or Richards only blurs the narrative focus, and diverts our attention for too long from the novel's central issues.

The Vanishing Point is on surer ground in portraying the white officials who run Indian Affairs. . . . Sanders, the doctor whose area includes Paradise Valley, is one of the few to recognize that it is the system itself, "the reserve-system slough—tepid with paternal help", which is sapping the strength of the native Indian. At the same time, the reserve does serve to protect the Indian, to maintain, however unsatisfactorily, a way of life which in many respects seems preferable to that led by the white man; Paradise may no longer be perfect, but its native inhabitants, poor and diseased as they may be, are more admirable, more enviable even, in Mitchell's view, than the pale-skinned, half-dead souls which dwell in the world of department stores, greenhouses and gas stations. (pp. 109-11)

Herbert Rosengarten, "Preferable Paradise" (reprinted by permission of the author), in Canadian Literature, *No. 61, Summer, 1974, pp. 109-11.*

CATHERINE McLAY

The place, the bald-headed prairie of southern Saskatchewan. . . . The time, the present . . . the principal characters, Jake and the Kid. And here, as the first episode in a new series

of radio plays by the Canadian writer W. O. Mitchell is the story of the Oldest Old-Timer. . . .

The date was Tuesday, June 27, 1950. And so began the radio series that was to run for six seasons and over two hundred and fifty scripts, and which was to make Crocus, Saskatchewan one of the enduring towns of the Canadian imagination. (p. 33)

The timing of Mitchell's series was apposite. By 1950 Canada's transition from a pioneering and agricultural country to a predominantly industrial and urban one was almost complete. By this date, the fears and anxieties of the Depression and the War years behind them, Canadians had settled down to peace and prosperity, ready and eager for diversion and entertainment. The Canadian Broadcasting Corporation, described as "a valuable instrument for national unity," was in its prime and Mitchell's Jake and the Kid has been described as its chief "cultural prop." The western setting was part of its appeal. . . . In Crocus, the Atheneum Literary Society can meet, geography can be changed by the advent of a "seaway" to make Crocus the "Venice of south central Saskatchewan," and rain may be made to fall by the intervention of the airplane and dry ice, but the old ways of life still go on, the eternal rhythms of birth, maturity and death in both the natural and the human world. In many ways, Jake's appeal is that of the original frontier hero: he is physically strong, self-reliant, practical, free, unburdened by wife or child, illiterate and uncultured but optimistic in his outlook on life and even one of "the true dreamers of the nation." Interestingly, the series was popular everywhere except on the prairies where, as one commentator notes, "the listeners thought that Mitchell was caricaturing them." (p. 334)

Indeed Mitchell's Crocus and its inhabitants appealed to the small-town hearts of Canada's urban population, and listeners across the breadth of the nation tuned in . . . to hear the new adventures of Crocus: "famous for number one hard wheat, number one tall tales, and Jake Trumper, number one hired man." . . . Crocus became a western Mariposa, a microcosm of the experience of many Canadians who had to leave their Mariposas in order to see them anew. The 50s in Canada provided a close parallel to the 20s and 30s in America where an interest in farm fiction reached its peak among the urban population who had left their farms for city comforts but who looked back nostalgically to their simpler and seemingly purer rural past with its rural virtues. (pp. 334-35)

In the adventures of Jake, the Kid, and the many other inhabitants of Crocus created by the fertile imagination of W. O. Mitchell, we experience again our own childhood and our own pastoral roots. (p. 335)

Mitchell's Crocus, unlike Sinclair Ross' Horizon and Upward, accents the joyousness of life, the will to live. . . . [We] see the town and its people from the inside, from the point of view of the child who accepts its limitations and petty rivalries with its exuberance. While Ross was to escape his little towns forever except in the pages of his fiction, Mitchell was to return and to celebrate their strengths while gently satirizing their weaknesses and foibles. (p. 336)

The characters of the fictional Crocus are varied and highly coloured, even Dickensian. Flat rather than round, each plays a set role already established by the first episode of the series. (p. 337)

[Many] are background characters who appear throughout the series but may be featured in one or two individual episodes. One commentator has estimated that about one fifth of the episodes deal with the adventures of Jake and the Kid, and the remainder with other townspeople. Where Jake is not the central character in the action, he usually provides the solution, sometimes by accident, usually by design. . . . A few of the episodes deal with significant issues such as racial prejudice. . . . But the racial issues do not undercut the essential comedy and these conflicts or tensions are dismissed in the final resolution.

In the week-by-week episodes, Mitchell employed not only national events and celebrations but also happenings of purely local significance. . . . But the rhythms of the seasons go on: autumn, winter, spring and summer, birth, courting, marriage and death. Against a background of national and international events, the local happenings of Crocus are both particular and universal, the concern of individuals everywhere for the everyday events and relationships that make up their own individual lives.

The Kid, like Ma, is given a generic name only. He is not simply Billy Mitchell but Everyboy. . . . The Kid is central to the series even though in many of the episodes he may play a minor role. He is Dr. Watson to Jake's Sherlock Holmes. He asks the right questions, exposes the right secrets; he believes Jake implicitly. Many of Jake's tall tales are told to entertain the Kid and it is the Kid who recounts these mythical adventures to Miss Henchbaw and others. (pp. 338-39)

But even in episodes where he plays a secondary role, the Kid controls the viewpoint. For Jake, Ma, Miss Henchbaw, and the whole of Crocus are seen essentially from his perspective. (p. 339)

Like Brian O'Connal of *Who Has Seen the Wind* and Keith Maclean of *The Kite,* the Kid is the sensitive child, the observer of man and nature alike. He recalls for us our childhood, our early years of life which bring the strongest memories of the freshness and wonder of the world. . . . But the boy is also aware of the negative side of nature, the menace, the awe of the numinous as felt by the young Wordsworth. He remarks "prairie's awful" and again "prairie's scary." . . . He sees the aging of the land which he compares to the aging of the human being, the prairie reclaiming its own. . . . (pp. 339-40)

The Kid also describes in some episodes the negative emotions of humanity, intensified by the newness of the child's perception. (p. 340)

[The] series evades the tragic possibilities which are occasionally introduced to complicate the action. . . . But the comic resolutions of all dilemmas, even the overt racism of much of Crocus society, is achieved not only by twisting or manipulating the action but also by the viewpoint of the child, as recreated by the man who was that child. Much of the pain and suffering is dulled by time and fading memory. Moreover, the figure of Jake, the giant who out-natures nature, gives us the sense of security which we feel we have left behind in childhood, the confidence that adults are all-powerful and usually benevolent, a projection of the self which we hope to become. (pp. 340-41)

Jake, Mitchell claims, is a composite of as many as ten originals, a kaleidoscope which grew from many bits of coloured glass. The most important sources were his Uncle Jim Mitchell, also the original of Uncle Sean in *Who Has Seen the Wind,* and an old horse gypsy, Jack Kelly, from whom he derived

much of Jake's colourful speech. A series of hired men also provided material to create Jake. (p. 341)

Part of Jake's attraction is his link with the living past of Saskatchewan history: he is described as "the sage of southern Saskatchewan and repository of all the history books left out." . . . (pp. 341-42)

Where Jake is not performing superhuman feats of strength or power, or telling of his many contributions to Canadian history, he is occupied in controlling events and relationships. . . . Jake becomes a type of Western Solomon for the daily problems of Crocus.

Jake is also most frequently associated with the tall tales characteristic of Mitchell humour in the series. (p. 343)

In these tales, as in the episodes in general, the language is a major source of humour. At one point in his career, Mitchell studied oratory and the prose shows his ear for dialogue, rhythm and local turns of speech. . . . The misuse of words is not simply quaint or folksy. It captures the very essence of the vernacular, translating into written language the full flavour of the oral tradition. (pp. 345-46)

Another comic technique is Mitchell's choice of names: "Crocus" itself is comically incongruous, as are the exotic names of surrounding towns—Khartoum, Conception Disraeli. The Crocus *Breeze* is a pun: it suggests the name of many a little town newspaper yet parodies them through implying they are, in the slang phrase, "shooting the breeze." In the manner of P. G. Wodehouse, dogs are called Mr. Churchill Two or Wilfred Laurier, a breed of cattle becomes the Duke of Waterdown, a boar is the Duke of Broomhead, horses are named Sodom and Go-more, and goats are named after the foremost ladies of the town. The pseudo-historical or Biblical references point up the incongruity of the comparison. Mitchell also gently parodies the self-importance of the townspeople through his titles: [for example,] The Burning Bush League of Knox Presbyterian Church. . . . (p. 346)

In reviewing the book *Jake and the Kid,* Margaret Laurence commented on the "thrill of recognition" which many Westerners had felt in hearing on radio tales of their own geography: "these stories were among the first that many of us who lived on the prairies had ever read concerning our own people, our own place, and our own time. . . . [We felt] *that's us; he's writing about us*" [see excerpt above]. But these stories are not merely local colour fiction nor are they factual transcriptions of prairie life of the day. To judge them by realistic standards is to misunderstand their intent. Like Leacock's Mariposa, Crocus is not a real place but a country of the imagination. (p. 347)

Catherine McLay, "Crocus, Saskatchewan: A Country of the Mind," in Journal of Popular Culture *(copyright © 1980 by Ray B. Browne), Vol. 14, No. 2, Fall, 1980, pp. 339-49.*

S. GINGELL

In studies of Canadian Prairie literature and in surveys of the development and outstanding achievements of Canadian fiction, W. O. Mitchell's novel *Who Has Seen the Wind* has been uniformly praised for its lyrically evocative style. (p. 221)

There are many passages in the novel that haunt the reader's imagination because of their rhythmic qualities and musical sounds. (p. 222)

The poetry of the prairies is nowhere better captured than in the description of the landscape on the final pages of the book. . . . The rhyme, alliteration, consonance and assonance, combined with both syntactical structures inverted for heightened rhetorical impact and metrical effects designed to enhance meaning, attest to a creator whose ear is finely attuned to sound. . . . (pp. 222-23)

Emotional intensity in the novel is established and sustained by a variety of devices employed by the lyric poet: Mitchell makes frequent use of synaesthesia, particularly striking imagery and figurative language and marries sound and sense as well. . . . His narrator characteristically fuses sensations of sight, touch, and sound. . . . (p. 224)

The striking originality of some of the images found in *Who Has Seen the Wind* can be illustrated by reference to the often quoted opening sentence of the book: "Here was the least common denominator of nature, the skeleton requirements simply, of land and sky—Saskatchewan prairie." . . . There is something approaching a metaphysical conceit in the notion that prairie sky is to the land below it as fractional numerator is to denominator. Furthermore, the idea that land and sky are the skeletal requirements of nature, leads to the implication that the human presence fleshes out prairie nature, gives it significance, and makes it truly come alive.

The lyric mode's subjective, personal, and imaginative view of a subject which is often expressed through figurative language is observable in the extended metaphor of sunset as fire in the penultimate paragraph of the last chapter of Part One. . . . The sunlight 'kindling' the edges of clouds is mirrored in a farmhouse window so that the glass 'blazes' until the flame subsides to its final form, a 'glowing' on the prairie's edge.

The visual effects of this metaphoric passage are paired with carefully contrived structures and sounds. The harmony of the parallel phrases "fades from cloud to cloud" and "dies from softness to softness" is supported by the half-rhyme of 'dies' and 'sky'. In the following sentence, the repetition of the 'b' sounds in 'briefly blazes' and 'bathes,' of 's' sounds in 'sinking sun,' and of 'g' sounds in 'golden glowing' helps strengthen the melodic effect produced by the immediately adjacent triple rhyming words 'mellower, yellower,' the middle rhyme of which is picked up in 'low' and 'glowing' in the latter part of the sentence. (pp. 224-25)

[Cycle] and the repetition of cyclic phenomena are the chief structural characteristics of the novel. In the metaphorical description of the prairie evening cited above, the dying of the light, itself part of a cyclic recurrence, appropriately follows the description of an animal death whose link with cycle is suggested by the "lazing circles" of the hawk: "In the summer sky there, stark blue, a lonely goshawk hung. It drifted low in lazing circles. A pause—one swoop—galvanic death to a tan burgher no more to sit amid his city's grained heaps and squeak a question to the wind." . . . This kind of observation of the fabric of natural life on the prairie is not merely lyric window dressing; it reinforces the sense of cycle and interconnectedness of life that is a primary thematic focus of the novel. . . .

[Motif] is one of the formal devices in which the novelist is most interested, but Mitchell has mixed success in handling motif. Recurrent images of entrapment provide an example of his penchant for *leitmotif*, but also an instance of stylistic concerns overriding thematic integrity. (p. 226)

While the motif of the cage or trap has the virtue of tying together several distinct incidents, the impact of the motif is considerably lessened by its being linked to situations that are qualitatively different. (p. 229)

Such betrayals of thematic integrity by stylistic concerns are rare, however; more commonly, Mitchell's lyric sense enriches and supports his thematic concerns while expressing his imaginative and emotionally charged view of the prairie and its life.

The Bible is the source of one of the most successfully handled motifs of *Who Has Seen the Wind,* scripture first entering the fabric of the novel through the epigraph from Psalm 103: 15-16: "As for man, his days are as grass: as a flower of the field, so he flourisheth. / For the wind passeth over it, and it is gone; and the place thereof shall know it no more." These verses both point up one of the major themes of the book, the beautiful but transitory nature of human existence, and call attention to several of the natural images which become *leitmotifs* themselves, the grass and flowers mutable and mortal, and thus symbolic of man, and the wind unchangeable and eternal, and therefore representative of God. The context of the verses from *Psalms* is important, because the next verse of Psalm 103 reads, "But the steadfast love of the Lord is from everlasting to everlasting upon those who fear him. . . ."

Mitchell was clearly thinking of the Psalm when he recorded Brian's thoughts about the prairie's being awful: "in his mind there loomed vaguely fearful images of a still and brooding spirit, a quiescent power unsmiling from everlasting to everlasting to which the coming and passing of the prairie's creatures was but incidental." . . . The verbal motif recurs when Brian tries to come to terms with his father's death, in the context of a passage which contrasts a series of 'forevers' and 'nevers,' the latter giving rise to the memory of the 'nevers' of Shakespeare's Lear. The most significant stylistic feature of the passage is, however, a lyric repetition of both words and syntactical structures, a repetition which here as elsewhere is designed to reflect the sense of cycle. . . . (pp. 229-30)

In the style and structure, motifs and music of *Who Has Seen the Wind* Mitchell's declared interests in the similarities between verbal lyricism and music find their fullest expression. If his undoubted success with these aspects of the novel had been matched by a corresponding success in the handling of theme and character, *Who Has Seen the Wind* would merit much more than the epithet 'minor classic' which best describes its place in the Canadian canon today. (p. 231)

S. Gingell, "The Lyricism of W. O. Mitchell's 'Who Has Seen the Wind'" (copyright by S. Gingell; reprinted by permission of the editors), in Canadian Studies in Literature, *Vol. 6, No. 2, 1981, pp. 221-31.*

MARTIN KNELMAN

Daddy Sherry [is] the hero of W. O. Mitchell's new play *The Kite,* based on his 1962 novel. Daddy is reputed to be the oldest human being in the world. As his birthday approaches, the media invade his home town in the foothills of Alberta. Daddy Sherry sits on the front porch of his great-great-granddaughter's house, taking it all in but refusing to play the game. He won't conform to the world's idea of how a distinguished ancient should behave. His rambling and bickering infuriate his family, and he embarrasses everyone by refusing to make nice for the TV cameras. . . . (p. 73)

Much to the consternation of those who hope to capitalize on his longevity, Daddy Sherry announces to the world that he's tired of living, and sets a date for his own death. "Dyin' ain't hard to do, you know," he explains. "All sorts of folks do it without no practice ner no talent an' most of'em gets it right the first time." . . .

Daddy Sherry is outrageous in a way that's meant to be ingratiating and lovable. Mitchell has always been flamboyant about waving the dung on his boots in his public's face, and Daddy Sherry is a champion of that tradition. He enjoys saying and doing exactly what must not be said or done. But Mitchell is careful to draw the line; he never risks having Daddy offend the kind of people who go to the theatre. Like Mitchell himself, Daddy is a raspy-voiced old character who loves attention and likes to get a rise out of people. (p. 74)

> *Martin Knelman, "Old Hams" (copyright © 1981 by Saturday Night; reprinted by permission of the author), in Saturday Night, Vol. 96, No. 9, October, 1981, pp. 73-4.*

PAUL ROBERTS

The story [of *How I Spent My Summer Holidays*], as you might expect from Mitchell, concerns a distant, rather happy childhood on the south Saskatchewan prairie. It differs from his previous accounts of similar childhoods in the discordant note set at the beginning—bizarre, darkly sexual. We are faced not so much with a story of the loss of innocence, as Mitchell claims, but with the revelation that behind the coyly innocent exteriors he previously depicted are lives torn by sadness, horror, and loss.

The tale revolves around the hero-worshipping relationship between a young boy, Hugh and a war hero, King Motherwell. "King sure was different from Mr. Mackey, or my mother, or any other adult I ever knew," says Hugh. He sure was. By the end of the book he has killed his wife and drunk himself into a lunatic asylum, where he eventually commits suicide. To a reader weaned on the saccharine *Jake and the Kid,* this will be as shocking as discovering that Peter Pan was a pedophile. . . .

[A] lack of clarity results from the narrative technique. Mitchell fails to see that what is ultimately interesting to the adult reader—and this book is not for children—is the adult world. Like many another author writing about childhood, he must have discovered that it is not one's memories of events that necessarily dim with age, but one's ability to stay in tune with childish perceptions. Thus, in order to keep his plot rolling, he's obliged to present us with certain adult facts, which he can't let his narrator fully comprehend. The reader, having been fed on a diet of hints and rumours, begins to jump to wild conclusions. Since all of Mitchell's novels are really vehicles for assorted anecdotes and mournfully evocative descriptions of the natural world, this perhaps does not trouble him.

What troubles me is Mitchell's lack of control. After the pseudo-Freudian mishmash at the start, we plunge into what promises to be a Wordsworthian search for identity, at which point the grown-up Hugh is jettisoned as narrator until the ending and we wade through little Hugh's school life, early pranks, and so on, eventually finding ourselves in the plot—which is fairly thin, and has to be interrupted by periodic forays into other subjects, none of which do much to deepen our understanding

of the characters. As the central story is resolved, or nearly resolved, the plot comes to an abrupt halt, and we leap the years in spurts as Hugh catches up with himself in age. "Finally I may have sorted it out," he says rather optimistically.

King Motherwell has the mark of a minor tragic hero, and it's easy to see how he came to dominate the book. There were always dark undertones to Mitchell's characters (the brutal intransigence of Daddy Sherry in *The Kite,* the empty boastfulness of Jake), but our forebodings were never justifiable. With King it's different. An alcoholic long before the tragedy strikes, he's a bootlegger involved with American gangsters, and his wife is an ex-prostitute. It's amazing, in fact, that people let him play with their kids, but within the convention of such childhood fictions it's perhaps unseemly to question why an adult should spend so much time with children. When the dénouement comes, we're more surprised that our suspicions were justified than at the way they're justified. The problem with seeing King through Hugh's eyes is that we do not really see him at all.

Despite the liberal sprinkling of expletives and the tentative exploration of early sexuality, Mitchell's childhood world remains rather coy and precious. *How I Spent My Summer Holidays* could have been an interesting departure in style and content; instead it lands in a limbo between Mitchell's old readers and those he might have gained had he been a more adventurous and meticulous writer.

> *Paul Roberts, "Mitchell in Limbo" (copyright © 1981 by Saturday Night; reprinted by permission of the author), in Saturday Night, Vol. 96, No. 10, November, 1981, p. 76.*

MARK ABLEY

[W. O. Mitchell's] first and most famous book, *Who Has Seen the Wind,* told the story of a sensitive boy growing up in a small Saskatchewan town. Later novels, notably *The Kite* and *The Vanishing Point,* explored the larger topics of time and old age. Now, at the age of 67, W. O. Mitchell has returned to the joys and bafflements of childhood, and his admirers will be delighted. A master of prairie fiction is up to his old tricks, and if you have forgotten Holy Rollers, swimming holes in the river or the sweet scent of willow smoke, *How I Spent My Summer Holidays* will remind you in the happiest possible way. Reading it, you begin to wonder whether this nostalgic string of boyhood escapades deserves to be called a novel. Until the last few chapters, that is, when you understand with a jolt just how shrewd a writer W. O. Mitchell really is.

How I Spent My Summer Holidays is narrated by a scrawny 12-year-old called Hughie, who bears more than a passing resemblance to Tom Sawyer. In the summer of 1924 he and an English boy . . . dig a secret cave beneath an empty expanse of prairie. . . . The boys spend part of their vacation learning such useful information as the correct method of building a fire, the true appearance of a naked woman and the embarrassing effects of eating shoveler ducks. They also learn about madness and, eventually, death. Here, at his least picturesque, Mitchell writes most forcefully.

His jaunty prose has many virtues, including a delicate, unpredictable sense of humor and a lively understanding of a child's perceptions: children in Mitchell's books never suffer the indignity of being portrayed as miniature adults. Unlike most contemporary texts, the novel could happily be read aloud;

it has something of the ease and leisure of oral storytelling, the unpretentious entertainment of street corners and porches, pubs and backyards. Nevertheless, it must also be said that some of the digressions are irritating rather than winning, that the book is slow to gather power, and that Mitchell hasn't entirely controlled his old weakness for melodrama. Occasionally, the breezy style seems at odds with an underlying bleakness. These pages are liberally sprinkled with madmen, whores, religious fanatics, prigs, bigots and drunkards. It's a clear-sighted vision of Saskatchewan, one of Canada's least understood and most surprising provinces.

In the end, the title is deliberately deceptive. Those who approach the book searching for lighthearted memories of a less complicated time than our own will find that Mitchell plays along with their expectations, then suddenly overthrows them.

> Mark Abley, "The Inquiring Heart of a Prairie Childhood," in Maclean's Magazine (© 1981 by Maclean's Magazine; reprinted by permission), Vol. 94, No. 44, November 2, 1981, p. 66.

GUY HAMEL

Mitchell has been much preoccupied with innocence. His sympathies have always attached themselves to those, whether children or not, who are subject to authorities imposed upon them by busybodies and boards, by custom and compact, by men of property and women of probity. . . .

[The] focus of innocence in *How I Spent My Summer Holidays* is Hugh, who tells his story, and who decides that its proper start is in the summer vacation of his twelfth year. The beginning of summer holidays represents the re-entry into a special temporal dimension. If it is possible to experience eternity, it is here. In their idle days Hugh and his friends conform to the evocative description given by Shakespeare's Polixenes: "lads that thought there was no more behind / But such a day tomorrow as to-day / And to be boy eternal." One of Mitchell's great strengths as a writer is his ability to remember and convey the condition of childhood. (p. 79)

[The story concerning Hugh and Peter's cave, however,] is a grown-up tale. Their action, as Hugh recognizes later, leads to "true war" with the adult world, different from the preceding "skirmishes and minor border engagements." Mitchell's sense of childhood is, again, acute in his description of Hugh's puzzled response to his parents and elders and his instinctive suspicion that adults are, perhaps despite themselves, the enemy. . . . The exception to the separation of estates is King Motherwell, a figure "both boy and adult," who moves with assurance in both worlds. Initially a vital ally, he becomes a tragic catalyst who brings about for Hugh the end of his childhood.

It is in large measure the destruction of King that makes the new novel so much more sombre in spirit, more pessimistic than any earlier books of Mitchell's. One can appreciate the extent of the change simply by recognizing that King's precursor in Mitchell's writing is Jake of the *Jake and the Kid* stories. Though Jake is a man and understands very well how to cope with the adult world, he is at heart a boy. . . . The vague eruption of sexual interest into Jake's life is treated as a comic aberration. King Motherwell, on the other hand, is a figure of passion and conviction whose values and sense of self-preservation have been perfected in the absolute testing ground of the first war trenches. His failure shows that the strains imposed by the compulsions of love and hate may be intolerable: if he fails, who may not? (pp. 80-1)

Mitchell uses form—in this, his most sophisticated novel formally—to admit the rich complexity of life. Near the end of *Huckleberry Finn* an inappropriate fictional mode intrudes to challenge the integrity of the novel: Tom Sawyer appears and realigns events so that they conform to the schemes of the pirate and swashbuckling tales that are his literary guides. The dislocation effected by Tom's presence is Twain's covert signal that there can be no "conclusion" to *Huckleberry Finn*. So long as Huck remains innocent, he is subject to authority, however misguided or debased, as children are; and there is no model by which the counterparts of his virtues may be expressed in the world of experience. In a way Mitchell pulls a similar trick.

How I Spent My Summer Holidays has an ending that is orthodox and formulaic: the mystery behind the crucial events of Hugh's adolescence is revealed and all the whatever-happened-to questions about the characters are answered. But the neatness of the ending points to the artificiality of the concept of closure. Early in his account, the narrator speaks of himself as "listening to my own voice coming to me not just from my own past but from much beyond that and from quite another world, the age of Jason or of Ulysses or of Aeneas." The implication that his story will conform to a universal shape or paradigm already shadowed in myth and fiction is borne out by the tidy arrestment of the end. The authority of the story-teller as artificer is also urged. . . . In looking upon his own past as a story, Hugh discovers the fixed identities of the presences in our lives represented by father and mother or their surrogates, by mentors, friends, rivals. But the dynamic consequences of their influence is constant and incalculable: retrospect itself gives any remembered occasion the force to work upon us anew. Hugh finds, as all of us really know, that any stopping place short of death is artificial, that once we were one person and now we are another while yet remaining in essence the same being and inescapably the heirs of our own beginnings, that the process working such variations upon us is, however marked by high events, continuous. (pp. 81-2)

> Guy Hamel, in his review of "How I Spent My Summer Holidays" (copyright by Guy Hamel; reprinted by permission of the author), in The Fiddlehead, No. 133, July, 1982, pp. 79-82.

Ted Mooney

1951-

American novelist.

Mooney's trendy first novel, *Easy Travel to Other Planets*, moves at a disjointed velocity which Mooney sees as characteristic of life in the not-too-distant future. With humor and insight, he portrays the effects of a rapidly changing world upon its human inhabitants.

PAUL GRAY

[In ***Easy Travel to Other Planets***] Melissa is a marine biologist who has become sexually involved with a dolphin named Peter. Jeffrey, Melissa's human lover, has given up a promising career as an architect to teach fifth-graders in the New York City public school system; he thinks of his students as "a kind of early warning system for what's next in the world." Meanwhile, their friend Nicole feels glum over the prospect of another abortion, her sixth. . . . Kirk, Jeffrey's twin brother, is taking parachute lessons in preparation for a photojournalistic assignment in Antarctica. The world, apparently, is ready to go to war over the natural resources under the South Pole.

If this does not sound like a recipe for trendy froth, then nothing can. But Author Ted Mooney adds some marijuana and gin, stirs and comes up with a substantial and moving first novel. For one thing, circumstantial whimsey is balanced against the pathos of characters trying to take their increasingly weird lives seriously. . . .

Everyone struggles with the barrage of data that is modern life. Memory no longer seems able to file everything that the senses receive. . . . A new disease has begun to spread: Information Sickness, a kind of systems-overload. . . . What with all the new vibes zinging through the air and the characters' craniums, a totally unprecedented emotion has also been reported. One student describes it: "It's like . . . I don't know, it's like being in a big crowd of people without the people. And you're all traveling somewhere at this incredible speed. But without the speed."

Although no one spells it out, this "new emotion" sounds like the tactile knowledge of what being alive now, thanks to science and space probes, means: sitting on a crowded planet that is moving very fast. . . . The author sometimes reaches for cosmic consciousness and produces more comedy than insights. . . . He also convincingly portrays a kind of ambitious anxiety that can erupt at any time in the here and now. At 29, he may well be an early warning system for what fiction in the '80s will be like.

> Paul Gray, "New Vibes," in Time (copyright 1981 Time Inc.; all rights reserved; reprinted by permission from Time), Vol. 118, No. 13, September 28, 1981, p. 85.

WEBSTER SCHOTT

Closing Ted Mooney's ***Easy Travel to Other Planets***, I remembered reading for the first time J. D. Salinger's *The Catcher*

in the Rye and James Purdy's *63: Dream Palace*. Mooney has different ideas about how we live and feel, and the style to make them seem important. . . .

Easy Travel involves principally two young couples, a late middle-aged couple, and a dolphin. The two most urgent of these characters are Melissa, a . . . marine biologist, and the dolphin, who is named Peter. . . .

Since ***Easy Travel*** is mostly about the effects of erotic liaisons, the Melissa-Peter combination is only the most unusual of several. . . .

Because ***Easy Travel*** is also about a general disjunction in American society, "being . . . thoroughly at the testy mercy of disorderly events," these emotional bondings tend to go nowhere except toward disaster. They become diluted by failures of talk and intention, existential angst, and the belief of the young that all alternatives are available and for unlimited time. . . .

Ted Mooney's waffling couples recall Walker Percy's despairing characters who are unaware of being in despair, or the early lovers of Ernest Hemingway who think things may or may not get better. They provoke speculation. They are real enough to learn from. Their values are new, like some of the drugs they take. But their personal strategies are as old as the seven deadly sins. Everything is permitted in their relationships. Therefore everything is open, right? Wrong. . . . The new-value environment of *Easy Travel to Other Planets* is vitalized by the same confusions psychological fiction has been observing for a hundred years.

Aside from its exposures of character, I think the most intriguing qualities of *Easy Travel* are Ted Mooney's various proposals about sensory perception and social condition. (p. 5)

Some of Mooney's accessory diversions—his fragments on "Use of the Ray Gun," "Time Measured by the Clapping of Hands," and his yarn about Freud's dog Fritz—are not only irrelevant but impudent. Mooney has a big bag of tricks. He wants to do them all in his first novel. It's unnecessary. He writes elegant sentences. He understands human motives. His ideas are large. (p. 7)

> *Webster Schott, "Love in the Shallows," in* Book World—The Washington Post *(© 1981, The Washington Post), October 4, 1981, pp. 5, 7.*

MEREDITH MARSH

The future is definitely upon [the protagonists of *Easy Travel to Other Planets*], but the people are recognizably ourselves and the time is very close to now: Mooney [uses] . . . imaginative devices to crystallize confusions that we already face. (p. 34)

[The reader] suffers a touch of information sickness by the time this hypnotic and compacted story ends. Along with the effects of rapid travel and communication, Mooney manages to pack in the fate of the family, the nature of art, the changing nature of science, twins, dolphins, death, and a brand new emotion, related to ESP. Even the moon itself glides on stage to deliver a few lines. Mooney is a deeply provocative writer, in all senses of the words, skilled enough at showing the ways in which these intellectual sounding subjects actually pump hearts that he could well have slowed down his plot to pay a little more attention to the motivations of the people. Instead they merely are like good cartoons, distinct at a glance but never developed. For this reason, although [the climax is] . . . beautifully written, [it is] . . . far less persuasive than the quiet scenes.

Perhaps the most surprising thing about so self-conscious a book is how unabashedly romantic it is, a tale of heroes and quests, with few of the usual ironic twists that assure the reader that the author knows it's all a game. This author, with his opening quotation from Levi-Strauss, does know perfectly well that it's a game, of course, but he plays it flat out and, on the whole, wins, sweeping us straight under the spell of his loquacious moon. Partly this is because, like his namesake, Mooney is such a beautiful and inventive stylist that he could make virtually any hocus-pocus work for a chapter or two, but it is mostly because he uses his taut style to convey a single emotion with relentless force, the same old dread of annihilation that is still, he makes clear, the fossil fuel that drives his pill-popping characters toward their high-speed futures. (pp. 34-5)

> *Meredith Marsh, "Auspicious Debuts," in* The New Republic *(reprinted by permission of* The New Republic; *© 1981 The New Republic, Inc.), Vol. 185, No. 16, October 21, 1981, pp. 33-5.**

JEFFREY BURKE

For the most part, Mooney's thoughtful treatment of the old problems prevents [*Easy Travel to Other Planets*] from being

reductively classed as science fiction. It must, however, be taken on its own peculiar terms, which involve some of the symptoms of information sickness: "disconnected speech, apparent disorientation, and the desire to touch everything." (p. 83)

Unfortunately, Mooney's bid for uniqueness began to try my patience. It's relatively easy to accept an Antarctic war or the extremities of information overload; and his "new emotion," perhaps a key to the novel, has the plausibility of a kind of psychological poetry while suggesting *Perelandra* and sounding like space travel. . . . [But] Mooney's provocations only tantalize me into trying to figure him out. Distracted, I've lost sight of his characters' abortions, tumors, and dreams.

Mooney's vision of the future is just a bit too strange and his manner of conveying it too strained for such traditional themes as he pursues in *Easy Travels*. . . . And the disconnected nature of his novel is potentially as distracting to a reader as the novel's "reality" is to its characters. Those characters are trivialized in a way that has little to do with the pace and incoherence of Mooney's future.

I end up with an impression of a very talented writer whose next novel will be as serious in intention as this one but less strained in form, avoiding particularly small nonsense effects like: "Twenty feet away Peter made a noise like a cocktail party heard through waxed paper." (p. 84)

> *Jeffrey Burke, "First Time Out," in* Harper's *(copyright © 1981 by* Harper's Magazine; *all rights reserved; reprinted from the November, 1981 issue by special permission), Vol. 263, No. 1578, November, 1981, pp. 82-4.**

THE NEW YORKER

[Mr. Mooney] is a deft and wily writer; his descriptions of how a dolphin may think (it would have 9,017 names for the taste of water) and how it sometimes sounds. . . are matched by his sense of how human communication can bound and rebound beyond words.

> *"Briefly Noted: 'Easy Travel to Other Planets'," in* The New Yorker *(© 1981 by The New Yorker Magazine, Inc.), Vol. LVII, No. 38, November 9, 1981, p. 206.*

PAUL STUEWE

[Ted Mooney's novel] is another roadside attraction of the Tom Robbins variety, and the betting here is on a very short run. Heavy promotion and ultra-trendy plot segments such as a girl-meets-dolphin affair may sell it to younger readers, but the book's inept construction and relentlessly cute prose guarantee a widely remaindered future. . . . *Easy Travel to Other Planets* is merely the latest in a series of failed attempts to feather an already fully occupied Robbins' nest.

> *Paul Stuewe, "From Bauhaus to the Issa Valley to Wesley's England," in* Quill and Quire *(reprinted by permission of* Quill and Quire*), Vol. 47, No. 12, December, 1981, p. 32.**

CHRISTOPHER LEHMANN-HAUPT

[Much] of **"Easy Travel to Other Planets"** is effective—the unusually vivid people that inhabit the story, its physical atmosphere of light and airiness, the sense it creates of the continuity of technology and people, the sense it creates of the growing discontinuity of human experience. One is especially struck by this sense of discontinuity, which Mr. Mooney achieves by mixing up his verb tenses, by disrupting the pace of the most ordinary action, and by inserting sudden, implausible scene changes. . . .

[However], there is a little too much that goes on in Mr. Mooney's novel, what with its slightly overbusy plot and its superabundance of formal experiments. Some readers may be troubled, too, by what they may construe as an excess of sentiment over the state of the environment. . . . One takes Mr. Mooney's title to be ironic: it is easy to travel to other planets, but it's not so simple to survive on earth.

Still, Mr. Mooney's experiment is strongly atmospheric and continually absorbing. The dolphin lore is very well done. There is a novelistic intelligence here, however much it may have been shaped by film and television. One gets the feeling that the author has tried to cram meaning into every word of **"Easy Travel."** When he relaxes a little more, something first-rate is likely to result.

Christopher Lehmann-Haupt, "Books of the Times: 'Easy Travel to Other Planets'," in The New York Times *(© 1981 by The New York Times Company; reprinted by permission), December 16, 1981, p. 23.*

Ezekiel Mphahlele

1919-

(Also writes as Es'kia Mphahlele and under pseudonym of Bruno Eseki) Black South African novelist, autobiographer, essayist, short story writer, editor, and poet.

Mphahlele is a major African author and a provocative critic. Both his writing and his life have been marked by the alienation and pain he felt as a citizen within his own country and the anguish he experienced in his self-imposed twenty-year exile. Mphahlele was born on a reserve and raised in an urban ghetto but managed to receive a higher education. He began his exile after his teaching was banned due to his opposition to apartheid.

Although his autobiographical novel, *The Wanderers*, describes the plight of exile, most of his writing is set in South Africa. *Down Second Avenue*, another fictional autobiography, is highly praised for its compassionate and realistic treatment of urban ghetto life, also the subject of his short stories. Many of these first appeared in *Drum*, a South African magazine for black readers, which Mphahlele helped edit.

Mphahlele's critical writings form an important part of his work. *The African Image* traces the portrayals of blacks in literature and discusses the cultural problems inherent in societies based on racial oppression. In *Voices in the Whirlwind* Mphahlele reaffirms his humanistic commitment to the formation of an indigenous literature based on Western aesthetics. He explains that his wariness of Negritude derives from his belief that cultural isolation would deprive the African of realizing his individuality within a world heritage.

Unable to forget his African roots, Mphahlele returned to South Africa in 1978, even though his works continue to be banned.

(See also *Contemporary Authors*, Vols. 81-84.)

© Lütfi Özkök

It is this theme which pulls the various essays of *The African Image* together.

"Passionate Scrutiny," in The Times Literary Supplement (© Times Newspapers Ltd. (London) 1962; reproduced from The Times Literary Supplement by permission), No. 3139, April 27, 1962, p. 279.

THE TIMES LITERARY SUPPLEMENT

Mr. Mphahlele is the most interesting writer to emerge from South Africa for some time. It is not that he possesses a high degree of technical accomplishment; the essays collected . . . [in *The African Image*] are loosely woven and the longest and most ambitious of them bears too many marks of its origin as a postgraduate thesis. What he does possess, to an extent unusual at the best of times and especially perhaps among exiles, is a capacity for combining passion with scrutiny. . . .

[For] all his anger he refuses to fall into fashionable African attitudes. He reveres Monsieur Senghor but pays no homage to *négritude;* he is carried away by President Nkrumah's oratory but remains sceptical about the African personality; he is a nationalist if nationalism means anti-tribalism, whether the tribe be black or white, but not if it means black fascism or chauvinism. He is against the ghetto, whatever the colour of the persons consigned to it, and for free communications and the interaction of cultures; and he is for and against these things equally passionately whether he is confronted by class distinctions in London, tribal distinctions in Ibadan or racial distinctions in Johannesburg.

JAMES R. FRAKES

If anger, first-hand experience, outrage, compassion, and topicality were the sole requirements for great literature, *The Wanderers* might well be one of the masterpieces of this declining part of the twentieth century. Ezekiel Mphahlele has been there and knows and cares. He is in charge of his emotions and convictions, and ofay doubters can step aside. . . .

But passionate involvement is simply not enough in itself, at least for fiction. What is sadly missing here is firm narrative line, convincing and full development of character, structural control. The reader wants very much to be swept along by the sheer urgency of subject and theme, to care deeply about teacher-journalist Timi Tabane and his family and friends, to read for more than information about what is still an exotic country to most Americans. And there is a lot to admire here: harrowing scenes of farm prison-labor in South Africa; hard discussions and dramatizations of "the creed of power," tribalism vs. nationalism, the plight of the liberal, the enigma of the Indian in Africa, caste and class, the inexorable influence of politics on every social and human relationship, withering cultural roots, mob fickleness. . . .

[However], Mphahlele introduces too many characters, both native and white, most of whom remain cartoon-ghosts, names without substance, largely indistinguishable. There must be at least twenty different dialects, most of them mystifying. . . .

What works best is the strange smoky atmosphere that permeates the prose, creating an almost kinetic effect of choking, gasping bewilderment.

> *James R. Frakes, "In South Africa," in* Book World— The Washington Post *(© 1971 Postrib Corp.; reprinted by permission of* Chicago Tribune *and* The Washington Post*), April 11, 1971, p. 2.*

BARNEY C. McCARTNEY

Because Mphahlele has established himself as a major African literary critic, cultural commentator, and short story writer, we awaited his first published novel with hopeful expectations. But we were somewhat disappointed [with *The Wanderers*].

Although Timi Tabane, the black exile and first person narrator, tells us, near the beginning of the novel, how his life and that of Steven Cartwright, the white South African exile, are "twined around each other", and although Mphahlele uses Steve as a first person narrator for some fifty pages, the story is primarily concerned with Timi's life as a reporter in South Africa and with his years in exile in Nigeria and Kenya. The shifts in narrator, using Timi, Steve, and an omniscient third person, seem contrived to show different points of view that might be expected to lead to a more complete picture of the exile's life. But they fail to do so.

The reader who has some knowledge of Mphahlele's life cannot avoid seeing the novel as largely autobiographical. . . . [We] feel certain, early in the work, that Mphahlele must have something to tell us of the life of the exile. And he does, but it is somehow not enough. We are kept waiting for something to happen in the story. We have the vivid sketches of life for the black man in the South African ghetto of Jericho township (which remind us much of Mphahlele's autobiography, *Down Second Avenue*); we have the episode concerning the reporter's mission to photograph the Goshen potato farm and investigate the fate of one of the prisoners sentenced to work there "for not being in possession of identity passbooks"; we read of and understand the situation which causes the central characters to leave South Africa; we feel with them the insecurity and rootlessness of the exile; we have portraits of other characters who live under conditions of apartheid in Johannesburg and social unacceptance or ostracism in Nigeria and Kenya. But the action and plot of the story still leave us wanting. (p. 41)

In Jamesian terms, Timi is not "interesting". But the life around him is. The book is certainly worth reading for the reportorial view it gives of life as an exile. It is also worth reading for Timi's philosophical discussions and Mphahlele's short digressions somewhat thinly disguised as Timi's musings on his condition. They remind us of Mphahlele's *The African Image;* here again we see the critical humanist, but in the character of Timi Tabane. Also, many of the episodes could stand by themselves as good short stories. (pp. 41-2)

The Wanderers is a curious mixture of a picture of life continually interesting, if appalling, to the westerner combined with an obvious failure to maintain a narrative to a point where we would unqualifyingly call it a novel. (p. 42)

> *Barney C. McCartney, "Book Reviews: 'The Wanderers'," in* East Africa Journal *(© East African Cultural Trust), Vol. VIII, No. 7, July, 1971, pp. 41-2.*

SAUNDERS REDDING

Reading *Down Second Avenue* and *The Wanderers,* one finds it easy to understand why the author, Ezekiel Mphahlele, and his books are banned in his native South Africa. *Down Second Avenue* is autobiography which covers Mphahlele's life down to his flight into exile in 1957. . . .

From the pen of another, less talented, less sensitive writer, *Down Second Avenue* could easily have become a sociological analysis of apartheid and/or a psychological explication of the effects of this "political" system upon its victims, black, white, colored and Indian. It is neither. One is made sharply aware of the operating sociological and psychological phenomena, not by the explication of them, but by the development of real life situations and especially by the presentation of striking real life characters. . . . (p. 78)

But it is impossible to do critical justice to a book that, while it meets the universally recognized literary canons, is at the same time meant primarily to serve a social function. . . . No work out of Africa since *Tell Freedom* by Peter Abrahams, which was published in 1954, has said so clearly that life for all people in South Africa is lived under social circumstances and in a spiritual temper so degrading as to destroy the hopes even of those who have been taught to believe—and do believe—that their salvation lies in the perpetuation of the "political" system called apartheid. This is the unstated thesis and the unspoken preachment: the world must save South Africa in spite of itself. Perception of this comes through the superb artistry of Mphahlele's storytelling, and the story itself, personal as it is, affirms man's common humanity and bridges the gap between one culture and another.

Though *The Wanderers* is presented as a work of fiction, the reader coming to it directly from *Down Second Avenue* suspects that many of the experiences it relates were the author's own. . . . But the similarity, which, anyway, is more apparent than real, does not erode the interest that the first page of *The Wanderers* arouses. Indeed, the interest grows and grows, though not because of the central story line, which works itself out in simple and dramatically logical ways.

The Wanderers takes its title from a group of rootless people, black and white, who, alienated by the social realities of South Africa, are forced into exile. . . . They seek more than refuge; they seek life—in Nigeria, in Kenya, in Tanzania. Recounting the wanderings of his characters provides an opportunity for the author to explore the milieu of these African countries, and what, among other things, you get is a panoramic view of almost the whole of the "dark continent."

If this makes it sound as if *The Wanderers* is some sort of travelogue, forget it. It is a carefully constructed work of fiction that brilliantly and imaginatively dramatizes man's irremediable alienation from the family of man and incidentally supplies insights into political, social and economic problems to which Africa is presently seeking solutions.

Ezekiel Mphahlele is one of a half dozen living South African writers, including Nadine Gordimer, Peter Abrahams, Bloke Modisane and Alan Paton, the value of whose work is vouched for by its rejection at home. (pp. 78-9)

> *Saunders Redding, "Out from Second Avenue," in* Africa Today *(© Africa Today Associates; reprinted by permission of* Africa Today, *Graduate School of International Studies, University of Denver, Denver, CO 80208), Vol. 18, No. 4, October, 1971, pp. 78-9.*

THE TIMES LITERARY SUPPLEMENT

[Ezekiel Mphahlele] writes a clear and serviceable, if unexciting—and sometimes too baldly didactic—prose, has a zest and a fair talent for the creation of a wide variety of characters from all races, and an occasional flair for narrative suspense which gives his story pace. Yet [*The Wanderers*], if always authentic and well-meant, remains too ordinary to make much that is new out of his range of bitter, touching or ironical experiences.

It gets off to a good enough start. . . . But two-thirds of this long novel of repression, discontent and wandering seem diffuse in their sheer documentary attention to political and racial situations. *The Wanderers* is too skilled and varied to be any kind of manifesto, but the novel interest—plot and character, insight into inward experience—loses the contest with the author's desire to render African realities with the very fidelity in which he excels.

> *"African Exile," in* The Times Literary Supplement *(© Times Newspapers Ltd. (London) 1972; reproduced from* The Times Literary Supplement *by permission), No. 3654, March 10, 1972, p. 265.*

EMINE SNYDER

Mphahlele's life has been constantly uprooted, a constant wandering over the earth as the partly autobiographical novel, *The Wanderers,* attests. . . .

For Mphahlele, the recalled nightmare of his early adult years in South Africa is synthesized in the image of the South African land scarred with terror. . . . (p. 260)

This image of South Africa becomes for the wanderer of the novel the symbol of his own interior landscape of desolation. The fate of a people is once more internalized in the drama of a single consciousness, that of Timi, the journalist-writer forced to exile himself from South Africa and to live an uprooted life in West Africa and East Africa. The historical conflict between traditional and modern society, between permanence and exile, are catalytic agents to the private conflict between Timi and his equally uprooted son Felang. Thus Mphahlele's *The Wanderers* is not only a powerful evocation of human imposition—the bestiality of the Apartheid system—but a study of the ensuing human alienation lived at a more private level, in the everyday life of one of its victims. Timi's problem is the possibility—or perhaps impossibility—of the transmutation of moral values in a world grown indifferent to all moral values. He is trying, he reflects, "to understand the forces I feel inside me, the relevance of the teaching of my forebears and of the reverence I have for them." But the very situation of exile transposes geography into ethics and metaphysics; for it is the human land, the human heaven, the final purification for modern man

(as in Soyinka, Armah, and Awoonor) which Timi and Mphahlele seek. (pp. 260-61)

> *Emine Snyder, "New Directions in African Writings," in* Pan-African Journal *(copyright © 1972 Pan-African Institute, Inc.), Vol. V, No. 2, Summer, 1972, pp. 253-61.**

ADDISON GAYLE, JR.

[The series of essays included in *Voices in the Whirlwind*] were written over a period of years. As a result, the statements concerning the Black Aesthetic, the Negritude and Pan-Africanist movements, the possibilities of *detente* between Black and white, and the possibilities of freedom under the Western Aesthetic, now appear to be outdated. However, when [Mphahlele] writes of the African situation, when he draws upon his own experiences while analyzing poets and novelists, when he throws over them his own personal—and he will not like the word—*angst*, he is most solid. He reveals here the spiritual anguish of a Black man who is both captive and admirer of Western culture. (p. 41)

This dualism leads Mphahlele to search for a synthesis, to attempt to bridge the gap between the old cultures and traditions of pre-urban Africa and the new cultures and traditions which result from urbanization. The bridge between the two is the culture of the West. . . . (p. 42)

What is there about Western culture which makes Black men forget those many thousands gone, the rape of Africa by major Western powers, the atrocities committed during the voyage through the Middle Passage, the holocaust undergone daily by Blacks in America and abroad, if not the mistaken idea that the West is, truly, the romanticized Canaan depicted in the verse of its poets: the birthplace of humanism, where men are concerned not with the parochial, but with the universal, not with man, but with mankind, and that this Eden, this mini-paradise offers man's only hope for liberty and freedom? To accept this thesis is, of course, to turn from one's own prophets, to deny one's own truth, to forget the admonition of Franz Fanon: "Let us waste no time in sterile litanies and nauseating mimicry. Leave this Europe where they are never done talking of man, yet murder men everywhere they find them, at the corner of every one of their streets, in all the corners of the globe. For centuries they have stifled almost the whole of humanity in the name of a so-called spiritual experience."

And thus Mphahlele's dilemma: the woman is beautiful, stately, desirable; she is also diseased. Does one court her, hoping for immunity from the disease, or does he search elsewhere for satisfaction? (pp. 42-3)

For Mphahlele is, after all, a Black man. . . . Wherever he goes in the West, he will be an outsider, an alien, never able to sing the songs of his fathers in any of its strange lands. The freedom he seeks from literary and racial restrictions are no more available to him outside South Africa than within. For what, after all, does freedom mean for the writer? It is not, as Mphalele seems to suggest, some metaphysical thing outside of any reference except the determination of one man to recognize the humanity of another. Instead, it is a shared experience, which, unless it be the experience of all men, is the experience of no man. And in a world where some Black men remain in bondage, freedom for the writer, as I have written elsewhere, is based upon an absurdity.

But Mphahele understands all of this. He recognizes the danger inherent in the ''élitism'' of Negritude and its companion movement, Pan-Africanism. The problem is that he deems these movements more capable of mind-enslavement than those of the West. . . . (p. 43)

Despite our own reservations about some aspects of the Negritude movement, we must not allow Mphahlele, like the overzealous prosecutor, to stack his case against the absent defendant. (p. 44)

[Predictably] Mphahlele demands of the Black Aesthetician a Hammurabi Code of literary conduct. Tell me, he asks of them, what you would reject in the Western Aesthetic. There are seven items which he wishes answers to, ranging from the question of ''form and structure'' to that which embodies ''the enriching of the reader's emotional experience out of the metaphorical or symbolic presentation of fact. . . .'' The questions are challenging and demand attention. However, at this point in time, they obscure the real issue: is there a necessity for a Black Aesthetic, and, if so, what is the major demarcation line between its literary emphasis and that of the Western Aesthetic?

To answer this question means to drive to the heart of Mphahlele's spiritual dilemma, for the answer which we give cannot comfort either him or those who seek a synthesis between the Western and the Black Aesthetics. We will not acquiesce in his attempt to render the Black Aesthetic Movement little more than the stepchild of the West. . . . (pp. 45-6)

For here is the problem in microcosm: The Western Aesthetic has created a system in which Blacks have either been left out or rigidly circumscribed. (p. 46)

[Finally], after long centuries of doubt and questioning, we have arrived at what we believe to be the great truth: that one cannot separate Zola from Napoleon, Goëthe from Adolph Hitler, Tolstoy from Joseph Stalin, or Henry David Thoreau from Richard Nixon; that we cannot dissociate the beauty of the Chartres Cathedral from the holocaust of the Middle Passage. . . . Look into the Western Aesthetic, if one will, for symbols and images of beauty and grandeur; search as one will for proclamations about the freedom and nobility of man. We, however, prefer to look elsewhere, and to pride ourselves that, as Imamu Baraka notes, we are not nationalists or Black Aestheticians because of the devil; we would be so if no devil existed.

We claim no moral superiority over Mphahlele. His spiritual quest in many respects is but a duplication of our own. He does not reject the concept of a Black Aesthetic, although he raises serious questions concerning it. He does, however, leave the major thesis untouched. The Black Aesthetic movement is the first literary movement in history dedicated to constructing images and metaphors which are meant to free men, rather than to enslave them; to elevate rather than to subjugate them. (p. 47)

I have read *Voices in the Whirlwind* twice; I will read it again. This, in addition to the fact that I have spent as much time arguing with Mphahlele as I have in evaluating his book, indicates something, I suppose, of how interesting and moving a document it is. . . . [But] the problems which face mankind are not to be solved by the Europeans, old or new; and the Black writer, if he is to begin the arduous task of creating a just and humane world, must step outside of the cultural history of the West, move away from literary and critical theories which enslave instead of liberate.

I believe this to mean nothing more than that I exercise the right to formulate my own truth—a truth which is in no way binding upon Mphahlele. For, in the final analysis, he has done his job well: he has written a moving critical document and asked the important questions; he has added to the storehouse of information which increases understanding. He has forced us to look anew at Africa, Europe, the Caribbean, and America; at Afro-Americans, Pan-Africanists and the proponents of Negritude and the Black Aesthetic. One senses from his book that he is both an honest writer and a good man. For one who has been so long involved with the West, this is a remarkable achievement. (pp. 47-8)

Addison Gayle, Jr., ''Under Western Eyes'' (reprinted by permission of the author; copyright, 1973 Addison Gayle in Black World, *Vol. XXII, No. 9, July, 1973, pp. 40-8.*

RHONDA JONES

Chinua Achebe and Ezekiel Mphahlele in various publications have addressed themselves to questions regarding the role of the African writer and his art. They view art as a craft that is responsible to African society, and as artists, regard themselves accountable to their societies. But there is often a contradiction between what they stated in articles, interviews, etc. . . . and what their early literatures actually express. It seems, that having realized this they are now working hard towards making their literatures committed to their society. (p. 119)

Unlike Achebe who adapts certain western aesthetics to an African context, Ezekiel Mphahlele uses it as a reference point in discussing his art. To him art is a craft and a vehicle for social criticism. Throughout his development as a critic and writer, he has demonstrated a reliance on western aesthetics. The chapter entitled, ''White on Black'', the subject of his B.A. thesis at the University of South Africa and which appears in *The African Image* . . . , reflects his feelings about art as expressing the paradoxes and complexities of life-concepts that have their roots in western aesthetics. . . . In ''White on Black'' he selects Joseph Conrad, E. M. Forster and William Faulkner as the three major white novelists who achieve a competency in depicting cultural groups other than their own. Mphahlele selects these authors primarily because they are able to go beyond the race problem in depicting human character, and into the more subtle aspects of human existence. There is no doubt that he identifies with literature that attempts to depict the complexities of life.

Prior to the publication of his work entitled *Voices in the Whirlwind*, . . . Mphahlele asks, ''Why should *la litterature engagée* be so spoiled as to want to be judged by different standards from those which have been tested by tradition?'' . . . In **''Voices in the Whirlwind''** Mphahlele addresses two literary audiences: those individuals from the western literary tradition, and those Black Americans who are attempting to define a new aesthetic, stressing that there is a standard of literary ideas and concepts, whose roots are in western culture, but which could take on another dimension when used by other cultural groups. Agreeing with the architects of western literary tradition that poetry has moral overtones and that the language of poetry is memorable, he concludes that the poetry of conflict by Black American poets expresses a deep-felt emotion. . . . Mphahlele infers that the uniquely black character that Black American literature is trying to assert may not be so unique. . . . Mphahlele then warns against the danger of ''finding ourselves'' having out of sheer crusading zeal, dismissed elements of Western aesthetics that are either built in our new modes of expression or have already been criticized by western critics. (pp. 121-22)

His attitude that literature is a criticism of life has much to do with his experiences in South Africa where the economic, political and social conditions of Blacks demands a response from black South African writers. Consequently his autobiographical novel, *Down Second Avenue* . . . "the autobiography of most Africans" criticizes and responds to the quality of life in South Africa. Employing a remarkably subtle yet alarming tone, Mphahlele is able to re-examine with seriousness and warmth past experiences from his life in South Africa. Chapters 1-2 present what life is like in the rural sector of the country. It is not only the poverty that arouses his memory, but the communal fellowship that he experienced with friends and family. Yet, in a scene around a fireplace, he is able to capture the disturbing realities that hover over this communal setting. . . . The following chapters describe what it is like to live in urban cities of South Africa. The references to poverty of black people in the townships carry a message and yet are well integrated into the framework of the story, thus increasing the impact. To illustrate the psychological damages that life in South Africa does to the black man, he describes one of his characters, Dinku Dikae as a man who trembles at the presence of the law but whose repressed fear ultimately surfaces leading to the murder of a policeman. Thus the quality of life under apartheid affects both blacks and whites.

Whereas Chinua Achebe and Ezekiel Mphahlele are very conservative and western oriented in their writings about the role of African writers and their art, their public pronouncements and their poems have gone the opposite direction, pointing the way their literary works hopefully would follow. (pp. 123-24)

For Mphahlele the language of poetry communicates on a personal as well as communal level. . . . His poem, **"Death II"** . . . demonstrates how art can serve a particular ethnic group within society. **"Death II"** asserts a positive image to the Black South African. It shows the growth of political consciousness of a young South African, beginning with him as a young boy looking at the statue of Paul Kruger. The statue, a symbol of the ruthless authority that came to South Africa and is now present in the country, instills fear in the youth. . . . As the poem progresses the history of the confrontation between Whites and Africans unfolds. The youth Masilo sees the illusion and the lies behind the history of the "master race" and recognizes the effects of the pillage and plunder of Kruger and his men. . . .

The final scenes of the poem show the present condition of the young man who is imprisoned for retaliating against the South African government. What has preceded has been a dream of the different levels of political consciousness that led to the open vengeance. At death Masilo's convictions are strong and his spirit appeased. (p. 126)

The socio-political conditions in South Africa have also influenced Ezekiel Mphahlele's concept of himself as an artist. At the beginning of his writing career in 1941, he was interested in writing about people as people and not as political victims. It was not until he became a teacher and felt the political pressures that his writing took a new direction. He wrote a number of things in *Drum* Magazine about the ghetto people and the political pressures over them. From this point on he consistently viewed his role as that of a social critic of society. In the chapter entitled, "Black on Black", of the *African Image* he feels that the South African writer has a dual responsibility.

The South African writer must act as a political man as well as practice his craft. . . .

Mphahlele's article, "African Writers and Commitment" . . . which appears in *Voices in the Whirlwind* states his views on the committed artist. He feels that a writer can take a stand without using propaganda. He then follows this statement by, "Every writer is committed to something beyond his art, to a statement of values not purely aesthetic—to criticizing life."

Mphahlele also sees the paradox of the committed artist who chooses to write rather than physically become involved in the struggle in South Africa. He asks himself, how can the African artist who deals with paradox, irony, symbols, images, reconcile a play of words with the urgent problems of poverty and racism in his society. Mphahlele has come to terms with this dilemma. He feels that working with images and symbols can help him understand the interconnectedness of life's experiences. The artist rather performs a cultural act. Literary technique is not useless because of its subject matter. (p. 129)

Rhonda Jones, "Art and Social Responsibility: Two Paths to Commitment," in UFAHAMU *(copyright 1976, Regents of the University of California), Vol. VI, No. 2, 1976, pp. 119-31.**

URSULA A. BARNETT

[*Man Must Live* is] Mphahlele's first collection of short stories. . . . (p. 17)

Although the characters in the stories are not as yet realistic portraits of the earthy people among whom he lived, *Man Must Live* already sets the pattern for Mphahlele's future writing in its dependence on personal experience. It is tempting in all Mphahlele's writing to spot the corresponding incident or character in his life, but this can obviously serve no useful purpose except to demonstrate authenticity. . . .

It is the mental, rather than the factual experience, however, that constitutes the material for his writing. "Whatever I write," he tells us, "will always be rooted in my boyhood experiences." These experiences, he says, helped to define his responses to life wherever he lived. This he calls the "tyranny of place," but a tyranny "that gives me the base to write, the very reason to write." (p. 19)

In these stories, as in his later fiction, Mphahlele often identifies with the chief characters and shares their thoughts and feelings. (p. 20)

Zungu, the hero of **"Man Must Live,"** makes a cult of the philosophy of survival to replace the ethics more acceptable to the world around him: "Let men accuse, deride and ridicule you in your actions; let them complain that you don't respect or fear them; let them say you don't earn your living honestly; but they too, sooner or later, will come down to the hard, cold and indisputable fact that man must live." (p. 22)

Mphahlele's characters know, or come to realize, that they must survive, not physically or communally, but spiritually as individuals, by strictly adhering to a moral code. This code is not necessarily identical with the morals accepted by the community in which they live. Courage, for example, does not have to mean facing the common enemy, but rather maintaining the truth as you yourself see it. (p. 23)

In **"Tomorrow You Shall Reap"** and in **"Unwritten Episodes"** the theme of survival does not motivate the characters. Rather, there is the conventional moral of virtue rewarded. It seems likely that these stories were written earlier, and it would have been better to exclude them. "Unwritten Episodes" is at times embarrassingly mawkish, and the language is stilted and often incorrect. The plot, in which love conquers all, could appear in a true confession periodical. . . .

There is little in this story, or in "Tomorrow You Shall Reap," that points to future creative ability. In the latter, Mphahlele does show some skill in conveying the feeling of simple love between a shy boy and a more sophisticated girl. The plot is even less convincing than that of "Unwritten Episodes," and far more melodramatic. (p. 25)

Mphahlele is . . . aware today of the amateurishness and sentimentality of the stories, but on the other hand he exaggerates in his mind the element of escapism. The protest, the struggle against oppressive external circumstances, is implied, even if the pressures have not as yet made him bitter. (p. 26)

Mphahlele's autobiography, Down Second Avenue, ends with his departure from South Africa. He wrote the first half in South Africa during 1956 and 1957 and completed it in Nigeria soon after he had settled there and begun to teach. In doing so, he was following a trend as well as making a notable contribution: autobiography became a popular form of expression among black South African writers during this time for several reasons. They needed to confirm a sense of identity, particularly those writers who had emerged from the slums and provided their own education. But they wrote the stories of their lives, and found publishers for them, chiefly because direct experience was far more exciting in content and characterization than anything they could invent. The outlets for short stories had practically all fallen away, and none of the writers felt that they had skill and experience sufficient for tackling a true novel. The Afro-American writers whom they admired, James Baldwin, Richard Wright, and others, had all written about themselves. (p. 50)

[In Down Second Avenue Mphahlele is] surprisingly reticent about many aspects of his personal life. The love story of his youth with a girl named Rebone is one of the weakest chapters, for instance, and we never get close to his wife, Rebecca. The search for identity is the theme of the book, but the author as self obtrudes only in occasional deeply personal revelations. This reticence is due to an innate shyness and consequent aloofness, which often led to an inability to communicate verbally with those closest to him and set him apart as a lonely and often unhappy figure. . . .

Yet, paradoxically, he succeeds in imparting the spirit of his experiences. The book was at first envisaged as a novel and is still sometimes regarded as such, in the same way as Camara Laye's The African Child and Herman Bosman's personal experiences in a South African prison, Cold Stone Jug, are catalogued under fiction. (p. 51)

Whether Down Second Avenue is strictly true in fact is of no importance. It is doubtless a true account in spirit of Mphahlele's life and that of the people around him. Even in his avowed fiction Mphahlele never compromises with the truth for the sake of dramatic effect or sentiment, as others are often tempted to do in their autobiographical writing. (p. 52)

What, then, is Down Second Avenue? We have examined its theme and its purpose. In contents it is a mixture of dramatic action, of sketches, of introspection and comments. It is typical of Mphahlele's writing other than his short stories, in that he

refuses to adhere to an established category; yet there is a considerable amount of unity. The story takes us from his earliest memories as a boy of five in the country to his departure from South Africa. . . .

It is the control and dramatization of his feelings, rather than the chronology of his life or the scheme to which the contents are loosely organized, that hold the book together. This he achieves without conscious effort. Action often becomes the vehicle of thought or emotional growth. Dramatization of bitter experiences helps him to keep the feeling of bitterness under control. (p. 53)

He is less successful when he cannot feel an incident as real, or identify with a situation emotionally. The tragic story of Dinku Dikae, who is terrified of policemen until the insults of one of them drives him to murder, seems beyond Mphahlele's powers. What should have been tragic climax to the love story of young Ezekiel and Dinku Dikae's daughter, Rebone, is recounted in retrospect and reads like a day-old newspaper story.

Most of the chapters start with a brief general description, followed by an incident which shows how his life is affected by the events or circumstances described. (p. 54)

Some of the incidents are written almost in the form of short stories, such as the chapter headed "Ma-Lebona" which became the short story "The Woman." . . .

Some of the stories or incidents are in a humorous vein. Most end tragically like the story of the sweet potato seller. Life is harsh, and it is here, on Second Avenue, that Mphahlele learns that man must live and make the best of his circumstances. (p. 55)

Once Mphahlele leaves Second Avenue, the work becomes more conventionally autobiographical. The interest for the reader now lies in his admiration for the achievements of the writer and for his political stand. There is no longer the spontaneity and aliveness of the earlier chapters. The narrative tends to ramble, and the ramifications of the political and the educational controversies are not sufficiently explained to make them clear from a distance in time and place. (pp. 57-8)

In the potpourri of theme and subject matter that is Down Second Avenue, one expects, and indeed finds, a variety of styles. When reliving periods of mental and spiritual conflicts and depression, the story seems to stagger and continue in small leaps. As bitterness becomes deeper and his despondency thickens, the writing becomes slower and laden, sometimes overladen, with imagery. . . . Yet there is always control. Bitterness and anger are never allowed to get out of hand. (p. 58)

As always, Mphahlele is at his best when describing the active world around him. Second Avenue is presented as it was almost without comment. (p. 59)

Down Second Avenue is by no means a static canvas painted in drab and monotonous tones of despair. It is the aliveness of the characters, and their efforts to rise above their circumstances, that distinguishes this work and sets it above the autobiographies of his contemporaries among black South African writers. Once again the individuals, major and minor, are, like Ma-Lebona, "there" and allow "you no room to forget [they were] born and [are] alive in flesh and spirit."

We learn to know them through incidents in which they are involved or through their casual encounters with each other.

Dialogue is always earthy and colloquial, and interspersed with proverbs and literal translations from the vernacular. This often has the effect of providing a touch of humor and further relieving the gravity of the account. (p. 60)

As the main character in a novel, if we are to regard the book as such, Ezekiel emerges without conscious effort. It is unlikely that Mphahlele even realized that he was drawing the portrait of a hero, a man brave and uncompromising when the situation demanded it, yet sensitive, a little aloof, a writer who in another time and place might have turned to nature for inspiration. We watch his emotional growth and his reaction to the forces that mold him. (p. 62)

Down Second Avenue is still as relevant today as it was in 1959. As a social record it is unique. As a human document it is more moving than anything that has come out of South Africa besides Alan Paton's *Cry, the Beloved Country* and Olive Schreiner's *Story of an African Farm*. (p. 65)

The stories in the collection *The Living and Dead and Other Stories* were all written in South Africa. . . .

The collection no longer has the autobiographical unity of *Down Second Avenue* or the unity of background of the "Lesane" stories [printed in Drum Magazine] and the stories in *Man Must Live*. (p. 70)

Most of the plots concern conflict between black and white. The stories represent the protest stage of Mphahlele's writing. Although they were written in South Africa, he selected them a year or two after he had left. They must thus be considered as reflecting his state of mind at the time: bitter, disillusioned. The race theme is predominant. Characters are black or white in character, according to the color of their skin. (pp. 70-1)

The title story of the collection, "The Living and Dead," suffers from the same disadvantage as most stories written in protest against a system. Plot and character have little chance to develop, either spontaneously toward a pleasing work of art, or according to the laws of probability and the principles of psychology. They have to suit a purpose extraneous to fiction. The theme thus becomes illustrative of the writer's outlook rather than arising out of it. . . .

In his protest writing Mphahlele's compassion for humanity leads to a flaw in understanding. He cannot envisage others not sharing his deep feeling for his fellowmen and can thus attribute the racial feelings of the South African white man only to guilt. Sadly, the major reason for racial hatred is fear, and for lack of understanding pure indifference. In the South African context the events and characters of "The Living and Dead" are impossible.

The main character is a white man, the Afrikaner Stoffel Visser. The only Afrikaners, or Boers as he prefers to call them, Mphahlele knew at this time were petty government officials on the other side of a counter, policemen, and employers with whom he had little personal contact and whom he regarded as "machines." Now, in order to portray them in fiction, Mphahlele had to animate such machines and visualize these cold and unfriendly people at home. The result is caricature. (p. 71)

Not only does Stoffel Visser remain an inanimate concept, but he is such a mass of contradictions that he cannot even function as a symbol. (p. 73)

The little action there is in the story tends to stall. The style of writing lacks the usual animation. The white men's dialogue, which covers the first few pages, is stilted to the point of being embarrassing. . . . (pp. 74-5)

Equally unsatisfactory both as a piece of fiction and as a study in race relations is "We'll Have Dinner at Eight." Miss Pringle, the principal white character, is a little more plausible than Stoffel, at least in so far as we learn to know her. . . . We are left in no doubt how we are to feel about Miss Pringle right from the beginning. Her efforts to win black friends were undertaken "with an eternal smile on her lips." Miss Pringle is hypocritical, self-deceiving, and sexually frustrated. Mzondi, who comes to the welfare institution to learn a trade, appears to Miss Pringle as an answer to her needs. He is poor and crippled, and therefore helpless and in need of her care; and he is a man whose "pathetic beautiful lips" and "steady eyes, almost expressionless" intrigue her. To befriend him becomes a passion with her.

Miss Pringle is utterly repulsive. Mphahlele may have intended to arouse our sympathy for her, but his dislike of a type prevented him from creating a character. The irony of her murder by the man she befriends therefore fails to appear tragic, and the theme of misunderstanding between black and white falls flat. (p. 75)

This is one of Mphahlele's few short stories with sexual overtones. The irony of the contrapuntal themes is promising, the spinster who hides her unconscious sexual longings behind the cloak of a dogooder and the lack of comprehension of the cripple to whom anyone who represents an unjust law and therefore danger. There is neither tragedy nor pathos, however, partly because of the poorly motivated murder . . . but mainly because of the lack of sympathy for or even interest in the two protagonists. No real attempt is made to explore either Mzondi's or Miss Pringle's human motives. These are merely hinted at and are not developed to the point where compassion can envelop both contenders.

What is the message of the story? There is condemnation of a legal system which is prejudiced against the black man. Mzondi is acquitted of the crime of theft he did commit, but the judge refuses to believe the story of his beating by the police in spite of the evidence. The conclusion one draws from the story is one of hopelessness in racial relations. If white shows signs of friendliness toward black, white's motives are suspect; black cannot accept such friendship under any terms, since it cannot be trusted. (pp. 76-7)

The ironic twists of life are . . . the subject of "The Suitcase." Here the irony is a little too obvious to make the plot plausible, although, ironically, Mphahlele says in *Down Second Avenue* that it is in essence a true story, told to him by his wife. . . . Timi, unemployed and desperate, is waiting for "sheer naked chance" to find a way of bringing a present to his wife on Old Year's Eve. He finds it on a bus when a woman passenger apparently forgets to take her suitcase. Another passenger sees Timi take it and reports him to the police. He is caught, and at the police station repeatedly swears that the case is his. But he has played with fate and lost. The case contains a dead baby.

Although unlikely, the plot is tight and the characters plausible. (p. 81)

The theme of this story is not the vagaries of fate, but the choices man has before him. Timi confuses the two component elements of chance. He speaks of taking advantage of a chance and of being provided with a lucky chance as though it were the same thing. It is this confusion between chance as fate and chance with an option that leads to his downfall. (p. 82)

Timi may not have the stature of a hero; his choice is not a matter of life and death and his downfall only an eighteen months' jail sentence. Nevertheless, this is tragedy in the classical sense. However far-fetched the plot, the theme arises spontaneously out of plot and characters, and the story is perhaps Mphahlele's most successful piece of fiction. (p. 83)

The only new stories [in Mphahlele's last collection of short stories, *In Corner B*] were "The Barber of Bariga," "Grieg on a Stolen Piano" (which contains incidents from *Down Second Avenue*), the title story, "A Ballad of Oyo," "A Point of Identity," and "Mrs. Plum."

As an African rather than a South African writer, Mphahlele very likely now felt that he must face the responsibility he mentions in *The African Image* of inventing plot and constructing characters outside the ready-made plots provided by the racial question. Yet only two of the stories are based outside South Africa, although Mphahlele had now been away for ten years. With South Africa as a background, the racial question is of course predominant, but in at least one of the new stories he goes far more deeply into the problems of racial attitudes than he has done before. The two non-South African stories show a certain unease. Mphahlele found it difficult to become emotionally involved in Nigerian affairs, while at the same time the enforced passivity probably made him unhappy.

Passivity in the face of the turmoil around him is the theme of ["The Barber of Bariga"]. Here Mphahlele expresses his reaction to the currents and cross-currents of life in an independent African state through his main character, the barber Anofi, a passive man who refuses to become emotionally involved in his surroundings. (p. 85)

[Such] withdrawal, Mphahlele makes it clear, is reprehensible. No one is entitled to go through life as a spectator as Anofi does, ignoring the throbbing world around him, the cavalcade of drum-beating masqueraders, of weddings and funeral processions that pass by the window of the barbershop, and the blaring, pulsating noise emanating from the radio shop across the road. (p. 86)

Yet one feels that Mphahlele, like Anofi, is not really involved in the life of the people in the story. As a result, the account seems suffused rather than neat and confined. It fails both to make a point and to uphold interest. (p. 87)

The only other story with a Nigerian background is "A Ballad of Oyo." . . .

The Yoruba markets of West Africa have fascinated both foreign and local writers through the years. To Mphahlele, as to others, there is poetry in the market that tingles and buzzes and groans, and never ceases, come rain, come blood, come malaria; its roar and chatter and laughter and exclamation and smells make a live symphony, quite independent of the people milling around it; the women behind the counters walk the black tarmac road to and from the market, walking, riding, the dawn, walking into sunrise, their bodies twisting at the hip.

"A Ballad of Oyo" is the story of one of the women, Ishola, also known as Mama-Jimi. (p. 88)

Mphahlele calls the story a ballad to emphasize the folk-tale element. He uses various devices to create the illusion of a tale by an observer who has fallen under the spell of the market. Words and phrases are repeated to simulate narrative verse,

for example: "And so goes the story of Ishola, Ishola, who was called Mama-Jimi, a mother of three children." . . .

These effects give the story the air of a tragic tale, something of importance. This, however, is not borne out by the story itself. Here we have a woman who is attractive, who is misused by her husband, and who decides to leave him for another man, but changes her mind when the call to traditional duty claims her. We never learn to know Ishola, and she thus fails to arouse our sympathy. Other characters are introduced to little purpose: Ishola's sister who encourages her to leave her husband, and the president of the court who accepts bribes but, for reasons not explained, hands them back.

The market, although ostensibly so important to the story as a background—it is the ballad of Oyo, the market of Oyo, not of Ishola and her problems—does not really become an integral part of it. The fact that Ishola sells vegetables and fruit there is irrelevant to what befalls her. There is no direction in either plot or setting. Thus it is with relief that we turn back to the South African stories in the collection. (p. 89)

"Grieg on a Stolen Piano" is perhaps Mphahlele's most successful attempt [to come to terms with a world of physical and mental violence]. He reverts to a background in which he is most at home. Once again he draws heavily on his own life. (p. 90)

"Grieg on a Stolen Piano" follows the earlier story "Man Must Live" in the collection. Like its predecessor, it also tells of the deterioration of a character, triggered off by circumstances beyond his control, but intrinsically arising out of his character. (p. 91)

Although "Grieg on a Stolen Piano," after the novella-length "Mrs. Plum," is the longest story in the collection, there is nothing extraneous to the serious theme of black intellectual struggle in the South African setting. It is a telling condemnation of a society in which a black man of intellect and integrity must founder. Scenes of black-white violent encounter are described realistically, and yet this is not a protest story in the same sense as "We'll Have Dinner at Eight." The protest in "Grieg" arises out of the action of the story.

Here is an economy of words which one does not always find in Mphahlele's writing. . . . The dialogue is always just right and captures South African speech idiom of both black and white. Even the few white characters speak idiomatically, instead of indulging in the stilted talk of "The Living and Dead." (pp. 93-4)

The similes and metaphors Mphahlele uses in ["Grieg"] are refreshingly unusual. (p. 94)

Neither cynicism nor sentimentality mars this successful sketch of a memorable character, which would easily have lent itself to either. . . .

In "A Point of Identity" Mphahlele deals more specifically with the political situation in South Africa. We are introduced to the laws that govern the lives of black people, and how they affect them. . . . Sardonically, the author describes the coldness of law and its remoteness from human feelings. (p. 95)

Mphahlele takes us back to Second Avenue in this story, but he sees it with a different eye. Karel may be a man whose whole physical being seemed to be made of laughter,'' but we only have the narrator's word for it. Karel is not funny in any way, neither in his talk nor in his actions. He has none of the vitality of the earlier township characters. He lacks, in fact, any kind of personality at all. Since the story concerns only his racial dilemma and ends with his death as a solution, it never arises above the political level. Mphahlele is justifiably bitter about South African laws and he is articulate in his protest, but he uses neither invention nor imagery to turn the narrative into imaginative fiction. It is a stirring record of injustice, but so are the many newspaper reports of similar cases, some even more tragic. The narrator's comments read like editorials.

By contrast Talita, in the title story ["**In Corner B**"], is alive, and the background of township life is woven into the story as an integral part of it. Whereas Karel Almeida is described for the reader, the characters in "**In Corner B**" and their background come to life through their actions. (p. 97)

Mphahlele does not use the convention of a narrator in this story, but comments freely as the author upon his characters and their lives. His "asides" from the dramatic action are full of affectionate humor about the people among whom he used to live. (pp. 97-8)

The plot of the story concerns the love between Talita and her husband. It is a simple and unembellished love story, tender without sentimentality. (p. 98)

Mphahlele has learnt the effect of and necessity for comic relief after a tense and dramatic scene. (pp. 99-100)

The alternation between scenes of the quiet and tender past and the noisy present provides a most effective contrast. Equally successful is the contrast between the reality of death and the humor of a scene in which a black constable drags in two disreputable young suspects in handcuffs for Talita to identify. (p. 100)

The more one reads Mphahlele's stories of township life, the greater becomes one's understanding of the term "acceptance" he uses to describe a phase in his fiction. This is not acceptance of township conditions or of life in South Africa; rather acceptance of the fact that human values of love, trust, and loyalty can continue even under impossible living conditions. In this story he calls it "surrender" rather than acceptance, a poetic surrender to life and death, underlying which is "the one long and huge irony of endurance."

The background is never allowed to obtrude for its own sake. At this time African writing was becoming popular with European readers, and many writers deliberately emphasized the un-European aspect of African life by giving lengthy anthropological explanations. With Mphahlele, on the other hand, African customs become an essential part of the story. Talita can lie back and indulge in her bittersweet memories because she knows that tradition and custom will take care of everything necessary for the wake and funeral. Interspersed with her thoughts are the inevitable acts and movements leading steadily toward the last rites for the dead. The story is static neither in the present nor in the past but leads toward their meeting place in organized rhythm.

Another well-organized story is the novella, "**Mrs. Plum.**" This is Mphahlele's most serious attempt to explore the relationship between white and black in South Africa. (pp. 101-02)

[A] subtle irony . . . raises this story, like "**Grieg on a Stolen Piano**" above the mere protest level. (p. 102)

[We] gradually realize that while Mrs. Plum's liberalism is quite genuine, unlike that of Miss Pringle, it is completely impersonal, directed at ideas rather than at people. Mphahlele dislikes this type so intensely because it lacks the one characteristic that is his own ruling passion: a feeling of compassion for one's fellowmen. (p. 103)

The story is a tragic one because of its inner and factual truth. It is the tragedy of South Africa. Here are two people, each representing her race in some of its better qualities, who genuinely try to understand each other, and fail miserably. (p. 107)

Mphahlele describes "**Mrs. Plum,**" still today as "the best thing I ever pulled off." (p. 110)

Mphahlele completed a new novel some time ago, but it is still awaiting publication. "Kwacha! A Bright New Day" was its original title [eventually changed to "**Chirundu**"]. . . .

The action takes place in the 1960's in Zambia, although the country is never named. By placing the action beyond the border of South Africa, Mphahlele is moving into the mainstream of African literature. (p. 158)

"**Chirundu**" is the story of the fall from power of a political figure, Chimba Chirundu, and of the dissolution of his marriage. Mphahlele professes to explore the dynamics of power in relation to domestic life, marital relations, the African's attitude toward polygamy, and the modern woman's rejection of it. At the same time it is a study of African independence and its effect of hope and disillusionment on several people bound together by circumstances or relationships. (p. 159)

We expect a writer of Mphahlele's standing to turn to a novel . . . only if he has something important to communicate, not merely to entertain. Yet at a first reading "**Chirundu**" seems almost trivial. It begins by introducing a cabinet minister as having committed a crime so petty that even his prisoners are contemptuous. The prisoners feel, however, that there must be something behind it, and it seems obvious that Mphahlele intended something deeper in the novel than the chicaneries of the vain, power-hungry, male-chauvinistic character of the title.

"**Chirundu**," it would appear, is a dirge for Africa, where anguished disillusionment is the keynote. Hope for a bright new day is dim indeed. At the beginning of the novel "*kwacha*" is the unreasoning faith of the simple-minded prison warden; at the end the losing battle against forces that destroy the hope of Africa is dismissed with a shrug. In *The Wanderers* the South African characters were searching for a better life. Here, in Zambia, with the arrival of independence, people thought that they had found it, but expectation turned to disillusionment and bitterness. (pp. 163-64)

By calling the novel "**Chirundu**," Mphahlele emphasizes the character rather than the theme. It might be better to revert to one of the earlier titles, the sardonic "**Bright New Day,**" or the symbolic "**House of Chirundu,**" since the portrayal of the title character is not a happy one. Chimba Chirundu embodies the African politician at the dawn of the independence era. The idealism—the fight for independence and social democracy—is already taken for granted and the practical aspect is emphasized. Chirundu lives in the present. He rejects Christianity along with all European ideas that had been dumped on Africa, as he puts it, but he believes in traditionalism only if it serves a purpose, or as individual choice, never as a stance. He is motivated entirely by a thirst for power, politically, personally, and sexually. Power to him is an area in which he can express himself. He loves it for its own sake and appears confident in his "profession." (p. 165)

Chirundu is a man filled with hate and guilt. In his childhood he saw his father disintegrate after conversion to Christianity. . . . The father abandons one wife while the other, Chimba's mother, later leaves him. Chimba makes his own way in life by clinging tenaciously to his grandfather's prediction that he was meant for great things. . . . Even after his downfall, when he has nothing left but his determination and faith in himself, he feels sure that he will make a come-back. We are reminded of Zungu in **"Man Must Live."** Has Mphahlele then come full circle, abandoning his search and his wanderings to conclude that all man can do is cling tenaciously to his faith in life and his destiny? This would be understandable, since Mphahlele is still in exile, displaced, with hope of a return to the country of his destiny as remote as ever.

If, however, we are being asked to admire Chirundu for this quality, then the character sketch is an abject failure. Chirundu is totally unsympathetic and repulsive. He is introduced in the novel as so contemptible to his enemies, the refugees he has imprisoned, that they cannot even hate him. Little follows to change this first impression. He rejects Christianity because of the enslaving institutions to which it gave rise, but does not accept faith in the ancestors, an alternative that would also have provided him with the sense of humility that his father had found wanting in him.

In love he is insensitive, callous, and entirely selfish. He tells the superintendent of the church school that he will not be pushed into marrying Tirenje (after he has made her pregnant) just to satisfy the church's scruples, but he does not seem to have considered the girl's feelings in the matter. He ignores the feelings of the two women entirely, and acts in the matter of his two marriages purely for his own purposes. Sometimes he feels guilt, but never real remorse.

Intelligent, capable, and ruthless, he has no difficulty in achieving his ambitions in love and in his career. (pp. 165-66)

Unpleasant as he is, Chirundu comes to life to a greater extent than the other characters. (p. 167)

Mphahlele does not seem to be deeply involved with [the characters] as he was with the people in *The Wanderers*. As a result they lack interest and tend to make the novel dull. Lack of tension is aggravated by the method of narration.

Mphahlele again favors the vehicle of several narrators, presumably to show various points of view, but this time it leads to confusion. (p. 168)

Mphahlele's style has become simpler and more colloquial. The dialogue, however, is often as stilted as in his very early fiction, and the slick sophisticated slang does not always flow easily from his pen. (p. 169)

This is Mphahlele's first truly African novel. He now accepts a background completely remote from the Christian-Western European townships of the Transvaal. The plot is based on the concept that polygamy, even if controversial, is psychologically and morally possible. In his earlier fiction characters had doubts about the church to which they belonged, but here he goes deeply into African religion and the effects of conversion to Christianity. The African's veneration of old age is clearly expressed and becomes a reality. . . .

The contrast between the dignity of the country and the corruption and superficiality of the city is also new in Mphahlele's fiction. It is personified by Chirundu's two women and appears again in a description of what happens after the death of Moyo's grandfather. (p. 170)

Starkly dramatic symbols are another innovation, though at times they appear Elizabethan rather than African. (p. 171)

[In all his writings, Mphahlele's main objective has been] to reproduce, grasp, and interpret what is essential and permanent in life and literature. A gentle man, he has turned his anguish and bitterness into an acceptance of a situation, not as one that he cannot change, but as an existing condition under which one can still find meaning in life. He has taught the younger writers that to know one's sorrow is to know one's joy. He has worked toward a balance between artistic integrity and social involvement. He not only talks about this in his essays and lectures, but demonstrates it in his fiction and autobiographical works. These, at their best, succeed through their vibrancy in translating his concepts into a living art. (p. 174)

> *Ursula A. Barnett, in her* Ezekiel Mphahlele *(copyright © 1976 by Twayne Publishers, Inc.; reprinted with the permission of Twayne Publishers, a Division of G. K. Hall & Co., Boston), Twayne, 1976, 195 p.*

ADRIAN ROSCOE

The problem of imagination in South African writing . . . is illustrated by the career of Ezekiel Mphahlele, scholar, teacher, lucid provocative critic, wanderer, and creative writer, a man whose experience in a rough world (badly treated even in independent Africa) has turned a deeply compassionate view of humanity into a conviction that only guns and violence can cure the cancer of apartheid in Vorster's Republic. It is not that Mphahlele lacks imagination. Far from it. Various collections of short stories such as *In Corner B* and *Let Live,* and *The Living & the Dead,* and a substantial though highly autobiographical novel *The Wanderers* . . . are evidence enough of an imaginative gift. Nor were the strengths of his first major critical book, *The African Image,* which added a wholly new dimension to African critical debates especially as they concerned negritude, underestimated, to say nothing of his most recent work, *Voices in the Whirlwind.* . . . It is simply that he feels that his autobiography *Down Second Avenue* . . . is the best book, presumably the most important book he has yet written; as if, in other words, the workaday South African scene is too fraught with pain and urgency for mere fiction, no matter how clever, to take precedence over the naked truth hauled up from the well of memory and set forth with care in an autobiography. Even his description of how the creative process worked in him while still at home makes a similar point about how close to daily reality the short stories are. Written in almost immediate response to sudden provocation, they have, on his own evidence, enjoyed little time for a slow steady fictive reworking of raw material where the fancy and imagination lift mundane stuff into the realms of literary art. Mphahlele strikes no poses [and] sees himself in the role of neither prophet nor messiah. . . . (pp. 228-29)

As individual pieces, the short stories are not always distinguished. Sometimes it is stretches of slack prose that reduce their impact; sometimes the standards of a professional teacher break through and impose a correctness and a propriety where 'fluency' should rule. Sometimes it is the very struggle between correctness and the desire to run free and capture the registers and dialect of the people that becomes obvious and therefore a weakness. But Mphahlele's stories as a group, a body, a collection, are excellent. From **'Man Must Live',** where a whole life span is squeezed into the strait-jacket tightness of the short story form, to **'A Point of Identity'**, which explores the tragi-comic complexities of the colour bar, to **'Mrs. Plum'** and **'The Living and the Dead'**, which play very deftly on the workings of the white South African mind, liberal or otherwise, the evidence accumulates that no other writer, with the exception of La Guma, can record with such delicacy the slow tragic harmonies that lie beneath the trivia, the unpolished surface of poor lives. The sad division among the various non-white groups which is subtly fostered by the white community is often reflected together with a plea for the kind of solidarity needed to unite all the oppressed groups against a common enemy. . . . The same note of needful solidarity and grim endurance rings through **'In Corner B'**, one of Mphahlele's finest stories. (pp. 229-30)

What the stories reveal constantly is the response to a brutal system of a mind fundamentally humane, free itself of brutality, and free too of racist blinkers. With the portrait of Stoffel Visser in **'The Living and the Dead'** there is even briefly canvassed the belief in white conversion; and despite the swelling bitterness of recent years . . . , Mphahlele's career is redolent with the signs of a soul that has laboured hard, nailing courage and hope to the mast of human decency and affirming the value of sacrifice. Even more, the most eloquent testimony of Mphahlele's writing is their author's basic and passionate concern not with himself but with other people, those he knew in his youth and childhood, whose difficulties and aspirations he shares and understands. This quality infuses all Mphahlele's writing and makes **Down Second Avenue** . . . perhaps the least ego-centric autobiography ever written. This is a remarkable if uneven work. . . . (p. 231)

Adrian Roscoe, "Central and Southern African Prose," in his Uhuru's Fire: African Literature East to South *(© Cambridge University Press 1977), Cambridge University Press, 1977, pp. 215-58.**

SAMUEL OMO ASEIN

There are a few African writers who have contributed much to the development of modern African literature and have had little written about them. Of the few, the black South African writer, Ezekiel Mphahlele, stands out rather pathetically as a much neglected, generally underestimated and often misjudged writer. (p. 38)

The reasons for the neglect which Mphahlele has suffered in the last decade seem obvious. I believe he is not 'popular', especially among the younger generation, because of his views, more often than not misinterpreted, on sensitive issues of race, inter-personal relationships and the destiny of the black man in the contemporary world. For well over thirty years, his integrationist attitudes as a person and as a writer have been progressively moulded into more definable shapes by a distinctly humanist vision which has its roots in Mphahlele's firm belief in the eternal value of a brotherhood that does not compromise man's essential humanity. It is that vision too which serves as the pivotal element in his artistic creations as well as the formative factor of his personality as an individual. Such indeed has been the close relationship between his two personalities as an artist and as individual that he could assert unequivocally the essential Mphahlele: "As for what I really am, and my place in the African revolution, I shall let my writings speak for me." Mphahlele's writings do provide us with just that testimony. (p. 39)

When he wrote his earliest short stories which subsequently appeared in the collection **Man Must Live**, his one absorbing interest was in "people as people rather than as political victims," and he sought to focus on ordinary South African blacks and coloureds "in their own ghetto life and their own little dramas and tragedies." His style and perspective followed in the humanist tradition which his mentors [Richard Wright and Langston Hughes] represented. In the last few years, Mphahlele has become visibly absorbed in the quest for a new socio-political order which would accommodate his vision and whose very foundation would rest on what he defines as a "more genuine cross-cultural nationalism."

Thus in his short stories his first interest usually centres on the human condition which they help him to illustrate. In these stories there is more often than not an articulate statement of what constitutes the reality of that condition and how it has in turn moulded the quality of life and fortunes of his protagonists. His characters, even when they appear to us as escapists, evoke a sympathetic response from us because we are aware of the fact that they are mere victims of situations in which we ourselves could be trapped irrespective of our background and racial or cultural affiliations. (p. 42)

The details of [the] . . . stories in **Man Must Live** exemplify the major features of the early Mphahlele: a ponderous style and somewhat apolitical humanism which borders on escapism; but there is nevertheless a concentration of sensibility in his consuming interest in the predicament of the individuals who inhabit his fictional world. In his later stories Mphahlele provides further illuminations of that world through both direct and implicit commentaries on the socio-political background of events and experiences. The political implications of these events and experiences emerge from the stories without his having to force into our hands a political banner.

Even when Mphahlele presents situations that are obviously political in nature he constantly strives to draw from the experiences yet another illustration of the frustrations and indignities which the black man is subjected to in South Africa. Thus his attention shifts inevitably from the event as a socio-political phenomenon to the human condition which it is meant to illustrate. **"The Suitcase"** is one of such stories; so also is **"Dinner at Eight."** . . . (p. 44)

Nowhere in Mphahlele's writings is his universalist vision or his humanism better illustrated than in his absorbing novel, **The Wanderers**, in which he provides a fictional framework for his socio-political ideal of harmonious co-existence of the various racial groups in South Africa. (pp. 45-6)

The main story itself focuses on Timi who is the central character, his wife, Karabo, their son, Felang, and the intermingling relationship between the Timi household on the one hand and other characters drawn from the racial communities in South Africa. (p. 46)

The Wanderers begins with reflections on Felang's death and ends with an account of how he met his death. Between the glimpses of that enigmatic character we are led through several landscapes and we are made to share in the anxieties and ordeals of the characters whose consciousnesses centre around a single problem of existence under the shadow of apartheid. It is their communal search for self-realisation which universalizes the central experience in the novel. The final act of commitment of Felang reflects Mphahlele's own modified views and his efforts to reconcile his humanist ideal with the socio-political imperatives of our time. (pp. 46-7)

Timi has completed the cycle of his growth. If we accept the reading that Timi is to a large extent a fictional projection of Mphahlele himself, it is easy to follow the pattern of his growth from the escapist and liberal humanist of his early writings through the period of vacillations trying to identify with a communal purpose to the pragmatist who, in seeking to reinforce the old foundations of his humanist ethos, now sees ultimate self-realisation in commitment to his land and the destiny of his people. This final resolution is evident in Mphahlele's almost mystical veneration of the harmony of a land and its people. To that extent his confessed longing for his lost homeland and his wish, in spite of the situation in South Africa, to return home and face death when it does come, is indicative of the same kind of attachment that he has sanctioned in the fictional world of *The Wanderers*. . . . (p. 47)

The question that does arise ultimately is: wherein lies the value of Mphahlele's humanism in the context of the South African situation and the contemporary experience in Africa as a whole? Where does Mphahlele stand in the on-going struggle in Southern Africa? He has directed us to his works for some of the answers, and our quest for those answers has yielded specific affirmatives. Mphahlele proposes an integrationist resolution, but it is a solution that must be based strictly on a firm guarantee of the humanity of the constituent groups in that society. (pp. 47-8)

[Mphahlele's] commitment is to the macrocosm; and the political realities in South Africa are a fragment of the totality of the human condition that is central to his thought. His vision encompasses a wider world and community of races. (p. 48)

A noticeable shortcoming of Mphahlele's formulations is the almost total neglect of a clearly defined strategy for realising the ideal framework, be it social, economic or political, within which his humanism will not be seen to be a mere intellectual indulgence. There can be no doubt that he believes in the value of his own vision of the South African reality and of the alternatives that his humanism has guided him to propose. This reservation notwithstanding, it is difficult to contest Mphahlele's claim to more serious attention in our study of African literature in the contemporary idiom. His significance is defined by the consistency of his thematic focus in his writings and utterances on the black-white issue, and as much by the complementarity of resonances both of his theories and of his practice as a writer. His persistent articulation of a humanist ideal which he sublimates from even the most overtly dated sketch cannot but be seen as a significant contribution to the heritage of ideas in contemporary African writing of which he is a distinguished pioneer. (pp. 48-9)

> *Samuel Omo Asein, "The Humanism of Ezekiel Mphahlele" (copyright Samuel Omo Asein; by permission of Hans Zell Publishers, an imprint of K. G. Saur Verlag), in Journal of Commonwealth Literature, Vol. XV, No. 1, August, 1980, pp. 38-49.*

GERALD MOORE

The advent of Ezekiel Mphahlele's first book, *Down Second Avenue* (1959), at the same moment that West African writing was beginning to assert itself, was a challenge to the understanding both of Western readers and of African readers themselves. There is hardly a single generalization which could be made about the predominantly peasant culture of West, East or Central Africa which would be equally applicable to the urban, industrialized Africa for which Mphahlele spoke. This

Africa of vast segregated modern cities, mine-dumps, skyscrapers and jazz-clubs was as alien and remote to the Nigerian or Senegalese reader of that time as Dallas or Harlem might have been. But the challenge to South African understanding by the new West African writers was equally great, for there was an almost insuperable temptation for them to lump together the tropical cultures of Africa as 'backward' (and perhaps backward-looking), because of certain characteristics which they shared with the rural and tribal remnants of South Africa itself—remnants often dismissed as 'blanket-Africans' by the city-dweller.

In truth, the black man in urban South Africa had then more in common with the North American blacks than with his neighbours in tropical Africa. Like the black American, he inhabits a society which is dominated by whites in a far grimmer and more universal sense than any tropical colony has ever been. And this domination is expressed not merely in the colonial ritual and pantomime satirized during that same decade by Mongo Beti, Ferdinand Oyono and Chinua Achebe, but in every department of his daily life. His residence, his movements, his place and grade of work, his education, his sexual and family life are all subject to intense regulation, all governed by an alien mythology about the black man's place in the natural scheme of things. He cannot even walk down a street at certain hours without breaking the law. An outcast in his own country, he has to scrutinize every doorway, every bench, every counter, to make sure that he has segregated himself correctly. He is permanently on the run. (pp. 41-2)

Partly as a result of his very exclusion, partly as a result of the far greater urbanization and industrialization of the South, and partly as a result of the impoverishment of the overcrowded 'Homelands', the black South African is oriented more and more towards a way of life which hysterically denies him admittance. A member of the most educated, Westernized and (patchily) prosperous black community in Africa, he asks only that he be accepted as such. No amount of official mystification about 'the Bantu' will induce him to look back to the tribe and the Bantustan as offering an adequate way of life. He is drawn irresistibly towards the cities, which need his labour but deny his civil existence. But in the cities he can exist only on sufferance and in circumstances which emphasize his helot status. (p. 42)

This is the supreme irony of the South African situation and the irony which, without specifically dwelling on it, Mphahlele makes manifest. His whole life has been an unrelenting struggle to achieve the way of life for which his urban upbringing and liberal education had prepared him. But to achieve that life, he had to become an exile. The logic of events drove him, through Nigeria, Paris, Kenya and Zambia to that urban black America whose similarity he had always recognized. But at the root of the dissatisfaction he felt for all these places lay a certain perverse nostalgia, and it must have been this very nostalgia which finally induced him to return to Vorster's South Africa. (p. 43)

Mphahlele was not yet fifteen when he suffered his first assault from a white constable. He learnt the full humiliation of his position as he cycled about the city, collecting the dirty washing of hostile and moody white customers. But somehow, at the sacrifice of any real life with her own children, his mother managed to save enough to put him through primary school. Though he rose daily at four to do the domestic chores or the washing round . . . he passed out in the first grade. So his mother strained an extra inch and sent him to St Peter's Secondary School in Johannesburg.

Mphahlele's fierce prose evokes all the strain of those years of adolescence. Both structure and style in *Down Second Avenue* show the attempt to enlarge the normal limits of autobiography, so that the book will be both a record of events, more or less chronological, in the author's life, *and* an immediate, impressionistic evocation of certain typical moods and moments which don't belong at any special place within it, but must be allowed to spill their fear and anguish over the book as a whole. These are evoked in the sections called Interludes, which contain some of Mphahlele's most angry and electric writing in the book. The search for immediacy has muted the common tendency for the writer (especially the exile) to see even the painful events of youth and childhood through a certain softening haze. In the Interludes we actually hear the steely clang of police boots in the yard, the thunder of hard knuckles on the door at dawn, the sirens, the cries and the sickening blows which authority rains upon the unprotected. . . . (p. 46)

In 1957 [Mphahlele left South Africa] for Nigeria, where he was to teach until 1961. (p. 51)

It was during those four years in Nigeria that Mphahlele achieved his greatest period of fertility as a writer. *Down Second Avenue*, presumably completed by 1958, was published in the following year. In 1961 the newly established Mbari Publishing House in Nigeria brought out a volume of his short stories entitled *The Living and Dead*. (p. 52)

[*The Living and Dead* contains the majority of Mphahlele's] best work in fiction. When I first wrote of these seven stories, in the first edition of the present work, I formed a strong impression that the title story and '**He and the Cat**' must be considerably later in composition than the others, and must represent a movement towards [the] . . . 'reconciliation of protest and acceptance' for which he was striving. However, the researches of Professor Bernth Lindfors have made it clear that '**He and the Cat**' was published as early as 1953. It nevertheless stands out from the stories which surround it by reason of its economy of means and its introspective quality, as the narrator, obsessed with his own problems, focuses slowly and with difficulty on what is around him.

It is a deceptively simple story. The narrator goes to a lawyer's office to seek help with a problem that is consuming him. He takes his place in the waiting-room with about twenty others. The clients gossip in snatches, the clerk comes to summon them one by one. At a table a little apart sits a man sealing envelopes, with the picture of a black cat on the wall behind him. Gradually this withdrawn figure becomes more and more important, until he dominates the whole room, the whole mood of the scene. . . . (pp. 53-4)

Whatever the chronology of its composition, this story shows a technical assurance not always evident in the rest of the collection. Here Mphahlele is content to write directly out of experience, without looking for the conventional type of 'plot'. The narrator's egocentric obsession with his legal anxieties is gently displaced by his slow awareness of the quiet presence of another man, more completely locked within the dark walls of his own experience than the narrator can ever be.

Several other stories in the collection show characters who, whether black or white, are borne helplessly along in a stream of events which they cannot master or understand. They seldom

act, and when they do, like Mzondi in '**We'll Have Dinner at Eight**' or Timi in '**The Suitcase**', they act disastrously. In the first-mentioned story there is a somewhat inadequately prepared murder: Mzondi kills the sentimental white employer who has invited him to dinner, because he mistakenly believes that she is pumping him on behalf of the police. In the second, a desperate man steals a suitcase which a girl has left beside him in a bus. He is taken to a police station on suspicion of theft and is there found to be carrying a dead baby around with him. Although the story of '**The Suitcase**' is apparently based on an actual event, these plots are rather too obtrusive in the neat way events are unfolded, and the stories suffer from a thinness of fictional texture.

'**The Master of Doornvlei**', first published in 1957 and reprinted in the same collection, is a more substantial story. The incident with the bull and the stallion which finally brings about the confrontation between Mfukeri and his master is convincing and appropriate, for this kind of projected conflict is precisely what we expect to find between two men who have no love for each other but have been held together by a certain mutuality of interest. The story is made all the stronger by the fact that the old, black foreman is not in himself at all a sympathetic character, though he comes to stand in sympathetic opposition to the Boer farmer.

But the other outstanding story in this collection is '**The Living and Dead**'. Unlike most of Mphahlele's stories, this one is not unidirectional, and its greater length gives it that degree of amplitude which is almost essential to real achievement in this form. The structure is daringly unorthodox for a story of only a few thousand words. Mphahlele begins with the thoughts and experience of two apparently unconnected people on a day in urban South Africa. Lebona, a railway sweeper, has just seen a man pushed backwards down the train steps and trampled to death by the rush-hour crowd. He has also picked up a letter which he found lying on the track. Thoughts of the letter and the casually abrupt death of the unknown man obsess him. Meanwhile Stoffel Visser, a middle-class white resident, has just completed a report to the Government urging that 'kaffir' servants should all be moved out of the white areas into their own locations. His obsession, very different from Lebona's, is the fear that white civilization will be swamped in a rising sea of black labour. But because his own servant, Jackson, has not returned in time from leave, Stoffel has overslept and has failed to send the report in time to the responsible Minister. A man comes to the door with a letter addressed to Jackson, saying that he found it on the railway line. He spills out a confused story of seeing a poor man killed at the station. Stoffel lends him half an ear, while impatiently longing for his departure. A moment later, Jackson's wife Virginia appears on the doorstep which Lebona has just vacated. She knows nothing of Jackson's whereabouts and is highly agitated by his disappearance. Stoffel fails to hand her the letter. Instead, he dismisses her and reports matters to the police, after which he guiltily opens the letter himself. By this time the reader has concluded that the dead man at the station is probably Jackson, and this suspicion is reinforced when the letter proves to be a desperate summons to Jackson from his dying father in Vendaland. He sends his son some photographs of his family for safe keeping and begs him to come and look after the farm. But the strength of the story is that the dead man turns out not to be Jackson and remains as unknown at the end of the story as at its beginning. (pp. 54-6)

It would have been easy to make this story the preparation for a reforming of Stoffel Visser, the breaking of a new light into his bleak corridor of bigotry. Mphahlele's ending is truer and, as we come to see it, inevitable. This is how things happen in a society dominated by racial mythologies. And the way in which Mphahlele draws his apparently random, anonymous threads together into a significant pattern of unacknowledged human relationship, unaccepted human responsibility, shows an altogether new power in his imaginative resources. (p. 57)

Critics and scholars have theorized for some years about the dearth of full-length fiction from black South Africans; on the face of it, this dearth is the more surprising in that South Africa made an early start with the novels of Mofolo, Phatje, Dhlomo and others, in the first thirty years of the century. Since then the considerable achievements in poetry, short fiction and autobiography have not been matched by any novel of major scale. To insist that writers like Peter Abrahams and Alex La Guma are 'coloured' rather than black may seem like participating in the racial obsessions of the authorities, but it remains true that the world of experience tapped in a work like La Guma's *A Walk in the Night* (which is in any case a short novel rather than a novel) is not the same as that revealed in the journalism and short stories of the black writers. To the voluntary segregation practised by most coloureds has been added the enforced segregation which puts them in different townships, different schools, different universities and a different range of jobs. Hence La Guma's work is centred upon the world he knows intimately, that of coloured slum-life in and around Cape Town. Although we may discern at a deep, unrealized level a phenomenon we can call 'South African literature', the absence of common experience, common education and common communication in a country so deeply and bitterly divided does force us to admit that a novel by a white, or Indian or coloured writer, however sensitive and perceptive, cannot be regarded as cancelling the expectations which attend upon a new black South African fiction.

It was into this atmosphere of expectancy that Mphahlele, certainly the best established black South African writer today, launched his novel *The Wanderers* in 1971. The first thing that must be said about this book is that it is simply not a novel. Rather, it is a thinly disguised autobiography, which extends the story of *Down Second Avenue* to cover the author's last couple of years in South Africa . . . and his subsequent wanderings in Africa and Europe. Comparison with the earlier book, however, can only damage *The Wanderers* as much as any insistence that it is a novel. As a novel it totally lacks shape and relevance; for the form of the novel demands rather more than an arbitrarily sawn-off section of the author's own experience. Incidents should be included only because they are important to the action, and not simply because they happened; events should be presented with some sense of their moral complexity, rather than in self-justification. The motive of self-justification is dangerously prominent in much of *The Wanderers.*

The range of experience presented in this book has faced Mphahlele with real problems of style. The prose of *Down Second Avenue* was angry and often abrupt, but, unlike the writing of many of *Drum*'s contributors, it never struck a note of wishful Americanism or a breathless striving for toughness of effect. Such a note does occasionally obtrude in *The Wanderers.* . . . (pp. 59-60)

The Wanderers comes nearest to having a life of its own in the earlier chapters, and particularly in the section dealing with the author's visit to a Boer potato farm in the effort to trace a girl's missing husband, who has been sent there for forced labour by the police. This lacks the immediacy of the late Harry Nxumalo's celebrated *Drum* articles on the potato farms of Bethel, but Mphahlele's dialogue is at its most successful when he is rendering Bantu speech. . . . The effect of such reporting is to give a certain human weight to even the most simple speech. Mphahlele, however, appears to have no ear for the mannerisms or accentuation of educated black South African talk. Everyone in this reach of society 'talks like a book', and there is an unintended effect of condescension when such characters are confronted by Indian or coloured speakers, whose mannerisms Mphahlele seems much more anxious to observe. (pp. 61-2)

The weaknesses of *The Wanderers* show as much in these kinds of detail as in its overall lack of fictional organization and authorial 'distance'. The disappointment is the greater in that this is the mature work of a good writer, the writer who above all might be expected to produce a black South African novel of real substance and achievement. Stories like **'Mrs Plum'** and **'The Living and Dead'** give us room to hope that Mphahlele will one day write a full-length work of fiction that displays a comparable power to organize and to project and develops more fully the style manifest in some of the short stories, now that the story of his wanderings has been told. (p. 63)

Mphahlele earns his place in this book because he is the most important black South African writer of the present age, by virtue of his all-round achievement and his lifelong commitment to literature. Others may have equalled or excelled him in autobiography, or in criticism, or in the short story. But Mphahlele's contributions in all three of these fields add up to a career of major distinction. If he cannot give us the great black South African novel which has been so long awaited, it seems probable that no one at present can. The fragmentation of creative achievement into the poems and short stories in which black South Africa has been so prolific must be seen as the obverse of those conditions which make major fiction so difficult of achievement there. The corpus of Mphahlele's work remains rich enough, however, in qualities of insight, compassion and intelligence. (pp. 65-6)

Gerald Moore, "Ezekiel Mphahlele: The Urban Outcast" (originally published in a different form in his Seven African Writers, Oxford University Press, London, 1962), in his Twelve African Writers (copyright © 1980 by Gerald Moore; reprinted by permission of Indiana University Press; in Canada by Hutchinson Publishing Group Limited), Indiana University Press, 1980, Hutchinson, 1980, pp. 41-68.

PETER SABOR

[*Chirundu*] traces the downfall of Chimba Chirundu, the corrupt, power-hungry minister of transport in an unnamed central African country. . . . Many urgent social and political problems are contained in Mphahlele's complex narrative web: the corruption of post-independence African governments; the struggle for workers' rights; the incompatibility of indigenous and colonially imposed laws; and the bitter impotence of exile. An eloquent work by a major African writer.

Peter Sabor, "Book Reviews: 'Chirundu'," in Library Journal (reprinted from Library Journal, November 15, 1981; published by R. R. Bowker Co. (a Xerox company); copyright © 1981 by Xerox Corporation), Vol. 106, No. 20, November 15, 1981, p. 2253.

MARTIN TUCKER

Mphahlele's story [*Chirundu*], about the self-made Chimba Chirundu, minister of transport and public works in an imaginary African country, is well crafted. The atmosphere conveys a sense of momentum; life is on the tracks in Mphahlele's fictional land, and the characters, while momentarily blocked by subterfuge, disappointment, or deception, do not lose their spirit. Chirundu is arrested on a charge of bigamy brought by his first wife. He defends his second marriage on the basis of Bemba tribal law. He has divorced his first wife because both realized their marriage was not working and because they have lived apart for some time. With this situation Mphahlele comes to grips with issues of modernism and tribalism, of new and old Africa, of individualism and communal responsibilities. He invests Chirundu with ambition and passion, even with a reluctant admiration for his Medea-like first wife.

Mphahlele tells his story through several narrators. . . . Their various points of view have cumulative force, and the reader senses the division and rich complexity of the independent nation Mphahlele is drawing. (pp. 25-6)

Chirundu is one of the new African breed—the men of power who order their suits from London tailors and drive in long, sleek limousines. We see that he is admirable as well as stubborn, intelligent as well as avaricious. But his fall is a result of the wish to "test" colonialist British law against tribal custom, or the new centralism against the traditional regionalism. This is a profoundly complex matter, but the author does not treat its ramifications. As a novelist Mphahlele is under no obligation to proselytize, but he must resolve what he introduces. Merely to leave the reader with a sense of these many layers of African society is to leave unfinished one's novelistic business.

Yet, if Mphahlele's novel seems unresolved, it also offers extraordinary insights into contemporary African life. Mphahlele is writing with a sense of command and a strong sense of his own identity. (p. 26)

Martin Tucker, "Books: 'Chirundu'," in Worldview *(© copyright 1982 Council on Religion and International Affairs), Vol. 25, No. 6, June, 1982, pp. 25-6.*

Christopher (Ifenayichukwu) Okigbo

1932-1967

Nigerian poet.

Critics consider Okigbo an important transitional poet in contemporary African literature. His studies in the classics enabled him to integrate within his work traditional elements of African culture with non-African influences such as Christianity and Western poetic techniques. His poetry is complex, partly because of obscure allusions, but critics nevertheless praise his work for its vivid imagery and rhythmic beauty.

Heavensgate **and** ***Limits*** **are works inspired by Okigbo's search for identity through an examination of his country's divided heritage. A later poem,** *Path of Thunder***, reveals the impact of the Nigerian civil war upon him. He was killed during that conflict while fighting for the Biafran cause.**

(See also *Contemporary Authors***, Vols. 77-80.)**

Lee Hunt

Drawing from a photograph; reproduced by permission of Heinemann Educational Books

O. R. DATHORNE

[The] process of transformation is the key to all of Okigbo's verse—how can human beings grow again into gods, how are they to regain their pristine state of spiritual innocence and yet retain their own sensuality? In order to deal with this problem Okigbo has forsaken the commonplace world and has chosen instead to reenact the entire cycle of birth, initiation and death. Because of the nature of his quest, his images tend to dwell on the disparity that exists between man's ambition and his puny attempts at becoming God.

Okigbo's verse shows man in the process of striving towards a god. The poet does not speak with an individual voice but with choral utterance, insisting on the infallibility of the statement and its divine nature. The five sections of *Heavensgate* demonstrate the technique. If Okigbo's poems are *about* anything, then *Heavensgate* attempts to work out the initiation into and the evolution of a religion. (pp. 82-3)

The five sections into which *Heavensgate* is divided clearly emphasize a striving—**PASSAGE, INITIATION, WATERMAID, LUSTRA** and **NEWCOMER. . . . PASSAGE** takes the reader to the childhood of the world and of the protagonist; it is both a time of 'dark waters of the beginning' and 'when we were great boys'. . . . The next section, **INITIATION**, rescues this vision of chaos 'in a symbolic interplay of geometric figures'. Here the angle, orthocentre, fourth angle, square, rhombus and quadrangle all suggest that a certain kind of order has been imposed; they form the series of intimations which the protagonist has had towards a complete harmony with himself and his world. The next section, **WATERMAID,** introduces the intercessor—a figure who is a mixture of a classical muse, the Virgin Mary, and a local priestess. She is described both as 'maid of the salt-emptiness, sophisticreamy, native' and as 'wearing white light about her'. At the end of this section the protagonist finds himself in a state of cosmic aloneness; he is completely alienated from everything he knows. . . . (p. 83)

LUSTRA suggests with appropriate Christian as well as African pagan imagery that there is hope which comes through a redeemer who is neither Christian nor pagan. . . . But the dramatic quality of the poem is spoilt by the last four pieces called **NEWCOMER** which are irrelevant and do little for the continuity of the piece. They are verses for the poet's teacher-friend and his niece, and were all written in a single afternoon. They betray a weak side in Okigbo, his tendency at times to be so very personal that there seems little room for any universal message.

The method of *Heavensgate* is to combine traditional African and modern modes and to fuse them into a synthesized whole. Both traditional oral and western forms of verse are used. In addition the poet deploys imagery so that African and non-African elements build up into a whole. The result is the invention of a personal style and creed, personal because it is intensely subjective, although meaning accumulates from various references that belong to the common store of all mankind. Diagrammatically, Okigbo's way is the imagistic construction of an inverted pyramid; he works outwards from the apex towards a broad base.

Dramatic progression from the traditional to the 'modern' and to the fusing of the two is seen in he quality of the utterance. The voice is at first choral, concerned with communal issues; later the private voice marks the emergence of an individual sensibility. The initial invocation to mother Idoto, the goddess of the poet's community in Ijoto, is in fact a praise-song. References to water and to the oil-bean situate mother Idoto, for her shrine is near a river and the oil-bean is her sacred totem. But the praise-song to the goddess is to a Judaic Christian god as well, and echoes of the psalms make this point with force and ease.

That the poet is working out a personal religion becomes apparent later on in the references to Leidan, Anna, and Kepkanly which the poet has invented himself. Allusions to St Paul, John the Baptist, the Pope, angels, God, and Christ illustrate the subtlety of the fusion that is taking place.

Creation myths have a place in the poem; in one place there is the piety of 'dark waters of the beginning', in another there is the sensuality of rain falling on a beach, 'Over man with woman'. The creation that is taking place is not simply that of man but that of the individual, freeing himself from tribal rigours, so as to crystallize the experience of humankind into a succinct and enigmatic form.

This is not to suggest that *Heavensgate* follows a chronological progression from creation, through birth, the fall, sin, redemption, crucifixion and ascension, but what the poem certainly affirms is that all these elements are present. Okigbo's purpose is not to chart a religious history of mankind but to enact a theatrical demonstration of the significance of these matters for the individual now. This is why after the opening choral 'I', the individual does not exist in the poem and the closest personal note is struck by 'we'. (pp. 84-5)

[The ending of *Heavensgate*] indicates that the absence of the agents of darkness has made the way for a confrontation with a private and agonizing truth; the truth about tribeless man existing amidst a limbo of contradictions. . . . The last line states a temporary triumph over Christian and pagan madness that would seek to inhibit self. The protagonist's transition is still only a vacation from the disaster that awaits him in the world. (p. 87)

It is clear now that it is the protagonist who is aspiring towards the last glory of flesh, to be a living god, and the final triumph over death, to be resurrected. At the end of the poem when 'the cancelling out is complete', one can be sure that he has come nearer this concept of godhead.

Images made familiar from *Heavensgate* re-appear in *Limits*. The bird becomes 'weaverbird', the watermaid is 'queen of the damp half light', a deity is identifiable. Flannagan and the Pope are once more mentioned and there are cryptic allusions to 'YUNICE at the passageway' and 'the twin-gods of IR-KALLA'. Solitude is the dominant mood and the search for redemption does not end in a period of transition as in *Heavensgate*, but with complete oblivion. On the whole *Limits* works through a more tenuous medium, almost like a trance, towards an indefinable elusiveness. The protagonist possessed body and soul in *Heavensgate;* in *Limits* his absence emphasizes his insubstantiality.

Although Okigbo's verse is not as straightforward as it has been made to sound, its theme is the quest for ultimate wisdom. Okigbo has himself helped to obscure the real issues relevant to an appreciation of his poetry, by emphasizing that he does not strive in his poetry towards meaning in the accepted sense of the term. (p. 89)

But . . . there is meaning in Okigbo's poetry even though it might be obscured by a too-ready desire to pun, or to exploit the more obvious devices of language for phonetic rather than semantic effects. . . .

The protagonist in Okigbo's poetry had not yet come to a full understanding of all that life is; it is as if Okigbo feels that his protagonist must always be aspiring towards an elusive something which is afterlife and art and Heaven and ideals, and the drama of a realization of this need is his quest for fulfilment. (p. 90)

O. R. Dathorne, "African Literature IV: Ritual and Ceremony in Okigbo's Poetry" (copyright O. R. Dathorne; by permission of Hans Zell Publishers, an imprint of K. G. Saur Verlag), in Journal of Commonwealth Literature, *No. 5, July, 1968, pp. 79-91.*

ROMANUS EGUDU

[Critics have] hinted that Christopher Okigbo . . . widely accepted as the greatest of modern African poets, was influenced by Ezra Pound. . . . [It is in the] technical aspects of style that Pound's influence on Okigbo can be fruitfully and meaningfully established.

What has often bothered me is the fact that Okigbo has always, whether deliberately or not, omitted Pound's name from the list of those who have influenced him; and yet Pound's influence on him is enormous. . . . It is because of the fact that Okigbo might, very likely, have deliberately kept silent about Pound and the fact that Pound's influence is vast and has, it seems to me, helped to make his poetry difficult that I consider this topic worth investigating. (pp. 144-45)

While Okigbo shows the same kind of tendency toward "imagemaking" and "melody-making" that Pound does, it cannot be argued that the former must necessarily have inherited this trait from the latter; for in the final analysis, imagery and sound are indispensable elements of good poetry. (p. 145)

The influence of Pound on Okigbo is more direct and obvious in other ways. First, both poets share the technique of having a descriptive or lyrical passage followed by a vivid image, which epitomizes and clinches the passage or resolves the mystery therein. It has been remarked that "Earl Miner, the closest student of Japanese influences on Pound, calls this the 'super pository method.'" (p. 146)

This method is used many times in Okigbo's work. The poem **"Passage 1"** demonstrates it. . . . The last line of this poem is a vivid image demonstrating not only the solitude of the poet mourning a lost "mother," or goddess (which is partially what the poem is about), but also the uncertainty that shrouds him as he is immersed in the "dark waters of the beginning." Although the theme of Okigbo's poem differs from those of Pound's, yet there is a similar atmosphere of solitude in both cases.

The poem **"Watermaid 1,"** which deals with the secrecy of love and the loneliness of a boy waiting in vain for the arrival of his girl friend, also employs the "super pository" style. . . . Okigbo's extraordinary power of image making can hardly be better illustrated by any other of his poems. All through the poem one gets the impression that the poet is in a secret, hollow, fragile situation. . . . It should be warned here that the peculiarity of this technique does not consist in the fact that the final images in the poems are charged or that they round off the poems neatly. This is not the point, for most poems (though by no means all) have this characteristic. What is peculiar to Pound and Okigbo after him is that their final images also rehearse ("repeat" is inadequate) and recapitulate dramatically and imagistically the themes and the atmosphere of the poems. (pp. 147-48)

Another stylistic trait that reflects Pound's influence on Okigbo is syntactic. This is the tendency to reverse the order of subject and verb. . . . Okigbo's poem **"Initiation 3"** is full of such syntactic arrangements (or rearrangements). . . . The second stanza's "where liveth / in the heart of Aguata / a minstrel" and the refrain's "Singeth jadum" illustrate this technique clearly. . . . Thematically, the poem satirizes the Catholic priests who dragged the poet into Catholicism in his childhood and whose preaching means to the poet nothing more than the rantings of the madman "Jadum." The validity of this interpretation can be fully realized by reading all five poems that make up **"Initiation."** Nonetheless, the last two lines of the poem, "and there are here / the errors of the rendering," directly point to the poet's opinion that the preachers of Catholicism have misinterpreted the church Christ originally founded.

Now we may take up the final technique, which can be called the artistic placenta linking Okigbo to Pound, and that is the use of tags from other authors and other languages. Pound's *Mauberley* and *The Cantos* are full of lines from Greek, Latin, and French. (pp. 150-51)

In the same way, Okigbo has taken many lines from other sources and languages. It is quite remarkable that he has practiced this technique of borrowing tags by exploiting Pound himself. In the first part of **"Limits 3,"** there is the refrain "& the mortar is not yet dry." . . . The refrain comes from Ezra Pound's Canto 8. The only change Okigbo has made is to substitute "&" for "As." In each case the line has the import of prohibition or caution. (pp. 151-52)

Furthermore, like Pound, Okigbo has borrowed tags from Latin. In his poem **"Lustra 3,"** for example, we see the phrases "Lacrimae Christi" and "Lumen mundi." . . . (p. 152)

It is thus clear that Ezra Pound bulks glaringly in the work of the African poet, Christopher Okigbo. But it should be much more clear that this is no mere accident. The continuation of a tradition is characteristic of English poetry, as T. S. Eliot has made abundantly clear in both his critical writing and his poetry. Okigbo, though he is African and because he is using the English language for his medium, has simply found Pound's tradition interesting enough to him that he considers it worth preserving and worth promulgating.

One must concede to both master and apprentice the power of creating wonderful images and sounds. But with regard to the effective organization of those images for the purpose of communicating thought, one must also note that at times Okigbo's style is almost too "beautiful" to communicate. The poet sometimes appears confused, carried away by his music and forgetful of his failure to make sense. Still, if to imitate Pound was one of the aims of his artistic endeavors, he has achieved a considerable success. And this has probably helped to widen his audience, for the fans of Pound will certainly appreciate most of Okigbo's poems. (pp. 153-54)

Romanus Egudu, "Ezra Pound in African Poetry: Christopher Okigbo," in Comparative Literature Studies (© 1971 by The Board of Trustees of the University of Illinois), Vol. VIII, No. 2, June, 1971, pp. 143-54.

PAUL THEROUX

There is no question about it: Okigbo is an obscure poet, possibly the most difficult poet in Africa. There are two ways of approaching him; one is to look at his poems, the other is to listen to his music.

By 'looking' I mean examining each word he uses, each echo from another poet (for there are many echoes; he was an extremely well-read person). To do this one would have to make a long list which would include such strange words as *kepkanly, anagnorisis, Yunice, Upandru, enki, Flannagan* and perhaps a hundred others. The meaning of these words would have to be found, and then it would be necessary to fit this meaning into the line, ignoring the word for the time being.

I tried this once and I was fortunate in having Okigbo a few feet away to correct my mistakes in interpretation. I was especially disturbed by 'Flannagan'; I could not find a reference to it. I asked Okigbo to tell me what it meant.

'Flannagan,' said Okigbo, 'was a priest that used to teach me in Primary School. He ran the Mission near my village.' (p. 135)

Many people have criticized Okigbo for writing as he did, and some of this criticism is well-founded. How can the average reader know that Flannagan is a priest? . . . A poet may present us with a mysterious little poem and teachers and critics may make a name for themselves by unravelling the mystery and showing us what exactly the poet meant to say or what he was getting at. It is possible that, in this exercise of interpretation, the critic may find more in the poem than the writer put in. This happens all the time, and it happens with Okigbo's critics more than others because there is often a smokescreen of obscurity thrown up which hides the meaning of the poem.

With Okigbo this must be accepted. There is not much use in saying that he is not obscure, because he certainly is, but once this has been accepted an approach to the poem can be made.

The approach can be made through the second method. That is, by listening. Looking is confusion: what we see in the poem may be an impenetrable mystery, and there are words and phrases in Okigbo's poetry that are nearly impossible to figure out. Listening is simpler and more rewarding; there is music in this poetry, and if we listen closely we hear three separate melodies: the music of youth, the clamour of passage (that is, growing up) and lastly, the sounds of thunder. (p. 136)

Okigbo was a careful craftsman; when he wanted someone to understand, when he considered something important enough to be made absolutely clear, he took pains to write with the utmost clarity. One could make too much of the obscurities, but as the poems stand—*Heavensgate, Limits, Silences, Distances*—there is plenty to digest without complicating the essential point: a man in search of purification, beset by visions and delays, fighting his way toward death. (p. 146)

Many biographies of Africans have been written, detailing the early rural life, the amazement at discovering education and political independence, the confusions and complexes wrought by urban life; and later the coups, the disappointment, the corrupt politics. In a much shorter space Okigbo has done all this; he has composed, in verse, an African autobiography, with all its pain and beauty, terror and mystery. At times it seems unfathomable, but the moment passes, and soon we are in familiar territory, the obscurity is like a cloud passing, it is brief but leaves an impression on us that we do not forget. Later, we may be able to piece this obscurity with something known and the result is often enlightenment.

'Path of Thunder' is a war poem; it is about the war that killed Okigbo himself. It is perhaps a testimony to his skill that even in this poem describing war's horrors, there is beauty. The end of this poem is also the end of the cycle of poems that began with *Heavensgate*. . . . ['**Path of Thunder**' describes] what Okigbo stood for, constantly hoping that against chaos there could be beauty and order. . . . (p. 150)

> Paul Theroux, "Christopher Okigbo," in Introduction to Nigerian Literature, *edited by Bruce King (© University of Lagos and Evans Brothers Limited 1971), University of Lagos, 1971, Evans Brothers Limited, 1971, pp. 135-51.*

DONATUS I. NWOGA

Interpretations of Okigbo's *Limits* have varied widely from the mystical, through the political, to the personal. All the divergence of opinion unfortunately cannot be attributed to the customary range of reactions which any poem of some complexity normally attracts. The root problem appears to me to have been that of technique: that there has been a tendency to circumvent the complexity by attaching interpretations to those elements of the poems which have fitted into preconceived theories and, therefore, move to conclusions without analysis and elucidation of the images of the poems and the total logic of those images. (p. 92)

I see the process of achieving meaning from the *Limits*, as from most of Okigbo's poetry, as dependent on two factors: firstly, an acquaintance with the very varied sources of Okigbo's imagery and symbolism: the many situations and myths of many cultures which to him become means with which to project his vision of his state and that of his society; secondly a realization of the aim of his composition and the method it has created. He said himself that he was not trying to convey any intellectually apprehensible meaning. . . . This attitude to 'meaning' has dominated the form and created the obscurity which makes the poetry incomprehensible when approached from a logical inquiry into its surface meaning. Technically, it is as if Okigbo, having caught the essence of an experience, casts around for sounds, images and symbols, most of them abstract, which are likely to evoke that experience in the reader. (pp. 99-100)

From [the experiences in each section of *Limits*] what emerges as a central theme or common concern of Okigbo at the time is the relationship between the poet/prophet/messiah figure and his community and its history. Parts of the poem may satisfactorily be related to specific incidents in Africa's or Nigeria's history. *Limits* **X** and **XI** have been accepted as a description of the colonial and missionary exploitation of Africa and the demise of African gods and values. There is also argument whether *Limits* is an allegory of 'the great political drama of Nigeria since Independence' or whether 'the Congo Crisis of 1960 would be a more relevant analogy'. A further argument is possible about whether Okigbo was reacting to the recent historical past of European exploitation of Africa or to the current situation of African exploitation of Africans. Debate or disagreement on these specific issues does not upset the balance of the poem because of the poem's emphasis on essence and pattern rather than on the particular incidents—a pattern is created which produces emotional response transcending the original impetus.

What varies in *Limits* then is the external stimulus and the emphasis rather than the central theme. '**Siren Limits**' is motivated from individual experience and the emphasis is on the poet's personal growth and frustration both within the com-

munity and in the love quest. '**Fragments out of the Deluge**' has a more general frame of reference. The consequences of failure to heed the voice of the prophet/messiah are therefore more destructive of the community. In spite of these changes of emphasis, there does come through the underlying theme of the validity and undying nature of the creative ideal and the fate of the group which rejects it. The applications may vary from the national to the international situation, from the physical to the religious level. Okigbo's achievement in *Limits* is that he has created, by taking images and symbols out of other mythologies, a myth with emotive force which is both a record of the African past and a warning and promise for the present and the future. *Limits* then may be taken as Okigbo's statement on the growth and nature of the poet, on his position in his community, and on the indestructible nature and continuing validity of the creative spirit. It is written in terms which evoke the African experience. But within it are elements which direct the reader to its significance in terms of patterns which are archetypal. (pp. 100-01)

> Donatus I. Nwoga, "Okigbo's 'Limits': An Approach to Meaning" (copyright Donatus I. Nwoga; by permission of Hans Zell Publishers, an imprint of K. G. Saur Verlag), *in* Journal of Commonwealth Literature, *Vol. VII, No. 1, June, 1972, pp. 92-101.*

SUNDAY O. ANOZIE

The four poems which Okigbo called *Canzones* and published in the journal *Black Orpheus*, No. 11, outline his earliest creative itinerary between 1957 and 1961. Considered as representative of the poet's *juvenilia*, two interesting observations can be made about *Four Canzones*. Firstly, these poems clearly indicate Okigbo's major physical displacements, all within the old Federation of Nigeria, since graduating from Ibadan University in 1956. Secondly, each of these physical displacements in time and space marks a new stage in Okigbo's poetic development and influence. (p. 24)

The central theme in Okigbo's *Four Canzones* is nostalgia. This is the result of successive impacts on a highly sensitive mind—hence the dual introspective and retrospective nature of these early poems. Okigbo's feeling of nostalgia is for the innocence of his childhood and for the peace and security of his birthplace. From both of these each successive growth or travel appears to him as a new physical as well as psychic displacement, in fact, a distancing into a form of alienation.

'**Song of the Forest**', the 1st Canzone, introduces into this central theme that of the *prodigal* or the *exile*, Okigbo's favourite protagonist. The poem itself is a bucolic *résumé* of an intensely introspective life. . . . Here the poet praises the pastoral ease and the security of village life in preference to the more complicated life in a modern city. Thus the poet insinuates (and here Okigbo is strongly partisan to the negritude tradition which he often criticizes) that the sole course open to the uprooted exile or prodigal is a return in humility and penitence to the original source of his being. . . . '**Debtors' Lane**', the 2nd Canzone, was written in 1959 at Fiditi. . . . As a rural hideout apparently responding well to the poet's nostalgia, Fiditi was conducive to quiet creative reflections. . . . Within such a setting the first sub-theme in '**Debtors' Lane**' emerges; the *rejection* of Lagos, its 'high societies' and 'mad generation', its sophisticated pleasures, its night clubs and cabarets. . . . The second sub-theme is that of personal *renunciation* of what the poet calls 'heavenly transports . . . of youthful passion' and the endless succession 'of tempers and moods'

This act of ascetic self-denial traces a ritualistic course throughout Okigbo's poetry and is invariably associated with cleansing and purification as a prelude to a new and creative life. . . . (pp. 25-7)

But 'rejection' and 'renunciation' simply are, within the present pale, themes within a still larger thematic structure: Okigbo's moralistic concern with the *individual* and the *society*. . . . His handling so early of the motif of individuals to whom 'repose is a dream unreal'—either because they are definite failures in life or just misfits in the urban context of it—clearly demonstrates Okigbo's didactic moral purpose as well as his awakening awareness of the consequences of social change in Nigeria. Thus the same themes which inform the city-based novels of Achebe, Ekwensi and Soyinka, the rise of individualism and moral liberalism with a concommitant increased range of preferential alternatives and a relaxation of traditional ties, are equally though implicitly present in Okigbo's poetry. (p. 27)

I have insisted rather heavily upon the social and moral thematic variations in the 2nd Canzone in order to emphasize the early encroachment of T. S. Eliot as a major poetic influence on Okigbo and to suggest that the two years spent at Fiditi mark a turning point in Okigbo's poetic career and thinking. From now on he is going to take poetry seriously as an art of creative self-expression embodying a personal vision of social reality.

The 3rd and 4th Canzones are forms of lament. The third, **'Lament of the Flutes',** was written in 1960. The occasion was Okigbo's revisit to his birthplace, Ojoto, a little village near Onitsha in Eastern Nigeria. Brief though it was, this visit contained just the experience necessary to create a feeling of *reconciliation* in the poet. . . . [Reconciliation] (here, synonymous with initiation) is to be effected through a process of purification rites. . . . [This] is a concentric motif in Okigbo's poetry. (pp. 27-9)

Love, particularly a child's first love with its secret pains and its transience, is the last of Okigbo's variations on the theme of nostalgia in his *Four Canzones.* This theme is introduced into the 4th Canzone, entitled **'Lament of the Lavender Mist',** where it is rescued from the usual banalities and romanticisms that surround poetic treatments of the Venus and Adonis motif by Okigbo's reticence and style of *griot* incantation. (pp. 29-30)

There are three levels to Okigbo's choice of images and symbols in *Four Canzones.* . . . There is, first of all, the *traditional* level, most noticeable in the 1st and 2nd Canzones which are strongly under the romantic and pastoral influence of the Roman poet, Virgil, or by logical extension the larger influence of the Greek poet, Theocritus of Syracuse, whose work in the same pastoral genre cannot have been unfamiliar to Okigbo. Then there is the *modern* level where Okigbo is concerned with modern actualities (**'Debtors' Lane'**) and also seeks to integrate elements from his readings in modern and contemporary poetry. Finally comes the *private* level where a deep subjective layer of experience (**'Lament of the Lavender Mist'**) compels the poet to use new forms of synthesis or association of ideas in order to arrive at a verbal approximation of his feeling. (pp. 32-3)

The formal unity of Okigbo's *Four Canzones* derives from the fact that they are originally intended (or seemingly intended) to constitute a kind of syncretic musical pattern. Okigbo's bold ambition is latent in the chosen title—'Canzones'. He means to go back to the ancient Italian and, surely, the pre-Petrarchan habit of arranging lyrical bits in a group of stanzas so that the verses and the rhymes are disposed in a specially predetermined and uniform order throughout. The result is that usually each 'canzonette' becomes a little Provençal song filled with popular refrains, with sentiment and gaiety. (p. 34)

After this rather synoptic survey, two tentative conclusions may be drawn *vis-à-vis* the nature of Okigbo's creative itinerary between 1957 and 1961 as represented in his *Four Canzones.* First is that at the beginning of his poetic career, Okigbo was not unaware of—in fact, was haunted by—a certain 'devil' that required to be exorcised, or at least propitiated. This may be easily dismissed as one of the perennial concerns of poets—just one of those emotions often recollected in tranquility. But the truth is, that the 'devil' can sometimes assume flesh and blood and, as in the 4th Canzone, become the secret 'Lady of the Lavender Mist'. It seems more probable in fact that the 'devil' is Okigbo's sensuality, and the 'lady' is allied to his 'watermaid' and 'lioness' (*Heavensgate*), the bearer of the mystical vision he is always striving to recapture. . . . (p. 36)

The second is that Okigbo's poetic language at the same period is both unoriginal and diffident, vacillating between different, often conflicting traditions, and adapting whichever poetic forms and diction may have appealed to his curious and impressionable mind. It is evidence of Okigbo's genius and labour that he practically overcame in his later poetry most of these difficulties and succeeded in creating a poetic technique and an idiom purely his own. (pp. 36-7)

Heavensgate is one long sustained poem, not several poems. It has no one defensible theme in the sense of a 'basic idea', but it is throughout informed by a dynamic ritualistic rhythm which indicates at least two possible levels of analogical interpretation. At one level the poem may be seen as a ritualistic exploration of the process of creative intuition; at another as a mythical projection of a personal experience of the poet. But these two streams are constantly infusing and diffusing into each other because myth is essentially correlative to ritual: myth is the spoken part of ritual, the story which the ritual enacts. (p. 41)

The progression from **'Passage'** to **'Initiations'**, and to **'Watermaid'**, **'Lustra'** and finally to **'Newcomer'**—all areas of experience into which the poet-hero in *Heavensgate* moves—is itself, like the stations of the cross during the Easter season, sufficiently indicative of the ritualistic pattern of the poem. (pp. 41-2)

Okigbo's whole poetic output tends to fit into the Malinowskian definition of myth as 'a narrative resurrection of a primeval reality, told in satisfaction of deep religious wants, moral cravings, social submissions, assertions, even practical requirements', yet it would be wrong to assert categorically that Okigbo sets out to construct a myth. Okigbo's poetry is a poetry of strong tensions and conflicts. It is not a conscious myth-making. In *Limits* this tension between creative intuition and personal experience, certainly too between myth and ritual, is tightened up, and that in a way compelling one to seek its possible resolution only in terms of religious and spiritual conflict. In fact, Okigbo's poetic attitude on the whole reveals a crisis between a messianic and an apocalyptic conscience: that is, its emotional pendulum swings unsteadily between an expression of hope and a negation of it. Sometimes it moves spiritually round a belief in the restoration of a peaceful social and moral order, a new epoch; sometimes it affirms a disintegration of all existing social and moral codes in favour of a new and more sublime creative reality. (pp. 63-4)

As a general statement on the theme of Okigbo's second volume of poetry, it may be said, provisionally, that *Limits,* despite its two parts (the **'Siren Limits'** and **'Fragments out of the Deluge'**), is a poem of ten movements. . . . The central tension of **'Fragments'** is, in plain prose, the burning down of a pagan shrine, either imaginary or real, by the agents of Christian missionaries. In the poetic sensibility this act acquires a new figurative colour and idiom. It becomes the raping of the god and goddess of Irkalla by a warrior 'fleet of eagles' and the killing of the Sunbird which had forewarned their approach. By a prophetic intuition the poet sees the reappearance of the killed god 'outside at the window' followed by the resurrection of the Sunbird whose song he now hears 'from the Limits of the dream'.

'Siren Limits' is, on the contrary, concerned with a problem at the same time more universal and more particular. Universal, because in this part Okigbo discusses the problem common to young poets—that of articulation, the union of soul and voice, the expression of the essential one-self. In other words, he examines the pre-creative psychology or predicament of a poet. But it is also particular, because as a 'Siren' it acts as a particular poem in relation to a particular poet-hero within his particular set of involvements. Thus throughout **'Siren Limits'** the impression is that the poet-initiate is taking stock of his conscience, rigorously examining his state of mind before he finally and devoutly goes to the confessional box. Indeed our hero is enacting a prelude to his homecoming. (pp. 64-5)

[The] note on which *Limits* begins is characterized decidedly by a new structural strength such as is lacking in its predecessor *Heavensgate*. This strength is revealed mostly in the tone or the voice that speaks in the poem. It is a tone which far from being reflective or sentimental . . . is neither conciliatory nor compromising. It is virile, almost sure of itself. This tonal strength which marks, we believe, a fresh advance in Okigbo's poetic technique, marks also the beginning of a clearer expression of his more genuine faith, an increasing commitment to a prophetic point of view—thus a new breadth of poetic intuition.

With *Limits II* we move into an area of ritual cleansing which is expressed symbolically and significantly in terms of vital reconciliation with the essence of light. The idea is worked out on two image patterns; say, for instance, the botanical image or the principle of plants' phototropism, and also the Neoplatonic image of the soul. (p. 67)

Okigbo's commentary has the quality of an insidious art. As in every good work of art, including poetry, certain categories of plastic and fine art and music (particularly classic symphony and modern jazz), such commentaries can only be insinuated through tonal variations, images and rhythmical curves. These demand of the reader, spectator or audience a certain amount of healthy awareness and imaginative participation. Especially in poetry like Okigbo's, which is poor in visual symbols but built up almost exclusively on a jazz-like infra-structure of sound, what is expected of the reader is a painstaking disposition coupled with a good ear. (p. 71)

Okigbo may safely be called an artist who, like James Joyce, prefers not to be committed to a fixed position within his own works. Okigbo's position is generally nowhere fixed in his poetry: at one time he is in the centre of it, at another on the fringe; sometimes he may simply be jesting or complaining, at others just silent or paring his fingernails. This will make rather difficult, or quite nonsensical as biographical criticism, an attempt to pin the poet down to any particular point in his poetry. (pp. 72-3)

But just as Eliot was before him, Okigbo seems to be concerned with the more immediate problem of the poet and his personality in relation to his work and art. In other words, Okigbo is concerned with the artist's ego and with the nature of the experiences in which this is generally manifested. . . . [For] the poet of *Ash-Wednesday* and *The Waste Land,* as for the author of *Limits* and *Distances,* the acceptance of an intense personal experience lived in a pattern of symbolic death and rebirth is the central truth of both religious and creative intuition. This is the central ritualistic experience or message which informs Okigbo's poetic world, and one which he comments upon in *Limits II.*

In that world, Eliot was Okigbo's favourite guide, as Dante had been Eliot's, as Virgil had been Dante's, as Homer had been Virgil's, and so on, since there are no frontiers to the continuity of human thought and artistic aspiration. Okigbo's is a world of dynamic relations and tensions. It is peopled, like Prospero's island, by strange echoes, solitudes, birds, beasts and silences—these for the poet may be various realities or aspects of one ideal mythical or symbolic reality. It is above all a world with two ends. At one end is the 'forest', meaning darkness, ignorance or the creative 'cloud of unknowing'; this is the world of debauched messianism. At the other is 'sunlight', meaning knowledge, experience and 'the limits of the dream'; this is the world of triumphant apocalypse. In between these two ends there is a continuum, a 'passageway' only to be found through the ritual of purification and by the power of music, art and memory. For Okigbo the true artist or poet is one who is caught up in this primordial continuum. (pp. 77-8)

A sense of religious piety and the principle of ritual death and rebirth constitute the dynamics of the second part of *Limits*— **'Fragments Out of the Deluge'.** Underlying this is the poet's feeling of a personal tragedy. Besides a common sense of mythology and a certain prophetic range of imagery there is hardly any continuity between the first and the second parts of *Limits* and they should best be treated as two separate poems. . . . **'Siren Limits'** is essentially expository in character whereas **'Fragments'** is narrative and dramatic. The first is exploratory of the process of artistic expression—hence the symbolic role of the 'weaverbird'; the second is a prophetic discovery of the fountain-head of creative intuition, hence the use of the 'Sunbird' as a symbol. If the former introduces a thesis on the process of art and creativity which has to be worked out and somehow concluded . . . , the latter simply posits a tragic axiom, in fact a universal *status quo.* (p. 85)

By its theme and craft *Path of Thunder* differs from [Okigbo's earlier poetry]. . . . This is so because in it Okigbo makes, for the first time ever, a forthright and direct political statement which itself undisguisedly defines the poet's own revolutionary option. But genetically speaking, *Path of Thunder* cannot be separated from the earlier poetry written by Okigbo, since it directly springs from the same parent stock or source of inspiration. (p. 174)

[In] Okigbo's poetic sensibility there seemed to exist a genetic struggle between a romantic pursuit of art for its own sake and a constantly intrusive awareness of the social relevance of art—its function, that is, as a means of embodying significant social comments. . . .

[It is possible] that Okigbo in 1962 was afraid of the possible consequences of committing to his poetry statements that would have direct political connotations in the Nigerian scene. This may mean also that he had not at that time fully resolved within himself the problem of whether art should be separated from politics or a poet be free from ideological commitments. (p. 175)

It is precisely at this juncture that *Path of Thunder* comes in, not as the beginning of a prophecy but as the end of one. In parts, therefore, it is the celebration of the end of a long period of socio-political *attente* and indecision, both on an individual and a national level, with all the hopes of renaissance and peace which this may imply. In this *Path of Thunder* does no more than reflect the contemporary mood of the Nigerian public. . . . Okigbo was one of the disenchanted but helpless 'John Citizens' but, unlike many, his own jubilation and hossanah cry, even as early as that time when it appeared a decisive turning-point had been made, was punctuated with sharp, sober warnings, reflective and suspicious. (p. 176)

Path of Thunder reflects the poet's own feeling of uncertainty about the political future of the country, a feeling which . . . amounts almost to a criticism of the new direction of events in Nigeria up to May 1966, when the poem itself was written. Nowhere is Okigbo's feeling of resentment more positively expressed than in the last of the poems written in May 1966, **'Elegy for Alto'**. In this 'Elegy' the poet's repeated insistence on 'robbers', 'eagles' and 'politicians' (his hatred for these symbols of imperialism goes as far back as the poems of *Heavensgate* and **'Fragments out of the Deluge'**) amounts to an unequivocal suspicion as well as fear of a return of events to the *status quo ante*, with all the implications that this might contain. . . . (pp. 176-77)

Path of Thunder is, by its very theme and time of composition, a description of the general euphoria which marked the public mood between January and May 1966, after the first military coup in Nigeria. But it is also a poem of a characteristically individual and mature reflection, written by a man who had just turned thirty-three and who was filled more and more with the desire for commitment through positive action as an antidote to the boring insulation and anonymity through fear which art had hitherto provided him. . . . The discarding of the cloak of impersonality, with its corresponding desire for positive commitment, is even more clearly revealed by the poet's deliberate self-insertion (the possibility of sheer conceit and self-immolation on the poet's part cannot be ruled out) into two of the poems in *Path of Thunder*. . . . (p. 177)

Christopher's revolt was an essentially artistic one, expressed by means of his poetry. Prophetic, menacing, terrorist, violent, protesting—his poetry was all these and at the same time it was humane, modest and often sentimental. But in a society such as Okigbo lived and wrote in, where the few leaders, including ministers of culture, could hardly afford the cheap luxury of reading the works of their writers, Christopher's scarring message was naturally and safely insulated, by its shrewd and learned obscurity, from comprehension and possible censorship.

The problem of identity thus emerges effectively as one of the dominant themes in Okigbo's poetry. We have seen this variously treated—with the poet's own awareness of the intrusive world outside—in *Heavensgate, Limits* and *Distances*, in the form of man's perennial quest for self-discovery, both on the artistic and the psychic levels. Hence we can conclude that in these poems there exists a deep-seated consciousness of certain shifts in the personality structure of the main characters (who may not necessarily be the poet himself), with the corresponding desire for fulfilment and integration. This may also account for the generally archetypal pattern in Okigbo's poetry, shown in his preference for exiles, for the uprooted or the prodigal

as protagonists, and also his use of myth and ritual to illustrate his ideal form of artistic experience. Thus a principle of creative intuition in art and poetry, by no means entirely original, is proposed for us and defined throughout Okigbo's poetry in terms of the individual artist's reconciliation of his first and second 'selves'. This refers to the capacity of every poet to rise above the inner contradictions of his personality and the existentialist *angst* imposed by his spiritual and physical worlds, in order to give forth an expression compatible with 'organic voice', the imprint, that is, of his own selfhood. The enactment of such a quest follows the well-known pattern of purification and initiation. It also outlines the course of true catharsis. (pp. 181-82)

The dilemma of Christopher Okigbo is that he never truly experienced this normal purgation of art. Every new artistic experience left, on the palate of his intuition, nothing but the sour taste of something raw and unfinished, a question mark and, therefore, a burning desire to start afresh. In other words, his poetic world is informed by a sense of the inscrutable absence of reconciliation of opposites. It is this that has shaped the puzzled syntax of his creative rhetoric. (p. 182)

Sunday O. Anozie, in his Christopher Okigbo: Creative Rhetoric *(© Sunday O. Anozie 1972), Evans Brothers Limited, 1972, 203 p.*

OMOLARA LESLIE

"The Lament of the Masks", one of Okigbo's last poems, was written in commemoration of the W. B. Yeats centenary. . . .

It was appropriate that Okigbo should write a poem to celebrate Yeats and his influence on other poets since contemporary African writers coming up then had been much influenced by the tradition of modern verse represented by Hopkins and Yeats, Eliot and Pound. Interestingly though, Okigbo does not use a modern English style in this poem; rather, he sings Yeats in the style of the traditional Yoruba praise song in which the attributes of a hero, ancestor or aristocrat are hailed in animal imagery and analogy from nature. . . . Section III of the Lament combines the direct address and the naming of the deeds of the hero, typical of the praise song with the use of special symbolism, "the white elephant". Such use of special symbolism occurs in the Yoruba praise song, where in contrast to Okigbo's use, the meaning of the symbol was known by all members (at least by the elders) in the community. . . . In Okigbo's **"Lament"**, the white elephant symbol serves a more Western poetic function because individual interpretation is permissible, even necessary. Yeats' white elephant could be many things: his poetic activity; his mystical ends expressed in his later poetry; even the cause of the Irish.

However, **"The Lament of the Masks"** is not in the style of poetry associated with Okigbo's name. It represents a new direction in his poetic style for after this poem he was to speak more and more in an African voice. In fact, by the time he writes his last poems, agonised outcries prophesying war, he had dropped all affectations and was using a poetic rendering of his own conversational voice combined with the style of traditional verse. With Okigbo's name comes to mind, a very personal poetry written in so recondite an idiom that it has given rise to critical debate as to its value; its effectiveness and even its nonsensical nature; and as to whether a reader is not a profane intruder into such hallowed and subjective verse. (p. 2)

Okigbo's earliest poems . . . are entitled *Four Canzones,* and they show the influence of his classical education. The first canzone **"Song of the Forest"** is modelled on the first verse of Virgil's First Eclogue. . . .

The poet Okigbo is sitting in Lagos gazing mentally back at the country, writing like Virgil for an urban reading public, musing about a modern Nigerian problem of alienation from the rural life. Okigbo has the good taste though, not to affect the pastoral device of the imitation of the action of actual shepherds. Okigbo's short exercise is nothing of the scope of Virgil's Eclogue. . . . Okigbo does not develop his eclogue; nor does he expatiate on public themes. He brings into the poem rather the personal subjectivity of the poet in the twentieth century; in this way imitating Virgil innovatively; therefore achieving a new approach to the pastoral in material and tone. (p. 3)

In fact, Okigbo's second canzone seems to be a variation of the pastoral device. Instead of two shepherds in a dialogue, there are two characters A and B who in solo and unison poetise about the misery of life, deciding to "rest with wrinkled faces / watching the wall clock strike each hour / in a dry cellar" until they choke and die rather "than face the blasts and buffets" of "the mad generation" presumably in the cities. Despite the imitation of Virgilian pastoral poetry and the echoes of Pound however, these early canzones also show some African traits. Firstly, three of them are written to be read or sung to musical instruments after the style of Senghor and in the tradition of the indigenous presentation of African oral poetry. Secondly, like Achebe in his novels, Okigbo reveals a partiality to the "goose pimpling" ogene. Thirdly, the poems voice neo-African themes, such as the contrast between the old and the new after colonialism; the traditional and rural in Africa contrasted with the urbanized and the Westernised; the alienation of the Westernised African; the Hobson's choice he faces between joining "the mad generation" in the filthy Westernised cities or remaining with the alienated and restless poor in the hinterland; the challenge posed by Western intellectual activity to African thought, in particular African religion. . . . (pp. 3-4)

"The Lament of the Masks" indicates a new development in style from the clear Virgilian statement of the first canzone to the subjective imagery of modern verse. . . . Despite the literary echoes . . . such as 'white lilies' and 'roses of blood'; 'woodnymphs' and 'snow-patch', the poem does show new confidence in the use of language . . . and a newly-expressed concern with the religion of his village in particular the female deity, Idoto, his **"Watermaid"**; his "lioness with the armpit fragrance," "white queen and goddess" whose worship provide some of Okigbo's most beautiful lyrics with their symbolism and imagic pattern as in *Heavensgate.* Most significantly, however, in **"The Lament of the Masks"** there emerges for the first time a poetic persona who is put to more than thematic use, who will now and subsequently in mythopoeic form explore the delicate labyrinths of the poet's subjectivity. . . . This poetic personality will be increasingly dramatised, placed always at the center of Okigbo's envisioned rituals and creative act. So much does Okigbo identify with this poetic self that in the last poems prophesying war, in particular in the poems, **"Hurrah for Thunder"** and **"Elegy for Slit-drum"**, the artistic self is inadequately subsumed into vision and experience. The face breaks through the mask.

The fourth canzone **"The Lament of the Lavender Mist"** carries forward the theme of memory as an important experiential dimension to our poet's imaginative vision. This theme is now more symbolically expressed than previously. In style, the canzone is more broken in rhythm than the earlier pieces. It is evocative of meaning cumulatively through phrase juxtapositions; repetitions and rephrasings; freely collocating images from Christianity and African religion. (p. 4)

Okigbo had attained his distinctive voice and his chosen stance towards the purpose and the doing of his art. From this lament onwards, the act of creation, the writing itself is a rite, transposed in medium. . . . The poet, as in Soyinka's early poems, is in a self-conscious act of creative ritual. The transposed rite is about experience, limned from memory and recast as ritual, while the poetic self is always at the dramatic center of the creative concentricity.

On one level, **"The Lament of the Lavender Mist"** can be read as the history of a love relationship; on another as an account of the poet's love for his art and his evolution as poet. It is the mythopoeic form employed in this Lament which is to energise Okigbo in [*Silences, Heavensgate* and *Limits*]. . . .

The first part of *Silences,* subtitled **"The Lament of the Silent Sisters"** was inspired . . . by the events of the day which were the Western Nigeria crisis and the death of Patrice Lumumba. This Lament shows the poet borrowing from all and sundry; taking poetic flight from any image which touched his imagination. . . . Not only does this lament reveal the rewards of predatory and eclectic reading, it indicates yet another new poetic direction, . . . towards the conscious and experimental use of the resources of the song form such as choruses, refrains, and repetitions; the conveyance of meaning through a contrapuntal use of assonance, dissonance and even pure sound itself. (p. 5)

The second part of **"the Silent Sisters"** entitled **"the Lament of the Drums"** is an agitated poem about deprivation and loss; unavoidable pain and mourning expressed through analogues of unanswered praise songs and unconsumated feasts, uncommencable journeys, and unanswered letters; unstemmable tears of wailing populations; and the lament of Ishtar for Tammuz. . . . *Silences* foreshadows orgies of violence and carnage on the national landscape. *Distances* [which follows] is a unified apocalyptic vision of consummation, rendered as a ritual of sacrifice involving the poet, who as victim and votive personage, walks the experiental stations of his cross, beyond "Death, herself . . . paring her fingernails" to his homecoming to which he is "sole witness".

Okigbo's last poems from **"The Lament of the Masks"** . . . to **"Path of Thunder"** . . . exploit, more than his earlier writing the attributes of African traditional poetry. Not only are popular proverbs and sayings, epigram and innuendo used, dramatic and situational African images abound such as the ritual of circumcision in **"Elegy of the Wind."** . . .

It is easy to see how Okigbo could move from exploiting music in general to using a specific musically expressive form such as African traditional poetry. The poems in *Path of Thunder* convey the rhythms of African verse in the long line and in the structural penchant for inculcating complete thoughts in single lines, best exemplified by **"Come Thunder"** and **"Elegy for Slitdrum"**: the latter being perhaps the most African poem of the group in its structure, and presentation; dramatic tensions and language. The imagination behind the poem is decidedly African. Yet these poems cohere in mythopoeic vision with the earlier ones. . . . The recurrent metaphor of iron, thunder, sentient elements and predatory life are compounded in an African mode to describe the violent political upheaval of the period. The favored elephant symbol reappears as the obdurate

Nigerian nation, among other meanings, stumbling towards its doom. (p. 6)

Okigbo's poetry will have to be evaluated in two sets since the published forms of his poems under the title *Labyrinths* are so dissimilar to their earlier published forms and so re-worked as to be completely new poems. His introduction to the volume sheds light on the artists who have influenced him. No mention however, is made of Senghor, to whom one finds similarities in poetic modes and in formal presentation; situational and verbal—the main difference being the stance of the poet protagonist.

Okigbo is significant because he did what most of the West African writers in English were doing in the 60's—a very personal poetry in a personal idiom—and he brought this mode to a virtuoso point. He represents their initially "art for art's sake" attitude which changed over time. His development therefore traces a West African pattern of artistic evolution from private anguish to public commitment. In addition, Okigbo exemplifies a neo-African wedding of the African to the Western poetic traditions to the rejuvenation of the effeteness and world weariness of the latter. He is, to my mind, one of the finest African poets in English, to be valued for the sheer beauty of his finely honed verse; his most delicate sensibility and the artistic discipline which informs the structure and the lyrical simplicity of his verse, a simplicity which conveys a false impression of facility. (p. 7)

> *Omolara Leslie, "The Poetry of Christopher Okigbo: Its Evolution and Significance," in* Studies in Black Literature *(copyright 1973 by Raman K. Singh), Vol. 4, No. 2, Summer, 1973, pp. 1-10.*

ROMANUS N. EGUDU

One of the worst effects of colonialism and colonial evangelization in West Africa has been the degradation of the indigenous West African culture in general and the indigenous religious worship in particular. The efforts of the early Christian missionaries were directed at estranging the natives from their indigenous religion and "planting" in them the imported Christian religion. Christopher Okigbo sees himself as a prodigal who has left this home religion for the foreign one. And, at a moment of mature realization, he returns to his original religion to revive and preserve the indigenous system of worship. This accounts for the satirical attitude to Christianity in his poetry.

Thus in Okigbo's poetry the themes of religious suppression, anti-Christianity, religious revival, and literary struggle are predominant. Besides these themes, however, he deals with love and with political issues, but only on a minor scale. (p. 3)

Early in *Heavensgate* ("Passage I"), Okigbo strikes a sad note. It is a note of mourning a dead mother. Like a "sunbird" the protagonist of the poem sings a song of woe. . . . To the poet the mother represents the indigenous culture. She is the same mother Idoto addressed in the poem "Idoto," who is a river goddess. And the poet's indigenous religion centers on the worship of this goddess. This goddess—mother—is, as it were, dead (*i.e.*, suppressed by the Christian religion), and the poet is mourning her.

The loss of the indigenous religion is a serious one, for it implies the loss of "innocence." Thus in the second part of **"Passage"** the poet responded to the song of the sunbird during the period of his innocence and that was before "white buck and helmet"—representing Christian missionaries—"pulled us thro innocence."

Christianity has waged a terrible war against the indigenous gods. (p. 4)

Okigbo's poetry reflects this kind of situation. **"Limits VII"** shows Flannagan, a Catholic missionary, preaching "the Pope's message". . . . The message is destruction; and there is the implication that it will be effective, for when fire is set to grass, the grass will naturally be burned clear.

In **"Limits X"** . . . the enemies of the indigenous gods are shown in action. These are the Christian missionaries or their agents. They first kill the "sunbird" which is sacred to the gods and then, entering the forest, find the twin gods living there. The malicious "scanning" of the forest points to savagery that will mark the vandalism of the invading "beasts". . . . Like the soldiers who cast lots on the garment of Christ after crucifying Him, the despoilers of Okigbo's twin gods divide among them the gods' "ornaments," "beads," "carapace," and "shell." The evocation of the Christian image (death of Christ) is a variation of the technique of juxtaposing Christian and indigenous images. . . . Besides, in this very incident of the killing of the twin gods the Christian and the pagan meet. The fertility ritual in which a god is killed or hanged—an old pagan practice—is reflected by Okigbo, though his context shows an antagonistic rather than a religious purpose. (pp. 4-5)

Christopher Okigbo reacts contemptuously and critically to the Christianity that has suppressed his native religion and its gods. For Christianity has done him two wrongs. First, it has estranged him from his indigenous system of worship for a long period of his life; and, secondly, it has nothing reasonable to offer him as a substitute. Because of his sad experiences in the Catholic religion, he satirizes the Catholic Church in his poems. (p. 6)

It should be noted that [Okigbo] is attacking the management of religion and politics . . . , not religion *per se* as an idea. After all, he is constantly defending his own indigenous religion against foreign corruption and desecration. He accepts that the "Mystery" (of religion) would be a witness to "the red-hot blade on the right breast / the scar of the crucifix" if only there were not the "errors of the rendering." In other words, to him the rulers of the church have misinterpreted the religion of Christ. (p. 8)

Since Christopher Okigbo could not be accommodated any longer in the Catholic religion, where he felt exiled, he decided to go back to the indigenous religion to revive it for himself and retain it. Thus in **"Idoto"** *(Heavensgate)* the poet stands before "mother Idoto" as "a prodigal" desiring to return to her who is his parent and deity, and praying to her to "give ear and hearken" to his "cry." . . . He is a prodigal, and outcast, an exile (the word "prodigal" is used three times in *Heavensgate*). And, having had an unsatisfactory experience with the imported Catholic religion, he, like the prodigal son of the Bible, comes back home now to his parent, begging for readmission into the family fold.

From now on, Okigbo's poems begin to teem with the apparatus of indigenous religious worship. (p. 9)

In **"Lustra (iii)"** *(Heavensgate* . . .), we get a mixture of Catholic and indigenous religious symbols. But while the Christian references are made satirically, the indigenous worship is carried out with genuine and serious intentions. . . . (p. 10)

There is a revolution of the spirit in Okigbo, but he is not trying to revolutionize the Catholic church with any view to making it better. This is not his aim; it is not even necessary for him. He has simply exposed this church with all the harm it has done to the indigenous values, which makes it unacceptable to him. The only choice left to him is "homecoming."

That homecoming is uppermost in his mind can . . . be illustrated by reference to **"Distances."** In this poem in which the refrain—"I am the sole witness to my homecoming"—runs from the beginning to the end, the idea of homecoming assumes a tone of uncertainty, for it is to a dream that the poet is returning. . . . Okigbo's period of exile in the Christian religion can as well be described as a period of "dark labyrinth"; and he is returning to a dream which will quickly become a reality. (p. 11)

Christopher Okigbo has struggled as much to establish his fame as a poet as to revive and preserve his indigenous religion. Like every artist he must have had to be cautious and wary, and must have had his difficult time with critics. His poetry is generally difficult and sometimes obscure. . . . Okigbo was sensitive about comments or questions about his poetry. . . . Thus, in some of his poems he has dealt with the problem of an artist struggling for survival.

Limits II is about this theme. It is packed full with images of the desire for growth, struggling for light, and the desire for expression. We have a whole picture of a tender child in the midst of giants, or of an equatorial forest where the gigantic trees form a canopy with their leaves on top, preventing a low undergrowth from getting light and rain for effective growth. (pp. 11-12)

The struggle to succeed as a poet in the face of other poets and critics and to attract publishers is quite a common literary experience. But in its usual extraordinary manner Okigbo's imagination has re-created the theme in such a way that one wonders if he meant to say anything beyond this. (p. 12)

The entire political scene in Nigeria comes under the surveying rays of Okigbo's poetic imagination. In the **"Elegy for Slit-drum"** and **"Elegy for Alta"** . . . the political corruption leading to the crisis of the later years is clearly shown. In the latter, politicians are represented as "robbers," parading their wealth and power. In the former we hear that "parliament is now on sale" and that "the voters are lying in wait." "The cabinet has gone to hell" and "ministers are now in gaol." The elephant symbol is very significant in the poem. It stands for all the old politicians who have fallen victims of the crises in the country. But the poet expresses some fear: the "thunder that has struck the elephant/the same thunder can make a bruise."

This is the warning that is central to the poem **"Hurrah for Thunder."** . . . Here the "elephant," who is a king of the jungle, is destroyed by the thunder that has been invoked by the "hunters." These hunters are warned by the poet to the effect that they themselves may also be victims of the same thunder. . . . It is in this prophetic function that the greatness of Okigbo as a poet of crises lies. And, besides, the clear and impeccable images in which Okigbo has couched his ideas not only confirm him as the purist image-maker, but also portray him as much more developed in tone and seriousness, precise in his visions, and clear in his expression. (pp. 16-17)

"Path of Thunder," particularly **"Come Thunder,"** has shown that Okigbo could handle a very complicated (political) issue without being unnecessarily obscure; and this clarity, coupled with effective imagery and appropriate emotional appeal, has made the poem one of the most successful of Okigbo's poems.

Christopher Okigbo is so famous for his craftsmanship that it is worthwhile to discuss his style separately. In fact, in his poetry as a whole, the art seems to matter more than the thought that is communicated. This does not mean that his style is always successful: it simply means that his preoccupation in poetic activity is craftsmanship. The dominant stylistic elements in his poetry are incantation, sound, imagery, and borrowing from other languages and other authors. (pp. 17-18)

The essence of this method lies in its emotional intensity, its lyricism and economy achieved by the use of effective short phrases instead of complete sentences. It is the method which Okigbo has inherited from the Igbo indigenous culture and literature. It is so pervading in his poetry that it is found in poems that have nothing to do with worship or invocation. In fact the main point of this book is to prove that the modern West African poets have creditably made use of the indigenous African poetic traditions as well as the British and other foreign traditions, and examples are rife to demonstrate the veracity of this thesis. Indeed, Okigbo has drawn some of his most significant modes of expression and stylistic elements from the traditional African linguistic and other experiences. (p. 18)

Okigbo is also noted for his music and sound effects. No African poet rivals him in this respect. Sound dominates his poetry so much so that in some of his poems it completely overshadows the meaning. (p. 19)

Not less important than sound or music in Okigbo's craftsmanship is image-making. (p. 20)

Very often Okigbo is so taken up with image-making that he loses sight of the fact that the images in a single poem do not make meaning or unity of thought. One does not see why such images should be grouped together to form the poem. . . . It is Okigbo's weakness, which arises from his greatness, that with his beautiful images, he only sets his readers guessing at what he means.

Finally, Okigbo has the habit of borrowing tags-lines from other languages and other authors. . . . This element in Okigbo's poetry is the least effective and least important. It is directly the influence of such foreign poets as Pound and Eliot on him.

Christopher Okigbo's poetry is that of agonized and excruciating experiences. His historical and social insight has created a labyrinth of life, from which the process of extrication is not easy. In his poetry the traditional and the foreign elements meet with equal force; and, in the exploration of his none-too-beautiful world, the poet "uses the type of broken melody perfected by T. S. Eliot to evoke the reproachful sadness of abandoned shrines and rotting images, symbols which quite naturally carry the whole weight of an African tradition which has always concentrated the expression of its values upon them." Okigbo's poetry is essentially a hodgepodge of many cryptic ingredients and this has naturally led to its tense obscurity—a quality by no means to its credit. (pp. 21-2)

Romanus N. Egudu, "Cultural Oppression: The Poetry of Christopher Okigbo," in his Four Modern West African Poets *(copyright by Romanus Egudu 1977), NOK Publishers International Ltd., 1977, pp. 1-22.*

Alan (Stewart) Paton

1903-

South African novelist, short story writer, biographer, auto-biographer, and essayist.

Paton is perhaps best known for his novels *Cry, the Beloved Country* and *Too Late the Phalarope*. Both of these works, as with the majority of his writing, expose and confront the South African situation. With a perceptive and sympathetic understanding, Paton examines the exploitation of nonwhites by the elite ruling class and reveals the effects this has not only on the exploited, but on the country as a whole.

It is with a religious rather than a political conviction that Paton devotes his life to the betterment of his country. Coming from a puritanical background heavily influenced both morally and stylistically by the Old Testament prophets, Paton approaches his cause with a quiet yet passionate eloquence. Some critics feel that the parable-like qualities of his writing—the spare and evenly biblical prose, the underdeveloped characters, the heavy thematic significance—detract from the literary value of his works. Others, however, feel that these points provide a classical, absorbing power which captivates the reader.

(See also *CLC*, Vols. 4, 10; *Contemporary Authors*, Vols. 15-16; *Contemporary Authors Permanent Series*, Vol. 1; and *Something about the Author*, Vol. 11.)

Photograph by Dennis Bughwan, Durban, South Africa

ALFRED KAZIN

Ever since he published **"Cry, The Beloved Country,"** a book which so passionately brought to the attention of the outside world the plight of the bitterly exploited native population of South Africa, Alan Paton has come to seem one of the few voices in that somber and menaced country that still speak out for liberal values. . . .

Mr. Paton, to put it mildly, is not a dangerous revolutionary, nor, to put it as simply and respectfully as possible, is he a writer of great originality. He writes as a sensitive liberal, placed in a situation whose ferocious depths plainly alarm him. . . . The humanity of his work and the limitations of his fiction are clearly marked in **"Too Late the Phalarope."**

Mr. Paton's subject here is the downfall of a South African hero, Pieter van Vlaanderen, a young police officer of the best Boer stock who represents what is legendary and noblest in South Africa; the book is in large part, I gather, to be taken as an allegory of South Africa today, in relation both to its past and to its cruel unawareness of inner weakness. Mr. Paton has something real to write about, which is why one wishes he had created characters strong enough in every detail to support the burden of meaning he puts on them.

Pieter's father is one of the great landowners, a leader in the Nationalist party and a harsh, somber man who reads nothing but the Bible, despises the English, and rules his wife and family with absolute authority. Pieter himself has a "tragic flaw" in him, to recall the classic formula for the Shakespearean hero; unfortunately, he is so evenly and perfectly split between his strength and weakness that it is hard to take him altogether seriously. . . .

The key to Pieter's isolation is his relation to his father—that is, to the past. The father has always distrusted and scorned in his son a tendency to sit and brood alone. . . .

On the old man's birthday Pieter buys him a book about South African birds. Although old van Vlaanderen never reads anything but the Bible, and is profoundly distrustful of anything in English, he has a passion for the birds of his country; and discovering that the English author of the book has not properly identified a particular bird, the phalarope, he tries in his stiff and clumsy way to win Pieter by going out into the high country with him to show his son what a phalarope really looks like.

They find one, but it is too late, the bird, like the fabulous open country in which they find it, is a symbol of the mythical innocence, freshness and excitement of early South Africa to which Pieter can never return. He has already prepared his downfall, has indulged wistfully his desire for "corruption" by relations with a young native girl. . . .

Under the "Immorality Act" of the country, sexual relations between whites and blacks are a legal offense. Pieter is sent to prison, his father strikes his name from the great family Bible and dies of shame, and the whole family withdraws from the community in horror at Pieter's crime "against the race." . . .

What is best in this novel . . . is the atmosphere Mr. Paton conveys of the sultry, brooding tension in South Africa itself. . . . The whole story prepares one for some terrible catastrophe, some mighty downfall, which seems to point to more than Pieter van Vlaanderen himself. (p. 1)

The book does this for us: it . . . gives us the local color, the taste and wildness of a new country. But Mr. Paton's characters, and his telling of the story in a too even biblical style, are finally much less satisfactory. Although he can give us an almost hypnotic sense of these people, they are, after all, just types. . . . Everything in such a story depends on the author's ability to make us believe in the hero's strength far more than in his flaw, which should *surprise* us; here the catastrophe is hinted at so steadily throughout the book that when it finally comes we are moved, but not enlightened. . . . (p. 24)

> Alfred Kazin, "Downfall of a South African Hero," in The New York Times Book Review (© 1953 by The New York Times Company; reprinted by permission), August 23, 1953, pp. 1, 24.

SHERIDAN BAKER

Too Late the Phalarope invites us to think of Alan Paton more simply as a novelist than as a kind of Christian plenipotentiary to South Africa. Not that *Cry the Beloved Country* is a religious tract, or natural accident—but the literary qualities of the first book, which seem to have sprung from the very ground, seem in the second imported. Though *Too Late the Phalarope* is no patchwork, its relative limitations can be detected. I think, squarely in the midst of its new 'literary' features.

Similarity to Paton's first book only emphasizes the defects. (p. 152)

Paton's symbology and psychology seem sound enough. A big and autocratic father may in effect emasculate the son, may make him half girl and half athlete. A timid wife may disappoint him. His need to prove himself a man may lead him to excel on the rugby field and in the police force, and to engage in the most primitive and dangerous sexual game available. And sexual intercourse with a black girl, at the very time that it enables the son to feel himself his father's equal in potency, has the further advantage of ultimate disobedience, of punishing the father at the cruellest extremity, and of caricaturing, as it were, the white domination of black for which he stands. But something is missing, and the earliest symptoms appear in the very technique.

To be sure, there are literary gains—in new territory, in plotting, in Paton's wonderful study of guilt—but we soon sense something vaguely familiar and slightly gratuitous. Jakob van Vlaanderen, for instance, has a game leg, the result of an accident. While it helps set his stiff character, is it really functional? One remembers the gouty patriarchs of English fiction and even, guiltily, *The Katzenjammer Kids*. And any viewer of TV will recognize the conventional stage business in the following:

> He took a step or two, then without turning called to his son; and for some reason I cannot give, that was a habit of his, to start to leave a room, and then to stop, and to talk with his back turned.
>
> —Pieter, have you ever seen the phalarope?
> —The what, father?
> —The phalarope.

Naturally Paton wanted to underline his symbol, as he brings it in here for the first time. But his significant moment seems to have inspired what looks distressingly like a second-rate theatrical—the pause without turning, then the laden speech.

The dramatics have been uncertain, however, from the first. Aunt Sophie's incantatory words open the story. She herself is writing it down, she says. . . . And though Paton does some fine things with Aunt Sophie, when she reports what she herself has seen—the birthday party, the group talking after church—competition between Paton and Aunt Sophie as storyteller repeatedly breaks the illusion. For instance, we get thoughts and actions (the captain's) which neither Sophie nor her nephew, the lieutenant, could have known. . . . (pp. 152-54)

Sophie is too clearly, for all her substance, a literary device, and a rather old-fashioned one at that. She is the Nelly Dean of *Wuthering Heights*, thinned down, brought into the family, and coloured up with Rosa Dartle. . . .

Paton brings Sophie a long way into reality, but he cannot make her narrative mechanics natural. (p. 154)

Why does Paton use Aunt Sophie at all? The first reason, I think, is that he wanted an authentic Afrikaner 'voice.' (p. 155)

I think the basic reason for Aunt Sophie, however, is Paton's inability to handle one of his central symbols: sexual union with a black girl. It seems, from the book itself, that he cannot quite imagine such a thing. Sophie enables him to stop short. (p. 156)

Almost the whole of the problem concerning Stephanie, the black girl, remains outside the reality of the book. After a passage of Paton at his best—a lyrical run into the heartland, talk with an old native who needlessly adjusts an old army coat, small black boys sitting and talking about him—we suddenly find ourselves right in broad day-dream. Stephanie has become a nymph. . . .

Now, this is a rather universal fancy. . . . But Paton cannot reconcile with his realistic tragedy this nymph of day-dream, even by treating her realistically in other scenes. Stephanie in the glade is not quite Stephanie in the street, saluting the *baas* with palm facing outwards and walking off with a little dance to her step.

Toward the end of the book, Paton seems to be trying to negotiate differences by making Pieter a kind of unfortunate satyr. . . . Paton, apparently, wants Stephanie nymphlike to excuse Pieter's temptation, and goes so far as almost to obliterate the problem of evil altogether. Stephanie under the waterfall is the very epitome of the evanescent world of nature. (p. 157)

Paton associates Stephanie rather closely . . . with the birdcry of all natural goodness in this transitory life. . . . She also represents that tender side of Pieter . . . which causes the antagonism and the tragedy. Somehow this shy bird of the native homeland is like the phalarope, which represents the missing tenderness between father and son.

But the design doesn't quite trace out, for Stephanie also represents the destructive anger Pieter's father stirs in him. . . . She graphically represents the black evil of Dutch authoritarianism, the black depths into which Pieter throws himself to pay back his father. Paton has not reconciled her two opposite meanings. He could have shown the union as good and natural in defiance of a repressive code, and written the openly romantic book he flirts with by the waterfall; or he could have made Stephanie convincingly attractive in her wickedness rather than in her innocence. He tries both, though in fact he seems to avoid the problem by giving Stephanie as little space as possible, and consequently Pieter's motives remain, at least for me, unconvincingly mixed and dimly realized. . . . (p. 158)

[Sex] is not Paton's subject. It has no deep and pervasive meaning for him as it does for, let us say, Lawrence. The agonizing need for love in a black-and-white world turns embarrassingly thin for him when translated into sexual terms, even implying that all would have been saved if Pieter's wife had just been a shade more aboriginal—which, I think, is not the point intended. Paton's real compassion, his real gift for life and for fiction both, finds in his second book nothing like the complete integration of his first. . . . [The] affairs of Pieter van Vlaanderen all too often turn Paton's compassion sentimental and his creative gift slick. His symbolic bird, the deep humanity he knows and wants to make viable, comes briefly and too late; it is too shy and is really not a native here. (p. 159)

> Sheridan Baker, "Paton's Late Phalarope," in English Studies in Africa, Vol. 3, No. 2, September, 1960, pp. 152-59.

JOHN BARKHAM

["**Tales from a Troubled Land**"] is a collection of ten tales, one superb, one first-rate, the remainder of lesser quality. To begin with the best, "**Life for a Life**" ranks with the most moving writing the author has ever done. It tells of the events that follow the murder of a rich Afrikaner farmer, as seen from the viewpoint of his colored laborers. . . . The writing is dark with the menace of approaching retribution. Once more the meekness of the colored folk is contrasted with the oafish brutality of the Afrikaner police. . . . The prose is Biblical in its power, and the whole terrifying episode is set down with a quiet ferocity which wells up not from the words, but in the heart of the reader. This is a story that shows Paton at his unapproachable best.

Hardly less poignant is the brief vignette he calls "**Ha'penny**." . . .

For many years before he became a writer, Paton served as head of a renowned reform school for colored boys. Most of the stories in this book are drawn from that experience. They vary in quality: some point up the peculiarities in African ratiocination, others are mere anecdotes which puzzle or amuse. The best of this group is "**Sponono**," about a Xosa boy who always meant well but invariably acted ill. If this story proves anything at all, it is only that the two races will probably never understand each other's thinking fully.

This reminiscent side of Paton is not one to bring out the best in him. Only when grappling with the massive themes which touch his conscience does the writer in him become most eloquent. It is this which stirs him in "**A Life for a Life**," and there are flashes of it, too, in the closing story, "**A Drink in the Passage**."

> John Barkham, "Meekness and Brutality," in The New York Times Book Review (© 1961 by The New York Times Company; reprinted by permission), April 16, 1961, p. 4.

NADINE GORDIMER

In terms of tragedy as the rest of the world knows it, there is a tragedy in Alan Paton's ***Too Late the Phalarope***—the private

tragedy of a man of fine instincts in conflict with an instinct that seems misplaced from some earlier, brutish existence. The writer takes care to endow his hero with noble attributes and virtues, and provides that he shall bring about his own downfall, thus fulfilling the classical conditions of tragedy. . . .

Peter van Vlaanderen is a Greek-godlike young man with [a fatal] flaw. It takes the form of lust, a terrible hunger of lust that, it is suggested (and as modern readers we require this sort of psychological explanation, though the Greeks would not have bothered), has grown out of all proportion to the rest of van Vlaanderen's nature through his father's stern suppression of the son's affectionate needs as a child. . . . Peter van Vlaanderen's lust takes as its object, as that of many men has done before him, an out-of-work servant girl. But she is black. The colour problem makes of this lust of van Vlaanderen's something hideous and unnatural, rather than an unfortunate venture into infidelity on the part of a strictly-brought-up young man. In terms of a morality outside South Africa, what he does would involve him in a private struggle, a private hurt and unhappiness between him and the wife whom he loves, and some social disapproval; but within the South African morality what he has done is dragged down the scale of sin to match the evilness of Humbert Humbert's relations with Lolita. (p. 521)

In the end, van Vlaanderen's relations with the girl are discovered, and he is undone; and all the consequences of tragedy fall upon him. But the morality of the novel—the morality of South Africa—claims tragedy on the wrong count. The thunderbolt misses; the explosion, like the moral truth, is off-centre. For lust can be a tragedy for a man, but it is not a national disaster. . . .

In ***Too Late the Phalarope*** there are two voices that speak outside the accepted morality of the book and they are not detached at all. The police captain who arrests van Vlaanderen says: "I know of an offence against the law, and, as a Christian, I know an offence against God; but I do not know an offence against the race." And when all normal ties of love and affection prove less strong than shame, and Peter van Vlaanderen's father closes his door to his son, and his wife is sent away back to her parents, the old aunt who has narrated part of the book says: "The truth is that we are not as other people any more." (p. 522)

> Nadine Gordimer, "The Novel and the Nation in South Africa," in The Times Literary Supplement (© Times Newspapers Ltd. (London) 1961; reproduced from The Times Literary Supplement by permission), No. 3102, August 11, 1961, pp. 520-23.*

D. D. CHAMBERS

It is not surprising that six of the ten ***Tales From A Troubled Land*** should be set within the framework and atmosphere of a reformatory, an environment at once the reflection and the microcosm of South Africa itself. Author Alan Paton is well acquainted with the setting that he uses, . . . but the "reformatory" stories are unfortunately and somewhat tediously similar in theme and texture. None really approaches the tender and almost "fey" quality of ***Cry The Beloved Country*** or ***Too Late The Phalarope***. The difficulty that the reader experiences in these stories may be with the rigid framework of warden and prisoner within reformatory walls, at times reminiscent of Thomas Mann at his worst, or it may be in the obstacle of accepting the carefree listlessness of the Africans themselves. It is nevertheless unmistakably difficult for the North American reader to accept or adapt himself to the position of either African delinquent or ''European'' principal in such stories as **"Sponono"** or **"The Elephant Shooter"**. And this acceptance is even more difficult in the English-Afrikaaner relationship dealt with in **"The Worst Thing In His Life"**.

Where the true brilliance of Paton's storytelling craft makes itself obvious is in the four other stories which take place outside the prison walls. . . .

It is with **"Debbie Go Home"** and **"A Drink In The Passage"** . . . that Mr. Paton's unmistakeable and intangible genius shines through. The first of these is a truly perceptive and luminous exposition within the setting of a family of the difficult and frustrating plight of the Cape Coloreds. Caught in the grip of the racial laws of South Africa between white and African, it acknowledges its desire for social recognition and prominence in the daughter while refusing the intrinsic inferiority and subservience inherent in such an acceptance in the son. **"A Drink In The Passage"**, however, goes beyond mere brilliance or compassion to supreme and enduring artistry and craftsmanship and that rare and almost apocalyptic moment of perceptivity that Wordsworth has called a ''spot of time'' and James Joyce an ''epiphany.'' In this story are all the tragic and almost inexpressible elements of the South African dilemma expressed with ultimate tenuousness and sensibility in terms of a single piece of sculpture and its implications. And in it, as much as in his two previous novels, is all Paton's haunting power and lyric genius.

> *D. D. Chambers, ''Books Reviewed: 'Tales from a Troubled Land','' in* The Canadian Forum, *Vol. XLI, No. 487, September, 1961, p. 144.*

EDMUND FULLER

Much has been published recently about the decline of tragedy, and the question has been asked whether tragedy can be written in this age. Offstage, during the discussion, Alan Paton went ahead and did it—in terms of the novel—in *Too Late the Phalarope*. It was the book that followed his much-acclaimed first novel, *Cry, the Beloved Country*. It offered him, therefore, all the notorious ''second book'' challenges, as well as the problems of tragedy. The two books are an interesting study in the tragic—and an element beyond. (p. 83)

The core of *Too Late the Phalarope* is classically simple: Pieter van Vlaanderen, a police lieutenant, honored in the community, breaks the iron law of the South African Immorality Act. Thereby he is destroyed and his family with him. A secret flaw has brought about the fall of a man of stature. He comprehends what has happened, and recognizes his own responsibility in it. Nevertheless, the story contains forces that become cumulative inevitabilities, helping to thrust him on an inexorable path. As in *Cry, the Beloved Country,* we are given a balanced picture of environmental influences coexistent with personal responsibility.

Four major factors—two of which are social and two, personal—produce the tragedy. The first of these is the psychotic rigidity of the Afrikaner community in South Africa. An illicit sexual encounter might cause varying degrees of trouble in marriage, family, and community anywhere. But it is not sex that destroys Pieter—it is race. . . . His name is destroyed irreparably and all who bear his name are consumed in the shame of it.

The second social element is puritanism, in the community and in Pieter's father, Jacob van Vlaanderen. The puritanism of the community, of course, has theological and historical roots that predate the race psychosis. But there has been a natural, inevitable absorption of the one strain into the other, so that they have become indissoluble and mutually reinforcing. Thus a deep emotional disturbance has been given the sanction of morality and the prejudice of man translated into the law of God.

It is such men as Jacob van Vlaanderen who make up the Afrikaner community, and it is partly the community that has formed Jacob van Vlaanderen, putting its own stamp upon those elements of character that are uniquely his. He is a good man in the letter of the law and of puritan moral codes, but praise of him, if such it be, must stop there. He is as hard and merciless a judge of men as any who ever walked in the line of Calvin and Knox in colonial America or puritan England.

The unyielding will and emotional insensitivity of Jacob are the root of the first of the personal disorders that prepare the long way for Pieter's fall: a deep hostility between father and son. (pp. 83-5)

Tante Sophie, who frankly calls herself a ''watcher,'' tells the tale in a generally direct way, though the limits of knowledge in first-person narration are occasionally strained. . . . In recurring passages of high rhapsodic tone—definitely conventionalized—she functions as chorus. It is both effective and slightly overdone. In the classic tragic manner, she reiterates the already accomplished doom, so that the suspense, which is great, is not the suspense of ''whether'' but the greater one of ''how.'' (pp. 85-6)

The fourth of the major destructive factors is the tension between Pieter and his wife, Nella. She is of a gentle and timorous nature, loving her husband but unable to venture into the depths of his mind and spirit where his dangerous conflicts rage. Also there is an inhibition upon their sexual life. Puritanism has conditioned Nella to believe in a sharp division between the bodily passions and the other elements of love, which in her eyes are essentially ''higher.'' She gives herself and then withdraws. Pieter longs for a sustained sexual harmony with her, based on an acceptance of the unity of all aspects of love. Failure to achieve this does contribute to Pieter's *swartgalligheid*, the deadly black mood. . . . (pp. 86-7)

The obsessive drive that carries Pieter to the secretly-smiling black girl, Stephanie, takes its rise from a constellation of factors which I would not presume to analyze clinically. Paton has captured the agony of obsession powerfully. But sex surely is more the operational means than the aim of it. A game of symbol-hunting might be played with the image of the bird and the name of the bird that is the occasion of a fleeting communication between this father and son. On the face of it, however, Paton, by his emphasis, has given this relationship the crucial place. He suggests that if some bond of emotion and interest had really united these two, in Pieter's boyhood, the tragedy would not have happened. (pp. 87-8)

A bitter, buried core of hostility is the explosive charge in Pieter. It takes its shattering force from the thick, hard casing of the social environment which provides the containing pressure that makes all great explosions. The immediate fuse is the sexual strain with Nella. (p. 88)

If it were simply consuming sexual hunger driving Pieter he could and would have found means to appease it, secretly and safely, within his own race. But "the thing that he hates," this "something that could bring no joy," is not only sexual, with the piquancy of a primitive, raw lust, it is also destruction and revenge. This is the one sure and deadly blow against his father, against Nella and his children, against Tante Sophie, and against the Afrikaner community. To this should be added— and against himself. These are his hates. He does not comprehend them; his real motivation is well below the level of his consciousness. He does not understand that he loves and hates at the same time. (p. 89)

Pieter cannot reach [Nella] in complete unity. . . . But that is not a total impasse and is not enough to drive him to the black girl. The basic trouble is, he cannot communicate his whole nature to Nella as he desperately needs to do. For expressing and exploring his rebellion against the communal code, her softness is as impermeable as his father's hardness. (p. 90)

Inevitably, comparisons with *The Scarlet Letter* and *Crime and Punishment* arise. Once Pieter has committed his act, there is no possible release for him but total exposure—a dilemma he shares in part with Arthur Dimmesdale and Raskolnikov. Paton gives us a long sequence of superb suspense, arising out of guilty misunderstandings of innocent natural coincidences. But just as the death wish is commonly unconscious, so Pieter suffers an agonized dread of discovery, unconscious of the fact that it is that exposure and its consequences that have motivated him from the start.

This, it seems to me, is what Paton has wrought intuitively. It is not made wholly clear to any of the persons in [*Too Late the Phalarope*] and it is not possible to say how far it was present in Paton's conscious intention, but it is at least intuitively unerring in all the elements as presented. (p. 92)

> *Edmund Fuller, "Alan Paton: Tragedy and Beyond," in his* Books with Men behind Them *(copyright © 1959, 1961, 1962 by Edmund Fuller; reprinted by permission of McIntosh and Otis, Inc.), Random House, 1962, pp. 83-101.*

HENRY HEWES

Although Alan Paton has come to be known as the poet of South African race relations, his point of greatest involvement often seems to be the more universal and eternal mystery of father-son relations. . . . [In his play *Sponono*] the same theme occasionally comes to the surface to capture our deeper interest in this admirable if routine portrait of life in a South African reformatory.

For while Mr. Paton and his collaborator, Krishna Shah, have with some success caught the whole panorama of a reformatory life that seems not essentially different from what it is in some American institutions of this kind, and have added to it a folk overtone unique to the conflict between tribal Africa and the ways of its European colonizers, it is in those moments when the principal attempts to break through to his most hopeful and difficult protégé, Sponono, that we are most moved. . . .

The truest problem of this play . . . is the exploration of Sponono's compulsions to good and evil and of the principal's parental necessity to be fair to all his sons as he patiently encourages their adjustment to an unjust society while trying to respond to one extraordinarily profound boy in his charge.

There can be no simple answer or even full understanding of such a boy, and the play wisely dismisses the traditional sociological excuses it briefly considers. It does suggest that the

principal's inability to believe one true statement among a pack of Sponono's lies set off the latter's self-destructive and antisocial transformation from good to evil. And insofar as all school principals and fathers find themselves unwilling or unable to sustain the degree of attention and faith required by this sort of boy, this constitutes a tragic fact of existence irrespective of the ultimate fate of either party.

> *Henry Hewes, "The Union 'from' South Africa," in* Saturday Review (© *1964 Saturday Review Magazine Co.; reprinted by permission), Vol. XLVII, No. 16, April 18, 1964, p. 31.*

DENNIS BRUTUS

[Alan Paton] started what seems to me almost a new era in South African writing. What is interesting about it is that other people had written not much less competently the sort of thing which Paton wrote in *Cry, the Beloved Country,* but somehow they did not set in motion the kind of cycle which Paton did. If you know *Cry, the Beloved Country,* you will know that it is a rather simple story. It is a narration of a black man in contact with a society which he doesn't really understand—a society in which he finds himself either unable to cope, or he finds himself sucked into the worst elements of that society. He ends as a criminal and the society is accused of having made him a criminal. All this is really very straightforward and, in a sense, almost trite—and I don't think Paton himself would mind if one described it in these terms.

One must not think in colour categories, but it is very difficult to resist thinking of Alan Paton as a white man, a sympathizing white man standing outside the South African society with all its complexities and dynamic tensions and reducing it to what is almost a parable, a simple little tale told with a certain lyricism which I think is sometimes false because it is almost like a kind of poetic prose; but telling a story which moved people, and caught people's attention. . . . It is almost as if a serious novel on the theme of the disintegration of African culture and society, a serious novel on the misfits in our culture, would not be accepted or would not be understood; but reduced to these simple, almost fabular, terms, it was intelligible and it made an impact. (pp. 95-6)

> *Dennis Brutus, "Protest Against Apartheid," in* Protest "and Conflict" in African Literature, *edited by Cosmo Pieterse and Donald Munro (copyright © 1969 by Cosmo Pieterse, Donald Munro and contributors; reprinted by permission of Africana Publishing Company, a division of Holmes & Meier Publishers, Inc., IUB Building, 30 Irving Place, New York, NY 10003), Africana, 1969, pp. 93-100.**

ANTHONY DELIUS

"I have been a teacher all my life", says the now septuagenarian Alan Paton in his absorbing *Towards the Mountain.* . . .

However, if after . . . much discouragement in confronting some of the most disturbing problems of our century—racism, nationalism, violence—this indefatigable man is still trying to teach us something, he has chosen the most engaging way of doing it. The account of his youth and early career as a science master, husband and lover against the background of the subtropical beauty of Natal, and his later career as a reformer of a reformatory for black delinquents outside Johannesburg, makes compelling reading, and culminates in the final excitement of

Paton's feverishly composing a best-seller while visiting penal institutions in Europe and America from Borstal to Alcatraz. He writes in a rigorously unmannered prose, lightened by gentle irony, sometimes breaking into comedy—to my mind this is his best writing yet.

He also presents his readers with a more rounded, interesting and entertaining character than he has succeeded in giving us in any previous novel, short story, play or biography. His honesty stops just this side of being obsessive—if he refrains from boring us with the whole truth, at least one feels he is telling nothing but the truth, without evasion.

> Anthony Delius, "Seeds on Stony Ground," in The Times Literary Supplement (© Times Newspapers Ltd. (London) 1981; reproduced from The Times Literary Supplement by permission), No. 4066, March 6, 1981, p. 250.

GRAHAM HOUGH

[Paton's *Cry, the beloved country*] is not merely a social record: it is the deeply imagined story of an individual life. And Paton has had to devise a language to tell the story in, for the simple Zulu parson who is the protagonist does not deal in the current coin of modern English speech. So that the literary question was as demanding as the historical one; the political act cannot be separated from the work of art. Now, after thirty years, comes *Ah, but your land is beautiful,* with similar themes and settings, the date of the action a few years later, the conflicts more distinctly those of the modern world. And though the continuity with Paton's earlier work is complete, this is a different kind of book. *Cry, the beloved country* is an exploration both of the racial problem and of personal suffering; and its quasi-Biblical language is a means of penetrating into a sorrowful and bewildered consciousness. *Ah, but your land is beautiful* is a panorama, a chronicle, with a wide variety of characters and the interest distributed between them. It is a less lyrical and more political book, in part an evident *roman-à-clef*. . . .

The story unrolls in a series of short episodes, each centred on a single character and the characters covering a wide spectrum of South African life. An Indian girl sits in a 'No Blacks' library and is arrested; a white school official becomes prominent in the Liberal Party; his life is threatened and shots are fired at his house; black farmers in white areas are evicted, their land taken and their houses destroyed; a 'Proud White Christian Woman' writes obscene letters to her political opponents; and an ironic chorus is provided by the correspondence of a petty Afrikaans civil servant, solemnly saluting the progress of apartheid and the triumph of the Nationalist cause. Paton's earlier writing is suffused with a plangent emotion. This is a drier and more objective book, with more variety of tone and manner. Each of the characters has his own style, and the imaginative equitableness we have come to associate with Paton is achieved by presenting each pretty much in his own terms. There is no distinct plot and no defined conclusion—partly because this is to be the first volume of a trilogy, partly because there is no conclusion to be seen. . . .

It is not an advantage to a novelist to be the champion of a cause that has rightly become a world-wide challenge. Paton's humanity, generosity and wisdom are apparent in everything he writes—and in the candour with which he reveals the complex social and racial alignments. But in the end all the right is on one side and all the wrong on the other, as probably it is. This is not the first instance we have seen in modern history. It may be that the political options are so inexorably black and white that the right public choice seems to subsume all the private virtues. But such a vision excludes the accidents, the mixture of motives, the inherited irrationalities that are the normal substance of daily life, and are not abolished by the great existential decisions. The modern imagination thrives on these ambiguities, and a novel where they are absent, even for the best of reasons, stands aside from the general course of imaginative fiction. It is probably meant to do so. (p. 16)

> Graham Hough, "Doomed" (appears here by permission of the London Review of Books and the author), in London Review of Books, December 3 to December 16, 1981, pp. 16-17.*

NADINE GORDIMER

In Paton's novels one hears voices. That is his method. It derives perhaps—fascinatingly—from the secret level at which the suprarational of creative imagination and the suprarational of religious belief well up together in him. In *Phalarope* a voice bore witness to the undoing of a young man by racist laws that made a criminal act out of a passing sexual infidelity. A loving relative watched what she was powerless to prevent; hers was the voice of compassion. In *Ah, But Your Land is Beautiful,* watcher has turned spy. Characters' actions are seen now by hostile, distorting eyes and recorded in the evil cadences of poison pen letters. Paton's technique remains the same, but his viewpoint has changed from sorrowful compassion to irony. Compare the hushed shock with which Paton described Pieter van Vlaanderen's "fall" (he has made love to a black girl) from the love of wife and family, honor, and self-respect in *Phalarope,* with the prurient cackle of Proud White Christian Woman. . . .

The phalarope, rare bird of understanding that came too late between father and son in the earlier novel, is recognized between the generations in the proud acceptance by the wealthy Indian family, the Bodasinghs, of their daughter's involvement in the Defiance Campaign against unjust laws. And, much later in the narrative, the bird figures again in the rise of internal moral conflicts and their liberal resolution within formerly self-righteous racists. . . . This type of happy-end conversion is sometimes difficult to believe and slightly embarrassing to read. Perhaps it is best taken as another symbol: that of Alan Paton the man's continued faith in the power of seeing the light, which is in tension with the writer's ironic doubt that its beam goes all the way to a change in power structure. Proud White Christian Woman's "conversion," on the other hand, is brought about by brutal circumstance that, alas, seems closer to the actualities of change in South Africa: the threat of her own death. She is dying of cancer, as there are signs that white society is beginning to know it can die of apartheid. (p. 36)

One cannot read this book without the total absorption that comes from recognition of its truth and admiration for the artistic truth into which that has been transposed. There are many characters, yet this is not so much a novel as a meditation on subjects and characters in a novel. Paton has made a meditation his own novelistic form. He seems more interested—and he succeeds in making the reader more interested—in his reflections on the characters and events than in these people and events themselves. When his characters speak—even the "voices," the marvelous ventriloquist's acts of Proud White Christian Woman and Van Onselen—it is quite simply Alan

Paton speaking. This was, I think, a fault in some of his earlier work. He did not always succeed in creating what Patrick White has called the "cast of contradictory characters of which the writer is composed." But this time, yes, Alan Paton is speaking, and such is his skill, so individual the music of his lyricism, the snap of his staccato, the beauty of his syntax, that what ought to be a failure becomes somehow the strength of the work. Style is a matter of finding the one way to say exactly what you have to say. What Paton wants to say here is so central to his own experience, at conscious and subconscious levels, that it is natural to hear it in his own voice.

Why a novel, then, and not just another volume of his autobiography . . .? Ah, but this is not *his* story; it is part of ours, the South Africans'. That demands an imaginative transposition. This one is achieved with shining intelligence and acerbity, a young man's book with the advantage of an old man's experience of the battle with life and words. (pp. 36-7)

> Nadine Gordimer, "Unconfessed History," in The New Republic (reprinted by permission of The New Republic; © 1982 The New Republic, Inc.), Vol. 186, No. 12, March 24, 1982, pp. 35-7.

JOHN ROMANO

"**Ah, But Your Land Is Beautiful**" shows no slackening of either [Paton's] hope or his realism. This novel is as vigorously and as exquisitely written as anything he has produced. It has the eloquence, the special commingling of sweetness and anger, the Orwellian force and lucidity, familiar to readers of "**Too Late the Phalarope**" . . . and several other volumes since. Its tone is quietly anguished. Its classical appeal is based on a direct and simple confidence that the facts of his country's moral disaster will move all men and women, all at once, in the same direction. (p. 7)

The cumulative anecdotal force of "**Ah, But Your Land Is Beautiful**" is difficult to convey. Considering its abundant violence, the passion of its advocacy, and the hatred it matter-of-factly reports, the book is remarkably gentle. . . .

Individual human dilemmas are never swallowed up or diminished by the overarching political context of the story he is telling. Paton is relentless in his faith in the moral meaning of individual human experience. . . . Paton's faith is not a religious one, but a faith in the function, the usefulness of personal sympathy. (p. 22)

> John Romano, "A Novel of Hope and Realism," in The New York Times Book Review (© 1982 by The New York Times Company; reprinted by permission), April 4, 1982, pp. 7, 22.

EDWARD CALLAN

For some years Paton's literary reputation rested on two successful novels and a handful of short stories. But the judgment of the future may rank his biographies of Jan Hofmeyr and Archbishop Geoffrey Clayton as well as his own autobiographical writings as a comparable literary achievement. (p. 92)

Paton's **Hofmeyr** is, essentially, about the moral and intellectual development of a man whose lot was to become deputy prime minister for a time and afterwards to be rejected because of his liberal views on civil rights. Although Paton had been Hofmeyr's friend, and a great admirer of his moral courage, the biography was not persevered with through years of dif-

ficulties simply out of friendship or admiration. There were those who thought that "of all the lives waiting to be written, Hofmeyr's was the least promising—dull, virtuous, conventional, with no wine, women, or song." Paton, with a novelist's discernment, realized that on the contrary Hofmeyr's life had "an inner drama as exciting as anything to be found in South Africa." This inner drama might have proved reason enough to undertake the work, but Paton had a more compelling reason. He was convinced that the story of Hofmeyr's life could reveal the true spirit of South Africa in our times more clearly than the biography of any other public figure. . . . (pp. 95-6)

Judged as a work of scholarship, Paton's biography has deficiencies. He is not meticulous about supplying exact references for source material, and he is overcareful in avoiding references to himself. His own name does not even appear in the index—although this may be a simple oversight. As a literary biography, however, it merits comparison with the best works in this genre. (p. 102)

[Archbishop Clayton's] witness against *apartheid* is memorialized in Paton's second major biography, **Apartheid and the Archbishop: The Life and Times of Geoffrey Clayton, Archbishop of Cape Town**. . . . (p. 104)

It seems likely that many biographers working on a life like that of Archboship Clayton would highlight the church-state conflict and perhaps find parallels in T. S. Eliot's dramatic representation of Archbishop Thomas à Becket in *Murder in the Cathedral*. Paton deals with the theme of church-state conflict in some degree, but he also gives four additional themes their due emphasis: the strange personality of the archbishop; the spiritual and human affairs of the Church of the Province which he guided; the politics of the times in South Africa; and the incompatibility between the Calvinist Dutch Reformed Churches and other Christian churches in South Africa—particularly the Anglo-Catholic Church of the Province.

This broad historical approach immediately suggests that Paton regarded **Apartheid and the Archbishop** not as simply representing the drama of one life, but as a sequel in some sense to **Hofmeyr,** his biography of South Africa's leading liberal statesman of the era before *apartheid*. Paton's **Hofmeyr** was . . . the portrait of a public man striving to act politically in conformity with his Christian conscience. His **Apartheid and the Archbishop** is a portrait of a spiritual man reluctantly forced by his Christian perspective to act in the political sphere. The common quality that his subjects share, in Paton's representation, is their will to rise above personal limitations, prejudices, and parochial presuppositions and to move, however falteringly, toward the vision of a just multi-racial society. Clayton was installed as Archbishop of Cape Town three weeks before Hofmeyr's death in December 1948, and Paton is explicit in identifying him as the successor to Hofmeyr's moral leadership. . . . (pp. 105-06)

[Besides] its themes of Church, State, and Race, and the Archbishop's personal pilgrimage, **Apartheid and the Archbishop** is of interest for what it reveals of the mind of Alan Paton, by affording a fresh perspective on themes consistently present in his work from the beginning. . . . [One] characteristic of Paton's way of seeing the world is the pervasive allegory of the Pilgrim Way—the coming out from various forms of darkness and ignorance into the light by which the exemplary characters in his works of fiction attempt to become something they were not before. (p. 110)

Paton had earlier taken up the theme of the Pilgrim Way in **For You Departed,** . . . his memorial for his first wife, Dorrie

Francis. This book was initially published in London as *Kontakion for You Departed*, a title drawn from the climactic passage: "And this book is done too, this Kontakion for you departed . . . it is a strange story and now it is done." A kontakion is an early Byzantine liturgical chant, elaborately composed of stanzas and linking refrains, performed (like a *Te Deum* in the Western church) to celebrate some public event or deliverance. (pp. 110-11)

For You Departed is composed of sixty-nine numbered passages varying in length from a few lines to several pages arranged antiphonally: passages set in the immediate present—at the time of his wife's death—alternate with passages that flash back in time to their earlier life. Dorrie Paton died in 1967, the year the Liberal party was dissolved in the face of the enactment of legislation making it illegal. Consequently Paton's literary method of moving backward and forward in time sets the events of their lives against a worsening climate of race relations in South Africa. (p. 111)

For You Departed was first made public when Paton read substantial portions of it in Rhodes University Theatre on 8 July 1969. Before beginning, he explained: "This document is a very intimate one; nevertheless I will read portions of it, because I think as you get older you don't wish to keep intimate things so close to yourself as you did when you were young." . . . Gradually, as the work's range of mood, humor, and movement emerged, there were stirrings of laughter at witty anecdotes followed by repeated wholehearted bursts of laughter during the reading of episode "Thirty"—a highly amusing narrative about a family card game at Diepkloof called Reformatory Bridge. The stillness returned as he read of detentions, house arrests, and searchings by the security police, but the sanity of humor pervaded even these somber recitals. (p. 112)

The problem of suffering and its acceptance is also the subject of other works Paton wrote about the same time as *For You Departed*—works that examine this profound subject in wider contexts than those of personal or South African experience. These works include **"Why Suffering,"** . . . [**"The Challenge of Fear,"** and *Instrument of Thy Peace,* a book of Lenten meditations prompted by the prayer of St. Francis of Assisi: "Lord make me an instrument of Thy peace"]. (p. 113)

It may be said of Paton's writings taken as a whole that their characteristic theme is the giving of thanks for the courage of others. Although deeply touched by personal emotion, *For You Departed* is less a cry of grief on the occasion of his wife's death than a thanksgiving for her courage in the often painful journey out from a relatively comfortable life among white South Africans in Ixopo and Pietermaritzburg to the unfamiliar prison world of Diepkloof, the uncertain world of a teacher turned writer in middle age, and the fearful world of anti-*apartheid* politics in the Liberal party. Finally it gives thanks for her courage to endure her final painful illness. (pp. 114-15)

Many of Paton's "Long View" articles are also direct tributes to the courage of others. . . . Furthermore, his autobiography measures milestones in his journey "Towards the Mountain" by examples of the courage of others. Here again, in *Towards the Mountain,* we encounter the example of the courageous public lives of Jan Hofmeyr, Alfred Hoernlè, and Archbishop Clayton. But there are examples of courage from more private lives, too . . . [such as that of] Railton Dent, a college friend of whom Paton says in *Towards the Mountain:* "He taught me one thing, the theme of which will run right through this book, with undertones (or overtones, I never know which) of victories, defeats, resolutions, betrayals, that life must be used in the service of a cause greater than oneself." . . . (p. 115)

In *Knocking on the Door* [editor] Colin Gardner has assembled Alan Paton's shorter writings that were either previously unpublished or had limited local circulation. . . . Gardner's arrangement enables us to see Paton as a man of consistent vision and integrity who has sought by every available means—as a practical penal reformer; as a novelist, biographer, and poet; and as a public speaker denied conventional political platforms—to convince his fellow South Africans that society has more to gain from freedom freely offered than from freedom denied, with its attendant prohibitions, prison bars, and iron laws. (pp. 119-20)

Edward Callan, in his Alan Paton *(copyright © 1982 by Twayne Publishers, Inc.; reprinted with the permission of Twayne Publishers, a Division of G. K. Hall & Co., Boston), revised edition, Twayne, 1982, 143 p.*

Raja Rao

1909-

Indian novelist, short story writer, and editor.

Rao, who was educated in India and England, is one of India's most outstanding authors writing in English. His distinctive style captures the rhythms of Indian speech and idiomatic expression. His writing is complex but poetic. Intensely philosophical, Rao examines, in his fiction, the religious and mythic roots of India, at times offering a comparison to Western thought.

Rao grew up during colonial India's struggle for independence and his first novel, *Kanthapura*, depicts the impact of Gandhi's passive resistance movement on a South Indian village. *The Serpent and the Rope*, considered his best work, describes the dissolution of a marriage between an Indian student and his French wife. It is semi-autobiographical, and because of its extensive symbolism and the nature of its philosophical discussion, it is considered a metaphysical novel. *The Cat and Shakespeare*, also metaphysical, is an allegory which has been variously interpreted. *The Cow of the Barricades and Other Stories* is a 1947 collection of some early short stories.

(See also *Contemporary Authors*, Vols. 73-76.)

© Jerry Bauer

MARTIN TUCKER

The Serpent and the Rope is much more than the description of the spiritual journey of an Indian visitor to a new land. . . . In his main character, Ramaswamy, the author has the East turn West in its search for one of the fulfilling mysteries of the universal quest. Rama comes to Europe to study the Albigensian heresy and to complete his doctoral thesis. During his immersion in his studies he meets and marries a beautiful French girl, Madeleine. . . .

Ostensibly, the story is about the dissolution of the marriage between Rama and Madeleine, told with "objectivity" (Rama's word) by an "historical scientist." . . .

[Madeleine] senses she must offer her womanhood, raise it to the point of a religious ecstasy if she is to hold on to Rama. Yet she cannot hold him. Something in her is rooted in the earth, and Rama is the air. Inevitably they separate, without having enunciated a quarrel. Characteristically, they understand the nature of their failure and do nothing but interpret it to each other and to themselves.

It is impossible to state the meaning of the novel, for to catch and hold onto the main thread one must tear the fabric. Where one ordinary stitch would do, Rao has woven thousands. (p. 471)

Rao does not merely confront East and West; he shows them working together and apart at the same instant. Yet the symbolism is easily apparent. Either one believes in the serpent or one believes in the rope. The serpent is the imagination; the rope is reality. Either the world is real and each man a part of it; or each man creates the world in his own image.

Rama believes in the serpent; Madeleine, in spite of her knowledge of Buddhist, Brahminic and Vedantio lore, and in spite of the fulfilment she has gained as a result of her forty-two-day fast, remains a believer in the rope. Madeleine needs a name and place for her knowledge to grow, while names and places must be destroyed before learning can exist for Rama. Thus, early in the novel, when Madeleine kisses Rama and feels she is "kissing a serpent or the body of death," the foreknowledge has its basis in their opposing personalities.

Rao has been widely acclaimed in his own land for the beauty of his style and thought. [*The Serpent and the Rope*], his first novel written directly in English, should contribute to his stature here, as it has already in England. (p. 472)

Martin Tucker, "Cultures in Conflict," in Commonweal *(copyright © 1963 Commonweal Publishing Co., Inc.; reprinted by permission of Commonweal Publishing Co., Inc.), Vol. LXXVII, No. 18, January 25, 1963, pp. 468-70.*

HORTENSE CALISHER

If Raja Rao's *The Serpent and the Rope* has a shape of its own, it is one altogether outside the duality of the Western mind. Such is both the intent and fascination of this first-person narration of a Hindu-French marriage in terms of the metaphysical quest on both sides. As one travels with it from France to India on its various threads of time-place description, seeing the persona at both the inner and the impersonal distance, participating in talk-reflection which ranges, with a scholar's emotion, from Judao-Christian ethic through all Vedanta lore, one is brilliantly seduced away from the *a priori* Western world into an Indian one that seems far more natural. . . . [The] ultimate sensation left by the book is deeper than instruction, and far and away from the fashion for such angularly repellent mimicry as Hesse's *Siddhartha* or even Mann's *Transposed Heads.* Rao's talent is to lead you as the two-dimensional creature was led in the mathematician Edwin Abbott's *Flatland,* into another dimension altogether, there to seat you, as you grow more Indian, at the round table of yourself. (p. 231)

> *Hortense Calisher, "Fiction: Some Forms Off-shore," in* The Nation *(copyright 1963 The Nation magazine, The Nation Associates, Inc.), Vol. 196, No. 11, March 16, 1963, pp. 229-32.**

LOIS HARTLEY

Whether writing of sophisticates or peasants, Raja Rao has a style that is slow-moving and difficult, and his texts require, for the ordinary reader, many notes of explication. Nevertheless, there are passages of immense beauty in his novels, and his notes are often delightful brief essays on Indian customs, history, philosophy and religion.

Raja Rao's *Kanthapura,* written almost 35 years ago, has been belatedly published in the United States. . . . [*Kanthapura*] must be recommended to all interested in a sensitive and compassionate story of an Indian village during the Gandhi movement for independence, and in fact to all who have any interest in India.

The narrator is an Indian woman of the village of Kanthapura, in South India. Raja Rao sustains superbly the viewpoint, the mannerisms, the ways of thought and speech of this villager so different from himself. At the beginning of the events there are rumors of the activities of Gandhi; but Kanthapura reclines in the passivities and rhythms of centuries. Then a young, dedicated Brahmin, inspired by the Mahatma to a vocation to his village, returns and slowly leads the villagers fully into the freedom movement. Eventually this hero turns from Gandhi to Nehru; but his villagers remain faithful to the primary religious and political vision of the Mahatma. A major irony is that the way of the Mahatma—a way of nonviolence and victory through love—leads Kanthapura into extremes of violence and destruction.

Kanthapura is told somewhat as an old wives' tale, and one suspects an element of the mythical in such a tale; but it is a book of extraordinary veracity in its details of village life in India.

> *Lois Hartley, "A Look at Spring Fiction: 'Kanthapura'," in* America *(reprinted with permission of America Press, Inc.; © 1964; all rights reserved), Vol. 110, No. 9, February 29, 1964, p. 290.*

EDWARD C. DIMOCK, JR.

To some schools of Indian religion the cat has a metaphorical significance. There are two theories of Grace: In the first, man's responsibility is to cling to God as a baby monkey clings to its mother in flight. In the second, man depends wholly upon God for his protection and progress, as a kitten depends upon its mother to carry it about by the scruff of its neck.

Raja Rao has used this latter metaphor as a point of departure for his third novel. . . . *The Cat and Shakespeare* is a tender and deceptively humorous story of a South Indian ration-office clerk called Govindan Nair, narrated by his friend Ramakrishna Pai. Raja Rao calls his book "a metaphysical comedy," and indeed his pungent and thoroughly delightful observations of South Indian middle-class life provide a counterpoint to a sometimes difficult allegory. (p. 27)

Raja Rao's book is itself a little like a cat. It has grace and beauty, dignity and a sense of humor, a certain mystery, and even a quality of insubstantiality. Its meaning comes to you of its own accord, and cannot be coaxed or wheedled. You reach out toward it, and it turns its back and stalks unconcernedly away, or even, with a Cheshire grin, fades into nothingness. Sometimes, too, for no apparent reason, it leaps stiff-legged into the air and charges up the draperies. (pp. 27-8)

The book requires multiple readings; one is not enough to follow the thought and at the same time to obtain a sufficient reward from Raja Rao's graceful and austere English and his striking and witty imagery. Only after one is able to relax a little can he give in to the charm of the picture of Ramakrishna Pai "sitting and listening to himself like a lizard," or be caught up by the image, rather than the meaning, of kittens walking sure-footedly along a garden wall between reality and unreality. Only then does one have time to reflect on the sub-themes, guilt and responsibility, causation and existence, which crowd in almost unobtrusively.

Raja Rao has given us a beautiful book. The "Shakespeare" of the title (though Shakespeare was a "natural man") may be somewhat gratuitous; it does however add the quality of a *mantra,* a truth-containing spell that has the power, in its sound perhaps more than in its lexical meaning, to reach beyond the mind to understanding. (p. 28)

> *Edward C. Dimock, Jr., "The Garden Wall between Worlds," in* Saturday Review *(copyright © 1965 by Saturday Review; all rights reserved; reprinted by permission), Vol. XLVIII, No. 3, January 16, 1965, pp. 27-8.*

AHMED ALI

[Raja Rao] published his first novel *Kanthapura* in 1938, which, but for its title, would have met with greater success than it did. It had a pictorial quality of its own both in word and style, and an approach to life and its problems more serious than had hitherto been made by any Indian writing in English, while it carried a sensibility and intelligence not found in many vernacular writers of the day. It centres round a small village in Mysore and the struggle for Independence through Satyagrah and non-cooperation started by Mahatma Gandhi and the Indian National Congress. But it has more to tell than the political vicissitudes of India. The inner stream of the novel, though not its whole canvas, concerns Tradition. . . .

Kanthapura narrates how the struggle for Independence came to this village, and tells of Moorthy and his band of *satyagrahis* in conflict with vested interests and the law. As compared with *The Serpent and the Rope* it has action. The characters have both shape and contour. They are living men and women, not mere symbols; and the story is not just a parable, but fiction. The telling may be strange, but it holds our interest. It is more satisfying than anything Indian that had appeared in English by 1938. (p. 17)

Indian that Raja Rao is, he is conscious, even over-conscious, of his Indian-ness. In *Kanthapura* he is also conscious of the fact that being an Indian he was writing in a language not his own, and that therefore his use of English was found to be different, akin to a dialect for, he said in the preface to that novel, 'one has to convey the various shades and omissions of a certain thought movement that looks maltreated'.

The emphasis, thus, right from the beginning in his writing, is on this thought movement. Only outlined in *Kanthapura* it is unfolded in his second and most considerable novel, *The Serpent and the Rope,* a 'serious and difficult book', in Raja Rao's own words, but which has made an understanding of the soul of the other India easier, the India free of the Fascist Jan Sangh movement which is blotting out the image of the real and traditional India. (pp. 18-19)

[The] form of *The Serpent and the Rope* is epic, sustained throughout, maintained at a pitch that carries the metaphysic in its train, the sweep of the rain-bearing clouds. Raja Rao is a superb narrator, and his narration carries with it wisdom, philosophy, scholarship, beauty of word and phrase and aphorism. The narrator in him is awake, ever moving, untired, even when the novelist, the weaver of tales, is asleep. His métier is the Vedas, not the *Ramayana,* that masterpiece of storytelling. . . . The machinery Raja Rao employs is weak—recourse to diaries and awkward manipulations of incidents. His powers of invention are negligible. There are false cries reported through the pages of the personalized diary, not different in tone from the rest of the book. There are abrupt introductions of extraneous characters . . . , whose only function is to provide an opportunity to enlarge on aspects of modern life, sex and frivolity. There are reflections on themes that have not found any place elsewhere in the book—contemporary European and Indian scenes with emphasis on the minor key in contrast to the high sensibility which throws the seriousness of thought and purpose Rama has inherited into carved relief. This method also serves the purpose (unnecessary in view of the main reflective theme of the novel) of showing the superiority of India by contrast. India does stand out, but the art, the fiction suffers. Such things are not part of the texture of the novel. It is, however, his power of narration and his sense of style that save him and carry him forward. Otherwise he skips, he jumps over from incident to narrative across time and space, though with a simplicity that is as sincere as it is disarming. (pp. 19-20)

In retrospect, the characters are unreal, except Georges perhaps, and the solutions of problems illusory—that of Madeleine in taking to Buddhism which was a revolt against Brahmanism and the Vedas; that of Savithri in accepting the bureaucracy and imperialism she had rebelled against: that of Rama in deciding to seek the Guru but giving up in tired hopelessness to relax in the plush chairs with his chocolate. As characters they could be said not to exist. . . . They are all moods or philosophizings, of motherhood and womanhood, body and soul in a losing conflict, religion, history. And yet, as the opposite is necessary for objectivity, contraries are essential for philosophy. Without Reality there would have been no Illusion. Without Madeleine and Savithri there would have been no *Serpent and the Rope.*

Things happen, but in the mind, not to the characters—awareness or affirmation, negation or failure. It's not the characters who stand out. It's the philosophy, and through the philosophy man's destiny, seen, however, not through the life of man but the mind of initiated Ramaswamy. Had it been presented through the men, the characters, *The Serpent and the Rope* would have been a great novel, and Raja Rao as great a novelist as Dostoevsky. As it is, *The Serpent and the Rope* is a reflective, a philosophical autobiography written in moments of deep contemplation. (p. 20)

The story of Tradition is left aside in his third and last novel with the curious name of *The Cat and Shakespeare.* It is different in tone and atmosphere—not so much a parable as a confession of faith. The frustrations of the last novel disappear. Their place is taken by a hope, as of Shantha, big with child, finding the happiness and fulfilment of becoming. Concern with Tradition is replaced by a conviction of Fate. Destiny plays the active role in this story as Tradition had done in *The Serpent and the Rope.* The writing is difficult, though more modern and resilient, the rhythm more staccato. (p. 27)

The Cat and Shakespeare contains the expression of inner joy embedded in Raja Rao's recent experiences, including the discovery of America and the re-discovery of the metaphysic of life in 'the way of the kitten'—surrender to Destiny. He calls it a 'metaphysical comedy'. (p. 28)

Ahmed Ali, ''Illusion and Reality: The Art and Philosophy of Raja Rao'' (copyright Ahmed Ali; by permission of Hans Zell Publishers, an imprint of K. G. Saur Verlag), in Journal of Commonwealth Literature, *No. 5, July, 1968, pp. 16-28.*

JANET P. GEMMIL

[*The Serpent and the Rope*] reflects the cultural synthesis effected in the mind of the author in his own encounter with Europe as epitomized by his intellectual French wife. Transcending these is his love for Savithri, a pseudonym for an Indian woman with whom Rao has maintained a Platonic relationship for some thirty years. To express the divine quality of their love, Rao borrows from the literature of Europe and India both, and the result is a monument to absolute love coupled with a series of metaphysical questions answerable only in terms of a lifelong philosophical quest. (p. 247)

In total, *The Serpent and the Rope* is an overwhelming novel, for Raja Rao a *tour de force* which encapsules and communicates a philosophical predicament which has occupied the better part of his life. In addition, this novel comprises a major synthesis of Eastern and Western cultures in the vast number of allusions to European and Indian literature, music and philosophy incorporated into the structure of the story. It further speaks to the eternal dichotomy between maleness and femaleness which is of concern periodically in the human cultural response to family and society. The novel as a whole represents a quest for an elusive unity, a resolution of the opposition between wisdom and goodness, East and West, male and female. It may be that these are polarities of human life which cannot be fully resolved, even through the means of Advaita Vedanta. As in every religious tradition, man continues to struggle with these conflicts, even though he knows of paths that offer him escape. If we are to accept Rao's third novel, *The Cat and Shakespeare,* as a resolution of sorts, we see that duality disappears only in play. But even then, we are reminded that duality is never resolved into oneness—only into nonduality. The distinction is a subtle one; the texture of the language is Eastern. It is a truth and therefore also a mystery. How can it be explained, except to say that in being one can know being?

This mysterious sense of non-duality, the possibility of some-thing other than suffering and illusion, lies at the heart of *The Serpent and the Rope*. Ramaswamy's quest is directed toward that end. The first-person point of view, heavy use of descrip-tion, and densely-textured language all work to create a strongly metaphysical atmosphere. In order to hint at the possibility of non-duality, the novelist can do little more than explain it in tautological terms and employ rhythmic patterns which offer a sense of some greater order beyond that of the story itself. For the reader who is himself searching for metaphysical so-lutions, it is worth the demands on his time and intellect to puzzle out the terms of such a possibility. *The Serpent and the Rope* is in effect a transmission of esoteric knowledge from writer to reader in the tradition of the Upanishads.

These scriptures, it should be noted, take the form of philo-sophical dialogues narrated as stories; with some exceptions, each has a protagonist who quests and makes mistakes and learns just as Ramaswamy does in Rao's novel. The meaning of *upanishad* in Sanscrit is "to sit near," and it is in this vein that the reader as student "sits near" the writer as teacher in order to learn of Truth. In such a context, the combination of strongly autobiographical and clearly metaphysical elements is particularly striking. Raja Rao's motive in writing the novel is akin to that of Augustine and Dante: having found Truth, he feels compelled to record the spiritual struggle which led him to that point. The line between reality and illusion, truth and fiction, is indeed a fine one. Obligated to record his ex-periences, the writer embroiders only slightly on the events of his own life and consequently presents the resulting story in a tone of utter seriousness.

The extreme lack of playfulness or humor in *The Serpent and the Rope* is . . . a characteristic of the metaphysical novel. . . . By taking seriously the events and insights that come his way, Ramaswamy forces us to do the same; at all costs, we must not laugh at him. This recognition is part of the compact which exists between writer and reader with a novel of this type. (pp. 256-57)

[*The Serpent and the Rope* concerns] the intellectual and spir-itual predicament of the modern Western-educated Indian. *The Serpent and the Rope* is therefore also a metaphysical novel of the sort which in the modern age fulfills the traditional function of religious scriptures. The story comprises a value structure and a metaphysical system which, if followed, would enable a hypothetical reader to cope with conflicts in his own exis-tence. This is not to say that Rao's novel replaces the Upan-ishads or Shankara's commentaries. Rather, it functions to point the reader toward the traditional scriptures by illustrating their relevance to the predicament of contemporary man. (p. 258)

> *Janet P. Gemmil, "Dualities and Non-Duality in Raja Rao's 'The Serpent and the Rope'," in* World Lit-erature Written in English *(© copyright 1973 WLWE-World Literature Written in English), Vol. 12, No. 2, November, 1973, pp. 247-59.*

R. SHEPHERD

In *The Cat and Shakespeare* (1965) the larger natural symbols of *The Serpent and the Rope* (1960) have been adapted for a deeper and more intensive examination of Truth, now sought in the familiar domestic details of the ordinary workaday life—houses, walls, cats, coffee, illness, and so on. These are the dominant symbols of the novel, which recur page after page. The wall defines a threshold between the physical and supra-physical worlds; the *bilva*-tree hangs over the wall, thereby sanctifying it through contiguity (as in the legend of the hunter explained at the beginning of the novel); the house of three storeys encompasses the three worlds, heaven, earth, and the underworld (according to one traditional interpretation of Hindu cosmology); the ration shop becomes a symbol of all mundane activity governed by clock time, while the cat stands for the fundamental regenerative and sustaining principle known var-iously as Brahman or the Great Mother. (p. 347)

[The cat] exists at two levels—at the level of actuality within time and space, and at a metaphysical level transcending time and space. At the level of actuality the cat figures as God Shiva, whose symbolic function is concerned with the creation, preservation and final dissolution of the physical universe. In the novel the cat presides over birth (creation), the course of law or *dharma* (preservation), and death (destruction). But Shiva also symbolizes what goes beyond Shiva; that is, the Brahman or Matrix. So at this metaphysical level the cat rep-resents the Great Mother of the universe. (pp. 350-51)

A good deal of the play or comedy in *The Cat and Shakespeare* arises from the direct participation of the cat in the main events, a kind of divine intervention after the manner of much tradi-tional literature. On the one hand, the cat is connected with the feminine principle, while on the other it is closely connected with Nair, who serves, so to speak, as the cat's apologist. Nair is a man who has learnt to understand the true (Vedantic) significance of symbols, and for him the cat stands as an ideal. (p. 351)

The cat too exists at several levels. At the naturalistic level its behaviour and cry are absurd, again reflecting the absurdity of life. When Nair says "All my language can be reduced to . . . meow, meow, meowooow," . . . he means that language too is hopelessly inadequate, hopelessly absurd. He improvises on Hamlet's famous soliloquy in a way that deliberately disturbs the beauty of the poetry in order to reveal some of this ab-surdity, to reveal the potential ugliness of language:

> To be or not to be. No, No. (He looks at the cat.)
> A kitten sans cat, kitten being the
> diminutive for cat. *Vide* Prescott
> of the great grammatical fame.
> A kitten sans cat, that is the
> question. . . .

At the same time he extends Shakespeare's meaning to embody a metaphysic that is strictly Indian. The famous question now becomes a question as to whether or not the finite world (kitten) can exist independent of, and unrelated to, the infinite universe (cat). Shakespeare epitomizes man's capacity for knowledge, understanding and expression but mainly within the realms of the physical world. The cat implies the possibility of a sus-taining principle beyond what can be ordinarily known. The novel's title links together the physical and supra-physical real-ities. The startling juxtaposition of symbols demonstrates the Advaitic premise that all difference is only apparent, that ev-erything can be ultimately related to everything else. (p. 352)

Both the absurdity and the profundity of the cat can be seen in the ration office and courtroom episodes. In the court it is the cat rather than the judge who presides over proceedings. The judge, as Nair proves, is not even certain of his own identity—that is, he does not know his own Self, in the meta-physical sense. . . . The cat is the focus of all attention. And yet its movements are by no means spectacular or even es-pecially unusual or interesting. Rather its movements are unexpected and difficult to explain. It is not a logical creature and in this sense it serves as an ideal paradigm in Nair's philosophy. The ways of God are inscrutable, often apparently downright absurd. But they offer the only proof we have of God's existence. (p. 353)

Raja Rao creates a world which symbolically closes in upon itself and in which all the usual sort of problems and contradictions of life are finally resolved in a vision of the beyond. He exploits, in novel form, one traditional Indian view of cosmic order, albeit a view that is peculiarly modern on account of a heightened sense of intellectual awareness. To describe the book's form as cyclic or as symphonic is helpful, but such a description does not go far enough. The subject of the novel is that relation of the physical and the supra-physical life, and the quest for self-identity. The formal elements of the novel reflect this preoccupation. Every symbol, wherever it occurs, seems to imply all other symbols connected either directly or indirectly. Each occurrence serves as a reminder of the beginning (of the universe, of the quest, of the novel) as well as of the end. The role played by Shiva in the varied aspects of cat, Nair and the world at large is reflected in the formal cycle (creation, preservation, destruction) of the story. Characters, places and events separate and then merge together in a convergent dialectic. The book itself becomes the universe in the same way that the Indian *mandala* becomes equivalent to the whole existential order in the eye of the beholder. (pp. 355-56)

R. Shepherd, "Raja Rao: Symbolism in 'The Cat and Shakespeare'," in World Literature Written in English *(© copyright 1975 WLWE-World Literature Written in English), Vol. 14, No. 2, November, 1975, pp. 347-56.*

CHARLES R. LARSON

[In *Kanthapura,*] Raja Rao has abandoned his position as story teller, giving it over to his fictive female persona [Achakka]. I can think of few other instances in Third World fiction where a male novelist has done this. (p. 134)

With the exception of Afro-American fiction, I would have to say that in most Third World novels female characters play lesser roles than their male counterparts—no doubt in large part because Western (romantic) love is missing as a theme. If women are present in any of these books, they tend to be of incidental importance, functional objects in an otherwise masculine-oriented world. . . .

[But in] *Kanthapura,* women are the vanguard for an entire revolutionary change. (p. 135)

Raja Rao's structural device of relinquishing his omniscient position to the [fictive narrator] within the story, coupled with that narrator's use of plural pronouns, is responsible for much of the effectiveness of the basic story and the rooting that it has in the communal consciousness. Not surprisingly, the reader learns very little about Achakka, the narrator. . . . We know that she owns a little land ("I have seven acres of wet land and twelve acres of dry land . . ." . . . and that she is a Brahmin, but these are the only facts directly revealed about her in the entire narrative.

The most significant of these characteristics undoubtedly are her Brahmin position and the fact that she is female. Achakka's Brahmin status initially presents some problems for her as a narrator, since her past education has told her to uphold the

caste system. . . . Since Achakka is much like the other villagers, she must learn to accept the changes that are taking place in Kanthapura. . . . Flexibility, however, typifies Achakka's character; quite early in the story she adopts Gandhi's teachings. In the riots that culminate at the end, Achakka is out there, proudly marching with the others—Brahmins and Pariahs, potters and weavers, coolies, even Mohammedans. Altogether, she becomes an admirable character—perhaps all the more surprising because she is no longer young.

The female point of view, however, is much more important than her Brahmin status, giving us, as I have already indicated, something atypical of most Third World fiction. Much of the novel's power is Raja Rao's determination to keep the viewpoint totally feminine. For this reason, it is especially important that the village protector is a goddess, Kenchamma, not a god. Her power resides in her past actions, and the origin of the village is attributed to her initial accomplishments. . . . Symbolically, Kenchamma's power, incarnated in the women of Kanthapura such as Achakka (engaging in a similar battle), brings about the great social change that radicalizes the village, for Gandhi and Moorthy are only the catalysts, the inspiration for what eventually happens. They become increasingly insignificant as the narrative continues, Moorthy even disappearing from the village itself. The women are the force, they bring about the real revolution, since their husbands have had to hide in the jungles around the village. Without the force of the women, there would not, in fact, have been a revolution in Kanthapura.

Achakka's entire story—her narrative of the events that take place in Kanthapura—is told in retrospect to other women listeners. There are constant references to these listeners who are identified as "sisters," but what is of more importance is that *Kanthapura* is thereby rooted in oral storytelling. The novel itself is one long oral tale, told by a mature woman who has survived the ordeal she is describing to her listeners. There are other tales also, usually digressions within the main narrative itself, tales related by Achakka that other people have told her. . . . Other oral characteristics of the narrative include the multiple use of songs and prayers and the more limited use of proverbs, mythology, and epic lists and catalogs. So strong is the oral tradition that if it were eliminated there would be no *Kanthapura.*

Stylistically, all of these aspects contribute a rather fast-paced quality to the prose itself, at times reminiscent of a kind of oral stream of consciousness or automatic writing because of the declarative sentences that go on and on, connected by conjunction after conjunction. (pp. 137-39)

[There] is a sense of a heightened pace—of time rushing by so quickly that it can never be recaptured. Most of the novel is told as a summary of past events, with endless digressions, as is often typical of longer oral narratives, and only limited use of dialogue. The combination of these aspects creates a style that is altogether breathless, vividly recapturing the abruptness of the social change within the culture itself. Time is not only marching on, but it is bringing about major social changes. (pp. 139-40)

Towards the end of the novel, when nothing can stop the women from marching against the soldiers sent in by the British, the change has been so complete that the women (in spite of the fact that many of them have been killed) make the voluntary choice to continue their protests. . . . The women envision a nationwide women's revolt, liberating all of India.

Kanthapura itself has become insignificant—it is simply the village where the riots began. That is why these same women decide to burn down what is left of the village, rather than return to it. For them, life can never again be as it was in Kanthapura. The revolution is now self perpetuating.

In retrospect, this change from passivity to activity is explained by Achakka as a kind of uncontrollable religious possession, growing out of the foundation of the villagers' beliefs. (pp. 140-41)

We have only to remember that *Kanthapura* was published in 1938—nine years before independence—to realize [its] revolutionary nature. . . . It is surprising that the novel was not banned in India or that its author was not imprisoned. (p. 141)

[*Kanthapura*] is built around several significant events in Gandhi's political career that eventually culminated in India's independence. Time is not presented through cyclical events in the novel, though there are some references to the natural seasons; we are not shown a closed system of which only the timeless present has any reality for the people. Rather, there is a sense of past and future—a sense of history marching on. Achakka herself is aware of this feeling as becomes apparent in her retrospective narrative of what has taken place. The other women also realize that they are a part of history on the march. No doubt much of this sense of historical time is a reflection of events in Gandhi's political life, plus the merging of his image with the oral tradition. Historically, for the Indians, Gandhi became a kind of myth in his own day, and this sense—almost of sainthood—permeates much of *Kanthapura*. . . . (pp. 141-42)

At the end of the story, when Range Gowda—one of the Pariah leaders who has gone back to Kanthapura to look at the site that was once the village—tells Achakka ' ''There's neither man nor mosquito in Kanthapura . . .''' . . . , it might be easy to conclude that what has taken place in Kanthapura is essentially negative. After all, the village no longer exists. Moorthy has run off and joined forces with the Communists, Gandhi has made a truce with the viceroy, and it is suspected that "the peasants will pay back the revenues, the young men will not boycott the toddy shops, and everything they say, will be as before." . . . It is then however that Achakka makes one of the most emphatic statements in the narrative, relating it to her comment about what has happened to their hearts: " 'No, sister, no, nothing can ever be the same again.' " . . . (p. 142)

In the concluding summary, Achakka expresses her beliefs that what has happened in Kanthapura is to be interpreted as essentially positive: "They say the Mahatma will go to the Red-Man's country and he will get us Swaraj" . . . , that is, independence. The time is propitious, the culture has been renewed, things will never again be as they were. The pessimism that has for so long been a controlling factor in Third World fiction has begun to shift toward optimism. Cultural renewal can only begin within the culture itself, from within its basic foundations: the village and the family. (pp. 142-43)

> *Charles R. Larson, "Revolt and Rebirth, Cultural Renewal: Raja Rao's 'Kanthapura', Kamala Mar-kandaya's 'Two Virgins'," in his* The Novel in the Third World *(copyright © 1976 by Charles R. Larson; reprinted by permission of the author), Inscape, Publishers, 1976, pp. 131-52 [the excerpts of Raja Rao's work used were originally published in his* Kanthapura *(copyright © 1963 by New Directions Publishing Corporation; reprinted by permission of New Directions), New Directions, 1963].**

RICHARD R. GUZMAN

Of the few [Third World] writers who have managed to synthesize forms and idioms out of the clash of the native and Western, one certainly thinks of Raja Rao, whom many consider the most brilliant Indian ever to write fiction in English. Forty years ago, in a preface to his first book *Kanthapura,* he wrote one of the first manifestos on Third World literary style.

> . . . English is not really an alien language to us. It is the language of our intellectual make-up—like Sanskrit or Persian was before—but not of our emotional make-up. . . . We cannot write like the English. We should not. We cannot write only as Indians. We have grown to look at the large world as a part of us. Our method of expression therefore has to be a dialect which will someday prove to be as distinctive and colorful as the Irish or the American. Time alone will justify it.

> After language the next problem is that of style. The tempo of Indian life must be infused into our English expression. . . . We, in India, think quickly, and when we move we move quickly. There must be something in the sun of India that makes us rush and tumble and run on. . . . The *Mahabharata* has 214,788 verses and the *Ramayana* 48,000. . . . Episode follows episode, and when our thoughts stop our breath stops, and we move on to another thought. This was and still is the ordinary style of our storytelling.

This 1937 preface remains to my mind the most eloquent and enticing guide to style a Third World writer can have, and Raja Rao's growing understanding of his own statement has manifested itself in two other celebrated works, *The Serpent and the Rope* (1960) and *The Cat and Shakespeare* (1967). Together with *Kanthapura,* they have become prime models in world literature, showing how profoundly one language can be made to serve the very soul of another culture.

Kanthapura is set in the early 30's, around the time Gandhi made his salt marches. Moorthy, a young Brahmin transformed by Gandhi's spirit into a revolutionary, comes back from the city to Kanthapura and attempts to cut across traditional boundaries of caste in order to create a unified front against the British. . . . Until he himself has a spiritual awakening . . . , his efforts remain relatively ineffectual. When Kanthapura finally is unified, it inspires more rebellion. The British retaliate, wasting the village and dispersing its inhabitants, but the impact has been made. Surprisingly, Raja Rao was not arrested for sedition, for he clearly meant tiny Kanthapura to be an example of the type of courage and unity that could expel the British.

Outwardly, the book's form is quite Western. It is told, first of all, by a narrator in the first person with a limited point of view. Most important, it has, in the tradition of Western historical narrative, a pointed, linear plot which Raja Rao has shaped with tight logic on a balanced curve which reaches its apex in chapter ten, the book's exact center. Chapter one is balanced with chapter 19, chapter two with 18, and so on. (p. 34)

Yet tight, logical structure is neither the first nor last impression *Kanthapura* makes. Rather the novel sprawls and digresses, and features, besides, 60 pages of notes on Indian culture and history arranged by chapter at the back of the book. At times these notes seem as interesting as the novel itself; so when the narrator, Achakka, mentions Ravanna, for example, one turns to the notes; and since Ravanna, or the Cauvery River, or Shakuntala is likely to be mentioned in a digression, the notes extend that digression, sometimes forcing slow movement through the text.

The text, however, does not move slowly, for Achakka, a fantastically garrulous old woman presumably telling her tale to a group addressed only as "sisters," is perhaps the fastest, most prolix talker in world literature. . . . She is something of a poet—especially in her descriptions of nature and evocations of Indian culture—but also a master gossip, telling us of squabbles, and houses, and who is jealous of whom (and why). Serious or frivolous, her words always pour forth in a near-breathless, near-torrential, near-endless rush which the American critic Charles Larson describes as an "oral stream of consciousness" [see excerpt above].

Another American critic says, however, that the book's style becomes monotonous over its 180-page length. The style is "dominated by *and, then, but, when,* and *now,*" says Robert J. Ray, and "one sequence follows another without emphasis or control." In fact, though Rao had promised just this relentless rush of words and episodes, he appears to have run into a problem that has plagued many other literary works, Third World or otherwise: the usually flat, repetitious syntax of such speakers is unable to buoy a long written narrative. In *The Serpent and the Rope* and *The Cat and Shakespeare* (which *are* better books) the narrators are quite sophisticated, and while the rhythm of Indian speech is still fully retained, the syntax of parataxis and simple coordination dominating *Kanthapura* gives way to what Robert J. Ray now describes as "paradoxical language patterns that are stunning, subtle, profound, and beautiful." Rao's artistic craft, says Ray, has become "the most profound in the history of Indo-Anglian literature, perhaps in the history of contemporary literature."

Ray's somewhat justified criticism of *Kanthapura* may be lessened, however, if we can learn to hear the rhythm and inflection of Indian speech and understand the peculiar literary synthesis Raja Rao is attempting. . . . *Kanthapura* is modeled not so much after the novel as the *shthala-purana,* or legendary history, which—oral or written—is chatty, digressive, amply laced with allusions, hymns, stories, and sayings. Even though *Kanthapura* has a few interesting characters and a tight, logical framework, Achakka's torrential, digressive voice overwhelms—and was meant to overwhelm—all and work against the sense of controlled, historical progress or sequence. For the real protagonist of *Kanthapura* has neither personal character nor history: it is India—the idea, the metaphysic. . . . (pp. 34-6)

The idiom of the sage has been the language of the venerable Sankara, of Sri Aurobindo, and Gandhi, and is based on the central text of Hinduism, *Tat tvam asi* (Thou art that). . . . *Tat tvam asi* gives rise to the doctrine of radical monism, which holds that all things are ultimately one. It rejects subject-object dualism, moves away from the object and from history, and believes the word illusory—not materially real, but arising from the perceptions of the self, which is ultimately identical with the Absolute Self whose highest expression is *ahimsa.* "Seeing oneself," says the central figure in *The Serpent and the Rope,* "is what we always seek; the world, as the great sage Sankara said, is like a city seen in a mirror." (p. 37)

To varying degrees each major leader of the Indian Revolution tried to blend the call for political unity with this sagely spirit of radical oneness found in the scriptures and rooted deeply in Indian culture. That spirit is India the idea, the metaphysic, and it is the connection between politics and *tat tvam asi* that Moorthy realizes during his awakening.

Only partially transformed by Gandhi's example, Moorthy is at first a mere modern trying to remake the traditional without the transcending power of the sagely vision. (p. 37-8)

In the end, feeling that Gandhi is not practical enough, Moorthy seems to turn away from the sagely vision and go to Nehru, the modern. But, as Raja Rao has said, Moorthy is immature and impatient: the only "practical" way, finally, is the way of the sage. Thus, except for a one-paragraph wrap-up by Achakka, *Kanthapura* ends not with Moorthy's tentativeness but with Gandhi's 1931 trip to England. That event, however, is not spoken of in historical terms, but, significantly, in terms of Indian myth and tradition. . . . The ever-present India mythos finally absorbs the characters and history it has all along been bathing and overwhelming.

For Raja Rao, myth is more real than fact, for myth leads fact out of itself, into the general, and finally into the realm of the nonmaterial Absolute, the One whose highest expression is *ahimsa. Tat tvam asi* gives to Indian aesthetics a movement diametrically opposed to the aesthetic tendencies of the West, especially as manifested in realism. (pp. 38-9)

In Raja Rao's synthesis . . . there is an exquisite contrariety of motion between establishing individuality on the one hand—as with the unforgettable Govindan Nair in *The Cat and Shakespeare*—and undermining that individuality with constant, overt pressure towards the general, towards the revelation that that individual is not himself but the Absolute. Of course, for Raja Rao the Absolute must prevail, and as he pursues the implications of *tat tvam asi* further and further, his style becomes more antirealistic in a way that is kin to, but, one should note, much more radical than the antirealism that animates so many of the classics of modern and contemporary literature in the West. . . . Revolted by both historical chaos and historical determinism, the West nonetheless remains historical, committed to redeeming history, or unwilling, at least, to consider it illusory. For Raja Rao the function of myth is to dispel history. Yet myth is only a halfway house to the real. "I want to bring myth up to the Real," says Rao, "not down to history."

Philosophy carries us beyond myth. Gabriel Marcel once told Rao that the Indians scared him because whereas the West went from philosophy to God, they went from God to philosophy. It is just this element of philosophical disquisition, generally absent from *Kanthapura,* that saturates the pages of *The Serpent and the Rope* and *The Cat and Shakespeare,* taking us further away from the object, from history, from the world.

The *mala* or threadlike storyline of *The Serpent and the Rope* concerns the breakup of a remarkable marriage between Rama, a Brahmin, and Madeleine, a Westerner and teacher of history. Rama, himself a history student and writing a dissertation for a French university, narrates the story, saying at one point:

> I am not telling a story here, I am writing the sad and uneven chronicle of a life, my life, with no art or decoration, but with the "objectivity," the discipline of the "historical sci-

ences,'' for by taste and tradition I am only an historian.

Yet to be thus dedicated to history is to be dedicated to the object, to the world, and Rama is uneasy about this. In fact, the tone of the book's first line constitutes an unconscious admission of this uneasiness: ''I was born a Brahmin,'' says Rama, ''—that is, devoted to Truth and all that.''

The Truth Rama is at first so tentative about concerns the relationship between the self and the world. The vision defined by *tat tvam asi* sees that the world persists because the ego persists, for the world is really only the self seen as the other. Thus *The Serpent and the Rope* revolves around the question, will one or will one not give up the world?—which is the same as asking, will one or will one not give up the self and see that one is not oneself, but the Absolute? Raja Rao's great achievement is to be able to pursue such questions with an almost manic philosophical drive without robbing them of the passion, pathos, and even sentimentality which must attend questions that threaten the realm of the self. (pp. 40-1)

Rama's dissertation has to do with possible connections between the Western, saintly Cathari and the Eastern, sagely Vedantin. The connections, however, exist only superficially, for although both sects forsake the world through the acquisition of knowledge and the practice of an extreme asceticism, the Cathari—whose doctrines descend from the Gnostics and Manichaens—base their attitudes on a fiercely maintained dualism. The ''West''—understood throughout the book not so much as a geographical term, but a shorthand term for the affirmation of the object—means something quite different when it speaks of giving up the world. It means, ultimately, ''The world must be more perfect or it must leave me alone.'' Yet the more intensely it rejects the world, the more intensely is the world's unsatisfying presence affirmed. (p. 42)

Even though he seems to understand the differences between Saint and Sage quite deeply, Rama still works at finding possible connections and confesses ''a tender heart for the Cathars.'' Indeed, tenderness of heart, rising from a deeply felt compassion for the difficulty of life, is one of his most endearing qualities. Because he is tender we respect his wavering between knowing the sagely vision true and desiring to affirm the world. And never does he waver so intensely between knowledge and desire than in his relationship to Madeleine. At times he feels that he and Madeleine can truly marry, become one, but at others he knows that the best he can do is possess her, play for her the hero as saint; for in her great love for Rama and India she longs to be made over in their images. ''Oh to be born in a country where tradition is so alive,'' she says. Yet Madeleine is the quintessence of the West: she can only reject the world, not truly give it up. Shortly after their second child is born, she writes a remarkable letter to Rama, whose father's death has forced him to return to India. The letter is the pure voice of the West addressing India. ''You people are sentimental about the invisible,'' she writes, ''we about the visible.'' ''I wondered,'' she continues, ''whether I could really love you—whether anyone could love a thing so abstract as you.'' She closes by saying she can, but this declaration is just bravura, for throughout, with great pathos and humor, she has been virtually confessing the opposite. (p. 43)

The Serpent and the Rope might be merely a short, touching, somewhat sentimental story were it not for the prodigious volume of philosophy that swells the book to more than twice *Kanthapura*'s length and brilliantly transforms the storyline

into small, seemingly ephemeral bits imbedded in vast realms of thought. (pp. 44-5)

As *Kanthapura* is, so to speak, centered on myth and tradition, and *The Serpent and the Rope* on philosophy, so *The Cat and Shakespeare,* while encompassing both myth and philosophy, is centered on the problem of perception. ''Freedom is only that you see that you see what you see,'' says Ramakrishna Pai, the book's main character. Merely to see is to affirm the object: to see you see is to affirm perception. But, untransformed in the beginning, Pai had said: ''Time ticks. You close your eyes and open. I want to be free,'' thereby echoing what Rama had said in *The Serpent and the Rope:* ''. . . all ends in our stomach. There must be a way out, Lord.''

The style of *The Cat and Shakespeare* rises out of its preoccupation with perception. Raja Rao intends his prose to be referentially difficult, ambiguous, as a way of de-emphasizing what is merely seen. Indeed, it is often difficult to figure out what, if anything, has happened, and Rao's determination to convey the vision of *tat tvam asi* deeply affects even the very grammar of written English. As in ''you close your eyes and open,'' he makes many sentences elliptical by dropping, appropriately, subjects and objects. Many sentences move by indirection, switching subjects or objects in mid-flow, using logical connectives to imply connections not there, winding up where they did not set out to go. Also, the contrariety of particularization and generalization, so lovely in Rao's works, operates here more pervasively than ever. One of the main symbols of the book, for example, is a wall which Ramakrishna Pai must learn to cross. . . . Ultimately the wall is only *ahankara*, the limitations of the ego, which keeps him from seeing what he sees he sees.

''The definition of Truth is simple,'' says Pai, ''—you wake up and you are in front of Truth.'' The book's plot is so tenuous because Truth is finally more a matter of what *is*, not what happens. It is not action, but recognition. *Ahankara*, however, blocks recognition by leading one to try to fulfill the longing for Truth with things which are lesser than the Truth. . . . Like Rama working on his dissertation, Ramakrishna Pai is involved in a project closely related to, but lesser than, his desire for freedom and Truth: he wants to build a three-story house.

Just as he begins seriously questioning his ability to do this, one of the great character creations in all literature makes his appearance. Govindan Nair, Pai's friend, easily jumps back and forth across the wall. ''Hey there, be you at home?'' he asks. A significant first question; for Govindan is really asking Pai how he conceives of his own being. Are you or are you not yourself? ''I tell you, God will build you a house of three stories.''. . . Govindan Nair is Ramakrishna Pai's guru, and for him the mother cat is symbol of Truth, of the Absolute.

In one of the book's most bizarre sequences, Nair's office mates present him with a cat they have placed in a rat cage. It is a joke of metaphysical proportions, and there ensues a weird parody on Hamlet's famous soliloquy. ''To be or not to be. No, no,'' says Govindan Nair. ''A kitten sans cat, that is the question.'' The vision shaped by *Tat tvam asi* sees that the world is but the play—*lila*—of the Absolute. Kittens *are* cats— the diminutive, playful aspect of cats, just as ''To be'' is the play of ''Not to be,'' or the serpent (the unreal) the play of the rope (the real). To choose, like Hamlet, is to affirm duality, to maintain the illusion that one is different from the other. To put a cat in a rat cage is to treat the Absolute like an object; and if the Absolute is an object, if it is not free, then there is no hope of freedom.

"We have no feline instinct. We live like rats," says Govindan in an atypical moment of despair. That is, we live as if we were objects. But on the whole Govindan Nair, like the book itself, exudes hope. In lovely accord with the concept of *lila,* *The Cat and Shakespeare* is a roguish, uproarious, but exceedingly gentle comedy which, despite its general abstruseness, strikes one with great warmth. "Life is so precious," says Pai near the end of the book, "I ask you why does not one play?" Man, like a kitten, plays because he perceives himself to be *lila,* and no one perceives this more profoundly and compassionately than Govindan Nair. One comes to love him not only for his delightful, teasing language but also for the fearless freedom with which he lives. (pp. 46-9)

The Cat and Shakespeare pulses with the very heartbeat of revolutionary India, for it is the most sophisticated extension to date of India as idea, as metaphysic. One may also sense in Govindan Nair's fearlessly free style something of the courage that animated Sri Aurobindo, and Gandhi, and so many of those early strugglers for freedom. To know that the world is but one's self seen as the other is to have, as Rama says, the courage "to dare annihilation." The metaphysic of *tat tvam asi* assures us that one's freedom is truly one's own creation. It is not, however, in one's hands: it is in one's eyes—in vision. (pp. 49-50)

> Richard R. Guzman, "The Saint and the Sage: The Fiction of Raja Rao," in The Virginia Quarterly Review (copyright, 1980, by The Virginia Quarterly Review, The University of Virginia), Vol. 56, No. 1 (Winter, 1980), pp. 33-50.

S. KRISHNAMOORTHY AITHAL and RASHMI AITHAL

Raja Rao's *The Serpent and the Rope,* the classic of Indo-English literature, portrays the encounter between East and West on the intimate plane of sex, love, and marriage. The recurring theme of interracial and intercultural relationships in Indo-English literature is explored in Raja Rao's novel with a set of variables not used elsewhere. . . .

Rama, who is a curious mixture of sensuousness and asceticism, is as strongly attracted by the beauty of Madeleine's body as by the virtues of her character. Being an Indian Brahmin, Rama is obviously impressed by Madeleine's active interest in Indian philosophy and religion and by her virtuous character; she is well known among her relatives and friends for being a person of great virtue and piety. Her cousins teasingly warn her that she will end up in a convent. She shares Rama's interest in the Cathars, because she finds in them kindred souls of purity. This streak of asceticism endears her to Rama, who never tires of talking about his purity and Brahminism.

Madeleine also combines a sensuous nature with her well-known asceticism, at least at the beginning. (p. 94)

The two love each other deeply and their married life is marked by mutual understanding, sympathy, and trust. They spend the early years of their marriage in playful fun and amusement, like children. Madeleine shows great concern for Rama's health and serves him with total devotion. Even when things cease to go well with them, their love remains unaffected. Rama continues to hold her in the highest regard, and Madeleine continues to think of his welfare. She initiates the action of divorce so that Rama can go back to the warmer climate of India which is good for his lungs; she also presents him with his freedom so that he can marry a young Hindu wife.

Rama and Madeleine are, broadly speaking, alike in temperament and character, and they seem to be made for each other. Looking at them from a distance, theirs will appear a marriage of true minds. They indeed enjoy a reputation among friends and relatives as an ideal couple. (p. 95)

The Serpent and the Rope contains numerous possible causes which could be cited for the dissolution of the marriage of Rama and Madeleine. What is, however, significant is that the novel does not show how any of the reasons given in it, separately or together, build up a crisis and bring about the breakup of the marriage.

First, there are problems created by the personality and makeup of the two. We know that Rama had lost his mother at an early age and had the feeling of being an orphan. . . . Madeleine was also an orphan, having lost both her parents at an early age. This shared situation probably arouses an initial sympathetic response in the hearts of Rama and Madeleine, which may be sympathy, but not the firm base for a marriage.

We are told that Madeleine is by nature a woman who can give herself to a cause. Rama knows this and thinks that Madeleine really loved him "partly because she felt India had been wronged by the British, and because she would, in marrying [him], know and identify herself with a great people." . . . (pp. 95-6)

When one examines the problems caused by cultural differences, one notices that Rama is unhappy with Madeleine's indifference to his gods and superstitions. He knows that to wed a woman one must wed her beliefs, and, after some inner struggle, he accepts them. He notices with regret, however, that she does not do the same.

Rama's love for Madeleine is, in a way, impersonal and abstract. The nature of this love is described in [the Indian philosopher] Yagnyavalkya's words: "For whose sake, verily, does a husband love his wife? Not for the sake of his wife, but verily for the sake of the Self in her." . . . Rama does not think that Madeleine could possibly appreciate this transcendental approach, for she "smelt the things of the earth, as though, sound, form, touch, taste, smell, were such realities that you could not go beyond them—even if you tried." . . .

To Madeleine, purity gradually comes to mean desisting from all physical and sexual contact. She implores Rama to practice the *brahmacharya* of his ancestors. She herself starts practicing a rigorous form of celibacy, and shrinks from the touch of even Rama. She would not expose any part of her body and certainly would not allow Rama to touch her. When Rama sees her sitting in her room in yogic posture with beads in hands and chanting mantras, he ruefully thinks, "This was the Madeline I had made." . . . Rama, on the other hand, could go to bed with Lakshmi, the wife of a friend of his, without violating his sense of purity. Similarly, he could receive the worship due to a husband from a wife from Savitri without any sense of guilt or infidelity. Purity is a mental and spiritual state to Rama, whereas it is a matter of physical touch to Madeleine.

In a similar way, Madeleine's India is not the same as Rama's. To Madeleine, India means saris, worship of cows, and Buddhism. Rama's India cannot be summed up neatly along these lines. It means many things to him, big and small, and evokes many feelings. It is a country with a rich tradition and culture. (p. 96)

Though Madeleine transcends her own cultural orientation to a certain extent, she is unable to acquire an inward knowledge of Rama's Indian culture. Though Rama quotes from Paul Valéry and gives beautiful lectures on French history, he cannot for a moment forget that he is an Indian Brahmin from Hariharapura of Mysore, and a grandson of Kittanna.

Important as some of these differences are, they are not accumulated and intensified so that a crisis forces the couple to separate. Further complications are caused by their declarations of everlasting love which occur right in the middle of the eruptions of their bitter thoughts. The reader's confusion is compounded by these expressions of love which continue even while their divorce arrangements progress.

The author himself is perhaps not very clear as to precisely what brought about the separation of Rama and Madeleine. Having chosen to present these sensitive, intelligent characters as two people who continue to show every possible consideration for each other's feelings in spite of their collapsing marital relations, the author does not seem to know how to explain their final estrangement. He reviews various events, thoughts, and words in the hope of finding the reason for separation. . . . When the book ends, neither Rama nor the author has resolved the problem.

The inconclusiveness referred to above need not, however, detract from Raja Rao's skill as an artist. He has chosen to present a difficult real life situation, one that does not always lend itself to logical explanations. The author should be commended for resisting the temptation to twist and turn situation or character, producing thereby a simple novel of East-West encounter.

The separation of Rama and Madeleine is a moving story. They respect one another, and yet they part. They are intelligent, mature, and enlightened; they are free from the usual narrow racial and cultural prejudices, and yet they cannot prevent themselves from drifting apart. The comforting aspect of this sad story of separation is that the end of marriage need not mean the end of love. Love between members of different races and cultures is possible, even if marriage is not. Having lived through the kind of situation presented in the novel in his own personal life, Raja Rao is able to give a point and force to his conclusion. (p. 97)

S. Krishnamoorthy Aithal and Rashmi Aithal, "Interracial and Intercultural Relationships in Raja Rao's 'The Serpent and the Rope'," in The International Fiction Review *(© copyright International Fiction Association), Vol. 7, No. 2, Summer, 1980, pp. 94-8.*

Piers Paul Read

1941-

English novelist and nonfiction writer.

Perhaps best known in America for *Alive*, a restrained account of the survivors of a 1972 Andes airplane crash, Read has also written several novels, including his recent *A Married Man* and *The Villa Golitsyn*. In these novels Read explores his moral and political concerns by focusing on the social and domestic life of the British upper-middle class.

Critics point to Read's plots as contrived and melodramatic because of the sensational events that often introduce or resolve his narratives. Read's style, even in his fiction, is characterized by its unimpassioned expression—an almost journalistic chronicling of events.

(See also *CLC*, Vols. 4, 10; *Contemporary Authors*, Vols. 21-24, rev. ed.; *Something about the Author*, Vol. 21; and *Dictionary of Literary Biography*, Vol. 14.)

Fay Godwin's Photo Files

DAVID CRAIG

Piers Paul Read's experimental novel [*Game in Heaven with Tussy Marx*] is an infuriating mixture of the trenchant and the perverse. . . . The novel spirals backwards—via satirical set-piece, heavenly interludes, jokes, straight fiction—to trace how revolutionary impetus was able to start up in the unpromisingly easy-osy conditions of Western Europe today. The devious irony at times cuts deep. . . . But pointful passages are outweighed by ones whose only aim seems to be to annoy the conventional reader. The revolt against exploitation becomes the impulse *pour épater le bourgeois*. . . . [All] Read can do is stand the conventional novel on its head. He cannot put his finger on any actual seed or source of revolution—of radical change—in the world he belongs to. For all the 'advanced' *cachet* sought by the title and the trappings, the book remains the furious shadow-boxing of someone trying to run a r-r-r revolutionary one-man-band in a situation where the only practicable line for the Left is cooperation and patience.

David Craig, "R-R-Revolutionary," in New Statesman *(© 1966 The Statesman & Nation Publishing Co. Ltd.), Vol. 71, No. 1838, June 3, 1966, p. 817.**

VERNON SCANNELL

Piers Paul Read's *The Junkers* is written in the first person, the narrator is roughly the same age as the author and the book is set in Germany where Read has lived, but you don't for a moment feel that he is dishing up a chunk of personal experience with himself at the centre of a group of his acquaintances dressed in false names and noses. The main character is a young British diplomat posted in the 1960s to Berlin where he falls romantically and credibly in love with a German girl, Suzi. . . . [Research into her] family's history provides a vivid account of the rise of the Nazis before the Second World War, some scenes of SS bestiality described with a careful restraint that intensifies the horror, and a penetrating and sympathetic study of the type of brave and patriotic German soldier who was also a devout Christian, agonised by his growing realisation that

his Fuehrer was not merely fallible but the incarnation of total evil. The flashbacks mesh smoothly with the development of the narrator's affair with Suzi and the novel is organised with unobtrusive but masterly skill. (p. 808)

Vernon Scannell, "Enjoying the Ride," in New Statesman *(© 1968 The Statesman & Nation Publishing Co. Ltd.), Vol. 75, No. 1944, June 14, 1968, pp. 808-09.**

DAVID REES

[*The Junkers* is an ambitious novel and inevitably leaves a] confused, fragmented impression as one realises towards the end of the book that the author has failed, honourably, in his task: that of attempting to give an artistic explanation of some of the Dionysian forces in the German collective psyche during the last forty years. Sensibly, Mr. Read has adopted as the framework for his novel the story of a single Pomeranian family, the Von Rummelsbergs. . . . (p. 75)

[Mr. Read tells] the tale through the eyes of a young British diplomat, a second secretary to the political adviser in West Berlin, who first falls in love with the city and then, perhaps romantically, with Suzi von Rummelsberg, so providing a means of exploring a story whose undertones are all the more effectively caught for the restraint and the insight with which it is treated. Yet the episodes created around the story of the death camps remind us this is no ordinary family chronicle.

If the denouement of *The Junkers* with its droll unmasking of interlocking mysteries, its curious understanding of Germany with which the narrator is completely involved, is unsatisfactory, that is to be expected, considering the complexity of the theme. (p. 76)

> David Rees, "Heroes of Our Time," in Encounter (© 1968 by Encounter Ltd.), Vol. XXXI, No. 4, October, 1968, pp. 74-6.*

RICHARD SULLIVAN

Technically, *The Junkers* is a fine achievement. Its agile handling of time-breaks gives it brisk coverage of half a century of intricate personal relationships, political complications and moral entanglements. The phrasing is bright, energetic; the craftsmanship, expert. Yet the overall effect is somehow diminished by the very characterization of the narrator. He simply isn't a storyteller who inspires confidence.

> Richard Sullivan, "Persons of Principle," in Book World—The Washington Post (© 1969 Postrib Corp.; reprinted by permission of Chicago Tribune and The Washington Post), May 18, 1969, p. 11.

EDWIN MORGAN

A year spent by [Piers Paul Read] in America seems to have tempted him into writing [*The Professor's Daughter,* a] low-keyed, unexciting account of the generation gap and revolution in American society. The approach—dutiful, lucid, schematic—simply does not match the theme, and the final liberal humanist retreat into a reactionary family-stability solution ('a family will always be the basic unit of society') hands us an old stone where new bread was never more needed. *The Professor's Daughter* begins well but soon becomes predictable.

> Edwin Morgan, "Dicey" (© British Broadcasting Corp. 1971; reprinted by permission of Edwin Morgan), in The Listener, Vol. 86, No. 2218, September 30, 1971, p. 453.*

CHRISTOPHER LEHMANN-HAUPT

[So] good is *The Professor's Daughter,* so intellectually engaging and compelling, that one must ask why this is not a novel of major importance instead of merely first-rate entertainment.

It can be argued that its ending is contrived—contrived, moreover, to give aid and comfort to middle-class, anti-revolutionary values. And there is justification for such a view: The domestic settlements that end it do seem trivial in the light of the questions it has raised; thus the ending does seem forced.

The trouble, however, does not lie in the ending itself, but in the fact that Mr. Read has staged his drama of social issues in a hermetic setting, as if he believed that issues that were once fought over in street warfare behind barricades could be solved in the drawing rooms of Brattle Street and the crash pads of Berkeley. . . .

But what does tend to trivialize this novel is its psychological literalness. . . .

[If] Mr. Read means us to take literally his story's assertion that the professor's incestuous yearnings, and his daughter's consequent nymphomania, are the results of the "rottenness" of mid-century American liberalism, then one begs to understand the precise psychological connection between liberalism and incest. But Mr. Read fails to explain. Which leaves gaping holes in his story, and some doubts about the truth of its conclusion.

But never mind that *The Professor's Daughter* falls short of mastery. At the rate Mr. Read's novels keep improving, one expects him to be equal to such problems in the not too distant future. In the meantime, he has given us some solid entertainment.

> Christopher Lehmann-Haupt, "Bedrooms on the Barricades," in The New York Times (© 1971 by The New York Times Company; reprinted by permission), October 27, 1971, p. 45.

CARL SENNA

The Professor's Daughter is a good fictional portrait of our American malaise. Here a father and his daughter find that their search for a meaningful cause is an oppressive condition. Their dilemma is that material wealth has deprived them of any social need. And this cunning, cynical tale suggests that our motivation for changing the status quo is frustrated by the freedom from want. (pp. 164-65)

The narrative smoothly alternates between events in the lives of father and daughter, interweaving and unifying them with a superb dramatic rhythm. On the basis of his two previous novels, *Monk Dawson* and *The Junkers,* Read has been compared to his compatriot, Graham Greene. At least from a technical view the comparison seems justified. Read has a fine sense of timing. The scenes in *The Professor's Daughter* are never boring; and at moments the action is almost sensational. But the Greene influence is definitely there; the professor and his daughter reflect an unmistakable concern for the moral fate of our affluent culture. . . . Read's message seems to be that life is not meaningful unless it is rational; and necessity, not possibility, makes it so. (p. 165)

> Carl Senna, "'The Professor's Daughter'," in Commonweal (copyright © 1971 Commonweal Publishing Co., Inc.; reprinted by permission of Commonweal Publishing Co., Inc.), Vol. XCV, No. 7, November 12, 1971, pp. 164-65.

CLANCY SIGAL

The Great Train Robbery co-ordinated the actions of 15 highly idiosyncratic thugs. It was supported by scores, if not hundreds, of underworld 'supply troops'. . . . Therefore, one way of looking at this 1963 'crime of the century' is as an expression of London working-class culture. . . .

This is one of the fascinating sidelights of Read's account [*The Train Robbers*], which he collected from the eager testimonies of the robbers who are out of prison. . . . Alas, like so much else of possible interest, it remains a sidelight to the main but conventional drama, a brisk re-run (yet again) of How It Was Done.

I don't know how much of the narrative to believe. . . . [According to the robbers interviewed, the train robbery] was financed by £80,000 from the Nazi adventurer, Otto Skorzeny. . . . One reason why [*The Train Robbers*] is more mystifying than necessary is that Read, at first taken in by the Skorzeny lie, presents it to us in the body of his story as factually true, and only in the last chapter exposes it as a collective fantasy dreamed up to make the whole proposition more commercially appealing. In other words, Read gives the facts as he was told them. He has made little apparent effort to do an independent investigation other than to nail the Skorzeny fable.

I was both mildly absorbed and disappointed by this account of how 15 squabbling, violent men robbed the Glasgow-to-London overnight mail of two-and-a-half million pounds. Chiefly what emerges is the general amateurishness of the thieves. . . .

The trouble is that Read, though an accomplished novelist, almost completely fails to characterise any of the robbers. . . . I had to keep turning back to the photographs rather than the text to follow who was whom. It is as if only the journalistic half of the writer's mind was at work.

However, he does retell the story of the robbery with brisk competence. . . .

One's attitude to this book may depend on one's personal experience. . . . I have never been badly robbed. But once, in hospital, I watched a bank guard, a rather nice old man, slowly die of head injuries caused by a coshing. It makes a difference.

> *Clancy Sigal, ''Money Talks'' (© British Broadcasting Corp. 1978; reprinted by permission of Clancy Sigal), in* The Listener, *Vol. 99, No. 2559, May 11, 1978, p. 616.*

PETER PRINCE

Mr Read's non-fiction approach, as we know from *Alive,* is to surround large and shocking events with understated prose. It seemed to work well for such a lurid subject as cannabalism. It works rather well [in *The Train Robbers*] too: this is a clean, steady, authoritative narrative. But given the familiarity of the material, at times one finds oneself wishing for a cruder, heavier brush and stronger colours; for some English Mailer who, for all the risks of buffoonery and bad taste, might give one a keener sense of the robbers' spectacular achievement, of the kind of glory that they won.

> *Peter Prince, ''The Biggs Boys,'' in* The Times Literary Supplement *(© Times Newspapers Ltd. (London) 1978; reproduced from* The Times Literary Supplement *by permission), No. 3972, May 19, 1978, p. 557.*

PAUL ABLEMAN

[In *A Married Man*] John Strickland finds the naked body of his wife, Clare, in the living-room of their country cottage and the corpse of her hitherto unsuspected lover in the bedroom upstairs [and] it gives him a nasty turn, especially as both have been demolished by shotgun blast. But he has set his heart on becoming a labour M.P. and is soon back at the hustings although warning his agent: 'I may be a little off form.'

His form declines still further when he discovers that the super-rich mistress, who is about to become his second wife, was responsible for Clare's messy end. He glumly breaks off the engagement but shows little other sign of being deeply affected. This uncanny poise is surely incompatible with humanity but not with the narrative since Strickland has long since ceased

to be human and has contracted to the dimensions of a symbolic figure in a theological tract. I personally have little taste for theology but it is a valid part of human culture and a scientific-materialist such as myself has no justification for attacking it per se. What a novel reviewer, however, whatever his religious convictions, has a sworn duty to smite with all the rhetoric at his command is theology that masquerades as fiction.

The tendentious plot—and it is a measure of Mr Read's skill that it takes some time for the reader to realise that it *is* tendentious—revolves around John Strickland, the husband of the title. . . .

[During] an idle hour one summer, John reads Tolstoy's 'Ivan Ilych' and the work, somewhat obscurely considering its actual contents, renders him dissatisfied with his way of life. He attempts, even more obscurely, to improve things by the disparate resorts of standing for parliament and acquiring a young mistress. At about this stage, it begins to be clear that Strickland is not really a free character in a free fictional universe but a football destined to be booted about by an author bent on scoring theological goals.

The work is set in the summer and early winter of 1973 when, as usual, there was trouble with the unions and the lights kept going out. John's grand friends are convinced that the communists are using the workers to foment revolution but subtle John himself realises that the workers are using the communists to get higher wage settlements. Behind these two parties lurks the immanent presence of the author telling us, in tone and allusion, that true salvation is not of this earth and that *any* material concern is prejudicial to spiritual redemption.

I would be happier with this message, even while rejecting it, if the author himself did not display that almost prurient obsession with class which has become the trade-mark of the post-war English novel. . . . One can almost feel a frisson flutter the pages of this book whenever words such as 'lord', 'sir' or 'servant' crop up while the unaristocratic background narrative remains as stagnant as a conservatory.

The letters exchanged between Clare and a Jesuit which John discovers after her death represent the true content of this book. They form a dialogue on the moral challenges of the contemporary world and, while stating some of the issues clearly, are neither profound nor passionate enough to sustain the inert superstructure. That the remainder of the novel *is* inert can be inferred from technical considerations as well as from overall impression. Thus at one moment Clare's brother is described as taciturn and the next minute no-one else can get a word in edgewise. He is just a football. John's son has given up his juvenile interest in trains but 100 pages later, in a toy-shop, he buys a new carriage for his train-set. Another football. Gordon, the left-wing journalist, orders a bottle of wine, talks non-stop for a minute and a half and then consumes 'what was left of . . . the wine'. An amazingly fast-drinking football. These are not quibbles about consistency but reproaches about integrity. Many major novels, and other works of art, harbour ludicrous breaches of consistency and some physicists would argue that the cosmos itself does too. But Mr Read's lapses are not those of a creator too impatient to gestate a living world to tie up boring loose ends but those of a forger who leaves out the water-mark. If God were reproached by a disillusioned theist with Heisenberg's uncertainty principle it would be open to Him to reply: 'What are you complaining about? The universe works, doesn't it?' Mr. Read, who has impermissibly appropriated the notation of reality in order to further what are essentially theological aims, can make no such excuse. His book doesn't.

Paul Ableman, "Booted About," in The Spectator (©1979 by The Spectator; reprinted by permission of The Spectator), Vol. 243, No. 7898, November 24, 1979, p. 21.

CHRISTOPHER LEHMANN-HAUPT

Mr. Read has outdone himself [in **"A Married Man"**], blending for the first time with absolute success his preoccupations with domestic, social and political upheavals, and creating as a result a story full of suspense and subtleties.

[Some] readers will argue that there's not much suspense involved here. Because Mr. Read is composing a domestic drama he introduces a very limited number of characters. Therefore, it's immediately apparent who the killer must be. (p. 30)

But, I submit, the suspense is not really supposed to involve who the killer may be, but rather what effect the revelation will have on Strickland. And this bit of suspense Mr. Read orchestrates to maximum effect. . . .

Few readers, on the other hand, will deny the subtlety with which Mr. Read has plied his craft. The skill with which he works into his plot England's 1973-74 political crisis, when the labor unions were literally causing the country's lights to dim; the way he dramatizes the fantasy of infidelity and then contrasts the dream with the sordid reality; the deftness with which the novel's many ideas are made to grow out of its characters—all attest to Mr. Read's growth from a two-dimensional storyteller into a novelist of depth.

I suppose the meaning of **"A Married Man"** is finally didactic, for it pushes a traditional Roman Catholic view that condemns marital infidelity and takes a dim view of radical politics. But if that is the message, it scarcely bangs us over the head with its righteousness. If the novel dramatizes a contest for John Strickland's soul between God and the Devil, then we learn a good deal more of the Devil's charms than we do of God's. But then where would fiction be if the Devil didn't get his due? (p. 31)

Christopher Lehmann-Haupt, "'A Married Man'," in The New York Times, Section III (© 1979 by The New York Times Company; reprinted by permission), December 21, 1979 (and reprinted in Books of the Times, Vol. III, No. 1, 1980, pp. 30-1).

MALCOLM BRADBURY

Piers Paul Read tells a latter-day version of [Leo Tolstoy's "The Death of Ivan Ilych"] in **"A Married Man."** . . .

The male menopause is a familiar enough modern story, yet this is not static feudal Russia but late bourgeois Britain in an age of decadent inconsistencies: it continues the practice of marriage while devaluing conventions and domesticity; it institutionalizes self-interest while thriving on middle-class guilt. . . . [Protagonist Strickland's] pursuit of freedom simply complicates his hypocrisy. He remains married, but half wishes for the death of his wife and marriage to the mistress who would assist his new ambitions. So his quest leads to new falsehoods, fresh failures of understanding, new illusions about the nature of his emotional ties—and finally to dreadful tragedy, very coolly enacted, very coolly told. . . .

Like Tolstoy, Mr. Read is a realist, a densely social novelist who knows that public and private worlds intersect at every point. His portrait of late bourgeois Britain in one of its crucial moments, when the boom in property and affluence continues while the social spaces widen, is compelling: a world on the verge of collapse, where personal amusements mask disconnection and disappointment.

But, like Tolstoy, Mr. Read uses realism for irony. The social world, which demands attention, is also a delusion, a source of inexhaustible hypocrisies. The world that Strickland takes as real is not quite real—not simply because he is a hypocrite, but because that society ignores larger and more lasting questions of life and death. Commitment to reform and freedom is also a form of self-interest, containing a deep desire to violate and abuse. It is this desire, deep in the culture, that explodes on Strickland in the book's dark, disturbing ending—which seems melodramatic compared to what has gone before, but brings the hypocrisy and emptiness full circle, as the illusions that he has pierced now begin to destroy him.

Mr. Read's irony, not unlike Tolstoy's, is cool and thorough. **"A Married Man"** is a sharp chronicle of England in an uneasy time. But it is also a chilling story about the modern age of affluent selfhood and self-interest. It confirms that Piers Paul Read, with seven novels now behind him, is one of Britain's most intelligent and disturbing writers.

Malcolm Bradbury, "A Case of Ilychitis," in The New York Times Book Review (© 1979 by The New York Times Company; reprinted by permission), December 30, 1979, p. 3.

THOMAS M. DISCH

The formula [for *A Married Man*] is familiar: a man of ordinary social dimensions is drawn inchmeal towards a pit of moral quicksand and then neatly pushed in. Usually the first step downward on this well-intentioned path is adultery, and so it is for Read's hero, John Strickland. . . .

This might seem to militate against a suspenseful narrative, but in fact *A Married Man,* after a slow start, becomes a proper page-turner. In part this may be due to the fascination inherent in watching a prophecy fulfilled, à la *Macbeth,* but surely most of the book's hold on our interest derives from its hypnotic believability. All of Read's considerable (though self-effacing) artistry is directed toward creating a wholly plausible fictional world. . . .

It is debatable whether the book succeeds in its main ambition—to make a drama of adultery that is also the moral analogue of the Condition of England. At the tasks of detailing the actual maneuverings of a parliamentary candidate and of showing the climate of political discourse at a moment of high tension (the election of 1974), Read is very persuasive. But if one seeks to interpret his foreground drama in the contextual light of heated-up class conflict, the moral of his novel would seem to be that the very rich are squeezing the middle classes out of existence with the tacit cooperation of a working class that Read represents as comprised by and large of career criminals. I remain unconvinced.

Perhaps Read doesn't mean his tale to bear such a weight of interpretation (though it surely invites it). Taken at face value, *A Married Man* is a satisfactory, civilized "good Read." . . .

Thomas M. Disch, "Taking up with Miss Wrong," in Book World—The Washington Post (© 1980, The Washington Post), January 27, 1980, p. 6.

JOHN MELLORS

Read does not make much of a case for Catholicism, or for religion at all, in [his early novel, *The Junkers*]. He writes with apparent approval of those ex-Nazis who have repented and are now (the mid-1960s) working for a unified Europe even if the unity can only be achieved by the spread of Communist principles and power. . . .

How far have Read's views changed since he wrote *The Junkers*? Neither author nor main character in Read's latest novel [*A Married Man*] seem to have any sympathies with Communism. John Strickland, family man, moderately successful barrister, takes up again at the age of 40 the Socialism in which he had first come to believe when he was an Oxford undergraduate. As a Labour candidate he wins a seat in the February 1974 General Election. . . . Moreover, at the end of the book Strickland quits even that moderate activism. His wife having been murdered, the crime master-minded by his mistress, Strickland decides that he must spend more time with his children: 'one's personal responsibilities come first'. (p. 131)

Between *The Junkers* and *A Married Man*, Read was less teasing, more dogmatic. The protagonist in *Monk Dawson* is a deeply religious man, determined to live his life in accordance with his beliefs. He concludes that the only way he can do that is by joining a monastic order. In *The Upstart*, the protagonist is more sinner than saint. Motivated by envy, seeking revenge for real or imagined wrongs, he cripples one adversary, ruins another financially, and shatters the marriage of a girl who had once been patronising to him. Thanks to what the author calls 'divine irony', *The Upstart* has a happy ending. It is as if Read had abandoned his responsibilities as a novelist and had asked God to take over. The *deus ex machina* figures prominently in Read's fiction. Acts of God, or of the devil, send his plots lurching into lurid melodrama. Murder and other crimes seem to have been introduced because they suit Read's thesis, even if they wreck his story. *The Upstart* is the worst instance, but the double murder of Strickland's wife and her lover, Strickland's old friend from Oxford days, engineered by Strickland's jealous mistress, comes as an inappropriate element in *A Married Man* and strains beyond breaking point the reader's willingness to suspend his disbelief. In *The Junkers*, there was no need to invent melodrama. It could be culled from the histories of Nazi war criminals. (pp. 131-32)

Read sees many of his characters as pilgrims struggling to overcome temptations and win through to the good life. Even non-Catholics are among them. . . . However, to Read, there is only one sure way of fulfilling oneself or saving one's soul, and that is through religion, through Roman Catholicism. It is better to be a monk than to meddle in politics, to emulate Dawson rather than Strickland.

Religion and morals are Read's chief preoccupations, but at times he seems almost equally interested in sex and class. Sexual love, he insists, delights and disgusts at the same time. . . . The similes and images which Read uses when he is dealing with sex could well be describing a disease. . . . (p. 132)

Class differences, snobbishness and feelings of social inferiority play large parts in Read's books. The many crimes and sins committed in *The Upstart* all stem from resentment of privilege and of the arrogant attitude adopted by the privileged. . . .

Read is hardly ever dull. He is a skilled storyteller, with a strong, unfussy narrative style and a good ear for dialogue. Not for nothing was he chosen to handle the truth-is-stranger-than-fiction stories of the train robbers and of the air-crash survivors who turned cannibal. But although he does not bore, he can often irritate. All is fine while he is carried away by the momentum of the tale he is telling. Unfortunately, he remembers every now and then that he has a preacher's task as well. Then the rot sets in and credibility flies out of the window. In *A Married Man*, nothing in Paula's character and behaviour leads us to believe that she would really sponsor the murder of Strickland's wife. She is ambitious, possessive, jealous, but she is not a convincing murderess, not even by proxy.

The murder happens because Read needs it to make points in his 'sermon'. He needs it to shock and shake Strickland out of his bland humanism and make him think that 'even I might believe in God . . . if He could show me the man I really am'. His other point is the importance of sincere repentance, even at the eleventh hour. (p. 133)

[*A Married Man*] is flawed because tale and tract are not fused. It is not a question of whether the argument is valid or not. Nor is it anything to do with the validity of the points of Catholic dogma which Read chooses to stress. His failure is a creative failure, a failure to make us believe that his characters would have behaved like that in real life. At some stage in a Read novel his people become puppets. Read is so near to being a first-rate novelist that his admirers must hope he will find a way of arguing a case without destroying the creative framework on which believability depends. (p. 134)

John Mellors, "Delight and Disgust," in London Magazine (© London Magazine 1980), Vol. 20, No. 112, April-May, 1980, pp. 131-34.

WILLIAM H. PRITCHARD

It is typical of Piers Paul Read that he should preface [*A Married Man*] with an Author's Note informing American readers about the difference in the English legal system between a solicitor and a barrister. Typical in that it recalls the generally sober, just-the-facts-please tone Read has assumed in previous novels like *Monk Dawson* and *The Professor's Daughter*, especially in the extended flatness of *Polonaise*. Read depends on the clarity and intelligence with which he states, rather than explores, his fictional materials. . . . Read contrives a shocker of a plot which convinced me of little more than that it was a shocker of a plot. For all the dispassionately careful observation in his writing, it's hard to escape the feeling that, in more than one sense, the hero has been fixed, his situation more relentlessly contrived than freely explored. (p. 259)

William H. Pritchard, "Fictional Fixes," in The Hudson Review (copyright © 1980 by The Hudson Review, Inc.; reprinted by permission), Vol. XXXIII, No. 2, Summer, 1980, pp. 256-70.*

SALLY EMERSON

In *The Villa Golitsyn* two old schoolfellows are invited to Willy Ludley's villa in Nice. Willy's wife Priscilla needs their help because Willy appears to be drinking himself to death. . . .

Before [Simon Milson] goes to Nice he is asked by his Foreign Office boss to discover from Ludley whether or not he was responsible for [an] act of treason back in 1963. The other suspect, Baldwin, is up for an important job and his name needs to be cleared before he gets it. Simon, who has little integrity, willingly agrees to spy on his old friend.

On the way to Nice Simon encounters a runaway English schoolgirl who joins the curious group of friends gathered around Willy at the Villa Golitsyn. Willy is a superbly drawn character. He is destructive, manipulative, witty and mesmerizing. He is also, Simon notes, obsessed by a sense of sin and guilt.

Piers Paul Reed brilliantly creates a mood of mystery and corruption where nothing is stable. . . .

In a superb ending, the novel twists and turns. Nothing is as expected. Piers Paul Read has created some remarkable characters and a story that examines the boundaries of right and wrong and the dangers of stepping beyond them.

> *Sally Emerson, "Recent Fiction: 'The Villa Golitsyn',"* in The Illustrated London News *(© 1981 The Illustrated London News & Sketch Ltd.), Vol. 269, No. 6999, October, 1981, p. 81.*

ANGELA HUTH

[In **The Villa Golitsyn** Mr. Read] skilfully infiltrates an air of menace, of intense unease, over the daily events that quicken towards the tragedy at the end. He juggles his characters with almost Murdochian dexterity: there's gambolling both hetero and homosexual; there's mystery, fear, banging shutters.

But, except for Willy, it is hard to feel very much sympathy for any of the characters: often they seem to be mouthpieces rather than flesh and blood. This is not Piers Paul Read at his strongest—as in **A Married Man**—but he never fails to be an elegant craftsman.

> *Angela Huth, "Thrills and Bills"* (© British Broadcasting Corp. 1981; reprinted by permission of Angela Huth), in The Listener, *Vol. 106, No. 2730, October 8, 1981, p. 412.*

ANDREW MOTION

"If I had to choose between betraying my country and betraying my friend, I hope I should have the guts to betray my country." Piers Paul Read's [**The Villa Golitsyn**] explores the implications of Forster's celebrated remark in a narrative of engrossing complexity. . . .

In summary, the plot sounds like a Famous Five adventure peopled by drunks and sexual frustrates. . . . But Piers Paul Read tries to dignify the extravagant element in his novel by drawing a number of parallels between its various worlds. As Milson tries to understand the secret of Ludley's past, issues raised by remote historical events are reflected in contemporary personal crises. The original question—how could Ludley behave so uncharacteristically as to betray a friend?—is mirrored in Milson's own worry about the rights and wrongs of seducing Priss, and in his wondering how youthful radicalism and energy can decline into middle-aged, boozy disillusionment. It is, in other words, the question of transformation that bothers him. . . .

Private morality, Piers Paul Read implies, is always subject to the brusque morality of the state. It is a conclusion which is made most resonant in **The Villa Golitsyn** when he uses a matter-of-fact style, and allows the oddities and ironies of his historical context to speak for themselves. But within the novel's plausibly factual framework is a more obviously "imaginative" fiction—and here, for all the plain language and cunning interweaving of past and present, extraordinary events like the storm seem stubbornly and freakishly melodramatic.

> *Andrew Motion, "F. O. Affairs,"* in The Times Literary Supplement *(© Times Newspapers Ltd. (London) 1981; reproduced from* The Times Literary Supplement *by permission), No. 4097, October 9, 1981, p. 1153.*

JOHN MELLORS

Breaches of etiquette come thick and fast in Piers Paul Read's **The Villa Golitsyn,** from insulting one's guests at dinner to talking about money—'it's too middle-class'—from drunkenness to incest and the seduction of a minor. Read has so many talents as a novelist that one is always expecting him to write a really first-class book and always feeling surprised as well as disappointed when he fails to live up to his promise. He is an entertaining storyteller. He is as interested in ideas as in people. He can explore other countries and cultures and seem quite at home in them. He plays well so many instruments; it is a pity that he falls down on the orchestration. Also, he is far too easily tempted into introducing the luridly melodramatic. (p. 95)

At the beginning of [**The Villa Golitsyn**] it seems as if the theme will be the nature of treason and the motives and afterthoughts of a traitor. However, that theme becomes submerged in the treatment of sex and the guilt that is rooted in the contravention of sexual taboos. (pp. 95-6)

> *John Mellors, "Breaches of Etiquette,"* in London Magazine *(© London Magazine 1982), Vol. 21, No. 11, February, 1982, pp. 93-6.*

Gregor von Rezzori
1914-

Rumanian novelist.

In his autobiographical fiction Rezzori, who now lives in Italy and writes in German, portrays the colorful and volatile milieu of central Europe after the First World War.

***Memoirs of an Anti-Semite*, his recent "novel in five stories," provides ironic and disturbing insight into the prevalent anti-Semitism of the pre-Second World War era by candidly examining Rezzori's own culturally inherited prejudices and values. *The Hussar*, an earlier novel, earned praise for the energetic and intricately textured prose with which Rezzori fashioned an imaginary city, Tchernopol, and its picturesque inhabitants.**

RICHARD PLANT

If there ever existed a melting pot, it was the city of Tchernopol, situated in some vague Eastern European country . . . , a place thriving on splendid feuds, relishing wit and stupidity, and living in four centuries simultaneously. Tchernopol, formerly imperial Austrian, now Polish or Czech—who knows? possesses an alert skepticism of everything, above all of itself. The city is the heroine of this strange, brilliant and exasperating novel ["**The Hussar**"] by Gregor von Rezzori. . . .

In many respects, this is a picaresque novel, abounding in knaves, rascals, innocent children and talkative bystanders. The scoundrels have the upper hand in every way, and the earlier chapters will lull readers into a false security: namely, that we are in for a delightful chronicle of roguery. But although the scalawags in Tchernopol deceive everyone except other scalawags, the author fools his readers, changes keys gradually and ends on a nearly tragic note. We must emphasize the word *nearly*—it is hard to say when the author wants us to take him seriously. Most of the time, he seems to be winking at the reader while relating the capricious doings of his bizarre characters. . . .

What about plot? What about heroes? Mr. Rezzori can't be bothered. He presents a mosaic of anecdotes, contemplations, lyrical hymns (descriptions of neglected gardens delight him forever), arguments, parodies, sketches and dialogues discussing all events described, plus others he has had no time to relate. He never catches up with himself. His inventiveness is as unlimited as his gusto and energy. He mixes the comic and the horrifying; he exalts the tender beauty of a feminine character on one page, and, on the next, spends as much time recounting a freakish business deal. . . .

To be truthful, Mr. Rezzori does not care much for connecting incidents. He is enamored of his language, which seems to produce all the characters and incidents. It is typical of the book that most of its people are enthusiastic talkers. . . .

Now and then, the author interrupts himself and promises to get on with the story, but he is not able to do so. In less experienced hands this nonchalance might have become fatal. Mr. Rezzori's narrative, gushing forth from the well of a boundless imagination, is never dull.

Richard Plant, "Scoundrels Had the Upper Hand in Every Way," in The New York Times Book Review *(© 1960 by The New York Times Company; reprinted by permission), April 10, 1960, p. 4.*

ROBERT C. HEALEY

In his childish innocence the nameless young narrator of this affectionate Old-World chronicle ["**The Hussar**"] had worshipped [a] colorful hussar as a quixotic white knight. . . .

[Gregor von Rezzori] uses the hussar as a wonderful excuse to explore the local folkways and to remember lovingly the wonder of growing up in . . . a heady and volatile atmosphere. As he doggedly follows the tenuous thread of Major Tildy's misfortunes, he introduces half the inhabitants of Tchernopol, where half a dozen nationalities and religions jostle for attention. Except for an ugly current of anti-Semitism, life is thoroughly relaxed and good-humored.

The leisurely and episodic narrative is dexterously held together by an engaging point of view that neatly blends the wide-eyed wonder of a child with the disenchantment of a remembering adult. The initial tone of gentle irony and satire melts into a mood of elegiac sadness for a city that could debase a proud hussar and allow a soccer match to explode into a short vicious pogrom. Though obviously autobiographical in inspiration, **"The Hussar"** is far more than a collection of scrappy memories. It is an extremely artful and frequently witty evocation of all the charms and contradictions of a bustling Central European city.

Robert C. Healey, "Sad, Witty and Charming," in New York Herald Tribune Book Review *(© I.H.T. Corporation; reprinted by permission), May 29, 1960, p. 8.*

CHRISTOPHER LEHMANN-HAUPT

How protected we are by our trust in the good manners of American publishers. We pick up Gregor von Rezzori's novel without batting an eye, knowing full well that its title, **"Memoirs of an Anti-Semite"** must be ironic, or at least ambiguous. And of course we are right. In the novel's fifth and final episode, called "Pravda" because it may be anything beside the truth, the narrator reflects from the vantage point of 1979 on his talents for declaring his past selves a fiction—"Indispensable talents, if you wanted to survive. For otherwise, how could you stand the look of your face of yesterday." Finally, the entire contents of these **"Memoirs"** are declared to be fiction.

On the other hand, the stories told in them are very close to autobiography, for the narrator strongly resembles the author. . . . And though the narrator is exceedingly hard on himself, the fact remains that he was raised to despise Jews by his aristocratic father. . . . [All] the complex causes of European anti-Semitism are anatomized in these pages. Nothing is made prettier than it was. Nothing is glossed over.

Still, though we never escape the theme of anti-Semitism, it is not what is uppermost in our minds when we turn the final pages. What we recall then is the breathtaking richness of the history it recounts and the extraordinary way it makes time pass by. (p. 416)

Yet it is not alone for the vividness of its settings and characters that we attend to **"Memoirs of an Anti-Semite."** We also savor the sound of the author's voice, an extraordinary blend of bitter self-denigration and sweet recollection. . . .

And of course we can never avert our eyes from the dissection of anti-Semitism that keeps going on in the background—a dissection that amounts to an anatomy of Central Europe in the 20th century. (p. 417)

Christopher Lehmann-Haupt, " 'Memoirs of an Anti-Semite'," in The New York Times, *Section III (© 1981 by The New York Times Company; reprinted by permission), July 1, 1981 (and reprinted in* Books of the Times, *Vol. IV, No. 9, September, 1981, pp. 416-17).*

V. S. PRITCHETT

Those who expect the sensational or a tract from Rezzori's title [**"Memoirs of an Anti-Semite"**] will find something very different. He might even be described as anti-Semite *manqué*, coming from a country where anti-Semitism—among other "anti" passions—was endemic by tradition. More accurately, like the arrogant young Jewish pianist whose gifts enchanted him but of whom he was violently jealous for other reasons when he was thirteen, Rezzori is an artist with a demon in him.

The episode with the young pianist occurs in the first of the four half-fictional disquisitional stories in which this vivid to-ing and fro-ing autobiography is enclosed. They are speculative dramatizations of the myths against which he rebelled in a youth that went adrift in the political catastrophes in the Middle Europe of his past. In an epilogue his mind scurries through a kind of reverie about some of the private disasters of his middle years which had not taken story form. This, I think, is a loss. But his conclusion revives a very generalized misanthropy which reminds one of Spengler's *Decline of the West:* the once confident Western "goys" themselves may, in their turn, become displaced persons, too gifted for a banal proletarian dispensation.

The word "troth" spoken by the most engaging and sisterly of the Jewish women the author has been in love with is at the heart of all his stories of a changing self. For his father, a minor landowner is Bukovina, troth means an inherited loyalty to the Austro-Hungarian Empire. . . .

The father's sense of caste brought boredom into the house, and as a boy the author suffered long spells of what the Russians call *skushno*, i.e., an ennui, a sense of "a spiritual void that sucks you in like a vague but intensely urgent longing." The longing is strongly influenced by the fact that the boy is the handsome pet of a frustrated mother. He will idealize and fear other women, especially women of his own class. As for the Jews who swarm in the countryside, he knows them well—he picks up Yiddish very fast—and does not hate them, but he does not *like* them. He is simply class-conscious: either they are too obsequiously poor or too flauntingly rich. Their chief "vice" is asking "personal questions." His boredom is also due to sexual frustration, and when at eighteen he rebels against his family and his class and runs off to Bucharest to earn his living—a notion repugnant to his parents—and has liaisons with Jewish women, who always attract him, he discovers that the Jews also have their troth.

This is the central theme of the episodes that follow: violent sexual desire—the "myth" of sex as he will call it; sex is not love—will surprise him by turning him into a Lothario, passionate but soon back in boredom. He will be left with guilt because he has betrayed the dreamed-of, lifelong "ideal" love, probably derived from his love of his mother. (That thought annoys Rezzori, who hates Freudian doctrine as "the Jewish disease.") . . .

His first experience of the Jewish "troth" is with an older woman who runs a pharmacy, and who is known to all the salesmen for her arrogance and rages—the hardheaded Black Widow. . . . Rezzori's erotic writing is at once tender and strongly carnal. Lust is no less an image-maker than love. He sees the Black Widow as "lovable" because of "the age-old Jewish sadness," as an archaic goddess. . . .

The liaison turns eventually into a sour comedy, and what brings about the inevitable break is not her Jewishness: he loves that, but he cannot bear it that she is petit bourgeois. He can tolerate her accent; he cannot bear her tastes. What is troth—a powerful myth or has it degenerated into the petty prejudices of manners and class? The final scene has that mingling of the cruel and grotesque which is overwhelmingly and marvelously done. It is he who is humiliated. He is less a man; she is more powerfully a woman.

The attraction of this early erotic career is Rezzori's very considerable gift for evoking the bazaar-like underground of Rumanian life, its half-Oriental, half-Slavonic crowds. (p. 12)

Whether his memoir is fact or hanging-in-the-air fiction, it is honest about his exasperation and his compelled affection for his—to him—peculiar Jewish friends, mistresses, and his two wives, half-Jewish and Jewish. He sees their lives and his own with detachment as tragicomedy in which he is the observant yet self-critical "floater." . . . (p. 13)

V. S. Pritchett, "Demon Lover," in The New York Times Book Review *(© 1981 by The New York Times Company; reprinted by permission), July 16, 1981, pp. 12-13.*

LEON WIESELTIER

Memoirs, not confessions: this anti-Semite asks not to be forgiven, he asks to be enjoyed [in *Memoirs of an Anti-Semite*]. Enjoying him is not hard; Gregor von Rezzori is a wizard of a writer. There is sin, but there is also style. Rezzori flaunts both. He will leave many readers in a muddle, and he will win many admirers. The man's malice is really elegant. His book is a new avenue through the century's most disgusting decades. It is the persecution of the Jews as told by a dandy.

Rezzori calls his book a novel, and he cannot be blamed for not calling it an autobiography. Fact or fiction, it is a book proudly consecrated to truth. (The last chapter, entitled "Pravda," is an apology for the author's embellishments, and for the author.) The impassioned protagonist of this chronicle of prejudice is Gregor, who was born during the Great War into an aristocratic Austrian family marooned in the Bukovina by the breakup of the empire. His father keeps faith with the imperial ideal; he fusses over a very ceremonial "Germanhood" and—the primary demonstration of his undefeated Austrian patriotism—he hunts. He instills his son with a fitting hatred of the Jews, and of the mind as Jews practice it. . . . [Gregor's] ambition was the sporting life, and sex; and he did not want for horses and women. Yet he is left with the memory of a life that has miscarried. His marriages fail, his son dies, his culture disappears.

What has all this to do with the Jews? Gregor has a hypothesis about his life. His memoir interprets his life according to the appearance in it of Jews at its most critical moments. Jews, especially the women, have been the instruments of his humiliation. It is a short fall from the amorist to the anti-Semite, because Gregor is a sucker for Jewish women. He is a philo-Semite in bed. He admires the "Oriental" charms of his accommodating Jewesses, and is deeply affected by the ancient tragedy he detects in their eyes. . . . [But when] the women disappoint, so does the race. (p. 29)

[Additionally], Jews who shook off the ghetto ran the risk . . . of being no longer fascinating. They could no longer provide the bored and embattled gentry what it needed most: color.

Color is what Rezzori believes in. Color in writing, color in people, color in history. The principle of his style, as he remarks, is "vividness," a dizzy accumulation of effects and allusions, which results in a kind of driven lyricism. The ethnic cacophony of Central Europe fills Rezzori with wonder. . . . He introduces his Ruthenians and Bessarabians and Armenians (and Jews, if they are still picturesque) with great relish, to exult in their differences; they are all so breathtakingly genuine. It is the tribute of a man who does not know who he is. At a time when *Mitteleuropa* has cast a new spell over many American intellectuals, Rezzori's book reminds that there was something morally and intellectually repulsive about all that root-

edness. The author's alienation is entirely appropriate. (pp. 29-30)

Gregor also longs for a mythic transfiguration. This is a familiar modern impertinence, for a man to conflate his grubby little life with a perfect world of old. The language, the characters, the myths—all are ornaments pitted against the ordinary. The struggle against ordinariness was a momentous psychological feature of what transpired in Europe between the wars. It issued in art, but more frequently it issued in politics.

There is no politics in Rezzori. . . . He has only an aesthetic attitude toward anti-Semitism. It is so *interesting*. It is not an evil, it is a subject. Rezzori has brilliantly captured the appearances of the prejudice, the way it looked and felt; he has changed the hatred in his heart into a spectacle. The imagination, for which nothing is final, will save him from the consequences of his emotional career. . . .

But Rezzori is not fooling around; he is fallen. Trapped in his own contemptible history, he smothers it with surfaces. He plays, rather insistently, the dreamer, dissociated from the catastrophe by the sovereign power of fantasy. He will give the truth, but as a dream. (It was not long in the century before Stephen Daedalus's nightmare could be easily topped.) There can be no doubt about the honesty of this man; his reader will be tempted to conclude that anybody big enough to own up to all this meanness can't be small enough to be this mean. But that is the book exactly: big, and very small. And never smaller than in this sentence: "The only dignity to be maintained in our time is the dignity of being among the victims." We have heard this before, but see who says it now. The anti-Semite wants to be taken for a Jew. Not so fast; those victims are yours. (p. 30)

Leon Wieseltier, "Sophisticated Barbarism," in The New Republic *(reprinted by permission of* The New Republic; *© 1981 The New Republic, Inc.), Vol. 185, No. 3, July 18, 1981, pp. 29-30.*

STANLEY KAUFFMANN

The jacket of this rich, disquietingly good book calls [**"Memoirs of an Anti-Semite"**] "a novel in five stories." Though these five long stories are independent, they are linked and dramatically cumulative. One can accept them as component parts of an organism, but there are reasons to examine the term "novel." . . .

Most of [the facts about the author] are also true of the book's protagonist, or are transparently touched up, and all the other facts of the book fit between or around them logically. Four of the five pieces are in the first person, whose name is Gregor. But I don't suggest that **"Memoirs of an Anti-Semite"** is simply autobiography costumed as a novel; nor is it a conventional autobiographical novel. It's a phenomenon more far reaching and refined—a novel as autobiography. In the last story the narrator says that though he "could look reality in the face, better than most other people," he had talents indispensable to survival. One of them is "the artful feat of always holding up a new possibility of himself, a fiction of himself." This connotes a great difference both from the formal autobiographical novel and from sheer fabrication. It is literature in which the author envisions himself as a character in a design arranged from the data of his life as another author might arrange items from fictitious notes.

Mr. von Rezzori's delicate method suits the book's central truth, which is indicated in its title. This is the story of an upper-class middle-European—of Italian ancestry, with Austrian loyalties and Rumanian influences—immersed in environmental attitudes, educated to regard Jews as aliens, threats, subordinates, rivals, curs. The possible exceptions were Jewish women, who might be seen as sport. (''A Jewess is no Jew'' was the common phrase.) Mr. von Rezzori's book does not recant or justify those views: It is the straightforward yet imaginative, often discomfiting, always enthralling ''novel'' of a life in which such attitudes provide the chief dynamics. (p. 7)

Conceived as the representative imaginings of a life, [the] stories are schematic only in that Mr. von Rezzori believes in destiny through conditioning. They are wonderfully intricate in character and texture, studded with observation, both factual and opinionated (e.g., the look of ''a typical immigrants' flat''; an ''Armenian preference for pink''). . . .

It is irrelevant—his title tells you so from the start—to draw up a ledger of the good and bad things that Mr. von Rezzori says about Jews and see how he comes out. (For instance, Gregor speaks Yiddish and knows more about some aspects of Jewishness than many of the Jews he meets; but this is offered only as a paradox.) It is as irrelevant to argue with Mr. von Rezzori's values as with Ferdinand Céline's or Knut Hamsun's. He is not of their stature, but he is an artist, devilishly honest, stubborn, the creator and the created of an art work about a survivor. It is through Mr. von Rezzori's art, rather than through any vanity or apology of Gregor's, that we are enlightened. Most of the millions who share Mr. von Rezzori's views don't even have the ability to face them as he does, let alone the gifts to reveal them with such disturbing, defiant clarity. (p. 17)

> Stanley Kauffmann, ''Imaginings of a Life,'' in The New York Times Book Review (© 1981 by The New York Times Company; reprinted by permission), July 19, 1981, pp. 7, 17.

VIVIAN GORNICK

Jews are the complicated walking symbol of von Rezzori's alienated state, the Jews of his boyhood and young manhood. Jews he has feared, loved, desired, betrayed, degraded and been degraded by, and of whom he has said to himself, ''Whatever else I am, at least I am not *that*, but why is it I can never get away from them?'' Jews he must scorn, patronize, flee from, merge with, drown in, be endlessly embroiled with. Jews he needs to separate from, cleanse himself of, extend recognition to, come to terms with. And never does. . . .

[*Memoirs of an Anti-Semite*] is composed of five pieces, four of which are highly shaped reminiscences of different periods of the author's life. Each reminiscence grows out of an experience with a Jew. . . .

The brilliance of these stories lies in von Rezzori's gift for evoking the special quality of the places in which they are set— the soft beauty of rural Bukovina in the 1920s, the teeming Easternism of Bucharest, the cafe life of prewar Vienna—and in his skill at painting the anti-Semitism that pervaded European life before the Second World War.

To an American Jew in her middle 40s, the Jew-hating texture of von Rezzori's prose is breathtaking: its seamless flow, the integration of its references, the ordinary, all-purpose, everydayness of it. (p. 151)

The personality behind *Memoirs of an Anti-Semite* both attracts and repels. It is savvy, literate, ardent, erotic; vain, shallow, purposeless, cruel. Von Rezzori's ''I'' is saved from caricature—the Middle European dandy of the prewar years, intellectually observant, spiritually listless, sexually exploitative— by the intelligence of his self-description, but as the stories progress there emerges the portrait of a man moving not toward engagement but rather toward a kind of misanthropic inertness he himself does not really understand and, moreover, does not wish to understand. Brilliant as these Jewish episodes of his life are, after a time they begin to read like the objective correlative to a condition of psychological sluggishness whose permanence has been assured from the first words of the memoir, an elaboration on *skushno*, the Russian word for boredom. . . .

The man at the center of these stories is always on the verge of breaking through to some open understanding of his feelings about Jews; he keeps coming close, but never arrives.

Instead, he tells his stories with the very particular unreflectiveness of a mind formed in the first decade of the century, out of a psyche that remained unresponsive to the years that followed. Von Rezzori's voice is both racy and literate, wonderfully rich in syntactical unexpectedness and the multilingual use of idiom, but he is essentially speaking from *inside* the world that originally shaped him—not, as he believes, from a point of informed removal. That world, at least insofar as literature is concerned, began with Schnitzler and ended with Céline, and can now deliver up only nostalgia, whether benign or malignant. . . .

The last chapter of the book—unfocused, bitter, nostalgic, abstract—only serves to underscore the deeper condition to which this skillful confession does not confess. This chapter is written in the third person instead of the first and set in the Rome of today; von Rezzori speaks here as a man in his late 60s, rapidly summing up. Bilious and confused, disappointed and a bit frightened, he clearly doesn't know what to make of the world around him, and he doesn't *want* to know. He openly longs for prewar Europe, the only world he can ever understand or value, and retreats before our eyes into the cocoon-like dislocation he has always wanted to occupy. (p. 152)

> Vivian Gornick, ''The Ultimate Other,'' in The Nation (copyright 1981 The Nation magazine, The Nation Associates, Inc.), Vol. 233, No. 5, August 22-29, 1981, pp. 151-52.

HAROLD SEGEL

To the individual dislocated by social change as much as by the upheaval of war, the memoir becomes less the literary retrieval of a past than a self-explication in terms of a value system irretrievably lost. The resources of fiction that can effectively be utilized for this purpose are handsomely exemplified by Czeslaw Milosz's *The Issa Valley* and Rezzori's *Memoirs*. The projection of the self as fictional hero lifts the constraints of linear narration, permitting changes of perspective (in Rezzori, through the fictionalization of the autobiographical ''I'') and the reordering of experience into the components of the novel.

For the landowning, hunt-loving (this above all), and class-conscious Austrian nobility among whom Rezzori grew up and whose outlook shaped and later collided with his own, anti-Semitism was a bedrock of society. . . .

In awaking to the preposterousness of prejudice, Rezzori discovered within himself the resources for a deflationary irony, both wry and comic. . . .

[The final chapter entitled "Pravda"] is the weakest of an otherwise entertaining and thought-provoking "novel in five stories," and not just because of the author's regurgitation of his Jewish marriage. In attempting to race through time to bring his readers up to date on the vicissitudes of his postwar career, Rezzori shifts gears from first to third person altering both narrative voice and rhythm for the worst. Forgiveness is in order, though; there are simply too many values of art and insight in the *Memoirs* to allow judgment to be misled by a late-appearing display of spleen or a backfired literary strategy.

An inherited class prejudice against Jews became the catalyst for Rezzori's rebellion against a static, moth-eaten, and more than slightly ridiculous world as doomed to oblivion as the Jews who were such a large part of it. The anti-Semitism of the lapsed aristocrat appears benign and bemused in the idiom of quasi-fiction, but the context of ultranationalistic pan-Germanism in which it unfolds, and which Rezzori at times delineates so tellingly, reinforces the grim awareness that it was indeed here that one of the greatest of human calamities was forged.

Harold Segel, "Goodbye to All That," in Book World—The Washington Post *(© 1981, The Washington Post), August 30, 1981, p. 11.*

PAUL GRAY

It matters little how much of *Memoirs of an Anti-Semite* may be autobiographical; the book's achievement overshadows its origins. These haunting stories portray history unwinding within a single skull, a cultivated, often charming mind being betrayed by a catastrophic flaw. They also show how such treason, magnified many millions of times, led civilization itself to the brink.

Paul Gray, "Divided Soul," in Time *(copyright 1981 Time Inc.; all rights reserved; reprinted by permission from* Time*), Vol. 118, No. 11, September 14, 1981, p. 100.*

Marilynne Robinson

1944-

© Jerry Bauer

American novelist.

Robinson's lyrical prose in her first novel, *Housekeeping*, caused Anatole Broyard to express "a delighted surprise at the unexpected capacities of language." The novel centers on efforts to cope with a world characterized by impermanence and loss. In it Robinson conveys an acceptance of transience that approximates celebration.

PAUL GRAY

Most small American towns have at least one: the "odd" house that everyone knows and gossips about, the old place going to seed on the outside while a hidden, perhaps unimaginable life transpires behind drawn shades or yellowing lace curtains. A home haunted by its occupants fascinates the neighbors and many, many writers; the phenomenon crops up from Poe to Faulkner to Harper Lee and beyond. That last category now includes Author Marilynne Robinson. Her unsettling first novel [*Housekeeping*] deals with the fall of yet another house, but from an unusual vantage. The story is told by an insider who helps pull down the roof.

Ruth Stone and her younger sister Lucille are deposited as small children at their grandmother's house in Fingerbone, an isolated community. . . .

When their grandmother dies, care of the castaway daughters eventually falls to their Aunt Sylvie. . . .

Lucille finally senses how peculiar the three of them look to the town and escapes from "Sylvie's dream." . . .

Sylvie and Ruth are passive, quicksilver characters, prone to skittering off at a hint of pressure. Having created wraiths without motives or accountable pasts, Author Robinson left herself a big problem: how to nudge them through a plot, make them interesting, worthy of attention, when they seem so indifferent about themselves. She solved it with language. Ruth's narrative is as colorful as she is pallid. For a self-confessed dreamer with a tenuous hold on reality, she shows a keen sense of the here and now, and of the right words to record it. . . .

Housekeeping has a few slack moments. Ruth occasionally meditates on a scene without sufficiently setting it. She sometimes meanders. But this first novel does much more than show promise; it brilliantly portrays the impermanence of all things, especially beauty and happiness, and the struggle to keep what can never be owned. . . .

> Paul Gray, "Castaways: 'Housekeeping'," in Time (copyright 1981 Time Inc.; all rights reserved; reprinted by permission from Time), Vol. 117, No. 5, February 2, 1981, p. 83.

LE ANNE SCHREIBER

Marilynne Robinson has written a first novel that one reads as slowly as poetry—and for the same reason: The language is so precise, so distilled, so beautiful that one doesn't want to

miss any pleasure it might yield up to patience. Miss Robinson's muse is clearly John Keats, and her theme, like his, the inextricability of pleasure and loss.

What sustains the lyricism of **"Housekeeping"** is the immovable melancholy of its narrator, a quiet dreamy girl named Ruth who becomes so used to loss so young that she cannot envision clinging to anything more permanent than a moment, a memory or a dream. (p. 14)

The controlled lyricism of Ruth's language, which had been anchored in sensuous detail, becomes unmoored [as tension mounts and the novel nears its end]. . . . Since Ruth is our narrator, when her imagination becomes fevered and hallucinatory, so does the novel, and it never quite regains its equilibrium.

This lapse is perhaps inevitable. None of the romantic poets ever fully managed to solve the problem of how to sustain lyric intensity over the course of a long narrative poem. (Even Keats left "The Fall of Hyperion" unfinished.) And there is only so much one can ask of a first novel, even one so generous in its accomplishments as the one Marilynne Robinson has given us. (p. 16)

> Le Anne Schreiber, "Pleasure and Loss," in The New York Times Book Review (© 1981 by The New

York Times Company; reprinted by permission), February 8, 1981, pp. 14, 16.

ANATOLE BROYARD

Here's a first novel that sounds as if the author has been treasuring it up all her life, waiting for it to form itself. It's as if, in writing it, she broke through the ordinary human condition with all its dissatisfactions, and achieved a kind of transfiguration. You can feel in the book a gathering voluptuous release of confidence, a delighted surprise at the unexpected capacities of language, a close, careful fondness for people that we thought only saints felt.

Marilynne Robinson's **"Housekeeping"** is not about housekeeping at all, but transience. It is about people who have not managed to connect with a place, a purpose, a routine or another person. It's about the immensely resourceful sadness of a certain kind of American, someone who has fallen out of history and is trying to invent a life without assistance of any kind, without even recognizing that there are precedents. It is about a woman who is so far from everyone else that it would be presumptuous to put a name to her frame of mind. (p. 132)

Miss Robinson works with light, dark, water, heat, cold, textures, sounds and smells. She is like the Impressionists, taking apart the landscape to remind us that we are surrounded by elements, that we are separated from one another, and from our past and future, by such influences.

At one point in **"Housekeeping,"** Ruth has grown so awkwardly tall that her sister, Lucille, knocks the heels off her shoes to help her stand and move more naturally. Marilynne Robinson, too, does something like this. She knocks off the false elevation, the pretentiousness, of our current fiction. Though her ambition is tall, she remains down to earth, where the best novels happen. (p. 133)

Anatole Broyard, '"Housekeeping','" in The New York Times, *Section C (© 1981 by The New York Times Company; reprinted by permission), January 7, 1981 (and reprinted in* Books of the Times, *Vol. IV, No. 3, March, 1981, pp. 132-33).*

HERMIONE LEE

[*Housekeeping* is] written with infinite care. It could easily be made to sound precious, and at times the fine style does become claustrophobic: 'For when does a berry break upon the tongue as sweetly as when one longs to taste it?' All the same, it is an exceptional, strange, alluring novel. . . .

The family life is finely done, from the grandmother's quiet ordinariness to Sylvie's abstracted love of air and darkness, her sad stories, her hoarding of useless things, her transient's habits. But all this depends on and is interwoven with the setting. The 'sharp watery smell' of the ploughed land, the depths in which the dead lie hidden under the busy water-life at the surface, the 'delicate infrastructure' of ice below the earth, the mysterious geography of mountains, shores, lake and bridge, are beautifully felt.

Gradually a satisfying analogy emerges between the house and the lake, the family memory and the geological layers: it is a novel about traces, flotsam, the perishable marks of 'every spirit passing through the world.' Marilynne Robinson's successful negotiation between the idea and its precise embodiment is an admirable, if very peculiar, achievement.

Hermione Lee, "Glaswegian Phantasmagoria," in The Observer *(reprinted by permission of The Observer Limited), No. 9888, March 1, 1981, p. 32.***

JULIE KAVANAGH

At the beginning of Marilynne Robinson's outstanding first novel [*Housekeeping*], set in a far-Western town by a glacial lake, domesticity is endowed with an almost spiritual aura. After the death of their father (the train he was on plunged into the lake), his three adolescent daughters cleave like infants to their mother, who encircles them with a kind of elemental warmth. The stability of their home is palpable: the girls sleep on starched sheets under layers of quilts, their mother makes cakes and apple sauce on rainy days and in summer mixes a pot-pourri of blown rose petals and spices. But the novel sets out to subvert this kind of tranquility, exposing it as illusory, and housekeeping subsequently becomes a gesture of despair.

Years later, when Helen, one of the daughters, returns home to Fingerbone to commit suicide by driving her car into the lake, her mother tries to restore order in the lives of the two children Helen leaves behind by adhering to household routine. . . . The two jittery maiden great-aunts who housekeep for Ruth and Lucille when their grandmother dies likewise take refuge in habit and familiarity as a way of handling a crisis. But their veneration of routine, of the need to make each day a replica of the next, is not to be reconciled with the vicissitudes of growing children ("Lucille and I perpetually threatened to cough or outgrow our shoes"). The aunts flee back to their basement room in a residential hotel, leaving Sylvie, Helen's vagrant sister to take over guardianship of the girls.

Housekeeping to Sylvie means a merging of love and squalor. . . . This good-natured eccentricity, however, has far more significance than is at first apparent. The sequinned velveteen ballet slippers Sylvie buys as school shoes for the girls represent not just her liking of fanciful gewgaws, but, spoiling as they instantly do on the muddy walk to school, are emblems of the novel's main theme—an acceptance of transience, an acceptance which Sylvie embodies: "To her, the deteriorations of things were always a fresh surprise." Lucille's growing desire to conform to the lives of ordinary people is expressed in her rejection of these slippers: she pulls the sequins off and demands red rubber boots: "Lucille saw in everything its potential for invidious change . . . Ruffles wilted, sequins fell."

Ruth and Lucille often come home after a day's truancy in the woods to find Sylvie sitting—and sometimes eating—in the dark. The habit not only exemplifies Sylvie's nonconformity, but is integral to the novel's thematic whole. Darkness on the one hand conveniently veils the dirt and clutter that Sylvie ignores, but it is also a kind of anodyne for her. . . . Then, again, darkness is given a mystical relevance. . . . Finally, all this is put in an oblique Christian context when, towards the end of the novel, an allusion to Christ cooking fish on the shore refers one back to [a] childhood incident, suggesting that Ruth's trance by the lake was a kind of religious experience, that the darkness was then, as in Eliot's paradox in *The Four Quartets*, "the darkness of God".

Rather as Eliot did in his poem, Ms Robinson incorporates seemingly mundane incidents and images in an overall metaphysical design. . . .

Though there is a vein of Christian faith running through this novel, it is not overt or over-schematic. Sylvie's transience can be taken as allegoric, but at the same time she is an original, fully-developed character in her own right. The growing rift between the sisters is also marvellously depicted, in a way that is both poignant and comic. . . . While Ruth, like Sylvie, clearly now feels, "the life of perished things" and knows that "what perished need not be lost", Lucille demands a solid home and predictable adolescent requirements like new jeans and nail polish. She goes to live with one of her schoolteachers, leaving Ruth and Sylvie to keep house in their own wayward fashion. When the tranquil understanding that now exists between them is threatened by meddlesome neighbours, who rightly assume that Sylvie is imposing her vagrancy on the girl, aunt and niece decide that rather than be separated, with Ruth committed into care, they should escape together, into a life of transience. They burn the house at night and cross the vast railway bridge that spans Fingerbone Lake.

The previously realistic narrative now begins to mirror the drifters' new freedom and to take the form of arcane, meandering reflections. That the pair have symbolically transcended the mundane by crossing the bridge is reiterated by a free—at times, inaccessible—prose-style. The flux which *Housekeeping* appears to endorse is also emphasized throughout by an abundance of similes, which contrive a sense of continual change and assist a dissolution of the actual. Ms Robinson will often use two or three similes at a time, and this, as well as the serpentine movement of her sentences, reflects the novel's themes of dematerialization and itinerary. . . . There is also in *Housekeeping* an aesthetic relish of words for their own sake, facilitated by Ms Robinson's exceptional command of language. Like Seamus Heaney in his essay "Mossbawn", she has the gift of evoking childhood through a graphic record of visual and tactile sensations. And like Nabokov in *Speak Memory* describing Pears Soap as topaz-like when held to the light, she achieves a lyrical colouring of everyday objects that is in itself a kind of poetry.

To call *Housekeeping* a novel is possibly to traduce it, since thematically and stylistically it offers itself as a long prose poem (that the magazine *Quarto* printed an extract from a chapter as a poem called "Loss" would seem to confirm this status). It is a complex work, and as such should be read slowly and carefully, but this is not to suggest that it is impenetrable or overintense. The author's control of plot, her eye for eccentricity, her clarity, quiet humour and delicate touch, invest the book with a lightness that successfully counterbalances the density of thought.

> *Julie Kavanagh, "Escaping into Flux," in* The Times Literary Supplement *(© Times Newspapers Ltd. (London) 1981; reproduced from* The Times Literary Supplement *by permission), No. 4070, April 3, 1981, p. 371.*

ALAN BROWNJOHN

Housekeeping is concerned with much more than the gentle account of the failure of [a] family to survive their battle with [an] insidiously hostile environment. Ruth and Lucille's last guardian, Aunt Sylvie, is given to lonely, eccentric confrontation of the lake [in which her father and her sister drowned]. . . . The water unmistakably draws her; and she takes Ruth on a wild expedition to a ruined house some miles along the lake shore where she hopes that the ghosts of its dead children might appear to them. And when Lucille leaves the household for a more stable one (to live, symbolically, with her Home Economics teacher), Sylvie takes Ruth away from prying police

and solid citizens into the world of transients and drifters. It is implied that this is perhaps better or at least no worse than the precarious Fingerbone community, where "not a soul there but knew how shallow-rooted it was." At any rate, Sylvie and Ruth's dangerous and triumphant crossing of the lake via the railway bridge on a dark, windy night is a conquest of darkness which all the "housekeeping" has never achieved—an escape to freedom.

There is hardly a "plot" in any conventional (or unconventional) sense in *Housekeeping*. Not much happens, no violent or unexpected action disturbs the weirdly even tenor of the households; and the tale is never less than enthralling. Marilynne Robinson has broken the rules, and succeeded, by doing something quite ordinary: by trusting the lucidity, intelligence, and at times sheer power of her prose. *Housekeeping* is simply one of the best-written novels I have read for a long time, and it's not a matter of acrobatic accomplishment or artificial stylishness. This is a prose which radiates a level perception both of character and of the currents of living in the eerie insecurity of this community. The writer understands profoundly just what is entailed in setting down to endure, perhaps even grow, in such a place (or possibly anywhere). The message of the book is not an easy one to take, if the only alternative to miserable insecurity in one place is cheerful drifting through many others. But I suspect that it will not be Miss Robinson's only note: to achieve something so impressive as *Housekeeping* with a first novel suggests a lot more surprises to come. (pp. 87-8)

> *Alan Brownjohn, "Breaking the Rules," in* Encounter *(© 1981 by Encounter Ltd.), Vol. LVI, No. 5, May, 1981, pp. 87-8.**

ROSEMARY BOOTH

Selfhood and shelter have had an intimate association in literature. . . . [The] notion of shelter is linked with an inner effort to forge a new self. (pp. 306-07)

[In] *Housekeeping,* Marilynne Robinson has exploited this familiar connection, immersing it in a story as riveting and taut as the plunge of a train from bridge tracks into lakewater below, the book's primal and haunting incident. While its homely title suggests domesticity, such a connotation is askew of the novel's design, which limns personal preservation as much as household maintenance, private as well as familial order. Yet the two themes are fundamentally inseparable, and "house" here *is* the self, product of toil and prey to destruction. In the end, both literal and figurative houses are intentionally destroyed, but out of ashes and dissolution a new self and life emerge. . . .

The underlying pilgrimage that impels the novel is . . . an ordinary one, the journey to self-consciousness or maturity. *Housekeeping* is an elementary book in another sense too, in that it is steeped in images of earth, water, air, and fire, which suffuse even minor details of each episode. . . .

Clarity and precision mark every level of writing in this work: its stark narrative incidents; its economical character portraits; and its spare tones of language. Though they are restrained, however, the details nonetheless resonate. . . .

Like Sylvie, Ruth has constructed a self which can confront oblivion and survive.

Housekeeping is an achievement of similar magnitude, a deft defiance of convention, a singular book. (p. 307)

Rosemary Booth, "Three Insiders, One Outsider: 'Housekeeping'," in Commonweal *(copyright © 1981 Commonweal Publishing Co., Inc.; reprinted by permission of Commonweal Publishing Co., Inc.), Vol. CVIII, No. 10, May 22, 1981, pp. 306-07.*

THOMAS LeCLAIR

[For] Marilynne Robinson in *Housekeeping*, style is metaphor: the identification of life with and through unusual language. The elegant, measured prose of *Housekeeping* transforms a year in the life of two small-town teenage girls into a profound meditation on loss, transiency, and the shelters we use for protection. The voice Robinson gives her narrator Ruth . . . is original, very much the sound of Ruth's inwardness, yet some comparisons help describe the qualities of this voice and the appeal of the book. *Housekeeping* has the sibling intimacy and domestic observation of Toni Morrison's *The Bluest Eye*, the beauty of threatening landscape and deep dream in John Hawkes's *Beetle Leg*, and the combination of quiet and excited sensibility found in Annie Dillard's *Pilgrim at Tinker Creek*. Best of all, though, is a distinctive rhythm—a matter of pace, syntax, and tone—that cannot be described but lingers after Robinson's equally wonderful visual effects wear off. William Gass has said he forgot the plot of *Middlemarch* a week after he read it but remembered its rhythms for years. The same is true of *Housekeeping*. (p. 88)

The elegant art of *Housekeeping* shames the journalistic realism of more popular fiction by women—and by men—for its metaphors examine the codes of sexual differentiation in ways no amount of brand names, uncouplings, and up-scale chatter can. Robinson is a subtle and lyrical writer but not "delicate," the write-off word for some work by women. *Housekeeping* has power because Robinson, like her narrator, goes her own way, watches, waits, and listens, distills a language that can cleanse the world, not just rearrange and tidy it. (p. 89)

Thomas LeClair, "Fiction Chronicle: January to June, 1981," in Contemporary Literature *(© 1982 by the Board of Regents of the University of Wisconsin System), Vol. 23, No. 1, Winter, 1982, pp. 83-91.**

Leon Rooke

1934-

American-born Canadian short story writer, novelist, and dramatist.

In his fiction, Rooke explores the lives and emotions of ordinary people in their reactions to a world becoming more and more impersonal. He often creates disturbing moods by combining intensely realistic detail with fantasy. The comic overtones present in his work often verge on black humor.

Last One Home Sleeps in the Yellow Bed, The Broad Back of the Angel, and *The Love Parlour,* Rooke's earliest short story collections, are evidence of a traditional style, even though sometimes modified by experimental techniques. In his later collections, *Cry Evil* and *Death Suite,* Rooke shows an increasing tendency to utilize the self-reflective, labrinthine techniques of postmodernism.

The release of his tragicomic novel *Fat Woman* has sparked a wide array of critical response. Some critics, for example, conclude that Rooke has merely expanded a short story into a short novel without a corresponding development of plot or character. Others, however, praise his fine portrayal of the protagonist, saying that it exemplifies Rooke's keen awareness of the psychology of human feelings.

(See also *Contemporary Authors,* Vols. 25-28, rev. ed.)

Photograph by Kim; courtesy of Leon Rooke

SALLY BEAUMAN

[There] is a feeling of frustration about [the stories in **"Last One Home Sleeps in the Yellow Bed"**], as if the writer felt his chosen keyboard were too small, and he was constantly flexing his fingers, eager to modulate from major to minor, throw in a few arpeggios and contrapuntal cross references; in short, as if he wanted to write, not short stories at all, but a novel. Not that it's such a bad fault to have themes which are too big for your medium. Most short-story writers seem to have themes which are too small—nasty, tight, neat little themes which can be cleverly exploited for 4,000 words and then rounded off with a cheap "point" or "twist"—the Somerset Maugham-Saki syndrome, you might call it. At least, Leon Rooke doesn't suffer from that.

There are five short stories in this collection, and one short novel, **"Brush Fire."** Two of the stories work; three of them suffer from a sort of intellectual and stylistic indigestion. **"When the Swimmers on the Beach Have All Gone Home,"** for instance, starts off well enough: an ex-lifeguard saves a girl who jumps off a bridge; it turns out she jumped, not to get away from him, but to find him; they go back to his apartment; they prevaricate; they end up in each other's arms. . . . The basic idea is good. Pinter, for instance, has written brilliant plays about relationships poisoned by gratefulness. But here too much else gets dragged in. . . . [Somehow] the originality of the idea erodes into cliché people, cliché postures. Mr. Rooke seems to sense the danger in this; and in the other two less successful stories, **"The Ice House Gang"** and **"The Alamo Plaza,"** he tries to combat the weakness of incident and characterization with the person and tone of his narrator, gutsy,

easy, almost jokey—a man sending up the romantic situations in which he finds himself.

But style is not something extra, a sauce that can disguise the flavor of the meat. In these stories, downbeat Holden Caulfield style modernity is poured over sad "B"-picture people and plots: the sauce is spicy, but it doesn't disguise the tired taste underneath.

Significantly, the two most effective stories are the simplest ones, and the ones that employ a different narrative technique. The title story is in the third person, and is about a man who commits spiritual suicide without realizing it; the other story **"The Daughters of the Vieux Carré,"** is narrated by a woman, and takes the form of an address to the man she met the evening before in New Orleans, and with whom she has just spent the night.

These two stories perfectly distill a mood: the one of despair that has lasted many years; the other of hope that has lasted an evening. **"Daughters of the Vieux Carré"** in particular, is totally accomplished and poised. . . . [The] people, and the style all mesh. And Mr. Rooke's strange, articulated, cinematic prose, which leaves out nothing, not the gesture of a hand, a noise from the street, comes into its own. He is not straining his medium; he modulates it to perfection. It will be interesting, when it comes out, to see how he handles his first novel. (pp. 42-3)

Sally Beauman, "A Past Like Fragments of a Movie," in The New York Times Book Review (© 1969 by The New York Times Company; reprinted by permission), March 2, 1969, pp. 42-3.

CHOICE

[Rooke's *The Last One Home Sleeps in the Yellow Bed* shows] that the author knows his craft: the careful pacing, the ability to capture and render a scene, and his fine eye for telling detail are all virtues of the conscious artisan. There are both good and exceptional stories in this collection of six. **"The Ice House Gang," "When Swimmers on the Beach Have All Gone Home,"** and the title story all rank as fine fictional achievements; and **"Brush-Fire,"** the longest story in the volume, is truly exceptional. The remaining two stories, however, seem to lack those virtues which Rooke demonstrates in the other stories. It may be that there is too much behind them that is not rendered. An impressive first collection. (pp. 1577-78)

"Humanities: 'Last One Home Sleeps in the Yellow Bed'," in Choice (copyright © 1970 by American Library Association), Vol. 6, No. 11, January, 1970, pp. 1577-78.

KENNETH BAKER

The most convincing stories in Leon Rooke's uneven collection [**"The Broad Back of the Angel"**] are those with a first person narrator. In **"Wintering in Victoria"** the composure with which the abandoned husband recounts his wife's madness is itself maddening. The angry female narrator of **"Dangerous Woman"** fills her story with resentful descriptions of the laundromat to the deliberate exclusion of two characters who demand her attention. And because a narrator constructs himself in telling his story, the crippled teller of the title story is the most compelling. His deformity finally becomes an incident in the story, as the narrator shapes his figurative anatomy into a figurative triumph over the zany life he has been passively witnessing. . . .

I get the feeling that Rooke is a more conventional writer than he would like to be. The humor of, say, the wife's list of things she hates about her husband in **"No Whistle Slow"** is irresistible. But when Rooke gets too arch, as in the **"Magician"** series, or too elliptical, as in **"The Third Floor,"** his writing drags like an interminable bad joke, despite its quick rhythms. Rooke's writing is full of good details (like a detergent called "Target") that are not always put to good use.

Kenneth Baker, "Fancy Fiction: 'The Broad Back of the Angel'," in The New York Times Book Review (© 1978 by The New York Times Company; reprinted by permission), January 1, 1978, p. 6.

JOHN MILLS

[Leon Rooke] writes excellent and sometimes poetic prose—which is enough to disqualify him from popular acclaim; he is an experimentalist—which is enough to create suspicion among those who read fiction; and he is not entirely successful at it—which is enough to damn him among the critics. Personally I wish he would write more. . . . [In *The Broad Back of the Angel,* three] stories about a magician are experimental,

and in my opinion they fail—there is a coy air of self-congratulation about them which brings to mind the *fin de siecle* affectations of *The Yellow Book* as does the title story and the frontispiece which illustrates it. Other than the Mexican pieces, **"Wintering in Victoria"** and **"Iron Woman"** seem to me to be the most successful. In the first an enraged woman leaves her husband taking their child with her. There seems, in the first few pages, every reason why she should do so—he is cold, hard, and cynical. As the story progresses, however, Rooke switches the reader's sympathies very cleverly. **"Iron Woman"** ought to interest feminists and be required reading for anyone who is not. It describes a nervous breakdown, and some of the revenge fantasies it generates very strikingly. It is here that Rooke's blending of the representational and the surreal works at its best.

John Mills, "Book Reviews & Review Articles: 'The Broad Back of the Angel'" (copyright by John Mills), in The Fiddlehead, No. 117, Spring, 1978, p. 127.

GEORGE GARRETT

[*Last One Home Sleeps in the Yellow Bed*] was a powerful, energetic, and original collection. Rooke has come (or gone) a ways since then, and *The Broad Back of the Angel* is very different, being more a unified collection of *tales* . . . than one of short stories; being also mildly surrealistic in matter and in manner, seeming, in style and vocabulary and syntax, to be like a translation, a slightly incoherent and inaccurate translation of a nineteenth-century Middle European novel; or, perhaps, a French surrealist movie of the late thirties, afflicted with poor subtitles. But Rooke is good at it and knows what he is doing well enough. A couple of tales, **"The Third Floor"** and **"Dangerous Women,"** are kin to the earlier stories. Perhaps the greatest difference is in the attitude toward character, the possibilities of individual being. It may be what has happened to the world in the decade since *The Yellow Bed* which has shabbily diminished the strength and dimension of character. (p. 468)

George Garrett, "Coming Out of Left Field: The Short Story Today," in The Sewanee Review (reprinted by permission of the editor; © 1978 by The University of the South), Vol. LXXXVI, No. 3, Summer, 1978, pp. 461-73.*

MICHAEL TAYLOR

I did not find [the stories in *The Love Parlour*] as disturbing as they were probably intended to be; partly because their avant-gardism . . . keeps them at a remove from immediacy, partly because of a certain slackness and attenuation, almost a languorous quality, in construction, particularly in the last group, **"For Love of Madeline," "For Love of Eleanor,"** and**"For Love of Gomez."** The trickiest of the stories, however, **"Memories of a Cross-Country Man,"** is a real *tour de force* whose savage apophthegms, expressed in an amusing and convincing Mexican English, memorably convey the bleak notion of this story, and that of most of the others, that "man is illness personified." . . . (p. 114)

Michael Taylor, "Old Soldiers Never Die: Some Canadian Short Stories" (copyright by Michael Taylor; reprinted by permission of the author), in The Fiddlehead, No. 120, Winter, 1979, pp. 111-15.*

LESLEY HOGAN

[*The Love Parlour*, published in Canada, and *The Broad Back of the Angel*, published in the United States,] show masterful control of a variety of techniques. Rooke's concern is with love and the importance of personal relationships in an ever-increasingly impersonal society. He writes of desperate situations in a comic and sympathetic manner.

The "For Love of" series or Mexican trilogy presents a beautifully subtle put-down of the American tourist who can think of the Mexicans as the foreigners in their own country. At the same time, the stories are also a much more complex statement about the nature of the banal world in which we, the "norteamericanos", live. (p. 222)

"For Love of Gómez" the third story, is found only in *The Love Parlour*, which is unfortunate for the American anthology, as this story explains Rooke's reasons for the trilogy. The story expresses more blatantly the subtle anti-Americanism of the other two. . . . The vain, belligerent, self-worshipping Madeline is contrasted to the patient, accepting, God-fearing Mexican. He is still tied to the land and finds a meaning to his life in that it is part of the divine plan of God. The spoilt brat, bitch-goddess Madeline meets her nemesis in Gómez who struggles to believe his priest's timid boast that God is in every person, even his obnoxious mistress. (p. 223)

The thirteen comic and bizarre stories of *The Broad Back of the Angel* show Rooke as a gifted story teller who reveals strange and puzzling situations. (p. 224)

Rooke probes our innermost feelings about love and death in a sensitive manner that is at once both humorous and tender. He maintains a delicate balance between the realms of reality and fantasy which gives his stories their double impact of strangeness and familiarity. (p. 225)

> *Lesley Hogan, "Book Reviews: 'The Love Parlour' and 'The Broad Back of the Angel'," in* The Canadian Fiction Magazine *(copyright © 1979 by The Canadian Fiction Magazine), Nos. 30-31, 1979, pp. 222-25.*

RUSSELL M. BROWN

Despite Rooke's versatility, there is something about all his fiction that remains identifiable, characteristic, and uniquely personal. Made out of internalized perceptions, his stories are typically ones in which the central character's mind becomes a reflecting pool through which we glimpse the external world. In the course of the story a few stones are dropped in, and as their ripples spread, the images we thought we had recognized reorganize themselves into intriguing new patterns which coalesce, vanish, and reappear, before giving way to something else again. The experience of stories such as these is perhaps closest to that of a particularly vivid dream: one is drawn into a dislocating scene, undergoes a puzzling but compelling experience, and is released somehow more troubled than enlightened.

I don't mean to suggest that Rooke's stories have not also had their own intense quality of reality, for they have. In their own way his first three collections have served to provide one man's records of life lived in the later twentieth century. This is less true, however, of *Cry Evil*.

From the very first words of [*Cry Evil*], Rooke's newest collection, ("Here's a story"), it becomes clear that we are dealing with a writer who is now trying out the self-conscious and self-reflexive mode of post-modernism. As we move through this book, we encounter something of the exhaustion, the labyrinths and the narrative games of writers like Barth. Indeed, the first story "The Deacon's Tale" defines not only the directions of the fiction which follows, but the reasons new directions are necessary. In the opening story Rooke's narrator is no longer as fluent as he has been. He now encounters trouble telling his tale, and reality intrudes as it has not before—especially in the form of his wife's voice, a voice which speaks for protesting readers and challenges his right to his story, complaining about the loss of conventional mimesis and asking for more clarity. The Deacon, as tale-teller from way back, is disturbed by these objections and yet acknowledges their force. . . . But in the story which closes the book "Adolpho's Disappeared and We Haven't a Clue Where to Find Him," the narrative has moved no closer to the conventions of reality and the narrator seems no less dispirited. (p. 36)

Between these two framing tales we are given a series of ingenious narrative variations that are evidence of the search for renewed creative energy. . . . "Friendship and Property," standing in the middle of the volume, . . . is more traditional than the others, a reminder of Rooke's earlier fiction (in fact a continuation of a series of stories begun in his last collection), and an indication of his unwillingness to abandon that mode entirely.

What then do we make of this work as a whole? Although not nearly so self-flagellatingly inventive as Barth's work, this book seems almost a gesture towards *Lost in the Funhouse:* the writer having arrived late on the modern scene and found that all the old stories have been told, invites us to observe instead his struggle with his craft and spends his time demonstrating his technical skills. But if this is all there is then the stories of *Cry Evil* themselves strike us as somewhat belated. After all it has been twelve years since Barth gave us those illustrations of the artist's plight. . . . (pp. 36-7)

This is not all there is: perhaps by emphasizing this aspect of these stories I have somewhat distorted *Cry Evil*. Rooke's experiments with technique are never so purely technical as Barth's were, or as others have been since, and there is still emotion embedded in these stories, still human compulsions and neuroses which lie under the words to trouble and intrigue us. There are, after all, depths that wit and cleverness do not sound—and Rooke seems to be a writer who cannot but choose to remind us of those depths, even in stories as ingenious as these newest ones. (p. 37)

> *Russell M. Brown, "Experiment and Compulsion," in* The Canadian Forum, *Vol. LX, No. 701, August, 1980, pp. 36-7.*

DAVID QUAMMEN

"Fat Woman" is a slim novel with a big heart and a sizable funnybone. Leon Rooke puts us inside the copious body of Ella Mae Hopkins . . . and we waddle with her through one traumatic day, sharing her secret worries and consolations, her routine travails, her battles of gastronomic will. . . . We share also her concern over a finger that is being choked gangrenous by her wedding ring and her curiosity as to why Edward, her husband, has begun nailing boards over the window of their bedroom. By novel's end there is resolution concerning the finger and the window—and that's the whole of the story. This admittedly sounds, in synopsis, like somniferous stuff; the small miracle about **"Fat Woman"** is that it remains entertaining despite its extreme simplicity of event.

One large reason for this is the richness and rhythms and humor of Southern country language, which Rooke has captured wonderfully, not just in the dialogue but throughout Ella Mae's reveries. We are swept through the novel on a gentle current of verbal comedy and quirky phraseology. (p. 15)

Beyond the charms of language and humor, **"Fat Woman"** is memorable for its portrayal of an exemplary and enduring love. . . . In fact this is one of the finer depictions of a functioning, vital marriage—with the ecstatic high moments, the desperate lows, the careenings between—that I can recall.

It is also, if Leon Rooke himself weighs anything under 270 pounds, a triumph of empathic imagination. (p. 24)

> *David Quammen, "Family Matters," in* The New York Times Book Review *(© 1981 by The New York Times Company; reprinted by permission), May 17, 1981, pp. 15, 24.**

TOM MARSHALL

[*Fat Woman*] is an enjoyable and absorbing read, and . . . has as a central aim an exploration of the dignity and even complexity of the lives of quite ordinary or socially marginal people. . . .

Both Ella Mae, the melancholy fat woman, and her thin and jocular husband Edward are vividly present in all their individual quirkiness and idiosyncrasy. (p. 120)

Fat Woman is a tour de force that could not be sustained at greater length. And though Ella Mae and Edward are utterly convincing as well as likeable, Rooke has (I feel) written *around* Ella Mae's relationship with her exceedingly bratty sons; he manages this evasive action skilfully, but something is felt to be lacking. Still, this is a minor flaw in a piece of writing that presents with considerable style and sensitivity a vulnerable and valuable human being trapped in the flesh and in a marginal rural existence. *Fat Woman* is a highly successful novel or novella of character; such plot as there is is best not revealed ahead of time to the reader. (pp. 120-21)

> *Tom Marshall, "Social Margins" (reprinted by permission of the author), in* Canadian Literature, *No. 89, Summer, 1981, pp. 120-21.**

JERRY WASSERMAN

Leon Rooke's *Cry Evil* is mostly unremitting in its sense of life as nasty and brutish. His stories are stocked with characters who, if they aren't mad or paranoid or perverse, are victims of the madness, paranoia, or perversity of others. Rooke tempers all this with hard-edged, self-conscious black humour, and even allows a few tentative affirmations. . . . With rare exceptions, though, the cry "evil" finds only further echoes in the labyrinth of the self. (p. 106)

[This collection is distinguished by Rooke's] intelligence, versatility, and craftsmanship. The stories in *Cry Evil* are . . . [baroque and make great] demands on the reader, echoing Barth and Borges, Dostoevsky, Kafka, and Poe. They are not recommended for chronic depressives. In theme and mood there is a dark sameness about them that is almost claustrophobic. However, the very extremity of Rooke's gloomy vision somewhat undermines its seriousness. With what seems like an

authorial wink, he has the nagging wife of the writer-protagonist in his opening story, **"The Deacon's Tale,"** complain of his work: "It won't make any of us feel any better. It won't make anyone want to rejoice that they are alive. So what if people like your ugly hero do exist, you think that's any excuse?" (p. 108)

> *Jerry Wasserman, "Fantasy Lives" (reprinted by permission of the author), in* Canadian Literature, *No. 91, Winter, 1981, pp. 106-09.**

STEPHEN SCOBIE

[One] feature of Rooke's fiction has been the way the ordinary lives of ordinary people coexist with the most extravagant and bizarre events and are presented in exuberantly experimental forms. . . .

Rooke's form *is* his content: that the wildness, the exuberance, the grotesqueness, and the sudden tonal shifts from fantasy to the catching and placing of realistic detail in the context of humdrum existence, are all as relevant thematically as they are dazzling technically. One key to such an approach is Rooke's insistence on *voice.* . . .

Whooping and hollering, cajoling or complaining, Rooke's characters meet the world at an interface of language; their perception *is* their rhetoric.

One of Rooke's central themes, then, is the way people become trapped in their rhetoric. Perception as speech and speech as perception form a vicious circle of solipsism. . . . [In] *Death Suite,* we find Mama Tuddi, the TV faith-healer-cum-Double-Ola-salesperson, caught inside a miasma of fundamentalist sales talk that cannot be pierced even by the realities of death or the challenge of a rival rhetoric. (p. 8)

In *The Magician in Love,* the rhetoric takes slightly different forms. The story is a fable, and the voice is not so much a character's as it is the author's, relating the story in a style that keeps realism at arm's length while never quite abandoning it, and maintains a tone of witty, slightly puzzled detachment. The Magician's love for his mistress, Beabontha, is based upon a rhetoric of illusion—fruit appears on the branches of the dead trees, rivals who shake hands are left holding flowers—and when it collapses it destroys not only the characters but the whole social fabric surrounding them. Yet what else is there, in fiction, except illusion? . . . And illusion itself, to complete once more the solipsistic circle, "is perception in reverse."

Rooke's art is one of performance, of impersonation, and the virtuoso brilliance of his writing . . . is again thematically essential, not merely entertaining and decorative, in two ways. First, he must depend upon the inventiveness and energy of the writing in order to enter into each of these "fully realized world[s] of appetite and speech"; his characters are themselves virtuosos of illusion and self-deception, and he must match their technique in order to portray them. But second, by playing the role of impersonator, or ventriloquist, for so many *different* voices, Rooke draws attention to his own "performing self" (in Richard Poirier's phrase), the author distinct from his creations. (pp. 8-9)

Consider a sentence like this, from *Death Suite:* "My Dream Girl, he say to friends, she like this: and he slice his hands through the air like what he really want is a Coca-Cola bottle." The observation is exact, as is the colloquial tone of speech;

the gesture is convincing, but so is the author's irony, the unstated comment on the confusion of ideals. (p. 9)

Stephen Scobie, "The Inner Voice," in Books in Canada, *Vol. 10, No. 9, November, 1981, pp. 8-10.*

BARBARA WADE

To give us such a clear understanding of the lives of the poor and the disaffected, western writer Leon Rooke must have spent a lifetime soaking up their mannerisms, their conversations, and learning to hear their private voices of disappointment and discontent. The result, in *Death Suite,* is a carefully crafted collection of tactile, poetic prose.

The book opens with **"Mama Tuddi Done Over,"** the longest story in the collection and an introduction both to the monologue style and to Rooke's spirit-world. (p. 75)

The choice of **"Mama Tuddi Done Over"** as the introductory story to *Death Suite* is a wise one, for the succeeding stories contain echoes of its eerie tone and its acute sense of language in the way one individual may use it. (p. 76)

Rooke seems best suited to describing the darker side of love relationships, as he does in **"Winter Is Lovely, Isn't Summer Hell," "Lady Godiva's Horse," "Standing In for Nita,"** and **"Hanging Out with the Magi."** What these stories have in common is that none of them are healthy, based as they are on neurotic, childish needs; and all of them are interesting. (pp. 76-7)

There is in *Death Suite* a three-part story called **"Murder Mystery,"** subdivided into "The Rocker Operation," "Do Something" and "The Strip." These compositions come the closest to reminding us of the death suite that is the book's title. We are taken from the scene of a murder, to the police precinct, to the house of a woman who is clearly one of the principals involved in the murder. It is the standard progression of scenes for a murder mystery, so, like true murder mystery readers, we expect it to be solved. We are, however, cleverly set up. The story is simply another medium for Rooke's exploration, through *Death Suite,* of how much gets thought, gets worried about, gets talked about, but how little gets done. (p. 77)

[The] spirit-world is *Death Suite*'s true domain, and it can be either constrictive or liberating, as it is in the final story, **"The Problem Shop."** This story of a downcast man's mysterious voyage out to sea is the only vaguely optimistic story in the collection. Rooke is perhaps ambivalent about the potential of the human imagination, but his understanding of it makes for a thoughtful, careful read. (pp. 77-8)

Barbara Wade, "Recourses of the Troubled Mind," in WAVES (© WAVES), *Vol. 10, No. 3, Winter, 1982, pp. 75-8.*

CATHLEEN HOSKINS

[In *Fat Woman*] Rooke gave us a strong dose of the macabre mixed with rollicking humor. Now, in his excellent collection of stories, *Death Suite,* he has upped the ante on the macabre. According to Rooke, life is a risky business, walking uncomfortably close to death. This ambivalent chumminess is the crux of his vision.

Not surprisingly, the opening story is set in a funeral home. Mama Tuddi, a tacky television personality, puts in a guest appearance at a young fan's funeral. The event slowly swerves

out of control, and Mama Tuddi finds herself caught up in as fine a crew of gospel shouters as any preacher could hope for. Rooke's hotshot black humor is a tour de force in *Mama Tuddi Done Over* (and in several other stories), but he never wastes his considerable comic sense simply to get laughs. His humor is like a searchlight freezing a criminal against a prison wall—in a single flash it can illuminate life's most sinister shadows. (p. 58)

Some of the stories offer no comic relief at all. Two of the strangest focus on the charged sexuality of adolescence. *Sixteen-Year-Old Susan March Confesses to the Innocent Murder of All the Devious Strangers Who Would Drag Her Down* is an obsessional monologue describing a beautiful girl's love for an unwary stranger. The piece is so steamy, breathless and overwhelming that, like drowning, there's the constant urge to come up for air. Rooke tosses off superb imagery with the largess of a king dispensing gold coins. . . .

In comparison, *Deer Trails in Tzityonyana* is more rarefied, understated and, finally, sinister. . . . The Gothic tale of sexual initiation is strung as tautly as a baroque melody.

In *Death Suite,* Rooke is best at his blackest. Stories such as *Winter Is Lovely, Isn't Summer Hell* and *The Problem Shop,* which offer an upbeat optimism, seem flabby with sentiment in the company of the other, darker tales. But when he's staring down the bleaker mysteries of life, Rooke is an exceptional storyteller. Then, like a knife in the stomach, his work is hard to ignore. (p. 59)

Cathleen Hoskins, "Laughter Trimmed in Basic Black," in Maclean's Magazine (© 1982 by Maclean's Magazine; *reprinted by permission), Vol. 95, No. 2, January 11, 1982, pp. 58-9.*

TIMOTHY DOW ADAMS

In light of the number and variety of his previous publications, it is surprising how amateurish the beginning of Rooke's first novel [*Fat Woman*] is. Many of the minor characters have names as stereotypical as their situations, despite topical references that suggest the book is set in the contemporary South. The fat woman of the title is Ella Mae Hopkins. . . .

At first this love story between an enormously overweight woman and her skinny husband, Edward, is told in a manner that echoes the worst of Southern fiction: slapstick humor . . . , [cornpone humor, stereotyped poverty, country fried religion], and a stock Big-Daddy whose unbelievable cruelty to Ella Mae as a child results in her poor self-image and obesity as an adult. . . .

In addition to these cliches, the first part of *Fat Woman* is slowed by a third-person point of view that tells us repeatedly what Ella Mae watches, thinks, feels, and does; filtered through this focus of narration, the story lacks the insight or interest to make us see the complexities that lie within the title character. For inside *this* fat person is a real character waiting to be fleshed out. And as the point of view begins to enter Ella Mae's mind directly, the real strength of the novel emerges: the depiction of the paradoxical agony of obesity which often combines a compulsive body-awareness and a resulting self-disgust with alternating denial of both fatness and responsibility for it. Rooke is at his best when portraying Ella Mae's justification for her weight. . . .

In contrast to her spoken utterances, Ella Mae's thoughts about her weight are presented in a language that is strong and lyrical, as authentic and individual as the best of Southern folk speech can be. . . .

The compassion and tender love of this contemporary Southern thin man and fat woman is genuinely humorous, compelling and well-crafted, once the novel shucks off its stock Southernisms and enters the rich mind of its title character. However, like its heroine, *Fat Woman* would have been easier to love if it were reduced by a third and tightened overall.

Timothy Dow Adams, "'Fat Woman'," in The American Book Review *(© 1982 by* The American Book Review*), Vol. 4, No. 3, March-April, 1982, p. 8.*

CHOICE

[*Death Suite*] shows Rooke in full command of his unique talents. His imagination moves agilely between the surreal and superreal, the kinky supernatural and the logically inexplicable, the banal and the familiar. His style can go from baroque black dialect, to breathless stream of consciousness, to laconic hard-boiled detective narrative. The stories focus on people at critical points-of-no-return in their lives. In Rooke's vision, people and society are corrupt, corrupting, and vicious, sometimes merely futile and vain, occasionally sublime. Perhaps the most exciting talent in Canadian fiction since Leonard Cohen.

"Language and Literature: 'Death Suite'," in Choice *(copyright © 1982 by American Library Association), Vol. 19, No. 8, April, 1982, p. 1071.*

Ntozake Shange

1948-

(Born Paulette Williams) Black American playwright, poet, novelist, essayist, and lecturer.

Shange's first major work, the choreopoem *For Colored Girls Who Have Considered Suicide/When the Rainbow Is Enuf*, depicts the emotional and often suicidal despair of black women in an oppressive society. A reflection of her own emotional pain, Shange's feminist stance urges self-realization and independence for black women. Most critics praised the exciting theatricality of *For Colored Girls* but were disappointed in her more conventional play, *Photography*. They also felt that her adaptation of *Mother Courage and Her Children* failed to realize the complexity of Brecht's original drama.

(See also *CLC*, Vol. 8 and *Contemporary Authors*, Vols. 85-88.)

TONI CADE BAMBARA

[Ntozake Shange's *For Colored Girls Who Have Considered Suicide When the Rainbow Is Enuf*] is a comfortably loose-strung series of portraits and narratives about women, black women. . . . (p. 36)

Blisteringly funny, fragile, droll and funky, lyrical, git down stompish, the play celebrates survival. The portraits are not case studies of stunning wrecks hollering about paid dues and criminal overcharges. The pieces are not booze-based blues and ballads about lost love and missing teeth. The Shange brand of keepin' on does not spring from the foot-caught-in-the-trap-gnawin'-ankle-free-oh-my-god school of moaning. She celebrates the capacity to master pain and betrayals with wit, sister-sharing, reckless daring, and flight and forgetfulness if necessary. She celebrates most of all women's loyalties to women.

One of the best orchestrated pieces on that dodgy subject involves three players who weave in and out of each other's lines, laying out a history of relationships: embrace, recoil, regather, resolve. (pp. 36, 38)

What is curious about the work is that though men appear exclusively as instruments of pain, there is no venom, no resorting to a Queen of Hearts solution—Off with his head! No godlike revenge, no godlike forgiving. Hell, some things are unforgivable. The women of the various pieces suck their teeth, storm, sass, and get on with the miracle of living. . . .

The "voice" of *Colored/Rainbow* defies and encourages theatrics. It contains a funkiness and a grand opera eloquence that we use when we self-consciously share pain. (p. 38)

> Toni Cade Bambara, "'For Colored Girls'—And White Girls Too," in Ms. (© 1976 Ms. Magazine Corp.), Vol. V, No. 3, September, 1976, pp. 36, 38.

MARTIN GOTTFRIED

Good is good, theater is theater and Shange's work ["**For Colored Girls Who Have Considered Suicide When the Rainbow Is Enuf**"] is the kind the stage was created for. There is

no comparing the trust and presence of its power with any other kind of art in any other medium (nor any need or sense in comparison anyhow).

The show . . . [contains] the author's narratives, poems and dialogues, all designed to, in one way or another, "sing a black girl's song. . . . sing a song of life, she's been dead so long."

The overriding tone of these monologues is bitter but assertive, imbued with a new-discovered pride, reaching toward exultation. The anger is over time and pain wasted rather than an expected, indefinite continuation of it.

There is some lack of variety in the selection of material; an excess of concern with romance and sex, music and dancing, even considering that the work is about young women. Within that limitation, however, the writing is regularly beautiful and often exquisite. The arrangement of the material for stage presentation is stage wise. . . .

The essence of the show remains its pure and perfectly captured blackness. Black language, black mannerisms, black tastes and black feelings have never been so completely and artistically presented in a Broadway theater except for Melvin van Peebles' "Ain't No Way to Die a Natural Death." This is truth, energy and strength, theater on the highest level, musical and choreographic to its roots.

Martin Gottfried, "'Rainbow' over Broadway," in New York Post (reprinted by permission of the New York Post; © 1976, New York Post Corporation), September 16, 1976, (and reprinted in New York Theatre Critics' Reviews, Vol. XXXVII, No. 16, September 13-19, 1976, p. 201).

RICHARD EDER

The poetry of perception is not the same as the poetry of drama. In ""**For Colored Girls**," Ntozake Shange arranged her acid and lyrical perceptions into a fine, loose-jointed set of meditations and sketches.

They had the design and rhythm of a song-cycle; the pieces were funny, exuberant or acrid, and Miss Shange's remarkable poetic diction took the role of music in binding them together. Themes would appear and reappear, but a formal dramatic structure was not attempted or needed.

Miss Shange is something besides a poet but she is not—at least not at this stage—a dramatist. More than anything else, she is a troubadour. She declares her fertile vision of the love and pain between black women and black men in outbursts full of old malice and young cheerfulness. They are short outbursts, song-length; her characters are perceived in flashes, in illuminating vignettes.

Some of these things are found in "**A Photograph; A Study of Cruelty**," her second major work. . . . But the work is forced, and finally broken by its form. The perceptions are made to do the donkey-work of holding up what attempts to be a whole dramatic structure, and they fail.

The central character in "**A Photograph**" is Michael. . . . She is clearly the personage with whom the author identifies; she is how the black woman in America is to be, and the other, inevitably shadowy characters, are misleaders or mistakes.

Michael is a free and sovereign spirit, loving but unsubmissive to men, ambition or the pressures of American society. . . .

She has settled . . . for Sean a photographer just on the brink of becoming rich and famous, and interviewed. It is his bitterness she loves, she says, but things are not so simple. Sean is surrounded by an array of tempters; all of them caricatures of how black people, as Miss Shange sees it, go wrong. . . .

Sean is vital and talented, but weak. His confidence rests upon his success. . . . and his success rests upon his photography.

The play's creaky plot deals with the collapse of his self-esteem. . . .

Everything, and every character, is really set up as a prop against which Michael can be wonderful. . . .

It is a grave and captivating seer that Miss Shange has created. But she didn't need an unconvincing play as background. . . .

Richard Eder, "Sovereign Spirit," in The New York Times, Section C (© 1977 by The New York Times Company; reprinted by permission), December 22, 1977, p. 11.

HARRIET GILBERT

[Ntozake] Shange's wit, her fierce anger, her sensuality and, most of all, her masterful, surprising use of language were of such potency that they bestrode, not only the Atlantic, but the gulf between her race and mine.

nappy edges, Shange's latest book of poetry resumes a great many of the themes of *for colored girls* . . . : love, lust, music, friendship, the condition of being a woman, of being black. It even contains three or four of the earlier poems, in a slightly altered form. . . . The three introductory pieces and several of the poems themselves are bloated almost beyond readability by Shange's current self-consciousness of herself as a celebrity and as an ambassador of black, feminist writing.

I do say "almost," however, because nothing that she writes is ever entirely unreadable, springing, as it does, from such as intense honesty, from so fresh an awareness of the beauty of sound and of vision, from such mastery of words, from such compassion, humor and intelligence. From this soil, no matter how entangled and confused they might grow, or how much pruning they might need, the plants must always be healthy.

And those many poems in *nappy edges* whose power has not become enmeshed in self-consciousness (the rhapsodic songs of love; the living portraits; the attacks, lethal in their wit and in the niceness of their observation, on male society, white society, hypocrisy and mediocrity) are at least as potent, impressive and astonishing as any in *for colored girls*. . . . . . (pp. 1, 4)

Shange's new book is crowded with such joys. That the reader must occasionally push through overgrowth in order to find them is due to no lack on Shange's part but rather to an overabundance—of talent, energy, cultural resources, ambition and daring. (p. 4)

Harriett Gilbert, "Somewhere over the Rainbow," in Book World—The Washington Post (© 1978, The Washington Post), October 15, 1978, pp. 1, 4.

CHRISTOPHER SHARP

Ntozake Shange's latest musical work . . . is a workshop production, and it looks it. "**Spell #7: A Geechee Quick Magic Trance Manual**" is a fecund garden that badly needs trimming. Curiously, the weaker scenes in this musical essay appear to be edited far better than the strong numbers. The best scenes are diluted by Shange's attempts to say one thing in many different forms as she can.

This musical evening is set in a bar-restaurant hangout for black theatrical performers. Although the work focuses on individual poetic soliloquys, . . . this is more of a play than anything Shange has had staged in the past. At least the actors are talking to each other here in intervals and suggesting that the words have some relevance to the action.

But Shange makes it clear that she values her verse much more than she values her characters. Thus the first act of the musical can be confusing when we see characters that show some promise suddenly change like chameleons when they deliver different kinds of soliloquys. But by the second act, we have learned what to expect and we see the lines finally leaving an impact on us.

Christopher Sharp, "'Spell #7: A Geechee Quick Magic Trance Manual'," in Women's Wear Daily (copyright 1979, Fairchild Publications), June 4, 1979 (and reprinted in New York Theatre Critics' Reviews, Vol. XL, No. 20, November 19, 1979, p. 109).

DON NELSEN

Ntozake Shange's "**Spell #7**" is black magic. It is a celebration of blackness, the joy and pride along with the horror of it. It is a shout, a cry, a bitter laugh, a sneer. It is an extremely fine theater piece.

The word that best describes Shange's works, which are not plays in the traditional sense, is power. Drama is inherent in each of her poetic sentences because the words hum with a vibrant urgency that shriek to be absorbed now, now, NOW! She writes as though there is not a moment to be lost and the nine players . . . deliver her ripostes to American life with a zeal that grabs and shakes the lapels.

The irony attendant upon being black in a white society is struck immediately. . . . [Player #1 provides the message:] You should rejoice in the richness that is yours even though it is different.

What follows is a tapestry of variations on this theme, akin in structure to Shange's **"For Colored Girls Who Have Considered Suicide,"** woven in a combination of dialogue, dance and song. . . . What divorces it from the ordinary is Shange's ability to make the word flesh, to fuse idea and character so that it comes out humanity. . . .

"Spell #7" is a piece of biting sorcery.

> *Don Nelsen, ''Shange Casts a Powerful 'Spell','' in* Daily News, *New York (© 1979, New York News, Inc.), July 16, 1979 (and reprinted in* New York Theatre Critics' Reviews, *Vol. XL, No. 20, November 19, 1979, p. 108).*

RICHARD EDER

Poetry is as contagious as poison ivy though less prevalent. Look at the response these days to the dramatic poems in Ntozake Shange's remarkable **"Spell No. 7."** . . . [The] sketches—lyrical, wry, painful and comically prosaic by turn—. . . invaded the audience. The place was alive with response, but it wasn't the ordinary applause or laughter of an audience that is pleased or moved. There was a kind of rumination, a repeating of lines, even a few tentative essays at embroidering them. . . .

[Sometimes] the springy rhetoric and response of these poetic vignettes about how it feels to be black . . . have the liveliness and stem-winding buildup of first-rate preaching. But if there is any event that Miss Shange's best work approaches, it is something more familiar in other countries—particularly the Soviet Union—than in this one. I am thinking of those highly charged poetry recitals in which a Voznesensky would advance toward the emotions of his audiences head-on, not merely giving words to what was buried or half-buried inside them, but providing them with the public emblem of a man speaking out.

Miss Shange's performers enter as if they were actors gathering in an after-hours bar, but under tutelage of . . . [the] *compere,* they hurl themselves into their poetic representations. . . . [The *compere*] has announced that he is the son of a magician who gave up his trade when a black child asked him to perform a spell to make him white. . . . [He then] proposes a different kind of spell: setting his performers to speaking, he will demonstrate that there is pride and rejoicing in being black. Poetry, of course, demonstrates nothing, not even rejoicing; but it can transmit it. Miss Shange's does, and not only to the black members of the audience. . . .

Miss Shange's vignettes proceed with excess, that of the classic tall story: an image is taken, worked up comically, exaggerated and blown up some more. Each vignette is a circus vehicle;

clown after clown climbs out, past all reasonable capacity. First they are comic clowns, then ironic clowns, and finally their message is pure pain; or would be except that art redeems the burden it carries by the raffishness with which it carries it.

> *Richard Eder, ''Miss Shange's Rousing Homilies,'' in* The New York Times *(© 1979 by The New York Times Company; reprinted by permission), July 22, 1979, p. D3.*

JOHN SIMON

Ntozake Shange, equally untalented as a poet and as a playwright, seems to have made it on the strength of being a black and a woman. Belonging to one formerly underprivileged class is an advantage; to two, a gold mine. Further, she thrives on the gap between poetry and drama. Poetry publishers may just think that she has solid achievements as a dramatist; if the drama critics raved about her *For Colored Girls* . . . , it was partly because they labored under the delusion that anything so sprawling, pretentious, and bellyaching must be poetry.

Indeed, Miss Shange has never even managed to write a real play. *A Photograph* came nearest to being one, but was laughed right off the boards even by reviewers benighted enough to have extolled *For Colored Girls.* The current *Spell #7* is every bit as bad as *For Colored Girls,* and though the cast is no longer all female, and the hatred of men not quite so obvious, the formula is the same: long monologues (occasionally dialogues, but nondramatic ones) recited or sung by a character or two, with the others intermittently chiming in—a directorial ruse meant to make recitation appear more theatrical. Dancing, too, is thrown in for the same purpose—with a dancer cavorting in front of a speaker, without any visible connection between the words and dance movements, except their shared triteness. . . .

[The various set pieces] are supposed to show, without magic, the beauty of blackness and the nobility of negritude; they are mostly gripes of one sort or another. The male characters are either projections of Shange herself (the Poet, the Magician) or, once again, unworthy: philanderers attempting to make black women traveling in Europe, a black youth trying to seduce a woman during a subway ride, and the like. The women tell various tales of woe, sometimes shot through with a bit of satire for which Shange has a slight aptitude. . . .

Most revealing is a monologue originally delivered, significantly, by Shange herself. . . . A woman who wants to have a child she would name Myself does have a boy and does so name him. But when, outside her body, Myself begins to live an independent life, she kills him. A maniacal egocentricity pervades *Spell #7* as it did *For Colored Girls.*

> *John Simon, ''Fainting Spell,'' in* New York Magazine *(copyright © 1979 by News Group Publications, Inc.; reprinted with the permission of* New York Magazine*), Vol. 12, No. 30, July 30, 1979, p. 57.*

MICHAEL S. HARPER

Ntozake Shange's **"Nappy Edges"** is too long a book; there are far too many poems that borrow from and reflect upon popular culture without dramatizing the inner conflicts of many of Miss Shange's characters. But she is a highly literate writer, capable of expressing anger at the mistreatment of women by means of an artful reference to some popular song or a scene from a movie.

[The] idiom is at once dramatic and restrained, but Miss Shange seldom offers insights as literate as those expressed in the epigraphs scattered through **"Nappy Edges,"** though one from Anaïs Nin—"all unfulfilled desires are imprisoned children"—is well chosen and brought to full life in the opening section of **"closets."** . . . Miss Shange's poetic mode consists of sharp, intense vignettes with a minimum of commentary; when she ventures into longer poems the lines become slack and prosaic, her references too private to express her themes.

> *Michael S. Harper, "Three Poets," in* The New York Times Book Review (© *1979 by The New York Times Company; reprinted by permission), October 21, 1979, p. 22.*

JOHN RUSSELL TAYLOR

[In *For Colored Girls Who Have Considered Suicide When the Rainbow Is Enuf*,] Ntozake Shange sets out to evoke the plight of black women and at the same time somehow to celebrate them and their triumphs in life through a series of monologues, usually taken straight by one of the seven players, sometimes illustrated by one while another speaks. She sees herself very much as a poet, and that may well be the case. But she is farthest from proving it when she most desperately strains to do so. Which, unfortunately, is often in the most prominent parts of the show, like the opening and closing numbers of the two parts.

In these, and every now and then elsewhere, she tends to fall into a loose, dithyrambic style that Dylan Thomas would have recognised. The words twist and turn in an anguish of frustrated communication, and it all sounds as phoney as hell. And yet when she relaxes a bit, comes down from her literary high horse and lets experience speak for itself, the result can be funny and touching and, yes, in its spare vividness actually poetic. Poetry, after all, comes from a fundamental poetic vision, not from trying to be a poet. (p. 16)

[*Colored Girls*] is clearly by a black, and about facets of the black experience; it is clearly by a woman, and about the experience of being a woman. But it is not much at any time, about the two together, functionally connected. In interviews Ntozake Shange talks about specifically black kinds of male chauvinism, about the problems of being a woman especially within Third World conditions and patterns of behavior. But little if any of that comes over in the show. It is as though she feels in some way that by following out her feminist logic she would be betraying blacks to the white audience by being specially critical of black men, while to sing uncomplicatedly the praises of negritude she would be betraying her special role as woman. This division of mind leaves whole areas mushy and unexplored. . . .

All the same Ms Shange, when not being too grand about her literary aspirations, is clearly a writer to watch. . . . (p. 17)

> *John Russell Taylor, "Reviews: 'For Colored Girls Who Have Considered Suicide When the Rainbow Is Enuf'* " (© *copyright John Russell Tayor, 1979; reprinted with permission of A D Peters & Co Ltd), in* Plays and Players, *Vol. 27, No. 3, December, 1979, pp. 16-17.*

MEL GUSSOW

Adaptations of classics are often based on a simple transfer in period; costumes and accents change, but almost everything else remains the same. In direct contrast, Ntozake Shange's new version of Brecht's "Mother Courage and Her Children," . . . is a true cultural and political transplant. . . .

[Miss Shange] has moved the play from Europe during the Thirty Years' War in the early 17th century to the American frontier during the Reconstruction in the late 19th century. Mother Courage is now a black woman . . . , twice emancipated and selling her canteen of wares to troops during the Plains wars against the Indians. Necessarily, there are certain relocation problems, but on her own terms Miss Shange has performed a venturesome feat of reinterpretation.

An adaptation must find equivalents to details of plot, character and atmosphere, and it is here where Miss Shange has been perspicacious. Scene by scene, almost line by line, she has translated Brecht into a black idiom, names, places, slang and aphorisms, without losing the essence of the play or of the heroine. This woman remains an unsinkable ship, making compromises but never forsaking first principles. A war profiteer, she is desperately trying to survive an endless siege—and to keep her family intact. Her "courage" is in her indomitability; nothing vanquishes her, not even the loss of her children. . . .

One shortcoming of Miss Shange's effort is that she is unable to probe the contradictory roles of the black man on the frontier, including the fact that he was fighting against the Indian, who should have been his natural ally. Racism on the plains would make a challenging subject for an original play. In this regard, Miss Shange is restricted, rather than released, by Brecht, although when possible she takes some liberty. . . .

Miss Shange's vision of "Mother Courage" can stand alone as a considerable dramatic achievement.

> *Mel Gussow, "Stage: 'Mother Courage'," in* The New York Times (© *1980 by The New York Times Company; reprinted by permission), May 14, 1980, p. 20.*

JOHN SIMON

Miss Shange was content to ruin one genre at a time, say poetry or drama. Now, [in *Mother Courage and Her Children*], she rewrites and makes ridiculous both American history and Bertolt Brecht at one foul swoop. Brecht plausibly perceived the Thirty Years' War as a nasty excuse for otherwise identical people who happened to be Protestants or Catholics to slaughter one another while ruthless and purblind speculators, such as the *vivandière* Mother Courage, made and lost their boodle, lost and lost their children. And learned nothing from it.

Shange has invented an American Thirty Years' War by gluing together a variety of discrete and diverse conflicts into one big Schwittersian collage. We never know who is fighting whom (North, South, blacks, whites, Indians, the U.S. Army, ranchers, the KKK appear among the combatants whom you cannot tell apart even *with* the program) or exactly what for—though, unlike in Brecht, there is value judgment: Blacks and Indians are felt to be superior to whites, though why they massacre one another is not gone into. In the late nineteenth century Courage's anachronistic wagon is already a sentimental, adorably quixotic conceit; *real* capitalism had already become very much bigger business. Issues are further muddied by one of this black Courage's children being half Indian, another half white. And, misunderstanding Brecht, Shange has made Courage into a basically lovable figure. (pp. 80-1)

John Simon, "Avaunt-Garde and 'Taint Your Wagon'," in New York *Magazine (copyright © 1980 by News Group Publications, Inc.; reprinted with the permission of* New York *Magazine), Vol. 13, No. 21, May 26, 1980, pp. 79-81.*

FRANK RICH

The text of Miss Shange's **"Mother Courage"** . . . raises some troubling questions. What are an adapter's responsibilities to the original work? What are a playwright's obligations to history? Is it right to call a play **"Mother Courage"** when it in many ways violates the spirit of the drama we associate with that title? The motivations behind Miss Shange's adaptation may well be pure, but the result is a case study of what can happen when an exercise in literary adaptation goes wildly astray.

Certainly the adaptation cannot be objected to in principle. Brecht would have approved; he was found of rewriting classic theatrical texts himself. And certainly Miss Shange . . . would seem the ideal candidate to redo **"Mother Courage."** Like Brecht, she is a poet with a radicalized political consciousness. It can even be argued that Miss Shange is entitled to move the play's setting from 17th-century middle Europe to another time and place; it all depends on how and why the relocation is done. By resetting Brecht's play in post-Civil War America and making the title character an emancipated slave, Miss Shange has landed in a quagmire. She ends up betraying Brecht and distorting American history. (p. D5)

[Miss Shange's] **"Mother Courage"** is set in the Southwest territories of 1866-1877, and it principally concerns a disconnected series of skirmishes in which American troops completed the clearing of the West by slaughtering the Indians.

In contrast to Brecht's Thirty Years War—a religious struggle waged by equally culpable antagonists who together wreaked havoc on a helpless peasantry—the battles of Miss Shange's play are conflicts involving clearly defined good guys and bad guys. This immediately alters Brecht's point in a substantial way. In his "Mother Courage," war (or, for that matter, peace) is a meaningless state that serves no purpose except to perpetuate a malevolent ruling class. It doesn't matter which side Mother Courage has financial dealings with, for both sides are the enemy. Everyone is out to grind her down; she is the trapped, innocent victim of an entire system.

In Miss Shange's version, Mother Courage is thrust into a class and racial war where the antagonists are anything but interchangeable. The bad guys are the government soldiers, the ruling class, and their victims are a defenseless proletariat, the Indians. As a result, Miss Shange's protagonist, unlike Brecht's, *does* have a moral choice. And for her Mother Courage, the choice should be clear; she has, after all, just lived through the Civil War. If she now does business with the oppressive Army, she is a villain; if she refuses, she is a heroic resister. Either way, Brecht's complex work is transformed into a simplistic melodrama about right and wrong.

Worse still, Miss Shange's Mother Courage, as well as her two sons, capitulate to the bad guys. The sons (one of whom is half-Indian, no less) join up with the Colored Cavalry—the so-called Buffalo Soldiers who were recruited by whites to fight against the Indians—and the mother does business with their superiors. While these actions parallel the text of the original play, their meaning becomes quite different in the context Miss Shange has chosen. When Brecht's Mother Cour-

age says "in business you ask what price, not what religion," it is a nihilistic fact of life. When Miss Shange's Mother Courage, at the same point in the play, implies that she would just as soon trade with rebel whites as anyone else, she is consciously siding against her own interests. She is no longer a pawn of historical forces beyond her control but an active counter-revolutionary siding with whites against her own people.

Perhaps Miss Shange would insist that her Mother Courage had to capitulate to whites to survive, just as Brecht's Mother Courage had to serve all comers to keep going. But is it really true that freed slaves, in the aftermath of the Civil War, had no option but to become collaborators in a new campaign of white genocide against the Indians? It would take a rather jaundiced reading of American history to claim so. (pp. D5, D33)

How did Miss Shange paint herself into this corner? To fulfill her mission of resetting **"Mother Courage"** in black America, she seems to have seized on some events that superficially correspond to those of Brecht's play without carefully considering how those events would square with the true meaning of the original text. Once the events were chosen, they became an *idée fixe* from which she refused to depart. By grafting far-from-representative black sellouts on to the epic theater of **"Mother Courage,"** Miss Shange has condemned a whole generation of black people by inference. If a white had written this play, he would have, quite rightfully, been accused of racism.

If Miss Shange had reshaped the entire work, she might have solved some of these problems. But she has not done that; she has only retranslated the play into black English. Perhaps if there were major white characters in this **"Mother Courage"**—her versions of [Southern] landowners and capitalists or the greedy bigots of Lillian Hellman's "Little Foxes"—we could see why some blacks did have no choice but to become collaborators with their enemy. This fact can't be explained away by the social system dramatized in Brecht's play—which is still the only one to be found in Miss Shange's version—because the system that prevailed in the Thirty Years War is not an accurate description of Reconstruction America. So confusing is Miss Shange's mixture of Brecht and Indian wars that on the night I saw her play, an audience of blacks and whites was actually cheering Mother Courage at the end. This shouldn't happen in an honest production of Brecht's drama—one that upholds the writer's so-called "alienation effect"—and it certainly shouldn't happen in Miss Shange's version, where Mother Courage is demonstrably evil.

However much the audience might blamelessly misread it in the theater, it seems that Miss Shange really did set out to concoct a "Mother Courage" that vilified its central characters. In an article in The Village Voice of May 19, she says so. . . .

She adds that by tackling Brecht she would also resolve a personal dilemma: She had forgotten about her own work and was involved "in fruitless combat with myself" about "the works of dead white men." On this point she is entirely right. Such combat *is* fruitless. A black writer indeed has no obligation to answer to white writers, living or dead, and for Ntozake Shange it seems a waste of talent and energy to do so. (p. D33)

Frank Rich, "'Mother Courage' Transplanted," in The New York Times, *Section 2 (© 1980 by The*

*New York Times Company; reprinted by permission),
June 15, 1980, pp. D5, D33.*

CAROL P. CHRIST

A gutsy, down-to-earth poet, Ntozake Shange gives voice to
the ordinary experiences of Black women in frank, simple,
vivid language, telling the colored girl's story in her own speech
patterns. Shange's gift is an uncanny ability to bring the experience of being Black and a woman to life. Those who hear
or read her choreopoem *for colored girls who have considered
suicide / when the rainbow is enuf* may feel overwhelmed by
so much reality, so much pain, so much resiliency, so much
life force. They may even feel they have actually lived through
the stories they have heard.

Like Adrienne Rich, Shange is acutely aware of the nothingness
experienced by women in a society defined by men. But Shange
is also aware of a double burden of pain and negation suffered
by women who are Black in a society defined by *white* men—
where Black women are not even granted the ambivalent recognition some white women receive for youth and beauty or
for being wives and mothers of white men. Shange's poem
also reflects the double strength Black women have had to
muster to survive in a world where neither being Black nor
being a woman is valued.

Though Shange's forte is the vivid re-creation of experience,
for colored girls is more than the simple telling of the Black
girl's story. It is also a search for the meaning of the nothingness experienced and a quest for new being. In Shange's poems
the experience of nothingness is born of the double burden of
being Black and a woman, but the stories she tells bring a
shock of recognition to every woman who has given too much
of herself to a man. The heart of the experience of nothingness
in *for colored girls* is a woman's loss and debasement of self
for love of a man. But what makes Shange's poems more than
just another version of *Lady Sings the Blues*—a theme of sorrow
and survival too familiar to Black women (and white women)—
is Shange's refusal to accept the Black woman's sorrow as a
simple and ultimate fact of life. She probes for a new image
of the Black woman that will make the old images of the colored
girl obsolete. Shange envisions Black women "born again"
on the far side of nothingness with a new image of Black
womanhood that will enable them to acknowledge their history
while moving beyond it to "the ends of their own rainbows."

For colored girls began as a series of separate poems, but as
it developed Shange came to view "these twenty-odd poems
as a single statement, a choreopoem." . . . In a sense the
dialogical form of Shange's play re-creates the consciousness-
raising group of the women's movement, where in sharing
experiences and stories, women learn to value themselves, to
recognize stagnant and destructive patterns in their lives, to
name their strengths, and to begin to take responsibility for
their lives. The sense of dialogue in Shange's choreopoem is
an invitation to the women in the audience to tell their stories.
What emerges is a tapestry of experiences, interwoven with a
sense of plurality and commonality.

The title of the choreopoem provokes questions. Why did Shange
use the outdated term "colored," which Black people abandoned as oppressive in the sixties? How is the rainbow enough?
And what does a rainbow have to do with suicide? In a television interview, Shange explained why she used "colored
girls" in the title of her poem. She spoke of the importance
of Black self-definition, of taking pride in dark skin and African

heritage. She said that her own name, "Ntozake," is an African
name she chose as a way of affirming her African roots. But,
she said, it was also important to affirm her American ancestors. She recalled that her grandmother's last words to her were
that she was a precious "little colored girl." Thinking about
this made Shange realize that "colored" was not only a term
used by whites to define Blacks, but also a term of endearment
in the Black community. To reclaim the name "colored girl"
was to reclaim her relationship to her grandmother, a part of
her story. The juxtaposition of "colored girl" with "rainbow"
enables Black women to see the varied tones of their skin as
a reflection of the glorious hues of the rainbow, not as a color
to be borne in shame. And, though colored girls have considered suicide because they have been abused by white society
and Black men, this need no longer be the case. "The rainbow"
is now understood as an image of their own beauty, and it "is
enuf."

Shange further explained the meaning of the enigmatic last line
of her title, when she said, "One day I was driving home after
a class, and I saw a huge rainbow over Oakland. I realized
that women could survive if we decide that we have as much
right and as much purpose for being here as the air and mountains do." Here Shange describes a kind of mystical insight—
being does not require justification, it just is. Within the poem,
Shange restates the last line of the title, "but are movin to the
ends of their own rainbows.". . . This restatement extends the
mystical insight further: after recognizing their grounding in
being, Black women must begin to create their own reality,
for example, by creating symbols like the rainbow to express
their infinite beauty.

For colored girls begins with a poem spoken by the lady in
brown about the importance of naming and celebrating experience in song and story. . . . Only when her song is sung,
her story told, will the Black woman know her potential. She
will be "born" as a human being for the first time, because
she will be aware of herself as a person with value and a range
of choices. (pp. 97-100)

In order to sing a colored girl's song, Shange must re-create
the language of her experience, a language which, in its concrete particularity, has almost never been spoken. Black wom-
en's voices have been negated by the standard (white) English
grammar that has forced Black people to fit their experiences
into alien language patterns. Black women's experiences have
also been negated by a literary tradition that celebrates the
experiences of white men. Shange ignores standard grammar
in her effort to capture the nuances of Black women's speech
patterns and experience. . . . The idiom of this Black girl's
life is reflected in speech patterns, choice of words, details of
description, spelling, and punctuation (or rather lack of it). . . .
Shange's poems also reflect her notion that Black speech is
close to music, an understanding expressed in the mixed genre
choreopoem in which music, dance, and spoken word are woven
together. (pp. 100-02)

The poems in *for colored girls,* when taken as a whole, describe
a spiritual journey through the particularities of a Black woman's experience. In this journey an alternation of joy, despair,
and reconstitution of self proceeds circularly, musically, rather
than linearly. Shange's women move through hope, defeat,
and rebirth in several of the poem sequences, until in the last
the lady in red experiences a crescendo of despair that leads
to a dramatic rebirth of self and a more certain awareness of
the self's grounding in larger powers of life and being. The
poems in *for colored girls* celebrate the Black woman's life

force and capacity for love. They confront her defeat and celebrate her resilience. They provide her with alternatives to the image of the Black woman as either helpless and defeated, a "sorry" colored girl, or as strong and resilient, "impervious to pain." . . . In her search for new images, the Black woman cannot simply adapt images from the white man, the Black man, or the white woman, because none of these images of being human reflect the fullness of her humanity, the affirmation of both her color and her sex. To search for new images of self is to ask anew the old questions: What is it to be human? Do we need relationships? Sex? What is the relation between body and soul? Shange seeks answers to these questions as she explores the Black woman's experience in her poems.

The first several poems in *for colored girls* create a mood of youthful optimism, playfulness, and joy in being alive. The serious note of the opening poem is interrupted by the singing of the childhood song, "mama's little baby," the reciting of a playful rhyme, and a game of tag. This lighter note, which carries over into the next two poems, expresses Shange's perception that the Black girl's childhood does not always prepare her for the struggles and hard times of her adult experience. (pp. 103-04)

["**Graduation nite**"] tells the story of a girl's first sexual initiation. While the girl's lower class and sometimes violent environment . . . is evident in her tale, the story is a positive one. Graduation was an exuberant rite of passage for her, and she sang inside. . . . (p. 104)

The following poem, "**now I love somebody more than,**" tells the story of the lady in blue's teen-age fascination with the Caribbean rhythms of Puerto Rican musician Willie Colon. Though this poem too has its serious moments, including a reference to Black self-hatred and color caste systems . . . , the poem as a whole is joyous. Beginning with the first "ola" . . . and moving through vivid descriptions of her dancing . . . , the poem is an invocation to the spirit of music and dance that has brought so much joy to a colored girl's life. (pp. 104-05)

While the first two poems celebrate Black women's life force, the next poem, "**no assistance,**" tells of their abuse. The lady in red tells how she loved a man who didn't appreciate her. . . . What makes the story of the lady in red more than the age-old female complaint about abuse by men is humor, anger, and insight. . . . Seeing her actions with humor creates a distance from pain and allows her to express her anger and to take responsibility for ending the affair. . . . Because she sees herself as responsible for letting herself be abused, she sees her power to refuse to be a victim. . . . The anger expressed in her last words to this man is the anger of a woman who has realized she doesn't need to waste her time on a man who doesn't value her. Her story calls up feelings of pain and outrage that such an obviously creative and funny woman has not been able to find a man to appreciate and love her. (pp. 105-06)

The next two poems speak of painful violations of women's bodies in rape and hack abortion. All the women speak the rape poem together, affirming that unfortunately this is not an individual story. . . . The picture created by Shange's poem is brutal but true. The stark simple lines of the poem and their harsh rhythm contrast effectively with the mood of joy expressed in the first two poems and deepen the feelings of pain and outrage that were introduced in "**no assistance.**" Shange creates a mood, preparing the audience to experience ever deeper nothingness in a Black woman's story.

In "**abortion cycle #1**" Shange re-creates a woman's terror during an illegal abortion. The poem begins cryptically as four of the women shriek "eyes," "mice," "womb," "nobody," evoking a feeling of terror. The rest of the poem, spoken by the lady in blue, is a collage of images of pain, disgust, fear, shame. . . . These images capture the feeling of violation, the pain of an abortion without anesthesia: it felt like something huge and powerful was inside her womb, like death was coming out of all her orifices. . . . This woman's secret shame recalls the opening poem, where it was stated that as long as the Black woman's story is not told, she will hear nothing but "maddening screams / / & the soft strains of death." . . . In sharing her story, the lady in blue can begin to break out of her isolation.

In the next several poems, "**sechita,**" "**toussaint,**" and "**one,**" Shange turns the audience to three individual stories which, while not without their own painful dimensions, are not as devastating as the stories of rape and back-room abortion. (pp. 106-08)

The alternation of naming Black women's strengths and naming their abuse and suffering continues in the next poem, "**i useta live in the world.**" In this poem Shange contrasts the universe of free Africa with its "waters ancient from accra / tunis / / cleansin me / feedin me" . . . with Harlem where "my ankles are covered in grey filth / / from the puddle neath the hydrant." . . . Black women in Harlem not only live in poverty and filth but also suffer verbal and physical abuse from men who assuage their shattered egos by abusing women. . . . The ultimate degradation she suffers is the knowledge that she must become violent like her surroundings if she is to survive. . . . (pp. 109-10)

The next poem, "**pyramid,**" considers women's complicity in their oppression. . . . It is an old story of women considering men more important than their friendships with each other. In this case, the women betray a close bond between each other for a man who doesn't even care about any of them. . . . Shange concludes the poem with the two women comforting each other. . . . The strongest love between them is their love for each other. . . . Shange celebrates the bond of sisterhood between women as a more reliable source of support than romantic fantasies about men.

In the next series of poems, "**no more love poems**" . . . , which form the reflective introspective center of the choreopoem, Shange explores the experience of nothingness created by women's dependence on men. In what to me is the most profound poem in *for colored girls*, the lady in orange (originally played by Shange) sings a "requium for myself / cuz i / / have died in a real way." . . . The death she suffered was caused by self-denial and self-deception. . . . In these lines Shange expresses an understanding of why women take abuse from men without complaining: it is just too painful to admit that men have the upper hand in many relationships and that they abuse the women who love them. The young Black girl who knows that she will suffer on account of her race often tries to deny that she will also suffer on account of her sex. However, to begin to admit the depth of her pain and experience of nothingness is the beginning of the road to self-acceptance for every woman. (pp. 110-11)

In the final poem of "**no more love poems,**" the poet confesses her inability to make her experience congruent with her philosophy. Indeed the disparity between her vision and her reality begins to drive her mad: "i've lost it / / touch with reality"

. . . , she confesses. She ponders again the alternatives and admits she does not have the answer. . . . Though she has not found a solution, she has achieved clarity about the problem and confidence in her own values and worth. She will not be likely again to deny her pain or to take abuse in relationships. She may not be able to find a man to love her, but she can at least refuse to be a victim, and this is an important step. The other women join her in her refusal to take abuse, asserting that their love is too "delicate," "beautiful," "sanctified," "magic," "saturday nite," "complicated," and "music" to have thrown back in their faces. Their joint affirmation has more power than an individual assertion because in celebrating their sisterhood with each other, each woman hears her value affirmed by the others.

Their resolution not to take abuse is put into practice in the next poem, the story of a woman who "made too much room" for a man and apparently considered herself worthless when he left her. The title line of the poem, "somebody almost walked off wid alla my stuff" . . . , is a metaphor that works on several levels. On the literal level it may refer to a man who stole some of a woman's things and attempted to sell them for money. On a sexual level, "stuff" is a euphemism for a woman's sexuality and refers to the man's failure to appreciate her giving of her body. And on the psychological level, the line refers to a man taking advantage of a woman's vulnerability and need for love. More than a lament, this poem is a celebration of a woman's self-respect and resolve not to abase herself for a man. The poem's humor stems from the literal elaboration of the central metaphor. . . . The lady in green enjoys her metaphor so much that she even begins to imagine this man has taken all her unique individuality, including her gestures and the identifying marks on her body. . . . In creating a catalogue of her "stuff" she comes to value herself in all her particularity. Instead of being turned in on herself, her anger is directed at the man who didn't appreciate what she had to offer. . . . Though rightly angry at the man, her anger is not a plea for him to love her as she thinks she deserves to be loved. Rather it is the anger of a woman who is learning finally to nurture and value herself. "My stuff," she says, "is the anonymous ripped off treasure // of the year." . . . Her list of what she treasures in herself is healing because she affirms her whole self, not just the self that has been primped and pampered to meet male approval. Shange deliberately celebrates aspects of her self that flout cultural ideals of female attractiveness: her immodesty, when she gives her crotch sunlight; her flawed body, including "calloused feet" and a "leg wit the // flea bite"; her unfeminine personality expressed in "quik language" . . . ; and her unfeminine female smells, when she "didnt get a chance to take a douche." . . . (pp. 112-14)

The lady in blue wonders what the lady will do if this man comes back saying he's sorry. This provokes the women to join together in creating a litany of excuses men give when they say they're sorry. . . . The lady in blue replies, "one thing i dont need // is any more apologies." . . . Instead of continuing to live out the forgiving female role, she expresses in yet another particular way the women's joint decision to take no more abuse.

At last able to affirm themselves as they are, colored, and sometimes sorry, open and in need of love, the women face a final challenge as the lady in red tells the story of Crystal and Beau Willie Brown. The story begins in the room of Beau Willie, a Vietnam veteran sent to "kill vietnamese children" . . . , who returned "crazy as hell" . . . and addicted to drugs.

Not unaware of the oppressive forces that turned Beau Willie crazy, the lady in red focuses on his tragic interaction with Crystal . . . , who with their children takes the brunt of Beau Willie's rage. (pp. 114-15)

The lady in red breaks the silence with her cry, "i waz missin somethin." . . . Her cry reminds everyone of the loss of her children. The other women deepen her cry, adding, "somethin so important," "somethin promised." . . . The lady in blue finally names what is missing—"a layin on of hands," to which the other ladies respond, "strong," "cool," "movin," "makin me whole," "sense," "pure," "all the gods comin into me / layin me open to myself." . . . Their words describe the sensations felt in a laying on of hands, an ancient healing ritual that is often practiced in evangelical sects in poor white and poor Black communities. The ladies explain that a laying on of hands is not sex with a man, or a mother's comforting touch, but a touching in which powers larger than the self are channeled into the one being healed. The laying on of hands ritual affirms the self's position in a community and in the universe, and suggests to her that she is not alone, that other humans—in this case women—and the very powers of being support her life and health. The laying on of hands in a community of women celebrates the power of sisterhood and sharing as one of the keys to a woman's moving through the experience of nothingness.

In the last poem, the lady in red describes how a woman, possibly Crystal, moves through nothingness to new being. Having contemplated suicide, this woman "fell into a numbness" . . . , but a mystical experience in nature brought her back to life. . . . Like Shange felt after her experience with the rainbow, the lady in red could conclude, "we are the same as the sky. We are here, breathing, living creatures, and we have a right to everything."

The final words of the lady in red, which are picked up and sung gospel style by the other women, are an incredible affirmation of her own power of being: "i found god in myself // and i loved her / i loved her fiercely." . . . These words express the affirmation of self, of being woman, of being Black, which is at the heart of *for colored girls*. . . . These final lines express Shange's conviction that the Black woman's quest for being is grounded in the powers of being. Though she has moments of despair that make her consideration of suicide logical, the powers of being in nature and sisterhood aid the Black woman in moving through nothingness. More than just a statement of self-affirmation, this woman's finding God in herself is an acknowledgement of her self's grounding in larger powers. (pp. 115-17)

To say "i found god in myself // and i loved her / i loved her fiercely" is to say in the clearest possible terms that it is all right to be a woman, that the Black woman does not have to imitate whiteness or depend on men for her power of being. This affirmation is a clear vision of new being on the far side of nothingness. (p. 117)

Carol P. Christ, "'I Found God in Myself . . . & I Loved Her Fiercely': Ntozake Shange," in her Diving Deep and Surfacing: Women Writers on Spiritual Quest *(copyright © 1980 by Carol P. Christ; reprinted by permission of Beacon Press), Beacon Press, 1980, pp. 97-118.*

SANDRA HOLLIN FLOWERS

There are as many ways of looking at Ntozake Shange's *For Colored Girls Who Have Considered Suicide / When the Rainbow*

Is Enuf as there are hues in a rainbow. One can take it as an initiation piece. . . . *Colored Girls* also might be seen as a black feminist statement in that it offers a black woman's movement. Still another approach is to view it as a literary coming-of-age of black womanhood in the form of a series of testimonies which, in Shange's words, "explore the realities of seven different kinds of women." Indeed, the choreopoem is so rich that it lends itself to multiple interpretations, which vary according to one's perspective and experiences.

I would suggest, however, that the least appropriate responses are those exemplified by reviewers who said that black men will find themselves portrayed in *Colored Girls* "as brutal con men and amorous double dealers", or that "The thematic emphasis is constantly directed at the stupid crudity and downright brutality of [black] men." Comments such as these are particularly misleading because they appear in reviews which contain generous praise for *Colored Girls*, thus suggesting that it is the condemnation of black men which gives the book its merit. Too, such comments have the effect of diminishing the work to nothing more than a diatribe against black men, when, quite the contrary, Shange demonstrates a compassionate vision of black men—compassionate because though the work is not without anger, it has a certain integrity which could not exist if the author lacked a perceptive understanding of the crisis between black men and women.

And there is definitely a crisis. Individually we have known this for some time, and lately black women as well as black men are showing growing concern about the steady deterioration of their relationships. Black literature, however, has lagged somewhat behind. The works which usually comprise Afro-American literature curricula and become part of general reading materials, for instance, show the position of the black man in America; but generally we see the black woman only peripherally as the protagonist's lover, wife, mother, or in some other supporting (or detracting) role. Certainly black women can identify with the predicament of black men. Black women can identify, for example, with the problems articulated in Ellison's *Invisible Man* because they share the same predicaments. But for black women the predicament of the black male protagonist is compounded by concerns which affect them on yet another level. This, then, is what makes *Colored Girls* an important work which ranks with Ellison's *Invisible Man*, Wright's *Native Son*, and the handful of other black classics— it is an artistically successful female perspective on a long-standing issue among black people. (p. 51)

[The poems **"Latent Rapists"** and **"Abortion Cycle #1"**], which seem to deal exclusively with women's issues, are of political significance to black men. It is difficult to politicize rape among black women, for instance, because the feminist approach began with a strongly anti-male sentiment, whereas the black community is highly male-identified. Furthermore, blacks have their own historical perspective on rape—the thousands of black men who were lynched for "rape" of white women. The history of these persecutions, however, does not remove the black woman's need for a political consciousness about rape, such as the traditionally feminist one Shange articulates. By the same token, Shange has sensitively portrayed the trauma of abortion, a trauma which, to some extent, probably exists in every case, no matter how strongly a woman might advocate the right to choose abortion. Still, the black movement's rhetoric linking birth control to genocide cannot be lightly dismissed. These considerations ought to make clear the delicate balance between blackness and womanhood which

Shange manages to strike in *Colored Girls*. Maintaining this balance is no easy task, and the black woman writer of some political consciousness is under tremendous pressure not to sacrifice issues of blackness to those of womanhood and vice versa.

As suggested, however, the primary focus of *Colored Girls* is on the quality of relationships between black women and their men. . . .

[An overt despair] is evident in **"A Nite with Beau Willie Brown."** . . .

Shange's compassion for black men surfaces most noticably in this poem and . . . her characterization of Beau Willie recognizes some of the external factors which influence relationships between black men and women. (p. 52)

This poem is purely political, although it has been misunderstood by critics. Here, we are again talking about a question of perspective, specifically an artist's perspective which can transform a passing incident into a poem of far-reaching and chilling significance. . . . [It] becomes apparent that Shange's anger is in response to the circumstances and impulses—whatever they are—which result in men brutalizing women. Consequently, while our sympathies might at first be entirely with Crystal, we ultimately come to understand that her pain is also Beau's and vice versa.

Finally, the significance of Beau Willie's and Crystal's children must not be overlooked. Their names—Naomi Kenya and Kwame Beau Willie—are important, for both contain elements of the African and the Western, the miscegenation which resulted in the Afro-American. Further, the girl and boy can be seen as nascent black womanhood and manhood. Literally and metaphorically, then, in dropping the children, Beau Willie is not only committing murder and—since they are his offspring—suicide; but he is also killing the hope of black manhood and womanhood. (pp. 52-3)

"No More Love Poems" is actually love poetry of the most explicit and poignant kind. Each poem exposes the persona so completely that one understands that she is basically defenseless and vulnerable as far as love is concerned. More important, in being so open, each woman takes an awesome risk: If her lover has a misguided notion of manhood, his response to her admissions may be terribly painful for her because he will not be able to drop the poses his self-image requires and allow himself to be equally open and vulnerable with her. The pathos of this group of poems is probably most evident in **"No More Love Poems #2"** Here the lady in purple, who, piteously, used to "linger in non-english speakin arms so there waz no possibility of understandin" . . . represents the epitome of the loveless love affair. Her inability to understand anything said by the person of the "non-english speakin arms" is symbolic of woman's attempts to understand man. He does not speak her language—which is to say that he is unable to express the kinds of feelings that she is capable of putting into words. At the same time, he lacks the ability to understand her and so she can never hope to make clear to him the things that are important to her. (p. 53)

Black men and women have not communicated successfully. It might even be said that they have tried everything imaginable to avoid articulating their needs—extended families, promiscuity, no-strings-attached fatherhood, getting/staying high together, even the Black Power Movement in which black people were all sisters and brothers, which meant that everyone *nat-*

urally had everyone else's welfare at heart and so there was no need to explain *anything*. . . .

Shange has given us an exquisite and very personal view of the politics of black womanhood and black male-female relationships. Too few black writers are doing that—perhaps because the truth is really as painful as that depicted in *Colored Girls,* and in telling it one opens oneself to charges of dividing the race and exposing blacks to ridicule by reinforcing stereotypes. That allegation has been levied against *Colored Girls,* which is unfortunate because the only thing of which Ntozake Shange is guilty is a sincere, eloquent rendering of what she has come to understand about black love relationships. Critics cannot afford to insist that black writers forgo expressing such visions simply because they are painful, embarrassing, or potentially divisive. If that is true, maybe it is because blacks have been so preoccupied with political and economic survival that they no longer know, if they ever did, how to confront their own responsibility for what happens between black men and women; in that case, blacks really *do* have a great need for *Colored Girls* and similar works. (p. 54)

Sandra Hollin Flowers, '' 'Colored Girls' : Textbook for the Eighties'' (© Indiana State University 1981; reprinted with the permission of the author and Indiana State University), in Black American Literature Forum, *Vol. 15, No. 2, Summer, 1981, pp. 51-4.*

Lee Smith

1944-

American novelist and short story writer.

Smith's fiction is set in the contemporary South. Her works are characterized by a tone of ironic humor, a fast narrative pace, and an eye for oddity in character and community. Her characters, often not developed past caricatures, struggle to accept the world's realities. Faced with truth, some of Smith's characters withdraw into fantasy, others into madness. This theme of "spiritual anemia" runs through all of Smith's works. It has prompted critic Leonard Rogoff to conclude that she "writes novels of limitations rather than possibilities."

Photograph by Susan Woodley Raines; courtesy of Lee Smith

MARTIN LEVIN

Mother is a Queen, sister is a Princess, and daddy is a cuckold, as seen by a 9-year-old Susan [in **"The Last Day the Dogbushes Bloomed"**]. One day a fierce Baron invades their castle in Dixie to take the Queen away to Splitsville in his big black car. Meanwhile, on the junior level, a dreadful little summer visitor forms a club to show the kids how to play doctor, and worse. The dogbushes, by the way, are not dogwood, but a place where a stray dog was found. Ah youth . . . youth, what novels are committed in thy name!

> Martin Levin, "Reader's Report: 'The Last Day the Dogbushes Bloomed'," in The New York Times Book Review (© 1968 by The New York Times Company; reprinted by permission), November 17, 1968, p. 82.

THE VIRGINIA QUARTERLY REVIEW

One aspect of Hemingway's technique is somewhat overworked in [Lee Smith's **Something in the Wind**, a yarn] about an eighteen year old girl on the loose as a freshman in college: even though the girl herself is the narrator and all manner of events affect her, readers are given few insights into her own character, her thinking, or her motivations. All we are really aware of is her meticulously cultivated approach to life, one that dissociates her from reality and permits her to regard herself as a separate being, thus able to participate in an action without personal involvement including endless copulations with a succession of strangers. If the heroine's intellectual solution to the problems of living in a contemporary world is marked by considerable vacuity, at least her methods are marked by abandon, despair, vengeance, and a subconscious wish to play Delilah to all men and symbolically emasculate each in turn, one by one.

> "Notes on Current Books: 'Something in the Wind'," in The Virginia Quarterly Review (copyright, 1971, by The Virginia Quarterly Review, The University of Virginia), Vol. 47, No. 3 (Summer, 1971), p. xcvi.*

MARTIN LEVIN

"Fancy strut," I learned from Lee Smith, is that stride of the drum majorette that resembles the goose-step. It's an important step for the town of Speed (Ala.), which aims to have its sesquicentennial parade led by its prize-winning high-stepper in the Tuscaloosa statewide competition. Other sesquicentennial events include an outdoor pageant ("The Song of Speed"), produced by an outdoor pageant promoter, a riot, a fire, a bungled suicide, a couple of seductions, and an acute case of senile dementia.

All the unscheduled events are in some way connected with the town's birthday carnival, which explodes into a display of comic fireworks that are pure delight. **"Fancy Strut"** is that rarity, a genuinely funny book that is satiric without being mean. Speed's social arbiter is a crazy lady possessed by delusions of past grandeur, and the rest of its power structure is afflicted with appropriate occupational diseases. I wouldn't want to live there, but Miss Smith makes it a great place to visit.

> Martin Levin, "New and Novel: 'Fancy Strut'," in The New York Times Book Review (© 1973 by The New York Times Company; reprinted by permission), October 7, 1973, p. 47.

LEONARD ROGOFF

Lee Smith's **Fancy Strut** marks a departure and homecoming. Her first novel—**The Last Day the Dogbushes Bloomed**—traces a Southern childhood, the story of Susan Tobey, who fancies a dreamworld of royalty and sunlight, even as her family disintegrates, even as her own imagination darkens and closes in on her. The second—*Something in the Wind*—is a novel of adolescence, Brooke Kincaid's, from boarding school in Virginia to university. Brooke too lives a vicarious life, through her friend and soul-mate Charles, who has died in a car crash. Brooke would also die to the world, embalmed in beer and shrouded in self-pity. She chooses not to understand, retiring in pain and madness. . . . Brooke's wish is to be left alone, not to "live in the world"; Susan Tobey would "see everything" but have "nothing . . . see me." Neither will feel or cry. Both would "live underground." . . .

In *Fancy Strut* Lee Smith expands the point of view and intrudes into other lives: a cheerleader, a demented spinster, a CPA. Unwilling or unable to transcend Brooke's special torment, Miss Smith has written a gently comic novel that is broader in sympathy but also less intense in feeling. Not confession but reporting, this is the portrait of a community: Speed, Alabama, 1965, the Year of the Sesquicentennial. If we care less for the businessmen and housewives of Speed than for Susan or Brooke, we recognize that they too are trying to make some sense of their world, however marginal their risks and niggling their victories. For despite the sternest efforts of these earnest, civic-minded townspeople to stage their pageant, events proceed without schedule and the Sesquicentennial program ends calamitously in a riot. The laughter is droll rather than sardonic; Miss Smith's penchant is for irony, but here it gleams far brighter than in her previous novels. Instead of visceral pain we have for once a laugh from the comic side of the absurd. If Susan and Brooke suffered privately, Speed's debacle is open to the public, and tickets sell quick and cheap. (p. 110)

Our laughter at [the people of Speed] is often disquietingly smug; however much the bric-brac of Speed clutters our own lives, we remain outsiders, detached, even as we feel ourselves strangers returning to our own hometowns. This is not Yoknapatawpha County but the New South. . . . (p. 111)

Miss Smith herself, however, is no tourist in Speed, and her irony is not totally deprecatory. Despite the surface banality— the suburban veneer—Miss Smith's habitual turn of mind inclines toward fantasy: all her novels occur on the borderline of reality, on the boundary of living. Susan makes her home in a Castle where her Mother reigns as Queen; Brooke clutches tightly to her paperback copy of *Ripley's Believe It or Not* as her guide through the freak show. In *Fancy Strut* the pattern also repeats itself, though the characters here are less threatened and threatening. Indeed, Miss Smith permits herself the luxury of affection. She is in control.

Though we know these people, have lived with them all our lives, we are never convinced of their reality. They live caricatures of lives, toying with authenticity. This comic pattern oftentimes vitiates their humanity. They wear their names as labels to their characters: Buck Fire, a stud, his libido flames; Manly Neighbors, . . . virile and chivalric, friendly and civic-minded. . . . And finally, Iona Flowers: an ancient relic, preserver of forms, as florid as the camellias adorning her Greek revival home.

The town's social arbiter and last surviving daughter of the Old South, Iona sees her fantasy life assaulted and sundered no less than Susan's or Brooke's. Miss Flowers lives according to an Idea of the Pageant: a regal theatrical event where Art Reigns in Queen Virtue's court. . . . Miss Flowers is an ob-

server of life, like Brooke, and as dead to the world—indeed she writes the town's obituaries. In her senility, in her devotion to the romantic imagination, she is as perpetual a child as Susan—and as lost.

In Miss Smith's novels the patterns swirl and dissolve. To set the time right, Brooke Kincaid would plot her future according to a Life Plan, choosing a model or a design as "a preparation for the world." In *Fancy Strut* the characters have arrived there: they live according to images of themselves—not honestly and openly with the dictates of their feelings. To that extent they scarcely live at all. (pp. 111-12)

The good people of Speed feel their way home: each has a place in the pageant, a center, a role to call his own. In their living rooms they have a friend in Johnny Carson to share the hard nights. These are the sort of homes from which Susan and Brooke would escape. . . .

Values in Speed are circumscribed, trivialized. Speed's world is far less terrifying than Susan's, far less tortured than Brooke's—as if the price for coming into knowledge of the world, for suffering through to maturity and achieving accommodation, is the withdrawal of mystery and death to the imagination.

Speed needs plasma, but the Pageant offers only a heady draught of Kool-Aid. (p. 113)

Ultimately, Miss Smith writes novels of limitations rather than possibilities. In *Fancy Strut* only two—possibly three—characters engage our sympathy. . . . But these are characters who suffer victory by defeat. And *Fancy Strut* accepts this defeat with resigned laughter. Finally, Speed fails, even as Brooke failed, from a kind of spiritual anemia, from values too weak in their origins, too exhausted in their ends, lending neither sustenance nor strength. As an amiable huckster proclaims to aspiring Sesquicentennial Queens, you win by losing. (p. 114)

Leonard Rogoff, "Reviews: 'Fancy Strut'," in Carolina Quarterly *(© copyright 1974 Carolina Quarterly), Vol. XXVI, No. 1, Winter, 1974, pp. 110-14.*

THE VIRGINIA QUARTERLY REVIEW

With their pubescent rotundities to the rear and impertinent little bosoms to the front, young majorettes twirling quite superfluous batons in the course of a sesquicentennial celebration by townsfolk in a medium-sized Southern city constitute the center of attraction in Lee Smith's newest novel [*Fancy Strut*], enabling her to disclose with admirable deftness the behind-the-scenes manipulations by promoters and participants alike, their petty chicaneries and their predatory pursuits of old-fashioned sin. Her book clips along at a lively pace and thus prompts the reader to hope she will presently develop material matching her innate capacities and engaging narrative skill.

"Notes on Current Books: 'Fancy Strut'," in The Virginia Quarterly Review *(copyright, 1974, by The Virginia Quarterly Review, The University of Virginia), Vol. 50, No. 1 (Winter, 1974), p. viii.**

CHRISTOPHER LEHMANN-HAUPT

The real heroine of Lee Smith's new novel, her fourth, is not doom-ridden Crystal Renee Spangler. . . . The real heroine of **"Black Mountain Breakdown"** is the narrator's voice, which turns Miss Smith's story into a country music ballad or a Southern Appalachian breakdown, in the sense of the word that means a tune played for a noisy dance, as in "Pike County Breakdown."

It is a voice that rushes its story forward in the present tense. . . .

It is a voice of many moods—from the delicate dreaminess of adolescence to the breathless cattiness of a smalltown gossip. . . .

Perhaps most impressive: it is a voice that reveals unhesitantly every banal and tawdry detail about her slightly hickish characters without for a moment patronizing them. Thus Lorene Spangler is made to capture all the pretentious dreams she has for daughter by calling her Crystal Renee, "the prettiest name she could think of." And yet behold, Crystal really is a bright and beautiful child who in her frantic search for an identity has every good reason to dream of a fairy-tale future. (p. 165)

The one major drawback to **"Black Mountain Breakdown"** has to do with its title being a pun, a heavy-handed one at that. Something happens to Crystal as an adolescent, when she goes out to the toolshed one evening to fetch her retarded uncle, Devere, for dinner. But we aren't certain what that something is because, in a glaring technical lapse, the narrator covers up the projector, figuratively speaking, so we can't see what is happening. Or rather the film is made to jump its track for a minute or two, and it's not for another 150 pages, when, years later, Crystal is reminded of Devere by the face of a patient in a psychiatric institute, that we learn how she was raped by her uncle in that interval.

Worse, the rape is so melodramatic and unnecessary that one nearly suspects the author of having added it as an afterthought to lend her story commercial pizzazz. A reflection of the single trauma view of mental disturbance that used to prevail in Hollywood films, it only serves to overspecify Crystal's difficulty and to transform her from a believable neurotic into a caricature. It would have been far more effective had Crystal only fantasized the rape, for then her neurotic character and eventual "breakdown" would have been more deeply rooted in her upbringing. And such a fantasy would have been entirely plausible since all the pressures on Crystal to imagine an assault have been so skillfully built up in the story.

The one redeeming feature of this plot complication is that the revelation of the rape is delayed so long. This lets us enjoy most of **"Black Mountain Breakdown"** for the book it could have been—one of those funny yet heartrending ballads that you hear on the country music stations—about a lovely young thing who just can't fit in anywhere. (p. 166)

Christopher Lehmann-Haupt, "'Black Mountain Breakdown'," in The New York Times, *Section 7 (© 1981 by The New York Times Company; reprinted by permission), March 29, 1981 (and reprinted in* Books of the Times, *Vol. IV, No. 4, April, 1981, pp. 165-66).*

ANNIE GOTTLIEB

[In *Black Mountain Breakdown*] Lee Smith does not show us life through a filter of literary allusions or devices. Instead, she gives us the sharp, sweet sensations of a life-hungry adolescent and the fresh poetry of Appalachian names. . . . There is no retrospective frame around the story of Crystal Spangler, so what happens to her is not a foregone conclusion. . . . We experience her life as she does, and it surprises us at every turn; we feel we are in the presence of someone "fully alive . . . more than real."

As a teen-ager in Black Rock, Va., Crystal is aroused to fear and ecstasy by the scary poems her father reads her in the darkened front room where he has withdrawn to drink and dream. After her father's death, and her rape by his retarded brother, Crystal is driven to seek out feelings of intensity: She sleeps with a "bad boy" from a nameless hollow, is "born again" at a revival meeting, has a vision. Her life fever impels her beyond Black Rock, away from her practical, enduring mother, her stolid best friend and her crazy-quilt of relatives, all the way to a New York burn-out from which she must come home to heal.

Lee Smith wisely observes Crystal's trajectory, like the departure and return of Halley's Comet, from the solid earth of Black Rock. In this novel, ordinary life has its own comforting poetry, but Crystal just isn't made for ordinary life. By living at home and teaching school she achieves an eggshell-like simulacrum of ordinary existence, but when well-meaning people force real life on her, she turns away to madness and to a beautifully implicit reunion with her dead father. Her withdrawal seems as much consummation as tragedy. She is not a failure but simply a stranger, one who, passing through life at a different angle, found it luminous. (pp. 15, 22)

Annie Gottlieb, "Three Hapless Heroines," in The New York Times Book Review *(© 1981 by The New York Times Company; reprinted by permission), March 29, 1981, pp. 14-15, 22.**

ROSANNE COGGESHALL

Lee Smith's fourth novel, *Black Mountain Breakdown,* stands in relation to her first three books . . . in much the same way that *Mrs. Dalloway,* Virginia Woolf's fourth novel, signals in her work new dimensions in vision as well as new stylistic and technical mastery. Smith has moved from her first narrative voice, that of nine-year-old Susan Tobey in *Dogbushes,* to a detached yet sympathetic and ironic third person omniscient narrator who reveals with equal ease the innermost musings of heroine Crystal Spangler, her "best friend" Agnes, her mother Lorene, her step-father Odell Peacock, and numerous other finely drawn and always interesting citizens of the Black Rock community.

We first meet Crystal when she is twelve years old, as she sits on the shore of the Levisa river, watching the lightning bugs that her friend Agnes expects her to be catching. Although "she could catch [them] . . . she doesn't; Crystal doesn't move." This passivity, this capacity for stillness, rare in a twelve-year-old, marks a quality in Crystal that makes her deserve her name. . . . [It] is this opening portion of the book, this scene of the youthful Crystal who can act but will not, whether from reverence for the beauty of the wild world she watches or from sheerest apathy we are never wholly certain, that we remember as we observe her growth and the metamorphoses, or seeming metamorphoses, that growth entails.

Despite the pervasiveness of Smith's always infectious humor, there remains an inescapable sombreness in Crystal Spangler's history. Is she, as her suicide-lover Jerold believed, "doomed" (as he was)? Or has she, in the end, reached a bliss that seems to us too fantastic to be real? Perhaps we are meant to conclude, as her step-father does, that the "Trouble with Crystal is, sometimes she almost makes you think something, but then she makes you stop and you never know what it was. You never get it thought through.''

Rosanne Coggeshall, ''Books in Brief: 'Black Mountain Breakdown','' in The Hollins Critic (copyright 1981 by Hollins College), Vol. XVIII, No. 2, April, 1981, p. 15.

KATHA POLLITT

For the heroines in this collection of Lee Smith's stories [Cakewalk], life happens on two levels. There are the half truths, pieties and conventions of Middle America, Southern division, and then there are the secret impulses of the heart. Sometimes this tension turns her women into lovable—maybe too lovable—eccentrics, like wild old Mrs. Darcy in **''Mrs. Darcy Meets the Blue-Eyed Stranger at the Beach,''** who hides her gift of healing from her worldly nagging daughters, or scatterbrained Florrie in the title story **''Cakewalk,''** whose disorderly household and fantastic homemade cakes express a full and innocent heart. Sometimes, too, they are not so lovable, like the iron-willed grandmother in **''Artists.''** . . . Others flounder, comically like Martha, the mad housewife of **''Dear Phil Donahue,''** whose ideas of love are straight out of a country western song and who is stranded by her low-life boyfriend in a Louisiana motel. (pp. 14, 24)

[Lee Smith] is to Southern writing what the New South is to the South. Hers is a South divested of mystery, of broodings about hellfire and race and fatal family history—indeed, of history, period. . . . Her heroines get their ideas from women's magazines and soap operas, and, if they are very daring, from Phil Donahue. They sustain themselves by their own pluck and warmth.

It would be wrong to claim too much for these stories. With the exception of two unsuccessful experimental efforts, they are not ambitious. But if they are sometimes too pat, too obvious in their sympathies—after all, how many wise eccentrics misunderstood by crass relatives can one book support?—they are also lively and compassionate. Miss Smith has a sharp ear for the rapid pithy speech of her neighbors and an amused eye for the sheer oddity of small-town popular culture, and these talents do much to animate even her most conventional stories. (p. 24)

Katha Pollitt, ''Southern Stories,'' in The New York Times Book Review (© 1981 by The New York Times Company; reprinted by permission), November 22, 1981, pp. 14, 24.

ROSANNE COGGESHALL

[Lee Smith's Cakewalk] works to confirm our conviction of the solidity, complexity, and downright delightfulness of her fiction. These fourteen stories, written over a period of eleven years . . . offer us worlds not necessarily unfamiliar yet charactered by Smith originals, men and women and children whose lives reveal the rarities too often left unnoticed in hour to hour existence. . . .

The force of Smith's stories (like the force of her novels) depends largely on [the] ranges and depths of vision, vision not just of character or narrator but of the author herself. Grounded always in the recognizable world of Krogers and ''Cool Club Rules,'' [Smith's] characters, through what they see and what they say, stretch and extend the boundaries of accepted reality,

and take us to existential borders we've never before imagined. Smith's characters, like friends we have lost touch with and yet cannot forget, restore to us insights too worthy and valuable for easy definition. . . .

Smith reveals intricacies of character and ambiguities of destiny that pull us back to contemplate her fictional world again and again, so here does she present us with lives never incredible and yet never simply apprehended. Much of the wonder of Smith's creations is derived from her mastery of the combination of the joyous and the awe-ful. Smith's Cakewalk commands first our attention, then our affection, and then our awe-filled delight.

Rosanne Coggeshall, ''Books in Brief: 'Cakewalk','' in The Hollins Critic (copyright 1981 by Hollins College), Vol. XVIII, No. 5, December, 1981, p. 17.

MARTHA ULLMAN WEST

Lee Smith has been pegged by a number of reputable reviewers writing in equally reputable publications as a regional writer, an author who can easily be mentioned in the same sentence as Carson McCullers, Eudora Welty, Harper Lee, Flannery O'Connor and Ellen Glasgow. . . .

[The stories in Cakewalk] do not deny the validity of the comparison, but such pigeonholing does not tell the whole story. Smith does set her fiction south of the Mason Dixon line, where she also happens to live, and she does indeed have a talent for replicating the embellishments of the mountain yarn. The best of the stories in this collection, however, go beyond regionalism, telling about people and their relationships in a way that transcends geographical location and regional temperament. While Smith's accent is authentically Southern, her style has none of the self-indulgent decadence of a Faulkner—magnificent as that style is—and her characters do not suffer from the distortions that we associate with those that people the work of McCullers and O'Connor.

Martha Ullman West, '''Cakewalk','' in San Francisco Review of Books (copyright © by the San Francisco Review of Books 1982), January, 1982, p. 13.

LUCINDA H. MacKETHAN

[In a story in Cakewalk], **''Artists,''** a young girl finds herself faced with a choice of identities that is reflected in the two pitched camps her family forms near her grandfather's deathbed; when the girl's father brings the dying old man's mistress to sit by his side, the family divides into those who are loyal to the grandmother, ensconced in frozen decorum downstairs in her Florida room painting cardinals and doves, and those who respect the mistress, a beauty shop proprietor who had been the one light of the grandfather's life for twenty years. ''The whole family had to take sides,'' Jennifer notes, yet she herself cannot. . . .

Which road to follow—high art and waist-length hair, suffering and self-willed isolation from such ''bestial'' . . . desires as midnight excursions to the refrigerator, or the ''beautician's'' entrenchment in rumpled realities of the flesh, page-boy curls, and kissing cousins? How to balance the longing after Beauty and Art with the necessary noises of the craft of life? Jennifer's decision in **''Artists''** (the plural form of the title reflecting the plurality of means to that end) suggests the value of openness and generosity and also indicates the value of balance that is central to Lee Smith's fiction. Not only do her works concern thematically the problem of choosing between or balancing the ordinary and the mysterious, the earthy and the ethereal, but technically, too, the stories and novels, most notably the last two books, strike a balance of effects, particularly in their choices of tone, point of view, and texture. (p. 3)

Three of the four novels and many of the stories collected in *Cakewalk* . . . chart the rites of passage of girl protagonists entering the world of womanhood and its consequences, from dawning sexuality, to commitments, to desertions, even to death. *The Last Day the Dogbushes Bloomed* . . . takes Susan Tobey from the beginning to the end of her ninth summer, concentrating on her exposure to a worldly, close to satanic boy whose growing influence over her parallels her growing awareness of the reality of her parents' dissolving marriage. . . . *Something in the Wind* . . . presents a more mature and deeper search in the story of Brooke Kincaid, a high school senior launched on a mission for an identity by the death of the boy friend who had always provided her roles and her certainties. *Black Mountain Breakdown* . . . builds from but goes far beyond Smith's first two novels, using a new point of view to allow the focus on Crystal Spangler to go deeper than her mind can take us. . . .

Susan Tobey, Brooke Kincaid, and Crystal Spangler are alike in that they are not so much actors as they are choosers, called upon to balance opposing demands, conflicting needs. They are watchers rather than catalysts, and in each book male friends supplant family ties, setting in motion incidents or delivering challenges that the girl or young woman initially accepts rather passively as a means to balance some lack in the patterns available through her life at home. (p. 4)

Yet while Crystal's long journey home might seem a continuation of quests tentatively glimpsed by Susan Tobey and firmly approached by Brooke Kincaid, *Black Mountain Breakdown* conceives of the initiation challenge not as a process to be undertaken only by the young, the romantically sensitive, the chosen, nor as a doorway that passes one only forward into the future. In Smith's latest novel, the inner life of the middle-aged wife and mother who loses her husband is chanted and probed, and the lonely career of the dependable, old-maid girlfriend becomes a counterpart, rich in its own reflectings, to Crystal's inverted odyssey. Additionally, Crystal's heritage—the small town milieu and the interrelations of her own family, not just parents, aunts, and uncles but pioneering grandfather and diary-keeping female ancestor, forms a tapestry of influence that proves Crystal's identity to have been formed in layers deeper than is her will or capacity to give them air in her own decreed time and place. *Cakewalk's* stories give brief glimpses of the same kind of uncovering of self for all kinds of protagonists; in addition to Jennifer in "**Artists**," the budding out of selfhood engages the well-appointed "society" columnist Joline Newhouse in "**Between the Lines**," the grave-demeanored, restless housewife Geneva in "**Heat Lightning**," as well as the free-spirited, abandoned teenager Debbi in "**Gulfport**," and the runaway, newly divorced soap opera fan Helen in "**All the Days of Our Lives**."

Fancy Strut . . . is not what we might consider calling Smith's other novels—an "initiation" story, yet in its own comically intricate style it is a satiric chronicle of the rite of passage of the entire town of Speed, Alabama, celebrating its "Roots" on the occasion of Sesquicentennial observances. . . . As is often the case with satire, underneath the ridicule of pretense

and pride we catch a mood of elegy, striking here for the child that the town once was.

While *Fancy Strut* is structured and narrated very differently from the first two novels, it abounds in a quality always present in Smith's writing and progressively more deftly handled—her eye for the richly comic possibilities of things belonging to a particular time and place. The time in which Smith embeds her things is a solid, contemporary Now that pulsates with the frighteningly fast rhythms of change. . . . And the place that Smith "catches ahold of" in her time, fixing upon it with an increasingly unerring ear for its rhythms, is the small southern town, carved from western Virginia mountain ridges or plains, Alabama river banks, shifting and absorbing the weight of progress, hanging on with dear life both to idiosyncrasies and distinctions. The gift for "seeing things in their time," as Eudora Welty has called it, involves an ability to create texture that Smith has welded into an art of balancing detail and meaning, particularly in her last two books. (pp. 5-6)

Fancy Strut relies more exclusively on details in their appropriate time and place than either of Smith's first two novels, and it represents an even clearer turning point in other technical areas of Smith's fiction, particularly the matters of tone and point of view. In this work we are introduced to a narrative position with sensibilities no less keen but definitely toughened, seeing the comic potential in small-town talk, hot local love affairs, aspirations and machinations of all sorts. Running like a sustaining thread through the novel is the chorus of good country people chatter, matchless as a means of capturing values and deflating egos as well. . . . Details are matched to essences of characters. . . .

While a mood evocative of the mystery and tentativeness of adolescent experience or young womanhood provides the tension for Smith's first two novels, the satiric strain of *Fancy Strut* will lead on in later works to a fully ironic tone, balancing satire with sympathy and matching a sense of the individual character's significance with the sense of humankind's ridiculousness. Crystal's story in *Black Mountain Breakdown* is one of tragic consequences, tracing as it does an eager spirit whose fate should be to go somewhere happily at last but which is frozen in the midst of its longings. . . . Her story becomes no long rehearsal of woe, though woes enough there are. . . . [Balancing] the moments of violence and loss are the inevitable rhythms of life in its daily measures, rhythms in which Crystal shares and has her being. (p. 7)

Several of the stories in *Cakewalk* also use a tone balancing satire and sympathy. None is a better example than the story which so effectively opens the collection. In "**Between the Lines**," Joline Newhouse seems to set herself up as a target for satire; in a story whose point of view is similar to that of Sister in Eudora Welty's "Why I live at the P.O.," Joline tells us, "That's me—I grew up smart as a whip, lively, and naturally good. Jesus came as easy as breathing did to me." . . . Such prattle would ordinarily be enough to doom any character, but Joline will not prove so easy to dismiss as purely a holier-than-thou gossip blinded by her own erroneous good opinion of herself. For all her seeming transparency, she begins her self-portrait by warning us that she writes "between the lines," . . . and we are forced to admit that her self-satisfaction has not been achieved without self-scrutiny. (p. 9)

When Joline asks, "Where will it all end? . . . All this pain and loving, mystery and loss," . . . she is identifying qualities of tone as well as life that will richly intermingle in the stories that follow in *Cakewalk*.

"**Between the Lines**" is a crucial story to consider in tracing the evolution of Smith's handling of point of view. Joline Newhouse, comically ironic in her pronouncements, lyrical as well as ludicrous, is far away, technically, from the first-person speakers of the first two novels. Susan Tobey's straightforward, earnest interpretations of her experiences are appropriate for her story; there Smith does not want a look back through memory but an actual reliving of what happened, which means that Susan reproduces the state of mind that existed in the past, rather than giving, as a retrospective, autobiographically-oriented narrator would, the double sense of being beyond as well as within the period being recalled. Growing up is the sensation intimately rendered, as we are meant to be held exclusively in the mind of the child in order to respond as she must, observing her limitations so as to have her experience, whole and authentic. With Joline Newhouse, however, we are told a story in which tone is as much a part of theme as the recounted experience is; how Joline talks matters more than what she says in the construction of her realities. Between the lines of her talk is irony wrought by a balancing of fact and strategy. We see her as she does not fully see herself, revealed through her talk; we read "between the lines" with her in ways as we would not consider doing in *The Last Day the Dogbushes Bloomed*. (pp. 9-10)

The use of an ironically limited first-person point of view to achieve a balance between inside and outside is a technique adapted for several stories in *Cakewalk*. Others in the collection, and *Black Mountain Breakdown* as well, apply what Smith has called a "close" third-person narrator to achieve much the same effect, yet greater control and flexibility. (p. 10)

The coupling of third-person point of view and present verb tense in *Black Mountain Breakdown* achieves a tension between closeness and distance crucial to both mystery and meaning in the novel. One of the most compelling stories in *Cakewalk* ["**Heat Lightning**"] uses the same device to much the same end. (p. 11)

The story "**Artists**" makes one other interesting variation with point of view that, again, involves a significant balance of effects. Jennifer tells the story in her own voice, yet she alternates present and past tense so that at certain times she is remembering while at others she is fully caught up in the reality of her past self. The earlier, recreated Jennifer is brought out, presented firmly in her own time and place. . . . The older, remembering narrator, who fully understands the significance of the past, controls our impressions of her younger, unenlightened image in a way that Brooke Kincaid, for instance, in *Something in the Wind*, is not permitted to do. (p. 12)

Flannery O'Connor wrote in a letter that "Everything has to operate first on the literal level," and Lee Smith's details obey this dictum, while increasingly they operate on other appropriate levels as well. A story such as "**Artists**" bears witness to her ability to supply depth to the texture of things in their time. In *Black Mountain Breakdown* . . . textures and patterns in literal things become a part of theme and significance. (pp. 12-13)

Lucinda H. MacKethan, "Artists and Beauticians: Balance in Lee Smith's Fiction," in The Southern Literary Journal (copyright 1982 by the Department of English, University of North Carolina at Chapel Hill), Vol. XV, No. 1, Fall, 1982, pp. 3-14.*

Martin Cruz Smith

1942-

(Born Martin William Smith; also writes as Martin Smith and under pseudonym of Simon Quinn) American novelist.

The publication in 1970 of *The Indians Won* marked the beginning of Smith's prolific writings. Since then, he has published over thirty crime and detective novels. Although fairly popular, none of these works generated as much critical and popular acclaim or were as important to his career as his 1981 novel of adventure and intrigue, *Gorky Park*.

Smith's work is noted for the detailed descriptions of often unusual settings. *Gorky Park*, for example, has been praised repeatedly for its depiction of Soviet lifestyles and manners. Smith also has the distinctive ability to build credible stories around seemingly odd combinations of people and places. His thriller, *Nightwing*, for instance, has been commended for its realistic presentation of Hopi Indian society within the context of a vampire story. In his early "Gypsy" series, Smith portrays a gypsy detective whose territory is New York City.

(See also *Contemporary Authors*, Vols. 85-88 and *Contemporary Authors New Revision Series*, Vol. 6.)

NEWGATE CALLENDAR

When Martin Smith's **"Gypsy in Amber"** was published, . . . it made a strong impression, an impression now reinforced by **"Canto for a Gypsy."** . . . Roman Grey, the gypsy antiques dealer who is the hero of Smith's series, is to the gypsy world what Harry Kemelman's Rabbi David Small is to Judaism. Both solve crimes that confront them; both are walking encyclopedias about their people and their way of life and thought. And all this is not supererogatory; it is germane to the mystery at hand and helps solve it. . . .

Smith is a smooth operator. He plots well, maintains tension, and creates believable characters. There is an underlying menace in his books that hits at the racial subconscious. Gypsies, tea-leaves, reading the future, forgotten mysteries of mankind: nonsense, we say. Except that after putting down **"Canto for a Gypsy,"** our superior smile may be a little weaker. Smith hits very hard.

> *Newgate Callendar, "Criminals at Large," in* The New York Times Book Review *(© 1973 by The New York Times Company; reprinted by permission), January 21, 1973, p. 26.**

WALTER CLEMONS

[Martin Cruz Smith] has a rare capacity to make the flesh crawl. The horrors in **"Nightwing"** are too vaguely set in motion: a Hopi medicine man, sickened by the intrusion of developers and tourists, resolves to "end the world." Vampire bats begin to rampage. Better the disruption of the natural order were entirely inexplicable, as in Hitchcock's "The Birds." But Smith has a fresh locale, arresting social detail about whites and Indians and a truly sickening ability to portray death in desert country. . . .

© Jerry Bauer

The wipe-out of human life in the Western desert is averted, but the possibility seems very real: the bats and fleas have much greater vitality than the human characters. The leathery rustle of wings becomes unnerving; the activity of fleas under a microscope provides one of the book's best scenes. An imperfect thriller, **"Nightwing"** is a nightmare of natural history. (p. 100A)

> *Walter Clemons, "Flesh Crawlers," in* Newsweek *(copyright 1977, by Newsweek, Inc.; all rights reserved; reprinted by permission), Vol. XC, No. 23, December 5, 1977, pp. 100-100A.**

CHRISTOPHER LEHMANN-HAUPT

[If] you stop and consider it objectively, **"Gorky Park"** winds down to a rather clichéd international shoot-'em-up, complete with murky speculations on the difference between American and Soviet justice, bewildering shifts in the various characters' apparent motivations and the somewhat shopworn implication that modern state bureaucracies spend more time double-crossing each other than they do looking out for the people they are supposed to serve.

But in truth we don't really look at the end of this novel too objectively. We are still under the spell of its beginning and middle, because for its first two-thirds . . . **"Gorky Park"** is superb.

It is superb in its sense of mystery. . . .

It is superb in its pacing, in the way it knits together coincidence and logical consequence to form a pattern of steadily accelerating excitement. Most of all, it is superb in its evocation of the Moscow atmosphere—or at least what this American imagines to be the Moscow atmosphere. . . . (p. 251)

At times, one can almost hear Mr. Smith chortling between the lines with delight over the way his Moscow has come to life and the way his characters move in it and express themselves. . . .

Perhaps it was his lack of familiarity that enabled him to imagine [the locales of his story] so vividly. Comparing the final section of **"Gorky Park"** with what precedes it, one has to regret that Mr. Cruz, who lives in New York, does not know as little about his native city, or of the conventional denouements of iron-curtain thrillers. (p. 252)

> *Christopher Lehmann-Haupt, "'Gorky Park',"* in The New York Times, *Section III (© 1981 by The New York Times Company; reprinted by permission), March 19, 1981 (and reprinted in* Books of the Times, *Vol. IV, No. 6, 1981, pp. 251-52).*

PETER OSNOS

Among the many very good qualities of Martin Cruz Smith's *Gorky Park,* the best is its sense of place. From the opening page . . . , the tension is palpable in every scene.

More perhaps than any other recent work of American fiction, this one conveys a feeling for the Soviet Union, its capital, its moods and its people—which is all the more remarkable because Smith spent a total of two weeks in Moscow in 1973. . . . He manages, nonetheless, to portray cops, robbers, suspects and victims with an uncanny authenticity. . . .

Most novels about the Soviets tend to caricature them into sinister stick figures: spies, dissidents, generals, political commissars. Not this one. The hero, homocide investigator Arkady Renko is, in his way, a Russian-style Sam Spade, skilled yet vulnerable, solitary yet capable of love. Humphrey Bogart would have been a natural for a film of the book.

The point is that *Gorky Park* is not at all a conventional thriller about Russians. It is to ordinary suspense stories what John Le Carré is to spy novels. The action is gritty, the plot complicated, the overriding quality is intelligence. You have to pay attention or you'll get hopelessly muddled. But staying with this book is easy enough since once one gets going, one doesn't want to stop. . . .

There is no reason to spin out the intricacies of the plot here. Sufficient to report, that the murders are motivated by a greed that no one coming to this book would readily predict. The choice of villains should tickle readers who prefer not to see every Soviet-American encounter end predictably with the trench-coated American downing a bourbon and branch water after the subdued (or eliminated) SMERSH agent gets his just desserts. There is enough villainy in *Gorky Park* to be shared all around. . . .

> *Peter Osnos, "Three Faceless Corpses,"* in Book World—The Washington Post *(© 1981, The Washington Post), March 29, 1981, p. 4.*

ROBERT LEKACHMAN

Gypsy in Amber and *Canto for a Gypsy,* two earlier thrillers by Martin Cruz Smith, demonstrated several comparatively rare virtues of this genre, particularly feeling for unusual milieus. . . . Both were written with grace and humor and without gratuitous violence or sadism. Nonetheless, all that the experienced consumer of this literature could reasonably have expected was a superior series, featuring the exploits of Police Sergeant Isadore. In the best of such series, the curve of inspiration is downward because the hero is a stable character, an old but predictable friend like Nero Wolfe, Ellery Queen, or the even more insufferable Lord Peter Wimsey. All parties—author, hero, readers, even villains—show signs of weariness as routine adventure succeeds routine adventure. The proprietor of the series turns into a *rentier* and the readers into addicts.

Gorky Park is a pleasant, even a stunning surprise, for its author has leaped several literary leagues onward into the company of genuine novelists. Although the murders, mutilations and episodes of minor violence are numerous enough to gratify the cravings even of those fed on contemporary best sellers, *Gorky Park* is only incidentally a murder story. It is a genuinely absorbing picture of certain aspects of Russian and American life, neither automatically anti-Soviet in the style of *Commentary* nor anti-American in the weary manner of the aging New Left.

The message seems to be that it is hard to behave well in a wicked world. . . .

The solution of the mystery is almost too pat and the ironies too symmetrical. Yet this is a good novel rather than a merely outstanding thriller because Smith has invented some genuinely complicated individuals [particularly Arkady and Kirwell] and placed them in challenging ethical predicaments. (p. 406)

Smith does less well with his women, who are types rather than people. Zoya is the model of a good Soviet citizen. Irina, the tormented rebel against Soviet fate, is from beginning to end simply too good to be true—a romantic fantasy of courage and beauty. At the end of the tale, Zoya and Irina act and talk much as they did at its start. . . .

Gorky Park, [however,] . . . passes one of the novel's tougher tests: its major characters will linger in memory for quite a while. All in all, this is a first-class job. . . . (p. 407)

> *Robert Lekachman, "A Wicked World, East and West,"* in The Nation *(copyright 1981 The Nation magazine, The Nation Associates, Inc.), Vol. 232, No. 13, April 4, 1981, pp. 406-07.*

PETER ANDREWS

Just when I was beginning to worry that the large-scale adventure novel might be suffering from a terminal case of the Folletts, along comes **"Gorky Park"** by Martin Cruz Smith, a book that reminds you just how satisfying a smoothly turned thriller can be. Mr. Smith fulfills all of the requirements of the adventure novel and then transcends the genre. **"Gorky Park"** is a proper novel, illuminated with fascinating glimpses of contemporary Russian life, a story dappled with flashes of irony. . . .

[In] essence, **"Gorky Park"** is a police procedural of uncommon excellence. Martin Cruz Smith has managed to combine the gritty atmosphere of a Moscow police squad room with a story of detection as neatly done as any English manor-house puzzlement. I have no idea as to the accuracy of Mr. Smith's descriptions of Russian police operations. But they ring as true as crystal. (p. 1)

If "Gorky Park" suffers from a flaw, it is one that is common among even the best examples of the genre. There is a falling-off at the end, when the plot turns about three notches more than my credulity is prepared to be stretched. But the first 340 pages were splendid. (p. 30)

> *Peter Andrews, ''Murder in Moscow, Arkady Renko on the Case,'' in* The New York Times Book Review *(© 1981 by The New York Times Company; reprinted by permission), April 5, 1981, pp. 1, 30.*

KAREN STEINBERG

Suspense novels can either be cut-and-dried thrillers, or they can strike deeper chords through the interweaving of universal themes and concerns with plot. "Gorky Park" . . . belongs to the latter category of espionage novels.

While the story that unfolds in "Gorky Park" provides enough intricacy and suspense for the most demanding aficionado, it is not primarily details of plot that engage our attention. Rather, within the context of this specialized genre, Martin Cruz Smith has succeeded in rendering very believable, realistic, and gripping portrayals of certain segments of Soviet society and of man's search for meaning. . . .

Certain scenes in the novel are particularly nicely done: A cat-and-mouse conversation between Arkady and his prime suspect is strongly reminiscent of the verbal sparring between Raskolnikov and police inspector Porfiry Petrovich in Dostoevsky's "Crime and Punishment."

While numerous gruesome details make this novel unsuited to the fainthearted, "Gorky Park" has much to recommend it. Far more than a mere espionage novel, "Gorky Park" is a vivid depiction of one man's struggle for meaning and truth within the Soviet system.

> *Karen Steinberg, ''Murder Thriller Set in Moscow'' (reprinted by permission of the author), in* The Christian Science Monitor, *April 13, 1981, p. B8.*

JOHN R. DUNLAP

Mr. Smith's dramatic stitching [in *Gorky Park*] is astonishingly plausible—neatly tailored to the grim reflections of Solzhenitsyn and to the grimly hilarious observations of Voinovich. It takes quite an imaginative leap, but, given the suppleness of the human spirit and the imbecility of the police state, a character like Chief Investigator Arkady Renko follows. . . .

In a totalist police state, the ordinary policeman is no less oppressed than the hapless citizen, and one of the minor feats of *Gorky Park* is that it exposes—incidentally and therefore powerfully—the very core of the totalitarian social order: a system that tacitly encourages its captive people to hate each other.

But the major feat is the characterization of Arkady Renko. . . .

Kingsley Amis once remarked that a critic should resist the temptation to call a fine writer a "creative artist." The writer may believe it, and his writing may consequently go to hell. . . .

[*Gorky Park*] wavers beyond a consistently expert craftsmanship toward genuine art. . . .

I shinny out on a critic's limb to note a scintillating creative flair about *Gorky Park:* not a single constipated sentence, not a trace of the intrusive artistic temperament, not a page lacking that telltale suggestion of the effortless, which, for the writer, follows only on great effort wed faithfully to minute detail. *Gorky Park* invites more than one reading, and reads as if there's more and maybe even better to come. (p. 34)

> *John R. Dunlap, ''Book Reviews: 'Gorky Park','' in* The American Spectator *(copyright © The American Spectator 1981), Vol. 14, No. 9, September, 1981, pp. 32-4.*

CAROLINE MOOREHEAD

[What gives Martin Smith's *Gorky Park*] its force is the stunning assurance of his descriptions. Some are simple trivialities: how pine martens are caught in trees, the way the black market works, the prostitutes on Kazan station who chalk their price on their toe caps. Others are entire reconstructions of organisations: the militia; the Siberian fur trade; the Moscow metro. They may not all be true, but they sound right.

More so, perhaps, than do the characters. Arkady is no party-liner, no grey pillar of the Moscow intelligentsia, but the classic hero, the good cop in a corrupt and evil institution. . . . He is sympathetic, wry, scruffy—but he also seems to be immortal, recovering with surprising ease from a stabbing, several months' interrogation in a Soviet psychiatric hospital, and a shoot-out in which only the innocent are spared. The minor characters come alive through their vanities and confusions. It is the major figures who are weak. . . . (p. 22)

There are, however, some compelling scenes and some strong passages of description, as well as dialogue that is fresh and often funny. . . . Martin Smith has an ear for the double-talk of Russian bureaucracy. The images remain, long after the intricacies of plot fade.

Gorky Park is certainly an intricate, even over-elaborate book. Apart from Arkady, all the characters are playing several games. As one phase of the action comes to an end another opens, like unpeeling an artichoke. There seems to be no heart. Why is Osborne allowed to go on manipulating everyone? Why, above all, is Arkady allowed to live? The concluding pages of this long book are unsatisfactory, as if only a James Bond solution of pyrotechnics—all car chase and bullets and whirling snow—could tie up a story that has got out of hand.

These criticisms are possibly churlish. *Gorky Park* is a marvellously readable book, alert, tense, even touching. It may be that it draws some of its power from the novelty of its Russian setting, but I do not think much. It is, of course, a thriller, but it also belongs among those books which are not quickly labelled, the mavericks, the writers' books, where the voice is somehow different. (pp. 22-3)

> *Caroline Moorehead, ''Double-Talk,'' in* The Spectator *(© 1981 by The Spectator; reprinted by permission of* The Spectator), *Vol. 247, No. 7992, September 12, 1981, pp. 22-3.**

HOWARD LACHTMAN

What is truly fascinating [about *Gorky Park*] is not Smith's Byzantine plot (it's about fur-smuggling, icon-forging, and dissident activities), but the absolute reality of the illusion that we have entered into Soviet life. Scenes and characterizations leap off the page with the clarity and coherence of photographs. . . .

The first police procedural novel to be set in the Soviet Union, *Gorky Park* is spellbinding in its view of an obstructive bureaucracy and destructive KGB at war with a lone detective. Renko's competence poses the kind of internal threat to the Soviet justice system which makes him vulnerable. The question of his vulnerability assumes a major role in the reader's expectations, and this concern for Renko's safety gradually creates a close bond between reader and hero. But Smith also earns our admiration by allowing us the fun of trying to outguess the shrewd Renko. If the Russian sleuth never quite takes us into his confidence, we understand how a man in his position, with an unfaithful wife, a questionable mistress, and a double-crossing department, must play his cards close to the vest.

Smith's gift for character-drawing begins with Renko and branches out to a wonderful cast of supporting players who have plausibility, wit, and irony to recommend them. . . .

If the book has a flaw, it's the downward spiral of events that occur once Renko is relocated in America. Something of the magic seems to be lost in the long leap from Gorky Park to Central Park. And in the inevitable shoot-out at the end between agents and cops of two nations, Smith opts for a Wild West climax, a blur of gunsmoke and identities.

These flaws undercut the credibility, but not the achievement, of a novel whose distinction is that it provides us with a new kind of detective from a most unexpected source. Renko's public investigation and private life illumine not only the heart and soul of the Russian nation but the sorrow and pity of our times. On any level—mystery, psychology, espionage, sociology—*Gorky Park* is a reading experience which ought not to be missed. (p. 362)

Howard Lachtman, "Current Reviews: 'Gorky Park'," in The Armchair Detective *(copyright © 1981 by* The Armchair Detective*), Vol. 14, No. 4, 1981, pp. 361-62.*

Stevie Smith

1902-1971

(Born Florence Margaret Smith) English poet, novelist, short story writer, essayist, and scriptwriter.

Smith is most noted for her light, comic verse and unorthodox writing style. Her poems—many of which combine elements from nursery rhymes, songs, and hymns—are characterized by a simplicity of diction and a youthful, lively wit. They are not, however, whimsical or fey. Underneath their surface gaiety lurks a stunning intellectual clarity. Obsessed with thoughts of death and religion throughout her life, Smith's poems fluctuate between moods of dark, cynical speculation and frivolous abandon.

Although definitely not confessional, Smith's novels, like much of her poetry, are somewhat autobiographical. *Novel on Yellow Paper*, *Over the Frontier*, and *The Holiday* have as a central character a young girl who, like Smith in her youth, works in a London office and lives in a suburb with an aunt. These novels, like Smith's poetry, are full of humor but are also strung through with notes of despair and portraits of lonely people aware of the quick, sometimes brutal movement of life. With the recent republication of several of Smith's early works and the publication of *Me Again: Uncollected Writings of Stevie Smith*, new comment on this unusual writer is beginning to appear. Critics are once again expressing their feeling that Smith's work is difficult to classify. Many are also reiterating the belief that it is nonetheless among the most intriguing and original of its day.

(See also *CLC*, Vols. 3, 8; *Contemporary Authors*, Vols. 17-20, Vols. 29-32, rev. ed. [obituary]; and *Contemporary Authors Permanent Series*, Vol. 2.)

CALVIN BEDIENT

Stevie Smith had a wonderfully various mind and her work is a forest of themes and attitudes. In large part it was her intelligence and honesty that led to this—to the protean, compound substance we all are. She was rather fierce about the truth—a modern peculiarity. The encouragement the age gives to both acceptance and doubt, the way it leaves us with the museum of everything without much trust in any of it, made her at once diverse and sardonic. '. . . we are born in an age of unrest', observes Celia, the narrator of her third novel, *The Holiday* (1949), 'and unrestful we are, with a vengeance.' Evidently Smith was prone to be sardonic anyway. Perhaps because her father had deserted to a life on the sea when she was young, she was quick to turn 'cold and furious' about anything selfish or unjust. Calling the heroines of her novels after Casmilus, 'shiftiest of namesakes, most treacherous lecherous and delinquent of Olympians', she seems also to have been nagged by a sense of unworthiness that may have gained strength from the same experience. In any case, fatherless, she would be 'nervy, bold and grim'; she would fend for herself. And clever as the next person, in fact cleverer, she would be nobody's fool, nor suffer foolishness. All this gives a wickedly unstable and swift slashing quality to her work. She herself is not to be trusted—except to be formidable, unpredictable, remorseless.

To a degree, however, Death stood in for Smith's father; she looked up to it, ran to it when she was hurt, needed its love. In *Novel on Yellow Paper* (1937), the heroine, Pompey, is sent to a convalescent home at age eight and there appalled by a maid's 'arbitrary' motherly feeling; 'it was so insecure, so without depth or significance. It was so similar in outward form, and so asunder and apart, so deceitful and so barbarous in significance.' Soon after, she becomes afraid for her mother, who suffers from heart disease—and terrified once again for herself, since there is nothing she can do: she is reduced to 'fury and impotence', 'a very hateful combination'. Thus startled into distrust of life, she discovers the great trustworthiness of death. 'Always the buoyant, ethereal and noble thought is in my mind: Death is my servant.' Let life do its worst, the black knight can be summoned. Indeed, what could be more liberating for the mind, keep it 'so quick and so swift and so glancing, and so proud'?

Thus allied, this clever poet was free to dance around life rather mockingly. (pp. 139-40)

Smith's combination of honesty and 'wicked bounce' makes her work a tonic. Considering the risks she ran, she wrote remarkably few poems that are clever or zany for their own sake. If her novels are too clever by half, the poems are as clever as they should be—clever beyond reasonable expecta-

416

tion. Much as she plays with her moods and insights, much as she remains sprightly and astonishingly inventive in poem after poem from the first volumes of the late Thirties to the posthumous *Scorpion and Other Poems* (1971), her work has almost always the dignity of disciplined seriousness. Of course like the sketches that often accompany them, many are slight—but they are frankly *hors d'oeuvres,* and justified by their unique tone or epigrammatic incisiveness. (p. 140)

Smith's secret bethrothal to death [did not] keep her from delight in life—from loving friends or the earth with 'the waters around [it] curled'. Indeed, she was blessed with a capacity for careless, innocent joy—an 'instinctuality', in words from *The Holiday,* that brought 'with it so much glee . . . so much of a truly imperial meekness'. The child in her, prematurely replaced by the adult, seems to have followed her like a shadow through her days, as a memory, a promise, of unlimited pleasure. It was not, in fact, Death she revered but the fountaining impulse of being. Indeed, she proved in certain poems—several of them among her best—one of the rare celebrators of what Blake called 'Eternal Delight'. If her bounce was often 'wicked' it was only because and in so far as this essential, transcendent joy was thwarted by circumstance or some inherent curse, some Original Contradiction.

But certainly it *was* thwarted and perhaps no poet's work has ever seemed so much a quarrel of classical scepticism and romantic liberation. Smith was open to every likelihood and perhaps finally partial to none. Few [are] so skilful at opening a crevasse between two truths. Is it wise to abandon hope wholly? 'No, it is not wise'. Is it wise to endure when Death's a prize easy to carry? 'No, it is not wise.' Certainty of this kind is worse than the uncertainty it resembles; it is wisdom past cure.

Just as the truth is mixed for Smith, so her poems are frequently startling and seemingly extempore mixtures of elements. She likes particularly to combine the archaic and the contemporary, the measured and the runaway. Often she brings a breezy or nervously colloquial manner to old-fashioned themes or traditional stories. . . . Where archaic measure avers assurance, Smith's rapid contemporary line, often long and unbound, dashes through silence as if uncertain of its right to interrupt it. Occasionally it rattles dramatically, abruptly, impatiently, out of a metrical opening, and then it may simulate the brusque, offhand dealings of life itself. (pp. 140-42)

About all we can count on in reading Smith is that she will be as surprising as she is skilful, her finesse equal to her boldness. And we can also count on hearing a voice—a 'talking voice', as Pompey says, pointed 'with commas, semi-colons, dashes, pauses', a voice held 'alive in captivity'. Indeed, Smith is so instinctively a dramatist of voice that she endows even the verse essay with necessity. And this is all the more remarkable in that her language is anyway that of a writer of verse. She remains almost always outside and above her words; they are smaller than she is, her instruments. And yet they are not only exact, they live, because they are quick with voice. It is in entering delightedly and inventively into idiom, rhythm, attitude, intonation, that Smith's imagination is most alive. Hence where most versifiers merely deck their morals in metre, Smith, cadenced and dramatic, converts hers into personality. . . . (p. 144)

Still, authoritative and captivating as Smith's voice usually is, it is never so impelling as when it invests an immediate situation or world. If the poet cannot put her imagination of voice aside, she can put both imagined space and the moment into her voice, as iridescence is in the bubble, as a mirrored face or world is there. . . . [In *Scorpion*] as against the voiced opinion, the thematic nakedness, of **'Thoughts about the Christian Doctrine of Eternal Hell',** is all the poignancy of a voice's rage to be silenced. It is still the complex, shifting intonation to which we respond—the blend of spite, longing, and fondness, the uncompromising emphasis (how the sharpened tail jerks about!), the wry intensity of *so* in the final line. But the poem fills out, as well, with the pressure of undeniable reality, the immediacy of an individual fate. And though sea and grass are subordinate to the speaker's impatient need for them, they are nonetheless there at the periphery, adding a horizon of appearance, a sense of the earth. (p. 145)

Yet just as the poems of immediate scenes and situations touch us more nearly than those of sharply voiced thought, so they pale, in turn, beside the finest poems in still another group, those of magic and romance: poems not only luminous with personality and weighted by matter but also dipped in the fabulous. Here the ordinary world, struck by a haloed moon of transcendental fantasy, lies under a spell, whether lovely or troubling. For finally Smith could not be held down and, in escaping the limitations of the earth, took it with her. Like Forster, Yeats, Dylan Thomas, and Isak Dinesen, she raised it felicitously into the marvellous. (p. 147)

None of Stevie Smith's poems summarize her view of life, for finally she had no view, only views. She knew perhaps everything the emotions can know with a knowledge as heavy as the earth and a brilliance as light as the air. She could touch any subject and give it truth. Bold and queer mixture of vivacity and honesty that she was, author of numerous poems of wit, force, and unexpectedness, we may find ourselves saying of her: it was improbable that such a poet should ever happen along, but now that she is with us she is indispensable. (p. 158)

Calvin Bedient, ''Stevie Smith,'' in his Eight Contemporary Poets: Charles Tomlinson, Donald Davie, R. S. Thomas, Philip Larkin, Ted Hughes, Thomas Kinsella, Stevie Smith, W. S. Graham *(copyright © 1974 by Oxford University Press, Inc.; reprinted by permission), Oxford University Press, New York, 1974, pp. 139-58.*

STEPHEN TAPSCOTT

From the first poems in [her **Collected Poems**], Smith's jingling eccentric rhythms and *faux naifs* social observations seem as finished and as edgy as the later, more familiar poems. The pieces are blunt, whimsical with an acidic toughness that belies their nursery-rhymed, chatty forms. Consciously resembling Blake's *Songs of Innocence and Experience,* Smith's poems purport to be innocent, or at least unaware of the final reaches of their suggestiveness. (Like Blake, too, she illustrates her own poems—with wobblingly childish line-drawings.) But the tightness of her forms avoids external emotionalizing or sentiment: the prancing rhythms and the obsessive, even nonsensical rhymes make the childishness of the form more penetrating, more subtly half-familiar, than a booming rhetoric or a free-verse profundity would do. And like Theodore Roethke, for instance, who in his ''Lost Son'' poems returns to nursery rhymes and to clinking rhythms in order to increase the terrors of childhood in the philogenic adult mind, Smith uses the childishness of the form to deal with adult obsessions. Surprisingly, the result is neither coy nor sentimental. . . . (pp. 448-49)

Pithy and compassionate, jauntily conversational, modest in their specific gravity and in their refusal to overreach in rhetoric or in gesture, Smith's poems stay at home, worrying the everyday circumstances and demanding a clear look at the spiritually unavoidable. And the mystery seems always to seep through the closed door, the telephone, the mailslot: Smith is, consciously, an Emily Dickinson figure, caught like Dickinson in the modern tug between the self-denigrating faith of an Edwards and the congratulatory self-reliance of an Emerson. For Smith the tension is even greater, if that is possible, because the terms of the split have become culturally more overt. In this tension she may become silly at times, but even that occasional tone of forced whimsy also bespeaks her tautly honest sense of the modern importance of the single individual. And like the obsessive internal rhyming of Sylvia Plath's best (late) poems, Smith's formal integrity saves the poems from self-indulgence and deepens the terror of the quotidian. . . . (p. 449)

Stephen Tapscott, "Book Reviews: 'The Collected Poems of Stevie Smith'," in The Georgia Review *(copyright, 1978, by the University of Georgia), Vol. XXXII, No. 2, Summer, 1978, pp. 446-50.*

MARK STOREY

The kind of poet Stevie Smith is begins to emerge from a close look at the **Collected Poems.** She does not develop, in any helpful sense of the word: the first handful of poems announce her concerns as clearly as do the final, posthumous poems. The consistency of technique and craftsmanship is as sure in 1937 as it is in 1969. To say that, though, is to acknowledge the inconsistency too, in that quite often the reader is left wondering whether Stevie Smith knew or cared when she had written a poem not quite true to her Muse. The answer to that sort of nagging doubt is probably that she knew but didn't care all that much. There is a deliberate carelessness in much of her writing which reflects her own rather cavalier attitude both to the world and to poetry, and this carelessness is something the reader has to confront, because it becomes, oddly enough, one of her peculiar strengths. . . . Stevie Smith is sufficiently sure of herself to throw at her audience quite a lot of what, in another context, she calls 'balsy nonsense', in the knowledge that, when she has to, she can redeem herself. This process of giving with one hand what she takes away with the other operates through all her work, and it is one which is itself disturbing for readers and critics. We do, after all, like our poets to develop, and to take themselves seriously. But the tendency to see all poets in terms of growth towards maturity, however natural and understandable, is not always illuminating: Keats has suffered because of it, so too has John Clare. Clare in fact provides a useful pointer in the argument, in that he has endured a fate similar to Stevie Smith's at the hands of critics prepared to acknowledge his presence but unwilling to absorb him into their patterns of critical discourse. You will not find Clare getting much of a mention in surveys of the Romantics and Victorians, and this is as much a hint as to his true stature as an indication of his supposedly minor significance. Furthermore, Clare evinces the same sort of inconsistency. Stevie Smith likewise stands outside any tradition of the day, and in so doing acts as a comment on what is happening elsewhere; she becomes a touchstone, just as to read Clare is to see him apart from his contemporaries and to see them in a new light.

The comparison with Clare is especially illuminating if we think of Clare's asylum poetry, where his lyricism achieves its fullest and most self-contained flight. Song after song spills out of the notebooks in a profusion that seems to challenge the rigours of critical analysis. It is in the asylum poems that Clare comes closest to Blake. It seems to me significant that Blake, too, can be heard behind and through several of Stevie Smith's poems, and these allusions help to clarify the nature of the critical problem. For, alongside the innocence of Clare, alongside the small cluster of recurrent preoccupations which mark Clare's work and Stevie Smith's, there is the simple directness of Blake as he appears in the *Songs of Innocence and of Experience.* (pp. 42-3)

Stevie Smith cultivates a particular type of simplicity which has its echoes of Blake especially, but the temptation to move towards greater abstruseness and complexity is always there, and a number of poems can be seen to fail when they succumb in this way. The risks of simplicity, so far as the poet is concerned, are enormous, particularly in an age which distrusts what is simple, which easily perceives when the simple becomes the simplistic. The arch, the knowing, the coy—simplicity attracts such labels. It seems to me that one of Stevie Smith's most important qualities is her determination to persevere within the confines of simplicity, as though at the back of her head all the time is Coleridge's urging of the poet to keep alive in adulthood the simplicity of the child. (pp. 43-4)

Stevie Smith's art often depends on what seems to be a carefully contrived carelessness, with respect to life as well as to art. . . . [For her] life is a matter of pain, of lost love, of desperation—and these things urge humour for their control. It is as though she engages us in the halting gait of a *danse macabre* where love and death and solitude hold hands; the music she dances to is generally quiet, off-beat—or, if it is noisy, the din rings slightly hollow. One of her poems celebrates Miss Pauncefort who 'sang at the top of her voice. . . . And nobody knew what she sang about' (which did not stop her singing in her manic way). The Muse for Stevie Smith tends to be quiet, even timid. . . . This relationship between Muse and poet is central to her vision, and to how Stevie Smith sees herself as a poet: it helps to explain her gait, her step at once firm and tentative. (pp. 44-5)

[In her poem, **'The Word',**] Stevie Smith is making a connection between her dramatised experience and her role as poet, and in doing this she is going beyond Blake, who rarely, even in the dourest Songs of Experience, suggests that the agonised and terrified consciousness is his. That is the difference between his poem 'Little boy lost' and Stevie Smith's of the same name. . . . [Smith's] poem does not work because ultimately the little boy lost is transparently a surrogate of a poet without bearings. Much more successful is **'Little boy sick',** where the Blakean idiom is recreated, and at the same time the dramatised utterance retains its integrity. The little lamb of Innocence has become a mangy tiger, his former glory departed utterly. Here is something of Stevie Smith's surprising virtuosity—surprising in that she would be the first to disclaim virtuosity. . . . The range of voices [in **'Little boy sick'**] is wide, but never so much so that the poem gets out of control: we are constantly brought back to the tautness of Blake's 'Tyger', its impressed syntax. At the epicentre of the poem lies the audacious line 'O God I was so beautiful when I was well' which echoes, if anything, the stark cry in a Brecht/Weill song, 'Surabaya Johnny, my God, and I love you so', and has the same chokingly dramatic effect: typically the cry to God is both colloquial blasphemy and desperate appeal. Once again, Blake's world of experience is the one which has its special meaning for Stevie Smith; it is characteristic of her deep-seated pessimism that she should choose the only optimistic poem in Blake's canon of Experience as a jumping-off point for an exploration of her own desolation. (pp. 47-9)

An early poem **'Night-time in the cemetery'** is one of her most moving poems because it acknowledges the bitterness of death even as it recognises the affinity. Here Stevie Smith strives to deserve the death she is to court more stoically elsewhere. It is not fanciful to hear Blake and Clare behind this poem, even Emily Dickinson; yet at the very core is the unmistakeable figure, the Stevie Smith whose colloquial twang explains the Clare-like insistence on peculiarity and strangeness. . . . This poem is a triumph of Stevie Smith's idiosyncratic art, and we learn not to be surprised by the fact that it comes so early in the canon: she returns to this world repeatedly, to weave variations of the subtlest and most lyrical kind on the theme of death and oblivion. She knows that the theme is inexhaustible, and that it is necessary, however hard that acknowledgement, when it would be so much easier, as in her dreams, to run away from it all. The reader of Stevie Smith finds himself making a long list of the memorable poems: there are far more poems announcing their authority than I have been able to hint at. It is ironic that a poet so concerned with scrupulosity, with the quietness of the Muse's voice, should be so fecund. She herself worries at this a lot, often referring to the parable of the talents. In the last resort her claim on posterity rests on this extraordinary combination of the minimal and the generous. In one sense, her work is a burden to her, something she lands herself with:

> I can call up old ghosts, and they will come,
> But my art limps,—I cannot send them home.

But she accepts the limp, learns to live with the ghosts that haunt her, until she is able to celebrate them. (pp. 54-5)

> *Mark Storey, "Why Stevie Smith Matters," in* Critical Quarterly *(reprinted by permission of Manchester University Press), Vol. 21, No. 2, Summer, 1979, pp. 41-55 [the excerpt of Smith's poetry used here was originally published in her* The Collected Poems of Stevie Smith *(copyright © 1972 by The Estate of Stevie Smith; reprinted by permission of New Directions Publishing Corporation, as agents for the Estate of Stevie Smith), Allen Lane, 1975].*

MICHAEL SCHMIDT

The most striking characteristic of [Stevie Smith's] work is the rhythm, a speech rhythm slipping naturally into metre and out again, a rhythm so strong that it overrides considerations of syntax and punctuation and—in releasing language from its formal structures—finds new forms, new tones. Language thus released from traditional bonds and held tenuously in new bonds of rhythm, doggerel rhyme, assonance, and tone of voice, becomes capable of a range of expression unusual in more traditional usage—though she forfeits certain formal effects, of course.

As she treats language, so she treats our common reality. Her fanciful vision illuminates our world and elements of our common experience. It disengages emotions and situations from their actual contexts and presents them distilled in a fanciful context. Her world of fancy is not escapist. It is like a mask through which she trains her eyes on actual experience; her transmutations of actual experience clarify it with knowing innocence and seldom sentimentalize it. The fanciful world is a cruel one—of fairy tales, legends and myths peopled by princes, princesses, ogres and ghouls, neurotic animals and

good spirits whose emotions and frustrations are ours. It is a world where guilt is out of place. In effect, she creates a modern pastoral. The short story poems about aristocrats or legendary people are another aspect of the same fanciful pastoralism. Her themes grow powerful through 'enchantment'—rhythms and the voice persuade us emotionally. Human self-deception is an evil enchantment; against it Stevie Smith marshals the beneficent enchantment of poetry, which throws the self-deception into relief. Her aim is ethical and didactic as well as to entertain. (pp. 203-04)

[Stevie Smith's] attitude to her models —for many of the poems have specific models, particularly nineteenth-century British and American poems, hymns and popular tunes, and plainsong conventions—is ambivalent. Some she approaches in the spirit of parody, writing a poem about a swinging ape to the tune of 'Greensleeves'. At other times she depends on our recollection of the strong rhythms of an earlier poem to lend resonance to her own poem. Her individual voice speaks above the rhythm of another poet, defying and then confirming our expectation. Her models do *not* include Emily Dickinson, a poet with whom she has often been compared. Where Emily Dickinson took rhythm as her constant and concentrated on the effective combination of carefully chosen words, Stevie Smith takes her vocabulary—which is generally simple and similar throughout her work—for granted and expends most of her energy on the rhythm.

Edgar Allan Poe echoes through much of her verse. **'The Stroke'**, **'The True Tyrant'**, and **'November'** contain specific echoes of Poe and each poem develops his rhythms. Stevie Smith seems to have been haunted by 'Ulalume' and 'Annabel Lee' and the underwater kingdom of some of Poe's poems. Many of her characters drown, and several watery gods preserve the victims as relics, deep and dead, but seeming asleep and pricelessly beautiful. She must have sensed a justice and ghostly permanence in rivers and the sea, as Poe did. Poe also suggested some of the odd and macabre names she uses. And though she builds on him with a mixture of dependence and parody, her power often derives from his rhythms, though the speaking voice is her own. (p. 204)

The poems, then sending down taproots into some text or musical tune, have an authority not entirely their own and yet not plagiarized either. In **'The Grange'** we hear Kipling, in **'Our Bog is Dood'** we hear the Blake of the 'Book of Thel' and in **'A Fairy Story'** and a number of short-lined poems we hear the Blake of the 'Songs of Innocence and Experience'. Cowper and Browning are there too, and Tennyson of the *Idylls* and 'The Lady of Shalott'. Coleridge with the cadences of 'Christabel' and 'Kubla Khan' announces himself from behind several poems. Hymn tunes and rhythms, prayer book and Biblical echoes can be heard. Hence the poems that reveal the passing of love, or of life, or of social orders, are nostalgic not in diction or specific content, but in the echoes the rhythms suggest, hinting at other sources and analogues.

Given the preponderance of Victorian models, her use of often antiquated diction littered with 'Oh' and 'Alas', her quaintness, her painful mock-Victorian doggerel rhymes, how is it that she evades banality? How does she manage to revitalize an outworn poetic language by means of the language itself? The answer lies in her humour—not irony but wit which refreshes the language and makes it meaningful again. If one says 'alas' glumly, one is being banal. If one says 'alas' slyly, the humour and the lament coexist, if the context is correct. Her humour redeems the outworn language. The unexpected intrusion into her poems of arch malapropisms and modern colloquialisms is often effective. The humour does not wear thin on re-reading. (p. 205)

Michael Schmidt, "Stevie Smith," in his A Reader's Guide to Fifty Modern British Poets *(© Michael Schmidt 1979; by permission of Barnes & Noble Books, a Division of Littlefield, Adams & Co., Inc.), Barnes & Noble, 1979, pp. 200-06.*

JOHN BAYLEY

The impression of Stevie Smith in [*Me Again: Uncollected Writings*] is overwhelming, almost too much so: it is not so much a question of her putting a head round the door and trilling Whoopee here I am again, as of plumping herself down in one's lap. That is an impression she would not have wished to make. She was not only an intensely professional writer but a sort of Parnassian, whatever contrary impression the idiom of her poems may give. Her sweetest songs were those which tell of saddest thought, but tell of it by odd contraries. . . .

The originality of her poems seems like isolation made visible. They are childish in the sense in which Henry James's children are childish, little images of dispossession which have a quality all their own. Like such children she is never on the Side of Life, but of the fatigue which for many people is the only way of making a success of it. . . .

From the admirable introduction by Jack Barbera and William McBrien—in itself a wholly adequate substitute for any biography—we learn that Sylvia Plath much admired Stevie's poems. The letter Plath wrote . . . is touching in its simple wish for contact and comfort. She was hoping, in November 1962, to move with her babies to a London flat. . . . It was not to be, however; Sylvia Plath killed herself three months after writing the letter. . . .

From the editors' unobtrusive annotations to Stevie's letters we learn that she herself attempted suicide at the office in 1953, a month or two after writing **"Not Waving but Drowning"**. . . . The poem has become, alas, her "Lake Isle of Innisfree", and gives no indication at all of how subtle and beautiful the sheer *density* of her poetry is (particularly in **Harold's Leap,** the preceding collection. . . . The critic would have to admit that in general there is a difference, and a disconcerting one, between the poems of Stevie Smith that "come off" and the ones that don't; but some none the less can come off too well, too obviously, like the one in the present volume which ends "But I forgive you Maria, / Kindly remember that." Most of the poems here, though, are aborted pieces which their author would hardly have wished to see in print. . . .

"Beside the Seaside" is probably the best of the ten . . . [stories] included in this volume. . . . **"Goodnight"** [is a poem] which she wrote about a married couple, friends of hers. They used to sit late in Stevie's room, apparently reluctant to withdraw into spousality. . . . Though she was adept at hitting off daily dolours like this, and especially those concerning "the woe that is in marriage", the solitary fancy of her muse does not soar in such a context. Much more memorable is the cry of the wife in **"Lightly Bound"**. . . .

Some of the poems will none the less have a special interest for the Stevie Smith addict, particularly a highly accomplished exercise in Miltonics, **"Satan Speaks"**, which she wrote when hardly more than a schoolgirl. . . .

John Bayley, "The Must of the Daily Dolours," in The Times Literary Supplement *(© Times Newspapers Ltd. (London) 1981; reproduced from* The Times Literary Supplement *by permission), No. 4101, November 6, 1981, p. 1289.*

VICTORIA GLENDINNING

She once ended a letter with 'lots of buoyant love and hollow laughter'—words that set the tone for this volume of Stevie Smith's uncollected writings. It consists of reviews, essays, poems, stories, letters and a radio play. The letters are lively, witty and affectionate; it is they, with the reviews and essays, that are the most worthwhile things in [*Me Again: Uncollected Writings*].

There is perhaps a little too much space given to her evocations of Palmer's Green, the North London suburb where she spent virtually her whole life and which she loved to describe. But on life within the house she is original and celebratory in her own throw-away, ironic manner. (p. 660)

[The] poems collected up here will not detract from, but will not add anything to, her reputation. So often she expected the heavy traffic of her own thoughts on the Deity, Nature, herself, to fit into a context as twee as the pram to which she whimsically, horrifically, longs to return in a poem called '**Surrounded by Children**'. Writing in prose, she was prepared to push prams over cliffs. In the essay '**My Muse**' she wrote: 'All the poems Poetry writes may be called "Heaven, a detail", or "Hell, a detail".' (She only writes about heaven and hell.) In a story '**Sunday at Home**,' the Stevie-figure says repeatedly that 'Hell is a continuation of policy'—which strikes an oddly topical note. Heaven and hell absorbed her. She said she was a 'religious-minded agnostic', and some of the simplest, sharpest prose writing here is about Christianity, which fascinated her and in which she could never quite believe.

She was a tightrope-walker in religion as in everything else. She seemed to walk a tightrope between life and death, flirting with both, but committing herself to neither. (pp. 660-61)

Another perpetual tightrope was that of personal relationships. There are no revelations about her private life in this volume. . . . But that she knew the pains of love is evident from all she wrote. . . .

The stuff of life and the stuff of death, 'her rhymes, her wit, her obsessions', as her editors say, are loud in this collection. Only Queen Victoria among Englishwomen has ever had such a personal, emphatic, epistolary or pseudo-epistolary style. In 1971 Stevie Smith died from a brain tumour. In the preceding months she lost control over the shape and meaning of words, but even in this disintegration she had grace and a sort of unearthly wit. (p. 661)

Victoria Glendinning, "Nuts on Death" (© British Broadcasting Corp. 1981; reprinted by permission of Victoria Glendinning), in The Listener, *Vol. 106, No. 2737, November 26, 1981, pp. 660-61.*

PENELOPE FITZGERALD

Stevie Smith said that she was straightforward, but not simple, which is a version of not waving but drowning. She presented to the world the face which is invented when reticence goes over to the attack, and becomes mystification. If you visited Blake and were told not to sit on a certain chair because it was for the spirit of Michelangelo, or if Emily Dickinson handed you a single flower, you needed time to find out how far the mystification was meant to keep you at a distance, and to give you something to talk about when you got home. Eccentricity can go very well with sincerity, and, in Stevie's case, with shrewdness. She calculated the effect of her collection of queer hats and sticks, her face 'pale as sand', pale as her white stockings, and also, I think, of her apparent obsession with death. She was interested in death, and particularly in its willingness to oblige, she had survived a suicide attempt in 1953, she was touched by the silence of the 'countless, countless dead': but when in her sixties she felt the current running faster and 'all you want to do is to get to the waterfall and over the edge,' she still remained Florence Margaret Smith, who enjoyed her life, and, for that matter, her success. Her poetry, she told Anna Kallin, was 'not *at all whimsical*, as some asses seem to think I am, but serious, yet not aggressive, and fairly cheerful though with melancholy patches'. The melancholy was real, of course. For that reason she gave herself in her novels the name of Casmilus, a god who is permitted to come and go freely from hell. . . .

Among the ten stories [in *Me Again: Uncollected Writings of Stevie Smith*] is perhaps the most lyrical of all, '**Beside the Seaside**', a languorous *fin-de-saison* holiday impression, the pebbles of the beach still warm to the touch but deeply cold underneath, and her friends' tempers just beginning to fray. There is a variable delicate friction between the interests of wives, husbands and children, and between human beings and nature—one might say between the seaside and the sea. Helena (the Stevie of this story) detaches herself, unable to help doing so, and wanders away inland across the marshes, returning 'full of agreeable fancies and spattered with smelly mud' to confront the edginess of the party with her artist's sense of deep interior peace. In '**The Story of a Story**' she again defends herself as an artist. This wiry situation comedy shows why Stevie sometimes longed, in her character as Lot's wife, to be turned into a pillar of asphalt, since she seemed to give offence so often. Her friends did not want to become her material, as they had in '**Sunday at Home**' . . . , and her publisher hesitated, afraid of libel. 'The morning, which had been so smiling when her employer first spoke, now showed its teeth.' Sitting alone in the rainswept park, the unhappy authoress regrets the loss of friends, but much more the death of her story. She had worked on it with love to make it shining and remote, but also with 'cunning and furtiveness and care and ferocity'. These were the qualities which went into Stevie's seemingly ingenuous fiction.

About the poems . . . I am not so sure, since she herself presumably didn't want them included in the collected edition of 1975. Stevie Smith had a remarkable ear ('it's the hymns coming up, I expect') and when she was manipulated by whatever force poetry is, she knew that all she had to do was listen. She produced then a kind of counterpoint between the 'missed-shot tunes' that haunted her and the phrasing and pauses of her own speaking voice. Not all the verses in *Me Again* seem quite to reach this, although you can hear her distinctive note of loneliness, which, as she pointed out, 'runs with tiredness', in '**None of the Other Birds**' and '**Childhood and Interruption**'.

In the end, one of Stevie's greatest achievements was to be not only a connoisseur of myths, but the creator of one. Out of an unpromisingly respectable suburb at the end of the apparently endless Green Lanes she created a strange Jerusalem.

Penelope Fitzgerald, "Jerusalem" (appears here by permission of the London Review of Books *and the author), in* London Review of Books, *December 3 to December 16, 1981, p. 13.*

CAROLE ANGIER

Because of the play and film *Stevie*, many people know a bit about the poet and novelist Stevie Smith. *Me Again* is a good and welcome book, telling us more. Not much more, because Stevie Smith, though she wrote so clearly out of her own life, never gave much of herself away. But here are her stories and essays, her previously uncollected poems, and a few letters, all in her particular, sharpish voice, full of her particular wit and her particular loneliness. . . .

Several of the short stories in *Me Again*—and they are very good, perhaps the best things in it—are classics of the visitor's point of view. Here are quarrelling, loving couples, and marvellous monstrous children; the visitor half envies and half mocks, and is glad in the end she isn't them. She loves life, but she is afraid of it; she hugs to herself the thought of death as the ill-at-ease visitor comforts herself with the thought of the door. Her humour is not quite black, but grey. . . . She is honest and intelligent. But perhaps she did not allow herself to experience enough; she kept herself essentially a child—a wise child, detached, alarming, sad. . . . *Me Again* is her last wave, and, like the others it is rather small, brave and moving. (p. 187)

Carole Angier, "English Miscellaneous Writings: 'Me Again: Uncollected Writings of Stevie Smith'," in British Book News (© British Book News, 1982; courtesy of British Book News), *March, 1982, p. 187.*

LISA MITCHELL

The uncollected work assembled for "**Me Again**" is not a case of spinning a deceased artist's old notes to the milkman into timely gold. This collection, though imperfect, holds treasures. . . .

Stevie—nee Florence Margaret—Smith constantly "blurred distinctions between one form of writing and another." She quoted her poems in her stories and essays, transplanted ideas (sometimes word for word across years) from her essays to her book reviews and drew heavily from her own life in almost everything she wrote.

The stories in "**Me Again**"—and these are all of Stevie Smith's stories—are an uneven lot. The opener, "**Beside the Sea**," has shining moments but fails in its stilted speech and obvious set-ups for the Stevie character, a writer named Helen, to talk her beliefs and recite her poems at a friend. "**In the Beginning of the War**" . . . is an artful piece of eavesdropping that deliciously re-creates dialogue among some liberals of the period. And it's hard to imagine a writer among us today unable to identify with Stevie/Helen's angst in "**Story of a Story**." Having written a thinly veiled piece based on friends ("**Sunday at Home**"), she not only lost the friends, she was threatened with a libel accusation. . . .

The essays show her stunning intelligence, wit, perversity. She is sensitive, scrupulous, wise. Also smug as all get-out. She'll hang on to an idea with the grip and growl of a dog at tug-of-war, as in "**Some Impediments to Christian Commitment**." Here, and elsewhere, particularly in the poems, we see that she is almost as obsessed with Christ, with what she can and cannot accept about Christianity, as she is with death. . . .

Her book reviews . . . made up my favorite section. A reviewer for 30 years, she is emphatic, direct; enviably concise, graceful, personable. How can we not love the Stevie who wrote of Simone Weil: "It is perhaps the humility of laziness she lacks?" . . .

With the exception of **"On the Dressing gown lent me by my Hostess the Brazilian consul in Milan, 1958,"** most of [the poems] do not match the style or content of her more familiar **"Away, Melancholy"** or **"Not Waving But Drowning."** Those will be found tucked inside essays here, though there's no index to tell you that. . . .

In the last of [the letters collected here], Stevie wrote to a friend about the symptoms of an illness. But did she ever learn that they were caused by the brain tumor that was to kill her? Did she ever know she was dying? And if she did, had anyone heard what this woman, who so relentlessly welcomed Death with her pen, had to say once she actually found its hand on her shoulder? **"Me Again"** does not answer or even ask these questions.

"All the writer can do . . . ," Stevie wrote in 1956, "is offer his life, which seems to him so shadowy and inconsiderable, to some god or other . . . to chew upon and make the best of." **"Me Again"** lets Stevie Smith continue her offer.

Lisa Mitchell, "*Decades of Poetry in Anticipation of Death*" (reprinted by permission of the author), in Los Angeles Times Book Review, *July 18, 1982, p. 7.*

QUENTIN CRISP

Anyone who is what Sylvia Plath called herself—a "Smith-addict"—will find [*Me Again: Uncollected Writings of Stevie Smith*] completely absorbing. . . .

The final item in this collection—the radio play—at first appears to be a hoax, a poetry reading masquerading as drama. Gradually, however, it transpires that the Interviewer is Death, the author's "earliest love." From then on I was spellbound. One speech begins, "There is little laughter where you are going and no warmth." It reads like a translation from Rilke. A few moments such as this fully compensate for a prevailing defect that is signaled to us by the very title of the book.

Elizabeth Lutyens said that Miss Smith adopted a "deliberate 'child*ish*' manner," and added with some asperity, "Who in hell wants 'innocence' from an adult—or a child?" Innocence is the opposite of guilt and is commendable in a person of any age. What is difficult to stomach is tweeness—a crude and unscrupulous bid for praise or, at least, pardon by means of a parade of helplessness that relies heavily for its success on the notion that incompetence is the same as sincerity. This ruse affects Miss Smith's style rather than her thoughts, and the text is riddled with the fault. . . . In contrast to the sloppiness of syntax, the author's ideas are sharp—even acid. . . . Moreover, there are descriptions in this book that, even when clumsily expressed, are almost as evocative as the writing of Katherine Mansfield. (p. 52)

I recommend to everyone these bright glimpses of a woman full of sweetness but without mercy, sometimes highly talented, sometimes maddeningly inept, and always fascinating. (p. 56)

Quentin Crisp, "A Sort of Innocence: 'Me Again: Uncollected Writings of Stevie Smith' " (reprinted by permission of the author), in New York Magazine, Vol. 15, No. 29, July 26, 1982, pp. 52, 56.

JOYCE CAROL OATES

[The] heroine of **"Novel on Yellow Paper"** muses to herself, by way of alleviating—or tabulating—the "orgy of boredom" to which her soul is committed: though the voice, the quirky, rambling, ingenuous, stubborn, funny-peculiar voice, could as easily be that of any other Stevie Smith heroine. In fact, Pompey Casmilus—christened Patience—is the narrator of both **"Novel on Yellow Paper"** and **"Over the Frontier";** and the slightly more subdued Celia of **"The Holiday"** is clearly a close relation. And each chatty voice bears a close resemblance to that of Stevie Smith's own in her numerous essays, reviews and BBC talks.

Since her death in 1971 at the age of 69, Stevie Smith has been honored by considerable acclaim, both in her native England and elsewhere. Her **"Collected Poems"** has been reissued several times; a handsome gathering of her short stories, essays, drawings and reviews, **"Me Again,"** was recently published in this country; and her three novels, long out of print, have [recently] been reissued. . . . Though differing in virtually every other way from the late Jean Rhys and the late Barbara Pym, Stevie Smith shares with them a posthumous fame that shows no signs of abating and is certainly well deserved. . . . An idiosyncratic talent, invariably deemed "eccentric," very much an acquired taste: a matter, it should be said, of tone, of rhythm, of voice, that appeals to some readers immediately and to others not at all. For Stevie Smith is all talk, all bright brash forthright confession, and no pretense is made of larger poetic or novelistic ambitions. . . .

"Novel on Yellow Paper" is refreshing in its insouciance, perhaps, and in its refusal to attempt any traditional narrative technique; but the resolutely clever talking voice never varies through the 60,000 words, and the charge Stevie Smith made against James Thurber (that his tone and humor quickly became "monotonous") certainly applies to her. Initially, however, Pompey Casmilus surprises us with her directness, for it is quite as if we are given the privilege of overhearing private thoughts. . . . (p. 11)

"Novel on Yellow Paper" is a gallimaufry of opinions on such subjects as Medea, D. H. Lawrence, Racine, Goethe, Christianity and Nazism. It deals in its slapdash manner with "women's issues." . . . The chatter is occasionally sobered by thoughts of Pompey's mother's death and by thoughts of death in general. Like all improvised works, this literary curiosity strikes some inspired notes and others less inspired. Its value mainly lies in the fact that it was written by Stevie Smith at the age of 34 and that Stevie Smith went on to establish a distinct name for herself in poetry.

Yet if one looks for a self-portrait here—or in **"Over the Frontier"** and **"The Holiday"**—one is likely to be disappointed, for Stevie Smith rarely "sees" herself, and efforts at characterization are minimal. No doubt the narrator's claims for strong emotion are authentic, if we read Pompey as Stevie, but since they are not dramatized within the fictional context of the novel, they fall flat indeed. (pp. 11, 26)

"Over the Frontier," . . . continues Pompey's observations, but shifts, surprisingly and I'm afraid not altogether plausibly, to an adventure-espionage tale (or dream) that carries her "over the frontier" into war. . . . Like **"Novel on Yellow Paper,"** it is studded with small, quick, deft insights and perceptions; its thumbnail sketches of characters (like Colonel Peck, forever in search of his spectacles) will make it worthwhile reading for admirers of Stevie Smith but difficult going for others. . . .

"The Holiday," written during wartime, was not published until 1949 and was Stevie Smith's own favorite among her novels, though a contemporary reader is likely to find it too whimsical, too disjointed, too low-keyed to hold his interest except in patches. It seems to have served its author as a kind of daybook in which she could record passing opinions and memories, awkwardly linked with an ongoing "narrative." . . .

Stevie Smith wrote novels with the left hand and made no claims otherwise. She is justly celebrated for her remarkable poetry, which magically combines the rhythms of light verse (upon occasion, even greeting card verse) with the unyielding starkness of a tragic vision. She has, as Robert Lowell noted, a "unique and cheerfully gruesome voice"; and this voice is most skillfully expressed by short, tightly knit forms where insouciant rhythms can be made to dramatically serve serious subjects. One has only to read a few of her characteristic poems—**"Thoughts About the Person from Porlock," "Away Melancholy,"** the much anthologized **"Not Waving but Drowning"**—to fall under her eery spell. Here is a childlike sensibility informed by a cold, cold eye, an inimitable, because poetically constrained, voice. (p. 26)

> *Joyce Carol Oates, "A Child with a Cold, Cold Eye," in* The New York Times Book Review *(© 1982 by The New York Times Company; reprinted by permission), October 3, 1982, pp. 11, 26.*

Scott Sommer

1951-

American novelist and short story writer.

Sommer writes with a clear vision of the effects of society on contemporary youth. In prose that is alternately comic and brooding, he portrays young people coming to terms with life, love, and self in worlds that are often confusing and impersonal.

Sommer's first novel, *Nearing's Grace*, attempts to capture the nuances of the adolescent sensibility. His grasp of the vernacular and psychology of his characters supply the reader with insights into the pill-popping generation.

Sommer's astute understanding of the difficulties of being young in a rapidly changing world comes into play again in his second novel, *Last Resort*. In this work, a new college graduate faces the reality that he has no career goals and little personal security. As is true of all of Sommer's fiction, *Last Resort* moves beyond the perimeters of its story to make observations on the morality of contemporary society.

(See also *Contemporary Authors*, Vol. 106.)

© Kelly Wise

PAUL ABLEMAN

Naturally, the kids will love [Scott Sommer's *Nearing's Grace*]. It is every switched-on adolescent's private phantasy. But what of the grown-up reader? Does *Nearing's Grace* offer anything to him? The disconcerting answer is: a great deal. Because Scott Sommer turns out to be a natural writer and every discriminating reader, young or old, will derive from his book the joy of words used to illuminate, tease, delight and amuse, will, in other words, find in these pages a true, if slight, work of literature. I would like to quote a passage that will reveal Mr Sommer at his substantial best. But it is difficult because the book is written in a spaced-out vernacular that ambles along and then suddenly soars into lyricism, psychological insight and even compassionate understanding. Perhaps the best I can do is quote three metaphors from three consecutive pages. 'Memory bullied its way into my thoughts like a cop into a crowd.' 'Even as a young boy I could feel her loneliness screaming desperately as a crow.' And the charmingly indelicate: 'When she kissed me, my testicles did pushups.' It is, of course, too early to say if Mr Sommer will succeed in harnessing his talent to broader and more urgent themes in the future but this, his maiden flight, is a joy to behold.

> *Paul Ableman, "Maiden Flight," in* The Spectator *(© 1980 by* The Spectator; *reprinted by permission of* The Spectator*), Vol. 245, No. 7935, August 9, 1980, p. 21.*

PETER KEMP

Nearing's Grace by Scott Sommer is a . . . mature book: in fact, it is partly about what constitutes genuine maturity. Narrated in the first person by a college drop-out with a nice line in irony, it inevitably calls to mind *The Catcher in the Rye*— especially as Henry Nearing also shares Holden Caulfield's

preoccupation with death: he rides a motor-bike called Thanatos and writes imaginary letters to his dead mother. The world he sardonically surveys, however, is very different from Holden Caulfield's. College sex is no longer a matter of heavy petting but strenuous all-night sessions fuelled by coke and Quaaludes.

For all their sexy rompings, the book's characters finally emerge as forlorn. Their hectic hedonism increasingly seems a panic-flight from the pressures of reality. . . .

Nearing himself is a virtuoso of irony—it is his real grace. Thanks to it, the book's sad facts are given very funny formulations.

> *Peter Kemp, "Sicker Roses" (© British Broadcasting Corp. 1980; reprinted by permission of Peter Kemp), in* The Listener, *Vol. 104, No. 2675, August 21, 1980, p. 249.**

JONATHAN BAUMBACH

A kind of hip, post-1960's despair informs ["**Lifetime,**" an] impressive collection of two novellas and three stories, the charm of the style in counterpoise to the anguish of the experience. To survive, Scott Sommer's characters take refuge in booze, drugs, sex, madness—anything to take the edge off loneliness and pain. All relationships in the corrupted world of these fictions are transient. In **"Waiting for Merna,"** the temporary absence of the unemployed narrator's lover seems a rehearsal for an inevitable, permanent loss. The distraught older son in **"Sickness,"** abandoned by wife and child, has returned to the madhouse of his parents' home. Mahoney, the hero of the title novella, has lost a woman he loves before the story starts and loses three more before the story is over. Love, which is of limited duration in this fictional world (and illusory perhaps even then), ends characteristically in disrepair and regret.

If the strategy of these stories tends to be post-modern in its imaginative use of literary form, the sensibility is romantic in the way of J. D. Salinger and F. Scott Fitzgerald. The brilliant **"Entrapped and Abandoned"** is presented as an imaginary love letter from the narrator, Taplinger, to a woman named Felice, whom he has provoked into leaving him. The narrator's nostalgia is the occasion of the story. . . .

The compressed form of **"Lifetime"**—the action takes place over seven days and seven nights—and the surprise of the language permit the novella to transcend its near bathetic resolution. **"Lifetime"** has the resonance of a full-length novel and is the most ambitious fiction in this collection. The pleasures of the style are not the least of its rewards. (p. 7)

The longest piece, **"Crisscross,"** narrated by an astonishingly precocious 10-year-old named Christopher, is the virtuoso performance of the collection. Set in Key West, **"Crisscross,"** like "The Adventures of Huckleberry Finn" and "The Catcher in the Rye," offers us an innocent's view of a casually depraved world. Abandoned by his father and mostly neglected by his childlike alcoholic mother, Christopher participates in the bizarre life around him like a parody of an adult. . . . Christopher's lot as a child bereft of childhood is implicitly poignant, but the action (the boy's misadventures in dope traffic) never quite moves us. The self-insistent charm of the narration works against the novella's deeper impulses, distracts us from its seriousness.

Despite a facility that tends to call attention to itself, Scott Sommer is a genuine discovery. He is a young writer—**"Lifetime"** is his second book—of exceptional resources of language and vision, an ironic chronicler of social depravity among fallen innocents. While these sad dazzling fictions are a legacy of growing up cool in the 60's, they are also—the other side of that sensibility—old-fashionedly romantic, disarming dirges for a world hopelessly lost. (p. 37)

Jonathan Baumbach, "Among Fallen Innocents," in The New York Times Book Review (© 1981 by The New York Times Company; reprinted by permission), April 12, 1981, pp. 7, 37.

ROBERT TOWERS

Even low-rent tragedies demand characters of some definition and grit. Those who populate *Lifetime,* a collection of three stories and two novellas by Scott Sommer, are, with one exception, too undone, too disintegrated or amorphous, to put up a fight. (p. 38)

Too often Sommer seems to be indulging in *Schadenfreude* at the expense of his characters; the laying on of woe becomes too easy, like the rhyming of *Hertz* and *Schmertz* in German Romantic poetry.

The only protagonist not totally defeated by life is the ten-year-old narrator of **"Crisscross."** Eerily precocious, Coke tells us about the goings-on among the drug-obsessed inhabitants of a sordid Key West hotel and his own involvement—at first innocent and then "street-wise"—in the cocaine traffic. Though he too is a victim—fatherless, and to all effects abandoned by his promiscuous, drug-besotted mother—the fact that Coke at least is still able to stand up and fight lends a certain hectic vitality to this curious novella. He has some language, too, that rises above the low-keyed monotone of heartbreak that prevails elsewhere. (pp. 38-9)

Sommer is not yet a master of his art. He has not found a voice of his own that he can use with real confidence. He is given to certain jarring mannerisms and a tendency to undermine his effects by cool, throwaway comments and self-consciously literary intrusions. . . . Above all, he is unable to persuade me that his vision of universal bleakness is fully earned. But in each of the pieces with the exception of **"Sickness,"** which I found vapid and unconvincing, there are passages of real power and incisiveness, phrases that one would like to have written; and two of the stories—**"Waiting for Merna"** and **"Crisscross"**—succeed well enough to make Scott Sommer's work worth following. (p. 39)

Robert Towers, "Low-Rent Tragedies," in The New York Review of Books (reprinted with permission from The New York Review of Books; copyright © 1981 Nyrev, Inc.), Vol. XXVIII, No. 8, May 14, 1981, pp. 37-40.*

SANDRA SALMANS

[In *Nearing's Grace,* Scott Sommer has] made the mistake of straining for profundity where none exists. The result is a book that never quite lives up to its ambitions, either comic or cosmic, and even in the short space of 175 pages manages to lapse all too frequently into tedium. . . .

[Henry Nearing], like most of the characters in the book, is neither dislikeable nor particularly interesting. . . .

In fact, although he is the narrator of *Nearing's Grace,* Henry has never really come alive; with no distinguishing physical or psychological marks, he is less vivid than most of the other characters, including the oversexed Grace and her lacrosse stick-swinging boyfriend Lance. Sommer's most successful character is Merna, a would-be songwriter who is afraid that she may be the last virgin in suburbia. Her much-publicized availability—she acquires simultaneously a diaphragm and birth-control pills—is one of the nicer touches in the book.

Sandra Salmans, "The High School Hedonists," in The Times Literary Supplement (© Times Newspapers Ltd. (London) 1981; reproduced from The Times Literary Supplement by permission), No. 4039, August 22, 1981, p. 930.

BARRY TARGAN

[The title story of Scott Sommer's *Lifetime*] is far richer in ironies and complexities and characters than a brief description can convey. And it is richer in this sense than the other admirable stories in the collection because thematically it ranges more widely, reaches up into the possibility and the condition of love and the chance for a kind of personal salvation even as it measures the more terrifyingly bleak likelihoods.

In Sommer's other stories we are not always sure enough about why his characters have succumbed so completely or so quickly to their self-destructive (and self-pitying) condition. Surely there are people ''like this,'' yet they are not simply or widely representative of life's options. Surely life does not fail so completely. But I do not think that the narrowed focus of the stories should be mistaken for Sommer's deeper idea. He is not saying that we are all like this—freakish malcontents, drug pushers, whores, 10-year-old burnt-out cases, seething sufferers. Rather I think he intends for us to realize that he is looking at an infection (the sick disease of modern life) and the prognosis is not good. If Sommer's fiction is, as I believe, socially diagnostic, then his method and style are fitting, where often we see and hear a dispassionate, tough reporting, a seeing but not necessarily a judging, a level presentation of characters who are themselves often not level or calm, who are often outrageous or glibly sardonic or teeth-grindingly angry or simply stupid. Colorfully vapid. Sommer's approach is to present the texture more than the shape of the consequences of three-quarters of a century of human debasement.

> *Barry Targan, ''In the Province of the Story,'' in* Book World—The Washington Post *(© 1981, The Washington Post), August 30, 1981, p. 10.**

TODD WALTON

Scott Sommer's second novel, **''Last Resort,''** might have been better as a longish short story. As it stands, the book contains more padding than substance. . . .

[Most] of Scott Sommer's writing is uneven, his syntax sometimes atrocious: ''The sun was upon us. By way of apology, I wanted to steal some of its mercy and give it to Leah, wrapped in ribbon.'' I don't think this was supposed to be New Wave prose, but if it was, that could explain it.

What, then, was the idea that spawned **''Last Resort''**? I think it might have been the question: What would happen if a boy / man met the perfect woman (whatever that means) *before* he was ready for her? How would he feel and what would he do? Scott Sommer's answer seems to be: Not much. The perfect woman will love the boy / man no matter how selfish and insensitive he is, even if he never changes. (p. 12)

> *Todd Walton, ''Love with Complications,'' in* The New York Times Book Review *(© 1982 by The New York Times Company; reprinted by permission), April 25, 1982, pp. 12, 16.**

JOAN SILBER

Tramp Bottoms [protagonist of *Last Resort*] is getting nowhere trying to be a rock star, won't marry his terrific girlfriend because he knows he'll just make her miserable, and has come home to the Jersey shore to brood about the whole thing. ''How at twenty-five my whole life had come to absolutely nothing was a mystery for which I needed a clue. You get older, I suppose, and things have a way of slipping through your fingers.'' So far (that quote appears on page one) the hero is not likely to get sympathy from anyone over 26.

But if the central dilemma never seems all that urgent, Sommer's writing is skilled enough to give the book some occasional lyric flashes. . . . He also has a knack for varieties of stylized dialogue, and even his broader characterizations are clever without being really mean; the tone is humane, if a little glibly forlorn. (pp. 54, 109)

[Still, there] is something naïve in Tramp's desire for worldly success (which is too easily satisfied by the end of the book), and even in his true-blue fondness for Leah, who has been his sweetheart since childhood. . . . [Sommer] seems unclear about how much distance he has on his character, and how much we are meant to take Tramp's darkly crabby speculations about life as real wisdom. In the end, despite Tramp's claim that he has made it to adulthood without the benefit of any usable models or ''tyrannies of custom or habit,'' his self-absorption remains the controlling tone of the book, a kind of rippling inventiveness within narrow limits. (p. 109)

> *Joan Silber, ''Brief Encounters: 'Last Resort''' (reprinted by permission of* The Village Voice *and the author; copyright © News Group Publications, Inc., 1982), in* The Village Voice, *Vol. XXVII, No. 18, May 4, 1982, pp. 54, 109.*

RICHARD PEABODY, JR.

It's a truism of contemporary life that a man's career often comes before family and friends. Scott Sommer's [*Last Resort*] explores this predicament and its effects on an aspiring rock 'n' roll singer-songwriter named Tramp Bottoms. . . .

Despite the tragic elements, and the fatalistic commentary on the nuclear family in America today, Sommer can't help but paint an optimistic picture. Tramp's prideful conflict with Leah—his career in music is promising only as compared to her relative success landing a book contract—seems ludicrous. Leah's love for Tramp appears equally unjustified but we come to appreciate his irresistible incompetence.

Well drawn adults buffer the star-struck children. The novel's poignancy is provided by Tramp's crippled sister (who, like all seondary women in Sommer's fiction, is loyal, supportive, and wise), and by his father's desperate pursuit of childhood with radio-controlled ships and planes. The dialogue is fast-paced. Sommer expects the reader to be familiar with the names of rock groups and songs. If you're not, you may miss some of the humor.

Success might have come too easily for Sommer. His writing has a wonderful vitality but little discipline. Naming the main characters Tramp Bottoms, Leah Summit, and Owen Chance is *too* cute. And dividing the book into three-parts—Breakups, Breakdowns, and Breakthroughs—is a failure of imagination. The song lyrics that wend their way throughout the book are weaker still. And yet, Owen Chance—Tramp's hip bisexual manager—is unforgettable. . . . If the 31-year-old Sommer hasn't peaked too soon he may yet write something worthy of his talent.

> *Richard Peabody, Jr., ''Fiction: 'Last Resort','' in* Best Sellers *(copyright © 1982 Helen Dwight Reid Educational Foundation), Vol. 42, No. 4, July, 1982, p. 133.*

James Tate

1943-

American poet.

Tate's literary career began with a flourish; his first volume of poems, *The Lost Pilot,* earned him the Yale Series of Younger Poets Award in 1966, as well as an enthusiastic critical interest. His poems were hailed for their striking surreal images, their unpretentious natural grace, and the balance between a comic lightness of surface tone and an underlying depth of somber suggestion.

In the decade following *The Lost Pilot,* Tate published several volumes of poetry. Critics noted throughout this period Tate's creative invention of metaphor, his frequent use of dream images, and his dramatic vocabulary. Noted too, were his self-assured manner and his cynical tone aimed at a wide range of contemporary ills. In his recent collections, *Viper Jazz* and *Riven Doggeries,* Tate continues to move toward the notion that communication and connection with the world outside the individual's mind are impossible.

(See also *CLC,* Vols. 2, 6; *Contemporary Authors,* Vols. 21-24, rev. ed; and *Dictionary of Literary Biography,* Vol. 5.)

Photograph by Edward T. Bissell, Northampton, MA

THE VIRGINIA QUARTERLY REVIEW

Missing, from ["**Notes of Woe**"], is the kind of emotional directness found in the title poem of Tate's first collection, "**The Lost Pilot.**" More in evidence is this young poet's great virtuosity. In consequence, the book is flawed. The desperation here (as reflected in the title, from Blake) is not always convincing: it has too much style. The reader is fascinated by what Tate can do with language, but the poems too often just remain on that level. Nevertheless, there is no lack of wit and brilliance, and some poems do everything; for example, "**Camping in the Valley.**" . . . (pp. xciv, xcvi)

> "*Notes on Current Books: 'Notes of Woe',*" *in* The Virginia Quarterly Review *(copyright, 1969, by* The Virginia Quarterly Review, *The University of Virginia), Vol. 45, No. 2 (Spring, 1969), pp. xciv, xcvi.*

STEPHEN DOBYNS

James Tate's *Torches* was a complete disappointment, which at first just irritated and then angered me. It seemed as if Tate had gathered up unused images, put them into a machine, and ground out poems like inferior sausages. Any poet has a fondness for his weak poems, but this is no excuse for finding them comfortable homes. They should be strangled, and the poet should move on.

I'm sure I wouldn't have been so disappointed if I hadn't read Tate before. The book has a few good poems, but none of them are up to other things he has done. . . .

The ending of [*The Sleepers*], and of most of the poems in this book, seems gratuitous. It's quite easy to compile any number of images, tack on a line like James Wright's "I have wasted my life," and call it a poem. At best the endings in this book

don't add to the poems. At worst they don't have anything to do with them.

The images themselves are neither very original nor very striking. . . . It is quite an accomplishment to bore a reader in an eight line poem. (p. 396)

> *Stephen Dobyns, "Five Poets," in* Poetry *(©1971 by The Modern Poetry Association; reprinted by permission of the Editor of* Poetry*), Vol. CXVII, No. 6, March, 1971, pp. 392-98.**

VICTOR HOWES

The poems [in *Viper Jazz* by] . . . James Tate occupy the tenuous borderland between nonsense and disaster. Whether he is spoofing a cosmic ultimatum . . . or blowing up a microcosmic annoyance . . . , his poems, like Halloween masks, elicit a double response. Do we laugh or cry?

Tate is concerned with everything from alienation to ecological mismanagement, from exploitation to automation. His keen awareness of the unfitness of things shows up in his absurd handling of language. . . .

Traditionally, absurdist art is accused of lacking seriousness. Like his contemporaries in the world of wackiness, Vonnegut and Barthelme, Tate often allows his fascination with ideas to carry him further than anyone wants to go. . . .

Still, there is a fine blend of lightness and sadness that plays across the face of these poems, a comic sense of the "tears of things" that prompts us to say, as Kent said of the songs and riddles of King Lear's court jester, "This is not altogether fool, My Lord."

> Victor Howes, "Tate: Wacky Seriousness," in The Christian Science Monitor (reprinted by permission from The Christian Science Monitor; © 1976 The Christian Science Publishing Society; all rights reserved), October 28, 1976, p. 27.

STANLEY PLUMLY

James Tate is a poet of fine intuitive intelligence. His quick-hit/near-miss use of the poetic punch line has led him into wider imaginative territory and more cul-de-sacs than any other poet of his generation. His risks are a vital part of the take. That is why, for a lot of readers, Tate presents problems. He is a genius of the double take, double-think, whether it is humor needling despair or platitude succumbing to perception. He can edit an experience down to its most evocative chord. . . . But Tate can also be an adolescent, unable or unwilling to resist the easy turn, the silly contrivance, Rimbaud at thirteen. . . . Both categories are from the poet's latest collection, *Viper Jazz*. And although this new book, on the whole, represents Tate's most mature work, it still suggests that certain destructive impulses in much of the earlier poetry have yet to be resolved. Perhaps the "fault" is not entirely Tate's. He is one of the few younger poets with a following. One sometimes senses that at strategic points in many of his poems—for whatever complex of reasons—he chooses entertainment over engagement. Consciously or not, he acknowledges his audience, or plays to that part of his nature that would put his readers on. At any rate, he indulges himself at the poetry's expense. Tate's poems begin in pain, not emotional fudge. At some of these moments when the absurdities become all too clear, and in frustration with the facts, he tends to opt for fun. The ambiguities break down. The rewards for fancy, one supposes, are more immediate than those of imagination. What is required is an art that Tate himself is so often master of: to never allow the intensity to be in debt to the comedy. It is a story as old as satire, and, finally, Tate may come to be regarded chiefly in such a hybrid contemporary coincidence: tragical satire. Because the underpinning of the best work in *Viper Jazz* is an *angst* that demands analogy at the deepest imaginative level, while keeping its "difficult balance" at the top. . . . The maturity of the new poems is the result of a consistency of vision in which the double-think does not lose its poise. Overall, Tate is more sure of and more open about what his real concerns are. If the potential for insidiousness as suggested by the book's title is in apparent contradiction to the vulnerability in most of the poems, we must assume there is method in it. Viper Jazz is not simply the presiding metaphor, it is the book's prevailing attitude: it is Tate's gloss of his relationship to his material. . . . Tate has never said his say better. . . . [He] has been praised and blamed too long for the populist surrealism of Rock. He is a satirist, perhaps even a satyr, whose absurdist targets range wide around a persona whose tragic mask keeps slipping—and sad without hands, and unable to speak for the wind that chips away at him. (pp. 45-6)

> Stanley Plumly, "Books: 'Viper Jazz'" (copyright ©1976 by World Poetry, Inc.; reprinted by permis-

sion of Stanley Plumly), in The American Poetry Review, Vol. 5, No. 6, November-December, 1976, pp. 45-6.

WILLIAM LOGAN

The allegiance James Tate announced in *The Lost Pilot*, his first book, was to a surrealism that would inform and interpret the familiar. In his subsequent work, though that early pledge has not been forsworn, there has appeared with increasing frequency an acknowledgment of failure, a suggestion that nothing, not even surrealism, will work as a method any longer, even that language, or communication its bastard son, has become impossible. . . . It is typical of Tate's perversity that he defines absence in the terms of presence, but his method has always been devoted to the conjugation of opposites: the surreal with the real, the colloquial with the serious, entropy with energy. His non-sequiturs may become violently yoked aphorisms. More than any of his books, *Viper Jazz* celebrates the notion that no thing may refer to anything else, that the lines of communication are all down, that continuity may no longer be possible. Nothing is certain. . . . No single conjunction of word and meaning may be less valid than any other.

Viper Jazz is an uneven book, but Tate's method is uneven. His jazzy, improvisatory technique consists of luminous moments of virtuosity played against a flurry of accretion, a blizzard of one-liners. When the poems succeed, they succeed despite their method, as would the classics if composed by computers. The fortunate poems inform despite failures of communication; they flirt with the actual despite a marriage to negation. Their victories are startling, then, because of method, and for subject they often claim nothing more than method—they are about their own inability to communicate.

Tate's intelligence is fascinating and brittle; if one is impatient with it, his poems frustrate. These new poems eschew control in exchange for a possible pregnancy of meaning and association impossible when the subject shapes the form. They witness a despair, a desperate struggle against language, against subject, against the successes of the past. The sense of looming failure at the heart of composition, that desperation that can both engender writing and spoil it, is the energy on which Tate's poems subsist. . . . These poems have few of the skills of poetry, but many of prose. Tate can write unbelievably badly. He is incomprehensible . . . and incoherent . . . , merely silly . . . and banal. . . . His lunacy and slapstick, however, can be fruitful; they throw the reader off-guard, and allow Tate to stumble sometimes into a moment quite wonderful. . . . (pp. 221-22)

In a book of sixty-eight poems, there are perhaps a dozen that pass safely across the thin ice, intense utterances that defeat the negation they are formed from. Those poems, including *A Voyage from Stockholm, Liaisons, A Radical Departure, Many Problems, A Box for Tom*, and *Disease*, imply in their titles the connections, physical and social, that are the circuits of their success. Otherwise, it is just one damned poem after another, a hell of small conceptions and maniacal blitherings. (p. 223)

> William Logan, "Language against Fear," in Poetry (©1977 by The Modern Poetry Association; reprinted by permission of the Editor of Poetry), Vol. CXXX, No. 4, July, 1977, pp. 221-29.*

STEPHEN KIRKPATRICK

[The] poet, and this I think applies to James Tate, can slip into a private world where his unique juxtapositions and fresh imagery are often meaningless to the reader. . . . There is no way the poet can judge the potential of his imagery except in relation to other elements of the poem. And here is the main problem I find with Tate's poetry [in *Viper Jazz*]; for he works with startling phrases and uncommon imagery almost exclusively. If they don't work there's little else in the poem to save it; more importantly, with little else working—rhythm, sound— readers are denied access points to what otherwise might be effective imagery for them. The sense element of poetic composition, however, is working in Tate's poetry. The active and intelligent voice, with a self-assured casualness, is the contrary of his surreal metaphorical devices, and the dynamic of the two generates great power in the imagery when it does work. . . .

*Stephen Kirkpatrick, "Trade Reviews: 'Viper Jazz',"
in* AB Bookman's Weekly *(© 1977 by A B Bookman
Publications, Inc.), Vol. 60, Nos. 2 & 3, July 11-
18, 1977, p. 142.*

THE VIRGINIA QUARTERLY REVIEW

Tate's [*Riven Doggeries*] is disturbingly defensive. The central characteristic of these poems is their impenetrability, at best ordering experience through savage parodies, wordplay, and grotesque wit; at worst assaulting the reader and denying any kind of meaning, linguistic or existential. In this extreme form of expressionism, neither narrative nor visual logic is possible; incoherence and solipsism are the rule. Futility of action, failure of love, and lack of spiritual comfort form depressing themes, yet Tate never loses his self-effacing humor and even, in his more successful poems, an elegiac tone.

"Poetry: 'Riven Doggeries'," in The Virginia Quarterly Review *(copyright, 1980, by* The Virginia Quarterly Review, *The University of Virginia), Vol. 56,
No. 1 (Winter, 1980), p. 26.*

JAMES FINN COTTER

Nothing at all controls James Tate's choice of metaphors, similes, images, or statements in his new book of poetry. The title poem, **"Riven Doggeries,"** reads like a page from the comics. . . . Like verbal doodling, whatever pops into the poet's mind crops up in the poem. Tate has a fine ear for inane colloquialisms and absurd figures of speech, but this volume is a far cry from the austere beauty of *Absences* and its probing of the Self. Perhaps success, which gives even the most sensitive poet second thoughts about his own seriousness, has caused Tate to become too cunning and whimsical. . . . Sometimes a ray of satire peeps through, as in **"The Life of Poetry"** . . . , but even here the humor becomes sophomoric. (p. 140)

James Finn Cotter, "Poetry, Ego, and Self," in The
Hudson Review *(copyright © 1980 by The Hudson
Review, Inc.; reprinted by permission), Vol. XXXIII,
No. 1, Spring, 1980, pp. 131-45.**

CALVIN BEDIENT

Tate has been visible as a poet so long . . . that one is dismayed to find him still stuck in adolescence [with the poems in *Riven Doggeries*]. The silliness, defiance of "authority," high spirits, blurted obscenities, and puerile cleverness of his poetry are perhaps confused, by some, with spunky American originality. . . .

What might save Tate for poetry? Perhaps doses of Indian poems . . . , for at moments Tate already writes in their happy animistic spirit . . . . But unlike, say, the Swampy Cree with their ancient imaginative culture, Tate has only his manically riven wits to sustain him, and the path he has chosen—his will-never-say-Uncle manner—cannot be easy to go down alone, especially if one is skipping with a vengeance. In any event the one thing Tate needs to take seriously is the triviality of mere nose-thumbing at seriousness. (pp. 484-85)

Calvin Bedient, "New Confessions," in The Sewanee Review *(reprinted by permission of the editor;
© 1980 by The University of the South), Vol.
LXXXVIII, No. 3, Summer, 1980, pp. 474-88.**

WILLIAM H. PRITCHARD

James Tate's . . . [*Riven Doggeries*] contains few surprises, is thoroughly in the mode of his increasingly extravagant previous work . . . , and [from the start of the title poem] we are off and running into an art which not only resists paraphrase but actively cultivates the resistance. Tate's practice is nowhere less than professional, his manner always self-assured even when (as is usually the case) not much of a future for the self is seen. . . . (p. 295)

Tate is not one to stay around for a long conversation with the reader. If his brisk insouciance is appealing . . . , it can also feel a bit relentless. One wonders if perhaps he's all "outer," and whether since the "inner" has been thoroughly suppressed or unexpressed, there is as much play in the poems as first appears. . . . Admirers of John Ashbery will perk up their ears. . . . But when it's all surprise, never a line but what one could never have predicted, it becomes all too easy to take in anything without blinking. So the surprise gets dissipated; it's just James Tate, doing his thing once more. (p. 296)

William H. Pritchard, "Play's the Thing," in Poetry
*(© 1980 by The Modern Poetry Association; re-
printed by permission of the Editor of* Poetry), *Vol.
CXXXVI, No. 5, August, 1980, pp. 295-304.**

MARK RUDMAN

Riven Doggeries is James Tate's most accessible book since his first, *The Lost Pilot*, but not necessarily his best. *Absences* still moves me more than anything else he's written. In it he retains elements of despair, anger, rage: it is surrealism with a razor-edge and transcends the boundaries of any *ism*. By comparison *Riven Doggeries* is surrealism with a dacquiri. . . .

Tate's way to the sublime is *through* the ridiculous because, for him, the sublime is ridiculous. His struggle has been to make language counteract the banality of everyday life and the threat of "oblivion." Tate's aesthetic position is such that even if we could make sense out of our experience we couldn't express it in words since expressive language and poetic diction consist of two components, both negative—cliches and hyperboles—and he uses them so unusually that he highlights their absurdity. (p. 42)

Inventing new metaphors is Tate's gift. It is this ability that gives his work its intermittent unity and integration and allows him to get a multitude of dictions into his poems. It is the freshness of his metaphors that creates the context necessary for him to experiment with language in the way he does. He knows the secret pleasures of words as things in themselves, is fascinated by topicality, revels in novelty, and avoids the randomness that could so easily afflict one who possessed less art. . . .

Even the titles of his books are complex, multi-leveled metaphors that operate like codes and until you break them his whole enterprise in books like **The Oblivion Ha-Ha** and **Riven Doggeries** could appear impenetrable, deceptive as a "ha-ha." . . . **Riven Doggeries** is the verbal equivalent of this optical trick. Tate manages to find words with many shadings. "Riven," with its connotations of being divided, rent, torn asunder, is a clue to the feeling that permeates this book—ambivalence. A word like "doggeries," linked to a book of poems immediately makes you think of doggerel. He's counting on you to think this but the word really means foul or obscene language, mean or contemptible behavior, doglike practices, mischievous doings. So that the title **Riven Doggeries** suggests a merging of the sublime and the ridiculous, of hieratic speech and doggerel.

Tate writes as though he were born as a Surrealist, as though Surrealism were not the lens through which he chose to see the world, his adopted aesthetic. . . . What John Berger has to say about Surrealism as it stood just after World War I still holds true: "The Surrealists were wry commentators on a reality that was already outbidding them." . . .

And the problem with surrealism as Tate employs it in **Riven Doggeries** is that the method itself contains a total denial of history. What seemed to be a radical aesthetic ten years ago is utterly conservative now. The clarity, for example, of Charles Reznikoff, makes us look up from the page and see the awesome, beautiful and horrible strangeness of most everything that surrounds us; whereas the straining after weird effects in many of Tate's poems rubs salt into the wound to the point of numbness. Shock tactics have ceased to shock. Black humor has turned bilious. It's like sticking your hand into an empty can—it touches nothing—doesn't hurt—but still comes out bloody. . . .

It is one thing to be a surrealist out of a belief in the irrational and another to believe that the irrational may be the biggest joke of all—*and it may be.* . . . It's not so much the sourceless terror that I object to but the hollow laughter that Tate seems intent on eliciting. A kind of humor pervades most of the poems but sometimes pure nihilism is masked as vision masked as projection.

At this point cynicism is Tate's response to the human condition. It's as though in order to escape the feeling of dread (which is necessary anyway if poetry is to exist) he's walled off all possibilities, the good as well as the bad. Used in this way cynicism doesn't admit to any possible alteration of the state of things; it is a mask, a defense against emotion. By denying the possibility of change Tate also denies the possibility of feeling, of certain feelings, and any felt need for action, or that we can have any effect on our destiny whatever. No moral universe remains. What if, after all, there really is, in the end, nothing. (p. 43)

Tate's perceptions of what is wrong with the world are acute but instead of saying "No! in thunder!" in response to the way things are he retreats to the sidelines and mocks the mockers.

His response to experience that might elicit grief in others is equivalent to a refusal or incapacity to mourn. . . .

But the defense mechanism of cynicism is not the issue here. It's an easy posture to adopt and a difficult one to live with. The stance of the cynics (and I want to use this term now as an aesthetic as well as an emotional one) is that they know in advance how everything is going to end and it doesn't really matter what happens between now and then. Tate retains some elements of satire yet even so the cynicism outweighs the rage. . . .

Tate refuses to be duped by false necessities or seduced by easy attainments. He is decisively against sententiousness and raids the territories that are most prone to this flaw. . . . Tate continually poses interesting formal problems for himself to solve. What I like about the kind of difficulty we encounter in such language-based poetry is that each time we decipher another element the meaning accretes.

"River's Story" is a good instance of how Tate's imagination works when it's working well and I found it to be one of the most compelling poems in the book. I can't locate any self behind the "I" in most of these poems but an authentic voice comes through here where the "I" is submerged in the guise of a playful narrative, a story about the idea of "story," in a poem that evolves out of and is a variation on the words "river" and "lake." Even the movement of the poem is consistent with the way a river flows into a lake: notice how it builds—plashing, rushing, widening, contracting. (p. 44)

Tate is writing about a world without comfort or haven, but he and "river" are doomed to go on with this unpromising search for refuge. Tate makes us feel "river's" humiliation keenly. He's imagined a world full of thoughtless people who inflict pain without knowing what they're doing (without calculating the effect of, or taking responsibility for their actions) and the arbitrariness of their behavior makes him (his persona and stand-ins) jumpy. . . .

Tate is never complacent and he's not feigning pain. His teeth have always been set on edge and I only wish he would vent his rage more openly. He has the capacity to catch us off guard, question our assumptions, make us laugh and hurt—long after we've read the poems. But if he allows the severance between language and emotion to get any wider he's in danger of falling through one of his own trapdoors, and his poetry will cease to communicate. I won't accept "'Incipient autism'" (**"I Got a Little Flat Off 3rd & Yen"**) as an excuse for his meandering too far from human concerns. Tate has too much going for him; he's quick-witted, spontaneous, and knows how to think on his feet. And these are things that can't be taught. . . .

I think that **Riven Doggeries** is a transitional book and that Tate is trying to leaven his cynicism, work his way out of the maze, the shattered prism, the labyrinth of self and mind he's created, to gain the lightness necessary for genuine laughter and feeling. (p. 45)

Mark Rudman, "Private but No Less Ghostly Worlds" (copyright © 1981 by World Poetry, Inc.; reprinted by permission of Mark Rudman), in The American Poetry Review, *Vol. 10, No. 4, July-August, 1981, pp. 39-46.**

Alexander (Louis) Theroux

1939-

American novelist.

Theroux is known for his ornately stylized prose and elaborate word plays. Though his themes are serious, Theroux's presentation is in a comic, sometimes satiric, vein.

His novels are unique and critically controversial. His first novel, *Three Wogs*, for example, gives three accounts of racial prejudice in England in such an energetic style that it is called alternately "exasperating" and "refreshing." With Theroux's recent work, *Darconville's Cat*, the controversy continues. As the force of this novel lies in its style rather than in its content, some critics have accused Theroux of losing contact with his characters in cascades of verbalism, repetition, and obscure turns of phrase. Other critics, however, find a consistency between the matter and manner of Theroux's works, suggesting that *Darconville's Cat*, like *Three Wogs*, is as much about love, betrayal, and life as it is about words.

(See also *CLC*, Vol. 2 and *Contemporary Authors*, Vols. 85-88.)

© Kelly Wise

DIANE JOHNSON

"Wogs" are what English bigots call dark-skinned non-Englishmen. [Alexander Theroux's first novel *Three Wogs*] is a book in which types of English bigot— old ladies, aristocrats, working men—encounter three Wogs—a Chinese, an Indian, and an African. It is not a novel but three long stories, successful in varying degrees, given the initial romantic proposition that all Wogs are good, because they are uncorrupted by civilization. And all Englishmen, supposedly civilized, are bad, premises one doesn't really bother to challenge in a comic and highly stylized work like this. Because English bigots are uncomfortably like American ones, it is alarming enough without trying to be believable.

In the first story, Mrs. Proby, American Alexander Theroux's first target, "gets hers": a fatal blow-dart from Mr. Yunnum Fun, her grocer, to whom she has been systematically rude for years. This seems to me at least partly to justify her apprehensions about him ("He's sneaky"). In the third story a posh homosexual cleric tries to dissuade his African choirmaster from marrying. The best story describes an exchange between a young red-neck named Roland and a saintly little Indian named Dilip at a train depot. . . .

A cautionary word about the style, which at its best, offers happy surprises; at other times exasperation. . . . The language is always interesting and can be rewarding. But you have to be in the mood.

> Diane Johnson, "Wog Good, Us Bad," in Book World—Chicago Tribune (© 1972 Postrib Corp.; reprinted by permission of Chicago Tribune and The Washington Post), Vol. VI, No. 7, February 13, 1972, p. 8.

THE TIMES LITERARY SUPPLEMENT

There have been good modern novels written about the British by "outsiders", usually Indians and West Indians. *All About Mr. Hatterr* and *The Prevalence of Witches* are outstanding examples. Alexander Theroux is an American, and *Three Wogs* has the impact and the slightly fantastic quality shared by these two forerunners. Indeed, the proliferating energy of the style is the most remarkable thing about it, together with a love for words found only in the very largest dictionaries: "cep", "haptic", "syzygy", "mattoid", "benthic". . . .

The total effect is very refreshing. Such an original and beautifully written first novel doesn't come along often.

> "Colour Chart," in The Times Literary Supplement (© Times Newspapers Ltd. (London) 1973; reproduced from The Times Literary Supplement by permission), No. 3722, July 6, 1973, p. 783.

MILES DONALD

Three Wogs by Alexander Theroux apparently consists of three separate vignettes of racial prejudice in England. I say 'apparently' because the actual subject matter of the stories hardly counts; their real concern is Mr. Theroux's unrequited love affair with his own prose style. Since my accusation is of the kind which has been levelled by most philistines against most great stylists, let me quote one of the many sentences in which Mr. Theroux convicts himself of being drunk in charge of a thesaurus:

> It was high tea: the perfervid ritual in England which daily sweetens the ambiance of the discriminately invited and that nothing short of barratry, a provoked shaft of lightning, the King's own enemies, or an act of God could ever hope to bring to an end.

That of course has nothing to do with high tea, or the English; it merely reflects Mr. Theroux's narcissistic pleasure in his own powers of observation. Still, annoying as such a sentence may be, it doesn't come close to the central problem of the book, which is that it turns on an American's grotesque misapprehension of England, English life and that version of the English language spoken outside the United States. The central character of each story is a huge repository of unwanted and misplaced slang. Mr. Theroux's defence may be that he is attempting to parody; but parody like any other form has to select, to suggest, and when we encounter an upper-class cleric saying 'What I mean is, when she'll bubble, he'll squeak. Wouldn't that be more bang on?', I feel as if we are in at the start of some new and perverse form of lexical game, in which a prize is awarded for the most persistently unidentifiable assembly of idioms. And there is something particularly distasteful in putting important social issues to such a use.

Miles Donald, "Shaker Country," in New Statesman *(© 1973 The Statesman & Nation Publishing Co. Ltd.), Vol. 86, No. 2209, July 20, 1973, p. 95.**

JACK BEATTY

"None would wish it longer." Thus Dr. Johnson on *Paradise Lost.* Thus any reader not named Theroux on *Darconville's Cat.* Still, if you have a month to spare and want to put muscle on your vocabulary, you might dip into it, only go slowly, one toe at a time, as if the book were a Maine bay. It's actually a romance about a young professor at a Virginia girls' college who falls in love, as one might fall into the maw of Mount Saint Helens, with an even younger student, whom he courts, and is on the point of marrying when she calls it off. She (Isabel) loves a sailor, you see. Darconville, the spurned professor, takes revenge by writing this novel, which, among many other things, is a summa of misogyny. Darconville's bad luck in love is not the main source of this spleen; it is the teaching of Dr. Crucifer, a gypsy scholar who haunts the attic of Harvard's Adams House, where Darconville goes to teach after being jilted by Isabel. Dr. Crucifer is a self-administered eunuch, an erudite woman-hater, and a great snoring bore. He is a preposterous creation, and as he goes on and on and on, spewing his polysyllabic prejudices, even readers named Theroux must weary, stumble, finally fall, too exhausted to scale yet another immense, small-printed page. Page? Better call it a Calvary, for though this book begins in comedy, it ends in torture. Yet for the first 50 pages I thought I was scouting one of those oddball American masterpieces, like *Gravity's Rainbow,* which maul the categories of judgment. For one thing, the author had an extraordinary way with imagery. . . . For another, he displayed a Nabokovian gift for satiric invention. . . . (pp. 38-9)

[But even] on page 18, you can see signs of ennui coming like the flicker of truck lights breaking the perfect night of a western highway. (p. 39)

Mr. Theroux is just wild about words; in this respect, he makes his brother Paul (he of the train books), who favors onomatopoeic words like "canoodling," seem terse, when really he's more artful, more aware of how the sound of a word can lend a passage not merely color but mood. Alexander wants you to notice his words; Paul wants you to feel them. It's the difference between a show-off and an artist. Alexander simply cannot make his gaudy words evoke emotion. They just sit there on the page, inert, without suggestive power, like ostentatious thumbprints. Longing and betrayal are his subjects, but he doesn't realize these poignant feelings for us in the way that Nabokov, obviously his model, realizes Humbert's love for Lolita and his heartache over her preference for Quilty. Darconville's infatuation, Darconville's suffering, are described in spangling language; but it is all merely, well, words, words, and more words, which bring the musty smell of the dictionary into the text, and which never pass over into what Lawrence called "art-speech," that realm of expression where word, feeling, thought fuse at the highest pitch of intensity. And not only do Mr. Theroux's words fail to evoke what Nabokov called "human interest"; they also fail to quicken our sense of beauty. Reading *Darconville's Cat* is like looking at a vast abstract canvas that doesn't work. The artist is too conscious of his materials, and too deliberate; his will is doing his imagination's work. . . . This is not literature; it is not even good fiction; it is a 700-page attack of logorrhea. (pp. 39-40)

Jack Beatty, "Logorrhea!" in The New Republic *(reprinted by permission of* The New Republic; *© 1981 The New Republic, Inc.), Vol. 184, No. 14, April 4, 1981, pp. 38-40.*

EVE OTTENBERG

Alexander Theroux hates injustice. In his first book, *Three Wogs,* he swoops down on it with a savage indignation that outstrips the prose. The racism of the white Englishmen and women who parade through this novel is at once his target and motivation. He is constantly on the attack—relentless, merciless, nasty. He has high ideals which lead him always to present his characters at their worst. His unwillingness to compromise on how people should treat each other is only matched by his views on prose, expressed in his essay "Theroux Metaphrastes" and reconfirmed in his newest novel, *Darconville's Cat,* the style of which is ornate, copious, digressive, modeled on that of Sterne and Joyce. In short, he is a writer determined to prove his point—something essential in matters of style and social justice. As long as he was focusing his talents on how racism corrodes character, this determination yielded that rare pleasure in contemporary fiction of seeing a complete social world through luxurious prose. But in another context, the love story of *Darconville's Cat,* Theroux's avenging angels are a bit out of place. Indeed, at times they descend upon the reader like a pack of harpies. . . .

That Darconville could all but cohabitate with Isabelle for four years and yet have so little idea of who she is would, if such things didn't happen every day, be too incredible to be believed. The same could be said of Isabel. But since this novel is written mainly from Darconville's point of view, it takes the form of an attack on her character. Hence the harpies, i.e., the tirades of Dr. Crucifer, the devil's cohort, against women, that charge down on the reader throughout the last part of the book. This attack on Isabel is instructive—primarily because she is just not there. Her character is never developed.

If Isabel were fully realized, if she actually did something besides run away, perhaps *Darconville's Cat* would not seem so unjust.

This really is the only defect in the novel—that Theroux's outraged sense of justice is misplaced. There is something unintegrated about it, it clamors around in the book as if it didn't really belong there. It becomes all the more noticeable by contrast to the scorn he heaps on other objects. His ridicule of American anti-intellectualism and vulgarity brings Mencken to mind, while the passages on race relations in Quinsyburg, Virginia, are some of the best in the book. What makes Theroux's observations on this Southern black community even more telling is that they occur at a time when most novelists who consider themselves stylists are treating such matters as if they had been settled 20 years ago, if they are treating them at all. But nowhere is Theroux so much in his element as in his satire of that most eminent personage, the American Professor. . . .

Theroux's fiction is quite deliberately free of all the doctrines spawned by that wretched institution, the creative writing class, with the possible exception of the one regarding experience— the defects in the portrayal of the affair between Darconville and Isabelle somehow smack of an unreconstructed trauma in the life of the author. Otherwise the length and copiousness of *Darconville's Cat* are some of its strongest points. One never gets that all too common sense that the story was slapped together to meet a publishing deadline or that its unity was sacrificed to the moronic notion that unity is out of date. The style is rhetorical in the best sense, that is, the tropes are used and, for a change, consciously. And the diction—well, there is something hilarious about the nastiness of an attack that would send its objects scurrying to the dictionary in order to find out what was being said against them.

Eve Ottenberg, "'Also But Not Yet the Wombat Cries . . .'" (reprinted by permission of The Village Voice *and the author; copyright © News Group Publications, Inc., 1981), in* The Village Voice, *Vol. XXVI, No. 16, April 15-21, 1981, p. 46.*

BENJAMIN DeMOTT

I remember noticing at intervals as I read [Alexander Theroux's **"Three Wogs"**] that the author was a dictionary buff—a writer eager to use the precisely correct word even where literary prudence, that wonderfully self-denying sanity, would prefer imprecision to lower the authorial profile. But only at intervals. For most of its length **"Three Wogs"** was uncluttered with the egotistical sublime, directing the reader's eye toward a social scene at once freestanding and solidly alive. I don't recall an American fictional debut in the 1970's that created a stronger image of the writer as responsive man—lover of the human variousness that's Out There, natural enemy of self-enclosure.

Traces of the gifts that surfaced in **"Three Wogs"** are visible on some pages of **"Darconville's Cat."** . . . (p. 9)

I'm afraid, though, that **"Darconville's Cat"** will disappoint those whose expectations for this author were shaped by **"Three Wogs."** The reason is that the book seldom if ever breaks out of the self-idolizing mind of its hero. . . .

As for Darconville's mind: It "was like one of those Gothic cathedrals of which he was so fond, mysterious within, and filled with light. . . ." . . .

Somewhere inside all this celebration one senses a spirit of irony trying to learn how to breathe, but the air's too dense, the cloud of self-approval too oppressive. As a result, irony chokes on itself and dies, and with its passing, hope vanishes for a check on authorial self-indulgence. (p. 30)

The book is awash with lists and catalogues. . . . There's an endless (and unoriginal) disquisition on the interdependencies of good and evil. There's an obsession with parallels. Everywhere the plot thickens by doubling and trebling. Nowhere does the spiral top out and, for this reader, that meant a bottom line, as they say, of exhaustion not illumination.

Energy does indeed pump in many of these chapters. . . . And, touring the cathedral of Darconville's mind, you do encounter memorable observations. . . . But **"Darconville's Cat"** as a whole doesn't begin to be worthy of Alexander Theroux's substantial gifts: Here too, sadly, inflation's out of control. (p. 31)

Benjamin DeMott, "Awash with Lists and Catalogues," in The New York Times Book Review *(© 1981 by The New York Times Company; reprinted by permission), May 3, 1981, pp. 9, 30-1.*

JOHN LEONARD

Mr. Theroux can't get through a sentence, much less a paragraph, without sticking his thumb into the reader's eye with a word we've never heard or a word he just makes up. . . . After 100 pages [of **"Darconville's Cat"**] you will want to punch his face out with a thesaurus. Trying too hard is always having to say I'm sorry. . . .

Mr. Theroux, like P. G. Wodehouse and the lamentable Dickens, leans on names for humorous effect. Miss Xystine Chapelle, as student body president, is permissible, maybe. But shouldn't the line have been drawn at Guggenheim Grant? Mr. Theroux, in addition, puns promiscuously. His characters drink tea at the Seldom Inn. They dance to the music of a band named The Uncalled Four. They experience "a fete worse than death." It has, unsurprisingly, "been raining longer than Louis XIV." We need some anti-DeVries. Moreover: if he is going to use words like "wimpled," "quincunx" and "dopplerian," he should use them only once. (p. 368)

And now a few words about the structure of this book. Darconville, a wimp, falls in love with Isabel, a tub of goat's milk and sheep dip. On being rejected the first time, he licks his wounds in London while writing a book. On being rejected the second time—after Harvard has accepted him because of his book—he plots murder and fiddles with black magic. Aside from many descriptions of faces, all of them ugly, that's the narrative.

Narrative, however, is seduced by technique. Mr. Theroux is equally at home—indeed, he lolls—with 18th- and 19th-century British fiction, Greek myth, Elizabethan drama, Jacobean revenge, German romanticism, French sickliness, the fathers of the Church, various heresies, including Venice, logic, alchemy, philosophy, philology and Charlottesville. He descends to the sonnet, the sermon, the heroic couplet, nursery rhymes, a diary, questionnaires, a bibliography of misogynists, formal essays on love and hate and ears, and a genealogy, which one hopes is spurious, of the Theroux family.

Mr. Theroux is, you see, very tricky and showing off like that pool player in the television commercial for watered beer. Much of "Darconville's Cat" is immensely entertaining, and none of it is maladroit. I would complain that if he insists on savaging education in the South, and the entire South as well, he owes it to us to afflict his satiric gifts on Cambridge, Mass. He refrains, because in Cambridge, in the rafters of Adams House, he meets Dr. Cruciform, who is a eunuch, the devil, and Darconville's double. By this time, the novel is out of control and we drown in metaphysicians.

Darconville will die in a decaying Venetian palazzo, pretending to be a Proustian priest of art, singing, like a swan, his single song. Isabel will marry a sailor. Whether or not a murder occurs is up to the reader. Perhaps the cat dies. Perhaps you were wondering about that cat. That cat is art, vision, the erotic, Jesus, jealousy, memory, conscience and everything else that is silent and black and vanishes, like Shane. That cat is asked to be either Satan or a saint and, refusing to die for love, leaves town. That cat's name is Spellvexit.

And yet Mr. Theroux is serious. After rummaging through old trunks of Faulkner and Thomas Wolfe; trying to better the various novels of academe perpetrated by Nabokov, Mary McCarthy, Randall Jarrell and Bernard Malamud, not to mention Dorothy Sayers; after combining French farce and Italian opera and Gothic romance, his target is God. Dr. Cruciform, who is wholly unbelievable, explains to Darconville: "God, I tell you, is the center of the pathetic fallacy." Literature meets religion. A curtain is drawn. (pp. 368-69)

> *John Leonard, "'Darconville's Cat'," in* The New York Times, *(© 1981 by The New York Times Company; reprinted by permission), May 28, 1981 (and reprinted in* Books of the Times, *Vol. IV, No. 8, August, 1981, pp. 367-69).*

J. O. TATE

If Sidney's *Astrophel and Stella* had been composed by Urquhart of Cromarty; if Poe's "To Helen" had been written by the Melville of *Moby Dick;* if the cookie-cutter form of the Harlequin romance had been glossed by Boethius—then the

result might have been the sublime mulligan [*satura*>satire] served up to us by Alexander Theroux. (pp. 620-21)

The substance of *Darconville's Cat* is Boy Meets Girl, Boy Loses Girl. The end is Death in Venice. But the "novel" or "romance" breaks off into the form of Menippean satire, or anatomy, and proceeds by way of encyclopedic recapitulation of forms: a sonnet, a blank-verse dialogue, a formal oration, a formal essay, a vulgar sermon, etc., and a multitude of lists. Theroux is a master of tropes, schemes, and rhetorical devices; and for him as for Blake, the road of excess leads to the palace of wisdom. . . .

As in *Three Wogs,* in *Darconville's Cat* we discern the theme of revenge. But dark emotion is only one excess: we have as much of *amo* as of *odi.* The rhetor excels also in naming his lady's beauties, and exalting them. At the end, the struggle of Love and Hate is resolved in a superior synthesis: the last sentence gives the theme of the whole: "Sorrow is the cause of immortal conceptions." The work itself exemplifies the thought, and the ancient wisdom is made new. . . .

[Theroux] defies criticism: the hands holding *Darconville's Cat,* when they do not race to turn the page, pause to admire a beauty or examine an obscurity, or shake with the rebound of laughter. The theme of Love's transmutation into Art subsumes a plethora of side-dishes, including a digression on ears, a travelogue worthy of Marlowe, a catalogue of mercantile mottoes, a list of Southern girls' names. . . .

The book's satire on the one hand, and Jacobean efflorescences on the other, are sufficiently dazzling to tempt one to neglect its success as a "straight novel": we have the virtues of tangible setting and developed characters, the pleasures of suspense and even shock. Darconville and his perfidious Isabel . . . are as "real" as any characters in universal fiction. And in the person of Dr. Abel Crucifer, that demoniacal Coptic eunuch who would have enjoyed a confabulation with Dr. Dee and Aleister Crowley, we have a creature of intimidating power and resource.

Darconville's Cat may be the strongest work of fiction published in the United States since *Gravity's Rainbow*—and *Three Wogs.* (p. 621)

> *J. O. Tate, "Bedtime for Boethius," in* National Review *(© National Review, Inc., 1981; 150 East 35th St., New York, NY 10016), Vol. XXXIII, No. 10, May 29, 1981, pp. 620-21.*

James (Grover) Thurber

1894-1961

American short story writer, cartoonist, essayist, and dramatist.

Thurber is often described as one of the outstanding humorists of this century. A distinctive stylist in both his prose and his cartoons, he satirized modern middle-class life, often focusing on the tragicomic nature of male/female relations. The "Thurber man" is one bewildered by the nature and pace of modern living. He finds women, fate, animals, and machines baffling in their complexity.

Thurber began working at the *New Yorker* in 1927 and was associated with the magazine for the rest of his life. Influential in establishing the *New Yorker*'s distinctive style, he also had the opportunity to gain a wide audience for his writings published therein.

Blinded in one eye in a childhood accident, Thurber lost his vision completely in 1947. He nevertheless continued to publish prolifically. The recent publication of the *Selected Letters of James Thurber* provides some insight into his mind and art and into how both were affected by the deterioration of his vision. The letters, many of which are to long-term *New Yorker* friends, reveal a blunt, strong-minded, highly individualistic man, gifted with an unerring sense of the absurd.

(See also *CLC*, Vols. 5, 11; *Contemporary Authors*, Vols. 73-76; *Something about the Author*, Vol. 13; and *Dictionary of Literary Biography*, Vol. 4.)

Culver Pictures, Inc.

KENNETH BURKE

That skillful literary man, St. Augustine, has warned that one should never smite an opponent in bad grammar. Applying a loose interpretation, we could translate his wise teaching thus: If a man would carry a discussion through points A, B, C and D, don't let him think he has got anywhere, in the way of cogency, simply by lining up a good argument. For should he have a lisp, or should someone in his audience periodically sneeze in a notable way, or should there be an irrelevant voice echoing from the corridors, our hero is all Achilles' heel. Especially when there is a Thurber about.

In fact, if he should make a statement that requires as many as three sentences, and there is a Thurber about, he is as vulnerable. For Thurber may choose to hear only the first sentence, proceeding joyously and outrageously to build upon it. We generally think of funny men as irrational. But they are as rational as the constructor of a Mother Goose rhyme (who gets to his crooked house via a crooked man, crooked smile, crooked sixpence, crooked stile, crooked cat and crooked mouse). And one thing they learn early is that, if a thought requires three sentences for self-protective presentation, they would be disloyal to their method in hearing out the three. Where three parts are needed, the professional funny man just *knows* that he should stop at part one. His one Marquis of Queensberry rule is: Belts are to hit below.

A Thurber, having singled out part one, will next proceed, with perverse rational efficiency, to ponder this broken part. He will invent "case histories" with which to try it out—and of course, they won't fit.

But a mere bad fit is not enough. The funny man will also seek a situation such that his readers *want* a bad fit. If they are good Catholics, for instance, he knows it will be hard to make them meet him halfway should he decide to play havoc with an encyclical. He will lay off such dynamite, leaving it for the news itself to provide the outrageous incongruities, as when, reporting a Papal blast on communism at the time of Mussolini's triumph in Africa, the dispatch proceeded: "On the subject of Ethiopia, His Holiness was less explicit." On the other hand, readers of *The New Yorker*, in which all but two of the articles in *Let Your Mind Alone!* appeared, are likely to be less problematical when leftward-looking politics is the subject—so we get **"What Are the Leftists Saying?"** I thought it tearfully lame; but for all I know it may be judged by typical *New Yorker* readers the most devastating bit of fun since the discovery of the banana peel.

The first ten pieces, which give [*Let Your Mind Alone!*] its title, are a very amusing burlesque of psychoanalysis. The field offers a good opportunity for Thurber's phenomenal gifts. The study of the mind has brought to the fore many paradoxes. A man may *think* he is doing one thing when he is *actually* doing another. This state of affairs outrages common sense—the thought of it makes one uneasy—hence we are glad to meet that man halfway who will expend his jocular enterprise to vindicate the judgments of common sense.

There are pages that make one laugh very hard. One is glad that Thurber does his part to keep the leftward-lookers on their toes. I am even willing to concede him his constitutional right, as funny man, to start too soon, to remain dumb on purpose, dying that others may live—though he tends somewhat to flatter stupidity, making it a kind of accomplishment within reach of all, like getting drunk. . . . (pp. 55-7)

His drawings are good *always* for the perception his writing has *sometimes*. But I do wish he'd go after bigger game. He shoots too many cockroaches. To get such heightened value, I'd even be willing to hand him over to the reactionaries. Let him hound the "socially conscious" more consistently, in case he finds their attitude of "uplift" too much for his antinomian perversity. He need not join the author of "Redder Than the Rose." But let him at least make an indirect contribution, in serving to keep the statements of the Left alert (though they could never be alert enough to forestall all possibility of Thurberization). I have just been reading Jacques Barzun's book on theories of racial superiority. I think fondly of what a Thurber might do by examining these documents on crooked thinking and translating them into the idiom of hilarity. But that would be asking too much (at least until his waggish remarks on cocktail parties run out—and he is so ingenious and fertile with them that I doubt whether they ever will run out). So I am willing to have him become our Lord Macaulay of fun-making, a reactionary keeper-thin of the Left. Unction must be made difficult—so let him be the deunctifyer. But as things now stand, he too is purveying a patent medicine. The trivial has its medicinal aspect—but too often he expends his talents to load the trivial with all the traffic can bear. (pp. 57-8)

> Kenneth Burke, "Thurber Perfects Mind Cure," in his Thurber Perfects Mind Cure: "Let Your Mind Alone!" and Other More or Less Inspirational Pieces (copyright © 1937 by Editorial Publications, Inc.; reprinted by permission of the author), Editorial Publications, Inc., 1937 (and reprinted in The Critic As Artist: Essays on Books, 1920-1970, edited by Gilbert A. Harrison, Liveright, 1972, pp. 55-8).

WILFRID SHEED

Thurber was a marvelous comic writer, but alone among such he was able to sketch the phantasmagoric goo from which his funny ideas came. If Henry James or Dostoevsky had done their own illustrations, the results could hardly have been stranger or more illuminating. *Men, Women and Dogs* is like a writer's head with the back open; the fact that it's *funny* back there is as spooky as anything in Jung. Thurber did not make up his jokes in his mouth, like so many clowns, but somewhere between the optic nerve and the unconscious, an area where the slightest tilt can lead to torment and madness.

As it did, we now know, in his last years. But this book belongs to the sunny period before he literally lost his sight and had to move into his own skull for good, with no fresh images to lighten the nightmares. At this point his defective eyesight was still an asset conjuring up useful if scary visions of rear admirals on bicycles and dogs guarding window ledges. . . . (p. 229)

Although Thurber's prose had its own unique glories, it could not endure the loss of his sight . . . but fell off tragically and bewilderedly. There was a brief, gallant period in the early 1940s when he mustered his last clear visual memories and produced at frantic speed his finest work. Then a period of wild word-play in which he strove vainly to make the words do it all but couldn't quite swing it. And finally those last stories in which people pour drinks upon drinks, and the author can no longer *see* things for them to do.

So his comic genius hung by a thread to his flickering vision, which had already been cruelly reduced by a childhood accident involving a bow and arrow. His life was in fact a sickeningly literal enactment of The Wound and the Bow theory (namely, that to draw the magic bow of art, one must have a disabling wound). Thurber's wound gave him a funny-looking world to draw and write about, and then his wound took it away again.

Thus the beguilingly blurred figures undercut by the incisive voice of the half-blind man, perhaps not quite sure where he is even in his own drawings. Some of these pictures are downright accidental. The notorious first Mrs. Harris was supposed to be crouched on a staircase not a bookcase: but it seems the artist's perspective failed him into a masterpiece. No wonder Thurber downplayed his art. Yet an openness to the accidental is a mark of genius. And precisely because it is accidental, Thurber blunders into effects beyond the reach of controlled draftsmanship. (For the last months of Walt Kelly's noble life, someone else did his drawing for him. But who could imitate Thurber's mistakes?)

Yet if his eyes were a crucial part of his comic machine, they were not the only part; his ears were in there too. The blurry women who menace the Thurber male, and the shaggy dogs that comfort him, are respectively strident and quiet as snow. In real life, Thurber was surrounded by his share of menacing women, starting with his mother, who set the trend, and one imagines their voices crackling out of the fog as harshly as the blind man's crackles back at them. But it is too simple to say that Thurber hated women. A close look at the creatures he drew suggests a fondness and a bizarre companionship. If some of his women are a bit on the tough side, they need to be to help the Thurber male across the street. This would be a screaming grievance later when, in real life, he had to be led to the bathroom, but shouldn't be read back too far. In [*Men, Women and Dogs*] men and women carry each other inexplicably home about equally often, and the monsters are more than made up for by gentle spirits "from haunts of coot and hearn" and good-hearted blondes and nude pianists. Although the Thurber woman is most triumphantly herself as the back part of a house lunging toward an apprehensive male, she is not always herself.

At his crudest (**"Goddamn pussycats"**), Thurber reflects the hearty misogyny of the frontier, echoing Mark Twain and his own boss, Harold Ross, who periodically blamed the state of the nation on women schoolteachers. As such he is merely a footnote to social history: sensitive boys from the macho country, blaming their mothers for making them sissies and lunging around speakeasies getting even with Wellesley girls and other effete Easterners.

But his feeling for women is usually more complicated than that. Their abiding gift is the power to baffle; Thurber's women may be illogical, but they are seldom stupid—and there is always a sense that they are probably right, that they "know" something. This imputation of mystical qualities may still be maddening to feminists, but at least Thurber's women are never inferior, and his response to them is closer to fear than contempt.

Furthermore, in emphasizing his alleged hatred of women, commentators have overlooked his equal and similar hatred of men. Riffling through the cartoons again, one notes that the males are just as liable to wild flights of illogic and of fiendish malice as the females. The only constant is warfare, culminating in the crashing cadenza in the back, **"The War between men and women."** Yet even this is complicated by strange collusions and crossings of sex lines. The dreadful Thurber couple hunting in pairs puts in several appearances: e.g., the unholy twosome who have broken into someone's apartment to perform their mad dance. ("I don't know them either, dear, but there may be some very simple explanation.")

Checking with Thurber's prose pieces, one finds the same people with the gloves (Thurber's) off: the couples who stay all night, zestfully wrecking homes and marriages, the swinish practical jokers and dotty women poker players, and—significantly often—a goodly measure of men picking on men. Life for Thurber was as competitive as it was for any hustling Midwesterner or for those compulsive games players in the Algonquin set, but it was softened by his goofy eyesight; as he said of the drawing captioned "Touché," "there is obviously no blood to speak of in the people I draw."

In his stories they bleed and bleed, and without the gloss of the drawings he would be remembered as a sardonic provincial in the Ring Lardner manner—a valuable American tradition in its own right, but Thurber didn't bite clear through like Lardner. Yet the stories plus the drawings give us the extra angle that reveals a genius. The stories are like the engine behind the drawings. Thurber came east with his mouth as wide as Scott Fitzgerald's, and for a while he reveled in what he took to be the glamor of it all. But then under pressure of booze and intelligence the mouth collapsed in a snarl and he became unfathomably bitter. When his eyes closed for good, he lost his most cheerful feature and joined the Lardner-Fitzgerald stream of disappointed Americans—than whom there is no one in the world more disappointed.

But thank God, he compiled *Men, Women and Dogs* first, while youthful high spirits could still put funny hats on his nightmares and the intoxication of humorous invention was glamor enough. The dark themes are there in embryo—in especial, the husband and wife who, having exhausted the competition, round on each other for the finals, the death struggle, But he could still be diverted by jokes that had nothing to say about anything, and Thurber is at his best when he isn't saying anything about anything. (pp. 230-32)

> *Wilfrid Sheed, "Introduction" (reprinted by permission of the author; copyright © 1975 by Wilfrid Sheed), in* Men, Women and Dogs *by James Thurber, Dodd, Mead, 1975 (reprinted as "James Thurber: 'Men, Women and Dogs'," in* The Good Word and Other Words *by Wilfrid Sheed, E. P. Dutton, Inc., 1978, pp. 228-33).*

BRIAN ATTEBERY

[James Thurber's] work is often said to be in the line of Twain, Henry James, or T. S. Eliot, and, indeed, he shares traits with all three. In view of his literary standing and the evident sophistication of his themes and techniques, it may seem presumptuous to squeeze such a figure into the [tradition of fantasy writers like L. Frank Baum, author of *The Wizard of Oz*]. But there he belongs, as the fullest flowering of that tradition.

Thurber was content, for many years, to write fictionalized accounts of his Ohio past and his Connecticut present, along with assorted parodies and word games. Anything he had to say about marriage, character, and the imagination—principal early themes—could be said within those limits. Nevertheless, he had already begun toying with the stuff of fantasy, like a man who unconsciously rubs flax straws into fiber but has not yet thought of spinning them into thread. His toying was along two related lines, one dependent upon the ear, the other upon the eye, and both upon a unique and lively imagination. (p. 145)

In the 1940s, Thurber, troubled by darkening vision and a world situation even darker, made a break with the rational frame that had hitherto held his fantastic imagination in check, limiting it to flights of fancy and figures of speech. I can think of two possible reasons for his departure from the ordinary: one artistic, the other personal. First, he had always depended on close visual observation for his stories and sketches, even when he exaggerated what he saw. His reputation as a comic artist nearly equals his fame as a writer, and, just as his cartoons are fully developed stories caught at the moment of truth, his early stories are like sequences of cartoons, dependent as much upon gesture and composition as on dialog and plot. When Thurber could no longer see his subjects, he could not manipulate them: except for *The Thurber Album,* which reworks the materials of *My Life and Hard Times,* his later conventional sketches become increasingly circumscribed and static.

A more personal reason for a change of form is that Thurber began to want to say more than he could say in a contemporary, naturalistic setting. He felt increasingly that the world was on the wrong track, and he wanted to tell it so. Rather like Melville after *Typee* and *Omoo,* he was tired of recounting his adventures and was plumed for a flight of the imagination. The inner landscape he had been preparing for years now became the only world that was both accessible and satisfying. His mind's eye could still see, and it showed him a fairyland in which, unlike the real world, problems could still be overcome.

Thurber the fantasist emerged at the same time as Thurber the Jeremiah: indeed, the two are neatly combined in the pictorial fable *The Last Flower* and in the *Fables for Our Time.* . . . Those works led to the creation of his most sustained pieces of writing, *The White Deer* and *The 13 Clocks,* as well as to the slighter fairy tales *Many Moons, The Great Quillow,* and *The Wonderful O.*

In 1934, Thurber wrote an appreciation of L. Frank Baum. . . . In it, he praises the Oz stories for being "fairy tales with a difference." . . . (pp. 146-47)

Thurber first read *The Wizard of Oz* and *The Land of Oz* when he was ten. Forty years later their influence surfaced in the writing of *The White Deer.* It, too, along with *The 13 Clocks,* is a fairy tale "with a difference," a difference which extends to each of the five facets of fantasy.

First of all is the fantasy world. The worlds of both *The White Deer* and *The 13 Clocks* lie closer to traditional fairy tale settings than does Oz. We find castles, enchanted forests, dukes, and wizards, all much as we might find them in works of the literary followers of the brothers Grimm. Thurber was never particularly interested in landscape as such, not like Baum, who was an unconscious regionalist. He was content to let convention dictate his locale, up to a point. The level at which his world strikes out on its own is that of fine detail. The enchanted forest of *The White Deer* is a standard magical forest, dark and mysterious, full of wizards and eerie creatures. But a closer look shows the Thurberian imagination at work, altering a flower here, an animal there, to exploit the magical possibilities of its name or shape. . . . (pp. 147-48)

Between the time of *The White Deer* and that of *The 13 Clocks,* Thurber came to rely more on tricks of sound than on sight. Occasionally . . . sound repetition alone creates the effect of an entangling spell. . . .

Buried in the prose of both tales are strings of rhymes and metric feet. . . . Sometimes these regularities seem accidental, an eerie piling up of poetic coincidence. Other times they signify the formality of a spell or decree. . . . (p. 148)

The headiest verbal magic in *The White Deer* accompanies the labors of the three princes. In the first of these parallel episodes, Thurber turns toward Lewis Carroll, rather than Baum, as a guide. Prince Thag, like Alice in *Through the Looking Glass,* loses his name in a forest of confusion and meets a man with Humpty-Dumpty's disregard for linguistic norms. . . . (pp. 148-49)

The second Prince, Gallow, finds a different kind of nonsense in the Forest of Willbe: the destruction of meaning brought about by wrenching language to economic ends. (p. 149)

Prince Jorn's labor, on the other hand, moves from nonsense to sense. He finds the true witch's broom hidden in a clump of witches'-broom, solves a riddle, and, with help, discovers that counting a thousand thousands (part of his appointed task) is not the same as counting to a million.

The nonsensical lands encountered by the three Princes are not, as in Lewis Carroll, the whole fantastic universe. Rather they are isolated pockets of absurdity like the places Dorothy and her friends encounter in *The Emerald City of Oz.* . . . They help, through contrast, to define the norm, which is an orderly realm despite its surprises and inversions. . . . And . . . everything will come out right in the end, for that is the kind of world we are dealing with. Thurber has not departed so far from old-style fairy tale as to change that essential feature.

Nor does he drastically alter the fairy tale structure which leads to such a happy conclusion. Each of the fairy tales, as Charles S. Holmes points out, has approximately the same pattern. It begins with a problem—what Propp calls a lack or insufficiency—proceeds through several attempts at solution by false heroes, men of worldly importance; and ends with the true hero in triumph, with girl or kingdom or some more private reward, like the respect of his fellows.

The smaller movements within this overall scheme also derive from traditional *Märchen.* There are interdictions and violations of interdictions, announcements, departures, thresholds, deceptions, meetings with helpers, and confrontations with enemies, all in the prescribed sequence, though not every element occurs in every tale.

It seems that Thurber determined to follow the rules of his chosen form, just as he did with his fables. Like the fables, however, the fairy tales add something above and beyond the structure: a certain self-consciousness, a covert announcement that, yes, the form is antique, but the author has reasons for selecting it and no other. Those episodes mentioned earlier, the labors of the three princes, call attention to the fairy tale conventions by briefly violating them. Suddenly encountering

the twentieth century in the middle of the story is a shock that makes us more aware of, and grateful for, the return of an older, quieter world. Other things direct our notice from the story to things outside of it: references to "tarcomed" and "nacilbuper" and the "Forest of Artanis" (read them backward), echoes of popular songs, caricatures of people like *New Yorker* editor Harold Ross, figures of speech just short of anachronism, and unexpected playful turns, like a villain who feeds his enemies, not to pigs or dogs or tigers, but to geese.

Because of this self-consciousness, one is always aware, in reading Thurber's fantasies, that the happy ending is a fragile thing that depends very much on our accepting the conventions of the genre. It is different from the inevitable falling into place of a true *Märchen.* We can accept the idea that a fairy tale Prince and Princess will live happily ever after, but we are all too aware that we tarcomeds and nacilbupers will not. What we can do is to retell their stories and take courage and comfort from them.

The hero of a Thurber fairy tale is, in addition to being the prince or plucky commoner of *Märchen,* an artist of some sort. Prince Jorn is a musician and versifier, as is the nearly identical Prince Zorn of *The 13 Clocks.* Other Thurber heroes are poets, toymakers, and jesters. The fairy tale hero is common man in romantic guise, but the Thurber hero is uncommon man, the man of imagination and sensibility. There is a reflection of culture in this difference. Oppressed peasant storytellers tell how a youngest son or a soldier—someone of relatively low rank—can attain maturity and the dignity of marriage and property. Thurber tells how an artist—someone whose rank seemed to him to be low and sinking lower in mid-century America—can restore an ailing land and indeed is the only one who can do so.

Because Thurber's heroes are more imaginative than those around them, they are more in touch with the marvels of the fantasy world. They understand the linguistic and sensory playfulness represented by magic; it is just the sort of thing they themselves strive for in their art. Perhaps this is the reason that Thurber portrays magic primarily as a beneficent force in league with Jorn or Zorn or the great Quillow. For every hostile magical creature there are two or more that aid the hero in his task. . . . The less familiar creatures of *The 13 Clocks* waver interestingly between good and evil, but generally choose good. . . . (pp. 149-51)

In [Thurber's fantasies] he was working out for himself questions of love and honor, time and mortality, and the role of the artist in modern society. He uses fantasy as a kind of algebra, or a special language, in which to evaluate and debate all sides of the case. In order for his conclusions to be fair and valid, however, he must treat the fantasy form with the respect due any artistic endeavor, as he was well aware. . . . (p. 151)

As simple and brief as Thurber's fairy tales are, they are . . . packed with philosophy . . . , for philosophical inquiry pervades plot, characters . . . , and even the very language of each story. They are the natural vehicles for Thurber's qualified reaffirmation of faith in his craft and in mankind. (p. 152)

Brian Attebery, "The Baum Tradition," in his The Fantasy Tradition in American Literature: From Irving to Le Guin *(copyright © 1980 by Brian Attebery), Indiana University Press, 1980, pp. 134-53.**

JONATHAN YARDLEY

James Thurber was often an irascible and difficult man, but there is little of that side of his personality in these *Selected*

Letters. Here we find him for the most part sunny side up—and what a pleasure that is. This is a slender volume, evidently intended to be a representative rather than an inclusive selection of his correspondence, but it contains enough first-rate Thurber to be ranked among his better books.

Indeed, if justice is at work in the world these days, the publication of these letters may initiate a Thurber revival. It is my sense, based on nothing except intuition, that Thurber is not widely read these days—even though his friend, *New Yorker* colleague and occasional collaborator, E. B. White, remains perhaps the country's most beloved writer. Two decades after his death, Thurber seems to have been relegated to the status of "minor" writer: a humorist of the *New Yorker* school and the author of a handful of short stories that appear, even now, in anthologies.

But Thurber, as he himself well knew, was far more than that; his literary legacy is larger and more durable. . . .

Thurber's humor, as these letters at times brilliantly demonstrate, has a timeless quality that should guarantee him a readership far into the future. It is for one thing a deeply American humor, rooted not in the brittle style of *The New Yorker* but in his own native Ohio. . . . He loved the Anglo-American language, explored all its labyrinthine passages, and played with it constantly—yet his humor depended far less on facile wordplay than on deeper, more universal quirks of character and incident. (p. 3)

In these letters Thurber writes of many things. New York. . . . The new age. . . . Humor: "I write humor the way a surgeon operates, because it is a livelihood, because I have a great urge to do it, because many interesting challenges are set up, and because I have the hope that it may do some good."

Indeed it may. The humor of James Thurber probably had done as much "good" as that of any American writer of the 20th century. Certainly he ranks with those who influenced him. Twain and Lardner in particular, and far above those whom *he* influenced; in that crowd, only Peter De Vries comes close. Because he was possessed by what he described in *My Life and Hard Times* as "the damp hand of melancholy," he was all the more keenly aware of the need to bring forth the bright light of laughter. (p. 13)

Jonathan Yardley, "Amusements and Diversions from the Thurber Carnival," in Book World—The Washington Post *(© 1981, The Washington Post), November 8, 1981, pp. 3, 13.*

WILLIAM ZINSSER

Afflicted by bad eyesight and eventual blindness, James Thurber had good reason to bemoan the advancing darkness and the racing years, as, in ["**Selected Letters of James Thurber**"], he does. The miracle is that under such a burden he wrote 27 books (starting at the age of 35) that cheered millions of people with their humor and perpetual surprise. His drawings were uniquely antic; his prose was a marvel of sonority and warmth. In these public offerings the rest of us could glimpse some of the fears and bewilderments that vexed the private man, and because they were very much like our own fears and bewilderments—and our Mitty-like dreams—we cherished his writing.

But that was because Thurber had labored to turn ordinary life into art. He rewrote endlessly; he was obsessive about achieving control of his material. . . .

I think Thurber would squirm to see these first drafts of his prose and his mind spread out on public view. It is the ultimate loss of control. Old men are entitled, for instance, to their umbrages, and here the aging Thurber, in several long letters to White, is found bitterly assailing Harold Ross for his penurious treatment of New Yorker writers. Perhaps the editors of this collection . . . think they are holding up for our admiration a champion of underpaid artists. The display is unbecoming. Ross has been dead for 30 years and Thurber for 20. One of them founded a great magazine, the other helped to shape its greatness. Their monument is their work; the rest is litter.

Still, any touch of Thurber brightens the day, and inevitably in the gray mass of this book I found some zircons that glittered and made me smile. (p. 3)

William Zinsser, "A Touch of Thurber," in The New York Times Book Review *(© 1981 by The New York Times Company; reprinted by permission), November 8, 1981, pp. 3, 46.*

NORA SAYRE

Encounters—with unfriendly food, or machinery, or objects that took on a life of their own—were essential to [James Thurber's] vision of human existence as an obstacle race. The Thurber man's feeling of helplessness when faced with collapsing cots, stalled cars, computers gone beserk, falling ceilings, malign plumbing, situations beyond control, marriages, ghosts in the attic and global war had to seem hilarious—since the author's own perception of chaos was sometimes unbearable. As Graham Greene wrote about Charlie Chaplin, "The man who falls downstairs must suffer if we are to laugh; the waiter who breaks a plate must be in danger of dismissal. Human nature demands humiliation, the ignoble pain and the grotesque tear: the madhouse for Malvolio." No one understood that better than James Thurber. . . .

The kinship between wit and dejection always intrigued him; as he noted in the preface to *My Life and Hard Times,* "The little wheels of [comedy] are set in motion by the damp hand of melancholy." (In conclusion, he acknowledged that "the claw of the seapuss gets us all in the end.") His often gleeful pessimism is reflected in the *Selected Letters,* meticulously edited by Helen Thurber and Edward Weeks. (p. 531)

Although the Thurber man was usually meek, that essence was alien to the writer: "A little crotch-kicking is a good thing, if done in anger. I can't stand guys who are merely piqued by the unforgivable. . . ." While there is more of the genial Thurber than the fierce one in these letters, many of them muse on the painful complexities of writing. . . .

The letters bestow the gift of spending twenty-six years in Thurber's company, of learning what engrossed or appalled him. The focus ranges from telepathy to bloodhounds, revering Henry James, and aging. . . . (p. 532)

The letters reveal how clearly he could see in his sleep, and the host of magnificent drawings that enrich the book resurrect the eye and the hand and the mind that died exactly twenty years ago—which now seem more inspired than ever. (p. 533)

Nora Sayre, "Chiming and Striking," in The Nation *(copyright 1981 The Nation magazine, The Nation Associates, Inc.), Vol. 233, No. 17, November 21, 1981, pp. 531-33.*

CLANCY SIGAL

[James Thurber] was one of the funniest men alive, if you at all tuned in to his doggerel cartoons, with their barking seals and daffily aggressive women swooping on gloomily defenceless males, and his fables, like **'The Secret Life of Walter Mitty'** and **'The Night the Bed Fell'**, which were angry parables of despair and raging frustration.

Thurber was often like one of his own flopping, loping, terrified animals. His humour, occasionally a little too arch and fey, was redeemed by a cruel pessimism laced with a sort of loony provincialism (his roots in small-town Ohio were deep) which found its sharpest focus either in his sex-war cartoons, or in newly-coined myths that did horribly inventive things to the old archetypes. To say that something is 'Thurberesque' is a code for something quite complex and almost unexplainable, but it certainly has much to do with this nearly blind writer's luminous perceptions of the shapes and movements of our unadmitted fears, presumptions and pretensions. (p. 20)

My appreciation of [*Selected Letters of James Thurber*] in great measure depends on my taste for Thurber the artist. At one level there is little spectacular about them. . . . But, if you like Thurber, then the epistolatory style will be a solid addition to the corpus, revealing not so much his unknown intimate side as his ability, under personal stress, to issue personal communiqués of marvellous clarity, generosity and quietly mad jokiness. His throwaway lines can be piercingly accurate and funny. . . .

With his psuedo-fables and cartoons he both celebrated and damned a critical passage in American life, a change from an old sedateness to a new breathlessness, from leisurely straw-picking to hyped-up 'technics'. He made fun of the change, obliquely and at a subtle, wild angle. The present edition of the letters is a joy to have, but I strongly suspect that there is another, less tameable and genial fellow buried in personal letters deemed, by his editors, just a little too—er—Thurberesque to be allowed to roam freely in the public eye. (p. 21)

Clancy Sigal, "'The Great Party of the Twenties Seemed to End Too Soon for Him'," (© British Broadcasting Corp. 1982; reprinted by permission of Clancy Sigal), in The Listener, *Vol. 107, No. 2745, January 28, 1982, pp. 20-1.*

ALAN COREN

[The] wife who wants to bring out a volume of her deceased husband's correspondence has not one, but two, reputations to protect, if not, indeed, enhance. But in the case of James Thurber, this double-indemnity embraces a particular threat to candour.

Thurber was a man who spent much of his grafting life in the pockmarked redoubts of the marital front-line, sending back his withering dispatches from the Million Years War, the Ernie Pyle of the sexual barrage and the nuptial raid. Yet there is not one word among the 80,000 gummed together [in *Selected Letters of James Thurber*] to suggest that he enjoyed anything but snug serenity beneath the monogamous conterpane. The

man that Thurber must have been, if we base our reasonable assumptions upon the writer that he unquestionably was, is simply not here. Did he *never* write privately, to anyone, about lust or love or marriage or extra-marriage, to confide, or complain, or rejoice, or even merely to tell?

The question does not proceed from irrelevant prurience, but from honest literary curiosity: for Thurber's published writings across thirty years take the disordered relationships of men and women (or, as he would jot it, men versus women) as a constant theme. And what are a writer's letters for, if not for the elucidation of the printed stuff? Particularly since the humorist's trade is so often the refraction of experience, the fabrication of an alternative reality from material whose raw state he has used his best endeavours to conceal. Does the devoted reader of Thurber not yearn for a detective hour or two spent tiptoeing through The Unselected Letters? . . .

Certainly, what Helen Thurber and Edward Weeks have gathered together would not, I think, have passed Thurber's obsessively rigorous criteria, nor received Harold Ross's imprimatur. They are dull dogs, almost all, too much concerned with the sort of day-to-day trivia of interest only to the recipients, the keeping-abreast, the private jokes, the inquiries into mutual friends, the evocation of mutual memories. The writing itself, casual to the point of sloppiness, is utterly uncharacteristic of so self-punishingly meticulous a prosemaker, and the laughs are very few indeed. . . . Nor does it seem to me, setting aside the quality of the expression, to be much use as a companion volume: it will, surely, be bought only by those who already have a considerable knowledge and love of Thurber's humour . . . , [but] I cannot for the life of me see how their reading of the works or their understanding of the man will be enriched by these disappointing shards of correspondence.

Except where the Eye is concerned. The agony of the eye was something from which Thurber could manufacture scant comedy (although there was one wonderful exception, *The Admiral on the Wheel,* written in the years before the whole terror hit), and thus, commercially unparlayable, it occupies a frequent and prominent position in his letters. The Eye, in fact, hovers over this book like a masonic emblem; at times, the book itself feels like a biography of the Eye.

Not the left eye, dead before our story begins, shot out (or, more accurately, in) during one of those childhood games in which one child pretends to be William Tell Jr. and the other pretends to know what he's doing with a bow and arrow; but the right eye. For forty years, the right eye had to make its way in the world alone; it was a tenacious and a courageous way, but that its long struggle was, quite literally, unequal, these sad letters bear bitter testimony. . . . The Eye struggled to do the work both of itself and of its absent mate; which doomed it. From the moment that the arrow struck, the writing was on the wall for the bereft Eye, and fading fast. It finally failed in 1947, when its host was fifty-two, leaving him fourteen further years of, now pitch, darkness.

I anthropomorphize this Eye, I give it a separate identity, only because Thurber insists upon doing so himself. He saw it as slightly apart from him, with its own personality, its own destiny, indeed its own health; the Eye's life affected his, but it belonged more to the Eye than it did to him. He observed it from within, like a compassionate, concerned and frequently irritated friend, knowing that it would one day let him down and leave him to struggle inadequately on, alone. . . .

We cannot, obviously, evaluate [the challenge of coping with a handicap]; all we can do is evaluate the product of the challenged years, and there is no question but that there is more of the good and the true and the unquestionably Thurber in the writing of the last two, dark, decades than in the brighter two that preceded them. That all I have taken away with me from this dislocated cobbling of his letters is the reminder of the hell of his blindness, I should probably find deeply distressing, if that reminder did not also serve to astound me with the magnitude of the tragedy which Thurber overcame in order to produce the dazzling magnitude of his comedy. The example charges up the spirit, and humiliates one's own cheap grievances.

Alan Coren, "Coming to Terms with the Eye," in The Times Literary Supplement *(© Times Newspapers Ltd. (London) 1982; reproduced from* The Times Literary Supplement *by permission), No. 4113, January 29, 1982, p. 101.*

William Trevor

1928-

(Born William Trevor Cox) Irish short story writer, novelist, and dramatist.

Trevor is renowned as a superb craftsman whose vision is moral and intensely humane. In prose noted for its subtletly and control, he attempts to show the reader what is extraordinary about the seemingly ordinary lives that he portrays. He does so, in the opinion of many critics, with remarkable success. Trevor's characters have a quiet dignity and command our respect. They are "recognizably human," believable in the fullness of their portrayed lives.

Trevor's novels and short stories, narrated by detached observers, are often extremely funny. Their subjects, nevertheless, are quite serious. Trevor's characters are isolated people who live bravely but fear a disruption in the order they have imposed on their thoughts and emotions. Typically, some person or event leads them to reassess their lives and selves. In his acclaimed early novel *The Old Boys*, for instance, a class reunion is the starting point for reflections on old age and for revelations of the pretentions of some of its characters. In the ambitious novel *The Children of Dynmouth* and the recent *Other People's Worlds*, it is a person rather than an event that causes the epiphanic moment around which all of Trevor's fiction revolves.

Trevor is often described as a master of the short story. His interest in the small but powerful moments that can change a person's life is particularly well suited to the form. Collections like his *The Day We Got Drunk on Cake*, *The Ballroom of Romance*, and *Angels at the Ritz* contain stories that have been described as both perfectly constructed and unusually moving. As Trevor's characters face some simple but painful truth about themselves, readers, critics feel, are moved to recognize their own vulnerability.

(See also *CLC*, Vols. 7, 9, 14; *Contemporary Authors*, Vols. 9-12, rev. ed.; and *Contemporary Authors New Revision Series*, Vol. 4.)

Fay Godwin's Photo Files

JOHN LUCAS

William Trevor is an extremely accomplished writer, and *Other People's Worlds* is as accomplished as anything he's so far written. Trevor has the professional's knack of allowing key moments to make their effect without help of underlining. The villain-hero of his new novel, Francis Tyte, is a bit-part actor, full-time liar and fantasist who makes trouble for all the women he fastens and fattens on, without himself being troubled by anything more than rage that they're occasionally ungrateful to and unworthy of him. He has an illegitimate daughter by a shop assistant, Doris, and Trevor contrasts the drab meanness of their lives with that of Francis's. One scene ends with Doris spooning out tinned ravioli for her daughter before she notices that Joy is comatose with drugs. . . . The next scene begins: 'In the Rembrandt Hotel, in the restaurant called the Carver's Table, Francis ate roast beef, and drank half a bottle of last year's beaujolais.'

Obvious enough, perhaps. Nothing interferes with Francis's appetites. He's about to be married to a well-to-do middle-aged widow, Julia Ferndale, whom he'll desert on their honeymoon. Much later in the novel Julia finds herself with the responsibility of trying to help Doris and Joy. She goes to stay in the Rembrandt Hotel. 'In the restaurant called the Carver's Table she tried to eat roast beef but found she could not.' It's part of Trevor's accomplishment that he resists drawing attention to the echo.

Much of the novel's artful construction depends on echo, parallel, contrast. Which is perhaps not surprising, since *Other People's Worlds* is about the distinctions that have to be made between various realities and the illusion out of which Francis in particular builds his life. 'Make-belief is all we have,' he remarks at one point, and he's the complete artificer, acting out the various parts he's assigned himself. (He always wears make-up.) He may remind us of the sad fantasist of Elizabeth Taylor's *A Wreath of Roses*, but his flawless egotism is very much Trevor's invention.

The novel is fascinating when it's concerned with the intense egotism of acting. There's a particularly fine scene that deals with the rehearsal for a TV dramatisation of the famous case of Constance Kent, the Victorian supposed child murderer, in which Francis has a small part. Trevor brilliantly allows us to become involved in the pathos of Constance's history as it's presented in the play, before suggesting that this is art, and maybe not good art at that. There's a further twist. Francis himself steals things and tells lies. He also commits murder—in his imagination. For he fantasises about brutally killing his ex-mistress, a dressmaker, whom he has told Doris is his invalid wife and the reason why he and Doris can't marry. Very late in the novel Doris does kill her. Ordinary people can do extraordinary, terrible things. . . .

The first half of *Other People's Worlds* is very fine indeed. But as soon as Francis is out of the way matters begin to go wrong. The problem is the handling of Julia and Doris, who now take over. As the [recent] re-publication of *The Boarding House* reminds us, Trevor began as something of a *pasticheur*. The tone and style of *The Boarding House* recall both Patrick Hamilton's remarkable *The Slaves of Solitude* and early Angus Wilson; and there's something deeply fictional and conventional about the women of *Other People's Worlds*. Doris, in particular, suffers from this. With her genteel cockneyisms, her dream of married life with Frankie, her belief in silver linings in that cloudy sky, she belongs in an entirely fictional world, one that can be traced through *The Wrong Set*, say, all the way back to Forster's Jackie Bast.

The problem with Julia is rather different. . . . [Her revelation that she has 'lived too long in flower beds'] is meant to carry more conviction than it can. I don't see why we should be greatly interested in her sudden awareness of the real horrors of the world. . . . [By] the end of Trevor's novel we are asked to believe that Julia has become A Serious Woman. But to put it that way is to imply that something has gone wrong. And the fact is that the sufferings of others seem to be there for *her* sake, to show the acuteness of *her* feelings. . . . Joy's tragedy is somehow supposed to be more real now that it's Julia's as well. It's a bad mistake, and it indicates the way in which a pastiche of middle-class angst has taken over from that altogether more chilling and original fiction which lasts while Francis Tyte is at its centre.

John Lucas, "Carver's Table," in New Statesman (©1980 The Statesman & Nation Publishing Co. Ltd.), Vol. 100, No. 2572, July 4, 1980, p. 23.

TERENCE WINCH

William Trevor, like many of the characters in his novels and stories, is something of a con artist. The boring opening to his new novel, *Other People's Worlds,* is a setup. . . . That Trevor is willing to lull us for 20 or so pages, only to jolt us back awake by revealing that Francis Tyte, the intended groom [of Julia Ferndale] is in fact an impostor with the sinister mission of violating the peaceful contentment of Swan House, is the first of Trevor's tricks in this novel, one of many masterful strokes by which he shifts our perceptions. (p. 3)

On one level, this new novel is an old-fashioned, very readable, Gothic tale about the dialectic between good and evil, truth and illusion, innocence and guilt. Yet it is also a thoroughly contemporary work, not only in its details (this is an England of "Pizzaland" and television addiction), but in the ways it touches on our most up-to-date fears, most especially the fear of being vulnerable and compassionate in a predatory, violent world.

Trevor's prose seems careful, delicate, almost cautious at times. He builds his narrative by setting everything up, then knocking it down: the repeated use of facades and faces (and, finally, of demolition) in *Other People's Worlds* gives this technique a metaphorical scaffold. But he is never too careful, and it would be a distortion to reduce his work to formulas on how his self-admitted "obsessions" all add up in the end.

It would also be a distortion to leave the impression that Trevor's novel is a bleak, pessimistic work. Julia Ferndale, a sane, sympathetic person caught up in what often seems to be a world of comic-book horror, does not so much surrender her innocence as her naiveté. She holds on to her best qualities—her character, her trust in people—while qualifying them with a deeper sense of life's darker realities. Her spiritual survival is a source of hope. . . . (p. 10)

Terence Winch, "A Predator and His Prey," in Book World—The Washington Post *(© 1981, The Washington Post), February 1, 1981, pp. 3, 10.*

JACK BEATTY

The three aesthetic challenges of [*Other People's Worlds*] are to establish Julia's innocence on credible grounds, to show it first as weakness and then as strength, and to intimate, lightly, the sources of Francis's malignity. Trevor succeeds with Julia, but I think he goes too far in the direction of the explicit with Francis. Still, it is a real artistic dilemma; if he tells too little about Francis, then allegory will rear its blunt head; too much, and the mystery around Francis will dissipate, revealing a case history. In these matters, a little early Freud can be dangerous; and Trevor, I think, errs in furnishing us with the childhood seduction theory as the key to Francis's foul nature. This error grows out of an attempt to avoid the greater simplifications of allegory. But since the essence of Francis's evil is his sheer externality, furnishing him with this gross scar shifts our attention from surface to psyche. It would have been better to have kept us hunting in the shadows of human motivation.

Julia, on the other hand, is a triumph in a difficult field: the portrayal of good. Her goodness is not ethereal; the natural motion of her soul is to form ties of loyalty and love. This makes her vulnerable (she comes close to suicide when Francis leaves her on the first day of their honeymoon in Italy). But it is also the source of her vitality and it proves infectious. (p. 38)

I admire what Trevor wants to do with Doris [the mother of Francis's illegitimate daughter Joy]: he wants to show us how much economic facts matter in any life—how the lack of cash, the lack of the psychological capital that goes with birth in the middle classes, can make everything worse. Trevor even knows how sexual opportunity—leave out stability and love—depends on cash. **"Lovers of Their Time,"** the title story of his last collection, is about a shop girl and a philandering travel agent who are forced to consummate their affair in a vacant hotel bathroom because they haven't money for a room. In a Cheever story, that would be a cute detail; in Trevor, it reveals social essence.

Set Trevor, with his understanding of these things, against those novels and films about chic trysts on the Upper East Side, and you see his depth. Unlike so many of our American novelists these days, the Anglo-Irish Trevor is haunted by plights not his own. But how I wish he had not made Doris so pathetic! . . . [Why] did Trevor have to make her a thief; and why did he have to make the grim Joy the very picture of the pathetic—a 12-year-old who doesn't go to school, has sex, takes drugs, and can't read? London is full of such unfortunates, but one suspects that in painting Doris and Joy in these dire hues Trevor had his eyes not on life but on the flagrant scenes in Dickens. . . . We get the point, we want to tell Trevor; don't lay it on so thick. Your judgment of *Other People's Worlds* as a work of art—and only the highest standards apply to William Trevor—will depend on your feelings about the Doris element. To me, she is excessive. Other readers may feel the pathos of her plight as a powerful effect.

Lovers of Their Time, which Graham Green compared to *Dubliners,* sold fewer than 10,000 copies while the likes of *Sophie's Choice* soared. *Other People's Worlds* does not, it seems to me, show Trevor at his best. Still, it is a better book than ninetenths of the novels being published. Trevor is a major writer; he deserves your serious attention. (pp. 38-9)

Jack Beatty, "Hell Is Other People," in The New Republic *(reprinted by permission of* The New Republic; *© 1981 The New Republic, Inc.), Vol. 184, No. 6, February 7, 1981, pp. 38-9.*

JOHN UPDIKE

"Other People's Worlds," by William Trevor . . . is a shorter, more efficient novel than [Iris Murdoch's] "Nuns and Soldiers," but bears some resemblances. It, too, has for a heroine a widow who marries a young man financially beneath her, and it, too, demonstrates that such a union, however rashly contracted, cannot be lightly undone. Julia Ferndale, like [Murdoch's] Gertrude Openshaw, is plump but still handsome; like Anne Cavidge, she undergoes a struggle with religious doubt. Catholicism haunts both books, and both are at their best showing different social worlds impinging, with painful and revelatory effect. . . . Like Miss Murdoch, Mr. Trevor was born in Ireland, and he brings to the anthropology of their adopted England an affectionate and attentive outsider's eye. . . . [While] he is not the international star she is, Mr. Trevor has a solid reputation in Great Britain and a growing one [in America]. "Other People's Worlds" surely will boost this reputation; it is a dense and constantly surprising work, grimly humorous, total in its empathy, and pungent with the scent of evil and corruption. While Iris Murdoch's world has something incorrigibly sunny and donnish about it, and even her meanest characters have intellectual positions to articulate, Mr. Trevor's contains true depths, hells whose inhabitants do not know where they are.

Unlike Miss Murdoch, Mr. Trevor is a short-story writer as well as a novelist, and he has the habit of economy. His situations and characters are blocked in as quickly as a bricklayer lays a walk, and widely different milieus unfold almost dizzyingly. . . . His portrait of Francis's twisted psyche is sinisterly fine, but the centerpiece of [*Other People's World's*] is his characterization of Doris Smith. . . . (pp. 154-55)

When Doris descends into the ultimate London depths, the society of "meths drinkers," these derelicts, "like bundles of rags," yet rumble with a curious courtesy and pertinence. The author does what Joyce never quite does in his underworld scenes—he gives these murky presences a mythic dignity. . . . Mr. Trevor knows, and dramatizes, two principal truths about low life: it never utterly lies down, but persists in asserting claims and values of its own derivation; and it cannot be fenced off and disowned by the fortunate. There is indeed "infinite responsibility." As we watch Francis Tyte's derangement spread to Doris and Joy and thence to Julia Ferndale and her mother

and the picture-book village of Stone St. Martin, Julia herself begins to seem crazy. Looking at herself naked in the mirror, she wants to be desired; she recalls the moment in Pisa when Francis disillusioned her and even so "she wanted to caress away the pain she knew was there, to rescue him at last from his awful world." This "awful" the author has earned. (pp. 155-56)

John Updike, "Worlds and Worlds" (© 1981 by John Updike), in The New Yorker, *Vol. LVII, No. 5, March 23, 1981, pp. 148-57.**

MICHAEL GARVEY

Rarely do verbal precision, intelligence, imagination, and compassion converge to produce a talent as awesome as William Trevor's. His eleventh offering to a burgeoning and increasingly enthusiastic American audience further entitles aspiring writers of fiction to despise him a little.

Other People's Worlds, with the persuasive intricacy characteristic of Mr. Trevor's short stories, reveals the presence of the demonic in human affairs as most ordinary human beings encounter it. . . . The despicable Tyte is one of the byzantine monsters in western literature; his adventures, only gradually discovered by Julia, have left the wake of his careening will strewn with human debris. . . .

As Tyte's rapine, so sedulously depicted by Mr. Trevor, propels the narrative toward excruciatingly predictable horror, it becomes apparent that the Devil which here concerns Mrs. Ferndale, Mr. Tyte, and other victims, is not the dramatic and obvious steward of hydrogen bombs, terrorism, and concentration camps. This is the Devil Joseph Conrad describes, "of a pitiless and rapacious folly." Appropriately, Trevor's characters are never (certainly not here) the archetypes against which inferior fiction pits Great Satans. They are, instead, like Julia Ferndale and ourselves, disturbingly unique and imbedded in the particulars of the everyday. This characteristic alone suffices for a fine novel, but *Other People's Worlds,* in its realism and mystery, is a work of art. Those critics (and there are many) who deplore the state of fiction these days are obviously unacquainted with William Trevor's work. They shouldn't be.

Michael Garvey, " 'Other People's Worlds'," in The Critic *(© The Critic 1981; reprinted with the permission of the Thomas More Association, Chicago, Illinois), Vol. 39, No. 15, April 1, 1981, p. 5.*

PETER KEMP

From his first novel, *The Old Boys,* onwards, [William Trevor] has specialized in harrying gentility. His books regularly shepherd into view the well-bred and/or well-heeled: then, unleashing some aggressive predator at them, they depict with sprightly relish the bleating distress and panic-stricken swervings that ensue.

The clash between herbivores and carnivores fascinates Trevor. His last novel, *Other People's Worlds,* absorbedly watched a psychopath wreaking havoc in a nest of gentlefolk. The preceding one, *The Children of Dynmouth,* recorded the tremors shaking rectory and bungalow as a crazy blackmailer harassed the mild citizens of a sleepy Dorset town. Retailing prim pandemonium, the book archly savoured such spectacles as that of a disgraced pederast trying to placate his virgin wife with a cup of Ovaltine.

Trevor's fiction constantly brings together the disruptive and the decorous, the sordid and sedate. The title of his new book, *Beyond the Pale,* epitomizes his preoccupation with an oasis of propriety beleaguered by viciousness and savagery. Most of the twelve stories in it offer variations on the theme. The opening piece, **"The Bedroom Eyes of Mrs Vansittart"**, focuses—as is so often the procedure—on an initially picturesque scene. . . . True to form, squalor soon gains entry—in the shape of one of Trevor's fictional stand-bys, a petty blackmailer. Finally, comes the divulging of an ugly secret: the man thought to be an ideal husband is, in fact, another of Trevor's seedy paedophiles.

Clattering through similar routines, other stories also automatically discharge little piles of dirty linen. In **"Mulvihill's Memorial"**, a stolidly wholesome-seeming chap . . . is found, after his death, to have been a peeping tom and pornographic film buff (exposures turned up by this cause the usual genteel consternation, including the dropping of an agitated cup of Ovaltine).

"Sunday Drinks" moves into a particularly well-trodden sector of Trevor's fictional territory: an attractive garden that throws into damning relief the unhealthy goings-on amidst the flowers and sunshine. As a group of prosperous acquaintances enjoy *al fresco* aperitifs, a theatrically bitchy homosexual—another type Trevor is fond of—circulates with assiduous malice, letting it be known that the guests "weren't quite as they appeared to be". There is the customary cracking of façades. . . . [A] fainting fit reveals that, behind the cheery, chin-up exterior of the central character, there is, if not a skeleton in the cupboard, at least a ruined, drug-addicted son in a darkened bedroom.

The use of the garden to suggest an Eden which proves to be swarming with snakes is very characteristic of Trevor. Ever since *The Old Boys,* where mangled bird-remains were found amongst suburban antirrhinums, and senile delinquents perpetrated "malicious damage in the wallflower beds" of a residential hotel, this has been so. In *Beyond the Pale,* horticultural mayhem abounds. . . .

The use of mealy-mouthed locutions when dealing with sex (spoken of, in these stories, in terms of "congress" or "conjunctions") is [also] common in Trevor. It acts as a verbal equivalent of the counter-pointing of niceness and nastiness which his plots continually effect. Raised eyebrows and pursed lips pore spinsterishly over gamey behaviour: with the result that, though the fiction makes constant use of sexually *louche* material, it never convincingly portrays it (a supposedly hard-porn film in **"Mulvihill's Memorial"**, for instance, is said to feature a woman being "divested" of a "petticoat"). . . .

[In **"Beyond the Pale"**, a] man who has been involved with a female terrorist kills himself, on the hotel premises. Multiple breakdown follows: phychological collapse, fracturings of etiquette, the crumbling of the proprietors' professional affability, the splitting of the foursome. And through paragraphs of stilted hysteria, the one sympathetic character pronounces the familiar Trevor message about the insubstantiality of niceness. "Chaos and contradiction . . . were hidden everywhere beneath nice-sounding names", "blood . . . flowed around those nice-sounding names".

For all its gesturing towards something of larger significance, though, the story remains at the level of the toy shocker. While

Trevor seems to have abandoned his earlier habit of labelling characters with joky names—Turtle, Sole, Strap, Spanners, Tiles, Batt, Clapp and the like—he still mainly deals in types and caricatures. Only minimally individualized, they can't support the ponderous pronouncements about Evil he now loads upon them. Attempted excursions into the dark places of the psyche soon founder in shallow talk of how "evil breeds evil in a mysterious way". Typically, in *Beyond the Pale,* there is no explanation of the crucial process that turned the happy young creature we first hear of, romping amidst the flowers, into a bitter manufacturer of bombs. Instead, there is just the usual flat contrast, an automatically abrupt switch from attractive to repulsive. Ultimately, here and in the other stories, Trevor's small-scale world—two-dimensional and programmed to familiar routines—functions as a peep-show rather than a microcosm.

    Peter Kemp, "Cosiness and Carnage," in The Times Literary Supplement *(© Times Newspapers Ltd. (London) 1981; reproduced from* The Times Literary Supplement *by permission), No. 4098, October 16, 1981, p. 1193.*

ANATOLE BROYARD

I liked **"Lovers of Their Time,"** William Trevor's last collection of stories, better than **"Beyond the Pale."** I still remember with a feeling of pleased surprise a couple of images from that book. . . .

Yet in some of the other pieces in that book I felt that Mr. Trevor indulged himself in a sort of perverse minimalism, a kind of contest with himself to see how little he needed to make a story. Though everyone regards him as a master of understatement, I wonder whether it isn't conceited in a way to insist on writing such carefully removed stories, so breathlessly poised on the edge of non-existence.

At one time it might have been argued that these are the people who do not get written about, that they were born to blush unseen until Mr. Trevor saw them. But this is no longer the case, for I can think of half a dozen highly regarded writers who are doing the same thing. There's a whole school, in fact, that deals in the gray, the drab and the dull, in those who missed out and stand sighing down a long perspective.

Of course it takes art to make such stories work even as pallidly as they do, but isn't it sentimental, I wonder, to keep picking these threads off people's sleeves? What is Mr. Trevor's message? That each of us has a poem that droops somewhere unseen about us, as Whitman said? I'm not sure I believe it.

"Beyond the Pale" has fewer intensely realized moments than **"Lovers of Their Time."** In fact, I'm not sure it has any. I tried to feel something about a teen-aged girl who wonders whether her divorced father cries in his flat—but why? He had no more reason to cry than anyone else. But that's Mr. Trevor's trick: an assumption of universal pathos.

In another piece, four middle-aged people are on holiday at a seaside hotel. A young man, a stranger, approaches a woman in the party while she is alone, tells her of his sorrow and drowns himself before her eyes. Apart from the fact that it's a melodramatic premise, there are several things wrong with the story. The young man has been driven to despair by learning that a girl he once loved now makes bombs for terrorists. But that isn't the sort of thing that drives people to suicide—it does only in stories.

And then the woman to whom he had confided begins hysterically to exhort everyone to stop and think and grieve, as if the scales have suddenly fallen from her eyes and she has seen the meaning of life in a religious vision. Meanwhile her friends say "Do have a scone" or "Pull yourself together," as if they couldn't believe in the story either. . . .

Something ungenerous in me sees Mr. Trevor not as a master of understatement, but as a blocked writer, lurking at the edges of literature, a wallflower afraid to dance. He's like one of those people who try to attract attention by speaking in a barely audible voice. He can write—everybody agrees on that—but he seems to be wary of inviting full-blooded people into his stories, as if they might break up the delicate furniture of his art.

> Anatole Broyard, "Books of the Times: 'Beyond the Pale'," in The New York Times (© 1982 by The New York Times Company; reprinted by permission), February 3, 1982, p. C25.

JON PARELES

William Trevor's characters would be perfectly content to lead decorous, uneventful lives. They work in shops or offices, attend bridge socials and lawn parties, quietly raise quiet families in London or the Irish countryside. Yet calm eludes them. Unbidden and inevitable as physics or original sin, the past catches them up, impartial History tracing out consequences. Each of the dozen stories in *Beyond the Pale,* Trevor's fifth collection, gauges some repercussion of past on present. Small ones, mostly—remembered indiscretions, hints of family secrets—or larger ones muffled by distance, specifically the continuing war in Ireland. As brute facts intrude, Trevor's characters struggle to stay unruffled, because in their daily round civility equals sanity. They're forced to shift their internal balance of acceptance, forgetfulness, apology, and rationalization. Trevor at his best neither glorifies nor minimizes the struggle; without judging, he illuminates it life-sized.

The stories register flickers of emotion an EKG would miss: tacit pressures, unstated private bargains, suppressed passions. The best story, **"Downstairs at Fitzgerald's,"** shows Cecilia turning 13 and starting to sort out the fallibility of adults. Her divorced, remarried mother fascinates Cecilia's schoolmates. . . . [One of them] suggests to Cecilia that she actually resembles her stepfather, and at a post-birthday lunch she begins to realize that her father has become a horseplayer since the divorce. With matter-of-fact tenderness, Trevor captures puberty's disconnection and disillusion: "It would be ridiculous, now, ever to look after him in his flat."

Trevor's female characters are more vivid than his males, perhaps mirroring a culture in which women feel while men act. **"Mulvihill's Memorial,"** set in an old-line ad agency, winds up with a flippant O. Henry twist that chokes off empathy. More telling, and more open-ended, are **"Paradise Lounge,"** in which an aged spinster and a young adulteress envy each other, and **"Being Stolen From,"** in which Bridget, whose husband has left her, is asked to return the child she'd adopted to its now-married mother. Eventually, "weeping without making a noise," Bridget accepts the prospect. "She belonged with her accumulated odds and ends, as Betty belonged with her mother, and Liam with the woman he loved." Trevor's elegiac understatement makes the smallest actions revelatory.

Reticence serves Trevor well; his least dramatic stories are his most convincing. Oddly, he overshoots in **"Beyond the Pale"** itself. At a gracious Irish hotel far from the "troubles," an English foursome—R. B. and Cynthia Strafe, R. B.'s school chum Dekko, and R. B.'s secret mistress Milly—are taking their yearly vacation. A lone man shows up and kills himself, after confiding to Cynthia, a history buff given to melodrama, that he'd just murdered an ex-girlfriend who had been making IRA bombs in London. Cynthia then shakes up the hotel by speechifying about atrocities and publicly denouncing her companions. Trevor's themes—decorum as necessary hypocrisy, history taking its toll, unquiet Ireland—are hammered home but cheapened by overstatement. In fact, while none of the other stories in *Beyond the Pale* is quite so strident, the collection as a whole is diminished because Trevor uses death so frequently as a clarifier. (*Lovers of Their Time* makes a better introduction to Trevor's short stories.) Individually, however, stories in *Beyond the Pale* can stand with the finest, and most finely tuned, domestic chronicles in print. (pp. 54-5)

> Jon Pareles, "Brief Encounters: 'Beyond the Pale'," (reprinted by permission of The Village Voice and the author; copyright © News Group Publications, Inc., 1982), in The Village Voice, Vol. XXVII, No. 7, February 10-16, 1982, pp. 54-5.

TED SOLOTAROFF

William Trevor's reputation has been slow to establish itself in America. . . . **"Other People's Worlds,"** his most recent novel, received a good deal of praise for its radioactive portrait of a talented sociopath and his victims. Still, Trevor is probably best known for his stories, particularly among writers and critics who recognize a master when they see one. Graham Greene hailed his third collection, **"Angels at the Ritz,"** as perhaps the best in English since "Dubliners," an astute comment that calls attention to the qualities Trevor shares with the early Joyce. Both write that austere Irish prose that quietly charms and that can be adapted to portray various walks of life. Further, both Trevor and the early Joyce are geniuses at presenting a seemingly ordinary life as it is, socially, psychologically, morally, and then revealing the force of these conditions in the threatened individual's moment of resistance to them. This is the deeper realism: accurate observation turning into moral vision. With Trevor as with Joyce one often has the sense of gazing down through the lucid surface of a personality to the dark, ambiguous activity of the soul.

Good and evil are active principles in Trevor's fiction. He knows their force and persistency and complexity; he knows the subtle, perverse ways in which they infiltrate the will. In **"Being Stolen From,"** a story in [Trevor's recent collection **"Beyond the Pale,"**] Bridget Lacy, an Irish countrywoman who lives in London, has been raising a little girl she adopted six years ago from a troubled woman in the neighborhood. Bridget has since lost her husband to a younger woman; though it came out of the blue, her husband being a decent man, it also seemed a part of her fate. . . .

This is a generous art—one that welcomes the homely, the banal, the meager life that writers of Trevor's sophistication tend to pass by. He has filled Bridget with interest and savor, she is the salt of the earth. Trevor takes risks, for the stringencies of his realism require him to work out in the open, as it were, accountable to the ordinary and the probable, while creating Bridget's unique, mysterious core. To get the surface details and tonalities just right involves a perfect eye and ear and an exceptional degree of empathy: the ability, as Auden put it, to "be just with the just, filthy with the filthy too."

Trevor has fashioned a remarkable gallery of contemporary figures. His farmers and priests and men of the turf are as convincing and suggestive as his Hempstead esthetes, his suburban swingers, his old-boy homosexuals, his mod clerks and shopgirls. Nothing seems alien to him; he captures the moral atmosphere of a sleek advertising agency, of a shabby West End dance hall, of a minor public school, of a shotgun wedding in an Irish pub.

Such range and authority are not much in vogue today and may be facilely relegated to the bin of English social fiction—sensitive, humane but small. . . . Our important fiction today is typically concerned with the self-revelations of the writer and of the medium. We have become so habituated to a literature that uses the world as a mirror that we hardly know what else to look for.

It is just here that I think Trevor's fiction is especially valuable; it strengthens the human bond in an age desperately in need of that, a task that most great fiction writers of previous centuries have taken for granted. A case in point is the title story in **"Beyond the Pale."** (p. 7)

The story is typical of Trevor's means and ends, employing, as it does, a clever accuracy about the quotidian in order to move beyond it to the high-risk area of the extravagant and the extreme, where the hidden meanings are to be grasped. We might say that his skill at verisimilitude is meant to carry over and make Mrs. Strafe's bizarre speech convincing; but this is a superficial point. Trevor, again, wants to reach us at a deeper level than our assent; nothing closes us off more from the world, as V. S. Pritchett has observed, than a correct opinion about it. Trevor wants us to envision what Cynthia Strafe envisions, which we do through imagination and spirit and thereby lay bare our own ambiguous and equivocal complicity in these matters. The creature-comfort insulation and the sedating routines foster the indifference and selfishness of these characters and form an active principle of the privileged life as well as of the mentality and morality of colonialism. . . .

I hope many people will read William Trevor. He is a truly wonderful writer, and his criticism of life is sorely needed. (p. 34)

Ted Solotaroff, "The Dark Souls of Ordinary People," in The New York Times Book Review *(© 1982 by The New York Times Company; reprinted by permission), February 21, 1982, pp. 7, 34.*

PATRICK SKENE CATLING

A good short story, like a good poem, exists only in its expression. Its essence is irreducible and immutable. As William Trevor has written (in a review in praise of one of the writers of short stories he most admires, Sean O'Faolain), 'the better the short story the less easy it is to re-tell'. By this criterion, among others, Trevor's short stories are among the best in English. . . . I have just re-read 59 of [his] stories and I cannot imagine how any of them could be improved by any alteration. Every story seems as perfect (as Philip Larkin might put it) as an egg.

Perhaps [Trevor's] most important virtue, rare among all sorts of people, especially writers, is that he acknowledges without condescension the value of every human life, no matter how restricted, distorted or embittered: even the outwardly most ordinary person feels extraordinary; everyone is unique and marvellous and awful, alone at the centre of his world.

Trevor's subjects are home, family, love, duty, pride and other difficulties and torments that make life, even with alcohol, seem so long. . . .

He is an inexorable yet usually merciful observer of major weaknesses and minor vices, some not so minor. He is a keen appraiser of the surfaces and depths of people and things. He is a diligent listener, sometimes an eavesdropper, with an ear as accurately retentive as a tape-recorder and with the artistic sensibility and skill to edit the recordings to achieve, beyond verbatim realism, a heightened sense of the oddities of different manners of speech.

His calm, evenly weighted, ostensibly dispassionate style makes eccentricity seem normal and normality bizarre. He makes few comments—few are needed; there are no nudges or winks. He presents his observations with such subtle imbalance that he gives an impression of fairness. His malefactors can be understood and sympathised with and their poor, foolish victims can be forgiven. He depicts tragedy without mawkishness, absurdity without ridicule. . . .

He is compassionate but not sentimental, ironic but not cynical. He is a moralist who only implies morality. He never preaches sermons to people when they are down, or even when they are up. He simply offers readers opportunities to perceive aspects of themselves—punishment enough. He also provides the healing Irish consolation of the sort of humour that would enable you to smile if you slipped and twisted your ankle in a graveyard in the rain. He would have made an excellent priest. . . .

Having up to now divided his life almost equally between Ireland and England, he knows both countries intimately and, like some other Anglo-Irishmen, he is sufficiently alien in each to be able to write about them with detached, affectionate exasperation.

Trevor's fictional Ireland is dreary, parochial and frustrating; his England is a place of petty vain pretensions. Many of his stories are illustrations of these general notions, which may appear at first glance to be unprepossessing but have stimulated him to create a richly varied gallery of emotional grotesques, like the residents of any neighbourhood. Behing the lace curtains of terrace houses and maisonettes, it seems, psychopathological monsters writhe in an agony of domestic orthodoxy.

Whether the portraits and case histories of the middle-aged and the old are terrible or ludicrous or both by turns depends on Trevor's unexpected shifts of focus and emphasis and his sudden revelations of inner realities. His mastery is such that he can persuasively manipulate responses in astonishing zig-zags and U-turns in the space of only a few pages. There are novelists who write stories 20 times as long which say less. (p. 25)

Patrick Skene Catling, "The Genius of William Trevor," in The Spectator *(© 1982 by The Spectator; reprinted by permission of* The Spectator*), Vol. 249, No. 8035, July 10, 1982, pp. 25-6.*

Derek (Alton) Walcott

1930-

West Indian poet, dramatist, and critic.

Walcott's writing career began at age eighteen, with the publication of *Twenty-five Poems*. Since then, in addition to being considered a major modern poet, he has become a respected playwright and is regarded as a voice of West Indian culture and thought. His poems and plays have won many awards, among them an Obie in 1971 for his play *Dream on Monkey Mountain*.

His recurrent themes include the search for identity—both that of the West Indies and his own within it, isolation and estrangement, particularly of the artist, and the divisive elements in the social and personal self. These ideas accommodate Walcott's poetic vision in his four principal collections, *In a Green Night, The Castaway, Another Life,* and *The Gulf,* the last of which deals with the literal and figurative divisions of history, race, class, and language. One of the primary characterizations Walcott uses is that of the islander as Robinson Crusoe, as the New World Adam, as the Castaway, to whom is left a despoiled Eden in the aftermath of colonialism, from which he must create a new West Indian World.

Walcott's loyalty to both his English and his African backgrounds provides the major tension of his work. His written language is split between literary English in the poems and island patois in the plays, though in later efforts the two styles have tended to merge into one that uses more natural speech and rhythm patterns, and a more direct, open mode of expression. Classical influences, while still in evidence, are used more sparingly.

Walcott has been criticized for his interpretation of island experiences through European literary traditions and for his avoidance of definitive statements about his racial and political loyalties. Walcott, however, believes that his mixed heritage has enabled him to put personal experiences into universal contexts. Because of this, he is both at home and displaced wherever he goes, a condition which he elaborates upon in his recent *The Fortunate Traveller*.

(See also *CLC*, Vols. 2, 4, 9, 14; *Contemporary Authors*, Vols. 89-92; and *Dictionary of Literary Biography Yearbook: 1981*.)

HUGO WILLIAMS

If the most beautiful thing in the world is inherited wealth, Derek Walcott's poetry is rich. He has none of the self-made man's frugality. He is a natural with all the confidence of a capitalist: that words will never run short, that there will always be fresh pleasures, new colours. He is extravagant and his poems are beautifully illuminated. They make the mouth water. . . . We drink its vocables and become lightheaded, but we wake up without a hangover. His poems have an indestructible flavour like that of a summer holiday abroad: bright, congested, nostalgic. They send us far from the complexities of cities, but they return us safe and sound.

[*In a Green Night*] is Derek Walcott's first collection of poetry and the book is well packed and comprehensive, containing

poems written between 1948 and 1960. . . . I would rather have had a slightly more restricted choice. (pp. 77-8)

Most of the book is on a high level and some like *Allegre* . . . display an agreeable pessimism and are really tempting and evocative. He is continually searching for the true feeling of beauty, what it feels like to see, as well as how it looks, and this is why the self comes into these poems at unexpected moments. It is not always successful: . . . *Simply Passing Through,* tucked away at the back of the book, deserves no praise. One feels a pointlessness as of a documentary film about a foreign country. The weak associations show through as soon as the highly-coloured words become merely parts of speech, employed for sense as much as sound. At his muddiest, Mr. Walcott starts attacking us with a slightly self-pitying volubility rather like the blues. The chords become richer and richer until they melt and we fall into a dreamless sleep. More often the notes are clear and primary and one can tell when this is about to happen from the way the poem begins. First lines are important and revealing. (p. 78)

Last lines are equally important and his ten sonnets called *Tales of the Islands* are particularly well finished. The various legends make pictures as clear as stained glass and he manages the iambics with a light and versatile touch.

Reaching the end of *In a Green Night,* I begin to sense that Mr Walcott went through a fairly thorough rehabilitation quite a long time ago and that we have not been spared the poems he wrote before that time: that they have in fact been sprinkled sparsely enough among better and, let us hope, more recent work. The best that remains is the self-willed buoyancy of the natural poet. (p. 79)

Hugo Williams, "Selected Books: 'In A Green Night'," in London Magazine *(© London Magazine 1962), Vol. 2, No. 4, July, 1962, pp. 77-9.*

CAMERON KING and LOUIS JAMES

The title poem of [Derek Walcott's] second major collection, **The Castaway** . . . , portrays a lone man on a sand-bank looking out to sea for rescue. He is lost. The implications are pessimistic. Yet Walcott's progression has been towards greater self-discovery and achievement. It is this paradox that lies behind the work of the finest Caribbean poet writing in English today.

From his earliest published work Walcott turned a critical eye on the predicament of the West Indian. We may find that his attitudes were a little pretentious, but this is not simply because Walcott was a young man when he wrote them. The critical intelligence he turned on his world he turned also on himself. In the first poem of **In a Green Night**, **'Prelude'**, he placed himself in a relationship to his poetry that is in part self-mocking. . . . This is the stance expected of the young West Indian intellectual. It also has a more serious purpose. Such attitudes are a protective mask, necessary until experience forms deeper reactions to life. . . . The styles that embody his attitudes are also 'useful'. They are ways by which he may discover his personal voice. Every young poet has to use experiments in style as stalking horses to track down his true poetic medium, but it is particularly important for a West Indian passionately concerned with the craft of words in areas where there is no native poetic tradition. Walcott tries on mask after mask. . . . But the very consistency and thoroughness of Walcott's early experiment should warn the critic that here is not simply an imitative poet. And as Walcott's experiments continued, gradually but surely, we see his masks shimmering, dissolving, and a face, Walcott's poetic features, appearing through. (pp. 86-8)

Walcott has been accused of turning to the European culture and experience in order to interpret the West Indian and so betraying his own civilization. There are critics who would like to see him pursue his experiments with dialect, or the direct, uncomplicated speech we find, for instance, in **'A Letter from Brooklyn'**. . . . But the West Indies have no definitive and exclusive culture. Its peoples have come to the West Indies as travellers, forced or of their own will from Africa, Asia and Europe. Any claim that there is one West Indian voice, at least as yet, does not bear examination. Secondly, for better or for worse, although the great majority of West Indians have an African background, the peculiar circumstances of Caribbean history, its slavery and its emancipation, its educational and governmental systems, have all been within the European system. Further, the concept that 'European' culture has a nationalist identity in opposition to that of the Caribbean has the dangerous elements of racial mythology. The 'literature of England' reaches backwards and outwards to the cultures of Greece, Rome and medieval France. It touches the thought and civilizations of Europe, the new world, even Asia and Africa. Its preoccupation is with man as a human being, and for this reason a culture that becomes isolationist and inward looking can

paradoxically cut itself off from the means of knowing itself. It is not simply chance that the greatest nationalist writers in French and Spanish as well as English, in modern Africa as well as the West Indies, have been those who have been able most fully to come to their own predicaments through mastery of the European literary experience. Walcott is in this tradition and from the reader he demands the same sympathies, at least in his earlier poems. He expects his reader to recognize and expand allusions to the metaphysicals, Shakespeare, Baudelaire and many others.

This 'literary' approach can of course have its dangers, and the early Walcott could fall into them. . . . [Some of his lines] are pretty but precious. This is not characteristic Walcott. At his best Walcott is lead in his avoidance of the 'kiff-kaff', the loose volubility, of West Indian idiom, to its strength, the heady Elizabethan delight in the sound and potential of words. . . . Walcott's use of language is exploratory, creative, and a surprisingly large number of his lines have the ring of Shakespearean aphorism. They are coined phrases that do not devalue. . . . Walcott's first great love in literature was Shakespeare; Walcott has been as much a dramatist as a poet, . . . and his movement has been away from the lyrical to the dramatic mode of writing. This sounded earlier in his turgid imitations of Dylan Thomas, and has developed into a style that can express experience not as emotion recollected in tranquillity, but as possessing all the continuing tension of drama. . . . (pp. 89-91)

The same account of weaknesses and strengths can be made with regard to the content of Walcott's verse. Senghor declared 'emotion is negro', but Walcott's early verse was a deliberate attempt to avoid the clichés of passion that invest so many Caribbean literary works. (p. 91)

One has to compare Walcott's early poetry with other Caribbean verse of the period to realize how unusual was Walcott's formidable intelligence and technical control. But what has been said may have already suggested that in this early period Walcott could be a victim of his intelligence. It could raise a veil between Walcott and his subject. His writing about the Caribbean has little of the area's experienced presence. There is no hint of heat and intense light: they are filtered out in the 'green night' of Walcott's intelligence. (p. 92)

Walcott however is a formidably self-aware poet, and he has consciously developed out of the imprisoning shell of his intelligence. Not intellectual concepts, but the physical environment of the Caribbean, has become more and more the bedrock of his imagination. He accepts and explores the existence that lies beyond the subjective human consciousness. (pp. 93-4)

If Walcott has turned more and more to the Caribbean predicament in all its aspects, he has returned to the themes of his earlier poetry with deeper understanding. Sex, which he earlier attacks as a West Indian preoccupation, . . . is still seen as a destructive force, but in a poem like **'Goats and Monkeys'** he reaches towards the paradox that lies beyond the destructive futilities of sexual passion touched on in the near-perfect but minor **'A Careful Passion'**. (p. 96)

As Walcott reaches beyond the immediate context of the Caribbean which is his starting point into metaphysical concepts, so he explores towards the wider predicament of the Negro. We see this in **'The Glory Trumpeter'**. Eddie Calvert, in the lonely exultation of his playing, eyes sealed like a 'deacon at his prayer', pours out music created in the alembic of Negro suffering and history. But Walcott does not stand back with the balanced judgment shown in **'Ruins of a Great House'**. He shifts still further away from blame of others, to an acceptance in himself of his part in 'all whom race and exile have defeated'. . . . Only as the percipient, more mature poet does Walcott see the Negro music still appealing for the emancipation of the Caribbean Negroes' less privileged brothers in the States, and incriminating those who do not hear. (pp. 97-8)

But, ultimately, if Walcott escapes from the confines of his intellect in one direction, he only finds himself confronted with yet another coast. The image of 'the castaway' is one which bears deep and continual consideration. The strains inherent in the West Indian situation—where Walcott, unlike most West Indian writers, has insisted on remaining—are intensified for the serious artist. The artist confronts the imperfections and vagaries of life with the absolute standards of art. A writer like A. L. Hendriks can retire into a private world of formal perfection. Walcott refuses to do this, and so a perfect poem contradicts life, the experience of life contradicts the work of art. This is not just a matter of perfection against imperfection, but of the conflict between two different modes of being: the living experience is essentially different to the experienced art. In trying to express the totality of experience the poet finds himself caught, a castaway, against the radius of the possibilities of poetry. He is locked in the self-generated visions of the poet's brain. . . . Art is inadequate. But, an island within an island, the poet is inadequate even to his art. The craft moves beyond the man, at once more perfect, and infinitely less, than the creative personality. All this lies behind the poem **'The Castaway'**. Here Walcott portrays the poet lying isolated. . . . He does not state that in writing the poem he is in fact rescued; not released from the island predicament, true, but driven in the boat of the poem across the seas of the imagination, where to travel is to arrive. (pp. 98-9)

> *Cameron King and Louis James, "In Solitude for Company: The Poetry of Derek Walcott," in* The Islands in Between: Essays on West Indian Literature, *edited by Louis James (© Oxford University Press 1968; reprinted by permission of Oxford University Press), Oxford University Press, London, 1968, pp. 86-99.*

EDWARD BAUGH

Derek Walcott has always had, even in his rawest apprenticeship, a head for metaphor. From the merest pastiche, the occasional and wholly original metaphor would burst to signal a talent that would endure. This gift has been one of the chief constants in his development and in his adventures among various styles. . . . That gift has itself undergone some development. (pp. 47-8)

A few preliminary observations about Walcott are necessary to help establish a context for the discussion of metaphor in his poetry. The first may seem, initially at least, rather trivial. In his first major collection, *In a Green Night* . . . , there are only two poems in which he does not follow the old convention of beginning each line with a capital. In *The Castaway* . . . only seventeen of the thirty-three poems follow that convention, while in the latest book, *The Gulf*, . . . all the poems are in the new convention. These statistics indicate more than a readiness to be in line with typographical fashion. They indicate Walcott's general hankering after a kind of poetic plainness, after a simple, direct, "natural" style. His development in this

pursuit of plainness can be seen in a comparison of *In a Green Night* with *The Castaway* and *The Gulf*. . . .

[The] overall impression left by [*In a Green Night*] is not so much one of "crisp," "clear," "cold" verse, as of an exuberance of language, a delight in the rich music of words, in the grand and sonorous verbal gesture. (p. 48)

[Some] of his strongest early influences came from poets who excelled at sonorous vocables and the histrionic line, at intricate playing with the more obviously musical qualities of words—poets like Dylan Thomas, Hart Crane, the early Stevens, the early Lowell; and there is some of the grandeur of seventeenth-century poetry. I think of poems like **"A City's Death by Fire," "Steersman, my Brother," "Castiliane," "En Mi-Careme."** . . . Of course, it isn't just the sound of the words or the rhythm which carries the echoes, but also the imagery and the whole way of using language. This Walcott [is] tipsy on the sweet and heady wine of words. . . . (pp. 49-50)

Walcott has not abandoned the ringing line, and it would be a pity if he did, but he has come to use it with less prodigality and a greater functional discretion. He has been moving towards sparer yet, in a way, subtler rhythms, more angular perhaps, nearer to normal speech and prose rhythms, and to this extent we may say that he has been developing a more natural, a homelier style. (p. 50)

The verse forms of his later poetry are, on the whole, freer, more open, contributing to the overall effect of comparative directness and plainness. The rhetorical flourish and the rich melody are used now more discreetly, with more specific functional point. The title poem of *The Gulf* is a model of a firmly controlled blend of eloquence and rhythmic emphasis on the one hand and the plain-sounding and low-keyed on the other. . . . The three-line stanza pattern, giving a sense of order, seems to want to remember *terza rima,* but there is no attempt at any regular rhyme-scheme and there is great freedom of movement within the three-line structure. . . . (p. 51)

What I am talking about is not simply a question of "style." The stylistic obsession is a function of Walcott's relentless tracking of the elusive and perhaps purely imaginary animal the simple truth. He seems to believe sometimes that somewhere there are realities which one can call the essentials of life and which one can, if one is cunning enough, steal upon and transfix, and that they will be characterised by a startling plainness and simplicity. What he is charting is not just a style of writing, but a view of life. (p. 52)

Like many another poet who recognises a "sacred duty to the Word" of poetry, Walcott is stricken by a nagging mistrust of art, of the art of words. There is a fear that poetry is ultimately unsatisfactory as a mode of achieving the kind of being which he covets. (pp. 52-3)

This mistrust of the art of words expresses itself partly in a desire to get beyond metaphor. (p. 53)

Walcott recognises the life-and-death game which he is playing with metaphor. Here we have a poet who moves in metaphor as in his native element, straining after a style, a life past metaphor, past poetry, which is, I suggest, essentially metaphorical. The truth is that any simplicity, any plainness, any lucidity which he achieves must be qualified by an increasing subtlety and centrality of metaphorical language. . . . Perhaps the plain truths which he seeks are not so plain after all—they involve a kind of complexity—and perhaps, even if they *are* plain, it is impossible for mortal sight to see them in their plainness. Any declaration by Walcott that his aim is to write "clear," "crisp," "lucent" verse, verse glowing with "the hard coral light," must be taken with reservation. For this is the same Walcott who is fascinated by effects of opacity and of seeing things through glass. And there is no feeling that this state of affairs is simply what he wishes to get away from. On the contrary, he seems to accept it as a permanent condition of being. . . . (pp. 53-4)

I would say that in Walcott's poetry there is a tension between the ideas of simplicity/lucidity/directness and the ideas of complexity/opacity/obliquity. The true life of the poetry is within the ambience of that tension. The two sets of ideas are in reality inseparable, since truth is at once simple and complex. . . .

Metaphor affords the poet a powerful means of expressing the tension of which I speak. Metaphor simplifies and multiplies at one and the same time. The concentrating force of metaphor is the simplest way of expressing what is to be expressed, but the concentration is liberating rather than limiting. (p. 54)

Throughout Walcott's poetry we will find the memorable and illuminating metaphor. . . . Very often these metaphors are not essential in respect of the total meaning of the poem as a whole; their force is largely confined to the moment of their use and does not radically affect or modify the poem. The poem develops an idea or an argument by means of a rational logic. The argument can be fairly well paraphrased. Metaphors occur along the way. Their effect on the poem is chiefly cumulative. They do not themselves constitute *the* basic or essential mode of the poem's existence. I am thinking, for example, of such poems as **"Ruins of a Great House," "A Far Cry from Africa"** and **"A Lesson for this Sunday."** Sometimes we can perceive a pattern or interplay of images/metaphors suggesting itself, but that pattern is again largely additive and two-dimensional. (p. 55)

I think we can see that in some of the more recent poems, certain impulses of metaphor struggling for fulfilment in other, usually earlier poems, enjoy a kind of fulfilment. One can almost say that poems like **"The Almond Trees," "Crusoe's Island"** and **"The Gulf"** belong to an essentially different mode from poems like **"Ruins of a Great House," "A Far Cry from Africa"** and **"A Lesson for this Sunday,"** and the difference has to do with metaphor. (This is not to say that the modes are mutually exclusive in respect of these poems.) (p. 56)

Ultimately, and this should be true of any poem, the nature of the poem's structural being determines the quality of the poem as a comment on its chosen subject. . . . Further, one ought to be able to see that differences in the nature or quality (scope, richness, resilience, viability) of the comment between a poem like **"The Almond Trees"** and an earlier one like **"Ruins of a Great House,"** which is on a roughly similar theme, are intimately related to such differences as there are in the ways in which the two poems work. By trying in this essay to indicate something of the way in which Walcott makes poems and of his preoccupation with the nature and capacity of poetry, I hope that I have suggested a way of seeing any Walcott poem in its totality, whatever its theme, whether West Indian-ness or suffering or cruelty or beauty or exile or love or lust. . . . (p. 58)

Edward Baugh, "Metaphor and Plainness in the Poetry of Derek Walcott," in The Literary Half-Yearly *(© The Literary Half-Yearly), Vol. XI, No. 2, July, 1970, pp. 47-58.*

DENIS DONOGHUE

Mr. Walcott is a powerful writer, but many of his poems are trapped in the politics of feeling, knowing the representative fate they must sustain. It is enough for any poet that he is responsible for his own feeling; he answers to his scruple, his conscience, hard master. But Mr. Walcott's poems try to serve a second master, the predicament of his people. They tie themselves in historical chains, and then try to break loose. It is my impression that the poems [in *The Gulf*] are trying now to escape from the politics of feeling by an increasingly personal understanding, taste, truth. Fighting against rhetoric, he resorts to rhetoric, both Caribbean, inescapable. Besides, he has a weakness for grandeur, and he rushes into temptation by writing of exile, ancestral loss, historical plangencies, the gulf between man and man.

He is in a middle state, history at one extreme, sensibility at the other; history, meaning loss and bondage, . . . and sensibility, meaning a sense of responsibility to feeling, its validity and measure. . . .

In principle, Mr. Walcott wants a direct style. "All styles yearn to be plain as life," he says, but he will not let his own style yearn for that quality. . . . [Many] of Mr. Walcott's poems howl, their sensibility overwhelmed. Sometimes the abuse is his own fault, one violence answering another, and we have the feeling that Mr. Walcott is impatient to assume the world, he will not wait for the just word. . . .

In diction, Mr. Walcott is striking, but often what he strikes is a hard bargain, practicing usury in the transaction between language and feeling. He writes everything so large that the reader is inclined to deduct something, to keep the situation reasonable. An impression of excess arises from Mr. Walcott's poems, especially when they insist upon converting the natural forms into human terms. . . .

The finest poems are those in which Mr. Walcott's sensibility communes with centuries of historical experience, the long perspective of life in place and time. Perhaps in these poems the venom of his own promises, needs, and aspirations is dispelled; there have been thousands of years before now. My favorite among such poems is **"Air."** . . . It is a lovely poem, and there are other poems in the book almost as fine.

Denis Donoghue, "Waiting for the End," in The New York Review of Books *(reprinted with permission from* The New York Review of Books; *copyright © 1971 Nyrev, Inc.), Vol. 16, No. 8, May 6, 1971, p. 27.**

SAMUEL OMO ASEIN

Walcott's treatment of the theme of death and the inscrutable ultimate power that governs the universe, and his moral statements on the tussle between the God-head and the Devil in us are various extensions of a central concern with the precariousness of the human condition. The dominant theme in *The Sea at Dauphin* is the perennial struggle between life and death. The theme recurs in a less obvious form in *Ti-Jean and His Brothers, Malcauchon* and *Dream on Monkey Mountain.* In each case Death is presented as a perennial source of anxiety an intractable Force which man is constantly trying to reconcile himself with. (p. 70)

The most intriguing question which Walcott has continued to address himself to and which provides an immediate thematic link between his poetry and his plays is the theme of racial and individual identity. The best and most representative treatment of that subject is contained in Walcott's most accomplished dramatic work to date, *Dream on Monkey Mountain*. (pp. 73-4)

What Walcott tries to do in his writings, is to affirm a positive cultural identity for the West Indies; and his works to date might be said to add up to just such a cultural affirmation. The fact that many of Walcott's characters fail in their various quests goes to emphasize the precariousness of man's existence in an unsympathetic universe. But grim as the picture may appear, Walcott does not allow room for utter despair because he constantly reminds us of certain possibilities open to man. Man's dignity, he seems to be saying is determined not by the circumstances of his being *per se* but by the extent to which he succeeds in reconciling himself with his world without compromising the essentials of his being. The significance of his works derives largely from his intense feeling for man in his day to day struggles, and from his sustained exploration of the problem of being. In sum, they amount to a poetic statement of man's struggle for self-fulfilment and his attempt to attain a harmonius existence in nature. It is the profundity of that statement and its universal applicability which ultimately establish the pre-eminent value of his works and have found for him a just place among the ranks of the leading poets and playwrights of our time. (p. 78)

> *Samuel Omo Asein, "Derek Walcott: The Man and His Ideas," in* The Literary Half-Yearly *(© The Literary Half-Yearly), Vol. XVII, No. 2, July, 1976, pp. 59-79.*

BRUCE KING

The examination of the drama of his own life against that of his community and region has been one of Walcott's main themes. His individual experience has become part, if not necessarily typical, of what it means to be West Indian. (pp. 119-20)

[*Epitaph for the Young: XII Cantos,* an early volume published in Barbados,] is in an experimental modern style. The epic-like twelve divisions of *Epitaph,* the parallels and contrasts of a West Indian life with the classical past, are indebted to James Joyce's *Ulysses.* There are echoes of T. S. Eliot and Dylan Thomas. The emphasis on late adolescence and early manhood, in which maturation is seen as a condition of feverish dying, had been made popular by Thomas. While immature in both theme and craft, *Epitaph* is an attempt to move beyond the fragments of lyric poetry to a larger structure shaped around the inner life of the author. The speaker's voyage through life is that of a modern Ulysses, a West Indian who, no matter how much he makes use of European myth, is conscious of problems of ethnic identity and colour. . . . Alongside the concern with problems of young love in a multiracial society, and the attempt to master the idiom of European elite culture, an ironic awareness of falsity emerges. . . . The burden of Walcott's poetry will be to explore his dual inheritance, especially in the various forms it is found within the New World. (p. 120)

[Another early volume, *Poems,* published in Jamaica,] shows a concern with the racial, economic and cultural problems of the region. '**Montego Bay—Travelogue II**' contrasts the rich white American tourists with the poor black fishermen and waiters. . . . While Walcott's early verse reveals a consciousness of racial and social problems, the Jamaica poems are most striking for rhymed verse forms and witty puns that were fash-

ionable in American and British literary circles during the 1940s and '50s.

The distance between such early attitudes of irony and protest and the more fully thought out positions later identified with Walcott can be seen in his *Selected Poems*. . . . The now famous '**A Far Cry from Africa**' treats of the Mau Mau uprising in terms that mock the usual justifications for and criticisms of colonialism. The ironies are those of compassion in the face of abstractions. . . . Although the poem attacks 'the drunken officer of British rule' and the 'statistics' that 'justify' colonial policy, the second stanza introduces a more encompassing theme, using religious imagery, in which all forms of violence are seen as part of man's long cruelty towards, and wish to dominate others. . . . The poem is remarkable for its complexity of emotions. The elaborately rhymed stanzas and regular five-stress lines give formal order to what are essentially confused, irreconcilably opposed feelings: identification with black Africa, disgust with the killing of both white and black innocents, distrust of motives, love of the English language, and dislike of those who remain emotionally uninvolved.

Many of the poems of this period treat of the author's divided heritage in paradoxical celebrations—of compassion towards the dead slave owner, the dead conqueror, or in '**The Train**' towards his English grandfather. A recognition of a shared humanity, and more particularly of a common heritage of poetry, changes accusations of guilt to feelings of compassion. . . . There is, however, an abstract quality to the poetry of this period, as if Walcott were rather thinking about than feeling his subject-matter. . . . The fusion of races involves a mixture of guilty pasts, but from such a mixture rebirth is possible. (pp. 120-22)

Walcott knows that protest in itself cannot give birth to a vital West Indian society. Many of his poems attack the politicians and intellectuals who have turned protest into demagogy and who mistake expressions of anger for art. The complex rhymes, stanzas and subtle patterns of repetition, allusion and contrast in '**Laventville**' show that the best engaged writing results from a commitment to literary craft. But instead of the inherited forms of the early poems, Walcott's style has become much plainer and closer to his own speech patterns. . . . Walcott's poems in *The Castaway* . . . use the myth of Crusoe to suggest that the New World is a new beginning, a new Eden. Both white and black have been shipwrecked and while those of African descent suffer an amnesia of their racial past, it is from such forgetfulness that a new culture began. Walcott sees himself in the line of such poets of the Americas as Whitman, Neruda and St John Perse. Art will give form and self-awareness to this new society. But in '**Crusoe's Island**' Walcott admits the limitations of art replacing belief. (p. 124)

What is needed is the acceptance of being West Indian. . . . In contrast the governments of the islands promoted a folk art which has become sterile and artificial. The folk culture of the past cannot be resurrected. The Black Power intellectuals mimic foreign revolutions in urging the people 'to acquire pride which meant abandoning their individual dignity'; even the fury of the intellectual was 'artificially generated' by an imitation of foreign 'metropolitan anger'. Thus Walcott angrily attacks politicians and intellectuals in *The Gulf* [and *Sea Grapes*]. . . . (p. 125)

Part of the power of Walcott's long autobiographical poem, *Another Life,* . . . results from the setting of the author's life within his community, the sensitivity with which his childhood is shown, and the way the verse universalises the particularities of St Lucian society without sentimentalising or claiming a false dignity. Dialect and patois sit comfortably alongside Latin, rhyming prayers in French, and a variety of complex verse forms and rhythms which seem necessary to the range of experiences being expressed. Since the nineteenth century the confessional autobiography has replaced the epic; the author's spiritual development and relationship to his culture have taken the role formerly given to the warrior or exploring hero. Autobiography is particularly relevant to those in an emerging nation or rapidly changing society and has resulted in some of the best West Indian and African literature. Walcott's examination of the divided consciousness of the mulatto in a mixed community—the evocations of childhood, the stages of maturation, middle-class life, family, individuals in the community, school, the priest, local merchants, friendships, early loves—recreates a world of which the narrator is a product and in which he is still involved. By using the confessional mode which Robert Lowell made popular, Walcott has produced a classic of West Indian literature which celebrates the local landscape, the many races, mixed culture and languages of the islands. (p. 129)

> Bruce King, "West Indies II: Walcott, Brathwaite and Authenticity," in his The New English Literatures: Cultural Nationalism in a Changing World (© Bruce King 1980; reprinted by permission of St. Martin's Press, Inc.; in Canada by Macmillan London and Basingstoke), St. Martin's Press, 1980, pp. 118-39.*

ROBERT D. HAMNER

[The] study of Walcott's career as a dramatist must begin with the play he regards as his first, **Henri Christophe**—and it is written in verse. (p. 52)

The plot unfolds in Haiti and concerns black characters for the most part but there is little besides to mark the play as West Indian. A quotation from *Hamlet* and one from *Richard III*, heading respectively each of the two parts of the play, are in keeping with the language Walcott puts into the mouths of illiterate ex-slaves. . . . The major problem is with the Jacobean polish on words and images that seems inconsistent with the rough-hewn dignity of the characters being portrayed. When Christophe utters fine poetic lines about his grief the sentiment rings hollow more for the archaic language than for the fact that Christophe himself plotted Toussaint's destruction. Even allowing for poetic license, there is nothing in this play to show of the bodily sweat that Christophe celebrates shortly before his death. . . . (p. 53)

Noticeably lacking in Walcott's first play are modulation of feeling and differentiation of character. In his second drama he avoids these weaknesses and also the problem of the discrepancy between character and style of presentation. **Harry Dernier**, a tour de force for radio production, though markedly literary and metaphysical in tone, achieves greater unity by the expedient of having only one player and having him placed in an unidentifiable location. (p. 54)

Walcott's themes and attitudes in the plays, as in his early poetry, are predominantly weighty and somber, probing psychological motivations and philosophical questions. It is as though he skirts the middle ground, feeling comfortable only with the high seriousness of Jacobean English or the wry intellectualism of more recent European writers. The spelling

puns with words and names in **Harry Dernier**, for example, have to be seen and contemplated rather than heard to be appreciated. There is an emotional restraint, an abstract dryness, about **Henri Christophe** and **Harry Dernier** that prevents their taking on a full-bodied life. (p. 55)

By comparison, Walcott's third drama, **The Sea at Dauphin**, . . . is vibrant with the sounds of life. **The Sea at Dauphin** is Walcott's first folk play and it is also the most perfectly executed of his early dramas. It would be tempting to assume that the effectiveness derives from his turning to the setting of St. Lucia and to the language he has heard spoken since childhood. These are important factors; but far more crucial to him during this apprenticeship phase was his discovery of a precedent-setting model in the work of Irish writer John Millington Synge. Walcott has admitted his debt to *Riders to the Sea*, and he could hardly have found a more instructive example to follow. . . . In the West Indies, as in Synge's Ireland, the folk idiom and imagination continue to thrive. There is a current in plays like *Riders to the Sea* and **The Sea at Dauphin** that is elemental, close to the sources of life.

In these plays the sea represents the unpredictable forces of nature with which men have to contend for their lives. Theirs is a daily battle which, if unspectacular, is still no less heroic than the Promethean theft of fire from the gods. Such a comparison is not as unwarranted as it sounds on the surface. Walcott's Afa, a fisherman, works hard and receives little return; he recounts the litany of his failures and of the fishermen who have died, but even in the face of inevitable defeat he defies the sea and the God who ignores his prayers. (pp. 55-6)

[**Ione**] moves deeper into St. Lucian folk tradition with the introduction of a greater number of characters, including an old prophetess, Theresine. Passions run high in this play. . . . The central conflict is between two mountain families over land. Their uneasy peace turns to violence because of marital infidelity, pride, and the thirst for revenge. . . .

[In] spite of the concreteness of local setting, character, and idiom, there are also elements which generate a pervasive tone reminiscent of Grecian classics—the inevitability of brooding fate (personified in the oracle Theresine), the chorus of women, and the Greek names of several of the characters. Like Teiresias, Theresine can foresee but is helpless to prevent impending doom. (p. 57)

Walcott treats marital infidelity, familial strife, and personal pride within a remote mountain settlement with the same tragic high seriousness he accords Christophe. . . . Walcott ventures beneath the external simplicity of lives narrowly circumscribed by accidents of birth and history to explore their potential for great drama. The actions of despotic slave-kings and of downtrodden fishermen may be disparate in the impact of their influence on history, but they are equal in what they reveal about the dimensions of human behavior.

[**Drums and Colours**], Walcott's fifth play, exploits these dimensions by presenting characters of legendary proportion side by side with representatives of countless little men whose legacy is their ability to survive. The juxtaposition is subtle but effective, and quite revealing. (p. 58)

Drums and Colours, which marks Walcott's departure from the earlier apprenticeship plays, is a West Indian historical pageant commissioned for the opening of the First Federal Parliament of the West Indies in 1958. Because of the requirements of spanning 400 years of history, the play ranges too broadly to be well unified. To aid continuity, Walcott utilizes for the first time an element of West Indian life that has never entered into his earlier plays. In addition to the coin as a linking device and the character names that recur, he frames the episodic action of the basic plot and provides interludes between scenes with a band of carnival dancers. The songs, dances, and antics of these celebrants exemplify the panache of West Indian life that rises above the brutal history of the islands. By including fundamental properties of Carnival—music, dance, masking, pageantry, mime, and parody—Walcott moves significantly nearer to the kind of drama that is adequate to the rich diversity of his cultural experience.

Walcott's next play, *Ti-Jean and His Brothers,* was conceived in the same year with *Drums and Colours,* but except for their closeness in time and certain technical similarities the two plays belong to separate stages of Walcott's career. *Drums and Colours* is a loosely constructed, somewhat didactic pageant. In spite of good character studies and convincing scenes, it lacks the kind of concentration that is desirable in drama. Such weaknesses may be unavoidable, considering the purpose for which the play was written. It is important in Walcott's career for two reasons: for the first time he opens his stage to a vast array of visual and audile experiences; second, he brings together his most prevalent character types. (pp. 60-1)

Ti-Jean and His Brothers is based on a St. Lucian folktale, and Walcott succeeded well with his dramatized version in retaining the storyteller's simple, narrative force. At the same time the play is, as Walcott described it, "stylized." (p. 68)

No prose summation does justice to the color and movement, the dance, music, and humor of *Ti-Jean and His Brothers.* Since its message and manner of presentation are so uniquely West Indian in flavor, this play stands as Walcott's first technically integrated West Indian drama. It incorporates the major ingredients of his varied culture, including the prominent figures from Walcott's emerging gallery of character types. . . . [In] Ti-Jean himself is the character of the trickster hero, one of the most popular figures in West Indian stories. Unable to overcome by force of knowledge or physical might, he can endure like his enslaved ancestors by outwitting those who have power. Overall, the play exemplifies the kind of foot-, life-, and earth-asserting force that Walcott called for in "Meanings." It is perhaps his best play between *The Sea at Dauphin* and *Dream on Monkey Mountain.* (pp. 71-2)

[Walcott has said that *Dream on Monkey Mountain*] was about the West Indian search for identity, and about the damage that colonialism does to the soul. He felt that the situation he described was true not only in the Third World, but in any society where men have been reduced to a meaningless, purposeless existence. He feared that some people in attempting to find a way out of their predicament might end up escaping from reality itself. Such was the danger he saw in the movement popular among many Negroes of returning spiritually or physically to Africa. In another discussion . . . , he expressed the opinion that his countrymen were mistaken in diluting ". . . our real power, a human thing, with the hallucination of *sharing* it, either with Africa or America." His solution: to find a truly West Indian sense of belonging, "We must look *inside.*"

Dream on Monkey Mountain dramatizes that philosophy. It reappears five years later in . . . *O Babylon!* Walcott could hardly have selected a group that is farther removed than the Rastafarians are from the mainstream of modern Western cul-

ture. The sect practices abstention from the material trappings of civilization, making a virtue of poverty, until they can escape Babylonian exile and return to Africa. (p. 116)

In the triumphant finale, stress is placed on a heavenly Zion—perhaps too much stress, in light of Walcott's expressed concern about the hallucination of escaping from the real world. There are, however, explicit passages within the play where he makes it clear that Aaron's strength is in his growing sense of belonging. Aaron spends two days walking in the clear air of the mountains and he comes to love that part of his native Jamaica. At the moment when it seems that he has lost everything, he finds peace inside—where Walcott insists man must look to find his authentic identity.

In spite of the leveling influence of that central theme, and the revisions for more unified structure, *O Babylon!* is still an unsatisfying, somewhat romantic play. . . . Walcott would have done well to have developed those forces in Aaron's life that give him the strength to believe, rather than trail off into a nebulous vision of future rewards in Zion. There are fine poetic passages and moments of good theater, but in *O Babylon!* Walcott seems to be refining formal techniques and reworking old themes rather than exploring in any particular new direction. (p. 121)

[*Remembrance*] exhibits in its title the general tendency of Walcott's writing in the middle and late 1970s to conjure up the past. While he seems to be settling into a more concentrated form, he shows less diversity and a calmer, more measured pace.

Compared with most of his previous plays, there is not much physical action in *Remembrance.* The little music that occurs is primarily for supporting mood. Although the opening scene is a drawing room in contemporary Port-of-Spain, Walcott employs a flashback technique to start the main story many years earlier, before Trinidad became independent. His protagonist, Albert Jordan, has been induced after many requests from the editor of the *Belmont Bugle* to confide his thoughts to a tape recorder. Since Jordan—a retired, locally prominent schoolmaster and poet—was involved more or less inadvertently in the country's independence and Black Power movements, the *Bugle* wants a record of his views. With this convenient framework, Walcott accomplishes seamless traditions in time and place. (pp. 127-28)

Walcott manages to include a great deal of rhetoric and exposition in this play by having Jordan disclaim the philosophical tenets that he had lived by. The primary vehicle for drawing his essential ideas together is Thomas Gray's "Elegy Written in a Country Churchyard." In several brief sequences, Jordan is shown back in his classroom declaiming the virtues of Gray's message. Jordan's theme (Gray's and Walcott's as well) is that the individual human being is of worth despite his humble birth and provincial surroundings. (pp. 128-29)

Another play from this period which recalls the past, in a way slightly different from *Remembrance,* is *Pantomime.* . . . It is not retrospective in the sense of looking back at the past, but it revives once more Walcott's familiar Robinson Crusoe theme.

On the surface *Pantomime* appears inconsequential. The plot involves a running argument between Harry, English manager of a second-rate tourist hotel, and his black assistant Jackson, an erstwhile calypsonian. Their ostensible point of contention is the artistic propriety of a nightclub pantomime that Harry, who is a retired actor, wishes to perform for his seasonal patrons. In spite of its limited cast of two and its apparently light plot, however, the play comes close to delivering more than it promises at first. The narrative takes an ironic turn and quickly becomes seriously involved when Jackson suggests that they switch roles in their Crusoe skit, he becoming the master and Harry assuming Friday's place. (p. 130)

Pantomime appears to rely rather heavily on exposition and it seems too ambivalent in intention. (p. 131)

Remembrance and *Pantomime* are compact dramas and they ring true to life. They have a sure touch, but they lack the unified force of Walcott's best work—they do not fare well in comparison with *Ti-Jean and His Brothers, Dream on Monkey Mountain*, and *The Joker of Seville*. There is an air of stillness, if not of complacency, about these two plays that contributes to a general impression that Walcott might have been rounding off a certain phase of his career. (pp. 136-37)

> Robert D. Hamner, in his Derek Walcott *(copyright © 1981 by Twayne Publishers, Inc.; reprinted with the permission of Twayne Publishers, a Division of G. K. Hall & Co., Boston), Twayne, 1981, 175 p.*

HELEN VENDLER

[Derek Walcott's] voice was for a long time a derivative one. His subject was not derivative: it was the black colonial predicament. . . . But there was an often unhappy disjunction between his explosive subject, as yet relatively new in English poetry, and his harmonious pentameters, his lyrical allusions, his stately rhymes, his Yeatsian meditations. I first met his work in an anthology that had reprinted his **"Ruins of a Great House."** . . . It was clear that Walcott had been reading Yeats. . . . Walcott's piece did not seem to me then, and does not seem now, a poem, but rather an essay in pentameters. The emotional attitudes of Walcott's early verse were authentic, but shallowly and melodramatically phrased. . . .

It is always dangerous for a young poet's future when he begins, as Walcott did, with a subject. Language may become, then, nothing but the ornament to his message, the rhetoric for his sermon. Walcott did not escape this ornamental view of language (and his uncertainty as to his own genre caused him to spend twenty years writing for the theater, forming a theater company, and directing plays, the most direct and urgent form of literary communication).

But there were other aspects, not anthologized, to Walcott's early verse. One was the presence of island patois—unsteady, not well managed, but boldly there, confronting the Yeatsian poise. . . . Somewhat later, a shrewd social observation made itself felt in Walcott's work. . . .

Hart Crane, Dylan Thomas, Pound, Eliot, and Auden followed Yeats in Walcott's ventriloquism. It seemed that his learnedness might be the death of him, especially since he so prized it. . . .

Walcott's agenda gradually shaped itself. He would not give up the paternal island patois; he would not give up patois to write only in formal English. He would not give up his topic—his geographical place, his historical time, and his mixed blood; neither would he give up aesthetic balance. . . . He was in all things "a divided child," loyal to both "the stuffed dark nightingale of Keats" and the "virginal unpainted world" of the islands. . . . Walcott has written of "the inevitable problem of all island artists: the choice of home or exile, self-realization

or spiritual betrayal of one's country. Travelling widens this breach."

And yet Walcott's new book is called, not entirely ironically, *The Fortunate Traveller.* The degree to which Walcott is able to realize a poem still varies. He is still, even as a fully developed writer, peculiarly at the mercy of influence, this time the influence of Robert Lowell, as in the poem **"Old New England."** . . .

This represents Walcott's new apprenticeship to the American vernacular. . . . But no one can take on a new idiom overnight, and Walcott's pentameters stubbornly retain their British cadences. It is American words, and not yet American rhythms, that find their way unevenly into these new poems. They ruin some lines and enliven others. Since the only point of using colloquialisms is to have them sound colloquial, Walcott loses momentum when his Americanisms ring ill on the ear. (p. 23)

This sort of uncertainty in diction is disconcerting in Walcott, since he has many virtues: he is always thinking, he does not write sterile exercises in verse, he is working out a genuine spiritual history from his first volume to his current one, he keeps enlarging his range of style and the reaches of his subject. And when he errs, he often errs in a humanly admirable direction, the direction of literal truth. The trouble is, literal truth is often the enemy of poetic truth. . . .

The Fortunate Traveller is divided into portions called North, South, North, and the division is a symbolic one, putting the two terms into a continual dialectic rather than a sullen opposition. The patois poems in this new volume still seem to me unconvincing. . . . The experiment is worth trying (and Walcott has used patois in every phase of his play-writing, too) but, once again, however much it reflects the truth of Walcott's own divided mind and inheritance, it has not yet found a conclusive and satisfying aesthetic relation to his "high" diction. . . .

When Walcott's lines fall effortlessly and well, as in a remarkable poem of exile called **"The Hotel Normandie Pool,"** he seems the master of both social topic and personal memory. . . . This seems to me Walcott at his most natural, worldly, and accomplished. . . . [No] labored effects of unnatural diction mar the lines. (p. 26)

Walcott's steady ironies and his cultivated detachment in the midst of a personal plight make him an observer to be reckoned with; he will remain for this century one of its most candid narrators of the complicated and even desperate destiny of the man of great sensibility and talent born in a small colonial outpost, educated far beyond the standard of his countrymen, and pitched—by sensibility, talent, and education—into an isolation that deepens with every word he writes (regardless of the multitude by whom he is read). This is in part the story of many writers—it could be said to be the story of Beckett. But in Walcott's case the story is deepened by the added element of mixed blood, an unconcealable and inescapable social identity. This has driven Walcott to the theater, and to his tidal efforts against solitude. But these efforts recede, and the writer finds himself where he was, alone, with the brief moment of community and coherence dissipated by time and the dispersal of companions.

The wars between races and nations now seem permanent to Walcott as personal isolation is permanent; but just as a momentary incandescence of joint effort is possible, so, in a time of wars, there can be a merciful respite of quiet, a "season of phantasmal peace.'' It is, one could say, the lyric season when a hush falls on the epic conflict, and a chorus can be heard in the polyphony of song. And though one may quicken to the Walcott of observant sharpness, brusque speaking, and social passion, voiced in patois, it is the lyric Walcott who silences commentary. The best poem in this new collection is the poem Walcott placed last, **"The Season of Phantasmal Peace."** . . . The poem says nothing explicit about Empire and the oppression of colonies, about dialects of white English and island English, about the power to rise above the immediate that is conferred on a poet by his allegiance to song, about the social identification that a black poet especially feels for those who share dark holes in houses, or about the betrayals and desertions entailed in a life lived between black and white, empire and outpost, island and mainland. But the poem is the transcendent clarification of all that darkness; and it holds the darkness back for its own instant of phantasmal peace. It is unashamed in its debt to Shakespeare, Keats, and the Bible; but it has assimilated them all into its own fabric. (pp. 26-7)

Helen Vendler, "Poet of Two Worlds," in The New York Review of Books *(reprinted with permission from* The New York Review of Books; *copyright © 1982 Nyrev, Inc.), Vol. XXIX, No. 3, March 4, 1982, pp. 23, 26-7.*

NICHOLAS BROMELL

[*The Fortunate Traveller*] shows that a poet can deal in an illuminating way with . . . [the] problems of personal identity, aesthetic choice, and political commitment. (p. 12)

[Walcott's] travelling is not altogether fortunate. Imagine Robert Frost spending half of his time in Kuwait, teaching oil-rich Arabs. Or William Butler Yeats wintering in Mexico, giving workshops at an artists' colony. But Walcott's life as a commuter poet does at least dramatize the other ways in which he is a go-between, shuttling from one culture to another. He is a black man who writes for a largely white audience. He is "an islander and a colonial" who both resents and admires the language he must work in. He is in no official or acknowledged way the heir of Keats, Browning, Hopkins, or Yeats; his native culture is after all the victim, not the inheritor, of an expansionist and exploitative European empire. Yet there he stands on his seagirt island, immensely talented, enamored of the English language, intimate with the European literary tradition going back to the Greeks. What else can he do but work within that tradition and become, well, "one of us"?

Walcott has written many poems about this difficult process of assimilation, exploring most deeply, often at great cost to himself, the labyrinthine implications of race. As a consequence, his quest for self-definition has been remarkably, and profitably, explicit. His race, language, nationality, and calling all raise practical and worldly problems. They are susceptible, moreover, to description and analysis. Unlike many of us, Walcott doesn't have to languish in hopelessly vague perplexities about the meaning of self. For him, the issues are starkly drawn—in "black and white," as he would say, in the contrasting colors of skin and in the look of a printed page.

This concern with race, however, raises one difficulty many Americans will have with Walcott's work. We've been brought up, at least in the liberal culture, to regard race as something superficial, an accident of inconsequential genes. . . . The first step in understanding a poet like Walcott is to shed the presumption that race is a pseudo-problem, a convention or a

metaphor. For when Walcott writes about race, as he does in almost every poem, he makes clear that he [is] writing about one of the fundamental mysteries of human culture.

Of course, it would have been much easier for Walcott to pass over this mystery by merely dramatizing the contrast between black and white. Walcott could have defined himself purely in opposition to white culture. By thinking of himself as everything that is "not white" or "not capitalist" or "not north," he could have created a soul out of negatives. Instead, Walcott painstakingly attends to every trace of each race and culture in himself. He does not exclude. He incorporates. And at the same time, he records and preserves. (pp. 12-13)

Walcott's remarkable range of voice and mood is what enables him to embrace so much experience without destroying it. He can write with a tropical abundance of imagery and rhythm that recalls the prose of Garcia Marquez. He can compose lines of a chiselled coolness that make us think of Yeats. He can write Caribbean and New England dialects. He can do a fair imitation of Georges Seferis, and he can echo the very sound of Latin, with its flat fields of vowels and its sharp, dark cypresses of consonants.

But although Walcott easily speaks in a variety of voices, his underlying tone throughout this book is grave, elegiac, Roman. He stands at the margin of a great, dying empire, one whose armies have for centuries washed like surf across distant islands. . . . Though he may widen his own soul and strive to assimilate both the good and the evil of this dominant culture, he fears that he has been swallowed himself. The course of empire has gathered all the scattered islands of the world into its own destiny. There may no longer be a place "outside." (p. 13)

Nicholas Bromell, "Having to Ask: The Loss of Self in Contemporary Culture," in Boston Review *(copyright ©1982 by the Boston Critic, Inc.), Vol. VII, No. 2, April, 1982, pp. 9-13.**

KENNETH FUNSTEN

In **"Cantina Music,"** [from *The Fortunate Traveller*] Derek Walcott warns that poor people—like poor nations—may turn to violence and that lack of opportunity is responsible. . . .

Unfortunately for his message, Walcott's **"Traveller"** is not new art but a good example of tiresome "respected" poetry. Not that I disagree with what he says; but poetically, his voyage relies entirely on previous charts. There's no personal experiment or development of equipment; no new hazards—and often little precision. . . .

Walcott lags behind the artistic antennae of new work; nevertheless, he seems anxious to burst convention in a few poems, to sing what he knows. **"The Hotel Normandie Pool"** and especially **"early Pompeiian,"** about his wife's miscarriage, are touching examples in which he dares to be precise, to trust in and respect the real things words designate. These pieces, and in spots the title poem, evince strong narrative, respect for content and wariness of poetic rhetoric. They confirm Walcott's worth, that we are fortunate voyagers—when we read him at his best.

Kenneth Funsten, "In Verse: 'The Fortunate Traveller' " in Los Angeles Times Book Review *(reprinted by permission of the author), April 4, 1982, p. 13.*

PETER BLAND

Derek Walcott has been alternating for some years between his native West Indies and America. Meanwhile he has produced a steady flow of fine discursive poems—*Sea-Grapes* and *The Star-Apple Kingdom*—set in the Caribbean and full of a growing sense of Walcott's search for a new identity. In [*The Fortunate Traveller*] he seems to have found it. . . . But, as the title suggests, his new-found freedom is double-edged. He can look back and 'think of Europe as a gutter of autumn leaves / choked like the thoughts in an old woman's throat' but he also feels 'like lice, like lice, the hungry of this earth / swarm to the tree of life.' His increasing identification with 'suffering humanity' reminds me of some of James K. Baxter's later poetry, in feeling and conviction as well as in a certain Lowellish rhetoric. Walcott's poetry, always rich and full of feeling for the natural world, has opened out since he moved north. He breathes deeper and there's a greater sense of space and tranquillity in both speech and phrasing. I think he's essentially a poet of place, whether that place be London, the West Indies, Wales, or 'Belle Epoque Manhattan.' . . . Most poets of place are strongly earthed in one locality. Walcott's at home anywhere and everywhere. As a 'fortunate traveller' he sees the universal in the particular. . . . His imagery is as brilliant as ever. But it's always the islands of the Caribbean that call him home. (pp. 73-4)

> *Peter Bland, "Pale Assassin," in* London Magazine *(© London Magazine 1982), Vol. 22, No. 3, June, 1982, pp. 73-6 [the excerpt of Walcott's poetry used here was originally published in his* The Fortunate Traveller *(reprinted by permission of Farrar, Straus and Giroux, Inc.; copyright © 1980, 1981 by Derek Walcott), Farrar, Straus and Giroux, 1981, pp. 73-6].*

BLAKE MORRISON

The Fortunate Traveller is an impressive collection that moves lucidly and at times brilliantly between abstract notions of power and responsibility and visual notations of landscape, cityscape and sea. But it is only the title poem that comprehensively escapes Walcott's rational grip: elsewhere one is too aware of him press-ganging images into the service of an idea. This is especially true of his poems about the United States, which have too many smartly appropriate similes. . . . The poems that explore the guilt and regret of being away—**'North and South', 'The Fortunate Traveller', 'The Hotel Normandie Pool'**—are the ones in which he seems to me most fully at home.

Walcott's are sophisticated poems versed in the Anglo-American tradition, dedicated to the likes of Mark Strand, Anthony Hecht and Susan Sontag, and aimed primarily at a circle of readers in London and New York. (p. 16)

> *Blake Morrison, "Beach Poets" (appears here by permission of the* London Review of Books *and the author), in* London Review of Books, *September 16 to October 6, 1982, pp. 16-18.**

ALAN JENKINS

[Derek Walcott] dedicates many of the poems in *The Fortunate Traveller* to, presumably, friends—from Joseph Brodsky to Susan Sontag—but his dedications have an unmistakable air of name-dropping, of bandying cultural credentials. The cultures Walcott evokes on his travels . . . are many and varied—geographically and historically—and the range of ostensible literary connections or devotions is great. Yet it is clear from the first poem, **"Old New England",** whose voice it is that exercises the most powerful spell over Walcott. . . . The spire, the whale, hellfire—the progression and the terms are Robert Lowell's; the hectic tone, the densely-packed phrases and lunging alliterative lines, all early Lowell as well. The whole is a consummate piece of ventriloquism—except that Lowell would not have sunk to the simplistic equation . . . that Walcott makes here.

When Walcott moves beyond this slavish imitation of the master, his outsider's eye on New York (and, beyond that, on northern Europe) produces some arresting similes . . . but his commitment to a hectoring note of naive antipathy persists, along with his commitment to the rhetoric of excess. . . . (p. 62)

> *Alan Jenkins, "Private and Public Languages: New Poetry," in* Encounter *(© 1982 by Encounter Ltd.), Vol. LIX, No. 5, November, 1982, pp. 56-63.**

Angus (Frank Johnstone) Wilson

1913-

English novelist, short story writer, essayist, and critic.

Wilson is one of the most important English novelists of the postwar years. Seen as a group, his works form a chronicle of social changes that have taken place within English society in the twentieth century. Although often extremely funny, they also contain serious critiques of that society. Wilson's subjects are usually failed or wasted lives, individuals whose crises reflect the disintegration of a larger way of life.

While not a great innovator, Wilson has experimented over the years in narrative form. He began with portraits of upper-middle-class society in his short story collections *The Wrong Set and Other Stories* and *Such Darling Dodos*. In his early novels Wilson stayed within the tradition of English realism, varying his characters and experimenting with point of view. In his later novels Wilson moved away from traditionalism, presenting a contemporary fable that blends realism and fantasy in *The Old Men at the Zoo*, a generational family saga in *No Laughing Matter*, and a highly complex symbolical novel in his recent *Setting the World on Fire*. In this work, critics note a successful organizational design, a moving work of social criticism, and a dramatic force that emphasizes Wilson's theatricality. Although few critics consider this a completely satisfying novel, many believe that *Setting the World on Fire* is a testament to Wilson's importance to contemporary literature.

(See also *CLC*, Vols. 2, 3, 5; *Contemporary Authors*, Vols. 5-8, rev. ed.; and *Dictionary of Literary Biography*, Vol. 15.)

© Jerry Bauer

JONATHAN RABAN

Who would choose to live in a novel by Angus Wilson? His characters are constantly exposed to the cruel publicity of society: everyone finds himself involuntarily, often unwittingly, on show. He may ache for silence and privacy, yearn to cultivate his inner life like a secret garden, but here the most retiring and insignificant people are condemned to be public figures. . . . Husbands and wives, parents and children, discover that there is nothing more demandingly public than private life. They have to learn to be actors, with the actor's conscious, uneasy control of character and expression. Failure here is dreadfully easy: a small solecism mushrooms into a humiliating disaster; what starts as a polite giggle ends as a shriek. The lights are always on, there are no corners to hide in.

Either we conduct ourselves honourably in these terrible games, or we go mad or die. Death happens here insidiously casually, and every drawing room has its share of gibbering loonies who wear tweeds and tell funny stories. It is a profoundly apprehensive and pessimistic vision of life in society, and it's perhaps not surprising that Wilson's novels should have been persistently misread. For there is a customary, Boots Lending Library version of his work which represents it as cosy, gently ironic, and, oh, so *accurate* about middle-class people like us. Wilson's unhinged stare has been wilfully misinterpreted as a blandly humorous twinkle. He has written about madness and death at a time when madness and death have been passionate bourgeois cults; but the overwhelmingly polite reception given to his books indicates, I suppose, that there is nothing quite so stolidly ignorable as the presence of a corpse or a madman at your own dinner party. He has filled his novels with the noise of the English middle classes warding off Armageddon. What has mostly been heard has been the genteel tinkle of the Forsytes, unnaturally protracted forty years on. (p. 16)

Alexandra, the heroine of [*As If By Magic*] is a student of English Literature at a new university. She is also—to the alarm of some of the book's reviewers—a new kind of person. Alternately mawkishly childlike and ferociously sophisticated, she is a devout irrationalist. Her emotional life is storm-bound, a superstitious melodrama. She dresses up, she plays, she reads Tolkien and Lawrence; she is swept by bouts of optimism and despair. Her sensibility is as remote from that of her Hampstead parents as a tribal African's.

Her character is a brilliant combination of empathy, research, and myth-making. To create her, Wilson read what she would read, studied her clothes, her north-London-cum-hippie argot, her hotch-potch of mysticism and liberationism, with the relish of Flaubert gutting popular encyclopaedias for *Bouvard et Pécuchet*. His anthropological curiosity shows in the intricate web of small details in which she is clad—as if he had, indeed, reconstructed a strange, extinct human from his unearthed ar- tifacts. Alexandra is more than a character; she stands for her generation, and her outlines are suitably idealised and theo- retical. But at every point, Wilson manages to give her feelings an eerie particularity; her hurts and anxieties are entirely her own. Insofar as she is a creature of her society, she is metic- ulously painted in the colours of her kind—yet we never lose the sense of her as a uniquely scarred private animal. There are many novelists who can make their characters live on one or the other of these two levels: there are very few who can make both real at the same time. Wilson's power as a 'social novelist' (and the phrase has an unaccustomed bite when ap- plied to his work) is largely vested in this peculiar capacity to stand sufficiently far outside to make myths and large, shapely statements, at the very moment when he is most intimately inside a single character. Since 1949, when [his first work] *The Wrong Set* came out, he has been animating a vast, dis- turbing tableau of English society. It is a portrait of the kind of hell which vulnerable private people create when they at- tempt to live with each other. (p. 17)

Dividing up one's life and parcelling the bits into separate 'parts of society' is something which all Wilson's characters find themselves doing perforce. For in his novels, society is seg- mented like an orange, and each lith has its own skin, its own intricate tracery of conventions and rules. The Belgravia host- ess, the man of letters, the Cockney pickup, the hippie student, all belong to separate segments. They talk in the cosy slang of their set, they live and breathe unconsciously in the rarefied climate of its morality. But bits of themselves spill out, and Wilson becomes interested in them at just those moments when the skin breaks. . . . Again and again, Angus Wilson needles his people into leaving the safety of their sets, driving them into unfamiliar parts of society where they are tested in col- lisions with strangers. The novelist's knowledge is exemplary: *he* knows each segment of the orange, *he* has suffered these encounters and divides. He stands like a teacher in relation to his characters, at once instructing and examining them in the ways of a riven world.

Wilson's books present society as an elaborate series of sep- arate compartments, intermitted by stretches of intolerable va- cancy. In his own life, he has clearly moved much more than most men through this rather cheerless galaxy—first by the accident of his upbringing, later by deliberate choice. . . . I suspect that the one great reward of his childhood was the discovery that it might be possible, in a century and a society more hopelessly disconnected than any other, to be Proteus: to go everywhere, to try on the clothes, the manners and the feelings of everybody; to reconstruct the lost wholeness of society out of the conflicting strains of one man's experience. A bit of South African . . . a bit of gentility . . . a bit of rake . . . a bit of Kensington . . . a bit of Bexley . . . a bit of homosexual camp . . . a bit of army officer; could it not be that these fragments, contained in one sensibility, might form a model for a grand recreation of England and Englishness? Wilson does, I think, see himself as a whole family of different people, and, as he has shown in *No Laughing Matter*, it's a very short step from being a family to being a population and a culture. In that book, he made the Matthews family act out a panoramic charade of English history from before the First World War to 1967; but in parodic interludes of 'The Family Sunday Play' they act out each other's lives as well. Children play parents, brothers walk on as sisters, sisters as brothers. It is a dark and suggestive ploy. For if at one level the book attempts to encompass the recent history of a nation, at another

it hints that that history, those rifts and eddies of style and principle, might all take place inside the head of a single actor. Given the right script, anybody might play anyone else's part; and as the characters swap about, in and out of each other's roles, they hint at a monstrous histrionic arbitrariness, a version of history as a ventriloquist's farce.

There is an innate theatricality in Wilson's writing, in his vision of society, and in his own personal style. He is a very exact mimic. His lips purse into a prim *O,* and he turns into the shrill, piping lady proprietor of a bookshop; they slacken, and he becomes a beery, self-consciously *fils du peuple* sports- writer. What in life is witty, camp impersonation turns in his books into an amazing range of rich performances. The out- rageous, mincing *swami* in *As If By Magic;* Sukey Pasco in *No Laughing Matter,* the schoolmaster's wife who gives weekly talks on the Western Region Home Service, describing family holidays in Winnie the Wolseley; the plump and beastly Mrs Curry in *Hemlock and After;* Harold Calvert in *Late Call,* with his *Guardian* philosophy, his string of mangled quotations, and his lugubriously orotund family humour. These characters stand just to one side of the centre of the novels they appear in; somewhat larger, funnier and badder than life, they are bril- liantly-coloured pantomime creatures who walk side by side with the 'real' people who are Wilson's heroes and heroines. They are there to infect reality with the bold satire and lighting of theatre.

For this is a society in which, however seriously we take our- selves, and however complex our motives may appear, we are always on the brink of farce or melodrama. Wilson's ravish- ingly agile impersonations spring from a conviction that dress- ing-up, playing a part, acting out a charade, constitute the greater part of what is left of reality; that, in effect, society has become a heap of scripts, with matching props and cos- tumes. (pp. 19, 21)

Increasingly, especially in the two most recent novels, *No Laughing Matter* and *As If By Magic,* the main problem of being a character has been the difficulty of finding and defining what one is in this troublingly theatrical world. There are lines to speak, certainly, and clothes to put on; but what is there in experience which is *not* faked or secondhand? In both books, Wilson keeps his characters continually on the move, dragging them through a succession of theatrical and social sets, each with its own conditions of action. In *No Laughing Matter,* the movement is through a historical period; in *As If By Magic* it is across the underside of the world, through Africa and Asia. Between them, the two novels form something very close to an encyclopedia of life in society in the 20th century, an in- ventory of roles and stages. The Matthews family, Hamo Lang- muir and Alexandra Grant are commissioned by Wilson to undertake an epic journey; on the way, they are tested, hum- bled, made to take on parts for which they are grossly unsuited, forced into milieux of which they have no experience at all, dressed up, stripped, brought, finally, face to face with what little is left of themselves. These are Wilson's fatal *Jeux Sans Frontières;* few characters survive them, and those who do are ceremoniously garlanded at the end of the book. A number of reviewers have been bothered by the oddly triumphant finales with which Wilson has rounded off his work, but they are appropriate, I think: if you can come through an Angus Wilson novel still kicking, still human, then life can have little to offer which will be more damaging to your character.

The tests themselves are formal and stagey. Most of them are borrowed from literature. Alexandra, who has taken a seminar on Lawrence at her university, finds herself living out a Lawrence novel which, with a sudden vertiginous bounce, drops her into Tolkien's pixie-gothic, which blurs nightmarishly into Dickens. Hamo Langmuir starts in a drawing-room comedy, is projected into an orgy out of De Sade, parachutes in and out of a Feydeau farce, and turns up in a television documentary. Wilson says, 'I nearly always feel when I'm writing a scene that this has been written before.' But life itself tends constantly to the second-hand; our responses are so conditioned, our behaviour so stereotyped, that it is immensely hard for us to extricate ourselves from these literary precedents which plot the course of our own feelings and actions. Wilson's 'literariness' is unusual, and often puzzling, because, unlike the formal allusiveness of most modernist writing, it is the product of the way in which the characters feel about themselves. They have often read their literature crudely and badly, but they take it seriously. Their first response to any new situation tends to be, 'How would Birkin—or Myshkin, or Alice, or a Hobbit— have felt about this, how would they have dealt with it?' And their possessively quirky version of Lawrence or Dostoievsky is often wildly at odds with the official, professorial image of the writer on which formalist novelists like Muriel Spark and John Barth base their allusions. Wilson, by contrast, tends to see literature as a kind of invalid-carriage on which his wounded characters wheel themselves through a world which offers few other precedents or consolations. (p. 21)

In his early novels and stories, Wilson's characters were weighed down by their manners. One could predict how they were likely to behave by their accents, their clothes, and the current fashionable mores of the sets in which they moved. But people like the Matthewses and Hamo and Alexandra are, much more importantly, prisoners of language. The later novels are full of documents of every kind, ranging from works of literature to Hamo's stiff Civil Service memoranda and the homoerotic captions in an advertisement for blue films. . . . The 'Magic' in the title of Wilson's last novel is a universally enslaving force. His people are all possessed. To be held in thrall by a great book, by the spiel of a mystical fake, by an ideology, by some official linguistic convention or dialect, by a code of manners or a style of dress, comes down in the end to the same thing. What counts is the degree of thraldom, not the goodness or badness of what it is that enthralls. On the surface, Wilson's recent novels are superb anthologies of all the kinds of language to which people in society fall victim. The texture of each book changes from page to page, shifting from crafty imitation to genial parodic spoof. They manage to convey the rich, paradoxical weave of the world by incorporating the languages of the world, and the effect is unnerving. Dickens, Lawrence, Rhoda Broughton, Rod and Mack, Civil Service jargon, Feydeau and the Maharaj Ji are all stirred into the same pudding. Writing for which one has solemn admiration goes shoulder to shoulder with bogus cliché and pretentious hokum. The result is so dense, and has so much of the fudgy, uncertain weightiness of reality about it, that it is easy to mistake its cunning artifice for life itself. Hasty reviewers have consistently underrated both of Wilson's last novels simply because they have not grasped how fully written and worked they are. For Wilson gives one no single style to cling to, no guiding, subtly discerning narrative tone. He immerses one in a great pottage of different styles, challenging the reader, as he challenges the characters, to find his own footholds, to make his way as best he can.

There's always a danger of making Wilson sound more theoretical, more of a *nouveau romancier*, than he is. In fact, the questions raised by this crazy-quilting of styles are anguishedly old-fashioned ones. Is it possible to break free of our enslavement to a predetermined way of feeling? Can we be individuals, or are we condemned to being types and zombies? Is there any notion of good and evil left in a world so given over to tearaway relativism? Must characters in a mad charade live entirely according to the requirements of the plot, or can they, even while wearing their costumes and speaking from their scripts, retain at least a little moral dignity of their own?

For, reading the novels, one never loses the sense that the characters, for all their modish trappings, are private, easily-hurt creatures, with animal needs and animal graces. The novels, like society itself, drive them to unlovable depths, forcing them to adopt ever more grotesque and desperate affectations and disguises. Hamo, doing an inept travesty of 'Doctor Malcolm' of the University of London Examination Board, or Alexandra, miming a chicken in a dreadful underground student theatre group (she would get a rave notice from *Time Out*), are made to touch a rock-bottom of human absurdity. They are so absurd that they are past laughing at; one simply sweats vicariously for their humiliation, and detests them for not recognising their own silliness. They have fallen too far down for the 'sophisticated comedy' which Wilson's readers egg him on to do; they are unengagingly gross and pitiable.

Yet, because they are seen so thoroughly from the inside, we follow them to these levels. Even when they are hunted down, bloodied and tearful, or when death takes them with a sudden, arbitrary rabbit-punch, disturbing shreds of farce still adhere to them. The reader is never allowed the luxury of unequivocal tragedy—or, indeed, of unequivocal feeling of any kind. Hamo ends passed over the heads of a rioting Goanese mob, flung in a muddy river, and stoned. His last thought is: *It would never have done, women's bodies suck you in. I need the hard resistance of a youth.* Alexandra, surviving heroically to the final page, commits herself there to an expression of her newly discovered wisdom: *Damn English Literature! Damn the past and the future!* The last we hear of her, she is saying 'Abracadabra!' aloud. Heroes and heroines usually manage to do a little better than this. We feel cheated of sympathy and moral uplift. Wilson, ambitiously and dangerously, dares us to despise people whose claim to dignity is so frail that they cannot even manage a good exit; if we do, we run the risk of being despised ourselves. (p. 22)

[Wilson's novels hint at a] savage proposition: that people have to be humbled into foolishness before what happens to them becomes important. There is an element of cruelty in the writing, a relish for destruction. As the characters are driven to greater and greater extremes of discomfiture, one hears, from behind the scenes, the novelist's *tsk-tsk* of pleasure. Before these people are fit to love, or we fit to love them, we have to learn to regard them with both mockery and disgust. It is an odd, icy manoeuvre. Wilson, like Brecht, excludes his characters from the hearth of his readers' sympathies until they have learned to be ashamed of themselves. And it is their capacity for shame which saves them—their own exhaustion and disgust with the absurd string of roles which life, and the novel, have forced them to play. (pp. 22-3)

Wilson's 'irony' does not, in the conventional formulation, make the reader feel comfortably superior. It habitually takes a three-pronged form from which nobody escapes without a wound. The reader suffers anxiety for the character as he precipitates himself into a foolishness or an indiscretion; the character suffers both shame and bodily hurt for his clumsiness;

his hosts or audience are then dragged stumbling into contrition and awkward apology. In an early scene of *As If By Magic,* set in a drawing room, Hamo tries to play uncle to Alexandra. He is woefully stiff and inept. Through Alexandra'a eyes, we see him as a ludicrous figure, 'Hamo the Hamster'. Through his eyes, we see Alexandra as a disturbed child, an appealing, vulnerable hysteric. He tries to make her a present of £100 in an envelope; a considerate uncle's gift. She tears up the money, disgracing herself in an orgy of abuse. In his embarrassment, he trips over her skirt, smashes a Nymphenburg Harlequin, and lies bleeding on the floor, while Alexandra's mother wails over her broken china. It is a whirlpool of social awkwardness, artfully constructed to leave nobody out; if at one level it is low theatre, it is low theatre performed with an inwardness and a care for individual feeling that traps the reader and keeps him one stop short of laughter. These occasions are machines for making everybody feel bad about themselves; and they are airless and tightly-seamed. Embarrassment bursts in them and resounds without release. (pp. 23-4)

There is a great deal of playfulness in the way Wilson works the surface of his novels: a camp pun on the word 'chicken', for instance, trails through the entire length of *As If By Magic,* and he delights in word-games, puns, ironic echoes, private jokes. But these small verbal joints mock at the disjointedness of a world which can never really come together. The books end with survivors—Marcus and Margaret Matthews, Alexandra Grant. But we see Marcus and Margaret hopelessly at odds with each other; Margaret goes off alone to write, Marcus, transformed into a bitchy Moroccan potentate, retires to his scent factory. Alexandra, a millionairess now, takes a grand house in Highgate where she lives with her baby and a bevy of older female relations, none of whom have any comprehension of her feelings. The very qualities which have enabled all these people to survive in the novels have isolated them even further from the other characters. They have graduated to a degree of lonely understanding which makes them as private and remote as anchorites engaged in a silent communion with the world.

Something of this sticks to Wilson himself. Much more than most writers, he lives very fully in society; a diner-out, a sought-after speaker, a traveller, a host. But it is his intense privacy which impresses itself on one. His novels have mostly been acclaimed for the wrong reasons; few critics have properly explored their seriousness or the real intricacy of their design. He has been saddled with labels—like 'liberal', 'traditional', 'ironical'—which have obscured what he has actually done. He has written about the world as a terrible, destructive place, and been patted on the head for reproducing its manners *just so*. (p. 24)

Jonathan Raban, "Angus Wilson—A Profile," *in* The New Review (© TNR Publications, Ltd., London), Vol. 1, No. 1, April, 1974, pp. 16-19, 21-4.

BERNARD BERGONZI

Setting the World on Fire is an elaborately structured book; I am sure that academic commentators will soon find many . . . crafty parallels, convergences and contrasts in it. The fantasy in Wilson's earlier fiction is usually negative, cruel and evil. In this novel he has opened himself to hedonistic imaginings of beauty, wealth, glamour, energy and talent, giving them free rein, though with just enough control to turn fantasy into art; the result can reasonably be called baroque. It is noticeable that much of the energy goes into describing, often in elaborate and beautiful language, artifacts and performances: architecture, painting, theatrical and operatic productions, gardens. Writers on Wilson, like Peter Faulkner in his new study [see excerpt below], have emphasized the element of theatricality in his art, and in *Setting the World on Fire* it is dominant. But there is a price to be paid. Wilson has to tell a story moving forward in time, whereas his deep imaginative impulse seems to have been to present a static or spiralling enactment of the Phaethon myth, turning in and round on itself like the imagined baroque ceiling he describes so vividly. The human element and the business of storytelling tend to come off second-best, but the realistic novelist, who is interested in character and motives, cannot be wholly suppressed.

He emerges well on in the novel, with the account of a long, unhappy and intermittently funny family lunch party at Tothill House in 1957, reminiscent of comparable incidents in Wilson's earlier fiction. If this episode is rather less convincing, that may be because Wilson aims too widely in this novel. The shifts between fantasy and moderate realism are disconcerting for the reader, who is not always able to suspend disbelief when required; particularly not, to speak for myself, in respect of the violent conclusion, which struck me as quite unbelievable. . . .

Admiring the ingenuity and skill that has gone into this novel, I still found much of it crude and two-dimensional, particularly the Pratt-Vanbrugh, Palladian-baroque, classical-romantic oppositions that underlie its structure, and the over-insistent treatment of the Phaethon myth. Perhaps Wilson's commitment to this new departure in his art was not quite whole-hearted enough, tending to be impaired by the subdued but not silenced realistic observer of men and manners. It may be that such radical incorporations of myth and reconstructed history into fiction need something like the manic intensity of a Thomas Pynchon, which the ultimately sensible and sociable Wilson lacks. But one can have nothing but admiration for the courage which prompted him to this enterprise, as opposed to the easy attractions of self-imitation. . . .

It would be fair to describe this novel as profligate and luxuriant; whether or not people will be lost in it, I am uncertain. In fact, I am not sure how far there is room for people in it at all.

Bernard Bergonzi, "Chariot Wheels of Fortune," in The Times Literary Supplement (© *Times Newspapers Ltd. (London) 1980; reproduced from* The Times Literary Supplement *by permission*), No. 4033, July 11, 1980, p. 773.

PENELOPE LIVELY

Setting the World on Fire is Angus Wilson's richest, most complex novel, if, in the last resort, one of the least satisfying. Yet, that being said, the dissatisfaction seems unjustified; all the Wilson skills are displayed, all that imaginative power and reflective insight that makes him for me, possibly the greatest English novelist of the post-war years. So what has gone wrong? It is a deeply symbolic novel, operatic in its symbolism and deliberately so, and perhaps it is just this that is unsettling even for the most devoted Wilson reader; you think regretfully of the calmer texture of *Late Call* and *The Middle Age of Mrs Eliot*. The opulence of the conception seems to blur the more unobtrusive but crucial novelistic crafts for which Angus Wilson is distinguished.

The central symbolism is architectural. Tothill House, the mansion owned by the Mosson family which occupies a vast tract of central London stretching from Westminster Abbey to St. John's, Smith Square, was built by Sir Roger Pratt, a marvel of classical regularity; within the very centre of the house was inserted, in violent contrast, Vanbrugh's Great Hall, a triumph of baroque flamboyance which carries upon its walls and ceiling Verrio's painting of the Phaethon legend. The Hall, the painting, and Lully's opera *Phaethon* (originally written for production in the Hall itself but never performed) are the essential matter of the novel: the story that is told is the story of Piers Mosson's ambition—eventually and tragically realised—to stage the production at last.

The secondary symbolism lies in the dispositions of the two heroes—the Mosson brothers, Piers and Tom. They are small boys when we first meet them in 1948 in a powerful and enormously clever scene which at once introduces us to the house and the family and states the novel's theme and direction. Tom, aged six, is weeping with fear in the Great Hall, oppressed by its size and implications; Piers, slightly older, is exhilarated and intoxicated, embarked on his obsession with the place and its subject. Sir Hubert Mosson, the present heir to Tothill, consoles his nephew in the level-headed language with which he has already explained and diminished the myth. . . . (pp. 59-60)

Ice and fire, order and irregularity; Pratt and Vanbrugh; Phaethon ("tragic, wayward, ambitious living humanity") and Jove ("noble, ordered, smug, dead statuary"). The statements of contrast are threaded through the book, a rich, intricate and heady pattern. The brothers are set in apposition; the worthy, unimaginative Mossons, Hubert and Jackie, his American heiress mother, are complemented by their fiery, dashing Tothill ancestors and by the wealthy Italian, Marina Luzzi, whom Hubert intends to marry, carrying on the family tradition of injections of external wealth when it seems expedient. Marina Luzzi is a central figure, as crucial in her way as the Mossons themselves. The trouble is that she remains flat upon the page when so much else—the house, the Great Hall, most of the large cast of characters—shapes so satisfyingly to the mind's eye: the garden, the rooms, the paintings are seen, the vapid chatter of the boys' poor silly widowed mother Rosemary is heard. But Marina is given a grating idiom that does more to inter her than bring her to life, try as you may you cannot hear it. . . . (p. 60)

The end is unexpected, shocking and entirely successful. It is not there that the uneasiness lies. Rather, I think, it is with an internal discord between the grandeur of the imagery and the presentation of some of the characters—notably Marina Luzzi but to some extent also the even more vital figures of Tom and Piers, Pratt and Van as they call each other in recognition of their oppositeness. In the long central act of the novel their conversation seldom sounds like that of 17- and 18-year-olds—too measured, too considered surely even for clever public schoolboys with Oxford scholarships. It is as though the all-pervading symbolism has at this point been allowed to obscure the characters through whom it must be presented. They have drowned in it.

And yet, saying this, and it has to be said, one feels a carping wretch. Because there is so much to praise: the accuracy and economy with which we are taken from 1948 to 1956-7 to 1969; the wit; the dramatic force; the neat Wilsonian touches like Rosemary's cultivation of species roses in the late 1950s (Sir Angus has always been a dab hand at the sociology of

gardening). The novel gives pleasure—and excitement—on almost every page. Read it and see for yourself. My reservation is simply that the mixture is too rich, the fumes obscure the taste. Maybe such a criticism is in harmony with the language of the novel: structure against flamboyance, coherence against abandon. (pp. 60-1)

Penelope Lively, "Lifescapes," in Encounter *(© 1980 by Encounter Ltd.), Vol. LV, No. 5, November, 1980, pp. 58-64.**

ANNE TYLER

Angus Wilson's uncommon energy is demonstrated not only by the number of his books . . . but also by the very fiber of his writing. As a novelist he is tireless in his pursuit of each and every character. He pounces upon the slightest telltale gesture or turn of phrase. Elision—the gliding over of smaller occurrences, summation of random conversations or any other form of creative shorthand—appears to strike him as a kind of cheating. He is meticulous, exhaustive in building up his scenes, word by word and clink of china upon clink of china. The result is people so firmly defined that you feel you could count the stitches in their English lawn dresses—although, in fact, you could not, for it is by their speech and movements that he describes them. Manner is crucial. Color of coat, length of hair tell Angus Wilson less than a single scrap of nervous laughter. (p. 33)

Setting the World on Fire, if diagramed, would resemble one of those evergreen swags draped along a mantel at Christmastime: a taut moment, a long droop, another taut moment, and so on. When Piers goes on and on about his theatrical productions (several of which we witness, in varying degrees of completion), the combined weight of casting problems, costume frills, wig styles, acoustics, and placement of orchestra is enough to sink the whole novel. There are extended conversations so fidgety and detailed that the reader positively itches, and they're not for any ultimate purpose.

The sags are deepened by the fact that, although the brothers make . . . great leaps in time, they seem the same age throughout. . . . There's no real sense of movement, only of situations flowing past the brothers like so many wheeled stage-sets, while Piers and Tom remains stationary—the one eternally Vanbrugh-like, the other eternally Pratt-like.

Contributing to the general slowness is a style so complicated you're continually forced to stop and reread. Some of the sentences look like examples in a grade-school punctuation class. . . . Some are illogically constructed. . . . And occasionally, there's outright bad grammar. . . . (pp. 33-4)

On the other hand, in the book's taut sections we're riveted. . . .

[Wilson] does best of all at *internal* revelation: those rare, elusive shifts of vision that involve no outward action whatsoever. . . .

At moments like this, we recognize Angus Wilson's particular blend of vitality and control. *Setting the World on Fire* is not, by a long shot, his best work, but still it is a remarkable novel, alternately absorbing and exasperating, always deserving of our serious attention. (p. 34)

Anne Tyler, "The Tenants of Tothill House," in The New Republic *(reprinted by permission of* The New

Republic; © *1980 The New Republic, Inc.), Vol. 183, No. 19, November 8, 1980, pp. 33-4.*

ROBERT KIELY

[Although] the novel is old enough to have a "tradition," which some would like to mortify by calling "great," writers like Angus Wilson are more likely to be drawn to the form precisely for its vulnerability to shapelessness and its susceptibility to vulgarity than to its respectability. Such a writer exposes himself in the act of writing to the same dangers and possibilities his readers struggle with every day. He is not a superior specimen, but a gifted equal.

During his long and varied career, Angus Wilson has continually experimented with narrative techniques and searched for definitions of his craft that do not exclude the messy world of private and public experience any more than they exclude the ordered world of books. His fiction is an unusual combination of two familiar English traits: earnestness and irony. Part of him is uncertain, groping, tolerant; part of him is knowing and crisp. All of his work, including his earliest short fiction, is a curious mixture of rough spots and polish; yet ease of expression is not an end in itself. He never tries quite the same thing twice. He likes to move on. (p. 39)

Wilson's two most acclaimed and best-known works of the 1950's were ["**Anglo-Saxon Attitudes**" and "**The Middle Age of Mrs. Eliot**"]. . . . Both novels contain whole sections of glittering dialogue, wonderfully satiric imitations of academics, politicians, diplomats, artists, scientists. . . . But although, as Mr. Faulkner argues, Wilson is an expert mimic, he rarely in his mature works allows himself merely to indulge in easy play. In both of these important novels—and this does become a kind of trademark—he probes the inner lives and especially the disappointments of the "unheroic" figures who are the central characters in his fiction: an aging professor facing the end of his career and life, a middle-aged widow who suddenly finds herself with nothing to do.

In his novels since the 1950's ["**The Old Men at the Zoo**," "**No Laughing Matter**," and "**As If by Magic**"]. . . . Wilson not only explores the relationships among very different groups—large families, young children, the very old, bureaucrats, students—but he experiments more and more with narrative form. . . . What had earlier looked to him like formlessness and snobbery in [the work of Virginia Woolf] and that of other Modernist writers began to look different. . . . If Wilson's fiction of the 1960's and 70's does not have the sureness of touch of the earlier work, it can be seen as a deliberate and quite courageous reaching after something else by a writer who chose not to relax into a familiar mode.

Wilson's new novel, "**Setting the World on Fire**," is both the most successful of his departures from tradition and the most explicit dramatization of the conflicts that, in his opinion, make that departure necessary. As in many earlier Modernist works, art is a major theme. Most of the action takes place in a fictitious London estate, Tothill House, and centers on the plans for a production of Jean-Baptiste Lully's opera "Phaethon." . . . Although some characters in the book regard architecture, music and painting as just so much decor, as background for their ignorant pastimes, the young protagonists, Piers and Tom Mosson, are heirs as much to the artistic spirit of [Tothill House] as they are to the family genes and fortune. For them, the links between esthetic taste, temperament and moral character are powerful. (pp. 39-40)

Between the brothers, as within the house, two distinct conceptions of art are in a state of tension, and yet each is shown to be necessary to the other, to preserve its distinction, to protect it from excess.

Nearly all the other characters in the book represent conscious or unconscious threats to both order and vision, to Tom and Piers. Like Virginia Woolf in "Between the Acts," Wilson takes the considerable risk of representing various combinations of unruliness and tedium until the reader is virtually aching for artistry—understood in the deepest sense—to save the situation. . . . Like the Modernist writers he has come more and more to appreciate, Wilson leads the reader dangerously close to the edge of the abyss.

But though the effect may be disquieting and at points too close to real tedium for comfort, Wilson's rescue of his material—through the cooperative efforts of Tom and Piers—makes the final third of the book a uniquely dramatic defense of art. . . . [As] the pacing of the book quickens and the violence of the hostility intensifies, it becomes clearer and clearer that the moral courage of the two brothers, their love for one another and their faith that even the least promising members of the audience might be aroused from torpor are at the heart of their performance.

The novel, like Tothill House or Lully's opera, may or may not survive another hundred years. By forcing us to contemplate a world of forbidden productions, humdrum spoilers and petrified audiences, Angus Wilson reminds us with passion, of what we would be losing. (p. 40)

Robert Kiely, "An English Novelist," in The New York Times Book Review *(© 1980 by The New York Times Company; reprinted by permission), November 16, 1980, pp. 1, 39-40.*

DAPHNE MERKIN

Angus Wilson is a British writer of repute who doesn't rattle any skeletons. His latest novel, *Setting the World on Fire* . . . is about as old-fashioned—indeed, doddering—a literary gesture as you can get. The only fire is in its title. The book itself is so stodgy that one is led to wonder whether Wilson intended the stodginess to be taken ironically, as a flicker of defiance; after all, it is filled with snatches of intelligence, as English novels generally are. Unfortunately, the intelligence is creakily rooted in those ageless, civilized truths we all wearily assent to, so Wilson's novel never attains enough tension to be defiant. It seems merely out-of-step, lumbering instead of stately. . . .

Wilson's opening is much the best part of his book. . . .

This poetic and accurate rendition of the wendings of a child's mind appears to promise a work of sparkling imagination. Regrettably, the expectation is not fulfilled. Characterization, so deftly done here, loses its vigor after Part One; instead, Wilson proffers bits of pre-meditated *types*—one of this and a little of that. Once he ignores, or loses faith in his own unguided artistic instincts, the novel turns resolutely formulaic: Wilson leads us and perhaps himself firmly by the nose. . . .

Setting the World on Fire is startlingly unconvincing. It is hard to believe in anyone talking or thinking like the characters in this book; it is impossible to credit siblings in their 20s and 30s who call each other "darling heart." Moreover, the author's notions of the costs of Tom's sanity versus the risks of Piers' fancy flap around like an ill-fitting coat. One presumes

Wilson set out to write an old-fashioned novel of realism that joins form and content, but his goal eluded him. His attention to life is not keen enough to fill up the grandiose structure of myth that feebly animates the book. Had he loosened up and abandoned his quest for a polished performance, had he perhaps taken the present fragmentariness of the world into account, *Setting the World on Fire* might at least have kindled our interest. (p. 13)

Daphne Merkin, "Myths and Mazola," in The New Leader (© *1980 by the American Labor Conference on International Affairs, Inc.), Vol. LXIII, No. 21, November 17, 1980, pp. 12-13.**

DENIS DONOGHUE

It is well known that Wilson has been complicating his art in the later novels, beginning with *No Laughing Matter*. . . . His early novels, notably *Hemlock and After, Anglo-Saxon Attitudes,* and *The Middle Age of Mrs. Eliot,* sat comfortably if not comfortably within the tradition of English realism. They were about what they appeared to be about, no more and no less. Mainly, they were about the comedy, irony, and tragedy of social existence, of being present to oneself by being present, necessarily, to other people. Wilson showed a critical interest in his subject, observing the instances of personal and social life with an eye keen enough for every decent purpose but not self-consciously sharpened for the occasion. As in the short stories of *Such Darling Dodos,* what was observed was not humiliated by the mind that observed it. In *Hemlock and After* and the other early novels, Wilson was vigilant about characters when vigilance was what they deserved, but he did not imply that they existed only to be detected or to appease his ironic zeal. His eye for revealing detail, his ear for nuances and idiosyncrasies of speech were acute within the limits imposed by generosity: he did not presume to dispose of his characters merely by finding them fallible. Fallible in one degree or another, they were unfailingly interesting, it was easy to care about them.

Some of this interest is carried over into *Setting the World on Fire,* especially in a passage where Miss Lantry's "social certainty" meets social muddle in the person of Mr. Brownlow, who can only live by making exceptions, seeing things afresh, starting over. But very little of the new novel ministers to such expectations. A passage in *No Laughing Matter* alerts the reader to look out for a new relation among the constituents of Wilson's fiction: it comes when the writer Margaret Matthews is described as beginning something new, "something fuller, something that, instead of putting a sharp line under life's episodes, would capture the fusion of all the moments, happy, unhappy." Putting a sharp line under life's episodes is what Wilson's early short stories and novels were engaged in. Capturing the fusion of all the moments is evidently what he has been trying to do since *No Laughing Matter.*

The effort has involved, in *No Laughing Matter, As If By Magic* . . . , and the new novel [*Setting the World on Fire*], a more explicit relation between events and meanings. Wilson's art has always veered between confidence that the events shown will bring their meaning with them and determination that the meaning will be declared, at whatever cost to the vagary of the events. It is a problem of the relation between detail and pattern; detail so abundant that it threatens every possible pattern; pattern so resolute that it threatens to impoverish the detail.

I am afraid the new novel is all pattern, and that the fusion has not been achieved. You can't read a page of it without feeling the novelist nudging you to appreciate the meaning similitudes, contrasts, Tom and Piers, Pratt and Vanbrugh, the Great House containing its constituents in powerful balance, Vanbrugh and Lully as wild men thriving upon solid ground, classic and romantic, the King of France, "the parallel of Lully's brilliant art and Louis's solemn regality." And of course, the House, which is also the House of Fiction. To say that piers is Phaethon is to say also that he is more Phaethon than he is Piers; except that in the uplifting end he is saved from Zeus's thunderbolt. *Setting the World on Fire* achieves its portentous meaning at the cost of its life; meaning has done the work of the thunderbolt.

Emotion in Wilson's fiction has always been acute but limited, limited to its provocation by the social muddle, acute in the expression mainly of distaste. In his recent novels the distaste is directed against those in power, the old men at the zoo, running things and running them amok. What the recent novels have lacked is energy, so that even their intelligence seems weary of itself and its perceptions. There is some evidence that Wilson the novelist and Wilson the critic of the novel are thwarting each other. Teaching fiction, these days, is no help to the release of a powerful creative urge. I am aware that there is more to the urge than its release. No matter. My point is that Wilson seems to have allowed recent arguments about the theory of fiction to inhibit the spontaneity so clear in *Hemlock and After* and the other early novels. Teaching fiction, he is bound to ask himself: after such knowledge, what forgiveness?

It is well known that the assumptions of realism have been, as some critics like to say, put in question. The only quality of realism still in high standing with avant garde critics is its intermittent tendency to destroy itself. Many critics seem to be delighted to hand over the realistic enterprise to popular fiction, the TV drama, and the minor efforts of film. Till recently, these conveyances have mostly been French and American. But it is evident that many English novelists who have professed realism in one degree or another are now themselves losing faith. Normally, critics explain matters of style, form, and structure in terms ultimately metaphysical: we claim to discover a writer's ontology in his sentence. What is happening in English fiction seems to require rather a political explanation than anything as high as metaphysics. Wilson's querulousness, his contempt for our masters, his insistence on induced meanings and willed relations do not issue from a deep creative source but from post-imperial disappointment. The relation between the English novel, bourgeois liberalism, and the certitudes of empire is still unclear, but a tetchy sense of it as issuing chiefly in frustrated idealism and guilt seems to correspond to Wilson's new novel. (pp. 21-2)

Denis Donoghue, "You Better Believe It," in The New York Review of Books (*reprinted with permission from* The New York Review of Books; *copyright* © *1980 Nyrev, Inc.), Vol. XXVII, No. 18, November 20, 1980, pp. 20-2.**

PETER FAULKNER

Wilson expresses the problem of the contemporary novelist in a striking question: "How can we combine caring with shaping?" The remarkable feature of his own career as a writer has been the way in which, despite the nihilistic tendencies of the age, Wilson has retained his care for humanity while enriching the formal elements of his work—though the formal complexity of the early works is often under-estimated. . . . Wilson agrees with the suggestion that his later novels reveal a less solid world than the earlier ones, relating this to his growing sense of the fragility of our civilisation. Some people, like Wilson's central characters, try to come to an understanding of the situation, but many avoid the issue and play ''louder and louder games to disguise from themselves the earthquake surface on which we all live''. Again we are made aware of the serious concern for humanity at the centre of Wilson's art. Despite his awareness of the elements of role-playing in social situations, which give the opportunities for his brilliant exercises in mimicry, and his modernist awareness of the subjective basis of all utterances, which leads to the use of pastiche, Wilson still affirms that ''I do have a sense that there is something real'' under the social surface, and his sympathies are always with those who try to develop that reality rather than retreat from it into a purely social identity. . . . [There is] a paradox which is central to his achievement. And it is finally linked with what Wilson rightly emphasises as a newer element in his work—which we may look forward to seeing further developed in future novels—the sense that ''the London media world'' is limitingly narrow and that truer values must be sought in awareness of ''a wider world theatre'', including nature as well as man. (pp. 216-17)

Fortunately it would be pointless here to try to sum up Wilson's achievement with any finality. What can be said now is that he is a restless and ambitious novelist who has never repeated himself, and who has used his great powers of observation and mimicry both to illuminate the change of English society and to suggest the epistemological problems posed by all literary texts. Criticism probably fails to do justice to the brilliance of his wit, but it can at least point to the range of relevance of his work. For Wilson has written about many of the main issues of our time: freedom and bondage in human relationships; the dilemmas of liberalism; the limits of language; the relation between public and private life; the appeals of role-playing; the temptations of magic; and, pervasively, the violence of the world. The seriousness of Wilson's concern about the general problems of the novelist is clear from his numerous theoretical discussions. But his attitude remains intelligently eclectic, refusing the doctrinaire solutions of either Social Realism or the *nouveau roman*, and expressing itself in a fiction which registers with uncomfortable accuracy the tensions and uncertainties of our world. (pp. 219-20)

Peter Faulkner, in his Angus Wilson: Mimic and Moralist *(copyright © 1980 by Peter Faulkner; reprinted by permission of Viking Penguin Inc.; in Canada by Martin Secker & Warburg Limited), The Viking Press, 1980, Secker & Warburg, 1980, 226 p.*

Joseph Wittlin

1896-1976

(Also transliterated as Józef) Polish novelist, poet, and essayist.

Wittlin's most significant contributions to the literary world consist of *Hymny (Hymns)*, a collection of poems revealing his personal anguish over war, and *Sól ziemi (Salt of the Earth)*, the first volume of an unpublished trilogy with the planned title *Saga of the Patient Footsoldier*.

***Salt of the Earth* expands on the war themes evident in Wittlin's earlier works. It has elicited almost unanimous praise for its symbolic depiction of the Unknown Soldier in his struggles to adapt to the horror and chaos of war. Although Wittlin died before completing the third volume, and the manuscript of the second volume was lost in the turmoil of World War II, the first volume stands as a complete work of art. Wittlin's skill at combining in this work the elements of a historical saga and a contemporary novel led the Polish critic Jan Koprowski to call it "a record of the time and a piece of art of timeless significance."**

(See also *Contemporary Authors*, Vols. 49-52, Vols. 65-68 [obituary] and *Contemporary Authors New Revision Series*, Vol. 3.)

Courtesy of Halina Wittlin

ARTHUR PRUDDEN COLEMAN

Wittlin has often been called the Polish Andreev, and it is of Andreev one is reminded at once by the title of [Wittlin's planned trilogy, "**Saga of the Patient Footsoldier**"]; one thinks instinctively of Andreev's "Confessions of a Little Man during Great Days" and reflects that it is justifiable to link the Pole with the Russian, since Wittlin's work, if not the "Confessions of a Little Man," is unquestionably that "Little Man's" odyssey. Wittlin's hero, Peter, moreover, is certainly the very archtype of those masses of marching men in Andreev's *Red Laugh* who "did not know where they were going," nor "what the sun was for," who, in fact, "did not know anything."

Again, they call Wittlin the Polish Barbusse, and in a sense he is, for his Peter is the very flesh and blood and heart and soul of what Barbusse's *poilu*-hero would be if he were a Polish-Ukrainian Austrian like Peter. For Peter is a single individual who stands for all the individuals who, drawn from the "emptied towns and ruined villages" constitute the "material of war" crowded by Barbusse into *Le Feu*.

Some call Wittlin the Polish Remarque, and again with a certain amount of justification. Wittlin's saga, like Remarque's familiar "All Quiet on the Western Front," is conceived in pity and elaborated with fine-edged irony. . . .

But Wittlin differs from his Russian and French and German contemporaries despite the common denominator of background, which is the First World War, and of hero, which is the ordinary individual. Andreev surveyed the common scene and found the poor creatures who marched blindly down the sunbaked roads all mad. Barbusse saw the same men in the filthy trenches of France as instruments, some consciously but the majority without knowing it, of a purpose. Remarque saw the mass of those who fought for Germany as men lost beyond

possibility of reclamation. Wittlin saw them as simply—Peter, the Hucul railroad guard from the mountain hamlet of Topory-Czernielica whose single ambition in life was to wear the cap which was the sign and symbol of Imperial service.

Who is Peter? He is the Unknown Soldier. . . .

But what sort of being was this Unknown Soldier? Nobody can say. Nobody knows. He was as unknown humanly as if he had never existed within a human frame or drawn a human breath. (p. 10)

Wittlin knew . . . from his own participation in the twentieth century counterpart of the Greco-Trojan duel, that it is not the Ulysseses who make a war but the nameless, long-suffering soldiers who travel on foot. The idea of these men as heroes fused in Wittlin's mind with the idea of revealing the Unknown Soldier, and so the "**Saga of the Patient Footsoldier**," whose very name Niewiadomski means "Son of an Unknown Father," was born.

The quality which more than any other distinguishes Wittlin from contemporaries to whom he has been compared is his Biblicalness. His style is essentially that of the great stories in the Bible: clear, simple, and detached, worthy of significant deeds. His treatment of individuals is Biblical: each becomes a symbol and each is as completely evoked in his symbolic role as a Job or a Daniel. His manner of communicating mass emotion has a Biblical quality too. Wittlin realizes the emotion simply and poignantly through the gestures and sounds of striking and symbolic figures. . . . Wittlin's sense of the mystical unity of all life is Biblical too and nowhere more majestically brought into play than in the early scenes of the story where Peter is still in his native village above the mist-hung gorges of the Prut and the Czeremosz.

The Biblical quality of Wittlin's saga, as well also as that of his earlier war poems ("Hymns"), is by no means exclusively of the Old Testament, though the Old Testament is unquestionably Wittlin's first and greatest model. His attitude toward all humankind, . . . is Christian and New Testamental: he has regard for both the least and the greatest of men and he sees both deluded in equal measure by the very quality in themselves that makes them nobler than the beasts, the capacity men have for selfless devotion to another human being or to an ideal. (pp. 10-11)

> Arthur Prudden Coleman, *"Joseph Wittlin: Giant of Polish Letters," in* The Saturday Review of Literature (© 1941, copyright renewed © 1968, Saturday Review Magazine Co.; reprinted by permission), Vol. XXIV, No. 15, August 2, 1941, pp. 10-12.

STANLEY EDGAR HYMAN

["**Salt of the Earth**"] is the simple, vivid and quietly passionate story of an unknown Polish soldier in the early days of the last war, the Polish Everyman, the eternal fall guy. . . . It is an intimate and always ironic picture of the war, not on a canvas of titanic battles and vast strategic movements, but on the smallest canvas imaginable—Peter Neviadomski. . . .

The war picks him up, packs him off to some place called Hungary, claps him into a second-hand uniform and prepares him to die for a senile and foolish old man named Franz Josef, whom Peter has never seen but whom he regards with a decent peasant adoration. . . .

In a really magnificent beginning, the book focuses the war deliberately on Peter, for all the world like a good movie opening. Wittlin's camera first picks out the ominous black double-headed eagle of Austria-Hungary, shifts to the council of bewhiskered incompetents around Franz Josef as he signs the proclamation of war, moves outward to reactions throughout the vast empire, and slowly comes to rest on Peter in his tiny Huzul village, where it remains. Only toward the end of the book does a character as central as Peter appear, Regimental Sergeant-Major Bachmatiuk, the incredibly perfect military machine (he gets himself out of bed in the morning with whispered commands). Even he, although he may emerge in subsequent volumes as a secondary protagonist, seems to be no more in this volume than a brilliantly executed counterweight to Peter, the flint and steel to Peter's tinder. . . .

Wittlin has created a novel to rank easily with the best war literature of our time. (p. 559)

> Stanley Edgar Hyman, *"The Patient Foot-Soldier," in* The New Republic (*reprinted by permission of* The New Republic; © 1941 The New Republic, Inc.), Vol. 105, No. 17, October 27, 1941, pp. 559-60.

F. C. WEISKOPF

Not much has happened [by the end of *Salt of the Earth*]. But it is the way in which the story is told that will hold the reader captive. Joseph Wittlin is a master of intensive characterization. Gifted with an endless love for the distressed and heavy laden, for the "little man," he knows how to bring his hero unforgettably before the reader. . . . His prose is poetically beautiful and powerful. His metaphors are finished in their artistry. And he has another gift that is not too common: He is possessed of a delicate humor which brightens even the most tragic moments without ever growing banal. The patient infantryman Peter Niewiadomski . . . will doubtless take his place with immortal creations like the "good soldier Schwejk" or his predecessors, the private soldiers in Tolstoi's *War and Peace*.

> F. C. Weiskopf, *"Poetry and Fiction: 'Salt of the Earth'," in* Books Abroad (*copyright 1942 by the University of Oklahoma Press*), Vol. 16, No. 2, Spring, 1942, p. 160.

ZBIGNIEW FOLEJEWSKI

[Joseph Wittlin] is above all a genuine poet, sufficiently original and sufficiently talented so as not to have slavishly to follow any programs and manifestoes. In Poland between the wars there were many programs and many manifestoes, but what is even more important is the fact that at the very threshhold of political independence, a few years after Versailles, Polish poetry produced such magnificent phenomena as *Łąka* (Meadow) by Bolesław Leśmian, *Karmazynowy poemat* (Crimson Poem) by Jan Lechoń, *Czychanie na Boga* (To Ambush God) by Julian Tuwim, *Ballady* (Ballads) by Emil Zegadłowicz, *Parada* (Parade) by Antoni Słonimski, and . . . [*Hymns*] by Joseph Wittlin. The authors, all young poets, expressed their individual feelings, hopes and doubts, in forms which were more or less novatory, but each was sufficiently original and suggestive to gain its own position in Polish literature. (p. 69)

In Wittlin's *Hymns* the leading note which will stay with the poet all his life is a tone of fright at the thought of what the war and the post-war developments have done to men, fright at the thought of dehumanization, the nightmare of the twentieth century. What was expressed in poetic form in the *Hymns* will forty years later be echoed by the symbolic title of Wittlin's latest volume, *Orpheus in the Underworld of the 20th Century*.

There are many personal and quite a few objective, descriptive motives in his *Hymns*. The collection shows us a sensitive poetic personality, not pessimistic, but somewhat weary in his world outlook. Wittlin, like many of his contemporaries, watched his world emerge out of the misery of war, in the process of which too many human values had to be sacrificed. This amalgamation of bold dreams and prosaic details of daily reality, in which a "spoonful of soup" can become a symbol of life and death, is the poetic matter of this volume. The poem, "**Hymn to a Spoonful of Soup**," is perhaps the most shaking and the most revealing in the volume, both from the ideological and from the formal point of view. At the same time, the vision of the soldier whose human reactions are being reduced to the desire for a spoonful of soup will prove productive in Wittlin's later work. (pp. 69-70)

Wittlin remained a poet of few words. In each consecutive edition of his *Hymns* some new poems were added. Although Wittlin never published another volume of poetry, the few poems published during the war, were very impressive, many of them unsurpassed in lyrical depth. Wittlin's "**Stabat Mater**," for example, will certainly remain one of the most memorable patriotic lyrics in which the poet's personal and national sentiments are expressed in a simple and at the same time artful form. (p. 70)

The vision of the soldier from the **"Hymn about a Spoonful of Soup"** gradually developed into a full-length novel, [*Salt of the Earth*]. . . .

Salt of the Earth [is] one of the most meaningful and artistically accomplished novels in modern literature. . . . [Although] this novel belongs to a large group of works devoted to the problem of war, it is unique in its perception of what happens to human beings when they are caught in this gigantic, merciless machinery of modern war apparatus with bureaucratic rules, paragraphs, orders and counter-orders, where individuals are only numbers. In the main structural theme, the hero, a simple, barely literate railroad worker, is confronted with all the puzzles of the collective machinery and with the intricate balance between the serious and the ridiculous in the process which is supposed to change unruly individuals into efficient soldiers. There are, of course, many literary parallels that could be drawn here, but there are hardly any direct influences. The work closely parallels *The Brave Soldier Sveik* by Jaroslav Hasek. The device of revealing some of the author's convictions by seemingly naive, humoristic reactions of the uneducated hero is common to both these works. But there the analogy ends. The uniqueness of Wittlin's novel is strengthened by the poetic quality of his style. This note of lyricism, paired with a very carefully precise construction of the whole vision, accounts for the artistic effect of a fulfilled work of art. (p. 71)

There is a serious and melancholy concern in Wittlin's novel with a Franciscan love of life and a note of quiet humor in the story of this unheroic hero. This attitude, the ability to discover elements of human love and dignity in the midst of the miseries of war, exile, poetry and frustration, is found in all Wittlin's writing. Both in his early collections of essays [*War, Peace and the Soul of the Poet* and *Stages*] . . . and in the recent *Orpheus in the Underworld of the 20th Century* we can see the stages of the same road, the road of a modern Odysseus dreaming of his lost Ithaca. (pp. 71-2)

> Zbigniew Folejewski, "The Creative Path of Joseph Wittlin" (a revision of the foreword to a Polish program held at the Polish Club in Toronto, September 29, 1963), in The Polish Review (© copyright 1964 by the Polish Institute of Arts and Sciences in America, Inc.), Vol. 9, No. 1, Winter, 1964, pp. 67-72.

ZOYA YURIEFF

To paraphrase poetry is a difficult and ungrateful task. However, if we are to afford the foreign reader a real insight into the spiritual-creative world of [Joseph Wittlin], the author of the *Hymns,* we must resort to this device. We must begin by stating that they are pervaded with a sense of metaphysical longing, and intense personal experience: they read more like prayers than poems and they were so read by Wittlin's contemporaries. The *Hymns* are not devoid, however, of doubts and contradictions, even blasphemy. Their main theme is war, which forms a general background against which the above-mentioned feelings are dynamically developed. War and Death are great tryers of the spirit. Wittlin's *Hymns* appeal for peace and for mankind to abandon their weapons. The author calls for repentance and a return to faith in God, thereafter a new future for mankind. Some of his hymns reflect the spirit of a crusader (the crusaders, after all, did sing hymns!) and of a

penitent, rebellious, sinful, and yet blissful poet-prophet, who has experienced God's grace upon himself and his lyre, and would like to see others converted to the faith he has been granted. (pp. 22-3)

The tone of the *Hymns* ranges from one of despair, rebellion and blasphemy to that of psalmodic serenity and Christian humility. . . . [Wittlin] succeeds in harmonizing all these dissonant tones into an impressive and very musical whole. The change from a distracted cry to a quiet, intimate tone, almost that of a whisper, is reflected in the arrangement of Part I of the *Hymns*. . . .

The book is divided into three parts. In Part I a young and immature poet, unable and unwilling to restrain himself, cries out his feelings. . . . He is representative not only of his own generation but of the entire human race, which had endured the hell of war. (p. 23)

"The Hymn to a Spoonful of Soup" describes in simple, unadorned, but poignant diction the wretched plight of a foot soldier doomed to perish who has asked for a spoonful of hot soup, which the poet would have liked to give to him, but it was already too late. . . . An ironic reply to the question of why the simple foot soldier had to perish is given in the next hymn, **"Burying an Enemy."** . . . The author of the hymn was told to bury an enemy because the design of his cap and buttons are those of the enemy, even though his hand is as hurt and tired as the hand of a brother. The poet has been seized by a sudden sympathy for the unknown soldier. He feels that his heart has been poisoned, and that when the burial is finished he has turned into a stone. A blend of sympathy, grief, abhorrence, irony and scorn is artfully woven together in simple, poignant words and rhythms, which take on the musical structure characteristic of soldiers' songs and funeral marches. There is also a vision of a "peasant paradise," written in quasipastoral tones and framed in the characteristic three-line stanzas of Polish church songs, which sums up the essential message, of Wittlin's *Hymns*. It is a paradise in which everyone, people of all nations . . . will embrace each other. . . . Here Wittlin's youthful, utopian faith in the possibility of influencing people through poetry and song is still intact. But Part II of the *Hymns* already shows a waning of this belief. (pp. 24-5)

Part II of the *Hymns* . . . is devoted to more intimate, but no less explosive emotions. . . .

"A Hymn of Restlessness, Madness and Boredom" . . . gives poignant expression to the author's feelings of nausea, restlessness, and boredom. Although written 15 or more years before Sartre's celebrated *La Nausée* (1936), it already has an existentialist ring. The emotional intensity of the hymn is fully Expressionistic and the author's emotions are clad in plastic and dynamic images. He does not want to accept the world around him, he searches for its *raison d'être*, for a solution to his longings and his thoughts, only to find that there is no limit to either. He tries to seize the moment when the miracle he has waited for since childhood would occur. But in vain: the happiness for whose sake he has "learned how to think and speak" eludes him. There is no end to the anguish caused by his longings, no stilling of all the unknown forces which slumber in his body and soul. . . . (p. 27)

This mood of hopelessness and restlessness persists also in the **"Hymn of Fire."** . . . (p. 29)

Part III of the *Hymns* contains **"Non-Hymns"** as a counterpart to the Hymns. It shows the versatility of the young poet, whose lyre is capable of various tones and tunes. **"Non-Hymns"** point to the future line of Wittlin's development as a poet. . . . [However], the issues of faith and doubt, despair and serenity of soul, appear in the **"Non-Hymns"** as well. Three short epigrammatic poems close the volume. **"Blanks"** shows the poet's dissatisfaction with existing linguistic and artistic methods and devices, especially with worn-out words and rhymes. In this poem he uses blanks (. . .) for those cliché rhymes that everyone will be able to fill in without much thought. Wittlin has battled strenuously against words even slightly suspect of descending into "clichédom" and against the automatic repetition of "empty words" (the title of one of his essays). Some of these worn-out words were laughed out of existence precisely by Wittlin and others who were equally sensitive to the deadening of the living Polish language. Thus Wittlin developed the practice of putting "so-called" in front of every word or phraseological unit that has become worn out by over-usage. There is no end to the ironic effects he achieves in this way in his poems and essays alike. (p. 31)

The *Hymns* are oratorical or rhetorical in structure, though they have some narrative and descriptive features as well. It has been said that epic elements are more prevalent in them than lyrical ones but the *Hymns* contain so many emotional elements and lyrical apostrophes, so many "mindscapes," every description in them is so subordinated to the mood of the lyrical "I" that one should consider them as predominantly lyrical. . . . The world is portrayed in a synthetic way, typical of a lyrical presentation. There are only a few concrete, epic details and these are submerged beneath lyrical vehemence, grandiose poetic visions, symbols and images. Details are often exaggerated, in keeping with the poetics of Expressionism. The *Hymns* are directed to an imaginary audience or to specific individuals (cf. **"To the Adversary"**) with the aim of impressing them, trying to make them share the author's beliefs and even act accordingly (the Expressionists' goal). Wittlin's oratorical style is characterized by frequent parallelisms of various kinds (thematic, syntactic, lexical), by questions, exclamations, exhortations. It is often hyperbolic, saturated with images and similes, rather extended, made dramatic by plastic visions and metamorphoses (as in the **"Hymn of Hatred"**). The tone changes from lyrical-apostrophic to satirical-sarcastic, the volume from a shriek to a whisper. The unity of the structure is achieved by the unity of the themes which encompass God, War, the human soul after the war and the lyrical "I." (pp. 32-3)

Unity is also achieved by the composition of the whole. The basic device seems to be a repetition of the main motif or of several motifs which are closely related and it reminds one of a musical composition where a leitmotif appears, disappears and reappears in different variations. The basic motif may be given at the very beginning, in the opening verse (*capoverso*), as in **"Burying an Enemy,"** where the author says that "his heart is poisoned," and repeated at the very end with a variation, thus framing the whole structure: "In vain am I carrying around my poisoned heart. . . ." (p. 33)

The oratorical style presupposes the choice of solemn words, an archaic syntax, and an extensive use of tropes and figures. Wittlin uses archaic words and archaic syntactic constructions to a moderate degree, combining them for greater expressiveness with everyday and sometimes even vulgar words (cf. **"In Praise of the Sword"**). There are some dialectisms for the sake of stylization, as in **"Burying an Enemy."** Wittlin shows great mastery in creating clusters of words around the key words of the poem, thus extending their meaning, reinforcing the texture and making possible smooth transition between the stanzas. . . . Of all the various types of metaphor, Wittlin especially favors and shows unusual skill in using personifications. He possesses a mythic imagination even though both his precursors Homer and Kasprowicz use a great deal of anthropomorphization as well. . . . Personifications make Wittlin's poetic world highly dynamic, expressive and dramatic. Everything comes alive and acts—not only objects but the most abstract concepts: abstract words predominate over concrete in the *Hymns*. (pp. 35-6)

Wittlin uses free verse rhythms—in the appropriately chosen form of hymns with great mastery. His immediate models in the use of free verse were Kasprowicz and Verhaeren. His rhythms convey all the minute fluctuations of emotion, they carry its ebb and flow with great ease. He does not borrow ready-made rhythms; his blood longs for "new rhythms" and he often achieves them. His rhythms are usually appropriate to his subject matter. (p. 37)

The meaning of Wittlin's *Hymns*—indeed of his poetry as a whole—lies in their religious sense, in the yearning of a hard-pressed soul for happiness and communion with God. We constantly sense the poet's fear that the human soul as a result of World War was deteriorating and reaching the state which was described in an expressionistic way as "man's defection from God," as "the extreme consequence of lack of sympathy." (pp. 38-9)

Wittlin's [First World War] experiences became the core of [*The Salt of the Earth*] which was designed to examine and to destroy the war myth, to laugh it out of existence, by turning it into absurdity. (p. 70)

Comparisons have been drawn between *The Salt of the Earth* and *War and Peace*. Even at first glance, however, there are more observable differences between the two books than similarities. The most significant difference concerns the two writers' very dissimilar artistic techniques. Tolstoy is a meticulous collector of the details which make up life in all its rich variety; he thereby creates a vast complex artistic "field of vision." Wittlin, on the other hand, works as a poet: he synthesizes his material, crystallizing it into a few words which are sustained and accentuated by the rhythm of his language. This does not preclude a certain epic *rozlewnosc* (prolix style) nor a lyrical linking of material on the associative principle. Thus, to understand and to enjoy the depth of meaning and art of Wittlin's prose, we must read very attentively—just as attentively as we read poetry, without skipping a single word. . . . (p. 74)

Wittlin's book is an attempt to modernize the epic; he has chosen a familiar theme—the conduct of men during a great upheaval, treating it in a new way. The traditional epic devices such as prologue and epilogue, the commencement *in medias res*, the intrusion of supernatural powers, the use of dreams and omens, wide-ranging "broad-view" pictures, the leisurely presentation of details, *"die Totalität der Objekte"* (in Hegel's phrase), extended metaphors and similes, stock epithets, are all present in *The Salt of the Earth*, but they usually serve a different function. At times the grand style demanded by every definition of the epic is here applied to some insignificant events, thereby creating a tension between manner and matter; or, sometimes the language may be dignified and poetic, even shot through with pathos, and then, all of a sudden, display a mocking intent. In this respect Wittlin's style resembles that of the great nineteenth-century Russian writer Nikolai Gogol. (pp. 75-6)

In a manner imperceptible to the untrained eye, Wittlin introduces a mythology of his own. He is at his best not where he tries to be a scholar and meticulous researcher in the style of Flaubert, who liked to check every detail against scientific treatises or archaeological findings, but rather where he gives free rein to his imagination and reconstructs not the historical but the "mythico-historical process." (p. 77)

The poetic intensity and artful simplicity of *The Salt of the Earth* make it a powerful mode of persuasion (a traditional prerogative of poetry) without the author's forcing his own ideology upon us. Composing his work more like a saga than a novel, Wittlin achieves an almost lyrical cohesion and compactness by using the associative principle of linking and interweaving the component parts. Various motifs—those of the Unknown Soldier, of War, of Death and the Devil—are combined to merge with, and overlay, each other. Minor motifs like those of Fear, of Treason, of the right and the left hand, follow suit reinforcing the already tight and condensed structure. The author achieves tension through subtly underscoring the main points of his vision by abundant ironies and ambiguities. . . . [He] sets about creating from the very beginning of the book the atmosphere of a world on its way out, using various motifs and devices, and replacing the dynamics of plot with the dynamics of style and language. (p. 82)

As for the problems of the characters and the setting or background of the book, it is difficult to decide . . . who or what is the hero and who or what forms the background. Peter Niewiadomski is in such close communion with his natural environment that he and the other Huculs whose presence we feel are virtually inseparable from it. . . . Could not Peter and the other Huculs be thought of as a kind of setting, a background against which historical events are projected by the author? Is not the chief conflict of the book between the earth (and everything which is on it and which grows out of it) and war—the cataclysm which fatally affects this earth? (pp. 97-8)

The War, the historical event on which Wittlin focuses his attention, is portrayed by him with such vividness and plasticity that it assumes the shape of a real protagonist. . . . War is personified; it is even accompanied by the old symbol of evil—the snake. We notice this with the first appearance of Corporal Durek . . . and we see it also in the comparison of the war telegrams to snake coils. . . . We see the encroachment of war upon everything and everybody, its dynamic development, its sweeping over places and people alike, its "life" which in the two later volumes of the trilogy is to end in its "death," the date of which we know from history. . . . The War is afforded a more thorough treatment in the book than are other characters who are here not portrayed from birth to death, as is often done in novels. (pp. 99-100)

Wittlin's prose has the compactness of poetry. Every component is related to other components; all details eventually converge to compose a portrait or convey some symbolic meaning. . . . The density of Wittlin's prose, where every thread reinforces the texture, adding another link to the total continuity, makes it difficult to distinguish between the more and the less important elements in the book, or to define precisely the nature of his craftsmanship.

How does he, for instance, achieve his effects in revealing to us the psychological depths of a human soul? What about the characterizations, aside from the fact that they are so close to his background? Despite the fact that the two principal "heroes," Peter Niewiadomski and Rudolph Bachmatiuk, could

well be regarded as personified ideas at almost every turn of the book, their primary importance being as instruments to expose the absurdity of the institution of war from two opposed vantage points: that of one who knows nothing about war and that of one who knows all about it; they can also be seen, especially Bachmatiuk, as splendid character studies. They show the keenness of the author's observation and a fine insight into human or, in Bachmatiuk's case, inhuman nature. The latter has been drawn (overdrawn, perhaps) with masterful and prophetic strokes. The Bachmatiuks served in all armies not only in World War I but also in World War II with still more disastrous results. (pp. 100-01)

[In] his depiction of characters Wittlin does not use linguistic characterization and deliberately avoids dialogue. (p. 102)

However, in *The Salt of the Earth* we do have an "interior monologue" of Peter. It contains Peter's rationalizations concerning God and the Emperor. . . . This internal monologue contains several features of linguistic characterization which have been lost in translation.

The style of *The Salt of the Earth* remains its most striking feature for the native reader. Thus the "microanalysis" of Wittlin's text presents difficulties when based on a translation, for we cannot discuss sentence structure, rhythm and all the other sound effects which play a major role in the book. The varying length of sentences and clauses, the smooth and graceful placement of words (Polish unlike English, has no compulsory word order), his so-called inversions and repetitions (especially triple ones)—all this has a rhythmical impact on the native reader who is captivated by this particular kind of prose almost as much as he is by the hexameters of Wittlin's *Odyssey*. One could point to the use of leitmotifs; one could even speak of certain recurring rhythmical units of a kind usually considered the prerogative of poetry. Wittlin's prose is permeated with alliterations, assonances, anaphoras and other rhythmic and melodic effects. Leitmotifs frequently serve as links in the chain of continuity (The leitmotif of "waiting for the war's end" is repeated in several chapters). Sometimes they stress a thought of special concern to the author, or serve to reinforce the emotional impact of a phrase or image. Wittlin composed for the eye as well as for the ear; he tries to eternalize the living word, to strike the right tone in every sentence. This rhythmical organization of language helps the author to harmonize such diverse elements as archaisms, neologisms, dialect words and phrases, and to bring his prose close to poetry. So, too, does his highly poetic concentration, where almost every sentence has its point and the similes and metaphors extend and reverberate as they should in any good epic and poetic work. (pp. 103-04)

[Another element is Wittlin's] personification of war to the degree that it actually becomes a *dramatis persona* of the book. War which comes over to the embankment in black boots and confronts Peter . . . is a metonymy: it is not the war as such who comes but merely an official carrying the summons to war. But Wittlin's hand creates a new mythical figure not unlike a new god of war, or the messenger of a Greek god, who is geared with mocking irony by the author to the contemporary scene, revealing its bureaucratic and unpoetic nature as soon as he opens his mouth . . . with a golden tooth. Even before the war spreads metonymically, assuming different forms, the station master, who learns of its outbreak from the telegraph, disentangles himself from "coils of paper covered with Morse Code" and shakes "the war from his feet." . . . (p. 110)

Wittlin uses both metaphor and metonymy with equal effectiveness. He is especially good at substituting a state of mind or emotion for the people who are in its grip, thus creating from such an abstraction a separate entity imbued with ephemeral life. Terror, Fear, Aggression, Revolt, Treason, Language—all these live, move, act as if quite separate from those whom they characterize. (pp. 110-11)

In his role as a poet, however, Wittlin seems to be attracted more by metaphor, perhaps because it gives him an opportunity to exploit the multivocality and ambiguity of words, as is more often the case in poetry than in "straight" prose. The same ambiguity is at the root of puns which are quite frequent in *The Salt of the Earth*. (pp. 111-12)

Irony, parody, the grotesque, puns, as we find them in *The Salt of the Earth* would often be out of place in an old-fashioned epic, but they help to make this book a new kind of epic, an epic of the twentieth century. . . . Wittlin destroyed the myths of the mighty Emperor and of the "unknown soldier" as these have been officially propagated. In creating his saga of the patient foot-soldier he erected a fine monument to one of the sons of the "Hucul earth" and all the other "sons" for whom Peter stands. *The Salt of the Earth* is a finished work of art in which the whole structure and the compositional unity encompasses everything down to the minutest detail, in which all dissonances are resolved into harmony. Nothing is lost, nothing is too small for an author who knows how to achieve unity by manipulating microscopic particles into a whole. The coming of doom is evoked by means of "moribund" metaphors which point to the philosophy of the work, and not by the novelist's direct statements. In *The Salt of the Earth* the author knows how to preserve the "fiction" of a novel, even what appears to be a historical novel, by presenting events in chronological order and using many authentic details. But what the modern reader most values are some of the "moments" described; for example that of the signing of the Declaration of War in the Prologue, which seems to last forever and thereby to have become indelible. The reader will never forget the little station of Topory-Czernielica, a microcosm lovingly created by an artist who knew how to reproduce its soul, which grows in dimensions to represent the soul of the whole Austro-Hungarian Empire and perhaps even of the whole world. (pp. 112-13)

Zoya Yurieff, in his Joseph Wittlin *(copyright © 1973 by Twayne Publishers, Inc.; reprinted with the permission of Twayne Publishers, a Division of G. K. Hall & Co., Boston), Twayne, 1973, 175 p.*

JAN KOPROWSKI

[The protagonist of *Salt of the Earth*] embodies a modern epic of the Unknown Soldier, told in an idiom full of simplicity and humour and showing a profound and infallible sense of the human predicament. Impressive pictures, which sink deep into the mind, build up the dramatic story of the hero. . . . This 'patient foot-soldier' is not only an apotheosis of the man-in-the-street figure so beloved of interwar literature, but also deep and moving study of the human psyche, a record of the time, and a piece of art of timeless significance. (pp. 57-8)

Jan Koprowski, "Józef Wittlin," in Polish Perspectives, *Vol. XX, No. 1, January, 1977, pp. 57-61.*

Gene (Rodman) Wolfe

1931-

American science fiction and fantasy novelist and short story writer.

Wolfe blends the intellectual appeal of science fiction with the emotional appeal of fantasy to explore contemporary themes. Among Wolfe's major concerns are the isolation and alienation of the individual and the terrors of daily existence. Wolfe's stories are typically open ended, and his protagonists are often children or young men trying to make their way in the world.

Wolfe has only recently emerged as a popular storyteller, although critics have praised his writing since the publication of *The Fifth Head of Cerberus* in 1972. *Cerberus*, which explores identity and selfhood, and *The Book of the New Sun*, a tetralogy that examines a decaying planet and the myth of a new sun which may be that planet's only salvation, are ranked among the most important science fiction works written in the last decade.

(See also *Contemporary Authors*, Vols. 57-60; *Contemporary Authors New Revision Series*, Vol. 6; and *Dictionary of Literary Biography*, Vol. 8.)

JOANNA RUSS

Operation Ares by Gene Wolfe . . . is going to do the author's reputation a disservice someday. I know what Mr. Wolfe can do when he sets his mind to it; *Ares* is far below his best. It is a convincing, quiet, low-keyed, intelligent book which somehow fades out into nothing. The characters are surprisingly decent; time after time there are touches of good observation and well-textured realism, but in the end Mr. Wolfe doesn't really seem to care. The book uses an interesting technique of presenting things obliquely; big events happen offstage, and often the explanations of events will be given long after the events themselves—I don't mean that this is mystification but that the significance of many things only becomes apparent long afterwards. One of the best things in the novel is its intense concentration on the present moment—time after time one swallows stereotypes without realizing that's what they are (the rational, naive Martians, the emergency government that can only harass and annoy, the fear of scientific "heterodoxy"). But all in all, the novel is a failure, shadowy and inconclusive. Books like this are generally called "promising," but by the time you read this review, Mr. Wolfe will be as far above *Operation Ares* as *Ares* is above the worst science fiction hackwork.

> *Joanna Russ, "Books: 'Operation Ares'" reprinted by permission of Ellen Levine Literary Agency, Inc.; copyright © 1971 by Mercury Press, Inc.), in* The Magazine of Fantasy and Science Fiction, *Vol. 40, No. 4, April, 1971, p. 69.*

DOUGLAS BARBOUR

[Gene Wolfe] has shown a consistent growth in the understanding of his art. The three interconnecting novellas of *The Fifth Head of Cerberus* are his most multiplex work yet.

The title novella concerns a man's search for his selfhood. Like [Barry Malzberg, author of *Beyond Apollo*], Wolfe is fully aware of the many possibilities true speculative fiction offers. All three novellas are connected by their relationships to each other and to the twin planets of St. Anne and St. Croix where they occur. Yet all three are forms of documentation and not ordinary stories at all. The character who seeks some truth about his own life by writing it down is both protagonist and storyteller in "**The Fifth Head of Cerberus**"; Gene Wolfe is hidden behind him (is, in fact, well hidden behind all the fictional 'documents' that *are* all three novellas). This character is a cloned immortal (immortal insofar as the fact of his being a clone means he is in some fashion the same man as his father, grandfather, etc.). But is he quite the same person, or is he not? Wolfe uses the story to raise the deepest questions about identity. There is a dark heart of mystery to this story which is chilling in its integrity. By finding a new speculative approach to age old questions concerning selfhood and inheritence, Wolfe has created a truly gripping, if entirely open-ended story here.

Nevertheless, the other two stories ["'**A Story' by John V. Marsch**" and "**V.R.T.**"] move further into dark areas of human knowledge, and self-knowledge. St. Anne and St. Croix were originally settled by the French and then, after some war, an English garrison took over, in very different ways on the two planets (there are certain subtle parallels with the conquest of North America implied). The social consequences of the double settlement are explored, but Wolfe is after something more important: there were (possibly) aboriginal inhabitants on St. Anne, but there appear to be none now. The two novellas concern an Earth anthropologist's attempts to discover proof of their existence. This anthropologist, John V. Marsch, first appears peripherally in the first novella. The second one, titled **"'A Story' by John V. Marsch"** is a brilliant re-construction by him (creation by Wolfe) of the aliens' way of life before the first French arrived. There were many different kinds of abos it appears, and the possibility of earlier settlements by space travelling humanoids is suggested. Alexei and Cory Panshin have recently suggested that the 60's saw the re-introduction of mystery into s-f. Wolfe revels in mystery, for he recognizes that in the mystery, accepted as such, the most interesting and arresting fiction finds its life. **"'A Story'"** is a marvelously mysterious creation of a whole alien world.

"V.R.T.", the final novella, is a collection of Marsch's documents, most of which concern his work on St. Anne, some of which are his writings in prison on St. Croix where he has been interned for some putative political crime. They are under examination by an officer who must decide whether or not to free him, and who is obviously as confused by them as we are. (pp. 81-2)

Wolfe uses the various documents of **"V.R.T."** to make many subtle and profound comments on politics, on the destruction of aliens or aborigines, on the ways in which people use each other, and on the strengths individuals can find to help them survive. Despite its harsh ending, it is a story of deep, if often only probable, hope.

One of the really good things about *The Fifth Head of Cerberus* is that although each novella can stand alone as a powerfully wrought work of fiction, the whole is far and subtly greater than the mere sum of its parts. The book will repay many readings with a growing sense of the depth of its art, yet it is, like Malzberg's [*Beyond Apollo*], compulsively readable the first time through; which is one reason I praise it so highly. . . .

Both these books could, I am sure, appeal to many readers of the new fiction of Barth, Coover, Pynchon, et.al., if they could only get over their hang up on the label "science fiction". O yes, these are speculative fiction all right, they're s-f; but they both do what all good fiction does; they reveal the human heart and mind, the deeply human desire to know one's self; and they do it with verve and style. (p. 82)

Douglas Barbour, "Two New (and Major) Works of Speculative Fiction," in Riverside Quarterly *(© 1973 by Leland Sapiro), Vol. 6, No. 1, August, 1973, pp. 79-82.**

GERALD JONAS

One writer who has not neglected cultural variables in his flights of fancy is Gene Wolfe, whose *The Fifth Head of Cerberus* . . . draws great power from a deceptively simple device: the original settlers on his twin planets of Sainte Croix and Sainte Anne were French, not American. The societies that they founded are deliciously decadent, in a manner reminiscent of the French Algeria depicted by Camus. . . .

Wolfe's prose is appropriately resonant, hinting at layers of meaning behind each apparently straightforward statement of fact. The reader who falls under Wolfe's spell soon learns to

be as wary as the principal characters, who live in a culture where every "truth" is suspect because every "truth-teller" has something to conceal, for personal or political reasons. Under such circumstances, the search for self-knowledge— difficult at best—becomes truly heroic. Within a beautifully realized science-fiction setting, Wolfe shows what happens to those who dare to be heroes.

Gerald Jonas, "'Of Things to Come'," in The New York Times Book Review *(© 1976 by The New York Times Company; reprinted by permission), September 12, 1976, p. 46.**

ALGIS BUDRYS

[Gene Wolfe's *The Devil in a Forest*] may or may not be a fantasy; there is a passing reference to something that may have been a supernatural incident in objective fact, rather than simply something that haunted the troubled sleep of Mark, the weaver's apprentice. . . .

In any event, this tale of a catastrophic few days in a Medieval English hamlet is told so beautifully, and gathers power at such a nicely controlled pace, that there is no getting out of it once you get into it.

Wolfe is just amazing with milieu. . . . [He makes] real people out of personalities formed in no world of ours, clothing and housing them, causing them to move and speak with absolute fidelity to verisimilitude. In addition, every board has its creak, every footpath its heelmarks, every tree its leaves. The guy is just an unbelievably effective writer, and a hell of a researcher to boot. (pp. 28-9)

In addition to all that, Wolfe holds your interest throughout, using the viewpoint of young, unsophisticated Mark to tell you what appears to be a simple tale of a time when outlawry and ordinary life were not at all distinct from each other. Only toward the end does it develop that what he has been telling you all along was an inexorable buildup to events of such power, based on such profound superstition, and just possibly on one of the most central of all supernatural events, that you do, indeed, achieve that rare moment when mere words on paper can make your scalp prickle. (p. 29)

Algis Budrys, "Books: 'The Devil in a Forest'," in The Magazine of Fantasy and Science Fiction *(© 1978 by Mercury Press, Inc.; reprinted from* The Magazine of Fantasy and Science Fiction*), Vol. 54, No. 5, May, 1978, pp. 28-9.*

ALGIS BUDRYS

Gene Wolfe is, I think, without peer at his own kind of story, and has a particular gift for the depiction of cataclysmic events through the eyes of a naive central character, usually an adolescent boy. In [the case of *The Shadow of the Torturer*], he's Severian of the Torturers' Guild. . . .

The narrative is done in the style of an old man, a potentate, inscribing an account of his passage through a convoluted life in a decadently subtle culture of enormous complexity. . . .

[The] culture of Severian's world reflects occasional touches of contact with interstellar technology. But in the main it is a blend of medievalism underlain by references to an earlier Hellenistic view of life, which makes sense in terms of actual Terrestrial anthropology, and overlain by a Victorian prurience which differs sharply from the innocent bawdiness and casual violence of the Middle Ages but also makes a kind of sense given the proposed circumstances. (p. 26)

[With] its references to DeSade, Plato and Jack the Ripper, this is a fully realized culture, utterly strange and utterly believeable, as might be expected from the author of **"The Fifth Head of Cerberus."**

Severian, considered as a character, is handicapped by the fact that we know we are meeting only one-fourth of him; considering that, he does better than well enough. The Chatelaine Thecla, his prisoner and first love, puts me in mind of certain ladies I have known, and somewhat of Blanche DuBois. Agia the trickstress and her desperate brother are very nicely done. It is Dorcas, the waif of the Botanic Gardens, who will explode into a major situation somewhere in subsequent volumes.

The difficulty with taking full satisfaction with *The Shadow of the Torturer* is that one can't; some people write a series of four books and call it a tetralogy, but Wolfe is clearly writing one book with four aspects. Thus, while the whole will very likely be far greater than the sum of its parts, no one part is whole. It is also not dispensible.

Wolfe is asking a lot; he is asking us to read what will no doubt eventually be a quarter-million words while waiting for the full reward. But, you know, he's one of our very best. I think he deserves that much trust, because I think he'll repay it. (pp. 26-7)

Algis Budrys, "Books: 'The Shadow of the Torturer'," in The Magazine of Fantasy and Science Fiction *(© 1980 by Mercury Press, Inc.; reprinted from* The Magazine of Fantasy and Science Fiction), *Vol. 58, No. 5, May, 1980, pp. 26-7.*

JAMES GUNN

[*The Shadow of the Torturer* is] not quite science fiction and not quite fantasy. The distinction between science fiction and fantasy is seldom clear even to long-time readers and critics. . . . Without going far into definition, one might suggest that fantasy appeals to the emotions and science fiction to the intellect. Fantasy asks to be accepted on its own terms; science fiction, in terms of the real world. . . .

Today, in response to the growing popularity of fantasy (at one time publishers thought fantasy didn't sell), as evidenced by the success of Tolkien and Stephen King, much sf is appearing in the guise and emotional stance of fantasy. . . . [*The Shadow of the Torturer* takes] place in a galaxy in which humanity has built a far-flung empire among the stars and has subsequently lost much of its power and abilities. But this is only background, and its intellectual relationships play a minor part in the [narrative]. . . . [It] is only hinted at in *The Shadow of the Torturer,* which is, however, the first volume of a promised tetralogy, and more galactic background may appear in subsequent volumes. . . .

[Wolfe] has turned to the writing of long, well-textured, colorful science fantasy after an earlier career dedicated mostly to short fiction that was usually difficult, often ambiguous, sometimes obscure, and always skillfully written. . . . [The] reflections upon the nature of the world and the events that befall [Severian in *The Shadow of the Torturer*] are the product of a more mature experience and a surer writing hand. That protagonist is a man of principle even though he has been raised in the guild of Torturers. What happens to him in the novel is the result of his adherence to principle, even to the journey he

begins to far-off Thrax to become a simple executioner after his expulsion from the guild for giving a knife to a tortured victim he has come to love. Out of such difficult and unpromising beginnings (imagine, if you will, a hero who is a professional torturer!) Wolfe has fashioned the beginnings of a tale. . . .

[*The Shadow of the Torturer*] may not be science fiction in the Asimovian sense [which appeals to the intellect rather than the emotions], but it is an engrossing narrative and perhaps a book in which wisdom may be found.

James Gunn, "Science Fiction: 'The Shadow of the Torturer'," in Book World—The Washington Post *(© 1980, The Washington Post), May 25, 1980, p. 8.*

THOMAS M. DISCH

The Claw of the Conciliator is the second volume of a tetralogy-in-progress, *The Book of the New Sun,* which already seems assured of classic status within the subgenre of science fantasy. This alone would be faint praise, for science fantasy is a doubtful sort of hybrid in which the more decorative elements of science fiction proper—*Star Wars* hardware, dinosaurs, ape-men, etc.—cohabit with the traditional chimeras of myth and legend. Characteristically, writers of science fantasy set wind-up heroes in quest of some grail across a bedragoned landscape quite as though Cervantes had not long since laughed picaresque romance off the literary map. Even when practiced by writers I ordinarily admire—Ursula Le Guin, Michael Moorcock, Brian Aldiss—science fantasy strikes me as inauthentic, coy, and trivial—circus costumery and paste diamonds, the lot of it.

Insofar as it is possible to judge any tetralogy by its first two volumes, *The Book of the New Sun* is a vast exception to that rule. Gene Wolfe has managed to do what no science fantasy author has done heretofore—he's produced a work of art that can satisfy adult appetites and in which even the most fantastical elements register as poetry rather than as penny-whistle whimsey. Furthermore, he's done this without in any way sacrificing the showmanship and splashy colors that auger a popular success. . . .

In allegorical fantasies (and science fantasy is, in its nature, allegorical) it is only possible to achieve intensity and depth if each of the individual elements of the fantasy—the swords, ogres, magic jewels—bears a weight of meditated meaning that intensifies and deepens as the tale progresses. (In the manner, say, of Wagner's *Ring* cycle.) In most hands these props are deployed with the artless caprice of children trimming a tree with their family's heritage of Christmas ornaments. Wolfe, however, is a Wagnerian, not a tree trimmer; his allegory actually has something to say, and it is said with art, acuity, wisdom and wit.

At the risk of compressing it into extinction, I would submit that Wolfe's central theme is the nature of political authority and the use of terror as a necessary means to secure social stability in any society (but especially ours). "Here the master and I do our business still," says Severian, as he pantomimes his trade as torturer in a masque performed at the Autarch's court. "We do it still, and that's why the Commonwealth stands." This cannot be said to be his last word on the subject; rather, the first—the subject up for debate. Here at the center of the labyrinth it is impossible to second-guess the outcome of that debate, but that it will be satisfying can scarcely be doubted.

This is not to say that the web is flawless. I doubt that any tetralogy has ever been written in which the second volume didn't come off as second-best. There are chapters in *The Claw of the Conciliator* that venture perilously close to pulp magazine hugger-mugger, and other chapters—one long interpolated masque, in particular—that are too archly Significant, after the manner of Thornton Wilder's *The Skin of Our Teeth.* (Wilder is a writer whom Wolfe resembles in other, and happier, respects.)

The acclaim and attention that *The Book of the New Sun* is winning among both critics and readers should further consolidate the reputation Gene Wolfe has won as a writer of short fiction. Eighteen of his stories are assembled in *Gene Wolfe's Book of Days,* a collection that aspires to unity by the doubtful device of matching the separate tales to national holidays: for Lincoln's birthday a story about the reintroduction of slavery as a solution to the problem of over-crowded prisons; for Valentine's Day a whimsy about computer matchmaking; and so on through the calendar. Actually, the stories suit their occasions fairly well, but sometimes I suspected that Wolfe was dipping toward the bottom of his barrel in order to accommodate his format. Even so, there are many first-rate stories, most notably the selection for Labor Day, "Forlesen," a novella in which all the morose absurdities of a life devoted to middle management job dissatisfactions are compressed into one day of high-speed, low-keyed nightmare.

> Thomas M. Disch, "A Wizard of the Fabulous," in *Book World—The Washington Post* (© 1981, The Washington Post), March 22, 1981, p. 11.

ALGIS BUDRYS

[You] will be missing a major—a seminal—event in the development of SF if you don't allow yourself the pleasure of reading [*The Claw of the Conciliator*] and its predecessor [*Shadow of the Torturer*], . . . as long as you do so in the privacy of your mind, the enjoyment will not count against you socially.

As a piece of literature, this work is simply overwhelming. Severian is a character realized in a depth and to a breadth we have never seen in SF before; of all unlikely tin things, a detailed, likeable portrait of the skilled artisan as a young man is emerging here; courageous, professional—distasteful of the slavering onlookers as he breaks his victims' thighs deftly—rather wise but certainly unsophisticated, he is still being led around by his private parts. But that will change.

As a piece of craftsmanship, the work so far is so good that some of Wolfe's moves cannot be analyzed. All writing, fiction more than the rest, is organized illusion. We who are also in that guild each have a working knowledge of how illusion is generated, sustained, and brought to a climax. When we read the work of others, we can invariably detect how they do it, even when they don't do it the way we would. Or so I have always thought.

No more. I am in the presence of a practitioner whose moves I cannot follow; I see only the same illusions that are seen by those outside the guild. I know the cards are up the sleeve somewhere, but there are clearly extra arms to this person. I know the rabbit has been in the hat all along, but an instant ago the man had no hat. And though I saw him slip a rabbit at the last instant into a compartment that could hold only a rabbit, a gyrfalcon has come out.

And mind you, as craftsmanship and as literature, what we're talking about are attributes that are world-class as *prose,* not "just" as SF; we are in no further need of proof that "genre" SF is not essentially limited to genre standards. There's no question any longer but that all we were waiting for was practitioners smart enough and gifted enough.

As SF, *Claw* unveils a few mysteries left shrouded in *Shadow.* It now seems possible to be sure that the setting is Earth in a very far future—the accompanying news release says 'a million years,' which seems to be the handout writer's own guess and which may not be of a sufficient magnitude. We learn—or at least I learned—for the first time that some of the ruling class have access to air transportation. There appear to be several major facts which Wolfe is only now letting us in on, but which, as we look back, were implied in the earlier book or even stated, but stated in such a way that they didn't distract us. (pp. 49-50)

As a segment in a larger work, *Claw,* honest segment that it is, intertwines seamlessly with *Shadow,* fulfilling some of the temporarily disconnected threadings in the earlier volume. Dorcas, for instance, is developing nicely. New threads are also appearing; how can constant contact with the Claw not be affecting Severian himself? But when *Claw* has reached its natural length, it stops. . . . Wolfe is not being Dashiel Hammett, writing *The Dain Curse* with three false climaxes in order to satisfy readers who have come in at midpoint or might not have the patience to wait for next month's episode. We are not going to know whether *The Book of The New Sun* is a "good" book—ie., a totally understandable illusion with a suitably grand climax—until all four parts are in our hands. At that point, the best thing to do will be to re-read the first three before reading the fourth. And, very likely, to then pause for an interval, ruminate, and go back and read it all again.

This is not the sort of exercise which is normally sufficiently rewarding to be justified. And very rare is the work in which I'd recommend placing the faith to contemplate doing so much work as a reader. In reviewing *Shadow* [see excerpt above], I promised you that such patience was, for once, very likely to be justified. What we have in *Claw* is further documentation that it will be. (p. 50)

> Algis Budrys, "Books: 'The Claw of the Conciliator'," in *The Magazine of Fantasy and Science Fiction* (© 1981 by Mercury Press, Inc.; reprinted from *The Magazine of Fantasy and Science Fiction*), Vol. 60, No. 6, June, 1981, pp. 48-50.

THOMAS D. CLARESON

Gene Wolfe has scored again with *The Claw of the Conciliator.* . . . Successful as it is, however, it differs in tone from *The Shadow of the Torturer.* That first volume introducing Severian had a special intensity—in large part because Wolfe had to concentrate upon his protagonist in order to make him a convincing individual whose awareness acted as the catalyst giving significance to the novel. For that reason, Wolfe focused upon those events which led to Severian's exile; if one looks at the narrative carefully, one finds that most of the action takes place within a period of several days, while the setting is limited to the City Imperishable. In contrast, the effect of *The Claw of the Conciliator* is more diffuse, for the action is episodic as Severian journeys toward Thrax, The City of Windowless Rooms. Certainly Severian's presence—his first-person narrative and his inexhaustible memory—remains a dominating factor, but the function of this second volume differs from that of the first. For example, even after checking the novel closely, one cannot be certain how much time has passed. In a sense, this second part of *The Book of the New Sun* must prepare for the action which is to follow. Specifically, it must not only increase one's interest in (and concern for) Severian's fate, but it must emphasize the potential of the mysterious gem, "The Claw of the Conciliator," which is a powerful relic of the so-called Master of Power. Whether he is an historical or legendary figure, one cannot yet be certain; but one realizes at once that he is of mythic and religious proportions. (p. 196)

Wolfe skillfully broadens the stage which he introduced in *The Shadow of the Torturer;* Severian's quest for his destiny and his memories of his experiences—involving, as they do, total recall—are not ultimately an end in themselves. They provide the strategy through which Wolfe will record the actions leading to the birth of the New Sun. At this point in the narrative the symbolic potential is tremendous. To say that *The Claw of the Conciliator* prepares for what will come does not in the least detract from its power and artistry as a work complete within itself. One is tempted to compare it to one of the novellas making up *The Fifth Head of Cerberus;* each of those three add to the dimensions and impact of the total, although each is very different from the others. . . .

[*Gene Wolfe's Book of Days* has also been recently issued.] As a collection the stories reveal the diversity of Wolfe. The title comes about because Wolfe has assigned each story to a day—often a national holiday—which has special significance to American culture. Therein lies the freshness and added dimension to his wit and irony. . . . It may well be the most important collection of short stories by a single author published this year. And . . . it is another cornerstone in emphasizing how important a writer Gene Wolfe has been throughout his surprisingly brief career. His stature becomes apparent by reading a number of his works. Only in that way does one realize the skill and subtlety with which he brings a fresh perspective to established themes and situations. (p. 197)

Thomas D. Clareson, "Star Cluster: 'The Claw of the Conciliator' and 'Gene Wolfe's Book of Days'," in Extrapolation *(copyright 1981 by Thomas D. and Alice S. Clareson), Vol. 22, No. 2, Summer, 1981, pp. 196-97.*

SOMTOW SUCHARITKUL

[*Sword of the Lictor* is the third volume of the *Book of the New Sun* tetralogy] and it is a shattering tour de force. Those readers who have somehow avoided the previous two episodes in this elegant, comic, searing *Bildungsroman* of a deeply sympathetic young torturer, have done themselves an unconscionable disservice. (p. 16)

The tetralogy folds out like one of those endless Chinese wallets, always different, always seamless, always one. . . . To summarize [*Sword of the Lictor*] is absurd, but images of wonder and weirdness linger long in the memory: the monstrous alzabo, half vampire, half soul eater; the mad two-headed king; vast statues like the Memnons of myth whose arms follow the sunlight and out of whose eyeballs one can gaze upon vistas of curious terrain. And throughout the work there is the language: acerbic, sensuous, intricate. [Wolfe] has created a language of startling alienness for the tetralogy, in which neologisms mingle with resurrected antique words and chimerical hybridizations of Latin, Greek, Germanic roots, strange as the

gene-tailored mutants, remnants of older times, that populate the landscape. And yet there is a rightness about his vocabulary, as though he were plucking his words out of some half-conscious dream-memory; they sound like forgotten friends, not aliens: alzabo, fuligin, balucither, cacogen.

In a very real sense, it is this very familiarity, not the baroque weirdness of its textures, that makes *Sword of the Lictor* so powerful. For Wolfe never loses sight of his sources, his mythical resonances. It is his classical adherence to that most ancient of literary structures, the finding of self within a journey through fantastical and ever-widening landscapes, that pushes the book beyond eccentricity into greatness.

Sword of the Lictor seems the finest of the three books published so far in Gene Wolfe's tetralogy. It will be difficult to wait for the final volume. (pp. 16-17)

Somtow Sucharitkul, "A Certain Slant of 'I'," in Fantasy Newsletter *(copyright © 1981 by Florida Atlantic University), Vol. 4, No. 12, December, 1981, pp. 16-17, 32.**

PETER NICHOLLS

Gene Wolfe's *The Book of the New Sun* is masterly. In the swampy landscape of the 20th-century fantastic epic, it towers solidly like a mountain. . . .

It is rather difficult to say exactly what sort of novel *The Book of the New Sun* is, for Wolfe has quietly and without any fuss invented a new literary form, the continuously recursive picaresque. He has done for picaresque fantasy very much what Escher did for architectural drawing. Just as in an Escher picture, what seems at first to be a wall appears after the onlooker blinks to be a roof or a floor, while downhill stairways mount ever higher, so in Wolfe the surface elements of the picaresque (the hero sets out on a quest and has a series of adventures before becoming king) rearrange themselves in a most disturbing fashion in the reader's mind. The apparently straight-line development loops into helices and even into a kind of literary equivalent of the Klein bottle, whose inside is its outside.

Illusion is everywhere. It is now clear that *The Book of the New Sun,* originally touted as fantasy, is in fact straight science fiction, pure if not simple. The language is the language of fantasy, for in the dying earth which is the novel's setting, technology is ancient and strange, and generates none of the jargon used by those for whom, like us, it is mundane and fresh. Words here are measured, and resonant with an archaic gravity. . . .

The Sword of the Lictor takes Severian, the banished torturer, along with his lover Dorcas to the city of Thrax, his planned destination though not, as it turns out, his final end. Mysteries abound. . . .

The book is marvellously written throughout. Tiny, parenthetic details are often as important as the dramatic set pieces. Careful readers will pick up clues, seldom explained or even emphasized, that reveal a network of strange, half-concealed relationships between characters and between events.

In fact, there are two "Books of the New Sun." Out in the open is the wonderfully vivid and inventive story of a brave and lonely hero; below is the sea of allusion and juxtaposition, metaphors flitting their tails adroitly like fish, images looming and wavering just beyond the point of sharp focus while, almost out of earshot, a pungent debate on ontology, eschatology and the metaphysics of time is taking place. (p. 6)

                    Peter Nicholls, "The Rising of a New Sun," in Book
                    World—The Washington Post *(© 1982, The Wash-*
                    ington Post), January 24, 1982, pp. 6, 8.*

PAUL GRANAHAN

The Sword of the Lictor is the penultimate book in that striking science fantasy [tetralogy, **"The Book of the New Sun"**], and continues the adventures and revelations of its protagonist, Severian of the Order of Torturers. Sentenced to demean himself as a jailmaster and executioner in a backwater town for the crime of showing mercy to a "client" whom he had loved, Severian is our focus for discovering the mystery and richness of the "Urth" of a million years hence. Beyond this, he himself plays a pivotal role in a world swiftly approaching a little understood Eschaton. For Severian is the wielder of the archetypal jewel, the Claw of the Conciliator, the full significance of which is yet to be revealed. . . .

I found this novel a bit of a letdown from the previous entries in the series. Less controlled than the others, it didn't seem to possess quite their texture, but it is still head and shoulders above most current writing. I'm confident that Gene Wolfe—perhaps the most talented author writing in the SF field today (and one who deserves recognition far beyond it)—will not disappoint us in the upcoming conclusion to one of the most innovative works of speculative fiction ever conceived.

                    Paul Granahan, "Science Fiction: 'The Sword of the
                    Lictor'," in Best Sellers *(copyright © 1982 Helen*
                    Dwight Reid Educational Foundation), Vol. 42, No.
                    1, April, 1982, p. 14.

THOMAS D. CLARESON

While [science fiction fans] may continue to debate whether or not [*The Book of the New Sun* tetralogy] should be regarded as science fiction or fantasy, its recognition as a major work in the field has already been established. Its influence . . . should at least equal that of Asimov's Foundation Trilogy.

To begin with, Wolfe has created Urth, an imaginary world which matches, in the richness of its detail, those worlds of *The Left Hand of Darkness, Dune,* and *Lord Valentine's Castle.* His accomplishment cannot be too highly praised. The basic texture of the society centering upon Nessus, the City Imperishable, seems to be medieval, so that, coupled with a first person narrator, the world is immediately acceptable. Bit by bit, Wolfe includes details that remove Urth from the familiar until one readily accepts its strangeness. One learns that Nessus, the City Imperishable, which provides the background of *The Shadow of the Torturer,* has mushroomed along the banks of the River Gyoll in the southern hemisphere of the planet, but the city is so ancient that its earliest structures have long been abandoned and are now little more than ruins. At some time in the past Urth has known interstellar trade and visitors. Indeed, at present a variety of aliens still inhabit the world. Yet one learns that some of them (past and present) were the products of biological engineering, while in *The Sword of the Lictor* and *The Citadel of the Autarch,* especially, one discovers that some of these beings can travel in time, both past and present. Wolfe refers repeatedly to the "corridors" of time. His ability to mix effectively the familiar and strange is well illustrated in *The Shadow of the Torturer.* (pp. 270-71)

The sun of Urth has begun to grow cold, and, unless some change occurs, a new ice age will come and eventually all life and the planet itself will be destroyed. One result has been the creation of the myth of the New Sun; yet that myth has mystical overtones so that through the early novels, at least, one cannot be certain whether the new sun refers to the second coming of the legendary figure of the Conciliator or to an actual renewal of the solar star. Throughout the four novels Wolfe stresses Urth's decline from greatness; he creates a world caught in a dark, essentially barbaric, yet potentially transitional age.

The effective tension between the familiar and strange which brings the novels alive results in large part because of the success Wolfe achieves in having the reader share the experiences of his protagonist, Severian. *The Book of the New Sun* is the autobiography of this complex man who has total recall. *The Shadow of the Torturer* combines Severian's recollections of his youth and adolescence with the central actions following his expulsion from the Guild of Torturers—actions compressed into no more than a day and confined within the walls of Nessus. (p. 271)

In contrast, both *The Claw of the Conciliator* and *The Sword of the Lictor* record his odyssey northward as he attempts to return the Claw to the Pelerines and as he moves ever closer to the front lines of the warfare between the troops of the Commonwealth and the Ascians. (It seems a perpetual war; in the south it has become almost myth rather than reality.) *The Citadel of the Autarch* moves full circle, bringing Severian again to Nessus. Yet Wolfe escapes the restrictions of the here-and-now, so often a characteristic limiting autobiographical tales. Severian tells the story when he is, comparatively, an old man who has himself become the Autarch, the supreme ruler of the southern Commonwealth. Thus, in addition to his photographic memory which so vividly evokes past scenes and incidents, Severian can make allusions which foreshadow events yet to come and, increasingly in the later novels, especially *The Citadel of the Autarch,* can reflect upon both past and future events, thereby complicating them thematically. (He constantly refers to his ability to remember fully and frequently apologizes for his digressions—that is, his reflections.) In several conversations Wolfe has acknowledged the resemblance of Severian to Robert Graves' protagonist in *I, Claudius* and *Claudius the God,* stressing that both men are among the most unlikely to become absolute rulers and both are given to reflection. Although Wolfe has created an epic stage and although he permits his protagonist to travel extensively through the world, the emphasis is never upon external action for the sake of action; rather, the four novels become increasingly a study of Severian's reactions and musings. The result is that Gene Wolfe has created one of the richest and most complex characterizations in the field of fantasy and science fiction. (pp. 271-72)

One interesting aspect of all the novels which has been overlooked is that Wolfe does not completely absent himself from them. Not only does he make use of Dr. Talos's plays and, especially in *The Citadel of the Autarch,* intrude a number of stories which serve as commentaries upon the action, but to each novel he has appended a discussion of some phase of the society of Urth, be it "Social Relationships in the Commonwealth," "Provincial Administration," or "Money, Measures, and Time." This gives him, of course, a chance to introduce expository material, as well as allowing him to guide his readers' reflections. What is more important, however, it permits him to pretend that he is editing an actual manuscript, as when he says in the appendix to *The Citadel of the Autarch:*

"Nowhere are the manuscripts of *The Book of the New Sun* more obscure than in their treatment of weapons and military organization." Or again, in the same appendix, he refers to "my translations." Through this device he gains a double effect. On the one hand, he adapts—gives a freshness to—a convention as old as fantasy and science fiction in order to gain an aura of authority/authenticity. On the other, however, like such contemporary writers as Barth and Coover, he reminds the reader that these narratives are fictional constructs and should be read as fiction—that is, as entertainment, as metaphor and symbol. (p. 273)

> *Thomas D. Clareson, "The Book of Gold: Gene Wolfe's 'Book of the New Sun'," in* Extrapolation *(copyright 1982 by The Kent State University Press), Vol. 23, No. 3, Fall, 1982, pp. 270-74.*

BOOKLIST

[*The Citadel of the Autarch*] concludes Wolfe's masterpiece, *The Book of the New Sun.* Severian the Torturer completes his travels on Urth by becoming Autarch and preparing to embark on a journey to the stars. It is possible that we have not seen the last of Severian, but it is not necessary that we see any more for this series to loom as a major landmark of contemporary American literature. Once again, there is hardly a word out of place or an ill-chosen detail. And also once again, there is no purpose in even beginning this book without having read the first volumes of what is, in fact, a single gigantic novel. Wolfe has wrought a genuine marvel here. . . .

> *R. G., "Upfront, Advance Reviews: 'The Citadel of the Autarch'," in* Booklist *(reprinted by permission of the American Library Association; copyright © 1982 by the American Library Association), Vol. 79, No. 5, November 1, 1982, p. 337.*

BOB COLLINS

In *The Citadel of the Autarch,* Wolfe's hero indeed comes to the end of his narrative, though neither his life or career. . . . Severian, as Autarch, sees himself as "an ancient buzzing with antiquity as a corpse with flies," and the description is apt as well for the narrative, in which Wolfe reveals a cyclical theory of time and space, not incompatible with Plato's, and the myth of the New Sun is at last adumbrated.

Wolfe's achievement, though, is nothing less than the mythic conflation of the whole of human drama, something the "first reader" of such a book may sense, but no review can possibly summarize.

Let me say, instead, that the conclusion of Severian's story is both wondrous and intense, and marked by occasional passages of such elegant and evocative prose as to pass into poetry. . . .

I will not comment on the plot further than to say that Severian, as the Autarch himself, unravels most (not all) of the mysteries remaining from earlier books, and that despite a vision of Urth as glaciated waste, presented by a future scientist whose "probability" is "rooted" in Severian's present, the Autarch is convinced that his final mission, to survive a cosmic trial on behalf of humanity, will succeed, and a new sun bloom.

> *Bob Collins, "Conclusion of 'The Book of the New Sun'," in* Fantasy Newsletter *(copyright © 1982 by Florida Atlantic University), Vol. 5, No. 11, December, 1982, p. 36.*

FAREN MILLER

["**The Book of the New Sun**"] is a curiously elusive work. Throughout the tetralogy, the reader recognizes Wolfe's intelligence, questing spirit, and superb mastery of language. These attributes have earned the books praise as literary masterworks. The praise is deserved. And yet. . . .

From my first encounter with Volume Two, *The Claw of the Conciliator,* I've made my way through the tetralogy like a baffled amnesiac. Who are all these characters? What was it Severian the Torturer did in those towns he passed through? How have his experiences served to shape his life and its tale? The answers lie somewhere in the recesses of the hero's all-encompassing memory, but Severian's casual references to the past only accentuate my uncertainties. An obvious solution presents itself: Go back and read the entire tetralogy as a single unit. But that would not solve the riddle of the individual volumes. Why do they slide so quickly from the grasp?

"**The Book of the New Sun**" is not cast in the form of a four-part novel, or of four novels in sequence. Rather, the work follows the wandering paths of picaresque literature, presenting a hero who goes travelling and encounters many remarkable things. *The Shadow of the Torturer* is the most novelistic, self-contained, and comprehensible book of the group. The later volumes offer a profusion of characters (rarely appearing for more than a few chapters), events, interposed stories, and glimpses of the history of Wolfe's enigmatic Urth. *The Citadel of the Autarch* represents this mode perfectly. Severian wanders, leaving past companions behind and meeting new ones who disappear in their turn; several chapters are devoted to stories told by some of these people; Severian's journey loses all semblance of a quest and moves instead with the random tides of war; various mysteries are explained. By the end of the book, Severian has indeed become Autarch, as the earlier volumes indicated he would. But this achievement seems almost unconnected with his previous adventures. The honor (or duty) is bestowed through a combination of chance and Severian's innate characteristics—in other words, by Fate.

"**The Book of the New Sun**" can't be called a novel or an epic. It falls somewhere between fantasy and science fiction (though the trappings of sf appear more prominently in the last volume). It is full of delights, yet resists any attempt to hold it whole in the mind. It has gathered a faithful following and won numerous awards. Is it Wolfe's masterwork, or only an enigma on the road to somewhere else?

> *Faren Miller, "'Locus' Looks at Books: 'The Citadel of the Autarch'" (© 1983 by Faren C. Miller), in* Locus, *Vol. 16, No. 1, January, 1983, p. 26.*

JOHN CLUTE

[If] Gene Wolfe is to be taken seriously—and however thrilling or pleasing [*The Book of the New Sun*] may seem, there is simply no point at all in thinking of its author as a creator of mere speculative entertainment—then he must be taken as attempting something analogous to Dante's supreme effort [*The Divine Comedy*]. With great urgency, layer after layer, he has created a world radiant with meaning, a novel that makes sense in the end only if it is read as an attempt to represent the Word of God. How intimate—how dizzyingly remote—how comforting or alienating that Word can be, each reader will of course discover.

We are on Urth, millennia upon millennia hence. So densely impacted with millions of years of human life is this world that even commercial mines, dug however deep into the ransacked planet, produce only bone and brick and artifact and icon, layer upon layer of human meaning, most of it indecipherable at first or second glance (just like certain passages of *The Book*). So the very earth radiates significance, as do its inhabitants, who live awash in ancientness, but who seem to glow with the fabulousness of their environment, strangely youthful, strangely assured. They have the deep polish of the citizens of the legends of childhood. But Urth is dying. The sun is red; stars are visible in the dark sky of midday. The starships of earlier epochs have become the dwelling places and headquarters of guilds themselves ancient. The mountains of Urth have been carved into giant sculptures of Autarchs, themselves fossils unearthed from deep mines. (pp. 1-2)

It may be the case that for some readers Severian's [experiences in the three volumes preceding *The Citadel of the Autarch*] may have seemed picaresque, somewhat random in nature, though colorful enough. But inexorably it becomes more and more clear that nothing in Severian's narrative—he tells the whole tale himself some time after he has become Autarch of the land of his birth—is accidental. Everything in his life becomes substance, and the reader can feel at times a kind of sweet cold terror as the true shape of that life begins to come clear. Much that happens to Severian has been lived before (in a manner which the fourth volume reveals) and is therefore twice-told, a code reverently to be broken. But much has not happened before, and represents something new on Urth. New on Urth is the Severian who will redeem humanity by becoming the New Sun/Apollo, or the New Son/Christ.

A miracle is required. The miracle (as T. H. White, quoting Malory, once said of Lancelot) is that Severian is allowed to perform a miracle. Early in volume one [*The Shadow of the Torturer*], he has—it seems inadvertently—acquired from a passel of traveling nuns their most treasured relic, the Claw of the Conciliator. The Conciliator is a Redeemer of a past age who may come again. At first the Claw seems to be a kind of weapon, but slowly we come to realize that—in direct contradiction of all the habits of science fantasy—it does nothing but heal. And the land blossoms where Severian sleeps. Only in the fourth volume do we see that the Claw is not the miracle, that it merely releases in Severian his true nature. He returns the Claw to its keepers. He becomes Autarch, in a scene terrible with desire and hints of the burdens to come. Animate projections from his childhood tell him something of what he must face—it is one of the hoariest of all science fiction clichés that he will soon be pitting his wits against, but Wolfe somehow manages to transform it (as he transforms so much else) into something moving, and rich and strange. (pp. 2, 11)

Like Funes the Memorious in Borges' story, Severian cannot forget anything, so that *The Book* which tells his life is like a Theater of Memory, where everything stands for something else, where everything is a relic. Severian's life is a performance which he cannot help but memorize for any future occasion. He needs no prompting; he writes *The Book of the New Sun* to prompt us.

Volume four of this gift is harrowing, but is full of pleasures as well. There are four new-minted fables set into the text. There is Master Ash, who roots Yggdrasillike back through time to observe Severian's Urth. There is time travel, space travel, teleportation; there are laser duels and gentle Mammoths; and delirium and dreams and the tying-up of loose threads. *The Book* is a feast and a eucharist; layer after layer, we have just begun to know it. (p. 11)

John Clute, "The Urth and All Its Glory," in Book World—The Washington Post *(© 1983, The Washington Post), January 30, 1983, pp. 1-2, 11.*

Appendix

THE EXCERPTS IN CLC, VOLUME 25, WERE REPRINTED FROM THE FOLLOWING PERIODICALS:

AB Bookman's Weekly
Africa Today
America
The American Book Review
The American Poetry Review
The American Scandinavian Review
The American Scholar
The American Spectator
Arizona and the West
The Armchair Detective
The Athenaeum
The Atlantic Monthly
Best Sellers
Black American Literature Forum
Black World
Book Week—The Sunday Herald Tribune
Book World—Chicago Tribune
Book World—The Washington Post
Booklist
Books Abroad
Books in Canada
Boston Review
British Book News
The Bulletin of Atomic Scientists: a
   magazine of science and public affairs
The Canadian Fiction Magazine
The Canadian Forum
Canadian Literature
Canadian Studies in Literature
Carolina Quarterly
Choice
The Christian Science Monitor
The Chronicle Review
Commentary
Commonweal
Comparative Literature Studies
Contemporary Literature
The Critic

Critical Quarterly
Critique: Studies in Modern Fiction
Daily News, *New York*
The Dalhousie Review
Delap's Fantasy & Science Fiction Review
Dialogue: A Journal of Mormon Thought
East Africa Journal
Educational Theatre Journal
Éire-Ireland
Encounter
English Studies in Africa
Esquire
Extrapolation
Fantasy Newsletter
The Fiddlehead
The French Review
Foundation
The Georgia Review
Harper's
Harvard Educational Review
The Hollins Critic
The Hudson Review
The Illustrated London News
The International Fiction Review
Journal of Canadian Fiction
Journal of Commonwealth Literature
Journal of Popular Culture
The Kenyon Review
Library Journal
The Listener
The Literary Half-Yearly
Locus
London Magazine
The London Review of Books
Lone Star Review
Los Angeles Times
Los Angeles Times Book Review
Maclean's Magazine

Magazine of Fantasy and Science Fiction
The Malahat Review
MLN
Modern Austrian Literature
Modern Fiction Studies
The Modern Language Journal
Moons and Lion Tailes
MOSAIC: A Journal for the Comparative
   Study of Literature and Ideas
Mother Jones
Ms.
The Nation
National Review
New Boston Review
New England Review
The New Leader
The New Republic
The New Review
New Statesman
The New Statesman & Nation
New York
New York Herald Tribune
New York Herald Tribune Book Review
New York Herald Tribune Books
New York Herald Tribune Weekly Book
   Review
New York Post
The New York Review of Books
New York Theatre Critics' Reviews
The New York Times
The New York Times Book Review
The New York Times Magazine
The New Yorker
Newsweek
The North American Review
North Dakota Quarterly
Notes on Modern American Literature
The Observer

Pan-African Journal
Parnassus: Poetry in Review
Plays and Players
Poetry
Polish Perspectives
The Polish Review
Publishers Weekly
Punch
Queen's Quarterly
Quill and Quire
Riverside Quarterly
San Francisco Review of Books
Saturday Night
Saturday Review
The Saturday Review, *New York*
The Saturday Review of Literature
The Sewanee Review

Slavic and East European Journal
The Southern Literary Journal
The Southern Review
Soviet Studies in Literature
The Spectator
Stand
Starship
Studies in Black Literature
Theater
Theatre Arts Monthly
Theatre Journal
Threepenny Review
Time
The Times Educational Supplement
The Times Literary Supplement
Tribune
Tulane Drama Review

UFAHAMU
University of Toronto Quarterly
The Village Voice
The Virginia Quarterly Review
VLS
The Wall Street Journal
WAVES
West Coast Review of Books
Western American Literature
Wisconsin Studies in Contemporary
   Literature
Women's Wear Daily
World Literature Today
World Literature Written in English
Worldview
Yale French Studies
The Yale Review

THE EXCERPTS IN CLC, VOLUME 25, WERE REPRINTED FROM THE FOLLOWING BOOKS:

Adams, Agatha Boyd. Paul Green of Chapel Hill. *Edited by Richard Walser. The University of North Carolina Library, 1951.*

Anderson, Poul. Introduction to The Best of Fritz Leiber, *by Fritz Leiber. Ballantine Books, 1974, Doubleday, 1974.*

Anozie, Sunday O. Christopher Okigbo: Creative Rhetoric. *Evans Brothers Limited, 1972.*

Attebery, Brian. The Fantasy Tradition in American Literature: From Irving to LeGuin. *Indiana University Press, 1980.*

Barnett, Ursula. Ezekiel Mphahlele. *Twayne, 1976.*

Bedient, Calvin. Eight Contemporary Poets: Charles Tomlinson, Donald Davie, R. S. Thomas, Philip Larkin, Ted Hughes, Thomas Kinsella, Stevie Smith, W. S. Graham. *Oxford University Press, 1974.*

Berke, Roberta. Bounds Out of Bounds: A Compass for Recent American and British Poetry. *Oxford University Press, 1981.*

Birnbaum, Henrik, and Eekman, Thomas, eds. Fiction and Drama in Eastern and Southeastern Europe: Evolution and Experiment in the Postwar Period. *Slavica Publishers, Inc., 1980.*

Brown, John Mason. Seeing More Things. *McGraw-Hill, 1948.*

Brown, Lloyd W. West Indian Poetry. *Twayne, 1978.*

Brown, Terence. Northern Voices: Poets from Ulster. *Rowman and Littlefield, 1975.*

Buttel, Robert. Seamus Heaney. *Bucknell University Press, 1975.*

Callan, Edward. Alan Paton. *Rev. ed. Twayne, 1982.*

Christ, Carol P. Diving Deep and Surfacing: Women Writers on Spiritual Quest. *Beacon Press, 1980.*

Clark, Barrett H. Introduction to Lonesome Road: Six Plays for the Negro Theatre, *by Paul Green. Robert M. McBride & Company, 1926.*

Coale, Samuel. John Cheever. *Ungar, 1977.*

Colley, Iain. Dos Passos and the Fiction of Despair. *Macmillan, 1978.*

Cooke, M. G., ed. Modern Black Novelists: A Collection of Critical Essays. *Prentice-Hall, Inc., 1971.*

Davidson, Arnold E., and Davidson, Cathy N., eds. The Art of Margaret Atwood: Essays in Criticism. *House of Anansi Press, 1981.*

Duprey, Richard A. Just off the Aisle: The Ramblings of a Catholic Critic. *Newman Press, 1962.*

Dutton, Robert R. Saul Bellow. *Twayne, 1982.*

Egudu, Romanus N. Four Modern West African Poets. *NOK Publishers International Ltd., 1977.*

Esslin, Martin. Reflections: Essays on Modern Theatre. *Doubleday, 1969.*

Esslin, Martin. The Theatre of the Absurd. *Rev. ed. Doubleday, 1969.*

Evans, Gareth Lloyd. The Language of Modern Drama. *Everyman's University Library, J M Dent & Sons Ltd, 1977.*

Farrell, James T. Literary Essays: 1954-1974. *Edited by Jack Alan Robbins. Kennikat Press, 1976.*

Faulkner, Peter. Angus Wilson: Mimie and Moralist. *The Viking Press, 1980, Secker & Warburg, 1980.*

Fletcher, John, ed. Forces in Modern French Drama. *University of London Press, 1972.*

Fowles, John. Introduction to The Book of Ebenezer LePage, *by G. B. Edwards. Knopf, 1981.*

Frane, Jeff. Fritz Leiber. *Starmont House, 1980.*

Fuller, Edmund. Books with Men behind Them. *Random House, 1962.*

Gilkes, Michael. The West Indian Novel. *Twayne, 1981.*

Goetz-Stankiewicz, Marketa. The Silenced Theatre: Czech Playwrights without a Stage. *University of Toronto Press, 1979.*

Grace, Sherrill. Violent Duality: A Study of Margaret Atwood. *Edited by Ken Norris. Véhicule Press, 1980.*

Guicharnaud, Jacques. Modern French Theatre. *Yale University Press, 1967.*

Haight, Amanda. Anna Akhmatova: A Poetic Pilgrimage. *Oxford University Press, 1976.*

Hallberg, Peter. Halldór Laxness. *Translated by Rory McTurk. Twayne, 1971.*

Hamner, Robert D. Derek Walcott. *Twayne, 1981.*

Harrison, Gilbert A., ed. The Critic As Artist: Essays on Books, 1920-1970. *Liveright, 1972.*

Heywood, Christopher, ed. Aspects of South African Literature. *Africana, 1976.*

Hingley, Ronald. Nightingale Fever: Russian Poets in Revolution. *Knopf, 1981, Weidenfield and Nicolson, 1982.*

James, Clive. First Reactions: Critical Essays, 1968-1979. *Knopf, 1980.*

James, Louis, ed. The Islands In Between: Essays on West Indian Literature. *Oxford University Press, 1968.*

Jones, Peter, and Schmidt, Michael, eds. British Poetry since 1970: A Critical Survey. *Persea Books, 1980.*

Kerr, Walter. Thirty Plays Hath November: Pain and Pleasure in the Contemporary Theater. *Simon & Schuster, 1969.*

King, Bruce, ed. Introduction to Nigerian Literature. *University of Lagos, 1971, Evans Brothers Limited, 1971.*

King, Bruce. The New English Literatures: Cultural Nationalism in a Changing World. *St. Martin's Press, 1980.*

King, Bruce, ed. West Indian Literature. *Archon Books, 1979.*

Kunitz, Stanley. Foreword to Gathering the Tribes, *by Carolyn Forché. Yale University Press, 1976.*

Larson, Charles R. The Novel in the Third World. *Inscape Publishers, 1976.*

Lehrmann, Charles C. The Jewish Element in French Literature. *Translated by George Klin. Fairleigh Dickinson University Press, 1971.*

Leiber, Fritz. Afterword to The Best of Fritz Leiber, *by Fritz Leiber. Doubleday, 1974.*

MacAdam, Alfred. J. Modern Latin American Narratives: The Dreams of Reason. *University of Chicago Press, 1977.*

Mansfield, Katherine. Novels and Novelists. *Edited by J. Middleton Murry. Knopf, 1930.*

McCann, John J. The Theater of Arthur Adamov. *Chapel Hill, 1975.*

Miller, James E., Jr. The American Quest for a Supreme Fiction: Whitman's Legacy in the Personal Epic. *University of Chicago Press, 1979.*

Monk, Patricia. The Smaller Infinity: The Jungian Self in the Novels of Robertson Davies. *University of Toronto Press, 1982.*

Moore, Gerald. Twelve African Writers. *Indiana University Press, 1980, Hutchinson, 1980.*

Moskowitz, Sam. Seekers of Tomorrow: Masters of Modern Science Fiction. *World Publishing Co., 1966.*

New, William H. Articulating West: Essays on Purpose and Form in Modern Canadian Literature. *New Press, 1972.*

Oberg, Arthur. Modern American Lyric: Lowell, Berryman, Creeley, and Plath. *Rutgers University Press, 1978.*

Panshin, Alexei, and Panshin, Cory. SF in Dimension: A Book of Explorations. *Advent, 1976.*

Peyre, Henri. French Novelists of Today. *Rev. ed. Oxford University Press, 1967.*

Phillips, Robert. The Confessional Poets. *Southern Illinois University Press, 1973.*

Pieterse, Cosmo, and Munro, Donald, eds. African Literature. *Africana, 1969.*

Pilkington, William T., ed. Critical Essays on the Western American Novel. *G. K. Hall & Co., 1980.*

Pritchett, V. S. The Tale Bearers: Literary Essays. *Random House, 1980.*

Pronko, Leonard Cabell. Avant-Garde: The Experimental Theater. *University of California Press, 1963.*

Rabkin, Gerald. Drama and Commitment: Politics in the American Theatre of the Thirties. *Indiana University Press, 1964.*

Reilly, John H. Arthur Adamov. *Twayne, 1974.*

Roscoe, Adrian. Uhuru's Fire: African Literature East to South. *Cambridge University Press, 1977.*

Schmidt, Michael. A Reader's Guide to Fifty Modern British Poets. *Barnes & Nobles, 1979.*

Shapiro, David. John Ashbery: An Introduction to the Poetry. *Columbia University Press, 1979.*

Sheed, Wilfrid. The Good Word and Other Words. *E. P. Dutton, Inc., 1978.*

Sherrell, Richard E. The Human Image: Avant Garde and Christian. *John Knox Press, 1969.*

Silbersack, John. Introduction to *The Change War, by Fritz Leiber. Gregg Press, 1978.*

Sinyavsky, Andrei. For Freedom of Imagination. *Translated by Laslo Tikos and Murray Peppard. Holt, Rinehart and Winston, 1971.*

Sontag, Susan. Under the Sign of Saturn. *Farrar, Straus and Giroux, 1980.*

Souza, Raymond D. Major Cuban Novelists: Innovation and Tradition. *University of Missouri Press, 1976.*

Spivey, Ted. R. The Journey beyond Tragedy: A Study of Myth and Modern Fiction. *University Presses of Florida, 1980.*

Strakhovsky, Leonid I. Craftsmen of the World, Three Poets of Modern Russia: Gumilyov, Akhmatova, Mandelstam. *Harvard University Press, 1949, Greenwood Press, Publishers, 1969.*

Thomas, D. M. Introduction to Way of All the Earth, *by Anna Akhmatova. Translated by D. M. Thomas. Ohio University Press, 1979.*

Thurston, Robert. Introduction to The Big Time, *by Fritz Leiber. Gregg Press, 1976.*

Tynan, Kenneth. Curtains: Selections from the Drama Criticism and Related Writings. *Atheneum, 1961.*

Wagner, Linda W. Dos Passos: Artist As American. *University of Texas Press, 1979.*

Waldeland, Lynne. John Cheever. *Twayne, 1979.*

Young, Stark. Immortal Shadows: A Book of Dramatic Criticism. *Charles Scribner's Sons, 1948.*

Yurieff, Zoya. Joseph Wittlin. *Twayne, 1973.*

Ziolkowski, Theodore. Introduction to Pictor's Metamorphoses and Other Fantasies, *by Hermann Hesse. Edited by Theodore Ziolkowski. Translated by Rika Lesser. Farrar, Straus and Giroux, 1982.*

Cumulative Index to Authors

Cumulative Index to Critics

Aaron, Daniel
Thornton Wilder **15**:575

Aaron, Jonathan
Tadeusz Różewicz **23**:363

Aaron, Jules
Jack Heifner **11**:264

Abbey, Edward
Robert M. Pirsig **6**:421

Abbott, John Lawrence
Isaac Bashevis Singer **9**:487
Sylvia Townsend Warner **7**:512

Abeel, Erica
Pamela Hansford Johnson **7**:185

Abel, Elizabeth
Jean Rhys **14**:448

Abel, Lionel
Samuel Beckett **2**:45
Jack Gelber **6**:196
Jean Genet **2**:157
Yoram Kaniuk **19**:238

Abernethy, Peter L.
Thomas Pynchon **3**:410

Abicht, Ludo
Jan de Hartog **19**:133

Ableman, Paul
Brian Aldiss **14**:14
Beryl Bainbridge **22**:45
Jurek Becker **19**:36
William S. Burroughs **22**:85
J. M. Coetzee **23**:125
Len Deighton **22**:116
William Golding **17**:179
Mary Gordon **13**:250
Mervyn Jones **10**:295

Piers Paul Read **25**:377
Mary Renault **17**:402
Anatoli Rybakov **23**:373
Andrew Sinclair **14**:489
Scott Sommer **25**:424
D. M. Thomas **22**:419
Gore Vidal **22**:438

Abley, Mark
Margaret Atwood **25**:65
Harry Crews **23**:136
William Mitchell **25**:327
Agnès Varda **16**:560

Abraham, Willie E.
William Melvin Kelley **22**:249

Abrahams, Cecil A.
Bessie Head **25**:236

Abrahams, William
Elizabeth Bowen **6**:95
Hortense Calisher **2**:97
Herbert Gold **4**:193
Joyce Carol Oates **2**:315
Harold Pinter **9**:418
V. S. Pritchett **5**:352

Abrams, M. H.
M. H. Abrams **24**:18
Northrop Frye **24**:209

Abramson, Doris E.
Alice Childress **12**:105

Abramson, Jane
Peter Dickinson **12**:172
Christie Harris **12**:268
Rosemary Wells **12**:638

Acheson, James
William Golding **17**:177

Acken, Edgar L.
Ernest K. Gann **23**:163

Ackerman, Diane
John Berryman **25**:97

Ackroyd, Peter
Brian Aldiss **5**:16
Martin Amis **4**:19
Miguel Ángel Asturias **8**:27
Louis Auchincloss **6**:15
W. H. Auden **9**:56
Beryl Bainbridge **8**:36
James Baldwin **5**:43
John Barth **5**:51
Donald Barthelme **3**:44
Samuel Beckett **4**:52
John Berryman **3**:72
Richard Brautigan **5**:72
Charles Bukowski **5**:80
Anthony Burgess **5**:87
William S. Burroughs **5**:92
Italo Calvino **5**:100; **8**:132
Richard Condon **6**:115
Roald Dahl **6**:122
Ed Dorn **10**:155
Margaret Drabble **8**:183
Douglas Dunn **6**:148
Bruce Jay Friedman **5**:127
John Gardner **7**:116
Günter Grass **4**:207
MacDonald Harris **9**:261
Joseph Heller **5**:179
Mark Helprin **10**:261
Russell C. Hoban **7**:160
Elizabeth Jane Howard **7**:164
B. S. Johnson **6**:264
Pamela Hansford Johnson **7**:184
G. Josipovici **6**:270
Thomas Keneally **10**:298

Jack Kerouac **5**:215
Francis King **8**:321
Jerzy Kosinski **10**:308
Doris Lessing **6**:300
Alison Lurie **4**:305
Thomas McGuane **7**:212
Stanley Middleton **7**:220
Michael Moorcock **5**:294
Penelope Mortimer **5**:298
Iris Murdoch **4**:368
Vladimir Nabokov **6**:358
V. S. Naipaul **7**:252
Joyce Carol Oates **6**:368
Tillie Olsen **13**:432
Grace Paley **6**:393
Frederik Pohl **18**:411
Davi Pownall **10**:418, 419
J. B. Priestley **9**:441
V. S. Pritchett **5**:352
Thomas Pynchon **3**:419
Frederic Raphael **14**:437
Simon Raven **14**:442
Peter Redgrove **6**:446
Keith Roberts **14**:463
Judith Rossner **9**:458
May Sarton **4**:472
David Slavitt **5**:392
Wole Soyinka **5**:398
David Storey **4**:529
Paul Theroux **5**:428
Thomas Tryon **11**:548
John Updike **7**:488; **9**:540
Gore Vidal **8**:525
Harriet Waugh **6**:559
Jerome Weidman **7**:518
Arnold Wesker **5**:483
Patrick White **4**:587
Roger Zelazny **21**:469

Critic Index

Critic Index

Critic Index

Critic Index

Critic Index

Critic Index

Critic Index

Critic Index

Critic Index

Critic Index

Critic Index

Critic Index

Critic Index

Critic Index

Critic Index

Critic Index

Critic Index

Critic Index

Critic Index

Critic Index

Critic Index

Critic Index

Critic Index

Critic Index

Critic Index

Critic Index

Critic Index

Critic Index

Critic Index

Critic Index

Critic Index

Critic Index

Critic Index

Critic Index

Critic Index

Critic Index

Critic Index

Critic Index